R. Gupta's®

POPULAR MASTER GUIDE

BBA/BBS

Bachelor of Business Administration
Bachelor of Business Studies

Entrance Exam

Conducted by

Major Indian Universities &
Prominent Institutes

2027
EDITION

RAMESH PUBLISHING HOUSE, NEW DELHI

Published by

O.P. Gupta *for* Ramesh Publishing House

Admin. Office

12-H, New Daryaganj Road, Opp. Officers' Mess,
New Delhi-110002 ✆ 23275224, 23245124

E-mail: info@rameshpublishinghouse.com

For Online Shopping: www.rameshpublishinghouse.com

Showroom

- Balaji Market, Nai Sarak, Delhi-110006 ✆ 23282525 📱 9354373464
- 4457, Nai Sarak, Delhi-110006

Book Code: R-1535

ISBN: 978-93-5012-308-9

Price: ₹ 560

Printed by : Repro India Ltd.

Contents

Previous Years' Paper

(BBA) Bachelor of Business Administration

Entrance Exam-2025*

ENGLISH LANGUAGE

Directions (Qs. No. 1-4): *Read the given passage and answer the questions that follow:*

Virtues are the result of repeated actions, as habits lay the foundation of moral excellence. Right from the beginning of their lives, children are taught good habits by their parents and teachers. Magnanimity, helpfulness and sacrifice are great virtues which need to be well cultivated in human beings. Trees give shade for the benefit of others, while they themselves stand enduring the scorching heat of the sun. They selflessly bear the fruit which is consumed by birds, animals and human beings. Rivers travel hundreds of kilometers, irrigating the land and providing water for all living beings. Flowers spread their scent to make the environment pleasant. Nature teaches us to tolerate pain for the sake of service to others. Henna yields its reddish hue when ground into a paste. Sugarcane yields sweet juice when it is pressed. Flowers get pierced through with a needle to embellish us with garlands.

The character of virtuous men and women is also like the above things and elements of Nature. What is the use of this périshable and mortal frame if it is not used for the benefit of others? To live our life only for ourselves is to live like cats and dogs. People who are noble at heart do not abandon human virtues even if they have to lose their lives. A Sanskrit couplet says—"Whether men praise them or no, whether they get riches or no, whether they live long or soon die, the virtuous will never waver from the path of righteousness."

1. Which of the following is NOT mentioned in the passage?
1. Being truthful is the most important sign of virtuosity.
2. Nature teaches us to endure pain and serve others.
3. A self-centred existence is a bestial existence.
4. Not abandoning the right path even in the face of death.

2. In the passage, what is meant by "mortal frame"?
1. Nature
2. Animals
3. Land
4. Human body

3. According to the passage, which of the following is NOT true?
1. Parents and teachers inculcate good habits in children from the early stages.
2. There are parallels between the character of virtuous human beings and Nature.
3. Ethical behaviour is not dependent upon praise or reward.
4. The virtuous deviate from their path, if they aren't duly acknowledged.

4. Which of the following does not exemplify 'endurance', according to the passage?
1. Trees enduring the scorching heat of the Sun.
2. Sugarcane getting pressed to yield juice.
3. Trees bearing fruit and flowers spreading fragrance.
4. Henna being ground and turned into a paste.

*Conducted by CUET

Directions (Qs. No. 5-8): *Read the given passage and answer the questions that follow:*

Uma could not sing; but since learning to write, she had developed the habit of writing down any song she heard, to lessen the pain of not being able to sing it. Today the beggar woman was singing...

Resentful anguish welled up in Uma's heart. She called the singer secretly to her room, shut the door and began to write down the song in her eccentric spelling.

Tilakmanjari, Kanakmanjari and Anangamanjari observed everything through the crack in the door, and burst out, clapping their hands, "Boudidi, we've seen what you're doing!"

Uma quickly unfastened the door and began to plead with them, "Darling sisters, please don't tell anybody. I beg you, please don't. I'll never do it again. I'll never write again..."

At length, Uma noticed that Tilakmanjari was eyeing her exercise-book. She ran and clutched the book to her chest. Her sisters-in-law tried to take it away from her by force, but when they did not succeed, Anangamanjari went to summon her brother.

Pyarimohan arrived and sat down grimly on the bed. He said in a voice like thunder, "Give me the exercise-book."

The little girl clasped the exercise-book to her chest and directed a glance of utter supplication at her husband's face. But when she saw Pyarimohan was getting up to snatch the book from her, she flung it down, covered her face with her hands and collapsed on the floor.

5. Pyarimohan is bound to Uma by ....
  1. paternal-ties
  2. the bond of friendship
  3. marital-ties
  4. fraternal-ties

6. What is meant by "eccentric" in the passage?
  1. neat and beautiful
  2. strange and incorrect
  3. written in the upper case
  4. written in European languages

7. Why did Uma develop the habit of writing down any song she heard?
  1. To alleviate her anguish at her lack of skill at singing.
  2. To work upon and enhance her recently acquired skill at writing.
  3. To compile all the songs in her exercise book.
  4. To be able to learn to sing the song later.

8. What does the phrase <u>'a glance of utter supplication'</u> mean in the passage?
  1. an extremely angry and irritated look
  2. a look of total excitement
  3. a look showing celebration
  4. a look of request and prayer

Directions (Qs. No. 9-12): *Read the given passage and answer the questions that follow:*

Solace. He turned the roll of paper between his fingers and wondered if that had not been his error—to search always for solace when there was other game to hunt in the forest. Had he had more spirit, more nerve, more desire and ambition, then perhaps he would have instead hunted for success, distinction, magic. Perhaps he would have followed in pursuit of an art, published a book of poetry, earned a name for himself, a little fame, even gold bangles for Sarla...

But the thought was puerile that it was made him spit out a bitter shred of tobacco. Every effort he had made had ended in defeat: most of the poems he had written and sent to Murad had been rejected, his monograph never published; his wife and son eyed him with blatant disappointment; nor had he won the regard of his colleagues or students. The inherent weakness in his father that had made him an ineffectual, if harmless, teacher and householder, had been passed on to him. He felt it inside him like an empty hole, one he had been staring at all his years, intimidated by its blackness and blankness. Even his attempt to fill it with a genuine and heartfelt homage to a true poet, a man who had distinguished himself as he would have liked to do, had been defeated by all the obstacles that sprang up in his life like shards and pebbles sent up at every step. It was one more blow, and perhaps the bitterest of all.

9. Choose a word similar in meaning to the word- Puerile

1. childish
2. melancholy
3. cosmopolitan
4. precocious

10. What does the word 'game' in the given phrase symbolise, 'other games to hunt in the forest'

1. Wild animals in the forest
2. Desires or goals being pursued
3. Playful activities
4. Rules of a competition.

11. On the basis of your reading identify the tone of the passage.

1. Contemptuous
2. Mournful
3. Satarical
4. Disillusioned

12. Who does Deven blame for his failure in life?

1. His wife and son
2. His lack of creativity
3. His father's submissive and timid nature
4. His inherited activism and assertiveness

13. Arrange the parts in the correct sequence to form a meaningful sentence:

A. peeps into the dark abyss of human consciousness,
B. Neruda conceives poetry not as something which has
C. its deliberate relation with things of beauty, but rather as an art which
D. something which has the ability to perceive suffering

Choose the ***correct*** answer from the options given below:

1. B, C, A, D
2. A, D, C, B
3. C, A, B, D
4. D, B, C, A

14. Select the correct antonym for the word: HEGEMONY

1. Supremacy
2. Leadership
3. Prosperity
4. Independence

15. Arrange the following parts in the correct sequence to form a meaningful sentence:

A. the three best hypotheses
B. ask them to get together
C. the group has come up with
D. in fours and decide on

Choose the ***correct*** answer from the options given below:

1. A, D, C, B
2. C, B, D, A
3. B, D, A, C
4. D, B, C, A

16. Complete the idioms given in List-I with their second part given in List-II:

List-I (Idiom's first part)	**List-II (Idiom's second part)**
A. To hit the nail	I. to injury
B. To add insult	II. before the horse
C. To put the cart	III. in the air
D. To build castles	IV. on the head

Choose the ***correct*** answer from the options given below:

1. A-I, B-III, C-II, D-IV.
2. A-II, B-IV, C-III, D-I.
3. A-IV, B-I, C-II, D-III.
4. A-III, B-IV, C-I, D-II.

17. Select the correct synonym for the word: DISCONCERTING

1. Embarrasing
2. Comfortable
3. Suave
4. Adroit

18. Select the correct antonym for the word: Valiant

1. Nervous
2. Kind
3. Coward
4. Brave

19. Arrange the following parts in the correct sequence to form a meaningful sentence:

A. tell a lie to the teacher
B. he is between the devil
C. neither betray his friend nor
D. and the deep sea as he can

Choose the ***correct*** answer from the options given below:

1. A, C, B, D
2. B, D, C, A
3. C, B, D, A
4. D, A, B, C

20. Rearrange the following parts in the correct sequence to form a meaningful sentence
A. better known as the shifting cultivation
B. garia is a folk dance performed in
C. Tripura revolves around the Jhum culture,
D. Tripura where the life and culture of the people of

Choose the ***correct*** answer from the options given below:
1. C, A, B, D 2. D, C, B, A
3. A, B, D, C 4. B, D, C, A

21. Fill in the blank in the given sentence with the correct option:
The person who studies the structure and composition of the earth to know about its history and antiquity is called a ....
1. Botanist 2. Geologist
3. Cartographer 4. Geographer

22. The little priest was not an interesting man to look at, having stubby brown hair and a round and stolid face which did not give away anything.
The word STOLID in the above sentence means:
1. Frowning 2. Darkish
3. Emotionless 4. Hateful

23. Fill in the blanks in the sentences given in List-I with the appropriate words given in List-II.

List-I (Sentences)	**List-II (Words)**
A. The .... silence in the courtroom was broken only by the sound of a pen tapping.	I. eccentric
B. Her .... behaviour raised eyebrows at the otherwise formal event.	II. penetrating
C. The .... weather made the trek arduous for the beginners.	III. oppressive
D. The professor gave a .... analysis of the painting, revealing hidden layers of meaning.	IV. inclement

Choose the ***correct*** answer from the options given below:
1. A-I, B-III, C-II, D-IV
2. A-III, B-I, C-IV, D-II
3. A-II, B-IV, C-I, D-III
4. A-IV, B-II, C-III, D-I

24. Which of the following words does not refer to one of the movements of a horse?
1. Trotting 2. Cantering
3. Galloping 4. Spinning

25. Match the words given in List-I with the appropriate definitions in List-II.

List-I (Words)	**List-II (Definitions)**
A. Neurologist	I. one who treats heart diseases
B. Orthodontist	II. one who studies causes and diagnosis of diseases
C. Cardiologist	III. one who corrects and straightens irregular teeth
D. Pathologist	IV. one who cures nerve-related diseases

Choose the ***correct*** answer from the options given below:
1. A-I, B-III, C-IV, D-II
2. A-IV, B-III, C-I, D-II
3. A-II, B-IV, C-I, D-III
4. A-III, B-I, C-II, D-IV

26. Rearrange the following parts in the correct sequence to form a meaningful sentence
A. the lives of labourers
B. *Pahala Pandhav* is
C. Shrilal Shukla's
D. a realistic portrayal of

Choose the ***correct*** answer from the options given below:
1. A, B, C, D 2. A, B, D, C
3. B, A, D, C 4. C, B, D, A

27. Arrange the following parts in the correct sequence to form a meaningful sentence:

A. who is a doctor,
B. for his higher studies
C. has gone to America
D. my brother Jagan,

Choose the ***correct*** answer from the options given below:

1. A, D, B, C 2. B, C, D, A
3. D, A, C, B 4. C, A, D, B

28. Select the word closest in meaning to the word 'ARDUOUS' from the options given below:

1. Mysterious 2. Continuous
3. Supportive 4. Difficult

29. Match the words given in List-I with their corresponding definitions in List-II.

List-I (Words)	**List-II (Definitions)**
A. Meteorologist	I. One who studies election and trends in voting
B. Cosmologist	II. One who studies fossils and the history of life forms on the earth
C. Psephology	III. One who studies and predicts atmospheric phenomena
D. Paleontologist	IV. One who studies the universe, its origin, expanse etc.

Choose the ***correct*** answer from the options given below:

1. A-II, B-I, C-IV, D-III
2. A-IV, B-II, C-III, D-I
3. A-I, B-III, C-II, D-IV
4. A-III, B-IV, C-I, D-II

30. Rearrange the following parts in the correct sequence to form a meaningful sentence:

A. technology, political opinions, military capacities, education, lifestyle, inter alia
B. there has been growing awareness and rise in urge to be at par with
C. with increasing purchasing power and larger disposable incomes
D. current trends in different countries across the world in terms of science,

Choose the ***correct*** answer from the options given below:

1. D, B, C, A 2. A, B, C, D
3. C, B, D, A 4. C, A, B, D

31. Select the correct antonym for the word:

PLACATE

1. Provoke 2. Appease
3. Hate 4. Nullify

32. Select the correct antonym for the word:

PURGE

1. Contaminate 2. Truncate
3. Conceal 4. Complicate

33. Choose the correct synonym for the word:

DISDAIN

1. Astonish 2. Contempt
3. Destruction 4. Exhaustion

34. Select the correct expression to complete the sentence:

It .... since morning.

1. has been raining
2. has raining
3. will raining
4. rain

35. Rearrange the following parts in the correct sequence to form a meaningful sentence:

A. culture is a characteristic
B. the vision
C. way of life inspired by
D. and values of life.

Choose the ***correct*** answer from the options given below:

1. A, C, B, D 2. A, B, C, D
3. B, A, D, C 4. C, B, D, A

36. Select the correct antonym for the word:

BELLIGERENT

1. Brave 2. Friendly
3. Hostile 4. Bemused

37. Match the words given in List-I with the appropriate definitions in List-II.

List-I (Words)	List-II (Definitions)
A. Aviator	I. controls and operates the flight of an aircraft
B. Jurist	II. knows several languages, mainly foreign
C. Lexicographer	III. an expert in the legal field
D. Linguist	IV. writer of a dictionary

Choose the ***correct*** answer from the options given below:

1. A-I, B-II, C-IV, D-III
2. A-II, B-IV, C-III, D-I
3. A-I, B-III, C-IV, D-II
4. A-III, B-I, C-II, D-IV

38. Select the correct antonym for the word: Zenith

1. Horizon 2. Nadir
3. Savage 4. Sober

39. Select the correct expression to complete the sentence

What is the time .... ?

1. for your watch 2. at your watch
3. by your watch 4. from your watch

40. Choose the appropriate word to fill in the blank in the given sentence:

.... they had been waiting in line all night, I was sure they'd get the tickets for the show.

1. As though 2. Because of
3. Since 4. Until

41. Select the correct antonym for the word: INIQUITOUS

1. Unfair 2. Wicked
3. Virtuous 4. Hilarious

42. Choose the correct word from the given options to fill the blank in the sentence given below:

"Pakhom .... with him and the deal was closed at one thousand Rupees."

1. played
2. negotiated
3. disagreed
4. fought

43. Match the words given in List-I with their definitions in List-II.

List-I (Words)	List-II (Definitions)
A. Theology	I. A branch of philosophy that deals with the nature of existence
B. Epistemology	II. The study of the origin of the human race, its customs, beliefs and development
C. Ontology	III. A part of philosophy that deals with knowledge
D. Anthropology	IV. The study of religion and beliefs

Choose the ***correct*** answer from the options given below:

1. A-I, B-II, C-III, D-IV
2. A-I, B-III, C-II, D-IV
3. A-IV, B-III, C-I, D-II
4. A-III, B-IV, C-I, D-II

44. Match the idioms given in List-I with the underlined part of the sentences given in List-II.

List-I (Idioms)	List-II (Sentences)
A. turned over a new leaf	I. This unexpected new difficulty <u>roused me to do my best.</u>
B. set his face against	II. It is a matter of gratification that he <u>changed for the better.</u>

C. put me on my mettle	III. It is pointless to worry about the result before it's declared.
D. to meet trouble half-way	IV. As a social reformer, he sternly opposed child labour.

Choose the ***correct*** answer from the options given below:

1. A-I, B-II, C-III, D-IV
2. A-II, B-IV, C-I, D-III
3. A-II, B-I, C-IV, D-III
4. A-III, B-IV, C-I, D-II

45. Select the correct synonym for the word: BENEDICTION

1. benefit
2. forgiveness
3. blessing
4. calmness

46. Select the correct synonym for the word: EPHEMERAL

1. Putrid
2. Invisible
3. Temporary
4. Permanent

47. Rearrange the following parts in the correct sequence to form a meaningful sentence

A. producing harmones, proteins lend satiety, prevent
B. hunger pangs at bay, managing both weight and calories
C. apart from building muscle, repair tissues and
D. quick breakdown of sugar in the blood and keep

Choose the ***correct*** answer from the options given below:

1. C, A, D, B
2. A, B, C, D
3. D, C, A, B
4. D, B, C, A

48. Select the correct meaning of the underlined word in the sentence given below:

His desultory efforts at studying made it clear that he was not serious about passing the exam.

1. cautious
2. impetuous
3. guileful
4. unenthusiastic

49. Match the sentences given in List-I with the correct figures of speech given in List-II:

List-I (Sentences)	**List-II (Figures of speech)**
A. The wind whispered through the trees.	I. Alliteration
B. A plumber's house always has a leaking tap.	II. Oxymoron
C. She opened her eyes to the deafening silence	III. Irony
D. The buzzing bees drew attention.	IV. Personification

Choose the ***correct*** answer from the options given below:

1. A-IV, B-III, C-II, D-I
2. A-III, B-I, C-II, D-IV
3. A-I, B-IV, C-III, D-II
4. A-II, B-III, C-IV, D-I

50. Rearrange the following parts in the correct sequence to form a meaningful sentence:

A. had left before Namita
B. the large group
C. reached the venue for her performance
D. of Sattriya dancers

Choose the ***correct*** answer from the options given below:

1. B, C, A, D
2. B, A, D, C
3. B, D, A, C
4. C, B, D, A

BUSINESS STUDIES

1. Which of the following shows the relationship between planning and controlling?

1. Both reinforce each other
2. Both are unrelated to each other
3. Both are substitutes of each other
4. Both are seperable twins of management

2. Arrange the following steps involved in selection process in the proper sequence.

A. Preliminary screening
B. Employment interview
C. Reference and background checks
D. Selection test

Choose the ***correct*** answer from the options given below:

1. A, C, B, D 2. A, B, C, D
3. A, D, B, C 4. C, B, D, A

3. Which of the following is NOT a limitation of formal organisation?

1. No clear-cut structure
2. Social interaction
3. Personal satisfaction
4. Rigidly laid down policies

4. "Not being afraid of the risks associated with business and relying on one's capabilities to successfully manage these". Identify the entrepreneurial competency highlighted in the aforesaid statement.

1. Assertiveness 2. Persistence
3. Self-confidence 4. Systematic Planning

5. Which principle of management is violated if a worker takes orders from two or more superiors?

1. Unity of direction
2. Unity of command
3. Order
4. Discipline

6. Which of the following statements is NOT true?

1. Price is an important element of the marketing mix.
2. Marketing is a social process.
3. Use of agressive selling techniques to make customers buy their products is marketing.
4. Placement is described as the set of marketing tools that firms use in a target market.

7. Match List-I with List-II.

	List-I		**List-II**
A.	Standards	I.	Setting of Reduction of defects from 10 pc to 5 pc per lot
B.	Management by exception	II.	Assigning additional workers and equipment to the project.
C.	Critical Control Point	III.	An attempt to control everything results in controlling nothing.
D.	Corrective Action	IV.	Focusing on KRAs

Choose the ***correct*** answer from the options given below:

1. A-II, B-I, C-III, D-IV
2. A-I, B-III, C-IV, D-II
3. A-I, B-II, C-IV, D-III
4. A-III, B-I, C-IV, D-II

8. Which among the options given below is NOT a feature of management as a profession?

1. Restricted Entry
2. Professional Association
3. Service Motive
4. Personalised Application

9. Which of the following is a career oriented process?

1. Training
2. Development
3. Selection
4. Reference check

10. Arrange the following steps involved in the process of organising in logical sequence:

A. The activities which are similar in nature are grouped together.

B. Jobs are allocated to the members of each department in accordance to their skills and competencies.

C. Authority and reporting relationships are established to create a hierarchal structure.

D. The work is divided into manageable activities so that duplication can be avoided.

Choose the ***correct*** answer from the options given below:

1. A, C, B, D
2. A, B, C, D
3. D, A, B, C
4. C, B, D, A

11. The importance of the business environment includes:

A. Identifying first mover advantage

B. Improving business performance

C. Performance appraisal

D. Coping with rapid changes

Choose the ***correct*** answer from the options given below:

1. A, B, and D only
2. A, B, and C only
3. A, B, C and D
4. B, C, and D only

12. Match List-I with List-II.

	List-I		**List-II**
A.	Responsibility	I.	Right to command sub-ordinates and to give orders and exact obedience.
B.	Authority	II.	Downward transfer of authority from a superior to a subordinate.
C.	Accountability	III.	Obligation of a subordinate to perform the duty or tasks assigned to him.
D.	Delegation	IV.	Answerability for the accomplishment of the task assigned by the superior to his subordinate.

Choose the ***correct*** answer from the options given below:

1. A-II, B-I, C-III, D-IV
2. A-I, B-II, C-III, D-IV
3. A-III, B-I, C-IV, D-II
4. A-III, B-IV, C-I, D-II

13. Span of management refers to:

1. Number of subordinates at lower level
2. Total number of managers
3. Number of subordinates under a superior
4. Number of levels in the organisation

14. Match List-I with List-II.

	List-I (Dimensions of business environment)		**List-II (Elements)**
A.	Social	I.	Literacy rates
B.	Economic	II.	Public Debt (internal and external)
C.	Technological	III.	Monopolistic Restrictive Trade Practices Act
D.	Legal	IV.	Scientific improvements

Choose the ***correct*** answer from the options given below:

1. A-I, B-II, C-IV, D-III
2. A-II, B-I, C-III, D-IV
3. A-IV, B-II, C-I, D-III
4. A-III, B-IV, C-I, D-II

15. Match List-I with List-II.

	List-I		**List-II**
A.	Physiological needs	I.	Friendship
B.	Safety and Security needs	II.	Status
C.	Esteem needs	III.	Confirmed job
D.	Social needs	IV.	Food

Choose the ***correct*** answer from the options given below:

1. A-IV, B-III, C-II, D-I
2. A-I, B-II, C-III, D-IV
3. A-II, B-III, C-IV, D-I
4. A-III, B-IV, C-I, D-II

16. Identify the correct statements in the context of the planning.

A. Planning will be a futile exercise if it is not acted upon or implemented.

B. Planning implies a process which coordinates human efforts and assembles resources.

C. Planning is closely connected with creativity and innovation.

D. Planning is what managers at all levels do.

Choose the ***correct*** answer from the options given below:

1. A and B only
2. A, B and D only
3. A, C and D only
4. B and D only

17. Which of the following concepts is not related to F.W. Taylor?

1. Scalar Chain
2. Harmony, not discord
3. Standardisation and simplification of work
4. Cooperation, not individualism

18. In India, the advertisements for alcoholic beverages are banned, the dimension of business environment referred to here is:

1. Economic
2. Social
3. Political
4. Legal

19. Who is popularly known as the 'Father of Scientific Management'?

1. Frederick Taylor
2. A.H. Maslow
3. Douglas McGregor
4. Henry Fayol

20. Fayol says that discipline requires:

A. Good supervisors at all levels

B. Agreements should be clear and fair

C. Removal of the employee

D. Penalties should be fairly imposed

Choose the ***correct*** answer from the options given below:

1. A, B and D only
2. A, C and D only
3. A, B, C and D
4. B, C and D only

21. Arrange the following steps of the planning process in a logical sequence.

A. Establishing Objectives

B. Developing Premises

C. Evaluation of Alternatives

D. Selecting a Course of Action

Choose the ***correct*** answer from the options given below:

1. A, B, D, C
2. A, B, C, D
3. B, A, D, C
4. C, B, D, A

22. Management is considered as art because of which of the following features?

A. Systematized body of knowledge

B. Existence of theoretical knowledge

C. Personalized application

D. Being based on practice and creativity

Choose the ***correct*** answer from the options given below:

1. A, B and D only
2. A, B and C only
3. A, B, C and D
4. B, C and D only

23. When the demand of a product is inelastic, the firm is in a better position to fix?

1. Higher Prices
2. Lower Prices
3. Similar Prices
4. Competitive Prices

24. Money required for carrying out business activity is called:

1. Debt capital
2. Equity capital
3. Personal fund
4. Business Finance

25. To oversee the efforts of the workforce is the function of:

1. Supervisory level
2. Middle level
3. Top level
4. Top & middle level

26. Arrange the following steps involved in the process of financial planning in logical sequence.

A. Sales forecast is made.

B. Requirement of fixed capital and working capital is estimated.

C. Expected profits are estimated.

D. Sources of finance are identified.

Choose the ***correct*** answer from the options given below:

1. A, B, C, D
2. B, D, C, A
3. C, A, D, B
4. C, B, D, A

27. The criteria against which actual performance is measured in the process of controlling are called:

1. Grades
2. Classes
3. Standards
4. Appraisals

28. Arrange the following steps of controlling the process in a logical sequence.

A. Reporting of deviation and their causes after comparison.

B. Projecting the future and determining the goals and standards.

C. Taking corrective action at an appropriate level.

D. Measuring the work in terms of control standards.

Choose the ***correct*** answer from the options given below:

1. B, D, A, C
2. A, B, C, D
3. B, A, D, C
4. C, B, D, A

29. The nature of relationship of our country with foreign countries is an example of which dimension of the business environment?

1. Economic environment
2. Social environment
3. Legal environment
4. Political environment

30. Financial leverage is believed to be favorable if:

1. ROI is lower than cost of debt
2. ROI is higher than cost of debt
3. Debt is not easily available
4. If the interest rate is high

31. Match List-I with List-II.

	List-I		List-II
A.	Net Working Capital	I.	Investments in long term assets.
B.	Fixed Capital Decision	II.	Proportion of debt in the overall capital.
C.	Financial Leverage	III.	Excess of current assets over current liabilities.
D.	Trading on Equity	IV.	Increase in profit earned by the equity shareholders due to the presence of fixed financial charges.

Choose the ***correct*** answer from the options given below:

1. A-IV, B-II, C-III, D-I
2. A-I, B-II, C-III, D-IV
3. A-II, B-I, C-IV, D-III
4. A-III, B-I, C-II, D-IV

32. The process of earning profits and increasing wealth while posing characteristics such as risk taking, management, leadership and innovation is called:

1. Business development
2. Entrepreneurship
3. Planning
4. Business Process

33. "Planning requires logical and systematic thinking rather than guess work or wishful thinking". Identify the feature of planning highlighted in the aforesaid statement.

1. Planning is futuristic
2. Planning involves decision making
3. Planning is a mental exercise
4. Planning is pervasive

34. .... is an impersonal form of communication by a marketer to promote a product.

1. Personal Selling
2. Advertising
3. Labelling
4. Packaging

35. Identify the type of plan which provides the prescribed ways or manner in which a task has to be performed considering the objective?

1. Rules
2. Strategies
3. Method
4. Procedures

36. Which of the following is the importance of delegation?

A. High morale of subordinates
B. Develops initiatives among employees
C. Promotes centralisation
D. Dilutes span of management

Choose the ***correct*** answer from the options given below:

1. A, B and D only
2. A and B only
3. B and D only
4. B, C and D only

37. Under which method of the training, a trainee is put under the guidance of a master worker?

1. Apprenticeship programme
2. Internship training
3. Vestibule training
4. Job rotation

38. The process whereby an executive develops an orderly pattern of group effort among his subordinates and secures unity of action is known as:

1. Control
2. Coordination
3. Reporting
4. Organising

39. Classifying products into different groups on the basis of their important features is called:

1. Grading
2. Branding
3. Labelling
4. Packaging

40. "Marketing methods used" is an important factor affecting which 'P' of marketing mix?

1. Product
2. Place
3. Price
4. Promotion

Directions (Qs. No. 41-45): *Read the given passage and answer the questions that follow:*

Manoj purchased a car from DD Motors invoiced at 10 lacs. The company offered many attractive gifts, like free insurance for the first two years, free pick-up and drop facilities for free servicing of upto 20,000 km etc. But after a few days, he noticed that the pick-up of the car was not good and there was some problem with the engine of the car. The company serviced the car for free, but even then, Manoj was not satisfied with the performance of the car. Manoj again called the customer care services of DD Motors, but DD Motors did not give him the due response. So he filed a complaint with the District Commission after but was not satisfied with the decision. He was very disturbed and, after a month, decided to appeal against it.

41. Manoj filed a complaint with the District Commission but was not satisfied with the decision. To which authority can he file an appeal against the decision?

1. National Commission
2. National Law Commission
3. State Commission
4. Supreme Court

42. Which rights of Manoj are violated by DD Motors?

1. Right to be informed and Right to safety
2. Right to be heard and Right to seek redressal
3. Right to choose/be assured and Right to safety
4. Right to consumer education and Right to be heard

43. Which of the following relief is NOT available to Manoj?

1. To remove the defect in car
2. To replace the defective car with a new one
3. To return the car and get refund of the price paid for the car
4. To retain the car and get a refund of the price paid for the car

44. Which of the following ways/means of consumer protection has been indicated in the above case?
1. Self regulation by the business
2. Business associations
3. Consumer organisations
4. Consumer awareness

45. Identify the responsibility which Manoj kept in mind in the above case?
1. Read labels carefully
2. Obtaining Bill/Invoice
3. Focusing on gifts only
4. Having a driving license

Directions (Qs. No. 46-50): *Read the given passage and answer the questions that follow:*

Sarah is the manager of a customer service team at a growing e-commerce company. The company has recently faced an influx of customer queries due to an increase in online orders. As the manager, Sarah's role is crucial in ensuring her team is aligned with the company's goals and capable of meeting the growing demand.

To begin, Sarah holds a team meeting where she clearly communicates the new expectations for handling customer inquiries, including targets for response times and quality standards. She provides clear guidelines on how to manage the increased workload and sets specific deadlines for individual tasks. Sarah integrates employees' efforts and ensures that the team understands the importance of customer satisfaction and how it contributes to the company's reputation and success.

Additionally, Sarah motivates her team by recognizing their achievements, offering constructive feedback, and providing training sessions to improve their skills. She fosters open communication, encouraging her team to express any challenges they encounter. Her leadership style includes delegation of responsibilities, which helps employees feel trusted and empowered.

Under Sarah's direction, the team becomes more efficient, delivering timely and high-quality customer service, which ultimately boosts customer satisfaction and supports the company's growth.

46. Which of the following is a key responsibility of Sarah when directing a team?
1. Establishing budget
2. Planning company strategy
3. Preparing a setting for initiating action
4. Hiring new employees

47. Which element of directing, does Sarah follow in encouraging employees to meet performance standards?
1. Delegation
2. Decentralisation
3. Control
4. Motivation

48. The above case clearly depicts that directing is the heart of management because Sarah:
1. Ensures managers plan all the work
2. Empowers employees and improves their engagement
3. Reduces employee responsibility
4. Limits feedback opportunities

49. What is the primary purpose of directing in management?
1. Setting company goals
2. Communicating with employees and guiding their actions
3. Developing new products
4. Analyzing market trends

50. Effective communication of Sarah in directing helps to:
1. Align employee efforts with organizational goals
2. Create confusion
3. Increase turnover
4. Avoid delegating tasks

GENERAL TEST

1. Jatin is ninth from the front in a column of boys. There were thrice as many behind him as there were in front. How many boys are there between Jatin and the fifth boy from the end of the column?

1. 33 2. 20
3. 21 4. 19

2. Earth Hour, the voluntary one hour blackout observed by 187 countries on 23rd day of March every year, to mark a battle against global warming, was first organized by which organization of the following:

1. Green Peace
2. World Health Organization
3. World Wildlife Fund for Nature
4. People for Ethical Treatment of Animals

3. Which one of the following is credited as the 'pioneer of rocket technology' in India?

1. Haider Ali 2. Sher Shah Suri
3. Tipu Sultan 4. Alauddin Khilji

4. C is to the East of B, which is to the North of D. If A is to the South of D, then in which general direction of C is A?

1. South 2. South-West
3. North 4. North-East

5. Earthquake refers to the vibration on the earth's surface caused by catastrophic endogenetic forces.

A. The magnitude or intensity of energy released by an earthquake is not measured by the modified Mercalli Intensity Scale.
B. The place on the ground surface which is perpendicular to the focus is called the epicenter.
C. Seismology is the special branch of geology that deals with the study of earthquakes.
D. Shadow zones are some specific areas where earthquake waves do not occur or occur rarely.

Choose the ***correct*** answer from the options given below:

1. A, B and D only
2. A, C and D only
3. A, B and C only
4. B, C and D only

6. A, B, C, D, E, F and G are sitting around a circular table facing the center. E is second to the right of F, who is sitting on the immediate right of C. A & D are the only persons sitting between G & E.

A. B is third to the right of G.
B. C is the immediate right of G.
C. D is the immediate right of B.
D. G is second to the left of F.

Choose the ***correct*** answer from the options given below:

1. C. and D only 2. A, B and D only
3. A, B and C only 4. A, B, C and D

7. Arrange the sequence of national events in the order of their occurrence.

A. Inauguration of Prerna Sthal.
B. Droupadi Murmu takes oath as the 15th President of India.
C. Karpoori Thakur, referred to as 'Jan Nayak', became the 49th recipient of the Bharat Ratna.
D. India became the first country to prepare a full list of fauna, called 'Fauna of India'.

Choose the ***correct*** answer from the options given below:

1. A, B, C, D 2. B, A, D, C
3. B, C, A, D 4. C, B, D, A

8. A trader sells wheat at 10% profit and uses weight 10% less than the actual measure. What is his actual percentage gain?

1. 18.18% 2. 20%
3. 22.22% 4. 10%

9. Choose the number which is different from the others.

1. 295 2. 552
3. 729 4. 906

10. Which of the following is called the 'Tiger of the Ganges' along with the distinction of being the 'National Aquatic Animal'?

1. Ghariyal
2. Dolphin
3. Royal Bengal Tiger
4. Hippopotamus

11. How many degrees will the hour hand move, in the time within which the minute hand moves 240°?

1. 20° 2. 18°
3. 24° 4. 22°

12. 'Amar Sonar Bangla', the national anthem of present day Bangladesh was written by which of the following poets?

1. Bankim Das Chatterjee
2. Rabindra Nath Tagore
3. Ashfaq Ullah Khan
4. Sarojini Naidu

13. Who among the following emperors fought the 'First Battle of Panipat'?

1. Babur and Sikandar Lodhi
2. Akbar and Hemu
3. Humayun and Sher Shah Suri
4. Babur and Ibrahim Lodhi

14. When seen through a mirror, an analog clock shows quarter to four. The correct time shows by the clock:

1. 9:15 2. 9:45
3. 8:15 4. 8:45

15. If the slant height of a cone is decreased by 15 per cent and the radius of its base is increased by 20 per cent, then by what per cent will its curved surface area change?

1. 2 per cent decrease
2. 2.5 per cent decrease
3. 2.5 per cent increase
4. 2 per cent increase

16. Match the following missions to their respective purposes:

List-I (Mission)	**List-II (Purpose)**
A. Chandrayaan-3	I. Development and launch of a dual-frequency synthetic aperture radar satellite
B. Gaganyaan-3	II. Attempt for soft landing on moon
C. NISAR	III. Solar Observatory Mission
D. Aditya-L1	IV. India's first crewed (human) space mission

Choose the ***correct*** answer from the options given below:

1. A-II, B-IV, C-I, D-III.
2. A-I, B-III, C-II, D-IV.
3. A-IV, B-I, C-III, D-II.
4. A-III, B-IV, C-I, D-II.

17. Manish is eighteenth from the right end and Rahul is fifth from the left end in a row of boys. If there are seven boys between Manish and Rahul, how many boys are there in the row?

1. 29 2. 30
3. 31 4. 41

18. The partition of Bengal in 1905 was realized during the Viceroyship of:

1. Lord Mountbatten
2. Lord Dalhousie
3. Lord Irwin
4. Lord Curzon

19. Trace out the figure, from among the following options, in which the figure (X) is embedded:

(X)

1. 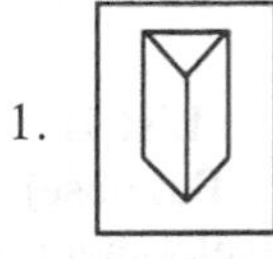
2. 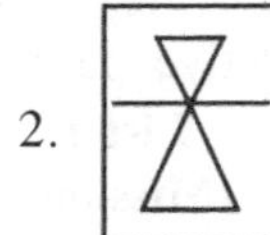
3. 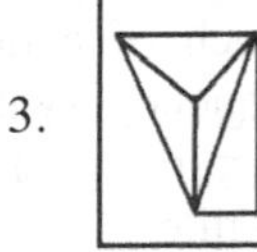
4. 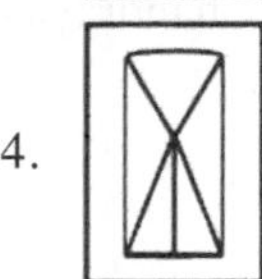

20. A bag contains 3 red, 2 blue, 5 green and 4 yellow balls. If two balls are picked at random, what is the probability that either both are red or both are blue?

1. 1/7
2. 3/91
3. 4/91
4. 5/91

21. The sum of n terms of the series

$$1+\frac{3}{2}+2+\frac{5}{2}+3+\frac{7}{2}+\ldots\ldots$$

1. $\frac{n(n+1)}{2}$
2. $\frac{n(n+3)}{4}$
3. $\frac{(n+1)(n+2)}{4}$
4. $\frac{n(n+3)}{2}$

22. The component of the blood which helps to fight infections is:

1. Erythrocytes
2. Plasma
3. Platelets
4. Leukocytes

23. A boy travels between point A and point B at a speed of 6 km/h and returns at a speed of 9 km/h. If the total time taken by him is 1 hour 15 min, the distance between A and B is:

1. 6.5 km
2. 5.5 km
3. 4.5 km
4. 9 km

24. In the given question, a statement is followed by two assumptions. You have to decide which of the assumptions is implicit in the statement and choose your answer accordingly.

Statement: Over The Top (OTT) platform has become indispensable for the entertainment of people.

Assumptions:

I. People enjoy watching content on OTT.
II. OTT is the only medium of entertainment.

1. Only assumption II is implicit.
2. Only assumption I is implicit.
3. Both I and II are implicit.
4. Neither I nor II is implicit.

25. In the letter series, some of the letters are missing, which are given in the alternatives A, B, C and D.

m n o n o p q o p q r _ _ _ _ s t u

A. r B. s
C. q D. p

Choose the ***correct*** sequence from the options given below:

1. C, B, D, A
2. A, B, C, D
3. B, A, D, C
4. B, D, C, A

26. The value of gravity (g) on the Moon is .... of that on the earth's surface.

1. 1/2
2. 1/3
3. 1/6
4. 1/9

27. In the given question, find out which of the following answer figures completes the figure matrix?

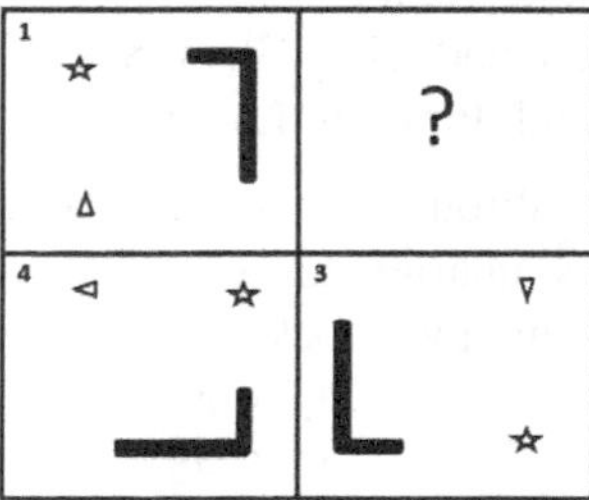

1. 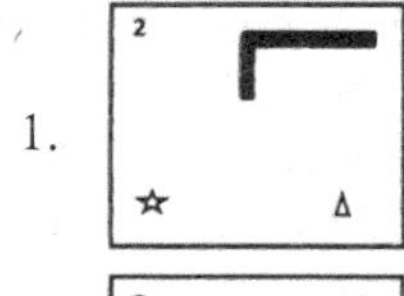
2. 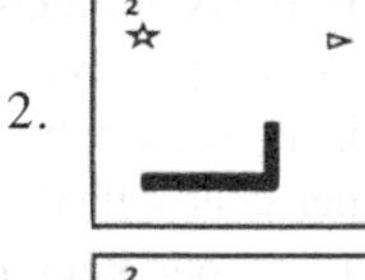
3. 
4. 

28. P and Q together can do a piece of work in 60 days. Q and R together can do it in 120 days. P and R together can do it in 90 days. In what time can Q alone do the same work?

1. 144 days
2. 720 days
3. 360 days
4. 720/7 days

29. Soap consists of:

1. Alkali salts of higher fatty acids
2. Calcium carbonate, aluminum silicate and gypsum
3. Sodium silicate and silicate of a base, like calcium or lead
4. Sodium silicate and ammonium nitrate

30. Match List-I with List-II.

List-I	List-II
A. Remainder when 17^{35234} is divided by 8	I. 0
B. Remainder when 4444 is divided by 9	II. 1
C. Unit's digit of $(34)^{15} + (34)^{16}$	III. 2
D. Unit digit of $7^4 - 9^3$	IV. 7

Choose the ***correct*** answer from the options given below:

1. A-II, B-IV, C-I, D-III.
2. A-I, B-II.. C-III, D-IV.
3. A-II, B-IV, C-III, D-I.
4. A-IV, B-II, C-I, D-III.

31. The number of diagonals in a Hexagon is:

1. 6
2. 7
3. 8
4. 9

32. The figures X, Y and Z given below show a sequence of folding of paper. The fig. (Z) shows the manner in which the folded paper has been cut. Choose from the answer figures given in options which would most closely resemble the unfolded form of fig. (Z).

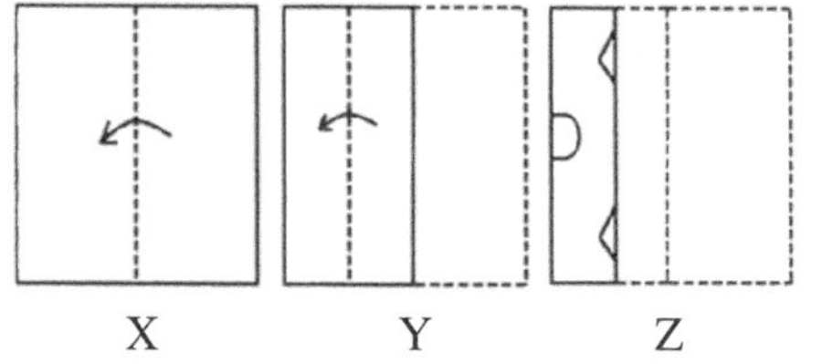

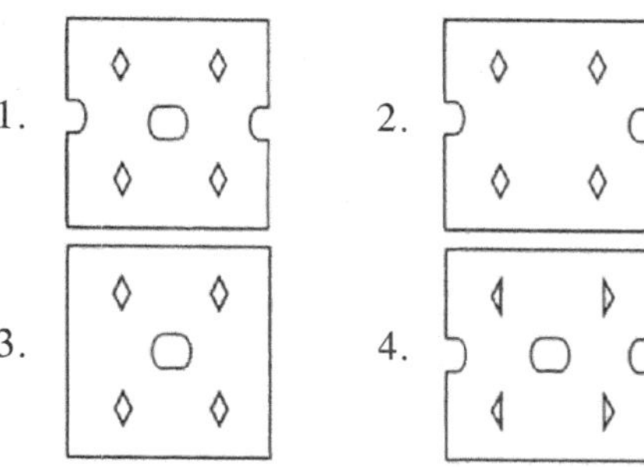

33. If the area of an equilateral triangle is $36\sqrt{3}$ cm^2, then the length of the side is:

1. 12 cm
2. 9 cm
3. 6 cm
4. 3 cm

34. Arrange the sequence of the stages of human progress in order of their occurrence.

A. The Palaeolithic Age
B. The Chalcolithic Age
C. The Neolithic Age
D. The Mesolithic Age

Choose the ***correct*** answer from the options given below:

1. A, B, C, D
2. B, A, D, C
3. D, A, B, C
4. A, D, C, B

35. Select a suitable figure from the answer figures which will substitute this question mark so that a series is formed in order.

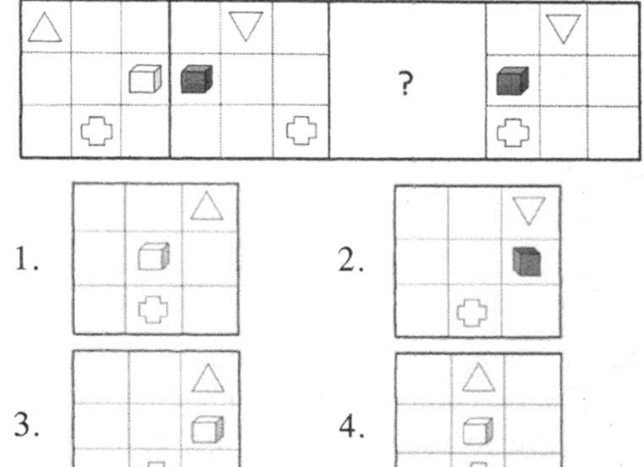

36. The sum of the digits of a 4-digit number is subtracted from the number. The resulting number is always:

1. divisible by 6
2. divisible by 9
3. divisible by 4
4. divisible by 8

37. Trace out the alternative figure from among the following options in which the figure (X) is embedded (rotation is not allowed):

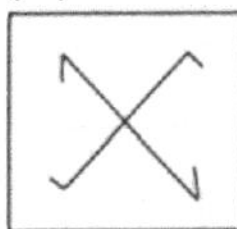

(X)

1. 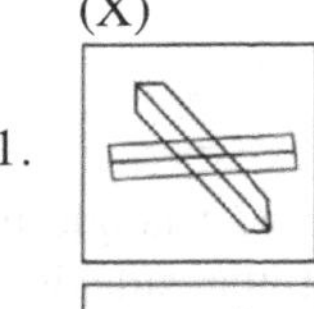
2. 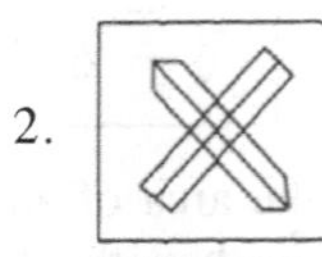
3. 
4. 

38. 3 men or 15 boys can do a piece of work in 30 days. In how many days will 2 men and 5 boys do this work?

1. 15 days
2. 25 days
3. 30 days
4. 40 days

39. The nearest integer to 6650 which is exactly divisible by 429 is:

1. 6864
2. 6435
3. 6436
4. 6535

40. Which of the following nicknames would you most likely relate to Thailand?

1. Land of Thousand Elephants
2. Land of Morning Calm
3. Land of White Elephants
4. Land of Tigers

41. If 10% of X = 15% of Y = 1/5 of Z, then X : Y : Z is:

1. 6 : 3 : 4
2. 10 : 15 : 18
3. 15 : 10 : 18
4. 6 : 4 : 3

42. In the given question, a statement is followed by two conclusions numbered I and II. You have to assume everything in the statement to be true, then consider the two conclusions together and decide which of them logically follows beyond a reasonable doubt from the information given in the statement.

Statement: Birds of same feather flock together.

Conclusions:

I. Similar people tend to associate with each other.

II. A group of birds have beautiful feathers.

1. Only conclusion I follows
2. Only conclusion II follows
3. Both I and II follow
4. Neither I nor II follows

43. Choose the correct water image of the given figure, amongst the following answer figures:

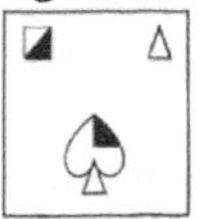

1. 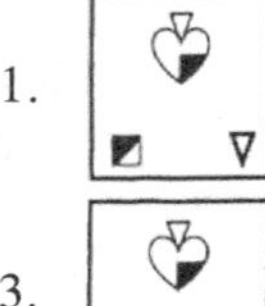
2. 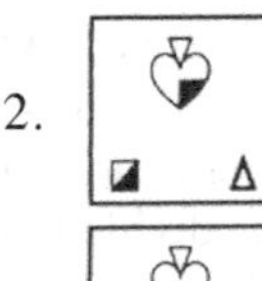
3. 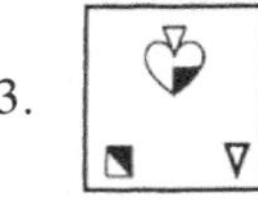
4. 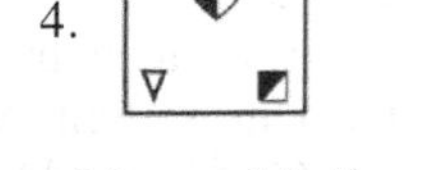

44. The relation between Mean, Median and Mode for symmetrical distribution is:

1. Mode = 2 Median – 5 Mean
2. Mode = 4 Median – Mean
3. Mean = Median = Mode
4. Mode = 2 Median = Mean

45. Which one of the following answer figures completes the figure matrix given below:

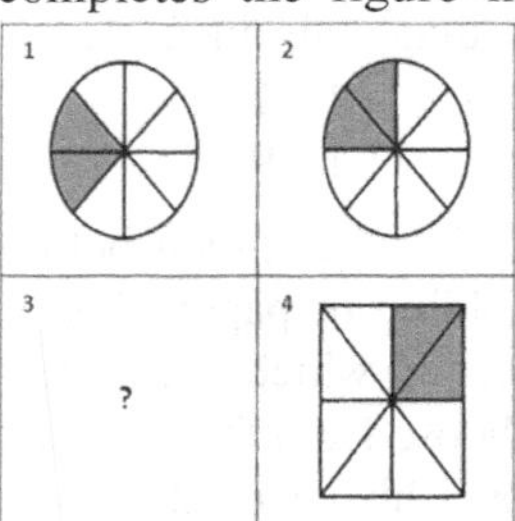

1. 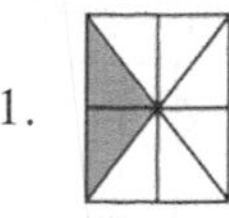
2. 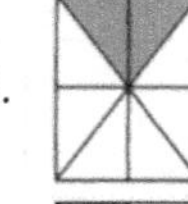
3. 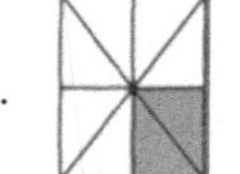 
4. 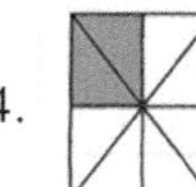

46. Mohiniyattam is a solo female dance form known for its rhythmic and unbroken flow of body movements.

A. The love and devotion to god Vishnu is usually the theme of this dance form.

B. This dance form belongs to the state of Andhra Pradesh.

C. Mohiniyattam has the grace and elegance of Bharatanatyam and the vigor of Kathakali.

D. The dancers attire in a beautiful white and gold bordered Kasavu sari with distinctive white jasmine flowers around a French bun at the side of her head.

Choose the ***correct*** answer from the options given below:

1. A, B and C only
2. A, B and D only
3. A, C and D only
4. B, C and D only

47. The question below consists of a question and two statements numbered I and II given below it. You have to decide whether the data provided in the statements is sufficient to answer the question.

The last Tuesday of February 2024 fell on which date?

I. The first Tuesday of that month fell on 6th.

II. The last day of that month was Thursday.

1. The data in the statement I alone is sufficient to answer the question.
2. The data in the statement II alone is sufficient to answer the question.
3. The data in both statements I and II together are necessary to answer the question.
4. The data either in statement I alone or in statement II alone are sufficient to answer the question.

48. By looking in a mirror, it appears that it is 6:05 on an analog clock. What is the actual time?

1. 11:30
2. 5:50
3. 5:55
4. 11:28

49. For what value of k, the system of equations $3x - ky - 3 = 0$ and $2x - 3y - 4 = 0$ has no solution?

1. 6
2. 9
3. 5
4. 9/2

50. Paris Olympics 2024 was held in the vicinity of which river?

1. Seine
2. Thames
3. Colorado
4. Nile

EXPLANATORY ANSWERS

ENGLISH LANGUAGE

1. **(1):** Being truthful is the most important sign of virtuosity: This point is not found in the passage. The author emphasizes virtues like magnanimity, helpfulness, sacrifice, and righteousness, but never mentions truthfulness as a key virtue Therefore, this option is correctly identified as not mentioned.

2. **(4):** The term "mortal frame" refers to the human body, which is described as perishable. The passage suggests that if the body is not used for the benefit of others, it serves no noble purpose. Thus, using one's life selflessly is seen as true virtue.

3. **(4):** The virtuous deviate from their path, if they aren't duly acknowledged: This is not true as per the passage. It clearly states that virtuous people stay committed to righteousness, regardless of praise, wealth, or life span. The Sanskrit couplet confirms this idea strongly.

4. **(3):** Trees bearing fruit and flowers spreading fragrance: These acts are beneficial but do not show "endurance" or suffering. The passage defines endurance through actions like facing the sun's heat or being pressed or pierced. Hence, this option does not truly reflect endurance.

5. **(3):** The passage identifies Pyarimohan as Uma's husband, especially when it says "a glance of utter supplication at her husband's face."

This clearly establishes that the bond between them is marital, not paternal or fraternal. His commanding tone and her pleading reaction further indicate a traditional husband-wife relationship.

6. **(2):** The word "eccentric" in "eccentric spelling" means that Uma wrote words in a peculiar and incorrect manner. Since she was newly literate, her spellings were likely unconventional. The passage implies she spelled words phonetically or in her own unique way, not neatly or correctly.

7. **(1):** Uma couldn't sing and felt deep pain because of it. She started writing songs she heard as a way to reduce this sorrow. The passage clearly states she developed this habit "to lessen the pain of not being able to sing," which makes option 1 the accurate reason.

8. **(4):** "Utter supplication" means a deep and humble plea. Uma looks at her husband with such a pleading expression, silently begging him not to take away her book. The tone is one of desperation and emotional appeal, fitting the meaning of request and prayer.

9. **(1):** The word "puerile" means childish or immature. In the passage, the thought that achieving fame and success could still be possible is called "puerile," indicating that Deven himself sees it as naive or juvenile, not grounded in reality.

10. **(2):** The phrase "other game to hunt in the forest" is metaphorical. Here, "game" symbolizes ambitions or goals like success, art, poetry, and fame that Deven feels he failed to pursue due to his constant search for solace or comfort.

11. **(2, 4):** Both "mournful" and "disillusioned" tones are present in the passage. The narrator expresses mournful regret over missed opportunities and failed ambitions. At the same time, there is a clear sense of disillusionment—he once hoped for recognition, poetry, success, and meaning, but now sees all those dreams shattered. He even calls his hope "puerile," showing that he no longer believes in it.

    Therefore, the combined tone is rightly described as mournful and disillusioned, and 2 & 4 is the correct answer.

12. **(3):** Deven blames his father's weakness, which he believes was passed on to him. He feels this inherited trait made both of them ineffectual in life. He sees it as a black hole inside him that prevented him from achieving anything meaningful.

13. **(1):** The correct sequence is: Neruda conceives poetry not as something which has (B), its deliberate relation with things of beauty, but rather as an art which (C), peeps into the dark abyss of human consciousness, (A), something which has the ability to perceive suffering (D). This order forms a logical and grammatically correct sentence describing Neruda's view of poetry.

14. **(4):** Hegemony means dominance or leadership, especially by one state or group over others. The opposite of dominance is independence, where no control or influence is exerted by another power. Hence, Independence is the correct antonym.

15. **(3):** The meaningful sentence is: Ask them to get together (B), in fours and decide on (D), the three best hypotheses (A), the group has come up with (C). This sequence maintains proper structure and meaning in a collaborative task context.

16. **(3):** (A) - (IV), (B) - (I), (C) - (II), (D) - (III)
    - (A) To hit the nail on the head (IV) – means to describe exactly what is causing a situation.
    - (B) To add insult to injury (I) – means to make a bad situation worse.
    - (C) To put the cart before the horse (II) – means to do things in the wrong order.
    - (D) To build castles in the air (III) – means to make unrealistic plans or dreams.

17. **(1):** The word "disconcerting" refers to something that causes discomfort, confusion, or embarrassment. It unsettles a person and makes them feel uneasy or awkward. Among the given options, "embarrassing" is the closest synonym in both tone and meaning.

18. **(3):** "Valiant" means showing courage, bravery, or heroism. Its direct opposite would be someone who lacks courage, i.e., a "coward." A coward avoids danger or challenge due to fear, which is the antonym of being valiant.

19. **(2):** The correct sentence is: He is between the devil (B), and the deep sea as he can (D), neither betray his friend nor (C), tell a lie to the teacher (A). This describes a dilemma with no good outcome.

20. **(4):** The meaningful sentence is: Garia is a folk dance performed in (B), Tripura where the life and culture of the people of (D), Tripura

revolves around the Jhum culture, (C), better known as the shifting cultivation (A). This forms a coherent and informative statement.

21. **(2):** A geologist studies the Earth's structure, materials, and processes to understand its history and formation. The question mentions learning about the Earth's structure and antiquity, which directly relates to the work of a geologist, not a geographer or cartographer.

22. **(3):** The term "stolid" means showing little or no emotion. In the sentence, the priest's face "did not give away anything," which supports the meaning of being unexpressive or emotionless.

23. **(2):** (A) - (III), (B) - (I), (C) - (IV), (D) - (II)
    (A) **Oppressive silence:** Refers to a tense, heavy quietness, often making people feel uncomfortable or pressured—common in intense places like courtrooms.
    (B) **Eccentric behaviour:** Means odd or unusual conduct; at a formal event, such behaviour would naturally draw attention.
    (C) **Inclement weather:** Describes harsh or severe weather—like rain, storms, or cold—making physical activity like trekking difficult.
    (D) **Penetrating analysis:** Means a deep and insightful examination that uncovers hidden details or meanings, often used in intellectual or academic contexts.

24. **(4):** Trotting, cantering, and galloping are standard horse gaits, each indicating a specific speed or movement pattern. Spinning, however, is not a recognized horse gait and does not describe movement used in equestrian contexts.

25. **(2):** (A) - (IV), (B) - (III), (C) - (I), (D) - (II)
    (A) **Neurologist:** treats nervous system disorders (IV)
    (B) **Orthodontist:** specializes in correcting teeth alignment (III)
    (C) **Cardiologist:** deals with heart-related issues (I)
    (D) **Pathologist:** studies disease causes and diagnosis (II)

26. **(4):** The correct sequence is: Shrilal Shukla's (C), *Pahala Pandhav* is (B), a realistic portrayal of (D), the lives of labourers (A). This forms a clear and meaningful sentence introducing the author and theme of the work.

27. **(3):** The sentence becomes: My brother Jagan, (D) who is a doctor, (A) has gone to America (C) for his higher studies (B). This flows smoothly and logically describes the subject and his action.

28. **(4):** The word "arduous" means something that is difficult, strenuous, or requiring great effort. It does not relate to mystery, supportiveness, or continuity, making "difficult" the correct synonym.

29. **(4):** (A) - (III), (B) - (IV), (C) - (I), (D) - (II)
    (A) Meteorologist - (III): A meteorologist studies and predicts weather and atmospheric conditions such as rainfall, storms, and temperature changes.
    (B) Cosmologist - (IV): A cosmologist is concerned with the study of the universe, including its origin, structure, and overall dynamics like the Big Bang theory.
    (C) Psephology - (I): Psephology is the branch of political science that deals with the study of elections and voting trends.
    (D) Paleontologist - (II): A paleontologist examines fossils and ancient life forms to understand Earth's biological history.
    Each word is matched with its correct scientific field, making Option 4 the correct answer.

30. **(3):** The sentence reads: With increasing purchasing power and larger disposable incomes (C), there has been growing awareness and rise in urge to be at par with (B), current trends in different countries across the world in terms of science, (D), technology, political opinions, military capacities, education, lifestyle, inter alia (A). This sequence builds logically from cause to effect and covers all aspects clearly.

31. **(1):** Placate means to calm, pacify, or soothe someone who is angry. The opposite of calming is to provoke, which means to stir up anger or annoyance. Therefore, provoke is the correct antonym.

32. **(1):** Purge means to cleanse or remove impurities. The opposite would be to make something impure or dirty, which is contaminate. So, contaminate is the correct antonym.

33. **(2):** Disdain means a strong feeling of dislike or contempt for someone or something considered unworthy. It does not relate to astonishment or exhaustion. Hence, contempt is the correct synonym.

34. **(1):** The sentence refers to a continuous action starting in the past and still ongoing, which calls for the present perfect continuous tense. So, "It has been raining since morning" is grammatically correct.

35. **(1):** The sentence reads: Culture is a characteristic (A), way of life inspired by (C), the vision (B), and values of life (D). This sequence is grammatically logical and meaningful.

36. **(2):** Belligerent means hostile or aggressive, especially in a confrontational way. The opposite of being aggressive is friendly, which indicates a peaceful and kind attitude. Hence, friendly is the correct antonym.

37. **(3):** (A) - (I), (B) - (III), (C) - (IV), (D) - (II)

(A) **Aviator – (I):** One who operates or flies aircraft.

(B) **Jurist – (III):** A legal expert or authority in law.

(C) **Lexicographer – (IV):** A person who writes or compiles dictionaries.

(D) **Linguist – (II):** Someone who knows or studies multiple languages, especially foreign ones.

38. **(2):** Zenith means the highest point or peak. Its antonym is nadir, which means the lowest point. The two are direct opposites in figurative and literal usage, making nadir the correct answer.

39. **(3):** The correct phrase is "What is the time by your watch?", which is the standard and idiomatic way of asking someone the time based on their watch. Other options are grammatically or idiomatically incorrect.

40. **(3):** The sentence is giving a reason for the speaker's certainty that the people would get the tickets. "Since" means because, which fits perfectly: "Since they had been waiting in line all night..." conveys both cause and context.

41. **(3):** Iniquitous means extremely wicked, immoral, or unjust. The correct antonym is virtuous, which refers to someone who is morally good, righteous, or ethical. Hence, virtuous is the correct opposite.

42. **(2):** The sentence "Pakhom .... with him and the deal was closed at one thousand Rupees" refers to reaching a deal. The word negotiated best fits here, as it means discussing terms to arrive at an agreement. Other options do not suit the context of closing a deal.

43. **(3):** (A) - (IV), (B) - (III), (C) - (I), (D) - (II)

(A) **Theology – (IV):** Theology is the study of religion and beliefs, focusing on divine concepts, scriptures, and spiritual matters.

(B) **Epistemology – (III):** Epistemology is a branch of philosophy that deals with knowledge—its nature, sources, and limits.

(C) **Ontology – (I):** Ontology studies the nature of existence and being, examining what entities exist and how they relate.

(D) **Anthropology – (II):** Anthropology is the study of human beings, including their origins, development, cultural customs, and evolution.

44. **(2):** (A) - (II), (B) - (IV), (C) - (I), (D) - (III)

(A) **Turned over a new leaf – (II):** This idiom means to reform or start afresh, which matches the sentence where someone changed for the better.

(B) **Set his face against – (IV):** This means to firmly oppose something, matching the context of sternly opposing child labour.

(C) **Put me on my mettle – (I):** Means to test someone's strength or ability, as in the sentence about a difficulty that made someone do their best.

(D) **To meet trouble half-way – (III):** Refers to anticipating or worrying about trouble before it happens, matching the idea of worrying before results are declared.

45. **(3):** Benediction means a blessing or expression of good wishes, especially at the end of a religious service. Among the options, blessing is the most accurate synonym.

46. **(3):** Ephemeral means lasting for a very short time. The best synonym among the options is temporary, which also refers to something not permanent or enduring.

47. **(1):** The sentence becomes:

(C) Apart from building muscle, repair tissues and

(A) producing hormones, proteins lend satiety, prevent

(D) quick breakdown of sugar in the blood and keep

(B) hunger pangs at bay, managing both weight and calories.

This arrangement logically explains the multiple roles of proteins in the body.

48. **(4):** Desultory means lacking a plan, purpose, or enthusiasm. In the sentence, it reflects that his studying was aimless and showed no real effort, making unenthusiastic the correct meaning.

49. **(1):** (A) - (IV), (B) - (III), (C) - (II), (D) - (I)
(A) The wind whispered... – Personification (IV): giving human traits to wind
(B) A plumber's house always has a leaking tap – Irony (III): unexpected contradiction
(C) Deafening silence – Oxymoron (II): two opposite terms used together
(D) Buzzing bees... – Alliteration (I): repetition of initial consonant sounds

50. **(3):** The correct sequence is:
(B) The large group
(D) of Sattriya dancers
(A) had left before Namita
(C) reached the venue for her performance.
This order forms a clear, grammatically correct sentence.

BUSINESS STUDIES

1. **(1):** Planning and controlling are interrelated and mutually reinforcing functions of management. Planning sets objectives and outlines what needs to be done, while controlling ensures that actual performance aligns with the planned objectives. If deviations are found during controlling, it leads to revision in plans, and thus, the cycle continues.

2. **(3):** The correct order of the selection process is:
(A) Preliminary Screening – initial shortlisting of applications,
(D) Selection Test – to evaluate candidate's aptitude or skills,
(B) Employment Interview – face-to-face assessment,
(C) Reference and Background Checks – verification of candidate's credibility and past records.

3. **(4):** A major limitation of formal organisation is its dependence on fixed rules, procedures, and rigidly laid down policies. This restricts flexibility and adaptability in decision-making. Employees must follow strict hierarchies and cannot easily take initiative or respond quickly to dynamic situations. While formal structure ensures order and clarity, its rigidity often reduces creativity and slows response to change.

4. **(3):** The statement highlights the entrepreneur's belief in their own ability to face business risks and manage successfully. This reflects self-confidence, which is a core entrepreneurial competency involving assurance in one's own decisions and actions.

5. **(2):** According to Fayol's principles of management, unity of command states that each employee should receive orders from only one superior. Violation leads to confusion, conflict, and inefficiency in operations.

6. **(3, 4): Use of aggressive selling techniques to make customers buy their products is marketing:** This statement is not true because marketing is a broader concept that focuses on identifying customer needs and satisfying them through value creation, not just pushing products through aggressive selling. Modern marketing emphasizes customer satisfaction, building relationships, and delivering value, whereas aggressive selling is a narrow and outdated view.
(4): Placement is described as the set of marketing tools that firms use in a target market: This is also not true. The set of marketing tools used by firms in a target market is known as the marketing mix, which includes Product, Price, Place (Placement), and Promotion — commonly referred to as the 4Ps. "Placement" alone refers only to distribution or the way the product reaches the consumer, not the entire set of tools. Hence, both options 3 and 4 are NOT true.

7. **(2):** (A) - (I), (B) - (III), (C) - (IV), (D) - (II):
(A) Standards – (I): Standards define the expected level of performance, such as reducing defects from 10 pc to 5 pc per lot.
(B) Management by Exception – (III): This principle says that trying to control everything is ineffective; focus should be on deviations or exceptions only.
(C) Critical Control Point – (IV): It involves identifying Key Result Areas (KRAs) where control is most effective.
(D) Corrective Action – (II): This refers to measures like assigning extra workers/ equipment to fix deviations from plans.

8. **(4):** Management as a profession is expected to follow a standardized and impersonal approach based on principles, codes of conduct, and professional ethics. While restricted entry, professional association, and service motive are accepted features of any profession, personalised application is not. Personal discretion or subjective decision-making based on personal bias goes against the professional nature of management. A profession is supposed to apply knowledge objectively and uniformly, not personally.

9. **(2):** Development is a career-oriented and long-term process focused on overall growth of the individual. It helps employees grow their capabilities for future responsibilities and roles. Unlike training, which is job-specific and short-term, development enhances conceptual, interpersonal, and decision-making skills that shape career progression. Selection and reference checks are hiring processes, not focused on career building.

10. **(3):** The correct logical sequence in the process of organising is:

(D) The work is divided into manageable activities so that duplication can be avoided: The first step is to identify and divide the total work into smaller tasks or activities. This is called division of work, and it helps avoid overlap and confusion.

(A) The activities which are similar in nature are grouped together: This step is known as departmentalisation, where related tasks are grouped into departments like finance, marketing, HR, etc.

(B) Jobs are allocated to the members of each department in accordance to their skills and competencies: This step involves assignment of duties. Each person is given a specific task that suits their skills.

(C) Authority and reporting relationships are established to create a hierarchal structure: This step creates the organizational structure by defining lines of authority, who reports to whom, and levels of responsibility.

Thus, the sequence D → A → B → C reflects the natural progression from planning the work to creating a structured hierarchy.

11. **(1):** The business environment is important for several reasons:

(A) **Identifying first mover advantage:** By analysing environmental trends, businesses can launch innovative products or services before competitors.

(B) **Improving business performance:** Understanding external factors helps in adapting better and making informed decisions, improving overall performance.

(D) **Coping with rapid changes:** A dynamic business environment requires quick adaptation. Awareness helps businesses survive and grow.

(C) **Performance appraisal,** however, is an internal HR activity, not directly linked to external business environment analysis.

12. **(3):** (A) - (III), (B) - (I), (C) - (IV), (D) - (II):

(A) Responsibility – (III): It is the obligation to perform assigned tasks.

(B) Authority – (I): It is the right to command and issue orders.

(C) Accountability – (IV): It is the answerability for fulfilling responsibilities.

(D) Delegation – (II): It is the downward transfer of authority from superior to subordinate.

These four are fundamental concepts in organizing and ensure clarity in task distribution and command relationships.

13. **(3):** Span of management, also called span of control, refers to how many subordinates report directly to one manager. A wider span means more subordinates per manager; a narrower span means fewer. It affects the structure of the organisation—wider spans create flatter structures, while narrow spans lead to more hierarchical levels.

14. **(1):** (A) - (I), (B) - (II), (C) - (IV), (D) - (III):

(A) Social – (I) Literacy rates: Social environment includes elements like education levels, lifestyles, and cultural values. Literacy rate is a key social factor.

(B) Economic – (II) Public Debt: Economic environment covers factors like national income, inflation, interest rates, and public debt.

(C) Technological – (IV) Scientific improvements: Technological environment includes research, innovation, and technological advancements.

(D) Legal – (III) Monopolistic Restrictive Trade Practices Act: Legal environment includes laws and regulations like MRTP Act, Consumer Protection Act, etc., which affect business operations.

15. **(1):** This is based on Maslow's hierarchy of needs:
   (A) Physiological needs – (IV) Food: Basic needs for survival like food, water, shelter.
   (B) Safety and Security needs – (III) Confirmed job: Includes job security, financial security, health, and safety.
   (C) Esteem needs – (II) Status: Desire for respect, recognition, and status.
   (D) Social needs – (I) Friendship: The need for belonging, love, and interpersonal relationships.

16. **(3):** (A), (C) and (D) only:
   (A) Planning becomes meaningless without execution. Action is essential to give effect to any plan.
   (C) Planning involves foresight, setting goals, and devising new ideas, which directly connects it to creativity and innovation.
   (D) Planning is a universal function performed by managers at all levels, from top to operational.
   (B) is incorrect because coordination and assembling resources relate more to organising, not planning.

17. **(1):** Scalar Chain is a principle given by Henry Fayol, not F.W. Taylor. Taylor's scientific management includes concepts like:
   - Harmony, not discord
   - Standardisation and simplification of work
   - Cooperation, not individualism

   These were part of Taylor's efforts to improve efficiency and reduce conflict in industrial settings.

18. **(4):** A ban on advertisements of alcoholic beverages refers to government regulations and legal restrictions imposed on business practices. This reflects the legal environment, which includes laws, rules, and legal policies affecting businesses.

19. **(1):** Frederick Winslow Taylor is known as the Father of Scientific Management. He introduced techniques like time study, motion study, standardisation, and functional foremanship to improve industrial productivity.

20. **(1):** Henri Fayol emphasized discipline as one of his 14 principles of management. According to him:
   (A) Good supervisors at all levels ensure proper guidance and rule enforcement.
   (B) Agreements should be clear and fair so employees understand expectations.
   (D) Penalties should be fairly imposed to maintain consistency and justice.
   (C) Removal of an employee is an extreme measure, not a direct requirement of discipline as per Fayol's principle.

21. **(2):** The correct sequence of the planning process is:
   (A) **Establishing Objectives:** First step—defining what the organisation wants to achieve.
   (B) **Developing Premises:** Assumptions about future conditions are made to base planning decisions.
   (C) **Evaluation of Alternatives:** Various options to achieve objectives are analysed.
   (D) **Selecting a Course of Action:** The most suitable alternative is chosen for implementation.

22. **(4):** Management is considered an art because:
   (B) It involves theoretical knowledge, but not in a rigid scientific format.
   (C) It requires personalized application, meaning each manager applies principles differently.
   (D) It is based on practice and creativity, as managers develop skills through experience.
   (A) It refers more to the science aspect of management, not the artistic side.

23. **(1):** When the demand is inelastic, it means that consumers will continue buying the product even if the price increases. In such cases, the firm has greater flexibility to fix higher prices without significantly affecting demand. This typically occurs for essential goods or products with no close substitutes.

24. **(4):** The money needed to carry out various business operations such as purchasing assets, paying salaries, or producing goods is collectively called business finance. It includes both short-term and long-term capital requirements from various sources like equity, debt, or retained earnings.

25. **(1):** The supervisory level of management is directly responsible for overseeing and guiding the efforts of workers. They ensure day-to-day operations run smoothly, maintain discipline, monitor work, and provide feedback to the workforce. This level acts as a link between workers and middle management.

26. **(1):** The correct logical sequence in the financial planning process is:

(A) **Sales forecast is made:** Estimating future sales is the first step as it influences other financial aspects.

(B) **Requirement of fixed and working capital is estimated:** Based on sales expectations, the capital needed for assets and operations is calculated.

(C) **Expected profits are estimated:** Profit projections depend on cost and revenue analysis.

(D) **Sources of finance are identified:** Once capital needs and profit potential are clear, suitable funding sources are chosen.

27. **(3):** In the process of controlling, performance is evaluated by comparing it to predefined standards. Standards act as benchmarks or criteria that define the expected level of performance. If actual performance deviates from these standards, corrective action is taken.

28. **(1):** The correct sequence of steps in the controlling process is:

(B) **Projecting the future and determining the goals and standards:** This is the first step where performance standards are set.

(D) **Measuring the work in terms of control standards:** Actual performance is measured.

(A) **Reporting of deviation and their causes after comparison:** Deviations are identified and analyzed.

(C) **Taking corrective action at an appropriate level:** Necessary actions are taken to fix the issues and align future performance.

29. **(4):** The relationship of our country with foreign nations reflects the political environment. This includes diplomatic relations, trade policies, stability of government, taxation policies on foreign investments, etc., all of which directly impact businesses operating internationally.

30. **(2):** Financial leverage is said to be favorable when the Return on Investment (ROI) exceeds the cost of debt. In such cases, the use of borrowed funds adds to the returns of shareholders, increasing the profitability of the firm. If ROI is lower than the interest on debt, leverage becomes unfavorable.

31. **(4):** (A) - (III), (B) - (I), (C) - (II), (D) - (IV):

(A) Net Working Capital – (III): It is calculated as Current Assets minus Current Liabilities, reflecting short-term liquidity.

(B) Fixed Capital – (I): Refers to investments in long-term assets like buildings, machinery, etc., essential for production.

(C) Financial Leverage – (II): Indicates the proportion of debt used in total capital structure.

(D) Trading on Equity – (IV): Occurs when fixed financial charges like interest on debt lead to increased earnings for equity shareholders due to higher return on capital employed than cost of debt.

32. **(2):** Entrepreneurship is the process of creating and running a business venture while taking risks and showing qualities like innovation, leadership, planning, and risk-taking. Its main aim is wealth creation and profit generation through new ideas or market opportunities.

33. **(3):** This feature highlights that planning is based on rational thinking, analysis, and forecasting, not guesswork or emotional decisions. It requires a logical and systematic approach, involving intellect and foresight to choose the best course of action.

34. **(2):** Advertising is an impersonal form of communication where a marketer communicates with a large audience to promote a product or service through mass media (TV, print, digital, etc.). Unlike personal selling, there is no direct interaction with individuals; the message is one-way and aimed at creating awareness or persuading buyers.

35. **(3):** A method is a specific and prescribed way of performing a task or activity. It is a type of plan that defines the step-by-step manner in which a job is to be done, considering the objectives. Methods are part of procedures and help in standardizing how activities are performed efficiently.

36. **(2):** The importance of delegation lies in empowering subordinates and building a capable workforce.

(A) High morale of subordinates: When responsibility and authority are delegated, it shows trust, which boosts confidence and motivation.

(B) Develops initiatives among employees: Delegation gives employees autonomy to take decisions, enhancing their decision-making and leadership skills.

(C) Promotes centralisation is incorrect because delegation actually supports decentralisation.

(D) Dilutes span of management is also not a key importance of delegation; rather, it helps manage workload but doesn't directly relate to altering span of control.

37. **(1):** In the apprenticeship training method, a trainee learns by working under the direct supervision of an experienced master worker. This method is commonly used in technical trades like carpentry, plumbing, and engineering, where practical, hands-on skills are essential and developed over a long period.

38. **(2):** Coordination refers to the process by which a manager ensures harmony of efforts among different individuals and departments to achieve common objectives. It involves aligning group efforts and maintaining unity of action, which is essential for organizational efficiency.

39. **(1):** Grading is the process of classifying products into different categories or classes based on their features, quality, size, or other characteristics. It helps in standardization and enables customers to easily compare and choose products of desired quality.

40. **(3):** The phrase "marketing methods used" influences the Price component of the marketing mix when it refers to how a company positions its product and uses different pricing techniques based on marketing strategies. For example, heavy promotional costs, premium branding, or niche targeting through marketing can lead to higher pricing decisions. Thus, the pricing strategy is often shaped by the marketing methods employed, such as cost-based pricing, value-based pricing, or competition-based pricing.

41. **(3):** Since Manoj first approached the District Commission and was not satisfied with its decision, he can appeal to the State Commission. As per the Consumer Protection Act, an appeal against the decision of the District Commission must be filed before the State Commission within the prescribed time.

42. **(2):** DD Motors ignored Manoj's complaints and did not respond adequately to his dissatisfaction. This violates his Right to be heard, which ensures that consumers can voice complaints and concerns. It also violates the Right to seek redressal, which ensures that consumers are entitled to fair settlement of genuine grievances.

43. **(4):** A consumer cannot retain the product and simultaneously claim a full refund, as it amounts to unjust enrichment. The legal relief includes repair, replacement, or return for refund—but not retention with full refund. Hence, this option is not a valid relief.

44. **(4):** The case shows that Manoj was aware of his consumer rights and proceeded to file a complaint and appeal—this reflects consumer awareness, a key way of consumer protection through individual vigilance and informed action.

45. **(2):** Manoj filed a formal complaint, which implies he had proper documentation like a bill/invoice. This reflects a responsible consumer behavior, as such proof is necessary to seek legal redressal in consumer forums.

46. **(3):** Sarah's role in holding meetings, setting expectations, assigning tasks, and guiding employees shows she is creating an environment where action can begin, which is a key part of the directing function in management. This prepares the team to act efficiently toward goals.

47. **(4):** By recognizing achievements, giving constructive feedback, and offering training, Sarah is encouraging employees to perform better. These are actions rooted in motivation, a vital element of directing that energizes individuals to achieve desired results.

48. **(2):** The passage emphasizes how Sarah delegates responsibilities, fosters open communication, and offers support, all of which empower the team and increase their involvement and commitment. This shows how directing is central to successful management.

49. **(2):** The main objective of directing is to guide, supervise, communicate, and lead employees so their actions align with the organization's goals. Sarah performs all these functions, highlighting the true purpose of directing in management.

50. **(1):** Sarah's clear communication regarding expectations, targets, and the importance of customer satisfaction ensures that employee actions are in sync with company goals, which is the core benefit of effective communication in directing.

GENERAL TEST

1. **(4):** Jatin is 9th from the front, so there are 8 boys ahead of him. According to the question, the number of boys behind him is three times the number in front:
$8 \times 3 = 24$ boys behind Jatin.
Therefore, total number of boys
= 8 (in front) + 1 (Jatin himself) + 24 (behind)
= 33 boys.
The fifth boy from the end will be at position number
$= 33 - 5 + 1 = 29$ from the front.
Jatin is 9th from the front.
The number of boys between Jatin (9th) and the fifth from end (29th) $= 29 - 9 - 1 = 19$ boys.

2. **(3):** Earth Hour was first initiated by the World Wide Fund for Nature (WWF) in 2007 in Sydney, Australia. It is observed annually on the 23rd of March in over 180 countries, encouraging individuals, communities, and businesses to turn off non-essential lights for one hour to raise awareness about global warming and environmental conservation.

3. **(3):** Tipu Sultan is regarded as the pioneer of rocket technology in India. He and his father Haider Ali developed iron-cased rockets which were used effectively during wars against the British, especially in the Anglo-Mysore wars. These Mysorean rockets influenced later European military rocket designs.

4. **(2):** C is to the east of B, and B is to the north of D, so C is northeast of D. A is to the south of D.
Thus, from C's position (northeast of D), A would lie toward the southwest.
Hence, A is in the south-west direction from C.

5. **(4):** (B), (C) and (D) only
(A) is incorrect because the Modified Mercalli Intensity Scale does measure the intensity of shaking, not magnitude, so the statement is factually wrong.
(B) is correct: the epicenter is the point on the earth's surface directly above the earthquake's focus.
(C) is correct: seismology is the branch of geology that studies earthquakes.
(D) is correct: shadow zones are regions where seismic waves are not recorded due to the wave refraction and absorption patterns inside Earth.

6. **(2):** We are given:
   - E is second to the right of F,
   - F is sitting on the immediate right of C,
   - A and D are the only persons sitting between G and E.

   Let's fix positions clockwise using the given information.
   Start by placing C at position P1, then:
   - F is to the immediate right of C ⇒ F at P2
   - E is second to the right of F ⇒ E at P4

   So far:
   P1 – C   P2 – F
   P3 – (unknown)   P4 – E
   Now use the clue: A and D are the only persons sitting between G and E.
   So G _ A D _ E (clockwise), placing A and D between G and E.
   Try placing:
   - E at P4
   - Then P5 = A, P6 = D, P7 = G

   Now filled:
   P1 – C   P2 – F
   P3 – B (only person left)   P4 – E
   P5 – A   P6 – D
   P7 – G
   Complete clockwise arrangement:
   C – F – B – E – A – D – G
   Now check each option:
   (A) B is third to the right of G
   From G (P7), count clockwise:
   1st = C (P1), 2nd = F (P2), 3rd = B (P3) ⇒ True
   (B) C is immediate right of G
   From G (P7), immediate right is P1 = C ⇒ True
   (C) D is immediate right of B
   From B (P3), immediate right is P4 = E ⇒ False
   (D) G is second to the left of F
   From F (P2), moving left:
   1st left = C (P1), 2nd left = G (P7) ⇒ True
   So, only (A), (B), and (D) are correct.
   Answer: 2: (A), (B) and (D) only.

7. **(3):** Let's arrange the events with year:
(B) Droupadi Murmu became President in July 2022

(C) Karpoori Thakur awarded Bharat Ratna in January 2024
(A) Prerna Sthal inaugurated in February 2024
(D) 'Fauna of India' list launched in March 2024

Correct sequence of occurrence:
(B) → (C) → (A) → (D)
Answer: 3: (B), (C), (A), (D).

8. **(3):** Let the trader claims to sell 1000 grams of wheat.
Cost Price (CP) per gram = Re. 1
So, actual CP of 1000 grams = ₹ 1000
However, he gives 10% less in weight.
That means he gives only 900 grams instead of 1000 grams.
So, actual cost to the trader = 900 × ₹ 1 = ₹ 900
He sells the wheat at 10% profit on the declared quantity (1000 grams), not on actual.
So, SP = 1000 × ₹ 1 × (1 + 10/100) = ₹ 1100
Thus, for 900 grams of wheat, the trader receives ₹ 1100.
His gain = ₹ 1100 – ₹ 900 = ₹ 200
Now calculate percentage gain:

$$\text{Percentage gain} = \frac{\text{Gain}}{\text{Actual CP}} \times 100$$

$$= \frac{200}{900} \times 100$$

$$= 22.22\%.$$

9. **(1 & 3):** This question allows for two valid interpretations, each highlighting a different number as the odd one out based on distinct logical reasoning:
Logic 1 – Perfect Power Logic:

- 729 is a perfect cube (9^3) and also a perfect sixth power (3^6), making it unique among the given numbers.
- 295, 552, and 906 are not perfect squares, cubes, or higher powers.

So, 729 stands out due to its special mathematical structure.
Logic 2 – Divisibility by 5:

- 295 ends in 5 ⇒ divisible by 5.
- 552, 729, and 906 do not end in 0 or 5, so they are not divisible by 5.

Thus, 295 is the only number in the group divisible by 5.
Since both logics are equally valid and highlight different numbers, both 295 and 729 are correct answers, depending on the reasoning applied.
Answer: 1 and 3: 295 and 729.

10. **(2):** The Ganges River Dolphin is referred to as the 'Tiger of the Ganges' due to its importance in the river ecosystem. It is also officially declared as the National Aquatic Animal of India by the Government.

11. **(1):** The minute hand of a clock moves 6° per minute (360° in 60 minutes).
To move 240°, time taken = 240 ÷ 6 = 40 minutes.
The hour hand moves 0.5° per minute (360° in 12 hours = 0.5° per minute).
So, in 40 minutes, hour hand moves = 0.5 × 40 = 20°.

12. **(2):** 'Amar Sonar Bangla' is the national anthem of Bangladesh. It was written by Rabindra Nath Tagore in 1905 during the Swadeshi movement, as a protest against the partition of Bengal by the British. The first ten lines of this song were adopted as the national anthem by Bangladesh in 1971.

13. **(4):** The First Battle of Panipat took place in 1526 between Babur, the founder of the Mughal Empire, and Ibrahim Lodhi, the last ruler of the Delhi Sultanate.
Babur's victory marked the beginning of Mughal rule in India and the end of the Lodhi dynasty.

14. **(3):** When a clock shows 3:45 in the mirror, the actual time is calculated by subtracting from 12:00.

12:00 – 3:45 = 8:15

Therefore, the actual time shown by the clock is 8:15.

15. **(4):** Curved Surface Area (CSA) of a cone

$= \pi \times r \times l$

Let original radius = 100, slant height = 100

$$\text{Original CSA} = \pi \times 100 \times 100 = 10000\pi$$

$$\text{New radius} = 100 + 20\% = 120$$

$$\text{New slant height} = 100 - 15\% = 85$$

$$\text{New CSA} = \pi \times 120 \times 85 = 10200\pi$$

$$\%\ \text{change} = \frac{10200 - 10000}{10000} \times 100 = 2\%$$

So, the curved surface area increases by 2%.

16. **(1):** Let's match the missions correctly:
(A) Chandrayaan-3 → (II) Attempt for soft landing on the moon: Chandrayaan-3 was ISRO's mission to achieve a successful soft landing on the Moon. It succeeded in August 2023.

(B) Gaganyaan-3 → (IV) India's first crewed (human) space mission: Gaganyaan aims to send Indian astronauts (Gagannauts) into space. Gaganyaan-3 is part of this human spaceflight programme.

(C) NISAR → (I) Development and launch of a dual-frequency synthetic aperture radar satellite: NISAR (NASA-ISRO Synthetic Aperture Radar) is a joint Earth observation mission with a dual-frequency radar for climate and disaster monitoring.

(D) Aditya-L1 → (III) Solar Observatory Mission: Aditya-L1 is India's first solar mission, launched to study the Sun's outer atmosphere (corona and solar wind).

Answer: 1: (A) - (II), (B) - (IV), (C) - (I), (D) - (III).

17. (2): Given:

- Manish is 18th from the right end
- Rahul is 5th from the left end
- 7 boys are between them

So, total boys = (Position of Manish from right) + (Position of Rahul from left) + (Number of boys between them) = 18 + 5 + 7 = 30.

18. (4): The Partition of Bengal was carried out in 1905 during the viceroyalty of Lord Curzon. The stated purpose was administrative efficiency, but it was widely seen as an attempt to divide and weaken nationalist sentiments in Bengal. The partition was strongly opposed and later annulled in 1911.

19. (4): The given figure (X) is a "Y" shaped structure — it consists of a vertical line with two diverging arms at the top, forming a symmetric "Y". Now let's carefully examine each option:

- **Option 1:** Contains a combination of hexagonal lines and verticals, but the structure does not form a Y shape. *(Incorrect)*
- **Option 2:** Has intersecting triangles forming an hourglass or "X" shape, which is not similar to figure (X). *(Incorrect)*
- **Option 3:** Shows a triangle with internal divisions but does not clearly form a Y-shaped structure. The lines do not match the alignment of figure (X). *(Incorrect)*
- **Option 4:** If you closely observe the center, you can clearly identify the "Y" shape embedded within. It consists of a vertical line with two lines diverging upwards, exactly as in figure (X). *(Correct)*

Therefore, figure (X) is correctly embedded in Option 4.

20. (3): Total number of balls in the bag
= 3 red + 2 blue + 5 green + 4 yellow = 14 balls

We are required to find the probability that either both balls are red or both are blue when two balls are drawn at random.

Total number of ways to choose 2 balls out of 14

$$= {}^{14}C_2 = \frac{14 \times 13}{2} = 91$$

Now, Number of ways to choose 2 red balls $= {}^{3}C_2 = 3$

Number of ways to choose 2 blue balls $= {}^{2}C_2 = 1$

So, favourable outcomes = 3 + 1 = 4

Therefore, required probability = 4/91.

21. (4): The given series is: $1 + \frac{3}{2} + 2 + \frac{5}{2} + 3 + \frac{7}{2} + \ldots$

Observe the pattern:

- Odd-positioned terms: 1, 2, 3, ... form an arithmetic sequence of natural numbers
- Even-positioned terms: $\frac{3}{2}, \frac{5}{2}, \frac{7}{2}, \ldots$ also form an arithmetic sequence

Let's calculate the sum of first few terms and test the formulas:

For $n = 1 : 1 \rightarrow$ Sum = 1

Check Option 2:

$$1 \times \frac{1+3}{2} = \frac{4}{2} = 2 \rightarrow \textit{(Incorrect)}$$

$n = 2$: $1 + \frac{3}{2} = \frac{5}{2}$

Option 2: $2 \times \frac{2+3}{2} = 2 \times \frac{5}{2} = 5$ → *(Incorrect)*

$n = 4$: $1 + \frac{3}{2} + 2 + \frac{5}{2} = \left(\frac{1}{2}\right) + \left(\frac{3}{2} + \frac{5}{2}\right)$
$= 3 + 4 = 7$

Option 2: $4 \times \frac{4+3}{2} = 4 \times \frac{7}{2} = 14 = 14$ → *(Correct)*

$n = 5$: $1 + \frac{3}{2} + 2 + \frac{5}{2} + 3 = (1 + 2 + 3) + \frac{3}{2} + \frac{5}{2}$
$= 6 + 4 = 10$

Option 2: $5 \times \frac{5+3}{2} = 5 \times \frac{8}{2} = 20$ → *(Correct)*

Hence, the formula that correctly represents the sum of n terms of the series is: $\frac{n(n+3)}{2}$.

22. **(4):** The component of blood that helps in fighting infections is known as Leukocytes, or white blood cells (WBCs).
They are part of the immune system and function to identify and destroy harmful pathogens like bacteria, viruses, and other foreign invaders.
Other options:

- **Erythrocytes (RBCs):** Carry oxygen
- **Plasma:** Transport medium for cells and nutrients
- **Platelets:** Help in blood clotting

Only leukocytes have the defensive role against infections.

23. **(3):** Let the distance between A and B be x km.
Time taken to go from A to B at 6 km/h

$$= \frac{x}{6} \text{ hours}$$

Time taken to return from B to A at 9 km/h

$$= \frac{x}{9} \text{ hours}$$

$$\text{Total time} = 1 \text{ hour } 15 \text{ minutes} = 1.25 \text{ hours}$$

So, $\frac{x}{6} + \frac{x}{9} = 1.25$

Take LCM of 6 and 9 = 18

$$\frac{3x + 2x}{18} = 1.25 \Rightarrow \frac{5x}{18} = 1.25$$

$$\Rightarrow x = \frac{1.25 \times 18}{5} = \frac{22.5}{5} = 4.5$$

Therefore, the distance between A and B is 4.5 km.

24. **(2):** Statement: "Over The Top (OTT) platform has become indispensable for the entertainment of people."

- **Assumption I:** People enjoy watching content on OTT — Implicit, because unless people find OTT entertaining, it wouldn't be considered indispensable.
- **Assumption II:** OTT is the only medium of entertainment — Not implicit, as the statement says OTT is indispensable, not exclusive.

Only the first assumption logically follows from the statement. Answer: 2: Only assumption I is implicit.

25. **(4):** Given sequence:
m n o | n o p | q o p | q r _ _ _ _ s t u
Break the series into overlapping trios:

- m n o
- n o p
- o p q
- p q r
- q r s
- r s t
- s t u

So, missing letters after "q r" must be:
s, t, p, q ⇒ But needs to fit full letter structure.
However, based on the pattern, after "q r", the correct 4-letter gap to reach "s t u" should be: s, t, u, v, but that conflicts.
Let's look again:
From "m n o", next trio = shift one forward each time:
n o p
o p q
p q r
q r s
r s t
s t u
So the missing letters are: s, t, u, v — but since the sequence given already ends at "s t u", the missing 4 letters just before that are: r, s, t, u
Therefore: The missing letters are: (B) s, (D) p, (C) q, (A) r.
But reordered correctly, matching pattern: (B), (D), (C), (A).

26. **(3):** The gravitational acceleration on the Moon is approximately 1/6th of that on Earth.

- Earth's gravity ≈ 9.8 m/s^2
- Moon's gravity ≈ 1.63 m/s^2

$$\frac{1.63}{9.8} \approx \frac{1}{6}.$$

27. **(4):** To solve this figure matrix, let's analyze both shapes and symbols row-wise and column-wise.

Step 1: Analyze arrow shapes (thick L-shapes):

- In the first row, images (1) and (2) both have an L-shape rotated differently.
- In the second row, images (4) and (3) also have L-shapes in different orientations.

Now observe the positions of the thick L-shapes:

- From left to right in the top row: shape rotates 90° clockwise from 1 to 2.
- From left to right in the bottom row: shape rotates 90° clockwise from 4 to 3.

So, following the same logic, the L-shape in the missing figure (top right) must be a 90° clockwise rotation of the shape in cell (2).
Looking at cell (2), the shape is a vertical L. Its 90° clockwise rotation is the horizontal L found in option 4.

Step 2: Analyze the small symbols (triangle, star, etc.):
Each box contains a triangle and a star, and their positions also follow a consistent diagonal symmetry or shifting across rows/columns.
Following the same position trend of symbols (as seen in cells 1, 2, 3, and 4), the triangle and star in the missing cell match the placement seen in option 4.
Thus, both the thick L-shape and the symbol positions match in option 4.

28. **(1):** Let the total work be 1 unit.
We are given:
- P and Q together can complete the work in 60 days ⇒ (P + Q)'s 1-day work = 1/60
- Q and R together can complete the work in 120 days ⇒ (Q + R)'s 1-day work = 1/120
- P and R together can complete the work in 90 days ⇒ (P + R)'s 1-day work = 1/90

Now, add all three equations:
(P + Q) + (Q + R) + (P + R)

$$= \frac{1}{60} + \frac{1}{120} + \frac{1}{90}$$

⇒ 2(P + Q + R) = LCM of 60, 120, 90 = 360

Convert each to a common denominator:

$$\frac{1}{60} = \frac{6}{360};\ \frac{1}{120} = \frac{3}{360};\ \frac{1}{90} = \frac{4}{360}$$

$$\Rightarrow \quad \text{Sum} = \frac{6+3+4}{360} = \frac{13}{360}$$

$$\text{So,} \quad 2(P + Q + R) = \frac{13}{360}$$

$$\Rightarrow \quad P + Q + R = \frac{13}{720}$$

Now subtract (P + R)'s work to get Q's work:

$$Q = (P+Q+R) - (P+R) = \frac{13}{720} - \frac{1}{90}$$

Convert 1/90 to denominator 720:

$$\frac{1}{90} = \frac{8}{720}$$

$$\Rightarrow \quad Q = \frac{13-8}{720} = \frac{5}{720}$$

Therefore, Q alone can complete the work in:

$$= \frac{720}{5} = 144 \text{ days.}$$

29. **(1):** Soap is formed by saponification, where alkali (such as NaOH or KOH) reacts with fatty acids or triglycerides.
This forms alkali salts of higher fatty acids, which we commonly call soap.
Other options refer to ingredients used in glass, ceramics, or fertilizers.

30. **(1):** Let's solve each part of List-I and match with the correct element from List-II:
(A) Remainder when $17^{(35234)}$ is divided by 8:
Use modulo patterns.
Since 17 ≡ 1 (mod 8), then $17^n \equiv 1^n \equiv 1$ (mod 8) for any n.
⇒ Remainder = 1 → Matches with (II)
(B) Remainder when 4^{4444} is divided by 9:
Powers of 4 modulo 9 cycle as:

$$4^1 \equiv 4 \pmod 9$$
$$4^2 \equiv 7 \pmod 9$$
$$4^3 \equiv 1 \pmod 9$$

Cycle: 4, 7, 1 (length 3)
Now, 4444 ÷ 3 gives remainder 1
⇒ So, $4^{4444} \equiv 4^1 \equiv 4 \pmod 9$ → Matches with (IV)
(C) Unit digit of $(34)^{15} + (34)^{16}$:
Look at unit digit pattern of 4:

$$4^1 = 4$$
$$4^2 = 16 \rightarrow \text{unit digit } 6$$

Cycle: 4, 6 (length 2)
For 4^{15} → odd ⇒ unit digit = 4
For 4^{16} → even ⇒ unit digit = 6
Sum = 4 + 6 = 10 ⇒ Unit digit = 0 → Matches with (I)
(D) Unit digit of $7^4 - 9^3$:
7^4: powers cycle → 7, 9, 3, 1 ⇒ 7^4 ⇒ unit digit = 1
9^3: powers cycle → 9, 1 ⇒ 9^3 ⇒ unit digit = 9
Now 1 − 9 = -8 ⇒ take unit digit = 2
→ Matches with (III)
Correct matching: (1): (A)-II), (B)-(IV), (C)-(I), (D)-(III).

31. **(4):** Formula for number of diagonals in an n-sided polygon $= \frac{n(n-3)}{2}$

For a hexagon (n = 6): $= \frac{6(6-3)}{2} = 6 \times \frac{3}{2} = 9$.

32. **(1):** Let's analyze the folding and cutting step by step:
- **Figure X:** The paper is first folded vertically in half, from left to right.

- **Figure Y:** Then the paper is again folded vertically from right to left, making a total of two vertical folds. So, the paper is folded into quarters (1/4th of its original width).
- **Figure Z:** Shows cuts made on the folded paper:
  One semicircular cut on the vertical edge (middle of the folded sheet)
  Two diamond-shaped cuts at the top and bottom

Now, when the paper is unfolded, the cuts will mirror along both fold lines.

- The semicircular cut, made at the center fold, will mirror to form two symmetrical semicircles on either side, resulting in two full circular notches on the middle of left and right edges.
- The diamond cuts on the folded sheet will replicate four times upon full unfolding (mirroring across both folds).

Among the options:

- Option 1 shows:
  4 diamond shapes — correctly placed due to mirroring
  2 semicircular edge notches — correct as per the central vertical cut

Thus, the unfolded paper must look like Option 1.

33. **(1):** We are given that the area of an equilateral triangle is: $36\sqrt{3}\ \text{cm}^2$

The formula for the area of an equilateral triangle with side length aaa is:

$$\text{Area} = \frac{\sqrt{3}}{4}a^2$$

Substitute the given area into the formula:

$$\frac{\sqrt{3}}{4}a^2 = 36\sqrt{3}$$

Divide both sides by $\sqrt{3}$:

$$\frac{1}{4}a^2 = 36$$

Multiply both sides by 4: $a^2 = 144$

Take the square root of both sides:

$$a = \sqrt{144} = 12$$

Therefore, the length of each side of the equilateral triangle is 12 cm.

34. **(4):** The correct chronological order of the prehistoric ages of human progress is:

(A) Palaeolithic Age – Old Stone Age: beginning of human tools and hunting

(D) Mesolithic Age – Middle Stone Age: transition phase, microliths used

(C) Neolithic Age – New Stone Age: agriculture, domestication begins

(B) Chalcolithic Age – Copper-Stone Age: early use of metal tools

Therefore, the correct sequence is:
Palaeolithic → Mesolithic → Neolithic → Chalcolithic.

35. **(3):** Let's analyze the movement and transformation of the three elements in the figure across the series from left to right:

Top row (Triangle) – 1st Item:

Pattern:

- It moves one step forward in each frame (left to right)
- It also alternates its orientation (inverted every time)

Sequence:

1. ▲ in column 1
2. ▼ in column 2
3. ▲ in column 3
4. ? → should be in column 4 and inverted ⇒ ▼
5. ▼ in column 5
6. ?

So, triangle in column 4, facing downward (▼)

Middle row (Cube) – 2nd Item:

Pattern:

- Moves 2 steps at a time, alternating forward and backward
- Also alternates color between white and black

Sequence (position and colour):

1. White cube in column 2
2. Black cube in column 3 (→ moved forward 1 step, and changed colour)
3. ? → Now should move 2 steps back, from column 3 → column 1, and colour switches to white
4. Then black cube reappears in column 2 in the next image

So, cube should be white, placed in column 1

Bottom row (Plus symbol) – 3rd Item:

Pattern:

- Remains in same shape and colour, and moves 1 step forward each time

Sequence:

1. Column 3 **2. Column 4**
3. Column 5

So, in the missing frame, it should be in column 6

But we are to find the missing figure before that — so before it reaches column 5, it was in column 4

→ It must be in column 4 in the missing image
Final Expected Configuration:

- Top row: ▼ in column 4
- Middle row: White cube in column 1
- Bottom row: White plus in column 4

Check which option matches:
Option 3 shows:

- ▼ (triangle) in column 4
- White cube in column 1
- White cross in column 4

Perfect match.

36. **(2):** Let the 4-digit number be represented as N.
Let the sum of its digits be S.
We are given: The number N – S is always divisible by a certain number.
General Rule: For any number, if you subtract the sum of its digits from the number itself, the result is always divisible by 9.
Why? Let's prove it algebraically:
Let the number be:
N = $1000a + 100b + 10c + d$ where a, b, c, d are the digits of the number
Sum of digits = $a + b + c + d$ = S
Then,
$$N - S = (1000a + 100b + 10c + d) - (a + b + c + d)$$
$$= 999a + 99b + 9c$$
Each term on the right-hand side is divisible by 9:
$999a = 9 \times 111a$, $99b = 9 \times 11b$, $9c = 9 \times c$
Hence, N – S is divisible by 9
This is a known divisibility property for all whole numbers.

37. **(2):** We are given a base figure (X), which consists of two intersecting thin lines forming an 'X' shape, where each line has a small outward bend at its ends. The figure is formed by two clean, curved strokes crossing each other.
The task is to identify which of the given options contain this exact figure embedded without rotation.
Let's analyze each option carefully:
Option 1:

- Contains thick, straight overlapping bands.
- The structure is geometrically rigid and lacks the distinctive outward curves found in figure (X).
- No accurate embedding of (X) is observed.

Not a match.
Option 2:

- Among all the lines in the structure, the inner intersecting lines are thin and angled, matching the curved outward strokes of figure (X).
- These lines exactly replicate the direction, style, and bending of figure (X) without rotation.

Perfect match
Option 3:

- Composed of thick, diagonal strips with squared ends.
- The distinctive curving ends of figure (X) are not present.
- The lines do not replicate the gentle bend seen in (X).

Not a match
Option 4:

- Similar to Option 3, features wide angular bands.
- No visible trace of the specific curve-ended X shape from figure (X).

Not a match
Hence, only Option 2 correctly embeds figure (X) without rotation and preserves the exact style, shape, and orientation of the curved intersecting lines.

38. **(3):** We are given:
3 men or 15 boys can complete the work in 30 days.
From this, we calculate total work:
Work = 3 men × 30 days = 90 men-days
This is the same as 15 boys × 30 days = 450 boys-days
We are asked: In how many days will 2 men and 5 boys complete the same work?
Let's convert all workers into a common unit, say man-days:
From the given, 3 men = 15 boys
⇒ 1 man = 5 boys
So, 1 boy = 1/5 man
Now, 2 men = 2 man
5 boys = 5 × (1/5) = 1 man
Total workforce = 2 + 1 = 3 men
Therefore, 2 men and 5 boys together are equivalent to 3 men, and since 3 men can do the work in 30 days,
2 men and 5 boys will also complete the work in 30 days.

39. **(1):** We are asked to find the nearest integer to 6650 that is exactly divisible by 429.
Step 1: Divide 6650 by 429
$$6650 \div 429 \approx 15.5$$
So, the two closest multiples of 429 are:

- 429 × 15 = 6435
- 429 × 16 = 6864

elected executive." M.K. Gandhi said about the Governor's office: "He would be an arbiter when there was a constitutional deadlock in the State and he would be able to play an impartial role." In the contemporary constitutional landscape, the Governor is expected to advance the cause of 'federalism' and 'democracy' which form a part of the basic structure of the Constitution.

21. Which of the following is the synonym of specious?
A. refined B. superficial
C. possible D. correct

22. What can be concluded from the paragraph 1?
I. The post of the governor is controversial yet unimportant.
II. The current case is typical example of a routine departure from norms.
III. The Governors are often abused.
A. Only II B. Only III
C. II and III D. None of the above

23. What is the tone of the author in the second paragraph?
A. Factual B. Understanding
C. Worried D. Pensive

24. What was the opinion of the Sarkaria Commission about the role of a Governor?
I. He would serve as an important link between the Union and State.
II. He would be the custodian of the constitution.
III. He is to be an arbiter in case of a deadlock in the state.
A. Only I B. Only III
C. Only I and II D. None of the above

25. Which of the following issues does the office of the governor is lacking currently?
I. Redundancy.
II. Autonomy.
III. Impartiality
A. Only I B. Only III
C. Only II and III D. None of the above

26. Which sport does Rhythm Sangwan, who was recently in the news, plays?
A. Wrestling B. Cricket
C. Shooting D. Hockey

27. Who is the author of the book "Yug Purush, Bharat Ratna, Atal Ji"?
A. Ramesh Pokhriyal
B. Praveen Kumar Pandey
C. Ramesh Datt Dikshit
D. Neeraj Srivastava

28. Tin Bigha Corridor is located on the border of which two countries?
A. India & Pakistan
B. India & Nepal
C. India & Bangladesh
D. India & Myanmar

29. Which of the following islands has been renamed after former President A.P.J. Abdul Kalam?
A. Barren Island B. Majuli Island
C. Katchal Island D. Wheeler Island

30. Which of the following is not among the major language families spoken in India?
A. Indo-European B. Altaic
C. Dravidian D. Sino-Tibetan

31. In which state/UT the village 'Mana', now being called as the first Indian village, is located?
A. Sikkim
B. Arunachal Pradesh
C. Uttarakhand
D. Jammu and Kashmir

32. Which one of the following state legislatures passed a law to enable factories to have working hours up to 12 hours per day ?
A. Tamil Nadu B. Kerala
C. Odisha D. West Bengal

33. In which city a Millets Experience Centre (MEC) which is first of its kind was inaugurated ?
A. Hyderabad B. New Delhi
C. Mysore D. Chennai

21. B	**22.** D	**23.** A	**24.** C	**25.** C	**26.** C	**27.** A
28. C	**29.** D	**30.** B	**31.** C	**32.** A	**33.** B	

34. Viksit Bharat Sankalp Yatra was flagged off by the Hon'ble Prime Minister from:
A. New Delhi B. Kunthi
C. Vadodara D. Varanasi

35. In which state was the Buland Bharat exercise conducted?
A. Tamil Nadu
B. Andhra Pradesh
C. Arunachal Pradesh
D. Rajasthan

36. Which festival is celebrated in north India when Pongal is celebrated in Tamil Nadu?
A. Holi B. Makar Sankranti
C. Diwali D. Baishaki

37. Lucknow Gharana and Jaipur Gharana are related to which dance?
A. Jatra B. Ghumar
C. Kathak D. OttanThullal

38. Which airport in India has been recognized as the world's most punctual airport, as per the recent report released by Cirium?
A. Kempegowda International Airport
B. Rajiv Gandhi International Airport
C. Indira Gandhi International Airport
D. Chhatrapati Shivaji Maharaj International Airport.

39. Which of the following was India's First Biosphere Reserves?
A. Sunderbans B. Nanda Devi
C. Nilgiri D. Pachmarhi

40. In 15th Asian shooting championship (2023), the winner was __________.
A. India B. China
C. South Korea D. Japan

41. Fiscal deficit for 2023-24, in Union Budget of India, was fixed at
A. 5.9% B. 4.9%
C. 4.2% D. 7.5%

42. As per the Union Budget of India 2023-24, individual income tax rate applicable for the annual income above 15 lacs in a year is:
A. 25% B. 30%
C. 40% D. 20%

43. The religion which is followed by nearly 30% of the world's population is ________
A. Islam B. Judaism
C. Hinduism D. Christianity

44. 'Sag Dawa' is a _________ festival and is one of the popular festivals of the state of ________
A. Buddhist ; Sikkim
B. Hindu ; Arunachal Pradesh
C. Buddhist ; Maharashtra
D. Tribal ; Jharkhand

45. Which of the following players won 'Orange Cap' in IPL 2023?
A. Rohit Sharma B. Hardik Pandya
C. Mohd. Shami D. Shubman Gill

46. 'Purple Cap' in IPL is awarded for
A. Taking maximum number of wickets in tournament
B. Hitting maximum number of sixes in tournament
C. Scoring maximum number of runs in tournament
D. Taking maximum number of catches in tournament

47. Who is the Governor of Reserve Bank of India?
A. Sh. A.K. Chawla
B. Sh. Rajiv Kumar
C. Sh. Shaktikanta Das
D. Sh Urjit Patel

48. Who is Chief Election Commissioner of India?
A. Sh. Rajiv Kumar
B. Dr. Sukhbir Singh Sandhu
C. Sh. Amitabh Kant
D. Sh. G.D. Marwah

34. B	**35.** C	**36.** B	**37.** C	**38.** B	**39.** C	**40.** B	**41.** A
42. B	**43.** D	**44.** A	**45.** D	**46.** A	**47.** C	**48.** A	

49. Ajanta caves are on the bank of river:
A. Krishna B. Penna
C. Cauvery D. Waghora

50. 'The India Story' is written by
A. Bimal Jalan B. Ruskin Bond
C. Rajnath Singh D. Shashi Tharoor

51. The average of marks of 13 papers is 40. The average of marks of the first 7 papers is 42 and that of the last 7 papers is 35. What are the marks of the seventh paper?
A. 17 B. 18
C. 19 D. 20

52. 50 is divided into two parts such that the sum of their reciprocals is $\frac{1}{12}$. Find the two parts.
A. 35 and 15 B. 30 and 20
C. 25 and 25 D. 10 and 40

53. If $3^{(x-y)} = 27$ and $3^{(x+y)} = 243$, then x is equal to:
A. 0 B. 2
C. 4 D. 6

54. Fresh grapes contain 80 per cent water while dry grapes contain 10 per cent water. If the weight of dry grapes is 250 kg what was its total weight when it was fresh?
A. 1000 kg B. 1100 kg
C. 1125 kg D. 1225 kg

55. A person purchases 90 toys and sells 40 toys at a gain of 10% and 50 toys at a gain of 20%. If he sold all of them at a uniform profit of 15%, then he would have got ₹ 40 less. The cost price of each toy is:
A. ₹ 50 B. ₹ 60
C. ₹ 80 D. ₹ 90

56. If two pipes function simultaneously, the reservoir will be filled in 12 hours. The second pipe takes 10 hours more than the first to fill the reservoir. How many hours does it take the second pipe to fill the reservoir?
A. 30 hrs B. 25 hrs
C. 20 hrs D. 35 hrs

57. Ram can row upstream at 20 kmph and downstream at 24 kmph. Find Ram's rowing speed in still water?
A. 22 kmph B. 24 kmph
C. 20 kmph D. 10 kmph

58. The rate at which a sum becomes four times of itself in 15 years at simple interest, will be
A. 15% B. $17\frac{1}{2}\%$
C. 20% D. 25%

59. A rectangular room can be partitioned into two equal square rooms by a partition 8 metres long. What is the area of the rectangular room in square meters?
A. 49 B. 147
C. 196 D. None of these

60. If the radius of a circle is increased by 75%, then its circumference will increase by
A. 25% B. 50%
C. 75% D. 100%

61. A circular road runs around a circular garden. If the difference between the circumference of the outer circle and the inner circle is 88 m, the width of the road is:
A. 12 m B. 13 m
C. 14 m D. 10 m

62. A dealer proposes to sell his goods at cost price but he uses a false weight of 950 grams for a kilograms. The gain per cent of the dealer is:
A. $4\frac{5}{19}\%$ B. 5%
C. $1\frac{5}{19}\%$ D. $5\frac{5}{19}\%$

49. D	**50.** A	**51.** C	**52.** B	**53.** C	**54.** C	**55.** C
56. A	**57.** A	**58.** C	**59.** D	**60.** C	**61.** C	**62.** D

63. 10 years ago, the average age of a family of 4 members was 24 years. Since then, two children having been born, still the average age of the family is the same today. If the two children differ in age by 2 years, find the present age of the younger child.

A. 3 years B. 2 years
C. 4 years D. 5 years

64. Rahul decided to donate 5% of his salary. On the day of donation, he changed his mind and donated ₹ 1687.50, which was 75% of what he had decided earlier. How much is Rahul's salary?

A. ₹ 33750
B. ₹ 37500
C. ₹ 45000
D. Cannot be determined

65. The speed of electric train is 25% more than that of steam engine train. What is the time taken by an electric train to cover a distance which a steam engine takes 4 hours 25 minutes to cover?

A. $3\frac{1}{10}$ *hr* B. $3\frac{11}{15}$ *hr*
C. $3\frac{11}{12}$ *hr* D. $3\frac{8}{15}$ *hr*

66. 1800, ?, 60, 15, 5, 2.5

A. 300 B. 600
C. 120 D. 240

67. Jay's house is 100 m North of his uncle's office. His uncle's house is located 200 m West of his uncle's office. Kailash is the friend of Jay and he stays 100 m East of Jay's house. The office of Kailash is located 100 m South of his house. Then, how far is his uncle's house from Kailash's office?

A. 200 m B. 300 m
C. 400 m D. 500 m

68. If 'P – Q', means 'Q is son of P', 'P × Q' means 'P is brother of Q', 'P ÷ Q' means 'Q is sister of P' and 'P + Q' means 'P is mother of Q', then which of the following is definitely true about 'N × K – M ÷ L'?

A. K is father of L and M
B. L is daughter of K and niece of uncle N
C. K is father of L and M, his son and daughter respectively
D. M is uncle of K's, brother N

69. Sachin read a book on Sunday. Shradha read that book one day prior to Amit but 4 days after Sachin. On which day did Amit read the book?

A. Friday B. Thursday
C. Tuesday D. Saturday

70. A watch, which gains uniformly, is 3 min slow at 12 noon on Sunday and is 5 min 36 sec fast at 4 pm on the next Sunday. At what time it was correct?

A. 12 am on same day
B. 12 pm on Monday
C. 12 am on Tuesday
D. 12 am on Wednesday

71. The letters in the word 'MORTIFY' are changed in such a way that the vowels are replaced by the previous letter in the English alphabet and the consonants are replaced by the next letter in the English alphabet. Which of the following will be in the middle of the third letter from the right end and third letter from left end of the new set of letters?

A. U B. H
C. G D. None of these

72. If all the digits in each of the numbers are arranged in descending order within the numbers, which of the following will be the highest number in the new arrangement of numbers?

A. 684 B. 385
C. 296 D. 437

63. A	**64.** C	**65.** D	**66.** A	**67.** B	**68.** B
69. A	**70.** D	**71.** A	**72.** C		

73. Some groups of letters are given, all of which except one, share a common similarity while one is different. Select the odd one.
A. GDA B. OLI
C. VSP D. WYZ

74. Ajay reaches at a certain place on Friday and found he reaches the place 3 days before. If he had reached the place on coming Sunday, then how many days before or after he would have reached the place?
A. One day before B. One day after
C. 2 days after D. 2 days before

75. A, Q, Y and Z are different persons. Z is the father of Q. A is the daughter of Y and Y is the son of Z. If P is the son of Y and B is the brother of P, then
A. B and Y are brothers
B. A is the sister of B
C. Z is the uncle of B
D. Q and Y are brothers

76. Founder of Tata group was
A. Dorabji Tata
B. J.R.D. Tata
C. Ratan Tata
D. Jamsetji Nusserwanji Tata

77. "Management is the process of designing and maintaining an environment in which individuals, working together in groups, efficiently accomplish selected aims." This definition is given by :
A. Robert L. Trewelly and M. Gene Newport
B. Harold Koontz and Heinz Weihrich
C. Kreitner
D. None of above

78. Government support for MSMEs often includes:
A. Increased tax burden
B. Subsidies and easier loan access
C. Stricter regulations and compliance
D. Limited marketing opportunities

79. Sources of Business Finance: Trade credit is a form of short-term financing provided by:
A. Banks
B. Venture capitalists
C. Suppliers
D. Government agencies

80. The General Agreement on Tariffs and Trade (GATT) aimed to:
A. Increase trade barriers
B. Reduce trade barriers between nations
C. Regulate international investments
D. Standardize product safety regulations

81. What is a key characteristic of a successful entrepreneur?
A. Risk aversion
B. Disorganized approach
C. Lack of innovation
D. Strong work ethic and vision

82. Which of the following is not a feature of a company?
A. Limited liability
B. Perpetual succession
C. Transferability of interest
D. Mutual agency

83. Equity capital can be raised by a company through which of the following?
A. Issue of bonds
B. Issue of debentures
C. Money market instruments
D. Public issue of shares

84. Which of the following is NOT a requirement for company registration in most countries?
A. Certificate of commencement of business
B. Memorandum of Association (MOA)
C. Articles of Association (AOA)
D. Minimum number of directors

85. The main difference between a business-to-consumer (B2C) and business-to-business (B2B) e-commerce model is the:
A. Payment methods used
B. Target customer base
C. Type of products or services offered
D. Technology platform used

73. D	**74.** A	**75.** B	**76.** D	**77.** B	**78.** B	**79.** C
80. B	**81.** D	**82.** D	**83.** D	**84.** A	**85.** B	

86. What is the primary goal of business ethics?
A. To maximize short-term profits
B. To create a fair and responsible business environment
C. To avoid government regulations
D. To prioritize shareholder interests

87. Businesses have a social responsibility to:
A. Act ethically and contribute to society
B. Maximize profits only
C. Minimize government regulations
D. Focus solely on customer satisfaction

88. Which of the following is NOT a type of public enterprise?
A. Departmental undertaking
B. Statutory corporation
C. Cooperative
D. Government company

89. Which of the following is NOT a core function of business?
A. Production of goods and services
B. Earning profits
C. Sustainability
D. Consumption of goods and services

90. What is the purpose of a marketing campaign?
A. To increase production costs
B. To create brand awareness and promote a product or service
C. To handle customer complaints
D. To manage a company's finances

91. Budget is ____________
A. A record of past financial transactions
B. A report on a company's financial performance
C. A legal document for borrowing money
D. A financial plan for the future

92. What is an example of a consumer right?
A. The right to be informed of product price
B. The right to buy the product at a reasonable price
C. The right against unwanted marketing calls
D. The right to warranty of a product.

93. What is the difference between market research and target marketing?
A. Market research is broader, target marketing is specific.
B. Target marketing is broader, market research is specific.
C. They are the same thing.
D. Market research focuses on sales, target marketing on branding.

94. The time value of money is:
A. The cost of borrowing money
B. The concept that money has different values at different times
C. The risk associated with investing
D. The amount of interest earned on savings

95. The 4Ps of marketing refer to:
A. Price, Place, Packaging, Promotion
B. Product, Price, People, Promotion
C. Positioning, Planning, Pricing, Promotion
D. Product, Price, Place, Promotion

96. Which statement best describes the relationship between directing and controlling?
A. Directing sets goals, and controlling ensures they are achieved.
B. Controlling provides direction for employees to follow.
C. Directing and controlling are independent functions.
D. Both directing and controlling involve motivating employees.

97. Which of the following is NOT a common method used for controlling in organizations?
A. Performance appraisals
B. Setting deadlines
C. Brainstorming new ideas
D. Budget monitoring

86. B	**87.** A	**88.** C	**89.** D	**90.** B	**91.** D
92. A	**93.** A	**94.** B	**95.** D	**96.** A	**97.** C

98. A manager provides clear instructions, assigns tasks, and offers feedback to a team working on a project. This is an example of:
A. Planning B. Directing
C. Controlling D. Organizing

99. Unity of Command refers to:
A. Having a clear reporting structure
B. Encouraging employee participation
C. Specialization of tasks
D. Focusing on short-term goals

100. The process of setting goals, outlining actions, and allocating resources is called:
A. Organizing
B. Staffing
C. Directing
D. Planning

EXPLANATORY ANSWERS

1. (C): The sentence "Sumit ________ to the wedding. He has an important engagement that day." is correctly completed by "can't go." This is because "can't go" correctly conveys that Sumit is unable to attend due to a prior engagement. The other options are incorrect: "could go" suggests possibility, not impossibility; "needed to go" implies obligation, not inability; and "haven't to go" is grammatically incorrect as it should be "don't have to go."

2. (D): The correct option is "May." The sentence "_________ I have your permission to leave the office early?" requires a formal and polite request, and "May" is the appropriate word for this context. "Would" and "Would not" are more about hypothetical situations or willingness, while "Can't" is negative and inappropriate for a polite request.

3. (C): The error in the sentence "Do you think you/should come over at/6 pm tomorrow?" is in part (C) "should come over at." The correct phrase should be "should come over by". The preposition "at" is incorrectly placed before the time, disrupting the sentence flow.

4. (D): The error in the sentence "Bismillah would play/the shehnai when/he was very young./No error" is in part (A) "Bismillah would play." It should be "Bismillah played" or "Bismillah used to play" to correctly convey past habitual action. "Would play" is incorrect in this context as it is generally used for future not the past.

5. (D): The error in the sentence "You can't borrow/my car if/you like to go for a drive./No error" is in part (*a*) "You can't borrow." The correct sentence should be "You can borrow my car if you like to go for a drive."

6. (A): The error in the sentence "You can listen to/what the doctor says/if you want to/get cured" is in part (*a*) "You can listen to." It should be "You should listen to" to imply recommendation or necessity rather than permission.

7. (B): The error in the sentence "I'm not sure./Kiran should/be in Delhi." is in part (*b*) "Kiran should." It should be "Kiran might" or "Kiran could" to indicate uncertainty. "Should" implies a sense of obligation or expectation, which doesn't fit the context of uncertainty.

8. (C): The correct option is "can't you." The sentence "Now you can make question

98. B	**99.** A	**100.** D

tags, __________?" requires a positive statement followed by a negative question tag. Therefore, "can't you" correctly follows the positive statement "Now you can make question tags."

9. **(A):** The correct option is "shall we." The sentence "Let us start now, _________?" requires the question tag "shall we" to seek agreement or confirmation in a polite manner. The other options are grammatically incorrect or inappropriate for this context.

10. **(B):** The correct option is "would." The sentence "He believed that he _____ turn out to be a cheat." uses "would" to indicate a belief about a future event in a past context. "Will" is incorrect because it suggests certainty in the future without the past context. "Should" and "must" imply obligation or necessity, which don't fit here.

11. **(C):** The correct option is "why." The sentence "Tell me the reason _______ they could not marry." requires "why" to explain the cause or reason. "That" would be used to introduce a clause, "so" implies a result, and "because" would make the sentence redundant. "Why" properly introduces the reason in this context.

12. **(C):** The correct option is "had seen." The sentence "He would have believed if he______ with his own eyes last week." requires "had seen" to correctly form a third conditional sentence, which expresses a hypothetical situation in the past. "Saw" and "have seen" do not fit the past perfect requirement, and "could see" is not appropriate here.

13. **(C):** The correct option is "he will." The sentence "As he is obstinate _____ not obey the instructions." requires "he will" to indicate the consequence of his obstinacy. "So he will" is redundant, "that he would" and "he must" imply a different meaning than intended. "He will not obey" correctly completes the sentence.

14. **(A):** The error in the sentence "Everybody was/ watching/ the TV,/ won't they?" is in part (A) "won't they." The correct question tag should be "weren't they" to match the past continuous tense "was watching." "Won't they" is incorrect as it does not match the tense and form of the main clause.

15. **(B):** The correct option is "through." The sentence "Your business is likely to fall _______ for want of sufficient investment." requires "through" to mean that the business is likely to fail due to insufficient investment. "Off," "down," and "at" do not convey the intended meaning of failure due to lack of investment.

16. **(C):** The correct option is "up." The sentence "Robert was cut ____ because he had been deceived by the shopkeeper." uses "up" to mean that Robert was very upset or emotionally disturbed. "Off," "down," and "out" do not accurately convey the emotional impact of being deceived.

17. **(B):** The synonym for "dainty" is "exquisite." "Dainty" refers to something that is delicately beautiful or fine. "Exquisite" similarly means beautifully made or designed. "Insipid" means lacking flavor, "deformed" means misshapen, and "spiritual" relates to the spirit, none of which are synonymous with "dainty."

18. **(C):** The meaning of "implacable" is "relentless." "Implacable" describes someone who cannot be appeased or pacified and is unyielding in their stance. "Considerate" and "empathetic" suggest understanding and kindness, while "friendly" indicates amiability, none of which are synonymous with "implacable."

19. **(A):** The word opposite in meaning to "niggardly" is "extravagant." "Niggardly" means miserly or stingy, while "extravagant" means spending much more than is necessary or lavish. "Shameful" means deserving or

bringing shame, "ruthless" means having no pity, and "pompous" means self-important, none of which are antonyms for "niggardly."

20. **(A):** A person who enjoys eating and eats large amounts of food is called a "Gourmand." A "Gourmand" refers to someone who has a great love for food and eats in large quantities. A "Hedonist" seeks pleasure, "Cuisines" refers to styles of cooking, and a "Bohemian" is an unconventional lifestyle, none of which specifically relate to eating large amounts of food.

21. **(B):** The correct option is "superficial." The word "specious" means something that appears to be true or correct, but is actually false or deceptive. In the context of the passage, "specious" describes justifications that seem plausible on the surface but lack real validity. "Refined" means elegant, "possible" means feasible, and "correct" means accurate, none of which convey the deceptive quality implied by "specious."

22. **(D):** The correct option is "None of the above." The passage indicates that the post of the governor is significant and often subject to controversy. It explicitly states that the recent case is not a routine departure from norms and does not suggest that governors are often abused. Therefore, none of the provided statements correctly summarize the passage.

23. **(A):** The correct option is "Factual." The tone of the second paragraph is factual as the author presents historical references and legal opinions about the role of the governor. The author cites the Sarkaria Commission and the Supreme Court ruling to provide an objective explanation of the governor's constitutional responsibilities, without displaying emotion or personal bias.

24. **(C):** The correct option is "Only I and II." The passage states that the Sarkaria Commission described the Governor as a "Constitutional sentinel and a vital link between the Union and the State," indicating that the Governor serves as an important link between the Union and State (I) and as a custodian of the constitution (II). The statement about the Governor being an arbiter in case of a deadlock is attributed to M.K. Gandhi, not the Sarkaria Commission, so option III is not correct in this context. Therefore, the correct conclusion includes both statements I and II.

25. **(C):** The correct option is "Only II and III." The passage discusses the lack of autonomy and impartiality in the governor's office, particularly highlighting the political endorsements that compromise neutrality. It does not suggest that the governor's office is redundant; instead, it underscores the importance of the governor's constitutional role. Therefore, the issues of autonomy and impartiality are the ones currently lacking.

26. **(C):** Rhythm Sangwan is a prominent figure in the sport of shooting. Recently, she has been in the news for her remarkable performances in national and international shooting competitions. Her achievements have garnered significant attention, highlighting her as a rising star in the field of shooting. This categorically sets her apart from other sports such as wrestling, cricket, and hockey.

27. **(A):** The book "Yug Purush, Bharat Ratna, Atal Ji" was authored by Ramesh Pokhriyal. The book is a tribute to the former Indian Prime Minister Atal Bihari Vajpayee, capturing his life, political journey, and contributions to the nation. Ramesh Pokhriyal, a seasoned politician and writer, provides an insightful look into Atal Ji's legacy, making this work a notable literary piece.

28. **(C):** The Tin Bigha Corridor is located on the border of India and Bangladesh. This corridor is a strip of land that connects the Bangladeshi enclave of Dahagram–Angarpota with mainland Bangladesh. It has been a subject of bilateral agreements between India and Bangladesh, aimed at resolving border disputes and facilitating the movement of people and goods.

29. (D): Wheeler Island has been renamed after former President A.P.J. Abdul Kalam. The island, located off the coast of Odisha, is home to the Integrated Test Range, where various missile tests are conducted. Renaming it Abdul Kalam Island honors Dr. Kalam's significant contributions to India's missile and space programs, cementing his legacy in the field of aerospace and defense.

30. (B): Altaic is not among the major language families spoken in India. The major language families in India include Indo-European, Dravidian, and Sino-Tibetan. Altaic languages are primarily spoken in regions of Central Asia and are not a part of the linguistic landscape of India. This distinguishes it from the other major language families listed.

31. (C): The village 'Mana', now being called the first Indian village, is located in Uttarakhand. Mana is situated near the India-China border, close to the famous Hindu pilgrimage site of Badrinath. Its designation as the first Indian village signifies its geographical and cultural importance, especially in the context of Indian border villages.

32. (A): Tamil Nadu is the state where the legislature passed a law to enable factories to have working hours up to 12 hours per day. This decision was part of labor reforms aimed at increasing productivity and providing more flexibility to industrial operations. The legislation faced significant debate regarding workers' rights and labor conditions.

33. (B): The Millets Experience Centre (MEC), the first of its kind, was inaugurated in New Delhi. This center aims to promote the consumption and benefits of millets, a group of highly nutritious and climate-resilient grains. The MEC serves as an educational hub, providing information about the health benefits of millets and encouraging their inclusion in diets.

34. (B): The Viksit Bharat Sankalp Yatra was flagged off by the Hon'ble Prime Minister from Kunthi. This initiative is part of a broader campaign to foster development and progress across various regions of India. The yatra symbolizes the government's commitment to achieving a developed India through sustainable and inclusive growth.

35. (C): The Buland Bharat exercise was conducted in Arunachal Pradesh. This military exercise involved various drills and maneuvers to enhance the operational readiness and coordination of the Indian armed forces. Conducting such exercises in Arunachal Pradesh is significant due to the strategic importance of the region, especially concerning border security.

36. (B): Makar Sankranti is the festival celebrated in North India around the same time as Pongal in Tamil Nadu. Both festivals mark the harvest season and are celebrated in January. Makar Sankranti signifies the transition of the sun into the zodiac sign of Capricorn. It is a major harvest festival celebrated with various regional customs and traditions, such as flying kites, preparing sweets made of sesame and jaggery, and taking holy dips in rivers.

37. (C): Kathak is the dance form associated with Lucknow Gharana and Jaipur Gharana. These gharanas or schools of Kathak have distinct styles and techniques. The Lucknow Gharana is known for its expressive, graceful, and intricate movements, while the Jaipur Gharana emphasizes complex footwork and spins. Kathak is one of the eight classical dance forms of India and has a rich tradition of storytelling through dance and music.

38. (B): Rajiv Gandhi International Airport in Hyderabad has been recognized as the world's most punctual airport, as per a recent report by Cirium. This recognition highlights the airport's efficiency in managing flight schedules and minimizing delays. The airport's punctuality is a testament to its operational excellence and commitment to providing timely services to passengers.

39. **(C):** The Nilgiri Biosphere Reserve was India's first biosphere reserve, established in 1986. It is located in the Western Ghats and Nilgiri Hills in South India. The reserve encompasses parts of Tamil Nadu, Kerala, and Karnataka. It is recognized for its rich biodiversity and is home to numerous endemic species of flora and fauna. The Nilgiri Biosphere Reserve plays a crucial role in conservation efforts and sustainable development in the region.

40. **(B):** China emerged as the winner of the 15th Asian Shooting Championship in 2023. This championship brought together top shooters from across Asia to compete in various shooting events. China's dominance in the competition reflects its strong training programs, investment in sports infrastructure, and the high skill level of its athletes.

41. **(A):** The fiscal deficit for 2023-24 in the Union Budget of India was fixed at 5.9%. This figure represents the gap between the government's total expenditure and its total revenue, excluding borrowings. A fiscal deficit indicates the extent to which the government is borrowing to meet its expenses. Managing the fiscal deficit is crucial for maintaining economic stability and ensuring sustainable public finances.

42. **(B):** As per the Union Budget of India 2023-24, the individual income tax rate applicable for annual income above 15 lakhs is 30%. This tax rate is part of the government's progressive tax structure, where higher income earners are taxed at a higher rate. The 30% tax rate applies to individuals earning more than 15 lakhs annually, ensuring that those with higher incomes contribute more to the nation's tax revenues.

43. **(D):** Christianity is followed by nearly 30% of the world's population, making it the largest religion globally. With approximately 2.3 billion adherents, Christianity has a significant presence across all continents. It is based on the teachings of Jesus Christ and has numerous denominations, including Catholicism, Protestantism, and Orthodoxy, each with its own doctrines and practices.

44. **(A):** 'Sag Dawa' is a Buddhist festival celebrated in the state of Sikkim. It marks the birth, enlightenment, and death of Lord Buddha. Celebrated with great reverence, Sag Dawa includes various rituals, prayers, and processions. The festival holds immense spiritual significance for the Buddhist community in Sikkim and is one of the state's most important religious events.

45. **(D):** Shubman Gill won the 'Orange Cap' in IPL 2023. The Orange Cap is awarded to the player who scores the most runs in a single season of the Indian Premier League. He scored 890 runs in 17 innings. Gill's consistent and high-scoring performances throughout the season earned him this prestigious title, highlighting his talent and skill as a top-order batsman.

46. **(A):** The 'Purple Cap' in IPL is awarded for taking the maximum number of wickets in the tournament. This award recognizes the leading wicket-taker of the season, celebrating their ability to consistently dismiss batsmen and contribute to their team's success. The Purple Cap is a symbol of excellence in bowling within the IPL.

47. **(C):** Shaktikanta Das is the Governor of the Reserve Bank of India (RBI). He has been serving in this position since December 2018. As the head of India's central bank, Shaktikanta Das plays a crucial role in shaping monetary policy, regulating financial institutions, and ensuring economic stability. His leadership is pivotal in navigating the country's financial landscape.

48. (A): Rajiv Kumar is a former IAS officer. On 15 May, 2022 he assumed the charge as the 25th Chief Election Commissioner of India, succeeding Sushil Chandra. Appointed in 2021, he oversees the Election Commission of India, which is responsible for administering elections in the country. The Commission ensures free and fair elections, upholds the democratic process, and maintains the integrity of the electoral system. Rajiv Kumar's role is vital in safeguarding India's democracy.

49. (D): The Ajanta Caves are located on the bank of the Waghora River. These ancient rock-cut caves in Maharashtra are renowned for their exquisite Buddhist art and architecture. Dating back to the 2nd century BCE, the Ajanta Caves feature intricate carvings, paintings, and sculptures that depict the life of Buddha and various Jataka tales. The Waghora River adds to the scenic beauty of this UNESCO World Heritage Site.

50. (A): "The India Story" is written by Bimal Jalan. The book provides an insightful analysis of India's economic journey, highlighting key developments and challenges faced by the country over the years. Bimal Jalan, an eminent economist and former Governor of the Reserve Bank of India, draws on his extensive experience to offer a comprehensive narrative on India's growth and transformation.

51. (C): The total marks of 13 papers

$= 13 \times 40$

$= 520 \quad \ldots(i)$

The total marks of first 7 papers

$= 7 \times 42 = 294$

and the total marks of the last 7 papers

$= 7 \times 35 = 245$

$\therefore$ The total marks of 14 papers

$= 294 + 245$

$= 539 \quad \ldots(ii)$

from (i) and (ii), we get

the marks of the 7th papers

$= 539 - 520 = 19$

52. (B): Let two parts of 50 be a and $(50 - a)$

Then, $\frac{1}{a} + \frac{1}{(50-a)} = \frac{1}{12}$

$\Rightarrow \frac{50 - a + a}{a\,(50-a)} = \frac{1}{12}$

$\Rightarrow \frac{50}{a\,(50-a)} = \frac{1}{12}$

$\Rightarrow 50a - a^2 = 600$

$\Rightarrow a^2 - 50a + 600 = 0$

$\Rightarrow a^2 - 20a + 30a + 600 = 0$

$\Rightarrow a\,(a - 20) - 30\,(a - 20) = 0$

$\Rightarrow (a - 20)\,(a - 30) = 0$

$\Rightarrow a = 20, 30$

Hence, two parts be $a = 30$,

and $(50 - a) = 20$

53. (C): Given,

$3^{(x - y)} = 27$

$\Rightarrow 3^{(x - y)} = 3^3$

$\Rightarrow x - y = 3 \quad \ldots(i)$

and $3^{(x + y)} = 243$

$\Rightarrow 3^{(x + y)} = 3^5$

$\Rightarrow x + y = 5 \quad \ldots(ii)$

Adding (i) and (ii), we obtain

$2x = 8$

$\Rightarrow x = 4$

54. (C): Quantity of pulp in dry grapes

$= 250 \times \frac{100 - 10}{100} = 250 \times \frac{90}{100} = 225$ kg

Let the total weight of fresh grape be x kg

Then,

$x \times \frac{100 - 80}{100} = 225$

$\Rightarrow x \times \frac{20}{100} = 225$

$\Rightarrow \frac{x}{5} = 225$

$\Rightarrow x = 5 \times 225$

$= 1125$ kg

Hence, the total weight of fresh grapes

$= 1125$ kg

55. (C): Let the cost price of each toy is ₹ x

Then, S.P. of 40 toys $= 40x \times \frac{110}{100}$

$= ₹\ 44x$

and S.P. of 50 toys $= 50x \times \frac{120}{100}$

$= ₹\ 60x$

and S.P. of 90 toys $= 90x \times \frac{115}{100}$

$= 90x \times \frac{23}{20}$

$= ₹\ \frac{207}{2} x$

$= ₹\ 103.5$

According to question

$44x + 60x - 103.5x = 40$

$\Rightarrow \quad 104x - 103.5x = 40$

$\Rightarrow \quad 0.5x = 40$

$\Rightarrow \quad x = ₹\ 80$

Hence the cost price of each toy is ₹ 80.

56. (A): Let the first pipe takes x hours to fill the reservoir.

Then, the second pipe takes $(x + 10)$ hours to fill the reservoir

$\therefore \quad \frac{1}{x} + \frac{1}{x+10} = \frac{1}{12}$

$\Rightarrow \quad \frac{x+10+x}{x(x+10)} = \frac{1}{12}$

$\Rightarrow \quad \frac{2x+10}{x^2+10x} = \frac{1}{12}$

$\Rightarrow x^2 + 10x = 12(2x + 10)$

$\Rightarrow \quad x^2 + 10x - 24x - 120 = 0$

$\Rightarrow \quad x^2 - 14x - 120 = 0$

$\Rightarrow \quad x^2 - 20x + 6x - 120 = 0$

$\Rightarrow \quad x(x - 20) + 6(x - 20) = 0$

$\Rightarrow \quad (x - 20)(x + 6) = 0$

either $\quad x - 20 = 0$ or $x + 6 = 0$

$\Rightarrow \quad x = 20$, or $x = -6$

Hence, the second pipe takes $(x + 10)$ hrs.

$= 20 + 10 = 30$ hrs. to fill the reservoir.

57. (A): Let Ram's rowing speed in still water be x kmph

and speed of the current be y kmph

Then,

$x - y = 20 \quad \ldots(i)$

$x + y = 24 \quad \ldots(ii)$

from adding (i) and (ii), we obtain.

$2x = 44$

$\Rightarrow \quad x = 22$ kmph

58. (C): At simple interest,

$\text{rate} = \frac{(n-1) \times 100}{\text{time}}$

$\Rightarrow \quad \text{rate} = \frac{(4-1) \times 100}{15}$

$= \frac{3 \times 100}{15} = 20\%$

Hence, required rate $= 20\%$

59. (D): Given, A rectangular room can be partitioned into two equal square rooms by a partition 8 m long.

$\therefore$ Side of a square room = 8 m

$\Rightarrow$ breadth of a rectangular room = 8 m

and length of a rectangular room

$= 8 + 8 = 16$ m

Hence, the area of the rectangular room

$= l \times b = 16 \times 8$

$= 128$ Sq. m

Now of the given options matches the answer.

$\therefore$ Answer is option (D)

60. (C): Let the radius of a circle be r

Then, circumference $= 2\pi r$

given, the radius is increased by 75%

$= r \times \frac{175}{100} = \frac{7}{4} r$

$\therefore$ Increase in circumference

$= 2\pi \frac{7}{4} r = \frac{7}{2} \pi r$

$\therefore$ Percentage increase $= \frac{\frac{7}{2}\pi r - 2\pi r}{2\pi r} \times 100$

$= \frac{\frac{3}{2}\pi r}{2\pi r} \times 100 = 75\%$

61. (C): Let the radius of outer circle be R and the radius of inner circle be r

Then,

$$2\pi R - 2\pi r = 88 \text{ m}$$

$$\Rightarrow \quad 2\pi (R - r) = 88$$

$$\Rightarrow \quad 2 \times \frac{22}{7}(R - r) = 88$$

$$\Rightarrow \quad \frac{44}{7}(R - r) = 88$$

$$\Rightarrow \quad (R - r) = 14 \text{ m}$$

Hence, the width of the road is

$$(R - r) = 14 \text{ m}$$

62. (D): The gain per cent of the dealer is

$$= \left[\frac{\text{Error}}{\text{True value} - \text{Error}}\right] \times 100$$

$$= \left[\frac{50}{1000 - 50} \times 100\right]$$

$$= \frac{50 \times 100}{950} = \frac{100}{19} = 5\frac{5}{19}\%$$

63. (A): 10 years ago,

The total age of a family of 4 members

$= 4 \times 24 = 96$ years

Now,

present age of family of 4 members

$= 96 + 40$

$= 136$ years

Since, 2 children having been born,

Still the average age of the family of 6 members = 24 years

Total age of the family of 6 members

$= 6 \times 24 = 144$ years

Present age of 2 children $= 144 - 136$

$= 8$ years

Let present age of younger child be x

Then, $x + (x + 2) = 8$

$$\Rightarrow \quad 2x = 6 \Rightarrow x = 3$$

Hence, present age of the younger child

$x = 3$ years

64. (C): Let Rahul's Salary = ₹ x

Then $\quad x \times \frac{5}{100} \times \frac{75}{100} =$ ₹ 1687.50

$$\Rightarrow \quad x \times \frac{1}{20} \times \frac{3}{4} = 1687.50$$

$$\Rightarrow \quad x = \frac{1687.50 \times 20 \times 4}{3}$$

$$\Rightarrow \quad x = 45000$$

Hence, Rahul's Salary = ₹ 45000

65. (D): Let the speed of steam engine train be x kmph then the speed of electric train

$$x \times \frac{125}{100} = \frac{5}{4}x \text{ kmph}$$

Now, distance travelled by steam engine

$$= \text{speed} \times \text{time} = x \times 4\frac{25}{60} \text{ km}$$

$$= x \times 4\frac{5}{12}$$

$$= \frac{53}{12}x \text{ km}$$

Hence, the time taken by an electric train to cover that distance

$$= \frac{\frac{53}{12}x}{\frac{5}{4}x} = \frac{53}{12} \times \frac{4}{5}$$

$$= \frac{53}{15} = 3\frac{8}{15} \text{ hr.}$$

66. (A): 1800 [300] 60 15 5 2.5

$\times\frac{1}{6}$ $\times\frac{1}{5}$ $\times\frac{1}{4}$ $\times\frac{1}{3}$ $\times\frac{1}{2}$

Hence ? = 300

67. (B):

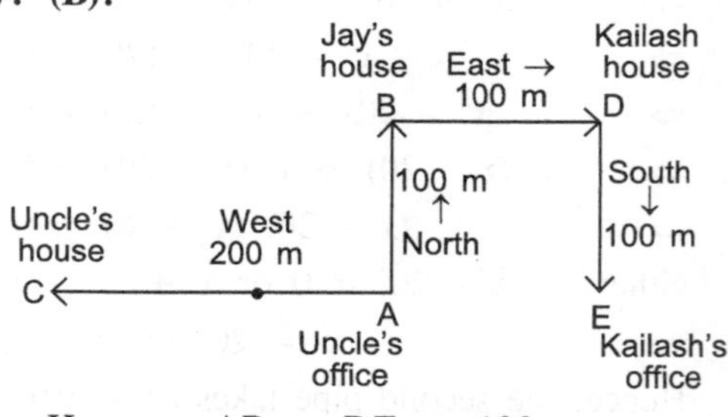

Here, $\quad AB = DE = 100$ m,

$\therefore \quad BD = EA = 100$ m

$$EC = EA + AC$$
$$= 100 + 200 = 300 \text{ m}$$

Hence, distance of his uncle's house from Kailash's office = EC = 300 m

68. (B): Given, N × K – M ÷ L

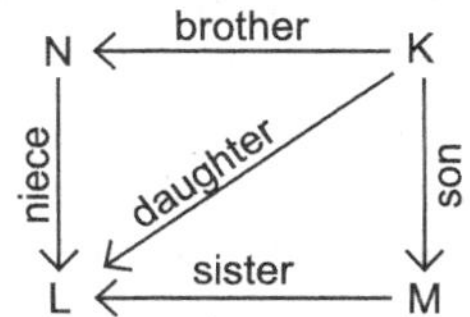

Hence, option (B) L is daughter of K and niece of uncle N is definitely true.

69. (A): Given,

Sachin —read a book→ Sunday
Shradha ——→ Thursday
Amit ——→ Friday

Hence, Amit read a book on Friday.

71. (A): Given, word "MORTIFY"
New set of letters : NNSUHGZ
↑ ↑

Here, 3rd letter from the right end = H and 3rd letter from left end = S
∴ the middle of H and S = U

72. (C): Given, New arrangement

A. 684 ⇒ 864
B. 385 ⇒ 853
C. 296 ⇒ 962
D. 437 ⇒ 743

Hence, option (C) 296 will be the highest number, in the new arrangement of numbers.

73. (D):

A. 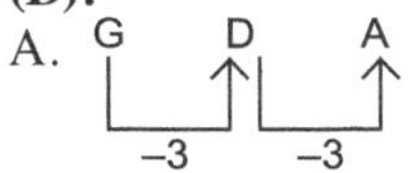

B. 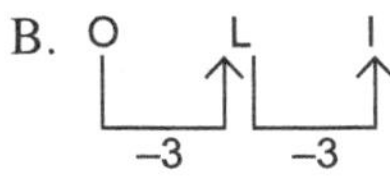

C. 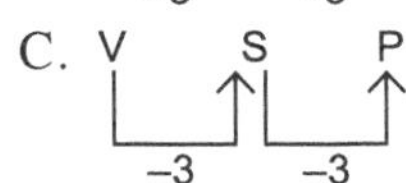

D. 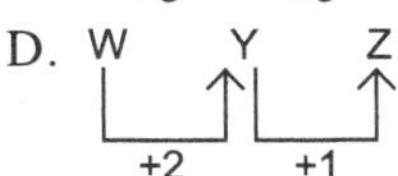

Here, option (D) is the odd one.

74. (A): Ajay reaches at a certain place on Friday which is 3 days earlier. It means the exact day of reaching was (Friday + 3 days) Monday. So when he reaches that place on Sunday, it means he would have reached the place (Monday – Sunday =) one day before.

75. (B):

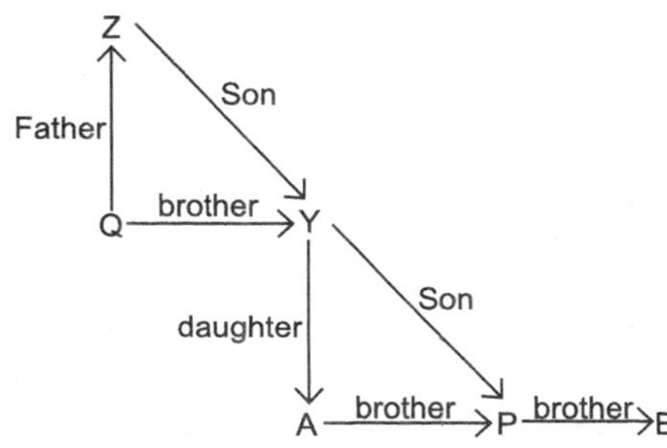

Here, option (B) A is the sister of B.

76. (D): The founder of the Tata Group was Jamsetji Nusserwanji Tata. He established the Tata Group in 1868 with a vision to contribute to India's industrial and economic growth. Jamsetji Tata is renowned for setting up the Tata Steel Company, which was India's first steel plant. His legacy includes pioneering efforts in various sectors such as textiles, hospitality, and steel, laying the foundation for one of India's largest and most respected conglomerates.

77. (B): The definition of management as "the process of designing and maintaining an environment in which individuals, working together in groups, efficiently accomplish selected aims" was given by Harold Koontz and Heinz Weihrich. They emphasized that management involves creating an environment conducive to achieving organizational goals through efficient teamwork and resource utilization. Their contributions to management theory and education have been influential in shaping modern management practices.

78. (B): Government support for MSMEs (Micro, Small, and Medium Enterprises) often includes subsidies and easier loan access. These measures are designed to encourage the growth and development of MSMEs, which are crucial for economic development, employment generation, and innovation. Subsidies can help reduce operational costs, while easier loan access improves financial liquidity, enabling MSMEs to expand and sustain their operations.

79. (C): Trade credit is a form of short-term financing provided by suppliers. It allows businesses to purchase goods or services on credit and pay for them at a later date. This type of financing is essential for managing cash flow and maintaining inventory levels without immediate outlay of cash. Trade credit terms typically vary, but common arrangements include 30, 60, or 90 days for payment.

80. (B): The General Agreement on Tariffs and Trade (GATT) aimed to reduce trade barriers between nations. Established in 1948, GATT sought to promote international trade by lowering tariffs, quotas, and other trade restrictions. The agreement facilitated a series of negotiations that led to substantial reductions in trade barriers, contributing to the expansion of global trade. GATT was succeeded by the World Trade Organization (WTO) in 1995.

81. (D): A key characteristic of a successful entrepreneur is a strong work ethic and vision. Successful entrepreneurs are typically characterized by their ability to work hard, persevere through challenges, and maintain a clear vision for their business. They are often innovative, adaptable, and willing to take calculated risks to achieve their goals. These traits enable them to navigate the complexities of starting and growing a business.

82. (D): Mutual agency is not a feature of a company. A company is characterized by limited liability, perpetual succession, and transferability of interest. Limited liability means shareholders are only liable up to the amount they invested. Perpetual succession ensures that the company continues to exist regardless of changes in ownership. Transferability of interest allows shareholders to transfer their shares. Mutual agency, where each partner can bind the business, is a feature of partnerships, not companies.

83. (D): Equity capital can be raised by a company through the public issue of shares. By issuing shares to the public, a company can attract investment from a wide pool of investors, thereby raising funds for its operations and growth. This method involves listing the company on a stock exchange, where shares can be bought and sold. Bonds, debentures, and money market instruments are other forms of financing but do not involve equity capital.

84. (A): A Certificate of Commencement of Business is not a requirement for company registration in most countries. The primary requirements for company registration typically include the Memorandum of Association (MOA), Articles of Association (AOA), and a minimum number of directors. The Certificate of Commencement of Business was previously required in some jurisdictions, but many have abolished this requirement to simplify the registration process and encourage entrepreneurship.

85. (B): The main difference between a business-to-consumer (B2C) and business-to-business (B2B) e-commerce model is the target customer base. B2C e-commerce involves transactions directly between businesses and individual consumers, offering products or services for personal use. B2B e-commerce, on the other hand, involves transactions between businesses, focusing on wholesale, manufacturing, or supply chain services. The nature of transactions, sales volume, and marketing strategies differ significantly between B2C and B2B models.,

86. (B): The primary goal of business ethics is to create a fair and responsible business environment. Business ethics involve the application of ethical principles to business situations to ensure fairness, transparency, and integrity. Ethical business practices build trust among stakeholders, improve the company's reputation, and contribute to long-term success. Unlike the short-term focus on profits, business ethics emphasize sustainable and socially responsible practices.

87. (A): Businesses have a social responsibility to act ethically and contribute to society. Social responsibility means that businesses should balance profit-making activities with activities that benefit society. This includes ethical labour practices, environmental stewardship, philanthropy, and community engagement. While maximizing profits is important, integrating social responsibility ensures sustainable growth and positive societal impact.

88. (C): Cooperatives are not a type of public enterprise. Public enterprises typically include departmental undertakings, statutory corporations, and government companies, which are owned and operated by the government to provide essential services and goods. Cooperatives, on the other hand, are autonomous associations of people united voluntarily to meet their common economic, social, and cultural needs through a jointly-owned and democratically-controlled enterprise.

89. (D): Consumption of goods and services is not a core function of business. Core functions of a business include the production of goods and services, earning profits, and ensuring sustainability. Businesses focus on producing and delivering value to customers, managing operations efficiently, and generating profits for growth. Consumption is the act of using goods and services, which is performed by customers, not the business itself.

90. (B): The purpose of a marketing campaign is to create brand awareness and promote a product or service. Effective marketing campaigns aim to reach the target audience, communicate the value proposition, and encourage customers to take action, such as making a purchase. Marketing campaigns utilize various strategies, including advertising, social media, and promotions, to increase visibility and sales.

91. (D): A budget is a financial plan for the future. It outlines expected revenues, expenses, and resource allocations over a specific period. Budgets help organizations plan for future financial needs, control costs, and ensure that funds are available for essential activities. They provide a framework for financial decision-making and performance monitoring, enabling organizations to achieve their financial goals.

92. (A): An example of a consumer right is the right to be informed of product price. Consumer rights are designed to protect buyers from unfair practices and ensure they have access to accurate information. This right ensures transparency in pricing, enabling consumers to make informed purchasing decisions. Other consumer rights include the right to safety, the right to choose, and the right to be heard.

93. (A): The difference between market research and target marketing is that market research is broader, and target marketing is specific. Market research involves collecting and analyzing data about the market, including consumer preferences, market trends, and competitive landscape. Target marketing, on the other hand, focuses on identifying and reaching a specific group of consumers who are most likely to buy the product or service, based on market research insights.

94. (B): The time value of money is the concept that money has different values at different times. This principle states that a sum of money received today is worth more than the same sum received in the future due to its potential earning capacity. This concept is fundamental in finance, influencing investment decisions, interest calculations, and discounting future cash flows.

95. (D): The 4Ps of marketing refer to Product, Price, Place, and Promotion. These elements form the marketing mix, which businesses use to achieve their marketing objectives. The product refers to what the company is selling, price is how much it will charge, place is where the product will be sold, and promotion involves the methods used to advertise and sell the product. These four elements are crucial for developing effective marketing strategies.

96. (A): The relationship between directing and controlling is that directing sets goals, and controlling ensures they are achieved. Directing involves guiding and motivating employees to meet organizational objectives. Controlling, on the other hand, involves monitoring performance, comparing it with set goals, and taking corrective actions if necessary. Together, these functions ensure that the organization stays on track to achieve its objectives efficiently.

97. (C): Brainstorming new ideas is not a common method used for controlling in organizations. Common controlling methods include performance appraisals, setting deadlines, and budget monitoring. These methods help ensure that organizational activities are aligned with planned goals and standards. Brainstorming is typically a creative process used for generating ideas and solutions, rather than for monitoring or controlling.

98. (B): A manager providing clear instructions, assigning tasks, and offering feedback to a team working on a project is an example of directing. Directing involves leading, guiding, and motivating employees to achieve organizational goals. It includes giving clear instructions, delegating tasks, providing feedback, and ensuring effective communication. This function is crucial for maintaining team productivity and achieving project objectives.

99. (A): Unity of Command refers to having a clear reporting structure. This principle ensures that each employee reports to only one manager, preventing confusion and conflicting instructions. Unity of Command is essential for maintaining order, discipline, and effective communication within an organization. It helps streamline decision-making processes and ensures accountability.

100. (D): The process of setting goals, outlining actions, and allocating resources is called planning. Planning involves defining organizational objectives and determining the best course of action to achieve them. It includes setting goals, developing strategies, and allocating resources to implement the plans. Effective planning provides direction, reduces uncertainty, and facilitates coordination within the organization.

Previous Paper (Solved)

BBA Entrance Exam 2023*

1. We have .... Eucalyptus tree in our garden.
   A. a B. an
   C. the D. no article
2. He knows a lot of people. Most of them are .... engineers.
   A. a B. an
   C. the D. no article required
3. Choose the correct option that represents the indirect speech for the following sentence:

   He said to his servant, "Why are you so lazy today?"
   A. He asked his servant why he was so lazy that day.
   B. He asked his servant why he had been so lazy that day.
   C. He asked his servant why he was being so lazy that day.
   D. He asked his servant that why he was so lazy today.
4. Choose the correct option that represents the passive voice of the following sentence:

   This book interests me.
   A. I have been interested by this book.
   B. I was interested in this book.
   C. I will be interested by this book.
   D. I am interested in this book.
5. Choose the correct option that represents the passive voice of the following sentence:

   The girl laughed at the beggar.
   A. The beggar was laughed by the girl.
   B. The beggar was being laughed by the girl.
   C. The beggar was laughed at by the girl.
   D. The beggar was being laughed at by the girl.
6. The antonym of the word 'agony' is ....
   A. Pain B. Excitement
   C. Ecstasy D. Peace
7. The antonym of the word 'quiescent' is ....
   A. mellifluous B. Exempt
   C. Restless D. Excitement
8. The correct meaning of the idiom/phrase 'Tooth and nail' is ....
   A. With all the might and strength
   B. Without any other weapon
   C. Resorting to violence
   D. Very cowardly
9. The correct meaning of the idiom/phrase 'In vogue' is ....
   A. In fashion
   B. Out of use
   C. Vaguely used
   D. Never used
10. Which part of the following sentence has an error:

    He is going everyday/for a morning walk/ with his friends and neighbours.
    A. He is going everyday
    B. for a morning walk
    C. with his friends and neighbours
    D. No error
11. Which part of the following sentence has an error:

    Such/rules do not apply/to you and I.
    A. Such
    B. rules do not apply
    C. to you and I
    D. No error

* *Exam held on 10-06-2023 (Conducted by GGSIPU)*

12. Choose the option that correctly represents the sentence 'Bringing about gentle and painless death from incurable disease'.

A. Suicide B. Euphoria
C. Gallows D. Euthanasia

13. Choose the option that correctly represents the sentence 'A person pretending to be somebody he is not':

A. Impostor B. Liar
C. Rogue D. Magician

14. Choose the correct option that can replace the italic part of the following sentence:

By such time you finish that chapter, I will write a letter.

A. The time when B. By the time
C. By that time D. The time

15. Choose the correct option that can replace the italic part of the following sentence:

No sooner *do the bells ring* than the curtain rose.

A. did the bell rang
B. did the bells ring
C. had the bell rang
D. had the bell rung

16. Which part of the following sentence has an error, if any.

He was debarred to attend (A)/the classes (B)/ for six months (C). /No error (D).

A. A B. B
C. C D. D

17. What to talk of (A)/running (B)/he cannot even walk (C). No error (D).

A. A B. B
C. C D. D

18. Choose the appropriate alternative which best expresses 'To struggle helplessly':

A. Flounder B. Founder
C. Fumble D. Finger

19. Choose the appropriate alternative which best expresses "The plants and vegetation of a region':

A. Fauna B. Flora
C. Landscape D. Ecosystem

20. Choose the alternative which best expresses the meaning of 'repartee'.

A. Refuse
B. Celebrate
C. Quick witty reply
D. Question

Directions (Qs. No. 21-25): *Read the following passage and answer the questions.*

The rise of social media has brought about a revolution in the way people communicate with one another. Social media platforms like Facebook, Twitter, and Instagram have made it possible for individuals to connect with each other across great distances, share their thoughts and experiences, and build communities around common interests.

While social media has many positive aspects, it also has its drawbacks. For example, research has shown that prolonged use of social media can lead to negative mental health outcomes, such as depression and anxiety. Additionally, social media can be a breeding ground for cyberbullying and misinformation, which can have serious consequences for individuals and society as a whole.

Despite these concerns, social media is likely to continue to play a prominent role in our lives in the comming years. As such, it is important for individuals to develop healthy habits around their social media use, such as limiting their time spent on these platforms and being vigilant about the quality and accuracy of the information they encounter.

21. What is social media?

A. A type of personal communication system
B. A platform for connecting with people across distances
C. A system for sharing personal information
D. All of the above

22. What are some potential negative outcomes of prolonged social media use?

A. Anxiety and depression

B. Breeds information
C. Decreased physical activity
D. Both (A) and (B)

23. What are some healthy habits individuals can develop around their social media use?
A. Limiting their time spent on social media
B. Being vigilant about the quality and accuracy of the information they encounter
C. Building communities around common interests
D. Both (A) and (B)

24. Which of the following is not a potential consequences of cyberbullying?
A. Building communities
B. Misinformation
C. Financial loss
D. None of the above

25. What is one potential consequence of misinformation on social media?
A. Negative impact on society as a whole
B. Increased physical activity
C. Improved mental health outcomes
D. None of the above

26. 'Yash Bharati' is instituted by which of the following states:
A. Madhya Pradesh
B. Uttar Pradesh
C. Bihar
D. Karnataka

27. Which of the following national parks is not a tiger reserve?
A. Ranthambore B. Jim Corbett
C. Kanha D. Keoladeo

28. Which of the following teams won IPL 2022?
A. Rajasthan Royals
B. Kolkata Knight Riders
C. Mumbai Indians
D. Gujarat Titans

29. National sports day is celebrated on ....
A. 29th August B. 22nd September
C. 3rd December D. 9th July

30. Which one of the following is Union Health Minister of India?
A. Giriraj Kishore
B. Prafful Patel
C. Dharmendra Pradhan
D. Mansukh Mandaviya

31. 'Kamakhya Temple' is situated in ....
A. Hyderabad B. Chennai
C. Guwahati D. Mysore

32. The nickname of Rabindranath Tagore was ....
A. Kaviguru B. Rashthra Pita
C. Rishivar D. Rajaji

33. Capital city of 'Tripura' is ....
A. Agartala B. Imphal
C. Shillong D. Guwahati

34. Which of the following is not a Union Territory?
A. Andaman and Nicobar Islands
B. Lakshadweep
C. Puducherry
D. Goa

35. The largest river (by length) in the world is ....
A. Amazon B. Nile
C. Mekong D. Volga

36. The largest country (in terms of total land area) in the world is ....
A. USA B. Canada
C. China D. Russia

37. Which country launched the world's first 5G service?
A. Japan B. South Korea
C. England D. China

38. Fear of illness is known as:
A. Iatrophobia B. Herpetophobia
C. Hypochondria D. Haemophobia

39. Which of the following International Tennis Tournaments is held on grass court?
A. US open
B. French open
C. Australian open
D. Wimbledon

40. The world famous 'Khajuraho' sculptures are located in:
A. Gujarat
B. Madhya Pradesh
C. Orissa
D. Jharkhand

41. Orange prize is given in the field of:
A. Sports
B. Medicine
C. Literature
D. All of the above

42. 'National Youth Day' is celebrated on which day?
A. January 15
B. January 14
C. January 17
D. January 12

43. The Olympic games in 2024 will be held at ....
A. Paris
B. New York
C. Barcelona
D. Shanghai

44. .... city is known as Mecca of Indian football?
A. Kolkata
B. Delhi
C. Sikkim
D. Chennai

45. Technophobia is the fear of :
A. Technology
B. Sleep
C. Thunder
D. Speed

46. Out of the following, which country is not a member of G20?
A. USA
B. India
C. China
D. Congo

47. World Environment Day is celebrated on:
A. 4th August
B. 5th June
C. 15th July
D. 6th December

48. Which city is known as 'Queen of Arabian sea'?
A. Mangaluru
B. Kakinada
C. Mumbai
D. Kochi

49. Periyar sanctuary is well-known for ....
A. Elephants
B. Lions
C. Tigers
D. Deers

50. Tamil is the official language of ....
A. Puducherry
B. Dadra and Nagar Haveli
C. Daman and Diu
D. Delhi

51. The difference between simple interest and compound interest at the same rate for ₹ 5000 for 2 years is ₹ 98 the rate of interest is:
A. 10%
B. 14%
C. 12%
D. 10.5%

52. John is twice as good a workman as Bob and together can finish a piece of work in 14 days. The number of days taken by John alone to finish the work is:
A. 11
B. 21
C. 28
D. 42

53. Tap A is 3 times faster than tap B and takes 32 min less than the tap B. When will the cistern be full if both the taps are opened together?
A. 12 min
B. 24 min
C. 30 min
D. Dara inadequate

54. If the ratio of x to y is 25 times the ratio of y to x, then what is the ratio of x to y?
A. 1 : 5
B. 5 : 1
C. 25 : 1
D. 1 : 25

55. Ratio of Asmita's age to Promila's age is 4 : 3. Asmita will be 26 years old after 6 years. How old is Promila now?
A. 18 years
B. 21 years
C. 15 years
D. 24 years

56. Ram purchased a chemical at ₹ 25/L. He diluted the chemical with water. He makes a profit of 25% by selling the diluted chemical at ₹ 20/L. In what ratio did he add water into chemical?
A. 12 : 15
B. 16 : 9
C. 13 : 16
D. 19 : 22

57. Sanjay covers half of a journey travelling at a speed of 4 km/hour. One third of the total journey is covered at a speed of 12 km/hour and remaining part of the journey is covered at 9 km/hour. It took 6 hour 12 minutes to complete the journey. What approximate distance did he cover during the entire journey?
A. 40 km
B. 153 km
C. 36 km
D. 28 km

58. Out of 8 consonants and 5 vowels, how many words can be made, each containing 4 consonants and 3 vowels?

A. 700 B. 504000
C. 3528000 D. 7056000

59. Three identical dice are rolled. What is the probability that same number will appear on each of them?

A. 1/6 B. 7/36
C. 1/12 D. 1/36

60. What is the number whose 20% is 30% of 40?

A. 90 B. 60
C. 80 D. 50

61. If the ratio of horizontal mean and geometric mean between two numbers A and B is 4:5, then the ratio of the two numbers will be:

A. 4:1 B. 5:1
C. 3:1 D. None of the above

62. If selling price is tripled and cost price doubled, the profit would be 65%. What is the present profit (in percent)?

A. 10 B. 15
C. 20 D. 25

63. A sum of money becomes 3 times in 5 years at simple interest. In how many years, will the same sum become 6 times at the same rate of simple interest?

A. 10 B. 12
C. 12.5 D. 10.5

Directions (Qs. No. 64-68): *Study the following information carefully and answer the questions that follow.*

Six friends—Ajay, Balbeer, Chetan, David, Ehsaan and Frank are sitting on a bench facing North. Chetan is sitting between Ajay and Ehsaan. David is not at the end. Balbeer is sitting to the immediate right of Ehsaan. Frank is not at the right end.

64. Who is the immediate right of Frank?

A. David
B. Ajay
C. Either David or Ajay
D. Cannot be determined

65. How many persons are there to the left of Chetan?

A. One B. Two
C. Three D. Four

66. Who is fourth from the left end?

A. Ajay
B. Chetan
C. Balbeer
D. Cannot be determined

67. Who is at the left end?

A. Frank
B. Ajay
C. Balbeer
D. Cannot be determined

68. Which of the following is sitting to one side of David?

A. Frank-Ehsaan B. Frank-Balbeer
C. Frank-Chetan D. None of these

69. Write Choose the correct alternatives.

Food : Stomach : : Fuel : ?

A. Plane B. Truck
C. Engine D. Automobile

70. Write Choose the correct alternatives.

Typist : Typewriter : : Writer : ?

A. Book B. Paper
C. Script D. Pen

71. Choose out the odd one.

A. Syringe B. Tweezer
C. Dropper D. Straw

72. If A = 26, SUN = 27, then CAT = ?

A. 24 B. 27
C. 57 D. 58

73. Deepak said to Nitin, "That boy playing football is the younger of the two brothers of the daughter of my father's wife." How is the boy playing football related to Deepak?

A. Son B. Brother
C. Cousin D. Nephew

74. If (i) P is taller than Q, (ii) R is shorter than P, (iii) S is taller than T but shorter than Q, then who among them is tallest?

A. P B. Q
C. S D. T

75. You go North, turn right, then right again and then go to the left. In which direction are you now?

A. North B. South

C. East D. West

76. Which of the following is not among the steps to active listening?

A. Contact B. Absorb

C. Transform D. Confirm

77. Communication is said to be the .... of an organization.

A. heart

B. soul

C. conscience

D. nervous system

78. Which of the following is not an element of communication process?

A. Sender B. Messenger

C. Encoding D. Receiver

79. Communication is essential because it facilitates ....

A. planning and control

B. development of team-spirit

C. greater managerial efficiency

D. All the above

80. Which of the following statements is/are true with respect to informal communication?

A. It is personal

B. It is systematic

C. Both (A) & (B)

D. Neither (A) nor (B)

81. Symbols used for communication have the potential to create ....

A. language barrier

B. status barrier

C. physical barrier

D. None of the above

82. Which of the following is/are considered as shareholders' meeting/s?

A. Statutory meeting

B. Class meeting

C. Both (A) & (B)

D. Neither (A) nor (B)

83. Primary industries comprise of ....

A. Synthetical industries

B. Processing industries

C. Genetic industries

D. Manufacturing industries

84. Which of the following is not a distinguishing character of a 'business activity'?

A. It is economic in nature

B. It involves exchange of goods or services

C. It enables earning a fixed return

D. It is aimed at profit making

85. Liability of all members of a Hindu Undivided Family (HUF) business, except *Karta* is ....

A. Defined and limited by an amount mutually agreed.

B. Unlimited

C. Defined and limited by the share of members in coparcenary property of business

D. None of the above

86. Which one of the following is considered to be a disadvantage of the company form of business organization?

A. Professional management

B. Oligarchic management

C. Perpetual existence

D. Separate legal entity

87. Which form of organization is among the forms that can be registered and governed under the provisions of Companies Act, 2013?

A. Government company

B. Statutory company

C. Both (A) and (B)

D. Neither (A) nor (B)

88. Which of the following is/are among the principles of insurance?

A. Utmost good faith

B. Subrogation

C. Mitigation

D. All of the above

89. Life insurance is a contract of ....

A. utmost good faith

B. indemnity
C. Both (A) & (B)
D. neither (A) nor (B)

90. Management aims to achieve ....
A. effectiveness
B. efficiency
C. Both (A) & (B)
D. maximum profit

91. Organizing is a management function which involves all the following except ....
A. grouping tasks
B. setting goals
C. establishing authority
D. allocating resources

92. Controlling includes ....
A. monitoring
B. measuring
C. comparing
D. All of the above

93. Coordination implies integrating the efforts of ....
A. individuals
B. departments
C. specialists
D. All of the above

94. Who among the following was an ardent supporter of standardization?
A. Abraham Maslow
B. Elton Mayo
C. Henri Fayol
D. F.W. Taylor

95. Fayol's Principles follow ....
A. A bottom-up approach
B. A top-down approach
C. 360 degrees approach
D. None of the above

96. Marketing is ....
A. an exchange process
B. a post-production process
C. a social process
D. an intra personal process

97. Selling focuses on ....
A. maximizing customer satisfaction
B. maximizing customer value
C. Both (A) & (B)
D. neither (A) nor (B)

98. The first stock exchange was set up in India in the year ....
A. 1850 B. 1875
C. 1956 D. 1991

99. Secondary markets promote capital formation ....
A. directly
B. indirectly
C. both directly and indirectly
D. neither directly nor indirectly

100. Currency and credit policies of India are made by ....
A. Ministry of Finance
B. Public Sector Banks
C. Parliament of India
D. None of these

ANSWERS

1. (A)	**2. (D)**	**3. (A)**	**19. (B)**	**20. (C)**	**21. (D)**
4. (A)	**5. (C)**	**6. (D)**	**22. (D)**	**23. (D)**	**24. (A)**
7. (D)	**8. (A)**	**9. (A)**	**25. (A)**	**26. (B)**	**27. (D)**
10. (A)	**11. (C)**	**12. (D)**	**28. (D)**	**29. (A)**	**30. (D)**
13. (A)	**14. (B)**	**15. (B)**	**31. (C)**	**32. (A)**	**33. (A)**
16. (A)	**17. (D)**	**18. (A)**	**34. (D)**	**35. (B)**	**36. (D)**

37. (B) **38. (C)** **39. (D)**

40. (B) **41. (C)** **42. (D)**

43. (A) **44. (A)** **45. (A)**

46. (D) **47. (B)** **48. (D)**

49. (A) **50. (A)**

51. (B): Given, Compound interest – simple interest = ₹ 98

$$\Rightarrow \quad p\left(1+\frac{r}{100}\right)^n - p - \frac{prt}{100} = 98$$

$$\Rightarrow \quad p\left[\left(1+\frac{r}{100}\right)^n - 1\right] - \frac{prt}{100} = 98$$

$$\Rightarrow \quad 5000\left[\left(1+\frac{r}{100}\right)^2 - 1\right] - \frac{5000r \times 2}{100} = 98$$

$$\Rightarrow \quad 5000\left[1+\frac{r^2}{10000}+\frac{2r}{100}-1\right] - 100r = 98$$

$$\Rightarrow \quad 5000\left[\frac{r^2}{10000}+\frac{2r}{100}\right] - 100r = 98$$

$$\Rightarrow \quad 5000 \times \frac{r}{100}\left[\frac{r}{100}+2\right] - 100r = 98$$

$$\Rightarrow \quad 50r\left[\frac{r}{100}+2-2\right] = 98$$

$$\Rightarrow \quad 50r \times \frac{r}{100} = 98$$

$$\Rightarrow \quad \frac{r^2}{2} = 98$$

$$\Rightarrow \quad r^2 = 196 = (14)^2$$

$$= r = 14\%$$

52. (B): Ratio of work efficiency

John : Bob = 2 : 1

Ratio of time (days)

John : Bob = 1 : 2

According to question

$$\frac{1}{x}+\frac{1}{2x} = \frac{1}{14}$$

$$\Rightarrow \quad \frac{2+1}{2x} = \frac{1}{14}$$

$$\Rightarrow \quad \frac{3}{2x} = \frac{1}{14}$$

$$\Rightarrow \quad 2x = 3 \times 14$$

$$\Rightarrow \quad x = 21$$

∴ John alone will take $x = 21$ days to finish the work.

53. (A): Ratio of efficiency, A : B = 3 : 1

⇒ Ratio of time, A : B = 1 : 3

According to question, $3x - x = 32$

$$\Rightarrow \quad 2x = 32 \Rightarrow x = 16$$

Part filled by tapes (A + B) in 1 min

$$= \frac{1}{x}+\frac{1}{3x}$$

$$= \frac{1}{16}+\frac{1}{48}$$

$$= \frac{3+1}{48} = \frac{4}{48} = \frac{1}{12}$$

Hence, both the taps will be full cistern in 12 minutes.

54. (B): Given, $\frac{x}{y} = 25\frac{y}{x}$

$$\Rightarrow \quad \frac{x}{y}\times\frac{x}{y} = 25$$

$$\Rightarrow \quad \frac{x^2}{y^2} = 5^2$$

$$\Rightarrow \quad \frac{x}{y} = 5$$

$$\Rightarrow \quad x : y = 5 : 1$$

55. (C): Let, Asmita's age = $4x$ years and

Promila's age = $3x$ years

then, after 6 years

Asmita's age = $4x + 6$

$\therefore \quad 26 = 4x + 6$

$\Rightarrow \quad 4x = 20 \Rightarrow x = 5$

$\therefore$ Promila's age how is $3x = 3 \times 5 = 15$ years.

56. (B): Given, cost price of the chemical = ₹ 25/L

Selling price of the mixture = ₹ 20/L

Profit = 25%

$\therefore$ cost price of the mixture = $\frac{20 \times 100}{125}$

$= 20 \times \frac{4}{5}$ = ₹ 16/L

So, while a liter of the mixture he is making a profit of = 25 – 16 = ₹ 9

$\because$ water is not monetary value

Hence, the ratio of water add into chemical

= 16 : (25 – 16)

= 16 : 9

57. (C): Let the total distance of journey = x km

Then, $\frac{\frac{x}{2}}{4}+\frac{\frac{x}{3}}{12}+\frac{\frac{x}{6}}{9}$ = 6 hours 12 minutes

$\Rightarrow \quad \frac{x}{8}+\frac{x}{36}+\frac{x}{54} = 6\frac{1}{5}$

$\Rightarrow \quad \frac{27x+6x+4x}{216} = \frac{31}{5}$

$\Rightarrow \quad \frac{37}{216}x = \frac{31}{5}$

$\Rightarrow \quad x = \frac{31}{5}\times\frac{216}{37}$

$\Rightarrow \quad x = \frac{6696}{185}$ = 36 km (approx.)

$\Rightarrow \quad x = 36$ km

58. (A): $\because$ 4 consonants out of 8 consonants can be selected in $^8C_4$ ways, 3 vowels out of 5 vowels can be selected in $^5C_3$ ways.

Therefore, by the fundamental principle of counting.

Number of words = $^8C_4 \times {}^5C_3$

$= \frac{\lfloor 8}{\lfloor 4 \lfloor 8-4} \times \frac{\lfloor 5}{\lfloor 3 \lfloor 5-3}$

$= \frac{\lfloor 8}{\lfloor 4 \lfloor 4} \times \frac{\lfloor 5}{\lfloor 3 \lfloor 2}$

$= \frac{8.7.6.5}{4.3.2} \times \frac{5.4}{2.1}$

$= 35 \times 20$

$= 700$

59. (D): Given, 3 identical dice are rolled

$\therefore$ number of sample space

$= n(S) = 6 \times 6 \times 6$

$\Rightarrow \quad n(S) = 216$

Let, E = same number will appear on each of them

then, E = {(1, 1, 1), (2, 2, 2), (3, 3, 3), (4, 4, 4), (5, 5, 5), (6, 6, 6)}

$\Rightarrow \quad n(E) = 6$

$\therefore \quad P(E) = \frac{n(E)}{n(S)} = \frac{6}{216} = \frac{1}{36}$

Hence, required probability = $\frac{1}{36}$

60. (B): Let the numbers be x

then, $x \times \frac{20}{100} = 40 \times \frac{30}{100}$

$\Rightarrow \quad x \times \frac{1}{5} = 12$

$\Rightarrow \quad x = 60$

61. (A): Given, two numbers be A and B

then, $\frac{\frac{2AB}{A+B}}{\sqrt{AB}} = \frac{4}{5}$

$\Rightarrow \quad \frac{2\sqrt{AB}}{A+B} = \frac{4}{5}$

$\Rightarrow \quad \frac{A+B}{2\sqrt{AB}} = \frac{5}{4}$

Applying componendo and dividendo

$$\frac{A+B+2\sqrt{AB}}{A+B-2\sqrt{AB}} = \frac{5+4}{5-4}$$

$$\Rightarrow \frac{\left(\sqrt{A}+\sqrt{B}\right)^2}{\left(\sqrt{A}-\sqrt{B}\right)^2} = \frac{9}{1}$$

$$\Rightarrow \frac{\sqrt{A}+\sqrt{B}}{\sqrt{A}-\sqrt{B}} = \frac{3}{1}$$

$$\Rightarrow 3\sqrt{A}-3\sqrt{B} = \sqrt{A}+\sqrt{B}$$

$$\Rightarrow 2\sqrt{A} = 4\sqrt{B}$$

$$\Rightarrow \frac{\sqrt{A}}{\sqrt{B}} = \frac{4}{2}$$

$$\Rightarrow \frac{\sqrt{A}}{\sqrt{B}} = 2$$

$$\Rightarrow \frac{A}{B} = \frac{4}{1}$$

$$\Rightarrow A : B = 4 : 1$$

Hence, the ratio of the two numbers will be 4 : 1.

62. **(A):** Let, C.P. = ₹ x and S.P. = ₹ y

Then, given C.P. = ₹ $2x$ and S.P. = ₹ $3y$

∴ by question,

$$2x \times \frac{165}{100} = 3y$$

$$\Rightarrow 2x \times \frac{55}{100} = y$$

$$\Rightarrow 2x \times \frac{11}{20} = y$$

$$\Rightarrow x \times \frac{11}{10} = y$$

$$\Rightarrow \frac{x}{y} = \frac{10}{11}$$

$$\Rightarrow x : y = 10 : 11$$

Now, the present profit % = $\frac{y-x}{x} \times 100$

$$= \frac{11-10}{10} \times 100 = 10\%$$

63. **(C):** Let, sum of money = ₹ p

then, A = ₹ $3p$,

t = 5 yrs

∴ Simple interest = $3p - p$

$= 2p$

$$\therefore \quad r = \frac{\text{S.I.} \times 100}{p \times t}$$

$$= \frac{2p \times 100}{p \times 5}$$

$= 40\%$

Again, A = $6p$

∴ S.I. = $6p - p = 5p$

$$\text{Now,} \quad t = \frac{\text{S.I.} \times 100}{p \times r}$$

$$= \frac{5p \times 100}{p \times 40}$$

$$= \frac{5 \times 5}{2} = \frac{25}{2}$$

$\Rightarrow$ t = 12.5 years.

Directions (Qs. No. 64-68):

From given information

Left Frank David Ajay Chetan Ehsaan Balbeer Right

64. **(A):** David is the immediate right of Frank.

65. **(C):** There are 3 persons to the left of Chetan.

66. **(B):** Chetan is fourth from the left end.

67. **(A):** Frank is at the left end.

68. **(D):** Frank-Ajay is sitting to one side of David.

69. **(C)** **70.** **(D)** **71.** **(D)**

72. (C): Given, A = 26

SUN = 27

$\Rightarrow$ 8 + 6 + 13 = 27

Similarly,

CAT = 24 + 26 + 7

$\Rightarrow$ CAT = 57

73. (B):

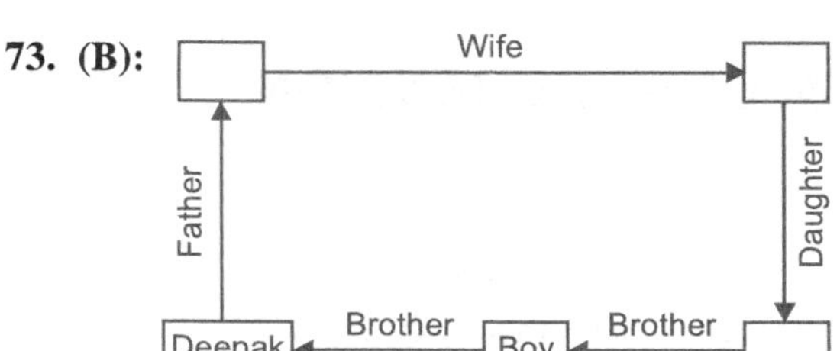

Here, boy is the brother of Deepak.

74. (A): Given, P > Q, P > R, Q > S > T

$\Rightarrow$ P > R, P > Q > S > T

Here, P is the tallest among them.

75. (C):

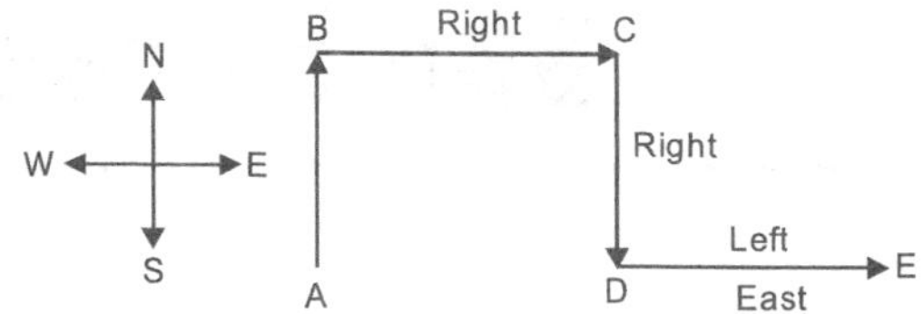

Here, you (E) are now in East direction.

76. (C)	**77.** (D)	**78.** (B)
79. (D)	**80.** (D)	**81.** (A)
82. (B)	**83.** (C)	**84.** (C)
85. (B)	**86.** (B)	**87.** (C)
88. (D)	**89.** (C)	**90.** (D)
91. (B)	**92.** (D)	**93.** (D)
94. (D)	**95.** (B)	**96.** (A)
97. (C)	**98.** (B)	**99.** (B)
100. (D)		

Previous Paper (Solved)

BBA Entrance Exam 2022*

ENGLISH LANGUAGE & COMPREHENSION

1. Which among the following options is the correct active voice of the sentence given below.

The students are taught by Mrs. Sethi

A. Mrs. Sethi teach the students
B. Mrs. Sethi teaches the student
C. Mrs. Sethi taught the students
D. Mrs Sethi teaches the students

2. Choose the correct sentence:

A. Suresh's teacher gave him many advise.
B. Suresh's teacher advised him.
C. Suresh's teacher gave him a piece of advice.
D. Suresh's teacher gave him a piece of advise.

3. Fill in the blank with appropriate word from the options below.

He does nothing but ______ .

A. Complaining B. To complain
C. Complained D. Complain

4. After he came back from his evening walk, he felt famished.

The meaning of the underlined word is:

A. Exhausted B. Hungry
C. Peevish D. Relaxed

5. Choose the correct sentence.

A. I gave the book to Sashi.
B. I gave to Shashi the book.
C. I gave Shashi to book.
D. I gave the book Shahi.

6. Read the sentence below and identify the part which contains a grammatical error.

At the request of the defense attorney (A)/ the jury were called (B)/and their individual verdicts were recorded. (C)

A. A B. B
C. C D. D

7. Read the sentence below and identify the part which contains a grammatical error.

Alam is (A)/ pupil of (B)/ the Green Valley School (C)/ in Delhi. (D)

A. A B. B
C. C D. D

8. Which of the words in the options below is closest to opposite in meaning to the underlined word in the following sentence:

How dare you desecrate an idol of this temple.

A. defy B. pollute
C. deify D. impious

9. Choose the correct sentence:

A. He told to his friends to visit to him tomorrow.
B. He told his friends to visit to him tomorrow.
C. He told to his friends visit him tomorrow.
D. He told his friends to visit him tomorrow.

* *Exam held on 23-06-2022 (Conducted by GGSIPU)*

10. Read the sentence below and identify the part which contains a grammatical error.

The owner (A)/ as well as his servants (B)/ is honest (C)/ No error (D).

A. A B. B
C. C D. No error

11. Choose the correct answer after changing the speech or narration of the following sentence:

They said, "We were waiting for Anushka to arrive."

A. They said that we were waiting for Anushka to arrive.
B. They say that they were waiting for Anushka to arrive.
C. They say that we were waiting for Anushka to arrive.
D. They said that they were waiting for Anushka to arrive

12. Change the voice of the following sentence.

The chief guest gave away the prizes.

A. The prizes are given away by the chief guest.
B. The prizes were given away by the chief guest.
C. The prizes had been given away by the chief guest.
D. The prizes had been given away by the prizes.

13. Select the option that has nearest meaning to the underlined word in the following sentence:

There was no ostensible reason for her being angry at her husband's remarks,

A. Hidden
B. Covert
C. Apparent
D. Secret

14. Fill in the blank with appropriate word from the options below. I could hear him ______.

A. Speaking
B. Speak
C. To speak
D. To have spoken

15. Read the sentence below and identify the part which contains a grammatical error.

A closed economy is identified (A)/ as a human community (B)/ which produces all it consumes (C)/ and consumed all it produces (D).

A. A B. B
C. C D. D

16. The opposite in meaning to the underlined word in the following sentence is:

Mrs Nimisha made a fervent appeal to the members of the club to maintain unity.

A. active B. impassive
C. cold D. passionate

17. We received them coldly. It means that:

A. it was cold when we received them.
B. we received them in an unfriendly manner.
C. our hands were cold when we received them.
D. we were happy to receive them

18. You'd better take off your shoes. You'd means in this sentence ______.

A. You should B. You would
C. You had D. You could

19. Fill in the blank with appropriate word from the options below.

They have gone to _____ church to pray.

A. a B. an
C. the D. No article required

20. Read the sentence below and identify the part which contains a grammatical error.

Kripa and Samarth had (A)/ been seeing (B)/ each other for years. (C)/ Been they? (D)

A. A B. B
C. C D. D

Directions (Qs. No. 21-25): *Read the passage carefully and answer the following questions.*

At noon, calmly and in a businesslike way she put the books around her bosom, and so skillfully and snugly that Yegor announced, smacking his lips with satisfaction:

"Sehr gut! As the German says when he has drunk a keg of beer. Literature has not changed you, granny. You still remain the good, tall, portly, elderly woman. May all the numberless gods grant you their blessings on your enterprise!"

Within half an hour she stood at the factory gate, bent with the weight of her burden, calm and assured. Two guards, irritated by the oaths and raillery of the working men, examined all who entered the gate, handling them roughly and swearing at them. A policeman and a thin-legged man with a red face and alert eyes stood at one side. The mother, shifting the rod resting on her shoulders, with a pail suspended from either end of it, watched the man from the corner of her eye. She divined that he was a spy.

21. The phrase 'a keg of beer' means:
A. A peg of beer
B. A tumbler of beer
C. A barrel of beer
D. Half a glass of beer

22. The word 'divined' means:
A. Understood
B. She had a revelation
C. Guessed
D. Knew it secretly

23. How many pails are suspended on the rod?
A. One B. Two
C. Three D. Four

24. The word 'raillery' means:
A. Hardships
B. Good-humoured teasing
C. Drudgery
D. Difficulty

25. The word 'snugly' means:
A. comfortably B. craftly
C. with expertise D. roughly

GENERAL AWARENESS

26. Which city is known as 'Queen of Arabian sea'?
A. Vizag B. Kakinada
C. Mumbai D. Kochi

27. Ghumot is indigenous traditional percussion instrument of _______ .
A. Andhra Pradesh B. Goa
C. Punjab D. Assam

28. Which of the following International Tennis Tournaments is held on grass court?
A. US open
B. French open
C. Australian open
D. Wimbledon

29. Who was the first Indian to be honoured with a lifetime achievement Oscar award?
A. Pandit Ravi Shankar
B. Bhimsen Joshi
C. Lata Mangeshkar
D. Satyajit Ray

30. Which of the following is called the storehouse of world-art collections?
A. National Archives of India
B. National Museum
C. National Modern Art Gallery
D. Salarjung Museum

31. Bihu is the festival that is observed in:
A. West Bengal B. Maharashtra
C. Assam D. Tamil Nadu

32. B.C. Roy award is given in the field of:
A. Sports B. Journalism
C. Medicine D. Economics

33. Which of the following programmes is being implemented by the National Bank for Agriculture and Rural Development (NABARD)?
A. Prime Minister's Rozgar Yojana (PMRY)
B. Swarnjayanti Gram Swarozgar Yojana (SGSY)
C. District Rural Industrial Project (DRIP)
D. Rural Employment Generation Programme (REGP)

34. The national income of a country for a given period is equal to the:

A. Total value of goods and services produced by the nationals
B. Sum of total consumption and investment expenditure
C. Sum of personal income of all individuals
D. Money value of final goods and services produced

35. Prime Minister Narendra Modi has launched India's first roll on-roll off or 'RoRo' ferry service in which state?

A. Sikkim B. Assam
C. Maharashtra D. Gujarat

36. Famous Rock Garden is located in which city?

A. Jaipur
B. Shimla
C. Chandigarh
D. Lucknow

37. Konkani is the official language of ______.

A. Chandigarh
B. Dadra and Nagar Haveli
C. Daman and Diu
D. Delhi

38. _________ city is known as Mecca of Indian football?

A. Kolkata B. Delhi
C. Sikkim D. Chennai

39. Which of the following is a major folk dance of Rajasthan?

A. Chhau B. Giddha
C. Ghumar D. Bihu

40. World Environment day is celebrated on ______.

A. 4th August B. 6th June
C. 15th July D. 6th December

41. Who is current Union Minister of Cooperation of government of India?

A. Shri Amit Shah
B. Shri Jyotiraditya Scindia
C. Shri Dharmendra Pradhan
D. Shri Giriraj Singh

42. Who among the following played the leading lady in the film 'Mission Mangal' that tells the dramatic true story of the women behind India's first mission to Mars?

A. Deepika Padukone
B. Vidya Balan
C. Kajol
D. Kareena Kapoor

43. National school of drama is situated in ______.

A. Agra B. New Delhi
C. Mumbai D. Pune

44. Fear of illness is known as:

A. Iatrophobia B. Herpetophobia
C. Hypochondria D. Haemophobia

45. *Vande Matram* was included in ______.

A. Rajtarangani
B. Anandmath
C. Akbarnama
D. Bharatdarshanam

46. Highway on which one has to travel to reach Vishakhapatnam from Vijayawada:

A. NH 9
B. NH 10
C. NH 47
D. None of the above

47. Toda tribes are found in the state of ______.

A. Andhra Pradesh B. Chhattisgarh
C. Jharkhand D. Tamil Nadu

48. Feroz Gandhi award is associated with:

A. Medical Research
B. Film direction
C. Sports
D. None of the above

49. Which of the following sanctuary is well-known for elephants?

A. Kanha B. Gir
C. Kaziranga D. Periyar

50. Where did the first ODI played in India?

A. New Delhi B. Ahmedabad
C. Kolkata D. Mumbai

LOGICAL AND ANALYTICAL ABILITY

51. If every alternate letter, starting with A, is removed from the alphabet, which letter among the remaining letters would be the third to the right of the fifth letter from the right?

A. X B. V
C. L D. J

52. In a queue, A is eighteenth from the front while B is sixteenth from the back. If C is twenty-fifth from the front and is exactly in the middle of A and B, then how many persons are there in the queue?

A. 45 B. 46
C. 47 D. 48

53. If in a certain code, ALMIRAH is written as BNPMWGO, which word would be written as DNRWLUA?

A. COSGOLT B. TOGSOLC
C. TOGCLOS D. CLOSGOT

54. A motorist travelled between two towns, which are 65 km past, in 2 hours and 10 minutes. Find the speed in metres per minute.

A. 200 B. 500
C. 600 D. 700

55. The value of $\frac{(75.8)^2 - (55.8)^2}{20}$ is:

A. 20 B. 40
C. 121.6 D. 131.6

56. A number consists of two digits. If the digits inter-change places and the new number is added to the original number, then the resulting number will be divisible by:

A. 3 B. 5
C. 9 D. 11

57. A speed of 30.6 km/hr is the same as:

A. 5.1 m/sec
B. 8.5 m/sec
C. 110.16 m/sec
D. None of these

58. The average of two numbers is 6.5 and square root of their product is 6. What are the numbers?

A. 11 and 2 B. 8 and 5
C. 9 and 4 D. 10 and 3

59. A boat goes 8 km in one hour along the stream and 2 km in one hour against the stream. The speed in km/hr of the stream is:

A. 2 B. 3
C. 4 D. 5

60. If A = 2, M = 26, Z = 52, then BET = ?

A. 44 B. 54
C. 64 D. 72

61. An urn contains 6 red, 4 blue, 2 green and 3 yellow marbles. If three marbles are picked up at random, what is the probability that 2 are blue and 1 is yellow?

A. $\frac{3}{91}$ B. $\frac{1}{5}$

C. $\frac{18}{455}$ D. $\frac{7}{15}$

62. Choose out the odd one.

A. Centaur B. Tortoise
C. Goat D. Lion

63. $\frac{1.6 \times 3.2}{0.08} = ?$

A. 0.8 B. 6.4
C. 8 D. 64

64. If an article is sold at 200 per cent profit, then the ratio of its cost price to its selling price will be:

A. 1 : 2 B. 2 : 1
C. 1 : 3 D. 3 : 1

65. If $x = a$, $y = b$ is the solution of the equations $x - y = 2$ and $x + y = 4$, then the values of a and b are, respectively:

A. 3, 5 B. 5, 3
C. 3, 1 D. −1, −3

66. A takes twice as much time as B of thrice as much time as C to finish a piece of work. Working together, they can finish the work in 2 days. B can do the work alone in:
A. 4 days
B. 6 days
C. 8 days
D. 12 days

67. The angle of elevation of the sun, when the length of the shadow of a tree is $\sqrt{3}$ times the height of the tree, is:
A. 30°
B. 45°
C. 60°
D. None of the above

68. In a joint family, there are father, mother, 3 married sons and one unmarried daughter. Of the sons, two have 2 daughters each, and one has a son. How many female members are there in the family?
A. 2 B. 3
C. 6 D. 9

69. What would be the simple interest obtained on an amount of ₹ 5890 at the rate of 6% per anum after 3 years?
A. ₹ 1060.20 B. ₹ 1063.80
C. ₹ 1336.80 D. ₹ 1666.80

70. I am facing east, I turn 100° in the clockwise direction and then 145° in the anticlockwise direction. Which direction am I facing now?
A. East B. North-east
C. North D. South-west

71. A room 5 m × 8 m is to be carpeted leaving a margin of 10 cm from each wall. If the cost of the carpet is ₹ 18 per sq. metre, the cost of carpeting the room will be:
A. ₹ 673.92 B. ₹ 682.46
C. ₹ 691.80 D. ₹ 702.60

72. If Atul finds that he is twelfth from the right in a line of boys and fourth from the left, how many boys should be added to the line such that there are 28 boys in the line?
A. 12 B. 13
C. 14 D. 20

73. 11, 13, 17, 19, 23, 25, ?
A. 26 B. 27
C. 29 D. 37

74. Five persons are standing in a line. One of the two persons at the extreme ends is a professor and the other a business man. An advocate is standing to the right of a student. An author is to the left of the business man. The student is standing between the professor and the advocate. Counting from the left, the advocate is at which place?
A. 1st B. 2nd
C. 3rd D. 5th

75. An urn contains 6 red, 4 blue, 2 green and 3 yellow marbles. If 4 marbles are picked up at random, what is the probability that at least one of them is blue?
A. $\frac{4}{15}$ B. $\frac{69}{91}$
C. $\frac{11}{15}$ D. $\frac{22}{91}$

MANAGEMENT APTITUDE AND COMMUNICATION SKILLS

76. Standup India Scheme is aimed at supporting entrepreneurs belonging to the following categories.
A. Women
B. SC/ST
C. Both A & B
D. Rural

77. Which of the following is not a sales promotion activity?
A. Discounts B. Contests
C. Free samples D. Publicity

78. Enterprises in tertiary sector ______ .
A. support enterprises in primary sector

B. support enterprises secondary sector
C. Both A & B
D. are independent and have no relationship with any other sector

79. What are the limitations of planning?
A. It is costly
B. It is time consuming
C. It reduces creativity
D. All the above

80. The term *laissez faire* means _______ .
A. freedom to government
B. government interference in solving economic problems
C. freedom from markets
D. non-interference of government in free markets

81. Which is the Goal 5 of Sustainable Development Goals (SDGs)?
A. Gender Equality
B. Elimination of Poverty
C. Quality Education
D. Good Health and Well-Being

82. Formal communication is _______ .
A. Authorized
B. Systematic
C. Planned
D. All the above

83. F.W. Taylor is called as _______ .
A. Father of modern management
B. Father of scientific research
C. Father of science and principles
D. None of the above

84. Product quality is not assured by the following:
A. BIS Hall Mark
B. AGMARK
C. Brand image
D. ISI Mark

85. Elements in communication process include among others _______.
A. Sender
B. Feedback
C. Decoding
D. All the above

86. ______ has greater significance in inter-personal communications
A. Verbal communication
B. Written communication
C. Gestural communication
D. Both verbal and non-verbal communications

87. Which of the following statements correctly reflect the prevailing and dominant view with respect to business?
A. Businesses sole responsibility is to earn profit
B. Profit may be a leading objective of business but not the sole objective
C. Businesses gain legitimacy by serving the poor and needy
D. Businesses exploit the consumers

88. Who among the following is the 11th richest person in the world according to the Forbes 2022 List?
A. Gautam Adani & family
B. Mukesh Ambani
C. Shiv Nadar
D. Kumar Birla

89. Which of the following is not a defining characteristic of business activity?
A. Exchange of goods and services
B. Uncertainty of return
C. Humanitarian aid
D. Risk

90. Trade Mark is _______ .
A. a brand name
B. a brand logo
C. a brand name and brand mark with legal protection
D. the name of the product given by traders

91. Which of the following is a non-durable consumer product?
A. Stationery items
B. Kitchen gadgets
C. Art items
D. None of the above

92. e-business compared to traditional business enables _______ .
A. flexible manufacturing
B. customization of products/services
C. Both A and B
D. Neither A nor B

93. Which of the following is/are among consumer rights?
A. Right to fair price of products & services
B. Right to easy access to products & services
C. Both A & B
D. Neither A nor B

94. Memorandum of Association contains the following clauses among others:
A. Name clause
B. Registered office clause
C. Capital clause
D. All of the above

95. In which of the following forms of business organizations the owners have unlimited liability due to failure of business?
A. Private company
B. Public company
C. Both partnership and sole proprietorship
D. Only in sole proprietorship

96. Which of the following Public Sector Banks was merged w ith Indian Bank?
A. Dena Bank
B. Allahabad Bank
C. Vijaya Bank
D. Union Bank of India

97. Which among the following are financial instruments for raising capital in international capital markets?
A. GDRs
B. ADRs
C. IDRs
D. All the above

98. Visual communication is attractive because it _______ .
A. has a stable effect on mind
B. is enhances complexity
C. Both A & B
D. Neither A nor B

99. The maximum number of members in a public company are _______ .
A. 200
B. 7
C. 15
D. None of the above

100. Citizens enjoy freedom to take economic decisions under the ______ .
A. Capitalist system
B. Socialist system
C. Constitutional system
D. Democratic system

ANSWERS

1. (D)	**2.** (C)	**3.** (D)	**25.** (A)	**26.** (D)	**27.** (B)
4. (B)	**5.** (A)	**6.** (B)	**28.** (D)	**29.** (D)	**30.** (D)
7. (B)	**8.** (C)	**9.** (D)	**31.** (C)	**32.** (C)	**33.** (D)
10. (D)	**11.** (D)	**12.** (B)	**34.** (D)	**35.** (D)	**36.** (C)
13. (C)	**14.** (B)	**15.** (D)	**37.** (C)	**38.** (A)	**39.** (C)
16. (B)	**17.** (B)	**18.** (C)	**40.** (B)	**41.** (A)	**42.** (B)
19. (D)	**20.** (D)	**21.** (C)	**43.** (B)	**44.** (C)	**45.** (B)
22. (C)	**23.** (B)	**24.** (B)	**46.** (D)	**47.** (D)	**48.** (D)

49. (D) **50. (B)**

51. (A): Given,

Here, the 5th letter from the right = R

∴ The 3rd to the right of R = X.

52. (C):

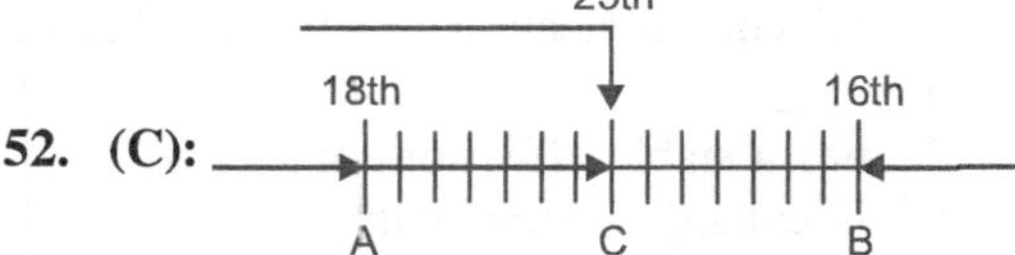

Hence, total number of persons in the que

= 18 + 6 + 1 + 6 + 16

= 18 + 13 + 16

= 47.

53. (D): Given,

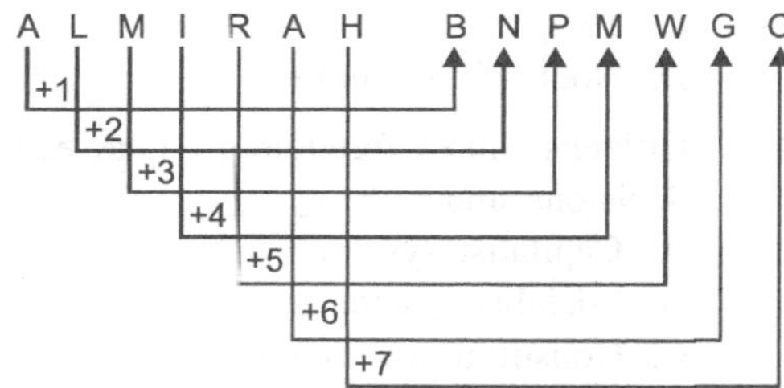

Similarly,

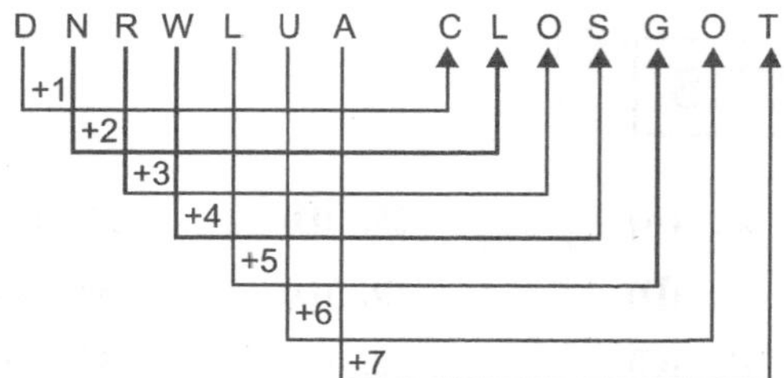

Hence, CLOSGOT is written as DNRWLUA.

54. (B): Distance = 65 km

= 65 × 1000 m

and Time = 2 hours and 10 minutes

= 2 × 60 + 10

= 130 minutes

Hence, the speed of motorist

$$= \frac{d}{t}$$

$$= \frac{65 \times 1000}{130} \text{ m/min}$$

= 500 meters/minutes.

55. (D): $\frac{(75.8)^2 - (55.8)^2}{20}$

$$= \frac{(75.8 - 55.8)(75.8 + 55.8)}{20}$$

$$= \frac{20 \times 131.6}{20} = 131.6$$

56. (D): Let the unit place and ten's place are y and x

Then, Number = $10x + y$

According to question,

Resulting number = $10x + y + 10y + x$

$= 11x + 11y$

$= 11(x + y)$

Hence, the resulting number will be divisible by 11.

57. (B): Speed = 30.6 km/hr

$$= \frac{30.6 \times 1000}{60 \times 60} \text{ m/sec}$$

$$= \frac{306}{36} \text{ m/sec}$$

= 8.5 m/sec.

58. (C): Let the two number are a and b

Then, $a + b = 6.5 \times 2$

$\Rightarrow$ $a + b = 13$ ...(*i*)

and $\sqrt{ab} = 6$

$\Rightarrow$ $ab = 36$ ...(*ii*)

$(a - b)^2 = (a + b)^2 - 4ab$

$= (13)^2 - 4 \times 36$

$= 169 - 144$

$= 25 = (5)^2$

$\Rightarrow \quad a - b = 5 \quad ...(iii)$

Adding (*i*) and (*iii*)

$2a = 18$

$\Rightarrow \quad a = 9$

From (*ii*), $\quad b = 4$

Hence, the numbers are 9 and 4.

59. **(A)**

60. **(B):** Given, $\quad$ A = 2,

M = 26,

Z = 52

$\therefore \quad$ BET = 4 + 10 + 40

= 54.

61. **(C):** Here, Total number of marbles

= 6 red + 4 blue + 2 green + 3 yellow

= 15

$\because$ 3 marbles are picked

$$\therefore \quad n(S) = {}^{15}C_3 = \frac{\underline{|15}}{\underline{|3}\,\underline{|12}} = \frac{15 \times 14 \times 13}{3 \times 2} = 5 \times 7 \times 13 = 455$$

Let E be the event of 2 blue and 1 yellow

$$\text{Then,} \quad n(E) = {}^{4}C_2 \times {}^{3}C_1 = \frac{\underline{|4}}{\underline{|2}\,\underline{|2}} \times \frac{\underline{|3}}{\underline{|1} \times \underline{|2}} = \frac{4 \times 3 \times 2}{4} \times \frac{3 \times 2 \times 1}{2} = 6 \times 3 = 18$$

Hence, the required probability

$$= \frac{n(E)}{n(S)} = \frac{18}{455}.$$

62. **(A)** Centaur is the only imaginary creature in the group.

63. **(D):**
$$\frac{1.6 \times 3.2}{0.08} = \frac{16 \times 32}{8} = 2 \times 32 = 64.$$

64. **(C):** Given, Profit = 200%

Let C.P. = ₹ 100

Then, $\quad$ S.P. = 100 + 200

= ₹ 300

Hence, the ratio of C.P. to S.P.

= 100 : 300

= 1 : 3.

65. **(C):** The given equation,

$x - y = 2 \quad ...(i)$

$x + y = 4 \quad ...(ii)$

Adding (*i*) and (*ii*), we get,

$2x = 6$

$\Rightarrow \quad x = 3$

Putting the value of x in (*i*), we get,

$y = x - 2$

$\Rightarrow \quad y = 3 - 2 = 1$

Hence, $\quad x = a = 3$

and $\quad y = b = 1$

$\Rightarrow \quad a = 3, b = 1.$

66. **(B)** $\because \quad$ A : B : C = 1 : 2 : 3

$$\text{(A + B + C)'s 1 day work} = \frac{1}{2}$$

$$\therefore \text{B's 1 day work} = \frac{1}{2} \times \frac{2}{6} = \frac{1}{6}$$

Hence, B can do whole work in 6 days.

67. **(A):** Let the height of the tree is x m.

Then, the length of the shadow of a tree

$= \sqrt{3}x$

$\because \quad AB = x$

$BC = \sqrt{3}x$

Angle of elevation = θ

In ΔABC,

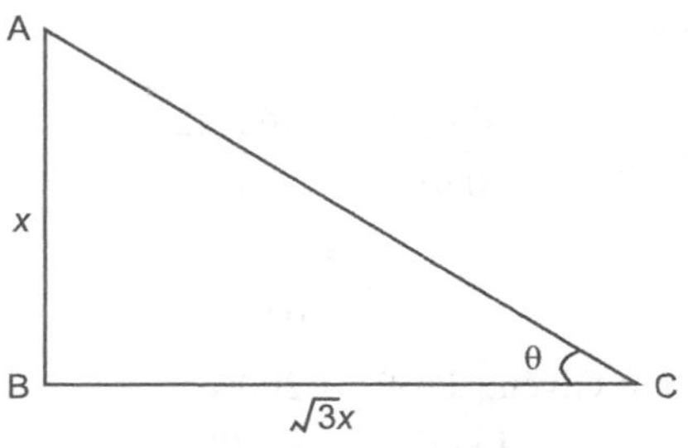

$$\tan\theta = \frac{AB}{BC}$$

$$\Rightarrow \quad \tan\theta = \frac{x}{\sqrt{3}x}$$

$$\Rightarrow \quad \tan\theta = \frac{1}{\sqrt{3}}$$

$$\Rightarrow \quad \tan 30^\circ = \frac{1}{\sqrt{3}}$$

$$\Rightarrow \quad \theta = 30^\circ$$

Hence, the angle of elevation of the sun $= 30^\circ$.

68. (D):

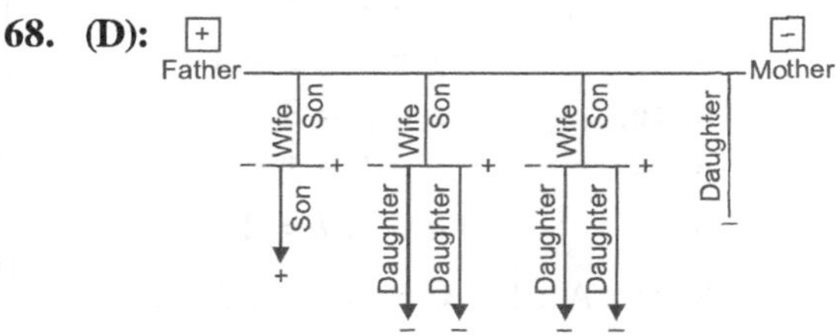

Hence, the number of female members in the family = 9.

69. (A): Given, P = ₹ 5890

r = 5% per annum

t = 3 years

$$\therefore \text{ Simple Interest} = \frac{Prt}{100}$$

$$= \frac{5890 \times 6 \times 3}{100}$$

$$= 58.9 \times 18$$

= ₹ 1060.20.

70. (B):

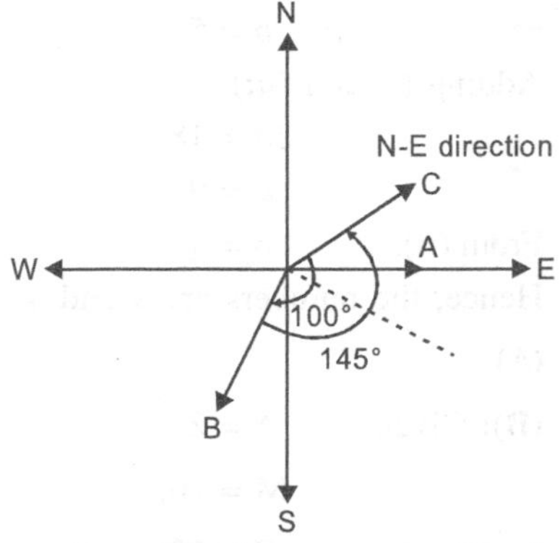

Hence, I am facing now in North-East direction.

71. (A): Given, Area of a room = 5 m × 8 m and leaving a margin of 10 cm from each wall

∴ Area of carpet

= (500 – 20) cm × (800 – 20) cm

= 480 cm × 780 cm

= 4.80 m × 7.80 m

= 4.80 × 7.80 m^2

Hence, the cost of carpeting the room

= ₹ 4.80 × 7.80 × 18

= ₹ 673.92.

72. (B): Here, the number of boys in the line

= 12 + 4 – 1 = 15

∴ The number of boys should be added to the line = 28 – 15 = 13 boys.

73. (C):

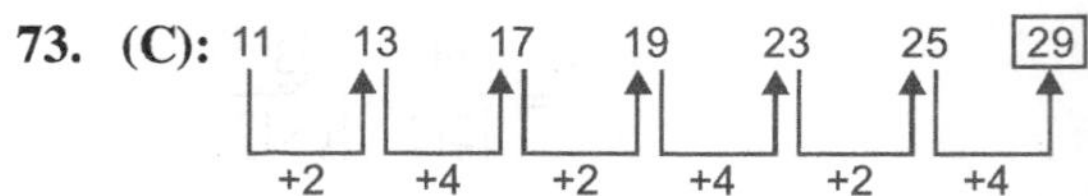

Hence, ? = the next number = 29.

74. (C):

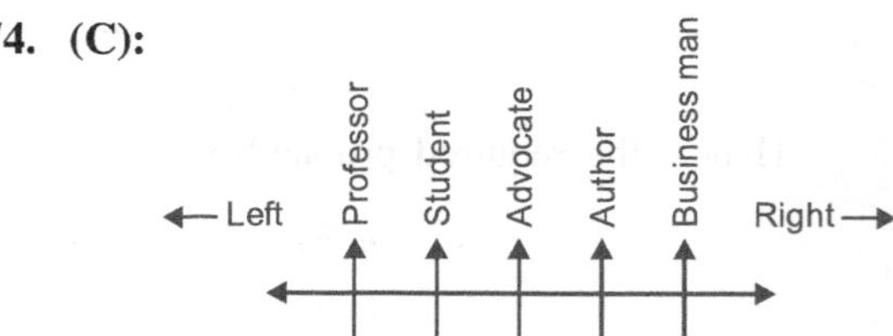

Hence, counting from left, the advocate at 3rd place.

75. **(B):** Total number of marbles

= 6 red + 4 blue + 2 green + 3 yellow

= 15

Given, 4 marbles are picked up

$$\therefore \quad n(S) = {}^{15}C_4$$

$$= \frac{\lfloor 15}{\lfloor 4 \lfloor 11}$$

$$= \frac{15.14.13.12}{4.3.2}$$

$$= 15 \times 7 \times 13$$

Let E be the event of atleast one blue marble then, $n(E)$

$$= {}^4C_1 \times {}^{11}C_3 + {}^4C_2 \times {}^{11}C_2 + {}^4C_3 \times {}^{11}C_1 + {}^4C_1 \times {}^{11}C_0$$

$$= 4 \times \frac{\lfloor 11}{\lfloor 3 \lfloor 8} + \frac{\lfloor 4}{\lfloor 2 \lfloor 2} \times \frac{\lfloor 11}{\lfloor 2 \lfloor 9} + 4 \times 11 + 1 \times 1$$

$$= 4 \times \frac{11.10.9}{6} + \frac{4.3.2}{4} \times \frac{11.10}{2} + 44 + 1$$

$$= 2 \times \frac{11 \times 10 \times 9}{3} + 12 \times 55 + 45$$

= 660 + 330 + 45 = 1035

Hence, required probability

$$P(E) = \frac{n(E)}{n(S)}$$

$$= \frac{1035}{15 \times 7 + 13}$$

$$= \frac{15 \times 69}{15 \times 91}$$

$$= \frac{69}{91}.$$

76. **(C)**	**77.** **(D)**	**78.** **(C)**
79. **(D)**	**80.** **(D)**	**81.** **(A)**
82. **(D)**	**83.** **(D)**	**84.** **(C)**
85. **(D)**	**86.** **(C)**	**87.** **(B)**
88. **(A)**	**89.** **(C)**	**90.** **(C)**
91. **(A)**	**92.** **(C)**	**93.** **(D)**
94. **(D)**	**95.** **(C)**	**96.** **(B)**
97. **(D)**	**98.** **(A)**	**99.** **(D)**
100. **(A)**		

Previous Paper (Solved)

BBA Entrance Exam 2021*

ENGLISH LANGUAGE & COMPREHENSION

1. Identify the correct idiom—When my dad bought me a computer, I was on cloud _______ .

A. Five B. Nine
C. Twice D. Seven

2. Choose the correct antonym for the given word:

Intentional

A. Deliberate
B. Accidental
C. Purposeful
D. Capricious

3. Although the fossils were well preserved, paleontologists were unable to _______ the identity of the mammal species.

A. Display B. Ascertain
C. Violate D. Embellish

4. Change the speech.

She said to her mother, "Please increase my pocket money."

A. She told her mother, "Please increase the pocket money."
B. She pleased her mother to increase my pocket money.
C. She requested her mother to increase her pocket money.
D. She asked her mother to increase her pocket money.

5. To err is ______, to forgive is divine.

A. Terror B. Sin
C. Satanic D. Human

6. Rearrange the following parts in proper sequence to obtain a correct sentence.

1. be, not what
2. Always be
3. whom you want to
4. others want to see

A. 1, 2, 4, 3 B. 3, 4, 2, 1
C. 2, 3, 1, 4 D. 4, 3, 1, 2

7. She broke the glass _____ many pieces.

A. into B. in
C. to D. from

8. Identify the type of sentence:

It was Sam who paid for the drinks.

A. Simple sentence
B. Complex sentence
C. Compound sentence
D. Interrogative sentence

9. Identify the correctly spelt word:

A. Survillance
B. Surveillance
C. Surveillence
D. Surveilance

10. Read the passage and answer the question that follows:

Policymakers must confront the dilemma that fossil fuels continue to be an indispensable source of energy even though burning them produces atmospheric accumulations of carbon dioxide that increase the likelihood of potentially disastrous global climate change. Currently, technology that would capture carbon dioxide emitted by power

* *Online exam held on 29-08-2021.*

plants and sequester it harmlessly underground or undersea instead of releasing it into the atmosphere might double the cost of generating electricity. But because sequestration does not affect the cost of electricity transmission and distribution, delivered prices will rise less, by no more than 50 per cent. Research into better technologies for capturing carbon dioxide will undoubtedly lead to lowered costs.

The passage implies which of the following about the current cost of generating electricity?

(*a*) It is higher than it would be if better technologies for capturing carbon dioxide were available.

(*b*) It is somewhat less than the cost of electricity transmission and distribution.

(*c*) It constitutes half of the delivered price of electricity.

(*d*) It is dwelt on by policymakers to the exclusion of other costs associated with electricity delivery.

A. (*b*) B. (*c*)
C. (*a*) D. None of the above

11. A person who has an urge to steal but without any intention of profit is called.
A. Claustrophobic B. Kleptomaniac
C. Pluviophile D. Agoraphobic

12. Identify the underlined word in the sentence:
'Kolkata is an old city.'
A. Noun B. Pronoun
C. Adjective D. Adverb

13. A row boat needs more than one ______.
A. oar B. ore
C. ode D. odd

14. Choose the correct synonym of the given word.
Gross
A. Common B. Shameless
C. Angry D. Sincere

15. Select the correctly punctuated sentence.
A. My friend who retires this year wants to live in Italy, or Mexico
B. My friend, who retires this year, wants to live in Italy or Mexico.
C. My friend who retires this year wants to live, in Italy, or Mexico.
D. My friend, who retires this year, wants to live, in Italy or Mexico.

16. In the question, four words are given, of which two words are most nearly the same in meaning. Mark the correct answer.
(*a*) Hectic (*b*) Risky
(*c*) Perilous (*d*) Stunning
A. (*a*)(*d*) B. (*b*)(*c*)
C. (*b*)(*d*) D. (*c*)(*d*)

17. Choose the option which gives the correct meaning for the given idiom:
A chip off the old block
A. Retaining inconsistencies of an earlier order.
B. Someone who is very similar in character to their father or mother
C. Presenting nothing novel or creative
D. Being orthodox or traditional

18. Change the word 'bold' into a verb:
A. Boldly B. Boldness
C. Embolden D. Bolder

19. Give one word for: The custom or practice of having more than one husband at same time
A. Polygyny B. Polyphony
C. Polyandry D. Polychromy

20. Write a one word substitution for:
Ability to understand and share the feelings of others
A. Sympathy B. Apathy
C. Pithy D. Empathy

21. Change the voice in the given sentence below:
Has a dog ever bitten you?
A. Have you ever being bitten by a dog?
B. Are you bitten by a dog?
C. Have you ever been bitten by a dog?
D. Has a dog ever bites you?

22. The speaker expressed his ______ to his senior's ______ for insulting his subordinates.
A. Interest, Interest
B. Liking, Desire
C. Aversion, Penchant
D. Views, Duty

23. Choose the statement(s) where the underlined word is used correctly:

(*a*) A prone is a dried plum.
(*b*) He was lying prone on the floor.
(*c*) People who eat a lot of fat are prone to heart disease.
(*d*) He is rather prone to making tactless remarks.

A. (*b*) (*c*) (*d*) B. (*a*) (*b*) (*c*)
C. (*d*) (*c*) (*a*) D. (*a*) (*b*) (*d*)

24. Out of the four alternatives suggested, select one which best expresses the same sentence in passive/active voice.
The burglar destroyed several items in the room. Even the carpet has been torn.

A. Several items were destroyed in the room by the burglar. Even the carpet was torn.
B. Several items were destroyed by the burglar. Even the carpet was torn in the room.
C. Including the carpet, several items in the room have been torn by the burglar.
D. The burglar, being destroyed several items in the room, also carpet has torn.

25. Choose the correct plural form of the word:
Cello

A. Celloes B. Celli
C. Cellos D. None of the above

GENERAL AWARENESS

26. Milkha Singh, who died recently was famously known as the:

A. Run machine B. Super Sikh
C. Flying Sikh D. Sprint king

27. Which of the following has become the first Gulf country to open embassy in Israel?

A. Bahrain B. Kuwait
C. UAE D. Oman

28. What does the abbreviation SEBI stand for?

A. Secret Examination Bureau of Investigation
B. Securities and Exchange Board of India
C. Sustainable Environment Board of Industries
D. Social and Economic Betterment Initiative

29. 'Azadi Ka Amrit Mahotsav' was launched to commemorate 91 years of:

A. Champaran Satyagraha
B. Non Cooperation Movement
C. Dandi March
D. Quit India Movement

30. The current Prime Minister of New Zealand is:

A. Jacinda Ardent B. Angela Merkel
C. Scott Morrison D. Kamal Harris

31. Facebook launched a new publishing tool called:

A. Newz B. Publisher
C. Channel D. Bulletin

32. The serving term of a member of the Rajya Sabha is:

A. 4 years B. 5 years
C. 6 years D. 7 years

33. Rickets is caused by lack of:

A. Vitamin C B. Vitamin D
C. Carbohydrates D. Iron

34. Which state has become the first rabies free-state in India?

A. Delhi B. Goa
C. Kerala D. Maharashtra

35. 'Good Friday' is:

A. The last Friday of the Christian Calendar
B. The day marking the crucifixion of Christ
C. The first Friday of the Christian Calendar
D. The day marking the birth of Christ

36. Which of the following is the official name of Indian variant of Covid 19 virus?

A. Covid-19 Delta Plus
B. Covid-19 Delta
C. Covid-21 Delta
D. Covid-Delta

37. 'Dehing' in the Dehing Patkai Wildlife Sanctuary in Assam is:

A. The name of a mountain
B. The name of a river
C. The name of a dam
D. The name of a local leader

38. What is the state Animal of Sikkim?
A. Stag B. Reindeer
C. Red Panda D. Flying Fox

39. QUAD group consists of:
A. India, USA, Australia and Japan
B. India, Russia, China, Australia
C. India, Australia, Singapore, Canada
D. India, France, USA, Germany

40. Rajatarangini (River of Kings) is an account of the history of:
A. Madhya Pradesh B. Rajasthan
C. Delhi D. Kashmir

41. Manduadih railway station renamed as _______ railway station.
A. Sardar Patel Railway Station
B. Narendra Modi Railway Station
C. Banaras Railway Station
D. Utkal Railway Station

42. In which category did Chanu Saikhom Mirabai win the Silver medal in weight lifting in the Tokyo Olympics, 2021?
A. 44 Kg B. 49 Kg
C. 55 Kg D. 67 Kg

43. Which of the following best described 'laissez-faire' economy?
A. Socialist Economy
B. Free market enterprise
C. State controlled
D. Dirigisme

44. Ngultrum is the currency:
A. Nepal B. Tibet
C. Mongolia D. Bhutan

45. Who is the author of the Harry Potter Series?
A. Roald Dahl B. J.K. Rowling
C. Enid Blyton D. Stephenie Meyer

46. 'The Jungle Book' was written by:
A. Samuel Richardson
B. Oscar Wilde
C. Benjamin Disraeli
D. Rudyard Kipling

47. 'A House for Mr. Biswas' is a famous novel:
A. Homi K. Bhabha
B. V.S. Naipaul
C. Gayatri Chakravorty
D. Mahasweta Devi

48. Savari, Ghumara, Painka and Munari are the folk dances of:
A. Tamil Nadu B. Assam
C. Chhattisgarh D. Odisha

49. Who was appointed as the first Vice Chancellor of the Delhi Sports University?
A. Karnam Malleswari B. P.T. Usha
C. Sarla Maheswari D. Sania Mirza

50. Who has launched an experiential learning portal for Cricket coaching named CRICURU?
A. Kapil Dev B. VVS Laxman
C. Sachin Tendulkar D. Virender Sehwag

LOGICAL AND ANALYTICAL ABILITY

Directions (Qs. No. 51-60): *The following table mentions production of various fruits and its consumptions. Answer the following questions according to the details given in the table.*

Fruit Varieties	Production in Tonnes	Country 1	Country 2	Domestic Consumption	Export
Apple	196,000	124,727	71,273	130,667	65,333
Orange	280,000	124,444	155,556	200,000	80,000
Banana	105,000	65,625	39,375	70,000	35,000
Strawberry	126,000	75,600	50,400	67,200	58,800
Papaya	210,000	95,455	114,545	100,000	110,000
Jack Fruit	126,000	50,400	75,600	70,000	56,000

51. The ratio of Strawberry produced for Domestic consumption to Papaya produced for Domestic consumption is:
A. (84 : 126) B. (84 : 125)
C. (87 : 125) D. (87 : 126)

52. The ratio of Jack Fruit produced for Domestic consumption to Apple produced for Export is:
A. (70000 : 65334) B. (70000 : 65333)
C. (70003 : 65333) D. (70003 : 65334)

53. What is the difference between Maximum value of Country 1 Production and the Minimum value of Country 1 Production?

A. 78,524 B. 79,452
C. 74,327 D. 77,651

54. What is the difference between Maximum value of Domestic consumption and the Maximum value of Export?
A. 80,000 B. 90,000
C. 60,000 D. 70,000

55. What is the Percentage of Export in the overall Production?
A. 37.64% B. 38.84%
C. 36.44% D. 39.24%

56. Which Fruit has the least number of Export?
A. Papaya B. Apple
C. Orange D. Banana

57. What is the difference between Maximum value of Domestic consumption and the Minimum value of Domestic consumption?
A. 142,500 B. 182,400
C. 132,800 D. 162,700

58. What is the Percentage of Country 1 Production in the overall Production?
A. 52.81% B. 53.61%
C. 54.71% D. 51.41%

59. Which Fruit has the highest number of Domestic consumption?
A. Orange B. Banana
C. Strawberry D. Apple

60. What is the difference between Maximum value of Country 1 Production and the Maximum value of Country 2 Production?
A. 28,782 B. 30,828
C. 32,578 D. 29,543

61. Angkor Wat is related to Cambodia in the same way as Borobodur is related to:
A. Malaysia B. Indonesia
C. Afghanistan D. Myanmar

62. Choose the word which is not similar in meaning of the given word.
Mandatory
A. Binding B. Compulsory
C. Obligatory D. Discretionary

63. If South-East becomes North, North-East becomes West and so on. What will West become?
A. East B. North
C. South-East D. South-West

64. Sowmya walked 20 m towards the north. Then she turned right and walks 30 m. Then she turns right and walks 35 m. Then she turns left and walks 15 m. Finally she turns left and walks 15 m. In which direction and how many meters is she from the starting position?
A. 15 m West B. 30 m East
C. 30 m West D. 45 m East

65. If MOBILITY is coded as 46293927, then EXAMINATION is coded as:
A. 45038401854 B. 56149512965
C. 57159413955 D. 67250623076

66. Identify a relationship between the given words and choose the word having similar relationship from the given choices:

Obliterate : Destroy : : Rigid : ?
A. Stiff B. Continue
C. Create D. Aid

67. If day after tomorrow is Tuesday, what was day before yesterday?
A. Thursday B. Friday
C. Saturday D. Monday

68. It was Sunday on January 1, 2006. What day of the week was January 1, 2010?
A. Sunday B. Saturday
C. Friday D. Wednesday

69. Arrange the following words in a meaningful sequence:
1. Probation 2. Interview
3. Selection 4. Appointment
5. Advertisement 6. Application
A. 123456 B. 562341
C. 654321 D. 132546

70. Which is the odd one out?
A. Orange B. Red
C. Yellow D. Blue

71. If 'table' is 'book', 'book' is 'pen', 'pen' is 'eraser', 'eraser' is 'sharpener', 'sharpener' is 'pencil' and 'pencil' is 'school', then what is used by student to sharpen a pencil?
A. sharpener B. pencil
C. pen D. eraser

72. **Directions:** Study the following question carefully and choose the right answer:

Statement: Do not lean out of the window of the bus—a warning in a school bus.

Assumptions:

I. Leaning out of a running bus is dangerous.

II. Children do not pay any heed to such warnings.

A. if only assumption I is implicit
B. if only assumption II is implicit
C. if either I or II is implicit
D. if neither I nor II is implicit

73. In certain code 'FROZEN' is written as 'OFAPSG'. Then how would 'MOLTEN' be written in that code?

A. OFPOMN
B. OFSMPN
C. OFUMPN
D. OFUNPM

74. Choose the correct order of the sentences marked A, B, C and D to form a logical paragraph.

(*a*) Along with Raj Kapoor and Dev Anand
(*b*) Born as Mohammad Yusuf Khan in Peshawar in 1922 in the home of a fruit merchant
(*c*) He went on to enjoy a career in the movies spanning five decades, blessed with a longevity enjoyed by few of his contemporaries.
(*d*) The reigning triumvirate of post-Independence Hindi cinema, Dilip Kumar's oeuvre reflects the social and political cross-currents of modern India.

A. (*b*) (*c*) (*a*) (*d*) B. (*b*) (*c*) (*d*) (*a*)
C. (*d*) (*a*) (*b*) (*c*) D. (*c*) (*d*) (*a*) (*b*)

75. If Z = 2197 and R = 729. How would J be written in that code?

A. 216 B. 124
C. 512 D. 125

APTITUDE RELATING TO THE FIELD OF MANAGEMENT AND COMMUNICATION SKILLS

76. Two numbers are in the ratio 2 : 5. If 8 is added to both the numbers, their ratio becomes 5 : 11. The numbers are:

A. 16, 40 B. 20, 50
C. 28, 70 D. 32, 80

77. Grapevine is a form of:

A. formal communication
B. channel of communication
C. informal communication
D. barrier to communication

78. Choose the most logical order of sentences from among the given choices to construct a coherent paragraph.

(*a*) Industrial Revolution and vast improvements in human technology, inanimate traction, productivity and demand led to mass production and conveyance of merchandise goods and people that resulted in cross-border integration.
(*b*) Pre-modern societies were above all else defined by localism and decentralisation.
(*c*) The rapid technological advances in information technology, and volatile capital flows have become new engines of growth.
(*d*) With the passing of pre-modern localism, improvements in maritime technology lead to the great age of maritime exploration.

A. (*a*) (*c*) (*d*) (*b*) B. (*c*) (*d*) (*b*) (*a*)
C. (*d*) (*c*) (*a*) (*b*) D. (*b*) (*d*) (*a*) (*c*)

79. Rearrange the following parts in order to make a correct sentence. Choose the right sequence.

(*a*) is priceless
(*b*) the sacrifice
(*c*) that healthcare professionals
(*d*) the safety and welfare of humanity
(*e*) have been making for

A. (*d*) (*b*) (*c*) (*e*) (*a*)
B. (*d*) (*c*) (*a*) (*b*) (*e*)
C. (*b*) (*e*) (*c*) (*d*) (*a*)
D. (*b*) (*c*) (*e*) (*d*) (*a*)

80. Which one of the following is not a principle of scientific management?
A. Functional foremanship
B. Development of personnel
C. Harmony, not discord
D. Maximum, not restricted output

81. Choose appropriate option to fill the blank:
'Avoid clichés in a formal letter.' 'Clichés' means ...
A. Jargon
B. Overused expressions
C. Ambiguous phrases
D. Discriminatory terms

82. Debits:
A. increase both assets and liabilities
B. decrease both assets and liabilities
C. increase assets and decrease liabilities
D. decrease assets and increase liabilities

83. Coordination is:
A. a management function
B. the essence of management
C. an objective of management
D. a social objective

84. To be a good communicator you should be able to:
A. Thank reasonably
B. Express your thoughts coherently
C. Express disagreements; whether it hurts is not your business
D. Make sure that you interrupt everyone to express your view

85. An unsolicited e-mail message sent to many recipients at once is a _____.
A. Virus B. Trash
C. Threat D. Spam

86. 'Webmercials' are:
A. Advertisements in print
B. Soap Operas
C. Advertisements on television
D. Internet advertisements

87. Subramanyam reached the ______ of his career at his early thirties when he got the ______ position of CEO of a software company.
A. Zephyr, Desired
B. Zenith, Coveted
C. Vale, Interesting
D. Plethora, Lucrative

88. 10 is the mean of a set of 7 observations and 5 is the mean of a set of 3 observations. The mean of the combined set is given by:
A. 7.5 B. 8.5
C. 10 D. 15

89. Which of the following is not a merit of written communication?
A. Can be kept as a record
B. Can be produced as a legal document
C. Is a form of formal communication
D. Serves as an oral record

90. Company selling goods 'play to the gallery' to boost their revenue. What does this mean?
A. Advertise a lot
B. Cater to the public taste
C. Play some games
D. Trick people

91. Which of the following is an attribute of an effective manager?
A. Procrastination B. Laziness
C. Sentimental D. Impartial

92. Sapna buys a glass, a pencil box and a cup and pays ₹ 42 to the shopkeeper. Aarti buys a cup, two pencil boxes and a glass and pays ₹ 56 to the shopkeeper. Sonam buys two glasses, a cup and two pencil boxes and pays ₹ 70 to the shopkeeper. The cost of 15 cups will be:
A. ₹ 120 B. ₹ 80
C. ₹ 150 D. ₹ 140

93. ______ denotes concentration of authority at the top level.
A. Decentralisation
B. Centralisation
C. Coordination
D. Delegation

94. A symbol or brand that is owned by the person who created it is:
A. property B. business
C. origin D. trademark

95. **Assertion (A):** Conservation of soil resources is critical to human sustenance.
Reason (R): Soil is home to many micro-organisms and contains minerals.
A. Both (A) and (R) are correct and (R) is the correct explanation of (A).
B. Both (A) and (R) are correct but (R) is not the correct explanation of (A).
C. (A) is true and (R) is false.
D. (A) is false and (R) is true.

96. Indicate the part containing an error:
(*a*) Many companies look for/ (*b*) candidates who already know/ (*c*) specific skills in order to save their time/ (*d*) in trained the new employees.
A. (*a*) B. (*b*)
C. (*c*) D. (*d*)

97. Apple IOS is a type of:
A. Operating System B. Compiler
C. Browser D. IP address

98. A train leaves Delhi at 5 am and reaches Kanpur at 9 am. Another train leaves Kanpur at 7 am and reaches Delhi at 10:30 am. At what time do the two trains cross each other?
A. 6 : 36 am B. 6 : 56 am
C. 7 : 00 am D. 7 : 56 am

99. There is no place for ______ in an accountant's job (fill in the most suitable word)
A. Money B. Errors
C. Assets D. Time

100. Choose the odd one in the following group:
1. Letter
2. Memorandum
3. Notice
4. Circular
5. Anecdote
A. 1 B. 2 and 3
C. 4 D. 5

ANSWERS

1	2	3	4	5	6	7	8	9	10
B	B	B	C	D	C	A	B	B	B
11	**12**	**13**	**14**	**15**	**16**	**17**	**18**	**19**	**20**
B	C	A	B	B	B	B	C	C	D
21	**22**	**23**	**24**	**25**	**26**	**27**	**28**	**29**	**30**
C	C	A	A	C	C	C	B	C	A
31	**32**	**33**	**34**	**35**	**36**	**37**	**38**	**39**	**40**
D	B	B	B	B	B	B	C	A	D
41	**42**	**43**	**44**	**45**	**46**	**47**	**48**	**49**	**50**
C	B	B	D	B	D	B	D	A	D
51	**52**	**53**	**54**	**55**	**56**	**57**	**58**	**59**	**60**
B	A	C	B	B	D	C	D	A	B
61	**62**	**63**	**64**	**65**	**66**	**67**	**68**	**69**	**70**
B	D	C	D	B	A	B	C	B	A
71	**72**	**73**	**74**	**75**	**76**	**77**	**78**	**79**	**80**
B	A	C	A	D	D	C	D	D	A
81	**82**	**83**	**84**	**85**	**86**	**87**	**88**	**89**	**90**
B	C	B	B	D	D	B	B	D	B
91	**92**	**93**	**94**	**95**	**96**	**97**	**98**	**99**	**100**
D	A	B	D	B	D	A	D	B	D

Previous Paper (Solved)

BBA Entrance Exam 2020 *

Directions (Q. Nos. 1-5): *Read the passages given below and answer the NEXT FIVE questions that follow:*

Globalization, liberalization and free market are some of the most significant modern trends in an economy. Most economists in our country seem captivated by the spell of the free market. Consequently, nothing seems good or normal that does not accord with the requirements of the free market. A price that is determined by the seller or for that matter, established by anyone other than the aggregate of consumers seems pernicious.

Accordingly, it requires a major act of will to think of price-fixing as both normal and having a valuable economic function. In fact, price-fixing is normal in all industrialized societies because the industrial system itself provides, as an effortless consequence of its own development, the price-fixing that it requires. Modern industrial planning requires and rewards great size. Hence a comparatively small number of large films will be competing for the same group of consumers. That each large firm will act with consideration of its own needs and thus avoid selling its products for more than its competitors' price is commonly recognized by advocated to free-market economic theories. But each firm will also act with full consideration of the needs that it has in common with the other large firms competing for the same customer. Each large firm thus avoid significant stable price cutting, because price-cutting will be prejudicial to the common interest in a stable demand for products.

Most economists do not see price-fixing when it occurs because they expect it to be brought about by a number of explcit agreements among large firms: it is not. Moreover, those economists who argue that allowing the free market to operate without interference is the most efficient method of establishing prices has not considered the economics of non-socialists countries. Most of these economies employ international price-fixing, usually in an overt fashion. Formal price fixing by carter and informal price fixing by agreements covering the members of an industry are common place. Were there something peculiarly efficient about the free market and inefficient about price-fixing, the countries that have avoided the first and used the second would have suffered drastically in their economic development. There is no indication that has.

Socialists industry also works within a framework of controlled prices. In early 1970s the Soviet Union began to give firms and industries some flexibility in adjusting prices that a more informal evolution has accorded the capitalist system. Economists in the USA have hailed the change as a return to the free market. But the Soviet firms were not in favour of the price established by a free-market over which they exercised little influence; rather. Soviet firms acquired some power to fix prices.

1. Author's primary objective of narration in writing the passage seems to:

A. Believe the popular belief that the free market helps enhance development of industrial societies.

B. Advocate that price-fixing is unavoidable and is beneficial to the economy of any industrialized society.

*Online exam held on 14-09-2020 conducted by GGSIPU Delhi.

C. Explain the methodology of fixing price to stabilize free-market.
D. Prove that price-fixing and free-market are compatible and mutually beneficial to industrialized societies.

2. What was the result of the then Soviet Union's change in economic polcity in 1970s?
A. Earned greater profits
B. Technologial up gradation
C. Less control over the market
D. None of these

3. The author feels that price fixed by seller seems pernicious because:
A. People don't have faith in large firms.
B. People don't want government of fix prices.
C. Most economists believe that consumers should determine prices.
D. Most economists believe that one group should determine price.

4. Which of the following statements are TRUE in the context of the information given in the passage? The information in the passage is helpful to:
I. Know some of the ways in which prices can be fixed.
II. Identify the products for which price fixing can be more beneficial.
III. Differentiate between the economies of various countries.

Select the most appropriate answer from the following:
A. Only I
B. Only II
C. Only III
D. Both I and II

5. Considering the literal meaning and connotations of the words used in the passage, the authors' attitude towards most economists can best be described as:
A. Spiteful and envious
B. Impartial and unbiased
C. Derogatory and antagonistic
D. Critical and condescending

Directions (Q. Nos. 6-10): *Read the passages given below and answer the NEXT FIVE questions that follow:*

Traditional Indian values must be viewed both from the angle of the individual and from that of the geographically delimited agglomeration of peoples or groups enjoying a common system of leadership which we call the 'state'. The Indian state's special feature is the peaceful or perhaps mostly peaceful co-existent of social groups of various historical provenances which mutually adhere in a geographical, economic and political sense, without ever assimilating to each other in social terms, in ways of thinking or ever in language. Modern Indian law will determine certain rules especially in realtion to the regime of the family, upon the basis of how the lion-cloth is tied or how the turban is worn, for this may identify the litigants as members of a rational group and therefore as participants in its traditional law, though their ancestors left the region three or four centuries earlier.

The use of the word 'State' above must not mislead us. There was no such thing as a conflict between the individual and the state at least before Foreign Governments became established, just as there was no concept of state sovereignty or of any church and state dichotomy. Modern Indian Secularism has an admittedly peculiar feature: It requires the state to make a fair distribution of attention and support amongst all religions.

These blessed aspects of India's famed tolerance (Indian kings so rarely persecuted religiously groups that the exceptions prove the rule) at once struck Portuguese and other European visitors to the West Coast of India in 16th century and the impression made upon them in this and other ways gave rise, at one remove to the basic Constitution of Thomas Mores Utopia. There is little about modern India that strikes one at once as Utopian but the insistence upon the inculcation of norms and the absence of bigotry and institutionalized exploitation of human or natural resources are two very different features which link the realities of India and her tradition with the essence of all Utopians.

6. Which of the following is a special feature of the Indian State?
A. Peaceful co-existence of people under a command system of leadership.
B. Peaceful co-existence of social groups of different historical provenances attached to each other in a geographical, economical and political sense.
C. Social integration of all groups.
D. Cultural assimilation of all social groups

7. The basic construction of Thomas More's Utopia was inspired by:
A. India traditional religious tolerance
B. Persecution of religious groups by Indian rulers
C. Social inequality in India
D. European perception of Indian state

8. The author uses the word 'state' to highlight:
A. Antagonistic relationship between the state and the individual throughout the period of history.
B. Absence of conflict between the state and the individuals upto a point in time.
C. The concept of state sovereignty
D. Dependence on religion

9. Which one is the peculiar feature of modern India 'secularism'?
A. No discrimination on religious considerations
B. Total indifference to religion
C. No space for social identity
D. Disregard for social law

10. What is the striking feature of modern India?
A. A replica of Utopian state
B. Uniform laws
C. Adherence to traditional values
D. Absence of bigotry

11. Captain is related to Soldier in the same way as Leader is related to ____.
A. Chair B. Party
C. Follower D. Minister

12. Correct the sentence(s) by appropriately choosing options given below:

He is too important **for tolerating** any delay.

A. to tolerate B. at tolerating
C. to tolerating D. with tolerating

13. What is the force of attraction between any two bodies by virtue of their masses called?
A. Electromagnetic force
B. Centripetal force
C. Gravitational force
D. Nuclear force

14. The authorization for the withdrawal of funds from the Consolidated Fund of India must come from:
A. President of India
B. Prime Minister of India
C. The Parliament
D. Union Finance Minister

15. Skirmish is related to War in the same way as Disease is related to ____.
A. Infection B. Patient
C. Epidemic D. Medicine

16. The famous hill station 'Kondaikanal' is located in:
A. Nilgiri Hills B. Palani Hills
C. Cardamom Hills D. Javadi Hills

17. Name the country, where the entire government has resigned after failing to achieve a key policy goal on social welfare and healthcare system in recent times?
A. Finland B. Sweden
C. Norway D. Austria

18. Select one word to describe the phenomenon narrated in the stem:

Story of old time Gods and Heroes is:
A. Lyric B. Epic
C. Legend D. Romance

19. Select one word to describe the phenomenon narrated in the stem:

A lady's umbrella is:
A. Parasol B. Granary
C. Epitaph D. Aviary

20. Select one word to describe the phenomenon narrated in the stem:

Commencement of words with the same letter is:

A. Pun
B. Alliteration
C. Transferred epithet
D. Oxymoron

21. Fill in the blanks from options given below to complete the sentence.

Please, come ____ the bathroom.

A. out of B. over
C. on D. in

22. 2019 Nobel Memorial Prize in Economics Sciences awarded to Michael Kremer. Abhijit Banerjee and Esther Duflo for their experimental approach to ______.

A. Wealth Creation
B. Poverty Alleviation
C. Equitable distribution of Wealth
D. Financial Inclusion

23. Select one word to describe the phenomenon narrated in the stem:

A person who renounces the world and practices self-discipline in order to attain salvation is:

A. Sceptic B. Ascetic
C. Devotee D. Antiquarian

24. IMF Chief economists Gita Gopinath is an alumnus of ______.

A. IIM-Ahmedabad B. IIM-Bangalore
C. IIM-Calcutta D. IIM-Lucknow

25. Fungi are plants that lack:

A. Oxygen B. Chlorophyll
C. Carbon dioxide D. None of these

26. In Union Cabinet, total number of ministers including the Prime Minister shall not exceed:

A. 20% members of Lok Sabha
B. 15% members of Lok Sabha
C. 25% members of Lok Sabha
D. 10% members of Lok Sabha

27. Which one of the following is the richest source of vitamin C?

A. Guava B. Orange
C. Pineapple D. Tomato

28. Correct the sentence(s) by appropriately choosing options given below:

The man **to whom I sold** my house was a cheat.

A. to whom I sell B. who was sold to
C. to who I sell D. to whom I sold

29. Which of the following indices is NOT released by the UNDP?

A. Human Development Index
B. Multidimensional Poverty Index
C. Gender Inequality Index
D. Environmental Quality Index

30. Who chaired the RBI expert committee to review its Extant Economic Capital Framework?

A. C. Rangarajan B. Bimal Jalan
C. L.C. Gupta D. Aditya Puri

31. Correct the sentence(s) by appropriately choosing options given below:

I need not offer any explanation regarding this incident-my behaviour **is speaking itself**.

A. will speak to itself
B. has been speaking
C. speaks for itself
D. speaks about itself

32. NBFCs stands for:

A. National Banking and Financial Companies
B. National Business and Finance Companies
C. Non-Banking Financial Companies
D. Non-Banking and Financial Companies

33. Choose the missing word in place of sign (?) on the basis of the relationship between the words given on the left/right hand side of the signs.

Doctor : Nurse :: ? : Follower

A. Worker B. Union
C. Employer D. Leader

34. 'Kathakali' is a folk dance prevalent in which Indian state?

A. Karnataka B. Orissa
C. Kerala D. Manipur

35. India's only active volcano is located in which Island?
A. Elephanta Island B. Havelock Island
C. Barren Island D. Car Nicobar

36. Which of the following is an air-borne disease?
A. Measles B. Pink eye
C. Typhoid D. Malaria

37. Fill in the blanks from options given below to complete the sentence.

Please, stop ______ so many mistakes.
A. to make B. make
C. making D. makes

38. Which city police has launched a mobile app 'digicop' to track the status of stolen two-wheeler and cell-phones?
A. Hyderabad B. Chennai
C. Bengaluru D. Pune

39. What makes the reptile a reptile?
A. Cold bloodedness
B. Non-hearing
C. Warm bloodedness
D. Egg-laying

40. Which three indicators are used in the Human Development Index?
I. Standard of Living
II. Education
III. Life Expectancy
IV. Environment Pollution
A. Only I, II and IV B. Only I and II
C. Only I, II and III D. All of the above

41. Who authored the 'Business@Speed of Thought'.
A. Dick Francis B. Bill Gates
C. Eon Musk D. Mark Zuckerberg

42. Choose the missing word in place of sign (?) on the basis of the relationship between the words given on the left/right hand side of the signs.

Food : Stomach :: Fuel : ?
A. Engine B. Rail
C. Automobile D. Aeroplane

43. Who founded the Ramakrishna Mission in 1896 to carry on humanitaration relief and social work?
A. Ramakrishna Paramahansa
B. Swami Vivekananda
C. Swami Dayananda Saraswati
D. Blavatsky and Olcott

44. Which Constitutional Amendment has provided Free and Compulsory Elementary Education to all children in the age group 6-14 years as a Fundamental Right?
A. 76th B. 72th
C. 86th D. 78th

45. Correct the sentence(s) by appropriately choosing options given below:

There are not many men who are so famous that they are frequently referred to by their **short names** only.
A. initials B. signatures
C. pictures D. middle names

46. Tree is related to Root in the same way as Smoke is related ______.
A. Cigarette B. Heat
C. Fire D. Chimney

47. Ratna says, "Gaurav's father is the only son of my father". How is Ratna related to Gaurav?
A. Grandmother B. Sister
C. Mother D. Aunt

48. Select one word to describe the phenomenon narrated in the stem:

A sad song is called:
A. Ditty B. Knell
C. Dirge D. Lay

49. Every year International Women's Day is celebrated on:
A. March 8 B. June 5
C. December 10 D. January 10

50. Sia introduced Raghav as the son of the only daughter of the father of her uncle. How is Raghav related to Sia?
A. Brother
B. Cousin
C. Nephew
D. Can't be determined

51. Who founded Satya Shodhak Samaj in 1873?
A. Shri Bharat Kumar
B. Bankim Chandra Chattophadhya
C. Purshottam Das Tandon
D. Jyotibha Phule

52. Correct the sentence(s) by appropriately choosing options given below:

The small child does whatever his father **was done**.
A. has done
B. did
C. does
D. had done

53. The fundamental duties were included in the Indian Constitution by which of the following Constitutional Amendment Acts.
A. 42nd B. 44th
C. 40th D. 43rd

54. Fill in the blanks from options given below to complete the sentence.

Our country is spiritual country, theirs ______ religious.
A. is B. are
C. have D. also

55. Fill in the blanks from options given below to complete the sentence.

Our sir teaches Mathematics ______ English.
A. across B. besides
C. beside D. both

56. Fill in the blanks from options given below to complete the sentence.

Please, don't laugh ______ those beggars.
A. for
B. against
C. at
D. from

57. Who assigns star ratings on electric goods in India on the basis of energy efficiency?
A. Finance ministry
B. Bureau of Energy Efficiency
C. Bureau of Indian Standards
D. Indian Standard Institute

Directions (Q. Nos. 58-62): *Read the following information carefully and answer the NEXT FIVE questions given below:*

Six members of a family G, H, I, J, K and L are Chemist, Clerk, Lawyer, Jeweller, Medico and Engineer but not in the same order.

I. Medico is he Grandfather of L and he is a Chemist
II. Clerk J is married to G
III. I, who is a jeweller, is married to lawyer
IV. There are two married couples in the family
V. H is the mother of L and K

58. How G is related to K?
A. Wife B. Grandmother
C. Father D. Grandfather

59. Who are the two couples in the family?
A. GJ and IH B. GK and JK
C. GH and IJ D. GI and HJ

60. What is the profession of K?
A. Medico B. Engineer
C. Clerk D. Physician

61. How many male members are there in the family?
A. Two
B. Four
C. Three
D. Can't be determined

62. What is the profession of G?
A. Lawyer B. Engineer
C. Clerk D. Medico

Directions (Q. Nos. 63-67): *Read the following information carefully and answer the NEXT FIVE questions given below:*

There are four friends Anju, Shyam, Rani and harsh. One of them is a cricketer and studies Chemistry and Biology. Anju and Shyam play football. Anju studies commerce. Both the football players study Mathematics. Harsh is a boxer. One football player also studies Physics. The boxer studies Mathematics and Accountancy. All the friednds study two subjects each and play one game each.

63. Who plays cricket?
A. Anju B. Rani
C. Shyam D. Harsh

64. Who study physics?
A. Anju B. Shyam
C. Rani D. Harsh

65. Name the person who is not a boxer, but studies both Chemistry and Biology?
A. Harsh B. Rani
C. Anju D. Shyam

66. Who study Commerce and does play football?
A. Harsh B. Shyam
C. Anju D. Rani

67. Who does not study Mathematics?
A. Rani
B. Harsh
C. Shyam
D. Both Rani and Harsh

Directions (Q. Nos. 68-72): *Read the following information and answer the NEXT FIVE questions that follow:*

In a school, there were five teachers, A and B were teaching Hindi and English. C and B were teaching English and Geography. D and A were teaching Mathematics and Hindi. E and B were teaching Hisotry and French.

68. Which of the following subjects were taught by A, B and C teachers?
A. Hindi B. English
C. Geography D. History

69. Which of the following teachers were teaching both Geography and Hindi?
A. A and B B. C and A
C. B and C D. None of these

70. Which of the following subject was taught by more than two teachers?
A. History B. French
C. Hindi D. Geography

71. D, B and A were teaching which of the following subjects?
A. English only
B. Hindi and English
C. Hindi only
D. English and Geography

72. Who among the teachers was teaching maximum number of subjects?
A. A B. C
C. D D. B

Directions (Q. Nos. 73-75): *In the next THREE questions, a statement is followed by two conclusions numbered 1 and 2 and responses are coded as:*

A. If only conclusion 1 follows
B. If only conclusion 2 follows
C. If neither 1 nor 2 follows
D. If both 1 and 2 follows

73. Statement:
Money plays most important role in politics.
Conclusion:
1. The poor can never become politicians.
2. All rich men take part in politics.

74. Statement:
Should there be only one University throughout India?
Conclusion:
1. Yes, this is the only way to bring about uniformity in the educational standards in the country.
2. No, this is administratively impossible.

75. Statement:
Morning walks are good for health.
Conclusion:
1. All healthy people goes for morning walks
2. Evening walks are not beneficial for health

76. Choose the option that completes the sentence most meaningfully and appropriately.

People in ancient Greece were so ____ with war and ____ of life that they preferred to kill their handicapped children at birth.
A. fraught; uncertainties
B. obsessed; frightened
C. busy; heartlessness
D. preoccupied; easiness

77. With growing sevice orientation of businesses, which of the following business activity has lost it sheen in recent times?
A. Marketing B. Market Research
C. Manufacturing D. Banking

78. Choose the option that completes the sentence most meaningfully and appropriately.

Some writers have claimed that Theocratic state is ____; they have even insisted that such a model of leadership is more ______.

A. repressive; authoritarian
B. division; plural
C. religious; tolerant
D. democratic; liberal

79. Choose the option that completes the sentence most meaningfully and appropriately.

People were charmed by his ______ appearance and ____ deportment.

A. ugly; haughty
B. handsome; dignified
C. cute; rude
D. shabby; snobbish

80. In digital transformations, which kind of business entities have suffered the most?

A. Service entities
B. Livestock entities
C. Agro based entities
D. Small business entities

81. Value creation is more challenging in which kind of business entities?

A. Agribusiness entities
B. Manufacturing entities
C. Mining entities
D. Service business entities

82. With growing digitization of business, which of the following has emerged as a key managerial skill in recent times?

A. Communication skill
B. Emotional intelligence
C. Appearance and soft skill
D. Data analysis skill

83. Social media and digital space often distract focused attention, is still visited by managers for:

A. Market making
B. Brand building
C. Both (A) and (B)
D. None of these

84. Choose the option that completes the sentence most meaningfully and appropriately.

The terrible disease a Mumbai doctor had ____ and declared the ____ demise of the eminent leader.

A. announced; eminent
B. suspected; unlikely
C. treated; suspected
D. diagnosed; imminent

85. Choose the option that completes the sentence most meaningfully and appropriately.

The women in India were kept under ____ until the new laws in free India ensured their ____ from the tentacles of orthodox society.

A. impression; education
B. shackles; exculpation
C. subjugation; emanicipation
D. pressure; release

Directions (Q. Nos. 86-90): *Study the passage given below and answer the NEXT FIVE questions that follow:*

If proof were needed that the organized sector of the Indian economy is globalised, look no further than the knee-jerk reaction of Jet Airways, which issued marching orders to 800 employees and then retracted following an adverse reaction, has now morphed into a strategic plan by companies to keep their heads above the rising waters. This strategy is predicted on the need to cut costs and protect profit margins as far as possible rather than look to increasing revenue in what is turning out to be a slowing market. Auto majors such as Tata Motors, Ashoka Leyland and Mahindra & Mahindra have began to cut back production and reduce man-hours at their plants across India in a bid to prevent inventory pile-up and tailor output to falling demand. It will not be long before auto component vendors follow suit, followed by firms across the product spectrum. Organized industry is learning to cope with the downside of a business cycle that first manifested itself last year in the wake of rising raw material and energy prices and in the lagged effects of high interest rates on consumer demand. In the last quarter of 2007-08, industry and manufacturing growth rates both slipped to around 5 per cent against 8.6 per cent and 9.6 per cent respectively in the previous quarter, which performance itself represented a decline from the high of 10 and 12 per cent in 2006-07.

Growth has been falling, therefore, all of 2007 -08 with the decline accelerating since January. Fiscal 2007-08 closed with a real GDP growth of 9 per cent mainly due to a double digit growth in services such as real estate, transport, hotel services and construction. With high albeit falling interest rates ad worse, a risk aversion among lenders impacting these sectors as much as they had manufacturing earlier, the overall growth momentum may slow even more than officially estimated. Against this backdrop, the best bet for policymakers and producers would be to turn the downturn into an opportunity for fresh strategizing. Manufacturing firms have begun the task of cutting costs in right earnest. The real estate sector is supposedly asking for relief and so will the shipping ad transport sectors, the government has to exercise discretion the way it did with the airline industry so as to encourage internal overhauling. The government will inevitably have to boost confidence and private investments at some future date through counter-cyclical spending. That future should start right away.

86. Which of the following is not implied in this passage?
   A. The economic slowdown should be perceived as an opportunity for strategizing by policymakers and producers.
   B. Growth rates in industry and manufacturing had been falling throughtout the year 2007–08.
   C. Jet Airways had to clear strategy behind sacking of 800 of its employees.
   D. Real estate and shipping, transport sectors are looking to the government for relief measures.

87. From which of the following factors does the slowdown in business become evident in the passage?
   A. Raw material and energy prices started rising last year.
   B. In the Jan-March 2008 quarter both the industry and manufacturing growth rates dropped to about 5%
   C. In fiscal 2007-08 consumer demand started to lag due to the high interest rates.
   D. All of the above

88. Which of the following points is implied in this passage?
   A. There is proof that India's organized sector may be affecting the global economy.
   B. The economic slowdown is a result to knee-jerk reactions of companies such as Jet Airways.
   C. Organized sector of the Indian economy is definitely globalised.
   D. None of the above

89. Which of the following captions would be the most apt for this passage?
   A. Government's role in boosting economy.
   B. Globalization of Indian economy.
   C. Cost-cutting is the cure for economic ills.
   D. Indian industry's impact on the global economy.

90. Given that the government will inevitably have to play a proactive role in boosting confidence and private investments in future:
   A. The corrective measures should begin right away.
   B. Atuto companies such as Tata Motor, Ashoka Leyland and Mahindra & Mahindra should cooperate with the government.
   C. The government should seek aid from World Bank.
   D. Organized industry should be encouraged to increase revenue.

Directions (Q. Nos. 91-95): *Study the passage given below and answer the NEXT FIVE questions that follow:*

'Don't disturb between 2 pm - 4 pm'. I have seen such boards outside many houses in Pune. I wondered why, until someone told me that people sleep at that time and they don't like to be disturbed by unwanted visitors. A siesta in Sanskrit is a luxury nowadays. But there are people who enjoy their 40 winks even at office. It's euphemistically called a 'power nap', which rejuvenates you. J F Kennedy loved this post lunch snooze so much so that there was a presidential order, not to disturb him for an hour during the daytime. The first Mughal emperor, Zahiruddin Babar, wrote in his autobiography, Tuzuk-e-Babri, that 'India's warm and humid climate makes one feel drowsy after having lunch.'

When it comes to siesta, Bengalis and Italians are number one in the world. I, however, am of the view that this is because of the food. Rice and pasta are sleep- inducing food items. Fish adds to it because it has phosphorous, which makes one feel sleepy. The practice of the siesta is also held responsible for the Parsi community's historic uprooting from Persia. According to legend, the Arabs who invaded Persepolis in modem-day Iran during the Islamic inclusions in the 10th century soon realized that the only way to conquer Zoroastrian warriors was to attack after the traditional Sunday lunch of Dhansaak the thick mutton stew served with cardamom-scented drowns rice is heavy enough to lull anyone into a long and peaceful siesta afterwards!

The word siesta is said to have originated from ancient Latin word 'siemete', which meant 'sleeping under tree', but not specified whether at night or during daytime. Even 'Sexta' in Spanish and Latin means the 6th hour, which is the time of rest. I have read that some corporate offices have sleeping rooms for their staff to have a power nap after lunch. But. it mustn't exceed 30 minutes. Siestas are very addictive. Just sleep one day for an hour after having lunch and next day exactly at that time, you'll feel sleepy and start yawning. There are people who're so fond of it that they can give a miss to all regular things in life of a few minutes of stolen slumber, as Allan Wanbridge aptly called it. After all, stolen moments, such as stolen kisses, are always the sweetest, aren't they?

91. Why is 'enjoying 40 winks at office' is called 'power nap'?
   A. Because it re-energizes the one who naps.
   B. Because it reduces the working hour in the office.
   C. Because the officials pretend that it gives them power.
   D. Because all those in power in the office can enjoy a nap inside the office.

92. What does the word 'siesta' mean?
   A. Sleeping late till late morning.
   B. Sleeping in the early afternoon.
   C. Sleeping in the late evenings.
   D. Sleeping late in the night.

93. What cause the Parsi community's historic uprooting from Persia?
   A. Their practice of the siesta every afternoon.
   B. Their having an afternoon siesta after eating sleep inducing mutton strews and brown rice on Sunday.
   C. Their inability to fight with their invaders because of their heavy and clumsy body.
   D. Their giving preference to delicious food and sleeping till late in the morning.

94. What out of the following, is cited as a reason for inducing sleep?
   A. The climate as it is in Bengal and Italy.
   B. Fatty junk food like pasta and pizzas
   C. Warm and humid climate and rice, pasta and fish.
   D. Humid climate and the food that contains sedative substances.

95. What is an example of addiction to siestas?
   A. One cannot resist it under any circumstances and will go to sleep hypnotized.
   B. One will tend to sleep again and again during the day.
   C. One will lose their normal sleep during the nights because of sleeping during the day.
   D. One will feel sleepy and start yawning at the same time every day and will tend to give a miss to all regular things for it.

Directions (Q. Nos. 96-100): *Study the passage given below and answer the NEXT FIVE questions that follow:*

On August 15, 1947, India was granted independence from British colonial dominance. This was an event of international significance. From this day onwards, the Indian Union assumed a role in world politics that was appropriate enough to modify the thinking of nations. Concepts like non-alignment, tolerance, non-violence and peaceful coexistence were introduced by India into international vocabulary. "Our dreams concern India" said the first Prime Minister of the country on the eve of achieving freedom, "but they also concern the whole world, for the world has become one". Mahatma Gandhi chose Nehru to become the first Prime Minister of Independent India. With his vision of unity of the nation, he became the architect of modem India. It was to be a federal state based on secularism- the commitment to an Indian identity, which was above all races, castes and religions. It was a vision of extraordinary dimensions.

Nehru as well as his daughter and successor, Smt. Indira Gandhi, were well aware that only a firm anchorage in the Indian identity could unite the nation and enable it to make an impact on the world. In these days of mutual independence, the western powers and America cannot afford to ignore what is happening in this region. It is possible that the fate of the Asian democracies would one day he decided on the banks of Ganges. If India fails to remain a democracy, this would trigger the fall of the whole of South and South-East Asia. That is why the Indian Prime Minister has to play a role that goes well beyond duties related to internal affairs only. It is of international political significance.

96. What does 'the fate of Asian democracies would one day be decided on the banks of the Ganges' mean in the context as it is used here?

A. If the Indian democracy grows, it will help other democracies in the region grow; if it fails, the countries of this region will fail.

B. The rulers of India sitting on the banks of the Ganges would control the Asian democracies.

C. India would come in a position to control the countries of the West and America because of its control over the democracies of Asia.

D. The seat of governance would shift from Delhi (which is on the banks of Yamuna) to Varanasi (which is on the banks of the Ganges).

97. What does the writer mean by 'in these days of mutual independence'?

A. Everyone in society is dependent on one another in one way or the other.

B. Each of the states of the country caimot do without the cooperation of the other states.

C. The countries of Asia, America and the West caimot exist without cooperating with one another.

D. The western powers and America cannot afford to ignore what is happening in Asia.

98. What does 'it was to be a federal state based on secularism' mean?

A. India was to be committed to the Indian identity.

B. India was to maintain its identity as a country of diverse groups with some autonomy to them and tolerance towards them.

C. Indian decided not to encourage races, castes and religions to grow.

D. India started the process of elimination of the bad practices of caste, race and communalism in the name of religion.

99. Which of the following mean same as the word 'trigger' as used in the passage?

A. Prevent B. Fail

C. Hit D. Bring about

100. How did the Indian Union modify thinking of nations?

A. It made the nations to accept it as an independent country.

B. It gave confidence to the countries which were still under colonial dominance to gain freedom by fighting.

C. It gave the world concepts like non-alignment, tolerance, non-violence and peaceful co-existence.

D. It gained freedom from the British colonial dominance and started providing leadership to the downtrodden nations of the world.

ANSWERS

1	2	3	4	5	6	7	8	9	10
B	D	C	A	B	B	A	D	A	D
11	**12**	**13**	**14**	**15**	**16**	**17**	**18**	**19**	**20**
C	A	C	C	C	B	A	C	A	B
21	**22**	**23**	**24**	**25**	**26**	**27**	**28**	**29**	**30**
A	B	B	C	B	B	B	D	D	B
31	**32**	**33**	**34**	**35**	**36**	**37**	**38**	**39**	**40**
C	C	D	C	C	A	C	B	A	C
41	**42**	**43**	**44**	**45**	**46**	**47**	**48**	**49**	**50**
B	A	B	C	A	C	D	C	A	D
51	**52**	**53**	**54**	**55**	**56**	**57**	**58**	**59**	**60**
D	C	A	A	B	C	B	D	A	B
61	**62**	**63**	**64**	**65**	**66**	**67**	**68**	**69**	**70**
D	D	B	B	B	C	A	B	D	C
71	**72**	**73**	**74**	**75**	**76**	**77**	**78**	**79**	**80**
C	D	C	B	C	A	C	A	B	D
81	**82**	**83**	**84**	**85**	**86**	**87**	**88**	**89**	**90**
D	D	C	D	C	C	D	C	B	A
91	**92**	**93**	**94**	**95**	**96**	**97**	**98**	**99**	**100**
A	B	B	C	D	A	C	B	D	C

Previous Paper (Solved)

BBA Entrance Exam 2019 *

GENERAL AWARENESS

Directions (Q. Nos. 1-37): *Choose the most appropriate option.*

1. Which of the following is the longest Railway tunnel in the world?
A. Standedge Tunnel
B. Laerdal Tunnel
C. Gotthard Base Tunnel
D. Seikan Tunnel

2. What is the art of Japanese flower arranging called?
A. Ikebana B. Feng Shui
C. Florabana D. Deribana

3. Which IIT has tied up with Pullela Gopichand Badminton Academy to develop training module?
A. IIT Tirupati B. IIT Kharagpur
C. IIT Hyderabad D. IIT Madras

4. Who won the Best actress award (Hindi language) in the 65th National Film awards in 2018?
A. Kangana Ranaut B. Sridevi
C. DIvya Dutta D. Vidya Balan

5. Which state of India has signed the Host City Contract with the Indian Olympic Association (IOA) to host the 39th National Games in 2022?
A. Assam B. Meghalaya
C. Manipur D. Negaland

6. RERA Act is related to:
A. Illegal selling of drugs
B. Real estate
C. Illegal possession of Arms
D. Benami property

7. The Kochon Prize is awarded annually to those have made significant contribution to combating which disease?
A. Leprosy B. Tuberculosis
C. Malaria D. Alzheimer's disease

8. Which among the following was the earliest drama of kalidasa?
A. Vikramorvishiyam
B. Malvikagnimitram
C. Abhijnanshakuntalam
D. Kumarasambhava

9. The Himalayan Hydro Expo 2018 was organized in
A. Nepal B. India
C. Burma D. None of the above

10. Which country among the following were suspended from voting in United Nations General Assembly (UNGA) in 2018-19 session for not paying dues to 193-member world body?
A. Marshall Islands B. Comoros
C. Somalia D. Guinea-Bissau

11. Who is the World Rugby Player of the year 2017?
A. Beauden John Barrett
B. Daniel William Carter
C. Brodie Allan Retallick
D. Kieran Read

* *Exam held on 11-05-2019. (Exam Conducted by GGSIPU Delhi)*

12. World Anti-Doping Agency (WADA) has its headquarter in
A. USA B. Canada
C. Switzerland D. Australia

13. Who was the captain of Indian hockey team for 1928 Olympic games?
A. Major Dhayanchand
B. Jaipal Singh Munda
C. K.D. Singh
D. Lal Shah Bokhari

14. "Controversially Yours" is an autobiography of
A. Shane Warne
B. Shoaib Akhtar
C. Muttiah Muralitharan
D. Manoj Prabhkar

15. National Sports day in India is celebrated on:
A. 29th August B. 29th March
C. 29th July D. 29th May

16. Which among the following is used as a moderator in nuclear reactor?
A. Radium B. Water
C. Graphite D. Thorium

17. ____ is a positively charged particle emitted by a radioactive element.
A. Alpha ray B. Beta ray
C. Gamma ray D. Cathode ray

18. "Fermi" is the unit of
A. Mass B. Frequency
C. Length D. Density

19. Which types of waves are used in the night vision devices?
A. Microwave B. UV rays
C. Short waves D. None of the above

20. A svedberg unit is a non-metric unit for
A. sedimentation rate B. viscosity
C. pressure D. density

21. Indigofera is a source of
A. dye B. vitamin
C. mineral D. protein

22. Which among the following is not a true fruit?
A. Grape B. Mango
C. Date D. Apple

23. Ribonucleic acid is responsible for
A. Protein synthesis B. Lipid synthesis
C. Oxygen synthesis D. All of the above

24. ____ can be deformed permanently by heat and pressure?
A. Thermoset B. Thermoplastic
C. Resin D. All of the above

25. What stone is called fool's gold?
A. Iron pyrite B. Iron sulphite
C. Both (A) and (B) D. Mercury iodide

26. What did Thomas Alva Edison invent?
A. the lightning rod
B. the telephone
C. the phonograph
D. Atom Bomb

27. Which among the following scripts of modern India have descended from the Sarda Script?
1. Gurmukhi
2. Dogri
3. Sindhi

Choose the correct option from the codes given below:
A. Only 1 B. Only 1 & 2
C. Only 2 & 3 D. 1, 2 & 3

28. The 'Saptanga Theory of State' (Theory of Seven Limbs of the State) was propounded by:
A. Kautilya in Arthashastra
B. Manu in Manusmriti
C. Kalhana in Rajatarangini
D. Banabhatta in Harshacharita

29. The evidences of 'pit-dwelling' have been discovered from which of the following ancient Indian sites?
A. Lothal and Kalibangan
B. Burzahom and Gufkaral
C. Ropar and Rangpur
D. Kalibangan and Surkotada

30. In 1837, James Princep deciphered an Inscription in Brahmi script referring to a king called 'Devanamapiya Piyadassi'. The celebrated monarch known by this epithet was:
A. Ashoka
B. Akbar
C. Kanishka
D. Chandragupta Vikramaditya

31. The harappans used intaglio seals, made mostly of carved and fired steatite.
A. As an export commodity
B. As a medium of exchange in place of coins
C. As amulets and charms to ward off evil spirits.
D. For marking their goods and property.

32. There is only one Rock Edict in which Asoka talks about taxation. Which among the following is that edict?
A. Bhabru Inscription
B. Nigalisagar Pillar Inscription
C. Rummindei Pillar Inscription
D. Barabar Cave Inscription

33. The temple of Konark was built by Narasimha of the:
A. Maratha Dynasty B. Chola Dynasty
C. Ganga Dynasty D. Vijaynagar Empire

34. Which among the following was used to create sculptures in the Mathura school of art that flourished around 1st century AD?
A. Marble B. State stone
C. Granite D. Red sandstone

35. Gandhara School of art is related to which of the following dynasties?
A. Shakas B. Kushanas
C. Guptas D. Greeks

36. In Vedic Era, Akhyani is the goddess of which of the following?
A. Peace B. Sacrifice
C. Forests D. Rivers

37. What was "Halivakara" in the Gupta Era?
A. A kind of Tax
B. A king of pay
C. A kind of Instrument
D. A king of Tribe

LOGICAL AND ANALYTICAL ABILITY

Directions (Q. Nos. 38-52): *Choose the most appropriate option.*

38. A man has a certain number of all boxes to pack into parcels. If he packs 3, 4, 5 or 6 in a parcel, he is left with one over; if he packs 7 in a parcel, none is left over. What is the number of boxes, he may have to pack?
A. 106 B. 301
C. 309 D. 400

39. In an examination, a student scores 4 marks for every correct answer and loses 1 mark for every wrong answer. If he attempts in all 60 questions and secures 130 marks the number of questions he attempts correctly is
A. 35 B. 38
C. 40 D. 42

40. If you write down all the numbers from 1 to 100; then how many times do you write 3?
A. 11 B. 18
C. 20 D. 21

41. In a city 40% of the adults are illiterate while 85% of the children are literate. If the ratio of the adults to that of the children is 2 : 3, then what per cent of the population is literate?
A. 20% B. 25%
C. 50% D. 75%

42. 12 years old Manick is three times as old as his brother Rahul. How cld will Manick be when he is twice as old as Rahul?
A. 14 years B. 16 years
C. 18 years D. 20 years

43. If A + B > C + D, B + E = 2C and C + D > B + E, then

A. A + B > 2E
B. A + B > 2C
C. A > C
D. A + B > 2D

44. If P means ×, R means +, T means ÷, and S means –, then 18T3P9S8R6 = ?

A. $-1\frac{1}{3}$
B. $\frac{2}{3}$
C. 46
D. 52

45. Ajay left home for the bus stop 15 minutes earlier than usual. It takes 10 minutes to reach the stop. He reached the stop at 08:40 am. What time does he usually leave home for the bus stop?

A. 08:30 am
B. 0.8:45 pm
C. 08:55 am
D. 08:15 am

46. Richard is fifteenth from the front in a column of boys. There were thrice as many behind him as there were in front. How many boys are there between Richard and the seventh boy from the end of the column?

A. 33
B. 34
C. 35
D. 30

47. How many combinations of two-digit numbers having 8 can be made from the following numbers:

8, 5, 2, 1, 7, 6

A. 9
B. 10
C. 11
D. 12

48. The letters L, M, N, O, P, Q, R, S and T in their order are substituted by nine integers 1 to 9 in that order. 4 is assigned to P. The difference between P and T is 5. The difference between N and T is 3. What is the integer assigned to N?

A. 4
B. 5
C. 6
D. 7

49. Thirty six vehicles are parked in a parking lot in a single row. After the first car, there is one scooter. After the second car, there are two scooters. After the third car, there are three scooters and so on. Work out the number of scotters in the second half of the row.

A. 10
B. 12
C. 15
D. 17

50. How many 5s are there in the following number sequence which are immediately preceded by 7 and immediately followed by 6?

7 5 5 9 4 5 7 6 4 5 9 8 7 5 6 7 6 4 3 2 5 6 7 8

A. One
B. Two
C. Three
D. Four

51. How many such pairs of letters are there in the word CLEARING each of which has two letters between them in the word as also in the alphabet?

A. Nil
B. One
C. Two
D. Three

52. A post man was returning to the post office which was in front of him to the North. When the post office was 100 metres away from him, he turned to the left and moved 50 metres to deliver the last letter. He then moved to the same direction for 40 metres, turned to his right and moved 100 metres. How many metres was he away from the post office?

A. 0 m
B. 90 m
C. 150 m
D. 100 m

Directions (Q. Nos. 53-57): *Find the odd word from the following:*

53. A. Insurance
B. Provident Fund
C. Salary
D. Shares

54. A. Mizoram
B. Sikkim
C. Kohima
D. Manipur

55. A. Amoeba
B. Bacteria
C. Germs
D. Microbes

56. A. Herring
B. Shark
C. Barracuda
D. Whale

57. A. Abundance
B. Plentiful
C. Copious
D. Ample

Directions (Q. Nos. 58-62): *In each of the following questions, select the one which is different from other three alternatives:*

58. A. 21 B. 60
C. 124 D. 210

59. A. (52, 142) B. (54, 126)
C. (56, 168) D. (58, 184)

60. A. (34 – 43) B. (62 – 71)
C. (55 – 62) D. (83 – 92)

61. A. (94 – 7) B. (42 – 6)
C. (35 – 5) D. (56 – 8)

62. A. (64 – 8) B. (80 – 9)
C. (7 – 49) D. (36 – 6)

Directions (Q. Nos. 63-67): *Find out the wrong number in the series.*

63. 6, 13, 18, 25, 30, 37, 40
A. 40 B. 25
C. 30 D. 37

64. 3, 5, 8, 11, 17, 23
A. 8 B. 11
C. 17 D. 23

65. 22, 33, 66, 99, 121, 279, 594
A. 33 B. 121
C. 279 D. 594

66. 6, 9, 12, 15, 18, 22
A. 12 B. 18
C. 22 D. 6

67. 6, 18, 36, 108, 216, 648, 1290, 3888
A. 36
B. 108
C. 1290
D. 648

Directions (Q. Nos. 68 and 69): *Choose the most appropriate option.*

68. A is B's brother, C is D's father, E is B's mother. A and D are brothers. How is E related to C?
A. Sister B. Sister-in-law
C. Niece D. Wife

69. Six members of a family namely A, B, C, D, E and F are travelling together. B is the son of C but C is not the mother of B. A and C are married couple. E is the brother of C. D is the daughter of A. F is the brother of B. How many male members are there in the family?
A. 3 B. 2
C. 4 D. 1

Directions (Q. Nos. 70-75): *In each of the following questions, a series is given, with one term missing. Choose the correct alternative from the given ones that will complete the series?*

70. 18, 24, 21, 27, ?, 30, 27
A. 33 B. 30
C. 24 D. 21

71. $\frac{2}{3}, \frac{4}{7}, ?, \frac{11}{21}, \frac{16}{31}$
A. $\frac{6}{11}$ B. $\frac{5}{9}$
C. $\frac{9}{17}$ D. $\frac{7}{13}$

72. 25, 50, 30, 45, 35, 40, ?
A. 30 B. 35
C. 40 D. 45

73. 5760, 960, ?, 48, 16, 8
A. 240 B. 192
C. 160 D. 120

74. 3, 15, 35, 63, ?
A. 77 B. 84
C. 99 D. 98

75. 22, 24, 28, ?, 52, 84
A. 46 B. 36
C. 38 D. 42

MANAGEMENT APTITUDE & COMMUNICATION SKILLS

Directions (Q. Nos. 76-112): *Choose the most appropriate option.*

76. Guess the tagline of Toyoto Innova?
- A. For You Luxury
- B. This is Style
- C. Feel the Comfort
- D. All you Desire

77. From the following which is CNBC TV 18 Tagline?
- A. Minting Money
- B. Business from it
- C. Make Profit
- D. Profit from it

78. "The Complete Man" is tagline of which brand/company?
- A. Mafatlal
- B. S. Kumars
- C. Vimal
- D. Raymonds

79. ICICI bank tagline?
- A. Hum hai aapke saath
- B. Aap ki khyal Humara
- C. Khyal Aapka
- D. Bharosa Hum se

80. The Tagline of Indian Overseas Bank?
- A. Right People to Grow with
- B. Good People to grow with
- C. Excellent People to Grow with
- D. A tradition of Banking

81. Which of the following is a set of activities used to implement a management orientation that stresses customer satisfaction?
- A. a control system
- B. customer management
- C. planning strategy
- D. marketing

82. Which of the following does not fall within the jurisdiction of MRTP commission?
- A. Prevention of Monopolistic Trade Practices
- B. Prevention of Restrictive trade Practices
- C. Prohibition of Unfair Trade Practices
- D. Regulation of Combinations

83. When a company taken over another one and clearly becomes the new owner, the action is called
- A. Merger
- B. Acquisition
- C. Strategic Alliance
- D. None of the above

84. Relaxing the restrictions and controls imposed on Business and industry means
- A. Liberalisation
- B. Privatisation
- C. Globalisation
- D. None of the above

85. 'Emerging market' refers to:
- A. Any developing country
- B. A fast-growing developing country
- C. Any growing consumer market
- D. China and India

86. Which of the following best describes the role of a company's directors:
- A. They take day-to-day management decisions.
- B. They have ultimate responsibility for how the company is run.
- C. They aim to maximize the wealth of the investors.
- D. They are the company's main investors.

87. Operations as a function within the company concerns:
- A. Controlling the revenues and outgoings of the business
- B. Making tangible products
- C. Delivering products to the customer
- D. The whole process of producing and delivering a product, a service, or the combination of both to a customer.

88. All but which one of the following is not an FDI investment?
- A. Acquisition of an existing company
- B. A joint venture with a foreign partner
- C. Exporting the company's products to new markets
- D. A green field project in another country

89. Which of the following is not linked with outsourced production?
A. Manufacturing under licence
B. Production in a low-cost country
C. Subcontracted manufacturing for a well-known brand
D. Franchising

90. Gross national income (GNI) is defined as:
A. The total income produced by business in the country, whether locally owned or owned by foreigners.
B. The country's total industrial output.
C. The total income from all the final products and services produced by the national economy, including income of national residents from their overseas investments.
D. The total income produced by the country's resident businesses.

91. Unemployment is defined as:
A. The section of the population that are on state benefits.
B. The section of the population willing to work but unable to find employment.
C. The section of the population that are waiting to be employed.
D. The section of the population that are without the skills needed by employers.

92. Where a single firm has control of the market it is called:
A. A monopoly
B. An oligopoly
C. An oligarchy
D. A monarchy

93. The G8 is made up of:
A. China, USA, France, UK, Germany, Italy, Russia and Japan.
B. EU, Asean Group, NAFTA, Russia, China, Japan and Canada.
C. UK, USA, Russia, Germany, France, Italy, Canada, Japan.
D. Japan, China, Italy, France, Germany, Russia, USA and UK.

94. "Environmental degradation" refers to environmental change caused by:
A. Businesses and their actions
B. Human activity
C. Actions by government
D. Factory emissions

95. Why are nuclear power plants controversial?
A. Because only a few companies have the relevant technology to build nuclear power stations
B. Because there is risk from the escape of radiation in the case of an accident
C. Because they are very expensive
D. Because they have high levels of greenhouse gas emissions

96. Ethics focuses on:
A. Differences between cultures
B. Principles of right and wrong
C. Values and norms of behaviour in different cultures
D. Universal standards of behaviour

97. Who was the first finance minister of (independent) india?
A. Morarji Desai
B. T.T. Krishnamachari
C. John Mathai
D. R.K. Shanmukham Chetty

98. Who was the first minister of commerce and industry (independent India)?
A. Shyama Prasad Mukherjee
B. Suresh Prabhu
C. Nitin Gadkari
D. Yashwant Sinha

99. Who is the current chairperson/chairman of the RBI?
A. Urjit Patel B. Raghuram Rajan
C. Manmohan Singh D. Arun Jaitley

100. The chairperson of Tata Sons Ltd. is ____.
A. Ratan Tata
B. Venu Srinivasan
C. Natarajan Chandrasekaran
D. Amit Chandra

101. The headquarters of the Aditya Birla Group is at _____.
A. New Delhi B. Kolkata
C. Chennai D. Mumbai

102. Who is the managing director and CEO of TCS?
A. Natarajan Chandrasekaran
B. Rajesh Gopinathan
C. Salil Parekh
D. U.B. Pravin Rao

103. The main objective of communication is
A. information and persuasion.
B. skill and personality development.
C. control and management.
D. need.

104. Example(s) of oral communication is/are _____.
A. letter B. e-mail
C. telephone D. fax

105. Gestures is an example for
A. body language B. grammar
C. speeches D. written

106. Posters fall under ____ communication.
A. oral B. visual
C. written D. spoken

107. Communication is the act of ______.
A. Transmitting and receiving information
B. Receiving information
C. Transmitting information
D. None of them

108. There is a paradox in communicating because ______.
A. I cannot expect that you will understand everything I tell you
B. I cannot expect that you will understand only what I tell you
C. Both (A) and (B)
D. We can't understand each other

109. Communication is ____.
A. Continuous
B. Complicated
C. Contextual
D. All of the above

110. Communication is affected by ____ context.
A. Psychological
B. Environmental
C. Cultural
D. All of the above

111. Communication is the process of ____.
A. Creating shared understanding
B. Speaking & listening
C. Understanding the opponent ideas
D. Making yourself clear

112. The first and most important reason for communicating is ______.
A. To build relationships with other people
B. To deliver a message
C. To understand the opponent ideas
D. To create shared understanding.

ENGLISH LANGUAGE AND COMPREHENSION

Directions (Q. Nos. 113-120): *Read the following passage carefully and choose the most appropriate option.*

The first battle to ever take place between ironclad naval vessels was the Battle of Hampton Roads, which occurred March 9, 1862, during the American Civil War. The ships engaged in the battle were the USS Monitor on the Union side and a captured and revampled northern vessel named the CSS Virginia on the Confederate side. Many accounts of the battle refer to the Virginia by its previous name of Merrimack. The Monitor and the Virginia were not history's first ironclads though they were the first ironclads to battle each other. The very first wooden ships to be armoured in iron date back to 16th century Korea, but the idea of using them for widespread naval warfare didn't really take off until the mid-19th century. During the Crimean was, the French used ironclad batteries to shell Russian forts, and they also built the first true ironclad oceangoing naval vessel, the Gloire, in 1856.

The Virginia began life in 1856 as a conventional steam frigate but was rebuilt as an ironclad ram when pressed into service for the Confederate Navy. The Monitor was built in 1862 as an armoured turret gunboat. On March 8 of that year, the CSS Virginia attacked a Union fleet of wooden warships in the channel near Newport News, Virginia, destroying the frigate Congress and the sloop Cumberland. At dawn on Match 9, The Virginia looked to resume the attack, this time going after the frigate Minnesota, which had run aground the previous day. Instead, the crew discovered that the Monitor had arrived during the night, so the two warships spent over four hours firing at each other. Finally, a shell from the Virginia hit the Monitor's pilothouse, temporarily blinding that ship's commander. By that time, the Virginia was running low on both ammunition and steam, so it headed back for the Norfolk shipyard, the battle ending in a draw.

On April 11, 1862, the two ships faced each other once again, but this time no shots were fired as the Monitor failed to lure the Virginia onto the open water and the Virginia couldn't get the monitor to re-enter the harbor. The Virginia only survived for one more moth, destroyed by the crew on April 11, after the Congederates were forced to about their Norfolk base and the ship proved too heavy to be moved up the James River. The Monitor was caught in a storm off the coast of Cape Hampton? North Carolina, later that year, and went down on December 31, drowing 16 crewmen.

113. What is not discussed in the article?
- A. The events of a battle in the American Civil War
- B. The ships involved in that battle
- C. Where those ships are now
- D. Ironclad ships from before that period

114. When the Battle of Hampton Roads began how old were the two ships involved?
- A. Less than a year old
- B. About six years old
- C. One was about six years old; the other was less than a year old
- D. There is insufficient information in the passage to answer the question

115. What surprising event improved the Union's prospects in the battle?
- A. The Monitor joining the battle
- B. The Minnesota running aground
- C. A shell striking a direct hit
- D. All of the above

116. Which of the ships survived into the following year?
- A. The Virginia
- B. The Monitor
- C. Both of the above
- D. None of the above

117. Which word in the passge means "upgraded"?
- A. Widespread
- B. Revamped
- C. Aground
- D. None of the above

118. Which word in the passage means "extensive"?
- A. Widespread
- B. Revamped
- C. Aground
- D. None of the above

119. Which word in the passage means "aboard"?
- A. Widespread
- B. Revamped
- C. Aground
- D. None of the above

120. Which word in the passage means "sink"?
- A. Sloop
- B. Frigate
- C. Lure
- D. None of the above

Directions (Q. Nos. 121-128): *For each question, find the sentence that has a mistake in capitalization or punctuation. If you find no mistakes, mark choice (D).*

121.
- A. This is someone elses coat.
- B. Which of these songs was recorded by Bruce Springsteen?
- C. That book must be yours.
- D. No Mistakes.

122.
- A. Don't stand in my way.
- B. Cecilia and I fought our way through the crowd.
- C. The vegetables were old rubbery and tasteless.
- D. No mistakes.

123. A. Remember to walk the dog.
B. "Don't run"! Mr. Ellington shouted.
C. It's supposed to snow today and tomorrow.
D. No mistakes.

124. A. Charleen's parents worried whenever she drove the car.
B. Who designed the Brooklyn Bridge?
C. Diseases like Smallpox and Polio have been eradicated.
D. No mistakes.

125. A. Can you find the Indian ocean on this map?
B. Which river, the Nile or the Amazon, is longer?
C. Lerner Avenue runs into the Thompson Parkway.
D. No mistakes.

126. A. He's the best dancer in the school.
B. We were planning to go, but the meeting was canceled.
C. "Okay," she said, I'll go with you."
D. No mistakes.

127. A. Does Judge Parker live on your street?
B. Twenty government officials met to deal with Wednesday's crisis.
C. The Mayor spoke at a news conference this morning.
D. No mistakes.

128. A. My brother Isaac is the best player on the team.
B. Because of the high cost; we decided not go.
C. Where's your new puppy?
D. No mistakes.

Directions (Q. Nos. 129-136): *Choose the most appropriate option to complete the sentence.*

129. The people who bought this old lamp at the auction ____ foolish.
A. was B. were
C. is D. has been

130. The little boy ____ himself down on the floor and threw a tantrum.
A. flings B. flinged
C. flung D. fling

131. There ____ three different ways to make perfect pie crust.
A. is B. are
C. was D. being

132. The noise from all the airplanes ____ louder in the afternoon.
A. gets B. get
C. have gotten D. are getting

133. I ____ the speech you gave last Thursday night, but I was in bed with flu.
A. will have heard B. would hear
C. might hear D. would have heard

134. In many popular movies today, the heroes are ____ armed than the villains
A. more heavily B. more heavy
C. heavier D. more heavier

135. That fine circus elephant now belongs to my sister and ____
A. I B. me
C. mine D. myself

136. The person ____ made these delicious candied figs has my vote.
A. that B. whom
C. who D. whose

Directions (Q. Nos. 137-144): *Part, or all, of each sentence is underlined. Following the sentence, four versions of the underlined portion are presented. Choice (1) repeats the original; the other choices are different. If you think a better sentence can be found in Choices (2) to (4), then choose one of them. If the sentence is correct as stated, your answer will be Choice (1).*

137. When making a chocolate torte, <u>only the best ingredients should be used</u>.
A. only the best ingredients should be used
B. you should use only the best ingredients.
C. the best ingredients only should be used.
D. one should have used only the best ingredients.

138. <u>If someone is looking</u> for the best car loan, you should compare interest rates at several banks.

A. If someone is looking
B. When one is looking
C. If you are looking
D. To have a person look

139. A corporation created by the federal government during the Great Depression, the Tennessee Valley Authority (TVA) is responsible for flood control, must generate electric power, and soil conservation.
A. flood control, must generate electric power, and soil conservation.
B. flood control, generating electric power, and for soil conservation.
C. controlling floods, generating electric power, and soil conservation.
D. flood control, the generation of electric power, and soil conservation.

140. With her book Coming of Age in Samoa, anthropologist Margaret Mead emphasized the role of culture, rather than biology, in shaping human behaviour.
A. rather than biology, in shaping human behaviour.
B. rather than biology with shaping human behaviour.
C. somewhat better than biology to shape human behaviour.
D. in shaping human behaviour, and not biology.

141. This was the fifth of the five speeches the mayor gave during this the month of May.
A. This was the fifth of the five speeches the mayor gave during this the month of May.
B. Of the five speeches the mayor gave during May, this was the fith one.
C. Thus far during the month of May, the mayor gave five speeches and this was the fifth.
D. This was the fifth speech the mayor has given during the month of May.

142. An American poet of the nineteenth century, Walt Whitman's collection of poems. *Leaves of Grass*, celebrates nature and individualism.
A. Walt Whitman's collection of poems, *Leaves of Grass*,
B. Walt Whitman published a collection of poems, *Leaves of Grass,* which
C. a collection of poems, *Leaves of Grass*, by Walt Whitman,
D. Walt Whitman published poems, collected as *Leaves of Grass*, that

143. We loved our trip to the desert where you could see the tall cactus, the blooming flowers, and the little desert animals.
A. desert where you could see
B. desert; you could see
C. desert; where we saw
D. desert; we saw

144. Opposite in what many financial analysts had predicted, the stock market rose by twenty two points this month.
A. Opposite in what many financial analysts had predicted,
B. Contrary to the predictions of many financial analysts,
C. As against the predictions of many financial analysts,
D. Contrasting of many financial analysts' predictions.

Directions (Q. Nos. 145-150): *Choose the option the answer that provides the best definition for each given word or is most similar to the given word.*

145. *quid pro quo*
A. to stop legislative action through the courts
B. to covertly meet with an opposition party
C. to give something in return for something of similar value
D. to acknowledge defeat

146. disenfranchise
A. to embrace into a political system
B. to desprive the rights of citizons especially the right to vote
C. to break apart from an estabalished political party
D. to vote exclusively for one candidate

147. nullify
   A. to validate
   B. to invalidate
   C. to elevate in standing
   D. to confirm voting results

148. alacrity
   A. sadness B. eagerness
   C. bitterness D. loneliness

149. consternation
   A. dismay B. constellation
   C. reservation D. disbelief

150. penury
   A. destitution
   B. punishment
   C. judgement
   D. agony

ANSWERS

1	2	3	4	5	6	7	8	9	10
C	A	B	B	B	B	B	B	A	A
11	**12**	**13**	**14**	**15**	**16**	**17**	**18**	**19**	**20**
A	B	B	B	A	B	A	C	D	A
21	**22**	**23**	**24**	**25**	**26**	**27**	**28**	**29**	**30**
A	D	D	D	C	C	D	A	B	A
31	**32**	**33**	**34**	**35**	**36**	**37**	**38**	**39**	**40**
D	C	C	D	B	C	A	B	B	C
41	**42**	**43**	**44**	**45**	**46**	**47**	**48**	**49**	**50**
D	D	B	D	B	C	B	C	C	A
51	**52**	**53**	**54**	**55**	**56**	**57**	**58**	**59**	**60**
C	B	C	C	A	D	A	A	C	C
61	**62**	**63**	**64**	**65**	**66**	**67**	**68**	**69**	**70**
A	B	A	B	C	C	C	D	C	C
71	**72**	**73**	**74**	**75**	**76**	**77**	**78**	**79**	**80**
D	C	B	C	B	D	D	D	C	B
81	**82**	**83**	**84**	**85**	**86**	**87**	**88**	**89**	**90**
D	D	B	A	B	C	D	C	B	C
91	**92**	**93**	**94**	**95**	**96**	**97**	**98**	**99**	**100**
B	A	C	B	B	B	D	A	A	C
101	**102**	**103**	**104**	**105**	**106**	**107**	**108**	**109**	**110**
D	B	A	C	A	B	A	C	A	D
111	**112**	**113**	**114**	**115**	**116**	**117**	**118**	**119**	**120**
B	D	D	C	A	D	B	A	D	D
121	**122**	**123**	**124**	**125**	**126**	**127**	**128**	**129**	**130**
A	C	B	C	A	C	D	B	B	C
131	**132**	**133**	**134**	**135**	**136**	**137**	**138**	**139**	**140**
B	A	D	A	B	C	C	C	B	A
141	**142**	**143**	**144**	**145**	**146**	**147**	**148**	**149**	**150**
D	B	C	B	C	B	B	B	A	A

EXPLANATORY ANSWERS

1. The Gotthard Base Tunnel is a railway tunnel through the Alps in Switzerland. It opened on 1 June 2016, and full service began on 11 December 2016. With a route length of 57.09 km, it is the world's longest railway and deepest traffic tunnel and the first flat, low-level route through the Alps. It lies at the heart of the Gotthard axis and constitutes the third tunnel connecting the cantons of Uri and Ticino, after the Gotthard Tunnel and the Gotthard Road Tunnel.

2. The word ikebana is usually translated as "the Japanese art of flower arrangement," but the materials of ikebana can include freshly cut branches, vines, leaves, grasses, berries, fruit, seeds, and flowers, as well as wilted and dried plants. In fact, any natural substance may be used, and in contemporary ikebana, glass, metal, and plastic are also employed. As one of the traditional arts of Japan, ikebana has developed a symbolic language as well as decorative concepts, and the use of natural, ephemeral flowers and branches makes the dimension of time an integral part of the creation.

3. IIT Kharagpur has signed a Memorandum of Understanding (MoU) with the Pullela Gopichand Badminton Academy (PGBA) to develop research and training module for the trainees of the Hyderabad-based sports facility. The thrust area of the collaboration is to promote health and wellbeing of sportspersons and coaches for enhancing the quality of performance and resilience. Players and coaches from PGBA will benefit from these programs. Further, the coaches will also be trained on how to use that knowledge while training players. Under the collaboration, IIT-KGP will also set up a sports academy in collaboration with Gopichand. The academy would promote collaborative research related to happiness in sports in general and badminton in particular, and science and technology in sports training. The scope would also include joint monitoring and use of materials used in general and badminton in particular by IIT Kharagpur and PGBA. A sum of Rs10 crore has been allocated to develop modern sports facilities at IIT-Kgp.

5. Meghalaya has signed the Host City Contract with the Indian Olympic Association (IOA) for hosting the 39th National Games in 2022 on January 3, 2018. The tripartite contract was signed between the IOA, the Meghalaya State Olympic Association, and the state government. With this, Meghalaya will host the National Games 2022 coinciding with the 50th year of the creation of the state. For these games, the central government will provide 30% of the total budget for the National Games while the remaining 70% funds would have to be raised by the state government on its own. Meghalaya will be the 3rd northeastern state after Manipur and Assam hosted the National Games in 1999 and 2007, respectively. It had co-hosted the 2016 South Asian Games with its neighboring Assam. Approx, 14,450 athletes and officials are expected to visit the state during the 2022 National Games.

6. RERA or Real Estate (Regulation and Development) Act, 2016 aims at protecting the home purchasers and also boosts the real estate investments. The bill of this Parliament of India Act was passed on 10 March 2016 by the Upper House (Rajya Sabha). The RERA Act was effective on and from 1 May 2016. During this time, Out of 92 sections, 52 were notified. All the other provisions were effective on and from 1 May 2017.

9. The Himalayan Hydro Expo 2018 has started at Kathmandu in Nepal on January 5, 2018. President of Nepal Bidya Devi Bhandari inaugurated the exhibition. The basic

objective of Expo is to unleash massive hydro power potential of Nepal and bring all stakeholders under one roof. According to experts Nepal has approximately 40,000 MW of economically feasible hydro power potential and so far it has developed just around 600 MW.

The delegates from various countries including India, China, Austria, Czech Republic and Norway are participating in the expo. Seminars, discussions and competitions for engineering students will also be organised during three day event.

11. Beauden John Barrett is a New Zealand rugby union player. He plays in the first five-eighth position (Fly-Half) for Taranaki and the Auckland based Super Rugby side, the Blues, and for New Zealand's national team the All Blacks. He was a key member of the 2015 Rugby World Cup winning team. Barrett also plays fullback and wing as demonstrated with Taranaki and the All Blacks. Barrett won the World Rugby Player of the Year award in 2016 and 2017, has also been a nominee for the award in 2018, and is only the second player to win the award in back-to-back years, after former teammate Richie McCaw.

12. At international level, the World Anti-Doping Agency (WADA) has been established in 1999 at Lausanne, Switzerland under the "Declaration of Lausanne" to coordinate, promote and monitor the fight against drugs in sports. Its headquarters are located at Montreal, Canada. At national level, many countries have their own anti-doping agencies. In India, such agency is called National Anti-doping Agency (NADA).

13. Jaipal Singh Munda (3 January 1903-20 March 1970) was a politician, prolific writer and sportsman. He was the member of the Constituent Assembly which debated on the new Constitution of the Indian Union. He captained the Indian field hockey team to clinch gold in the 1928 Summer Olympics in Amsterdam.

15. The National Sports Day is celebrated on August 29 in India to mark the birth anniversary of Dhyan Chand, the hockey player who won gold medals for India in the years 1928, 1932 and 1936.

20. A Svedberg unit (symbol Sv) is a non-metric unit for sedimentation coefficient. The Svedberg unit (S) offers a measure of a particle's size based on its sedimentation rate, *i.e.* how fast a particle of given size and shape 'settles' to the bottom of a solution. The Svedberg is a measure of time, defined as exactly 10^{-13} seconds.

26. Thomas Alva Edison (February 11, 1847–October 18, 1931) was an American inventor and businessman who has been described as America's greatest inventor. He developed many devices in fields such as electric power generation, mass communication, sound recording, and motion pictures. These inventions, which include the phonograph, the motion picture camera, and the long-lasting, practical electric light bulb, have had a widespread impact on the modern industrialized world. He was one of the first inventors to apply the principles of organized science and teamwork to the process of invention, working with many researchers and employees. He established the first industrial research laboratory.

33. The thirteenth-century Sun Temple (also known as the Black Pagoda), built in Orissa red sandstone (Khandolite) and black granite by King Narasimhadeva I (AD 1236-1264) of the Ganga dynasty. A World Heritage Site, the temple provides an exceptional look at India's religious heritage. The Konark Sun Temple had been built as one of the finest examples of Brahmin architecture and beliefs. Built to honor the Sun God, Arka, the temple complex displays the enormous wealth, talent, and spirituality of the Brahmin in Orissa. Hinduism, the world's oldest continuously practiced religion, presents a mixture of the spiritually sublime and the earthly erotic in the Konark Temple.

38. $\because$ LCM (3, 4, 5, 6) = 60

Required number of boxes = 60 K + 1

Then, least vlaue of K, as 60K + 1 is divisible by 7

K = 1, 61 (×)

K = 2, 121 (×)

K = 3, 181 (×)

K = 4, 241 (×)

K = 5, 301 (✓)

Hence, required number of boxes is 301.

39. Average marks = $\frac{130}{60} = \frac{13}{6}$

By Alligation Rule,

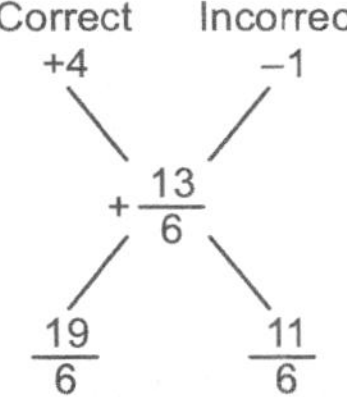

Then Correct question : Incorrect question

= 19 : 11

$\therefore$ Number of correct question

$$= 60 \times \frac{19}{19+11} = 38.$$

41. Let, number of adults = $2x$

and number of children = $3x$

Number of literatre adults

$$= 2x \times 60\% = \frac{6x}{5}$$

Number of literate children

$$= 3x \times 85\% = \frac{51x}{20}$$

$$\text{Required percentage} = \frac{\frac{6x}{5} + \frac{51x}{20}}{2x+3x} \times 100$$

$$= \frac{75x}{100x} \times 100 = 75\%.$$

43.

A + B > C + D ...(*i*)

B + E = 2C ...(*ii*)

C + D > B + E ...(*iii*)

From (*i*) and (*iii*),

A + B > C + D > B + E

$\therefore$ A + B > B + E

A + B > 2C.

44. 18 ÷ 3 × 9 − 8 + 6 = ?

According to BODMAS Rule

= 6 × 9 − 8 + 6

= 54 − 8 + 6

= 54 − 2 = 52.

45. Usual time − 15 minute = 8 : 40 − 10 minute

Usual time = 8 : 40 + 5 minute

Usual time = 8 : 45 am.

46. Number of boys in front of Richard = 14

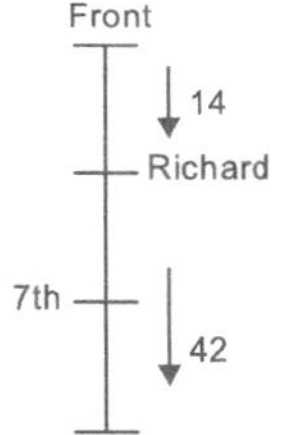

Number of boys behind Richard

= 3 × 14 = 42

Number of boys between Richard and the 7th boy from the end = 42 − 7 = 35.

47. There will be two case—

Case-I: When '8' at unit digit

5, 2, 1, 7, 6	8
$^5C_1$	1

Total combination = $^5C_1 \times 1 = 5$

Case-II: When 8 at tenth place

8	5, 2, 1, 7, 6

Total combination = $1 \times {}^5C_1 = 5$

$\therefore$ Required total combination

= 5 + 5 = 10.

48. Number assigned to P = 4

Number assigned to T = 9 (T − P = 5)

Number assigned to N = 6 (T − N = 3)

— — — $\underset{4th}{P}$ — $\underset{6th}{N}$ — — $\underset{9th}{T}$

Hence, the number assigned to N is '6'.

49. Let C and S denote car and scooter respectively

Then, the squence of parking is

C S C S S C S S S C S S S S C S S S | S S C S S S S S S C S S S S S S S C

Clearly number of scooters in second half of the row = 15.

50. 7 5 5 9 4 5 7 6 4 5 9 8 [7 5 6] 7 6 4 3 2 5 6 7 8

There is only one 5.

51. 3 12 5 1 18 9 14 7
C L E A R I N G

52.

Postman Final position ← 90 m → Post Office (N)

100 m | 100 m

W ← 40 m · 50 m → Postman Starting Point → E

deliver letter

S

54. Kohima is the capital of Nagaland.

56. Whale is a mammal.

57. Abundance is a Noun while all others are adjectives.

58. 21 is an odd number.

59. (56, 168) second number is divisible by first one.

60. Except (C) (55-62), difference between two numbers is '9'.

61. Except (A) in each group first number is divisble by second number.

62. Except (B) in each group one number is the square root of the other one.

63. 6 13 18 25 30 37 [40] (42)

+7 +5 +7 +5 +7 +5

64.

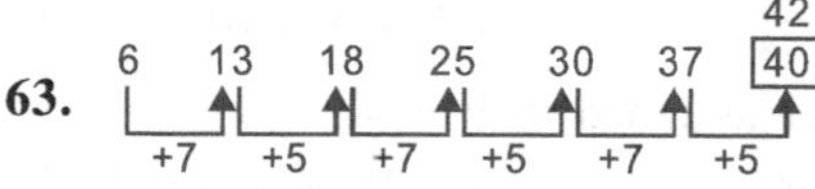

66.

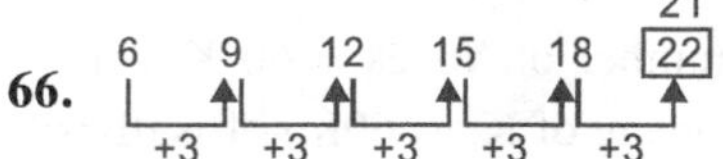

67.

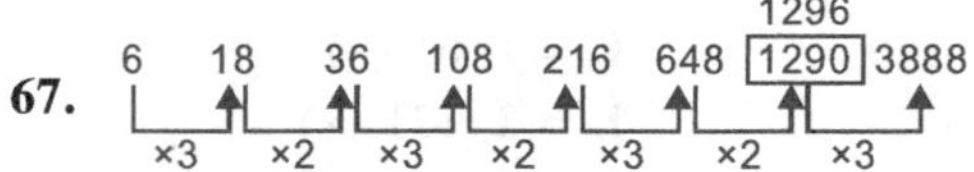

68.

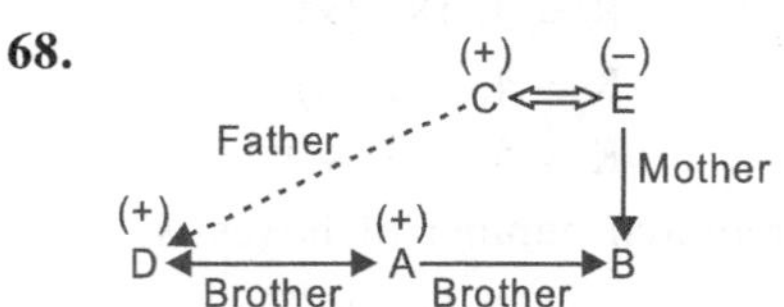

E is wife of C.

69. (Male) (+) E — Brother → (Male) (+) C ⟺ (–) A

C ↑ Son — B (+) (Male); A ↑ Daughter — D (–)

(+) F (Male) — Brother → B

There are four male members in the family.

70. 18 24 21 27 [24] (42) 30 27

+6 –3 +6 –3 +6 –3

71. $\frac{2}{3}$ $\frac{4}{7}$ [$\frac{7}{13}$] $\frac{11}{21}$ $\frac{16}{31}$

Numerators: +2 +3 +4 +5

Denominators: +4 +6 +8 +10

72. 25 50 30 45 35 40 [40]

+5 +5 +5; –5 –5

73. 5760 960 [192] 48 16 8

÷6 ÷5 ÷4 ÷3 ÷2

74. 3 15 35 63 [99]

$2^2 - 1$ $4^2 - 1$ $6^2 - 1$ $8^2 - 1$ $10^2 - 1$

75. 22 24 28 [36] 52 84

+2 +4 +8 +16 +32

Previous Paper (Solved)

BBA Entrance Exam 2018*

MANAGEMENT APTITUDE & COMMUNICATION SKILLS

Directions (Q. Nos. 1-37): *Choose the most appropriate option.*

1. What is the tagline of Amul?
A. The Taste of India
B. Millions Choice
C. Best of India
D. Favorite of India

2. "Beauty bar of Film stars" is tagline of which toilet soap brand?
A. Pears
B. Lux
C. Cinthol
D. Mysore Sandal

3. "Play the Game" is tagline of which of the following?
A. Indian Express
B. Business World
C. The Hindu Business line
D. Hindustan Times

4. "The Nations Bank on Us" is part of which bank tagline?
A. Bank of Maharashtra
B. Punjab National Bank
C. State Bank of India
D. Catholic Syrian Bank

5. "The bank that begins with U" is tagline of which bank?
A. UCO Bank
B. United Bank of India
C. Central Bank of India
D. Union Bank of India

6. What is the definition of marketing?
A. planning sales campaigns
B. selling
C. advertising and promotion activities
D. a philosophy that stresses customer satisfaction

7. Human resources management refers to:
A. all managerial activities
B. concepts and techniques used in leading people at work
C. concepts and techniques for organizing work activities
D. the management of people in organizations

8. By which act government checks restrictive trade?
A. Industrial Policy Act, 1991
B. MRTP Act
C. FEMA Act
D. None of these

9. Liberalization means
A. Reducing number of reserved industries from 17 to 8
B. Liberating the industry, trade and economy from unwanted restrictions
C. Opening up of economy to the world by attaining international competitiveness
D. Free determination of interest rates

10. In the following list of ways by which governments exert control over businesses, which one is out of place?

* *Exam Conducted by GGSIPU Delhi*

A. Full ownership of a company
B. Partial stake in a public company
C. Privatization of a nationalized company
D. Sovereign wealth fund

11. A business, whether national or international, contains the following activities of functions:
A. Operations, Human Resource Management, Accounting
B. Production, Human Resource Management, Accouning, Markeing, and Research and Development
C. Production, Human Resources, Finance, Sales and Marketing, Research and Development
D. Operations, Human Resource Management, Accounting, Sales, Research and Development

12. To which body within the company is the CEO answerable?
A. The board of directors
B. The employees
C. The shareholders' annual general meeting
D. The company's trade union representatives

13. Economic activity can be divided into which three broad types?
A. Retail sector, manufacturing sector, service sector
B. Primary production, secondary production and services
C. Agricultural sector, manufacturing sector and retail sector
D. First sector, second sector, third sector

14. Which of the following is a *push* factor which would influence a company to internationalize?
A. Difficulty in finding skilled staff in the home country
B. The need to be close to key resources
C. Low-cost labour in other countries
D. Financial incentives from governments in emerging markets

15. Strong economic growth is associated with all but which one of the following:
A. Rising standards of living
B. Industrialization
C. Sustainable development
D. Strong capital investment

16. Why is rising inflation a concern for government?
A. The country's exports will become less competitive in global markets
B. Workers will demand higher wages
C. Consumers will go deeper into debt
D. Unemployment will rise

17. An oligopoly is defined as:
A. A cartel
B. A few large producers who dominate a market
C. A group of consumers who can dictate conditions to the producers
D. A sector of the market dominated by game theory

18. Which of the following is a free trade area?
A. Mercosur
B. Ecowas
C. Nafta
D. The EU

19. Which best describes the United Nations (UN)?
A. World government
B. International law-making body
C. Group of sovereign states
D. International forum

20. Word "intrapersonal" means:
A. Within the person
B. Outside the person
C. Not personal
D. Impersonal

21. All of the following are the barriers to communication, EXCEPT:
A. Over communication
B. Conflicting information
C. Language difference
D. Composing message at proper level

22. Corporate Responsibility is:
A. The integration of social and environmental concerns into the daily business of the company
B. The same as business ethics
C. A theory about ethics
D. The title of a government committee

23. Which of the following statements best describes what economists mean by a merit good?
A. Goods which people deserve if they are work hard
B. Goods that it is felt people should own or have access to irrespective of ability to pay
C. Goods which rich people buy to demonstrate how rich they are
D. Goods which are impossible to be provided to one person without excluding other people from benefitting from its provision

24. Costs that do not vary with production or sales levels are called
A. fixed costs
B. variable costs
C. standard costs
D. independent costs

25. In an economy the sectors are classified into public and private on the basis of
A. employment conditions
B. nature of economic activities
C. ownership of enterprises
D. use of raw materials

26. Probing in a communication process is
A. an attempt to gain additional information
B. making judgements
C. an attempt to explain what the sender meant
D. None of the above

27. Which one of the following is not a part of electronic media?
A. Radio
B. Television
C. Film
D. Brochure

28. A brand includes
A. combination of name and symbol
B. design
C. logo or mark
D. All of the above

29. Consumer Protection Act is an act of Parliament of India enacted in
A. 1986 B. 1987
C. 1988 D. 1989

30. Relationship in marketing means
A. relation between salesperson
B. relation between buyer and seller
C. relation between company and consumer
D. All of the above

31. Face-to-face communication is a ....
A. visual communication
B. direct conversation
C. oral communication
D. written

32. You are a student and you didn't understand what the teacher just said but you didn't ask. So the conversation failed because ....
A. You don't like the teacher
B. You made assumptions before you ask
C. It was a wrong time to ask
D. Conversation never happened

33. Our relationship defines the .... of our conversation
A. Limits
B. Type
C. Time
D. Ease

34. Conversations can go too fast because ....
A. We become solution-oriented
B. Too much analysis is going on
C. The conversation becomes problem-entered
D. All of the above

35. To slow down a conversation, you ....
A. Reflect what the other person says
B. Summarize and close one stage of the conversation
C. Ask for new ideas and offer some new ones of your own
D. All of the above

36. In a company meeting, the high board members are talking about the company management system, the accountant tries to explain his point of view, but he was ignored. The conversation failed because ....
A. The accountant has a low rank
B. The high board members have high power upon him
C. The accountant was labelled to a specified role
D. All answers are wrong

37. When an expert holds a conversation with an amateur, the conversation may probably fail because ....
A. Completely different ranks
B. Absence of clear objective
C. The high power of one of the members affects the conversation
D. Both A and C

ENGLISH LANGUAGE AND COMPREHENSION

Directions (Q. Nos. 38-45): *Read the following passage carefully and choose the most appropriate option.*

"I was away from home for seven years – years full of hope of laborious studies of novel experience. Oh, that Allah would give back to me even though it were but one of those swift-fleeting years spent in Europe! But no, that were a vain longing, a futile prayers, a never-to-be fulfilled hope when we bid adieu to the university, we generally, with that, sigh forth a last farewell to all the fairest dreams of life, for then we are launched on our respectives careers, no longer to indulge in dreams, but to fight the realities of life."

"And realities how undeceiving they are! I had to select a career for myself and as all other avenues of advancement are either closed against us, or offer but meagre prospects or are even held in disfavour, I, like the majority of my countrymen, took to the study and eventually to the practice of law. To the observant law is a profession which reflects more of life and reveals more of human nature than does any other profession. It shows the reverse side of the medal the baseness, the ugliness the horror of actual life: nay more, it brings home to one the ignoble uses where to is not soldom put that divinest of all human institutions the administration of justice and it forces upon one the melonecholy reflection that in actual life things are not generally what they pretend to be."

"I secured first hand experience not only of law but also of the educational institutions of my country and I must confess that there too I found things different from what appeared on the surface. What struck me most forcibly was the painful lack of zest and zeal shown everywhere in the pursuit of learning. Learning was sought in no other spirit than that of mean trade and sordid gain. It was regarded as a mere commodity, with a market value attached to it. Everywhere where so ever I turned my attention, I was confronted with sham and counterfeit fraud and imposture. In religion, I found a set of forms a congeries of traditions a mere shadow of a shade. In social life I either found wicked lies in fullest bloom, or hideous anachronism supported by all the strength of enthusiastic ignorance."

Directions (Q. Nos. 38-41): *Answer the question that follows according to the contents of the passage.*

38. As per the passage the author enjoyed his life when he was:

A. in Europe
B. a student
C. a lawyer
D. in his own country

39. We can infer from the passage that the author is a
A. Psychologist
B. Philosopher
C. Reformist
D. Realist

40. The author's tone is:
A. Advisory
B. Argumentative
C. Descriptive
D. Introspective

41. Which of the following is ***not*** true as per the passage?
A. A student life is a life full of fairest dreams.
B. The author comes from an undeveloped country
C. The author is against the study of Law
D. The author found the educational institutions of his country unsatisfactory

Directions (Q. Nos. 42-45): *Choose the word which is most nearly the SAME in meaning of the word given in caps as used in the passage.*

42. SORDID
A. immoral
B. unpleasant
C. Inhuman
D. Irrational

43. COUNTERFEIT
A. Abuses
B. Indecent
C. Unauthentic
D. Opponent

44. CONGERIES
A. Dichotomy
B. Arrangement
C. Disorderly Collection
D. Conflate

45. ANANCHRONISM
A. Popular demand
B. Ambition
C. Affair
D. Inappropriate idea

Directions (Q. Nos. 46-50): *Pick out from the alternatives the one that gives the correct meaning of the idiom:*

46. Far and away
A. beyond imagination
B. completely beyond comparison
C. unreal
D. spiritual

47. To split hairs
A. to struggle hard
B. to observe minutely
C. to argue unnecessarily about trivial matters
D. to dissect

48. To fall in with
A. to fall in love
B. to develop intimacy
C. to lag behind
D. to meet with

49. To hark back
A. to return to a subject which has been dropped
B. to return back to the original point
C. to retaliate
D. to rebuke

50. To knuckle under
A. to escape
B. to hide
C. to deny
D. to submit

Directions (Q. Nos. 51-54): *Mark the option in which punctuation marks have been incorrectly applied, if there is no mistake mark (D).*

51. A. The tour guide asked us if we had any questions?
B. Lauren's father is an auto mechanic.

C. We asked if he could give us change for a dollar.
D. No mistakes.

52. A. Did you read that article in Newsweek?
B. My Uncle took us to Yankee Stadium
C. Christina has a Persian cat named Snow ball
D. No mistakes

53. A. "I'll come and stay with you, grandma," I said
B. "Don't ever tell a lie, he warned
C. "Why won't you play with us?" he asked
D. No mistakes

54. A. I always have a hard time getting up in the morning
B. We took: a tent, a cooler, and a sleeping bag
C. The fog was as thick as potato soup
D. No mistakes

Directions (Q. Nos. 55-62): *Fill in the blanks with the most appropriate option.*

55. On February 27, 1995, the City Fire Department responded to a blaze that .... at the Icarus Pulishing Co. warehouse.
A. breaks out
B. will break out
C. had broken out
D. is breaking out

56. On November 4, suspects Gary Talerino and Jennifer O'Brien were arrested on a charge of vandalism that .... at the local high school.
A. occurs
B. will occur
C. is occurring
D. occurred

57. I am trying to become more skilled at weaving before winter ....
A. arrived
B. will have arrived
C. will arrive
D. arrives

58. We have .... more of these strange pods since those people moved in next door.
A. saw
B. been seeing
C. been seen
D. see

59. While trying to .... his pet iguana from a tree, Travis Stevens fell and broke his ankle.
A. be rescuing
B. have rescued
C. rescue
D. rescuing

60. .... the gun down carefully.
A. Put B. Putted
C. Been putting D. To put

61. The main problem Jim had .... too many parking tickets.
A. will have been B. were
C. will have D. was

62. On Wednesday, Jamal and Jennifer were called to the principal's office and praised for helping a student who .... on the icy sidewalk.
A. falls
B. would fall
C. had fallen
D. has fallen

Directions (Q. Nos. 63-68): *Which of the phrases given as options means the same as (or is the most similar to) the phrase underlined in the sentence.*

63. A standardized extract made from the leaves of the ginkgo biloba tree <u>is proving to be effective in treating</u> mild to moderate Alzheimer's disease.
A. is proving to be effective in treating
B. has shown its proof of effectiveness with treating
C. may have proven effective treatment for
D. is effectively proving in treating

64. The citizens' action committee has accused the city counsel members with being careless with the spending of the taxpayers' money.

A. with being careless with the spending of
B. as to carelessness in the spending of
C. of carelessness in the spending of
D. of careless spending to

65. Aspirin was exclusively known as a painkiller until the time when cardiologists began prescribing it as a preventative for heart attacks.

A. as a painkiller until the time when cardiologists began prescribing it as a preventative for
B. to be a painkiller since when cardiologists prescribed it to be a prevention for
C. as a way to kill and stop pain until cardiologists began to prescribe it as a method for the prevention of
D. as a painkiller until cardiologists began prescribing it as a preventative for

66. The news reporter who had been covering the story suddenly became ill, and I was called to take her place.

A. had been covering the story suddenly became ill, and I was called
B. was covering the story suddenly becomes ill, and they called me
C. is covering the story suddenly becomes ill, and I was called
D. would have been covering the story suddenly became ill, and I am called

67. Lee Iacocca, the son of Italian immigrants, he worked his way to the top of the Ford Motor Company and later rescued Chrysler Corporation.

A. Lee Iacocca, the son of Italian immigrants, he
B. Lee Iacocca, being the son of Italian immigrants,
C. As he was the son of Italian immigrants Lee Iacocca
D. The son of Italian immigrants, Lee Iacocca

68. The troposphere is the lowest layer of Earth's atmosphere, it extends from ground level to an altitude of seven to ten miles.

A. atmosphere, extends
B. atmosphere; it extends
C. atmosphere. Extending
D. atmosphere, and extending

Directions (Q. Nos. 69-75): *Choose the option the answer that provides the best definition for each given word.*

69. totalitarian

A. government that encourages openness and freedom of expression
B. government that demands total submission of the individual to the needs of the state
C. government that encourages equal political, social, civil and economic rights for all
D. government that is comprised of freely elected representatives

70. laissez-faire

A. government that practices noninterference in business/economic affairs
B. government that practices state control over business/economic affairs
C. government that practices principles embraced in France
D. government that practices moderate control over business / economic affairs

71. anarchy

A. complete absence of government or control resulting in lawlessness
B. strict control over a country and its people by governmental authorities
C. government that practices noninterference in business and economic affairs
D. government that encourages equal political, social, civil and economic rights for all

72. precept

A. an official at a judicial hearing

B. a voting irregularity
C. a form of government that is represented by freely elected representatives
D. a rule or principle establishing standards of conduct

73. reactionary
A. a political conservative who opposes liberalism and/or progress
B. a political liberal who opposes traditional and/or conservative leadership
C. a professional protestor
D. a professional lobbyist

74. proscribe
A. to request in the form of a written document
B. to prohibit, forbid, banish, or outlaw
C. to vote in a secret legislative session
D. to stall a legislative vote

75. protocol
A. a political liberal
B. a vote during a legislative session
C. a ceremony or procedure regarding people's rank/status
D. an illegal act of Congress

GENERAL AWARENESS

Directions (Q. Nos. 76-113): *Choose the most appropriate option.*

76. Long March 3B rocket is associated with which country?
A. North Korea B. China
C. Russia D. USA

77. Abdel Fattah al-Sisi got re-elected as President for a second term in March, 2018 of which country?
A. Sudan
B. Syria
C. Greece
D. Egypt

78. The annual military exercise named 'Foal Eagle drill' takes place between
A. USA & South Korea
B. UK & India
C. India & Japan
D. France & Australia

79. Which country withdraws from United Nations Educational, Scientific and Cultural Organization (UNESCO)?
A. USA
B. India
C. Austria
D. South Korea

80. Vijay Keshav Gokhale has been recently appointed as India's
A. Foreign Secretary
B. Ambassador to north Korea
C. Chief Justice
D. Defence Secretary

81. NARI (In India) is a
A. web portal for empowerment of women
B. Mobile APP for women security
C. NGO
D. All of the above

82. Which company bagged the broadcast rights of 2018 Khelo India School Games (KISG)?
A. Sony B. Star Sports
C. ESPN D. Zee

83. Soumeylou Boubeye Maiga was appointed the new Prime Minister of
A. Mali B. Maldives
C. Seychelles D. Tunisia

84. Salil S. Parekh is the current chief executive officer and managing director of Infosys is graduate in
A. Mechanical engineering
B. Electrical engineering
C. Aeronautical Engineering
D. Civil engineering

85. Prime Minister's official Multilingual website - www.pmindia.gov.in — is currently available in how many languages?
A. 12 B. 10
C. 13 D. 14

86. Meteksan World Cup is associated with which sport?
A. taekwondo
B. archery
C. Jodo
D. rowing

87. Who among the following is ***not*** a swimmer?
A. Aaron Peirsol
B. Ryan Lochte
C. Stephan Hansen
D. Sandeep Sejwal

88. Sarah Attar is an American-born track and field athlete who competed at the 2012 Summer Olympics as one of the first two female Olympians representing
A. Iraq
B. Pakistan
C. Saudi Arabia
D. Iran

89. William George Morgan is the inventor of
A. basketball
B. volleyball
C. badminton
D. softball

90. James Naismith wrote the original rule book for which sport?
A. Basketball
B. Table tennis
C. Badminton
D. Lawn tennis

91. Choudhury Trophy is associated with Circumnavigating of the earth by car sport named after
A. Geeta and Pinky Chodhary
B. Babita & Krishna Choudhary
C. Naina & Tina Choudhary
D. Saloo and Neena Choudhury

92. In which year, Sir Chandrasekhara Venkata Raman was awarded Nobel Prize for Raman effect?
A. 1927 B. 1929
C. 1930 D. 1931

93. Which among the following is known for developing FM radio?
A. Edwin Howard Armstrong
B. Albert Abraham Michelson
C. Charles Thomson Rees Wilson
D. Hideki Yukawa

94. "Mach number" is a measure of which of the following?
A. liquid pressure
B. speed
C. heat
D. volume

95. A transition from the solid to gas phase with no intermediate liquid stage is called?
A. Evaporation
B. Sublimation
C. Diffusion
D. Osmosis

96. "APSARA" is India's oldest
A. Nuclear reactor
B. Space launch vehicle
C. GPS satellite
D. Coal generated electricity plant

97. Riboflavin, also known as
A. Vitamin B2
B. Vitamin B12
C. Vitamin B3
D. Vitamin B6

98. Chlorophyll was first isolated and named by
A. Joseph Bienaime Caventou & Pierre-Joseph Pelletier
B. Filip Neriusz Walter & Charles Courtice Alderton
C. Hubert Horatio Humphrey Jr. & John Stith Pemberton
D. Willis Harvey Ricketts & William Procter Jr.

99. Amoeba moves by
A. Podia
B. Pseudopodia
C. Cilia
D. None of the above

100. Polio is caused by
A. bacteria
B. virus
C. fungus
D. None of the above

101. Hydrogenation is done usually in the presence of a catalyst such as
A. Nickel
B. Lead
C. Copper
D. All of the above

102. Aluminium silicate is main chemical constituent of
A. Bakelite
B. Latex
C. Clay
D. All of the above

103. Buckyballs are basically the allotropes ....?
A. Sulphur
B. Calcium
C. Phosphorous
D. None of the above

104. The reign of Chandragupta Maurya:
A. B.C. 298-273
B. B.C. 324-299
C. B.C. 261-236
D. B.C. 280-255

105. The person who established British rule in India:
A. Robert Clive
B. Duplex
C. Mir-Jafer
D. Hestings

106. The official language of Pallavas was:
A. Tamil B. Pali
C. Sanskrit D. Harosti

107. The lines that adjoin different places with the same pressure are known as:
A. Contour
B. Isotherm
C. Isobar
D. Hythergraph

108. In India, the National Human Rights Commision was established in the year:
A. 1991 B. 1992
C. 1993 D. 1994

109. The person who was named as 'Tiger of Mysore':
A. Tippu Sultan
B. Hyder Ali
C. Sabdar Ali
D. Fadek Hyder

110. The science of constructing map is called:
A. Topography
B. Demography
C. Cartography
D. Geography

111. The Article which deals with 'Education for All':
A. Article 41
B. Article 43
C. Article 45
D. Article 44

112. The local Government in India was initially established by:
A. Lord Rippon
B. Lord Canning
C. Lord Curzon
D. Lord Dalhousie

113. 'Khajuraho' temple was built by:
A. Chandelas
B. Chauhans
C. Prathiharas
D. Khilji

LOGICAL AND ANALYTICAL ABILITY

Directions (Q. Nos. 114-118): *Read the following information carefully and choose the most appropriate option.*

A family has six members P, Q, R, S, T and U. There is only one married couple in the family. P has only two sons. Q is the mother of R. S is the brother of P. T is the sister-in-law of Q.

114. How is U related to Q?
A. mother B. daughter
C. son D. none

115. How is S related to U?
A. uncle B. nephew
C. father-in-law D. father

116. How many female members are there in the family?
A. four B. three
C. two D. one

117. How is T related to P?
A. sister-in-law B. mother
C. wife D. sister

118. Four of the following are alike in a certain way. Find the odd one out.
A. P B. T
C. U D. S

Directions (Q. Nos. 119-123): *Choose the most appropriate option.*

119. Mahesh started from his house toward south. After covering a distance of 16 km he turned towards right and covered a distance of 5 km. Then, he turned towards right and walked 4 more kilometers. What is the shortest distance now from his house?
A. 24 km B. 21 km
C. 18 km D. 13 km

120. Ajay is facing West. He turns 90° clockwise and again turns 180° clockwise and then 225° anti-clockwise. In which direction is he facing now?
A. East B. North
C. North-West D. South-West

121. In a certain code, NURSE is coded PWTUG and TRUST is coded as VTWUV. How will LEAST be coded in the same code?
A. MGDUT B. NHCVU
C. NGCUV D. OFBTK

122. In a certain code 'SEVEN' is written as '95454' and 'DONE' is written as '4545'. How is 'PERSON' written in the same code?
A. 658594 B. 685954
C. 658954 D. 658654

123. If 'DA' is related to 'IF', 'NK' will be related to:
A. SP B. PS
C. PR D. SR

Directions (Q. Nos. 124-128): *Choose the odd one out.*

124. A. SED B. MAD
C. QED D. WED

125. A. Anger B. Grief
C. Humorous D. Joy

126. A. Ranthambor B. Sunderban
C. Kaziranga D. Gangtok

127. A. Crust B. Mantle
C. Pangea D. Lithosphere

128. A. Stomata B. Gills
C. Lungs D. Trachea

Directions (Q. Nos. 129-133): *Pick up the pair that best illustrates a similar relationship.*

129. Nightingale : Warble : : Frog : ?
A. Yelp B. Croak
C. Cackle D. Squeak

130. Cheetah : Cub : : Cockroach : ?
A. Chick B. Larva
C. Foal D. Nymph

131. Birds : Feathers : : Fish : ?
A. Skin B. Fur
C. Scales D. Shell

132. Asteroids : Belt : : Owls : ?
A. Parliament
B. School
C. Deck
D. Gaggle

133. Language : Linguist : : Dictionary : ?
A. Plutocracy
B. Feminist
C. Lexicographer
D. Calligraphist

Directions (Q. Nos. 134-138): *Read the following information carefully and choose the most appropriate option.*

A, B, C, D, W, X, Y and Z are sitting around a square table facing the centre, not necessarily in the same order. Half of them sit at the corners of the table while the remaining sit in the middle of each of the four sides. Y is third to the right of W. C is second to the left of A who is second to the left of X. B is second to the right of D who is third to the right of X.

134. Who is sitting to the immediate left of Y?
A. Z B. X
C. D D. A

135. Who is sitting third to the right of Z?
A. Y B. D
C. B D. C

136. Who is sitting to the immediate right of A?
A. B B. W
C. X D. None of these

137. What is Z's position with respect to B?
A. Fourth to the left
B. Third to the left
C. Fifth to the left
D. Fifth to the right

138. In which of the following pairs is the first person sitting to the immediate right of the second person?
A. CB B. DY
C. WB D. XZ

Directions (Q. Nos. 139-150): *Choose the most appropriate option.*

139. Yatin is 24th from the left end in a row of 39 students. What is his position from the right end?
A. 15 B. 16
C. 12 D. 10

140. In a row, Mohan is 15th from the left and Shyam is 9th from the right. When they interchange their positions, Mohan becomes 27th from the left end. Find out the next position of Shyam from the right end of the row.
A. 21 B. 22
C. 23 D. 24

141. How many pairs of letters are there in the word 'TURMERIC' each of which has a many alphabets (forward and backward direction) between them as there are in the English alphabet?
A. One B. Two
C. Three D. Four

142. If '–' stands for addition
'+' stands for subtraction
'÷' stands for multiplication
'×' stands for division
then which one of the following equation is correct?
A. $50 \times 5 \div 2 - 30 + 25 = 25$
B. $50 - 30 + 5 \div 2 \times 30 = 25$
C. $40 + 35 \times 2 - 50 \div 30 = 95$
D. $30 \times 2 - 25 + 50 \div 5 = 100$

143. If one candle in box 1 is placed in box 2, then box 2 has twice the number of candles that box 1 has. If one candle from box 2 is placed in box 1, then box 2 and box 1 have the same number of candles. How many candles were there in box 1 and box 2?
A. 5, 7 B. 7, 5
C. 6, 4 D. 5, 3

144. If 2 × 16 = 8; 8 × 8 = 1; 6 × 12 = 2, then 12 × 144 = ?

A. 11 B. 12
C. 16 D. 24

145. Anil reached a place on Friday. He came to know that he was three days earlier than the scheduled day. If he had reached there on the following Sunday. How many days late/ early he would have been?

A. One day earlier
B. One day late
C. Two days late
D. Two days earlier

146. Mrs. Saxena celebrated her wedding anniversary on Tuesday, 30th September, 1997. When will she celebrate her next wedding anniversary on the same days?

A. 30th September, 2003
B. 30th September, 2004
C. 30th September, 2002
D. None of these

147. A clock with only dot markings 3, 6, 9 and 12 positions has been kept upside down in front of a mirror. A person reads the time in the reflection of the clock as 12:30, the actual that will be

A. 12 o'clock B. 12:30
C. 6 o'clock D. 03:45

148. In a shop, two clocks were brought for repairs. One clock has the Cuckoo coming out every sixteen minutes, while the other one has the cuckoo coming out every eighteen minutes. Both cuckoos come out at 12:00 noon. When will they both come out together again?

A. 02:06 pm B. 02:08 pm
C. 02:24 pm D. 02:32 pm

149. 1438, 1429, 1417, 1402, ?

A. 1378 B. 1384
C. 1387 D. 1392

150. 10, 100, 200, 310, ?

A. 400 B. 410
C. 420 D. 430

ANSWERS

1	2	3	4	5	6	7	8	9	10
A	B	B	C	B	C	C	B	B	C
11	**12**	**13**	**14**	**15**	**16**	**17**	**18**	**19**	**20**
D	A	B	D	C	B	B	C	D	A
21	**22**	**23**	**24**	**25**	**26**	**27**	**28**	**29**	**30**
D	A	B	A	C	A	D	D	A	C
31	**32**	**33**	**34**	**35**	**36**	**37**	**38**	**39**	**40**
B	D	D	D	D	C	D	B	D	D
41	**42**	**43**	**44**	**45**	**46**	**47**	**48**	**49**	**50**
C	A	C	C	D	B	C	D	A	D
51	**52**	**53**	**54**	**55**	**56**	**57**	**58**	**59**	**60**
A	D	B	B	C	D	D	B	C	A
61	**62**	**63**	**64**	**65**	**66**	**67**	**68**	**69**	**70**
D	C	A	C	D	A	D	B	B	A
71	**72**	**73**	**74**	**75**	**76**	**77**	**78**	**79**	**80**
A	D	A	B	C	B	D	A	A	A

81	82	83	84	85	86	87	88	89	90
A	B	A	C	D	B	C	C	B	A
91	**92**	**93**	**94**	**95**	**96**	**97**	**98**	**99**	**100**
D	C	A	B	B	A	A	A	B	B
101	**102**	**103**	**104**	**105**	**106**	**107**	**108**	**109**	**110**
A	C	D	B	A	A	C	C	A	C
111	**112**	**113**	**114**	**115**	**116**	**117**	**118**	**119**	**120**
C	A	A	C	A	C	D	C	D	C
121	**122**	**123**	**124**	**125**	**126**	**127**	**128**	**129**	**130**
C	C	A	B	C	D	C	A	B	D
131	**132**	**133**	**134**	**135**	**136**	**137**	**138**	**139**	**140**
C	A	C	A	D	B	A	B	B	A
141	**142**	**143**	**144**	**145**	**146**	**147**	**148**	**149**	**150**
B	A	A	B	A	A	C	C	B	D

EXPLANATORY ANSWERS

114-118.

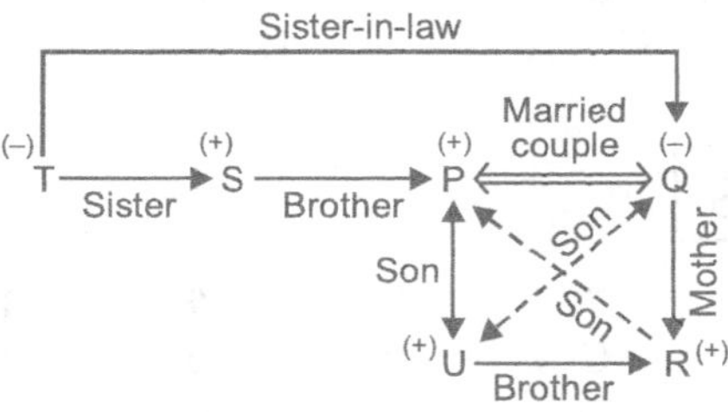

119.

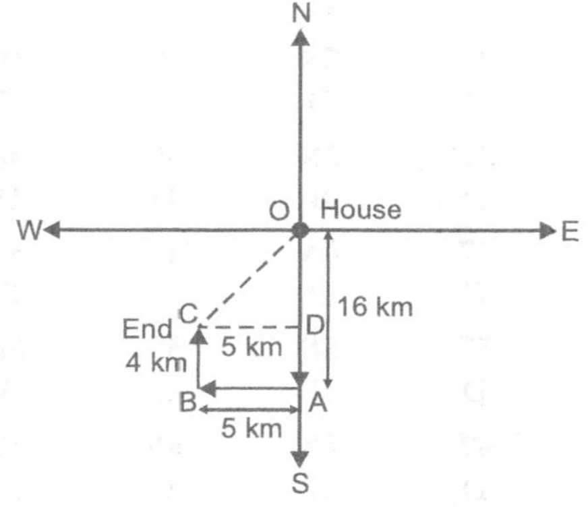

$\because \quad DA = BC = 4 \text{ km}$

$OD = OA - DA = 12 \text{ km}$

$CD = BA = 5 \text{ km}$

$$OC = \sqrt{OD^2 + CD^2}$$

$$= \sqrt{(12)^2 + (5)^2}$$

$$= \sqrt{144 + 25}$$

$$= \sqrt{169} = 13 \text{ km}$$

$\therefore$ Shortest distance between house and ending point = 13 km.

120.

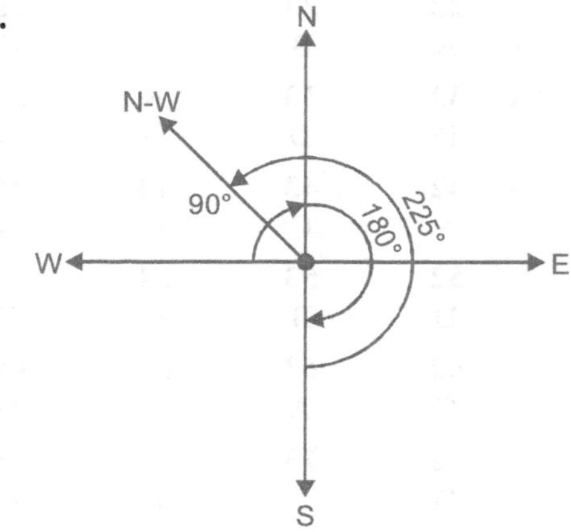

121. As, N U R S E → (+2 each) → P W T U G; T R U S T → (+2 each) → V T W U V

Similarly,

L E A S T → (+2 each) → N G C U V

122. As, S E V E N → 19 5 22 5 14 → 1×9 5 2×2 5 1×4 → (9) (5) (4) (5) (4)

D O N E → 4 15 14 5 → 4 1×5 1×4 5 → (4) (5) (4) (5)

Similarly,

P E R S O N → 16 5 18 19 15 14 → 1×6 5 1×8 1×9 1×5 1×4 → (6) (5) (8) (9) (5) (4)

123. As, D A → (+5 each) → I F

Similarly,

N K → (+5 each) → S P

124. Only (B) MAD is a meaningful word.

126. Except (D) Gangtok, all others are National Tiger Reserve.

127. Except (C) Pangea, all others are the internal structures part layer name of the earth.

128. Except (A) Stomata, all others are the respiratory organ name of different types of animal.

134-138.

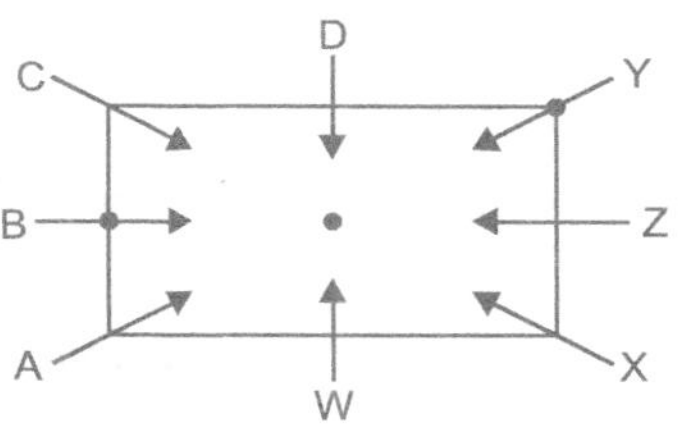

137. Fourth to the left.

139. Total students = Left + Right – 1

$39 = 24 + \text{Right} - 1$

$\text{Right} = 39 - 23 = 16$

140. Left — Mohan — Shyam — Right

15th Shyam (from left); 9th Mohan (from right); 27th (from left)

$\text{Total} = L + R - 1$

$= 27 + 9 - 1 = 35$

Again,

$\text{Total} = L + R - 1$

$35 = 15 + R - 1$

$R = 35 - 14 = 21$

Shyam is 21th position from the right end.

141. T U R M E R I C

Check the options.

142. $50 \div 5 \times 2 + 30 - 25$

$10 \times 2 + 30 - 25$

$20 + 30 - 25$

$50 - 25 = 25$

Hence, equation (A) is correct.

143. Let the number of candle in Box 1 and Box 2 are x and y

Then,

$x - 1 = 2(y + 1)$

$x - 1 = 2y + 2$

$$x - 2y = 3 \quad ...(1)$$

$$x + 1 = y - 1$$

$$x - y = -2 \quad ....(2)$$

After solving equations (1) and (2), we get

$$x = 5, \quad y = 7.$$

144. If we divide, second number from first number we get the result

As, $16 \div 2 = 8$

$8 \div 8 = 1$

$12 \div 6 = 2$

Similarly,

$144 \div 12 = 12.$

145. Scheduled day = Friday + 3 = Monday

If he reached on Sunday, then Anil would have been reached one day earlier.

146. 30th September 1997 – Tuesday

30th September 1998 – Wednesday (one day ahead)

30th September 1999 – Thursday (one day ahead)

30th September 2000 – Saturday (two days ahead)

30th September 2001 – Sunday (one day ahead)

30th September 2002 – Monday (one day ahead)

30th September 2003 – Tuesday (one day ahead)

147.

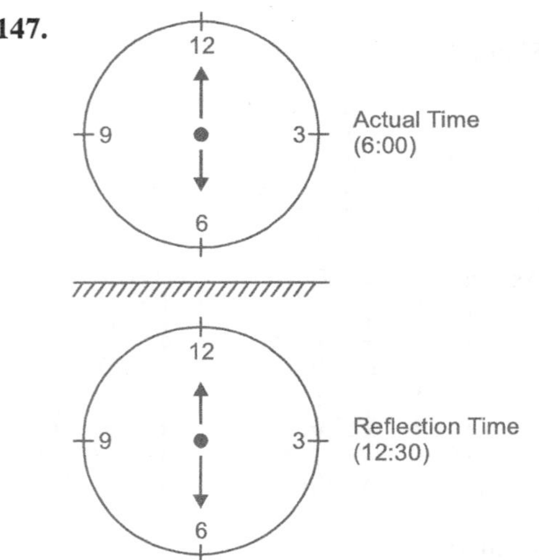

148. LCM (16 min, 18 min) = 144 min

$\therefore$ Both cuckoos come out after = 2 h, 24 min *i.e.*, 2 : 24 pm.

149. 1438 1429 1417 1402 [1384]

−9 −12 −15 −18

−3 −3 −3

150. 10 100 200 310 [430]

+90 +100 +110 +120

Previous Paper (Solved)

BBA Entrance Exam 2017*

MANAGEMENT APTITUDE & COMMUNICATION SKILLS

Directions (Q. Nos. 1-37): *Choose the most appropriate option.*

1. In verbal communication one's physical appearance affects the ....
A. Message B. Channel
C. Sender D. Status

2. What is involved in communication process?
A. Idea-encoding-channel-decoding-feedback
B. Idea-information-channel-receiver
C. Information-channel-receiver
D. Sender-receiver-channel

3. Word "intrapersonal" means:
A. Within the person
B. Outside the person
C. Not personal
D. Impersonal

4. In the USA, maintaining eye contact while talking with elders shows confidence, in Pakistan, it shows disrespect. What does this example depict?
A. The interpretation of body language is universal
B. The interpretation of body language is not universal
C. The interpretation of body language is same worldwide
D. The interpretation of body language is global

5. What does frequent eye contact show?
A. Tension B. Liking
C. Rejection D. Boredom

6. Poor retention either on the part of the sender or on the part of the receiver can create problems or lead to ....
A. Misunderstanding B. Hatred
C. Understanding D. Generosity

7. Which of the following is the first step in order to overcome communication barriers:
A. To recognize the most common barriers and then, understand their negative impact on communication
B. To recognize the most common barriers and then, find the positive aspects
C. To find the rare barriers and understand their negative impact
D. All of the given options

8. Which of the following is correct about human memory?
A. Not very sharp
B. Reconstructive
C. Poorly developed
D. All of the given options

9. All of the following are the barriers to communication, EXCEPT:
A. Over communication
B. Conflicting information
C. Language difference
D. Composing message at proper level

* *Exam Conducted by GGSIPU Delhi*

10. Self-confident individuals usually stand more erect than those:
A. Who lack confidence
B. Who are over-confident
C. Who are submissive
D. Who are arrogant

11. It is always easier to communicate at the ....
A. Peer level B. Differing status
C. Different position D. Different class

12. .... can also seriously impede the transmission of ideas.
A. Tolerance B. Broadsides
C. Prejudice D. Acceptance

13. By which act government checks restrictive trade?
A. Industrial Policy Act 1991
B. MRTP Act
C. FEMA act
D. None of these

14. Corporate Responsibility is:
A. The integration of social and environmental concerns in to the daily business of the company
B. The same as business ethics
C. A theory about ethics
D. The title of a government committee

15. What is 'whistleblowing'?
A. The practice of an employee informing relevant management or external organizations about malpractice in the corporation
B. The development of a company windband
C. The development of a marketing policy
D. The production of glass wind instruments

16. When a company takes over another one and clearly becomes the new owner, the action is called
A. Merger B. Acquisition
C. Strategic Alliance D. None of the above

17. The Globally Responsible Leadership Initiative (GRLI) was partly founded by:
A. Enron
B. The UN Global Compact
C. The World Health Organisation
D. Robert Maxwell

18. Which U.S. company was responsible for the explosion of a chemical plant in Bhopal in 1984?
A. Union Carbide B. Shell
C. BP D. Anglo American

19. What are the three modes of responsibility?
A. Theory, value and practice
B. The triple bottom line
C. Stakeholder, shareholder and environmental relationships
D. Agency, accountability and liability

20. Globalisation is the term used to describe process of removal of restriction on
A. Foreign Trade
B. Investment
C. Both A and B
D. None of the above

21. Any individual or group that is affected by the decisions of a business organization is known as a:
A. Shareholder B. Stakeholder
C. Citizen D. Customer

22. An oligopolistic market is:
A. Where there is only one supplier
B. Where there is only one buyer
C. Where there is a large number of small firms
D. Dominated by a small number of large firms

23. What key word can be used to describe the basic economic problem that all societies face?
A. Selfishness B. Greed
C. Inequality D. Scarcity

24. The idea that consumers are in charge of the economic system because their preferences drive business decisions about what to produce is referred to as:
A. Consumer activism
B. Consumer sovereignty
C. Consumerism
D. Consumer therapy

25. Environment degradation does not consist of:
A. Land degradation and soil erosion
B. Problem of over grazing and ecological degradation
C. Floods
D. None of the above

26. A multi-national corporation (MNC) is defined by:
A. Carrying out production in more than one country
B. Having sales in more than one country
C. Having a multi-ethnic workforce
D. Having suppliers in more than one country

27. The 'I' in BRIC stands for:
A. Indonesia
B. Ireland
C. India
D. Iceland

28. Which of the following is not a part of the opportunity cost of a university education for a full time student?
A. Any tuition fees payable
B. Cost of food
C. Income forgone from not working full time
D. Cost of textbooks

29. Which of the following statements best describes what economists mean by the term "scarcity"?
A. When unlimited needs and wants exist and yet resources are limited
B. When limited needs and wants exist and yet resources are unlimited
C. When people cannot afford to buy what they need to guarantee a minimum standard of living
D. When as a result of high demand prices of resources and commodities rise

30. Which of the following options is not an example of "market failure"?
A. Failure of a firm to maximize its profits
B. Failure to produce merit goods
C. Failure to produce public goods
D. Failure to account for externalities

31. Which of the following is an example of a primary form of business activity?
A. Hairdressing
B. Automobile Production
C. Banking
D. Forestry

32. Which of the following statements is most likely to be true?
A. As incomes rise the demand for agricultural goods in general will fall
B. As incomes rise the percentage of total income spent on agricultural goods in general tends to fall
C. As incomes rise the percentage of total income spent on agricultural goods in general tends to rise
D. As incomes rise total spending on agricultural products in general will fall

33. The economic policies as practised by President Reagan in the USA and Prime Minister Thatcher in the UK are most best associated with:
A. The Washington Consensus
B. The Keynesian Welfare Consensus
C. The Marshall Plan
D. The Industrial Revolution

34. Which of the following statements best describes what economists mean by a merit good?
A. Goods which people deserve if they are work hard
B. Goods that it is felt people should own or have access to irrespective of ability to pay
C. Goods which rich people buy to demonstrate how rich they are
D. Goods which are impossible to be provided to one person without excluding other people from benefitting from its provision

35. What is meant by the term 'economies of scale'?
A. That big firms will always be more efficient than small ones

B. That big firms can always invest more than small ones and so can spend more on resource and development
C. That bigger economies will always perform better than the smaller ones
D. That as markets grow in size businesses can adapt production techniques to meet increased demand and in the process lower average costs

36. The Division of Labour refers to:
A. The differences in skill levels between workers
B. The idea that if production can be broken down into specific tasks, with workers specializing in each task, then productivity can be increased. This is because each worker can become more efficient in their particular task
C. A division between the workers in a business and its owners
D. The idea that for profits to be generated it is important that business owners are separate from the labour force

37. What is meant by the term "comprador capitalism"?
A. A form of capitalism in developing countries whereby businesses in the developing countries try to copy the technology of the more developed ones.
B. A form of capitalism in developing countries whereby ruling elites and foreign commercial interests siphon off profits preventing these being re-invested into the businesses
C. A form of capitalism that ensures that growth will be "inclusive".
D. That capitalism is by its very nature highly competitive and it is this that gives the spur to competition.

ENGLISH LANGUAGE AND COMPREHENSION

Directions (Q. Nos. 38-45): *Read the following passage carefully and choose the most appropriate option.*

1. In its simplest terms, geothermal means earth-heat. It is related to the thermal energy of Earth's interior. On a large scale, the intensity of this thermal energy increases with depth, that is, the temperature of the Earth increases as we travel closer to its centre. A global average for Earth's geothermal gradient (temperature increase with depth) is approximately 30°C/km. For example, if we merely removed the outer 3 km of Earth's outer surface, it would be a sphere 5000°C at the core, and nearly hot enough to boil water on its surface. Earth contains an incredibly vast amount of thermal energy.

2. A vast majority of the world's power production involves the use of hot water. Sources like nuclear, coal and natural gas harness different processes (*i.e.,* radioactive decay, combustion) to heat water into steam, which is run through a turbine to generate electricity. Geothermal energy uses the escaping heat from Earth's core as a means to heat water and produce electricity. By drilling deep into the Earth's interior, we find temperatures suitably high to produce electricity.

3. Sometimes when we drill deep, there is hot water where the rock is porous (has space for fluids). In this case, we can extract the water from depth and through specialized equipment, use it to produce electricity (explained further on). If there is no water, but the rocks are very hot where we drill, it is possible to inject water to create an enhanced geothermal system (EGS) and hot water where it did not exist before. Using Earth's thermal energy to heat water instead of processes with harmful by-products like coal and nuclear, geothermal energy can produce clean, reliable electricity as long as heat continues to seep from Earth's interior (as it has for 4.5 billion years). Further, it is sustainable power because once we have extracted the thermal energy from the water or

steam, it can be continuously re-injected deep underground to obtain more geothermal heat.

4. Aside from producing power, we also use hot, geothermal water for heating pools (*i.e.*, hot springs), district heating, agriculture and laundries, to name a few. This is called direct-use geothermal because the heat is used directly from the water to serve a function.

5. Many countries including the United States, Mexico, Japan, Iceland and The Philippines are already taking advantage of their geothermal resources for electricity production. It is true that anywhere in world, at some depth below your feet exists enough geothermal heat to use for geothermal power. However, to reach that depth we must drill, and drilling costs increase exponentially with depth. At our present level of drilling technology, we are able to harness the highest quality geothermal resources, which are those located closest to Earth's surface.

38. According to what is said in the second paragraph what distinguishes geothermal power generation from other ways of generating electricity listed?
- A. Unlike geothermal power generation that uses heat escaping from the earth, the other processes need to first generate heat
- B. Other processes are much more expensive and hence not as feasible as geothermal power generation
- C. It is not possible to use geothermal power to generate electricity everywhere because of problems of availability
- D. Other processes are much better for the environment than geothermal power generation

39. What is direct-use geothermal?
- A. When electricity gets produced without human intervention
- B. When geothermal energy reaches homes directly through wires
- C. When geothermal water is used directly for heating purposes
- D. Geothermal power generation in India

40. Because the thermal energy from the water has been extracted it can be sent back underground to get heated again. This makes geothermal energy ....
- A. Achievable B. Perceivable
- C. Unredeemable D. Sustainable

41. If the word "thermal" means "of or relating to heat", what does the "geo" in "geothermal" mean
- A. Of or relating to cold
- B. Of or relating to the earth
- C. Of or relating to the sun
- D. Of or relating to nature

42. Which of the following means the opposite of the word "approximately", used in the first paragraph?
- A. Precisely B. Smoothly
- C. Simply D. Believably

43. Which of the following would be a good title for this passage?
- A. Geothermal Power: Uses, Ways of Using, and Difficulties
- B. Geothermal Power: New Zealand's Hot Water Springs
- C. Geothermal Power: Uses and Abuses
- D. Geothermal Power: Coal as a Source of Energy

44. Which of the following words from the passage above means the same as "dependable"?
- A. Sustainable B. Possible
- C. Reliable D. Advantage

45. Which of the following words from the passage above means the same as "to control and make use of"?
- A. Enhanced B. Direct-use
- C. Extract D. Harness

Directions (Q. Nos. 46-50): *Choose the most appropriate option to complete the sentence.*

46. The rain forest, ... large trees that provide shade to the vegetation below, is home to unique flora and fauna.
- A. has B. with its
- C. and D. although has

47. Despite the polar bear's tremendous weight and height, ... of sprinting at tremendous speed.
A. it is capable
B. is capable
C. it is able
D. ability

48. Patients on Interferon are adivsed ...., so that they can sleep through the night without noticing the flu-like symptoms that are characteristic of the drug.
A. just before going to sleep to inject themselves
B. to inject themselves just before going to sleep
C. to inject just before going to sleep themselves
D. injecting themselves just before going to sleep

49. The leaders of the two countries .... an agreement to avoid future conflicts.
A. have recently reach
B. recently reach
C. have reached recently
D. have recently reached

50. Instructors who .... teaching ability are prevalent at this university because publishing is one of the major criteria for tenure.
A. lack B. without
C. do not D. no have

Directions (Q. Nos. 51-55): *Choose the option that is most dissimilar to the given word.*

51. Laconic
A. Bright B. Cerebral
C. Precocious D. Verbose

52. Maladroit
A. Skillful B. Astute
C. Ephemeral D. Gauche

53. Mulish
A. Obdurate B. Murderous
C. Observant D. Acquiescent

54. Esprit
A. Dullness B. Established
C. Immanence D. Bizarre

55. Obstreperous
A. Calm B. Delectable
C. Fatuous D. Elated

Directions (Q. Nos. 56-60): *Rearrange the jumbled segments into the correct order to make meaningful sentences.*

56. to get some fruit (A)/ about (B)/going to the market (C)/ I was thinking (D)
A. DBCA B. DABC
C. BADC D. DACB

57. is a view that is (A)/is a completely objective social practice (B)/that science (C)/ progressively being dismantled (D)
A. ACDB B. CBAD
C. ABCD D. CBDA

58. that the child's mind (A)/ the teacher helps to unwind (B)/ it is imagined (C)/ is like a ball of string which (D)
A. BCDA B. DACB
C. CADB D. ACDB

59. these days (A)/ it is commonplace (B)/ we live in turbulent times (C)/ to say that (D)
A. ACBD B. CBDA
C. BADC D. ADBC

60. through planting a noxious weed (A)/ is the same as saying (B)/ your reasoning (C)/ that we can get a rose (D)
A. BDCA B. ACDB
C. CBDA D. DABC

Directions (Q. Nos. 61-65): *Choose the option that is most similar to the given word.*

61. Surmise
A. Inference B. Reference
C. Preference D. Celebrate

62. Berate
A. Deteriorate B. Articulate
C. Reprimand D. Hark

63. Broach
A. Arraign
B. Derail
C. Raise
D. Argue

64. Interregnum
A. Hiatus
B. Hayat
C. Hydras
D. Hydrous

65. Frugal
A. Thrifty
B. Crafty
C. Urban
D. Clammy

Directions (Q. Nos. 66-70): *Part, or all, of each sentence is underlined. Following the sentence, four versions of the underlined portion are presented. Choice (A) repeats the original; the other choices are different. If you think a better sentence can be found in Choices (B) to (D), then choose one of them. If the sentence is correct as stated, your answer will be Choice (A).*

66. Laura Ingalls Wilder published her first book and she was sixty-five years old then.
A. and she was sixty-five years old then
B. when she was sixty-five
C. being age sixty-five years old
D. upon the reaching of sixty-five years

67. Such of his novels as was humorous were successful.
A. Such of his novels as was humorous were successful
B. Such of his novels as were humorous were successful
C. His novels such as were humorous were successful
D. His novels were successful and humorous

68. Being that the plane was grounded, we stayed over until the next morning so that we could get the first flight out.
A. Being that the plane was grounded, we stayed over
B. In view of the fact that the plane was grounded, we stayed over
C. Since the plane was grounded, we stayed over
D. Because the plane was grounded, we stood over

69. He never has and he never will keep his word.
A. He never has and he never will
B. He has never yet and never will
C. He has not ever and he will not
D. He never has kept and he never will

70. The teacher felt badly because she had scolded the bright child who was restless for wand of something to do.
A. felt badly because she had scolded the bright child
B. felt badly why she had scolded the bright child
C. felt bad because she had scolded the bright child
D. felt bad by scolding the bright child

Directions (Q. Nos. 71-75): *If the sentence contains an error, select the one underlined part that must be changed to make the sentence correct. If the sentence is correct, select choice (D).*

71. The reason most Americans don't (A)/ pay much attention to rising (B)/ African nationalism is because (C)/ they really do not know modern Africa. No error (D).

72. There remains (A)/ many reasons for the animosity (B)/ that exists between (C)/ the Arab countries and Israel. No error (D).

73. The Aviation Administration ordered (A)/ an emergency inspection of several (B)/ Pan American planes on account (C)/ of a Pan American Boeing 707 had crashed on Bali, in Indonesia. No error (D).

74. A gang of armed thieves, (A)/ directed by a young woman, has raided (B)/ the mansion of a gold-mining millionaire near Delhi (C)/ late last night. No error (D).

75. I had (A)/ a male chauvinist pig dream (B)/ that the women of the world rose up and denounced the women's (C)/ liberation movement. No error (D).

GENERAL AWARENESS

Directions (Q. Nos. 76-112): *Choose the most appropriate option from the choices given.*

76. The republic state against which Ajatashatru fought was:
A. Koliya B. Sakya
C. Malla D. Vajji

77. The Age of consent bill in 1891 sought to increase the age of marriage for women from:
A. 8 to 10 B. 10 to 12
C. 12 to 14 D. 14 to 16

78. To whom did Mahatma Gandhi consider his spiritual guide?
A. The New Testament
B. The Quran
C. The Bhagvad Gita
D. The Ramayana

79. 'Loor' is a well-known folk song and dance of which State?
A. Haryana B. Bihar
C. Himachal Pradesh D. Assam

80. Who was the author of the book "Unhappy India" written as a response to the book "Mother India"?
A. Lala Lajpat Rai
B. Lala Hardayal
C. Mahatma Gandhi
D. B.G. Tilak

81. The Fort William College was established by
A. Warren Hastings
B. Lord Ripon
C. Lord William Bentinck
D. Lord Wellesley

82. In India, Crocodile breeding project started for the first time in
A. Tamil Nadu B. West Bengal
C. Odisha D. Goa

83. Which year was declared as International Year of Biodiversity?
A. 2002 B. 2010
C. 2020 D. 1972

84. Which one of the following ports has been developed on a lagoon?
A. Chennai B. Mumbai
C. Kochi D. Visakhapatnam

85. The scientist who first discovered that the earth revolves around the sun was:
A. Newton B. Dalton
C. Copernicus D. Einstein

86. Deficiency of Vitamin-D results in ....
A. night blindness B. rickets
C. scurvy D. hair fall

87. Which one of the following countries has decided in January 2014 to make military services compulsory for all its adult males?
A. North Korea B. UAE
C. Israel D. Turkey

88. When was the Berlin Wall demolished by East German demonstrators which was the chief symbol of the cold war?
A. 1989 B. 1990
C. 1991 D. 1994

89. Tripoli is the capital of ....
A. Gambia B. Mali
C. Libya D. Mauritius

90. The famous AI-Tehrir Square is in ....
A. Istanbul B. Damascus
C. Cairo D. Kabul

91. Dr. Henry Kissinger served as America's Secretary of State during the presidency of ....
A. Richard Nixon B. Gerald Ford
C. Both of them D. None of them

92. 'Prince of Wales Cup' is associated with the game of ....
A. Hockey B. Cricket
C. Golf D. Football

93. The oldest Oil field in India is ....
A. Bombay High, Maharashtra
B. Ankleshwar, Gujarat
C. Navagam, Gujarat
D. Digboi, Assam

94. In which one of the following years Great Depression occurred in the World?
A. 1929-39 B. 1935-36
C. 1939-40 D. 1941-42

95. Which of the following is correct about the Annual London Season?
A. It was meant for wealthy Britishers only
B. Organized for the working class
C. Organized for the exchange of news
D. Organized for political action

96. Which of the following groups of industries were the dynamic industries of England during its earliest phase of industrialization?
A. Cotton and metals
B. Cotton and silk
C. Silk and foot wears
D. Foot wears and glass

97. After reclamation how many islands were joined together to develop the city of Bombay (Mumbai)?
A. Seven B. Five
C. Three D. Ten

98. Who among the following developed the first known printing press in the 1430s?
A. Johann Gutenburg B. James Watt
C. New Commen D. Marconi

99. Who among the following is the author of the novel 'Hard Times'?
A. Leo Tolstoy B. Thomas Hardy
C. Charles Dickens D. Samuel Richardson

100. The first printing press came to India with which one of the following?
A. Portuguese Missionaries
B. Catholic Priests
C. Dutch protestants
D. East India Company

101. Who among the following is the author of the novel 'Pariksha Guru'?
A. Prem Chand
B. Srinivas Das
C. DevkiNandan Khatri
D. Chadu Menon

102. Which one of the following soil types is the most widely spread and important soil in India?
A. Laterite soils
B. Black soils
C. Alluvial soils
D. Red and Yellow soils

103. On which one of the following rivers Sardar Sarover Dam is built?
A. Kaveri B. Narmada
C. Krishna D. Satluj

104. Name the ancient theatre originated in Kerala.
A. Kuttiyatam B. Sattriya theatre
C. Sung theatre D. Cultural theatre

105. Name the ancient treatise that is a major source for dance, drama and theatre.
A. Silapaddikaran B. Manimekhalai
C. Natyashastra D. Ramayana

106. Gwalior gharana is known for which art form?
A. Style of dance B. Style of theatre
C. Style of music D. All of the above

107. In which classical dance form silk sari is used for making costume?
A. Kathak B. Garbha
C. Bharatnatyam D. Sattriya

108. Which Indian deity is known as lord of dance?
A. Vishnu B. Brahma
C. Indra D. Shiva

109. Vietnam, Cambodia and Laos were colonized by which European Power?
A. Germany B. France
C. Britain D. Portugal

110. Who was the founder of Indian Museum in Kolkata?
A. Prof. R.D. Bhandarkar
B. Sir William Jones
C. Sir Ashutosh Mukherji
D. Lord Carzon

111. How many independent emirates constitute the United Arab Emirates?
A. 5 B. 6
C. 7 D. 9

112. Who was also known as the 'Saint of Gutters'?
A. Baba Amte B. C.F. Andrews
C. Mother Teresa D. Jyotirao Phule

LOGICAL AND ANALYTICAL ABILITY

Directions (Q. Nos. 113-116): *Choose the most appropriate option.*

113. Malica : Spite :: Love : ....

A. Disregard B. Affection
C. Wedlock D. Hats

114. ACD : EGH :: IKL: ....

A. MNP B. MOP
C. MNO D. KLM

115. VW: .... :: DE : HI

A. BC B. XY
C. FG D. ZA

116. 5, 9, 6, 10, 7, 11, 8, 12, ...

A. 9 B. 10
C. 15 D. 13

Directions (Q. Nos. 117-119): *Choose the most appropriate option.*

117. In a code if A is written as Z, B is written as Y and C is written as X; then DEF will be written as:

A. ONM B. RST
C. SRQ D. WVU

118. In a certain language SUMAN is written as RTLZM, how will FRIEND be written in that code language?

A. EQHDMC B. EQHDMF
C. CMDHQE D. EQHEMF

119. In a certain code language CLEARING is written as BFMDFMHQ, how will SLIGHTED be written in that code language?

A. GSDCHJMT B. HJMTEFUI
C. HJMTCDSG D. TMJHCDSG

Directions (Q. Nos. 120-122): *Choose the most appropriate option on the basis of the information given below.*

In a certain code language, '481' means 'sky is blue', '246' means 'sea is deep' and '698' means 'sea looks blue'.

120. What number could be the code for 'sea'?

A. 2 B. 4
C. 6 D. 8

121. What number could be the code for 'blue'?

A. 1 B. 6
C. 8 D. 9

122. What number could be the code for 'deep'?

A. 1 B. 2
C. 4 D. 6

Directions (Q. Nos. 123-125): *Choose the most appropriate option on the basis of the information given below.*

Eight adults—A, B, C, D, E, F, G and H—are seated around the perimeter of a square table.

The following conditions are true about their seating: An equal number of adults sits on each side of the table.

A woman is always seated next to a man.

Half of the adults are women.

A woman is always seated between two men.

123. All of the following must be true EXCEPT.

A. People of the same sex sit directly across from each other
B. A man is seated between two women
C. Two men never sit in adjacent seats
D. A man is always seated directly across from a woman

124. Which of the conditions repeats information that may be inferred from the initial facts or previous conditions?

A. The first condition
B. The second condition
C. The third condition
D. None of the conditions

125. If a man changes places with a woman to his right, which of the following must now be true?

A. One side of the table will seat just men

B. One side of the table will seat just women
C. At least two sides of the table will seat a man and a woman
D. Two sides of the table will seat just men

Directions (Q. Nos. 126-131): *Choose the most appropriate option on the basis of the information given below.*

Five planets—A, B, C, D and E—are orbiting around a central sun, each in its own circular orbit but not necessarily in the order given. Each planet is in its own circular orbit, and none of the orbits cross paths.

- The smallest orbit is not planet A's or planet B's.
- Planet D has the largest orbit.
- Planet C is not in an orbit next to planet E's or D's.
- Planet E is closest to the sun.

126. Which of the following must be true?
A. Planet C's orbit is not second from the sun
B. Planet D's orbit is next to planet E's orbit
C. Planet A's orbit is next to planet B's orbit
D. Planet A's orbit is closer to the sun than planet B's orbit

127. Which of the following must be FALSE?
A. The orbit of planet C is between planet B's orbit and planet D's orbit
B. The orbit of planet B is between planet C's orbit and planet E's orbit
C. The orbit of planet D is between planet C's orbit and planet E's orbit
D. The orbit of planet E is smaller than planet D's orbit

128. Which of the following statements can be derived from the other four statements?
A. The smallest orbit is not planet A's or B's
B. Planet D has the largest orbit
C. Planet C is not in an orbit next to planet E's or D's
D. Planet E is closest to the sun

129. If planet B's orbit is next to planet C's orbit, which of the following must be true?
A. Planet A's orbit is closer to the sun than planet C's orbit
B. Planet B's orbit is closer to the sun than planet C's orbit
C. Planet A's orbit is next to planet B's orbit
D. Planet A's orbit is not next to planet B's orbit

130. If planet A's orbit is next to planet E's,
A. planet D's is next to planet E's
B. planet B's is next to planet D's
C. planet C's is next to planet E's
D. planet A's is between planet C's and planet D's

131. If a new planet is discovered, planet F, and its circular orbit around the sun is next to planet C's orbit, then planet F's orbit must be
A. between the orbits of planet B and planet C
B. between the orbits of planet A and planet B
C. between the orbits of planet C and planet D
D. between the orbits of planet C and planet E

Directions (Q. Nos. 132-139): *Choose the most appropriate option.*

132. 37.5% of ? = 375
A. 500
B. 800
C. 1000
D. 900

133. On the seven members panel sitting in a row X is to the left of Y, but on the right of O, P is on the right of Y but is on the left of N and M is on the left of Z, who is to the left of O. Find the member sitting right in the middle.
A. Z
B. P
C. O
D. X

134. $\sqrt{7} \div 7\sqrt{7} = ?$

A. 7 B. $\frac{1}{7}$

C. $\frac{1}{\sqrt{7}}$ D. $\sqrt{7}$

135. How many combinations of two-digit number having 8 can be made from the following numbers: 8, 5, 2, 1, 7, 6?

A. 9 B. 11
C. 10 D. 12

136. If 15th of the June falls 3 days after tomorrow, that is Friday, on what day will the last of the month fall?

A. Monday B. Tuesday
C. Wednesday D. Thursday

137. Ranga starts from his house towards South and walks 60 m then turns towards east and walks 40 m and turns towards north and walks 30 m and stops. How far is he away from his house?

A. 30 m B. 35 m
C. 40 m D. 50 m

138. Six boys are sitting in a row, Jose and Manu are sitting adjacent to Raju. Uday has Gopi and Ram as his adjacent. Gopi is not next to either Jose or Manu. Ram is not sitting next to Manu. Who are/is sitting adjacent to Jose?

A. Raju and Uday B. Raju and Manu
C. Raju and Ram D. Only Raju

139. Pick the 1st, 2nd, 4th, 5th and 6th letters in the word REASONING, form yet another word and then write the first and last letters of the word formed.

A. SE B. ES
C. NE D. OR

Directions (Q. Nos. 140-144): *In each of the following questions, three out of four given pairs of words have similar relationship. Find out the pair that is most different from the others.*

140. A. pen : nib B. bicycle : handle
C. water : boat D. monkey : tail

141. A. python : reptile
B. gold : metal
C. physics : chemistry
D. chair : furniture

142. A. hammer : paper
B. butter : cheese
C. curtain : shirt
D. brick : pottery

143. A. duck : swan
B. magazines : newspaper
C. oak : banyan
D. dog : whale

144. A. smile : frown
B. plan : win
C. cool : warm
D. caught : released

Directions (Q. Nos. 145-148): *Find the odd one out.*

145. A. idli B. dosa
C. bhatoora D. sambhar

146. A. cricket B. tennis
C. hockey D. badminton

147. A. Agra B. Allahabad
C. Kanpur D. Haridwar

148. A. knee B. elbow
C. wrist D. palm

Directions (Q. Nos. 149 and 150): *Choose the most appropriate option.*

149. The perimeter of a rectangle is 104 inches. The length is 6 inches less than 3 times the width. Find the length of the rectangle.

A. 13.5 inches
B. 37.5 inches
C. 14.5 inches
D. 15 inches

150. A certain sum of money amounted to ₹ 6000 in 3 years and ₹ 9000 in 6 years, interest being compounded. The sum is:

A. ₹ 4000 B. ₹ 2000
C. ₹ 1000 D. ₹ 3000

ANSWERS

1	2	3	4	5	6	7	8	9	10
B	A	A	B	B	A	B	B	D	A
11	**12**	**13**	**14**	**15**	**16**	**17**	**18**	**19**	**20**
A	C	B	A	A	B	B	A	D	C
21	**22**	**23**	**24**	**25**	**26**	**27**	**28**	**29**	**30**
B	D	D	B	D	A	C	B	A	A
31	**32**	**33**	**34**	**35**	**36**	**37**	**38**	**39**	**40**
D	B	A	B	D	B	A	A	C	D
41	**42**	**43**	**44**	**45**	**46**	**47**	**48**	**49**	**50**
B	A	A	C	D	B	A	D	D	A
51	**52**	**53**	**54**	**55**	**56**	**57**	**58**	**59**	**60**
D	A	D	A	A	A	B	C	C	C
61	**62**	**63**	**64**	**65**	**66**	**67**	**68**	**69**	**70**
A	C	C	A	A	B	B	C	A	C
71	**72**	**73**	**74**	**75**	**76**	**77**	**78**	**79**	**80**
C	A	A	B	C	D	B	C	A	A
81	**82**	**83**	**84**	**85**	**86**	**87**	**88**	**89**	**90**
D	C	B	C	C	B	B	A	C	C
91	**92**	**93**	**94**	**95**	**96**	**97**	**98**	**99**	**100**
A	C	D	A	A	C	A	A	C	A
101	**102**	**103**	**104**	**105**	**106**	**107**	**108**	**109**	**110**
B	C	B	A	C	C	C	D	B	B
111	**112**	**113**	**114**	**115**	**116**	**117**	**118**	**119**	**120**
C	C	D	B	D	A	D	A	C	C
121	**122**	**123**	**124**	**125**	**126**	**127**	**128**	**129**	**130**
C	B	B	C	C	A	C	D	D	B
131	**132**	**133**	**134**	**135**	**136**	**137**	**138**	**139**	**140**
A	C	D	B	B	C	D	C	A	C
141	**142**	**143**	**144**	**145**	**146**	**147**	**148**	**149**	**150**
C	A	D	B	C	A	A	A	B	B

EXPLANATORY ANSWERS

113. Malica and spite are antynomous words. Similarly, Love and Hats are antynomous words.

114. 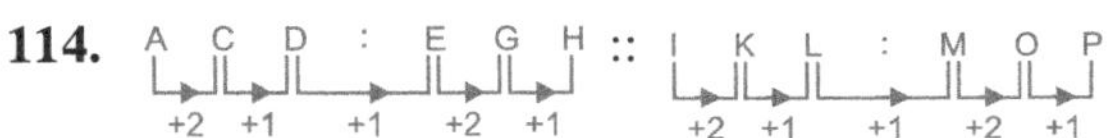

115. 

116. 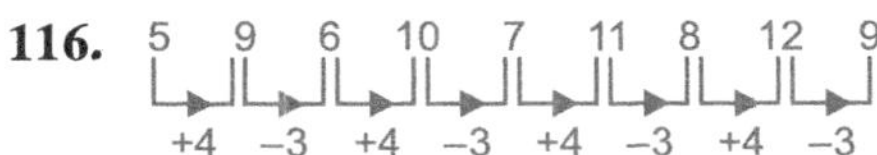

117. A is 1st letter in English alphabet.

Z is 1st letter in English alphabet in reverse order.

B is 2nd letter in English alphabet.

Y is 2nd letter in English alphabet in reverse order.

Similarly, DEF are 4th, 5th and 6th letters respectively in english alphabet.

Similarly, 4th, 5th and 6th letters in english alphabets in reverse order are WVU.

118.

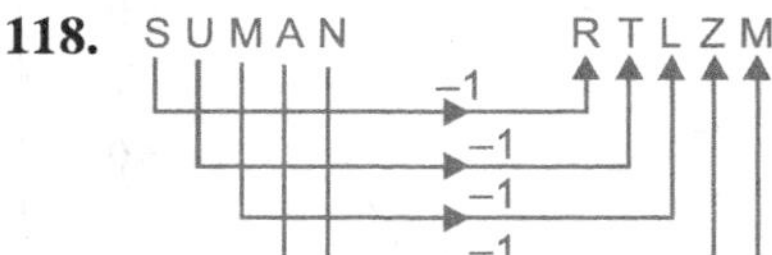

Similarly,

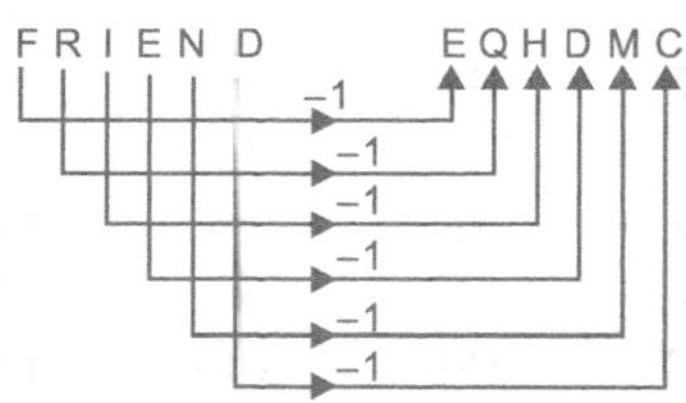

119.

Similarly,

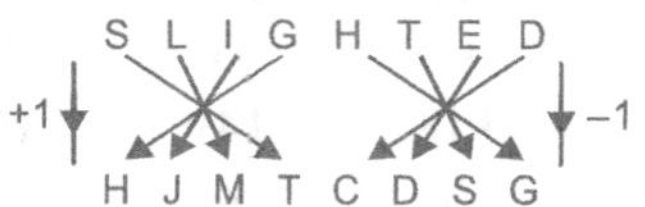

120-122.

△4	□8	1	—	sky	△is	□blue
2	△4	○6	—	○sea	△is	deep
○6	9	□8	—	○sea	looks	□blue

120. Code for 'sea' is '6'.

121. Code for 'blue' is '8'.

122. Code for 'deep' is '2'.

123-125.

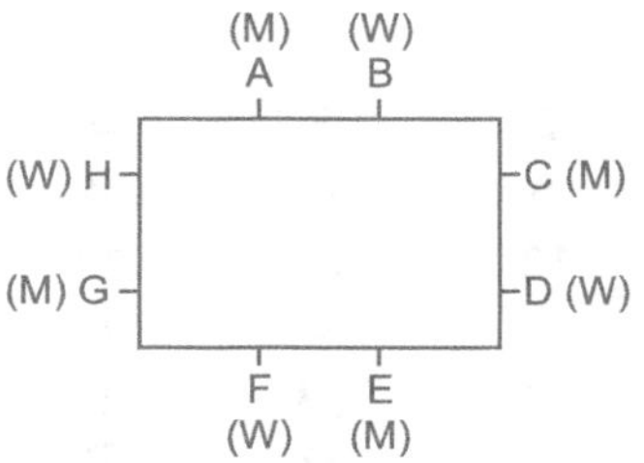

Let A, C, E and G are four men and B, D, F, H are four women in the group. According to the question, one of the possible seating arrangement will be like this:

Thus a man is seated between two women.

124. From previous conditions, we get that each side of square occupied by two adults, one men and other women. So there must be 4 women to occupy four side of the square.

Thus, Among 8 adults, half of the adults are women.

126-131.

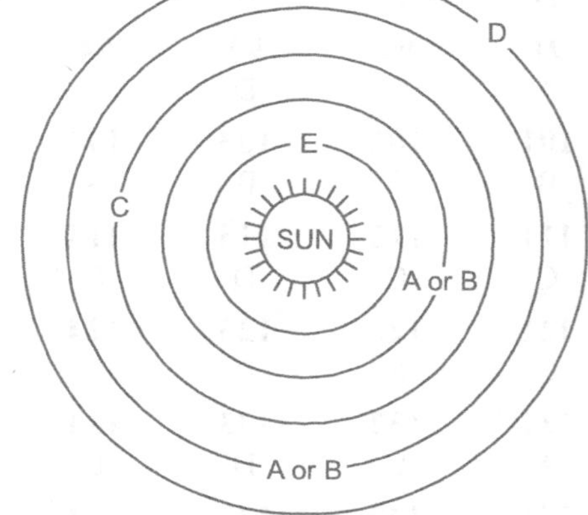

126. As, planet E orbit is closest to the Sun. So planet C orbit is not second from the Sun. This is a definetly true statement.

129. If planet B is next to planet C.

Then, planet A is not next to planet B is a correct statement.

130. If planet A is next to planet E. Then, order of the planet will be E, A, C, B, D.

Thus, planet B will be next to 'D'.

132. $\frac{37.5}{100} \times x = 375$

$$x = \frac{375 \times 100}{37.5} = 1000.$$

133. Sitting arrangement of seven members are like this:

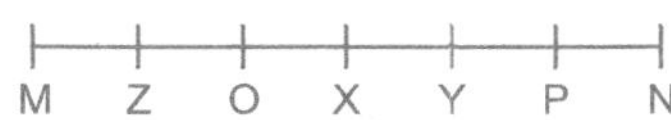

Hence, 'X' is in the right of the middle.

134. $\sqrt{7} \div 7\sqrt{7} = \sqrt{7} \times \frac{1}{7\sqrt{7}} = \frac{1}{7}.$

135. Number of 2 digits number having '8' at unit place

$$= {}^5P_1 = 5$$

and those numbers are 18, 28, 58, 68, 78

Number of 2 digits number having '8' at tenth place

$$= {}^5P_1 = 5$$

and those numbers are 81, 82, 85, 86, 87

Number of 2 digits having 8 at both place = 1 and that is '88'

Hence, number of such numbers

$$= 5 + 5 + 1 = 11.$$

136. Since, tomorrow is 11th of June and if 11th of June is Friday.

Therefore 18th and 25th of June is Friday also. And 30th of June will be Wednesday.

137.

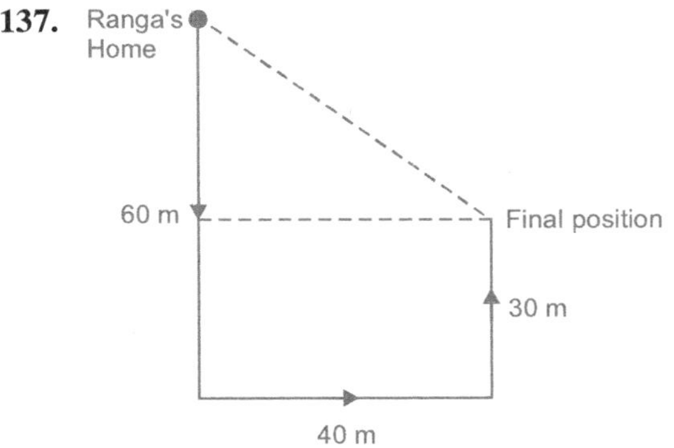

Ranga distance from his home

$$= \sqrt{(40)^2 + (60-30)^2}$$

$$= \sqrt{1600 + 900}$$

$$= \sqrt{2500}$$

$$= 50 \text{ m}.$$

138. Sitting arrangement of six boys are like this:

Gopi, Uday, Ram, Jose, Raju, Manu

Hence, Ram & Raju are adjacent to Jose.

139. R E A S O N I N G

| | | | | |

1st 2nd 4th 5th 6th

1st, 2nd, 4th, 5th and 6th letters are R, E, S, O, N respectively, from these letter a meaningful word will be 'SNORE'

So, first and last letter of that word is 'SE'.

140. Nib is a part of pen, handle is a part of bicycle, tail is part of monkey but boat is not a part of water.

141. Python belongs to reptile class, gold belongs to metal, chair is a kind of furniture but physics & chemistry are two different subjects in science stream.

142. Raw material used in butter-cheese, curtain-shirt, brick-pottery are same, where as hammer-paper are totally different kind.

143. Dog & Whale are different kind, whereas other three pairs belongs to same groups.

144. Smile-frown, cool-warm, caught-released are antonymous pair, whereas plan-win are not such pair.

145. Idli, dosa, sambhar are South Indian dishes, whereas Bhatoora is a North-Indian dish.

146. Tennis, Hockey & Badminton are play in the court/field, in which a single court/field is divided into two equal part, whereas in Cricket field is not divided into any part.

147. Agra is on the bank of Yamuna river whereas Allahabad, Kanpur & Haridwar on the bank of the Ganga river.

148. Elbow, Wrist and Palm are hand parts whereas Knee is a leg part.

149. Let, width of the rectangle is x meter

then, length of the rectangle = $(3x - 6)$ m

Perimeter of the rectangle

$$= 2\text{ (length + width)}$$

$$104 = 2(x + 3x - 6)$$

$$52 = (4x - 6)$$

Hence, $x = 14.5$ m

Length of the rectangle

$$= 3 \times 14.5 - 6$$

$$= 37.5 \text{ inches.}$$

150. Let, rate of interest is $r\%$ and amount is ₹ P

then, $$A = P\left(1+\frac{r}{100}\right)^n$$

So, $$9000 = P\left(1+\frac{r}{100}\right)^6 \quad ...(i)$$

and $$6000 = P\left(1+\frac{r}{100}\right)^3 \quad ...(ii)$$

On dividing we get,

$$\left(1+\frac{r}{100}\right)^3 = \frac{9000}{6000}$$

∴ From eq. (*ii*)

$$6000 = P\left(\frac{9000}{6000}\right)$$

$$P = \frac{6000 \times 6000}{9000}$$

$$= \frac{36000}{9} = 4000.$$

Previous Paper (Solved)

BBA/BBS Entrance Exam–2016*

Directions (Qs. 1-5) : *Read the article carefully and answer the questions that follow. Choose one answer from among the four choices given:*

Slower growth and deceleration in funding are making companies – including startups – across a range of sectors hire junior-level candidates in place of mid-level ones, according to multiple hiring platforms. In the case of tech firms, the trend is even more pronounced because, in addition to budget constraints, many of the new-age tech qualifications that companies need are more likely to be available among younger employees.

Online hiring firm Hiree has said that tech companies are now increasingly preferring people with experience of 1-3 years over those with experience of 3 years and more. It also noted that there's a 15% decline in the salary being offered to the junior-level employees. The data is based on the recruitment search patterns of over 400 companies, 60% of which comprised established startups, on the Hiree platform between October 2015 and February 2016. Almost 70% of the candidates surveyed were for tech roles by startups and corporates.

Mettl, an online assessment service that helps companies in recruitment, saw 40% of its assessments happening for candidates with 1-3 years of work experience in the January-March quarter, compared to 25% in the previous quarter. This was calculated from over 6 lakh assessments conducted by large and medium enterprises across IT, pharmacy, manufacturing, banking and automobile.... .

Hacker Earth, which organizes coding challenges for recruitment companies to understand the skillsets of candidates, also says hiring is shifting in favour of junior level candidates. "Also companies are now looking at particular skillsets rather than work experience. People with over six years of experience will not have technical expertise in Django or Python (programming languages needed for new-age tech apps)."

Ketan Kapoor, founder of Mettl, said companies are today a lot of more focused on the skills of the people, and on young people with lesser experience if they can deliver the required output. Sunil Goel, MD of recruitment agency Global Hunt, said the concept of junior and senior roles in organizations is changing. "The pyramid of hierarchies is getting flattened", he said.

— Times Business, April 15, 2016

1. Companies prefer to hire junior level candidates because:

A. They demand lower salaries and are willing to work longer hours

B. They have the required skill sets and cost less

C. They cost less and have 1-3 years experience

D. Mid level candidates do not have leadership abilities

2. To work with new-age tech apps, one needs to have:

A. Technical expertise in languages like Django and Python

B. Technical expertise in languages like Mettl and Hacker Earth

C. 1-3 years of experience

D. Access to online hiring firms.

* *Exam Conducted by Delhi University*

3. A word in the article which means the same as slow down, is:
   A. Constraints B. Increasingly
   C. Assessments D. Deceleration
4. A word in the article which means the opposite of horizontal, is:
   A. Hierarchies B. Pharmacy
   C. Skill-sets D. Multiple
5. The data used in this article comes from:
   A. Assessments conducted for tech roles by startups and corporates
   B. Assessments conducted by Hiree, an online hiring firm
   C. Assessments conducted by multiple hiring platforms
   D. Assessments conducted by Mettl and Hacker Earth

Directions (Qs. 6-10) : *Choose one pair of words, from among the four choices given, to complete the given sentences.*

6. Globalization, liberalization and free market .... some of the most significant modern trends in economies .... the world.
   A. is; around B. are; under
   C. are; around D. is; for
7. The writer's primary objective .... writing this seems to be a hatred .... lies and cheating.
   A. while; for B. for; with
   C. of; by D. while; in
8. Some prophets .... doom believe that we .... soon pollute ourselves to death.
   A. in; was B. at; have
   C. of; will have D. of; will
9. When I got .... the train at Guwahati, I .... welcomed by my host Mr. Baruah.
   A. in; will be B. off; was
   C. at; is D. on; were
10. After a gap of ten years, I .... to visit my old school again to see if anything .... changed.
   A. decide; have
   B. deciding, has
   C. will decide; will have
   D. decided; had

Directions (Qs. 11-14) : *Read the following sentences and replace the italicised part with the option closest in meaning:*

11. I shall have to *call on* her to show her the documents.
   A. Ring up B. Seek permission
   C. Visit D. Confront
12. They are *up in arms* to push the Bill for approval.
   A. Shoot B. Oppose
   C. Shout D. Impress
13. No political party in a democracy can ignore the *fourth estate* to gain power.
   A. The panchayat B. The city courts
   C. The police D. The press
14. *To spill the beans* is to violate a tacit contract.
   A. Giving away information
   B. Being negligent
   C. Condemning
   D. Passing critical remarks

Directions (Qs. 15 & 16): *Choose the* ***correct meaning*** *for the* ***euphemism*** *given in italics.*

15. "*In the sunset years*":
   A. Drunk B. Old
   C. Dead D. Young
16. "*To pass away*":
   A. To die B. To run
   C. To walk D. To step down

Directions (Qs. 17-19) : *Listed below are words given in italics. Choose the* ***correct synonym*** *from the given options.*

17. *Immaculate:*
   A. Immature B. Imperfect
   C. Immortal D. Spotless
18. *Recalcitrant:*
   A. Amenable B. Disobedient
   C. Docile D. Former

19. *Belligerent:*
A. Peaceful B. Believer
C. Diligent D. Aggressive

Directions (Qs. 20-25): *Choose the correct option for the italics part of each of the sentences given below:*

20. Her love for animals developed her career as a *specialist in animal diseases*.
A. Occulist B. Biologist
C. Veterinarian D. Paediatrician

21. A *soldier who fights for the sake of money* cannot be celebrated as courageous and patriotic.
A. Sinecure B. Honorary
C. Mercenary D. Equestrian

22. He is *working in return for being taught a trade.*
A. A pupil B. A disciple
C. An apprentice D. A sobriquet

23. Meena impressed all with her *persuasive and fluent speech*.
A. Discourse B. Expression
C. Eloquence D. Lecture

24. The *caretaker of a public building* needs to be a vigilant and an honest person.
A. Custodian B. Proctor
C. Watchman D. Dean

25. He found his duties increasingly *onerous*.
A. Easy B. Taxing
C. Interesting D. Frivolous

Directions (Qs. 26-30): *Read the following sentences in which S_1 and S_6 are the first and last sentences. P, Q, R and S are in jumbled order. Choose the correct option to form a coherent paragraph.*

26. S_1. India is a very old country with a great past.
P. Since August 1947, she has been in a position to pursue her own foreign policy.
Q. But it is a new country also, with new urges and new desires.
R. But even so, she cannot forget the lesson of her great leaders.
S. She is limited by the realities of the situation which cannot be ignored or overcome.
S_6. She has tried to adapt theory to reality.
A. PQRS B. QPSR
C. SRPQ D. RSPQ

27. S_1. When Galileo went home, he began to experiment with the pendulum.
P. When he showed it to his teachers, they were delighted.
Q. It was not long before physicians were all using the instrument to count the heart-beats of their patients.
R. Soon he had invented an instrument which marked the rate of pulse-beats.
S. Then the clock makers began to use the pendulum to keep time.
S_6. Today it has many other uses.
A. PQRS B. QRPS
C. SPQR D. RPQS

28. S_1. Pollution is one of the evils brought about by the growth of science.
P. Air Pollution has very harmful effects.
Q. They pollute the air and the atmosphere.
R. It is making the environment, water and air dirty.
S. Factories and Industries keep throwing out smoke which contains toxic gases.
S_6. People living in the surroundings breathe the impure air and are affected by diseases of the lungs and heart.
A. PSQR B. RPSQ
C. QPSR D. SPQR

29. S_1. Anna had longed to see her son.
P. "He will arrive at the station at 7o'clock", she said to herself.
Q. She prepared herself for it.
R. She looked at the clock.
S. There were only ten minutes left.

S_6. She rushed out of her house and hailed a taxi to reach the station in time.

A. QPRS B. SPRQ
C. PRQS D. QSRP

30. S_1. A rocket burns a fuel that makes a great deal of gas at the back of the rocket.
P. Ordinary fuel will burn only in air because it needs the oxygen in the air.
Q. A rocket can therefore travel outside the atmosphere in space where there is no air.
R. This gas pushes against the rocket and sends it forward.
S. However, rocket fuels have their oxygen in them and so they burn without air.
S_6. In fact, it will travel faster in space than in the air because the friction of the air is not there to slow it down.

A. QSRP B. RPSQ
C. SQPR D. PRQS

31. If '=' stands for 'addition', '×' stands for 'subtraction', '÷' stands for 'division', '+' stands for 'multiplication', '>' stands for 'equal to', '<' stands for 'greater than' and '–' stands for 'less than', state which of the following is true?

A. $3 = 2 \times 4 < 16 + 2 \div 4$
B. $5 + 2 \div 2 - 10 \times 4 = 8$
C. $3 = 4 + 2 > 9 \div 3 \times 3$
D. $5 = 3 \times 7 < 8 \div 4 = 1$

32. In a certain code, PLEADING is written as FMHCQMFB. How is SHOULDER written in that code?

A. KCDQTIPV B. QDCKVPIT
C. QDCKTIPV D. TIPVQDCK

33. In a History midterm test, D got more than A & C and B got less than E but more than D. Who got the maximum marks?

A. B B. E
C. D D. Both (A) and (C)

Directions (Qs. 34 & 35): *Read the information given below and answer the questions that follow.*

A team has to be selected from among five professors – A, B, C, D and E; six Engineers – P, Q, R, S, T and U; and seven Chartered Accountants – H, I, J, K, L, M and N. Among them C, D, E, R, S, T, J, K and L are females and the rest are males.

The formation of the team is subjected to the following conditions:

(*i*) Whenever there is a female professor in the team, there will be no male engineer.
(*ii*) Whenever there is a male chartered accountant in the team, there will be no female professor.
(*iii*) There can't be more than two male engineers in a team at a given time.

34. If a team consists of 2 engineers, 2 chartered accountants and 3 professors out of whom at least 2 professors are females, then which of the following teams is not possible?

A. CDERTJK B. CDARSJK
C. CDBRUJL D. DEBSTKL

35. If a team consists of 3 engineers, 3 chartered accountants and 2 professors, then which of the following teams are possible?

A. PRTJKLCD B. PQUHINAB
C. RSTKLMCE D. PQRHIMAB

36. Consider the following statements:
(*i*) Some students play basketball
(*ii*) To get scholarship in the school one must play basketball
(*iii*) All students getting scholarship are brilliant

Which of the following conclusions can be drawn from the above statements?

A. All brilliant students play basketball
B. All students who play basketball are brilliant
C. All students playing basketball get scholarship
D. No conclusion can be drawn

Directions (Qs. 37 & 38) : *Read the given information and answer the questions that follow:*

P, Q, R, S, T and U are sitting in a circle facing the center. P is facing S, while Q is sitting second to the right hand side of P. R is sitting between P and Q and U is sitting between T and P.

37. Who is sitting opposite to T?
A. P B. Q
C. R D. T

38. Who is sitting between R and S?
A. P B. Q
C. R D. T

39. Two positions of a dice are shown below:

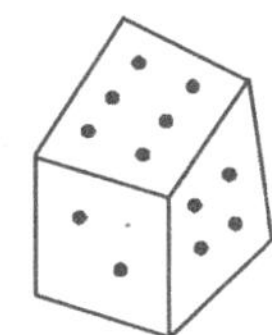

When three dots are at the top, how many will be at the bottom?
A. 1 B. 2
C. 4 D. 5

40. Which alternative will complete the series: DF, JL, PR, ?
A. ZX B. VX
C. PQ D. OR

Directions (Qs. 41) : *In the following question a statement is followed by two conclusions. Taking the statement to be true, decide which of the given conclusions definitely follows from the given statement. Indicate your answers as:*

A. If only statement one follows
B. If only statement two follows
C. If neither one nor two follows
D. If both statements follow

41. "Use of cosmetics is hazardous":
I. Cosmetics have got side effects
II. Cosmetics are expensive

42. If RENT is written as '÷ + × –', SAND is written as '* / × <', how is START written as:
A. '+ – / ÷ –' B. '* – / ÷ –'
C. '* ÷ / – +' D. '× – / ÷ –'

43. How many triangles are there in the figure?

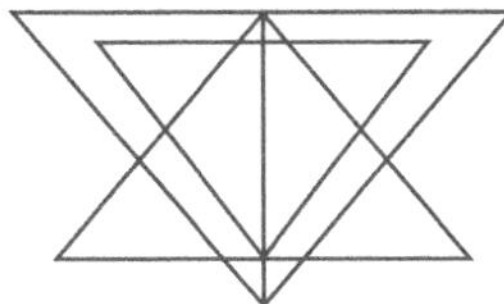

A. 25 B. 23
C. 21 D. 27

Directions (Qs. 44-48) : *Study the following and answer the questions that follow.*

Eight people: S, R, N, L, M, T, O and P are sitting in a circle facing the centre. All eight belong to different professions: journalist, doctor, cricketer, professor, accountant, shopkeeper, painter and supervisor. {They are not necessarily seated in the mentioned order}.

M is seated third to the left of O.

The doctor is to the immediate right of M.

M is not a journalist.

R is sitting fourth to the right of P.

Neither R nor P is an immediate neighbour of M.

T is a professor and is sitting third to the right of the doctor.

The shopkeeper is sitting second to the left of the professor.

The painter is sitting second to the left of M.

S, the cricketer is sitting exactly in the middle of T and P.

Accountant is sitting second to the right of cricketer.

N is sitting third to the left of the T.

44. Who is the journalist?
A. O B. L
C. N D. R

45. What is S's position with respect to R?
A. Third to the right of R
B. Second to the right of R
C. Third to the left of R
D. Second to the left of R

46. How many people are sitting between P and N when counted in anti-clockwise direction from N?
A. One B. Two
C. Three D. Four

47. The following pairs are alike in a certain way. Which of the following is odd one out:
A. Professor – painter
B. Supervisor – shopkeeper

C. Cricketer – journalist
D. Shopkeeper – doctor

48. Which of the following is false?
A. N is to immediate right of supervisor
B. Cricketer is third to the right of shopkeeper
C. Doctor is sitting exactly between supervisor and accountant
D. L is neither a professor nor a supervisor

Directions (Qs. 49 & 50): *In each of the following questions, there is some relationship between the two terms to left of :: and the same relationship continues between the two terms to its right. Also in each question, one term either to the right of :: or to the left of it is missing. This term is given as one of the alternatives given below each question. Find out the missing term.*

49. B : F : : E : ....
A. H B. T
C. I D. J

50. Ppk : kPP : : Llm : ....
A. mlL B. LmM
C. mLL D. lMl

51. If 'P + Q' means 'P is the father of Q', 'P × Q' means 'P is the brother of Q'; 'P – Q' means 'P is the mother of Q', then which of the following is true for C – A + B?
A. B is the son of A
B. A is the son of C
C. B is the father of A
D. C is the mother of B

Directions (Qs. 52-55) : *Read the information given below and answer the questions that follow:*

Six persons A, B, C, D, E and F were playing a game of cards. A's father, mother and uncle were in the group. There were two women. B, the mother of A, got more points than her husband. D got more points than E but less than F. Niece of E got lowest points. Father of A got more points than F but could not win the game.

52. Who won the game?
A. A B. B
C. D D. F

53. Who got the lowest points?
A. A B. B
C. C D. E

54. Who is the husband of B?
A. C B. D
C. E D. F

55. Who stood second in the game?
A. D B. B
C. C D. A

Directions (Qs. 56 & 57) : *Read the following information carefully and answer the questions given below:*

(*i*) Six children namely B, D, C, M, J and K are split into two groups of three each and are made to stand in two rows in such a way that a child in one row is exactly facing a child in the other row.
(*ii*) M is not at the ends of any row and is to the right of J, who is facing C. K is to the left of D, who is facing M.

56. Who is to the immediate left to B?
A. M B. J
C. D D. None of these

57. Which of the following groups of children is in the same row?
A. BDC B. KJM
C. MJD D. BMJ

58. Find the missing number :

8	3	4
7	6	1
2	4	?
13	5	4

A. 1 B. 3
C. 2 D. 4

59. In a certain code '526' means 'sky is blue'; '24' means 'blue colour' and '436' means 'colour is fun', which digit means 'fun'?
A. 2 B. 3
C. 4 D. 5

60. Statements:

All benches are cots.

No cot is lamp.

Some lamps are candles.

Conclusions:

1. Some cots are candles
2. Some candles are cots

A. If only conclusion 1 follows
B. If only conclusion 2 follows
C. If either conclusion 1 or 2 follows
D. If neither conclusion 1 nor 2 follows

61. Christine Lagarde was in the news recently. What was the reason behind it?

A. She got an extension for second term as IMF chief
B. She got an extension for second term as World Bank chief
C. She is designated as the next UN chief
D. None of the above

62. Match the following :

(*a*) Kiran Mazumdar Shaw	(*i*) Banker
(*b*) Chanda Kochhar	(*ii*) Journalist
(*c*) Tavleen Singh	(*iii*) Business Woman
(*d*) Mithali Raj	(*iv*) Cricketer

Code :

	(*a*)	(*b*)	(*c*)	(*d*)
A.	(*iv*)	(*iii*)	(*i*)	(*ii*)
B.	(*iii*)	(*i*)	(*ii*)	(*iv*)
C.	(*iv*)	(*ii*)	(*iii*)	(*i*)
D.	(*i*)	(*ii*)	(*iii*)	(*iv*)

63. On what date is the International Yoga Day celebrated?

A. 21st June B. 5th June
C. 24th September D. 31st January

64. Committee formed by Union Government to look into recent protest by Jat community in Haryana :

A. Prakash Singh committee
B. Yashwant Sinha committee
C. Nivedkar committee
D. Gadkari committee

65. Which one is not a component of composite Human Development Index (HDI)?

A. Per capita income
B. Literacy rate
C. Life expectancy
D. Infant mortality rate

66. Amartya Sen, an Indian economist was awarded Nobel prize in economics for his pioneering work in:

A. Microeconomics
B. Macroeconomics
C. Welfare economics
D. International economics

67. Which of the following books is not written by Dr. A.P.J. Kalam?

A. Wings of Fire
B. India 2020
C. Ignited Minds
D. The Argumentative Indian

68. Recently Reuben Brothers were in the news for:

A. They replaced Hinduja Brothers as the wealthiest persons of Britain
B. They are one of the franchisee of IPL
C. They are black listed by the enforcement director for fraud
D. They purchased the ownership of Flipkart

69. Who is the NRI businessman behind Liberty House that has expressed the desire to acquire one of the Tata Steel units in UK?

A. Sanjeev Gupta B. Sachin Bansal
C. Vijay Mallya D. Sanjeev Puri

70. The highest peace-time military gallantry award in India is:

A. Paramvir Chakra B. Ashok Chakra
C. Shaurya Chakra D. None of the above

71. Who is the Chief Executive Officer of Niti Aayog?

A. Bibek Debroy
B. Arvind Subramanium
C. Ramesh Chand
D. Amitabh Kant

72. Anshu Gupta won the Ramon Magsaysay Award for the year 2015. Who is he?

A. He is an Indian Forest Service officer who fought corruption in forests.
B. He is the founder of the NGO 'Goonj'.
C. He is the founder of the NGO 'Akshaya Patra'.
D. He is an RTI activist.

73. In 2015, which of the following sports persons has been appointed as the Goodwill Ambassador of the UNICEF?
A. Novak Djokovic
B. Maria Sharapova
C. Lionel Messi
D. Christino Ronaldo

74. Gennaro Bernile, Vineet Bhagwat and P. Raghavendra Rau won the 'Ig Nobel Prize' in Management for the year 2015. What is special about these 'Ig Nobel' awards?
A. They are given in fields like Management, Mathematics and Physiology and not in the usual Nobel Prize fields like Physics, Chemistry, Medicine etc.
B. They are given to Asian discoverers only.
C. They are given for unusual, trivial or humourous scientific discoveries or achievements.
D. They are given for business related discoveries only.

75. The Jain religious practice of a ritualistic fast unto death, which was in news recently because of a Supreme Court judgment, is known as:
A. Euthanasia B. Swetambara
C. Santhara D. Jallikattu

76. Which of the following is world's most powerful supercomputer?
A. Pleiades (USA) B. Jaguar (USA)
C. Nebulae (China) D. Tianhe-2 (China)

77. What do you understand by NOTA?
A. New and Old testament advice
B. National Organisation of the Anarchists
C. Not atheist
D. None of the above

78. In the year 2016, the chairmanship of the influential bloc BRICS has passed from which country to which?
A. From India to Russia
B. From India to Brazil
C. From Russia to India
D. From Russia to China

79. Tata Communications Payment Solutions Ltd became the first company in India to get RBI's permission to open White Label ATMs in India under the brand name 'Indicash'. How is a 'White Label ATM' different from a 'Brown Label ATM'?
A. White label ATM has a logo of a particular bank, say SBI or ICICI or Kotak; while Brown label ATM doesn't have any logo of a particular bank
B. White label ATM is operated by a banking company; while Brown label ATM is operated by a non-banking financial company
C. Both (A) and (B) are correct
D. Both (A) and (B) are wrong

80. Which of the following well known fashion designers has been recently appointed as the adviser to Khadi and Village Industries Commission for promotion of Khadi in India and across the world?
A. Ritu Beri
B. Rohit Bal
C. Wendell Rodrickes
D. Sabyasachi Mukherjee

81. As per the latest Forbes magazine rankings who is the second richest Indian billionaire following Mukesh Ambani at the top?
A. Shiv Nadar of HCL Technologies
B. Dilip Shanghvi of Sun Pharmaceutical Industries
C. Azim Premji of Wipro
D. Kumar Mangalam Birla of Aditya Birla Group

82. Which company launched the biggest Indian IPO of 2015?
A. InterGlobe Aviation (IndiGo Airlines)
B. Coffee Day Enterprises (cafe coffee day chain)

C. Dr. Lal Path Labs (medical diagnostics chain)
D. UFO Moviez India (digital cinema & in-cinema advertising)

83. "Inspired Living" is the advertisement tagline of which of the following companies/brands?
A. URBAN LADDER
B. LG
C. HAIER
D. PHILLIPS

84. In March 2016, the 13th edition of India-European Union Summit was held in:
A. London, UK
B. Paris, France
C. Brussels, Belgium
D. Zurich, Switzerland

85. Match the following :

	Movies		*Directors*
(*a*)	Mother India	(*i*)	Mira Nair
(*b*)	Sholay	(*ii*)	Ramesh Sippy
(*c*)	Salaam Bombay	(*iii*)	Mehboob Khan
(*d*)	Do Bigha Zameen	(*iv*)	Bimal Roy

Code :

	(*a*)	(*b*)	(*c*)	(*d*)
A.	(*iv*)	(*iii*)	(*i*)	(*ii*)
B.	(*ii*)	(*iii*)	(*i*)	(*iv*)
C.	(*iv*)	(*ii*)	(*iii*)	(*i*)
D.	(*iii*)	(*ii*)	(*i*)	(*iv*)

86. India foiled a bid by which of the following companies to patent Nutmeg extract based mouthwash formula at the European Patent Office, on the argument that the said herb 'Myristica Fragrans' was traditionally used for oral diseases in Indian System of medicine?
A. Glaxo Smith Kline plc
B. Hindustan Unilever Ltd.
C. Johnson & Johnson Ltd.
D. Colgate Palmolive Ltd.

87. Who won the prestigious lifetime achievement award at the Annual Asian Business Leadership Forum in Dubai 2015?
A. Hinduja Brothers
B. Brij Mohan Lall Munjal
C. Nandan Nilekani
D. Arun Jaitley

88. The ore of Aluminium is :
A. Bauxite B. Charcopyrites
C. Hematite D. Fluorspar

89. Which of the following became the first Indian brand to be endorsed by the International sports icon Lionel Messi?
A. Oppo phones B. Indian Oil
C. Tata Motors D. Dabur

90. Subir Gokarn recently got appointed as Executive Director of the IMF. He earlier served as:
A. Deputy Governor of RBI
B. Chief Economic Advisor to Govt. of India
C. Deputy Chairman, Planning Commission of India
D. Vice Chairman of Niti Aayog

91. The set of real values of x satisfying the inequality $|x^2 + x + 6| < 6$ is:
A. $(-\infty, \infty)$
B. $(-1, 0)$
C. $(-\infty, -1) \cup (0, \infty)$
D. $(-\infty, -1] \cup [0, \infty)$

92. The number of real solutions of the equation $e^x = x$, is:
A. 1 B. 2
C. 0 D. None of these

93. On the set of natural numbers, a relation R is defined so that p is related to q if and only if the GCD of p and q is 2, then R is:
A. Reflexive but not symmetric
B. Symmetric only
C. Equivalence
D. Neither reflexive nor symmetric but transitive

94. The inverse of the function $f : \mathrm{R} \to \{x \in \mathrm{R} : x < 1\}$, where R is the set of real numbers, given by $f(x) = (e^x - e^{-x})/(e^x + e^{-x})$ is:
A. $\frac{1}{2}\log\frac{1+x}{1-x}$ B. $\frac{1}{2}\log\frac{2+x}{2-x}$
C. $\frac{1}{2}\log\frac{1-x}{1+x}$ D. None of these

95. If the first, second and the last term of an AP are a, b, c respectively, then the sum of n terms of the AP is:

A. $(a + b)(a + c - 2b)/2(b - a)$
B. $(b + c)(a + b - 2c)/2(b - a)$
C. $(a + c)(b + c - 2a)/2(b - a)$
D. None of the above

96. In a GP of positive terms, any term is equal to the sum of the next two terms. Then, the common ratio of GP is:

A. $\frac{(\sqrt{5}-1)}{2}$ B. $\frac{(\sqrt{5}+1)}{2}$
C. $-\frac{(\sqrt{5}+1)}{2}$ D. $\frac{(1-\sqrt{5})}{2}$

97. If $b > a$, then the equation $(x - a)(x - b) - 1 = 0$, has :

A. Both roots in $[a, b]$
B. Both roots in $(-\infty, a]$
C. Both roots in $[b, \infty)$
D. One root in $(-\infty, a)$ and other in (b, ∞)

98. The number of six digit numbers that can be formed using three digits 0, 1, 2, is:

A. 3^6 B. 2×3^5
C. 3^5 D. None of these

99. If A = $\begin{pmatrix} \alpha & 2 \\ 2 & \alpha \end{pmatrix}$ and determinant $(A^3) = 125$, then the value of α is:

A. ± 1 B. ± 2
C. ± 3 D. ± 5

100. If P(A) = 2/3, P(B) = 1/2, P(A $\cup$ B) = 5/6 then events A and B are :

A. Mutually exclusive
B. Independent as well as mutually exclusive
C. Independent
D. Dependent only on A

101. The number of points equidistant to three given distinct non-collinear points is:

A. 0 B. 1
C. 2 D. Infinite

102. The lines $2x - 3y - 5 = 0$ and $3x - 4y = 7$ are diameters of a circle :

A. $x^2 + y^2 + 2x + 2y - 62 = 0$
B. $x^2 + y^2 + 2x - 2y - 47 = 0$
C. $x^2 + y^2 - 2x + 2y - 47 = 0$
D. $x^2 + y^2 - 2x - 2y - 62 = 0$

103. $\lim_{x \to a} \frac{x-a}{|x-a|}$ equals:

A. a B. 0
C. 1 D. None of these

104. The Set $(A \cap B) \cup (A \cap B')$ refers to the set :

A. A B. B
C. Universal Set D. Null Set

105. If $f(x) = \frac{1-x}{1+x}$ then:

A. $f(-x) = f(x)$ B. $f(x)\,f(-x) = 2$
C. $f(1/x) = f(x)$ D. $f(1/x) = -f(x)$

106. If p, q are roots of the equation $x^2 + pq = (p + 1)x$ then q is equal to:

A. −1 B. 1
C. 2 D. −2

107. The length of a side of a square is ‘a’ metres. A second square is formed by joining the middle points of this square. Then a third square is formed by joining the middle points of the second square and so on. Then, the sum of the area of squares, carried up to infinity is:

A. a^2 B. $2a^2$
C. $3a^2$ D. $4a^2$

108. Three letters are written to three persons and addresses on the envelopes are also written. One letter is placed randomly in each envelope. The chances that the letters go into right envelopes are:

A. 1/9 B. 1/6
C. 1/27 D. None of these

109. The number of ways in which we can post 5 letters in 10 letter boxes is :

A. 50 B. 5^{10}
C. 10^5 D. None of these

110. The sum of the coefficients in the expansion of $(5p - 4q)^n$ is:

A. 1 B. −1
C. 9 D. None of these

111. It was calculated that 50 persons could complete a piece of work in 15 days. But before the start of work, 25 persons more joined the work. How long will it take to complete the work?

A. 5 days B. 10 days
C. 12 days D. None of these

112. In an exam, the average was found to be 60 marks. After it was found that marks of 10 candidates were wrongly written 50 in place of 70 and after correction the average became 65. The total number of candidates who took the exam are:

A. 45 B. 40
C. 35 D. 30

113. Sum of the series $\frac{2}{1!}+\frac{3}{2!}+\frac{4}{3!}+....$ to ∞ is:

A. $2e$ B. $2e - 1$
C. $2e + 1$ D. $2(e + 1)$

114. If $|\vec{x}|$ represents length of vector $\vec{x}$ and if $|\vec{\alpha}+\vec{\beta}|=|\vec{\alpha}-\vec{\beta}|$ then :

A. $\vec{\alpha}$ is parallel to $\vec{\beta}$

B. $\vec{\alpha}$ is perpendicular of $\vec{\beta}$

C. $|\vec{\alpha}|=|\vec{\beta}|$

D. None of these

115. If each element of a matrix of order 3 × 3 has determinant of value A. If each element of this matrix is multiplied by 2, then the determinant of the new matrix is equal to:

A. A B. 3A
C. 8A D. 9A

116. A shopkeeper buys a number of books for ₹ 80. If he had bought four more books for the same amount, each book would have cost him ₹ 1 less. Then the number of books he had bought is:

A. 15 B. 16
C. 17 D. 18

117. If $\frac{1}{x+1}+\frac{2}{x+2}=\frac{5}{x+4}$, $(x \neq -1, -2, -4)$. Then x is equal to:

A. 2 B. 3
C. 4 D. 5

118. If the coefficients of the second, third and fourth terms in the expansion of $(1 + x)^n$ are in A.P. then n is equal to:

A. 5 B. 6
C. 7 D. 8

119. The length of shadow of a vertical pole on the horizontal ground is $\frac{1}{\sqrt{3}}$ times of its height, then the angle of elevation of the sun is:

A. 15° B. 30°
C. 45° D. 60°

120. $(\log_3 2) \cdot (\log_5 5) \cdot (\log_4 9)$ is equal to :

A. 1 B. 4
C. 3 D. 2

ANSWERS

1	2	3	4	5	6	7	8	9	10
B	A	D	A	C	C	A	D	B	D
11	**12**	**13**	**14**	**15**	**16**	**17**	**18**	**19**	**20**
C	B	D	A	B	A	D	B	D	C
21	**22**	**23**	**24**	**25**	**26**	**27**	**28**	**29**	**30**
C	C	C	A	B	B	D	B	A	B
31	**32**	**33**	**34**	**35**	**36**	**37**	**38**	**39**	**40**
B	C	B	C	D	D	C	B	C	B

41	42	43	44	45	46	47	48	49	50
A	B	D	A	A	D	D	C	C	C
51	**52**	**53**	**54**	**55**	**56**	**57**	**58**	**59**	**60**
B	B	A	A	C	A	D	A	B	D
61	**62**	**63**	**64**	**65**	**66**	**67**	**68**	**69**	**70**
A	B	A	A	D	C	D	A	A	B
71	**72**	**73**	**74**	**75**	**76**	**77**	**78**	**79**	**80**
D	B	A	C	C	D	D	C	D	A
81	**82**	**83**	**84**	**85**	**86**	**87**	**88**	**89**	**90**
B	A	C	C	D	D	A	A	C	A
91	**92**	**93**	**94**	**95**	**96**	**97**	**98**	**99**	**100**
B	C	B	A	C	A	D	B	C	C
101	**102**	**103**	**104**	**105**	**106**	**107**	**108**	**109**	**110**
B	C	D	A	D	B	B	B	C	A
111	**112**	**113**	**114**	**115**	**116**	**117**	**118**	**119**	**120**
B	B	B	B	C	B	A	C	D	A

EXPLANATORY ANSWERS

31. = Stands for +
× Stands for –
÷ Stands for ÷
+ Stands for ×
> Stands for =
< Stands for >
– Stands for <

(A) $3 + 2 - 4 > 16 \times 2 \div 4$
$1 > 8$ which is not true.

(B) $5 \times 2 \div 2 < 10 - 4 + 8$
$5 \times 1 < 18 - 4$
$\Rightarrow 5 < 13$ which is true.

(C) $3 + 4 \times 2 = 9 \div 3 - 3$
$\Rightarrow 3 + 8 = 3 - 3$
$\Rightarrow 11 = 0$ which is not true

(D) $5 + 3 - 7 > 8 \div 4 + 1$
$\Rightarrow 8 - 7 > 2 + 1$
$\Rightarrow 1 > 3$ which is not true.

Hence, option (B) is true.

37 and 38.

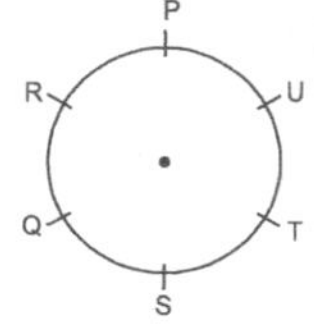

37. R is sitting opposite to T.

38. Q is sitting between R and S.

42. ∵ R E N T is written as
↓ ↓ ↓ ↓
÷ + × –

S A N D is written as
↓ ↓ ↓ ↓
* / × <

∴ S T A R T is written as
↓ ↓ ↓ ↓ ↓
* – / ÷ –

Hence, option (B) is correct.

58.

8	3	4
7	6	1
2	4	?
13	5	4

$(8 + 7) - 13 = 2$
$(3 + 6) - 5 = 4$
$(4 + 1) - 4 = 1$

Hence, the required missing number = 1.

91. $|x^2 + x + 6| < 6$

$-6 < x^2 + x + 6 < 6$

$x^2 + x + 6 < 6$

$\Rightarrow \quad x^2 + x < 0$

$x(x + 1) < 0$

$\therefore \quad x = (-1, 0)$

Set of real values of $x = (-1, 0)$.

94. Let, $y = f(x) = \dfrac{(e^x - e^{-x})}{(e^x + e^{-x})}$

$$y = \frac{e^x - e^{-x}}{(e^x + e^{-x})}$$

By compenendo & dividendo,

$$\frac{1+y}{1-y} = \frac{(e^x + e^{-x}) + (e^x - e^{-x})}{(e^x + e^{-x}) - (e^x - e^{-x})}$$

$$= \frac{2e^x}{2e^{-x}} = e^{2x}$$

Taking log on both sides, we have

$$\log\left(\frac{1+y}{1-y}\right) = \log e^{2x}$$

$$\log\left(\frac{1+y}{1-y}\right) = 2x$$

$$x = \frac{1}{2}\log\left(\frac{1+y}{1-y}\right)$$

$\therefore$ Inverse of the function $= \dfrac{1}{2}\log\left(\dfrac{1+x}{1-x}\right)$.

95. We have 1st term $= a$

2nd term $= b$

$\therefore$ d = common difference $= b - a$

It is given that last term is c

$$c = a + (n - 1)d$$

$$= a + (n - 1)(b - a)$$

$$\Rightarrow \quad \frac{c-a}{b-a} = n - 1$$

$$\Rightarrow \quad n = \frac{c-a}{b-a} + 1 = \frac{c-a+b-a}{b-a}$$

$$= \frac{b+c-2a}{b-a}$$

$$S_n = \frac{b+c-2a}{2(b-a)}\left\{2a + \left(\frac{b+c-2a}{b-a} - 1\right)d\right\}$$

$$= \frac{b+c-2a}{2(b-a)}\left[2a + \left(\frac{b+c-2a-b+a}{b-a}\right)(b-a)\right]$$

$$= \frac{b+c-2a}{2(b-a)}[2a+b+c-2a-b+a]$$

$$= \frac{b+c-2a}{2(b-a)} \times (c+a)$$

Sum of n terms of AP $= \dfrac{(a+c)(b+c-2a)}{2(b-a)}$

96. Let, $\langle a_n \rangle$ be a G.P. with common ratio r. Then,

$a_n = a_{n+1} + a_{n+2}$ (given)

$\Rightarrow \quad a_1 r^{n-1} = a_1 r^n + a_1 r^{n+1}$

$\Rightarrow \quad a_1(r^{n-1}) = a_1(r^n + r^{n+1})$

$\Rightarrow \quad r^{-1} = 1 + r \Rightarrow \dfrac{1}{r} = 1 + r$

$\Rightarrow \quad r^2 + r - 1 = 0 \quad \Rightarrow \quad r = \dfrac{-1 \pm \sqrt{5}}{2}$

$\Rightarrow \quad r = \dfrac{\sqrt{5}-1}{2}$ [$\because$ $r > 0$ given].

98.

1 or 2					

↑ 1st digit

1st digit can be placed in 2 ways

As repetition of the digit is allowed

So, remaining 5 digits can be formed in $(3)^5$ ways

$\therefore$ Number of Numbers $= 2 \times (3)^5$.

99. $A = \begin{pmatrix} \alpha & 2 \\ 2 & \alpha \end{pmatrix}$

$$A^2 = \begin{pmatrix} \alpha & 2 \\ 2 & \alpha \end{pmatrix}\begin{pmatrix} \alpha & 2 \\ 2 & \alpha \end{pmatrix}$$

$$= \begin{pmatrix} \alpha^2+4 & 2\alpha+2\alpha \\ 2\alpha+2\alpha & 4+\alpha^2 \end{pmatrix}$$

$$= \begin{pmatrix} \alpha^2+4 & 4\alpha \\ 4\alpha & \alpha^2+4 \end{pmatrix}$$

$$A^3 = \begin{pmatrix} \alpha^2+4 & 4\alpha \\ 4\alpha & \alpha^2+4 \end{pmatrix}\begin{pmatrix} \alpha & 2 \\ 2 & \alpha \end{pmatrix}$$

$$= \begin{pmatrix} \alpha(\alpha^2+4)+8\alpha & 2(\alpha^2+4)+4\alpha^2 \\ 4\alpha^2+2\alpha^2+8 & 8\alpha+\alpha(\alpha^2+4) \end{pmatrix}$$

$$= \begin{pmatrix} \alpha^3+12\alpha & 6\alpha^2+8 \\ 6\alpha^2+8 & \alpha^3+12\alpha \end{pmatrix}$$

$$= (\alpha^3 + 12\alpha)(\alpha^3 + 12\alpha) - (6\alpha^2 + 8)(6\alpha^2 + 8)$$

$$= (\alpha^3 + 12\alpha)^2 - (6\alpha^2 + 8)^2$$

For $\alpha = \pm 3$

$$\left((\pm3)^3 + 12(\pm3)\right)^2 - \left(6(\pm3)^2 + 8\right)^2 = 125.$$

100. $P(A \cup B) = P(A) + P(B) - P(A \cap B)$

$$\frac{5}{6} = \frac{2}{3} + \frac{1}{2} - P(A \cap B)$$

$$P(A \cap B) = \frac{2}{3} + \frac{1}{2} - \frac{5}{6}$$

$$= \frac{4+3-5}{6} = \frac{2}{6} = \frac{1}{3}$$

$$P(A \cap B) = \frac{1}{3}$$

$$P(A)\cdot P(B) = \frac{2}{3}\cdot\frac{1}{2} = \frac{1}{3}$$

$\therefore$ $P(A \cap B) = P(A)\cdot P(B)$

Hence, events A and B are independent events.

102. Point of intersection of two unparallel diameter gives centre of the circle.

$$2x - 3y - 5 = 0$$

$\Rightarrow$ $2x - 3y = 5$ ...(*i*)

$3x - 4y = 7$ ...(*ii*)

From (*i*) and (*ii*),

$\{2x - 3y = 5$ ...(*i*)$\} \times 4$

$\{3x - 4y = 7$ ...(*ii*)$\} \times 3$

$$8x - 12y = 20$$
$$9x - 12y = 21$$
$$- \quad + \qquad -$$

$-x = -1 \quad \Rightarrow x = 1$

$$2(1) - 3y = 5$$
$$-3y = 5 - 2 = 3$$
$$y = -1$$

Thus, centre of the circle = (1, –1)

From the given circle equation,

$$x^2 + y^2 - 2x + 2y - 47 = 0$$

$$\text{Centre of the circle} = \left(\frac{-(-2)}{2}, \frac{-2}{2}\right) = (1, -1).$$

105.

$$f(x) = \frac{1-x}{1+x}$$

$$f\left(\frac{1}{x}\right) = \frac{1-\frac{1}{x}}{1+\frac{1}{x}} = \frac{x-1}{x+1}$$

$$= -\left(\frac{1-x}{1+x}\right) = -f(x)$$

$$\therefore \quad f\left(\frac{1}{x}\right) = -f(x).$$

106. $\because$ p, q are the roots of the equation

$$x^2 + pq = (p + 1)x$$

$\Rightarrow$ $x^2 - (p + 1)x + pq = 0$

$$\text{Sum of the roots} = -\frac{b}{a}$$

$\Rightarrow$ $p + q = p + 1$

$\Rightarrow$ $q = 1$

Hence, value of $q = 1$.

107.

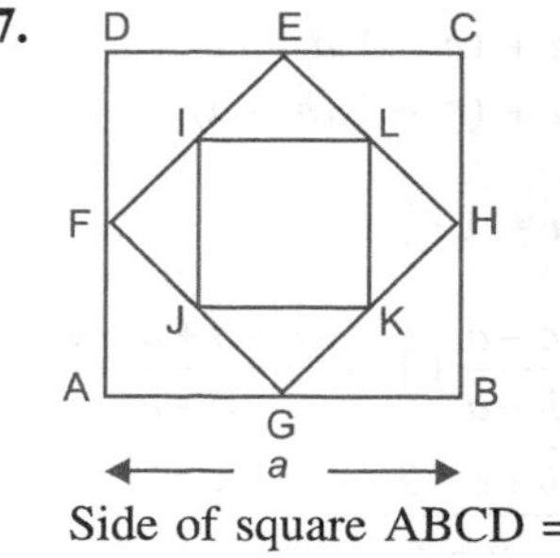

Side of square ABCD = a

Area of square ABCD = a^2

Side of square EFGH = $\sqrt{\left(\frac{a}{2}\right)^2+\left(\frac{a}{2}\right)^2}$

$= \sqrt{\frac{a^2}{4}+\frac{a^2}{4}}$

$= \sqrt{\frac{2a^2}{4}} = \sqrt{\frac{a^2}{2}} = \frac{a}{\sqrt{2}}$

Area of square EFGH = $\left(\frac{a}{\sqrt{2}}\right)^2 = \frac{a^2}{2}$

Side of square IJKL = $\sqrt{\left(\frac{a}{2\sqrt{2}}\right)^2+\left(\frac{a}{2\sqrt{2}}\right)^2}$

$= \sqrt{\frac{a^2}{8}+\frac{a^2}{8}}$

$= \sqrt{\frac{2a^2}{8}} = \sqrt{\frac{a^2}{4}} = \frac{a}{2}$

Area of square IJKL = $\left(\frac{a}{2}\right)^2 = \frac{a^2}{4}$

$\therefore \quad a^2 + \frac{a^2}{2}+\frac{a^2}{4} + \text{.........} \infty$

$$S = \frac{a}{1-r} = \frac{a^2}{1-\frac{1}{2}} = \frac{a^2}{\frac{1}{2}} = 2a^2.$$

108. Number of ways of placing a letter in the envelop = ${}^3P_2 = 3 \times 2 = 6$ ways

Out of the 6 ways, there is only one way to place all letters into write envelop = $\frac{1}{6}$.

109. The total no. of ways can post 5 letters in 10 boxes

= 10 × 10 × 10 × 10 × 10 ways

= 10^5 ways.

110. Required Sum = $(5 - 4)^n = (1)^n = 1$.

111. 50 workers can do a work in 15 days

1 worker can do a work in 50 × 15 days

75 workers can do a work in $\frac{50\times15}{75}$ days

= 10 days.

112. Let, no. of students = x

Total marks of x candidates = $x \times 60 = 60x$

Increased no = (70 – 50) × 10

= 20 × 10 = 200

New total no. = $x \times 65 = 65x$

$(65x - 60x) = 200 \Rightarrow 5x = 200$

$\Rightarrow \quad x = \frac{200}{5} = 40.$

113. From expansion of e^x, we have

$$e^x = 1 + x + \frac{x^2}{2!}+\frac{x^3}{3!}+\frac{x^4}{4!}+\ldots\infty$$

$$x\cdot e^x = x+x^2+\frac{x^3}{2!}+\frac{x^4}{3!}+\frac{x^5}{4!}+\ldots\infty$$

Differentiating both sides w.r.t. x, we have

$$\frac{d}{dx}(x\cdot e^x) = 1+2x+\frac{3x^2}{2!}+\frac{4x^3}{3!}+\ldots\infty$$

$$e^x + x\cdot e^x = 1+2x+\frac{3x^2}{2!}+\frac{4x^3}{3!}+\ldots\infty$$

for $\quad x = 1$

$$e + e = 1+2+\frac{3}{2!}+\frac{4}{3!}+\frac{5}{4!}+\ldots\infty$$

$$2e - 1 = 2+\frac{3}{2!}+\frac{4}{3!}+\frac{5}{4!}+\ldots\infty.$$

114. $\because \quad |\vec{\alpha}+\vec{\beta}| = |\vec{\alpha}-\vec{\beta}|$

$\Rightarrow \quad |\vec{\alpha}+\vec{\beta}|^2 = |\vec{\alpha}-\vec{\beta}|^2$

$|\vec{\alpha}|^2 + |\vec{\beta}|^2 + 2|\vec{\alpha}|\cdot|\vec{\beta}|$

$= |\vec{\alpha}|^2 + |\vec{\beta}|^2 - 2|\vec{\alpha}|\cdot|\vec{\beta}|$

$= 4|\vec{\alpha}|\cdot|\vec{\beta}| = 0.$

$\Rightarrow \vec{\alpha}$ is perpendicular to $\vec{\beta}$.

115. When a matrix of order $(n \times n)$ has determinant of value A is multiplied each element by constant k.

Then, determinant of new matrix $= (k)^n \cdot A$

Here, $k = 2$ and $n = 3$

$\therefore$ Determinant of new matrix

$$= (2)^3 \cdot A = 8A.$$

116. Let no. of books bought $= x$

$\because$ Cost of x books $=$ ₹ 80

$\therefore$ Cost of 1 book $=$ ₹ $\frac{80}{x}$

Now, cost of $(x + 4)$ books $=$ ₹ 80

$\therefore$ Cost of 1 book $=$ ₹ $\frac{80}{x+4}$

According to the question,

$$\frac{80}{x} - \frac{80}{x+4} = 1$$

$$\Rightarrow \frac{80x + 320 - 80x}{x(x+4)} = 1$$

$$\Rightarrow x^2 + 4x - 320 = 0$$

$$\Rightarrow x^2 + 20x - 16x - 320 = 0$$

$$\Rightarrow x(x + 20) - 16(x + 20) = 0$$

$$\Rightarrow (x - 16)(x + 20) = 0$$

$$\Rightarrow x = 16 \text{ or } x = -20$$

Hence, number of books bought $= 16$.

117.

$$\frac{1}{x+1} + \frac{2}{x+2} = \frac{5}{x+4}$$

$$\Rightarrow \frac{x+2+2x+2}{(x+1)(x+2)} = \frac{5}{x+4}$$

$$\Rightarrow \frac{3x+4}{x^2+2x+x+2} = \frac{5}{x+4}$$

$$\Rightarrow \frac{3x+4}{x^2+3x+2} = \frac{5}{x+4}$$

$$\Rightarrow 5x^2 + 15x + 10 = 3x^2 + 12x + 4x + 16$$

$$\Rightarrow 2x^2 - x - 6 = 0$$

$$\Rightarrow 2x^2 - 4x + 3x - 6 = 0$$

$$\Rightarrow 2x(x - 2) + 3(x - 2) = 0$$

$$\Rightarrow (2x + 3)(x - 2) = 0$$

$$\Rightarrow 2x + 3 = 0$$

$$\Rightarrow 2x = -3 \Rightarrow x = -\frac{3}{2}$$

Or $x - 2 = 0 \Rightarrow x = 2$

Hence, value of $x = 2$.

118. $(1 + x)^5 = {}^nC_0 1^5 + {}^nC_1(1)^4(x) + {}^nC_2(1)^3(x)^2 + {}^nC_3(1)^2(x)^3$

$$= 1 + \frac{5\times4!}{4!} + \frac{5\times4\times3!}{3!\times2} + \frac{5\times4\times3!}{3!\times2}$$

$$(1 + x)^6 = {}^nC_0 + {}^nC_1 + {}^nC_2 + {}^nC_3$$

$$= 1 + \frac{6\times5!}{5!} + \frac{6\times5\times4!}{4!\times2} + \frac{6\times5\times4\times3!}{3!\times3\times2}$$

$$(1 + x)^7 = 1 + \frac{7\times6!}{6!} + \frac{7\times6\times5!}{5!\times2} + \frac{7\times6\times5\times4!}{4!\times3\times2}$$

$$21 - 7 = 14$$

And $35 - 21 = 14$

Hence, $n = 7$.

119.

$$\tan\theta = \frac{h}{\frac{h}{\sqrt{3}}} = \sqrt{3}$$

$$\tan\theta = \tan 60°$$

$$\therefore \theta = 60°$$

Hence, the angle of elevation of the sum $= 60°$.

120. $(\log_3 2) \cdot (\log_5 5) \cdot (\log_4 9)$

$$= \frac{\log 2}{\log 3} \times \frac{\log 5}{\log 5} \times \frac{\log 9}{\log 4}$$

$$= \frac{\log 2}{\log 3} \times \frac{\log 5}{\log 5} \times \frac{2\log 3}{2\log 2} = 1$$

Previous Papers (Solved)

BBA/BBS Entrance Exam, 2015*

ENGLISH LANGUAGE

PASSAGE-I

Twenty-first-century readers can be broadly divided into two categories: those who read e-books (in an electronic, digital format) and those like me who prefer to curl up with the original printed version. And so what if the world's largest online retailer Amazon announced that it was selling 105 e-books for every 100 print books? Amazon also announced that sales of print books were going up. Going to bed with a paperback or hardcover may be old-fashioned, but you can fall asleep while reading without worrying about the battery life on the e-reader. "As we get older, we get honester," goes the first line of Yevgeny Yevtushenko's 1956 Russian poem, *Zima Junction.* As we get older, we also get more sleepless. And for those who like to read, nothing can be as sooting as a book that makes you forget the problems that keep you awake and takes you away to a different world until you fall asleep. Even the most sophisticated e-reader is not as user-friendly as a paperback or a hardcover that you can carry in all kinds of weater (from snowstorms to tsunamis) and wherever you go (from the office, the park and the zoo, to the hospital or even the metro that has just started rolling in India's pensioner's paradise-turned-Silicon Plateau). You can even take a book to war. A copy to *Three Men in a boat* (one of the funniest books in English literature, first published in 1889) was found in the knapsack of a British soldier who was killed at Spion Kop during the Boer War of 1900. Watch a telecast of any cricket match anywhere in the world and the camera invariably zooms in on that one male or female spectator who is reading a printed book, with the cameraman voyeuristically trying to give the viewers a glimpse of the cover and title. Maybe, one day, someone will publish a book titled 'What to read at the match!' In the very first summer after World War-II ended and cricket resumed in England, the poet-turned-sports commentator John Arlott wrote a book, '*Off for the cricket*', which perhaps explains why Arlott was called the voice of summer. Books remain the ideal gift for all occasions and festivals. I have forgotten much of what they taught me at schools, but I remember the books presented to me at annual prize distribution functions.

1. Which of the following statements could be inferred from the passage?
   A. Sales of books is increasing, although sales of print books is declining
   B. E-books are surely going to phase out print books in the not-too-distant future
   C. Sale of e-books is higher than the sale of print versions
   D. All these

2. The author believes that books make the ideal gifts because
   A. they are inexpensive and affordable
   B. they could be presented on all occasion includeing festivals
   C. books remain with you forever even through memories may fade away with time
   D. they could be on a myriad of topics

3. Where all do people possible carry books to read, as per the author?
   1. To war
   2. To cricket matches
   3. To office

* Held on 09/05/2015

A. 2 only B. 2 and 3
C. 3 only D. 1, 2 and 3

4. What are the advantages offered by print over e-books, as outlined in the passage?
1. These help you forget the worries that make you sleepless.
2. These are more portable.
3. These cost less money than buying an e-reader.

A. 2 only B. 2 and 3
C. 1 and 2 D. 1, 2 and 3

5. It is implied from the passage that ....
A. People are more turning towards e-books than printed books
B. With the modern civilisation, printed books are selling more than e-books but in less amount
C. e-books have become the ideal gift for all occassions and festivals
D. None of the given options is true

PASSAGE-II

Climatic conditions are delicately adjusted to the composition of the Earth's atmosphere. If there were a change in the atmosphere, for example, in the relative proportions of atmospheric gases, the climate would probably also change. A slight increase in water vapour, for instance, would increase the heat-retaining capacity of the atmosphere and would lead to a rise in global temperatures. In contrast, a large increase in water vapour would increase the thickness and extent of the cloud layer, reducing the amount of solar energy reaching the Earth's surface.

The level of carbon dioxide, CO_2, in the atmosphere has an important effect on climatic change. Most of the Earth's incoming energy is short-wavelength radiation, which tends to pass through atmospheric CO_2 easily. The Earth, however, reradiates much of the received energy as long wavelength radiation, which CO_2 absorbs and then remits toward the Earth. This phenomenon, known as the green house effect, can result in an increase in the surface temperature of a planet. An extreme example of the effect is shown by Venus, a planet covered by heavy clouds composed mostly of CO_2, whose surface temperatures have been measured at 430°C. If the CO_2 concentration were halved, the Earth would become completely covered with ice. Another equally respectable theory, however, states that halving of the CO_2 concentration would lead only to a reduction in global temperatures of 3°C.

I because of an increase in forest fires or volcanic actitity, CO_2 content of the atmosphere increased, a warmer climate would be produced. Plant growth, which relies on both the warmth and the availability of CO_2, would probably increase. As a consequence, plants would use more and more CO_2. Eventually, CO_2 levels would diminish and the climate, in turn, would become cooler. With reduced temperatures many plants would die; CO_2 would thereby be returned to the atmosphere and gradually the temperature would rise again. Thus, if this process occurred, there might be a longest magnitude. Some climatologists argue that the burning of fossil fuels has raised the level of CO_2 in the atmosphere and has caused a global temperature increase of at least 1°C. But a supposed global temperature rise of 1°C may in reality be only several regional temperature increases, restricted to areas where there are mainly meteorological stations and caused simply by shifts in the pattern of atmospheric circulation. Other areas, for example, the Southern Hemisphere oceanic zone may be experiencing an equivalent temperature decrease that is unrecognized because of the shortage of meteorological recording stations.

6. The passage supplies information for answering which of the following questions?
A. Why are projections of the effects of changes in water vapour levels on the climate so inaccurate?
B. What are the steps in the process that take place as CO_2 absorbs long-wavelength radiation?
C. How can our understanding of the green house effect be improved if the burning of fossil fuels decrease?
D. What might cause a series of regular increase and decrease in the amount of CO_2 in the atmosphere?

7. The author is primarily concerned with
   A. explaining the effects that the burning of fossil fuel might have on climate
   B. illustrating the effect of CO_2 on atmospheric radiation
   C. discussing effects that changes in the CO_2 level in the atmosphere might have on climate
   D. challenging hypotheses about the effects of water vapour and CO_2 on climate

8. The passage suggests that a large decrease in the amount of CO_2 in the atmosphere would result in
   A. at least a sligth decrease in global temperature
   B. at the most a slight increase in short wavelength radiation reaching the Earth
   C. a slight long-term increase in global temperatures
   D. a large long-term increase in the amount of volcanic activity

9. The author refers to Venus primarily in order to
   A. show the inherent weakness of the green house effect theory
   B. show that the green house effect works on other planets but not on Earth
   C. show the extent to which Earth's atmosphere differs from that of Venus
   D. support the contention that as water vapour increases, the amount of CO_2 increases

10. What according to some climatologists is the reason of global temperature increase of 1°C and increased level of CO_2?
   A. Increasing population
   B. Increase in water vapour
   C. Long wave length radiation
   D. Burning of fossil fuels

Directions (Qs. 11 to 13): *Fill in the blanks.*

11. The term "rare earth's" is in fact a ...., for, paradoxically, the rare-earth elements are in actuality .... being present in low concentration in virtually all minerals.
   A. truism, essential
   B. misnomer, ubiquitous
   C. disclaimer, ephemeral
   D. metaphor, figurative

12. The columnist was very gentle when he mentioned his friends, but was bitter and even .... when he discussed people who .... him.
   A. laconic, infuriated
   B. acerbic, irritated
   C. remorseful, encouraged
   D. militant, distressed

13. She conducted the interrogation not only with dispatch but with ...., being a person who is .... in manner yet subtle in discrimination.
   A. elan, enthusiastic
   B. equanimity, abrupt
   C. finesse, expeditious
   D. zeal, doctrinaire

Directions (Qs. 14 to 18): *Choose the word of phrase nearly similar in meaning to the given word.*

14. Self-esteem
   A. Self-respect   B. Dignity
   C. Decorum   D. Self-awareness

15. Conformity
   A. Consensus   B. Relevance
   C. Compatibility   D. Consistency

16. Insolent
   A. Defiant   B. Attack
   C. Impudent   D. Charge

17. Sobriety
   A. Abstinence   B. Sober
   C. Moderate   D. Dry

18. Analogy
   A. Ratio   B. Similarity
   C. Associate   D. Relevant

Directions (Qs. 19 to 23): *In these questions, four parts of a sentence are marked as A, B, C and D and are in sequence. Select the part which is not acceptable in standard written English.*

19. A. His all daughters   B. are uneducated
   C. so they   D. cannot be married

20. A. In no circumstances
B. will the Principal
C. permit students
D. to be absent

21. A. The professor B. emphasised on
C. the point D. again and again

22. A. The reason B. of his failure
C. is due to D. his negligence

23. A. You will reach B. on time
C. because the train D. is running in time

Directions (Qs. 24 to 26): *Choose the correctly spelt word.*

24. A. Pediatrician B. Paeditrician
C. Peditirician D. Peditrician

25. A. Cannebalism B. Cannebelism
C. Cannebilism D. Cannibalism

26. A. Numereology B. Numerology
C. Numbereology D. Numeriology

Directions (Qs. 27 to 31): *In each of these questions, a sentence is given with four underlined portions marked as A, B, C and D. Select the option that has an error.*

27. Shyam had (A)/ atleast (B)/ four hundred (C)/ of books. (D)
A. A B. B
C. C D. D

28. Thirty kilometres (A)/ are (B)/ a (C)/ long way to walk. (D)
A. A B. B
C. C D. D

29. We have (A)/ just lost (B)/ an (C)/ irreparable colleague. (D)
A. A B. B
C. C D. D

30. The cat chased (A)/ a bird who (B)/ few and perched itself (C)/ on a branch of a tree. (D)
A. A B. B
C. C D. D

31. Mr. Malhotra, along (A)/ with (B)/ his friends were (C)/ invited to dinner. (D)
A. A B. B
C. C D. D

Directions (Qs. 32 to 36): *In the following questions a sentence is given. Some parts of the sentence have been jumbled up. You are required to rearrange these parts which are labelled as P, Q, R and S to produce the correct sentence. Choose the most appropriate answer option.*

32. Since
P : life has now become intensely competitive.
Q : not only by the grades he obtains.
R : but also by his skill of observation and logical reasoning.
S : We judge a person's intellectual worth.
The proper sequence should be:
A. SQRP B. PSRQ
C. PQRS D. PSQR

33. It is known that
P : the world's greatest men
Q : becoming rich
R : with a view to
S : have not laboured
The proper sequence should be:
A. PRQS B. RQPS
C. PSRQ D. RQSP

34. By the time
P : known to everyone
Q : we appeared on the scene
R : he had already become an institution
S : who had ever stayed at Anand Bhawan
The proper sequence should be:
A. QPRS B. PSQR
C. QRPS D. RSQP

35. I can guarantee
P : as a medical representative
Q : without any doubt
R : for the post for which he has applied
S : that this candidate will be successful
The proper sequence should be:
A. SPRQ B. SRQP
C. PSRQ D. QSPR

36. The broker said the
P : a person
Q : should shop carefully
R : who buys a house
S : for the lowest interest rate

The proper sequence should be:
A. SPRQ B. PRQS
C. SPQR D. PSRQ

Directions (Qs. 37 to 40): *Each sentence consists of a word or a phrase which is printed in bold. It is followed by four words. Select the word which is closest to the opposite in meaning to the bold part.*

37. I took a **durable** pair of shoes when I went on the trip.
A. worn out B. fragile
C. light D. delicate

38. He was **erroneous** in his assessment of her character.
A. justified B. impartial
C. sincere D. correct

39. His father was generally **gratified** with his examination report.
A. displeased B. worried
C. surprised D. disheartened

40. There is a **fair** chance that we might win the game.
A. distant B. unlikely
C. remote D. bare

NUMERICAL & DATA ANALYSIS

41. A micro organism doubles itself numerically every 24 hours. At the end of 30 days, its number was 84 lakh. On which day, it was 21 lakh?
A. 14th day B. 20th day
C. 28th day D. 29th day

42. The average age of 10 students is 15 years. When 5 new students joined, the average age rose by one year. The average age, in yeas, of the new students is ....
A. 18 B. 16
C. 15 D. 17

43. If one-seventh of a number exceeds its one-eleventh by 100, then the number is ....
A. 770 B. 1925
C. 1825 D. 1200

44. A spherical structure of diameter 10 meters is to be painted on the outer surface. Approximately, what amount would required to paint it @ ₹ 80 per sq. metre?
A. ₹ 25140 B. ₹ 40220
C. ₹ 10550 D. ₹ 12780

45. A ladder 50' long is placed in a lane such that it reaches a window 40' high. On turning the ladder to the other side, keeping the feet at the same place, it reaches a point 30 ft high. What is the breadth of the lane?
A. 50 ft B. 60 ft
C. 80 ft D. 70 ft

46. A and B have some money in the ratio of 3 : 5. After A spends ₹ 40 and B spends ₹ 90, the money left with A and B is in the ratio of 7 : 11. The amounts they respectively had in the beginning were ....
A. ₹ 285, ₹ 475 B. ₹ 225, ₹ 425
C. ₹ 270, ₹ 450 D. ₹ 300, ₹ 500

47. A shopkeeper mixes two kinds of flours, one costing ₹ 3.50 per kg and the other ₹ 2.25 per kg, so that the price of the mixture is ₹ 2.75 per kg. The ratio of the first kind of flour to that of the second kind is ....
A. 4 : 3 B. 3 : 4
C. 3 : 2 D. 2 : 3

48. In an examination 900 candidates were boys and 600 were girls. If 30% of the boys and 40% of the girls passed the examination, then the percentage of total number of candidates that failed in the examination is ....
A. 42% B. 34%
C. 58% D. 66%

49. In an examination, there are 3 papers of Mathematics of 100 marks each. A boy secures 60% in the first paper, and 70% in the second paper. In order to secure 70% in the aggregate, the percentage of marks he should secure in third paper will be ....

A. 90% B. 80%
C. 75% D. 70%

50. A manufacturer sold an article at a profit of 4% to the wholesaler. The wholesaler sold the same at 5% profit to the retailer. If the retailer paid ₹ 273 for the articles then the cost price of manufacturer is ....
A. ₹ 250 B. ₹ 260
C. ₹ 270 D. ₹ 280

51. A salesman's commission is 5% on all sales upto ₹ 10,000 and 4% on all sales exceeding this. He remits ₹ 31,100 to his parent company after deducting his commission. His sales worth (in ₹) were ....
A. 32,500 B. 35,000
C. 35,100 D. 36,100

52. In a town, the population was 8000. In one year, male population increased by 10% and female population increased by 8% but the total population increased by 9%. Number of males in the town was ....
A. 4500 B. 6000
C. 5000 D. 4000

53. Three persons, whose monthly salaries together amount to ₹ 14,400, spend 80%, 85% and 75% of their salaries respectively. If their savings are in the ratio of 8 : 9 : 20, their salaries (monthly) are ....
A. ₹ 3200, ₹ 4800, ₹ 6400
B. ₹ 4800, ₹ 3200, ₹ 6400
C. ₹ 4800, ₹ 6400, ₹ 3200
D. ₹ 6400, ₹ 4800, ₹ 3200

54. A number when divided by 32 leaves the remainder is 29. This number when divided by 8 will leave the remainder ....
A. 3 B. 5
C. 7 D. 29

55. A man has ₹ 480 in the denominations of one rupee notes, five rupee notes and ten rupee notes. The number of notes each denomination is equal. What is the total number of notes he has?
A. 45 B. 60
C. 75 D. 90

56. The number of grams of water needed to reduce 9 grams of shaving lotion containing 50% alcohol to a lotion containing 30% alcohol, is ....
A. 4 B. 5
C. 6 D. 7

57. A, B and C together can complete a piece of work in 10 days. Al the three started working at it together and after 4 days, A left, then, B and C together completed the work in 10 more days. A alone could have completed the work in
A. 15 days B. 16 days
C. 25 days D. 50 days

58. The ratio between the rates of walking of A and B is 2 : 3. If the time taken by B to cover a certain distance is 36 minutes, the time in minutes taken by A to cover that much distance is ....
A. 24 B. 38
C. 48 D. 54

59. The wheel of an engine, metres $7\frac{1}{2}$ metres in circumference makes 7 revolutions in 9 seconds. The speed of the train in km per hour is ....
A. 150 B. 132
C. 130 D. 135

60. At an election, a candidate secures 40% of the votes but was defeated by the other candidate by a margin of 298 votes. The total number of votes recorded were ....
A. 1360 B. 1490
C. 1520 D. 1602

Directions (Qs. 61 to 65): *Study the stacked bar graph carefully to answer these questions.*

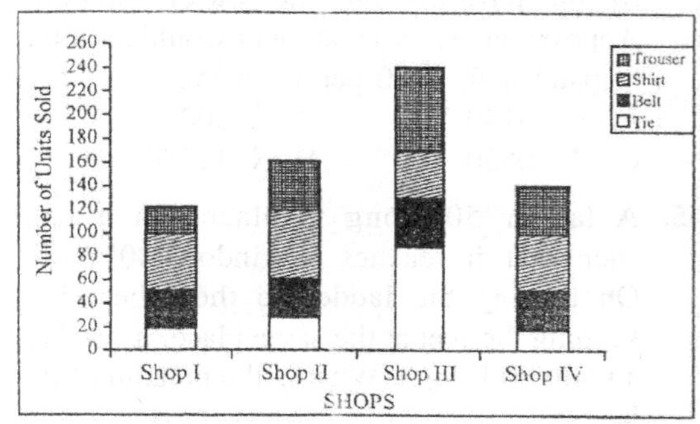

61. The total number of items sold in all shops is ....
A. 660
B. 540
C. 740
D. Cannot be determined

62. If shop I were to sell twice the number of ties and thrice the number of all other items, then the total number of items sold by it would be ....
A. 300 B. 225
C. 340 D. 475

63. If every item sold earns a profit of ₹ 10 on which a tax of 50% is levied, the profit after tax of shop IV is ₹ ....
A. 500 B. 700
C. 750 D. 1025

64. The total number of trousers sold by all shops is ....
A. 108 B. 125
C. 95 D. 160

65. Total sales of ties are how much greater than the total sales of shirts?
A. 15% B. 31%
C. 35% D. 40%

Directions (Qs. 66 to 70): *The gross investments of Life Insurance Corporation of India (In crores of rupees) in different sectors are shown in the Pie Chart given below.*

Answer the questions on the basis of information given in the pie chart.

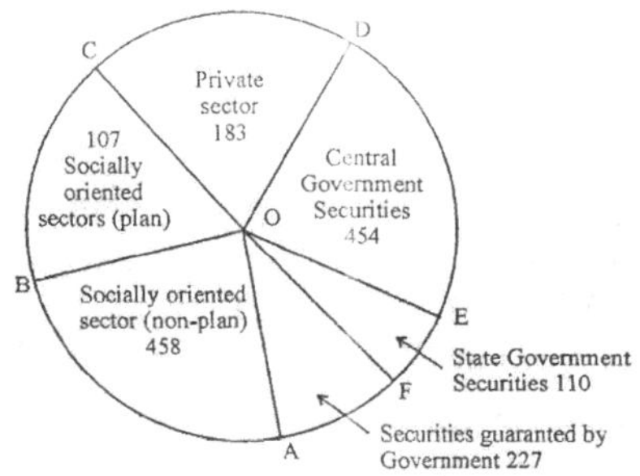

66. The percentage of gross investment in State Government Securities is nearly ....
A. 7.1% B. 7.8%
C. 8.6% D. 9.2%

67. The magnitude of ∠AOC is nearly ....
A. 123° B. 132°
C. 126° D. 115°

68. The investment in socially oriented sectors (plan and non plan) is .... than the investment in Government Securities (Central and State) by ....
A. more, 4 crore B. more, 1 crore
C. more, 111 crore D. less, 106 crore

69. The investment in private sectors is nearly .... percent higher than the investment in State Government Securities.
A. 66 B. 54
C. 46 D. 40

70. The ratio of the area of the circle above COF to the area of the circle below it, is nearly ....
A. 1 B. 0.966
C. 0.94 D. 0.92

REASONING AND INTELLIGENCE

Directions (Qs. 71 to 74): *Study the Information given below to answer these questions.*

P, Q, R, S, T, V and W are travelling in three different vehicles. There are at least two passengers in each vehicle I, II and III and one of them is a lady. There are two engineers, two doctors and three teachers among them. R is a lady doctor and she does not travel with the pair of sisters P and V. Q, a male engineer travels with only W, a teacher in vehicle I. S is a male doctor. Two persons belonging to the same profession do not travel in the same vehicle. P is not an engineer and travels in vehicle II.

71. What is V's profession?
A. Engineer B. Teacher
C. Doctor D. Data inadequate

72. In which vehicle does R travel?
A. I
B. II
C. III
D. II or III

73. Which of the following represents the three teachers?
A. WTV
B. WTP
C. WTV or WTP
D. Data inadequate

74. Which of the following is not correct?
A. T-Male-Teacher
B. Q-Male-Engineer
C. P-Female-Teacher
D. V-Female-Teacher

Directions (Qs. 75 to 78): *In each of these questions, a series is given with one term missing. Choose the correct alternative from the given ones that will complete the series.*

75. 125, 235, 345, 455, (.........)
A. 465
B. 565
C. 575
D. 665

76. 15, 16, 20, 29, (.........)
A. 42
B. 45
C. 54
D. 38

77. V, T, (.........), P, N
A. S
B. Q
C. O
D. R

78. (.........), HJL, NPR, TVX, ZBD
A. BDF
B. BFD
C. BED
D. CFI

Directions (Qs. 79 to 82): *Below are given role numbers of some candidates registered at different centres for an examination. The first two digits from the left stand for the centre code and the next four for the serial number of the candidates registered at the centre. Now answer the questions based on this sample of numbers.*

A	B	C	D
181927	817929	887386	332896
333782	651923	888325	513338
887325	474312	511927	888187
651200	336378	338379	475347
474321	184320	184843	814752
812783	882345	817131	189901

79. Which of the following centres has highest serial number?
A. 47
B. 18
C. 88
D. 81

80. Which of the following centres has lowest serial number?
A. 51
B. 88
C. 65
D. 33

81. Which one of the following centre pairs had some common serial numbers?
A. 88 and 81
B. 33 and 51
C. 65 and 47
D. 18 and 51

82. Which centre code is represented maximum no. of times?
A. 88
B. 33
C. 51
D. 18

Directions (Qs. 83 to 85): *Select the one which is different from the other three responses.*

83. A. Book
B. Magazine
C. Journal
D. Paper

84. A. YWU
B. PRT
C. DFH
D. IKM

85. A. 11
B. 13
C. 17
D. 21

Directions (Qs. 86 to 89): *Read the following information and answer the questions that follow.*

There is a family of six persons A, B, C, D, E and F. They are Lawyer, Doctor, Teacher, Salesman, Engineer and Accountant. There are two married couples in the family. D, the salesman is married to the Lady Teacher. The Doctor is married to the Lawyer. F, the Accountant is the son of B and brother of E. C, the Lawyer is the daughter-in-law of A. E, is the unmarried Engineer. A, is the grandmother of F.

86. How is E related to F?
A. Brother
B. Sister
C. Cousin Brother
D. Cannot be determined

87. Which of the following is the profession of B?
A. Teacher
B. Doctor
C. Lawyer
D. Cannot be determined

88. Which of the following is the profession of A?
A. Lawyer
B. Teacher
C. Doctor
D. Cannot be determined

89. Which of the following is one of the couples?
A. F D B. D B
C. E A D. None of these

Directions (Qs. 90 to 92): *A cube is coloured red on three adjacent faces. It is then cut into four cuboids of equal size. Each of these cuboids is coloured green on all the uncoloured faces and is then cut into four cubiods of equal size.*

90. How many cuboids have three red faces each?
A. 1 B. 2
C. 4 D. 8

91. How many cuboids have two green faces each?
A. 3 B. 5
C. 6 D. 9

92. How many cuboids have three green faces each?
A. 4 B. 5
C. 7 D. 9

Directions (Qs. 93 to 94): *The two given items have a definite relationship. Find out the set with similar relationship from the options given.*

93. Postcard : inland
A. pillow : cot B. shirt : blouse
C. flower : bunch D. boat : oars

94. stare : glance
A. gulp : sip B. confide : tell
C. hunt : stalk D. step : walk

Directions (Qs. 95 to 100): *There are four answer options to each question. Choose the correct answer.*

95. Ramesh, Rahim and Robert play a game of cards. Ramesh says to Rahim "If I give you 5 cards and you give me 3 cards and Robert gives me 4 cards and one to you, you will have twice as many cards as yours." If the total number of cards be 45, how many cards does Rahim have initially?
A. 3 B. 7
C. 10 D. 28

96. If two-third of three-fourth of a number added to three-fourth of the four-fifth of the number is x times the number, the value of x is ....
A. 11/10 B. 1/11
C. 10/11 D. 9/11

97. In a queue, Sohan is 9th from the back. Ramesh's place is 8th from the front. Radhey is standing in between the two. What could be the minimum number of boys standing in the queue?
A. 8 B. 10
C. 12 D. 14

98. In a certain code 'FORGET' is written as 'DPPHCU'.
How would 'DOCTOR' be written in that code?
A. BPAUMS B. BPAUPS
C. EMDRPP D. BPARPP

99. If the first and the second letters in the word INORDINATE were interchanged, also the third and the fourth letter, the fifth and sixth and so on, which letter would be eighth counting to your left?
A. A B. D
C. N D. R

100. From a given piece of cloth 10 cm × 10 cm, the maximum number of 3 cm × 3 cm pieces that one can cut out of it would be
A. 9 pieces. B. 10 pieces.
C. 11 pieces. D. 12 pieces.

GENERAL KNOWLEDGE

101. Purest water is
A. river water B. tube well water
C. rain water D. ocean water

102. Jnanpith Award is awarded for
A. sports B. social work
C. literature D. music

103. Typhoid fever is caused by
A. bacteria B. allergy
C. fungus D. virus

104. Capital of Manipur is
A. Guwahati B. Shillong
C. Imphal D. Itanagar

105. With which of the following sports is the Subroto Cup associated?
A. Hockey B. Cricket
C. Tennis D. Football

106. Head quarters of International Labour Organisation are situated at
A. Geneva B. New York
C. Washington D. Paris

107. .... is known as Nightingale of India.
A. Mother Teresa
B. Sarojini Naidu
C. M.S. Subba Laxmi
D. Lata Mangeshkar

108. Lord Budha died at
A. Patna B. Gaya
C. Kushi Nagar D. Lumbini

109. Where is the Indian Military Academy located?
A. Hyderabad B. Chennai
C. Khadakwasla D. None of these

110. India has been a member of the United Nations since ....
A. 1945 B. 1946
C. 1947 D. 1951

111. Which country is known as the 'Land of the Rising Sun'?
A. Japan B. Bangladesh
C. Norway D. Australia

112. The instrument which can record accurate time is called
A. Hydrometer B. Anemometer
C. Chronometer D. None of these

113. Which of the following is the dance form of Kerala?
A. Kathak B. Kathakali
C. Kuchipudi D. Bharat Natyam

114. The UN body concerned with the welfare of children is
A. UNICEF B. UNCTAD
C. UNIDO D. UNESCO

115. National Anthem was written by
A. B.C. Chatterjee B. Prem Chand
C. Sarojini Naidu D. None of these

116. Who among the following said "Independence is our birht right"?
A. Mahatma Gandhi
B. Jawaharlal Nehru
C. Lala Lajpat Rai
D. Bal Gangadhar Tilak

117. 'Ashes' is the term associated with which of the following sports?
A. Football B. Hockey
C. Cricket D. Basket ball

118. Hirakud Dam is situated in
A. Andhra Pradesh B. West Bengal
C. Orissa D. Assam

119. Panchatantra was written by
A. Kalidas B. Vishnu Sharma
C. Tulsidas D. Jaydev

120. Which state does not have Atomic Power Project?
A. Rajasthan B. Maharashtra
C. Uttar Pradesh D. Punjab

121. Ritu Kumar is a well known
A. Painter B. Fashion designer
C. Musician D. Architect

122. Which among the following states has been declared recently as the first 'total banking state' in India?

A. Kerala B. Karnataka
C. Punjab D. Gujarat

123. Where is India's first operational Special economic Zone (SEZ) located?
A. Indore B. Bombay
C. Ahmedabad D. Surat

124. National education Day is celebrated in India in ....
A. 11 November B. 11 December
C. 21 November D. 21 December

125. Which of the following countries is the biggest trading partner of Russia?
A. China B. India
C. USA D. Ukraine

126. The country that accounts for nearly one-third of the total teak production in the world is ....
A. India B. Sri Lanka
C. Myanmar D. Pakistan

127. Monte Carlo is a leading Indian brand of ....
A. Winter wear and apparels
B. Casual wear only
C. Formal wear only
D. Fashion accessories

128. MYCK is a leading Indian made brand of ....
A. jewellery B. cosmetics
C. photofilm D. None of these

129. 'United Colours of Benetton' is a leading brand of ....
A. apparel B. cosmetics
C. photofilm D. None of these

130. The longest train journey in India is between ....
A. Trivandrum-Jammu Tawi
B. Dibrugarh-Chennai
C. Mumbai-Kolkata
D. Kanyakumari-Dibrugarh

ANSWERS

1	2	3	4	5	6	7	8	9	10
C	B	D	C	A	D	C	A	C	D
11	**12**	**13**	**14**	**15**	**16**	**17**	**18**	**19**	**20**
B	D	C	B	D	C	A	B	A	C
21	**22**	**23**	**24**	**25**	**26**	**27**	**28**	**29**	**30**
D	C	B	A	D	B	D	B	D	C
31	**32**	**33**	**34**	**35**	**36**	**37**	**38**	**39**	**40**
C	D	C	C	D	B	B	D	A	C
41	**42**	**43**	**44**	**45**	**46**	**47**	**48**	**49**	**50**
C	A	B	A	D	A	D	D	B	A
51	**52**	**53**	**54**	**55**	**56**	**57**	**58**	**59**	**60**
A	D	A	B	D	C	C	D	A	B
61	**62**	**63**	**64**	**65**	**66**	**67**	**68**	**69**	**70**
A	C	B	D	A	A	B	A	A	C
71	**72**	**73**	**74**	**75**	**76**	**77**	**78**	**79**	**80**
A	C	B	D	B	B	D	A	B	C
81	**82**	**83**	**84**	**85**	**86**	**87**	**88**	**89**	**90**
A	A	D	A	D	D	B	B	D	A
91	**92**	**93**	**94**	**95**	**96**	**97**	**98**	**99**	**100**
C	C	C	C	A	A	B	A	C	A

101	102	103	104	105	106	107	108	109	110
C	C	A	C	D	A	B	C	D	A
111	**112**	**113**	**114**	**115**	**116**	**117**	**118**	**119**	**120**
A	C	B	D	D	D	C	C	B	D
121	**122**	**123**	**124**	**125**	**126**	**127**	**128**	**129**	**130**
B	A	A	A	A	C	A	D	A	D

Some Selected Explanatory Answers

41. $\because$ At the end of 30 days the number of micro organisms = 84 lakh

$\therefore$ 29th day no. of micro organism = 42 lakh

Hence, 28th day no. of micro organism = 21 lakh.

42. Total age of 10 students

$= 10 \times 15 = 150$ years

Total age with new 5 students

$= 15 \times 16 = 240$ years

$\therefore$ Total age of new 5 students

$= 240 - 150 = 90$ years

$\therefore$ Average age of new students $= \frac{90}{5}$

$= 18$ years.

43. Let the number $= x$

According to the question,

$$\frac{1}{7}x = \frac{1}{11}x+100$$

$$\Rightarrow \quad \frac{x}{7}-\frac{x}{11} = 100$$

$$\Rightarrow \quad \frac{11x-7x}{77} = 100$$

$$\Rightarrow \quad 4x = 7700$$

$$\Rightarrow \quad x = \frac{7700}{4} = 1925$$

Hence, the number = 1925.

44. Surface area of sphere $= 4\pi r^2$

$$= 4\times\frac{22}{7}\times5\times5$$

$$= \frac{2200}{7} m^2$$

cost of 1 m^2 = ₹ 80

cost of $\frac{2200}{7} m^2$ = ₹ $\frac{2200}{7}\times 80$

$= \frac{176000}{7}$ = ₹ 25142

= ₹ 25140 (Approx.)

45.

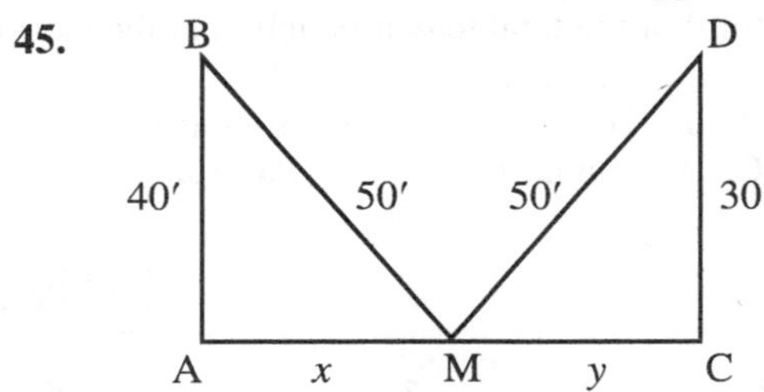

In ΔABM, $x = \sqrt{(50)^2-(40)^2}$

$= \sqrt{2500-1600} = \sqrt{900} = 30'$

In ΔDCM, $y = \sqrt{(50)^2-(30)^2}$

$= \sqrt{2500-900}$

$= \sqrt{1600} = 40'$

$\therefore \quad x + y = 30 + 40 = 70$ feet

Hence, breadth of the lane = 70 feet.

46. Let amount of A = ₹ $3x$

and amount of B = ₹ $5x$

According to the question,

$$\frac{3x-40}{5x-90} = \frac{7}{11}$$

$$\Rightarrow \quad 35x - 630 = 33x - 440$$

$$\Rightarrow \quad 2x = 190$$

$$\Rightarrow \quad x = 95$$

Amount of A $= 3x = 3 \times 95$ = ₹ 285

Amount of B $= 5x = 5 \times 95$ = ₹ 475.

47. 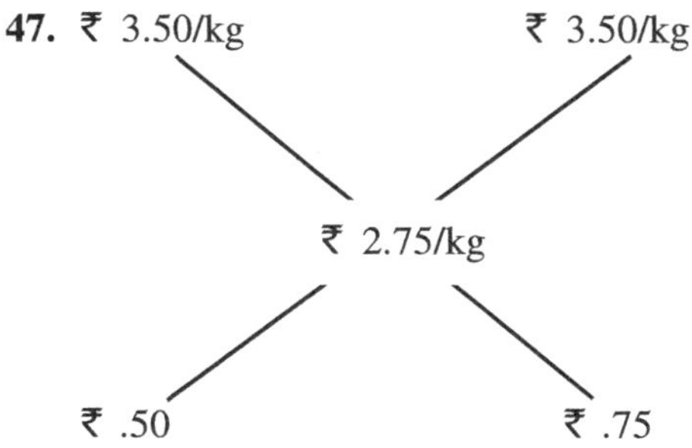

Required ratio = $\frac{.50}{.75}$ = 2 : 3.

48. No. of boys passed in the examination

$= \frac{30}{100} \times 900 = 270$

No. of girls passed in the examination

$= \frac{40}{100} \times 600 = 240$

Total no. of students passed in the examination
= 270 + 240 = 510

Total no. of studends appear in the examination
= 900 + 600 = 1500

Total no. of students failed in the examination
= 1500 – 510 = 990

% no. of students failed in the examination

$= \frac{990}{1500} \times 100 = 66\%.$

49. Total marks obtained in two paper
= 60 + 70 = 130

Total mark obtained in three papers

$= \frac{70}{100} \times 300 = 210$

Marks obtained by boy in third paper
= 210 – 130 = 80

He should secure % marks in third paper
= 80%.

50. Let cost price of manufacture = ₹ 100

Cost price of wholesaler = 100 + 4 = ₹ 104

Cost price of retailer = $\frac{5}{100} \times 104 + 104$
= 5.20 + 104
= ₹ 109.20

When cost price of retailer ₹ 109.20 then cost price of manufacture = ₹ 100

When cost price of retailer ₹ 273 then cost price of manufacture

$= \frac{100}{109.20} \times 273$

$= \frac{100 \times 100 \times 273}{10920}$

= 25 × 10 = ₹ 250.

51. Let his total sales be ₹ x

Now, Total sales – commission = ₹ 31100

$\therefore \quad x - \left[\frac{5}{100} \times 10000 + \frac{4}{100}(x - 10000)\right] = 31100$

$\Rightarrow \quad x - 500 - \left(\frac{x - 10000}{25}\right) = 31100$

$\Rightarrow \quad x - \frac{x}{25} = 31200$

$\Rightarrow \quad 24x = 25 \times 31200$

$\Rightarrow \quad x = \frac{25 \times 31200}{24}$

$= 32500$

Hence, total sales = ₹ 32500.

52. Let no. of males in the town = x

$\therefore$ No. of female = 8000 – x

$\frac{10x}{100} + \frac{8}{100}(8000 - x) = \frac{9}{100} \times 8000$

$\Rightarrow \quad 10x + 64000 - 8x = 72000$

$\Rightarrow \quad 2x = 8000$

$\Rightarrow \quad x = 4000$

Hence, no. of males in the town = 4000.

53. From the given option,

Expend. = $\frac{80}{100} \times 3200$
= 80 × 32 = 2560

Saving = 3200 – 2560
= ₹ 640

Expend. = $\frac{85}{100} \times 4800$
= 85 × 48 = 4080

Saving = 4800 – 4080 = 720

Expend. = $\frac{75}{100} \times 6400$

= 75 × 64 = 4800

Saving = 6400 – 4800

= ₹ 1600

= 640 : 720 : 1600

= 64 : 72 : 160

= 8 : 9 : 20

Hence, their monthly salaries are ₹ 3200, ₹ 4800 and ₹ 6400.

54. ∵ The number is divided by 32 gives remainder = 29

When 29 is divided by 8 gives remainder = 5

Hence, the number is divided by 8 gives remainder = 5

55. According to the question,

$1x + 5x + 10x = 480$

⇒ $16x = 480$

⇒ $x = 30$

Hence, total number of notes

= 30 + 30 + 30

= 90.

56. Quantity of alcohol in 9 ml lotion

$= \frac{50}{100} \times 9 = 4.5$ ml

Let the water to be added by x ml

Then, $\frac{4.5}{9+x} = \frac{30}{100}$

⇒ $270 + 30x = 450$

⇒ $x = 6$ ml.

57. Work done by A, B and C in 4 days

$= \frac{1}{10} \times 4 = \frac{2}{5}$

Remaining work $= 1 - \frac{2}{5} = \frac{3}{5}$

Now, $\frac{3}{5}$ work is done by B and C in 10 days

whole work will be done by B and C in

$10 \times \frac{5}{3} = \frac{50}{3}$ days

(A + B + C)'s 1 day work $= \frac{1}{10}$

(B + C)'s 1 day work $= \frac{3}{50}$

A's 1 day work $= \left(\frac{1}{10} - \frac{3}{50}\right)$

$= \frac{2}{50} = \frac{1}{25}$

∴ A alone could complete the work in 25 days.

58. Ratio of speeds of A and B = $2x$ and $3x$

Ratio of time taken $= \frac{1}{2} : \frac{1}{3} = 3 : 2$

If B takes 2 min. then A takes 3 min

If B takes 36 min. then A takes

$\left(\frac{3}{2} \times 36\right)$ min = 54 min.

59. Circumference of the wheel $= \frac{15}{2}$ m

Path covered by wheels in 7 revolutions

$= \frac{15}{2} \times 7 = \frac{105}{2}$ m

Time taken = 9 seconds

∴ Speed of the train $= \frac{105}{2 \times 9}$ m/s

$= \frac{105}{18} \times \frac{18}{5}$ km/hr

= 21 km/hr.

60. 60% of x – 40% of x = 298

⇒ 20% of x = 298

⇒ $\frac{20}{100} \times x = 298$

⇒ $x = 298 \times 5$

= 1490

Hence, total number of votes = 1490.

61. Total number of items sold in all shops

= 120 + 160 + 240 + 140

= 660.

62. No. of ties = 20 × 2 = 40

No. of other items = 100 × 3 = 300

Total no. of items sold by shop I
$= 300 + 40 = 340.$

63. Profit = 140 × 10 = ₹ 1400

Tax = 50% of ₹ 1400

$$= \frac{50}{100} \times 1400 = 700$$

Profit after tax = 1400 – 700 = ₹ 700.

64. Total number of trousers sold by all shops is 160.

65. Required % = 15%.

66. $$\text{Required } \% = \frac{110}{1539} \times 100$$

$$= \frac{11000}{1539} = 7.1\% \text{ (Approx.)}$$

67. The magnitude of ∠AOC

$$= \frac{974}{1539} \times 360° = \frac{974 \times 8}{57}$$

$= 136° \cong 132°$ (Approx.)

68. Total investment in socially oriented sectors (plan and non-plan)

= 107 + 458 = 565 crores

Total investment in Government securities (Central and State)

= 454 + 110 = 564 crores

Difference = 1 crores

Hence, investment in socially oriented sectors is more than the investment in government securities (central and state) by 4 crores.

69. The investment in private sectors

= 183 crores

The investment in state government securites

= 110 crores

Difference = 183 – 110 = 73 crores

$$\text{Required\%} = \frac{73}{110} \times 100$$

$$= \frac{730}{11} = 66\% \text{ (Approx.)}$$

Hence, the investment in private sectors is nearly 66% higher than the investment in state Government securities.

70. The ratio of the area of the circle above COF to the area of the circle below = 0.94 (Approx.)

71-74.

Based on the given information, the passanger travelling on three vehicles:

	Vehicle-I	Vehicle-II	Vehicle-III
Engineer	Q (Male)	V (Female)	
Doctor		S (Male)	R (Female)
Teacher	W (Female)	P (Female)	T (Male)

75-78.

75.

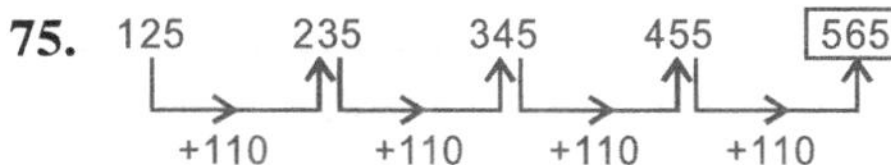

76. 15 16 20 29 45

+(1)² +(2)² +(3)² +(4)²

77. V T R P N

–2 –2 –2 –2

78. B D F H J L N P R T V X Z B D

+2 +2 +2 +2 +2 +2 +2 +2 +2 +2 +2 +2 +2 +2

79.

Centre Code	Serial Number (Highest)
18	9901 (Highest)
33	8379
47	5347
65	1923
81	7929
88	8325

80.

Centre Code	Serial Number
51	3338
88	8325
65	1923 (Lowest)
33	8379

84. Y W U P R T D F H I K M

–2 –2 +2 +2 +2 +2 +2 +2

85. 11, 13 and 17 are prime numbers, whereas 21 is not a prime number.

86-89.

(Salesman) D ←Spouse→ A (Teacher)

A ↑ Daughter-in-law — C

(Doctor) B ←Spouse→ C (Lawyer)

B ← Son — F

(Engineer) E ←Brother→ F (Account)

A — Grandmother → F

95.

	Ramesh	**Rahim**	**Robert**
Initially, No. of cards	x	y	z
Card transfer	–5 +3 +4	+5 –3 +1	 –5
Net No. of Card	$x + 2$	$y + 3$	$z - 5$

From question, $(y + 3) = 2y$

$$y = 3.$$

Hence, Number of Cards Rahim had initially = 3.

96. Let, the number is P.

Then, $\frac{2}{3}$ of $\frac{3}{4}$P + $\frac{3}{4}$ of $\frac{4}{5}$P = xP

$$\left(\frac{1}{2}+\frac{3}{5}\right)P = xP$$

$$\frac{11}{10}P = xP$$

$$x = \frac{11}{10}.$$

98. 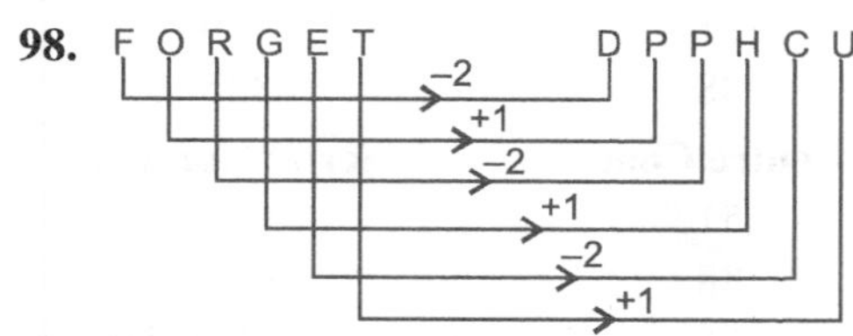

Similarly,

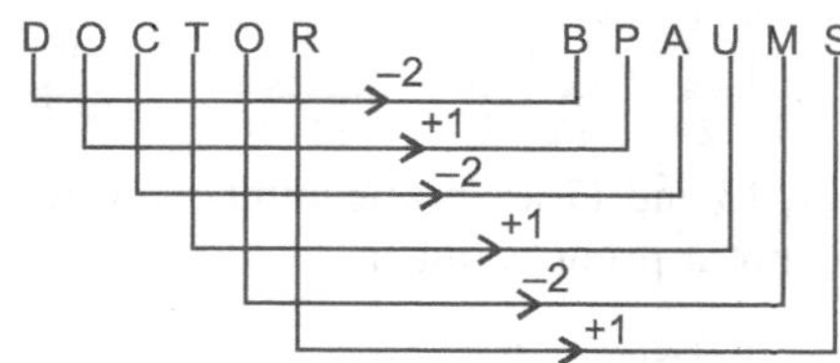

99. Given word: I N O R D I N A T E

After interchanging: N I R O I D A N E T

↑

8th Letter

102. The **Jnanpith Award** is a literary award in India. Along with the Sahitya Akademi Fellowship, it is one of the two most prestigious literary honours in the country. The award was instituted in 1961. Eligibility is restricted to any Indian citizen who writes in one of the 22 languages listed in Schedule Eight of the Indian constitution. It is presented by the Bharatiya Jnanpith, a trust founded by the Sahu Jain family, the publishers of the newspaper *The Times of India.*

103. **Typhoid fever** is an acute illness associated with fever caused by the *Salmonella typhi* bacteria. It can also be caused by *Salmonella paratyphi*, a related bacterium that usually causes a less severe illness. The bacteria are deposited in water or food by a human carrier and are then spread to other people in the area.

105. **Subroto Cup Football Tournament** is one of the famous inter-school football tournament in India, named after the Indian Air Force Air Marshal Subroto Mukerjee. It started in 1960 and has been conducted every year since then.

111. Japan is an archipelago, or a group of islands, about 100 miles east of the Asian mainland. The ancient Japanese knew about China and Korea, but they did not know of any land east of their islands. They believed theirs was the first land awakened by the rising sun. The Japanese call their land Nippon, meaning "Land of the Rising Sun".

112. A **marine chronometer** is a timepiece that is precise and accurate enough to be used as a portable time standard; it can therefore be used to determine longitude by means of celestial navigation.

115. **"Jana Gana Mana"** is the national anthem of India. Written in highly Sanskritised (Tatsama) Bengali, the first of five stanzas of a Brahmo hymn composed and scored by Nobel laureate Rabindranath Tagore. Underlying message of the Jana Gana Mana is pluralism.

Previous Paper (Solved)

BBA/BBS Entrance Exam, 2014

BUSINESS APTITUDE AND MANAGEMENT

1. The 'Hukumchand jute industry' was incorporated in the year

A. 1999 B. 1998
C. 2000 D. 1997

2. The process that turns marketing strategies and plans into marketing actions in order to accomplish strategic marketing objectives is called

A. marketing strategy
B. marketing control
C. marketing analysis
D. marketing implementation

3. Costs that do not vary with production or sales levels are called

A. fixed costs B. variable costs
C. standard costs D. independent costs

4. Which are the elements in personal selling?

A. Human behaviour B. Empathy
C. Persuasiveness D. All of the above

5. The difference between the export and import of services is called

A. Balance of Trade
B. Balance of Capital Account
C. Balance of Current Account
D. Balance of Invisible

6. Bad loans in banking terminology are generally known as

A. BPOs B. Prime Asset
C. NPAs D. CBS

7. Ashok Leyland is owned by the

A. Tatas B. Birlas
C. Hinduja D. None of these

8. Which is not the stage of product life cycle?

A. Introduction B. Increase
C. Decline D. Maturity

9. 'Functional Finance' is associated with

A. Adacns B. Abba P Lerner
C. Adolph Wogner D. Adam Smith

10. In an economy the sectors are classified into public and private on the basis of

A. employment conditions
B. nature of economic activities
C. ownership of enterprises
D. use of raw materials

11. Which is the characteristics of an entrepreneur?

A. Ability to innovate
B. Capacity to face uncertainties
C. It is a creative activity
D. All of the above

12. A speech designed to change or reinforce the audience's beliefs or actions. This is an example of

A. informative speech B. ceremonial speech
C. persuasive speech D. None of these

13. Probing in a communication process is

A. an attempt to gain additional information
B. making judgements
C. an attempt to explain what the sender meant
D. None of the above

14. Which one of the following is not a part of electronic media?

A. Radio B. Television
C. Film D. Brochure

15. Which one is not a function of money?
A. Price stabilisation
B. Value measurement
C. Transfer of value
D. Store of value

16. What is context?
A. Verbal and non-verbal responses to message
B. A physical and psychological environment for conversation
C. An interference with message reception
D. Effective communication

17. A brand includes
A. combination of name and symbol
B. design
C. logo or mark
D. All of the above

18. Downward communication flows from people at higher levels to those at lower levels in an organisation. Primary function of downward communication is to provide
A. organisation policies and procedures
B. feedback about employee's performances
C. organisation goal and objectives
D. All of the above

19. Consumer Protection Act is an act of Parliament of India enacted in
A. 1986 B. 1987
C. 1988 D. 1989

20. In context of mutual fund, SIP stands for
A. Special Income Plan
B. Systematic Investment Plan
C. Specific Investment Plan
D. Special Investment Plan

21. Capital budgeting is related to
A. long-term planning
B. short-term funding
C. profit making
D. dividend policy

22. ETOP stands for
A. Entry Threats and Opportunity Position
B. Environmental Technology Opportunities Portal
C. Energy Table On Price
D. None of the above

23. In a disappointing newsletter
A. it is important to apologise
B. apology can be made with reason
C. no apology is offered for the decision
D. None of the above

24. In marketing term, attitude can best be defined as
A. rude behaviour of sales person
B. rude behaviour of consumer
C. mental state of consumer
D. ego of the merketing executive

25. The characteristics of a group include
A. activities or tasks
B. common objectives
C. membership or association with group
D. All of the above

26. Digjam is a product of
A. Oswal Enterprise
B. Tata Enterprise
C. Reliance Enterprise
D. Birla Enterprise

27. In which year, 'The Banking Regulation Act' was passed?
A. 1947 B. 1948
C. 1949 D. 1961

28. In general grapevine is related to learn something informally by means of
A. gossip B. rumour
C. Both A and B D. None of these

29. A .... communication is the traditional form of communication in which employees sent messages to their seniors.
A. bottom down B. lower up
C. lower down D. bottom up

30. Business activity is primarily concerned with making profit by
A. marketing
B. production
C. distribution exchange
D. All of these

31. The tagline 'The Edge is Efficiency' is used by
A. BSE B. NASDAQ
C. NYSE D. EURONEXT

32. Which of the following does not come under Maharatna status?
A. Bharat Heavy Electrical Limited
B. Coal India Limited
C. Bharat Electronics Limited
D. Steel Authority of India Limited

33. 'Sugar Free' is a leading brand of artificial sweetner in India. It is owned by
A. Cadila B. Ranbaxy
C. Dr. Reddy's D. Cipla

34. Non-financial incentives consist
A. reward B. recognition
C. opportunity D. All of these

35. .... refers to the degree of highness or lowness of a sound.
A. Pitch B. Speed
C. Volume D. Rate

36. Relationship in marketing means
A. relation between salesperson
B. relation between buyer and seller
C. relation between company and consumer
D. All of the above

37. GAIL was conferred with Maharatna status in the year
A. 2011 B. 2012
C. 2013 D. 2010

ENGLISH LANGUAGE AND COMPREHENSION

Directions (Qs. Nos. 38-45) : *Read the passage carefully and answer the questions given below.*

Although speech is generally accepted as the most advanced form of communication, there are many ways of communicating without using words. In every known culture, signals, signs, symbols and gestures are commonly utilised as instruments of communication. There is a great deal of agreement among communication scientists as to what each of these methods is and how each differs from the others. For instance, the basic function of any signal is to impinge upon the environment in such a way that it attracts attention, as, *e.g.*, the dots and dashes that can be applied in a telegraph circuit. Coded to refer to speech, the potential for communication through these dots and dashes—short and long intervals as the circuit is broken—is very great. Less adaptable to the codification of words, signs also contain agreed upon meaning, that is, they convey information in and of themselves. Two examples are the hexagonal red sign that conveys the meaning of stop and the red and white swirled pole outside a shop, that communicates the meaning of barber.

Symbols are more difficult to describe than either signals or signs because of their intricate relationship with the receiver's cultural perceptions. In some cultures, applauding in a theater provides performers with an auditory symbol of approval. In other cultures, if done in unison, applauding can be a symbol of the audience's discontent with the performance. Gestures such as waving and handshaking also communicate certain cultural messages.

Although signals, symbols and gestures are very useful, they also have a major disadvantage in communication. They usually do not allow ideas to be shared without the sender being directly adjacent to the receiver. Without an exchange of ideas, interaction comes to a halt. As a result, means of communication intended to be used across long distances and extended periods must be based upon speech. To radio, television and the telephone, one must add fax, paging systems, electronic mail and the internet and no one doubts but that there are more means of communication on the horizon.

38. Applauding was cited as an example of
A. a signal B. a sign
C. a symbol D. a gesture

39. The word 'intricate' in second paragraph could best be replaced by which of the following?
A. Inefficient B. Complicated
C. Historical D. Uncertain

40. The word 'potential' in first paragraph could be replaced by
A. range B. advantage
C. organisation D. possibility

41. The word 'it' in paragraph first refers to
A. function B. signal
C. environment D. way

42. The phrase 'impinge upon' in first paragraph is closest in meaning to
A. intrude B. improve
C. vary D. prohibit

43. What does the author say about speech?
A. It is the only true form of communication
B. It is dependent upon the advances made by inventors
C. It is necessary for communication to occur
D. It is the most advanced form of communication

44. Which of the following would be the best title for the passage?
A. Signs and Signals
B. Gestures
C. Communication
D. Speech

45. Why were the telephone, radio and TV invented?
A. People were unable to understand signs, symbols and signals
B. People wanted to communicate across long distances
C. People believed that signs, signals and symbols were obsolete
D. People wanted new forms of entertainment

Directions (Qs. Nos. 46-52) : *Read the passage carefully and answer the questions given below.*

A leading Indian industrialist in a recent article on ways to strengthen India's economy has drawn attention to the problems of inflation and industrial sickness among other things. One of the main reasons for industrial sickness in our country has been the fact that business and industrial managers, have not been able to look beyond the immediate future. They have been too preoccupied with their attempts to report favourable results for the current year-higher profits and larger dividends to the share holders. The planning horizon has hardly ever exceeded five years. Investments have been inadequate for new plants and towards diversification and expansions. Modernisation and as set creation has seriously lagged behind. In business, growth is needed for survival, one has to grow if one does not want to be wiped out. This is particularly true today with liberalisation of imports and increasing competition. Moreover, growth and higher productivity create employment and higher employment creates larger markets both for industrial and consumer products. It was Henry Ford, who brought home the need for the creation of a larger and a more stable middle class, that is, a larger number of people who can afford more and more of goods and services. Even after forty years of independence our industrialists have not been able to shed the petty shopkeeper's mentality and our highly educated management has tagged along merrily and without concern.

46. 'The planning horizon has hardly ever exceeded five years' implies
A. planning should not be for a period of less than five years
B. the planning process is very time consuming
C. planning should take care of all probable ups and downs in the next five years period
D. Five year period is too short for successful implementation of plans

47. Why did Henry Ford stress the need for a more stable middle class?
A. They are mostly service oriented
B. They do not have shopkeeper mentality
C. They can afford to buy more and more expensive goods
D. They are most unstable

48. In order to improve the condition of Indian industries, the industrialist should do all of the following except
A. giving up the narrow mentality which very small shopkeepers generally have
B. striving to earn long term profits
C. encouraging competition from industrialists within the country and from abroad
D. resorting to long term planning for industrial growth and expansion in diverse fields

49. The leading industrialist attributes industrial sickness mainly to
- A. lacunae in five year plans
- B. preoccupations of managers with matters unrelated to business
- C. higher profits and larger dividends to shareholders
- D. lack of foresight among managers

50. According to the passage, growth and increasing productivity leads to
- A. imposition of restrictions on imports
- B. employment and thus provide an outlet to industrial and consumer products
- C. encouragement to export of excess consumer goods
- D. disproportionate surplus of commodities

51. According to the passage, the net gains pursued by managers are at the cost of
- A. diversification, modernisation and asset creation
- B. availability of markets for industrial and consumer products
- C. inflation and industrial sickness
- D. liberalisation of imports and increasing competition

52. Which of the following shortcomings of Indian industrialists has been highlighted by the author?
- A. They invest unreasonable high amount on diversification and expansion
- B. They are more concerned for immediate net gains than for developmental activities
- C. They are reluctant to maintain the shopkeeper mentality
- D. They are less concerned for payment of dividends to shareholders

Directions (Qs. Nos. 53-58) : *In each of the following questions, out of the given alternatives, choose the one which best expresses the meaning of the given word.*

53. IMMACULATE
- A. refined B. pure
- C. faithful D. splendid

54. EBULLIENT
- A. Gilted B. Enthusiastic
- C. Luscious D. Arrogant

55. IGNOMINIOUS
- A. shameful B. fruitful
- C. unexpected D. expected

56. INNOCUOUS
- A. harmless B. insidious
- C. insolvent D. invasion

57. CHICANERY
- A. choleric B. cogent
- C. trickery D. confess

58. CHAGRINED
- A. frustrated B. annoyed
- C. disappointed D. tired

Directions (Qs. Nos. 59-64) : *In the following questions, choose the word opposite in meaning to the given word.*

59. SERVILITY
- A. bravery B. prudence
- C. insolence D. slavery

60. KNOTTY
- A. involved B. intricate
- C. easy D. assuming

61. DEARTH
- A. extravagance B. scarcity
- C. velocity D. abundance

62. VEHEMENCE
- A. apathy B. passion
- C. eagerness D. ascent

63. PLACATE
- A. antagonize B. pity
- C. amuse D. embroil

64. PEJORATIVE
- A. soothing B. appreciative
- C. smoothing D. critical

Directions (Qs. Nos. 65-69) : *Fill in the blanks in the following sentences by selecting the most appropriate alternative from amongst the given choices under each sentence.*

65. The police confronted the thief .... the accusers.
- A. with B. at
- C. upon D. to

66. Civilization, in real sense of the term consists not in the .... but in the deliberate and voluntary .... of wants.
A. increasing .... decreasing
B. increment .... decrement
C. multiplication .... reduction
D. hoarding .... dehoarding

67. That rumour has no foundation .... fact.
A. of B. up
C. to D. in

68. In all these and a thousand other details you and I please ourselves and ....
A. ask of no one's leave
B. ask no one's leave
C. ask leave of no one
D. ask from any one no leave

69. They praised him ....
A. and pointed out it was a good hit
B. and exclaimed it was a good hit
C. and said that it was a good hit
D. and showed that it was a good hit

Directions (Qs. Nos. 70-72) : *In the following questions six sentences are given. The first and the sixth sentences are numbered 1 to 6. The 2nd, 3rd, 4th and 5th sentences are not in proper sequence and named P, Q, R and S. Select the correct sequence of these four sentences from the responses given below each question.*

70. 1. The Ganga is a holy river to the Hindus
P. Every Hindu wishes to die on the bank of the holy Ganga, so that he may reach heaven.
Q. It comes from the Gangotri mountains in the Himalayas.
R. It is one of biggest rivers in India.
S. The Hindus call the Ganga 'Mother Ganga'.
6. At Haridwar, it leaves the mountains and enters the plains.
A. SQRP B. PRQS
C. RSQP D. SPRQ

71. 1. The two men who were following
P. and who were separated from the tigress by the rock,
Q. when they saw me stop
R. a few yards behind me
S. stood still
6. and turn my head
A. RPSQ B. QPSR
C. RQPS D. RQSP

72. 1. Science improves our living conditions, but
P. rejecting or accepting anything, provided
Q. and not be afraid of
R. teach us to think straight
S. it should also
6. there are sufficient reasons for doing so.
A. SRQP B. SRPQ
C. RSPQ D. PQSR

Directions (Qs. Nos. 73-75) : *In each of the following questions, a word has been written in four different ways out of which only one is correctly spelt. Find the correctly spelt word.*

73. A. Kalidoscope B. Kaleidoscope
C. Kalaidoscope D. Kaliedoscope

74. A. Rapprochment B. Repprochment
C. Raproachment D. Rapprochement

75. A. Strategam B. Strategem
C. Stratagem D. Stratagam

GENERAL AWARENESS

76. Dr. S. Chandrashekhar was the Indian who got Nobel Prize in
A. Economics B. Literature
C. Piece D. Physics

77. World laughter day is celebrated on ....
A. January 15 B. January 1
C. January 30 D. January 10

78. 'Green Index' has been developed by
A. United Nations Environment Programme
B. International Monetary Fund (IMF)
C. World Bank
D. None of the above

79. 'World Ozone Day' is celebrated on
A. September 16 B. April 21
C. December 25 D. January 30

80. 'NEERI' is located at
A. Nagpur B. Mumbai
C. Chennai D. Bengaluru .

81. The world movement of Jews aimed at finding a home state for the Jews in the world is called ....
A. Juisim B. Zionism
C. Juadism D. None of these

82. The topmost crust of the Earth on which stand our continents and ocean basins are called ....
A. Stratosphere B. Lithosphere
C. Autosphere D. Hemisphere

83. Limnology is the study of ....
A. Waterfalls B. Lakes
C. Lime stones D. Oceans

84. The currency of Suriname is called ....
A. Guilder B. Taka
C. Deutsch D. Dollar

85. Alexander defeated Porus in the Battle of ....
A. KhyberPass B. Panipat
C. Kalinga D. Hydaspas

86. Who wrote the book 'The Flight of Pigeons'?
A. Ruskin Bond B. Khushwant Singh
C. O.V. Vijayan D. V.S. Naipaul

87. Who invented Antiseptic?
A. Sir William Ramsay B. Dr. C.F. Brush
C. Dr. Felix Hoffman D. Dr. Joseph Lister

88. The capital of Switzerland is ....
A. Damascus
B. Geneva
C. Swiss Confederation
D. Bern

89. The Headquarters of International Red Cross is at ....
A. Geneva B. Paris
C. London D. Washington

90. Who invented Electric fan?
A. GottFried Leibniz
B. Wheeler
C. Thomas Alva Edison
D. W.H. Selley

91. The Headquarters of Common Wealth of Independence State (CIS) is
A. Rome B. Manila
C. Cairo D. Kirava

92. Autoecology is the study of
A. Species B. Ecology
C. Environment D. None of these

93. .... a written public declaration of the intentions, opinions or motives of sovereign of a leader, party or body.
A. Policy recommendation
B. Manifesto
C. Charter of demands
D. Mandate

94. The first Shuttle to go in space was
A. Columbia B. Viking-I
C. Space Group I D. None of these

95. The first Indian to cross English Channel
A. Nagender Singh B. Mihir Sen
C. S. Mukherjee D. Sukumar Sen

96. Workers Day with the slogan 'workers of the world unite' is celebrated on
A. First day of April
B. First day of June
C. First day of May
D. First day of December

97. .... is an order from the Supreme Court or a High Court to restrain a person from acting in an office to which he is not entitled.
A. Quorum B. Quisling
C. Quarantine D. Quo Warranto

98. .... rocks are originally igneous and sedimentary but have been changed by pressure, heat or action of water.
A. Salt Rocks B. Weathering Rocks
C. Metamorphic Rocks D. None of these

99. After how many years 'Mahakumbh' is held?
A. 12 year B. 10 year
C. 9 year D. 6 year

100. 'Panchtantra' is originally written by
A. Kalidas B. Vishnu Sharma
C. Tulsidas D. Raidas

101. .... is an instrument for measuring the strength of direct current.
A. Tele Galvanometer
B. Telemeter
C. Tangent Galvanometer
D. Simple Galvanometer

102. The Headquarters of Officers Training Academy is at ....
A. Pune B. Chennai
C. Dehradun D. Kolkata

103. Who wrote 'All Under Heaven'?
A. J.K. Galbraith B. Wilson John
C. Pearl S. Buck D. Vikram Seth

104. Chhau is the famous dance of ....
A. Karnataka B. Kerala
C. West Bengal D. Gujarat

105. The currency of Syria is called
A. Syrian Sia B. Syrian Dollar
C. Syrian Pound D. Syrian Aleppo

106. Trapping and taming operations against wild elephants in Karnataka style is called ....
A. Khalida B. Operation giant
C. Operation elephant D. Khedda

107. In Battle of Haldighati, Akbar defeated
A. Rani Laxmi Bai
B. Maharana Pratap
C. Maharaja Ranjit Singh
D. None of these

108. The Capital of Sudan is
A. Cape Town B. Jaffna
C. Khartoum D. Paramaribo

109. The first National Park, established in India, is
A. Namdapha National Park
B. Corbett National Park
C. Dudhwa National Park
D. Guinady National Park

110. Rovers cup is associated with .... sport.
A. Table Tennis B. Polo
C. Roving D. Football

111. .... awards are given in the field of Medical Sciences.
A. Shanti Swarup Bhatnagar Award
B. Iqbal Samman
C. R.D. Birla Award
D. Tansen Award

112. The largest peninsula of the world ....
A. Southern India B. Alaska
C. Arabia D. Greenland

113. The World Disabled Day falls on ....
A. March 15 B. December 3
C. March 19 D. December 14

LOGICAL AND ANALYTICAL ABILITY

114. In a code language 'Sil Fin Kil' means 'money one problem', 'Tin Sil Fis' means 'problem secret danger' and 'Kil Tip Ne' means 'one strange traveller'. What does 'Tip' stand for in the same code language?
A. Traveller
B. Strange
C. One
D. Cannot be determined

115. If 'ZOOM' is coded as 13, 'PUSA' will be coded as
A. 15 B. 16
C. 17 D. 18

116. If 'CORRESPONDENCE' is coded as 'NUTTRAXUPQRPNR' in a certain code, how will 'SCOPE' be coded?
A. AUXNR B. ANUXR
C. RNUXA D. XUPAR

Directions (Qs. Nos. 117-120) : *In the questions given below establish the relationship between the two words. Then, from the given options select one which has the same relationship as of the given two words.*

117. DAYBREAK : BEDSTEAD
A. Earthen : Brazen
B. Fresh : Tired
C. Nocturnal : Diurnal
D. Eyeglass : Landmark

118. HOPE : ASPIRES
A. Film : Flam B. Fake : Ordinary
C. Fib : Lie D. Spirits : Soar

119. ANCIENT : MODERN
A. Often : Seldom B. Often : Frequent
C. Often : Always D. Often : Never

120. 08 : 28 : : 15 : ?
A. 63 B. 126
C. 65 D. 124

Directions (Qs. Nos. 121-125) : *In each of the following questions there is a series. The one term is missing in the series. Find out the missing term.*

121. M L O N Q P R ?
A. R B. O
C. Q D. L

122. Find out the wrong number in the series.
15, 45, 90, 360, 1080, 2160, 6480
A. 90 B. 360
C. 6480 D. 2160

123. –yyx–xxyx–yxyx–y
A. yxxy B. xyxy
C. yxyx D. xyyx

124. 7776, 1296, 216, 36, 6, ?
A. 6 B. 0
C. 3 D. 1

125. K P A, L Q B, M R C, N S D, ...
A. T O E B. O E T
C. E T O D. O T E

Directions (Qs. Nos. 126-128) : *In each of the questions given below which one of the answer figures should come in place of question mark, if the sequence were continued.*

126. Problem solving

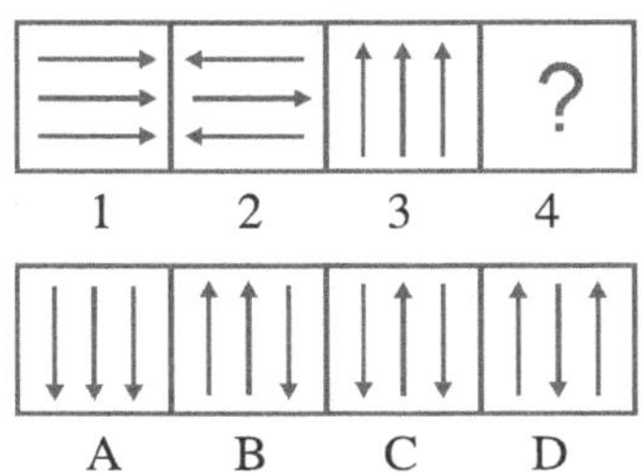

127. Problem Solving

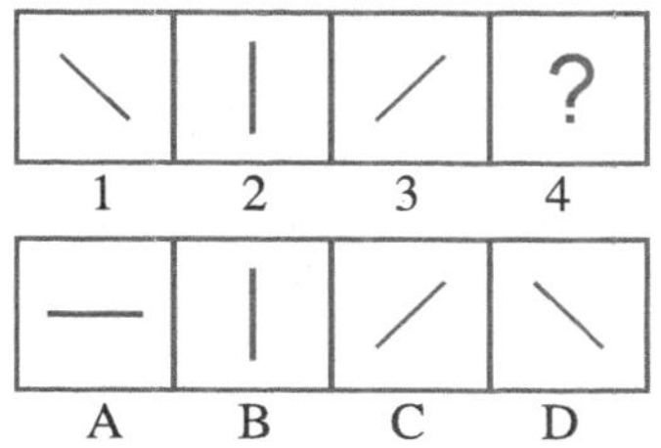

128. Problem Solving

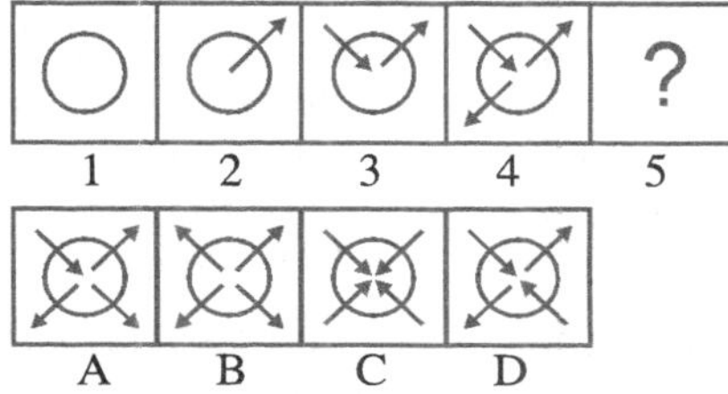

Directions (Qs. Nos. 129-131) : *In the following questions, select the right answer from the given options to depict the correct direction/distance.*

129. Arjun goes 30 m North, then turns right and walks 40 m, then again turns right and walks 20 m, then again turns right and walks 40 m. How many metres is he from his original position?
A. 9 B. 10
C. 20 D. 40

130. A train runs 120 km in West direction, 30 km in South direction and then 80 km in East direction before reaching the station. In which direction is the station from the train's starting point?
A. South-West B. North-West
C. South-East D. South

131. Ramesh was facing East. He walked 14 km forward and then after turning to his right walked 13 km. Again, he turned to his right and walked 14 km. After this he turned back. Which direction was he facing at that time?
A. East B. West
C. North D. South

Directions (Qs. Nos. 132-134) : *In the following questions, there are four alternative answers out of which one is correct.*

132. 'D' is the son of 'J' who is son of 'F' and 'P' is the daughter of 'R'. If 'N' is the sister of 'P' and daughter of 'J' what is 'J' 's relationship with 'R'?

A. Husband B. Brother
C. Father D. Uncle

133. Madhuri is the wife of Rajesh and Rajesh is the brother of Mahesh. Mahesh is the uncle of Pranav. What is Pranav's relation with Madhuri?

A. Daughter B. Nephew
C. Sister-in-law D. Niece

134. Introducing a women, a man said, 'Her mother's husband's sister is my aunt.' How is the man related to the woman?

A. Nephew B. Brother
C. Uncle D. Cousin

Directions (Qs. Nos. 135-138) : *Read the following information carefully and answer the questions given below it.*

Five friends Ramesh, Suresh, Mahesh, Dinesh and Ganesh are sitting on a bench.

(*i*) Ramesh is sitting next to Suresh.
(*ii*) Mahesh is sitting next to Dinesh
(*iii*) Dinesh is not sitting with Ganesh
(*iv*) Ganesh is on the left end of the bench.
(*v*) Mahesh is on second position from right.
(*vi*) Ramesh is on the right side of Suresh and to the right side of Ganesh.

135. What is the position of Suresh?

A. Second from right B. Centre
C. Extreme left D. Second from left

136. At what position is Ramesh sitting?

A. Between Suresh and Mahesh
B. Between Dinesh and Mahesh
C. Between Ganesh and Dinesh
D. Between Mahesh and Ganesh

137. What is the position of Dinesh?

A. Extreme left B. Extreme right
C. Third from left D. Second from left

138. Who is sitting at the centre?

A. Ramesh B. Suresh
C. Mahesh D. Dinesh

139. Akash was born on 3rd March 1980. Sanjiv was born 4 days before Akash. The Republic day that year fell on Saturday. Which day was Sanjiv's birthday?

A. Wednesday B. Friday
C. Thursday D. Tuesday

140. Which of the following is a leap year?

A. 1982 B. 1978
C. 1704 D. 1945

141. If 15 apples and 20 oranges cost as much as 20 apples and 15 oranges. How do you compare the costs of two?

A. Apples are as costly as oranges
B. Oranges are costly than apples
C. Apples are costly than oranges
D. None of the above

142. A, B, C, D and E distribute some cards among themselves in a manner that A gets one less than B, C gets 5 more than D, E gets 3 more than B while D gets as many as B. Who gets the least number of cards?

A. B B. C
C. D D. A

143. What number in the dice, given below will on the side opposite to 6?

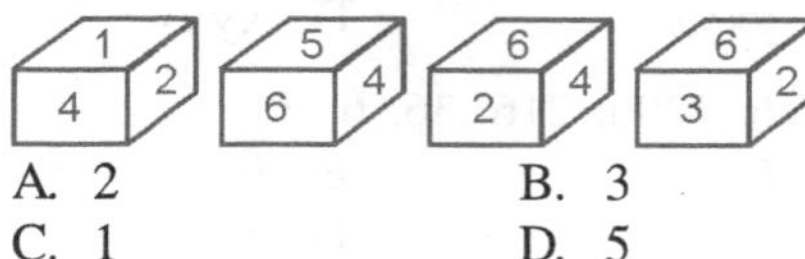

A. 2 B. 3
C. 1 D. 5

Directions (Qs. Nos. 144-146) : *In the following questions, there are four options. Find out the one that is correct in verification of the given statement.*

144. Escalators help in

A. vertical movement only
B. horizontal movement only
C. vertical and horizontal movement
D. circular movement only

145. Which one of the following is always associated with 'Justice'?

A. Hypocrisy B. Magnaninity
C. Legitimate D. Diminutiveness

146. Which one of the following is always in the 'Sentiment'?

A. Cruelty B. Insight
C. Neutrality D. Emotion

Directions (Qs. Nos. 147-148) : *In the following questions, find out the most suitable answer.*

147. The Selection Board call the candidates for the interview because
- A. they want to see the candidate's physical appearance
- B. it is then easier to decide which candidate is fit for the job
- C. the members of the Selection Board have no other work during office hours
- D. None of the above

148. Now a days many young people use high heeled shoes because
- A. these shoes increase the heights of the young people
- B. it comes under fashion
- C. it is safer for them to wear these types of shoes
- D. they practice to balance their bodies after wearing such shoes

149. At what angle the hands of a clock are inclined at 15 min pasts 5?
- A. $72\frac{1}{2}^\circ$
- B. $67\frac{1}{2}^\circ$
- C. $58\frac{1}{2}^\circ$
- D. 64°

150. Today is Wednesday, what will be the day after 94 days?
- A. Monday
- B. Tuesday
- C. Wednesday
- D. Sunday

ANSWERS

1	2	3	4	5	6	7	8	9	10
C	D	A	D	D	C	C	B	B	C
11	**12**	**13**	**14**	**15**	**16**	**17**	**18**	**19**	**20**
D	C	A	D	A	B	D	D	A	B
21	**22**	**23**	**24**	**25**	**26**	**27**	**28**	**29**	**30**
A	B	C	A	D	A	C	C	D	D
31	**32**	**33**	**34**	**35**	**36**	**37**	**38**	**39**	**40**
A	C	A	D	A	C	C	C	B	D
41	**42**	**43**	**44**	**45**	**46**	**47**	**48**	**49**	**50**
B	A	D	C	B	D	C	C	D	B
51	**52**	**53**	**54**	**55**	**56**	**57**	**58**	**59**	**60**
A	B	B	B	A	A	C	C	C	C
61	**62**	**63**	**64**	**65**	**66**	**67**	**68**	**69**	**70**
D	A	A	B	A	C	D	A	B	D
71	**72**	**73**	**74**	**75**	**76**	**77**	**78**	**79**	**80**
A	A	B	D	C	D	D	C	A	A
81	**82**	**83**	**84**	**85**	**86**	**87**	**88**	**89**	**90**
B	B	B	D	D	A	D	D	A	B
91	**92**	**93**	**94**	**95**	**96**	**97**	**98**	**99**	**100**
D	A	B	A	B	C	D	C	A	B
101	**102**	**103**	**104**	**105**	**106**	**107**	**108**	**109**	**110**
D	B	C	C	C	D	B	C	B	D
111	**112**	**113**	**114**	**115**	**116**	**117**	**118**	**119**	**120**
A	C	B	D	C	B	B	C	A	C
121	**122**	**123**	**124**	**125**	**126**	**127**	**128**	**129**	**130**
C	C	D	D	D	C	A	D	B	A
131	**132**	**133**	**134**	**135**	**136**	**137**	**138**	**139**	**140**
A	A	B	B	D	A	B	A	C	C
141	**142**	**143**	**144**	**145**	**146**	**147**	**148**	**149**	**150**
A	D	C	C	C	D	B	A	B	D

SOME SELECTED EXPLANATORY ANSWERS

114. 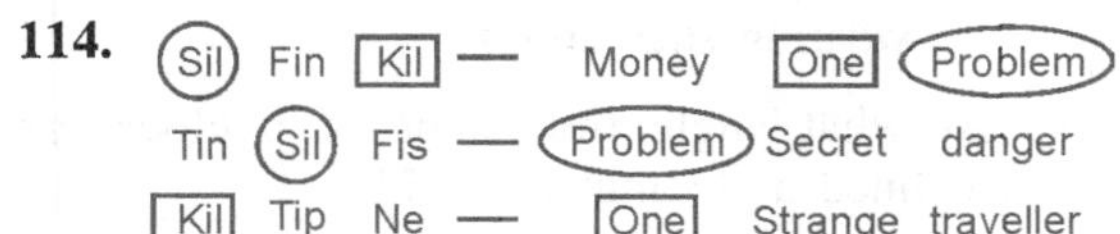

Code 'Tip' means either strange or traveller.

115. Letter Positions :

Z O O M
↓ ↓ ↓ ↓
26 15 15 13

= (26 + 15) – (15 + 13) = 13.

Letter Position :

P U S A
↓ ↓ ↓ ↓
16 21 19 1

= (16 + 21) – (19 + 1) = 17.

116. Code :

C O R R E S P O N D E N C E
↓ ↓ ↓ ↓ ↓ ↓ ↓ ↓ ↓ ↓ ↓ ↓ ↓ ↓
N U T T R A X U P Q R P N R

Hence, Code for

S C O P E
is ↓ ↓ ↓ ↓ ↓
A N U X R

120. 08 : 28 : : 15 : 65

↓ ↓ ↓ ↓

$(3^2 - 1) : (3^3 + 1) : : (4^2 - 1) : (4^3 + 1)$

121. M L O N Q P R Q

–1 –1 –1 –1

122. 15 45 90 360 1080 2160 ~~6480~~ 8640

×3 ×2 ×4 ×3 ×2 ×4

123. The series is xyyx, yxxy ....

124. 7776 1296 216 36 6 1

÷6 ÷6 ÷6 ÷6 ÷6

125. K P A L Q B M R C N S D O T E

+1 +1 +1 +1

+1 +1 +1 +1

+1 +1 +1 +1

126. First and third arrow rotated by 180°.

127. In every next figure the line is rotated by 45° clockwise.

129. 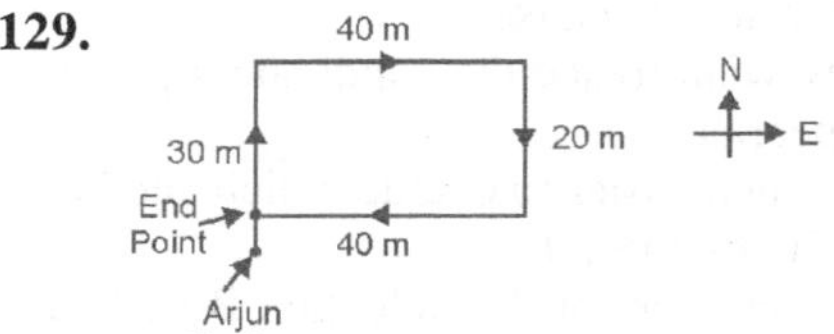

Hence, distance from starting point
= 30 – 20 = 10 m.

131. 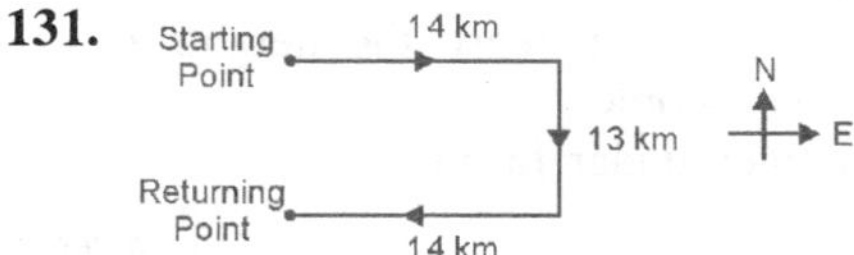

After returned back, Ramesh is facing East.

135-138. Left to right sitting arrangement.

Ganesh Suresh Ramesh Mahesh Dinesh

141. Let cost of an apple is x and cost of an orange is y.

then, from question,

$$15x + 20y = 20x + 15y$$
$$20y - 15y = 20x - 15x$$
$$5x = 5y$$
$$x = y$$

Hence, cost of apple = cost of orange.

142. Let B gets 100 Cards. Then,

Persons:	A	B	C	D	E
No. of Cards	(100 – 1) = 99	100	100 + 5 = 105	100	100 + 3 = 103

Hence, A gets least number of Cards.

143. From the figures of dice, pair of numbers on opposite faces are (1 – 6), (2 – 5) and (3 – 4).

149. In 60° minutes, minute hand rotates 360°
so, in 15 minutes, minute hand rotates

$$\frac{360°}{60°} \times 15 = 90°$$

In 12 hours, hour hand rotates 360°
so, in 5.25 hours, hour hand rotates

$$= \frac{360°}{12} \times 5.25 = 157.5°$$

Hence, angle between two hands
= 157.5° – 90° = 67.5°.

Quantitative Aptitude

1 Simplification

Simplification is a mathematical operation by which a complex expression of numbers or fractions is converted into a simpler or less difficult form. It is erroneous to solve this type of questions on random basis and a very appropriate method is to apply BODMAS Rule for arriving at the solution of such problems. Each of the letters of the word 'BODMAS' when explained serially, has following implications:

1.	B	→	Bracket	$[\{(\overline{\ })\}]$
2.	O	→	of	of
3.	D	→	Division	÷
4.	M	→	Multiplication	×
5.	A	→	Addition	+
6.	S	→	Subtraction	–

Therefore, for simplification, we should remove the brackets first. Thereafter operation for 'of', then for 'division', after that the operation for 'multiplication' and thereafter for 'addition' and at last operation for 'subtraction' should be carried out.

Important Notes

(a) In mathematical operations the word 'of' indicates multiplication.

(b) While removing brackets, first of all bar bracket '–' and after that small bracket '( )' is removed. Thereafter the curly bracket '{ }' and at last square bracket [ ] is removed.

EXAMPLES

Example 1. : Simplify the following expression:

$800 \div 8 \text{ of } 4 \times [40 - \{35 - (\overline{20-10} \div 2) + 6\}]$

Solution: For simplifying the given expression we will first remove bar bracket '–', then the small bracket '( )', thereafter the curly bracket '{ }' and at last the square bracket '[ ]'. 'BODMAS' Rule is applied to solve the expression.

$\therefore 800 \div 8 \text{ of } 4 \times [40 - \{35 - (\overline{20-10} \div 2) + 6\}]$

$= 800 \div 8 \text{ of } 4 \times [40 - \{35 - (10 \div 2) + 6\}]$

$= 800 \div 8 \text{ of } 4 \times [40 - \{35 - 5 + 6\}]$

$= 800 \div 8 \text{ of } 4 \times [40 - \{41 - 5\}]$

$= 800 \div 8 \text{ of } 4 \times [40 - 36] = 800 \div 8 \text{ of } 4 \times 4$

$= 800 \div 32 \times 4$

$= \frac{800}{32} \times 4 = 100$

Example 2: Simplyfy:

(a) $\frac{2.8 \times 2.8 - 1.2 \times 1.2}{2.8 - 1.2}$

(b) $(6.8)^2 + 6.8 \times 6.4 + (3.2)^2$

Solution:

(a) $\because \frac{2.8 \times 2.8 - 1.2 \times 1.2}{2.8 - 1.2} = \frac{(2.8)^2 - (1.2)^2}{2.8 - 1.2}$

$= \frac{(2.8 + 1.2)(2.8 - 1.2)}{2.8 - 1.2} = 2.8 + 1.2 = 4$

$[\because a^2 - b^2 = (a + b)(a - b)]$

(b) $\because (6.8)^2 + 6.8 \times 6.4 + (3.2)^2$

$= (6.8)^2 + 2 \times 3.2 \times 6.8 + (3.2)^2$

$= (6.8 + 3.2)^2 = (10)^2 = 100$

$[\because a^2 + 2ab + b^2 = (a + b)^2]$

Example 3: Simplify : $7680 \div 256 \div 64 \div 8$

Solution: $7680 \div 256 \div 64 \div 8 = \frac{7680}{256} \div 64 \div 8 =$

$30 \div 64 \div 8$

$= \frac{30}{64} \div 8 = \frac{15}{32} \div 8 = \frac{15}{32 \times 8} = \frac{15}{256}$

Example 4: Simplify:

$$b-\left[b-(a+b)-\left\{b-\left(b-\overline{a-b}\right)\right\}+2a\right]$$

Solution:

$$b-\left[b-(a+b)-\left\{b-\left(b-\overline{a-b}\right)\right\}+2a\right]$$

$$= b-\left[b-(a+b)-\{b-(b-a+b)\}+2a\right]$$

$$= b-\left[b-a-b-\{b-b+a-b\}+2a\right]$$

$$= b-\left[b-a-b-\{a-b\}+2a\right]$$

$$= b-\left[b-a-b-a+b+2a\right]$$

$$= b-b$$

$$= 0.$$

EXERCISE

1. If $75^2 - 65^2 = 2x$, then value of x is:

(a) 715 (b) 700
(c) 688 (d) 711
(e) None of these

2. What will be the value of $\dfrac{\frac{1}{3}\times 20 \div 4}{\frac{1}{4}\times 25 \div 5}$?

(a) $\frac{7}{3}$ (b) $\frac{2}{3}$
(c) $\frac{5}{3}$ (d) $\frac{10}{3}$
(e) $\frac{4}{3}$

3. Which of the following is the standard form of $\dfrac{(24\times 13)+(28\div 7)}{(24+13)-\left(\frac{14}{3}\text{ of }\frac{5}{8}\right)}$?

(a) $\frac{3792}{409}$ (b) $\frac{4792}{309}$
(c) $\frac{3792}{411}$ (d) $\frac{3092}{409}$
(e) None of these

4. What will be the value of $\dfrac{\left(\sqrt{6}+\frac{1}{\sqrt{6}}\right)^2}{\frac{1}{2}\text{of } 18 + 4} + \dfrac{2}{3}$?

(a) $\frac{101}{78}$ (b) $\frac{104}{71}$
(c) $\frac{101}{88}$ (d) $\frac{99}{57}$
(e) None of these

5. $\dfrac{(.08)^3 + (.011)^3}{(.08)^2 - .08\times .011 + (.011)^2} = ?$

(a) .087 (b) 0.91
(c) .077 (d) .067
(e) 0.0091

6. What is the value of

$22 \div \left[(28-13)\div\{(32-8)\div\left(5+\frac{1}{3}\right)\}\right]$?

(a) 7.9 (b) 6.8
(c) 6.6 (d) 5.7
(e) None of these

7. What is the value of $\dfrac{\left(20^2-10^2\right)\div 5\times 3+10}{\frac{1}{3}\text{ of } 27+10\div 2+1}$?

(a) $10\frac{2}{3}$ (b) $14\frac{1}{3}$
(c) 15 (d) $12\frac{2}{3}$
(e) None of these

8. What is the value of $11^2 - 6^2 \div 6 \times \frac{5}{2}$ + 2 of 10?

(a) 126 (b) 108
(c) 110 (d) 125
(e) None of these

9. What is the value of $\frac{19}{17}$ of $\frac{28}{5}$ of $\left(\frac{17}{3} \div \frac{5}{3} \text{ of } 6\frac{1}{3}\right)$?

(*a*) $4\frac{9}{25}$ (*b*) $3\frac{8}{23}$

(*c*) $3\frac{9}{24}$ (*d*) $3\frac{8}{25}$

(*e*) $3\frac{9}{25}$

10. What is the value of $\left(17^{\frac{3}{2}} + 11^{3/2}\right)\left(17^{\frac{3}{2}} - 11^{3/2}\right)$?

(*a*) 3852 (*b*) 3582
(*c*) 3782 (*d*) 3258
(*e*) None of these

11. What is the value of $3 - [9 + \{14 - (6 - \overline{3 - 21})\}]$?

(*a*) 0 (*b*) 4
(*c*) 18 (*d*) 6
(*e*) None of these

12. $\dfrac{4\frac{1}{7} - 2\frac{1}{4}}{3\frac{1}{2} + 1\frac{1}{7}} \div \dfrac{1}{2 + \dfrac{1}{2 + \dfrac{1}{5 - \frac{1}{5}}}} = ?$

(*a*) 3 (*b*) $\frac{1}{8}$

(*c*) 8 (*d*) 1
(*e*) None of these

13. 25 – 5 [2 + 3 {2 – 2 (5 – 3) + 5} –10] ÷ 4 = ?

(*a*) 5 (*b*) 25
(*c*) 23.25 (*d*) 23.75
(*e*) None of these

14. $\dfrac{(6+6+6+6) \div 6}{4+4+4+4 \div 4} = ?$

(*a*) $3\frac{6}{13}$ (*b*) $\frac{4}{13}$

(*c*) $\frac{3}{2}$ (*d*) 1

(*e*) None of these

15. 18 – [5 – {6 + 2 (7 – 8 – 5)}] = ?

(*a*) 32 (*b*) 27
(*c*) 15 (*d*) 13
(*e*) None of these

16. A student was asked to solve the fraction $\dfrac{\frac{7}{3} + 1\frac{1}{2} \text{ of } \frac{5}{3}}{2 + 1\frac{2}{3}}$ and his answer was $\frac{1}{4}$.

By how much was his answer wrong?

(*a*) $\frac{23}{44}$ (*b*) $\frac{3}{44}$

(*c*) $1\frac{5}{44}$ (*d*) $\frac{23}{40}$

(*e*) None of these

17. 7 is added to a certain number, the sum is multiplied by 5 the product is divided by 9 and 3 is subtracted from the quotient. The remainder left is 12. Find the number.

(*a*) 60 (*b*) 40
(*c*) 30 (*d*) 20
(*e*) None of these

18. If $2 = x + \dfrac{1}{1 + \dfrac{1}{3 + \frac{1}{4}}}$, then the value of x is:

(*a*) $\frac{21}{17}$ (*b*) $\frac{18}{17}$

(*c*) $\frac{13}{17}$ (*d*) $\frac{12}{17}$

(*e*) None of these

19. The value of $\dfrac{2 + \dfrac{1}{3\frac{4}{5}}}{2 + \dfrac{1}{3 + \dfrac{1}{1 + \frac{1}{4}}}}$ is:

(*a*) $\frac{8}{7}$ (*b*) $\frac{3}{7}$

(c) $\frac{1}{7}$ (d) 1

(e) None of these

20. $\dfrac{1}{1+\dfrac{\frac{2}{3}}{1+\frac{2}{3}+\dfrac{\frac{8}{9}}{1-\frac{2}{3}}}}$ is equal to:

(a) $\frac{15}{13}$ (b) $\frac{13}{11}$

(c) $\frac{13}{15}$ (d) $\frac{11}{13}$

(e) None of these

21. $\frac{3}{4}\left(1+\frac{1}{3}\right)\left(1+\frac{2}{3}\right)\left(1-\frac{2}{5}\right)\left(1+\frac{6}{7}\right)\left(1-\frac{12}{13}\right)$ is simplified to:

(a) $\frac{1}{8}$ (b) $\frac{1}{7}$

(c) $\frac{1}{6}$ (d) $\frac{1}{5}$

(e) None of these

22. $\left(1+\frac{1}{2}\right)\left(1+\frac{1}{3}\right)\left(1+\frac{1}{4}\right)\ldots\left(1+\frac{1}{120}\right)$ is simplified to:

(a) 121 (b) 85.5

(c) 40.5 (d) 30

(e) None of these

23. $999\frac{995}{999}\times 999$ is simplified to:

(a) 999824 (b) 998999

(c) 999996 (d) 990809

(e) 998996

24. $\frac{3}{1^2.2^2}+\frac{5}{2^2.3^2}+\frac{7}{3^2.4^2}+\frac{9}{4^2.5^2}+\frac{11}{5^2.6^2}+\frac{13}{6^2.7^2}+\frac{15}{7^2.8^2}+\frac{17}{8^2.9^2}+\frac{19}{9^2.10^2}$ is simplified to:

(a) $\frac{101}{100}$ (b) 1

(c) $\frac{99}{100}$ (d) $\frac{1}{100}$

(e) None of these

25. $1+\frac{1}{4\times 3}+\frac{1}{4\times 3^2}+\frac{1}{4\times 3^3}$ is simplified to:

(a) $\frac{11}{18}$ (b) $\frac{121}{108}$

(c) $\frac{3}{2}$ (d) $\frac{31}{2}$

(e) None of these

26. $\frac{1}{1\cdot 2\cdot 3}+\frac{1}{2\cdot 3\cdot 4}+\frac{1}{3\cdot 4\cdot 5}+\frac{1}{4\cdot 5\cdot 6}$ is simplified to:

(a) $\frac{17}{30}$ (b) $\frac{13}{30}$

(c) $\frac{11}{30}$ (d) $\frac{7}{30}$

(e) None of these

27. $\dfrac{\left(\frac{3}{5}\right)^3-\left(\frac{2}{5}\right)^3}{\left(\frac{3}{5}\right)^2-\left(\frac{2}{5}\right)^2}$ is simplified to:

(a) 1 (b) $\frac{21}{25}$

(c) $\frac{25}{19}$ (d) $\frac{1}{5}$

(e) $\frac{19}{25}$

28. $\dfrac{(13)^3+7^3}{(13)^2+7^2-?}=20$

(a) 91 (b) 81

(c) 100 (d) 64

(e) None of these

29. $$\frac{\left(1+\frac{1}{1+\frac{1}{100}}\right)\left(1+\frac{1}{1+\frac{1}{100}}\right)-\left(1-\frac{1}{1+\frac{1}{100}}\right)\left(1-\frac{1}{1+\frac{1}{100}}\right)}{\left(1+\frac{1}{1+\frac{1}{100}}\right)+\left(1-\frac{1}{1+\frac{1}{100}}\right)}$$

is simplified to:

(a) $\frac{101}{200}$ *(b)* 101

(c) 200 *(d)* $\frac{200}{101}$

(e) None of these

30. $$\frac{\left(3\frac{2}{3}\right)^2-\left(2\frac{1}{2}\right)^2}{\left(4\frac{3}{4}\right)^2-\left(3\frac{1}{3}\right)^2}\div\frac{3\frac{2}{3}-2\frac{1}{2}}{4\frac{3}{4}-3\frac{1}{3}}$$ is simplified to:

(a) $\frac{97}{74}$ *(b)* $\frac{74}{97}$

(c) $\frac{37}{97}$ *(d)* $\frac{97}{37}$

(e) None of these

ANSWERS

1	2	3	4	5	6	7	8	9	10
(b)	*(e)*	*(a)*	*(a)*	*(e)*	*(c)*	*(d)*	*(a)*	*(e)*	*(b)*
11	**12**	**13**	**14**	**15**	**16**	**17**	**18**	**19**	**20**
(b)	*(d)*	*(d)*	*(b)*	*(b)*	*(e)*	*(d)*	*(a)*	*(d)*	*(c)*
21	**22**	**23**	**24**	**25**	**26**	**27**	**28**	**29**	**30**
(b)	*(e)*	*(e)*	*(c)*	*(b)*	*(d)*	*(e)*	*(a)*	*(d)*	*(b)*

SOME SELECTED EXPLANATORY ANSWERS

1. $\because \quad 75^2 - 65^2 = 2x$

$\Rightarrow (75 + 65)\ (75 - 65) = 2x$

$[\because a^2 - b^2 = (a + b)\ (a - b)]$

$\Rightarrow \quad 140 \times 10 = 2x$

$\Rightarrow \quad x = 70 \times 10 = 700$

$\therefore$ Value of x is 700.

2. $$\because \frac{\frac{1}{3}\times 20\div 4}{\frac{1}{4}\times 25\div 5}=\frac{\frac{1}{3}\times 5}{\frac{1}{4}\times 5}=\frac{\frac{5}{3}}{\frac{5}{4}}=\frac{4}{3}.$$

3. $$\because \frac{(24\times 13)+(28\div 7)}{(24+13)-\left(\frac{14}{3}\text{ of }\frac{5}{8}\right)}$$

$$=\frac{312+4}{37-\frac{35}{12}}=\frac{316}{\frac{409}{12}}=\frac{3792}{409}.$$

4. $$\therefore \frac{\left(\sqrt{6}+\frac{1}{\sqrt{6}}\right)^2}{\frac{1}{2}\text{ of }18+4}+\frac{2}{3}$$

$$=\frac{\left(\sqrt{6}\right)^2+\left(\frac{1}{\sqrt{6}}\right)^2+2.\sqrt{6}\frac{1}{\sqrt{6}}}{9+4}+\frac{2}{3}$$

$$=\frac{6+\frac{1}{6}+2}{13}+\frac{2}{3}=\frac{\frac{49}{6}}{13}+\frac{2}{3}=\frac{49}{78}+\frac{2}{3}=\frac{101}{78}.$$

8. $11^2-6^2\div 6\times\frac{5}{2}+2\text{ of }10$

$= 11^2 - 6^2 \div 6 \times \frac{5}{2} + 20$

$= 11^2 - 6 \times \frac{5}{2} + 20$

$= 11^2 - 15 + 20 = 121 + 5 = 126.$

11. $3 - [9 + \{14 - (6 - \overline{3-21})\}]$
$= 3 - [9 + \{14 - (6 + 18\}]$
$= 3 - [9 + \{14 - 24\}]$
$= 3 - [9 - 10] = 3 + 1 = 4.$

13. $25 - 5\ [2 + 3\ \{2 - 2\ (5 - 3) + 5\} - 10] \div 4$
$= 25 - 5\ [2 + 3\ \{2 - 4 + 5\} - 10] \div 4$
$= 25 - 5\ [2 + 9 - 10] \div 4$

$$= 25 - 5 \times 1 \times \frac{1}{4} = 25 - \frac{5}{4} = \frac{95}{4} = 23.75.$$

15. $18 - [5 - \{6 + 2\ (7 - \overline{8-5})\}]$
$= 18 - [5 - \{6 + 2\ (7 - 3)\}]$
$= 18 - [5 - \{6 + 8\}]$
$= 18 - [5 - 14] = 18 + 9 = 27.$

16. $$\frac{\frac{7}{3} + \frac{3}{2} \text{ of } \frac{5}{3}}{2 + \frac{5}{3}} = \frac{\frac{7}{3} + \frac{5}{2}}{\frac{11}{3}} = \frac{29}{6} \times \frac{3}{11} = \frac{29}{22}$$

Required difference

$$= \frac{29}{22} - \frac{1}{4} = \frac{58-11}{44} = \frac{47}{44} = 1\frac{3}{44}.$$

17. Let, $\frac{5\,(x+7)}{9} - 3 = 12$

$\Rightarrow \quad \frac{5\,(x+7)}{9} = 15$

$\Rightarrow \quad x + 7 = \frac{9 \times 15}{5} = 27$

$\therefore \quad x = 20.$

20. $$\frac{1}{1 + \frac{\frac{2}{3}}{1 + \frac{2}{3} + \frac{8/9}{1-2/3}}} = \frac{1}{1 + \frac{\frac{2}{3}}{1 + \frac{2}{3} + \frac{8}{9} \times 3}}$$

$$= \frac{1}{1 + \frac{\frac{2}{3}}{1 + \frac{10}{3}}} = \frac{1}{1 + \frac{2}{3} \times \frac{3}{13}} = \frac{1}{\frac{15}{13}} = \frac{13}{15}.$$

21. $$\frac{3}{4}\left(1+\frac{1}{3}\right)\left(1+\frac{2}{3}\right)\left(1-\frac{2}{5}\right)\left(1+\frac{6}{7}\right)\left(1-\frac{12}{13}\right)$$

$$= \frac{3}{4} \times \frac{4}{3} \times \frac{5}{3} \times \frac{3}{5} \times \frac{13}{7} \times \frac{1}{13} = \frac{1}{7}.$$

22. $$\left(1+\frac{1}{2}\right)\left(1+\frac{1}{3}\right)\left(1-\frac{1}{4}\right)\ldots\left(1+\frac{1}{120}\right)$$

$$= \frac{3}{2} \times \frac{4}{3} \times \frac{5}{4} \times \ldots \times \frac{121}{120} = \frac{121}{2} = 60.5.$$

24. $$\frac{3}{1^2.2^2} + \frac{5}{2^2.3^2} + \frac{7}{3^2.4^2} + \frac{9}{4^2.5^2} + \frac{11}{5^2.6^2}$$

$$+ \frac{13}{6^2.7^2} + \frac{15}{7^2.8^2} + \frac{17}{8^2.9^2} + \frac{19}{9^2.10^2}$$

$$= 1 - \frac{1}{4} + \frac{1}{4} - \frac{1}{9} + \frac{1}{9} - \frac{1}{16} + \frac{1}{16} - \frac{1}{25} + \frac{1}{25}$$

$$- \frac{1}{36} + \frac{1}{36} - \frac{1}{49} + \frac{1}{49} - \frac{1}{64} + \frac{1}{64} - \frac{1}{81} +$$

$$= 1 - \frac{1}{100} = \frac{99}{100}.$$

❑❑❑

2 L.C.M. & H.C.F.

L.C.M.

Multiple : A number is said to be multiple of other when it is exactly divisible by the other.

Common multiple : A common multiple of two or more numbers is a number which is exactly divisible by each of them. For example, for 2 and 3, common multiples are 6, 12, 18, 24 and so on.

Consider the two numbers 2 and 3

Multiple of 2 are 2, 4, 6, 8, 10, 12, ...

Multiple of 3 are 3, 6, 9, 12, 15, ...

∴ Common multiples are 6, 12, 18, ...

Least Common Multiple (L.C.M.) : L.C.M. of two or more given numbers is the least number which is exactly divisible by each of them. For example,

6 is a common multiple of 2 and 3

12 is also common multiple of 2 and 3

Methods to find out L.C.M.

L.C.M. of two or more given numbers is determined by following two methods:

1. By prime factorization method

2. By division method

1. **By prime factorization method :** Resolve the given numbers into their prime factors and then find the product of the highest power of all the factors that occur in the given numbers. This product will be the L.C.M.
2. **By division method :** This is the quicker method to find the prime factors and hence L.C.M.

   For determining L.C.M. of the numbers 40, 50, 60 and 80, following process of division is adopted:

2	40, 50, 60, 80
2	20, 25, 30, 40
2	10, 25, 15, 20
5	5, 25, 15, 10
	1, 5, 3, 2

Now required L.C.M.

$$= 2 \times 2 \times 2 \times 5 \times 5 \times 3 \times 2 = 1200$$

L.C.M. of decimal : First of all, we find out the L.C.M. of numbers without decimal and then, we see the number in which decimal is given in the minimum digit from right to left. We put the decimal in our result which is equal to that number of digits.

Example : Find the L.C.M. of 0.6, 9.6 and 0.36.

Sol : The given numbers are equivalent to 0.60, 9.60 and 0.36.

Now, we find out the L.C.M. of 60, 960 and 36, which is equal to 2880.

Hence, the required L.C.M. = 28.80.

L.C.M. of fraction : The L.C.M. of two or more fractions is the least fraction or integer which is exactly divisible by each of them.

If $\frac{a}{b}, \frac{c}{d}, \frac{e}{f}$ be the proper fractions, then their L.C.M. is given by

$$\frac{\text{L.C.M. of numerators } a, c, e}{\text{H.C.F. of denominators } b, d, f}$$

H.C.F.

Factor : One number is said to be a factor of other when it divides the other exactly. Hence, 5 and 7 are factors of 35.

Common factor : A common factor of two or more numbers is a number that divides each of them exactly. Hence, 5 is a common factor of 15, 25, 35 and 55.

Highest Common Factor (H.C.F.) : H.C.F. of two or more numbers is the largest number by which each given number is divisible without leaving any remainder.

An example : It is required to find the H.C.F. of 6 and 8. Factors of 6 are 1, 2, 3, 6 and Factors of 8 are 1, 2, 4, 8.

The common factors are 1, 2, but highest of these is 2. Hence, 2 is the H.C.F.

We can find H.C.F. by two methods:

1. By prime factorization method :

An example : Find the H.C.F. of 144, 336 and 2016.

Sol : $144 = 2 \times 2 \times 2 \times 2 \times 3 \times 3$

$= 2^4 \times 3^2$

$336 = 2 \times 2 \times 2 \times 2 \times 3 \times 7$

$= 2^4 \times 3 \times 7$

$2016 = 2 \times 2 \times 2 \times 2 \times 2 \times 7 \times 3 \times 3$

$= 2^5 \times 7 \times 3^2$

$\therefore$ H.C.F. of given numbers $= 2^4 \times 3 = 48$.

2. By division method

Divide the greater number by the smaller number, divide the divisor by the remainder, divide the remainder by the next remainder, and so on until no remainder is left. The last divisor is the required H.C.F.

H.C.F. of Decimals : First of all find the H.C.F. of the given numbers ignoring decimals and then put decimal at maximum digits from right to left.

An example : Find the H.C.F. of 0.0012, 1.6 and 2.8.

Sol : First we find the H.C.F. of 12, 16 and 28, which comes to 4.

So, H.C.F. of 0.0012, 1.6 and 2.8 will be 0.0004.

H.C.F. of Fractions :

If $\frac{a}{b}, \frac{c}{d}, \frac{e}{f}$, ... be the proper fraction, their H.C.F. is

equal to $\frac{\text{H.C.F. of numerators}}{\text{L.C.M. of denominators}}$

EXAMPLES

Example 1 : Find the H.C.F. of 8, 9 and 16.

Solution:

```
8 )  9 ( 1
     8
    ---
     1 ) 8 ( 8
         8
        ---
         ×
```

$\therefore$ H.C.F. of 8 and 9 is 1.

Now, we will have to find out the H.C.F. of 1 and 16.

```
1 ) 16 (16
    16
   ---
    ×
```

$\therefore$ H.C.F. of 1 and 16 is 1

Hence, the required H.C.F. of 8, 9 and 16 is 1.

Example 2 : Find the L.C.M. of 11, 33, 77 and 121.

Solution:

```
11 | 11, 33, 77, 121
   |  1,  3,  7,  11
```

Hence, required L.C.M. $= 11 \times 3 \times 7 \times 11 = 2541$

Example 3 : Determine the H.C.F. of $\frac{54}{9}, 3\frac{9}{17}$ and $\frac{36}{51}$.

Solution: $\frac{54}{9} = \frac{6}{1}, 3\frac{9}{17} = \frac{60}{17}$ and $\frac{36}{51} = \frac{12}{17}$

Now, H.C.F. of $\frac{6}{1}, \frac{60}{17}$ and $\frac{12}{17}$

$= \frac{\text{H.C.F. of 6, 60 and 12}}{\text{L.C.M. of 1, 17 and 17}}$

$\because$ H.C.F. of 6, 60 and 12 = 6

and L.C.M. of 1, 17 and 17 = 17

$\therefore$ Required H.C.F. $= \frac{6}{17}$

Example 4 : Find the L.C.M. of $4\frac{1}{2}$, 3 and $10\frac{1}{2}$.

Solution: $4\frac{1}{2} = \frac{9}{2}, 10\frac{1}{2} = \frac{21}{2}$

$\therefore$ L.C.M. of $\frac{9}{2}, \frac{3}{1}$ and $\frac{21}{2} = \frac{\text{L.C.M. of 9, 3 and 21}}{\text{H.C.F. of 2, 1 and 2}}$

$\because$ L.C.M. of 9, 3 and 21 = 63

and H.C.F. of 2, 1 and 2 = 1

Hence, required number $= \frac{63}{1} = 63$

EXERCISE

1. The L.C.M. of 6, 8, 10 and 12 is
   (a) 120 (b) 60
   (c) 240 (d) 130
   (e) None of these

2. The H.C.F. of $\frac{5}{6}, \frac{6}{7}, \frac{7}{8}, \frac{8}{9}$ and $\frac{9}{10}$ is
   (a) $\frac{1}{2420}$ (b) $\frac{1}{2520}$
   (c) $\frac{1}{2660}$ (d) $\frac{1}{2540}$
   (e) None of these

3. The L.C.M. of two numbers is 85 and their product is 1020. Their H.C.F. will be
   (a) 16 (b) 27
   (c) 12 (d) 22
   (e) None of these

4. L.C.M. of 24, 28, 36 and 44 is a multiple of 24 and which of the following numbers?
   (a) 441 (b) 368
   (c) 337 (d) 197
   (e) 231

5. H.C.F. of 420, 315 and 462 is
   (a) 24 (b) 28
   (c) 27 (d) 21
   (e) None of these

6. The largest three-digit number, when divided by 6, 9 and 12 leaves 1 as remainder in each case, will be
   (a) 887 (b) 987
   (c) 973 (d) 730
   (e) None of these

7. Two numbers are in the ratio of 8 : 15. If their H.C.F. is 4, the numbers are
   (a) 32 and 60 (b) 16 and 30
   (c) 80 and 150 (d) 64 and 120
   (e) None of these

8. The largest number that will divide 226 and 272 leaving 1 and 2 as remainders respectively, is
   (a) 36 (b) 45
   (c) 55 (d) 59
   (e) None of these

9. The product of two numbers is 2160 and their H.C.F. is 12. How many such pairs of numbers can be possibly formed?
   (a) 3 (b) 1
   (c) 5 (d) 2
   (e) 2

10. The greatest number that will divide 33, 64 and 80 leaving 3, 4 and 5 as remainders respectively, is
    (a) 10 (b) 20
    (c) 15 (d) 22
    (e) None of these

11. The greatest four-digit number completely divisible by 2, 3, 4 and 5 is
    (a) 9960 (b) 9690
    (c) 8990 (d) 9980
    (e) None of these

12. Three bells ring respectively at an interval of 15 seconds, 20 seconds and 24 seconds. If they ring continuously for 12 minutes then how many times, during this period, will they ring together?
    (a) 2 times (b) 6 times
    (c) 5 times (d) 3 times
    (e) None of these

13. The smallest number, on being successively divided by 5, 6, 8, 9 and 12 leaves 1 as remainder in each case and is completely divisible by 13, will be
    (a) 4603 (b) 6305
    (c) 4503 (d) 3601
    (e) None of these

14. HCF of $4 \times 27 \times 3125$, $8 \times 9 \times 25 \times 7$ and $16 \times 81 \times 5 \times 11 \times 49$ is
    (a) 1260 (b) 540
    (c) 360 (d) 240
    (e) 180

15. The LCM of $2^3 \times 3^2 \times 5 \times 11$, $2^4 \times 3^4 \times 5^2 \times 7$ and $2^5 \times 3^3 \times 5^3 \times 7^2 \times 11$ is :
    (a) $2^5 \times 3^4 \times 5^3$
    (b) $2^3 \times 3^2 \times 5$
    (c) $2^5 \times 3^4 \times 5^3 \times 7^2 \times 11$

(d) $2^3 \times 3^2 \times 5 \times 7 \times 11$
(e) None of these

16. H.C.F. of 3240, 3600 and a third number is 36 and their L.C.M. is $2^4 \times 3^5 \times 5^2 \times 7^2$. The third number is

(a) $2^3 \times 3^5 \times 7^2$
(b) $2^5 \times 5^2 \times 7^2$
(c) $2^2 \times 5^3 \times 7^2$
(d) $2^2 \times 3^5 \times 7^2$
(e) None of these

ANSWERS

1	2	3	4	5	6	7	8	9	10
(a)	(b)	(c)	(e)	(d)	(c)	(a)	(b)	(e)	(c)
11	**12**	**13**	**14**	**15**	**16**				
(a)	(b)	(d)	(e)	(c)	(d)				

SOME SELECTED EXPLANATORY ANSWERS

1. $6 = 2 \times 3;\ 8 = 2 \times 2 \times 2$
$10 = 2 \times 5;\ 12 = 2 \times 2 \times 3$

It is clear that 2 occurs as prime factor maximum three times, 3 one time and 5 one time.

Hence, required L.C.M. $= 2 \times 2 \times 2 \times 3 \times 5 = 120$

2. H.C.F. of $\frac{5}{6}, \frac{6}{7}, \frac{7}{8}, \frac{8}{9}$ and $\frac{9}{10}$

$$= \frac{\text{H.C.F. of 5,6,7,8 and 9}}{\text{LCM of 6,7,8,9 and 10}}$$

Now H.C.F. of 5, 6, 7, 8 and 9 = 1

and L.C.M. of 6, 7, 8, 9 and 10 = 2520

$\therefore$ Required H.C.F. $= \frac{1}{2520}$

3. L.C.M. of two numbers × H.C.F. of the numbers = Product of the numbers

$\therefore \quad 85 \times \text{H.C.F.} = 1020$

$\therefore \quad \text{H.C.F.} = \frac{1020}{85} = 12$

9. Product of two numbers = their HCF × their LCM

$2160 = 12 \times \text{LCM}$

$\therefore \quad \text{LCM} = \frac{2160}{12} = 180$

Therefore such pairs of numbers in which product of numbers is 2160 and HCF is 12 will be only 2.

i.e., 12×180 and 36×60.

10. $33 - 3 = 30$, $64 - 4 = 60$ and $80 - 5 = 75$

Now, HCF of 30, 60 and 75:

$30 = 2 \times \underline{3 \times 5}$

$60 = 2 \times 2 \times \underline{3 \times 5}$

$75 = \underline{3 \times 5} \times 5$

$\because$ Common factor $= 3 \times 5 = 15$

$\therefore$ Required largest number = 15.

13. LCM of 5, 6, 8, 9 and 12 = 360. Hence, the smallest number which when divided by 5, 6, 8, 9 and 12 leaves 1 as remainder in each case will be 360 + 1 = 361. But 361 is not completely divisible by 13. Hence, on considering $360 \times 2 + 1$, $360 \times 3 + 1$,... , $360 \times n + 1$, we conclude that $360 \times 10 + 1 = 3601$ is the required number.

14. $4 \times 27 \times 3125 = 2^2 \times 3^3 \times 5^5$

$8 \times 9 \times 25 \times 7 = 2^3 \times 3^2 \times 5^2 \times 7$

$16 \times 81 \times 5 \times 11 \times 49 = 2^4 \times 3^4 \times 5 \times 7^2 \times 11$

$\therefore \quad \text{HCF} = 2^2 \times 3^2 \times 5 = 4 \times 9 \times 5 = 180$

15. $2^3 \times 3^2 \times 5 \times 11;\quad 2^4 \times 3^4 \times 5^2 \times 7$
and $\quad 2^5 \times 3^3 \times 5^3 \times 7^2 \times 11$

$\therefore \quad \text{LCM} = 2^5 \times 3^4 \times 5^3 \times 7^2 \times 11$

❑❑❑

3 Surds & Indices

SURDS

If x is a rational number and n is a positive integer, such that $x^{1/n} = \sqrt[n]{x}$ is irrational, since $\sqrt[n]{x}$ is called a surd of order n.

Laws of Surds:

(i) $\sqrt[n]{x} = x^{1/n}$ (ii) $\left(\sqrt[n]{x}\right)^m = \sqrt[n]{x^m}$

(iii) $\sqrt[m]{\sqrt[n]{x}} = \sqrt[mn]{x}$ (iv) $\left(\sqrt[n]{x}\right)^n = x$

(v) $\sqrt[n]{xy} = \sqrt[n]{x} \times \sqrt[n]{y}$ (vi) $\sqrt[n]{\dfrac{a}{b}} = \dfrac{\sqrt[n]{a}}{\sqrt[n]{b}}$

We know that $x \times x = x^2$, $x \times x \times x = x^3$, $x \times x \times x \times x = x^4$ ..., $x \times x \times x \times x \times x$ ... n times $= x^n$.

In the given quantity x^n, x is called **base** and n is called **exponent** or **index** or **power**. We read x^n as x raised to the power n or, nth power of x.

Laws of Indices:

Law 1: *When m and n are natural numbers or positive integers and x is a non-zero real number, then* $x^m \times x^n = x^{m+n}$.

Law 2: *When m and n are natural numbers or positive integers and x is a non-zero real number, then* $x^m \div x^n = \dfrac{x^m}{x^n} = x^{m-n}$, *if* $m > n$ *and* $\dfrac{x^m}{x^n} = \dfrac{1}{x^{n-m}}$, *if* $n > m$.

Law 3: *When m and n are natural numbers or positive integers and x is a non-zero real number, then* $(x^m)^n = x^{mn}$.

Law 4: *When m and n are natural numbers or positive integers and x and y are non-zero real numbers, then* $(xy)^m = x^m \times y^m$.

ROOT

If 'x' is a positive real number, 'n' an integer and 'a' is a natural number such that $x^n = a$, then it means nth root of a is x. It is generally denoted as:

$$x^n = a \text{ or } x = \sqrt[n]{a} = a^{\frac{1}{n}}$$

Similarly, if x is a positive real number, 'p' an integer and 'q' is a natural number such that $x^{p/q} = a$ (where a is a non-zero real number) then it means that qth root of x is equal to pth root of 'a'.

$$i.e., x^{\frac{p}{q}} = a \Rightarrow \left(x^{\frac{1}{q}}\right)^p = a \Rightarrow x^{\frac{1}{q}} = a^{\frac{1}{p}} \Rightarrow$$

$$\sqrt[q]{x} = \sqrt[p]{a}$$

Important Note: *If x is any rational number other than zero, then* $x^0 = 1$

When the base is a non-zero real number and exponent is negative integer: Here, we shall find out the value of x^{-n} (where $x \neq 0$ and a positive integer).

From the first law of exponent,

$$x^{-n} \times x^n = x^{-n+n} = x^0$$

$$\Rightarrow \quad x^{-n} \times x^n = 1 \ (\because x^0 = 1)$$

Dividing both sides by x^n,

$$x^{-n} = \frac{1}{x^n},$$

Similarly, $$x^n = \frac{1}{x^{-n}}$$

Hence, x^{-n} means the reciprocal of x^n.

EXAMPLES

Example 1: Simplify the following using laws of exponents.

(a) $24\, a^7\, b^5\, c^2 \div 3a^5\, b^3\, c^4$

(b) $\dfrac{x^{-2}y^{-4}}{x^{-3}y^{-1}} \div \dfrac{y^{-2}}{x^{-1}}$

Solution:

(a) $24\, a^7\, b^5\, c^2 \div 3a^5\, b^3\, c^4$

$$= \frac{24a^7b^5c^2}{3a^5b^3c^4} = 8\left(\frac{a^7}{a^5}\right)\left(\frac{b^5}{b^3}\right)\left(\frac{c^2}{c^4}\right)$$

$$= 8\, a^{(7-5)}\, b^{(5-3)}\left(\frac{1}{c^{4-2}}\right) = \frac{8a^2b^2}{c^2}$$

(b) $\because \dfrac{x^{-2}y^{-4}}{x^{-3}y^{-1}} \div \dfrac{y^{-2}}{x^{-1}}$

$$= \frac{\dfrac{x^{-2}y^{-4}}{x^{-3}y^{-1}}}{\dfrac{y^{-2}}{x^{-1}}} = \frac{x^{-2}.y^{-4} \times x^{-1}}{x^{-3}.y^{-1} \times y^{-2}} = \frac{x^{-3}y^{-4}}{x^{-3}.y^{-3}}$$

$$= y^{-4+3} = y^{-1}$$

$$= \frac{1}{y}$$

Example 2: Evaluate the following:

$$\left[\left(\frac{2^{-1}}{3^{-4}}\right)^7 \div \left(\frac{3^{-5}}{2^{-2}}\right)^{-5}\right] 2^{-4}\ 3^{-2}$$

Solution :

$$\because \left(\frac{2^{-1}}{3^{-4}}\right)^7$$

$$= \frac{2^{-1\times 7}}{3^{-4\times 7}} = \frac{2^{-7}}{3^{-28}}$$

$$= \frac{3^{28}}{2^7} \text{ and } \left(\frac{3^{-5}}{2^{-2}}\right)^{-5} = \frac{3^{-5\times -5}}{2^{-2\times -5}} = \frac{3^{25}}{2^{10}}$$

$$\therefore \left[\left(\frac{2^{-1}}{3^{-4}}\right)^7 \div \left(\frac{3^{-5}}{2^{-2}}\right)^{-5}\right] 2^{-4}.3^{-2}$$

$$= \left(\frac{3^{28}}{2^7} \div \frac{3^{25}}{2^{10}}\right) 2^{-4}.3^{-2} = \frac{3^{28} \times 2^{10} \times 2^{-4} \times 3^{-2}}{2^7 \times 3^{25}}$$

$$= 3^{28-25-2} \times 2^{10-4-7} = 3^1 \times 2^{-1} = \frac{3}{2}$$

Example 3: If $5\sqrt{5} \times 5^3 \div 5^{-3/2} = 5^{a+2}$, what is the value of a?

Solution: $5\sqrt{5} \times 5^3 \div 5^{-3/2} = 5^{a+2}$

$$\Rightarrow \frac{5 \times 5^{\frac{1}{2}} \times 5^3}{5^{-3/2}} = 5^{a+2}$$

$$\Rightarrow 5^{1+\frac{1}{2}+3+3/2} = 5^{a+2}$$

$$\Rightarrow 5^6 = 5^{a+2} \qquad \Rightarrow 6 = a + 2$$

$$\Rightarrow \qquad a = 6 - 2 = 4$$

EXERCISE

1. $(x^{2/3})^{-3/4}$ is equivalent to:

(a) $\dfrac{1}{x}$ (b) $\dfrac{1}{\sqrt{x}}$

(c) $\dfrac{1}{x^2}$ (d) $\dfrac{1}{x^{-2}}$

(e) None of these

2. The value of $\left(-\dfrac{1}{125}\right)^{-\frac{2}{3}}$ is:

(a) $\dfrac{1}{25}$ (b) 125

(c) 5 (d) $\dfrac{1}{5}$

(e) 25

3. The value of $27^3 \times 3^4 \div 3^{10}$ is equal to:
(a) 9 (b) 3
(c) 81 (d) $\frac{1}{27}$
(e) 27

4. The expression $\frac{(-1)^{132}}{5^{-1}+3^{-1}}$ is equivalent to:
(a) $\frac{16}{9}$ (b) $-\frac{15}{8}$
(c) $\frac{15}{8}$ (d) $\frac{17}{8}$
(e) None of these

5. $\sqrt{\frac{1}{\left(\frac{3}{4}\right)^{-2}}}+\sqrt[3]{\frac{27}{64}}$ is equivalent to:
(a) $\frac{2}{3}$ (b) $\frac{4}{5}$
(c) $\frac{13}{12}$ (d) $\frac{3}{2}$
(e) None of these

6. $\sqrt[3]{x^6} \div \sqrt[6]{x^{12}} \times x^{-3} \times \sqrt[3]{x^9}$ is equivalent to:
(a) $2x$ (b) 1
(c) $\frac{1}{3x^2}$ (d) $\frac{1}{x}$
(e) None of these

7. $\left[\left(2a^2\right)^3\right]^3 \left[\left(3a^3\right)^2\right]^2 \div \left[\left(6a^6\right)^2\right]^2$ is equivalent to:
(a) $36a^6$ (b) $32a^6$
(c) $32a^4$ (d) $34a^5$
(e) None of these

8. $\frac{\left[\left(3^{-2}\right)^{-5}\right]^{1/5}+\left[\left(4^{-3}\right)^{-6}\right]^{1/6}-1}{\left[\left(2^{-3}\right)^{-4}\right]^{1/4}}$ is equivalent to:
(a) 9 (b) 8
(c) 27 (d) $\frac{1}{3}$
(e) None of these

9. $\frac{3^{n+3}-3^{n+1}+3^n}{2\left(3^{n-1}\right)}+2^{-1}$ is equivalent to:
(a) 32 (b) 39
(c) 35 (d) 38
(e) None of these

10. $\left(\frac{x^a}{x^{-b}}\right)^{a^2-ab+b^2}\left(\frac{x^b}{x^{-c}}\right)^{b^2-bc+c^2}\left(\frac{x^c}{x^{-a}}\right)^{c^2-ca+a^2}$ is equivalent to:
(a) $x^{(a^2+b^2+c^2)}$ (b) $x^{2(a^3+b^3-c^3)}$
(c) $x^{2(a^3-b^3-c^3)}$ (d) $\frac{1}{x^{2(a^3+b^3+c^3)}}$
(e) None of these

11. The value of $\frac{(243)^{0.13}\times(243)^{0.07}}{(7)^{0.25}\times(49)^{0.075}\times(343)^{0.2}}$ is:
(a) $2\frac{2}{7}$ (b) $1\frac{3}{7}$
(c) $\frac{7}{3}$ (d) 3/7
(e) None of these

12. $\left(\frac{x^b}{x^c}\right)^{(b+c-a)}\cdot\left(\frac{x^c}{x^a}\right)^{(c+a-b)}\left(\frac{x^a}{x^b}\right)^{(a+b-c)}=?$
(a) x^{a+b+c} (b) $x^{ab+bc+ca}$ (c) 1
(d) x^{abc}
(e) None of these

13. $\frac{1}{1+x^{(b-a)}+x^{(c-a)}}+\frac{1}{1+x^{(a-b)}+x^{(c-b)}}+\frac{1}{1+x^{(b-c)}+x^{(a-c)}}=?$
(a) x^{a+b+c} (b) x^{a-b-c}
(c) 1 (d) 0
(e) None of these

14. If m and n are whole numbers such that $m^n = 121$, then find the value of $(m-1)^{n+1}$.
(a) 1000 (b) 121
(c) 10 (d) 1
(e) None of these

15. If $10^{0.48} = x$, $10^{0.70} = y$ and $x^z = y^2$, then what is the approximate value of z?

(*a*) 3.7 (*b*) 1.73

(*c*) 1.88 (*d*) 1.45

(*e*) 2.9

16. Given that $2^x = 4^y = 8^z$ and $\left(\frac{1}{2x}+\frac{1}{4y}+\frac{1}{6z}\right) = \frac{24}{7}$, then find the value of z.

(*a*) $\frac{7}{64}$ (*b*) $\frac{7}{48}$

(*c*) $\frac{7}{32}$ (*d*) $\frac{7}{16}$

(*e*) None of these

ANSWERS

1	2	3	4	5	6	7	8	9	10
(*b*)	(*e*)	(*e*)	(*c*)	(*d*)	(*b*)	(*b*)	(*a*)	(*d*)	(*e*)
11	**12**	**13**	**14**	**15**	**16**				
(*d*)	(*c*)	(*c*)	(*a*)	(*e*)	(*b*)				

SOME SELECTED EXPLANATORY ANSWERS

1. $\left[x^{2/3}\right]^{-\frac{3}{4}} = x^{\frac{2}{3}\times\frac{-3}{4}} = x^{-\frac{1}{2}}$

$$= \frac{1}{x^{\frac{1}{2}}} = \frac{1}{\sqrt{x}} \quad \left[\because \left(x^m\right)^n = x^{mn}\right]$$

4. $\dfrac{(-1)^{132}}{5^{-1}+3^{-1}} = \dfrac{\left((-1)^2\right)^{66}}{5^{-1}+3^{-1}} = \dfrac{(1)^{66}}{5^{-1}+3^{-1}}$

$$= \frac{1}{\frac{1}{5}+\frac{1}{3}} = \frac{1}{\frac{3+5}{15}} = \frac{1}{\frac{8}{15}} = \frac{15}{8}$$

5. $\sqrt{\dfrac{1}{\left(\frac{3}{4}\right)^{-2}}} + \sqrt[3]{\dfrac{27}{64}} = \sqrt{\left(\frac{3}{4}\right)^2} + \sqrt[3]{\dfrac{3\times3\times3}{4\times4\times4}}$

$$= \sqrt{\left(\frac{3}{4}\right)^2} + \sqrt[3]{\left(\frac{3}{4}\right)^3}$$

$$= \frac{3}{4}+\frac{3}{4} = \frac{6}{4} = \frac{3}{2}$$

7. $[(2a^2)^3]^3\ [(3a^3)^2]^2 \div [(6a^6)^2]^2 = (8a^6)^3.\ (9a^6)^2$

$$\div (36a^{12})^2 = \frac{(8)^3.a^{18}.(9)^2.a^{12}}{(36)^2.a^{24}} = 32a^6$$

9. $\dfrac{3^{n+3}-3^{n+1}+3^n}{2\left(3^{n-1}\right)} + 2^{-1} = \dfrac{3^n\cdot3^3-3^n\cdot3+3^n}{2.3^n.3^{-1}} + 2^{-1}$

$$= \frac{3^3-3+1}{2.3^{-1}} + 2^{-1} = \frac{3^4-3^2+3}{2} + \frac{1}{2}$$

$$= \frac{81-9+3}{2} + \frac{1}{2} = \frac{76}{2} = 38$$

11. $\dfrac{(243)^{0.13}\times(243)^{0.07}}{(7)^{0.25}\times(49)^{0.075}\times(343)^{0.2}}$

$$= \frac{\left(3^5\right)^{0.13}\times\left(3^5\right)^{0.07}}{(7)^{0.25}\times\left(7^2\right)^{0.075}\times\left(7^3\right)^{0.2}}$$

$$= \frac{(3)^{0.65}\times(3)^{0.35}}{(7)^{0.25}\times(7)^{0.15}\times(7)^{0.6}}$$

$$= \frac{(3)^{(0.65+0.35)}}{(7)^{(0.25+0.15+0.6)}} = \frac{3^1}{7^1} = \frac{3}{7}$$

❑❑❑

4 RATIO & PROPORTION

RATIO

In ratio we compare two quantities of the same kind and consider what multiple, part or parts one is of the other. In comparing 8 with 4, observe that it is 2 times 4. This comparison can be represented as $8 \div 4$ or $\frac{8}{4}$.

Hence, *ratio is that relation between two numbers which is expressed by the fraction, the numerator is which is the measure of the first quantity and denominator is the measure of the second quantity.*

If the terms of a ratio be multiplied or divided by the same quantity the value of the ratio remains unaltered.

Thus, 3 : 4 is the same as 9 : 12 and 9 : 12 is the same as 3 : 4.

PROPORTION

The equality of two ratio is called proportion.

Consider the two ratios:

Ist ratio   2nd ratio

5 : 15   7 : 21

Since, 5 is one-third of 15 and 7 is one-third of 21, the two ratios are equal. The equality of two ratios is called proportion and the numbers 5, 15, and 7, 21 are said to be in **proportion.**

The proportion may be written as

5 : 15 : : 7 : 21 (5 is to 15 as 7 is to 21)

$\Rightarrow 5 : 15 = 7 : 21$

$$\Rightarrow \frac{5}{15} = \frac{7}{21}$$

The numbers 5, 15, 7 and 21 are called the terms. 5 is the first term, 15 the second, 7 the third, and 21 the fourth.

The first and fourth terms, *i.e.*, 5 and 21 are called extremes (end terms), and the second and the third terms, *i.e.*, 15 and 7 are called the **means** (middle terms), 21 is called the fourth proportional.

EXAMPLES

Example 1 : Find the third proportional to 5 and 15.

Solution: Suppose the third proportional to 5 and 15 is x.

$$5 : 15 :: 15 : x$$

But the product of the extremes is equal to the square of the mean.

$$\Rightarrow \quad 5 \times x = 15 \times 15$$

$$\Rightarrow \quad x = \frac{15 \times 15}{5} = 45$$

The required third proportional = 45

Example 2 : An amount is to be divided among A, B and C in the ratio of 3 : 5 : 6 respectively. If the difference between A and B's share is ₹ 600, what is C's share?

Solution: Trick : $\frac{A}{3} = \frac{B}{5} = \frac{C}{6}$

$$\Rightarrow \quad A = \frac{C}{2}, B = \frac{5C}{6}$$

$$B - A = 600$$

$$\Rightarrow \quad \frac{5C}{6} - \frac{C}{2} = 600 \Rightarrow C = ₹\ 1800$$

Example 3 : Sand and cement were mixed in the ratio 3 : 1 to make 100 tonnes. How much sand must be added to make the ratio 6 : 1?

Solution: The quantity of sand $= \frac{3 \times 100}{3+1}$

= 75 tonnes

and the quantity of cement = $\frac{1 \times 100}{3+1}$

= 25 tonnes

Suppose we add x tonnes of sand to make the ratio 6 : 1,

then $\frac{75 + x}{25} = \frac{6}{1}$

$\Rightarrow$ $75 + x = 150$

$\therefore$ $x = 150 - 75 = 75$ tonnes

EXERCISE

1. If A : B = 6 : 7 and B : C = 8 : 9, then A : B : C is:

(a) 24 : 28 : 63 (b) 48 : 28 : 63
(c) 48 : 56 : 63 (d) 24 : 56 : 63
(e) None of these

2. The sum of two numbers is 20 and their difference is $2\frac{1}{2}$. What is the ratio of the numbers?

(a) 11 : 7 (b) 9 : 11
(c) 7 : 9 (d) 7 : 11
(e) None of these

3. If 10% of x is the same as 20% of y, then $x : y$ is equal to :

(a) 1 : 2 (b) 2 : 1
(c) 5 : 1 (d) 10 : 1
(e) None of these

4. One man adds 3 litres of water to 12 litres of milk and another 4 litres of water to 10 litres of milk. What is the ratio of the strenghts of the milk in the two mixtures?

(a) 15 : 25 (b) 25 : 28
(c) 28 : 25 (d) 15 : 28
(e) None of these

5. ₹ 425 is divided among 4 men, 5 women and 6 boys such that the share of a man, a woman and a boy may be in the ratio of 9 : 8 : 4. What is the share of a woman?

(a) ₹ 34 (b) ₹ 24
(c) ₹ 44 (d) ₹ 37
(e) None of these

6. A and B are two alloys of gold and copper prepared by mixing metals in proportions 7 : 2 and 7 : 11 respectively. If equal quantities of the alloys are melted to form a third alloy C, the proportion of gold and copper in C will be

(a) 5 : 9 (b) 5 : 7
(c) 7 : 5 (d) 9 : 5
(e) None of these

7. The contents of two vessels containing water and milk are in the ratio 1 : 2 and 2 : 5 are mixed in the ratio 1 : 4. The resulting mixture will have water and milk in the ratio:

(a) 21 : 54 (b) 31 : 74
(c) 27 : 74 (d) 23 : 27
(e) None of these

8. The monthly salary of A, B, C is in the proportion of 2 : 3 : 5. If C's monthly salary is ₹ 1200 more than that of A, then B's annual salary is:

(a) ₹ 14400 (b) ₹ 24000
(c) ₹ 12000 (d) ₹ 2000
(e) ₹ 1200

9. The ratio between the ages of Kamla and Savitri is 6 : 5 and the sum of their ages is 44 years. The ratio of their ages after 8 years will be:

(a) 5 : 6 (b) 7 : 8
(c) 6 : 7 (d) 14 : 13
(e) 8 : 7

10. Vinay got thrice as many marks in Maths as in English. The proportion of his marks in Maths and History is 4 : 3. If his total marks in Maths, English and History is 250 then, what is his marks in English?

(a) 120 (b) 90
(c) 40 (d) 80
(e) None of these

11. A certain amount was divided between Kavita and Reena in the ratio 4 : 3. If Reena's share was ₹ 2400, the amount is:

(a) ₹ 5600 (b) ₹ 3200
(c) ₹ 9600 (d) ₹ 3800
(e) None of these

12. A circle and a square have same area. Therefore, the ratio of the side of the square and the radius of the circle is :

(*a*) $\sqrt{\pi}:1$ (*b*) $1:\sqrt{\pi}$
(*c*) $1 : \pi$ (*d*) $\pi : 1$
(*e*) None of these

13. A, B and C can do a work in 20, 25 and 30 days respectively. They undertook to finish the work together for ₹ 2220, then the share of A exceeds that of B by:

(*a*) ₹ 120 (*b*) ₹ 180
(*c*) ₹ 300 (*d*) ₹ 600
(*e*) None of these

14. A bag contains 25 paise, 10 paise and 5 paise coins in the ratio 1 : 2 : 3. If their total value is ₹ 30, the number of 5 paise coin is:

(*a*) 50 (*b*) 100
(*c*) 135 (*d*) 200
(*e*) None of these

15. If ₹ 782 be divided into three parts, proportional to $\frac{1}{2}:\frac{2}{3}:\frac{3}{4}$; then the first part is:

(*a*) ₹ 204 (*b*) ₹ 196
(*c*) ₹ 190 (*d*) ₹ 182
(*e*) None of these

16. Two numbers are in the ratio 1 : 2. If 7 is added to both, their ratio changes to 3 : 5. The greater number is:

(*a*) 32 (*b*) 28
(*c*) 26 (*d*) 24
(*e*) None of these

17. A fraction which bears the same ratio to $\frac{1}{27}$ that $\frac{3}{11}$ does to $\frac{5}{9}$, is equal to:

(*a*) 55 (*b*) $\frac{3}{11}$
(*c*) $\frac{2}{11}$ (*d*) $\frac{1}{55}$
(*e*) None of these

18. If ₹ 510 be divided among A, B, C is such a way that A gets $\frac{2}{3}$ of what B gets and B gets $\frac{1}{4}$ of what C gets, then their shares are respectively:

(*a*) ₹ 150, ₹ 300, ₹ 60
(*b*) ₹ 120, ₹ 240, ₹ 150
(*c*) ₹ 60, ₹ 90, ₹ 360
(*d*) ₹ 120, ₹ 90, ₹ 300
(*e*) None of these

ANSWERS

1	2	3	4	5	6	7	8	9	10
(*c*)	(*e*)	(*b*)	(*c*)	(*a*)	(*c*)	(*b*)	(*e*)	(*e*)	(*c*)
11	**12**	**13**	**14**	**15**	**16**	**17**	**18**		
(*a*)	(*a*)	(*b*)	(*e*)	(*a*)	(*b*)	(*d*)	(*c*)		

SOME SELECTED EXPLANATORY ANSWERS

2. $$\text{Ratio} = \frac{20+\frac{5}{2}}{20-\frac{5}{2}}$$

$$= \frac{22.5}{17.5} = \frac{225}{175} = \frac{9}{7}$$

$= 9 : 7.$

3. 10% of x = 20% of y

$$\Rightarrow \quad \frac{10}{100}x = \frac{20}{100}y$$

$$\therefore \quad \frac{x}{10} = \frac{y}{5} \quad \Rightarrow \frac{x}{y} = \frac{10}{5}$$

$$= \frac{2}{1} \Rightarrow x:y = 2:1.$$

4. Strength of milk in the first mixture

$$= \frac{12}{12+3} = \frac{12}{15}$$

Strength of milk in the second mixture

$$= \frac{10}{10+4} = \frac{10}{14}$$

$\therefore$ The ratio of their strengths

$$= \frac{12}{15} : \frac{10}{14}$$

$$= 12 \times 14 : 15 \times 10 = 28 : 25.$$

5. The ratio of shares of group of men, women and boys

$$= 9 \times 4 : 8 \times 5 : 4 \times 6 = 9 : 10 : 6$$

$\therefore$ Share of 5 women

$$= \frac{425}{9+10+6} \times 10 = ₹\ 170$$

$\therefore$ Share of 1 woman

$$= \frac{170}{5} = ₹\ 34.$$

6.
$$\text{Gold in C} = \left(\frac{7}{9} + \frac{7}{18}\right) = \frac{21}{18} = \frac{7}{6}$$

$$\text{Copper in C} = \left(\frac{2}{9} + \frac{11}{18}\right) = \frac{15}{18} = \frac{5}{6}$$

$\therefore$ Gold : Copper $= \frac{7}{6} : \frac{5}{6} = 7 : 5.$

8. Let the monthly salary of A, B, C be $2x$, $3x$ and $5x$

Then, $5x - 2x = 1200$

or, $3x = 1200$

$\therefore$ $x = 400$

B's monthly salary

$= 3x = 3 \times 400 = ₹\ 1200.$

9. Let their ages be $6x$ and $5x$ years.

$\therefore$ $6x + 5x = 44$

$\Rightarrow$ $11x = 44$

$\Rightarrow$ $x = 4$

So, their present ages are 24 years and 20 years

$\therefore$ Ratio of their ages after 8 years

$= 32 : 28 = 8 : 7.$

11. Let their shares be ₹ $4x$ and ₹ $3x$

Then, $3x = 2400 \Rightarrow x = ₹\ 800$

$\therefore$ Total amount $= 7x = 7 \times 800 = ₹\ 5600.$

12. Let the side of the square be x and the radius of the circle be y. Then,

$$x^2 = \pi y^2$$

$$\Rightarrow \frac{x^2}{y^2} = \pi \qquad \Rightarrow \frac{x}{y} = \sqrt{\pi}$$

$$\therefore \quad x : y = \sqrt{\pi} : 1$$

14. Ratio of their values

$$= \frac{1}{4} : \frac{2}{10} : \frac{3}{20} = 5 : 4 : 3$$

$\therefore$ Value of 5 paise coins

$$= ₹\left(30 \times \frac{3}{12}\right) = ₹\ 7.50$$

$\therefore$ Number of 5 paise coins

$$= \frac{750}{5} = 150.$$

15.
$$\text{Here ratio} = \frac{1}{2} : \frac{2}{3} : \frac{3}{4} = 6 : 8 : 9$$

Hence, Ist part $= \frac{6}{6+8+9} \times ₹\ 782$

$$= \frac{6}{23} \times ₹\ 782 = ₹\ 204$$

17. Let the fraction be x

Then, $x : \frac{1}{27} = \frac{3}{11} : \frac{5}{9}$

$$\Rightarrow \quad x \times 27 = \frac{3}{11} \times \frac{9}{5}$$

$$\therefore \quad x = \frac{3}{11} \times \frac{9}{5} \times \frac{1}{27} = \frac{1}{55}.$$

5 AVERAGE

The average of any number of quantities of the same kind can be found by dividing their sum by their number. Thus,

$$\text{Average} = \frac{\text{Sum of quantities}}{\text{No. of quantities}}$$

$$\text{Sum of quantities} = \text{Their average} \times \text{Their number}$$

$$\text{Number of quantities} = \frac{\text{Sum of quantities}}{\text{Their average}}$$

When a body covers the same distance at two different speeds p km/hr and q km/hr, then its average speed for the whole journey is $\frac{2pq}{p+q}$ km/hr.

EXAMPLES

Example 1 : The average score of a cricketer for 10 matches is 38.9 runs. If the average for the first six matches is 42, find the average for the last 4 matches.

Solution: Total runs of the last four matches = 10 × 38.9 – 6 × 42 = 137

$\therefore$ Average = $\frac{137}{4}$ = 34.25 run

Example 2 : The average of 13 numbers is 52. The average of first seven of these numers is 48 and the average of the last seven numbers is 58. What is the seventh number?

Solution: Seventh number = (7 × 48 + 7 × 58) – 13 × 52 = 742 – 676 = 66

Example 3 : The average age of 8 persons increases by 2 years when a person comes in place of another person who is 24 years old. What is the age of the new person?

Solution: Age of new person = 8 × 2 + 24 = 16 + 24 = 40 years

Example 4 : The average age of 33 students and their teacher is 18 years. If the class teacher is 51 years old, what would be the average age of the students?

Solution: Average age of the students

$$= \frac{18 \times 34 - 51}{33} = \frac{612 - 51}{33} = 17 \text{ years}$$

Example 5 : The average salary of Prakash, Jayesh and Kailash is ₹ 1100. The average salary of Prakash and Kailash is ₹ 900. What is Jayesh's salary?

Solution: Total salary of Prakash, Jayesh and Kailash

= ₹ (1100 × 3) = ₹ 3300

Total salary of Prakash and Kailash

= ₹ (900 × 2) = ₹ 1800

$\therefore$ Salary of Jayesh = ₹ (3300 – 1800) = ₹ 1500

Example 6 : The average weight of 45 passengers on board of an aircraft is 50 kg. If the weight of 5 members of the crew is added, the average is reduced by half kilogram. What is the average weight of the crew members?

Solution: Total weight of 45 passengers

= 45 × 50 = 2250 kg

and the total weight of 45 passengers and the 5 crew = 50 × 49.5 = 2475 kg

$\therefore$ Total weight of 5 crews = 2475 – 2250

= 225 kg

$\therefore$ Average weight of 5 crews = $\frac{225}{5}$ = 45 kg

Example 7 : The average of Mukesh's marks in 7 subjects is 75. His average in 6 subjects excluding Science is 72. How many marks did he get in Science?

Solution: Marks in Science

$= 7 \times 75 - 6 \times 72 = 525 - 432 = 93$ marks

Example 8 : The average of 10 numbers is calculated as 15. It is discovered later on that while calculating the average one number, namely 36 was wrongly read is 26. Find the correct average.

Solution: Sum of numbers

$= (10 \times 15 - 26 + 36) = 160$

$\therefore$ Correct average $= \dfrac{160}{10} = 16$

Example 9. The average of 25 results is 18; that of first twelve is 14 and of last twelve is 17. Find the thirteenth result.

Solution: Thirteenth result

$= (25 \times 18 - 12 \times 14 + 12 \times 17) = 78$

EXERCISE

1. The average of first nine multiples of 3 is
   (*a*) 12.0 (*b*) 12.5
   (*c*) 15.0 (*d*) 18.5
   (*e*) None of these

2. The average of 13 numbers is 68, the average of first 7 numbers is 63 and the average of last 7 numbers is 70. What is the 7th number?
   (*a*) 43 (*b*) 45
   (*c*) 46 (*d*) 49
   (*e*) 47

3. Average age of 8 persons increased by 2 years, when two men whose ages are 20 and 24 years are replaced by two women. What is the average age of women?
   (*a*) 30 years (*b*) 31 years
   (*c*) 28 years (*d*) 33 years
   (*e*) None of these

4. A man had seven children. When their average age was 12 years, the child who was 6 years of age died. What was the average of the surviving children 5 years after the death of the child?
   (*a*) 15 years (*b*) 16 years
   (*c*) 17 years (*d*) 18 years
   (*e*) None of these

5. A batsman has a certain average of runs for 16 innings. In the 17th innings, he makes a score of 85 runs thereby increasing his average by 3. What is the average after the 17th inning?
   (*a*) 33 runs (*b*) 34 runs
   (*c*) 37 runs (*d*) 36 runs
   (*e*) None of these

6. The average of marks obtained by 120 candidates was 35. If the average of marks of passed candidates was 39 and that of failed candidates was 15, the number of candidates who passed the examination is
   (*a*) 100 (*b*) 110
   (*c*) 120 (*d*) 150
   (*e*) None of these

7. Out of three numbers, the first is twice the second and is half of the third. If the average of the three numbers is 56, the three numbers in order are
   (*a*) 48, 96, 24 (*b*) 48, 24, 96
   (*c*) 96, 24, 48 (*d*) 96, 48, 24
   (*e*) None of these

8. The average age of an adult class is 40 years. 12 new students with an average age of 32 years join the class, thereby decreasing the average by 4 years. The original strength of the class was
   (*a*) 10 (*b*) 11
   (*c*) 13 (*d*) 15
   (*e*) None of these

9. The average age of 24 students in a class is 10. If the teacher's age is included, the average increases by one. The age of the teacher is
   (*a*) 25 (*b*) 30
   (*c*) 35 (*d*) 40
   (*e*) None of these

10. If *a*, *b*, *c*, *d*, *e* are five consecutive odd numbers, their average is
    (*a*) $5(a + 4)$ (*b*) $\dfrac{abcde}{5}$
    (*c*) $5(a + b + c + d + e)$ (*d*) $(a + 4)$
    (*e*) None of these

11. The average of four positive integers is 72.5. The highest integer is 117 and the lowest integer is 15. The difference between the remaining two integers is 12. Which integer is higher of these two remaining integers?

(a) 85 (b) 84
(c) 73 (d) 70
(e) None of these

12. A student was asked to find the average of the numbers 3, 11, 7, 9, 15, 13, 8, 19, 17, 21, 14 and x. He found the average to be 12. What should be the number in place of x?

(a) 31 (b) 17
(c) 7 (d) 3
(e) None of these

13. If a, b, c, d, e are five consecutive numbers, their average is:

(a) $5(a + b + c + d + e)$ (b) $(a + 2)$
(c) $\dfrac{abcde}{5}$ (d) $5\ (a + 2)$
(e) None of these

14. The average of a, b, c is M and $ab + bc + ca = 0$, then the mean of a^2, b^2, c^2 is:

(a) $9M^2$ (b) $6M^2$
(c) $3M^2$ (d) M^2
(e) None of these

15. The average of five numbers is 27. If one number is excluded, the average becomes 25. The excluded number is

(a) 37 (b) 30
(c) 27 (d) 25
(e) None of these

ANSWERS

1	2	3	4	5	6	7	8	9	10
(c)	(e)	(a)	(d)	(c)	(a)	(b)	(e)	(c)	(d)
11	**12**	**13**	**14**	**15**					
(a)	(c)	(b)	(c)	(e)					

SOME SELECTED EXPLANATORY ANSWERS

1. Average

$$= \frac{3(1 + 2 + 3 + 4 + 5 + 6 + 7 + 8 + 9)}{9}$$

$$= \frac{135}{9} = 15.$$

6. Let the number of candidates who passed = x

$\Rightarrow 39 \times x + 15 \times (120 - x) = 120 \times 35$

$\Rightarrow \quad 24x = 4200 - 1800$

$\therefore \quad x = \dfrac{2400}{24} = 100.$

9. Age of the teacher = $(25 \times 11 - 24 \times 10)$ years = 35 years.

10. Average $= \dfrac{a + (a + 2) + (a + 4) + (a + 6) + (a + 8)}{5}$

$= (a + 4).$

11. Let the remaining two positive integers be x and $x + 12$

Now, $117 + x + 12 + x + 15 = 4 \times 72.5$

$\Rightarrow \quad 2x + 144 = 290$

$\Rightarrow \quad 2x = 146 \ \therefore\ x = 73$

Hence, required number $= x + 12$

$= 73 + 12 = 85.$

12. Here,

$$\frac{3 + 11 + 7 + 9 + 15 + 13 + 8 + 19 + 17 + 21 + 14 + x}{12} = 12$$

$\Rightarrow 137 + x = 144 \ \therefore\ x = 7.$

13. Here, a, b, c, d and e are five consecutive numbers.

then, $b = a + 1$; $c = a + 2$; $d = a + 3$ and $e = a + 4$

Now, Their average

$$= \frac{a + b + c + d + e}{5} = \frac{a + a + 1 + a + 2 + a + 3 + a + 4}{5}$$

$$= \frac{5a + 10}{5} = \frac{5(a + 2)}{5} = (a + 2).$$

❑❑❑

6 PERCENTAGE

The word 'per cent' or 'percentage' means 'for every one hundred'. In other words, it gives an indication of rate per hundred.

It is denoted by the symbol %.

For example, 5% means 5 out of one hundred or $\frac{5}{100}$.

Remember :

(i) For converting a per cent into a fraction, divide it by 100.

(ii) For converting a fraction into a per cent, multiply it by 100.

(iii) For converting a per cent into a decimal, shift the decimal point two places to the left.

(iv) For converting one given quantity (x) as a percentage of another given quantity (y), find $\frac{x}{y} \times 100$.

(v) There is no unit of percentage.

Important Facts:

For quickly solving the problems related to percentage, remember following rules:

(a) Of the given two numbers if the first is x% more than the second, then the second will be $\left(\frac{100 \times x}{100 + x}\right)$% less than the first.

(b) Of the given two numbers if the first is x% less than the second, then the second will be $\left(\frac{100 \times x}{100 - x}\right)$% more than the first.

(c) If two numbers are respectively x% and y% more than a third number, then the first number will be $\left(\frac{100 + x}{100 + y} \times 100\right)$% of the second.

(d) If two numbers are respectively x% and y% less than a third number, then the first number will be $\left(\frac{100 - x}{100 - y} \times 100\right)$% of the second.

EXAMPLES

Example 1: The population of a town is 45000. $\frac{11}{18}$th of them are males and the rest females, 40% of the females are married. Find the number of married males.

Solution: Number of males

$$= \frac{11}{18} \times 45000$$
$$= 27500$$

$\therefore$ No. of females = 45000 − 27500
= 17500

Thus, No. of married females
= 40% of 17500 = 7000

$\Rightarrow$ The number of married males = 7000

Example 2: The population of a town is 40,000. If the population increases 20% every year, find the population after 3 years.

Solution: Population after 3 years

$$= 40000\left(1 + \frac{20}{100}\right)^3$$
$$= 40000 \times \frac{6}{5} \times \frac{6}{5} \times \frac{6}{5}$$
$$= 69120$$

Example 3 : In an examination 60% of the candidates passed in English, 55% in Mathematics and 25% failed in both subjects. Find the pass percentage.

Solution: Those failing in mathematics

$= 100 - 55 = 45\%$

Those failing in English

$= 100 - 60 = 40\%$

Failing in both = 25%

Failing in one or both the subjects

$= (45 + 40 - 25) = 60\%$

$\therefore$ Pass % = $100 - 60 = 40\%$

Example 4: Atul's marks in Science are 20 less than 60% of the total marks obtained by him in Science and Maths together. If his total marks are 250, what are his marks in Maths?

Solution: Marks obtained in Science = 60% of 250

$$- 20 = \frac{60}{100} \times 250 - 20 = 130$$

$\therefore$ Marks obtained in Maths = 250 – 130 = 120

EXERCISE

1. If x is 90% of y, then what per cent of x is y?

(a) 90 (b) 190
(c) 101.1 (d) 111.1
(e) None of these

2. The price of an article is cut by 10%. To restore it to the former value, the new price must be increased by :

(a) 10% (b) $9\frac{1}{11}\%$
(c) $10\frac{1}{9}\%$ (d) 11%
(e) $11\frac{1}{9}\%$

3. The income of a broker remains unchanged though the rate of commission is increased from 4% to 5%. The percentage of slump business is :

(a) 8% (b) 1%
(c) 12% (d) 80%
(e) 20%

4. 5% income of A is equal to 15% income of B and 10% income of B is equal to 20% income of C. If income of C is ₹ 2000, then total income of A, B and C is :

(a) ₹ 6000 (b) ₹ 18000 (c) ₹ 20000 (d) ₹ 14000
(e) None of these

5. A student who secures 20% marks in an examination fails by 30 marks. Another student who secures 32% gets 42 marks more than those required to pass. The percentage of marks required to pass is:

(a) 20 (b) 25
(c) 28 (d) 30
(e) None of these

6. In a college election, a candidate secured 62% of the votes and is elected by a majority of 144 votes. The total number of votes polled is:

(a) 600 (b) 800
(c) 925 (d) 1200
(e) None of these

7. The price of an article has been reduced by 25%. In order to restore the original price, the new price must be increased by :

(a) $33\frac{1}{3}\%$ (b) $11\frac{1}{9}\%$
(c) $9\frac{1}{11}\%$ (d) $66\frac{2}{3}\%$
(e) None of these

8. The price of cooking oil has increased by 25%. The percentage of reduction that a family should effect in the use of cooking oil so as not to increase the expenditure on this account is :

(a) 25% (b) 30%
(c) 20% (d) 15%
(e) None of these

9. In 40% of the people read newspaper X, 50% read newspaper Y, and 10% read both the papers. What percentage of the people read neither newspaper?

(a) 10% (b) 15%
(c) 18% (d) 25%
(e) 20%

10. The population of a town increases by 5% annually. If its population in 2008 was 138915, what it was in 2005?

(a) 110000 (b) 100000
(c) 120000 (d) 90000
(e) None of these

11. The population of a village is 4500. $\frac{5}{9}$th of them are males and rest females. If 40% of the males are married, then the percentage of married female is :

(a) 35 (b) 40
(c) 50 (d) 60
(e) None of these

12. A mixture of 40 litres of milk and water contains 10% water. How much water must be added to make water 20% in the new mixture?

(a) 10 litres (b) 7 litres
(c) 5 litres (d) 3 litres
(e) None of these

13. If $z = \frac{x^2}{y}$ and x, y both are increased in value by 10%, then the value of z is :

(a) unchanged
(b) increased by 10%
(c) increased by 11%
(d) increased by 20%
(e) None of these

14. If the price of a television set is increased by 25%, then by what percentage should the new price be reduced to bring the price back to original level?

(a) 15% (b) 18%
(c) 25% (d) 30%
(e) 20%

15. A candidate needs 35% marks to pass. If he gets 96 marks and fails by 16 marks, then the maximum marks are :

(a) 250 (b) 320
(c) 300 (d) 425
(e) None of these

ANSWERS

1	2	3	4	5	6	7	8	9	10
(d)	(e)	(e)	(b)	(b)	(a)	(a)	(c)	(e)	(c)
11	**12**	**13**	**14**	**15**					
(c)	(c)	(b)	(b)	(b)					

SOME SELECTED EXPLANATORY ANSWERS

1. $x = 90\%$ of y

$\Rightarrow \quad x = \frac{90}{100} y$

Required percentage $= \frac{y}{9y/10} = \frac{10}{9} \times 100$

$= 111.1\%$

2. Required percentage $= \frac{10}{100 - 10} \times 100$

$= \frac{10}{90} \times 100 = 11\frac{1}{9}\%$

8. Required reduction $= \left[\frac{r}{(100 + r)} \times 100\right]$

$= \left(\frac{25}{125} \times 100\right)\% = 20\%$

9. Number of people read either one or both

$= 40 + 50 - 10 = 80\%$

Hence, number of people read neither newspaper $= 100 - 80 = 20\%$.

12. Water $= 10/100 \times 40 = 4$ litres

Let x litres of water be added,

Then, $x + 4 = \frac{20}{100}(40 + x)$

$\Rightarrow \quad 5x + 20 = 40 + x$

$\Rightarrow \quad 4x = 20$

$\therefore \quad x = 5$ litres.

14. Required reduction $= \frac{25}{100 + 25} \times 100 = 20\%$.

❑❑❑

7 PROFIT AND LOSS

A consumer who goes to the market and buys certain goods. The buyer is called a customer and the shopkeeper who sells the goods to him is called a retailer. The retailer purchases goods in turn in bulk from a wholesaler who keeps a large stock of goods and in this case, the retailer becomes the customer.

1. **Cost price (C.P.) :** Cost price is that price at which a particular article is bought. Profit and loss both are marked at cost price.
2. **Selling Price (S.P.) :** Selling price is that price at which a particular article is sold.
3. **Overheads :** The expenses incurred on transportation, maintenance, packaging, advertisements and the like are included as *Overhead.* These overheads and the profit when added to the cost price determine the selling price.
4. **Profit or Gain** : Whenever a person sells an article at price greater than the cost price he is said to have made a profit or gain.
   Profit or Gain = S.P. – C.P.
5. **Loss :** If S.P. is less than the C.P. there is loss.
   Loss = C.P – S.P

Some Basic Formulae :

(i) $\text{Gain \%} = \dfrac{\text{Gain} \times 100}{\text{C.P.}}$

(ii) $\text{Loss \%} = \dfrac{\text{Loss} \times 100}{\text{C.P.}}$

From these we can write direct expressions for S.P. and C.P.

(iii) $\text{S.P.} = \left(\dfrac{100 + \text{Gain\%}}{100}\right) \times \text{C.P.}$ in case of gain or profit

(iv) $\text{S.P.} = \left(\dfrac{100 - \text{Loss\%}}{100}\right) \times \text{C.P.}$ in case of loss

These can be rewritten as

$$\text{C.P.} = \frac{100}{100 + \text{Gain\%}} \times \text{S.P. in case of profit}$$

$$\text{C.P.} = \frac{100}{100 - \text{Loss\%}} \times \text{S.P. in case of loss}$$

(v) If the C.P. of x goods = S.P. of y goods, then

(a) $\text{Gain \%} = \dfrac{x - y}{y} \times 100$ [In case of $x > y$]

(b) $\text{Loss \%} = \dfrac{y - x}{y} \times 100$ [In case of $y > x$]

EXAMPLES

Example 1: A dishonest dealer professes to sell his goods at cost price, but he uses a weight of 950 gm for the kg. weight. Find his gain per cent.

Solution: $\text{Gain \%} = \dfrac{\text{Error}}{\text{True value} - \text{Error}} \times 100$

$= \dfrac{50}{950} \times 100 = 5.26\%$

Example 2: A man buys 5 apples for ₹ 3 and sold each for ₹ 2. What did he gain or loss?

Solution: C.P. of apples = ₹ 3 and S.P. of apples = ₹ 2 × 5 = ₹ 10

∴ Gain = ₹ 10 – ₹ 3 = ₹ 7

∴ $\text{Gain \%} = \dfrac{7}{3} \times 100 = 233\dfrac{1}{3}\%$

Example 3: I lose 20% by selling a watch for ₹ 64. What per cent shall I gain or loss by selling it for ₹ 100?

Solution: ₹ 64 = 80% of C.P.

∴ ₹ 100 = $\dfrac{80}{64} \times 100\%$ of C.P.

= 125% C.P.

Hence, Gain = 25%

Example 4: A radio dealer marks a radio with a price which is 20% more than the cost price and allows a discount of 10% on it. Find the gain per cent.

Solution: Let C.P. = ₹ 100 and Marked price = ₹ 120

Since, S.P. = 90% of ₹ 120 = ₹ 108

(∵ Discount = 10%)

∴ Gain% = (108 – 100)% = 8%.

EXERCISE

1. Ashok bought 25 kg of rice at the rate of ₹ 6 per kg and 35 kg of rice at the rate of ₹ 7 per kg. He mixed the two and sold the mixture at the rate of Rs. 6.75 per kg. What was his gain or loss in the transaction?
(*a*) ₹ 16 gain (*b*) ₹ 16 loss
(*c*) ₹ 10 loss (*d*) ₹ 12 gain
(*e*) ₹ 10 gain

2. A horse and a cow were sold for ₹ 12000 each. The horse was sold at a loss of 20% and the cow at a gain of 20%. The entire transaction resulted in
(*a*) no loss no gain (*b*) loss of ₹ 1000
(*c*) gain of ₹ 1000 (*d*) loss of ₹ 2000
(*e*) None of these

3. Profit after selling a commodity for ₹ 425 is same as loss after selling it for ₹ 355. The cost of the commodity is :
(*a*) ₹ 285 (*b*) ₹ 390
(*c*) ₹ 295 (*d*) ₹ 400
(*e*) None of these

4. Ram bought 4 dozen apples at ₹ 12 per dozen and 2 dozen at ₹ 16 per dozen. He sold all of them to earn 20%. At what price per dozen did he sell the apples?
(*a*) ₹ 14.40 (*b*) ₹ 16.00
(*c*) ₹ 16.80 (*d*) ₹ 16.20
(*e*) None of these

5. Jimmy bought paper sheets for ₹ 7200 and spent ₹ 200 in transport. Paying ₹ 600 he had 330 boxes made, which he sold at ₹ 28 each. What is his profit percentage?
(*a*) 15.5 (*b*) 40
(*c*) 50 (*d*) 30
(*e*) None of these

6. A owns a house worth ₹ 10000. He sells it to B at a profit of 10% based on the worth of the house. B sells the house back to A at a loss of 10%. In this transaction A gets:
(*a*) no profit no loss
(*b*) profit of ₹ 1000
(*c*) profit of ₹ 1100
(*d*) profit of ₹ 1200
(*e*) None of these

7. At what price must Kantilal sell a mixture of 80 kg sugar at ₹ 6.75 per kg with 120 kg at ₹ 8 per kg to gain 20%?
(*a*) ₹ 7.50 per kg (*b*) ₹ 8.20 per kg
(*c*) ₹ 8.35 per kg (*d*) ₹ 9 per kg
(*e*) None of these

8. Subhash purchased a taperecorder at $\frac{9}{10}$ of its selling price and sold it at 8% more than its S.P. His gain is :
(*a*) 8% (*b*) 10%
(*c*) 18% (*d*) 20%
(*e*) None of these

9. A dealer marks his goods 20% above cost price. He then allows some discount on it and makes a profit of 8%. The rate of discount is:
(*a*) 12% (*b*) 10%
(*c*) 6% (*d*) 4%
(*e*) None of these

10. Tarun bought a T.V. with 20% discount on the labelled price. Had he bought it with 25% discount, he would have saved ₹ 500. At what price did he buy the T.V.?
(*a*) ₹ 5000 (*b*) ₹ 8000
(*c*) ₹ 9000 (*d*) ₹ 12000
(*e*) ₹ 10000

11. While selling a watch, a shopkeeper gives a discount of 5%. If he gives a discount of 7%, he earns ₹ 15 less as profit. The marked price of the watch is :
(*a*) ₹ 697.50 (*b*) ₹ 712.50
(*c*) ₹ 787.50 (*d*) ₹ 750.50
(*e*) None of these

12. Kabir buys an article with 25% discount on its marked price. He makes a profit of 10% by selling it at ₹ 660. The marked price is :

(*a*) ₹ 600 (*b*) ₹ 700
(*c*) ₹ 1000 (*d*) ₹ 885
(*e*) ₹ 800

13. A tradesman sells one kind of sugar at ₹ 3 per kg and loses 20 per cent and another kind of sugar at ₹ 5 per kg and gains 25 per cent. He mixes them together in equal proportion and sells the mixture at ₹ 6 per kg. What is his gain %?

(*a*) $53\frac{26}{31}\%$ (*b*) $51\frac{31}{26}\%$
(*c*) $54\frac{26}{31}\%$ (*d*) $55\frac{26}{31}\%$
(*e*) None of these

14. A fan is listed at ₹ 1400 and the discount offered is 10%. What additional discount must be given to bring the net selling price to ₹ 1200?

(*a*) $4\frac{16}{21}\%$ (*b*) 5%
(*c*) 6% (*d*) $16\frac{2}{3}\%$
(*e*) None of these

15. Samir purchased 150 quintals of wheat. One-fourth of the total quantity, he sold at a loss of 10%. At what gain per cent should he sell the remaining wheat to gain 10% on the whole transaction?

(*a*) $14\frac{1}{2}\%$ (*b*) $15\frac{2}{3}\%$
(*c*) $16\frac{2}{3}\%$ (*d*) $18\frac{2}{3}\%$
(*e*) None of these

16. If the cost price of 24 articles is equal to selling price of 21 articles, find the percentage gain or loss.

(*a*) 12.5 gain (*b*) 12.5% loss
(*c*) $14\frac{2}{7}\%$ gain (*d*) $14\frac{2}{7}\%$ loss
(*e*) None of these

17. The profit obtained after selling an article for ₹ 1,186 is the same as loss incurred after selling the same article for ₹ 1,098. Find the cost price of the article.

(*a*) ₹ 1100 (*b*) ₹ 1135
(*c*) ₹ 1142 (*d*) ₹ 1146
(*e*) None of these

18. A merchant professes to sell tea at the cost price but uses a false weight of 900 gm for a kilogram. His profit per cent in the transaction is:

(*a*) $9\frac{1}{11}\%$ (*b*) 10%
(*c*) $10\frac{2}{7}\%$ (*d*) 20%
(*e*) $11\frac{1}{9}\%$

19. The difference in selling a coat at profits of 4% and 6% is ₹ 12. The cost price of the coat is:

(*a*) ₹ 150 (*b*) ₹ 300
(*c*) ₹ 450 (*d*) ₹ 600
(*e*) None of these

20. A shopkeeper marks his goods at a price that would give him 20% profit and allows a discount of 10% in the sale on the marked price. What is his profit or loss per cent in the transaction?

(*a*) 8% profit (*b*) 12% profit
(*c*) 30% profit (*d*) 10% loss
(*e*) None of these

ANSWERS

1	2	3	4	5	6	7	8	9	10
(*e*)	(*b*)	(*b*)	(*b*)	(*a*)	(*c*)	(*d*)	(*d*)	(*b*)	(*e*)
11	**12**	**13**	**14**	**15**	**16**	**17**	**18**	**19**	**20**
(*d*)	(*e*)	(*c*)	(*a*)	(*c*)	(*d*)	(*c*)	(*e*)	(*d*)	(*a*)

SOME SELECTED EXPLANATORY ANSWERS

1. C.P. of 60 kg mixture

$= ₹\ (25 \times 6 + 35 \times 7)$

$= ₹\ 395$

S.P. of 60 kg mixtire

$= ₹\ (60 \times 6.75) = ₹\ 405$

$\therefore$ Gain $= ₹\ (405 - 395) = ₹\ 10$

3. Let C.P. $= ₹\ x$

Then, $425 - x = x - 355$

$\Rightarrow 2x = 780$

$\therefore x = ₹\ 390$

6. Final C.P. for A $= \frac{110}{100} \times \frac{90}{100} \times ₹\ 10000$

$= ₹\ 9900$

Hence, profit for A

$= \frac{10}{100} \times ₹\ 10{,}000 + ₹\ (10{,}000 - 9900)$

$= ₹\ 1100.$

8. Let S.P. $= ₹\ 100;$

C.P. for Subhash $= \frac{9}{10} \times 100$

$= ₹\ 90$ and

S.P. $= ₹\ 108$

Hence, gain % for Subhash

$= \frac{108 - 90}{90} \times 100$

$= 20\%.$

11. Let the marked price $= ₹\ x$

Then, $\frac{7x}{100} - \frac{5x}{100} = 15$

$\Rightarrow \frac{x}{50} = 15 \quad \therefore x = ₹\ 750.$

13. C.P. of both kinds of sugar of 1 kg each

$= \frac{100}{80} \times 3 + \frac{125}{100} \times 5 = \frac{15}{4} + 4$

$= ₹\ \frac{31}{4}$

Hence, C.P. of 1 kg mixture

$= ₹\ \frac{31}{8};$

then, Gain $= 6 - \frac{31}{8} = ₹\ \frac{17}{8}$

$\therefore$ Gain% $= \frac{17/8}{31/8} \times 100 = \frac{1700}{31} = 54\frac{26}{31}\%.$

14. Let second discount $= x\%$; then

$\frac{90}{100} \times \frac{(100 - x)}{100} \times 1400 = 1200$

$\Rightarrow (100 - x) = \frac{2000}{21}$

$\therefore x = 100 - \frac{2000}{21}$

$= \frac{100}{21} = 4\frac{16}{21}\%.$

18. Required pofit per cent

$= \frac{1000 - 900}{900} \times 100 = 11\frac{1}{9}\%.$

19. Here $2\% = 12$

$\therefore 100\% = \frac{12}{2} \times 100 = ₹\ 600$

Hence, cost price of coat $= ₹\ 600.$

❑❑❑

8 Simple & Compound Interest

INTEREST

Interest is the money paid for the use of money borrowed, *i.e.*, extra money paid for using other's money is called *interest.*

The sum borrowed is called the principal. The sum of interest and principal is called the *Amount.*

If the interest on a certain sum borrowed for a certain period is reckoned uniformly, then it is called simple interest, denoted by S.I.

Thus, if A = Amount, P = Principal,
I = Interest, T = Time (in year),
R = Rate per cent per annum, then

(*a*) $I = \dfrac{P \times R \times T}{100}$ (*b*) $P = \dfrac{100 \times I}{R \times T}$

(*c*) $T = \dfrac{100 \times I}{P \times R}$ (*d*) $R = \dfrac{100 \times I}{P \times T}$

(*e*) $P = \dfrac{100\,A}{100 + RT}$ (*f*) $A = P + I$.

COMPOUND INTEREST

In business transaction if interest as it becomes due is not paid to the lender but is added on to the principal, the money is said to be lent at *compound interest* and the total sum owed after a given time is called the amount at compound interest for that time.

After a certain period, the difference between the amount and the original principal is called the compound Interest (C.I.).

Some Important Formulae :

Let Principal = P
Time = *n* years
Rate = *r*% p.a.

then, the amount,

(*a*) when interest is compounded annually:

then, $\text{Amount} = P\left(1 + \dfrac{r}{100}\right)^n$

(*b*) when interest is compounded half yearly:

then, $\text{Amount} = P\left(1 + \dfrac{r/2}{100}\right)^{2n}$

(*c*) when interest is compounded quarterly :

then, $\text{Amount} = P\left(1 + \dfrac{r/4}{100}\right)^{4n}$

(*d*) when rates are $r_1\%$, $r_2\%$ and $r_3\%$ for Ist, IInd and IIIrd year respectively;
then, Amount =

$$P\left(1 + \frac{r_1}{100}\right)\left(1 + \frac{r_2}{100}\right)\left(1 + \frac{r_3}{100}\right)$$

EXAMPLES

Example 1: If a certain sum of money at simple interest amounts to ₹ 2642 in 3 years and to ₹ 3235 in 4 years, what is the sum and rate of interest?

Solution: Here, P + 3I = 2642; P + 4I = 3235
Then, I = 3235 – 2642 = ₹ 593
Since, P = 2642 – 3 × 593
= ₹ 863

Hence, $R = \dfrac{593 \times 100}{863 \times 1} = 68.71\%$

Example 2: In what time does a sum of money become four times at the simple interest rate of 5% per annum?

Solution: Let principal = ₹ *x*; then amount = 4*x*
Since, I = 4*x* – *x* = ₹ 3*x*

Hence, $T = \dfrac{3x \times 100}{x \times 5} = 60$ years

Example 3: A sum was put at SI at a certain rate for 2 years. Had it been put at 3% higher rate, it would have fetched ₹ 300 more. Find the sum.

Solution: If R = 3%, T = 2 years;

then I = ₹ 300

Hence, $P = \frac{300 \times 100}{3 \times 2}$ = ₹ 5000

Example 4: Find the difference between the compound interest and the simple interest for the sum ₹ 2000 at 5% p.a. for 2 years.

Solution: Required difference

$$= 2000\left[\left(1+\frac{5}{100}\right)^2 - 1\right] - \frac{2000 \times 5 \times 2}{100}$$

$$= 2000 \times \frac{41}{400} - 200 = 205 - 200 = ₹\ 5$$

Example 5: If a sum of ₹ 13040 is to be paid back in two equal annual instalments at $3\frac{3}{4}\%$ per annum, what is the amount of each instalment?

Solution: Let each instalment be ₹ x; then,

$$\frac{x}{\left(1+\frac{15}{4 \times 100}\right)} + \frac{x}{\left(1+\frac{15}{4 \times 100}\right)} = 13040$$

$$\Rightarrow x.\frac{80}{83} + x.\left(\frac{80}{83}\right)^2 = 13040$$

$$\Rightarrow x.\frac{80}{83}\left(1+\frac{80}{83}\right) = 13040$$

$$\Rightarrow x\ .\frac{80}{83}.\frac{163}{83} = 13040$$

$$\therefore x = \frac{13040 \times 83 \times 83}{80 \times 163} = ₹\ 6889$$

Example 6: Find the compound interest on ₹ 1000 for 3 years at 5% p.a.

Solution:

$$\text{C.I.} = 1000\left[\left(1+\frac{5}{100}\right)^3 - 1\right] = 1000\left[\left(\frac{21}{20}\right)^3 - 1\right]$$

$$= 1000\left[\frac{9261 - 8000}{8000}\right]$$

$$= 1000 \times \frac{1261}{8000} = ₹\ 157.63$$

EXERCISE

1. If the simple interest on a certain sum of money at 6% per annum for 3 years is ₹ 90, the sum will be:
   (a) ₹ 500 (b) ₹ 450
   (c) ₹ 525 (d) ₹ 560
   (e) None of these
2. If the simple interest on Re. 1 for 1 month is 1 paise, the rate per cent p.a. will be :
   (a) 10% (b) 8%
   (c) 12% (d) 6%
   (e) None of these
3. A sum of money doubles itself in 20 years. In how many years will it triple itself at the same rate of simple interest?
   (a) 30 years (b) 50 years
   (c) 40 years (d) 45 years
   (e) None of these
4. The simple interest on a certain sum of money is $\frac{25}{64}$ of the sum and the number of years equals the rate per cent p.a. The rate per cent p.a. will be :
   (a) $7\frac{1}{2}\%$ (b) $5\frac{1}{4}\%$
   (c) $6\frac{3}{4}\%$ (d) $6\frac{1}{4}\%$
   (e) None of these
5. If the simple interest on a certain sum of money at 6% p.a. for 4½ years is ₹ 81, the sum will be:
   (a) ₹ 325 (b) ₹ 225
   (c) ₹ 300 (d) ₹ 340
   (e) None of these
6. A sum of ₹ 1850 lent out for 5 years at 3% p.a. simple interest will amount to:
   (a) ₹ 2227.75 (b) ₹ 2127.50
   (c) ₹ 2137.50 (d) ₹ 2086.50
   (e) None of these

7. A lent a sum of ₹ 1250 to B at a certain rate of interest for 3 years and a sum of ₹ 1500 to C at the same rate of interest for 2 years. If he was paid total ₹ 258.75 as interest in both cases, find the rate of interest at which money was lent by him.

(a) $4\frac{1}{6}\%$ (b) $6\frac{1}{4}\%$

(c) $2\frac{1}{7}\%$ (d) $3\frac{5}{6}\%$

(e) None of these

8. What annual instalment should be paid to clear the debt of ₹ 645 in 4 years at the rate of 5% p.a. simple interest?

(a) ₹ 160 (b) ₹ 185

(c) ₹ 180 (d) ₹ 190

(e) None of these

9. A borrowed ₹ 2500 at a certain rate of simple interest and ₹ 1500 at 3% higher rate of interest. If after 4 years the interest paid by him in both cases is ₹ 1140, the former rate of interest was :

(a) 5% (b) 8%

(c) 8½% (d) 5½%

(e) None of these

10. A and B borrowed an equal sum of money from a moneylender at the rate of 8% and 5½% p.a. respectively. If to clear the debt after 4 years, A paid Rs. 550 more than B, the total sum of money taken by them was :

(a) ₹ 12500 (b) ₹ 11000

(c) ₹ 11500 (d) ₹ 10500

(e) None of these

11. A sum of ₹ 2444 is divided among three parts in such a manner that simple interest on the three divided parts at 6% p.a. after 3, 4 and 5 years respectively remains equal. Such three parts will be:

(a) ₹ 780, ₹ 1040, ₹ 624

(b) ₹ 1040, ₹ 780, ₹ 624

(c) ₹ 624, ₹ 780, ₹ 1040

(d) ₹ 940, ₹ 880, ₹ 624

(e) None of these

12. If the sum of 8097 is divided among A, B and C in such a manner that amount received from these parts at 4% p.a. simple interest after 4, 5 and 6 years respectively remains equal, then A's part will exceed the B's part by :

(a) ₹ 85 (b) ₹ 87

(c) ₹ 75 (d) ₹ 63

(e) None of these

13. What will be the compound interest on ₹ 8000 for 3 years at 5% p.a.?

(a) ₹ 1361 (b) ₹ 1341

(c) ₹ 1260 (d) ₹ 1250

(e) ₹ 1261

14. What will be the amount if a sum of ₹ 2500 is invested for 1 year at 4% per annum compound interest, interest being compounded half-yearly?

(a) ₹ 2625 (b) ₹ 2601

(c) ₹ 2830 (d) ₹ 2901

(e) None of these

15. After how many years will ₹ 3375 become ₹ 4096 at $6\frac{2}{3}\%$ per annum compound interest?

(a) 4 years (b) 2 years

(c) 2½ years (d) 3 years

(e) None of these

16. A certain sum of money placed at compound interest amounts to ₹ 110 in 1 year and to ₹ 121 in 2 years. The rate of interest per annum is :

(a) 5% (b) 10%

(c) 8% (d) 4%

(e) None of these

17. The present population of a city is 80,000. If the rate of growth is 5% per year, find its population after 3 years.

(a) 88,100 (b) 95,600

(c) 92,610 (d) 84,600

(e) None of these

18. The difference between compound and simple interest on a certain sum of money for 2 years at 5% per annum is ₹ 21. Find the sum.

(a) ₹ 7200 (b) ₹ 8400

(c) ₹ 9200 (d) ₹ 8500

(e) None of these

19. In how many years will a sum of ₹ 19200 placed at 10% per annum compound interest yield an interest of ₹ 4032?

(a) 1½ years (b) 2½ years
(c) 2 years (d) 3 years
(e) None of these

20. A sum of money lent out at a certain rate of simple interest amounts to ₹ 6600 in 2 years and to ₹ 6900 in 3 years. What will be the compound interest on the same sum of money if lent out at the same rate for 2 years?

(a) ₹ 605
(b) ₹ 715
(c) ₹ 615
(d) ₹ 595
(e) None of these

21. A man deposits ₹ 1200 in a bank on the 1st day of each year. If the bank pays 5% per annum compound interest on deposited sum of money, what will be the amount to his credit on the 10th day of the second year?

(a) ₹ 2560 (b) ₹ 2210
(c) ₹ 2370 (d) ₹ 2860
(e) ₹ 2460

22. Two friends A and B jointly lent out ₹ 81,600 at 4% per annum compound interest, payable annually. 2 years after A gets the same amount as B gets after 3 years. The investment made by B was :

(a) ₹ 30,000 (b) ₹ 40,000 (c) ₹ 45,000 (d) ₹ 38,000
(e) None of these

ANSWERS

1	2	3	4	5	6	7	8	9	10
(a)	(c)	(c)	(d)	(c)	(b)	(d)	(c)	(e)	(b)
11	12	13	14	15	16	17	18	19	20
(b)	(e)	(e)	(b)	(d)	(b)	(c)	(b)	(c)	(c)
21	22								
(e)	(b)								

SOME SELECTED EXPLANATORY ANSWERS

1. $P = \frac{90 \times 100}{6 \times 3} = ₹\ 500.$

2. $\text{Rate} = \frac{1 \times 100}{100 \times \frac{1}{12}} = 12\%.$

5. $P = \frac{81 \times 100 \times 2}{6 \times 9}$

$= ₹\ 300.$

6. $I = \frac{1850 \times 3 \times 5}{100} = ₹\ 277.50.$

$\therefore$ Amount = ₹ 1850 + ₹ 277.50

= ₹ 2127.50

7. $\frac{1250 \times R \times 3}{100} + \frac{1500 \times R \times 2}{100} = 258.75.$

$\Rightarrow \quad 6750R = 25875$

$\therefore \quad R = \frac{25875}{6750} = \frac{23}{6} = 3\frac{5}{6}\%.$

8. Let annual instalment be ₹ x; then

$x + \frac{x \times 3 \times 5}{100} + x + \frac{x \times 2 \times 5}{100} + x + \frac{x \times 1 + \times 5}{100} + x$

$= 645 + \frac{645 \times 4 \times 5}{100}$

$\Rightarrow \quad 4x + \frac{3x}{10} = 774$

$\Rightarrow \quad \frac{43x}{10} = 774$

$\therefore \quad x = \frac{774 \times 10}{43} = ₹\ 180.$

9. Here, $\frac{2500 \times R \times 4}{100} + \frac{1500 \times (R+3) \times 4}{100}$

$= 1140 \Rightarrow 160R = 960$

$\therefore \quad R = \frac{960}{160} = 6\%$.

10. Here, $\frac{P \times 8 \times 4}{100} - \frac{P \times 11 \times 4}{100 \times 2} = 550$

$\Rightarrow \frac{8P}{25} - \frac{11P}{50} = 550 \quad \Rightarrow \frac{P}{10} = 550$

$\therefore \quad P = 5500$

Hence, total sum of money

$= 2P = 2 \times 5500 =$ ₹ 11000.

12. Let parts of A, B and C are ₹ a, ₹ b and ₹ c respectively; then,

$a + \frac{a \times 4 \times 4}{100} = b + \frac{b \times 4 \times 5}{100} = c + \frac{c \times 4 \times 6}{100}$

$\Rightarrow \frac{29a}{25} = \frac{30b}{25} = \frac{31c}{25}$

Hence, $a : b : c = 930 : 899 : 870$

Sum of proportionals

$= 930 + 899 + 870 = 2699$

$\therefore$ Out of 8097, A's part

$= \frac{930}{2699} \times 8097 =$ ₹ 2790;

B's part $= \frac{899}{2699} \times 8097 =$ ₹ 2697

Hence, it is clear that A's part exceeds B's part by ₹ 2790 – ₹ 2697 = ₹ 93.

13. $\therefore \quad$ C.I. $= 8000\left[\left(1+\frac{5}{100}\right)^3 - 1\right]$

$= 8000\left[\left(\frac{21}{20}\right)^3 - 1\right]$

$= \frac{8000 \times 1261}{8000} =$ ₹ 1261.

14. $A = 2500\left(1+\frac{2}{100}\right)^2$

$= 2500\left(\frac{51}{50}\right)^2$

$= \frac{2500 \times 51 \times 51}{50 \times 50} =$ ₹ 2601.

15. Here, $4096 = 3375\left(1+\frac{20}{3 \times 100}\right)^n$

$\Rightarrow \frac{4096}{3375} = \left(1+\frac{1}{15}\right)^n$

$\Rightarrow \left(\frac{16}{15}\right)^3 = \left(\frac{16}{15}\right)^n$

$\therefore \quad n = 3$ years.

17. Population of the city after 3 years

$= 80{,}000\left(1+\frac{5}{100}\right)^3$

$= 80{,}000 \times \frac{21}{20} \times \frac{21}{20} \times \frac{21}{20} = 92610.$

19. Amount = ₹ 19200 + ₹ 4032 = ₹ 23232

Now, $23232 = 19200\left(1+\frac{10}{100}\right)^n$

$\Rightarrow \frac{23232}{19200} = \left(\frac{11}{10}\right)^n \Rightarrow \frac{121}{100} = \left(\frac{11}{10}\right)^n$

$\Rightarrow \left(\frac{11}{10}\right)^2 = \left(\frac{11}{10}\right)^n$

$\therefore \quad n = 2$ years.

21. Required amount $= 1200\left(1+\frac{5}{100}\right) + 1200$

$= 1200 \times \frac{21}{20} + 1200$

$= 1260 + 1200$

= ₹ 2460.

❑❑❑

9 Alligation or Mixture

Alligation deals with calculation of values or properties of a mixture. Alligation is the rule that enables us—

(1) to find the proportion in which the two or more ingredients at the given prices must be mixed to yield a mixture at the given price. This is termed as "Alligation Alternate".

(2) to calculate the average or mean value of a mixture when the prices of two or more ingredients which are to be mixed together and proportion in which they are to be mixed are given. This is termed as "Alligation Medial".

Rule of Alligation:

$$\frac{\text{Amount of Cheaper ingredient}}{\text{Amount of Dearer ingredient}} = \frac{\text{Cost price of Dearer} - \text{Mean Price}}{\text{Mean Price} - \text{Cost Price of Cheaper}}$$

Here cost price of unit quantity of the mixture is called the *Mean Price.*
The above rule may be represented schematically as under:

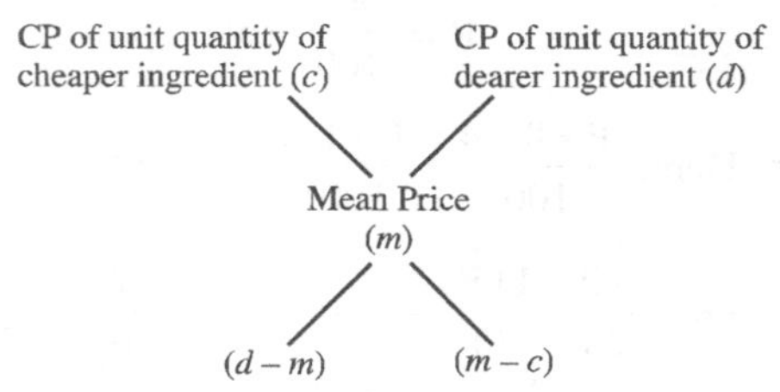

(Cheaper quantity) : (Dearer quantity) = $(d - m) : (m - c)$

This relationship is very helpful in solving problems on mixture involving percentage values, rates, prices, speeds etc.

2. m gm of sugar solution has $x\%$ sugar in it. To increase the sugar content in the solution to $y\%$, quantity of sugar need to be added

$$= \frac{m(y-x)}{100-y}$$

3. A vessel contains x litres of liquid A. y litres are withdrawn and replaced by liquid B. Next y litres of the mixture is withdrawn and again replaced by liquid B.
This operation is repeated n times.

$$\frac{\text{Quantity of liquid A left after } n\text{th operation}}{\text{Whole quantity of liquid A initially present}}$$

$$= \left(\frac{x-y}{x}\right)^n \text{ or } \left(1-\frac{y}{x}\right)^n$$

EXAMPLES

Example 1: 12 litres of a mixture has wine and water in the ratio 2 : 3. How much water must be added to get wine to water ratio of 3 : 7 in the resultant mixture?

Solution: Fraction of water in the given mixture

$$= \frac{3}{5}$$

For water to be added, fraction = 1

Fraction of water in the resultant mixture = $\frac{7}{10}$

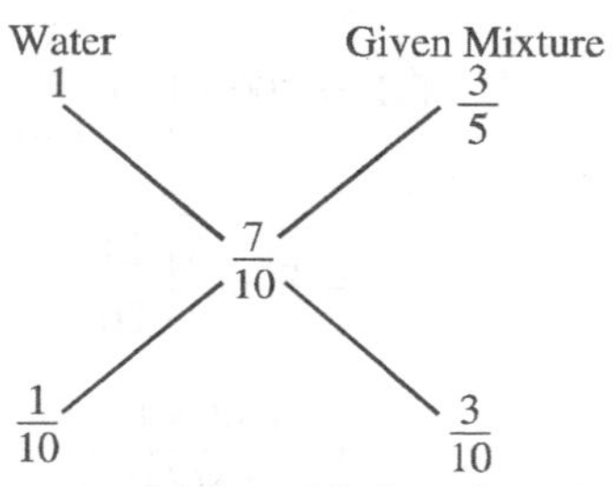

So, water must be added to the mixture in the ratio 1 : 3

Quantity of water to be added

$$= \frac{1}{3} \times 12 = 4 \text{ litres.}$$

Example 2: A person bought two tables for ₹ 2200. He sells one at 5% loss and the other at 6% profit and thus on the whole he neither gains nor loses. Find the cost price of each.

Solution:

CP of the table sold at 5% loss

$$= \frac{6}{6+5} \times 2200$$

= ₹ 1200

CP of the table sold at 6% profit

$$= \frac{5}{6+5} \times 2200$$

= ₹ 1000.

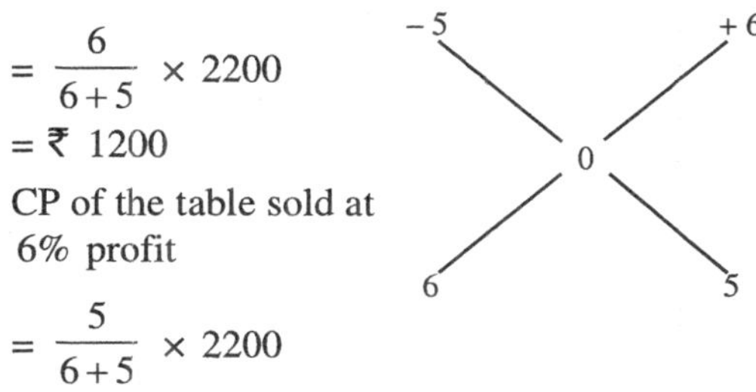

EXERCISE

1. In what proportion must tea at ₹ 62 per kg be mixed with tea at ₹ 72 per kg in order to obtain the mixture worth ₹ 65 per kg?
   (a) 4 : 6 (b) 7 : 3
   (c) 2 : 3 (d) 4 : 7
   (e) None of these

2. Find the quantity of rice @ ₹ 10 per kg. which should be mixed with 25 kgs of rice @ ₹ 8 per kg, so that on selling the mixture @ 15 per kg there is 80% profit.
   (a) 6 kgs (b) 7 kgs
   (c) 3 kgs (d) 5 kgs
   (e) None of these

3. A shopkeeper buys 26 kgs of milk @ ₹ 16 per kg. He also buys from another source an inferior quality of milk @ ₹ 10 per kg. How much quantity of the latter should he buy to mix it with the former so that he can sell the mixture @ ₹ 14 per kg without making any loss?
   (a) 13 kgs (b) 12 kgs
   (c) 14 kgs (d) 16 kgs
   (e) None of these

4. Two vessels A and B contain milk and water in the ratio 7 : 5 and 17 : 7 respectively. In what ratio mixtures from two vessels should be mixed to get a new mixture containing milk and water in the ratio 5 : 3?
   (a) 1 : 2 (b) 1 : 3
   (c) 2 : 3 (d) 3 : 2
   (e) None of these

5. Two vessels A and B contain mixture of milk and water in the ratio 4 : 1 and 9 : 11 respectively. They are mixed in the ratio of 3 : 2. Find the ratio of milk : water in the resulting mixture.
   (a) 34 : 16 (b) 33 : 17
   (c) 16 : 34 (d) 17 : 33
   (e) None of these

6. A person has two solutions of sugar with 30% and 50% concentration respectively. In what proportion should he mix two solutions to get 45% concentration in the resulting mixture?
   (a) 1 : 3 (b) 3 : 1
   (c) 2 : 3 (d) 3 : 2
   (e) None of these

7. 6 litres of milk and water mixture has 75% milk in it. How much milk should be added to the mixture to make it 90% pure?
   (a) 8 litres (b) 11 litres
   (c) 10 litres (d) 12 litres
   (e) None of these

8. In what ratio must water be added to spirit to gain 25% by selling it at cost price?
   (a) 1 : 4 (b) 4 : 1
   (c) 3 : 4 (d) 4 : 3
   (e) None of these

9. A shopkeeper has 50 kgs of rice. He sells a part of it at 20% profit and the rest at 40% profit. If he gains 25% on the whole, find the quantity of each part.
   (a) 12.5 kgs and 37.5 kgs
   (b) 37.5 kgs and 12.5 kgs
   (c) 23.5 kgs and 21.5 kgs
   (d) 21.5 kgs and 23.5 kgs
   (e) None of these

10. A shopkeeper has 100 kgs of tea. He sells a part of it at 20% profit and the rest at 5% loss. If his overall profit is 10%, find the quantity for each part.

(a) 20 kgs, 80 kg *(b)* 25 kgs, 75 kg
(c) 30 kgs, 70 kg *(d)* 60 kg, 40 kgs
(e) None of these

ANSWERS

1	2	3	4	5	6	7	8	9	10
(b)	*(d)*	*(a)*	*(e)*	*(b)*	*(a)*	*(e)*	*(a)*	*(b)*	*(d)*

SOME SELECTED EXPLANATORY ANSWERS

2. Cost price of the mixture

$$= 15 \times \frac{100}{180} = ₹\frac{25}{3} \text{ per kg}$$

8 10

$\frac{25}{3}$

$\frac{5}{3}$ $\frac{1}{3}$

$$\frac{\text{Quantity of rice @ Rs. 8 per kg}}{\text{Quantity of rice @ Rs.10 per kg}} = \frac{5/3}{1/3} = \frac{5}{1}$$

Quantity of rice @ ₹ 10 per kg

$$= 25 \times \frac{1}{5} = 5 \text{ kgs.}$$

3. 16 10

14

4 2

or 2 : 1

$$\frac{\text{Quantity of milk @ Rs.10 per kg}}{\text{Quantity of milk @ Rs. 16 per kg}} = \frac{1}{2}$$

So, quantity of milk @ ₹ 10 per kg.

$$= \frac{26}{2} = 13 \text{ kgs.}$$

5. Fraction is

A : $\frac{4}{5}$ $\frac{1}{5}$

B : $\frac{9}{20}$ $\frac{11}{20}$

$$(3A + 2B) = A \text{ and } B : \left(\frac{12}{5} + \frac{9}{10}\right) \left(\frac{3}{5} + \frac{11}{10}\right)$$

$$\frac{33}{10} \qquad \frac{17}{10}$$

So, Ratio of milk : water in the resulting mixture = 33 : 17.

8. Let cost price of spirit be Re. 1 per litre.

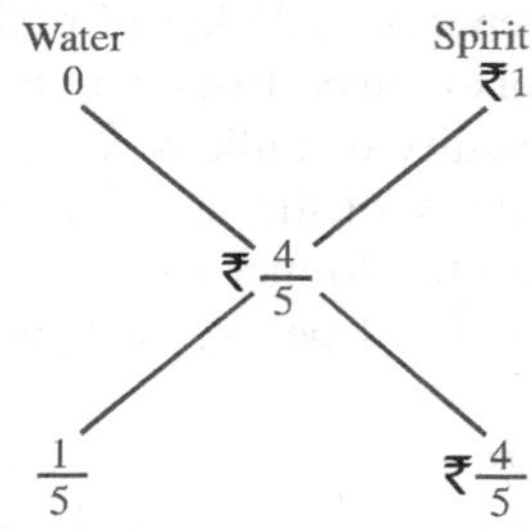

Then SP of mixture = ₹ 1 per litre
Gain = 25%

So, CP of mixture $= 1 \times \frac{100}{125} = ₹\frac{4}{5}$

We assume that CP of water is zero.
Using alligation rule on cost price,
Water should be mixed to spirit in the ratio

$\frac{1}{5} : \frac{4}{5}$ or 1 : 4.

❑❑❑

10 Time, Speed & Distance

Important Formulae:

1. Speed = Distance ÷ Time
2. Distance = Time × Speed
3. Time = Distance ÷ Speed
4. x km/hr $= \left(x \times \frac{5}{18}\right)$ m/sec
5. x metres/sec $= \left(x \times \frac{18}{5}\right)$ km/hr.
6. If the speed of a body is changed in the ratio $m : n$, then the ratio of the time taken changes in the ratio $n : m$.
7. When a man covers a certain distance with a speed of x km/h and another equal distance at the rate of y km/h, then for the whole journey, the average speed is given by

$$\text{Average speed} = \frac{2xy}{x+y} \text{ km/h.}$$

Important Facts:

1. The time taken by a train in passing a signal post or a telegraph pole or a man standing near a railway line $= \dfrac{\text{Length of the train}}{\text{Speed of the train}}$
2. The time taken by a train of length x passing a railway bridge or a platform or a tunnel or a train of length y at rest $= \dfrac{x+y}{\text{Speed}}$
3. (*a*) Time taken by faster train of length x and speed u to pass the slower train of length y and speed v in the same direction $= \dfrac{x+y}{u-v}$

   (*b*) Time taken by the trains in passing each other while moving in opposite direction $= \dfrac{x+y}{u+v}$
4. (*a*) Time taken by the train of length x and speed u to cross a man moving with speed v in same direction $= \dfrac{x}{u-v}$

   (*b*) Time taken by the train to cross a man moving in the opposite direction $= \dfrac{x}{u+v}$

When we simply say speed of a boat and swimmer, it usually means speed in still water. If the boat or the swimmer moves against the stream, then it is called *Upstream* and if it moves with the stream, it is called *Downstream*.

Hence, if x km per hour be the man's rate in still water, and y km per hour the rate of the current then

$x + y$ = man's rate with the current (called the downstream)

$x - y$ = man's rate against the current (called the upstream)

$$x = \frac{1}{2} \text{ (downstream + upstream)}$$

$$y = \frac{1}{2} \text{ (downstream − upstream)}$$

EXAMPLES

Example 1: A man covers a certain distance between his house and office on scooter. Having an average speed of 30 km/h, he is late by 10 min. However, with a speed of 40 km/h, he reaches his office 5 min. earlier. Find the distance between his house and office.

Solution: Let the distance between the house and the office be x km.

Difference of time

$$= 5 - (-10) = 15 \text{ min} = \frac{1}{4} \text{ hr.}$$

Here, $\frac{x}{30}-\frac{x}{40}=\frac{1}{4} \Rightarrow \frac{x}{120}=\frac{1}{4}$

$\therefore\ x=\frac{120}{4}$ = 30 km.

Example 2: A car can complete a journey in 6 hours if it travels at 45 km/hr. At what speed (in km/hr) must it travel in order to complete the journey in 5 hours?

Solution: Distance covered by the car in 6 hours at 45 km/hr = 45 × 6 = 270 kms.

∴ In the second case speed of the car should be

$\frac{270}{5}$ = 54 km/hr.

Example 3: A train 100 m long takes 9 seconds to cross a man walking at 5 km/h in the direction opposite to that of the train. Find the speed of the train.

Solution: Let the speed of the train be x km/h.

Relative speed $=(x+5)$ km/h

$=\frac{5(x+5)}{18}$ m/sec

Now, $\frac{100}{\frac{5(x+5)}{18}}=9 \Rightarrow x+5=\frac{20\times 18}{9}$

$\therefore\ x=35$

Hence, speed of the train = 35 km/h.

Example 4: A platform is 131 metre long. If the speed of the train of 67 m long is 45 km/h, how long will it take to pass the platform?

Solution: Total distance = 131 + 67 = 198 m

and speed of the train = 45 km/h

$=45\times\frac{5}{18}=\frac{25}{2}$ m/s.

∴ Time taken to pass the platform

$=198\times\frac{2}{25}=15.84$ sec.

Example 5: A boat can travel 35 km downstream in 5 hours. If it covers the same distance upstream in 7 hours, find the speed of the boat in still water.

Solution: Speed of the boat downstream

$=\frac{35}{5}=7$ km/hr.

and speed of the boat upstream

$=\frac{35}{7}=5$ km/hr.

Speed of the boat in still

water $=\frac{1}{2}$ (downstream + upstream)

$=\frac{1}{2}(7+5)=6$ km/h

EXERCISE

1. A car moving at 48 km/hr completes a journey in 10 hours. By how much the speed of this car should be increased so as to do this journey in 8 hours?
   (a) 8 km/hr (b) 12 km/hr
   (c) 10 km/hr (d) 15 km/hr
   (e) None of these
2. Starting from a point at a speed of 4 km/hr a man reaches at a cerain place and returns back to the point from where he had started journey on bicycle at the speed of 16 km/hr. His average speed during the entire journey will be :
   (a) 6.4 km/h (b) 8.4 km/h
   (c) 5.4 km/h (d) 10 km/h
   (e) None of these
3. A motorist covers a certain distance at a average speed of 48 km/h in 45 minutes. What speed in km/h he must maintain to cover the same distance in 30 minutes?
   (a) 66 km/h (b) 79 km/h
   (c) 80 km/h (d) 72 km/h
   (e) None of these
4. Two points A and B are 150 km apart. A man completes his onward journey from A to B in 3 hours 20 minutes and return journey from B to A in 4 hours 10 minutes. His average speed during the entire journey will be less than his

average speed during the journey from A to B by :

(a) 5 km/h (b) 7.5 km/h

(c) 9 km/h (d) 3 km/h

(e) None of these

5. A policeman saw a thief at a distance of 200 m. The policeman and the thief started running at the same time. If the policeman runs at a speed of $4\frac{1}{6}$ m per second and the thief at a speed of $3\frac{1}{3}$ m per second, after what time the policeman will catch the thief?

(a) 12 min (b) 10 min

(c) 9 min (d) 4 min

(e) None of these

6. Kanchan walks from her home at 4 kms per hour and reaches her school 5 minutes late. If she walks at 5 kms per hour, she reaches the school 2½ minutes earlier. How far is the school from her home?

(a) 3.5 kms (b) 2.5 kms

(c) 2.75 kms (d) 3.2 kms

(e) None of these

7. A monkey wants to climb up a glazed pole. He climbs 12 metres in 1 minute and then he slips back 3 metres in the next minute. If the pole is 63 metre high, how long does he take to climb at the top of the pole?

(a) $11\frac{1}{4}$ min (b) $12\frac{1}{2}$ min

(c) $12\frac{3}{4}$ min (d) $14\frac{3}{4}$ min

(e) None of these

8. A and B start walking at the same time on a circular path with circumference 35 metre. If they walk in the same direction at 4 km/hr and 5 km/hr respectively, after what time will they meet together?

(a) 35 hours (b) 27 hours

(c) 24 hours (d) 40 hours

(e) None of these

9. A car covers four consecutive extensions of 3 km each at the speeds of 10 km/hr, 20 km/hr, 30 km/hr and 60 km/hr. Its average speed of journey is:

(a) 30 km/hr (b) 25 km/hr

(c) 20 km/hr (d) 10 km/hr

(e) None of these

10. A train is scheduled to cover the distance between two stations 70 km apart in an hour. If it travels the first 30 km at 60 km/hr can it complete the journey in time without exceeding a speed restriction of 80 km/hr?

(a) yes

(b) no

(c) can't be determined

(d) Data insufficient

(e) None of these

11. A train runs at 45 km per hour. How far does it go in 6 seconds?

(a) 72 m (b) 60 m

(c) 75 m (d) 70 m

(e) None of these

12. A motorist covers a distance of 39 km in 45 minutes, by moving at a speed of x km/hr for the first 15 minutes, then moving at double the speed for the next 20 minutes and then again moving at his original speed for the rest of journey. Then x is equal to :

(a) 31.2 (b) 42

(c) 40 (d) 52

(e) 36

13. If a train running at 72 km/hr crosses a coconut tree standing by the side of the track in 7 seconds, the length of the train is :

(a) 104 m (b) 140 m

(c) 504 m (d) 540 m

(e) None of these

14. Two trains are moving in the same direction at 45 km/hr and 25 km/hr. The faster train crosses a passenger travelling in the slower one in 18 seconds. The length of the faster train is :

(a) 100 m (b) 120 m

(c) 150 m (d) 180 m

(e) None of these

15. Two trains are moving at 50 km/hr and 70 km/hr in an opposite direction. Their lengths are 150 m and 100 m respectively. The time they will take to pass each other completely is :

(a) 3 seconds (b) $4\frac{1}{2}$ seconds

(c) 5 seconds (d) $7\frac{1}{2}$ seconds

(e) None of these

16. A train leaves Delhi at 9 A.M. at a speed of 30 km/hr. Another train leaves at 2 P.M. at a speed of 40 km/hr on the same day and in the same direction. How far from Delhi, will the two trains meet?

(a) 300 km (b) 400 km

(c) 600 km (d) 650 km

(e) None of these

17. Two trains are running in opposite direction with the speed of 62 km/hr and 40 km/hr respectively. If the length of one train is 250 metres and they cross each other in 18 seconds, what will be the length of the other train?

(a) 125 m (b) 250 m

(c) 260 m (d) 280 m

(e) None of these

18. The distance of earth from sun is 141,000,000 km and light travels from latter to former in 7 minutes and fifty seconds. Find the velocity of light per second.

(a) 30000 km (b) 3000 km

(c) 300000 km (d) 300 km

(e) None of these

19. If the speed of a boat in still water is 5 km/hr and its speed against the current is 2.5 km/hr, then what is its speed in the direction of the current?

(a) 7.5 km/hr (b) 12 km/hr

(c) 10 km/hr (d) 11.5 km/hr

(e) None of these

20. The speed of a motorboat in still water is 9 km/hr and the speed of the stream is 2.5 km/hr. Find the time taken by the motorboat to go 9.1 km against the stream.

(a) 1 hour 40 minutes

(b) 2 hours 24 minutes

(c) 3 hours 24 minutes

(d) 4 hours 24 minutes

(e) None of these

21. The boat goes 40 km upstream in 8 hours and 36 km downstream in 6 hours. Find the speed of the boat in still water.

(a) 5 km/hr (b) 6 km/hr

(c) 6.5 km/hr (d) 7 km/hr

(e) None of these

22. A boat goes 6 km upstream and back to the starting point in 2 hours. If the current of the stream runs at the rate of 4 km/hr, find the speed of the boat in still water.

(a) 6 km/hr (b) 8 km/hr

(c) 10 km/hr (d) 12 km/hr

(e) None of these

23. A man can swim 3 km/hr in still water. If the velocity of the stream be 2 km/hr, find the time taken by him to swim to a point 10 km upstream and back.

(a) 12 hours (b) 10 hours

(c) 8 hours (d) 6 hours

(e) None of these

24. A boat covers 24 km upstream and 36 km downstream in 6 hours, while it covers 36 km upstream and 24 km downstream in 6½ hours. Find the speed of the current.

(a) 3 km/hr (b) 4 km/hr

(c) 6 km/hr (d) 8 km/hr

(e) None of these

ANSWERS

1	2	3	4	5	6	7	8	9	10
(b)	(a)	(d)	(a)	(d)	(b)	(c)	(a)	(c)	(a)
11	**12**	**13**	**14**	**15**	**16**	**17**	**18**	**19**	**20**
(c)	(e)	(b)	(a)	(e)	(c)	(c)	(c)	(a)	(e)
21	**22**	**23**	**24**						
(e)	(b)	(a)	(e)						

SOME SELECTED EXPLANATORY ANSWERS

1. Let he has to increase his speed by x km/hr for given condition; then,

$$(48 + x) \times 8 = 48 \times 10$$
$$\Rightarrow \quad 48 + x = 60$$
$$\therefore \quad x = 12 \text{ km/hr}$$

2. Average speed during the entire journey

$$= \frac{2xy}{x+y} = \frac{2 \times 4 \times 16}{4+16}$$
$$= \frac{8 \times 16}{20} = 6.4 \text{ km/hr.}$$

3. Let required speed be x km/hr; then

$$x \times \frac{1}{2} = 48 \times \frac{3}{4}$$
$$\therefore \quad x = 48 \times \frac{3}{4} \times 2 = 72 \text{ km/hr.}$$

5. Suppose the policeman will catch the thief after t seconds

$$\text{then,} \left(\frac{25}{6} - \frac{10}{3}\right)t = 200 \quad \Rightarrow \frac{5}{6}t = 200$$
$$\therefore \quad t = \frac{200 \times 6}{5} = 240 \text{ sec} = 4 \text{ min.}$$

8. The two persons walk in the same direction
$\therefore$ Their relative speed = 5 – 4 = 1 km/hr
Distance covered in 1 round on the circular path = 35 km

$\therefore$ They will meet after $\frac{35}{1}$ = 35 hours.

10. Time taken in covering 30 km $= \frac{30}{60} = \frac{1}{2}$ hr
Remaining distance = 70 – 30 = 40 km

Hence, the train has to cover 40 km in $\frac{1}{2}$ hr

Hence, speed of the train = 40 × 2 = 80 km/hr
So, the train can complete the journey in time without exceeding a speed restriction of 80 km/hr.

11. Speed = 45 km/hr = $45 \times \frac{5}{18} = \frac{25}{2}$ m/s

Hence, distance covered $= \frac{25}{2} \times 6$ = 75 m.

13. Length of the train $= 72 \times \frac{5}{18} \times 7$ = 140 m.

14. The length of the faster train

$$= (45 - 25) \times \frac{5}{18} \times 18 = 20 \times 5 = 100 \text{ m.}$$

15. Required time

$$= \frac{(150+100)}{(50+70) \times \frac{5}{18}} = \frac{250 \times 18}{120 \times 5} = \frac{15}{2} = 7\frac{1}{2} \text{ sec.}$$

16. Let they will meet after t hours from starting the first train.

Then, $t \times 30 = (t - 5)40$
$\Rightarrow \quad 40t - 30t = 200$
$\Rightarrow \quad 10t = 200$
$\therefore \quad t = 20$

Hence, required distance from Delhi
$= 30 \times 20 = 600$ km.

18. Time = 7 min 50 sec. = 470 sec.
Velocity of light per second

$$= \frac{141{,}000{,}000}{470} = 300000 \text{ km.}$$

19. Let the speed of the boat downstream = x km/h.

$$\text{Now,} \quad 5 = \frac{1}{2}(x + 2.5)$$
$$\Rightarrow \quad x = 10 - 2.5 = 7.5 \text{ km/hr.}$$

21. Upstream speed $= \frac{40}{8}$ = 5 km/hr;

Downstream speed $= \frac{36}{6}$ = 6 km/hr

Hence, speed of the boat in still water

$$= \frac{1}{2}(6+5) = \frac{11}{2} = 5.5 \text{ km/hr.}$$

23. Downstream speed = (3 + 2) = 5 km/hr
Upstream speed = (3 – 2) = 1 km/hr

$$\text{Required time} = \frac{10}{1} + \frac{10}{5} = 12 \text{ hrs.}$$

❑❑❑

11 TIME, WORK & WAGES

Important Facts:

1. If A can do a piece of work in n days, then work done by A in 1 day $= \frac{1}{n}$.
2. If work done by A in 1 day $= \frac{1}{n}$; then A can finish the whole work in n days.
3. If A is twice as good a workman as B then; Ratio of work done by A and B = 2 : 1.
   Ratio of times taken by A and B to finish a work = 1 : 2.

EXAMPLES

Example 1: A can do a piece of work in 6 days. B can do the same work in 3 days. How long would both of them take to do the same work?

Solution: Here, A's 1 day's work $= \frac{1}{6}$ and also B's

1 day's work $= \frac{1}{3}$

Hence, (A + B)'s 1 day's work $= \frac{1}{6}+\frac{1}{3}=\frac{1}{2}$

So, (A + B) could do the same work in 2 days.

Example 2: A, B and C working together can complete a piece of work in 24 days. C alone can complete this work in 48 days. A works twice as fast as B. How long would A take to finish the work working alone?

Solution: Here, (A + B + C)'s 1 day's work $= \frac{1}{24}$; C's

1 day's work $= \frac{1}{48}$

Ratio of work done of A and B = 2 : 1

Hence, ratio of their time taken = 1 : 2

Let A and B can finish the work x and $2x$ days respectively.

Now, $\frac{1}{x}+\frac{1}{2x}+\frac{1}{48}=\frac{1}{24} \Rightarrow \frac{3}{2x}=\frac{1}{48}$

$\therefore$ $x = 72$ days

Example 3: A contractor undertakes to complete a work in 20 days. He employs 18 labourers on this job but after 12 days he finds that only half of the work has been done. How many more labourer should he employ to complete the work within the scheduled period?

Solution: Here, remaining part of the work $= \frac{1}{2}$ and

remaing number of days = 20 − 12 = 8 days

Hence, $8 \times x = 12 \times 18 \therefore x = \frac{12 \times 18}{8} = 27$

So, number of more labourers = 27 − 18 = 9

EXERCISE

1. 12 boys can do a piece of work in 16 days. In how many days can 6 boys do the same work?
   (*a*) 16 days (*b*) 32 days
   (*c*) 23 days (*d*) 24 days
   (*e*) None of these
2. A can do a piece of work in 8 days while B can do the same work in 16 days. If they start working together, how long would they take to complete half portion of this work?
   (*a*) $2\frac{2}{3}$ days (*b*) $3\frac{5}{7}$ days
   (*c*) $4\frac{1}{2}$ days (*d*) $3\frac{1}{2}$ days
   (*e*) None of these

3. A can do a piece of work in 4 days. B is 50% more efficient than A. How long would B alone take to finish this work?

(a) $3\frac{1}{3}$ days *(b)* $5\frac{1}{4}$ days

(c) $2\frac{2}{3}$ days *(d)* $1\frac{2}{3}$ days

(e) None of these

4. A and B working together complete a work in 35 days. If A takes 60 days to complete it, how long would B alone take to complete it?

(a) 64 days *(b)* 72 days
(c) 81 days *(d)* 84 days
(e) None of these

5. A few children working together can do a piece of work in 18 days. If the number of children employed on the work is made double, how long would they take to complete half of the work?

(a) $4\frac{1}{2}$ days *(b)* $2\frac{1}{3}$ days

(c) $8\frac{3}{4}$ days *(d)* $6\frac{1}{2}$ days

(e) None of these

6. 10 men or 18 boys can do a piece of work in 15 days. In how many days would 25 men and 15 boys complete the same work working together?

(a) $5\frac{1}{2}$ days *(b)* $4\frac{1}{2}$ days

(c) $6\frac{2}{3}$ days *(d)* $2\frac{1}{3}$ days

(e) None of these

7. Two persons A and B can complete a piece of work in 8 hours and 16 hours respectively. If they work at it alternately for an hour, A starting first, in how many hours will the work be finished?

(a) $9\frac{1}{3}$ hours *(b)* $10\frac{1}{2}$ hours

(c) $11\frac{1}{2}$ hours *(d)* $8\frac{1}{2}$ hours

(e) None of these

8. A cistern is filled by a tap in $3\frac{1}{2}$ hours. Due to a leak in the bottom of the cistern, it takes half an hour longer to fill the cistern. If the cistern is full, how long will it take the leak to empty it?

(a) 28 hours *(b)* 29 hours

(c) $31\frac{1}{3}$ hours *(d)* 38 hours

(e) None of these

9. A is twice as good a workman as B and thrice as good a workman as C. If C alone can do a piece of work in 24 days, how long would the three persons take to finish the work working together?

(a) $3\frac{3}{11}$ days *(b)* $4\frac{4}{7}$ days

(c) $4\frac{4}{11}$ days *(d)* $3\frac{4}{11}$ days

(e) None of these

10. Two pipes can fill a tank in 8 hours and 12 hours respectively whereas an escape pipe can empty it in 6 hours. If the three pipes are opened at 1 p.m., 2 p.m. and 3 p.m. respectively, at what time will the tank be filled?

(a) 7.00 a.m. *(b)* 8.00 a.m.
(c) 5.00 a.m. *(d)* 7.30 a.m.
(e) None of these

11. Working 7 hours daily 24 men can complete a piece of work in 27 days. In how many days would 14 men complete the same piece of work working 9 hours daily?

(a) 32 days *(b)* 31 days
(c) 36 days *(d)* 39 days
(e) None of these

12. Two men undertake to do a piece of work for ₹ 1400. First man alone can do this work in 7 days while the second man alone can do this work in 8 days. If they working together complete this work in 3 days with the help of a boy, how should money be divided?

(a) ₹ 600, ₹ 500, ₹ 300
(b) ₹ 600, ₹ 525, ₹ 275
(c) ₹ 600, ₹ 550, ₹ 250

(d) ₹ 500, ₹ 525, ₹ 375
(e) None of these

13. Amit takes twice as much time as Aryan and thrice as much as Ram to finish a piece of work. Together they finish the work in 1 day. What is the time taken by Amit to finish the work?
(a) 6 days (b) 5 days
(c) 3 days (d) 4 days
(e) None of these

14. A works twice as fast as B. If B can complete a piece of work independently in 12 days. Find in how many days A and B together can complete the work?
(a) 8 days (b) 6 days
(c) 4 days (d) 18 days
(e) None of these

15. The daily wages of a worker is ₹ 100. Five workers can do a work in 10 days. If you pay ₹ 20 more daily they agree to do 25% more work daily. If the proposal is accepted the total amount could be saved is:
(a) ₹ 500 (b) ₹ 300
(c) ₹ 250 (d) ₹ 200
(e) None of these

16. 12 men take 36 days to do a work while 12 women complete $\frac{3}{4}$th of the same work in 36 days. In how many days 10 men and 8 women together will complete the same work?
(a) 27 days (b) 12 days
(c) 6 days (d) 16 days
(e) Data inadequate

17. X and Y can do a work in 12 days, Y and Z in 15 days and Z and X can do the same work in 20 days. How long will they take to complete the work if all the three working together?
(a) 10 days (b) 9 days
(c) 8 days (d) $7\frac{1}{2}$ days
(e) None of these

18. A and B can do a piece of work in 30 days, while B and C can do the same work in 24 days and C and A in 20 days. They all work together for 10 days when B and C leave. How many days more will A take to finish the work?
(a) 36 days (b) 30 days
(c) 24 days (d) 18 days
(e) None of these

ANSWERS

1	2	3	4	5	6	7	8	9	10
(b)	(a)	(c)	(d)	(a)	(b)	(b)	(a)	(c)	(a)
11	**12**	**13**	**14**	**15**	**16**	**17**	**18**		
(c)	(b)	(a)	(c)	(d)	(a)	(a)	(d)		

SOME SELECTED EXPLANATORY ANSWERS

1. ∵ 12 boys can do a piece of work in 16 days.
∴ 1 boy will do the same piece of work in 16 × 12 days.
∴ 6 boys will do the same piece of work in $\frac{16 \times 12}{6}$ days = 32 days.

3. A's 1 day's work $= \frac{1}{4}$; Hence, B's 1 day's work $= \frac{150}{100} \times \frac{1}{4} = \frac{3}{8}$

So, B will do the whole work in $\frac{8}{3} = 2\frac{2}{3}$ days.

5. Let number of children be x;
Now x children can do the work in 18 days.
Hence, $2x$ children will do $\frac{1}{2}$ of the work in $\frac{18 \times x}{2x \times 2} = \frac{9}{2}$ days
$= 4\frac{1}{2}$ days.

8. In 1 hour $\frac{2}{7}$ cistern is filled by the tap.

Hence, in $\frac{1}{2}$ hour $\frac{2}{14}=\frac{1}{7}$ cistern is filled by the tap.

So, $\frac{1}{7}$ cistern is emptied by the leakage in 4 hours.
So, 1 cistern will be emptied by the leakage in 28 hours.

9. Here, ratio of efficiency of A, B and C = $1 : \frac{1}{2} : \frac{1}{3}$
So, ratio of their time taken to complete the work = 1 : 2 : 3
Now C completes the work in 24 days, so A and B will complete the work in 8 and 16 days respectively.
Hence, (A + B + C)'s 1 day's work

$$= \frac{1}{8}+\frac{1}{16}+\frac{1}{24}=\frac{11}{48}$$

Therefore, (A + B + C) will complete the work in $\frac{48}{11}=4\frac{4}{11}$ days.

11. Working 7 hours a day 24 men can do the work in 27 days.

Hence, working 9 hours a day 14 men will do the work in $\frac{27\times24\times7}{9\times14}$ = 36 days.

13. Let Amit, Aryan and Ram can finish the work in $x, \frac{x}{2}$ and $\frac{x}{3}$ days respectively, then
(Amit + Aryan + Ram)'s 1 day's work

$$= \frac{1}{x}+\frac{2}{x}+\frac{3}{x}=\frac{6}{x}$$

Now, $\frac{6}{x}=1$ $\quad\therefore x = 6$
Hence, Amit will finish the work in 6 days.

15. 25% more work daily means
10 days' work ≡ 8 days' work
Hence, saved amount
= ₹ 10 × 100 × 5 – ₹ 8 × 120 × 5
= ₹ 5000 – ₹ 4800 = ₹ 200

16. Ratio of work of a man and a woman = $1 : \frac{3}{4}$
= 4 : 3
Ratio of their time taking = 3 : 4
Hence, 4 women ≡ 3 men
∴ 8 women ≡ 6 men
Now, 10 men + 8 women ≡ 10 men + 6 men = 16 men
Again, 12 men can complete the work in 36 days
Hence, 16 men will complete the work in $\frac{12\times36}{16}$ = 27 days.

17. 2(X + Y + Z)'s 1 day's work

$$= \frac{1}{12}+\frac{1}{15}+\frac{1}{20}=\frac{12}{60}=\frac{1}{5}$$

Hence, (X + Y + Z)'s 1 day's work = $\frac{1}{10}$
Hence, they all together will complete the work in 10 days.

18. 2 (A + B + C)'s 1 day's work

$$= \frac{1}{30}+\frac{1}{24}+\frac{1}{20}=\frac{15}{120}=\frac{1}{8}$$

Hence, (A + B + C)'s 1 day's work = $\frac{1}{16}$

Now, A's 1 day's work = $\frac{1}{16}-\frac{1}{24}=\frac{1}{48}$

Again, (A + B + C)'s 10 days' work

$$= 10 \times \frac{1}{16}=\frac{5}{8}$$

Remaining part of work = $1-\frac{5}{8}=\frac{3}{8}$, which will be done by A alone.
Hence, time taken by A to complete the remaining work = $\frac{3/8}{1/48}=\frac{3}{8}\times48$ = 18 days.

❑❑❑

12 PARTNERSHIP

When two or more than two persons agree to invest money to run a business jointly, this association or deal is called *partnership* and those who invest money are called *partners*. The total investment is called the *capital*.

Kind of Partners

There are two kinds of partners.

1. **Working or active partner :** When a partner devotes his time for the business in addition to invest his money, he is called a working partner. With mutual agreement, the active partners get some fixed percentage of profit as *working allowance*.
2. **Sleeping or non-active partner :** A partner who simply invests money, but does not attend to the business is called a sleeping partner.

Kind of Partnership :

(i) **Simple partnership :** If the capitals of several partners are invested for the same period, it is called a simple partnership.

(ii) **Compound or complex partnership :** If the capitals of the partners are invested for diffrent intervals of time, the partnership is called compound or complex.

EXAMPLES

Example 1: If A and B enter into a partnership, A contributes ₹ 7000 and B contributes ₹ 10000. If the profit at the end of the year amounts to ₹ 7310, what would be the share of B in the profit?

Solution: Ratio of their capitals= 7000 : 10000
= 7 : 10

Hence, share of B = $\frac{10}{17} \times 7310 =$ ₹ 4300

Example 2: Gulshan and Tarun invested ₹ 3900 and ₹ 4200 respectively in a business. If at the end of the year there was a profit of ₹ 2025 in the business, what will be the gain of Gulshan?

Solution: Ratio of the capitals of Gulshan and Tarun
= 3900 : 4200 = 13 : 14

Hence, Share of Gulshan in the profit

$= \frac{13}{27} \times 2025 =$ ₹ 975.

Example 3: A started a business with an investment of ₹ 80000. After 3 months, B also joined him with an investment of ₹ 50000. If at the end of the year total profit is ₹ 23,500, what profit will each of them get?

Solution: Ratio of Capitals of A and B
= (80000 × 12) : (50000 × 9) = 32 : 15

∴ A's profit = $\frac{32}{47} \times 23500 =$ ₹ 16000

B's profit = $\frac{15}{47} \times 23500 =$ ₹ 7500.

Example 4: Rajesh and Suresh invested ₹ 8000 and ₹ 1000 respectively in a business. After 6 months Naresh also joined them with an investment of ₹ 6000. If at the end of 3 years total profit is ₹ 9660, what profit will each of them get?

Solution: Ratio of their capitals
= (8000 × 36) : (1000 × 36) : (6000 × 30)
= 8 : 1 : 5

Share of Rajesh in the profit

$= \frac{8}{14} \times 9660 =$ ₹ 5520

Share of Suresh in the profit

$= \frac{1}{14} \times 9660 =$ ₹ 690

Share of Naresh in the profit

$= \frac{5}{14} \times 9660 =$ ₹ 3450

Example 5: A and B invested ₹ 2600 and ₹ 2800 respectively in a business. If at the end of 6 months, there was a profit of ₹ 1350 in the business, what will be the gain of A?

Solution: Ratio of their capitals

= 2600 : 2800 = 13 : 14

Share of A in the profit

$$= \frac{13}{27} \times 1350 = ₹\ 650.$$

Example 6: A and B start a business with the investment of ₹ 7500 and ₹ 6000 respectively. B is an active partner and therefore he gets 12½% of the profit separately for supervision of the trade. If total profit of the business is ₹ 2160, what will be the profit of B?

Solution: Separate profit of B for supervision of the

$$\text{trade} = \frac{25}{200} \times 2160 = ₹\ 270$$

Remaining profit = ₹ 2160 – ₹ 270

= ₹ 1890

Ratio of capitals of A and B

= 7500 : 6000 = 5 : 4

$$\text{B's share in the profit} = \frac{4}{9} \times 1890 = ₹\ 840$$

Hence, total profit of B = ₹ 840 + ₹ 270

= ₹ 1110.

Example 7: A, B and C together make a profit of ₹ 7200 in a business. If A invested ₹ 8000 in the business and A and C make profit of ₹ 1920 and Rs. 2880 respectively. What did B invest in the business?

Solution: Total profit in the business = ₹ 7200

B's profit = 7200 – (1920 + 2880)

= ₹ 2400

A's capital = ₹ 8000,

A's profit = ₹ 1920

$$\therefore \text{Capital invested by B} = \frac{8000}{1920} \times 2400 = ₹\ 10000$$

EXERCISE

1. A and B started a business with the investment of ₹ 80000 and ₹ 60000 respectively. At the end of the year total profit in the business will be divided between them in the ratio of :
(a) 2 : 3 *(b)* 3 : 4
(c) 2 : 1 *(d)* 4 : 3
(e) None of these

2. A and B started a business in partnership with the investment of ₹ 4000 and ₹ 6000 respectively. If at the end of the year total profit is ₹ 2250, what will each of them get?
(a) ₹ 900, ₹ 1350 *(b)* ₹ 800, ₹ 1450
(c) ₹ 1000, ₹ 1250 *(d)* ₹ 1200, ₹ 1050
(e) None of these

3. Sonu, Monu and Mohit together start a business with the investment of ₹ 1800, ₹ 1500 and ₹ 1600 respectively. If at the end of the year, Monu gains a profit of ₹ 900 the total profit in the business is :
(a) ₹ 2880 *(b)* ₹ 2940
(c) ₹ 3200 *(d)* ₹ 3240
(e) None of these

4. Omdutt started a business with a capital of ₹ 8000. After six months, Sanjay joined him with investment of some capital. If at the end of the year each of them gets equal amount as profit, how much did Sanjay invest in the business?
(a) ₹ 18000 *(b)* ₹ 17500
(c) ₹ 16000 *(d)* ₹ 16500
(e) None of these

5. A, B and C buy a farm for ₹ 100000. A contributes ₹ 40000 in it. They sell it, and from the profit B gets ₹ 2750 and C gets ₹ 1750. What would be the profit of A?
(a) ₹ 2780 *(b)* ₹ 3000
(c) ₹ 3280 *(d)* ₹ 2785
(e) None of these

6. A and B jointly invest ₹ 2100 and ₹ 3100 respectively in a firm. A is an active partner and hence he gets 25% of the profit separately. If their business yields them total ₹ 1040 as profit, what will be the gain of each of them?
(a) ₹ 415, ₹ 625 *(b)* ₹ 415, ₹ 575

(c) ₹ 515, ₹ 525 (d) ₹ 560, ₹ 480
(e) ₹ 575, ₹ 465

7. Two partners invested ₹ 12500 and ₹ 8500 respectively in a business and decided that 60% of the profit incurred from the business will be equally divided between them while remaining profit will be assumed as interest on their capitals. If one of the partners gets ₹ 300 more profit than the other, what is the total profit in the business?
(a) ₹ 3937.50 (b) ₹ 4940.50
(c) ₹ 3936.50 (d) ₹ 4156
(e) None of these

8. Neeraj and Birju are partners in a business. They divide between them the profit incurred in the business in such a proportion that $\frac{2}{5}$th portion of the profit gained by Neeraj is equal to $\frac{1}{3}$rd portion of the profit gained by Birju. If total profit in the business is ₹ 1210, find the profit earned by Birju.
(a) ₹ 780 (b) ₹ 660
(c) ₹ 680 (d) ₹ 590
(e) None of these

9. A, B and C together took under lease a pasture ground for ₹ 888. If in this pasture ground A put his 20 sheep out to graze for 2½ months, B put his 30 sheep out to graze for 4 months and C put his 36 sheep out to graze for 3½ months, find the lease amount paid by each of them.
(a) ₹ 205, ₹ 315, ₹ 378
(b) ₹ 228, ₹ 360, ₹ 378
(c) ₹ 170, ₹ 360, ₹ 358
(d) ₹ 228, ₹ 360, ₹ 300
(e) ₹ 150, ₹ 360, ₹ 378

10. A, B and C started a business with the investment of ₹ 5000, ₹ 6000 and ₹ 4000 respectively. A is an active partner and therefore he gets 30% of the profit separately. Rest of the profit is divided in the ratio of their capitals. If at the end of year, A's profit is ₹ 200 more than the sum of the profits made by B and C, find the profit made by each of them.
(a) ₹ 1620, ₹ 1242, ₹ 1178
(b) ₹ 1720, ₹ 1252, ₹ 1228
(c) ₹ 1510, ₹ 1187, ₹ 1133
(d) ₹ 1600, ₹ 840, ₹ 560
(e) None of these

ANSWERS

1	2	3	4	5	6	7	8	9	10
(d)	(a)	(b)	(c)	(b)	(e)	(a)	(b)	(e)	(d)

SOME SELECTED EXPLANATORY ANSWERS

2. Ratio of capitals of A and B

$$= 4000 : 6000 = 2 : 3$$

A's share in the profit

$$= \frac{2}{5} \times 2250 = ₹\ 900$$

B's share in the profit

$$= \frac{3}{5} \times 2250 = ₹\ 1350$$

3. Ratio of their capitals

$= 1800 : 1500 : 1600 = 18 : 15 : 16$

Sum of proportionals $= 18 + 15 + 16 = 49$

Monu's profit = ₹ 900

∴ Total profit in the business

$$= \frac{900}{15} \times 49 = ₹\ 2940$$

4. Investment by Omdutt for 1 month

$$= ₹\ 8000 \times 12 = ₹\ 96000$$

Let Sanjay invested ₹ x for 6 months

∴ Capital of Sanjay for 1 month

$$= ₹\ x \times 6 = ₹\ 6x$$

Now, $6x = 96000$

∴ $x = ₹\ 16000$

5. Here, ratio of capitals of A and (B + C)

$= 40000 : 60000 = 2 : 3$

Profit of (B + C) = 2750 + 1750 = ₹ 4500

Hence, A's profit $= \frac{4500}{3} \times 2 =$ ₹ 3000

7. Ratio of their capitals = 12500 : 8500

$= 25 : 17$

Hence, sum of their ratios

$= 25 + 17 = 42$

and difference of ratios

$= 25 - 17 = 8$

Now total profit taken as interest

$= \frac{300}{8} \times 42 =$ ₹ 1575

Hence, total profit in the business

$= \frac{100}{40} \times 1575 =$ ₹ 3937.50

8. Let shares of Neeraj and Birju in profit are ₹ x and ₹ y respectively; then,

$$\frac{2}{5}x = \frac{1}{3}y$$

$\therefore \quad x : y = 5 : 6$

Hence, share of Birju

$= \frac{6}{11} \times 1210 =$ ₹ 660

9. Ratio of their shares

$= (20 \times 5/2) : (30 \times 4) : (36 \times 7/2)$

$= 25 : 60 : 63$

Sum of proportionals

$= 25 + 60 + 63 = 148$

Total lease amount

= ₹ 888

$\therefore$ Amount paid by A

$= \frac{25}{148} \times 888 =$ ₹ 150

Amount paid by B

$= \frac{60}{148} \times 888 =$ ₹ 360

Amount paid by C

$= \frac{63}{148} \times 888 =$ ₹ 378

10. Ratio of capitals of A, B and C

$= 5000 : 6000 : 4000 = 5 : 6 : 4$

Let total profit in the business = ₹ x; then

$$\frac{30x}{100} + \frac{5}{15} \times \frac{70x}{100} - \frac{(6+4)}{15} \times \frac{70x}{100} = 200$$

$$\Rightarrow \quad \frac{8x}{15} - \frac{7x}{15} = 200$$

$\therefore \quad x =$ ₹ 3000

Hence, A's profit $= \frac{8 \times 3000}{15} =$ ₹ 1600;

B's profit $= \frac{6}{15} \times \frac{7 \times 3000}{10} =$ ₹ 840;

C's profit $= \frac{4}{15} \times \frac{7 \times 3000}{10} =$ ₹ 560.

❑❑❑

13 PROBLEM BASED ON AGE

IMPORTANT FACTS

1. The present age of the father is x times the age of his son. T years hence, the father's age become y times the age of his son. Then the present ages of the father and his son are:

Present age of the son = $\frac{(y-1)T}{x-y}$ years and

age of the father = $\frac{(y-1)\,T \times y}{x-y}$ years

2. T years ago, the father's age was x times that of his son and at present the father's age is y times the age of his son. Then their present ages are:

Son's age = $\frac{T(x-1)}{x-y}$ years;

Father's age = $\frac{T(x-1)}{x-y} \times y$ years.

EXAMPLES

Example 1: The sum of the ages of a son and father is 56 years. After 4 years, the age of the father will be three times that of the son. What is the age of the son?

Solution: Let ages of the son and father be x and $(56 - x)$ years respectively.

Then, $\frac{x+4}{56-x+4} = \frac{1}{3} \Rightarrow 3x + 12 = 60 - x$

$\Rightarrow 4x = 48 \qquad \therefore x = 12$

Hence, age of the son = 12 years.

Example 2: The age of Ram is 4 times the age of Shyam. If 5 years hence, Ram's age would be $1\frac{1}{2}$ times that of Shyam. What are their present ages?

Solution: Let the present age of Ram and Shyam be $4x$ and x years; then

$\frac{4x+5}{x+5} = \frac{3}{2} \Rightarrow 8x + 10 = 3x + 15$

$\Rightarrow 5x = 5 \qquad \therefore x = 1$

Hence, $4x = 4 \times 1 = 4$ years and $x = 1$ year

Example 3: The ratio of ages of the father and his son at present is 12 : 5. The difference of their age is 28 years. What will be the ratio of their ages after 8 years?

Solution: Let the present ages of father and his son be $12x$ and $5x$ years respectively; then

$12x - 5x = 28 \Rightarrow 7x = 28 \quad \therefore x = 4$

Now, $12x = 12 \times 4 = 48$ years and

$5x = 5 \times 4 = 20$ years

After 8 years their age will be 48 + 8 = 56 years and 20 + 8 = 28 years

Hence, their ratio = 56 : 28 = 2 : 1

EXERCISE

1. The present ages of Sunil and Anil are 40 and 60 years respectively. How many years ago was the ratio of their ages 3 : 5?

(a) 5 years *(b)* 10 years

(c) 12 years *(d)* 15 years

(e) None of these

2. The ratio of present ages of two brothers is 1 : 2 and 5 years ago the ratio was 1 : 3. What will be the ratio of their ages after 5 years?

(a) 1 : 4 *(b)* 2 : 3

(c) 3 : 5 *(d)* 5 : 6

(e) None of these

3. The ratio of ages of A and B is 3 : 11. After 3 years the ratio becomes 1 : 3. What are the ages of A and B?
   (a) 9 years, 33 years *(b)* 10 years, 40 years
   (c) 9 years, 27 years *(d)* None of these
   (e) None of these

4. Two years ago, the ratio of Ram's and Mohan's age was 3 : 2 and at present 7 : 5. What are their present ages?
   (a) 14 years, 10 years *(b)* 15 years, 10 years
   (c) 13 years, 9 years *(d)* None of these
   (e) None of these

5. One year ago, the ratio of Yamini and Gamini's was 6 : 7 respectively. Four year hence, the ratio would become 7 : 8. Find the age of Gamini?
   (a) 30 years *(b)* 32 years
   (c) 36 years *(d)* 40 years
   (e) None of these

6. The ratio of the present ages of Suresh and his daughter is 2 : 1. Six years hence, the ratio of their ages would be 23 : 13. Find the present age of Suresh?
   (a) 35 years *(b)* 40 years
   (c) 45 years *(d)* 50 years
   (e) None of these

7. The ages of Surabhi and Neerja are in the ratio of 6 : 7 respectively. After 6 years the ratio of their ages will be 15 : 17. Find the age of Neerja.
   (a) 24 years *(b)* 26 years
   (c) 27 years *(d)* 32 years
   (e) None of these

8. The present age of Deepak is 3 times the present age of his son. Five years hence, the ratio of their ages will be 34 : 13 respectively. The present age of Deepak is:
   (a) 58 years *(b)* 60 years
   (c) 63 years *(d)* 68 years
   (e) None of these

9. A mother is 25 years older than her daughter. Five years ago, the age of the mother was 6 times the age of the daughter. What is the present age of mother?
   (a) 25 years *(b)* 29 years
   (c) 32 years *(d)* 35 years
   (e) None of these

10. The mother is five times older than her son. After 4 years, the sum of their ages will be 44 years. What is the present age of the son?
   (a) 5 years *(b)* 5½ years
   (c) 7 years *(d)* 8 years
   (e) None of these

11. The respective ratio of the ages of Shami, Nammi and Pammi is 3 : 4 : 5. The sum of their ages is 48 years. What will be the respective ratio of their ages 8 years hence?
   (a) 4 : 5 : 6 *(b)* 5 : 6 : 7
   (c) 5 : 7 : 8 *(d)* 6 : 7 : 8
   (e) None of these

ANSWERS

1	2	3	4	5	6	7	8	9	10	11
(b)	*(c)*	*(a)*	*(a)*	*(c)*	*(b)*	*(e)*	*(c)*	*(d)*	*(e)*	*(b)*

SOME SELECTED EXPLANATORY ANSWERS

1. Let x years ago, the ratio of their ages was 3 : 5, then

$$\frac{40-x}{60-x} = \frac{3}{5}$$

$\Rightarrow$ $200 - 5x = 180 - 3x$

$\Rightarrow$ $2x = 20$ $\therefore x = 10$ years

2. Let their present ages be x and $2x$ years; then

$$\frac{x-5}{2x-5} = \frac{1}{3}$$

$\Rightarrow$ $3x - 15 = 2x - 5$ $\therefore x = 10$

Hence, their present ages 10 years and 20 years

Required ratio $= \frac{10+5}{20+5} = \frac{3}{5} = 3 : 5$

3. Let the ages of A and B be $3x$ and $11x$ years; then

$$\frac{3x+3}{11x+3} = \frac{1}{3}$$

$$\Rightarrow \quad 9x + 9 = 11x + 3$$

$$\Rightarrow \quad 2x = 6 \quad \therefore x = 3$$

Hence, their present age,

$$3x = 3 \times 3 = 9 \text{ years};$$

$$11x = 11 \times 3 = 33 \text{ years}$$

4. Let the present ages of Ram and Mohan are $7x$ and $5x$ years; then

$$\frac{7x-2}{5x-2} = \frac{3}{2}$$

$$\Rightarrow \quad 14x - 4 = 15x - 6$$

$$\therefore \quad x = 2$$

Hence, their present ages : $7 \times 2 = 14$ years and $5 \times 2 = 10$ years.

5. Let one year ago the ages of Yamini and Gamini were $6x$ and $7x$ years respectively; then

$$\frac{6x+5}{7x+5} = \frac{7}{8}$$

$$\Rightarrow \quad 48x + 40 = 49x + 35$$

$$\therefore \quad x = 5$$

Hence, present ago of Gamini

$$= 7x + 1 = 7 \times 5 + 1$$

$$= 36 \text{ years.}$$

6. Let the present ages of Suresh and his daughter be $2x$ and x years respectively; then

$$\frac{2x+6}{x+6} = \frac{23}{13}$$

$$\Rightarrow \quad 26x + 78 = 23x + 138$$

$$\Rightarrow \quad 3x = 60 \quad \therefore x = 20$$

Hence, present age of Suresh $= 2 \times 10$

$$= 40 \text{ years.}$$

7. Let the present ages of Surabhi and Neerja are $6x$ and $7x$ years respectively; then,

$$\frac{6x+6}{7x+6} = \frac{15}{17}$$

$$\Rightarrow \quad 102x + 102 = 105x + 90$$

$$\Rightarrow \quad 3x = 12$$

$$\therefore \quad x = 4$$

Hence, present ages of Neerja

$$= 7 \times 4 = 28 \text{ years.}$$

8. The present age of Deepak and his son be $3x$ and x years respectively; then

$$\frac{3x+5}{x+5} = \frac{34}{13}$$

$$\Rightarrow \quad 39x + 65 = 34x + 170$$

$$\Rightarrow \quad 5x = 105$$

$$\therefore \quad x = 21$$

Hence, present age of Deepak

$$= 3x = 3 \times 21 = 63$$

9. Let the present ages of mother and her daughter are $(x + 25)$ and x years respectively; then

$$6(x - 5) = x + 25 - 5$$

$$\Rightarrow \quad 6x - 30 = x + 20$$

$$\Rightarrow \quad 5x = 50$$

$$\therefore \quad x = 10$$

Hence, the age of the mother

$$= 10 + 25 = 35 \text{ years}$$

10. Let the present ages of mother and her son be $5x$ and x years respectively; then

$$5x + 4 + x + 4 = 44$$

$$\Rightarrow \quad 6x = 36$$

$$\therefore \quad x = 6 \text{ years.}$$

11. Let the present ages of Shami, Nammi and Pammi are $3x$, $4x$ and $5x$ years respectively; then,

$$3x + 4x + 5x = 48$$

$$\Rightarrow \quad 12x = 48 \quad \therefore x = 4$$

Hence, their present ages are 12, 16 and 20 years respectively.

So, required ratio

$$= (12 + 8) : (16 + 8) : (20 + 8)$$

$$= 20 : 24 : 28 = 5 : 6 : 7.$$

❑❑❑

14 Mensuration

In this part of mensuration we often have to deal with the problem of finding the areas and perimeters of plane figures.

Triangle

1. Perimeter = 3 × side (Equilateral triangle)
2. Area = $\frac{1}{2} \times \text{base} \times \text{height}$, or

   Area = $\sqrt{s(s-a)(s-b)(s-c)}$

   where a, b, c, are the lengths of the sides of triangle and $s = \frac{a+b+c}{2}$

Right Angled Triangle : It is one whose one of the angles is right angle, *i.e.*, 90°.

1. $(\text{Hypotenuse})^2 = (\text{Perpendicular})^2 + (\text{Base})^2$
2. Area = $\frac{1}{2} \times \text{Base} \times \text{Perpendicular}$

Equilateral Triangle : All three sides are equal in length and all three angles are equal to 60°.

1. Area = $\frac{\sqrt{3}}{4} \times (\text{Side})^2$
2. Area = $\frac{(\text{Height})^2}{\sqrt{3}}$
3. Height = $\frac{\sqrt{3}}{2} \times \text{side}$
4. Perimeter = 3 × side

Isosceles Triangle : Two sides are equal in lengths.

1. Area = $\frac{b}{4}\sqrt{4a^2 - b^2}$

   where a = lengths of equal sides
   b = length of unequal side
2. In an isosceles right triangle,

   (*a*) Hypotenuse $= \sqrt{2} \times \text{congruent side (a)}$

   (*b*) Area = $\frac{1}{2} \times a^2$

   (*c*) Perimeter = $\sqrt{2} \times a(\sqrt{2}+1)$

Rectangle

1. Area = length(l) × breadth(b)
2. Perimeter = $2(l + b)$
3. Diagonal = $\sqrt{l^2 + b^2}$

Square

1. Area = $(\text{Side})^2$
2. Perimeter = 4 × side
3. Diagonal = $\text{side} \times \sqrt{2}$

Parallelogram: In parallelogram opposite sides are parallel and equal. The two diagonals are not always equal but they bisect each other at the point of intersection.

Area = Base × Height.

Trapezium : It is a quadrilateral whose one pair of opposite sides is parallel. Other two opposite sides are oblique.

Area $= \frac{1}{2} \times \text{Height} \times (\text{Sum of parallel sides})$.

Here, height is the distance between the two parallel sides.

Rhombus : It is parallelogram whose all sides are equal and diagonals are bisect each other at right angle.

1. Area = $\frac{1}{2} \times \text{Product of diagonals}$
2. Side = $\sqrt{\left(\frac{d_1}{2}\right)^2 + \left(\frac{d_2}{2}\right)^2}$, where d_1 and d_2 are diagonals
3. Perimeter = 4 × side

Quadrilateral : Area $= \frac{1}{2} \times \text{One diagonal} \times$ (Sum of perpendicular to it from the opposite vertices),

$$= \frac{1}{2} \times d \times (a+b)$$

Circle :

1. Diameter = 2 × Radius
2. Area = $\pi r^2 = \frac{\pi}{4} d^2$;

   where d = diameter = $\sqrt{\frac{4A}{\pi}}$

Polygon :

1. Interior angle + Exterior angle = 180°
2. Each interior angle = $\left(\frac{2n-4}{n}\right) \times 90°$

   where n = number of sides
3. Sum of Exterior angles = 360°
4. Perimeter = Number of sides × Length of side.
5. For an equilateral triangle of side 'a' *(a)* radius of inscribed circle $= \frac{a}{2\sqrt{3}}$ and side of the triangle = $2\sqrt{3}r$, *(b)* radius of circumcircle = $\frac{a}{\sqrt{3}}$
6. Area of regular polygon = $\frac{1}{2}$(No. of sides) (Radius of the inscribed circle)
7. Area of regular hexagon = $\frac{3\sqrt{3}}{2}(\text{side})^2$

   = 2.598 $(\text{side})^2$
8. Area of a regular octagon

   $= 2(\sqrt{2}+1)(\text{side})^2$ = 4.828 $(\text{side})^2$
9. Area of quadrilateral,

   $A = \sqrt{s(s-a)(s-b)(s-c)(s-d)}$

   where, $s = \frac{a+b+c+d}{2}$

Volume and Surface Area

In mensuration we often have to deal with the problem of finding the volume of solid figure.

Cuboid : A cuboid has six faces, each one a ractangle. It has 12 edges. For example, a rectangular brick.

Let Length = l, Breadth = b and Height = h, then,

1. Volume = (Length × Breadth × Height)
2. Whole Surface Area = $2(lb + bh + lh)$
3. Diagonal = $\sqrt{l^2 + b^2 + h^2}$
4. Area of 4 walls of a room = $2 \times h\,(l + b)$

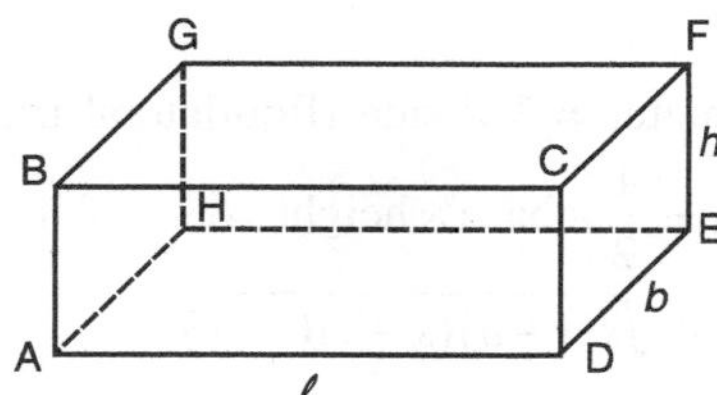

Cube : In a cube, Length = Breadth = Height

1. Volume = $(l)^3$
2. Length = $\sqrt[3]{\text{Volume}}$
3. Whole Surface Area = $6\,l^2$
4. Diagonal = $l \times \sqrt{3}$
5. Lateral Surface Area = $4\,l^2$

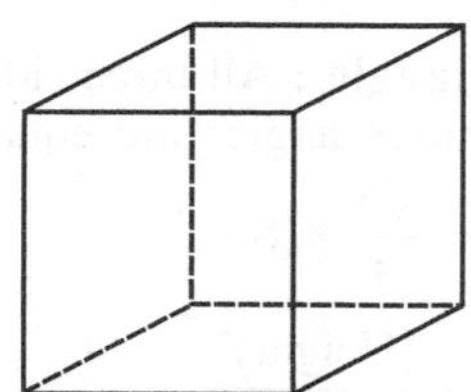

Cylinder :

1. Volume = $\pi r^2 h$
2. Curved Surface Area = $2\pi rh$
3. Total Surface Area = $2\pi r(r + h)$

   where r = radius, h = height

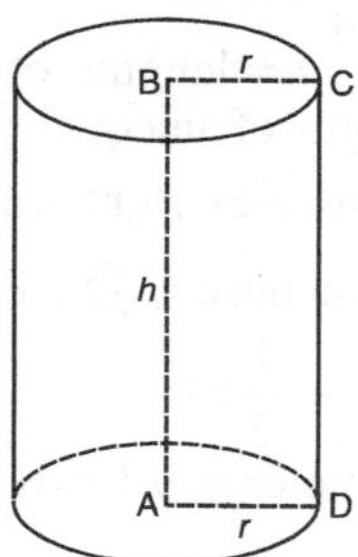

Spherical Cell :

1. Volume $= \frac{4}{3}\pi\left(R^3 - r^3\right)$
2. Total Surface Area $= 4\pi(R^2 - r^2)$

   where R = Outer radius

   r = Inner radius

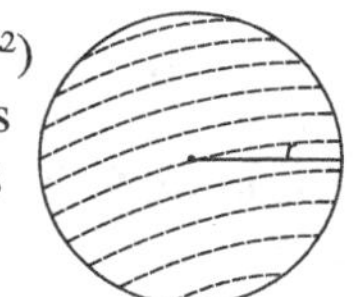

Sphere :

1. Volume $= \frac{4}{3}\pi r^3$
2. Surface Area $= 4\pi r^2$

Semi-sphere :

1. Volume $= \frac{2}{3}\pi r^3$
2. Curved surface area $= 2\pi r^2$
3. Total surface area $= 3\pi r^2$

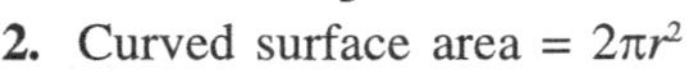

Cone :

1. Slant height $(l) = \sqrt{r^2 + h^2}$
2. Volume $= \frac{1}{3}\pi r^2 h$
3. Curved surface area $= \pi r l$
4. Total surface area $= \pi r\,(l + r)$
5. If the depth of the frustum of a cone be k and the radii of its ends are r_1 and r_2, then

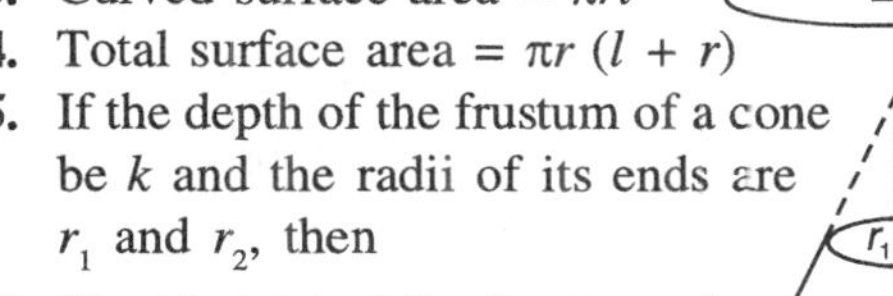

(i) Slant height of the frustum of a cone $= \sqrt{k^2 + (r_1 - r_2)^2}$

(ii) Curved surface of the frustum $= \pi(r_1 + r_2)\,l$.

(iii) Volume $= \frac{\pi k}{3}\left(r_1^2 + r_1 r_2 + r_2^2\right)$

EXAMPLES

Example 1: Area of a rectangular field is 1600 sq. metre. If its length is four times its width, find the length of this rectangular field.

Solution: Suppose the length and the width of this field is $4x$ metres and x metres respectively.

$\therefore$ Area of the field $= 4x \times x = 4x^2$ sq. metre

Since, $4x^2 = 1600 \Rightarrow x^2 = 400$

$\Rightarrow x = \sqrt{400} \Rightarrow x = 20$

$\therefore$ Length of the rectangular field

$= 4 \times 20 = 80$ m.

Example 2: Perimeter of the rectangular floor of a room is 100 m. If its length and breadth are in the ratio 3 : 2, find the area of this rectangular floor.

Solution: Suppose the length and the breadth of this rectangular floor are $3x$ metre and $2x$ metre respectively.

The perimeter of the floor $= 2 \times (l + b)$

$= 2(3x + 2x)$

$= 2 \times 5x = 10x$ metre

Since $10x = 100 \therefore x = \frac{100}{10} = 10$

$\therefore$ Length of the floor $= 3 \times 10 = 30$ m

And breadth of the floor $= 2 \times 10 = 20$ m

$\therefore$ Area of the floor $= 30 \times 20 = 600$ sq. m.

Example 3: The diagonal of a quadrilateral is 140 m and the offsets on it are 100 m and 30 m respectively. Find the area of this quadrilateral.

Solution: Area of the quadrilateral

$= \frac{1}{2} \times \text{diagonal} \times \text{sum of the offsets}$

$= \frac{1}{2} \times 140 \times (100 + 30)$

$= \frac{1}{2} \times 140 \times 130 = 9100$ sq. m.

Example 4: A circular path 3.5 m wide runs round outside a circular garden. If the circumference of the garden is 44 m, find the cost of levelling the path at 15 paise per sq. metre.

Solution: Circumference of the circular garden

$= 2\pi R = 44$ m

$\therefore$ Radius of the garden $= \frac{44}{2\pi} = \frac{44 \times 7}{2 \times 22} = 7$ m

Radius of the (garden + path)

$= 7 + 3.5 = 10.5$ m

$\therefore$ Area of the (garden + path) $= \frac{22}{7} \times (10.5)^2$

$= 346.5$ sq. m.

Area of the garden $= \frac{22}{7} \times 7 \times 7 = 154$ sq. m.

$\therefore$ Area of the path $= 346.5 - 154$

$= 192.5$ sq. m.

Hence, Cost of levelling the path at 15 paise per sq. metre $= 192.5 \times 0.15 =$ ₹ 28.88.

Example 5: Find the side and surface area of a cube whose volume is 729 cu cm.

Solution: Here, $(\text{side})^3 = 729$

$\Rightarrow (\text{side})^3 = (9)^3$

$\Rightarrow \text{side} = 9$ cm

Since, surface area $= 6 \times (9)^2 = 6 \times 81$

$= 486$ sq. cm.

Example 6: How many cubical blocks can be packed in a carton of size 10 m × 6 m × 4 m, if the volume of each cubical block is 15 cu metre?

Solution: Volume of the carton

$= l \times b \times h$

$= 10 \times 6 \times 4 = 240$ cu m

∴ Number of cubical blocks that can be packed in the carton $= \dfrac{240}{15} = 16$

Example 7: A 1100 cu cm iron cube is to be melted and recast into a iron rod in the form of a right circular cylinder. If diameter of the rod is kept 4 cm, what will be the length of this rod?

Solution: Suppose length of the rod = h cm

Radius of the rod $= \dfrac{4}{2} = 2$ cm

Here, Volume of the rod

= Volume of the iron cube

$\therefore \dfrac{22}{7} \times (2)^2 \times h = 1100$

$\Rightarrow h = \dfrac{1100 \times 7}{22 \times 4} = 87.5$ cm

∴ Rod will be 87.5 cm long.

Example 8: An open box is made of wood 3 cm thick. Its external length is 1.46 m, breadth is 1.16 m and height is 83 cm. Find the cost of painting the inner surface of the box at 50 paise per 100 cm^2.

Solution: Here, Internal length = 146 – 2 × 3 = 140 cm; Internal breadth = 116 – 2 × 3 = 110 cm and also, internal height = 83 – 3 = 80 cm

Since, Inner surface area of the open box

= 140 × 110 + 2 × (140 + 110) × 80

= 15400 + 40000

= 55400 cm^2

Required cost of painting

$= ₹ \dfrac{50}{100} \times \dfrac{1}{100} \times 55400 = ₹\ 277$

Example 9: The diameter of a roller 120 cm long is 84 cm. If it takes 500 complete revolutions to level a playground, determine the cost of levelling at the rate of 30 paise per m^2.

Solution: Area of the playground

$= 500 \times \dfrac{22}{7} \times 42 \times 120$

$= 15840000$ cm^2 $= 1584$ m^2

Since, cost of levelling = Rs. $\dfrac{30}{100} \times 1584$

= ₹ 475.20

Example 10: Some solid metallic circular cones, each with radius of the base 3 cm and height 4 cm, are melted to form a solid sphere of radius 6 cm. Find the number of right circular cones.

Solution: Let number of right circular cones be n; then,

$n \times \dfrac{1}{3} \pi \times 3^2 \times 4 = \dfrac{4}{3} \pi \times 6^3$

$\therefore n = \dfrac{4 \times 6 \times 6 \times 6}{3 \times 3 \times 4} = 24$

Example 11: If the ratio of volumes of two cones is 2 : 3 and ratio of radii of their bases is 1 : 2, then what will be the ratio of heights?

Solution: Here, $\dfrac{V_1}{V_2} = \dfrac{2}{3}$ and $\dfrac{r_1}{r_2} = \dfrac{1}{2}$; then

$$\frac{\frac{1}{3}\pi.(1)^2 \times h_1}{\frac{1}{3}\pi.(2)^2 \times h_2} = \frac{2}{3}$$

$\therefore \dfrac{h_1}{h_2} = \dfrac{2}{3} \times \dfrac{4}{1} = \dfrac{8}{3}$

Hence, required ratio = 8 : 3

EXERCISE

1. A field is in the form of a square whose perimeter is 580 m. Area of this field is
   (a) 21025 sq. m. *(b)* 20225 sq. m.
   (c) 30025 sq. m. *(d)* 19975 sq. m.
   (e) None of these
2. Area of a circle is 154 sq. cm. Its circumference will be
   (a) 37 cm *(b)* 48 cm

(c) 54 cm (d) 68 cm
(e) None of these

3. Perimeter of a rectangular field is 760 m and its length and breadth are in the ratio 11 : 8. Area of this rectangular field is
(a) 35200 sq. m. (b) 34700 sq. m.
(c) 35600 sq. m. (d) 45200 sq. m.
(e) None of these

4. If side of a square is reduced by 50%, its area will be reduced by
(a) 50% (b) 75%
(c) 80% (d) 60%
(e) None of these

5. If perimeter of a right angled triangle is six times its smallest side, then the three sides of this triangle are in the ratio of
(a) 13 : 5 : 12 (b) 12 : 13 : 5
(c) 12 : 5 : 13 (d) 13 : 5 : 10
(e) 13 : 12 : 5

6. If each side of a square is doubled, its area will become
(a) double (b) four times
(c) three times (d) eight times
(e) None of these

7. The difference between the areas of two squares is 225 sq. metres and each side of the bigger square is 25 metres. The side of the smaller square is
(a) 18 m (b) 21 m
(c) 20 m (d) 22 m
(e) None of these

8. If the circumference of a circle is equal to the perimeter of a square, then their areas are in the ratio of
(a) 14 : 11 (b) 7 : 8
(c) 14 : 13 (d) 13 : 11
(e) None of these

9. Three sides of a triangle are in the ratio of 17 : 15 : 8. If the perimeter of this triangle is 40 m, find its area
(a) 50 sq. m. (b) 49 sq. m.
(c) 60 sq. m. (d) 69 sq. m.
(e) None of these

10. If the length of a rectangle is increased by 20% and width is decreased by 15%, then its area
(a) decreases by 4% (b) increases by 2%
(c) decreases by 2% (d) increases by 3%
(e) None of these

11. Each side of a given square is 5 cm and assuming the two opposite sides of this square as diameters, two semicircles are drawn in the inside of the square. If these semicircles are cut out from the square, then the area of the remaining portion of the given square will be
(a) $(9 - 6.25\pi)$ sq. cm.
(b) $(24 - 6.25\pi)$ sq. cm.
(c) $(25 - 4.25\pi)$ sq. cm.
(d) $(36 - 6.25\pi)$ sq. cm.
(e) $(25 - 6.25\pi)$ sq. cm.

12. Two adjacent sides of a parallelogram are 40 m and 30 m respectively. If one diagonal of the parallelogram measures 50 m, find its area.
(a) 1100 sq. m. (b) 1300 sq. m.
(c) 1400 sq. m. (d) 1500 sq. m.
(e) None of these

13. Four sides of a trapezium are 50 cm, 17 cm, 25 cm and 12 cm respectively. If the first of the four sides is parallel to the third, find the area of this trapezium.
(a) 280 sq. cm. (b) 810 sq. cm.
(c) 270 sq. cm. (d) 225 sq. cm.
(e) None of these

14. A chord AB of a circle of radius 10 cm makes a right angle at the centre of the circle. The areas of the major and minor segments are:
(a) 220 cm^2; 30 cm^2
(b) 280 cm^2; 30 cm^2
(c) 285.5 cm^2; 28.5 cm^2
(d) 280.5 cm^2; 38.5 cm^2
(e) None of these

15. The parallel sides of a field which is in the shape of trapezium are 20 m and 41 m and the remaining two sides are 10 m and 17m. Find the cost of levelling the field at the rate of ₹ 30 per m^2.
(a) ₹ 7150 (b) ₹ 7220
(c) ₹ 7430 (d) ₹ 7350
(e) None of these

16. The difference between the length and breadth of a rectangle is 23 m. If its perimeter is 206m, then its area is:
(*a*) 1520 m^2 (*b*) 2420 m^2
(*c*) 2480 m^2 (*d*) 2520 m^2
(*e*) None of these

17. What will be the cost of building a fence around a circular field with area equal to 18,634 m^2; if the cost of building the fence per metre is ₹ 365?
(*a*) ₹ 1,76,660 (*b*) ₹ 1,86,680
(*c*) ₹ 2,10,660 (*d*) ₹ 2,76,660
(*e*) None of these

18. A solid in the form of a cuboid is 4 cm × 3 cm × 2 cm. Its volume will be
(*a*) 20 cu cm (*b*) 22 cu cm
(*c*) 28 cu cm (*d*) 24 cu cm
(*e*) None of these

19. Surface area of a cube is 1014 sq. cm. Its volume will be
(*a*) 2197 cu cm (*b*) 2297 cu cm
(*c*) 2179 cu cm (*d*) 2117 cu cm
(*e*) None of these

20. Two spheres have their surface areas in the ratio 9 : 16. Their volumes are in the ratio of
(*a*) 64 : 27 (*b*) 27 : 64
(*c*) 16 : 27 (*d*) 11 : 27
(*e*) None of these

21. Circumference of the base of a cylinder is 88 cm and height of the cylinder is 42 cm. Its volume is
(*a*) 25872 cu cm (*b*) 28572 cu cm
(*c*) 25870 cu cm (*d*) 22584 cu cm
(*e*) None of these

22. If a solid sphere of 3 cm radius is melted and recast into a right circular cone whose base radius is same as that of the sphere, the height of the cone will be
(*a*) 8 cm (*b*) 12 cm
(*c*) 6 cm (*d*) 5 cm
(*e*) None of these

23. Diameter of a roller is 2.4 m and it is 1.68 m long. If it takes 1000 complete revolutions once over to level a field, the area of the field is
(*a*) 12672 sq. m (*b*) 12671 sq. m
(*c*) 12762 sq. m (*d*) 11768 sq. m
(*e*) None of these

24. If each edge of a cube is increased by 10%, then by how much per cent will the surface area of this cube be increased?
(*a*) 21% (*b*) 18%
(*c*) 15% (*d*) 20%
(*e*) None of these

25. Height and base radius of a solid cylinder are 14 m and 4 m respectively. It is melted and recast into a solid cone of the same base radius as that of the cylinder, what will be the height of the cone?
(*a*) 21 m (*b*) 42 m
(*c*) 48 m (*d*) 54 m
(*e*) None of these

26. If the base radius of a cylinder is decreased by 25% and height is increased by 10%, then the curved surface area
(*a*) Decreases by 17.5%
(*b*) Increases by 16.5%
(*c*) Increases by 17.5%
(*d*) Decreases by 11.5%
(*e*) None of these

27. If the whole mass of a sphere can be tightly placed in a cube, then the volume of the cube and the volume of the sphere are in the ratio
(*a*) 7 : 12 (*b*) 22 : 21
(*c*) 21 : 11 (*d*) 20 : 7

28. A cone and a sphere have the same radius and the same volume. The ratio of the diameter of the sphere to the height of the cone is
(*a*) 1 : 3 (*b*) 3 : 2
(*c*) 2 : 1 (*d*) 2 : 3
(*e*) 1 : 2

29. A sphere of maximum volume is cut out from a hemisphere of radius *r*. Find the ratio of the volume of the hemisphere to that of the sphere.
(*a*) 2 : 1 (*b*) 3 : 1
(*c*) 3 : 2 (*d*) 4 : 1
(*e*) None of these

ANSWERS

1	2	3	4	5	6	7	8	9	10
(a)	(e)	(a)	(b)	(e)	(b)	(c)	(a)	(c)	(b)
11	**12**	**13**	**14**	**15**	**16**	**17**	**18**	**19**	**20**
(e)	(e)	(c)	(c)	(e)	(d)	(a)	(d)	(a)	(b)
21	**22**	**23**	**24**	**25**	**26**	**27**	**28**	**29**	
(a)	(b)	(a)	(a)	(b)	(a)	(c)	(e)	(d)	

SOME SELECTED EXPLANATORY ANSWERS

1. Here, $4 \times \text{side} = 580 \Rightarrow \text{side} = \frac{580}{4} = 145$ m

$\therefore$ Area = $(\text{side})^2 = (145)^2 = 21025$ sq. m.

2. Area of the circle $= \pi r^2 \Rightarrow \pi r^2 = 154$

$\Rightarrow r^2 = \frac{154 \times 7}{22} \Rightarrow r = 7$ cm

$\therefore$ Circumference of the circle $= 2\pi r$

$= 2 \times \frac{22}{7} \times 7 = 44$ cm.

3. Suppose length and breadth of the rectangular field are $11x$ m and $8x$ m.

$\therefore$ Perimeter of the field $= 2(11x + 8x) = 2 \times 19x = 38x$ m.

Now, $38x = 760$

$\Rightarrow x = \frac{760}{38} = 20$

$\therefore$ Length of the field $= 11 \times 20 = 220$ m

Breadth of the field $= 8 \times 20 = 160$ m

$\therefore$ Area of the field $= 220 \times 160 = 35200$ sq. m.

6. Area of the square $= x^2$ sq. m

Now, area of the new square $= (2x)^2 = 4x^2$ sq. m

Hence, it is clear that if side of a square is doubled, its area becomes four times.

7. Area of smaller square, $x^2 = 25^2 - 225 = 625 - 225 = 400$

$\Rightarrow x = \sqrt{400} = 20$ m

$\therefore$ Side of the smaller square = 20 m.

8. Here, $2\pi R = 4x \Rightarrow R = \frac{2x}{\pi}$

$\therefore$ Ratio between the areas of the circle and the square $= \pi R^2 : x^2$

$$= \pi \times \left(\frac{2x}{p}\right)^2 : x^2 = \frac{4x^2}{\pi} : x^2 = 4 : \frac{22}{7} = 14 : 11$$

11. Area of the remaining portion of the square

$$= 5^2 - 2 \times \frac{1}{2} \pi \times \left(\frac{5}{2}\right)^2$$

$$= 25 - \frac{25}{4}\pi$$

$= (25 - 6.25\pi)$ sq. cm.

12. Here, $50^2 = 40^2 + 30^2$

$\therefore$ Two triangles, *i.e.*, ΔABC and ΔADC are right angled triangle.

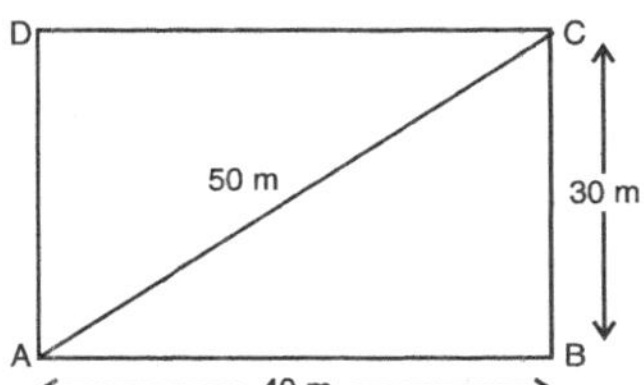

$\therefore$ Area of parallelogram ABCD $= 2 \times$ Area of Δ ABC $= 2 \times \frac{1}{2} \times 40 \times 30 = 1200$ sq.m.

14. Area of circle $= \frac{22}{7} \times (10)^2 = \frac{2200}{7}$ cm$^2 \approx 314$ cm^2

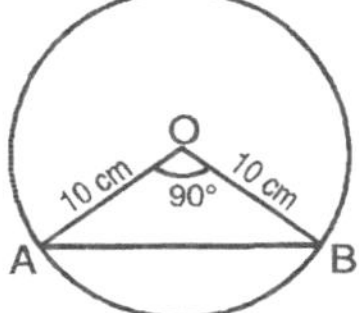

Area of minor segment

$$= \frac{90}{360} \times \frac{22}{7} \times 10^2 - \frac{1}{2} \times 10 \times 10$$

$$= \frac{550}{7} - 50$$

$$= \frac{200}{7} = 28.57 \approx 28.5 \text{ cm}^2$$

16. Here, $l - b = 23$ ...(i)

and also, $2(l + b) = 206 \quad \therefore l + b = 103$ ...(ii)

Hence, $l = \frac{1}{2}(103 + 23) = 63$ m;

$b = \frac{1}{2}(103 - 23) = 40$ m

Since, $A = 63 \times 40 = 2520$ m²

17. Radius of the circular field

$$= \sqrt{\frac{18634 \times 7}{22}} = \sqrt{847 \times 7} = 77 \text{ m}$$

Circumference $= 2 \times \frac{22}{7} \times 77 = 484$ m²

Required cost = 484 × ₹ 365 = ₹ 1,76,660

18. Volume of the cuboid

$$= l \times b \times h$$
$$= 4 \times 3 \times 2 = 24 \text{ cu. cm.}$$

19. Here, $6 \times (\text{side})^2 = 1014$

$$\Rightarrow (\text{side})^2 = \frac{1014}{6} = 169$$

$\therefore$ side $= \sqrt{169} = 13$ cm

Hence, Volume of the cube $= (\text{side})^3 = (13)^3$

$= 2197$ cu cm.

20. Here, $4\pi r_1^2 : 4\pi r_2^2 = 9 : 16 \Rightarrow r_1^2 : r_2^2 = 9 : 16$

$$\Rightarrow \left(\frac{r_1}{r_2}\right)^2 = \left(\frac{3}{4}\right)^2 \quad \Rightarrow r_1 : r_2 = 3 : 4$$

$$\Rightarrow \frac{r_1^3}{r_2^3} = \frac{27}{64} \quad \Rightarrow r_1^3 : r_2^3 = 27 : 64.$$

Therefore, ratio of their volumes

$$= \frac{4}{3}\pi r_1^3 : \frac{4}{3}\pi r_2^3 = r_1^3 : r_2^3 = 27 : 64$$

21. Here, $2\pi r = 88$

$$\therefore \quad r = \frac{88}{2\pi} = \frac{88 \times 7}{2 \times 22} = 14 \text{ cm}$$

Since, volume of the cylinder

$$= \pi r^2 h = \frac{22}{7} \times (14)^2 \times 42$$
$$= 22 \times 2 \times 14 \times 42$$
$$= 25872 \text{ cu cm.}$$

23. Surface area of the roller $= 2\pi rh$

$$= 2 \times \frac{22}{7} \times 1.2 \times 1.68$$
$$= 12.672 \text{ sq. m}$$

In one complete revolution, the roller covers 12.672 sq. m.

$\therefore$ It will cover in 1000 revolutions

$$= 12.672 \times 1000$$
$$= 12672 \text{ sq. m}$$

Hence, area of the field

$$= 12672 \text{ sq. m.}$$

24. Percentage increase in the surface area of the cube

$$= \left(x + y + \frac{xy}{100}\right)\%$$

$$= \left(10 + 10 + \frac{10 \times 10}{100}\right)\%$$

$$= 21\%.$$

26. Change in the curved surface of the cylinder

$$= \left(-25 + 10 + \frac{-25 \times 10}{100}\right)\%$$

$$= (-15 - 2.5)\% = -17.5\%$$

$\therefore$ Curved surface of the cylinder will be decreased by 17.5%.

28. Here, $4/3\pi r^3 = \frac{1}{3}\pi r^2 h$

$\Rightarrow 4r = h$

$\Rightarrow 2d = h$

$\therefore \frac{d}{h} = \frac{1}{2}$

Hence, required ratio = 1 : 2

29. Required ratio $= \dfrac{\frac{2}{3}\pi r^3}{\frac{4}{3}\pi r^3} = \frac{8}{2} = \frac{4}{1} = 4:1$

❑❑❑

15 DATA INTERPRETATION (TABLE)

Data Interpretation is one of the easy sections of Bank PO Examination. It is an extension of Mathematical skills and accuracy. Data Interpretation is nothing but drawing conclusions and inferences from a comprehensive data presented numerically in tabular form by means of an illustration, viz., Graph, Pie chart etc. Sound knowledge of quantitative techniques is a prerequisite for good performance in this section. The thumb rule, as in the case of reading comprehension—read the passage rapidly but carefully and comprehend it at the same time—applies in this section too. However, unlike reading comprehension where one can afford to skip irrelevant portions of the passage, here even the minutest of details cannot be overlooked.

A good grasp of basic geometric as well as arithmetic formulae is must to score high in this section. Since such questions may require a fair amount of calculations, one should be able to multiply and divide quickly using short-cut methods. Familiarity with graphical representation of data like venn diagrams, graphs, pie diagrams, histogram, polygon etc. should be thorough. Once the data are grasped well, questions based on tables and graphs take little time.

In some Bank PO Exams data are presented in more than one table or graph. The aim is to test not only quantitative skills but also relative, comparative and analytical ability. The crux of the matter is to find a relationship between the two tables or graphs before attempting the questions.

EXERCISE

Directions (Qs. 1 to 5): *Study the following tables carefully and answer the questions given below:*

Number of Males and Females staying in various societies

Societies	Males	Females
A	250	350
B	400	150
C	300	275
D	280	300
E	180	250
F	325	300

Percentage of Children (Males and Females) in the societies

Societies	Children	Males	Females
A	25%	40%	60%
B	40%	75%	25%
C	16%	25%	75%
D	25%	80%	20%
E	40%	50%	50%
F	24%	46%	54%

1. What is the respective ratio of the number of the adult females to the total number of female children staying in all the societies together?

(*a*) 82 : 243
(*b*) 243 : 82
(*c*) 71 : 112
(*d*) 112 : 71
(*e*) None of these

2. What is the respective ratio of the total number of adult males in the societies A and B together to the total number of adult males in the societies E and F together?

(*a*) 14 : 17
(*b*) 17 : 14
(*c*) 75 : 79
(*d*) 79 : 75
(*e*) None of these

3. What is the difference between the number of male children in society B and the number of male children in society F?
(*a*) 14 (*b*) 26
(*c*) 84 (*d*) 96
(*e*) None of these

4. What is the total number of female children staying in all the societies together?
(*a*) 314 (*b*) 343
(*c*) 410 (*d*) 433
(*e*) None of these

5. What is the total number of members staying in all the societies together?
(*a*) 3000 (*b*) 3360
(*c*) 4100 (*d*) 4289
(*e*) None of these

Directions (Qs. 6 to 10): *Study the following table carefully and answer the questions given below:*

Quantity of Rice produced by Various states over the years (Quantity in Tonnes)

States ↓	YEARS					
	2003	2004	2005	2006	2007	2008
A	1500	1480	1620	1700	1540	1650
B	1250	1190	1400	1450	1320	1380
C	1160	1190	1310	1300	1340	1360
D	1520	1500	1480	1590	1630	1580
E	1440	1350	1430	1280	1380	1400
F	1600	1620	1510	1610	1580	1590

6. In which state has the production of rice increased continuously over the years?
(*a*) B (*b*) C
(*c*) D (*d*) A
(*e*) None of these

7. Which state produced the lowest quantity of rice over the years?
(*a*) A (*b*) C
(*c*) D (*d*) E
(*e*) None of these

8. Rice produced by State C in the year 2006 is approximately what per cent of the rice produced by State A in the same year?
(*a*) 69% (*b*) 72%
(*c*) 76% (*d*) 82%
(*e*) None of these

9. In which year was the production of rice the highest in all the states together?
(*a*) 2005 (*b*) 2006
(*c*) 2007 (*d*) 2008
(*e*) None of these

10. What is the respective ratio of the average quantity of rice produced by State D to the average quantity of rice produced by State F over the years?
(*a*) 69 : 79 (*b*) 138 : 155
(*c*) 276 : 317 (*d*) 310 : 317
(*e*) None of these

ANSWERS

1	2	3	4	5	6	7	8	9	10
(*b*)	(*b*)	(*d*)	(*c*)	(*b*)	(*e*)	(*b*)	(*c*)	(*d*)	(*d*)

SOME SELECTED EXPLANATORY ANSWERS

1. **In society A:**
Number of children

$$= \frac{25}{100} \times (250 + 350) = \frac{1}{4} \times 600 = 150$$

$$\text{Number of male children} = \frac{40}{100} \times 150 = 60$$

$$\text{Number of female children} = 150 - 60 = 90$$

In society B:

Number of children

$= \frac{40}{100} \times (400 + 150) = \frac{2}{5} \times 550 = 220$

Number of male children $= \frac{75}{100} \times 220 = 165$

Number of female children

$= 220 - 165 = 55$

In society C:

Number of children $= \frac{16}{100} \times (300 + 275)$

$= \frac{4}{25} \times 575 = 92$

Number of male children $= \frac{25}{100} \times 92 = 23$

Number of female children $= 92 - 23 = 69$

In society D:

Number of children $= \frac{25}{100} \times (280 + 300)$

$= \frac{1}{4} \times 580 = 145$

Number of male children $= \frac{80}{100} \times 145 = 116$

Number of female children

$= 145 - 116 = 29$

In society E:

Number of children

$= \frac{40}{100} \times (180 + 250) = \frac{2}{5} \times 430 = 172$

Number of male children $= \frac{50}{100} \times 172 = 86$

Number of female children $= 172 - 86 = 86$

In society F :

Number of children

$= \frac{24}{100} \times (325 + 300) = \frac{6}{25} \times 625 = 150$

Number of male children $= \frac{46}{100} \times 150 = 69$

Number of female children $= 150 - 69 = 81$

Hence, total number of female children
$= 90 + 55 + 69 + 29 + 86 + 81 = 410$

Total number of adult females
$= (350 + 150 + 275 + 300 + 250 + 300) - 410$
$= 1625 - 410 = 1215$

Hence, required ratio $= 1215 : 410 = 243 : 82$

2. Total number of adult males in the society
A and B $= (250 + 400) - (60 + 165)$
(As shown in solution : 1)
$= 650 - 225 = 425$

Total number of adult males in the society
E and F $= (180 + 325) - (86 + 69)$
(As shown in solution : 1)
$= 505 - 155 = 350$

Hence, required ratio $= 425 : 350 = 17 : 14$

3. Male children in society B = 165
Male children in society F = 69
(As shown in solution : 1)
Hence, their difference $= 165 - 69 = 96$

4. Total number of female children = 410
(As shown in solution : 1)

5. Number of members
$= (250 + 350) + (400 + 150) + (300 + 275) + (280 + 300) + (180 + 250) + (325 + 300)$
$= 600 + 550 + 575 + 580 + 430 + 625$
$= 3360$

6. It is clear from the table that none of the state has the production of rice increased continuously over the years.

7. Production of rice by different states over the years:

A → 1500 + 1480 + 1620 + 1700 + 1540 + 1650 = 9490 tonnes

B → 1250 + 1190 + 1400 + 1450 + 1320 + 1380 = 7990 tonnes

C → 1160 + 1190 + 1310 + 1300 + 1340 + 1360 = 7660 tonnes

D → 1520 + 1500 + 1480 + 1590 + 1630 + 1580 = 9300 tonnes

E → 1440 + 1350 + 1430 + 1280 + 1380 + 1400 = 8280 tonnes

F → 1600 + 1620 + 1510 + 1610 + 1580 + 1590 = 9510 tonnes

Hence, the State C produced the lowest quantity of rice.

8. Required percentage $= \frac{1300}{1700} \times 100$

$= 76.47\% \approx 76\%$

9. Production of rice in different years by all states together:

2003 → 1500 + 1250 + 1160 + 1520 + 1440 + 1600 = 8470 tonnes

2004 → 1480 + 1190 + 1190 + 1500 + 1350 + 1620 = 8330 tonnes

2005 → 1620 + 1400 + 1310 + 1480 + 1430 + 1510 = 8750 tonnes

2006 → 1700 + 1450 + 1300 + 1590 + 1280 + 1610 = 8930 tonnes

2007 → 1540 + 1320 + 1340 + 1630 + 1380 + 1580 = 8790 tonnes

2008 → 1650 + 1380 + 1360 + 1580 + 1400 + 1590 = 8960 tonnes

Hence, in year 2008 the production of rice was the highest.

10. Average quantity of rice produced by State D

$= \frac{9300}{6} = 1550$ tonnes

(As shown in soluton : 7)

Average quantity of rice produced by State F

$= \frac{9510}{6} = 1585$ tonnes

(As shown in soluton : 7)

Hence, required ratio

= 1550 : 1585

= 310 : 317

❑❑❑

16 DATA INTERPRETATION (BAR GRAPHS AND PIE CHART)

BAR GRAPHS

A bar graph may be either horizontal or vertical. The important point to note about bar graphs is their bar length or height; the greater their length or height, the greater their value. Bar graphs usually present categorical and numeric variables grouped in class intervals. They consist of an axis and a series or labelled horizontal or vertical bars. The bars depict frequencies of different values of a variable or simply the different values or simply the different values themselves. The numbers on the x-axis of a bar graph or the y-axis of a column graph are called the scale.

PIE CHARTS

A pie chart is a way of summarising a set of categorical data or displaying the different values of a given variable (*e.g.*, percentage distribution). This type of chart is a circle divided into series of segments. Each segment represents a particular category.

EXERCISE

Directions : *Shown below is the multiple bar diagram depicting the changes in the student's strength of a college in four faculties from* 2000-01 *to* 2002-03. (*Scale* 1 *cm* = 100)

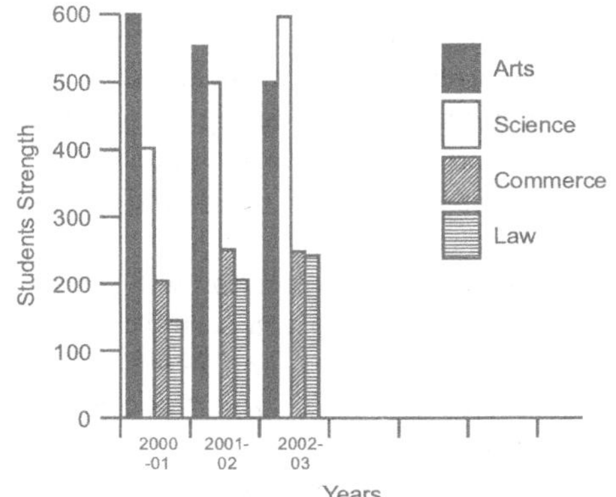

Study the above multiple bar chart and mark a tick against the correct answer in each of the following questions.

1. The percentage of students in science faculty in 2000-01 was :
   (*a*) 26.9 % (*b*) 27.8 %
   (*c*) 29.6 % (*d*) 30.2 %
   (*e*) None of the above
2. The percentage of students in law faculty in 2002-03 was :
   (*a*) 18.5 % (*b*) 15.6 %
   (*c*) 16.7 % (*d*) 14.8 %
   (*e*) None of the above
3. How many times the total strength was of the strength of commerce students in 2001-02?
   (*a*) 3 times (*b*) 4 times
   (*c*) 5 times (*d*) 6 times
   (*e*) None of the above
4. During which year the strength of arts faculty was minimum?
   (*a*) 2000-01 (*b*) 2001-02
   (*c*) 2002-03 (*d*) 2003-04
   (*e*) None of the above
5. How much per cent was the increase in science students in 2002-03 over 2000-01?
   (*a*) 50% (*b*) 150%
   (*c*) $66\frac{2}{3}\%$ (*d*) 75%
   (*e*) None of the above
6. A regular decrease in students' strength was in the faculty of
   (*a*) Arts (*b*) Science
   (*c*) Commerce (*d*) Law
   (*e*) None of the above

ANSWERS

1	2	3	4	5	6
(*c*)	(*b*)	(*d*)	(*c*)	(*a*)	(*a*)

SOME SELECTED EXPLANATORY ANSWERS

1. Total number of students in 2000-01
$= (600 + 400 + 200 + 150) = 1350$
Number of science students in 2000-01 was 400.
Percentage of science students in 2000-01
$= \left[\frac{400}{1350} \times 100\right]\% = 29.6\%$
So, answer (*c*) is correct.

2. Total number of students in 2002-03
$= (500 + 600 + 250 + 250) = 1600$
Number of law students in 2002-03 is 250.
Percentage of law students in 2002-03
$= \left[\frac{250}{1600} \times 100\right]\% = 15.6\ \%$
So, answer (*b*) is correct.

3. Total strength in 2001-02
$= (550 + 500 + 250 + 200) = 1500$
So, $\frac{\text{Total strength}}{\text{Strength of commerce students}} = \frac{1500}{250} = 6.$

4. A slight look indicates that the strength in arts faculty in 2000-01, 2001-02 and 2002-03 was 600, 550 and 500 respectively. So, it was minimum in 2002-03.
So, answer (*c*) is correct.

5. Number of science students in 2000 - 01 was 400.
Number of science students in 2002 - 03 was 600.
Percentage increase $= \left(\frac{200}{400} \times 100\right)\% = 50\%$
Answer (*a*) is correct.

EXERCISE

Directions (Qs. 1 to 5) : *Examine the following graph carefully and answer the questions given below it.*

Production of Cotton bales of 100 kg. each in lacs in States during 2005-2006, 2006-2007, 2007-2008

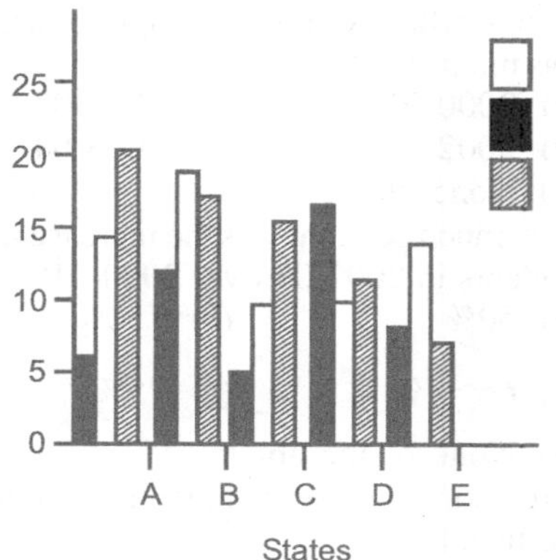

1. The production of State *D* in 2007-2008 is how many times its production in 2006-2007?
(*a*) 1.33 (*b*) 0.75
(*c*) 0.56 (*d*) 1.77
(*e*) None of these

2. In which states is there a steady increase in the production of cotton during the given period?
(*a*) *A* and *B* (*b*) *A* and *C*
(*c*) *B* only (*d*) *D* and *E*
(*e*) None of these

3. How many tonnes of cotton was produced by State *E* during the given period?
(*a*) 2900 (*b*) 290000
(*c*) 29000 (*d*) 2900000
(*e*) None of these

4. Which of the following statements is False?
(*a*) States *A* & *E* showed the same production in 2006-2007.
(*b*) There was no improvement in the production of cotton in State *B* during.
(*c*) State *A* has produced maximum cotton during the given period.
(*d*) Production of states *C* and *D* together is equal to that of State *B* during 2006-2007.
(*e*) None of these

Directions (Qs. 5 to 9): *Study the graph carefully to answer the questions that follow:*

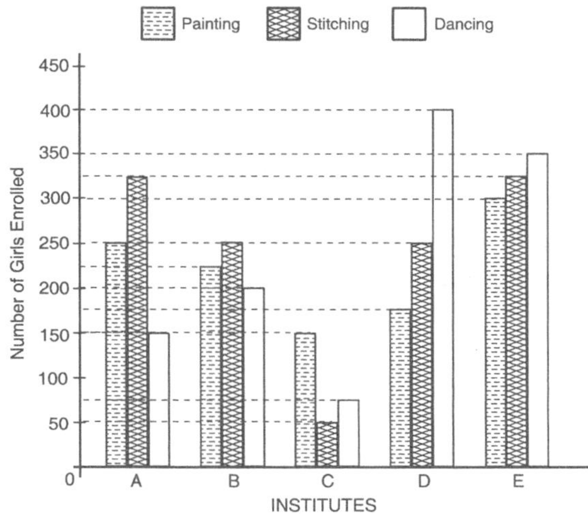

5. What is the respective ratio of total number of girls enrolled in Painting in the institutes A and C together to those enrolled in Stiching in the institutes D and E together?
   (a) 5 : 4 (b) 5 : 7
   (c) 9 : 8 (d) 16 : 23
   (e) None of these
6. What is the respective ratio of total number of girls enrolled in Painting, Stiching and Dancing from all the Institutes together?
   (a) 43 : 47 : 48 (b) 44 : 47 : 48
   (c) 44 : 48 : 47 (d) 47 : 48 : 44
   (e) None of these
7. What is the total number of girls enrolled in Painting from all the Institutes together?
   (a) 1100 (b) 1150
   (c) 1200 (d) 1275
   (e) None of these
8. Number of girls enrolled in Stitching in Institute B forms approximately what per cent of the total number of girls enrolled in Stitching in the Institutes together?
   (a) 21%
   (b) 29%
   (c) 33%
   (d) 37%
   (e) None of these
9. Number of girls enrolled in Dancing in Institute A forms what per cent of total number of girls enrolled in all the Hobby classes together in that Institute?
   (a) 17.76% (b) 20.69%
   (c) 31.23% (d) 33.97%
   (e) None of these

Directions (Qs. 10 to 14): *Study the following graph and table carefully and answer the questions given below it:*

Distribution of Candidates appeared in a competitive examination from seven states Total Candidates appeared = 3 lakh

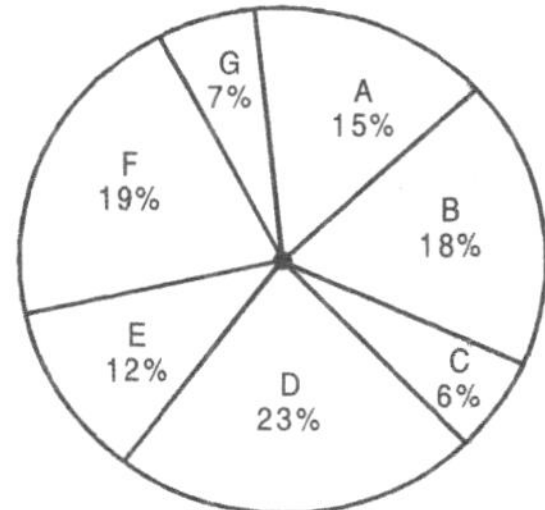

State-wise percentage and ratio of male and female qualified candidates

S		
A	49	4 : 5
B	61	6 : 4
C	54	7 : 8
D	45	3 : 2
E	65	7 : 6
F	57	11 : 8
G	48	9 : 11

10. What is the number of male candidates qualified from State 'G'?
    (a) 4536 (b) 4568
    (c) 5454 (d) 5544
    (e) None of these
11. Which of the following pair of states have equal number of qualified male candidates?
    (a) A and E (b) B and F
    (c) C and E (d) C and G
    (e) None of these

12. What is the total number of candidates qualified from states E and D together?
(a) 45540 (b) 54410
(c) 54450 (d) 54540
(e) None of these

13. What is the total number of female candidates qualified from states A and B together?
(a) 24526 (b) 25426
(c) 26426 (d) 26526
(e) None of these

14. What is the percentage of candidates qualified from states 'A' and 'B' together of the total candidates appeared?
(a) 16.23% (b) 18.33%
(c) 22.23% (d) 25.33%
(e) None of these

Directions (Qs. 15 to 19): *Study the following graph carefully and answer the questions given below it.*

Per cent profit earned by two Companies A and B over the years

Profit = Income – Expenditure

$$\text{Profit\%} = \frac{\text{Profit}}{\text{Expenditure}} \times 100$$

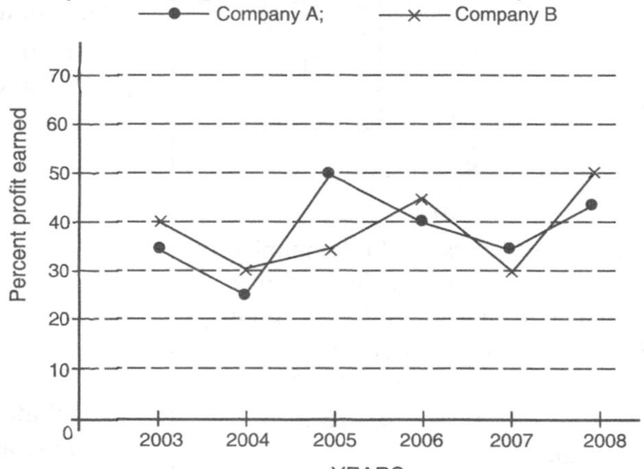

15. If the income of company A in 2005 was ₹ 1,42,500, what was its expenditure in that year?
(a) ₹ 95000 (b) ₹ 95500
(c) ₹ 99,500 (d) ₹ 1,05,000
(e) None of these

16. If the expenditure of Company 'A' in 2004 was ₹ 75 lakhs and income of Company A in 2004 was equal to its expenditure in 2005. What was the total income (in lakhs ₹) of the Company A in 2004 and 2005 together?
(a) 131.25 (b) 175
(c) 218.75 (d) 234.37
(e) None of these

17. Total expenditure of companies A & B together in 2008 was ₹ 13.5 lakhs. What was the total income of the two companies (in lakh Rs.) in that year?
(a) 19.75
(b) 20.25
(c) 19.575
(d) Cannot be determined
(e) None of these

18. Expenditure of company 'B' in 2006 was 90% of its expenditure in 2005. Income of Company 'B' in 2006 was what per cent of its income in 2005?
(a) $96\frac{2}{3}$ (b) $99\frac{1}{3}$
(c) 121.5 (d) 130.5
(e) None of these

19. Expenditure of company 'B' in years 2003 and 2004 were in the ratio of 5 : 7 respectively. What was the respective ratio of their incomes?
(a) 8 : 13 (b) 10 : 13
(c) 11 : 14 (d) 13 ; 14
(e) None of these

ANSWERS

1	2	3	4	5	6	7	8	9	10
(b)	(b)	(b)	(c)	(d)	(c)	(a)	(a)	(b)	(a)
11	12	13	14	15	16	17	18	19	
(d)	(c)	(b)	(b)	(a)	(d)	(d)	(a)	(b)	

SOME SELECTED EXPLANATORY ANSWERS

1. Suppose, it is x times

$$x = \frac{12}{9} = \frac{4}{3}$$

2. It is clear by graph.

3. 8 + 14 + 7 = 29 lakhs

$$\text{Its weight} = \frac{29 \times 100000}{1000} \times 100$$

4. State B = 48 lakh bales State A = 41 lakh bales

5. Total number of girls enrolled in Painting in the Institutes A and C

= 250 + 150 = 400

Total number of girls enrolled in Stitching in the Institutes D and E

= 250 + 325 = 575

Required ratio = 400 : 575 = 16 : 23

6. Total number of girls enrolled in Painting

= 250 + 225 + 150 + 175 + 300 = 1100

Total number of girls enrolled in Stitching

= 325 + 250 + 50 + 250 + 325 = 1200

Total number of girls enrolled in Dancing

= 150 + 200 + 75 + 400 + 350 = 1175

Hence, required ratio

= 1100 : 1200 : 1175 = 44 : 48 : 47

7. Total number of girls enrolled in Painting

= 250 + 225 + 150 + 175 + 300 = 1100

8. Number of girls enrolled in Stitching in Institute B = 250

Total number of girls enrolled in Stitching in all the Institutions

= 325 + 250 + 50 + 250 + 325 = 1200

Hence, required percentage

$$= \frac{250}{1200} \times 100 = 20.83 \approx 21\%$$

9. Number of girls enrolled in Dancing in Institute A = 150

Total number of girls enrolled in all the Hobby classes together in Institute A

= 250 + 325 + 150 = 725

Hence, required percentage

$$= \frac{150}{725} \times 100 = 20.69\%$$

10. Number of candidates qualified from State

$$G = \frac{48}{100} \times \frac{7}{100} \times 3{,}00{,}000 = 10080$$

Number of male candidates qualified from State

$$G = \frac{9}{9+11} \times 10080 = \frac{9}{20} \times 10080$$

$$= 4536$$

11. Qualified Male Candidates from different states:

$$A \rightarrow \frac{4}{9} \times \frac{49}{100} \times \frac{15}{100} \times 300000 = 9800$$

$$B \rightarrow \frac{6}{10} \times \frac{61}{100} \times \frac{18}{100} \times 300000 = 19764$$

$$C \rightarrow \frac{7}{15} \times \frac{54}{100} \times \frac{6}{100} \times 300000 = 4536$$

$$D \rightarrow \frac{3}{5} \times \frac{45}{100} \times \frac{23}{100} \times 300000 = 18630$$

$$E \rightarrow \times \frac{7}{13} \times \frac{65}{100} \times \frac{12}{100} \times 300000 = 12600$$

$$F \rightarrow \frac{11}{19} \times \frac{57}{100} \times \frac{19}{100} \times 300000 = 18810$$

$$G \rightarrow \frac{9}{20} \times \frac{48}{100} \times \frac{7}{100} \times 300000 = 4536$$

Hence, states C and G have equal number of qualified male candidates.

12. Required number of candidates

$= \frac{65}{100} \times \frac{12}{100} \times 300000 + \frac{45}{100} \times \frac{23}{100} \times 300000$

= 23400 + 31050 = 54450

13. Required number of female candidates

$= \frac{5}{9} \times \frac{49}{100} \times \frac{15}{100} \times 300000 + \frac{4}{10} \times \frac{61}{100}$

$\times \frac{18}{100} \times 300000$

= 12250 + 13176 = 25426

14. Number of candidates qualified from states A and B together

$= \frac{49}{100} \times \frac{15}{100} \times 300000 + \frac{61}{100} \times \frac{18}{100} \times 300000$

= 22050 + 32940 = 54990

Required percentage $= \frac{54990}{300000} \times 100$

= 18.33%

15. Let expenditure of Company A in 2005 = ₹ x; then

$x + \frac{50}{100} \times x = 1{,}42{,}500 \quad \Rightarrow \frac{3x}{2} = 1{,}42{,}500$

$\therefore x = \frac{2 \times 1{,}42{,}500}{3} =$ ₹ 95000

16. In 2004, expenditure of Company 'A'

= ₹ 75 lakh

Since, income of the Company 'A' in 2004

$= 75 + \frac{25}{100} \times 75 =$ ₹ 93.75 lakhs

Now, expenditure of the Company 'A' in 2005 = ₹ 93.75 lakhs

Since, income of the Company A in 2005

$= 93.75 + \frac{50}{100} \times 93.75$

= ₹ 140.62 lakhs

Hence, total income for both the years

= 93.75 + 140.62 = ₹ 234.37 lakhs

17. Here total expenditure of both companies are given while their individual expenditures are needed to determine their incomes. So, the total income of the two companies cannot be determined by the given datas.

18. Let expenditure of Company B in 2005 = ₹ x; then

I_1 (Income) $= x + \frac{35}{100} x = \frac{27x}{20}$

Since, expenditure of Company B in 2006

$= \frac{90}{100} \times$ ₹ $x =$ ₹ $\frac{9x}{10}$, then

I_2 (Income) $= \frac{9x}{10} + \frac{45}{100} \times \frac{9x}{10}$

$= \frac{9x}{10} + \frac{81x}{200} =$ ₹ $\frac{261x}{200}$

Hence, required percentage

$= \frac{261x/200}{27x/20} \times 100 = \frac{290}{3} = 96\frac{2}{3}\%$

19. Let expenditures of Company B in 2003 and 2004 are ₹ $5x$ and ₹ $7x$ respectively; then their income in 2003, I_1

$= 5x + \frac{40}{100} \times 5x =$ ₹ $7x$

Also their income in 2004,

$I_2 = 7x + \frac{30}{100} \times 7x =$ ₹ $\frac{91x}{10}$

Hence, the required ratio $= 7x : \frac{91x}{10}$

= 10 : 13.

❑❑❑

17 PERMUTATION & COMBINATION

IMPORTANT RESULTS

(*i*) Number of permutations of n distinct things taken r at a time, $0 \le r \le n$

$= n(n-1)(n-2)\ldots(n-r+1)$

$= n!/(n-r)! = {}^nP_r$.

This is equivalent to filling r places by r objects taking from n distinct objects.

(*ii*) The number of permutations of n distinct objects taken all at a time $= n!$

(*iii*) The number of combinations of n objects taken r at a time, $0 \le r \le n = {}^nC_r$

$$= \frac{n!}{(n-r)!.r!}.$$

(*iv*) The number of permutations of n dissimilar things taken r at a time when each thing can be repeated any number of times $= n^r$.

(*v*) The number of combinations of n distinct objects taken r at a time when any object may be repeated any number of times

$=$ coefficient of x^r in $(1 + x + x^2 + \ldots + x^r)^n$

$=$ coefficient of x^r in $(1-x)^n = {}^{n+r-1}C_r$.

(*vi*) Number of combinations of n distinct things taken r at a time when p particular things always occur $= {}^{(n-p)}C_{(r-p)}$.

(*vii*) The number of permutations of n distinct things taken r at a time when p particular things always occur $= {}^{(n-p)}C_{(r-p)}.r!$.

(*viii*) Number of combinations of n distinct things taken r at a time when p particular things never occur $= {}^{(n-p)}C_r$.

(*ix*) Number of permutations (arrangements) of n distinct things taken r at a time when p particular things never occur $= {}^{(n-p)}C_r.r!$.

(*x*) Number of permutations of n things, taken all at a time when p_1 are alike of one kind, p_2 are alike of second kind, ..., p_r of them are alike of the rth kind $p_1 + p_2 + \ldots + p_r \le n$, and remaining things are all different $= n!/\{p_1!p_2! \ldots p_r!\}$.

(*xi*) If $3n$ things are to be divided into three equal groups, then the number of ways

$$= \frac{(3n)!}{n!.n!.n!.3!}.$$

(*xii*) If $3n$ things are to be divided equally between 3 persons (*i.e.*, division of $3n$ things into 3 equal groups with permutation of groups) then the number of ways

$$= \frac{(3n)!}{(n!)^3}.$$

(*xiii*) Greatest value of ${}^nC_r$

${}^nC_r$ is greatest when

$r = n/2$ if n is even

$r = (n-1)/2$ or $(n+1)/2$ if n is odd.

(*xiv*) ${}^nC_r = {}^nC_{n-r}$.

(*xv*) ${}^nC_r + {}^nC_{r+1} = {}^{n+1}C_{r+1}$.

(*xvi*) ${}^nC_r = {}^nC_s$

$\Rightarrow r = s$ or $r + s = n$.

(*xvii*) The number of circular permutations of n different things taken all at a time $= (n-1)!$

(*xviii*) The number of arrangements of n persons on a round table $= (n-1)!$.

(*xix*) The number of arrangements of n flowers to make a garland $= \frac{1}{2}(n-1)!$.

EXAMPLES

Example 1: In how many different ways can the letters of the word 'PRIDE' be arranged ?

Solution: Required number of arrangements

$= {}^5P_5 = 5! = 120$

Example 2: In how many different ways can the letters of the word 'PRAISE' be arranged ?

Solution: Required number of ways

$= {}^6P_6 = 6! = 720$

Example 3: On a shelf there are 4 books on Economics, 3 books on Management and 4 books on Statistics. In how many different ways can the books be arranged so that the books on Economics are kept together ?

Solution: Required number of different ways

$= {}^8P_8 \times {}^4P_4 = \underline{|8} \times \underline{|4}$

$= 40320 \times 24$

$= 967680$

Example 4: In how many different ways can the letters of the word 'PRETTY' be arranged?

Solution: Required ways $= \frac{\underline{|6}}{\underline{|2}} = 360$

Example 5: In how many different ways can the letters of the word 'PEANUT' be arranged ?

Solution: Required ways $= {}^6P_6 = \underline{|6}$

$= 6 \times 5 \times 4 \times 3 \times 2 \times 1 = 720.$

EXERCISE

1. How many seven digit numbers can be made from the number 3428651, using each digit only once?
   (*a*) 49 (*b*) 180
   (*c*) 5040 (*d*) 2520
   (*e*) None of these
2. How many words can be formed from the letters of the word 'DIRECTOR' so that the vowels are always together?
   (*a*) 2106 (*b*) 1206
   (*c*) 360 (*d*) 2160
   (*e*) None of these
3. In how many ways a committee of 5 members can be selected from 6 men and 5 ladies, consisting of 3 men and 2 ladies?
   (*a*) 120 (*b*) 220
   (*c*) 200 (*d*) 320
   (*e*) None of these
4. In how many ways can the letters of the word 'APPLE' be arranged?
   (*a*) 720
   (*b*) 120
   (*c*) 60
   (*d*) 180
   (*e*) None of these
5. How many words can be formed by using all the letters of the word. 'ALLAHABAD'?
   (*a*) 3780 (*b*) 1890
   (*c*) 7560 (*d*) 2520
   (*e*) None of these
6. How many words can be formed from the letters of the word 'SIGNATURE' so that the vowels always come together?
   (*a*) 720 (*b*) 1440
   (*c*) 2880 (*d*) 17280
   (*e*) None of these
7. In how many different ways can the letters of the word 'BANKING' be arranged so that the vowels always come together?
   (*a*) 120 (*b*) 240
   (*c*) 360 (*d*) 720
   (*e*) None of these
8. In how many ways can a group of 5 men and 2 women be made out of a total of 7 men and 3 women?
   (*a*) 63
   (*b*) 90
   (*c*) 126
   (*d*) 45
   (*e*) None of these

9. In a group of 6 boys and 4 girls, four children are to be selected. In how many different ways can they be selected such that at least one boy should be there?
(*a*) 159 (*b*) 194
(*c*) 205 (*d*) 209
(*e*) None of these

10. A box contains 2 white balls, 3 black balls and 4 red balls. In how many ways can 3 balls be drawn from the box, if at least one black ball is to be included in the draw?
(*a*) 32 (*b*) 48
(*c*) 64 (*d*) 96
(*e*) None of these

11. In how many ways can a team of 3 boys and 3 girls be selected from 5 boys and 4 girls?
(*a*) 14 (*b*) 40
(*c*) 18 (*d*) 140
(*e*) None of these

12. The number of ways of selecting 9 balls from 6 red, 5 white and 5 blue if each selection consists of 3 balls of each colour is :
(*a*) 1200 (*b*) 20000
(*c*) 2200 (*d*) 2000
(*e*) None of these

13. In how many ways can we select 4 red balls and 3 blue balls from 8 red balls and 9 blue balls?
(*a*) 8550 (*b*) 5850
(*c*) 5880 (*d*) 8580
(*e*) None of these

14. Find the number of diagonals of a decagon
(*a*) 45 (*b*) 35
(*c*) 55 (*d*) 25
(*e*) None of these

15. In how many ways can a student choose a programme of 5 courses if 9 courses are available and 2 specific courses are compulsary for every student?
(*a*) 53 (*b*) 14
(*c*) 35 (*d*) 28
(*e*) None of these

16. Seven different lecturers are to deliver lectures in seven periods of a class on a particular day. A, B and C are three of the lecturers. The number of ways in which a routine for the day can be made such that A delivers his lecture before B, and B before C, is
(*a*) 420 (*b*) 120
(*c*) 210 (*d*) 840
(*e*) None of these

17. The number of words that can be made by rearranging the letters of the word APURBA so that vowels and consonants alternate is
(*a*) 18 (*b*) 35
(*c*) 36 (*d*) 24
(*e*) None of these

18. The number of ways in which the letters of the word ARTICLE can be rearranged so that the even places are always occupied by consonants is
(*a*) 576 (*b*) ${}^4C_3 \times (4!)$
(*c*) 2(4!) (*d*) 288
(*e*) None of these

19. The number of ways in which a couple can sit around a table with 6 guests if the couple take consecutive seats is
(*a*) 1440 (*b*) 720
(*c*) 5040 (*d*) 2880
(*e*) None of these

20. The number of ways in which 20 different pearls of two colours can be set alternately on a necklace, there being 10 pearls of each colour, is
(*a*) $9! \times 10!$ (*b*) $5(9!)^2$
(*c*) $(9!)^2$ (*d*) $(18!)^2$
(*e*) None of these

21. There are 4 mangoes, 3 apples, 2 oranges and 1 each of 3 other varieties of fruits. The number of ways of selecting at least one fruit of each kind is
(*a*) 10! (*b*) 9!
(*c*) 4! (*d*) 5!
(*e*) None of these

22. The number of ways in which 6 different balls can be put in two boxes of different sizes so that no box remains empty is
(*a*) 62 (*b*) 64
(*c*) 36 (*d*) 60
(*e*) None of these

23. The number of arrangements of the letters of the word BHARAT taking 3 at a time is

(*a*) 72 (*b*) 120
(*c*) 14 (*d*) 48
(*e*) None of these

24. Find the number of different permutations of the letters of the word BANANA.

(*a*) 16 (*b*) 60
(*c*) 61 (*d*) 36
(*e*) None of these

25. A box contains two white balls, three black balls and four red balls. In how many ways can three balls be drawn from the box if at least one black ball is to be included in the draw?

(*a*) 16 (*b*) 32
(*c*) 64 (*d*) 128
(*e*) None of these

26. All the letters of the word EAMCET are arranged in possible ways. The number of such arrangement in which not two vowels are adjacent to each other is:

(*a*) 360 (*b*) 144
(*c*) 72 (*d*) 54
(*e*) None of these

27. The number of arrangements which can be made by using all the letters of the word LAUGH, if the vowels are adjacent, is:

(*a*) 10 (*b*) 24
(*c*) 48 (*d*) 120
(*e*) None of these

28. There are 10 lamps in a hall. Each one of them can be switched on independently. The number of ways in which the hall can be illuminated is:

(*a*) 10^2 (*b*) 1023
(*c*) 210 (*d*) 10!
(*e*) None of these

29. Everybody in a room shakes hands with everybody else. The total number of hand shakes is 66. The total number of persons in the room is:

(*a*) 11 (*b*) 12
(*c*) 8 (*d*) 14
(*e*) None of these

30. 20 persons are invited for a party. The number of ways in which they and the host can be seated at a circular table, if two particular persons be seated on either side of the host, is equal to:

(*a*) 18! . 2! (*b*) 18! . 3!
(*c*) 19! . 2! (*d*) 19! . 3!
(*e*) None of these

31. The number of ways in which 5 prizes be distributed among 4 boys, while each boy is capable of having any number of prizes is:

(*a*) 6^4 (*b*) 4^5
(*c*) $4! \cdot 2^4$ (*d*) 6 . (4!)
(*e*) None of these

32. In an examination there are three multiple choice questions and each question has 4 choices. Number of ways in which a student can fail to get all answers correct, is:

(*a*) 11 (*b*) 12
(*c*) 27 (*d*) 63
(*e*) None of these

33. 7 men and 7 women are to sit round a table so that there is a man on either side of a woman. The number of seating arrangement is:

(*a*) $(7!)^2$ (*b*) $(6!)^2$
(*c*) $6! \times 7!$ (*d*) 7!
(*e*) None of these

34. Three men have 4 coats, 5 waist coats and 6 caps. In how many ways can they wear them?

(*a*) 178200 (*b*) 172000
(*c*) 172800 (*d*) 1720800
(*e*) None of these

35. To fill 12 vacancies there are 25 candidates of which 5 are from scheduled castes. If 3 of the vacancies are reserved for scheduled caste candidates while the rest are open to all, find the number of ways in which the selection can be made.

(*a*) 4974200
(*b*) 4947200
(*c*) 4972400
(*d*) 4927400
(*e*) None of these

ANSWERS

1	2	3	4	5	6	7	8	9	10
(*c*)	(*d*)	(*c*)	(*c*)	(*c*)	(*d*)	(*d*)	(*a*)	(*d*)	(*c*)
11	**12**	**13**	**14**	**15**	**16**	**17**	**18**	**19**	**20**
(*b*)	(*d*)	(*c*)	(*b*)	(*c*)	(*d*)	(*c*)	(*a*)	(*a*)	(*b*)
21	**22**	**23**	**24**	**25**	**26**	**27**	**28**	**29**	**30**
(*c*)	(*a*)	(*a*)	(*b*)	(*c*)	(*c*)	(*c*)	(*b*)	(*b*)	(*a*)
31	**32**	**33**	**34**	**35**					
(*b*)	(*d*)	(*c*)	(*c*)	(*a*)					

SOME SELECTED EXPLANATORY ANSWERS

1. Required number of ways

$$= {}^7P_7 = \underline{|7} = 5040$$

2. In the given word, we treat the vowels IEO as one letter.

Thus, we have DRCTR (IEO).

This group has 6 letters of which R occurs 2 times and others are different.

Number of ways arranging these letters

$$= \frac{6!}{2!} = 360.$$

Now 3 vowels can be arranged among themselves in $3! = 6$ ways.

∴ Required number of ways

$$= (360 \times 6) = 2160.$$

3. (3 men out of 6) and (2 ladies out of 5) are to be chosen.

∴ Required number of ways

$$= ({}^6C_3 \times {}^5C_2)$$

$$= \left(\frac{6 \times 5 \times 4}{3 \times 2 \times 1} \times \frac{5 \times 4}{2 \times 1}\right) = 200.$$

4. The word 'APPLE' contains 5 letters, 1A, 2P, 1L and 1E.

∴ Required number of ways

$$= \frac{5!}{(1!)(2!)(1!)(1!)} = 60.$$

5. The word 'ALLAHABAD' contains 9 letters, namely 4A, 2L, 1H, 1B and 1D.

∴ Required number of words

$$= \frac{9!}{(4!)(2!)(1!)(1!)(1!)} = 7560.$$

6. The word 'SIGNATURE' contains 9 different letters.

When the vowels IAUE are taken together, they can be supposed to form an entity, treated as one letter.

Then, the letters to be arranged are SGNTR (IAUE).

These 6 letters can be arranged in

$${}^6P_6 = 6! = 720 \text{ ways.}$$

The vowels in the group (IAUE) can be arranged amongst themselves in

$${}^4P_4 = 4! = 24 \text{ ways.}$$

∴ Required number of words

$$= (720 \times 24) = 17280.$$

7. In the word 'BANKING', we treat the two vowels AI as one letter. Thus, we have BNKNG (AI).

This has 6 letters of which N occurs 2 times and the rest are different.

Number of ways of arranging these letters

$$= \frac{6!}{(2!)(1!)(1!)(1!)(1!)} = 360.$$

Now, 2 vowels AI can be arranged in

$2! = 2$ ways.

$\therefore$ Required number of ways

$= (360 \times 2) = 720.$

8. Required number of ways

$= ({}^7C_5 \times {}^3C_2)$

$= ({}^7C_2 \times {}^3C_1)$

$= \left(\frac{7 \times 6}{2 \times 1} \times 3\right) = 63.$

9. We may have (1 boy and 3 girls) or (2 boys and 2 girls) or (3 boys and 1 girl) or (4 boys).

$\therefore$ Required number of ways

$= ({}^6C_1 \times {}^4C_3) + ({}^6C_2 \times {}^4C_2) + ({}^6C_3 \times {}^4C_1) + ({}^6C_4)$

$= ({}^6C_1 \times {}^4C_1) + ({}^6C_2 \times {}^4C_2) + ({}^6C_3 \times {}^4C_1) + ({}^6C_2)$

$= (6 \times 4) + \left(\frac{6 \times 5}{2 \times 1} \times \frac{4 \times 3}{2 \times 1}\right) + \left(\frac{6 \times 5 \times 4}{3 \times 2 \times 1} \times 4\right) + \left(\frac{6 \times 5}{2 \times 1}\right)$

$= (24 + 90 + 80 + 15) = 209.$

10. We may have (1 black and 2 non-black) or (2 black and 1 non-black) or (3 black)

$\therefore$ Required number of ways

$= ({}^3C_1 \times {}^6C_2) + ({}^3C_2 \times {}^6C_1) + ({}^3C_3)$

$= \left(3 \times \frac{6 \times 5}{2 \times 1}\right) + \left(\frac{3 \times 2}{2 \times 1} \times 6\right) + 1$

$= (45 + 18 + 1) = 64.$

13. 4 red balls from 8 red balls can be selected in ${}^8C_4$ ways

3 blue balls from 9 balls can be selected in ${}^9C_3$ ways

$\therefore$ Total number of selection

$= {}^8C_4 \times {}^9C_3$

$= \frac{8 \times 7 \times 6 \times 5}{1 \times 2 \times 3 \times 4} \times \frac{9 \times 8 \times 7}{1 \times 2 \times 3}$

$= 70 \times 84 = 5880.$

14. A decagon has 10 vertices.

Join any two vertices in ${}^{10}C_2$ lines 10 lines will be sides.

$\therefore$ Number of diagonals

$= {}^{10}C_2 - 10$

$= \frac{10 \times 9}{1 \times 2} - 10$

$= 45 - 10 = 35$

16. As the order of A, B and C is not to change they are to be treated identical in arrangement. So, the required Number of ways

$= \frac{7!}{3!}.$

$= \frac{7 \times 6 \times 5 \times 4 \times 3 \times 2 \times 1}{3 \times 2 \times 1} = 840.$

18. The number of ways to fill the three even places by 4 consonants $= {}^4P_3$.

After filling the even places, remaining places can be filled in ${}^4P_4$ ways.

So, the required number of words

$= {}^4P_3 \times {}^4P_4$

$= 4! \times 4! = 24 \times 24 = 576.$

19. A couple and 6 guests can be arranged in $(7 - 1)!$ ways. But the two people forming the couple can be arranged among themselves in $2!$ ways.

$\therefore$ The required number of ways

$= 6! \times 2!$

$= 720 \times 2 = 1440.$

20. Ten pearls of one colour can be arranged in 1/2 $(10 - 1)!$ ways. The number of arrangements of 10 pearls of the other colour in 10 places between the pearls of the first colour $= 10!$.

$\therefore$ The required number of ways

$= \frac{1}{2} \times 9! \times 10!$

$= 5 \times 9! \times 9! = 5(9!)^2.$

22. Each ball can be put in 2 ways (either in one box or the other).

$\therefore$ 6 balls can be put in $2 \times 2 \times \ldots$ to six times, *i.e.*, 2^6 ways. But in two of the ways one box is empty. So, the required number of ways $= 2^6 - 2 = 62.$

24. BANANA

3A's, 2N's, B, i.e., 6 letters, 3 alike of one type and 2 of another type. Number of words taken all at a time is $\frac{6!}{3!\,2!} = \frac{6 \times 5 \times 4}{2} = 60.$

25. The required number of ways $= {}^3C_1 \times {}^6C_2 + {}^3C_2 \times {}^6C_1 + {}^3C_3 = 64.$

26. First we place 3 consonant in 3! ways and then at four places (2 between them and 2 on sides) 3 vowels in which one vowels is repeated can be placed in ${}^4P_3/2!$ ways.

Hence, required number = $3!\ {}^4P_3/2! = 72.$

27. Considering two vowels together as a letter, there are 4 letters in all which can be arranged in 4! ways while 2 vowels can also be arranged in 2! ways.

$\therefore$ Total number of arrangements = 4! . 2! = 48.

28. Each bulb has two choices, either switched on or off.

$\therefore$ Required number $= 2^{10} - 1 = 1023$

(Since in one way, when all switches are off, the hall will not be illuminated.)

29. Let there be n persons in a room.

$\therefore$ Total no. of shakehands

$$= {}^nC_2 = 66$$

$$\Rightarrow \quad \frac{1}{2}n(n-1) = 66$$

$$\Rightarrow \quad n^2 - n - 132 = 0$$

$$\Rightarrow \quad (n + 11)(n - 12) = 0$$

$$\Rightarrow \quad n = 12 \qquad (\because n \neq -11)$$

30. Host can sit on any seat. Two particular guests can sit on either sides of host in 2! = 2 ways and remaining 18 guests in (18)! ways.

Hence, total ways = 2.(18)!.

31. Since every prize can be given by any of the four boys, so number of ways $= 4 \times 4 \times 4 \times 4 \times 4 = 4^5.$

32. Each question can be answered in 4 ways and all questions can be answered correctly in only one way, so the required number of ways $= 4^3 - 1 = 63.$

33. First the seven women sit round the table in 6! ways and then seven men will sit in the spaces between every pair of two women in 7! ways.

$\therefore$ Required seating arrangements = 6! × 7!.

34. ${}^4P_3 \times {}^5P_3 \times {}^6P_3 = 172800.$

35. ${}^5C_3 \times {}^{22}C_9 = 4974200.$

❑❑❑

18 Probability

1. **Random Experiment:** If the result of an experiment is not certain and is any one of the several possible outcomes, the experiment is called a trial or a random experiment.

2. **Sample Space:** The set of all possible outcome of an experiment is called the sample space provided no two or more of these outcomes can occur simultaneously and exactly one of these outcomes must occur whenever the experiment is conducted.

3. **Events:** The outcomes of an experiment, *i.e.*, sample points of the sample space are usually known as simple events and any subset of the sample space 'S' is called an event.

   Thus throwing of a dice is an experiment, S = {1, 2, 3, 4, 5, 6} is the sample space, {1}, ... {6} are simple events and {1, 2}, etc., are events. The empty set ϕ is also an event as $\phi \subset S$ and it is called an impossible event. The sample space S is also a subset of S and so it is also an event. S represents the sure event, *i.e.*, certainty.

4. **Equally Likely Events:** A set of events is said to be equally likely if taking into consideration all the relevant factors there is no reason to expect one of them in preference to others.

   For example, when a fair coin is tossed, the occurrence of a tail or a head are equally likely.

5. **Exhaustive Events:** A set of events is said to be exhaustive if the performance of the experiment always results in the occurrence of atleast one of them.

   For example, if we throw a dice, then the events A_1 = {1, 2}, A_2 = {2, 3, 3} are not exhaustive as we can get 5 as outcome of the experiment which is not the member of any of the events A_1 and A_2. If we consider the events E_1 = {1, 2, 3} and E_2 = {2, 4, 5, 6}, then the set E_1, E_2, is exhaustive.

6. **Mutually Exclusive Events:** A set of events is said to be mutually exclusive if they have no point in common, *i.e.*, happening of one of them eliminates the happening of any of the remaining events. Thus E_1, E_2, E_3, ... are mutually exclusive iff $E_i \cap E_j = \phi$ for $i \neq E_1$ and E_2 are mutually exclusive.

7. **Complement of An Events:** The complement of an event A, denoted by $\overline{A}$, A' or A^c, is the set of all sample points of the space other than the sample points in A.
   e.g., In the experiment of throwing a fair dice, S = {1, 2, 3, 4, 5, 6}. If A = {1, 3, 5, 6},

   then $\overline{A}$ = {2, 4}

   Note that $A \cap \overline{A} = S$.

8. **Classical Definition of Probability:** If there are n exhaustive mutually exclusive and equally likely outcomes of an experiment and m of them are favourable to an event A, the probability of the happening of A is defined as the ratio m/n.

   Thus, denoting the probability of the happening of an event A by p, we have $p = m/n$.

   Clearly p is a positive number not greater than unity, so that $0 \leq p \leq 1$.

   Since the number of cases in which the event A will not happen is $n - m$, the probability q that the event will not happen is given by $q = \frac{(n-m)}{n} = 1 - \frac{m}{n} = 1 - p$. $\therefore p + q = 1$

If probability of happening of an event A is 1, then A is certain event and if probability of happening of an event A is 0, then A is impossible event.

9. Odds in Favour and Odds against an Event: As a result of an experiment if a of the outcomes are favourable to an event E and b of the outcomes are against it, then we say that odds are a to b in favour of E or odds are b to a against E.

Thus, odds in favour of an event E

$$= \frac{\text{number of favourable cases}}{\text{number of unfavourable cases}}.$$

Similarly, odds against an event E

$$= \frac{\text{number of unfavourable cases}}{\text{number of favourable cases}}.$$

If odds in favour of an event are $a : b$ then the probability of the occurrence of that event is $\frac{a}{a+b}$ and the probability of the non-occurrence of that event is $\frac{b}{(a+b)}$.

Addition Theorem:

(*a*) If 'A' and 'B' are any two events in a sample space S, then

$$P(A \cup B) = P(A) + P(B) - P(A \cap B).$$

(*b*) If 'A' and 'B' are mutually exclusive then

$P(A \cap B) = 0$ so that

$$P(A \cup B) = P(A) + P(B).$$

(*c*) If A is any event in S, then $P(A') = 1 - P(A)$.

Total Probability Theorem:

The probability that one of several mutually exclusive events $A_1, A_2, ..., A_n$ will happen, is the sum of the probabilities of the separate events. In symbol,

$$P(A_1 + A_2 + ... + A_n) = P(A_1) + P(A_2) + ... + P(A_n).$$

Conditional Probability:

The probability of B under the assumption that A has occurred is called the conditional probability of B under the condition that the event A has taken place and is denoted by P(B/A). P(B/A) is read as "probability at the event B given A^B."

Conditional Probability Theorem:

If A and B are any two events in the sample space S, the conditional probability of B relative to A is given by

$$P(B/A) = \frac{P(B \cap A)}{P(A)}$$

$$= \frac{n(B \cap A)}{n(A)}$$

$$A \neq \phi.$$

Some Important Remarks about Coins, Dice and Playing Cards:

(*a*) **Coins:** A coin has a head side and a tail side. If an experiment consist of more than a coin, coins are considered to be distinct if not otherwise stated.

(*b*) **Dice:** A die (cubical) has six faces marked 1, 2, 3, 4, 5, 6. We may have tetrahedral (having four faces 1, 2, 3, 4) or pentagonal (having five faces 1, 2, 3, 4, 5) die. As in the case of dice, if we have more than one die, all dice are considered to be distinct if not otherwise stated.

(*c*) **Playing Cards:** A pack of playing cards usually contain 52 cards.

There are 4 suits (spade, heart, diamond and club) each having 13 cards. There are two colours — red (heart and diamond) and black (spade and club) each having 26 cards.

In thirteen cards of each suit, there are 3 face cards namely king, queen and jack, so there are in all 12 face cards (4 kings, 4 queens and 4 jacks).

Also there are 16 honours cards, 4 of each suit namely ace, king, queen and jack.

EXAMPLES

Example 1: A bag contains 7 Red balls, 4 Green balls and 5 Yellow balls. What is the probability that 3 balls drawn at random are either Green or Yellow?

Solution: Total ways = $^{16}C_3 = \dfrac{\underline{|16}}{\underline{|13}\ \underline{|3}}$

$= 560$

Favourable ways = $^4C_3 \times {}^5C_3$

$= \dfrac{\underline{|4}}{\underline{|3}\ \underline{|1}} \times \dfrac{\underline{|5}}{\underline{|3}\ \underline{|2}}$

$= 4 \times 10 = 40.$

$\therefore$ Reqd. Probability $= \dfrac{40}{560} = \dfrac{1}{14}.$

Example 2: A basket contains three Red and four Green balls. If four balls are drawn at random from the basket, what is the probability that two are Red and two are Green?

Solution: Reqd. Probability

$$= \frac{^3C_2 \times {}^4C_2}{^7C_4} = \frac{3 \times 6}{35} = \frac{18}{35}.$$

Example 3: A box contains 8 Red, 16 Blue, 4 Yellow and 12 Black bolls. Two balls are picked up randomly. What is the chance that both are Red?

Solution: Total results = $^{40}C_2 = \dfrac{40 \times 39}{2} = 780$

and favourable results = $^8C_2 = \dfrac{\underline{|8}}{\underline{|2}\ \underline{|6}} = \dfrac{8 \times 7}{2}$

$= 28.$

$\therefore$ Required probability $= \dfrac{28}{780} = \dfrac{7}{195}.$

Example 4: A bag contains 8 Red, 16 Blue, 12 Black and 4 Yellow marbles. One marbles is picked up randomly. What is the probability that it is not Blue?

Solution: Total results = $^{40}C_1 = 40$

Favourable results when it is Blue

$= {}^{16}C_1 = 16.$

$\therefore$ Favourable results when it is not Blue

$= 40 - 16 = 24$

$\therefore$ Reqd. probability $= \dfrac{24}{40} = 0.6.$

EXERCISE

Directions (Qs. 1 to 3) : *Study the information carefully to answer the questions that follow.*

A bucket contains 8 Red, 3 Blue and 5 Green marbles.

1. If 4 marbles are drawn at random, what is the probability that 2 are Red and 2 are Blue?

(a) $\frac{11}{16}$ (b) $\frac{3}{16}$

(c) $\frac{11}{72}$ (d) $\frac{3}{65}$

(e) None of these

2. If 2 marbles are drawn at random, what is the probability that both are Green?

(a) $\frac{1}{8}$ (b) $\frac{5}{16}$

(c) $\frac{2}{7}$ (d) 0

(e) None of these

3. If 3 marbles are drawn at random, what is the probability that none is Red?

(a) $\frac{3}{8}$ (b) $\frac{1}{16}$

(c) $\frac{1}{10}$ (d) 0

(e) None of these

Directions (Qs. 4 to 5) : *Study the information and answer the questions that follow.*

A basket contains 3 Red balls, 5 Blue balls and 2 Green balls.

4. If three balls are drawn at random, what is the probability that none is Blue?

(a) $\frac{1}{6}$ (b) $\frac{1}{12}$

(c) $\frac{1}{5}$ (d) $\frac{3}{10}$

(e) None of these

5. If four balls are drawn at random, what is the probability that at least one is Green?

(a) $\frac{2}{3}$ (b) $\frac{1}{2}$

(c) $\frac{1}{3}$ (d) $\frac{2}{5}$

(e) None of these

6. If two balls are drawn at random, what is the probability that both are Red?

(a) $\frac{1}{5}$ (b) $\frac{3}{10}$

(c) $\frac{3}{5}$ (d) $\frac{1}{15}$

(e) None of these

7. A dice is thrown once. Find the probability of getting a number greater than 3.

(a) $\frac{2}{3}$ (b) $\frac{1}{3}$

(c) $\frac{1}{2}$ (d) $\frac{3}{2}$

(e) None of these

8. A bag contains 5 Red balls, 8 White balls, 4 Green balls and 7 Black balls. If one ball is drawn at random, find the probability that it is Black.

(a) $\frac{7}{24}$ (b) $\frac{5}{24}$

(c) $\frac{5}{6}$ (d) $\frac{1}{4}$

(e) None of these

9. Find the probability that a number selected from the numbers 1 to 25 is not a prime number when each of the given number is equally to be selected.

(a) $\frac{9}{25}$ (b) $\frac{16}{25}$

(c) $\frac{21}{25}$ (d) $\frac{14}{25}$

(e) None of these

10. A bag contains 3 Red balls and 5 Black balls. A ball is drawn at random from the bag. What is the probability that the ball drawn is not Red?

(a) $\frac{3}{8}$ (b) $\frac{5}{8}$

(c) $\frac{1}{8}$ (d) $\frac{7}{8}$

(e) None of these

11. A die is thrown once. Find the probability of getting an odd number.

(a) $\frac{1}{2}$ (b) $\frac{3}{2}$

(c) $\frac{2}{3}$ (d) $\frac{1}{3}$

(e) None of these

12. A letter is chosen at random from the word REED the probability of choosing an E is –

(a) $\frac{3}{4}$ (b) $\frac{1}{2}$

(c) $\frac{1}{4}$ (d) $\frac{2}{3}$

(e) None of these

13. A card is drawn at random from a well-shuffled deck of playing cards. Find the probability that the card drawn is a card of spade or an ace.

(a) $\frac{11}{13}$ (b) $\frac{1}{26}$

(c) $\frac{4}{13}$ (d) $\frac{9}{13}$

(e) None of these

14. If a letter is chosen at random from the word TRIANGLE.
What is the probability that it a vowel?

(a) $\frac{3}{8}$ (b) $\frac{5}{8}$

(c) $\frac{1}{4}$ (d) $\frac{3}{4}$

(e) None of these

15. What is the chance that a leap year, selected at random, will contain 53 Sundays?

(a) $\frac{52}{365}$ (b) $\frac{52}{366}$

(c) $\frac{2}{7}$ (d) $\frac{5}{7}$

(e) None of these

16. In a book of 300 pages, if a page is opened at random; find the probability that the sum of the digits in its number is 10.

(a) $\frac{8}{15}$ (b) $\frac{9}{15}$

(c) $\frac{7}{75}$ (d) $\frac{14}{15}$

(e) None of these

17. A die is thrown once. Find the probability of getting an even number.

(a) $\frac{1}{3}$ (b) $\frac{1}{2}$

(c) $\frac{1}{4}$ (d) $\frac{1}{6}$

(e) None of these

18. Two friends were born in the year 2000. What is the probability that they have the same birthday?

(a) $\frac{1}{500}$ (b) $\frac{1}{730}$

(c) $\frac{1}{365}$ (d) $\frac{1}{366}$

(e) None of these

19. A number is chosen at random from among the first 30 natural numbers. The probability of the number chosen being prime is :

(a) $\frac{1}{3}$ (b) $\frac{3}{10}$

(c) $\frac{1}{30}$ (d) $\frac{11}{30}$

(e) None of these

20. The probability that a number selected at random from the set of numbers {1, 2, 3, 4, ..., 100} is a cube is :

(a) $\frac{1}{25}$ (b) $\frac{2}{25}$

(c) $\frac{3}{25}$ (d) $\frac{4}{25}$

(e) None of these

21. A single letter is selected at random from the word 'COLLEGE'. Find the probability of getting a vowel.

(a) $\frac{3}{7}$ (b) $\frac{4}{7}$

(c) $\frac{5}{7}$ (d) $\frac{2}{7}$

(e) None of these

22. A box contains 5 Red balls, 4 Green balls and 7 White balls. A ball is drawn at random from the box. Find the probability that the ball drawn is neither Red nor White.

(a) $\frac{2}{7}$ (b) $\frac{3}{4}$

(c) $\frac{1}{4}$ (d) $\frac{1}{2}$

(e) None of these

23. In a cricket match, a batsman hits boundary 8 times out of 40 balls he plays. Find the probability that he didn't hit boundary.

(a) 0.8 (b) 0.6

(c) 0.5 (d) 0.4

(e) None of these

24. Two coins are tossed simultaneously. The probability of getting atmost one head is :

(a) $\frac{1}{4}$ (b) $\frac{3}{4}$

(c) $\frac{1}{2}$ (d) $\frac{1}{4}$

(e) None of these

25. A bag contains 50 coins and each coin is marked from 51 to 100. One coin is picked at random. The probability that the number on the coin is not a prime number is :

(a) $\frac{1}{5}$ (b) $\frac{3}{5}$

(c) $\frac{2}{5}$ (d) $\frac{4}{5}$

(e) None of these

26. In a football match, a player makes 4 goals from 10 penalty kicks. The probability of converting a penalty kick into a goal by the player, is :

(a) $\frac{1}{4}$ (b) $\frac{1}{6}$

(c) $\frac{1}{3}$ (d) $\frac{2}{5}$

(e) None of these

27. Three unbiased coins are tossed. What is the probability of getting at least 2 heads?

(a) $\frac{1}{4}$ (b) $\frac{1}{2}$

(c) $\frac{1}{3}$ (d) $\frac{1}{8}$

(e) None of these

28. In a simultaneous throw of two dice, what is the probability of getting a total of 7?

(a) $\frac{1}{6}$ (b) $\frac{1}{4}$

(c) $\frac{2}{3}$ (d) $\frac{3}{4}$

(e) None of these

29. What is the probability of getting a sum 9 from two throws of a dice?

(a) $\frac{1}{6}$ (b) $\frac{1}{8}$

(c) $\frac{1}{9}$ (d) $\frac{1}{12}$

(e) None of these

30. Tickets numbered 1 to 20 are mixed up and then a ticket is drawn at random. What is the probability that the ticket drawn bears a number which is a multiple of 3?

(a) $\frac{3}{10}$ (b) $\frac{3}{20}$

(c) $\frac{2}{5}$ (d) $\frac{1}{2}$

(e) None of these

31. A card is drawn from a pack of 52 cards. The probability of getting a queen of club or a king of heart is :

(a) $\frac{1}{13}$ (b) $\frac{2}{13}$

(c) $\frac{1}{26}$ (d) $\frac{1}{52}$

(e) None of these

32. Two cards are drawn together from a pack of 52 cards. The probability that one is a spade and one is a heart, is :

(a) $\frac{3}{20}$ (b) $\frac{29}{34}$

(c) $\frac{47}{100}$ (d) $\frac{13}{102}$

(e) None of these

33. A bag contains 6 white and 4 red balls. Three balls are drawn at random. What is the probability that one ball is red and the other two are white?

(a) $\frac{1}{2}$ (b) $\frac{1}{12}$

(c) $\frac{3}{10}$ (d) $\frac{7}{12}$

(e) None of these

34. A box contains 20 electric bulbs, out of which 4 are defective. Two bulbs are chosen at random from this box. The probability that at least one of these is defective, is :

(a) $\frac{4}{19}$ (b) $\frac{7}{19}$

(c) $\frac{12}{19}$ (d) $\frac{21}{95}$

(e) None of these

35. Two dice are tossed. The probability that the total score is a prime number is :

(a) $\frac{1}{6}$ (b) $\frac{5}{12}$

(c) $\frac{1}{2}$ (d) $\frac{7}{9}$

(e) None of these

ANSWERS

1	2	3	4	5	6	7	8	9	10
(*d*)	(*a*)	(*a*)	(*b*)	(*c*)	(*d*)	(*c*)	(*a*)	(*b*)	(*b*)
11	**12**	**13**	**14**	**15**	**16**	**17**	**18**	**19**	**20**
(*a*)	(*b*)	(*c*)	(*a*)	(*c*)	(*c*)	(*b*)	(*d*)	(*a*)	(*a*)
21	**22**	**23**	**24**	**25**	**26**	**27**	**28**	**29**	**30**
(*a*)	(*c*)	(*a*)	(*b*)	(*d*)	(*d*)	(*b*)	(*a*)	(*c*)	(*a*)
31	**32**	**33**	**34**	**35**					
(*c*)	(*d*)	(*a*)	(*b*)	(*b*)					

SOME SELECTED EXPLANATORY ANSWERS

1. Total number of ways

$$= {}^{16}C_4 = \frac{\lfloor 16}{\lfloor 12 \lfloor 4} = 1820$$

And favourable number of ways

$$= {}^{8}C_2 \times {}^{3}C_2$$

$$= \frac{\lfloor 8}{\lfloor 6 \lfloor 2} \times \frac{\lfloor 3}{\lfloor 1 \lfloor 2} = 84$$

$$\therefore \text{ Reqd. probability} = \frac{84}{1820} = \frac{3}{65}.$$

2. Total number of ways

$$= {}^{16}C_2 = \frac{\lfloor 16}{\lfloor 14 \lfloor 2} = 120$$

And favourable number of ways

$$= {}^{5}C_2 = \frac{\lfloor 5}{\lfloor 3 \lfloor 2} = 10$$

$$\therefore \text{ Reqd. probability} = \frac{10}{120} = \frac{1}{12}.$$

3. Total number of ways

$$= {}^{16}C_3 = \frac{\lfloor 16}{\lfloor 13 \lfloor 3} = 560$$

Total number of ways when all the marbles are Red

$$= {}^{8}C_3 = \frac{\lfloor 8}{\lfloor 5 \lfloor 3} = 56$$

∴ Probability when all the three are Red

$$= \frac{56}{560} = \frac{1}{10}$$

∴ And probability when none is Red

$$= 1 - \frac{1}{10} = \frac{9}{10}.$$

4. Probability that none is blue

$$= \frac{{}^{5}C_3}{{}^{10}C_3} = \frac{10}{120} = \frac{1}{12}$$

5. Probability that none is green

$$= \frac{{}^{8}C_4}{{}^{10}C_4} = \frac{70}{210} = \frac{1}{3}$$

∴ Probability that at least one is green

$$= 1 - \frac{1}{3} = \frac{2}{3}$$

6. Probability that both are red

$$= \frac{{}^{3}C_2}{{}^{10}C_2} = \frac{3}{45} = \frac{1}{15}$$

7. Sample space S = {1, 2, 3, 4, 5, 6} ; n(S) = 6

Let A = "getting a number grater than 3" then

A= {4, 5, 6} ; n(A) = 3

$$P(A) = \frac{n(A)}{n(S)} = \frac{3}{6} = \frac{1}{2}.$$

9. We are given numbers from 1 to 25.

n(S) = 25.

Prime numbers from 1 to 25 are 2, 3, 5, 7, 11, 13, 17, 19, 23.

These are 9 prime numbers.

Let E denote the event 'Number drawn is not prime'.

$\therefore$ $$n(E) = 25 - 9 = 16$$

$$p(E) = \frac{n(E)}{n(S)} = \frac{16}{25}.$$

10. Total number of balls in the bag = 3 + 5 = 8

Let E denote the event 'ball drawn is red'.

$\therefore$ $n(E) = 3$ and $n(S) = 8$.

(*i*) $$p(E) = \frac{n(E)}{n(S)} = \frac{3}{8}$$

(*ii*) $$p(\text{not red}) = p(\bar{E})$$

$$= 1 - p(E) = 1 - \frac{3}{8} = \frac{5}{8}.$$

11. Sample S = {1, 2, 3, 4, 5, 6} ; $n(S) = 6$

Let F denote the event 'getting an odd number'.

$$F = \{1, 3, 5\} \; ; \; n(S) = 3$$

$\therefore$ $$P(F) = \frac{n(F)}{n(S)} = \frac{3}{6} = \frac{1}{2}.$$

12. The sample space is {R, E_1, E_2, D}

There are 2 ways to choose the letter E from the four letters

$\therefore$ $$P(E) = \frac{2}{4} = \frac{1}{2}.$$

13. There are 52 cards in a deck of 52 playing cards.

There are 13 spades and 4 aces in 52 playing cards. Out of 13 spades there is one ace.

$\therefore$ Favourable no ways for the card drawn to be spade or an ace = 13 spades + 3 aces = 16.

$\therefore$ P(a card of spade or an ace) = $\frac{16}{52} = \frac{4}{13}$.

14. Since there are 3 vowels out of a total of 8 letters, the probability of choosing a vowel is 3/8.

15. A Leap year has 366 days. In a leap year, here are 52 complete weeks (52 Sundays) and 2 days over these two days can be as follows.

Sunday and Monday, Monday and Tuesday, Tuesday and Wednesday, Wednesday and Thursday, Thursday and Friday, Friday and Saturday, Saturday and Sunday.

Out of these 7 possibilities, only two (Saturday and Sunday; Sunday and Monday) are favourable for having 53 Sundays)

Required chance = $\frac{2}{7}$.

17. A die is thrown once. Its sample space is

$$S = \{1, 2, 3, 4, 5, 6\}, n(S) = 6$$

Let E : an even number,

then E = {2, 4, 6} Number of favourable cases = $n(E) = 3$

$\therefore$ $$P(E) = \frac{n(E)}{n(S)} = \frac{3}{6} = \frac{1}{2}.$$

18. Year 2000 is a leap year. There are 366 days in the year 2000. Total number of cases in which two friends can be born on the same day are 366.

Out of 366 days, number of favourable ways in which two friends have the same birthday = 1

$\therefore$ Required probability = $\frac{1}{366}$.

19. The prime numbers from first 30 natural numbers are 2, 3, 5, 7, 11, 13, 17, 19, 23, 29.

We find that there are 10 prime numbers from 1 to 30.

$\therefore$ Probability that the number chosen being prime is = $\frac{10}{30} = \frac{1}{3}$.

20. From the natural numbers 1 to 100 the four number 1, 8, 27 and 64 are cubes

$\therefore$ Required Probability = $\frac{4}{100} = \frac{1}{25}$.

23. Let A denote the event that the batsman did not hit a boundary.

We have, Total number of trials = 40

Number of trials in which the event A happened

$= 40 - 8 = 32$

$\therefore \quad P(A) = \frac{32}{40} = \frac{4}{5} = 0.8.$

27. Here S = {HH, HT, TH, TT}.

Let E = Event of getting at least one head = {HT, TH, HH}.

$\therefore P(E) = \frac{n(E)}{n(S)} = \frac{4}{8} = \frac{1}{2}.$

28. We know that in a simultaneous throw of two dice,

$n(S) = 6 \times 6 = 36.$

Let E = Event of getting a total of 7 = {(1, 6), (2, 5), (3, 4), (4, 3), (5, 2), (6, 1)}.

$\therefore P(E) = \frac{n(E)}{n(S)} = \frac{6}{36} = \frac{1}{6}.$

29. In two throws of a die,

$n(S) = (6 \times 6) = 36.$

Let E = Event of getting a sum 9 = {(3, 6), (4, 5), (5, 4), (6, 3)}.

$\therefore P(E) = \frac{n(E)}{n(S)} = \frac{4}{36} = \frac{1}{9}.$

30. Here, S = {1, 2, 3, 4, ..., 19, 20}.

Let E = Event of getting a multiple of 3 = {3, 6, 9, 12, 15, 18}.

$\therefore P(E) = \frac{n(E)}{n(S)} = \frac{6}{20} = \frac{3}{10}.$

31. Here $n(S) = 52$.

Let E = Event of getting a queen of club or a king of heart.

Then, $n(E) = 2$.

$\therefore P(E) = \frac{n(E)}{n(S)} = \frac{2}{52} = \frac{1}{26}.$

32. Let S be the sample space. Then,

$n(S) = {}^{52}C_2 = \frac{(52 \times 51)}{(2 \times 1)} = 1326.$

Let E = Event of getting 1 spade and 1 heart.

$\therefore n(E)$ = Number of ways of choosing 1 spade out of 13 and 1 heart out of 13

$= ({}^{13}C_1 \times {}^{13}C_1) = (13 \times 13) = 169.$

$\therefore P(E) = \frac{n(E)}{n(S)} = \frac{169}{1326} = \frac{13}{102}.$

33. Let S be the sample space. Then,

$n(S)$ = Number of ways of drawing 3 balls out of 10

$= {}^{10}C_3 = \frac{(10 \times 9 \times 8)}{(3 \times 2 \times 1)} = 120.$

Let E = Event of drawing 1 red and 2 white balls

$\therefore n(E)$ = Number of ways of drawing 1 red ball out of 4 and 2 white balls out of 6

$= ({}^{4}C_1 \times {}^{6}C_2) = \left(4 \times \frac{6 \times 5}{2 \times 1}\right) = 60.$

$\therefore P(E) = \frac{n(E)}{n(S)} = \frac{60}{120} = \frac{1}{2}.$

34. P (None is defective)

$= \frac{{}^{16}C_2}{{}^{20}C_2} = \left(\frac{16 \times 15}{2 \times 1} \times \frac{2 \times 1}{20 \times 19}\right) = \frac{12}{19}.$

P (at least one is defective) $= \left(1 - \frac{12}{19}\right) = \frac{7}{19}.$

35. Clearly, $n(S) = (6 \times 6) = 36.$

Let E = Event that the sum is a prime number.

Then, E = {(1, 1), (1, 2), (1, 4), (1, 6), (2, 1), (2, 3), (2, 5), (3, 2), (3, 4), (4, 1), (4, 3), (5, 2), (5, 6), (6, 1), (6, 5)

$\therefore n(E) = 15$

$\therefore P(E) = \frac{n(E)}{n(S)} = \frac{15}{36} = \frac{5}{12}.$

❑❑❑

19 Logarithms

Definition of Logarithms

If a is a positive real number ($\neq 1$) and $a^x = m$, then the exponent x is called the logarithm of the number m to the base a and is written as $\log_a m = x$

Similarly $10^2 = 100 \quad \therefore \log_{10} 100 = 2$

Here 10 is the base and 2 is the logarithm of 100 or the logarithm of 100 to the base 10 is 2 and is read as log 100 to the base 10 is equal to 2.

Thus
$$2^3 = 8 \quad \therefore \quad \log_2 8 = 3$$
$$3^5 = 243 \quad \therefore \quad \log_3 243 = 5$$
$$4^4 = 256 \quad \therefore \quad \log_4 256 = 4$$
$$7^3 = 343 \quad \therefore \quad \log_7 343 = 3$$
$$5^4 = 625 \quad \therefore \quad \log_5 625 = 4$$
$$4^6 = 4096 \quad \therefore \quad \log_4 4096 = 6$$
$$2^{-2} = \frac{1}{4} \quad \therefore \quad \log_2 \frac{1}{4} = -2$$
$$\left(\sqrt{5}\right)^6 = 125 \quad \therefore \quad \log_{\sqrt{5}} 125 = 6$$

Hence the logarithm of a number to a given positive real number base $\neq 1$ is index or the power to which the base must be raised in order to make it equal to the given number.

Common Logarithms

Any number except zero or unity, can be taken as the base of logarithms. But in practice all logarithms are calculated to the base 10. These are called 'Common Logarithms'. Usually the base 10 is not written but it is understood.

Thus log10 3296 is written as log 3296 with 10 omitted.

Some common logarithms are given below :
$$10^1 = 10 \quad \therefore \quad \log 10 = 1$$
$$10^2 = 100 \quad \therefore \quad \log 100 = 2$$
$$10^3 = 1000 \quad \therefore \quad \log 1000 = 3$$
$$10^4 = 10000 \quad \therefore \quad \log 10000 = 4$$
$$10^5 = 100000 \quad \therefore \quad \log 100000 = 5$$

However, all numbers are not integral powers of 10. For example, 593 can not expressed as power of 10. But 593 lies between 100 and 1000. So logarithm of 593 must be between 2 and 3.

EXERCISE

1. The characteristic of the logarithm of 0.00145 is:

(a) 1 *(b)* –2
(c) –3 *(d)* 0
(e) None of these

2. The characteristic of the logarithm of 0.00000531 is:

(a) 4 *(b)* –6
(c) –3 *(d)* –2
(e) None of these

3. If $\log_{10} 3 = 0.4771$, what is $\log_{10} 30^4$?

(a) 1.9084 *(b)* 4.771
(c) 5.9084 *(d)* 19.084
(e) None of these

4. The value of $\log_{1296} 6$ is:

(a) 4 *(b)* Between 5 and 6
(c) 0.25 *(d)* 216
(e) None of these

5. If $2 \log (a + b) = \log 9 + \log a + \log b$, then $a^2 + b^2$ is:

(a) 5 ab *(b)* 7 ab
(c) 9 ab *(d)* 11 ab
(e) None of these

6. The number of digits in 2^{64} is (given $\log_{10} 2 = 0.3010$)

(a) 20 *(b)* 25
(c) 30 *(d)* 33
(e) None of these

7. If log 27 = 1.431, then log 9 is equal to:
(a) 0.934 (b) 0.945
(c) 0.954 (d) 0.958
(e) None of these

8. If log x – 5 log 3 = –2, then x equals:
(a) 0.81 (b) 1.25
(c) 2.43 (d) 3.20
(e) None of these

9. If $\log_{10} m = b - \log_{10} n$, then m equals:
(a) bn (b) $10n - 10^b \cdot n$
(c) $b - 10^n$ (d) $\frac{10^b}{n}$
(e) None of these

10. If log 8 = 0.9031 and log 9 = 0.9542, then the value of log 6 is:
(a) 0.3010 (b) 0.4771
(c) 0.7781 (d) 1
(e) None of these

11. If log 2 = 0.3010 and log 3 = 0.4771, then the value of log (3240) is:
(a) 0.6020 (b) 2.9084
(c) 3.5104 (d) 4.5321
(e) None of these

12. The value of $\log_5\left(\frac{(125)(625)}{25}\right)$ is:
(a) 5 (b) 6
(c) 725 (d) 3135
(e) None of these

13. If $\log_{10} 2 = a$ and $\log_{10} 3 = b$, then $\log_5 12$ equals:
(a) $\frac{a+b}{1+a}$ (b) $\frac{2a+b}{1+a}$
(c) $\frac{a+2b}{1+a}$ (d) $\frac{2a+b}{1-a}$
(e) None of these

14. The value of $[\log_{10}(5\log_{10}100)]^2$ is:
(a) $\log_{10} 50$ (b) 10
(c) 2 (d) 1
(e) None of these

15. Given that log 8 = 0.9031 and log 9 = 0.9542, then the only logarithm that can not be found without the use of tables is:
(a) log 17 (b) $\log\left(\frac{5}{4}\right)$
(c) log (15) (d) log (600)

16. If log 2 = 0.3010 and log 3 = 0.4771, then the value of x that satisfies the equation $3^{x+3} = 135$ is approximately:
(a) 5.0 (b) 1.8
(c) 1.7 (d) 1.5
(e) None of these

17. $\log 8 \div \log\frac{1}{8}$ equals:
(a) 6 log 2 (b) log 2
(c) 1 (d) 1
(e) None of these

ANSWERS

1	2	3	4	5	6	7	8	9	10
(c)	(b)	(c)	(c)	(b)	(a)	(c)	(c)	(d)	(c)
11	**12**	**13**	**14**	**15**	**16**	**17**			
(c)	(a)	(d)	(d)	(a)	(d)	(d)			

❑❑❑

20 LINEAR AND QUADRATIC EQUATION

REMEMBER

1. An equation of the form $ax^2 + bx + c = 0$, $a \neq 0$ in which the highest power of x is 2 and a, b, c are any three numbers free from x but $a \neq 0$ is called a *quadratic equation* or second *degree equation* in x.
2. A quadratic equation is satisfied by two values of x, *i.e.*, there are two roots of the quadratic equation.
3. The formula for solving a quadratic equation $ax^2 + bx + c = 0$ is:

$$x = \frac{-b \pm \sqrt{b^2 - 4ac}}{2a}$$

where $b^2 - 4ac$ is called *discriminant.*

(*i*) If $b^2 - 4ac > 0$, the two roots are real and different.

(*ii*) If $b^2 - 4ac = 0$, the two roots are real and equal.

(*iii*) If $b^2 - 4ac < 0$, the two roots are imaginary.

(*iv*) If $b^2 - 4ac$ is a perfect square and a, b, c are rational, the two roots are rational.

(*v*) If $b^2 - 4ac$ is not a perfect square and a, b, c, are rational, then the two roots are irrational.

4. *Linear Equations in two variables* : The equation of the form $ax + by + c = 0$, where a, b, c are real constants, is called a linear equation in two variables x and y. Two equations

$$a_1x_1 + b_1y_1 + c_1 = 0$$

and $$a_2x + b_2y + c_2 = 0$$

which satisfy the same values of x and y are called linear simultaneous equations in two variables.

Important Rule:

(*i*) The solution is unique, if $\frac{a_1}{a_2} \neq \frac{b_1}{b_2}$.

(*ii*) The solutions are infinite, if $\frac{a_1}{a_2} = \frac{b_1}{b_2} = \frac{c_1}{c_2}$.

(*iii*) No solution, if $\frac{a_1}{a_2} = \frac{b_1}{b_2} \neq \frac{c_1}{c_2}$.

The equation $a_1x - b_1y = c$ and $a_2x^3 + b_2y^3 = c_2$ say are non-linear simultaneous equations in x and y.

EXAMPLES

Example 1: *Solve the equation:*

$$2(x - 3) = 9 + 3(x - 9)$$

Solution: $2(x - 3) = 9 + 3(x - 9)$

or $2 \times x - 2 \times 3 = 9 + 3 \times x - 3 \times 9$

or $2x - 6 = 9 + 3x - 27$

or $2x - 3x = 9 - 27 + 6$

or $-x = -12$

$\therefore$ $x = 12$

Example 2: *Find two numbers whose sum is 64, and whose difference is 16.*

Solution: Let the smaller number be x.

Then another number $= 64 - x$

Difference, $(64 - x) - x = 16$

$\Rightarrow$ $64 - 2x = 16$

$\Rightarrow$ $-2x = 16 - 64$

$= -48$

$\therefore \qquad x = \frac{-48}{-2} = 24$

$\therefore$ Second number = 64 – 24 = 40.

Example 3: *Solve:* $x^2 + (1 - p)x - p = 0$.

Solution: $x^2 + (1 - p)x - p = 0$

$\Rightarrow \qquad x^2 + x - px - p = 0$

$\Rightarrow \qquad x(x + 1) - p(x + 1) = 0$

$\Rightarrow \qquad (x + 1)(x - p) = 0$

$\Rightarrow \qquad x + 1 = 0$

or $\qquad x - p = 0$

$\therefore \qquad x = -1$

or $\qquad x = p$

Thus, the two roots of the quardratic equation are -1 and p.

Example 4: *If the equations* $4x + 7y = 10$ *and* $10x + ky = 25$ *represent coincident lines, then find value of k.*

Solution: Since the two lines $y = -\frac{4}{7}x + \frac{10}{7}$, $y = -\frac{10}{k}x + \frac{25}{k}$ represent coincident lines.

$$-\frac{10}{k} = -\frac{4}{7}$$

$$\therefore \qquad k = \frac{70}{4} = \frac{35}{2}$$

Example 5: *If the quadratic equation* $2x^2 + 3x + p = 0$ *has equal roots, then find the value of p.*

Solution: Since the given equation has equal roots,

$b^2 - 4ac = 0$

or $\qquad 3^2 - 4.2.p = 0$

or $\qquad 9 - 8p = 0$

$\therefore \qquad p = \frac{9}{8}$

EXERCISE

1. The value of x in the equation $\frac{x+2}{x-1} = \frac{5}{2}$ is:

(a) 3 (b) 7
(c) 5 (d) 9
(e) None of these

2. 32 is divided into two parts such that if the larger is divided by the smaller, the quotient is 2 and the remainder is 5. The larger part is:

(a) 9 (b) 18
(c) 23 (d) 27
(e) None of these

3. If the sum of the roots of the equation $qx^2 + 2x + 3q = 0$ is equal to their product, then the value of q is:

(a) $-\frac{2}{3}$ (b) $\frac{3}{2}$
(c) 3 (d) -6
(e) None of these

4. If $(x - 2)(x + 6) \geq 0$, then the solution set is:

(a) $\{x : x \geq 2\}$
(b) $\{x : x \leq 6\}$
(c) $\{x : x \leq -6\}$
(d) $\{x : x \geq 2 \text{ or } x \leq -6\}$
(e) None of these

5. If α, β are the roots of the quadratic equation $4x^2 - 4x + 1 = 0$, then $\alpha^3 + \beta^3$ is equal to:

(a) $\frac{1}{4}$ (b) $\frac{1}{8}$
(c) 16 (d) 32
(e) None of these

6. If the roots of the equation:

$$\lambda^2 + 8\lambda + \mu^2 + 6\mu = 0$$

are real, then μ lies between:

(a) -2 and 8 (b) -3 and 6
(c) -8 and 2 (d) -6 and 3
(e) None of these

7. The values of x satisfying the equation $5^{2x} - 5^{x+3} + 125 = 5^x$ are:

(a) 0 and 2 (b) -1 and 3
(c) 0 and -3 (d) 0 and 3
(e) None of these

8. Two students while solving a quadratic equation in x, one copied the constant term incorrectly and got the roots 3 and 2; while the other copies the constant term and coefficient of x^2 as -6 and 1 respectively. The correct roots are:

(a) 3, -2 (b) -3, 2

(c) –6, –1 (d) 6, –1
(e) None of these

9. For a given value of k, the product of roots of $x^2 - 2kx + 3k^2 - 4 = 0$ is 5. The roots may be characterised as:
(a) integral
(b) rational but not integral
(c) irrational
(d) imaginary
(e) None of these

10. If the roots of the equation $x^2 - 6x + 10 = 0$ are α and β, then $\alpha^2 + \beta^2$ is:
(a) –16 (b) 4
(c) 60 (d) 16
(e) None of these

11. Total salary of A and B is equal. If A gets 65% allowance of his basic salary and B gets 80% of his basic salary. If the basic salary of B is ₹ 1,100, then the basic salary of A is:
(a) ₹ 1,200 (b) ₹ 1,980
(c) ₹ 1,800 (d) ₹ 1,100
(e) None of these

12. The length of a field is twice its breadth. If the length is reduced by 5 metre and breadth is increased by 3 metre, the area remains as before. The length of the field is:
(a) 15 m (b) 30 m
(c) 12 cm (d) 25 m
(e) None of these

13. A student starts for a hostel 24 km away from his house on bicycle. If he increases his speed by 2 km per hour, he reaches 2 hours early. His speed in km/hour is:
(a) 8 (b) 6
(c) 4 (d) 3
(e) None of these

14. Ravi, after giving away 80% of his pocket money to Komal and 6% of the remaining to Kavita, has ₹ 47 left with him. The money with Ravi in the beginning was:
(a) ₹ 200 (b) ₹ 250
(c) ₹ 500 (d) ₹ 700
(e) None of these

15. The solution of the simultaneous linear equations $2x - 3y = 3$ and $4x - y = 11$ is:
(a) $x = 1, y = 1$ (b) $x = 3, y = 2$
(c) $x = 2, y = 3$ (d) $x = 3, y = 1$
(e) None of these

ANSWERS

1	2	3	4	5	6	7	8	9	10
(a)	(c)	(a)	(d)	(a)	(c)	(d)	(d)	(d)	(d)
11	12	13	14	15					
(a)	(b)	(c)	(b)	(d)					

SOME SELECTED EXPLANATORY ANSWERS

1.
$$\frac{x+2}{x-1} = \frac{5}{2}$$
$$2(x + 2) = 5(x - 1)$$
$$2x + 4 = 5x - 5$$
$$2x - 5x = -5 - 4$$
$$-3x = -9$$
$$x = \frac{-9}{-3} = 3$$

2. Let smaller number = x

$\therefore$ larger number = $32 - x$

According to the condition given,

larger number = 2 × smaller number + 5

$\Rightarrow$ $(32 - x) = 2 \times x + 5$

$\Rightarrow$ $3x = 32 - 5 = 27$

$\therefore$ $x = 9$

$\Rightarrow$ larger number = 32 – 9 = 23

3.
$$\alpha + \beta = \alpha\beta$$
or
$$\frac{-2}{q} = \frac{3q}{q} = 3$$
$\Rightarrow$
$$q = \frac{-2}{3}$$

4. $(x-2)(x+6) \geq 0$

$\Rightarrow$ $(x-2) \geq 0$ and $(x+6) \geq 0$

$\Rightarrow$ $x \geq 2$ and $x \geq -6$

Also $(x-2)(x+6) \geq 0$

$\Rightarrow$ $(x-2) \leq 0$ and $(x+6) \leq 0$

$\Rightarrow$ $x \leq 2$ and $x \leq -6$

5. $\alpha + \beta = \frac{4}{4} = 1, \alpha\beta = \frac{1}{4}$

$\therefore$ $\alpha^3 + \alpha^3 = (\alpha + \beta)^3 - 3\alpha\beta(\alpha + \beta)$

$= 1^3 - 3 \times \frac{1}{4} \times 1 = 1 - \frac{3}{4} = \frac{1}{4}$

6. $\lambda^2 + 8\lambda + \mu^2 + 6\mu = 0$ (quadratic in λ)

Since roots are real,

$b^2 - 4ac \geq 0$

or $8^2 - 4(\mu^2 + 6\mu) \geq 0$

$\Rightarrow$ $\mu^2 + 6\mu - 16 \leq 0$

$\Rightarrow$ $(\mu + 8)(\mu - 2) \leq 0$

$\Rightarrow$ $\mu \geq -8$ and $\mu \leq 2$

or $\mu \leq -8$ and $\mu \geq 2$

It means μ lies between –8 and 2.

7. $5^{2x} - 5^{x+3} + 125 = 5^x$

or $5^{2x} - 5^x(125 + 1) + 125 = 0$

or $5^x(5^x - 125) - 1(5^x - 125) = 0$

or $(5^x - 1)(5^x - 125) = 0$

$\therefore$ $5^x - 1 = 0$

or $5^x - 125 = 0$

or $5^x = 1 = 5^0$

$\therefore$ $x = 0$

or $5^x = 125 = 5^3$

$\therefore$ $x = 3$

8. Suppose the correct equation be

$ax^2 + bx + c = 0$

Taking c and the correct roots α and β, wrong roots as 3 and 2.

$\therefore$ $\alpha + \beta = 3 + 2 = 5$ ...(*i*)

Also $a = 1$ and $c = -6$,

$\alpha\beta = c/a = -6$ ...(*ii*)

Solving, we get the correct roots are 6 and –1.

9. By hypothesis,

$3k^2 - 4 = 5$

or $3k^2 = 9$

$\Rightarrow$ $k^2 = 3$

Disc. $= 4k^2 - 4(3k^2 - 4)$

$= -8 < 0$

Hence, roots are imaginary.

10. $x^2 - 6x + 10 = 0$ ...(1)

$\therefore$ $x - (\alpha + \beta)x + \alpha\beta = 0$ ...(2)

{$\because$ α, β are the roots of (1)

Comparing (1) and (2),

$\alpha + \beta = 6$ and $\alpha\beta = 10$

$\therefore$ $\alpha^2 + \beta^2 = (\alpha + \beta)^2 - 2\alpha\beta$

$= 6^2 - 2 \times 10$

$= 36 - 20 = 16$

11. Let the basic salary of A = x

$\therefore$ A's total salary

$= x + 65\%$ of x

$= x + x \times \frac{65}{100} = x + \frac{65x}{100}$ ...(*i*)

B's total salary

$= 1{,}100 + 80\%$ of $1{,}100$

$= 1{,}100 + \frac{80 \times 1{,}100}{100}$

$= 1{,}100 + 880 = 1{,}980$ ...(*ii*)

A's total salary = B's total salary (given)

$\Rightarrow$ $x + \frac{65x}{100} = 1{,}980$

$\Rightarrow$ $100x + 65x = 1{,}980 \times 100$

$\Rightarrow$ $165x = 1{,}980 \times 100$

$\therefore$ $x = \frac{1{,}980 \times 100}{165}$

= ₹ 1,200

12. Let the breadth of the field = x metre

$\therefore$ length of the field = $2x$ metre

and area of the room = $2x \times x = 2x^2$ metre^2 ...(*i*)

New area = $(2x - 5)(x + 3) = 2x^2 + x - 15$ ...(*ii*)

Comparing (*i*) and (*ii*),

$$2x^2 = 2x^2 + x - 15$$

$\Rightarrow \quad x - 15 = 0$

$\therefore \quad x = 15$

Hence, length = 2 × 15 = 30 metre

13. Let the speed of the student be x km/hour

$\therefore$ Time taken to cover 24 km

$$= \frac{24}{x} \text{ hour} \qquad ...(1)$$

When speed is $(x + 2)$ km/hour

Then time taken to cover 24 km

$$= \frac{24}{x+2} \text{ hours} \qquad ...(2)$$

According to the condition given,

$$\frac{24}{x} - \frac{24}{x+2} = 2$$

$\Rightarrow \quad 24(x + 2) - 24x = 2x(x + 2)$

$\Rightarrow \quad 24x + 48 - 24x = 2x^2 + 4x$

$\Rightarrow \quad 2x^2 + 4x - 48 = 0$

$\Rightarrow \quad x^2 + 2x - 24 = 0$

$\Rightarrow \quad (x + 6)(x - 4) = 0$

$\therefore \quad x = -6$ or $x = 4$

neglecting negative value, the speed of the student is 4 km/hour.

14. Let the pocket money be x

$\therefore \quad 80\%$ of $x = \dfrac{80x}{100} = \dfrac{4x}{5}$

$$\text{Balance} = x - \frac{4x}{5} = \frac{x}{5}$$

Again 6% of $\dfrac{x}{5} = \dfrac{6}{100} \times \dfrac{x}{5} = \dfrac{3x}{250}$

The amount left with Ravi $= \dfrac{x}{5} - \dfrac{3x}{250} = 47$

$\Rightarrow \quad \dfrac{50x - 3x}{250} = 47 \Rightarrow \dfrac{47x}{250} = 47$

$\therefore \quad x =$ ₹ 250

15. $2x - 3y = 3 \qquad ...(1)$

$4x - y = 11 \qquad ...(2)$

Multiply equation (2) by (3), which gives

$12x - 3y = 33 \qquad ...(3)$

Subtracting equation (1) from (3), we get

$10x = 30$

$\therefore \quad x = 3$

Substituting this value of x in (2), we have

$4 \times 3 - y = 11$

$\therefore \quad y = 12 - 11 = 1$

21 TRIGONOMETRY

Trigonometery

1. In a right Δ the side between the reference angle and the right angle is treated as the **base**, the side opposite to the right angle as the **hypotenuse** and the remaining side is taken as the **perpendicular.**

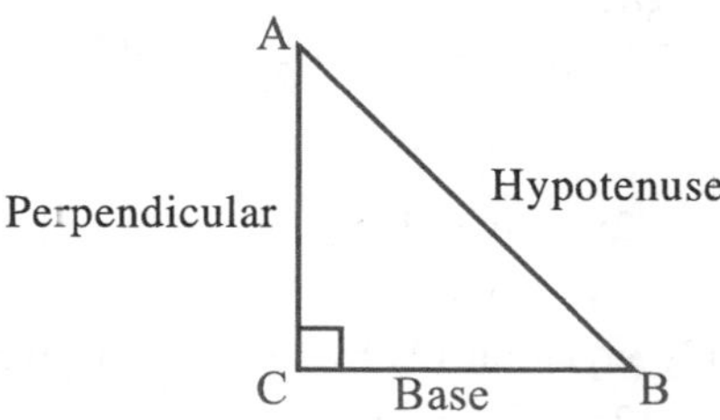

2. Trigonometric Ratios

Let **perpendicular** be **P, base** be **B** and **hypotenuse** be **H.** Then,

$\sin\theta = \frac{P}{H}$ $\qquad$ $\frac{B}{P} = \cot\theta$

$\cos\theta = \frac{B}{H}$ $\qquad$ $\frac{H}{B} = \sec\theta$

$\tan\theta = \frac{P}{B}$ $\qquad$ $\frac{H}{P} = \operatorname{cosec}\theta$

3. Reciprocals of Trigonometric Ratios

$\sin\theta = \frac{1}{\operatorname{cosec}\theta}$ $\qquad$ $\frac{1}{\sin\theta} = \operatorname{cosec}\theta$

$\cos\theta = \frac{1}{\sec\theta}$ $\qquad$ $\frac{1}{\cos\theta} = \sec\theta$

$\tan\theta = \frac{1}{\cot\theta}$ $\qquad$ $\frac{1}{\tan\theta} = \cot\theta$

$\cot\theta = \frac{1}{\tan\theta}$ $\qquad$ $\frac{1}{\cot\theta} = \tan\theta$

$\sec\theta = \frac{1}{\cos\theta}$ $\qquad$ $\frac{1}{\sec\theta} = \cos\theta$

$\operatorname{cosec}\theta = \frac{1}{\sin\theta}$ $\qquad$ $\frac{1}{\operatorname{cosec}\theta} = \sin\theta$

$\frac{\sin\theta}{\cos\theta} = \tan\theta$ $\qquad$ $\frac{\cos\theta}{\sin\theta} = \cot\theta$

4. Trigonometric Ratios of Complementary Angles

$\sin\theta = \cos(90-\theta)$ $\qquad$ $\cos\theta = \sin(90-\theta)$

$\tan\theta = \cot(90-\theta)$ $\qquad$ $\cot\theta = \tan(90-\theta)$

$\sec\theta = \operatorname{cosec}(90-\theta)$ $\qquad$ $\operatorname{cosec}\theta = \sec(90-\theta)$

$\sin(90-\theta) = \cos\theta$ $\qquad$ $\cos(90-\theta) = \sin\theta$

$\tan(90-\theta) = \cot\theta$ $\qquad$ $\cot(90-\theta) = \tan\theta$

$\sec(90-\theta) = \operatorname{cosec}\theta$ $\qquad$ $\operatorname{cosec}(90-\theta) = \sec\theta$

5. Trigonometric Identities

$\sin^2\theta + \cos^2\theta = 1$

$\sin^2\theta = 1-\cos^2\theta = (1-\cos\theta)(1+\cos\theta)$

$(1-\cos\theta)(1+\cos\theta) = 1-\cos^2\theta = \sin^2\theta$

$\cos^2\theta = 1-\sin^2\theta = (1-\sin\theta)(1+\sin\theta)$

$(1-\sin\theta)(1+\sin\theta) = 1-\sin^2\theta = \cos^2\theta$

$1+\tan^2\theta = \sec^2\theta$

$\tan^2\theta = \sec^2-1 = (\sec\theta-1)(\sec\theta+1)$

$$(\sec\theta-1)(\sec\theta+1)=\sec^2\theta-1=\tan^2\theta$$

$$1=\sec^2\theta-\tan^2\theta=(\sec\theta-\tan\theta)(\sec\theta+\tan\theta)$$

$$(\sec\theta-\tan\theta)(\sec\theta+\tan\theta)=\sec^2\theta-\tan^2\theta=1$$

$$1+\cot^2\theta=\text{cosec}^2\theta$$

$$\cot^2\theta=\text{cosec}^2\theta-1=(\text{cosec}\,\theta-1)(\text{cosec}\,\theta+1)$$

$$(\text{cosec}\,\theta-1)(\text{cosec}\,\theta+1)=\text{cosec}^2\theta-1=\cot^2\theta$$

$$1=\text{cosec}^2\theta-\cot^2\theta=(\text{cosec}\theta-\cot\theta)(\text{cosec}\theta+\cot\theta)$$

$$(\text{cosec}\theta-\cot\theta)(\text{cosec}\theta+\cot\theta)=\text{cosec}^2\theta-\cot^2\theta=1$$

6. Trigonometric Values

	0°	30°	45°	60°	90°
$\sin\theta$	0	$\frac{1}{2}$	$\frac{1}{\sqrt{2}}$	$\frac{\sqrt{3}}{2}$	1
$\cos\theta$	1	$\frac{\sqrt{3}}{2}$	$\frac{1}{\sqrt{2}}$	$\frac{1}{2}$	0
$\tan\theta$	0	$\frac{1}{\sqrt{3}}$	1	$\sqrt{3}$	∞
$\cot\theta$	∞	$\sqrt{3}$	1	$\frac{1}{\sqrt{3}}$	0
$\sec\theta$	1	$\frac{2}{\sqrt{3}}$	$\sqrt{2}$	2	∞
$\text{cosec}\,\theta$	∞	2	$\sqrt{2}$	$\frac{2}{\sqrt{3}}$	1

Approximate Values

$\sqrt{2}=1.414;$ $\sqrt{3}=1.732;$

$\frac{1}{\sqrt{2}}=0.707;$ $\frac{1}{\sqrt{3}}=0.577;$

$\frac{\sqrt{3}}{2}=0.866;$ $\frac{2}{\sqrt{3}}=1.154$

7. Sum and Difference Formulae

$$\sin(A+B)=\sin A\cos B+\cos A\sin B$$

$$\sin(A-B)=\sin A\cos B-\cos A\sin B$$

$$\cos(A+B)=\cos A\cos B-\sin A\sin B$$

$$\cos(A-B)=\cos A\cos B+\sin A\sin B$$

$$\tan(A+B)=\frac{\tan A+\tan B}{1-\tan A.\tan B}$$

$$\tan(A-B)=\frac{\tan A-\tan B}{1+\tan A.\tan B}$$

8. Multiple and Submultiple Angles

$$\tan 2x=2\sin x\cos x$$

$$\cos 2x=\cos^2 x-\sin^2 x=2\cos^2 x-1$$

$$=1-2\sin^2 x$$

$$\sin 2x=\frac{2\tan x}{1-\tan^2 x}$$

$$\sin 3x=3\sin x-4\sin^3 x$$

$$\cos 3x=4\cos^3 x-3\cos x$$

$$\tan 3x=\frac{3\tan x-\tan^3 x}{1-3\tan^2 x}$$

9. Trigonometric Ratios of Some Important Angles

$$\sin 15°=\frac{\sqrt{3}-1}{2\sqrt{2}}=\frac{\sqrt{6}-\sqrt{2}}{4}=\cos 75°$$

$$\cos 15°=\frac{\sqrt{3}+1}{2\sqrt{2}}=\frac{\sqrt{6}+\sqrt{2}}{4}=\sin 15°$$

$$\tan 15°=\frac{\sqrt{3}-1}{\sqrt{3}+1}=2-\sqrt{3}=\cot 75°$$

$$\cot 15°=\frac{\sqrt{3}+1}{\sqrt{3}-1}=2+\sqrt{3}=\tan 15°$$

HEIGHTS AND DISTANCES

(a) $a = c\cot\theta = b\cos\theta$

$b = c\operatorname{cosec}\theta = a\sec\theta$

$c = b\sin\theta = a\tan\theta$

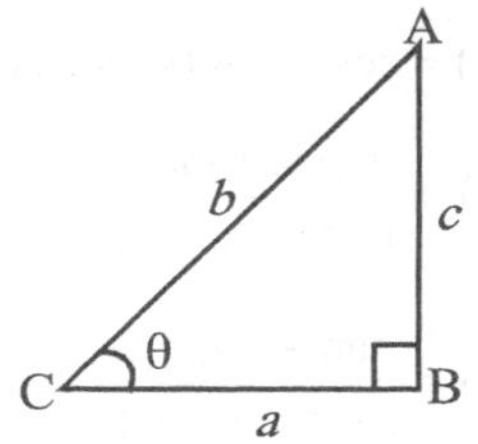

(b) $x = h(\cot\theta + \cot\alpha)$

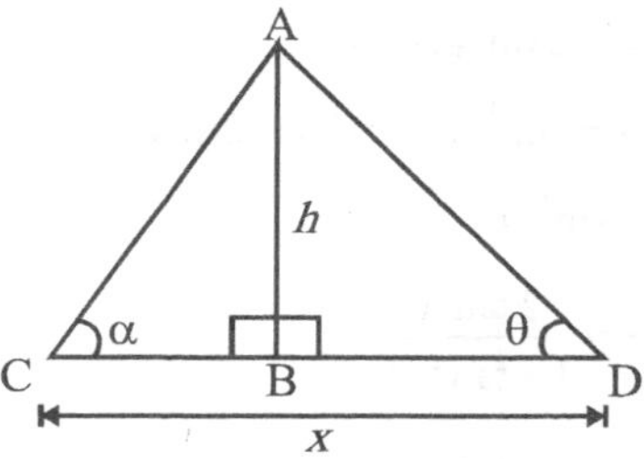

(c) $x = h(\cot\theta - \cot\alpha)$

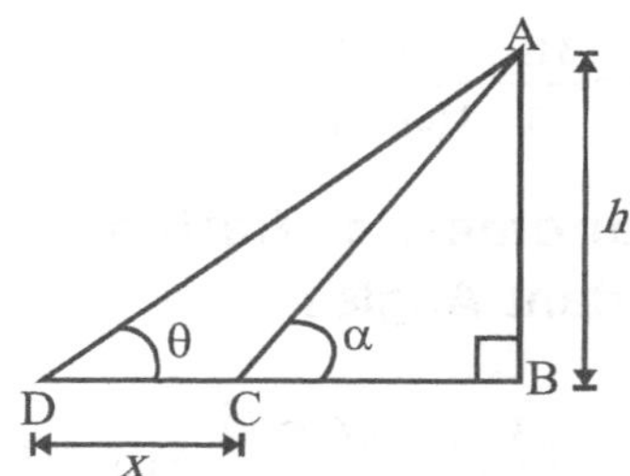

(d) $x = h(\cot\theta + \cot\alpha)$

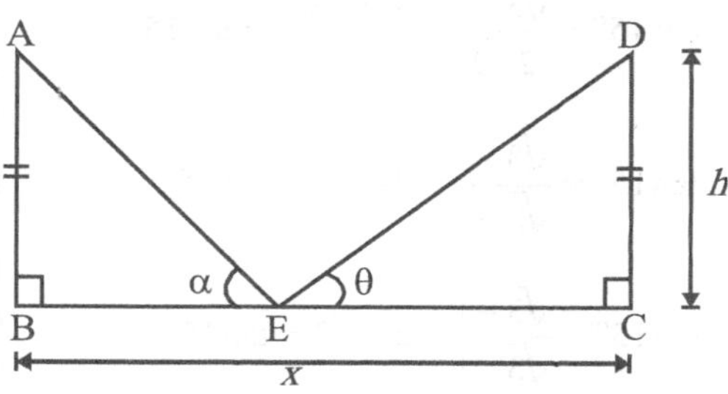

(e) $h\cot\theta = H\cot\alpha$

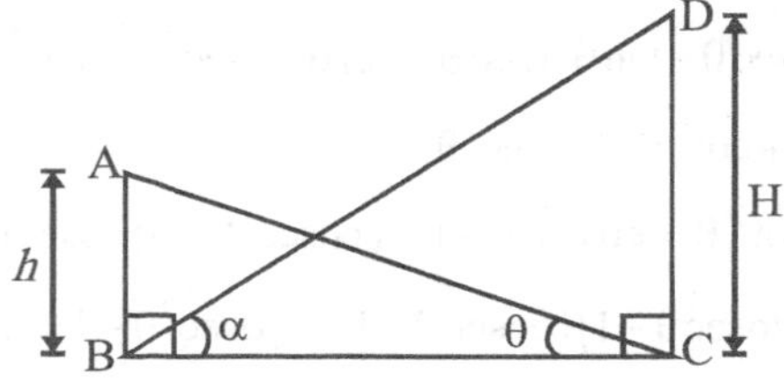

(f) $h = x(\tan\alpha - \tan\theta)$

$h\cot\alpha = H(\cot\theta - \cot\alpha)$

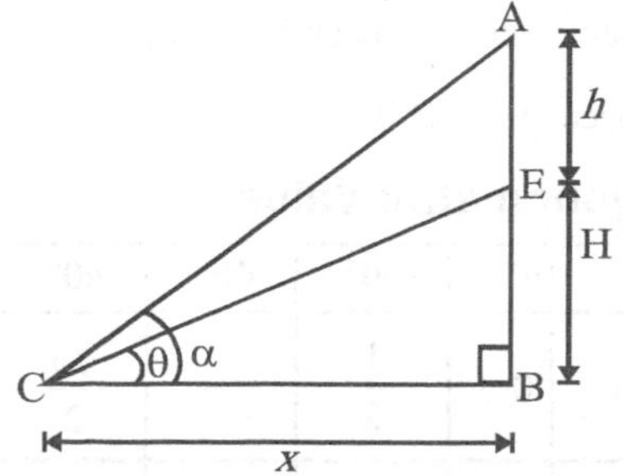

(g) $h\cot\theta = H(\cot\theta - \cot\alpha)$

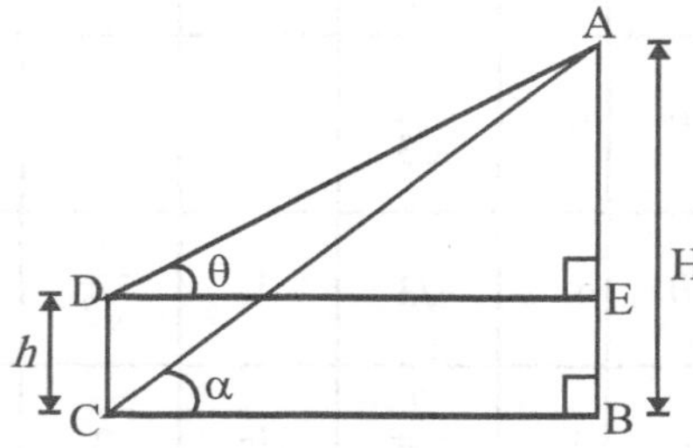

(h) $x = h\cot\alpha$

$h(\cot\alpha + \cot\theta) = H\cot\theta$

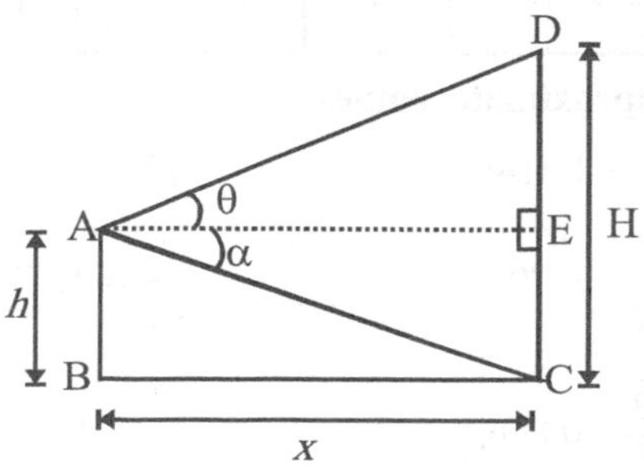

(i) $x = h(\cot\theta - \cot\alpha)$

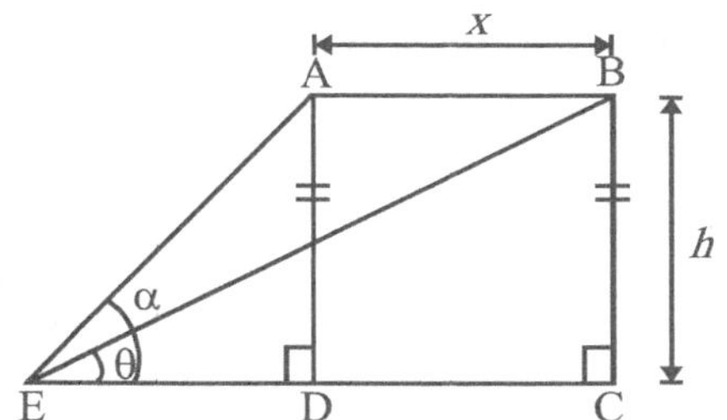

(j) $h = x\left(\dfrac{\tan\alpha + \tan\theta}{\tan\alpha - \tan\theta}\right)$

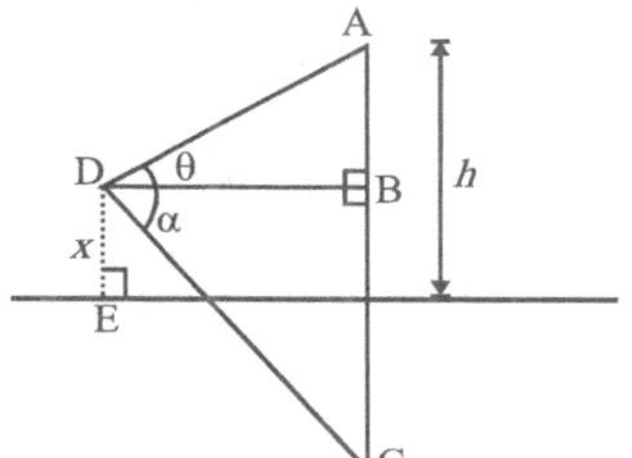

EXAMPLES

Example 1 :

If $\tan\theta = \dfrac{4}{5}$, then $\dfrac{1-\cos\theta}{1+\cos\theta} = ...$

(a) $\dfrac{1}{2}$ (b) $\dfrac{1}{8}$

(c) $\dfrac{1}{16}$ (d) $\dfrac{1}{4}$

Sol.

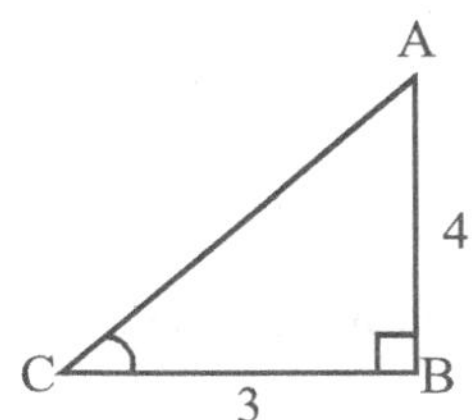

$\tan\theta = \dfrac{4}{3} \Rightarrow AB = 4, BC = 3$

$\Rightarrow AC^2 = 3^2 + 4^2 = 25$

$\Rightarrow AC = 5$

$\Rightarrow \cos\theta = \dfrac{3}{5}$

$$\frac{1-\cos\theta}{1+\cos\theta} = \frac{1-\frac{3}{5}}{1+\frac{3}{5}} = \frac{2}{8} = \frac{1}{4}$$

Hence, option (d) is correct.

Example 2 :

$3\sin^2 30° + 2\cos^2 45° - 5\tan^2 30° = ...$

(a) $\dfrac{1}{2}$ (b) $\dfrac{1}{12}$

(c) $\dfrac{1}{6}$ (d) $\dfrac{1}{3}$

Sol. L.H.S = $3\times\left(\dfrac{1}{2}\right)^2 + 2\times\left(\dfrac{1}{\sqrt{2}}\right)^2 - 5\times\left(\dfrac{1}{\sqrt{3}}\right)^2$

$= 3\times\dfrac{1}{4} + 2\times\dfrac{1}{2} - 5\times\dfrac{1}{3} = \dfrac{1}{12}$

Hence, option (b) is correct.

Example 3 :

If $\sqrt{3}\cot\theta = 1,\quad 0 \le \theta \le 90°$,

Then the value of $\cos^2\theta - \sin^2\theta$ is

(a) $\dfrac{1}{2}$ (b) $-\dfrac{1}{2}$

(c) $\dfrac{1}{\sqrt{2}}$ (d) 0

Sol. $\cot\theta = \dfrac{1}{\sqrt{3}} \quad \Rightarrow \theta = 60°$

Then, $\cos^2 60° - \sin^2 60° = \left(\dfrac{1}{2}\right)^2 - \left(\dfrac{\sqrt{3}}{2}\right)^2$

$= \dfrac{1}{4} - \dfrac{3}{4} = -\dfrac{1}{2}$

Hence option (b) is correct.

Example 4 :

If $2\sec^2 60° + x\cos^2 30° - \frac{3}{4}\cot^2 60° = 10$, then the value of x is

(a) 3 (b) –3

(c) 2 (d) 0

Sol. $2(2)^2 + x\left(\frac{\sqrt{3}}{2}\right)^2 - \frac{3}{4}\left(\frac{1}{\sqrt{3}}\right)^2 = 10$

$\Rightarrow\ 8 + \frac{3}{4}x - \frac{1}{4} = 10$

$\Rightarrow\ \frac{3}{4}x = 10 - 8 + \frac{1}{4}$

$\Rightarrow\ x = \frac{9}{4} \times \frac{4}{3} = 3$

Hence, option (a) is correct.

Example 5 :

If $2\cos 3\theta = 1$ then $\theta =$ ....

(a) 20° (b) 40°

(c) 25° (d) None of these

Sol. $2.\cos 3\theta = 1 \Rightarrow\ \cos 3\theta = \frac{1}{2} = \cos 60°$

$\Rightarrow\ 3\theta = 60°$

$\Rightarrow\ \theta = 20°$

Hence, option (a) is correct.

Example 6 :

If $x^2 \tan^2 45° + 3\cos^2 60° - 7\sin^2 30° = 99$, then x = ...

(a) $\pm\frac{1}{2}$ (b) $\pm\sqrt{2}$

(c) ± 1 (d) ± 10

Sol. $x^2 (1)^2 + 3\left(\frac{1}{2}\right)^2 - 7\times\left(\frac{1}{2}\right)^2 = 99$

$\Rightarrow\ x^2 + \frac{3}{4} - \frac{7}{4} = 99$

$\Rightarrow\ x^2 = 100$

$\Rightarrow\ x = \pm 10$

Hence, option (d) is correct.

Example 7 :

If $2x\sin 60° - 3y\tan 45° = 0$ and

$x\tan 60° + \sqrt{2}y\,\text{cosec}45° = 5$

then value of x and y respectively are

(a) $\sqrt{3}$ and $\frac{1}{2}$ (b) $\frac{1}{\sqrt{3}}$ and 1

(c) $\sqrt{3}$ and 1 (d) None of these

Sol. $\begin{cases} 2x\frac{\sqrt{3}}{2} - 3y.1 = 0 \\ x\sqrt{3} + \sqrt{2}y.\sqrt{2} = 5 \end{cases}$

$\Rightarrow\ \sqrt{3}x - 3y = 0$

$\sqrt{3}x + 2y = 5$

solving $x = \sqrt{3}, y = 1$

Hence, option (c) is correct.

Example 8 :

If $\tan\theta = \frac{2}{\sqrt{5}}$, then $\frac{\text{cosec}^2\theta - \sec^2\theta}{\text{cosec}^2\theta + \sec^2\theta} =$ ....

(a) $\frac{1}{9}$ (b) $\frac{1}{8}$

(c) $\frac{1}{7}$ (d) $\frac{1}{6}$

Sol. Dividing numerator and denominator by $\text{cosec}^2\theta$

We get $\dfrac{1 - \dfrac{\sec^2\theta}{\text{cosec}^2\theta}}{1 + \dfrac{\sec^2\theta}{\text{cosec}^2\theta}}$

However $\frac{\sec\theta}{\text{cosec}\,\theta} = \left(\frac{1}{\cos\theta}\right)\left(\frac{\sin\theta}{1}\right) = \tan\theta = \frac{2}{\sqrt{5}}$

The value of expression is

$\dfrac{1 - \frac{4}{5}}{1 + \frac{4}{5}} = \frac{1}{9}$

Hence, option (a) is correct.

Example 9 :

$(\sin A - \cos A)^2 + (\cos A - \sin A)^2 = ...$

(a) 2 (b) −2
(c) 1 (d) 0

Sol. $\sin^2 A + \cos^2 A - 2\sin A\cos A + \cos^2 A$
$+ \sin^2 A + 2\sin A\cos A$

$= 2\sin^2 A + 2\cos^2 A$

$= 2(\sin^2 A + \cos^2 A)$

= 2

Hence, option (a) is correct

Example 10 :

$\sqrt{1-\cos^2\theta} = \frac{\sqrt{3}}{2}$ and $0 \le \theta \le 90°$ then $\theta = ...$

(a) 60° (b) 30°
(c) 15° (d) 75°

Sol. $\sqrt{1-\cos^2\theta} = \sqrt{\sin^2\theta} = \sin\theta$

$\sin\theta = \frac{\sqrt{3}}{2} \Rightarrow \theta = 60°$

Hence option (a) is correct

Example 11 :

$\sin^6 A + \cos^6 A = ...$

(a) $1 + 3\sin^2 A\cos^2 A$

(b) $3\sin^2 A\cos^2 A - 1$

(c) $1 - 3\sin A\cos A$

(d) None of the above

Sol. $(\sin^2 A)^3 + (\cos^2 A)^3$

$= (\sin^2 A + \cos^2 A)^3 - 3\sin^2 A\cos^2 A$
$(\sin^2 A + \cos^2 A)$

$= 1 - 3\sin^2 A\cos^2 A$

none of the option (a), (b) or (c) are correct. Hence option (d) is the correct answer.

Example 12 :

$\frac{\cot\theta + \text{cosec}\theta - 1}{\cot\theta - \text{cosec}\theta + 1} = ...$

(a) $\frac{1+\sin\theta}{\cos\theta}$ (b) $\frac{1-\sin\theta}{\cos\theta}$

(c) $\frac{1+\cos\theta}{\sin\theta}$ (d) $\frac{1-\cos\theta}{\sin\theta}$

Sol. Substitute 1 in the numerator only by $\text{cosec}^2\theta - \cot^2\theta$

LHS $= \frac{\cot\theta + \cos\text{ec}\theta - (\text{cosec}^2\theta - \cos^2\theta)}{(\cot\theta - \text{cosec}\theta + 1)}$

$= \frac{(\cot\theta - \text{cosec}\theta + \cot\theta)(\text{cosec}\theta - \cot\theta)}{(\cot\theta - \text{cosec}\theta + 1)}$

$= \frac{(\cot\theta + \text{cosec}\theta)(1 - \text{cosec}\theta + \cot\theta)}{(1 - \text{cosec}\theta + \cot\theta)}$

$= \cot\theta + \text{cosec}\theta$

$= \frac{1+\cos\theta}{\sin\theta}$

Hence option (c) is correct.

Example 13 :

$\frac{1}{\sec A - \tan A} - \frac{1}{\cos A} = ...$

(a) $\frac{1}{\sec A} - \frac{1}{\sec A - \tan A}$

(b) $\frac{1}{\cos A} - \frac{1}{\sec A + \tan A}$

(c) $\frac{1}{\cos A} + \frac{1}{\sec A - \tan A}$

(d) None of the above

Sol. LHS $= \frac{1}{\sec A - \tan A} \times \frac{\sec A + \tan A}{\sec A + \tan A} - \frac{1}{\cos A}$

$= \frac{\sec A + \tan A}{\sec^2 A - \tan^2 A} - \frac{1}{\cos A}$

$= \sec A + \tan A - \sec A$

$= \tan A$

$= \sec A - \sec A + \tan A$

$= \sec A - (\sec A - \tan A)$

$$= \sec A - \frac{(\sec A + \tan A)(\sec A + \tan A)}{\sec A + \tan A}$$

$$= \frac{1}{\cos A} - \frac{1}{\sec A + \tan A}$$

Hence, option (b) is correct.

Example 14 :

$\cot 7°.\cot 23°.\cot 67°.\cot 83° = ...$

(a) -1 (b) 1

(c) 0 (d) $\sqrt{3}$

Sol. $\cot 83° = \tan(90-83)° = \tan 7° = \frac{1}{\cot 7°}$

similarly $\cot 67° = \frac{1}{\cot 23°}$

$\Rightarrow$ LHS $= \cot 7°.\cot 23°.\frac{1}{\cot 23°}.\frac{1}{\cot 7°} = 1$

Hence, option (b) is correct

Example 15 :

Maximum and minimum value of $5\sin x + 3\cos x$ respectively are

(a) -8 and $+8$

(b) 2 and 8

(c) $-\sqrt{34}$ and $+\sqrt{34}$

(d) None of the above

Sol. A = 5, B = 3

maximum value $= \sqrt{A^2+B^2} = \sqrt{5^2+3^2} = \sqrt{34}$

minimum value $= \sqrt{A^2+B^2} = -\sqrt{34}$

Hence option (c) is correct.

Example 16 :

A vertical flagstaff is surmounted on the top of avertical tower. From a point on the ground the angle of elevation of the top and bottom of the flagstaff are 30° and 15° respectively. If the tower is 20 m high, the height of the flagstaff is

(a) 10.72 m

(b) 5.36 m

(c) 9.38 m

(d) None of the above

Sol.

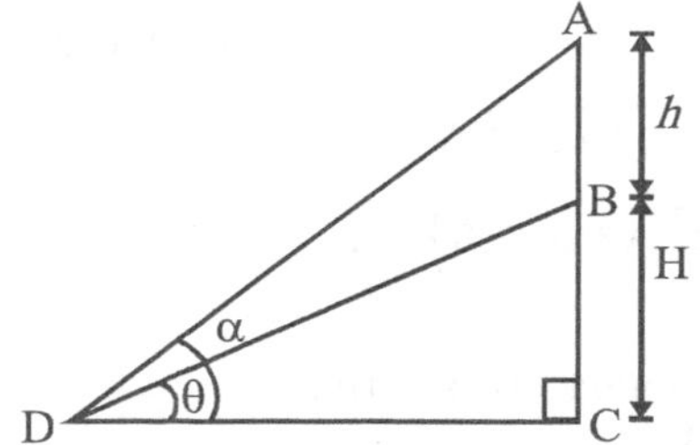

$\theta = 15°$, $\alpha = 30°$,

H = 20 m, h = ?

but $h = \frac{H(\cot\theta - \cot\alpha)}{\cot\theta}$

$$\Rightarrow h = \frac{20(\cot 15° - \cot 30°)}{\cot 15°} \text{m}$$

$$\Rightarrow h = \frac{20(2+\sqrt{3}-\sqrt{3})}{2+\sqrt{3}} \text{m}$$

$$\Rightarrow h = \frac{40}{2+\sqrt{3}} \times \frac{2-\sqrt{3}}{2-\sqrt{3}} \text{m}$$

$\Rightarrow h = 40(2-\sqrt{3})\text{m}$

$\Rightarrow h \approx 40(2-1.732)\text{m}$

$\Rightarrow h \approx 10.72\text{m}$

Hence, option (a) is correct.

Example 17 :

An aircraft flying parallel to the ground is observed at an instant at an elevation of 30°. After 9 seconds the elevation changed to 60°. If the speed of the plane is 360 km/hr then the height at which it is flying is

(a) 450 m (b) $600\sqrt{3}$ m

(c) $900\sqrt{3}$ (d) $450\sqrt{3}$ m

Sol. Speed $= 360\dfrac{\text{km}}{\text{hr}} = 360\times\dfrac{5}{18}\text{ m/sec} = 100\text{ m/sec}$

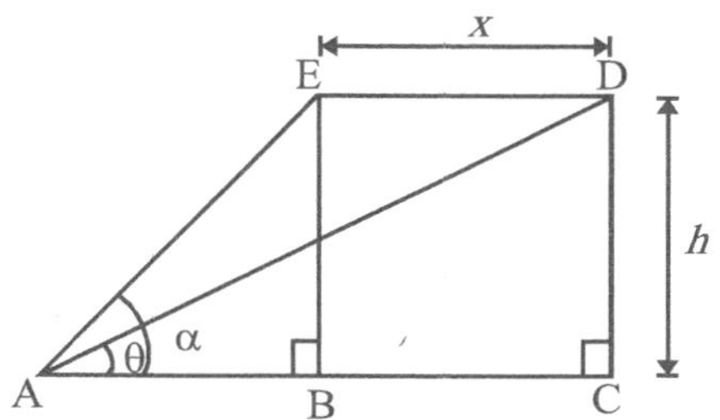

distance : $x = 100\times 9\text{ m} = 900\text{ m}$

$x = 900,\quad \theta = 30°,\quad \alpha = 60°,\quad h = ?$

but $h = \dfrac{x}{\cot\theta - \cot\alpha}$

$\Rightarrow\ h = \dfrac{900}{\cot 30° - \cot 60°}\text{m}$

$\Rightarrow\ h = \dfrac{900}{\left(\sqrt{3} - \dfrac{1}{\sqrt{3}}\right)}\text{m}$

$\Rightarrow\ h = 900\times\dfrac{\sqrt{3}}{2}\text{m}$

$\Rightarrow\ h = 450\sqrt{3}\text{ m}$

Hence option (d) is correct

Example 18 :

Two boats on either side of a light house observe the angles of elevation of the top to be 30° and 45° respectively. If the tower is 50m high and the boats and the light house are in same straight line, then the distance between the boats is

(a) 36.6 m (b) 366 m
(c) 236.6 m (d) 246.6 m

Sol.

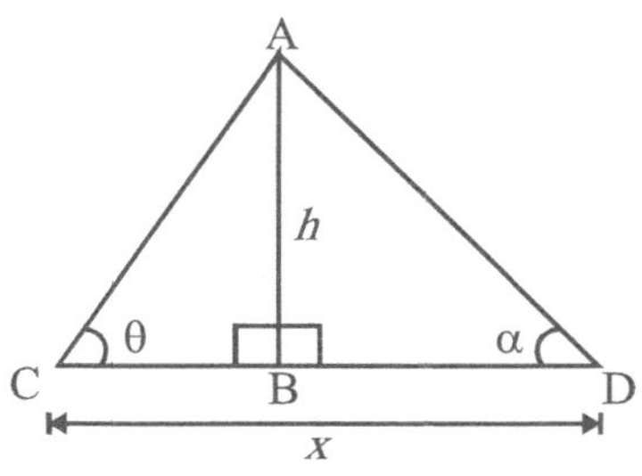

$\theta = 45°,\quad \alpha = 30°,\quad h = 50\text{m},\quad x = ?$

but $x = h(\cot\theta + \cot\alpha)$

$\Rightarrow\ x = 50(\cot 45° + \cot 30°)\text{m}$

$\Rightarrow\ x = 50\left(1 + \sqrt{3}\right)\text{m}$

$\Rightarrow\ x \approx 50(1 + 1.732)\text{m}$

$\Rightarrow\ x \approx 236.6\text{m}$

Hence, option (c) is correct

Example 19 :

A tower in a city is 150 m high and a multistory hotel at the city centre is 20 m high. The angle of elevation of the top of the hotel is 5°, A building h meters high stands on the straight road connecting the tower and the hotel at a distance of 1.2 km from the tower. If the top of the hotel, top of the building and top of the tower are in a same straight line, then the distance of the tower from the hotel is

[use $\tan 5° = 0.0875, \tan 85° = 11.43$]

(a) 1386 m (b) 1486 m
(c) 1468 m (d) 1528 m

Sol.

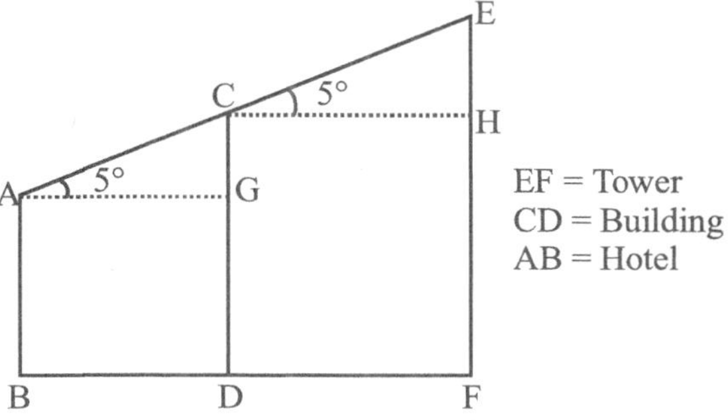

EF = 150 m; AB = 20 m; CD = h;
DF = 1.2 km = 1200 m; BF = ?
CH = DF = 1200 m
from Δ CHE, EH = $1200\tan 5°$
$= 1200\times 0.0875 = 105$
CD = FH = 150 − 105 = 45 m
$GC = 45 - 20 = 25\text{m}$ [Note GD = AB]

From ΔAGC, $AG = 25 \cot 5°$

$= 25 \tan 85° = 286$ m

Hence, $BF = 1200 + 286 = 1486$ m

Hence option (b) is correct

Example 20 :

A boy standing on ground on flying a kite with a 100 m long string. The string is inclined to the ground at an angle of 30°. Another boy is standing on the roof of a 10 m tall building and is flying a kite making an angle of elevation of 43° with the horizontal. If both the boys are on same side of the kites then the length of the string the second boy must have so that the two kites meet is ...... [Use cosec 43° = 1.466]

(a) 50.65 m (b) 58 m

(c) 58.64 m (d) None of the above

Sol.

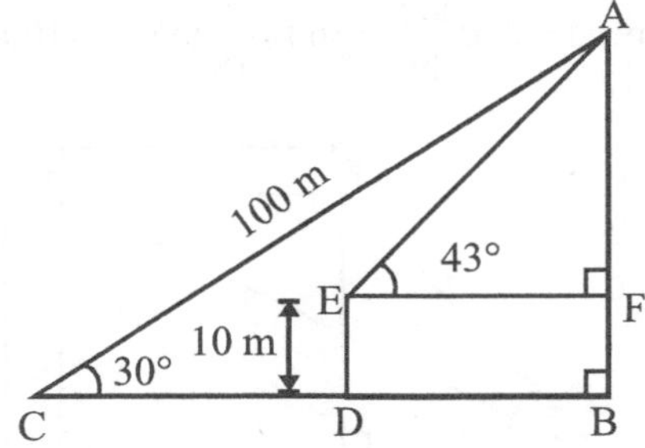

$AB = 100 \sin 30° = 50\text{m};$

$FB = DE = 10\text{m}; \quad \Rightarrow AF = 40\text{m}$

$AE = AF\text{cosec}43°$

$AE = 40 \times 1.466\text{m}$

AE = 58.64 m

Hence, option (c) is correct.

❑❑❑

Logical & Analytical Reasoning

1. LETTER SERIES

In letter series, the letters follow a definite order. The given series of letters can be in natural order or in reverse order or combination of both. The letters may be skipped or repeated or consecutive. The given series may be single or may even comprise of two different series merged at alternate positions. While attempting questions on letter series one should note the pattern of alphabet series.

Alphabets in natural series are :

A B C D E F G H I J K L M N O P Q R S T U V W X Y Z

A ↓ 1st, E ↓ 5th, J ↓ 10th, O ↓ 15th, T ↓ 20th, Y ↓ 25th

Alphabets in reverse series are :

Z Y X W V U T S R Q P O N M L K J I H G F E D C B A

Z ↓ 1st, V ↓ 5th, Q ↓ 10th, L ↓ 15th, G ↓ 20th, B ↓ 25th

Note : On reaching Z, the series restarts from A and on reaching A, it restarts from Z.

EXERCISE

Directions : *In each of the following series determine the order of the letters. Then from the given options select the one which will complete the given series.*

1. B Y C X D W E ?
(*a*) S (*b*) T
(*c*) U (*d*) V

2. B A F E J I P O ? U
(*a*) V (*b*) T
(*c*) S (*d*) Q

3. B A D C ? H G J I
(*a*) EF (*b*) FE
(*c*) FG (*d*) DF

4. ADG, XVT, BEH, WUS, ?
(*a*) VTR (*b*) CFI
(*c*) DFJ (*d*) STU

5. GMSY, IOUA, KQWC, ?
(*a*) MSYE (*b*) NSYE
(*c*) MTYE (*d*) MSYF

6. ADG, GJM, ?, SVY
(*a*) MPS (*b*) MQR
(*c*) MQS (*d*) SPM

7. XYZ, UVW, ?, OPQ
(*a*) RST (*b*) STU
(*c*) QRS (*d*) TUV

8. JOBS, KMEO, LKHK, ?, NGNC
(*a*) MJLH (*b*) LIKG
(*c*) MIKG (*d*) MNGM

9. AZ, GT, MN, ?, YB
(*a*) KF (*b*) TS
(*c*) RX (*d*) SH

10. BMY, DNW, FOU, ?
(*a*) HPT (*b*) HPS
(*c*) HQS (*d*) GPS

11. AZ, CX, EV, ?
(*a*) HU (*b*) GS
(*c*) GT (*d*) HT

12. DMP, FLN, HKL, JJJ, ?
(*a*) MIH (*b*) III
(*c*) LIH (*d*) MII

13. ECA, JHF, OMK, ?, YWU
(*a*) TRP (*b*) LNP
(*c*) QPN (*d*) RPT

14. ABP, CDQ, EFR, ?
(*a*) GHS (*b*) HGS
(*c*) GHR (*d*) GHT

15. BEH, KNQ, TWZ, ?
(*a*) IJL (*b*) BDF
(*c*) CFI (*d*) ADG

16. EJO, TYD, INS, XCH, ?
(*a*) MRW (*b*) NRV
(*c*) MRV (*d*) NRW

17. ABP, CDQ, EFR,?
(*a*) GHS (*b*) GIS
(*c*) GGS (*d*) GJS

18. NRA, PRC, RRE, TRG, ?
(*a*) USI (*b*) VRI
(*c*) WRJ (*d*) TRI

19. FJKP, ILMQ, LNOR, OPQS, ?
(*a*) RQTV (*b*) RQSS
(*c*) RRST (*d*) RTTU

20. DQCP, EPEN, FOGL, GNIJ, ?
(*a*) HNLG (*b*) HLJG
(*c*) HOMI (*d*) HMKH

21. DFST, FSTD, STDF, ?
(*a*) TSFD (*b*) FDTS
(*c*) TDFS (*d*) SFDT

22. IXT, MAV, QDX, ?
(*a*) WGX (*b*) VHY
(*c*) UGZ (*d*) YHZ

23. QYK, ?, ISG, EPE
(*a*) NWJ (*b*) MVI
(*c*) NVI (*d*) MVJ

24. JMC, CLT, KND, ?, LOE, GPX
(*a*) ENV (*b*) DMX
(*c*) EOU (*d*) DRX

25. ZDV, XGS, VJP, ?
(*a*) SNM (*b*) TMM
(*c*) TNR (*d*) SNT

EXPLANATORY ANSWERS

1. (*d*) : There are two alternate series.

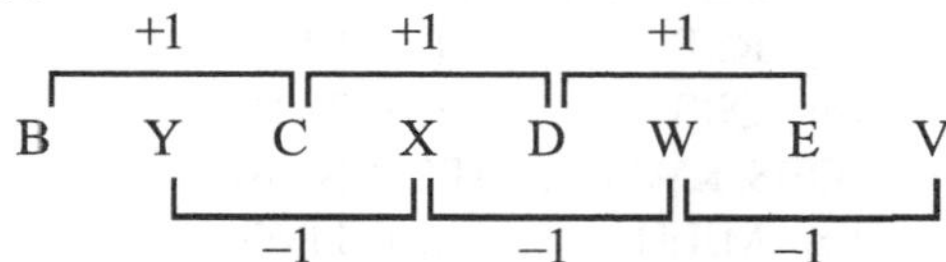

Series I : BCDE (natural order)
Series II : YXWV (reverse order)

2. (*a*) : Each vowel (AEIOU) is preceded by the letter that comes next to it in the natural alphabetical series.

B A F E J I P O V U

3. (*b*) : The letters in natural series are divided into sections of two letters each. The letters in each section are written backward.

<u>BA</u> <u>DC</u> <u>FE</u> <u>HG</u> <u>JI</u>

4. (*b*) : There are two alternate series.

ADG XVT BEH WUS CFI

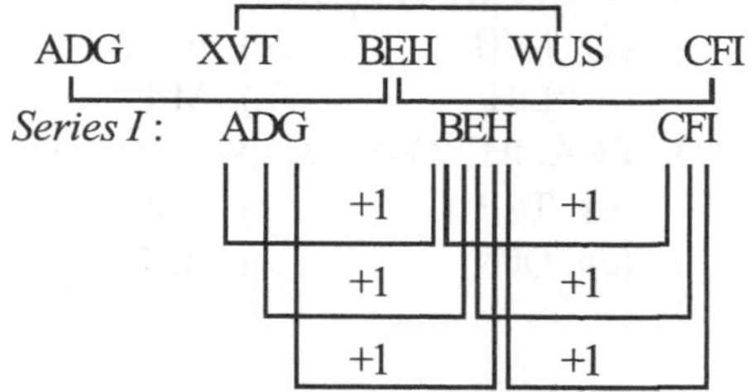

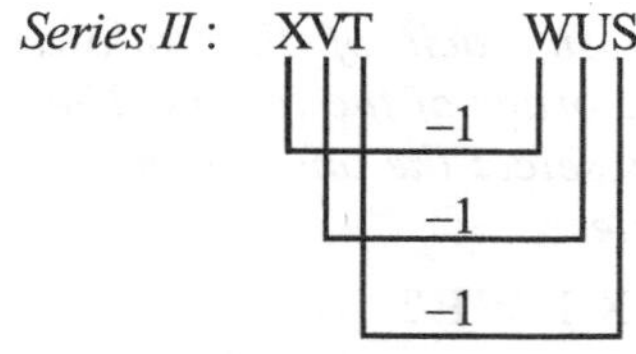

5. (*a*) : The series is formed by moving each letter two steps forward from one group to the next.

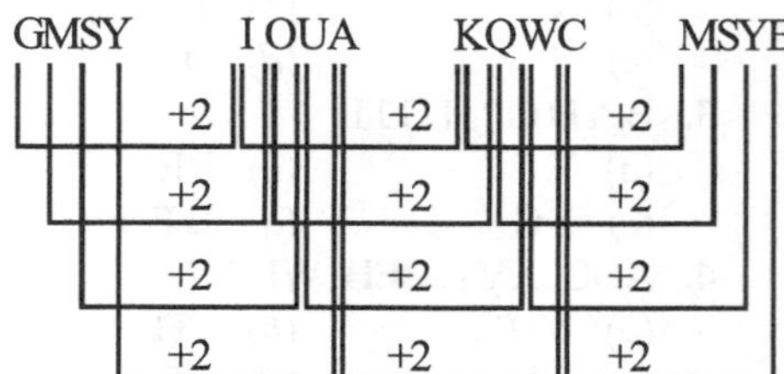

(The series restarts from A on reaching Z)

6. (*a*) : In each group of three letters the alphabet is in the succession of +3. The next group begins with the last alphabet of the previous group.

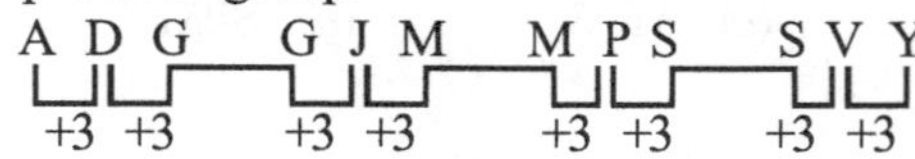

7. (*a*) : The alphabet from one group to the next are in recession of –3, *i.e.*,

XYZ UVW RST OPQ

–3 –3 –3
–3 –3 –3
–3 –3 –3

8. (*c*) : The alphabets in each group follow the pattern +1, –2, +3 and –4 respectively from one group to the next group.

9. (*d*) : The letters in one group correspond to the letters in the next group in the manner +6, –6 respectively, *i.e.*,

AZ GT MN SH YB

+6 +6 +6 +6
–6 –6 –6 –6

10. (*b*) : The letters in one group correspond to the letters in the next group in the manner +2, +1, -2 respectively, *i.e.*,

BMY DNW FOU HPS

+2 +2 +2
+1 +1 +1
–2 –2 –2

11. (*c*) : The letters in each group correspond to the letters in the next group in the manner +2, –2 respectively, *i.e.*,

AZ CX EV GT

+2 +2 +2
–2 –2 –2

12. (*c*) : The alphabets in each group correspond to the alphabets in the next group in the manner +2, –1, –2 respectively, *i.e.*,

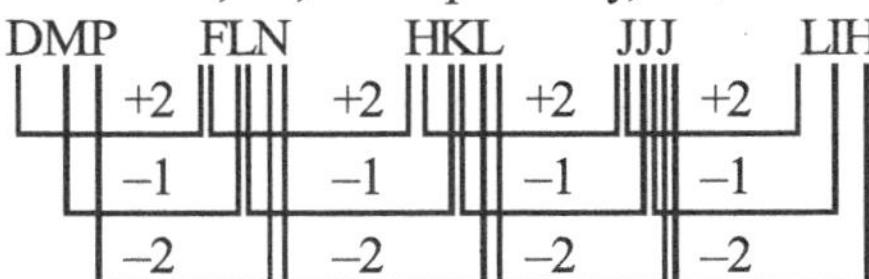

13. (*a*) : The alphabets in each group are moved five steps forward, *i.e.*,

ECA JHF OMK TRP YWU

+5 +5 +5 +5
+5 +5 +5 +5
+5 +5 +5 +5

14. (*a*) : The letters in one group correspond to the letters in the next group in the manner +2, +2, +1 respectively, *i.e.*,

ABP CDQ EFR GHS

+2 +2 +2
+2 +2 +2
+1 +1 +1

15. (*c*) : All the letters in each group are moved nine steps forward.

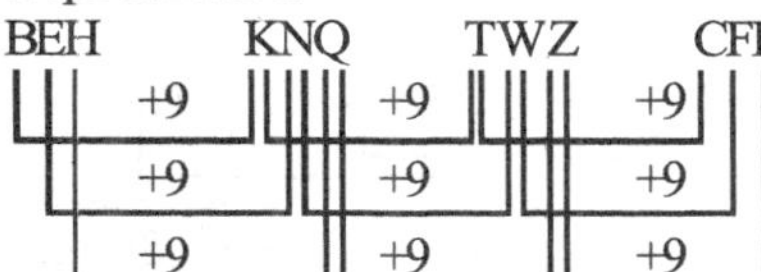

16. (*a*) : There are two alternate series :

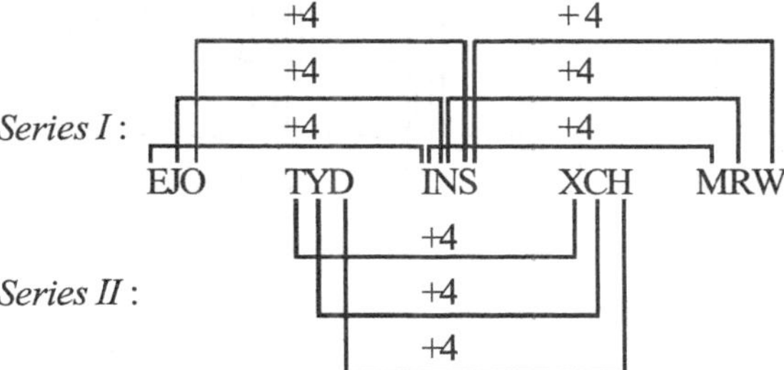

17. (*a*) : The letters in one group correspond to the letters in the next group in the manner +2, +2, +1 respectively, *i.e.*,

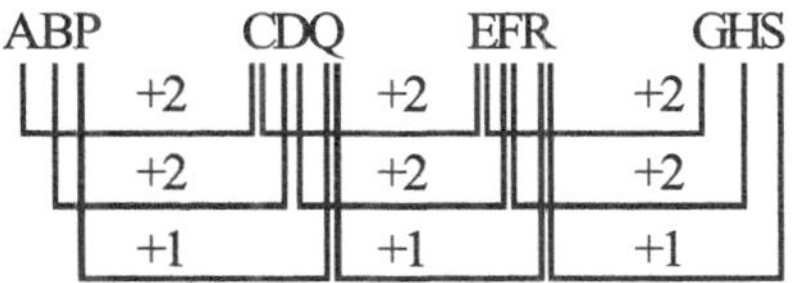

18. (*b*) : The first and third letters are moved two steps forwards while the middle letter remains unchanged, *i.e.*,

NRA PRC RRE TRG VRI

+2 +2 +2 +2
+2 +2 +2 +2

19. (*c*) : The four letters are moved 3, 2, 2, 1 steps forward respectively, *i.e.,*

FJKP ILMQ LNOR OPQS RRST

+3 +3 +3 +3

+2 +2 +2 +2

+2 +2 +2 +2

+1 +1 +1 +1

20. (*d*) : The letters in one group correspond to the letters in the next group in the manner, +1, –1, +2 –2 respectively, *i.e.,*

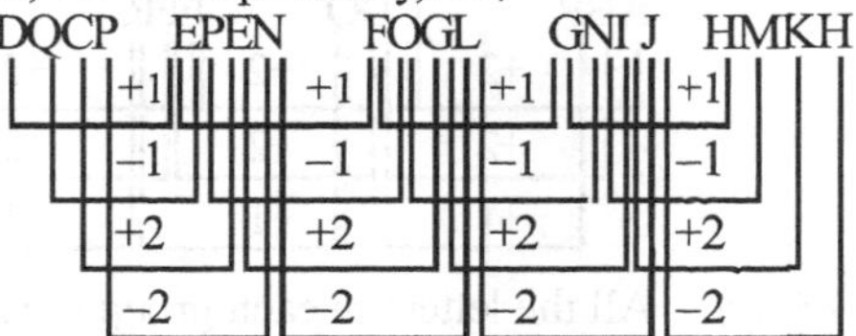

21. (*c*) : The first letter in each group is the last letter in the next group, *i.e.,*

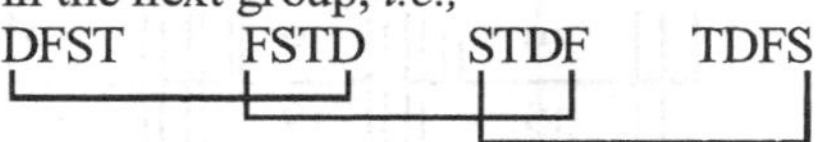

22. (*c*) : The three letters in each group are moved 4, 3 and 2 steps forward respectively, *i.e.,*

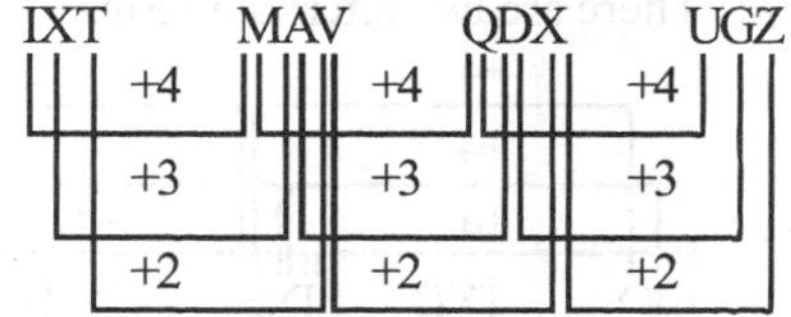

23. (*b*) : The three letters in each group are moved 4, 3 and 2 steps backward respectively, *i.e.,*

QYK MVI ISG EPE

–4 –4 –4

–3 –3 –3

–2 –2 –2

24. (*a*) : There are two alternate series :

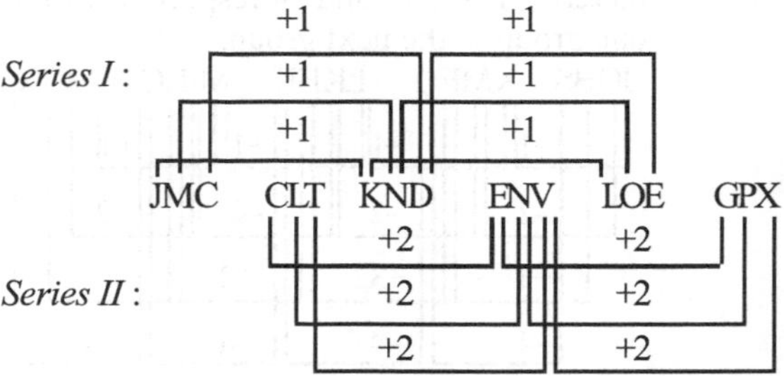

25. (*b*) : The letters in one group correspond to the letters in the next group in the manner –2, +3 –3 respectively, *i.e.,*

ZDV XGS VJP TMM

–2 –2 –2

+3 +3 +3

–3 –3 –3

2. Wrong Letter Series

In this type of series, the candidates are not required to find the letter or group of letters which will complete the given series but, they have to identify the letter or number which is wrong or misfit in the given series.

SOLVED EXAMPLE

1. Which of the following letters in the given series is wrong?
J M P T V Y
(*a*) J (*b*) P (*c*) T (*d*) Y
Ans. (*c*) : The letters in this series are moved three steps forward, *i.e.*,
J M P S V Y
+3 +3 +3 +3 +3
Letter 'T' should have been 'S'.

EXERCISE

Directions : *Which letter(s) in each of the following series is wrong or is misfit in the series?*

1. A E H O U
(*a*) U (*b*) O
(*c*) H (*d*) E

2. C H M S W B
(*a*) C (*b*) S
(*c*) B (*d*) W

3. X S N I C Y
(*a*) Y (*b*) C
(*c*) S (*d*) I

4. Z A W B X C
(*a*) D (*b*) C
(*c*) X (*d*) W

5. M L O N Q P R
(*a*) R (*b*) O
(*c*) Q (*d*) L

6. D K R Y F L
(*a*) L (*b*) D
(*c*) R (*d*) Y

7. L N Q T W Z C F
(*a*) C (*b*) Q
(*c*) L (*d*) F

8. XW, DC, CB, NM, PQ
(*a*) NM (*b*) CB
(*c*) PQ (*d*) XW

9. B E I N S A I
(*a*) A (*b*) E
(*c*) S (*d*) I

10. Z T P K H F
(*a*) Z (*b*) P
(*c*) T (*d*) F

EXPLANATORY ANSWERS

1. (*c*) : The series is made with vowels only. AEIOU. I should be in place of H.

2. (*b*) : The letters in the series are moved five steps forward.

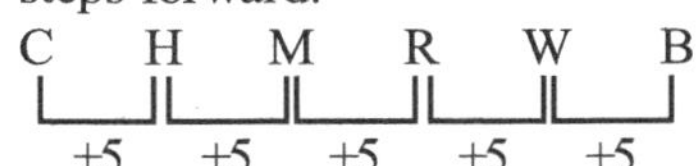

R should be in place of S
(The series restarts from A on reaching Z)

3. (*b*) : The pattern in the series is –5, *i.e.*,

D should be in place of C.

4. (*d*) : There are two alternate series

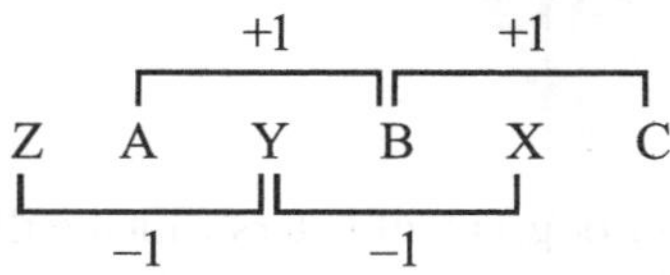

Series I : ZYX (reverse series)
Series II : ABC (natural series)
Y should be in place of W.

5. (*a*) : Two consecutive letters are written backwards.

ML ON QP SR

S should be in place of R.

6. (*a*) : The pattern in this series in moving the letters seven steps forward.

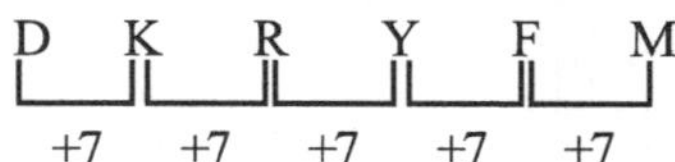

M should be in place of L.

7. (*c*) : The pattern in the series is +3

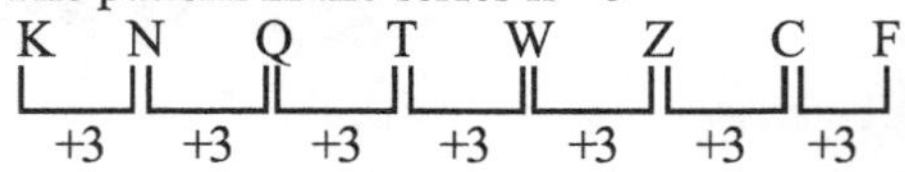

K should be in place of L.

8. (*c*) : The series is made with any two consecutive letters written backwards.

XW DC CB NM QP
← ← ← ← ←

Q should come before P in the series.

9. (*c*) : The difference between the letters is increased by one at each step.

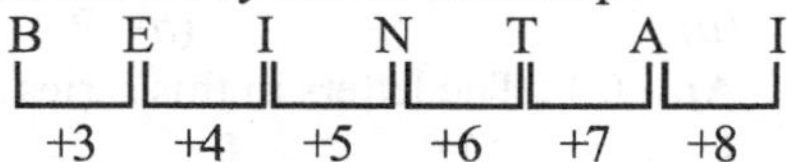

T should be in place of S.

10. (*b*) : The difference between the letters is decreased by one at each step.

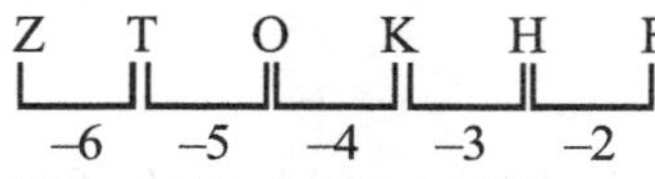

O should be in place of P.

---

3. Repeat Series

In this type of series, small letters of the alphabet are used to make a set of letters which are repeated. The candidate has to find the set of letters which will fit the blanks left in the given series in such a manner that one section of the series is further repeated in the same manner.

SOLVED EXAMPLE

1. Which of the following groups of letters will complete the given series?
ba-b-aab-a-b
(*a*) baab (*b*) abba (*c*) abaa (*d*) babb
Ans. (*b*) : The series is baab, baab, baab. Here the section 'baab' is repeated in the series.

Solving steps **:** The candidate has to look for clues to solve such series pattern. 'aab' in the Series indicates that 'b' in this series is preceded by two 'a' so, the first blank and the last blank will be filled by 'a'. Now the first set is formed, *i.e.,* 'baab' in the beginning. This set is repeated, so the second and third blanks will have 'b' filling them. Now, solve the exercise given below to know the different ways in which these series are formed.

EXERCISE

Directions : *Which of the following groups of letters will complete the given series?*

1. ab---b-bbaa-
(*a*) babba (*b*) abaab
(*c*) abbab (*d*) baaab

2. aa-ab--aaa-a
(*a*) baaa (*b*) abab
(*c*) aaab (*d*) aabb

3. -baa-aab-a-a
(*a*) baab (*b*) abab
(*c*) aaba (*d*) aabb

4. -a cca-ccca-acccc-aaa
(*a*) ccaa (*b*) acca
(*c*) caac (*d*) caaa

5. c-bbb--abbbb-abbb-
(*a*) abccb (*b*) bacbb
(*c*) aabcb (*d*) abacb

6. ac-cab-baca-aba-acac
(*a*) bcbb (*b*) aacb
(*c*) babb (*d*) acbc

7. --aba--ba-ab
(*a*) abbab (*b*) bbaba
(*c*) baabb (*d*) abbba

8. --babbba-a--
(*a*) bbaba (*b*) babbb
(*c*) baaab (*d*) ababb

9. k-mk-lmkkl-kk-mk
(*a*) lklm (*b*) lkmk
(*c*) lkmm (*d*) lkml

10. abc-d-bc-d-b-dd
(*a*) decdb (*b*) dadac
(*c*) cdabe (*d*) bacde

11. b-abbc-bbca-bcabb-ab
(*a*) acba (*b*) acaa
(*c*) cacc (*d*) cabc

12. aca-ac--a-ac
(*a*) babc (*b*) aaac
(*c*) cacc (*d*) caca

13. ba-cb-b-bab-?
(*a*) acbb (*b*) bcaa
(*c*) cabb (*d*) bacc

14. ab-aa-caab-aab-a
(*a*) bcbc (*b*) bbca
(*c*) cbcc (*d*) caba

15. -bbcaa-bcaa-bc-a-bca
(*a*) bacab (*b*) abbab
(*c*) abcba (*d*) bcaab

16. a-bccb-ca-cca-baab-c
(*a*) accab (*b*) abcaa
(*c*) bacaa (*d*) ababc

17. b-dabbcd-b-c-ab
(*a*) cabd (*b*) bcad
(*c*) dcba (*d*) acbd

18. a-ba-caacb-bc-
(*a*) acbb (*b*) cbab
(*c*) cbaa (*d*) cbba

19. c-baa-aca-cacab-acac-bca
(*a*) acbaa (*b*) cbaac
(*c*) bccab (*d*) bbcaa

20. -bcc-ac-aabb-ab-cc
(*a*) bacab (*b*) abaca
(*c*) aabca (*d*) bcaca

21. ab-ccca-bccc-bbcc-
(*a*) abbc (*b*) bbac
(*c*) bbca (*d*) cabc

22. -cbc-a-bcaac-ca
(*a*) aaba (*b*) caab
(*c*) bcab (*d*) aacb

23. ab-ba--ba-
(*a*) abba (*b*) baab
(*c*) baba (*d*) abab

24. yx-yx-yxz-xzy-zyxz
(*a*) zzyx (*b*) xxzy
(*c*) yyzx (*d*) yzxz

25. xxxy-y-xxy-yxx-
(*a*) xyxy (*b*) yxyx
(*c*) yyxx (*d*) xxyy

EXPLANATORY ANSWERS

1. (*d*) : The series is abbaab, abbaab.
2. (*c*) : The series is aaaaba, aaaaba.
3. (*b*) : The series is aba, aba, aba, aba.
4. (*d*) : The series is c,a,cc,aa, ccc, aaa, cccc, aaaa.
5. (*a*) : The series is cabbbb, cabbbb, cabbbb.
6. (*b*) : The series is acac, abab, acac, abab, acac.
7. (*a*) : The series is ab, ab, ab, ab, ab, ab.
8. (*b*) : The series is bababb, bababb.
9. (*d*) : The series is klmk, klmk, klmk, klmk.
10. (*b*) : The series is abcdd, abcdd, abcdd.
11. (*d*) : The series is bcab, bcab, bcab, bcab, bcab.
12. (*c*) : The series is ac, ac, ac, ac, ac, ac.
13. (*d*) : The series is babc, babc, babc.
14. (*c*) : The series is abca, abca, abca, abca.
15. (*b*) : The series is abbca, abbca, abbca, abbca.
16. (*d*) : The series is aabcc, bbcaa, ccabb, aabcc.
17. (*a*) : The series is bcdab, bcdab, bcdab.
18. (*c*) : The series is acbabca, acbabca.
19. (*a*) : The series is cabaac, acabca, cabaac, acabca.
20. (*a*) : The series is bbccaa, ccaabb, aabbcc.
21. (*b*) : The series is abbccc abbccc.
22. (*d*) : The series is acbca acbca acbca.
23. (*d*) : The series is ab ab ab ab ab.
24. (*a*) : The series is yxz yxz yxz yxz yxz yxz.
25. (*b*) : The series is xxx yyy xxx yyy xxx.

4. NUMBER SERIES

In this type of series, the set of given numbers in a series are related to one another in a particular pattern or manner. The relationship between the numbers may be (i) consecutive odd/even numbers; (ii) consecutive prime numbers; (iii) squares/cubes of some numbers with/without variation of addition or subtraction of some number; (iv) sum/product/difference of preceding numbers; (v) addition/subtraction/multiplication/division by some number; and (vi) many more combinations of the relationships given above.

EXERCISE

Directions : *In the following questions, select the number(s) from the given options for completing the given series.*

1. 7776, 1296, 216, 36, 6, ?
(*a*) 6 (*b*) 0
(*c*) 3 (*d*) 1

2. 29282, 2662, 242, 22, ?
(*a*) 1 (*b*) 2
(*c*) 0 (*d*) 11

3. 1, 2, 2, 4, 16, ?, 65536
(*a*) 276 (*b*) 64
(*c*) 256 (*d*) 198

4. 3, 5, 9, 15, 23, ?, 45
(*a*) 37 (*b*) 35
(*c*) 31 (*d*) 33

5. 7, 21, 35, 49, 63, ?
(*a*) 70 (*b*) 77
(*c*) 81 (*d*) 108

6. 10, 14, 23, 39, 64, ?, 149
(*a*) 78 (*b*) 128
(*c*) 103 (*d*) 100

7. 6, 24, 29, 116, 121, ?, 489
(*a*) 468 (*b*) 484
(*c*) 243 (*d*) 363

8. 5, 50, 45, 450, 445, ?, 4445
(*a*) 4450 (*b*) 4600
(*c*) 4550 (*d*) 4500

9. 6.25, 9, 12.25, 16, 20.25, 25, 30.25?
(*a*) 36 (*b*) 32
(*c*) 28.25 (*d*) 40.25

10. 243, 5, 81, 15, 27, 45, 9, ?
(*a*) 5 (*b*) 15
(*c*) 135 (*d*) 27

11. 2, 7, 14, 23, ?, 47
(*a*) 31 (*b*) 38
(*c*) 28 (*d*) 34

12. 0, 1, 8, 27, 64, ?
(*a*) 125 (*b*) 128
(*c*) 256 (*d*) 121

13. 37, 47, 58, ?, 79, 95
(*a*) 71 (*b*) 69
(*c*) 68 (*d*) 67

14. 4, –8, 14, –22, 32, ?
(*a*) –44 (*b*) 42
(*c*) –42 (*d*) 44

15. 6, 7, 9, 11, 15, 15, 24, 19, ?
(*a*) 32 (*b*) 34
(*c*) 36 (*d*) 37

16. 2, 6, 12, 20, 30, ?
(*a*) 42 (*b*) 36
(*c*) 41 (*d*) 40

17. 1, 4, 5, 11, 9, 18, ?, 25
(*a*) 12 (*b*) 13
(*c*) 19 (*d*) 23

18. 27, 45, 9,15, 3, 5, ?
(*a*) 1 (*b*) 1/3
(*c*) 1/5 (*d*) 1/9

19. 3, 1/3, 14, 1/14, 25, 1/25, ?
(*a*) 1/36 (*b*) 34
(*c*) 35 (*d*) 36

20. 1/2, 3/4, 5/8, 7/16, ?
(*a*) 10/17 (*b*) 9/32
(*c*) 11/34 (*d*) 12/35

21. 4, 8, 7, 14, 12, 22, 19, ?, 28
(*a*) 12 (*b*) 24
(*c*) 28 (*d*) 32

22. 96, 90, 78, ?, 36, 6
(*a*) 60 (*b*) 72
(*c*) 48 (*d*) 54

23. 6, 3, 11, 8, 18, 15, 27, 24, ?, ?
(*a*) 36, 33 (*b*) 36, 35
(*c*) 38, 35 (*d*) 38, 34

24. 1, 6, 15, ?, 45, 66, 91
(*a*) 25 (*b*) 26
(*c*) 27 (*d*) 28

25. 1, 2, 5, 12, 27, 58, 121, ?
(*a*) 246
(*b*) 247
(*c*) 248
(*d*) 249

EXPLANATORY ANSWERS

1. *(d)* : The numbers in this sequence are divided by 6 each time.

2. *(b)* : The numbers in the series are divided by 11 at each step.

3. *(c)* : The number in the series is product of all the numbers preceding it.

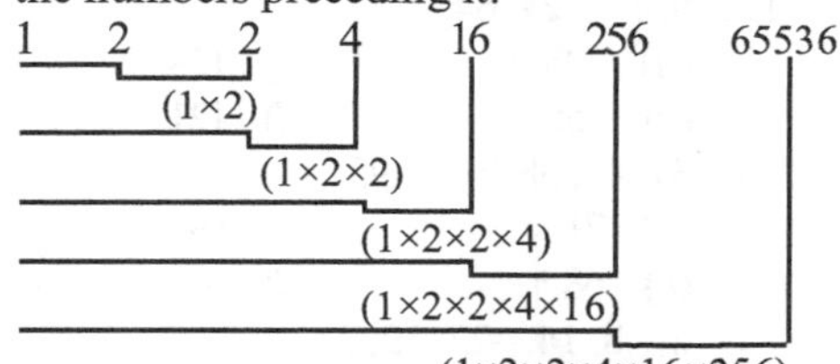

4. *(d)* : The difference between consecutive numbers increases by 2 at each step.

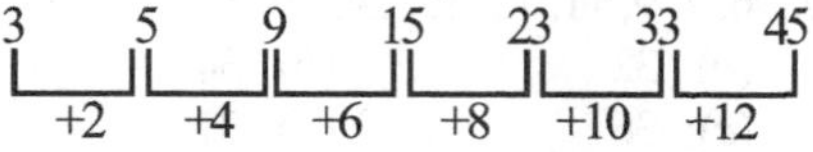

5. *(b)* : The series is multiplication of 7 by odd numbers starting from 3.

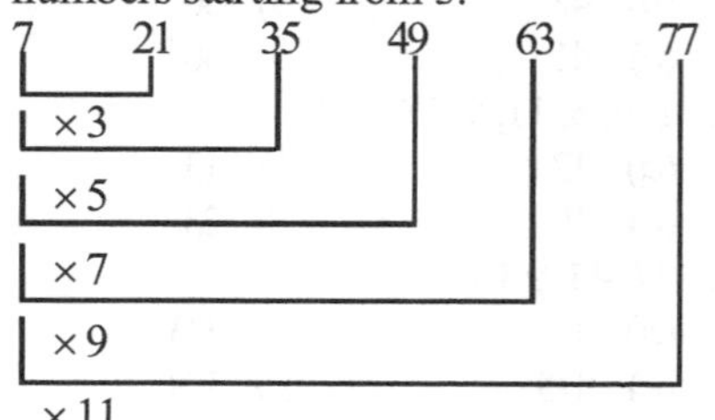

6. *(d)* : The number plus the square of numbers in natural order starting from 2 gives the next number in the series.

10 14 23 39 64 100 149

$+2^2$ $+3^2$ $+4^2$ $+5^2$ $+6^2$ $+7^2$

7. *(b)* : The sequence in the series is ×4, +5, which is repeated.

8. *(a)* : The sequence in the series is ×10, –5, which is repeated.

9. *(a)* : There are two alternate series :

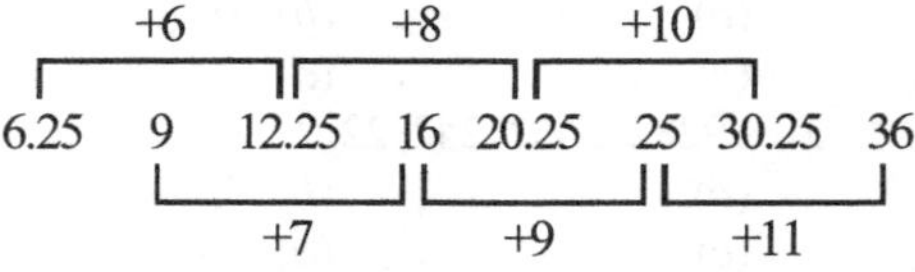

Series I : 6.25, 12.25, 20.25, 30.25 (sequence is +6, +8, +10)
Series II : 9, 16, 25, 36 (sequence is +7, +9, +11)

10. *(c)* : There are two alternate series :

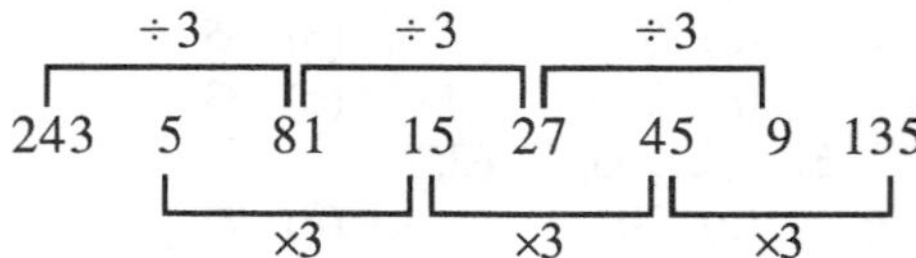

Series I : 243, 81, 27, 9 (division by 3)
Series II : 5, 15, 45, 135 (multiplication by 3)

11. *(d)* : The difference between two consecutive numbers is increasing by 2 starting from 5.

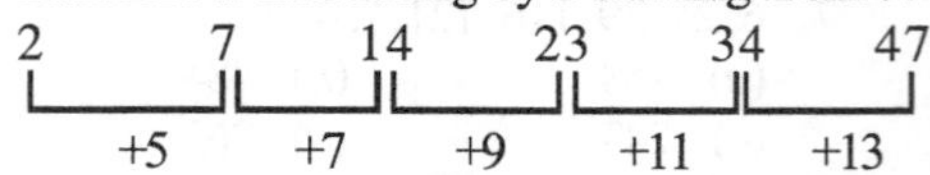

12. *(a)* : The numbers are cubes of numbers in natural order.

13. *(a)* : The sum of the digits of the number is added to the number to obtain the next number in the series.

37 47 58 71 79 95

+(3+7) +(4+7) +(5+8) +(7+1) +(7+9)

14. *(a)* : Alternate numbers are marked positive and negative, but the difference between their magnitude increases by 2 at each step.

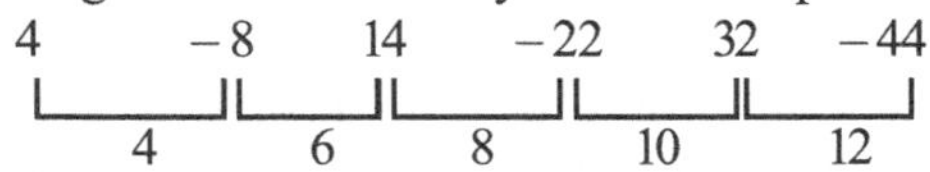

15. *(c)* : There are two alternate series :

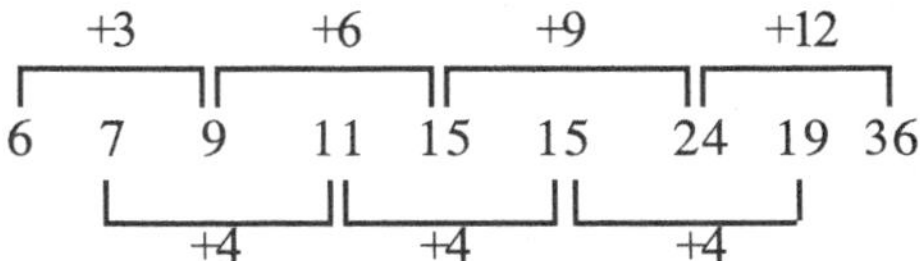

Series I: 6, 9, 15, 24, 36 (sequence is +3, +6, +9, +12)
Series II : 7, 11, 15, 19 (addition of 4 at each step)

16. *(a)* : The difference between the consecutive numbers in the series increases by 2 at each step.

2 6 12 20 30 42

+4 +6 +8 +10 +12

17. *(b)* : There are two alternate series :

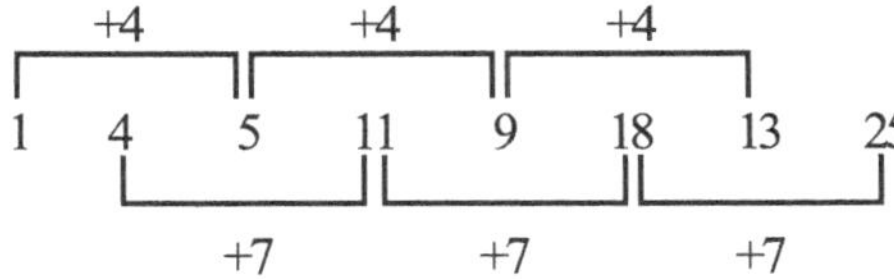

Series I: 1, 5, 9, 13 (addition of 4)
Series II : 4, 11, 18, 25 (addition of 7)

18. *(a)* : There are two alternate series :

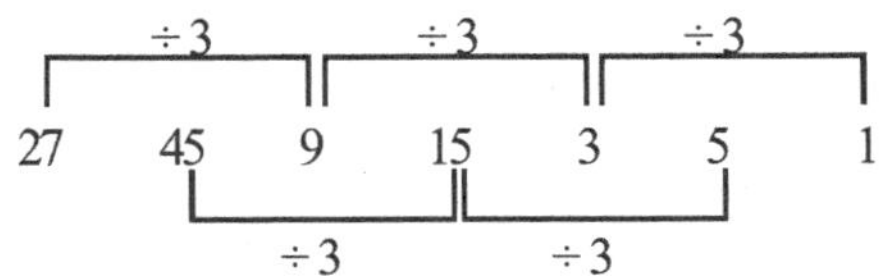

Series I : 27, 9, 3, 1 (division by 3)
Series II : 45, 15, 5 (division by 3)

19. *(d)* : Two consecutive numbers form a pair. The difference between the numbers placed at odd places increases by 11 and the second number is the fraction part of the number.

$3 \quad \frac{1}{3} \quad 14 \quad \frac{1}{14} \quad 25 \quad \frac{1}{25} \quad 36$

+11 +11 +11

20. *(b)* : In this fraction series the numbers on the top are increased by 2 and at the bottom, multiplied by 2.

21. *(d)* : There are two alternate series :

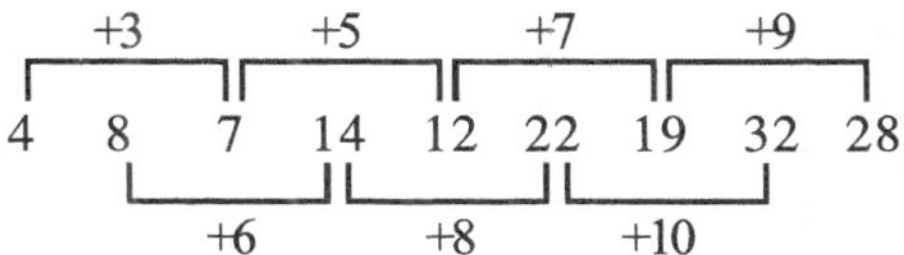

Series I : 4, 7, 12, 19, 28 (sequence is +3, +5, +7, +9)
Series II : 8, 14, 22, 32 (sequence is +6, +8, +10)

22. *(a)* : The series is formed by multiples of 6 in this manner :

6×16	$= 96$		
6×15	$= 90$	$(16 - 1)$	$= 15$
6×13	$= 78$	$(15 - 2)$	$= 13$
6×10	$= 60$	$(13 - 3)$	$= 10$
6×6	$= 36$	$(10 - 4)$	$= 6$
6×1	$= 6$	$(6 - 5)$	$= 1$

23. *(c)* : There are two alternate series :

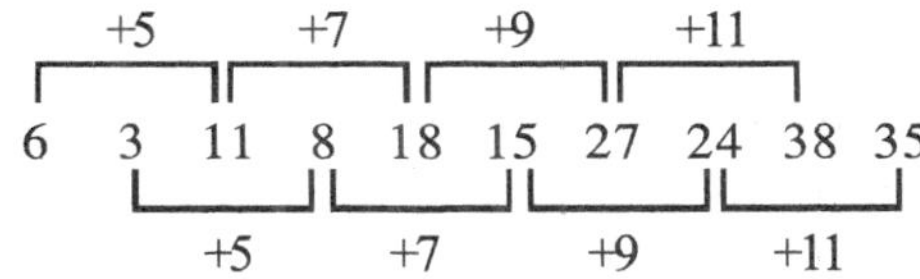

Series I : 6, 11, 18, 27, 38
Series II : 3, 8, 15, 24, 35
(Both series follow the pattern +5, +7, +9, +11)

24. *(d)* : The difference between the numbers in this series is increased by 4 at each step.

1 6 15 28 45 66 91

+5 +9 +13 +17 +21 +25

25. *(c)* : The sequence in this series is number into 2 plus the numbers in natural order starting from 0.

1 2 5 12 27 58 121 248

(1×2)+0 (2×2) +1 (5×2)+2 (12×2) +3 (27×2)+4 (58×2)+5 (121×2)+6

5. Wrong Number Series

In this type of series, the given series may be complete but what needs to be identified is the number in the given completed series which is disturbing the sequential pattern of that series and does not fit in with the relationship shared between the other numbers.

EXERCISE

Directions : *In the given series find the number which is wrong.*

1. 5, 25, 120, 625, 3125, 15625
(*a*) 15625 (*b*) 625
(*c*) 120 (*d*) 5

2. 4, 8, 11, 22, 18, 36, 24, 50
(*a*) 8 (*b*) 22
(*c*) 36 (*d*) 24

3. 2, 4, 12, 24, 72, 142, 432
(*a*) 432 (*b*) 12
(*c*) 142 (*d*) 72

4. 2, 3, 4, 4, 6, 8, 9, 12, 16
(*a*) 3 (*b*) 9
(*c*) 6 (*d*) 12

5. 97, 91, 86, 83, 79, 77, 76, 76
(*a*) 86 (*b*) 76
(*c*) 91 (*d*) 83

6. 7, 11, 11, 9, 15, 7, 19, 5, 23, 1
(*a*) 5 (*b*) 7
(*c*) 1 (*d*) 9

7. 3, 7, 12, 28, 48, 118, 192, 448
(*a*) 12 (*b*) 118
(*c*) 28 (*d*) 7

8. 10, 100, 1100, 11000, 111000, 1210000
(*a*) 1210000 (*b*) 11000
(*c*) 100 (*d*) 111000

9. 24576, 6144, 1536, 386, 96, 24
(*a*) 386 (*b*) 6144
(*c*) 96 (*d*) 1536

10. 11, 13, 15, 17, 19, 23, 29, 31, 37
(*a*) 13 (*b*) 23
(*c*) 15 (*d*) 31

11. 36, 43, 49, 54, 60, 61, 63, 64
(*a*) 60 (*b*) 63
(*c*) 54 (*d*) 43

12. 3, 10, 41, 206, 1236, 8660
(*a*) 10 (*b*) 41
(*c*) 206 (*d*) 1236

13. 17, 25, 37, 50, 65, 82, 101
(*a*) 25 (*b*) 17
(*c*) 101 (*d*) 65

14. 12, 20, 38, 42, 56, 72
(*a*) 20 (*b*) 38
(*c*) 56 (*d*) 72

15. 5, 6, 11, 22, 42, 88, 176
(*a*) 5 (*b*) 42
(*c*) 176 (*d*) 11

16. 905, 180, 175, 35, 30, 6, 1
(*a*) 6 (*b*) 1
(*c*) 175 (*d*) 905

17. 5040, 840, 160, 42, 14, 7
(*a*) 7 (*b*) 160
(*c*) 14 (*d*) 840

18. 3, 32, 363, 3993, 43923
(*a*) 363 (*b*) 3
(*c*) 32 (*d*) 43923

19. 3, 18, 38, 78, 123, 178, 243
(*a*) 78 (*b*) 3
(*c*) 123 (*d*) 18

20. 0, 1, 2, 2, 4, 4, 6, 8, 8, 10
(*a*) 6 (*b*) 0
(*c*) 1 (*d*) 10

21. 5, 12, 16, 24, 27
(*a*) 12 (*b*) 16
(*c*) 24 (*d*) 27

22. 27, 36, 45, 60, 71, 99
(*a*) 27 (*b*) 45
(*c*) 60 (*d*) 71

23. 81, 64, 49, 35, 25, 16
(*a*) 64 (*b*) 35
(*c*) 25 (*d*) 16

24. 625, 125, 25, 5, 0
(*a*) 0 (*b*) 125
(*c*) 5 (*d*) 625

25. 25, 19, 17, 13, 11, 7
(*a*) 25 (*b*) 17
(*c*) 13 (*d*) 7

EXPLANATORY ANSWERS

1. (*c*) : The numbers in the series are multiplied by 5 to get the next number.
∴ 125 should be in place of 120.

2. (*d*) : Two numbers form a pair. The first number increases by 7 for the next pair and the second number is the double of first number.

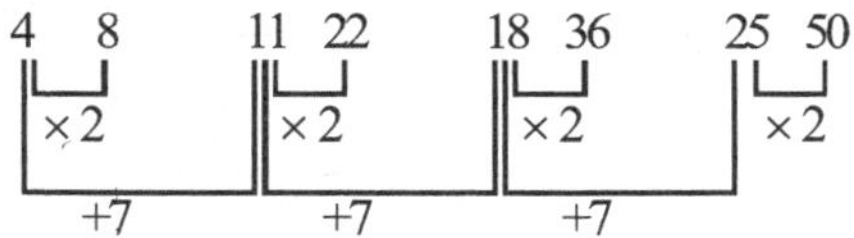

∴ 25 should be in place of 24.

3. (*c*) : There are two alternate series and in each series, the numbers are multiplied by 6 to get the next number.

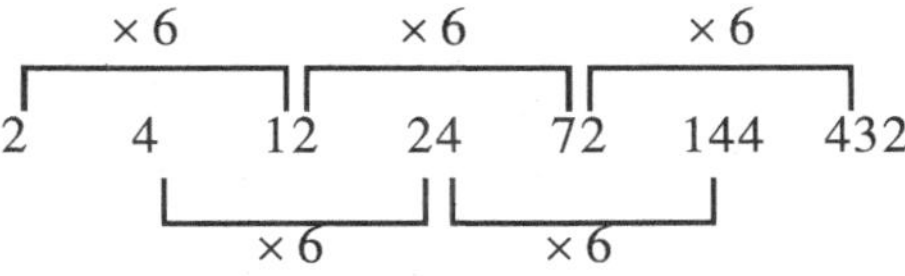

∴ 144 should be in place of 142.

4. (*b*) : There are three alternate series and in each series, the numbers are multiplied by 2 to get the next number.

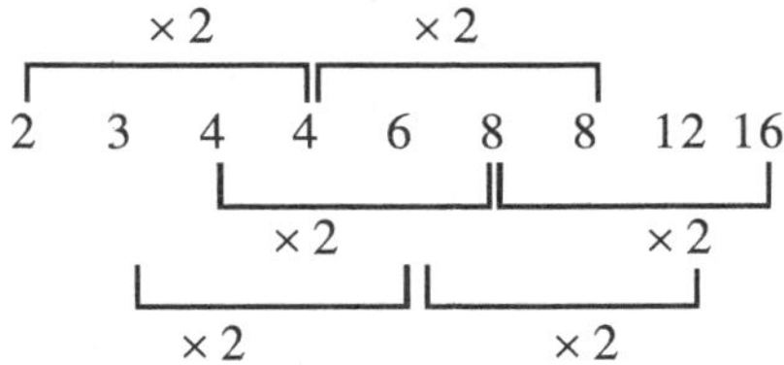

Series I : 2, 4, 8
Series II : 3, 6, 12
Series III : 4, 8, 16
∴ 8 should be in place of 9.

5. (*d*) : The difference between the consecutive numbers in the series decreases by 1 at each step.

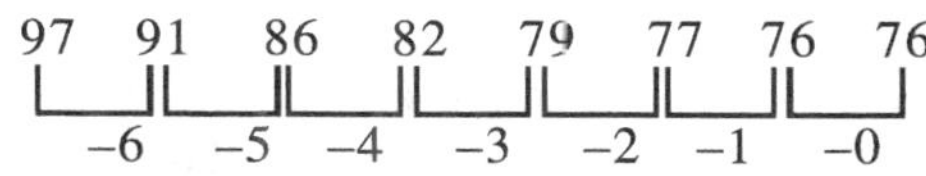

∴ 82 should be in place of 83.

6. (*c*) : There are two alternate series :

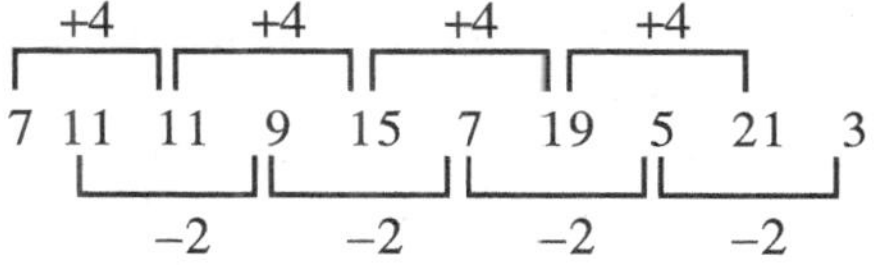

Series I : 7, 11, 15, 19, 23 (addition of 4)
Series II : 11, 9, 7, 5, 3 (subtraction of 2)
∴ 3 should be in place of 1.

7. (*b*) : There are two alternate series and in each series, the numbers are multiplied by 4 to get the next number.

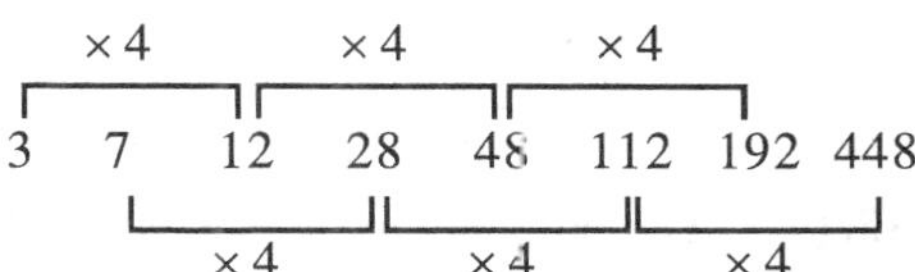

∴ 112 should be in place of 118.

8. (*d*) : The numbers in this series are multiplied by 10 and 11 alternately is, *i.e.*, × 10, × 11.

10 100 1100 11000 121000 1210000
× 10 × 11 × 10 × 11 × 10

∴ 121000 should be in place of 111000.

9. (*a*) : The numbers in this series are divided by 4 to get the next number.

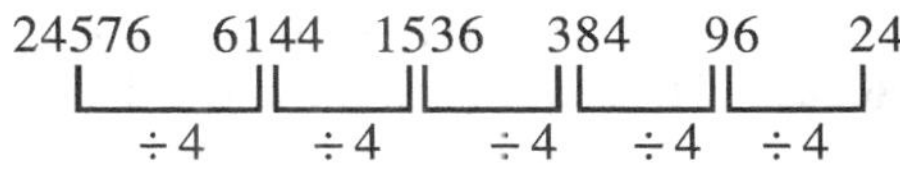

∴ 384 should be in place of 386.

10. (*c*) : The series comprises of prime numbers in increasing order. Only 15 is an exception.

11. (*a*) : The difference between two consecutive numbers is decreasing by 1 at each step.

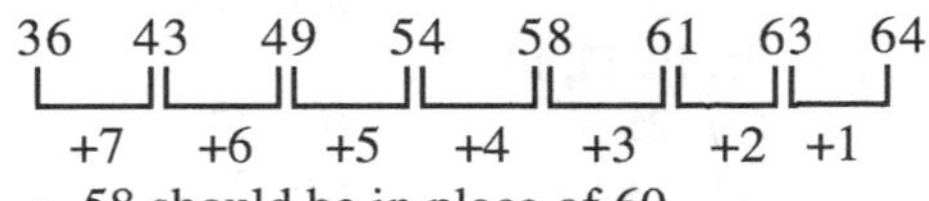

∴ 58 should be in place of 60.

12. (*d*) : The sequence followed in this series is :

$3 \times 3 + 1 = 10$
$10 \times 4 + 1 = 41$
$41 \times 5 + 1 = 206$
$206 \times 6 + 1 = 1237$; and
$1237 \times 7 + 1 = 8660$

∴ 1237 should be in place of 1236.

13. (*a*) : The numbers in the series are 1 plus the squares of numbers in natural order starting from 4.

17	26	37	50	65	82	101
↓	↓	↓	↓	↓	↓	↓
$4^2 + 1$	$5^2 + 1$	$6^2 + 1$	$7^2 + 1$	$8^2 + 1$	$9^2 + 1$	$10^2 + 1$

∴ 26 should be in place of 25.

14. (*b*) : The sequence followed in this series is :

$3 \times 4 = 12$
$4 \times 5 = 20$
$5 \times 6 = 30$
$6 \times 7 = 42$
$7 \times 8 = 56$
$8 \times 9 = 72$

∴ 30 should be in place of 38.

15. (*b*) : The numbers in the series are the sum of all the numbers preceding them.

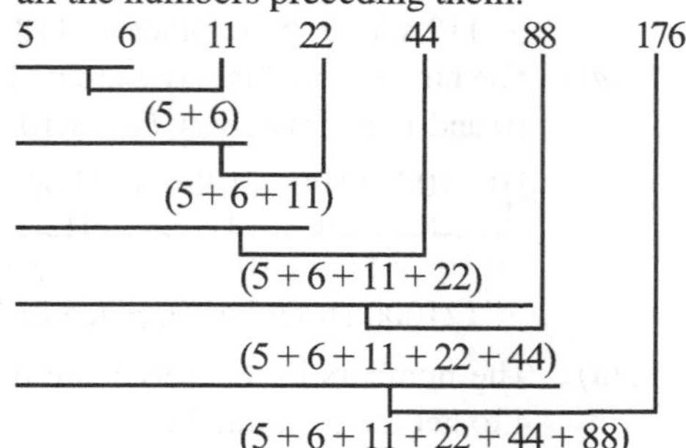

∴ 44 should be in place of 42.

16. (*d*) : The sequence followed in the series is ÷ 5, – 5 which is repeated.

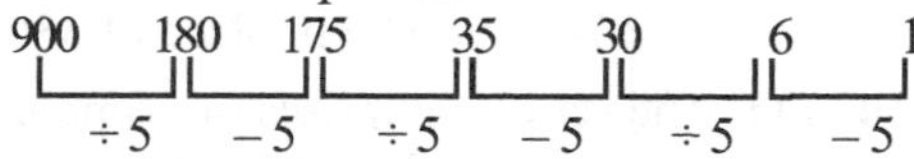

∴ 900 should be in place of 905.

17. (*b*) : The numbers in the series are divided by numbers in reverse order starting from 6 to get the next number.

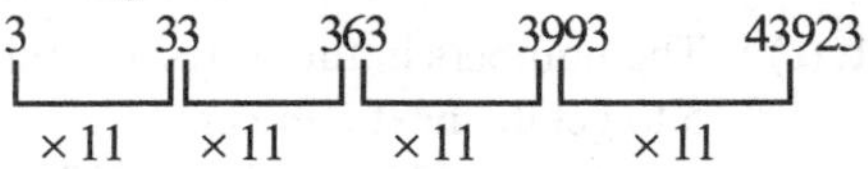

∴ 168 should be in place of 160.

18. (*c*) : The numbers in this series are multiplied by 11 to get the next number.

3	33	363	3993	43923
× 11	× 11	× 11	× 11	

∴ 33 should be in place of 32.

19. (*b*) : 3 is the only prime number in the series.

20. (*d*) : There are two alternate series :

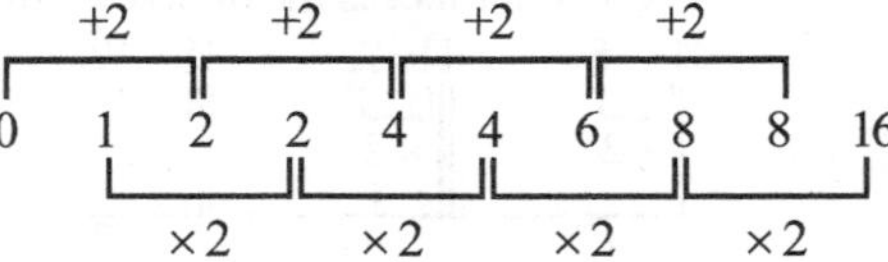

Series I : 0, 2, 4, 6, 8, (addition of 2)
Series II : 1, 2, 4, 8, 16 (multiplication by 2)

∴ 16 should be in place of 10.

21. (*c*) : The sequence in the series is +7, +4 which is repeated, *i.e.*,

5	12	16	23	27
+7	+4	+7	+4	

∴ 23 should be in place of 24.

22. (*d*) : All other numbers are divisible by 3.

23. (*b*) : The sequence is the square of the number in decreasing order starting from 9, *i.e.*,

$9^2 = 9 \times 9 = 81$
$8^2 = 8 \times 8 = 64$
$7^2 = 7 \times 7 = 49$
$6^2 = 6 \times 6 = 36$
$5^2 = 5 \times 5 = 25$
$4^2 = 4 \times 4 = 16$

∴ 36 should be in place of 35.

24. (*a*) : The number in the series are divided by 5 to get the next number

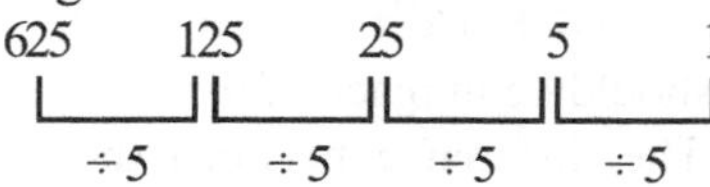

∴ 1 should be in place of 0 digit.

25. (*a*) : Other numbers are prime numbers.

6. WORD ANALOGY

In Analogy Tests, the relationship between two given words is established and then applied to the other words. The type of relationship may vary, so while attempting such questions the first step is to identify the type of relationship, which can be any one of the following.

EXERCISE

Directions : *In the questions given below one term is missing. Based on the relationship of the two given words find the missing term from the given options.*

1. HUNGER : FOOD : : THIRST : ?
(*a*) Water (*b*) Drink
(*c*) Tea (*d*) Coffee

2. HUNTER : GUN : : WRITER : ?
(*a*) Book (*b*) Pen
(*c*) Poem (*d*) Page

3. WOOL : SHEEP : : SILK : ?
(*a*) Saree (*b*) String
(*c*) Silkworm (*d*) Moth

4. FOOD : STOMACH : : FUEL : ?
(*a*) Engine (*b*) Automobile
(*c*) Rail (*d*) Aeroplane

5. WATER : SAND : : OCEAN : ?
(*a*) Island (*b*) River
(*c*) Desert (*d*) Waves

6. ADULT : BABY : : FLOWER : ?
(*a*) Seed (*b*) Bud
(*c*) Fruit (*d*) Butterfly

7. WRITER : READER : : PRODUCER : ?
(*a*) Creator (*b*) Contractor
(*c*) Creature (*d*) Consumer

8. ENTRANCE : EXIT : : LOYALTY : ?
(*a*) Treachery (*b*) Patriotism
(*c*) Fidelity (*d*) Reward

9. MOTHER : MATERNAL : : FATHER : ?
(*a*) Eternal (*b*) Detrimental
(*c*) Paternal (*d*) Formidable

10. PEARL : NECKLACE : : FLOWER : ?
(*a*) Plant (*b*) Garden
(*c*) Petal (*d*) Bouquet

11. ALPHABET : WORD : : WORD : ?
(*a*) Sound (*b*) Music
(*c*) Sentence (*d*) Dictionary

12. LIFE : DEATH : : HOPE : ?
(*a*) Cry (*b*) Pain
(*c*) Despair (*d*) Sad

13. GOOD : BAD : : VIRTUE : ?
(*a*) Blame (*b*) Sin
(*c*) Despair (*d*) Vice

14. BIRD : FLY : : SNAKE : ?
(*a*) Timid (*b*) Clatter
(*c*) Crawl (*d*) Hole

15. CAT : MOUSE : : BIRD : ?
(*a*) Cage (*b*) Trap
(*c*) Eagle (*d*) Worm

16. STATE : EXILE
(*a*) Police : Arrest
(*b*) Judge : Convict
(*c*) Constitution : Amendment
(*d*) Church : Excommunicate

17. CAPRICIOUSNESS : RELIABILITY
(*a*) Extemporaneous : Predictability
(*b*) Unreliable : Inhuman
(*c*) Tenacious : Practicality
(*d*) Arbitrary : Whimsical

18. LOATH : COERCION
(*a*) Detest : Caressing
(*b*) Irritate : Caressing
(*c*) Irate : Antagonism
(*d*) Reluctant : Persuasion

19. SCALES : FISH
(*a*) Lady : Dress (*b*) Tree : Leaves
(*c*) Bird : Feather (*d*) Skin : Man

20. TREE : SAPLING
(*a*) Hut : Mansion
(*b*) Giant : Dwarf
(*c*) Horse : Foal
(*d*) Ant : Elephant

21. CHALK : BLACKBOARD
(*a*) Door : Handle
(*b*) Table : Chair
(*c*) Ink : Paper
(*d*) Type : Paint

22. PRIMEVAL : MEDIEVAL
(*a*) Dinosaur : Dragon
(*b*) Gorilla : Soldier
(*c*) Evolution : Revelation
(*d*) Thorn : Rose

23. TRILOGY : NOVEL
(*a*) Rice : Husk
(*b*) Milk : Cream
(*c*) Fabric : Weaving
(*d*) Serial : Episode

24. PEDANT : ERUDITION
(*a*) Prude : Modesty
(*b*) Blunt : Politician
(*c*) Diplomats : Tactless
(*d*) Enemy : Friendly

25. FURY : IRE
(*a*) Convulsion : Spasm
(*b*) Amusement : Happiness
(*c*) Joke : Laugh
(*d*) Dispassion : Emotion

26. BaBy : TaTa : : LiLy : ?
(*a*) PooL (*b*) ROse
(*c*) HaNd (*d*) DoWN

27. BCDA : STUR : : KLMJ : ?
(*a*) VWXU (*b*) EFHG
(*c*) SRTU (*d*) QSRP

28. AEI : LPT : : CGK : ?
(*a*) OSV (*b*) RUY
(*c*) TXC (*d*) FJN

29. RUX : TRP : : BEH : ?
(*a*) SQN (*b*) QON
(*c*) QOM (*d*) QNL

30. CART : ART : : FOUR : ?
(*a*) RUN (*b*) TWO
(*c*) QUE (*d*) OUR

31. FIK : JGO : : DFR : ?
(*a*) BIO (*b*) HDV
(*c*) GCU (*d*) FLP

32. LJH : KKI : : CIA : ?
(*a*) BJB (*b*) DHB
(*c*) BJC (*d*) BBJ

33. ACE : HIL : : MOQ : ?
(*a*) SVW (*b*) TUX
(*c*) RTW (*d*) WUS

34. BCDE : WVUT : : QRST : ?
(*a*) EFHG (*b*) JIHG
(*c*) POML (*d*) GEDC

35. PNLJ : IGEC : : USQO : ?
(*a*) HJLN (*b*) LNJH
(*c*) NLJH (*d*) JHNL

36. DIMO : DMIO : : JUVR : ?
(*a*) JVRU (*b*) JRVU
(*c*) JVUR (*d*) JUVR

EXPLANATORY ANSWERS

1. *(a)* : Hunger is satiated by food, thirst by water.

2. *(b)* : Weapon of a hunter is a gun, weapon of a writer is a pen.

3. *(c)* : Wool is obtained from sheep, silk is obtained from silkworm.

4. *(a)* : Food is consumed in stomach, fuel is consumed in engine.

5. *(c)* : The related words are near opposites.

6. *(b)* : The youngone of an adult is a baby and that of a flower is a bud.

7. *(d)* : A writer aims to please the readers by his writings, a producer aims to please the consumers by his products.

8. *(a)* : The related words are opposites.

9. *(c)* : Relations on the mother's side are maternal and on the father's side paternal.

10. ***(d)*** **:** Many pearls make a necklace, many flowers make a bouquet.

11. ***(c)*** **:** More than one alphabet make a word, more than one word make a sentence.

12. ***(c)*** **:** The related words are opposites.

13. ***(d)*** **:** The related words are opposites.

14. ***(c)*** **:** Birds fly, snakes crawl.

15. ***(d)*** **:** Cat chases the mouse, bird chases the worm.

16. ***(d)*** **:** Punishment of leaving the State is exile, punishment of leaving the Church is excommunication.

17. ***(c)*** **:** The related words are antonyms.

18. ***(d)*** **:** Loathing is the result of constant coersion, reluctance is the result of constant persuasion.

19. ***(d)*** **:** Covering of the fish is scales, covering of man is skin.

20. ***(c)*** **:** Young tree is a sapling, young horse is a foal.

21. ***(c)*** **:** Chalk is used to write on blackboard, ink is used to write on paper.

22. ***(a)*** **:** The related words represent almost the same time period and answer option represents almost the same sized creatures.

23. ***(d)*** **:** Trilogy is section of a novel, episode is a section of a serial.

24. ***(a)*** **:** The related words are synonyms.

25. ***(b)*** **:** Fury causes ire, amusement causes happiness.

26. ***(c)*** **:** In each group the alternate letters are capitals.

27. ***(a)*** **:** In each group the first three letters are consecutive and they follow the fourth letter.

ABCD : RSTU : : JKLM : UVWX

28. ***(d)*** **:** In each group the letters jump three letters between them, *i.e.,* they are moving to the fourth letter.

AEI : LPT :: CGK : FJN

+4 +4   +4 +4   +4 +4   +4 +4

29. ***(c)*** **:** The letters in first set are jumping two letters, *i.e.,* moving three steps forward and in the second they are jumping one letter, *i.e.* moving two steps backward.

RUX : TRP :: BEH : QOM

+3 +3   –2 –2   +3+3   –2 –2

30. ***(d)*** **:** The first set of letters drop the first letter to get the second set.

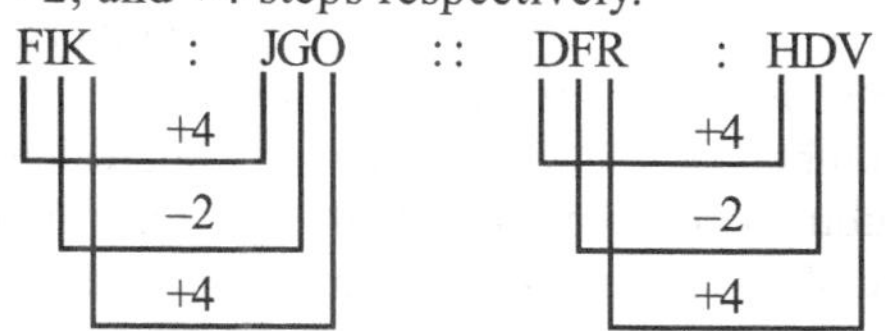

31. ***(b)*** **:** The three letters in first set are moved +4, –2, and +4 steps respectively.

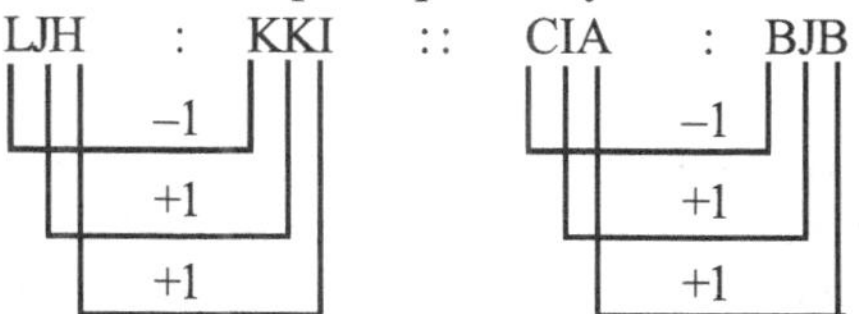

32. ***(a)*** **:** The letters in the first set are moved –1, +1 and +1 steps respectively.

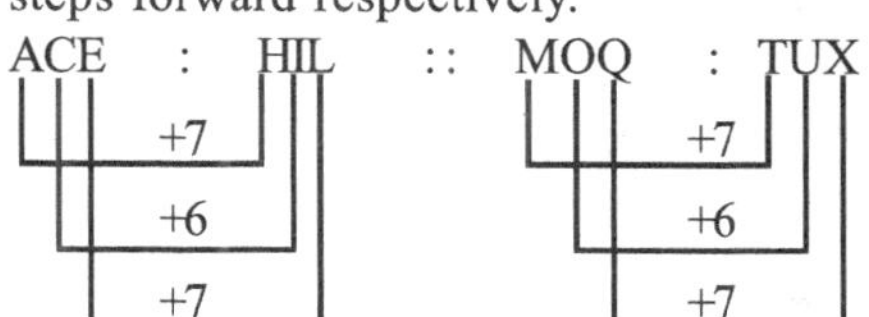

33. ***(b)*** **:** The three letters are moved +7, +6 and +7 steps forward respectively.

ACE : HIL :: MOQ : TUX

+7, +6, +7   +7, +6, +7

34. ***(b)*** **:** The consecutive letters in the first set are in natural order and in the second set, they are in reverse order.

BCDE : WVUT :: QRST : JIHG

35. ***(c)*** **:** The letters are moved seven steps backwards.

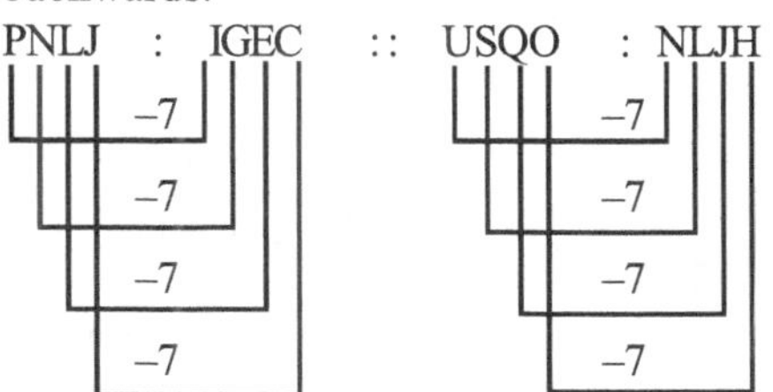

36. ***(c)*** **:** Only the middle letters are reversed to obtain the second set of letters.

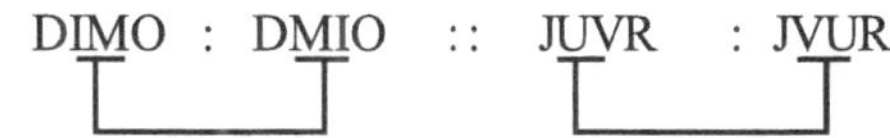

7. Number Analogy

In number analogy also, the relationship between the given numbers is detected and then applied to the second part to find the missing numbers. This relationship between the numbers can be based on any of the following patterns : *(i)* numbers can be odd/even/prime numbers; *(ii)* numbers can be multiples of one number; *(iii)* numbers can be squares/cubes of different numbers; *(iv)* some numbers can be added to/ subtracted from/multiplied to/divided into the first number to get the second number; *(v)* the second number can be the sum/product/difference of the digits of first number; and *(vi)* combinations of any mathematical calculations given above can apply to the relationship between the two given numbers.

EXERCISE

Directions : *In the following questions, select the number from the given options which follows the same relationship as shared between the first two numbers.*

1. 1 : 11 : : 2 : ?
(*a*) 20 (*b*) 22
(*c*) 24 (*d*) 44

2. $\frac{1}{7} : \frac{1}{14} :: \frac{1}{9} : ?$
(*a*) $\frac{1}{88}$ (*b*) $\frac{1}{80}$
(*c*) $\frac{1}{81}$ (*d*) $\frac{1}{18}$

3. 0.16 : 0.0016 : : 1.02 : ?
(*a*) 10.20 (*b*) 0.102
(*c*) 0.0102 (*d*) 1.020

4. 663 : 884 : : 221 : ?
(*a*) 332 (*b*) 554
(*c*) 773 (*d*) 442

5. 16 : 0.16 : : ?
(*a*) 2 : 0.02 (*b*) 7 : 0.007
(*c*) 1.3 : 0.13 (*d*) 0.01 : 0.001

6. $3 : \frac{1}{3} :: ?$
(*a*) 6 : 12 (*b*) 5 : 2/15
(*c*) 8 : 1/8 (*d*) 9 : 27

7. 65 : 13 : : 180 : ?
(*a*) 93 (*b*) 36
(*c*) 133 (*d*) 102

8. 125 : 27 : : 343 : ?
(*a*) 729 (*b*) 64
(*c*) 216 (*d*) 512

9. 357 : 73 : : ?
(*a*) 429 : 94 (*b*) 201 : 21
(*c*) 138 : 38 (*d*) 93 : 39

10. 731 : 902 : : 655 : ?
(*a*) 646 (*b*) 800
(*c*) 793 (*d*) 556

11. 162 : 9 : : 310 : ?
(*a*) 33 (*b*) 27
(*c*) 16 (*d*) 4

12. 13 : 17 : : 15 : ?
(*a*) 19 (*b*) 11
(*c*) 21 (*d*) 16

13. 225 : 15 : : 256 : ?
(*a*) 26 (*b*) 16
(*c*) 20 (*d*) 28

14. 46 : 48 : : 54 : ?
(*a*) 59 (*b*) 40
(*c*) 67 (*d*) 62

15. 33 : 36 : : 21 : ?
(*a*) 9 (*b*) 18
(*c*) 25 (*d*) 32

16. 123 : 149 : : 201 : ?
(*a*) 202 (*b*) 404
(*c*) 401 (*d*) 227

17. 7 : 105 : : 5 : ?
(*a*) 97 (*b*) 83
(*c*) 75 (*d*) 61

18. 11 : 101 : : 73 : ?
(*a*) 153 (*b*) 330
(*c*) 543 (*d*) 703

19. 4 : 32 : : 8 : ?
(*a*) 34 (*b*) 68
(*c*) 92 (*d*) 128

20. 94 : 26 : : 62 : ?
(*a*) 16 (*b*) 22
(*c*) 39 (*d*) 48

EXPLANATORY ANSWERS

1. *(b)* : The first number is repeated to obtain the second number.

2. *(d)* : The first fraction is multiplied by half to obtain the second fraction.

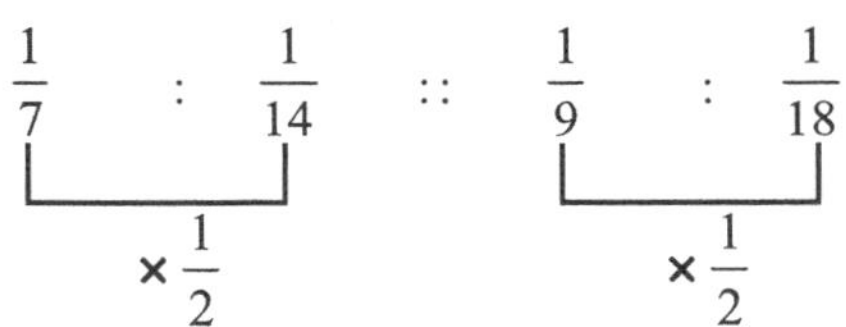

3. *(c)* : The decimals are divided by 100.

4. *(d)* : The digits at tens and hundreds place is same but the digit at the units place is half the other identical digits.

66 3 : 88 4 : : 22 1 : 44 2

5. *(a)* : Of the two related numbers, the second number is the result of first number divided by 100.

6. *(c)* : Of the two related numbers, the second number is the part fraction of the first number, *i.e.* 3 is related to one-third $\left(\frac{1}{3}\right)$. Similarly, 8 will be related to one-eighth $\left(\frac{1}{8}\right)$.

7. *(b)* : The first number is divided by 5 to get the second number.

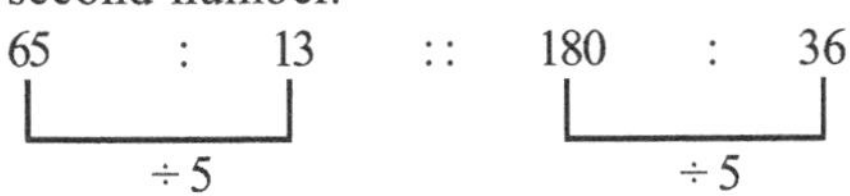

8. *(a)* : The numbers are cubes of different odd numbers.

125 : 27 : : 343 : 729
↓ ↓ ↓ ↓
5^3 3^3 7^3 9^3

9. *(a)* : The central digit of the first number is left out and the corner digits written in reverse order to get the second number.

357 : 73 : : 429 : 94

10. *(a)* : The sum of the digits of both the numbers is same.

$731 : 902 \rightarrow 7 + 3 + 1$
$= 9 + 0 + 2$ *i.e.* $11 = 11$
$655 : 646 \rightarrow 6 + 5 + 5$
$= 6 + 4 + 6$ *i.e.* $16 = 16$

11. *(d)* : The sum of the digits of the first number is the second number.

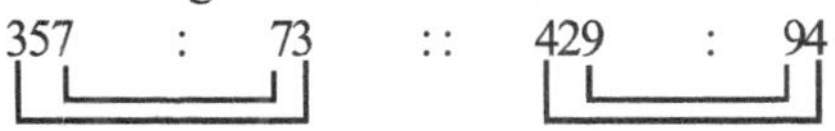

12. *(a)* : First number plus 4 gives the second number.

13 : 17 : : 15 : 19
+4 +4

13. *(b)* : The root of first number is the second number.

225 : 15 : : 256 : 16
$\sqrt{225}$ $\sqrt{256}$

14. *(b)* : The product of the digits of first number is multiplied by 2 to get the second number.

15. *(a)* : The square of the sum of the digits of the first number is the second number.

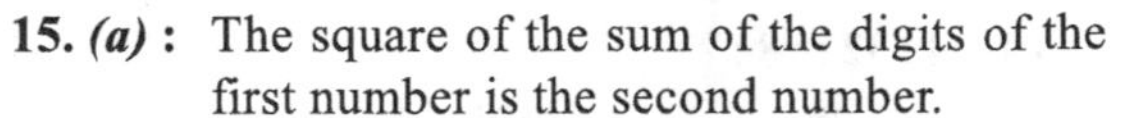

33 : 36 :: 21 : 9

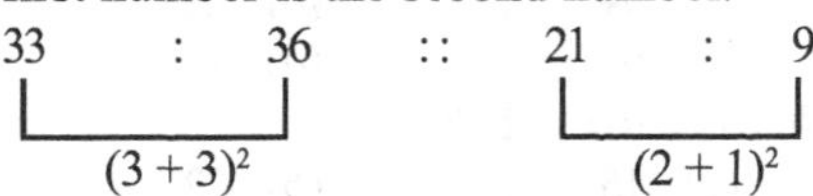

$(3+3)^2$ $(2+1)^2$

16. *(c)* : Each digit of the first number are squared to get the digits of the second number.

123 : 149 :: 201 : 401

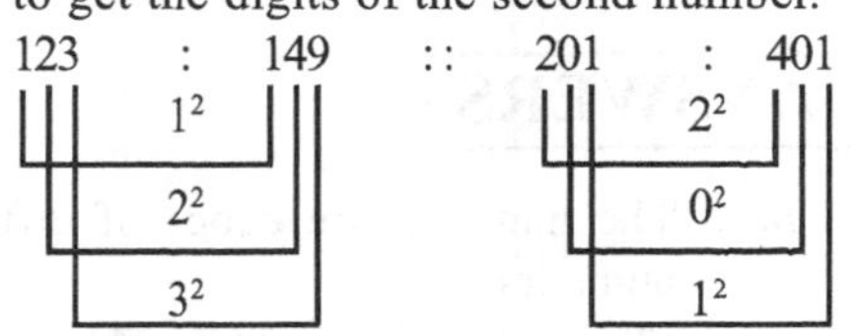

1^2 2^2 3^2 2^2 0^2 1^2

17. *(c)* : The first number is multiplied by 15 to get the second number.

7 : 105 :: 5 : 75

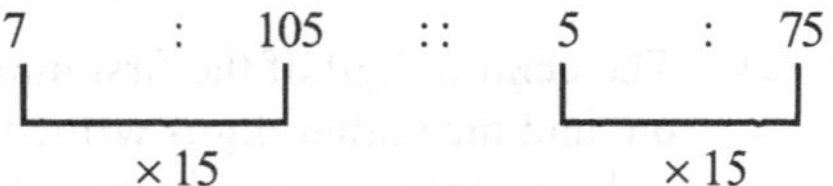

$\times 15$ $\times 15$

18. *(d)* : Zero is inserted in between the digits of the first number to get the second number.

11 : 1$\underline{0}$1 :: 73 : 7$\underline{0}$3

19. *(d)* : Double the first number multiplied by the number itself gives the second number.

4 : 32 :: 8 : 128

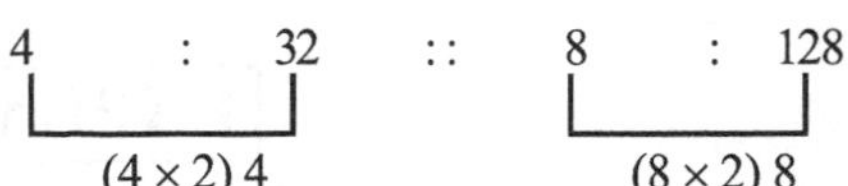

$(4 \times 2)\,4$ $(8 \times 2)\,8$

20. *(a)* : The sum of the digits of the first number multiplied by two gives the second number.

94 : 26 :: 62 : 16

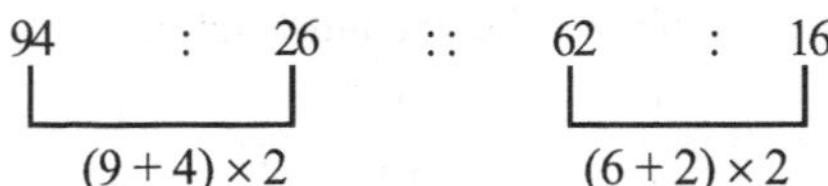

$(9+4) \times 2$ $(6+2) \times 2$

8. Odd One Out

In this type of classification, four words are given out of which three are almost same in matter or meaning and only one word is different from the common three. One has to find out the word which is different from the rest.

EXERCISE

Directions : *In each of the following questions, three words are alike in some manner. Spot the odd one out.*

1. (*a*) Green (*b*) Red (*c*) Colour (*d*) Orange

2. (*a*) Stable (*b*) Hole (*c*) Canoe (*d*) Sty

3. (*a*) Nose (*b*) Eyes (*c*) Skin (*d*) Teeth

4. (*a*) Venus (*b*) Moon (*c*) Pluto (*d*) Mars

5. (*a*) Happy (*b*) Gloomy (*c*) Lively (*d*) Cheerful

Directions : *Three of the following four in each question are alike in a certain way and so form a group. Select the group of letters that does not belong to that group.*

6. (*a*) ACE (*b*) LOR (*c*) GIK (*d*) VXZ

7. (*a*) TSR (*b*) LKJ (*c*) PQO (*d*) HGF

8. (*a*) EF LM (*b*) KJ SR (*c*) XW HG (*d*) ED YX

9. (*a*) JOPK (*b*) BOPC (*c*) QOPR (*d*) TOPS

10. (*a*) DfH (*b*) MoQ (*c*) UwY (*d*) lnO

Directions : *In each of the following questions, there are four options. Three numbers, in these options, are alike in certain manner. Only one number does not fit in. Choose the one which is different from the rest.*

11. (*a*) 1948 (*b*) 2401 (*c*) 966 (*d*) 1449

12. (*a*) 182 (*b*) 169 (*c*) 130 (*d*) 158

13. (*a*) 129 (*b*) 130 (*c*) 131 (*d*) 132

14. (*a*) 3215 (*b*) 9309 (*c*) 4721 (*d*) 2850

15. (*a*) 1776 (*b*) 2364 (*c*) 1976 (*d*) 3776

Directions : *In the following questions select the pair which is different from the other three.*

16. (*a*) Chair - Furniture
(*b*) Shirt - Garment
(*c*) Necklace - Jewellery
(*d*) Bogie - Engine

17. (*a*) Crayon - Paper
(*b*) Pencil - Lead
(*c*) Pen - Ink
(*d*) Brush - Paint

18. (*a*) War - Peace
(*b*) Real - Natural
(*c*) Premiere - First
(*d*) Wrath - Anger

19. (*a*) Finger - Thimble
(*b*) Head - Cap
(*c*) Waist - Tiara
(*d*) Foot - Shoe

20. (*a*) Day - Night
(*b*) Clever - Foolish
(*c*) Clear - Blurred
(*d*) Arrive - Come

Directions : *In the following questions, which of the following pair of letters is different from the other three?*

21. (*a*) FGH - HIJ (*b*) PQR - RST (*c*) MNO - OPQ (*d*) CDE - DEF

22. (*a*) JuM - jUm (*b*) iLo - Ilo (*c*) PSa - psA (*d*) ZeX - zEx

23. (*a*) NQT - JMP (*b*) CFI - RUX (*c*) ADG - FGH (*d*) SVY - ORU

24. (*a*) DXD - XDX (*b*) KUK - UKU (*c*) FHF - EHE (*d*) RSR - SRS

25. (*a*) AYT - BZU (*b*) FNG - EMF (*c*) RWO - QVN (*d*) HJD - GIC

Directions : *Which of the following pair of numbers is different from the other three pairs?*

26. (*a*) 28, 4 (*b*) 63, 7 (*c*) 56, 8 (*d*) 35, 5

27. (*a*) 3, 11 (*b*) 8, 16 (*c*) 5, 13 (*d*) 14, 24

28. (*a*) 13, 156 (*b*) 12, 144 (*c*) 15, 180 (*d*) 16, 176

29. (*a*) 32, 13 (*b*) 46, 20 (*c*) 51, 24 (*d*) 72, 45

30. (*a*) 5, 25 (*b*) 9, 81 (*c*) 4, 64 (*d*) 6, 36

31. (*a*) 91, 10 (*b*) 57, 12 (*c*) 69, 15 (*d*) 72, 13

32. (*a*) 20, 10 (*b*) 45, 27 (*c*) 15, 12 (*d*) 30, 18

33. (*a*) 7, 3 (*b*) 13, 9 (*c*) 11, 7 (*d*) 17, 8

34. (*a*) 10, 20 (*b*) 40, 50 (*c*) 30, 40 (*d*) 50, 60

35. (*a*) 16, 26 (*b*) 3, 4 (*c*) 26, 24 (*d*) 27, 25

EXPLANATORY ANSWERS

1. (*c*) : All others are types of colour.

2. (*c*) : Canoe is a boat. Others are resting places of birds/animals.

3. (*d*) : All others are sense organs.

4. (*b*) : All others are planets.

5. (*b*) : All others are expressions of joy.

6. (*b*) : The sequence in each group is +2. Only option (*b*) has sequence in +3, *i.e.,*

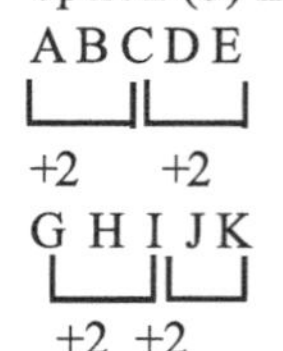

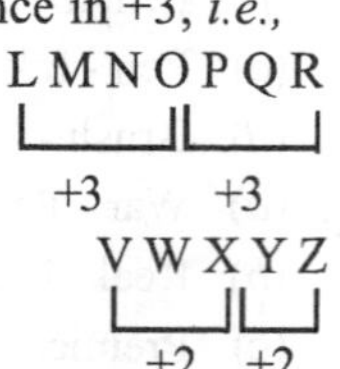

7. (*c*) : The sequence of alphabet in each group is in reverse order. Only option (*c*) has sequence in disturbed order.

8. (*a*) : Two consecutive alphabet in each group are in reverse sequence (–1), *i.e.,*

KJ SR; XW HG; ED YX
–1 –1 –1 –1 –1 –1

Only in option (*a*) the sequence is in natural order (+1), *i.e.,*

9. (*d*) : In each group, letters 'OP' are common. The two corner alphabet are in natural order (+1); *i.e.,*

JOPK ; BOPC ; QOPR
+1 +1 +1

Only in option (*d*) they are in reverse order (–1); *i.e.,*

TOPS
–1

10. (*d*) : In other groups, only the alphabet in the centre is of lower case. In this option letter 'L' on the left is also in lower case.

11. (*a*) : Other numbers are divisible by 7.

12. (*d*) : Other numbers are multiples of 13.

13. (*c*) : 131 is a prime number.

14. (*b*) : In other numbers, no digit is repeated.

15. (*b*) : In other numbers, the last two digits are same.

16. (*d*) : Bogie is a part of train which is a type of conveyance. Chair, Shirt and Necklace are types of furniture, garment and jewellery respectively.

17. ***(a)*** **:** The medium used for writing with pencil is lead, with pen it is ink and with brush, it is paint. With crayon it should be wax.

18. ***(a)*** **:** The pair of words are opposite. Other pairs are synonyms.

19. ***(c)*** **:** Tiara is worn on the head.

20. ***(d)*** **:** Other words are opposite to each other.

21. ***(d)*** **:** In all other groups, the letters are in natural series and the last letter of first part is the first letter of the second part.

22. ***(b)*** **:** In all other groups, only the vowel is in lower case in the first part and in second part the case is reversed.

23. ***(c)*** **:** In all other groups, the letters jump two letters in between them.

24. ***(c)*** **:** In all other groups, the single letter in first part is repeated in the second and vice versa.

25. ***(a)*** **:** In all other groups, the letters in the first part are one step forward than the corresponding letters in the second part.

26. ***(b)*** **:** In all other pairs 7 times the second number is the first number. In this option 9 times 7 is the first number.

27. ***(d)*** **:** In all other groups, the difference between the two numbers is 8.

28. ***(d)*** **:** In other groups 12 times, the first number is the second number. In this option 11 times the first number is the second number.

29. ***(a)*** **:** 13 is a prime number.

30. ***(c)*** **:** In all other pairs, the second number is a perfect square of the first.

31. ***(d)*** **:** In all other pairs, the second number is the sum of the digits of the first number.

32. ***(a)*** **:** In all other pairs, the numbers are divisible by 3.

33. ***(d)*** **:** In other groups, the difference between the numbers is 4.

34. ***(a)*** **:** In this option, the second number is double the first number. In other groups the difference between the two numbers is 10.

35. ***(a)*** **:** In other groups, the first digits of the two numbers are same (consider 3 and 4 as 03 and 04).

9. Coding and Decoding

Coding is a secretive language which is used to change the representation of the actual term/word/value. This coded language can be framed by *(i)* moving the letters one or more steps forward or backward; *(ii)* substituting numbers for letters and vice–versa; *(iii)* writing the letters of the given word in reverse order in part or in whole; and *(iv)* replacing the letters in their natural series by the same positioned letters in their reverse series.

There is variety in ways of coding. Coding language is not only for words and numbers but also for hiding a group of words, statements or even sentences. This form of coding pattern may appear to be confusing but after solving only a few questions it is very easy to understand. Questions based on this coding pattern require no moving of steps or straining efforts of calculations, but only quick tallying or comparing ability. The codes can be letters or numbers.

EXERCISE

Directions : *In the following questions select the right option which indicates the correct code for the word or letter given in the question.*

1. If MUSK is coded as 146816, then ZERO will be coded as :
   (*a*) 113811 (*b*) 122912
   (*c*) 15915 (*d*) 2651815
2. If BAD is coded as 7, HIS as 9, LOW will be coded as :
   (*a*) 50 (*b*) 8
   (*c*) 23 (*d*) 5
3. In a certain code LIBERATE is written as 56403170, TRIBAL will be written in the same code as :
   (*a*) 734615 (*b*) 736415
   (*c*) 136475 (*d*) 034615
4. In certain military code, SYSTEM is written as SYSMET, and NEARER as AENRER, what will be the code for FRACTION?
   (*a*) CRAFNOIT (*b*) FRCAITNO
   (*c*) CARFNOIT (*d*) FRACNOIT
5. If CRUDE is written as BSTED, then MOIST will be coded as :
   (*a*) NNJRU (*b*) LNHRS
   (*c*) NPJTU (*d*) LPHTS
6. In a certain code ALPACA is written as ACAPLA. How will ANIMAL be written in that code?
   (*a*) LAMINA (*b*) ALAMIN
   (*c*) LAMNIA (*d*) AAMLIN
7. In a certain code FINGER is written as DGLECP. What will be the code for KIDNEY?
   (*a*) IGBLCW (*b*) IGCLBW
   (*c*) IBCGLE (*d*) IGBKCV
8. In a certain code QUESTION is written as NXBVQLLQ. How will REPLY be coded?
   (*a*) YHMOV (*b*) OBMVI
   (*c*) VHSOB (*d*) OHMOV
9. If in a certain code SKEW is coded as PNCY, then what will JXQV will stand for?
   (*a*) MUTS (*b*) MUST
   (*c*) MTSU (*d*) STUM
10. In a certain code LONDON is written as MPOEPO. What will IVOHSZ mean in the same code?
    (*a*) HUNGRY (*b*) HUNDRY
    (*c*) GRUNHY (*d*) HONDUS
11. In a certain code language 8514 is a code for HEAD, 3945 for RIDE and 057 for BEG. What will be the code for GRADE?
    (*a*) 71345 (*b*) 73415
    (*c*) 74135 (*d*) 73145

12. If MOTHERLAND is coded as 9501623748, how will DREAM be coded?

(*a*) 82697 (*b*) 86297
(*c*) 82769 (*d*) 82679

13. If OATH is coded in a certain language as TEYL, then how will WORD be coded?

(*a*) BWRH (*b*) HRWB
(*c*) BSWH (*d*) CSXI

14. If FINANCE is coded as GKQESIL, then how will BANK be coded in the same manner?

(*a*) CBOL (*b*) CDRP
(*c*) CCQO (*d*) CCPN

15. PLANNING is coded in a certain language as UFFHSCSA. How will AUTHORITY be coded in the same language?

(*a*) FOYBTLNND
(*b*) FYOTBNNLT
(*c*) FBOYTLNTN
(*d*) FBOYTNLTN

Directions : *In the following questions study the coded patterns and then select the right option from the given alternatives.*

16. In a certain language, (a) 'go ju mi' stands for 'plenty of money'; (b) pao ju go nei vu' for 'money creates lots of problems'; (c) 'kol vu nei' for 'problems create tension'; and (d) 'sol tun ju haw' for 'still money is needed'. Which of the following words stand for 'money'?

(*a*) nei (*b*) ju
(*c*) haw (*d*) go

17. In a certain language, (a) 'FOR' stands for 'old is gold'; (b) 'ROT' stands for 'gold is pure'; (c) 'ROM' stands for 'gold is costly'. How will 'pure old gold is costly' be written?

(*a*) TFROM (*b*) FOTRM
(*c*) FTORM (*d*) TOMRF

18. In a certain code '415' means 'milk is hot'; '18' means 'hot soup'; and '895' means 'soup is tasty'. What number will indicate the word 'tasty'?

(*a*) 9 (*b*) 8
(*c*) 5 (*d*) 4

19. In a certain code '643' means 'she is beautiful', '593' means 'he is handsome', and '567' means 'handsome meets beautiful'. What number will indicate the word 'meets'?

(*a*) 5 (*b*) 3
(*c*) 7 (*d*) 6

20. In a certain code language, (a) 'dugo hui mul zo' stands for 'work is very hard'; (b) 'hui dugo ba ki' for 'Bingo is very smart'; (c) 'nano mul dugo' for 'cake is hard', and (d) 'mul ki qu' for 'smart and hard'. Which of the following words stand for 'Bingo'?

(*a*) jalu (*b*) dugo
(*c*) ki (*d*) ba

Directions : *Read the given coded information and choose the correct answer from the given options.*

21. If 'water' is called 'blue', 'blue' is called 'red', 'red' is called 'white', 'white' is called 'sky', 'sky' is called 'rain', 'rain' is called 'green', 'green' is called 'air' and 'air' is called 'table', which of the following is the colour of milk?

(*a*) white (*b*) rain
(*c*) sky (*d*) green

22. If 'light' is called 'dark', 'dark' is called 'green', 'green' is called 'blue', 'blue' is called 'red', 'red' is called 'white' and 'white' is called 'yellow', what is the colour of blood?

(*a*) red (*b*) dark
(*c*) white (*d*) yellow

23. If 'sky' is called 'sea', 'sea' is called 'water', 'water' is called 'air', 'air' is called 'cloud' and 'cloud' is called 'river', then what do we drink when thirsty?

(*a*) sky (*b*) air
(*c*) water (*d*) sea

24. If 'yellow' means 'red', 'white' means 'green', 'red' means 'orange', 'blue' means 'white' and 'green' means 'blue', then the colour of sky is :

(*a*) white (*b*) green
(*c*) blue (*d*) yellow

25. If 'land' is called 'sky', 'sky' is called 'air', 'air' is called 'water', 'water' is called 'sand' and 'sand' is called 'solid', where do fishes swim?

(*a*) air (*b*) sky
(*c*) water (*d*) sand

EXPLANATORY ANSWERS

1. (b) : The coded number signifies the position of the alphabet in its reverse order of the alphabetical series (ZYXW...)

M U S K → MUSK
↓ ↓ ↓ ↓
14th 6th 8th 16th → 146816

Similarly,

Z E R O → ZERO
↓ ↓ ↓ ↓
1st 22nd 9th 12th → 122912

2. (d) : The coded number is the sum of number digits signifying the position of the alphabet in the natural order.

B A D
↓ ↓ ↓
2nd 1st 4th *i.e.,* 2 + 1 + 4 = 7

Similarly,

H I S
↓ ↓ ↓
8th 9th 19th *i.e.,* 8 + 9 + 19 = 36
further, 3 + 6 = 9

Also,

L O W
↓ ↓ ↓
12th 15th 23rd *i.e.,* 12 + 15 + 23 = 50
further, 5 + 0 = 0

3. (b) : The letters of the word TRIBAL are picked from LIBERATE. So will be the coded numbers.

L I B E R A T E → given word
5 6 4 0 3 1 7 0 → codes

Similarly,

T R I B A L → word to be coded
7 3 6 4 1 5 → answer codes

4. (c) : The word is divided into two equal parts and the letters of each part are written in reverse order.

SYS TEM SYS MET NEA RER AEN RER

Similarly,

FRAC TION CARF NOIT

5. (d) : The code is formed by moving the letters one step backwards and one step forward alternately.

CRUDE BSTED
−1
+1
−1
+1
−1

Similarly,

MOIST LPHTS
−1
+1
−1
+1
−1

6. (a) : The letters of the word are written backwards.

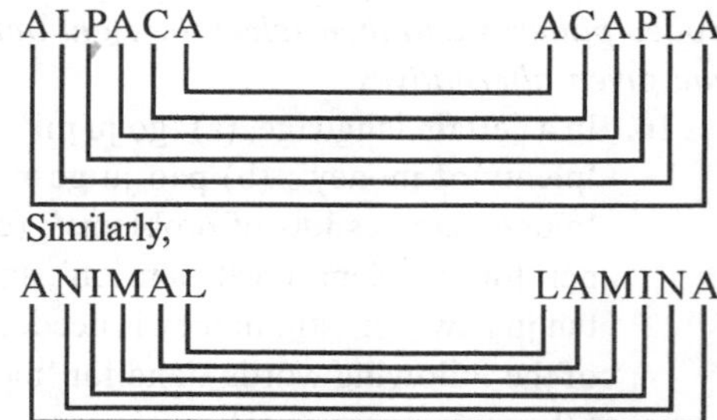

Similarly,

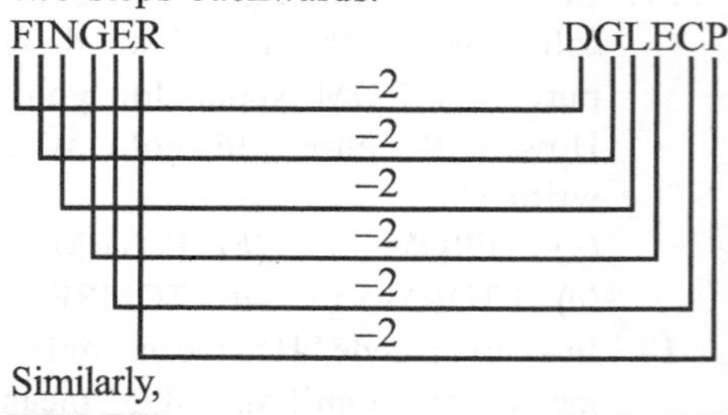

7. (a) : The word is coded by moving the letters two steps backwards.

FINGER DGLECP
−2
−2
−2
−2
−2
−2

Similarly,

KIDNEY IGBLCW
−2
−2
−2
−2
−2
−2

8. *(d)* : The letters of the word are coded by moving three steps backward and three steps forward alternately.

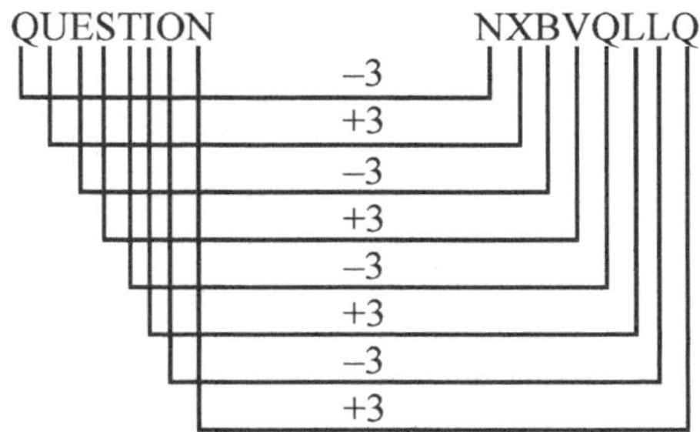

Similarly,

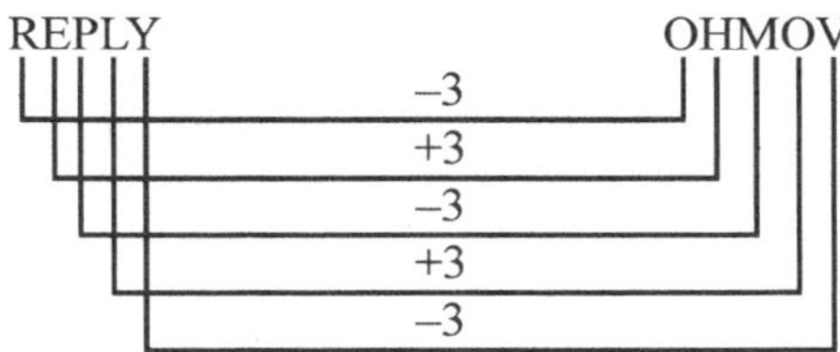

9. *(b)* : The letters are decoded by moving the letters +3, –3, +2 and –2 steps respectively.

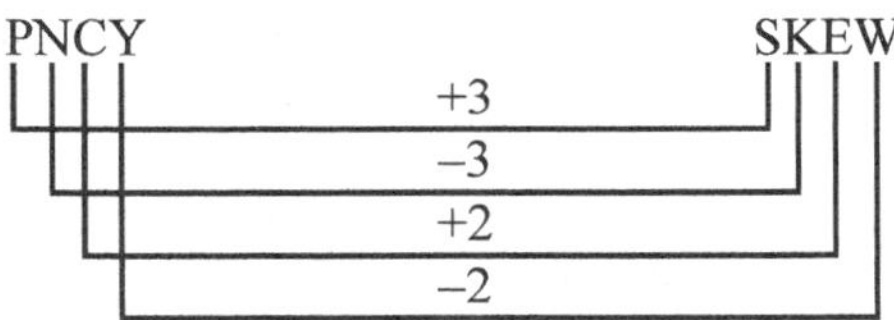

Similarly,

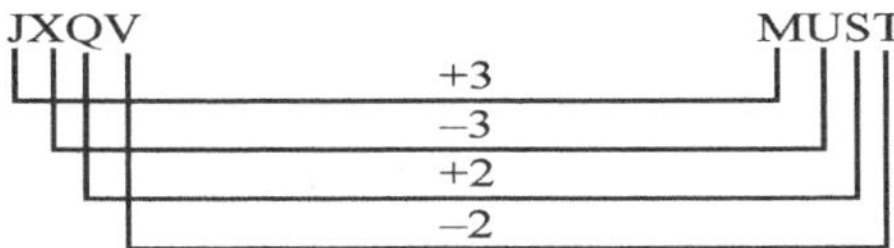

10. *(a)* : The letters of the coded word are moved one step backward.

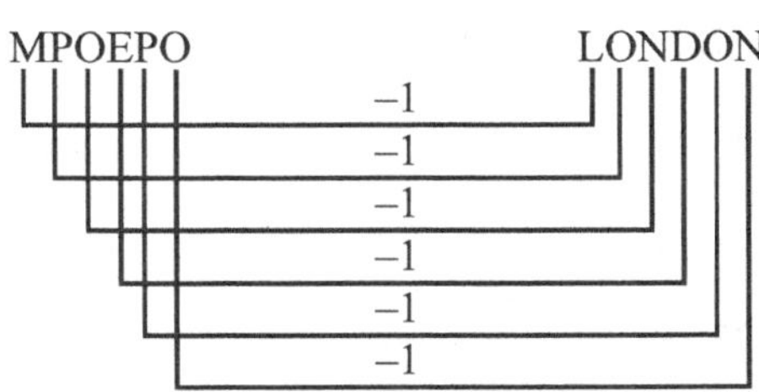

Similarly,

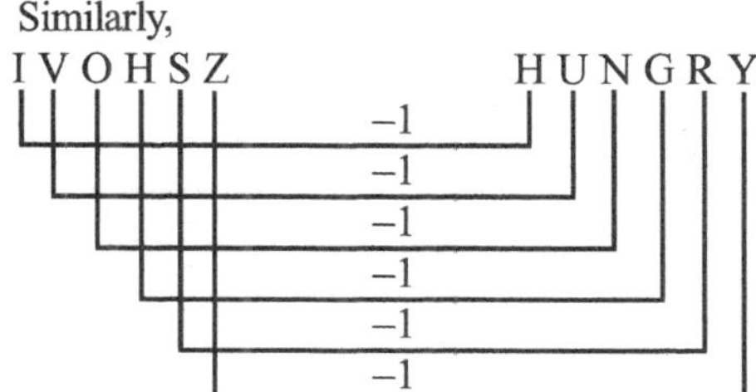

11. *(d)* : The word GRADE is framed by letters in the given words. So, in order to find the code for GRADE select the respective number codes.

H E A D R I D E B E G → letters
8 5 1 4 3 9 4 5 0 5 7 → codes

So,

G R A D E →letters
7 3 1 4 5 →answer codes

12. *(d)* : The letters of the word are coded by numbers. So to find the code for DREAM select the respective numbers.

M O T H E R L A N D → letters
9 5 0 1 6 2 3 7 4 8 → codes

So, D R E A M → letters
8 2 6 7 9 → answer codes

13. *(c)* : The letters are coded by moving five and four steps forward alternately.

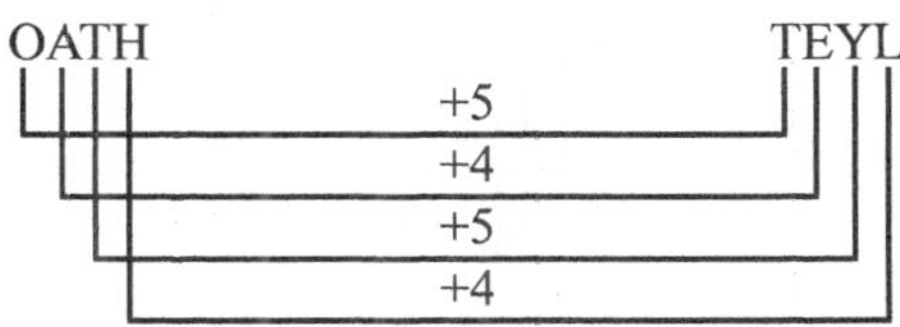

Similarly,

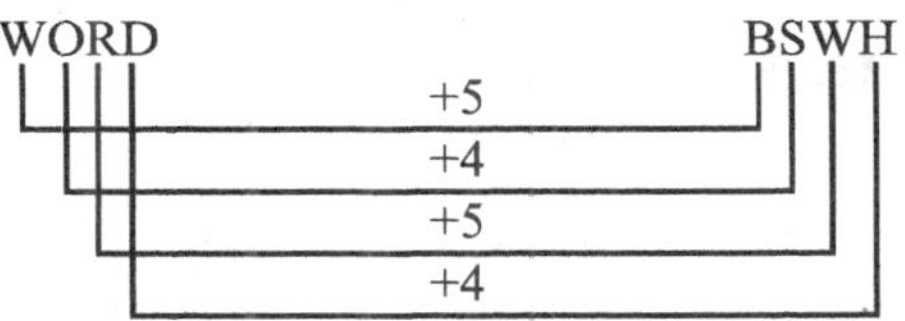

14. *(c)* : The letters of the word are coded by moving one step ahead and increasing the difference by one.

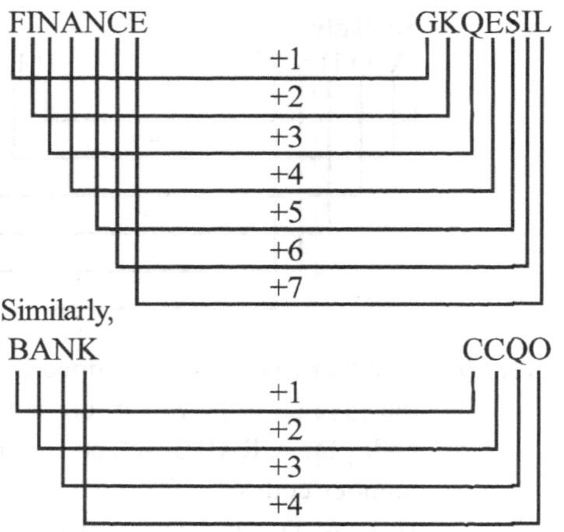

15. *(a)* : The letters of the word are coded by moving five steps forward and six steps backward alternately.

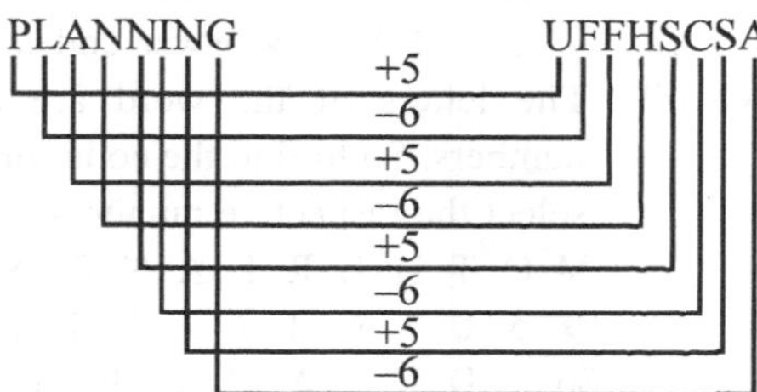

Similarly,

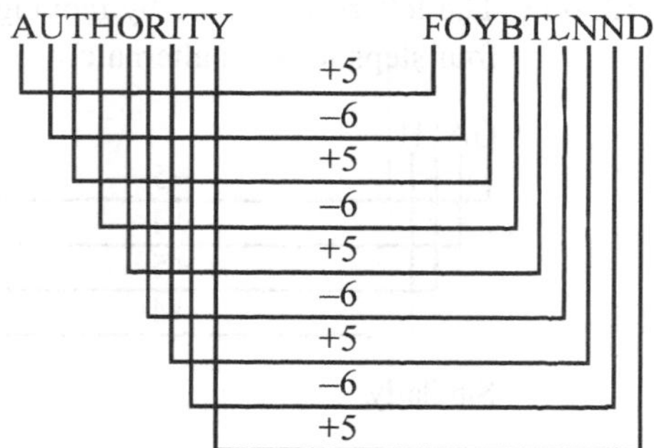

16. *(b)* :

	Code	*Sentence*
1.	go *ju* mi	plenty of *money*
2.	pao *ju* go nei vu	*money* creates lots of problems
3.	kol vu nei	problems create tension
4.	sol tun *ju* haw	still *money* is needed

In 1st, 2nd and 4th codes and their sentences the word 'ju' is repeated and so is 'money'.

17. *(a)* :

	Code	*Sentence*
1.	FOR	old is gold
2.	ROT	gold is pure
3.	ROM	gold is costly

Therefore,

F stands for old
O stands for is
R stands for gold
T stands for pure
M stands for costly

So, 'pure old gold is costly' will be written as 'TFROM'.

18. *(a)* :

	Code	*Sentence*
1.	415	milk is hot
2.	18	hot soup
3.	895	soup is *tasty*

From 3rd code and its sentence neither number '9' is repeated nor the word 'tasty'.

19. *(c)* :

	Code	*Sentence*
1.	643	she is beautiful
2.	593	he is handsome
3.	567	handsome *meets* beautiful

From 3rd code and its sentence, neither number '7' nor the word 'meets' is repeated.

20. *(d)* :

	Code	*Sentence*
1.	*dugo hui* mul zo	work *is very* hard
2.	*hui dugo* **ba** *ki*	**Bingo** *is very smart*
3.	nano mul *dugo*	cake is *hard*
4.	mul *ki* qu	*smart* and hard

From 2nd code and its sentence, neither 'ba' nor 'Bingo' is repeated.
(Words repeated are in italics)

21. *(c)* : Colour of milk is 'white' and 'white' is called 'sky'.

22. *(c)* : Colour of blood is 'red' and 'red' is called 'white'.

23. *(b)* : We drink 'water' when we are thirsty and 'water' is called 'air'.

24. *(a)* : Colour of sky is 'blue' and 'blue' means 'white'.

25. *(d)* : Fishes swim in 'water' and 'water' is called 'sand'.

10. Statement Analysis

In these type of questions, a few statements are given. Certain facts are broken up and mentioned in these statements. What is required is to analyse the statements, arrange and sort out the given facts and then answer the questions related to the given statements.

EXERCISE

1. Among five friends, A is heavier than B; C is lighter than D; B is lighter than D but heavier than E. Who among them is the heaviest?

(*a*) B (*b*) C
(*c*) A (*d*) Can't say

2. Pune is bigger than Jhansi, Sitapur is bigger than Chittor. Raigarh is not as big as Jhansi, but is bigger than Sitapur. Chittor is not as big as Sitapur. Which is the smallest?

(*a*) Jhansi (*b*) Pune
(*c*) Chittor (*d*) Sitapur

3. Ajay works more than Ram. Alok works as much as Raju. Pankaj works less than Alok. Ram works more than Alok. Who works the most of all?

(*a*) Ajay (*b*) Ram
(*c*) Alok (*d*) Raju

4. Among five friends P, Q, R, S and T, who is the youngest? To arrive at the answer which of the following information given in the statements (A) and (B) is sufficient?

(A) R is younger than P and T.
(B) S is younger than Q.

(*a*) Only A alone is sufficient
(*b*) Either A or B is sufficient
(*c*) Both A and B together are needed
(*d*) Both A and B together are not sufficient

5. A is elder to B while C and D are elder to E who lies between A and B. If C be elder to B, which one of the following statements is necessarily true?

(*a*) E is elder to B
(*b*) A is elder to C
(*c*) C is elder to D
(*d*) D is elder to C

6. Suresh is as much older than Kamal as he is younger than Prabodh. Navin is as old as Kamal. Which of the following statements is wrong?

(*a*) Suresh is older than Navin
(*b*) Kamal is younger than Suresh
(*c*) Prabodh is not the oldest
(*d*) Navin is younger than Prabodh

Directions (Qs. 7 to 9) : *Ram, Sohan and Mohan play football, hockey and cricket. Ram, Ramesh and Mohan play hockey, cricket and basketball. Ram, Sohan, Rahim and Mohan play football and cricket. Now answer the following questions based on the above statements :*

7. Which game is played by all the boys?

(*a*) Football (*b*) Hockey
(*c*) Cricket (*d*) Basketball

8. Which two boys play all the games?

(*a*) Ram, Sohan (*b*) Ram, Ramesh
(*c*) Sohan, Mohan (*d*) Ram, Mohan

9. Who does not play football?

(*a*) Ramesh (*b*) Sohan
(*c*) Rahim (*d*) Mohan

Directions (Qs. 10 to 12) : *Read the following directions and answer the questions given below :*

There are five persons in a group. Out of these two are men. Only three persons know swimming, of which one is a man. There is a couple, of which the husband knows swimming. A is the younger sister of D and B is the husband of E. C is a swimming champion.

10. Who is the other man in the group?
(*a*) C (*b*) B
(*c*) A (*d*) D

11. The two women who know how to swim are:
(*a*) A and C (*b*) C and D
(*c*) D and E (*d*) A and E

12. The two persons who do not know how to swim are :
(*a*) B and D (*b*) D and E
(*c*) A and E (*d*) A and D

Directions (Qs. 13 to 15) : *Read the following statements and answer the questions given below :*

Rajat, Sushil and Nagesh play football, hockey and cricket. Rajat, Ramu and Nagesh play hockey, cricket and basketball. Rajat, Sushil, Mayank and Nagesh play football and cricket.

13. Which game is played by all the boys?
(*a*) Hockey (*b*) Basketball
(*c*) Football (*d*) Cricket

14. Who does not play football?
(*a*) Rajat (*b*) Nagesh
(*c*) Sushil (*d*) Ramu

15. Which of the following two boys play all the games?
(*a*) Nagesh, Rajat
(*b*) Mayank, Ramu
(*c*) Ramu, Nagesh
(*d*) Sushil, Mayank

Directions (Qs. 16 to 20) : *Read the following information and answer the questions given below:*

(i) P, Q, R, S, T and U are six members in a family in which there are two married couples.
(ii) T a teacher is married to the doctor who is mother of R and U.
(iii) Q the lawyer is married to P.
(iv) P has one son and one grandson.
(v) Of the two married ladies one is a housewife.
(vi) There is also one student and one male engineer in the family.

16. Who among the following is the housewife?
(*a*) Q (*b*) P
(*c*) S (*d*) T

17. Which of the following represents the group of females in the family?
(*a*) QTR (*b*) PSR
(*c*) PSU (*d*) Data inadequate

18. Which of the following is true about the granddaughter in the family?
(*a*) She is a student
(*b*) She is an engineer
(*c*) She is a lawyer
(*d*) Data Inadequate

19. How R is related to U?
(*a*) Brother
(*b*) Sister
(*c*) Brother or Sister
(*d*) Data inadequate

20. How is P related to R?
(*a*) Grandfather (*b*) Mother
(*c*) Sister (*d*) Grandmother

EXPLANATORY ANSWERS

1. *(d)* : The five friends in descending order of weight are : A/D, B/C, E or A/D, B, C/E. Either A or D is the heaviest.

2. *(c)* : The order of cities in descending order of size is : Pune, Jhansi, Raigarh, Sitapur, Chittor.

3. *(a)* : On the basis of doing work, the descending order will be : Ajay, Ram, Alok/Raju, Pankaj.

4. *(d)* : Statements are not inter-related.

5. *(a)* : The order in descending seniority will be : A/C/D, E, B.

6. *(c)* : On the basis of age the descending order will be : Prabodh, Suresh, Kamal/Navin.

Chart for Answers 7 to 9

Boy	*Games Played*
Ram	Football, Hocky, Cricket, Basketball
Sohan	Football, Hockey, Cricket
Mohan	Football, Hockey, Cricket, Basketball
Ramesh	Hockey, Cricket, Basketball
Rahim	Football, Cricket.

7. ***(c)*** **8.** ***(d)*** **9.** ***(a)***

For Answers 10 to 12 the information chart will be :

A. Woman ((younger sister of D); knows swimming.

B. Man (husband of E); knows swimming

C. Woman; Swimming champion

D. Man (brother of A)

E. Woman (wife of B)

From the couple B & E, B (husband) knows swimming. C is a swimming champion. Three persons know how to swim of which only B is a man. So, the two women who know how to swim are C and A (the younger sister of D). There are two men in the group of five. One is B and the other will be D.

10. ***(d)*** **11.** ***(a)*** **12.** ***(b)***

Chart for Answers 13 to 15

Boy	*Games Played*
Rajat	— Football, Hockey, Cricket, Basketball
Sushil	— Football, Hockey, Cricket, Basketball
Nagesh	— Football, Hockey, Cricket, Basketball
Ramu	— Hockey, Cricket, Basketball
Mayank	— Football, Cricket

13. ***(d)*** **14.** ***(d)*** **15.** ***(a)***

Chart for Answers 16 to 20

P (female/housewife) — Q (male/lawyer) *Grandparents*

T (male/teacher) — S (female/doctor) *Parents*

R, U Children

(of R and U, one is a male engineer and one is a student)

16. ***(b)*** **:** One married lady S who is mother of R and U is a doctor. Q the lawyer is married to P. Of the two married ladies one is a house-wife. As Q is a lawyer the other married lady who is a housewife should be P.

17. ***(d)*** **:** Sex of R and U is not given.

18. ***(a)*** **:** P has one son T and one grandson either R or U one of whom is an engineer. So, the granddaughter is a student.

19. ***(c)*** **:** Sex of R and U is not given, but as both are children of S and one is a male engineer, the relationship between the two is of brother and sister.

20. ***(d)***

11. Place Arrangement

Place arrangement generally refers to the positioning of persons or objects in a manner indicated by set of information given. One has to understand the order of placement and then attempt questions following the given information.

EXERCISE

Directions : *In the following questions, understand the arrangement pattern and then select the right answer from the given options :*

1. Five boys are sitting in a row. Raghu is not adjacent to Shyam or Amit. Ajay is not adjacent to Shyam. Raghu is adjacent to Mayank. If Mayank is at the middle in the row, then Ajay is adjacent to whom out of the following?

(*a*) Amit (*b*) Raghu
(*c*) Mayank (*d*) Shyam

2. Mini is to the right of Rajni but to the left of Ananta. Saya is to the right of Mini but to the left of Jaya. Who is on the extreme left if all the girls are facing North?

(*a*) Jaya (*b*) Mini
(*c*) Rajni (*d*) Saya

3. O, P, Q, R, S and T are standing on a bench according to their height. P is taller than O but shorter than S. Only S is taller than T. R is shorter than P but taller than Q. Who is the shortest?

(*a*) O (*b*) Q
(*c*) P (*d*) Cannot be said

4. Five personalities are living in a multistoried building. Mr. Effortless lives in a flat above Mr. Active, Mr. Charge lives in a flat below Mr. Diligent, Mr. Active lives in a flat above Mr. Diligent and Mr. Behaved lives in a flat below Mr. Charge. Who lives in the topmost flat?

(*a*) Mr. Charge (*b*) Mr. Diligent
(*c*) Mr. Effortless (*d*) Mr. Behaved

5. Six friends are sitting in a circle and playing cards. Kenny is to the left of Danny. Michael is in-between Bob and John. Roger is in between Kenny and Bob. Who is sitting to the right of Michael?

(*a*) Danny (*b*) John
(*c*) Kenny (*d*) Bob

6. Four girls A, B, C and D are sitting in a circle. B and C are facing each other. Which of the following is definitely true?

(*a*) A is to the left of C
(*b*) D is to the left of C
(*c*) A and D are facing each other
(*d*) A is not between B and C

7. Brijesh, Jayesh, Amar and Praveer are playing a game of cards. Amar is to the right of Jayesh who is to the right of Brijesh. Who is to the right of Amar?

(*a*) Brijesh
(*b*) Praveer
(*c*) Brijesh or Praveer
(*d*) Jayesh

8. In a pile of 10 books there are 3 of History, 3 of Hindi, 2 of Maths, and 2 of English. Taking from above there is an English book between a History and Maths book, a History book between a Maths and an English book, a Hindi book between an English and a Maths book, a Maths book between two Hindi books, and two Hindi books between a Maths and a History book. Book of which subject is at the sixth position from the top?

(*a*) English (*b*) Hindi
(*c*) History (*d*) Maths

9. Five persons A, B, C, D and E are sitting in a row facing you such that D is on the left of C and B is on the right of E. A is on the right of C and B is on the left of D. If E occupies a corner position, then who is sitting in the centre?

(*a*) A (*b*) B
(*c*) C (*d*) D

10. Six friends A, B, C, D, E and F are standing in a circle. B is between F and C; A is between E and D; F is to the left of D. Who is between A and F?

(*a*) C (*b*) B
(*c*) D (*d*) E

EXPLANATORY ANSWERS

1. *(b)* : The order of sitting is :
Amit, Shyam, Mayank, Ajay, Raghu
or
Ajay, Raghu, Mayank, Amit, Shyam

2. *(c)* : The order in which the girls are positioned is :
Rajni, Mini, Ananta, Saya, Jaya
or
Saya, Jaya, Ananta
or
Saya, Ananta, Jaya

3. *(d)* : In descending order of height, the standing positions are :

S		S
T		T
P	*or*	P
R		R
O		Q
Q		O

Either O or Q is the shortest. The informa-tion given is not enough to clarify the answer.

4. *(c)* : The personalities living in flats in multi-storied building are in order given below :
Mr. Effortless
Mr. Active
Mr. Diligent
Mr. Charge
Mr. Behaved

5. *(d)* : The order in which the friends are sitting is :

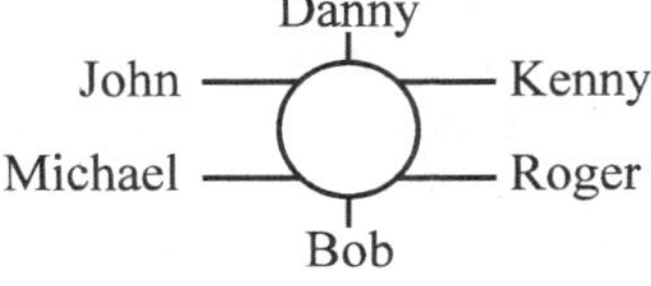

6. *(c)* : The sitting positions are :

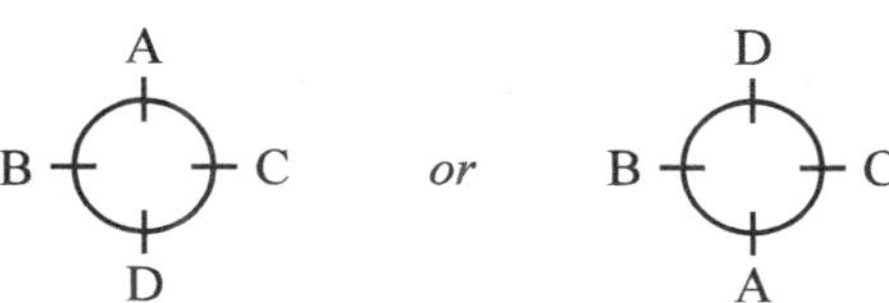

7. *(b)* : The order from left to right is :
Brijesh, Jayesh, Amar, Praveer

8. *(b)* : The pile of books is in the order :

1st — History
English
Maths
History
English
6th — Hindi
Maths
Hindi
Hindi
10th — History

9. *(d)* : Sitting order while facing us is :
A, C, D, B, E

10. *(c)* : The pattern of standing is :

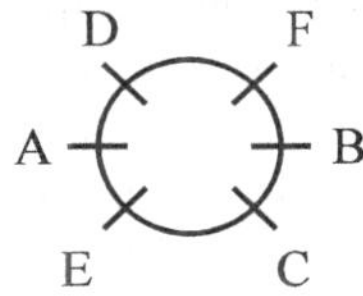

12. Direction Sense

In these type of tests, the directions in questions needs to be perceived. Such questions are based on the direction chart.

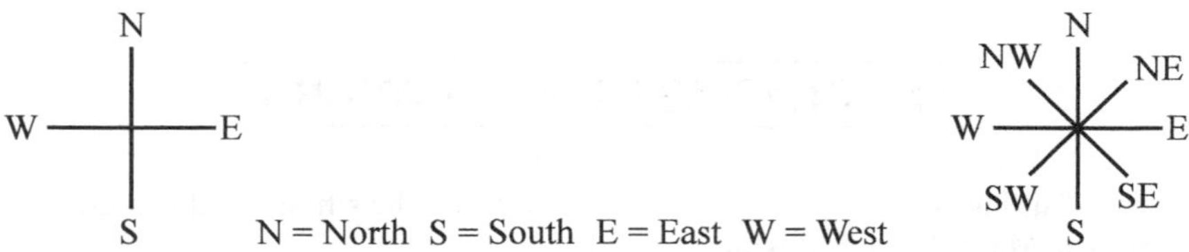

The sense of the different directions are guided by the left and right turns or angular turns.

EXERCISE

Directions : *In the following questions, select the right answer from the given options to depict the correct direction/distance.*

1. Kittu walks towards East and then towards South. After walking some distance he turns towards West and then turns to his left. In which direction is he walking now?

(*a*) North (*b*) South
(*c*) East (*d*) West

2. A person is driving towards West. What sequence of directions should he follow so that he is driving towards South?

(*a*) left, right, right
(*b*) right, right, left
(*c*) left, left, left
(*d*) right, right, right

3. Richa drives 8 km to the South, turns left and drives 5 km. Again, she turns left and drives 8 km. How far is she from her starting point?

(*a*) 3 km (*b*) 5 km
(*c*) 8 km (*d*) 13 km

4. Dingi runs 40 km towards North then turns right and runs 50 km. He turns right and runs 30 km, and once again turns right and runs 50 km. How far is he from his starting point?

(*a*) 90 km (*b*) 50 km
(*c*) 10 km (*d*) 5 km

5. If North is called North-West, North-West is called West, West is called South-West and so on. What will South-East be called?

(*a*) East (*b*) West
(*c*) North-East (*d*) South-East

6. A man travels 100 km towards South. From there he turns right and travels 100 km and again turns right to travel 50 km. Which direction is he in from his starting point?

(*a*) North (*b*) North-East
(*c*) East (*d*) South-West

7. A train runs 120 km in West direction, 30 km in South direction and then 80 km in east direction before reaching the station. In which direction is the station from the train's starting point?

(*a*) South-West (*b*) North-West
(*c*) South-East (*d*) South

8. Facing the West direction, Priya jogs for 20 m, turns left and goes further 40 m. She turns left again and jogs for 20 m. Then she turns right to go 20 m to reach the park. How far is the park from her starting point and in which direction?

(*a*) 20 m South (*b*) 40 m West
(*c*) 60 m South (*d*) 100 m East

9. If all the directions are rotated, *i.e.,* if North is changed to West and East to North and so on, then what will come in place of North-West?
(*a*) South-West (*b*) North-East
(*c*) East-North (*d*) East-West

10. A and B start together from one point. They walk 10 km towards North. A turns left and covers 5 km whereas B turns right and covers 3 km. A turns left again and covers 15 km whereas B turns right and covers his 15 km. How far is A from B?
(*a*) 18 km (*b*) 10 km
(*c*) 5 km (*d*) 8 km

11. Tarun is walking towards East. What direction he should not follow if he should walk towards North?
(*a*) right, right, left, right, right
(*b*) right, right, left, left, left
(*c*) right, right, right
(*d*) right, left, right, left

12. Sony and Moni start walking from a point. Sony walks in West direction and Moni in South direction. After covering 20 km, Soni turns left and walks 15 km. Moni walks 10 km, turns left and walks 5 km. Soni, then turns left again and walks 25 km, whereas Moni turns right and walks 5 km. How far are Sony and Moni from each other?
(*a*) 5 km
(*b*) They are back at the starting point
(*c*) They are at same place at the finishing point
(*d*) Data is insufficient

13. I was walking in South-East direction. After a while I turned 90° to the right and walked ahead. Later I turned 45° to the right. In which direction am I walking now?
(*a*) North (*b*) North-East
(*c*) South-West (*d*) East

14. Two friends Jack and Bunny start a race, and together they run for 50 mts. Jack turns right and runs 60 mts while Bunny turns left and runs 40 mts. Then Jack turns left and runs 50 mts while Bunny turns right and runs 50 mts. How far are the two friends now from each other?
(*a*) 60 mts (*b*) 100 mts
(*c*) 20 mts (*d*) 150 mts

15. A policeman left his police post and proceeded south 4 km, after hearing a loud sound from point A. On reaching the place he heard another sound and proceeded 4 km to his left to the point B, only to find that the sound was coming from left of B. From B he proceeded left to reach that place 4 km away. In which direction he has to go to reach his police post?
(*a*) North (*b*) South
(*c*) East (*d*) West

EXPLANATORY ANSWERS

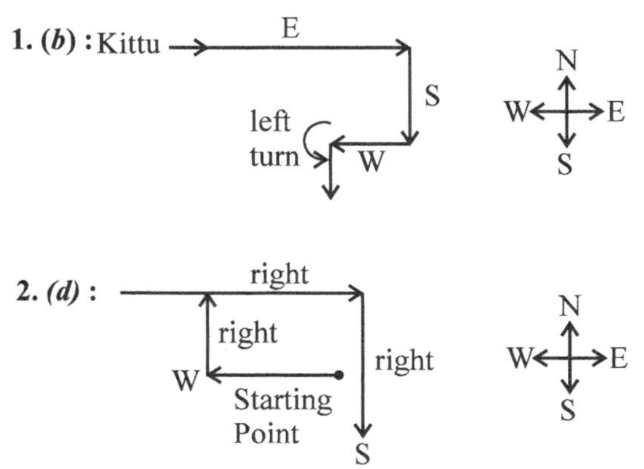

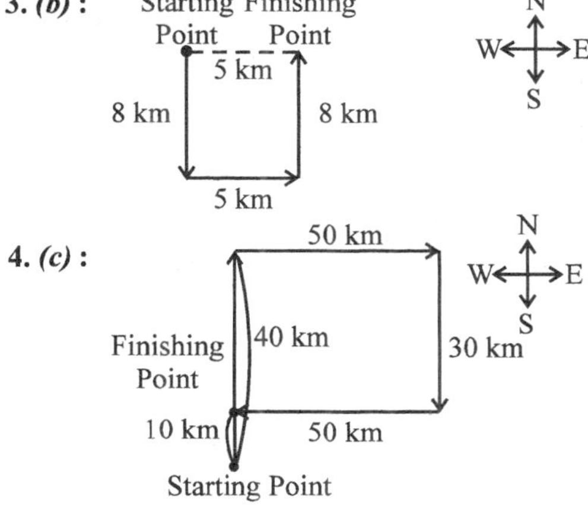

5. ***(a)*** **: Original Directions**

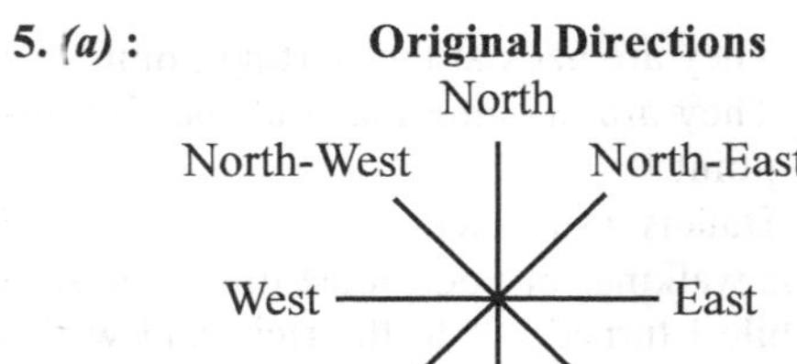

Changed Directions

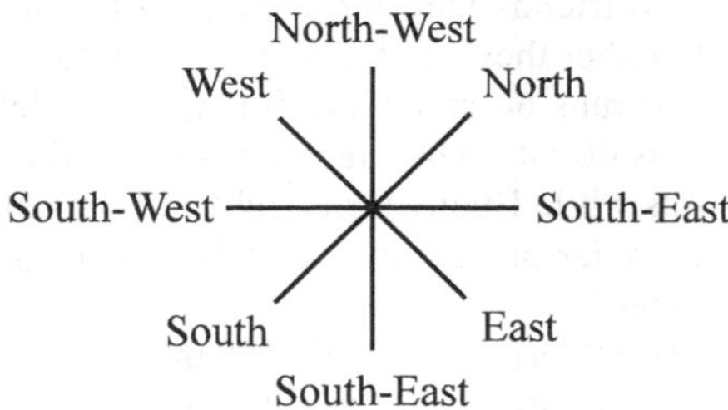

6. ***(d)*** **:**

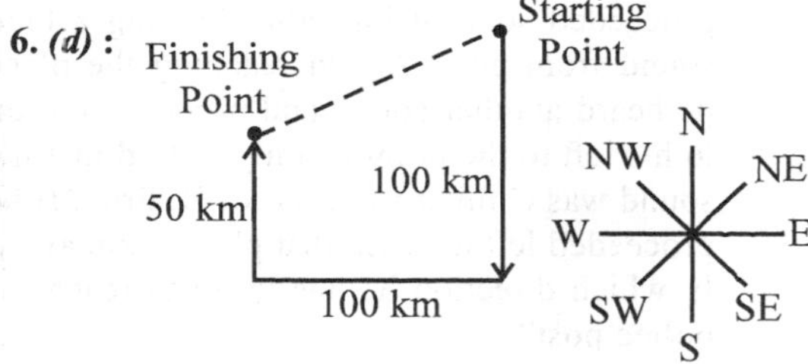

7. ***(a)*** **:**

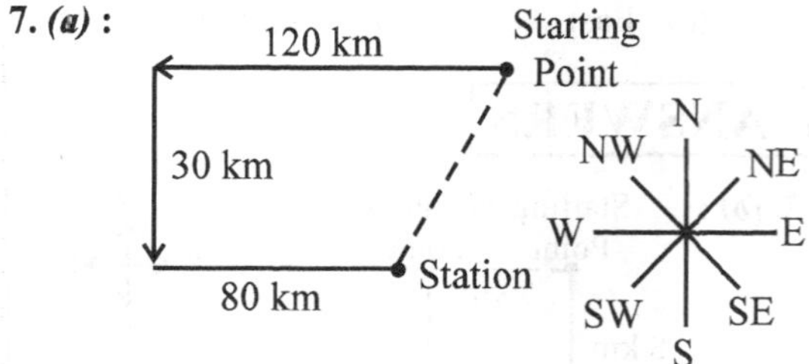

8. ***(c)*** **:** (40 + 20) = 60 metres South

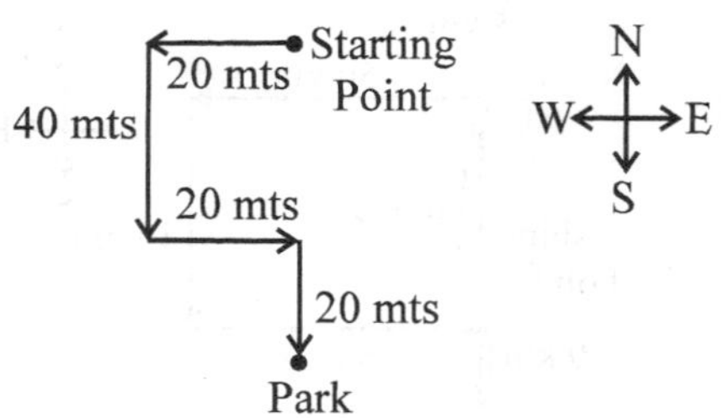

9. ***(a)*** **: Original Directions**

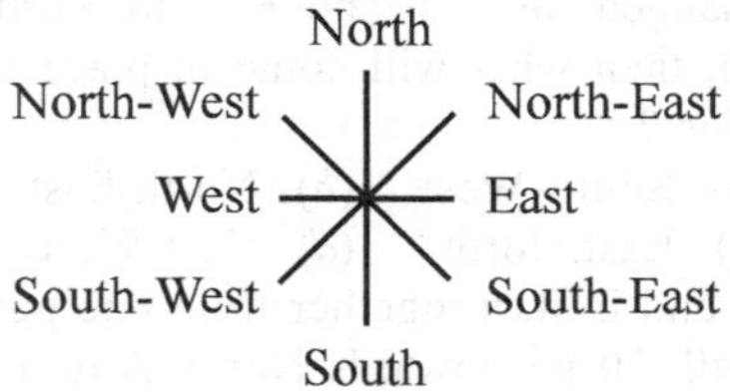

Changed Directions

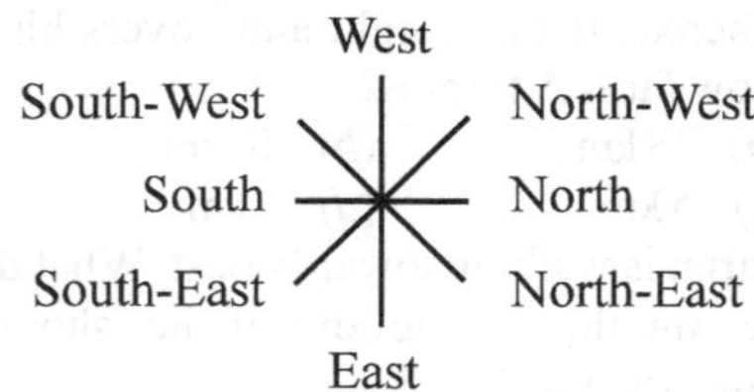

10. ***(d)*** **:**

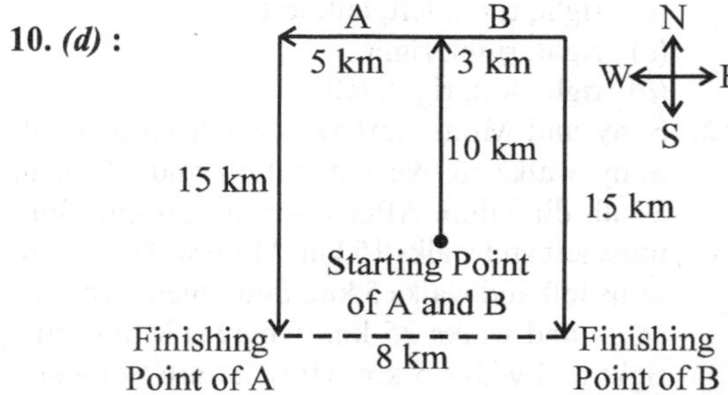

11. ***(d)*** **:**

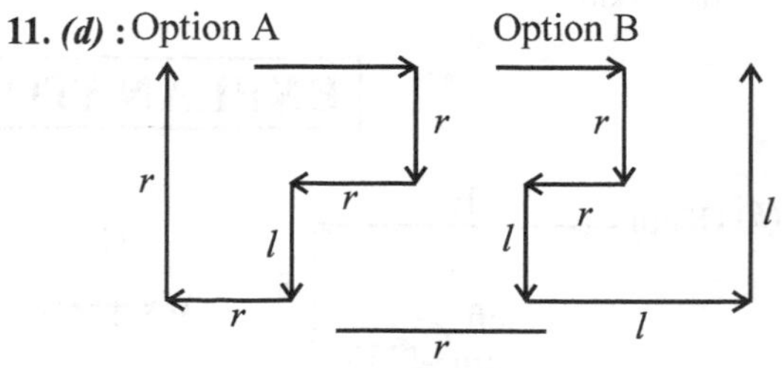

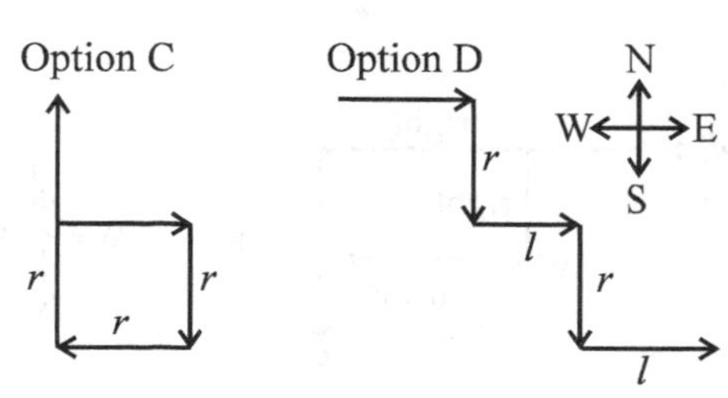

12. ***(c)*** **:**

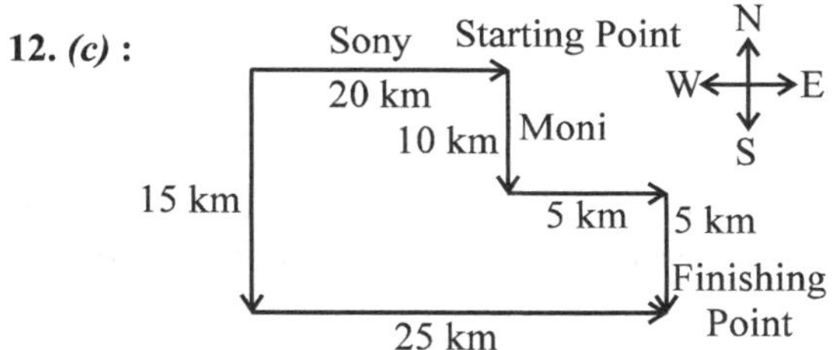

13. ***(a)*** **:** The direction of the movement is :

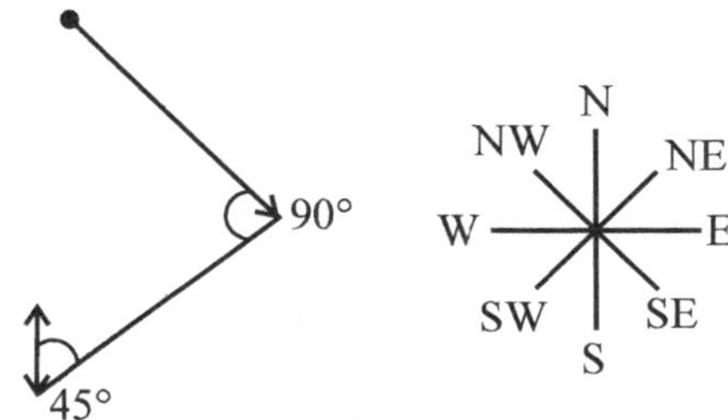

14. ***(b)*** **:** The track of both the friends is :

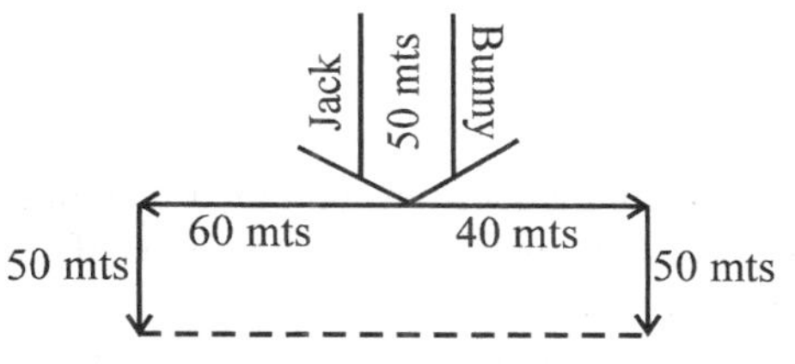

The two friends are 60 + 40 = 100 mts apart

15. ***(d)*** **:**

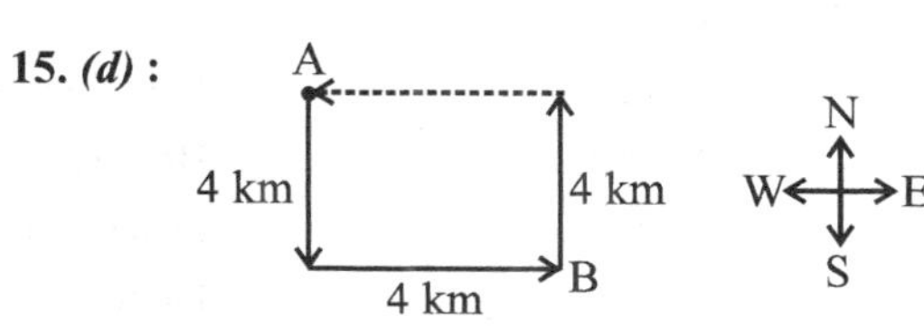

13. Blood Relationships

While attempting questions on blood relations, one should be clear of all the relation patterns that can exist between any two individuals. These type of questions are given mainly to test one's relationship ability.

Very well-known relations are :

Mother	Grandmother
Father	Grandfather
Son	Grandson
Daughter	Granddaughter
Brother	Brother-in-law
Sister	Sister-in-law
Niece	Father-in-law
Nephew	Mother-in-law
Uncle	Son-in-law
Aunt	Daughter-in-law
Husband	Cousin
Wife	

The patterns of some relationships which help in solving questions in these tests are :

Father's *or* Mother's Father	—	Grandfather (Paternal *or* Maternal)
Father's *or* Mother's Mother	—	Grandmother (Paternal *or* Maternal)
Father's *or* Mother's Son	—	Brother
Father's *or* Mother's Daughter	—	Sister
Father's Brother	—	Paternal Uncle
Father's Sister	—	Paternal Aunt
Mother's Brother	—	Maternal Uncle
Mother's Sister	—	Maternal Aunt
Uncle *or* Aunt's Son *or* Daughter	—	Cousin
Son's Wife	—	Daughter-in-law
Daughter's Husband	—	Son-in-law
Husband's *or* Wife's Brother	—	Brother-in-law
Husband's *or* Wife's Sister	—	Sister-in-law
Brother's Wife	—	Sister-in-law
Sister's Husband	—	Brother-in-law
Brother's Son	—	Nephew
Brother's Daughter	—	Niece

EXERCISE

Directions : *In each of the following questions keenly study the relationship mentioned between the persons, and then from the given options select the right relationship as the answer.*

1. A lady said, "The person standing there is my grandfather's only son's daughter". How is the lady related to the standing person?
(*a*) Sister
(*b*) Mother
(*c*) Aunt
(*d*) Cousin

2. Ajay is the brother of Vijay. Mili is the sister of Ajay. Sanjay is the brother of Rahul and Mehul is the daughter of Vijay. Who is Sanjay's Uncle?
(*a*) Rahul
(*b*) Ajay
(*c*) Mehul
(*d*) Data inadequate

3. A man introduced the boy coming with him as "He is son of the father of my wife's daughter". What relation did the boy bear to the man?
(*a*) Son-in-law
(*b*) Son
(*c*) Brother
(*d*) Father

4. If Amit's father is Billoo's father's only son and Billoo has neither a brother nor a daughter, what is the relationship between Amit and Billoo?
(*a*) Uncle — Nephew
(*b*) Father — Daughter
(*c*) Father — Son
(*d*) Cousins

5. Pointing to a woman in the photograph a man said, "She is the daughter of my grand-mother's only son. How is the woman related to the man?
(*a*) Mother (*b*) Daughter
(*c*) Sister-in-law (*d*) Sister

6. Pointing to a photograph, a woman said, "She is the only daughter of my mother's father." How is the woman related to the person in the photograph?
(*a*) Mother
(*b*) Grandmother
(*c*) Daughter
(*d*) Cannot be determined

7. Ram is the brother of Shyam and Mahesh is the father of Ram. Jagat is the brother of Priya and Priya is daughter of Shyam. Who is the uncle of Jagat ?
(*a*) Shyam
(*b*) Mahesh
(*c*) Ram
(*d*) Data insufficient

8. Introducing a man, a woman said, "His wife is the only daughter of my father". How is the man related to the woman?
(*a*) Husband
(*b*) Father
(*c*) Father-in-law
(*d*) Brother

9. If Maya is the only daughter of Richa's grandmother's brother, how is Maya's daughter related to Richa?
(*a*) Niece
(*b*) Cousin
(*c*) Aunt
(*d*) Mother

10. Pointing to a woman, a man said, "Her husband's mother is the wife of my father's only son". How is the man related to the woman?
(*a*) Son
(*b*) Brother-in-law
(*c*) Uncle
(*d*) Father-in-law

EXPLANATORY ANSWERS

1. (*a*) : Grandfather

Father
(only son)

Daughter ⟶ Lady
(standing person) (sister)

Lady's grandfather's son is lady's father and father's daughter will only be lady's sister.

2. (*d*) : 1. Mili ⟶ (sister) Ajay ⟶ (brother) Vijay ↓ Mehul (daughter)

2. Sanjay ⟶ (brother) Rahul

There are two sets of relationship. Information given is incomplete and no relation can be established between the two sets.

3. (*b*) : The relationship chart based on problem is :

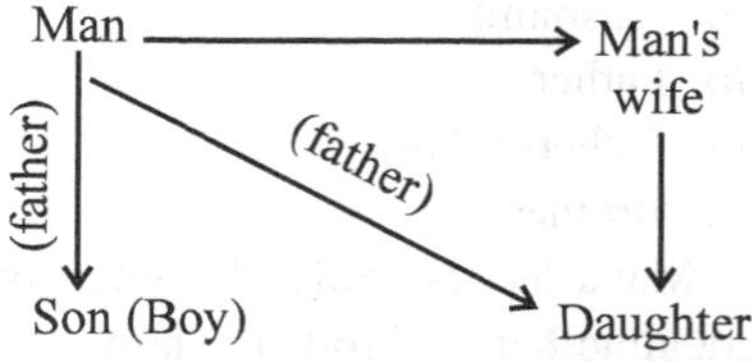

'Father of the man's wife's daughter' is the man himself and the boy in question is the man's son.

4. (*c*) : The relationship chart based on problem is :

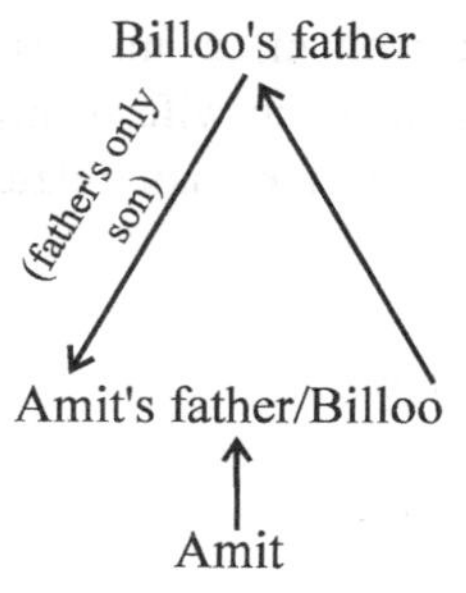

Amit's father is Billoo's father's only son means Billoo is the only son in question also, he is the father of Amit. It must be noted that Billoo has no brother which means he is single and also, when he has no daughter, Amit is his only son.

5. (*d*) : Man's Grandmother
↓
Grandmother's only son
A
↓
Man ⟵ (sister) Daughter

'My grandmother's only son' is the father of the man, and 'daughter of my grandmother's only son' is the sister of the man.

6. (*c*) : Woman's mother's father
↕
Person in photograph
(woman's mother/only daughter)
↑ (daughter)
Woman

'Only daughter of my mother's father' is the person in the photograph and she is also the mother of the woman. So, the woman is the daughter of the person in the photograph.

7. (*c*) :

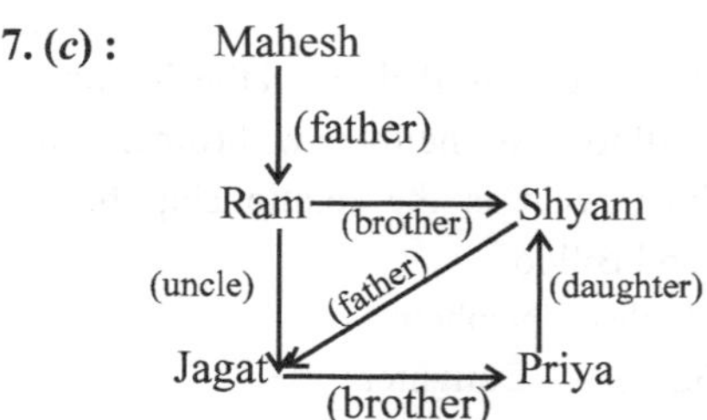

Jagat is brother of Priya and Priya is daughter of Shyam. So Shyam is also the father of Jagat. Ram is the brother of Shyam. So, Jagat's father's brother Ram is the uncle of Jagat.

8. (*a*) :

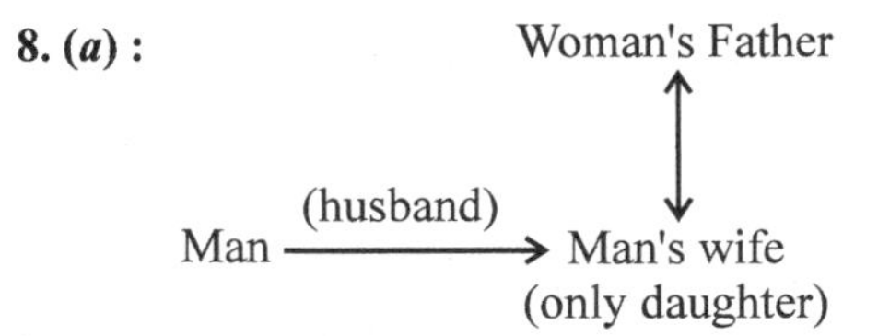

'Only daughter of my father' is the woman herself and the man is her husband.

9. (*b*) :

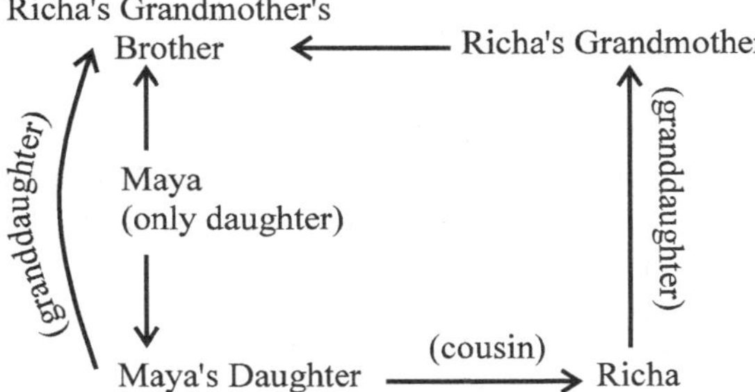

Both Maya's Daughter and Richa are granddaughters of a brother and a sister respectively. So Maya's daughter is the cousin of Richa.

10. (*d*) :

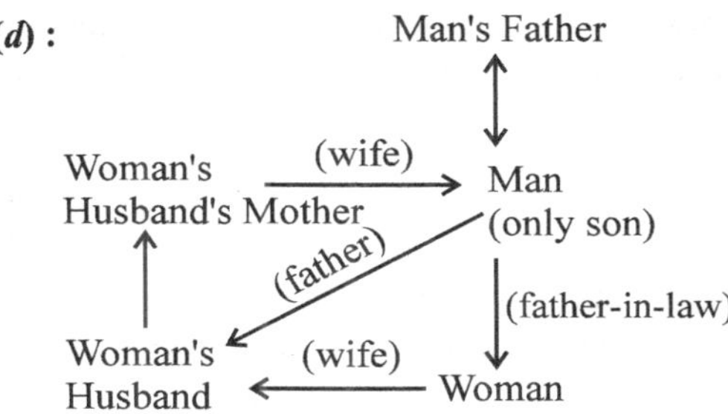

'My father's only son' is the man himself. 'Her husband's mother' is the wife of the man and so the man is the father of the woman's husband. As the woman is the wife of man's son, the man is the father-in-law of the woman.

14. Rows and Ranks

These type of problems need easy calculations to find out the number of objects in a row, lane or queue or to find a person's rank in a class of certain number of students; or to find the total number of students.

EXERCISE

1. In a row of trees, one tree is fifth from either end of the row. How many trees are in the row?
(*a*) 11 (*b*) 8
(*c*) 10 (*d*) 9

2. Jaya ranks 5th in a class of 53. What is her rank from the bottom in the class?
(*a*) 49th (*b*) 48th
(*c*) 47th (*d*) 50th

3. Mohan ranks twenty-first in a class of sixty-five students. What will be his (Mohan's) rank if the lowest candidate is assigned rank 1?
(*a*) 44th (*b*) 45th
(*c*) 46th (*d*) Data inadequate

4. If Rahul finds that he is 12th from the right in a line of boys and 4th from the left, how many boys should be added to the line such that there are 28 boys in the line?
(*a*) 12 (*b*) 14
(*c*) 20 (*d*) 13

5. In a row of boys, Rajan is tenth from the right and Suraj is tenth from the left. When Rajan and Suraj interchange their positions, Suraj will be twenty-seventh from the left. Which of the following will be Rajan's position from the right?
(*a*) Tenth
(*b*) Twenty-sixth
(*c*) Twenty-ninth
(*d*) None of these

6. Mahesh and Suresh are ranked 11th and 12th respectively from the top in a class of 41 students. What will be their respective ranks from the bottom?
(*a*) 32nd and 33rd
(*b*) 29th and 30th
(*c*) 30th and 31st
(*d*) 31st and 30th

7. Uma ranked 8th from the top and 37th from bottom in a class. How many students are there in the class?
(*a*) 47 (*b*) 46
(*c*) 45 (*d*) None of these

8. In a queue, Sadiq is 14th from the front and Joseph is 17th from the end, while Jane is in between Sadiq and Joseph. If Sadiq be ahead of Joseph and there be 48 persons in the queue, how many persons are there between Sadiq and Jane?
(*a*) 5 (*b*) 6
(*c*) 7 (*d*) 8

9. Rohan ranked eleventh from the top and twenty-seventh from the bottom among the students who passed the annual examination in a class. If the number of students who failed in the examination was 12, how many students appeared for the examination?
(*a*) 48
(*b*) 49
(*c*) 50
(*d*) Cannot be determined

10. Some boys are sitting in a row. P is sitting fourteenth from the left and Q is seventh from the right. If there are four boys between P and Q, how many boys are there in the row?
(*a*) 19 (*b*) 21
(*c*) 25 (*d*) 23

EXPLANATORY ANSWERS

1. (*d*):

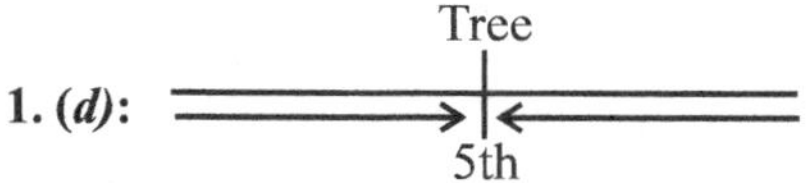

Total number of trees in the row are :
$(5+5)-1=9$.

2. (*a*) :

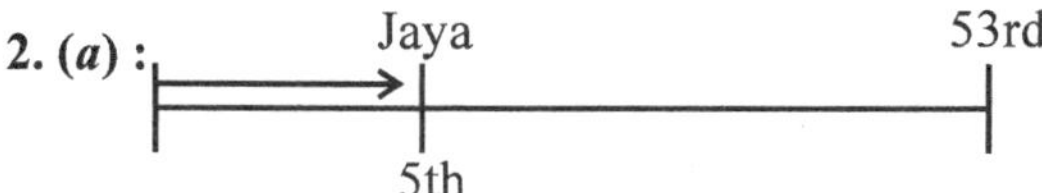

Jaya's rank from the bottom is :
$(53-5)+1=49$th.

3. (*b*) :

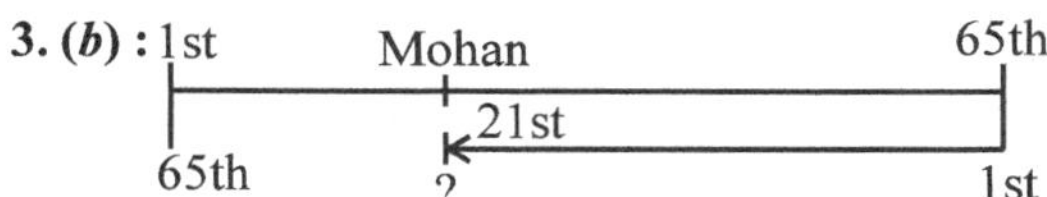

Note : Mohan's rank from the last or the question asked means the same.

Mohan's rank is $(65-21)+1=45$th.

4. (*d*) :

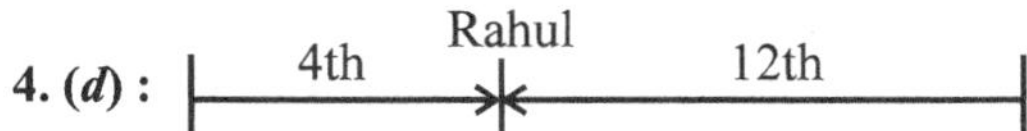

The number of boys in the line are :
$(4+12)-1=15$

To make a line of 28 boys, $(28-15)$ *i.e.* 13 more boys are needed.

5. (*d*) :

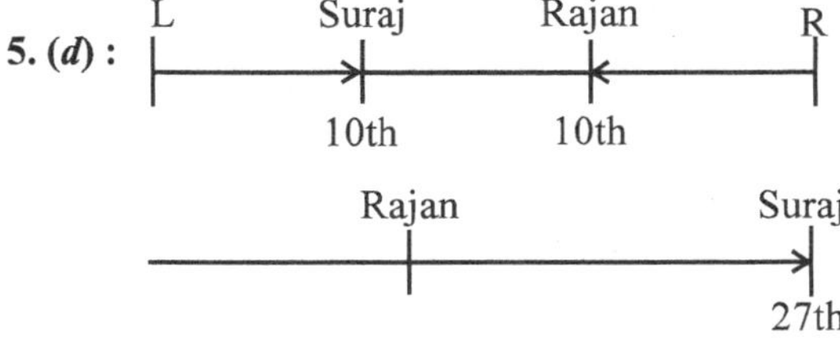

As the position of boys is equal from both ends, Rajan will also be 27th from the right after changing positions.

6. (*d*) :

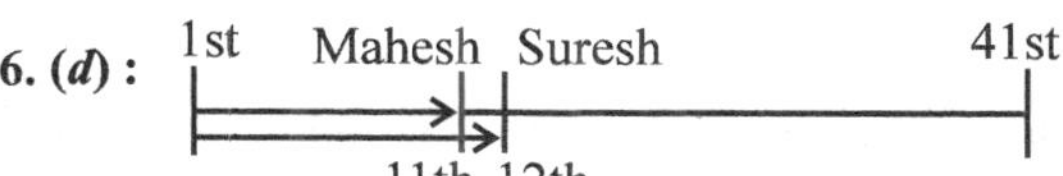

Mahesh's position from bottom is :
$(41-11)+1=31$st

Suresh's position from bottom is :
$(41-12)+1=30$th.

7. (*d*) :

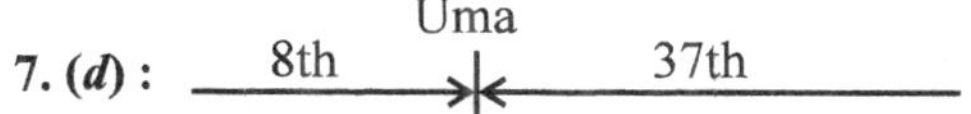

Total number of students in the class are :
$(8+37)-1=44$.

8. (*d*) : 1st Sadiq Jane Joseph 48th

14th 23rd 17th

Sadiq's position from front : 14th

Joseph's position from last :
17th or $48-17+1=32$nd from front.

Middle postion between Sadiq & Joseph

$$=\frac{(32-14)}{2}+14=23 \text{ rd.}$$

Hence, Jane position is 23rd from front

Person between Sadiq & Jane
$=23-14-1=8$.

9. (*b*) : Rohan

11th 27th

Number of students who passed the examination $(11+27)-1=37$

Those who failed $=12$

Total number of students who appeared in the examination $=37+12=49$.

10. (*c*) : P Q

14th 4 7th

The number of boys in the row are :
$(14+4+7)=25$.

15. Permutations and Combinations

In these type of questions, the only factor essential is alertness. In every question, a word is given. By using the letters of this given word the options are formed. The candidates are required to find from the given options the word *(i)* which cannot be formed by using the letters of the given word or *(ii)* which can be formed by using the letters of the given word.

EXERCISE

Directions : *Find out the one word among the options which cannot be formed by using the letters of the word as given in each question.*

1. ROTATION
(a) TORN *(b)* NOTE
(c) TART *(d)* RAIN

2. PHILOSOPHY
(a) SOIL *(b)* SHIP
(c) SOLO *(d)* SPIN

3. SLAVATION
(a) SNORT *(b)* LATVIA
(c) SALIVA *(d)* AVAIL

4. ACADEMY
(a) DEMY *(b)* MACE
(c) DIRE *(d)* MADE

5. INCOGNITO
(a) GOING *(b)* INACTION
(c) IGNITION *(d)* TONGO

6. JUDICIARY
(a) INJURY *(b)* CADDY
(c) DICY *(d)* ACRID

7. DOCTRINE
(a) CRUST *(b)* DOCTOR
(c) TIRED *(d)* CREED

8. EDUCATED
(a) DATE *(b)* CUTE
(c) EAST *(d)* DUCT

9. INSUFFICIENT
(a) ENTICE *(b)* SCENT
(c) SUFFICE *(d)* THENCE

10. DECEMBER
(a) REDEEM *(b)* DECREE
(c) BRACED *(d)* MEMBER

11. FUGITIVE
(a) EXIT *(b)* FIVE
(c) GIVE *(d)* GIFT

12. CATASTROPHE
(a) TASTE *(b)* CHEAP
(c) POUCH *(d)* STARE

13. TORRENTIAL
(a) TRAIL *(b)* MENTAL
(c) LEARN *(d)* RETAIL

14. INFRASTRUCTURE
(a) RAPTURE *(b)* INSECURE
(c) CRAFTS *(d)* STRUCTURE

15. RECOMMEND
(a) MEND *(b)* ROME
(c) CANE *(d)* OMEN

Directions : *Find out the one word among the options which can be formed by using the letters of the word as given in each question.*

16. INVESTIGATE
(a) INVERT *(b)* GLIDE
(c) STING *(d)* ACTED

17. MAJORITY
(a) MORE *(b)* JURY
(c) READ *(d)* TRAY

18. WATERMELON
(a) MAKER *(b)* WRITE
(c) TOWER *(d)* NOVEL

19. PREDICTION
(a) DESIRE *(b)* CREDIT
(c) ACTION *(d)* PICKED

20. BARGAIN
(a) GRAIN *(b)* BARGE
(c) ANGRY *(d)* TRING

21. THERMOSTAT
(a) MOTHER *(b)* STAMEN
(c) THRUST *(d)* HOIST

22. LEARNED
(a) DREAM *(b)* CLEAR
(c) ELDER *(d)* DRAPE

23. ADVENTURE
(a) AWARE *(b)* EVENT
(c) TRUCE *(d)* DRIED

24. THANKSGIVING
(a) AVENGE *(b)* HAUNTS
(c) GRAINS *(d)* SAVING

25. NOCTURNAL
(a) CRUST *(b)* TRAIL
(c) CORAL *(d)* OCEAN

ANSWERS

1	**2**	**3**	**4**	**5**	**6**	**7**	**8**	**9**	**10**
(b)	*(d)*	*(a)*	*(c)*	*(b)*	*(a)*	*(a)*	*(c)*	*(d)*	*(c)*
11	**12**	**13**	**14**	**15**	**16**	**17**	**18**	**19**	**20**
(a)	*(c)*	*(b)*	*(a)*	*(c)*	*(c)*	*(d)*	*(c)*	*(b)*	*(a)*
21	**22**	**23**	**24**	**25**					
(a)	*(c)*	*(b)*	*(d)*	*(c)*					

16. Symbol Substitution

Questions in these category are easy to attempt. Candidates must be quick in substituting symbols and calculations. The common pattern of questions asked are given below.

EXERCISE

1. If "+" means "–"; "–" means "×"; "×"means "÷" and "÷" means "+", then
$15 \times 5 \div 10 + 5 - 3 = ?$
(a) 9.5 *(b)* 0
(c) –2 *(d)* 24

2. If "+" means "×"; "–" means "÷"; "÷"means "+" and "×" means "–", then what will be the value of $20 \div 40 - 4 \times 5 + 6 = ?$
(a) 60 *(b)* 1.67
(c) 150 *(d)* 0

3. If $\times$ stands for addition, $<$ for subtraction, $+$ stands for division, $>$ for multiplication, $-$ stands for equal to, $\div$ for greater than, and $=$ stands for less than, state which of the following is true?
(a) $5 \times 3 < 7 \div 8 + 4 \times 1$
(b) $3 \times 4 > 2 - 9 + 3 < 3$
(c) $5 > 2 + 2 = 10 < 4 \times 8$
(d) $3 \times 2 < 4 \div 16 > 2 + 4$

4. If $\rightarrow$ stands for subract, $\leftarrow$ stands for add, $\uparrow\uparrow$ stands for multiply, $\downarrow\downarrow$ stands for divide, $\leftrightarrow$ for greater than, $\longleftrightarrow$ stands for equal to, then which of the following alternatives is true?
(a) $4 \leftarrow 6 \uparrow\uparrow 2 \longleftrightarrow 3 \rightarrow 12 \leftarrow 12$
(b) $10 \downarrow\downarrow 5 \uparrow\uparrow 5 \longleftrightarrow 9 \rightarrow 3 \leftarrow 4$
(c) $15 \uparrow\uparrow 2 \rightarrow 5 \longleftrightarrow 12 \downarrow\downarrow 4 \leftarrow 3$
(d) $13 \downarrow\downarrow 13 \leftarrow 1 \leftrightarrow 20 \rightarrow 5 \uparrow\uparrow 2$

5. If Δ denotes $=$; $+$ denotes $>$, $-$ denotes $<$, $\square$ denotes $\neq$, $\times$ denotes $>$ and $\div$ denotes $<$ then $a + b - c$ denotes
(a) $b \,\Delta\, c \,\square\, a$
(b) $b \,\square\, a \div c$
(c) $a \div b \times c$
(d) $b - a + c$

6. If '$\ast$' denotes '×', 'Δ' denotes '÷', '$\square$' denotes '–', '$\bullet$' denotes '+', 'α' denotes '=' and 'β' denotes $\neq$, then which of the following euations is correct?
(a) $2 \,\square\, 10 \ast 4 \,\Delta\, 5 \,\alpha\, 5 \bullet 12 \,\Delta\, 6$
(b) $27 \,\Delta\, 9 \bullet 6 \,\beta\, 3 \ast 6 \,\square\, 9$
(c) $4 \,\Delta\, 2 \ast 0 \,\alpha\, 7 \,\Delta\, 1 \ast 0$
(d) $5 \bullet 6 \,\Delta\, 3 \,\square\, 2 \,\alpha\, 8 \,\Delta\, 4 \ast 3$

7. If $\downarrow$ stands for '÷', $\uparrow$ stands for '×', $\rightarrow$ stands for '+' and $\leftarrow$ stands for '–', then
$25 \downarrow 5 \rightarrow 3 \uparrow 6 \leftarrow 8 = ?$
(a) 9 *(b)* 12
(c) 16 *(d)* 15

8. If the + and × signs of the following equations are interchanged, which will be the correct equation?
(a) $7 \times 5 + 3 = 20$
(b) $4 + 9 \times 1 = 42$
(c) $6 \times 5 + 8 = 46$
(d) $2 + 11 \times 4 = 28$

9. If '+' stands for multiplication, '×' stands for addition, '÷' stands for subtraction and '–' stands for division, then what will be the result of the following equation?
$7 \times 4 \div 10 \times 2 + 5 = ?$
(a) 7 *(b)* 0
(c) 11 *(d)* 15

10. If 'A' means '÷', 'B' means '+', 'C' means '×' and 'D' means '–', then
12 C 4 A 24 D 10 B 1 = ?
(a) $11\frac{1}{3}$ *(b)* 23
(c) –7 *(d)* $16\frac{4}{5}$

EXPLANATORY ANSWERS

1. (c) : $15 \div 5 + 10 - 5 \times 3$
$3 + 10 - 15 = -2$

2. (d) : $20 + 40 \div 4 - 5 \times 6$
$20 + 10 - 30 = 0$

3. (c) : *(a)* $5 + 3 - 7 > 8 \div 4 + 1$
$1 > 3$
(b) $3 + 4 \times 2 = 9 \div 3 - 3$
$11 = 0$
(c) $5 \times 2 \div 2 < 10 - 4 + 8$
$5 < 14$
(d) $3 + 2 - 4 > 16 \times 2 \div 4$
$1 > 8$

4. (b) : *(a)* $4 + 6 \times 2 = 3 - 12 + 12$
$16 = 3$
(b) $10 \div 5 \times 5 = 9 - 3 + 4$
$10 = 10$
(c) $15 \times 2 - 5 = 12 \div 4 + 3$
$25 = 6$
(d) $13 \div 13 + 1 > 20 - 5 \times 2$
$2 > 10$

5. (d) : What is given is $a > b < c$
The equations are :
(a) $b = c \neq a$ which is wrong
(b) $b \neq a < c$ which is wrong
(c) $a < b > c$ which is wrong
(d) $b < a > c$ which is correct
Therefore, *(d)* is the answer.

6. (c) : The solved equations will be :
(a) $2 - 10 \times 4 \div 5 = 5 + 12 \div 6$
$2 - 8 = 5 + 2$
$-6 = 7$ which is wrong
(b) $27 \div 9 + 6 \neq 3 \times 6 - 9$
$3 + 6 \neq 18 - 9$
$9 \neq 9$ which is wrong
(c) $4 \div 2 \times 0 = 7 \div 1 \times 0$
$2 \times 0 = 7 \times 0$
$0 = 0$ which is correct
(d) $5 + 6 \div 3 - 2 = 8 \div 4 \times 3$
$5 = 6$ which is wrong

7. (d) : $25 \div 5 + 3 \times 6 - 8$
$5 + 18 - 8 = 15$

8. (c) : After interchanging the signs the equations are :
(a) $7 + 5 \times 3 = 22$ which is wrong
(b) $4 \times 9 + 1 = 37$ which is wrong
(c) $6 + 5 \times 8 = 46$ which is correct
(d) $2 \times 11 + 4 = 26$ which is wrong

9. (c) : $7 + 4 - 10 + 2 \times 5$
$7 + 4 - 10 + 10 = 11$

10. (c) : $12 \times 4 \div 24 - 10 + 1$
$2 - 10 + 1 = -7$

17. MISSING NUMBERS

Playing with numbers and mathematical skills are needed to attempt these type of tests. The candidates have to work out the right combination of arithmetical symbols to arrive at the answer options which will take the place of the interrogation sign in the given questions.

EXERCISE

Directions: *In each question given below which one number can be placed at the sign of interrogation?*

1.

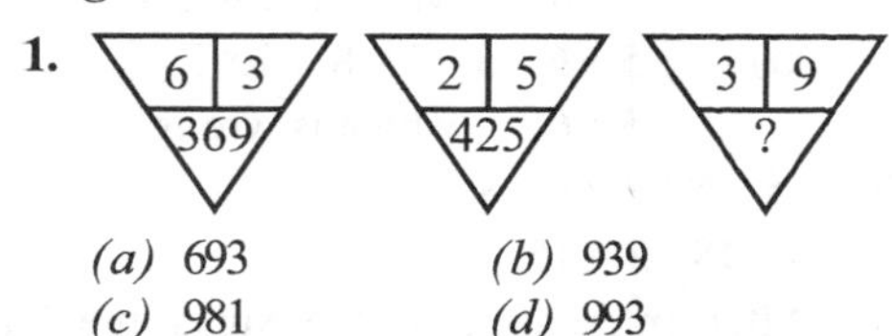

(a) 693 (b) 939
(c) 981 (d) 993

2.

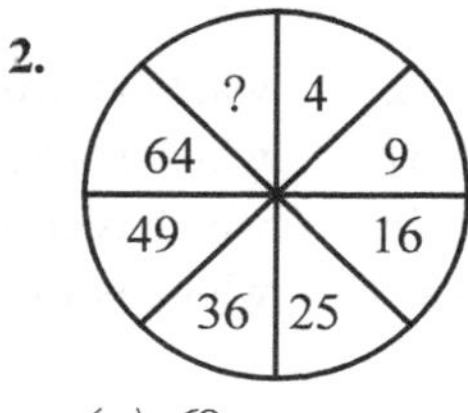

(a) 68 (b) 100
(c) 72 (d) 81

3.

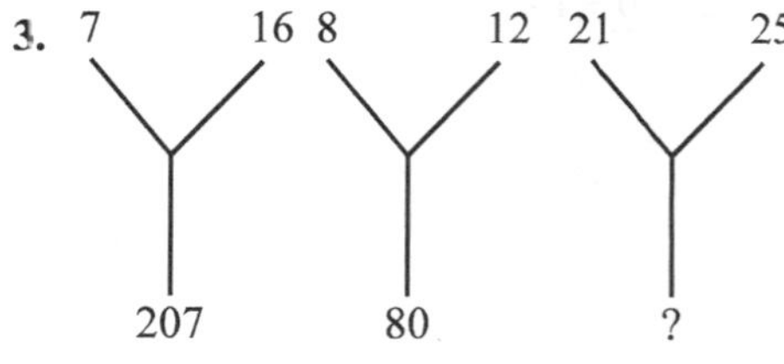

(a) 425 (b) 184
(c) 241 (d) 210

4.

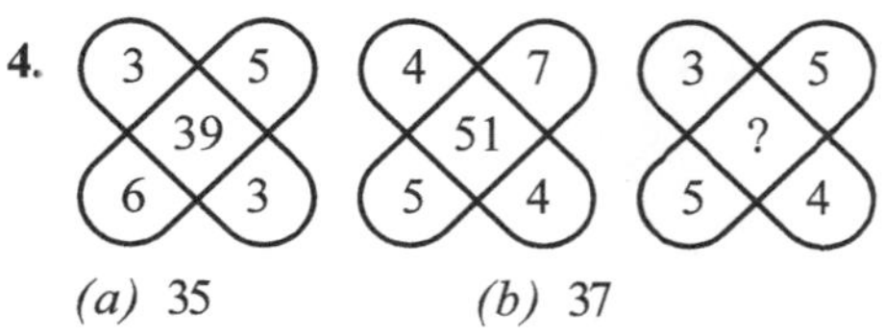

(a) 35 (b) 37
(c) 45 (d) 48

5.

7	5		5	21		24	4
6			13			?	

(a) 4 (b) 8
(c) 20 (d) 14

6.

14	9	4
12	7	2
10	5	0
16	11	?

(a) 9 (b) 6
(c) 3 (d) 7

7.

29, 27, 39, 80, 33, 45, 43   29, 30, 42, 70, 31, 43, 44   59, 40, ?, 80, 10, 39, 20

(a) 69 (b) 49
(c) 50 (d) 60

8.

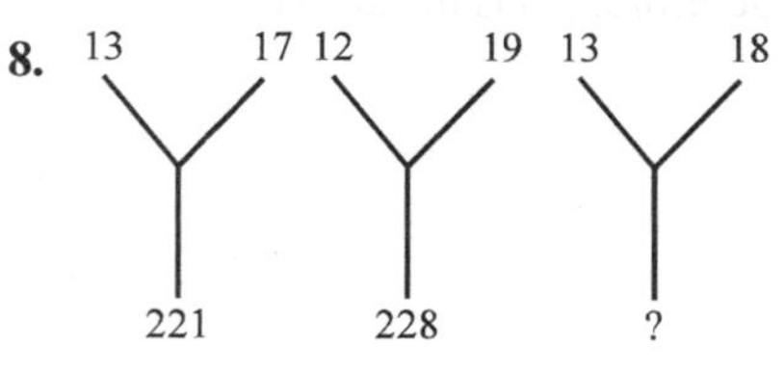

(a) 31 (b) 229
(c) 234 (d) 312

9.

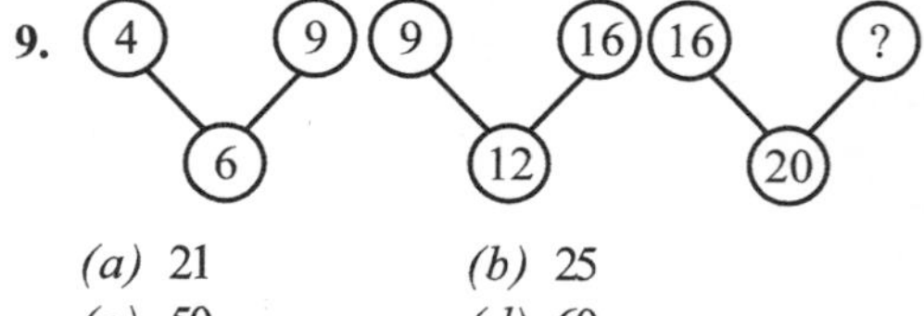

(a) 21 (b) 25
(c) 50 (d) 60

10.

51	(11)	61
64	(30)	32
35	(?)	43

(a) 25 *(b)* 27
(c) 32 *(d)* 37

11.

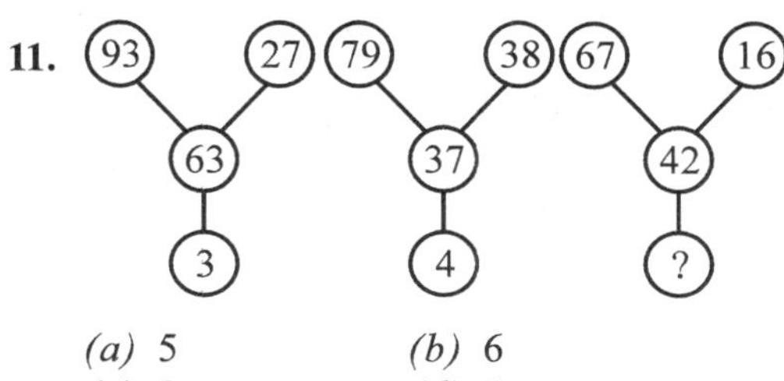

(a) 5 *(b)* 6
(c) 8 *(d)* 9

12.

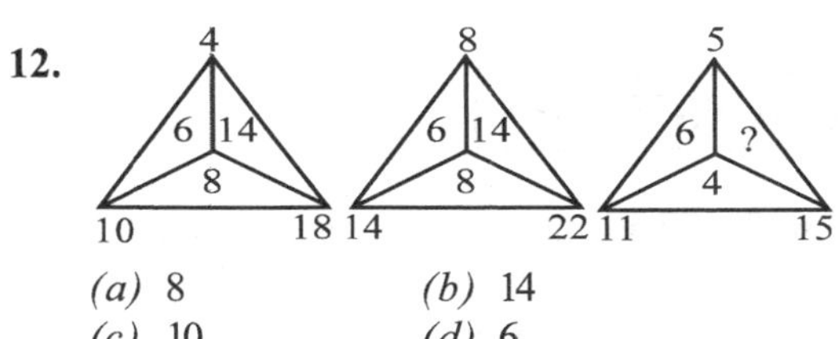

(a) 8 *(b)* 14
(c) 10 *(d)* 6

13.

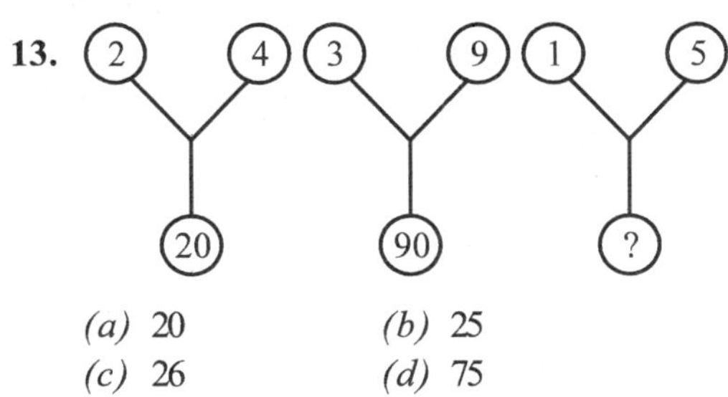

(a) 20 *(b)* 25
(c) 26 *(d)* 75

14.

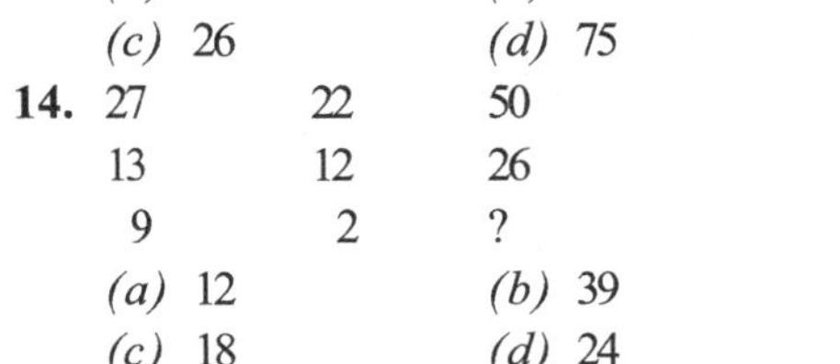

27	22	50
13	12	26
9	2	?

(a) 12 *(b)* 39
(c) 18 *(d)* 24

15.

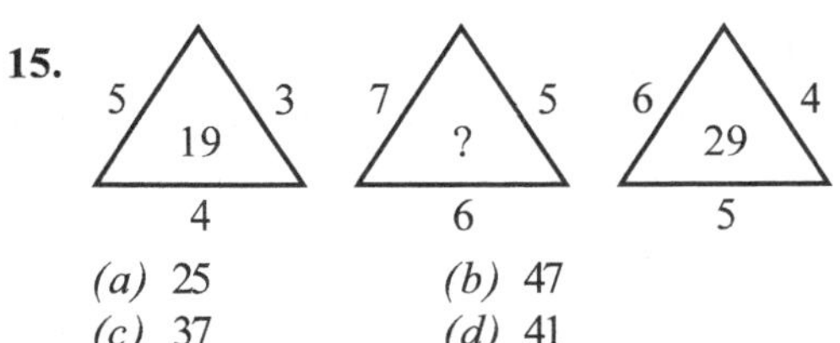

(a) 25 *(b)* 47
(c) 37 *(d)* 41

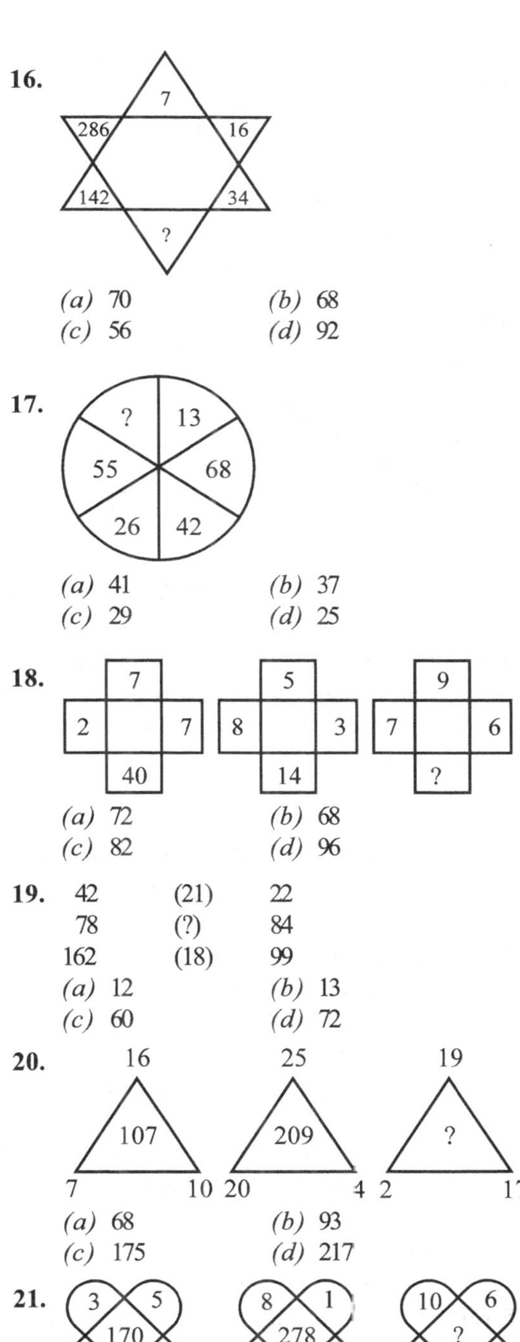

16.

(a) 70 *(b)* 68
(c) 56 *(d)* 92

17.

(a) 41 *(b)* 37
(c) 29 *(d)* 25

18.

(a) 72 *(b)* 68
(c) 82 *(d)* 96

19.

42	(21)	22
78	(?)	84
162	(18)	99

(a) 12 *(b)* 13
(c) 60 *(d)* 72

20.

(a) 68 *(b)* 93
(c) 175 *(d)* 217

21.

3 5 / 170 / 6 2 8 1 / 278 / 9 4 10 6 / ? / 2 7

(a) 960 *(b)* 628
(c) 830 *(d)* 492

22.

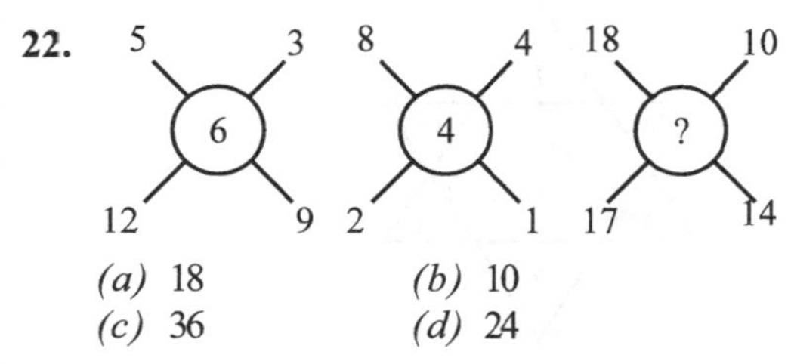

(*a*) 18 (*b*) 10
(*c*) 36 (*d*) 24

23.

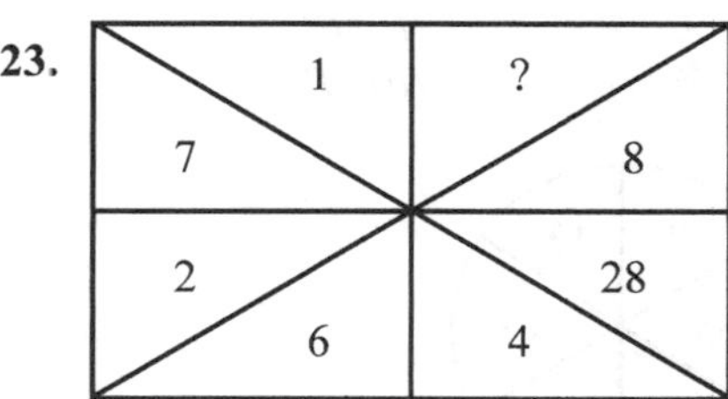

(*a*) 24 (*b*) 10
(*c*) 32 (*d*) 12

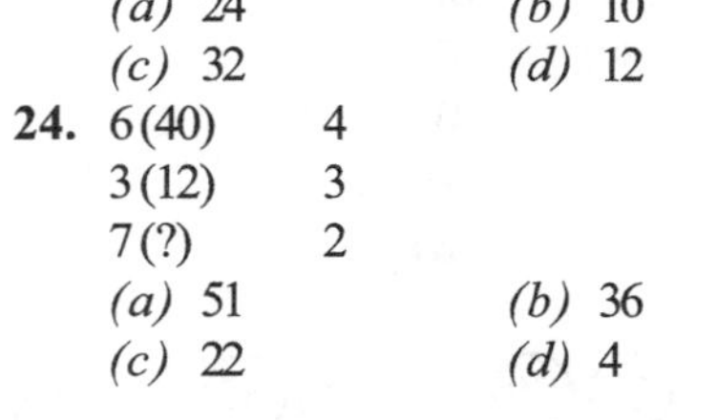

24.

6 (40)	4
3 (12)	3
7 (?)	2

(*a*) 51 (*b*) 36
(*c*) 22 (*d*) 4

25.

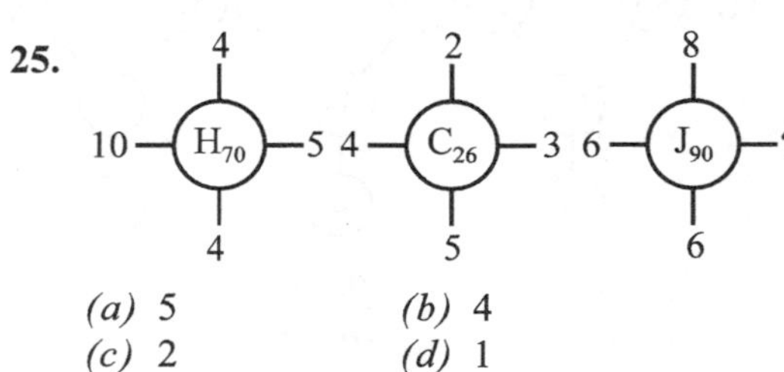

(*a*) 5 (*b*) 4
(*c*) 2 (*d*) 1

EXPLANATORY ANSWERS

1. *(c)* : The squares of two numbers on the top placed side by side gives the number inside the bottom triangle, *i.e.*,
6^2 and $3^2 = 369$
2^2 and $5^2 = 425$, similarly
3^2 and $9^2 = 981$.

2. *(d)* : Starting from number 4 the numbers are the squares of numbers in natural order *i.e.*, $2^2 = 4, 3^2 = 9, 4^2 = 16 \ldots\ldots 9^2 = 81$.

3. *(b)* : The number at the bottom is the difference of the squares of two numbers at the top, *i.e.*,
$16^2 - 7^2 = 256 - 49 = 207$
$12^2 - 8^2 = 144 - 64 = 80$, similarly
$25^2 - 21^2 = 625 - 441 = 184$.

4. *(b)* : The number in the centre is the sum of the products of diagonal numbers, *i.e.*,
$(3 \times 3) + (5 \times 6) = 39$
$(4 \times 4) + (7 \times 5) = 51$, similarly
$(3 \times 4) + (5 \times 5) = 37$.

5. *(d)* : Sum of two numbers on the top divided by 2 gives the third number, *i.e.*,
$(7 + 5) \div 2 = 6$
$(5 + 21) \div 2 = 13$, similarly
$(24 + 4) \div 2 = 14$.

6. *(b)* : The numbers in 2nd and 3rd columns are 5 less than the nunbers in 1st and 2nd columns respectively, *i.e.*,
$14 - 5 = 9$ and $9 - 5 = 4$
$12 - 5 = 7$ and $7 - 5 = 2, \ldots$ similarly
$16 - 5 = 11$ and $11 - 5 = 6$.

7. *(a)* : The sum of 3 numbers in each line in one figure is same, *i.e.*,
$29 + 80 + 43$ or $39 + 80 + 33$
or $45 + 80 + 27 = 152$
$29 + 70 + 44$ or $42 + 70 + 31$
or $43 + 70 + 30 = 143$,
similarly $59 + 80 + 20$ or $39 + 80 + 40 = 159$.
The missing number is :
$159 - (80 + 10) = 69$.

8. *(c)* : The number at the bottom is the product of two numbers at the top, *i.e.*,
$13 \times 17 = 221$
$12 \times 19 = 228$, similarly
$13 \times 18 = 234$.

9. *(b)* : Square of number at the bottom is equal to the product of two numbers at the top, *i.e.*,
$6^2 = 4 \times 9$, *i.e.*, 36
$12^2 = 9 \times 16$, *i.e.*, 144, similarly
$20^2 = 16 \times ?$, *i.e.*, 400. The missing number is $400 \div 16 = 25$.

10. *(b)* : The sum of the products of the digits of numbers in 1st and 3rd columns is the number in the 2nd column, *i.e.*,
$(5 \times 1) + (6 \times 1) = 11$
$(6 \times 4) + (3 \times 2) = 30$, similarly
$(3 \times 5) + (4 \times 3) = 27$.

11. *(d)* : The sum of numbers on right and centre subtracted from the number on the left gives the number at the bottom, *i.e.*,
$93 - (27 + 63) = 3$
$79 - (38 + 37) = 4$, similarly
$67 - (16 + 42) = 9$.

12. *(c)* : The number inside each triangle is the difference of the numbers at its base *i.e.*
$10 - 4 = 6$, $18 - 4 = 14$ and $18 - 10 = 8$
$14 - 8 = 6$, $22 - 8 = 14$ and $22 - 14 = 8$, similarly
$11 - 5 = 6$, $15 - 5 = 10$ and $15 - 11 = 4$.

13. *(c)* : The sum of squares of two numbers at the top gives the third number below, *i.e.*,
$2^2 + 4^2 = 20$
$3^2 + 9^2 = 90$, similarly
$1^2 + 5^2 = 26$.

14. *(a)* : The sum of numbers in 1st and 2nd column plus 1 is the number in the 3rd column, *i.e.*,
$27 + 22 + 1 = 50$
$13 + 12 + 1 = 26$, similarly
$9 + 2 + 1 = 12$.

15. *(d)* : The product of numbers on either side of the triangle plus the number at the base is the number inside the triangle, *i.e.*,
$(5 \times 3) + 4 = 19$
$(6 \times 4) + 5 = 29$, similarly
$(7 \times 5) + 6 = 41$.

16. *(a)* : Clockwise starting from number 7, the next number is obtained by doubling the number and adding 2, *i.e.*,
$(7 \times 2) + 2 = 16$
$(16 \times 2) + 2 = 34 \ldots$, similarly
$(34 \times 2) + 2 = 70$
$(70 \times 2) + 2 = 142$
$(142 \times 2) + 2 = 286$.

17. *(c)* : The difference between the numbers in opposite sectors is 13, *i.e.*,
$26 - 13 = 13$
$68 - 55 = 13$, similarly
The missing number is $42 - 13 = 29$
($42 + 13 = 55$ is not given as option).

18. *(b)* : The number at the bottom is obtained by subtracting the sum of two numbers in the centre grid line from the square of the number at the top, *i.e.*,
$7^2 - (2 + 7) = 40$
$5^2 - (8 + 3) = 14$, similarly
$9^2 - (7 + 6) = 68$.

19. *(b)* : The number inside the brackets is obtained by multiplying the number on the left by 2 and then dividing the product by the sum of digits of number on the right, *i.e.*,
$(42 \times 2) \div (2 + 2) = 21$
$(162 \times 2) \div (9 + 9) = 18$, similarly
$(78 \times 2) \div (8 + 4) = 13$.

20. *(a)* : Subtracting the sum of squares of two numbers at the base from the square of number at the apex gives the number inside the triangle, *i.e.*,
$16^2 - (7^2 + 10^2) = 107$
$25^2 - (20^2 + 4^2) = 209$, similarly
$19^2 - (2^2 + 17^2) = 68$.

21. *(c)* : The number in the centre is the product of all the 4 numbers minus 10, *i.e.*,
$(3 \times 5 \times 2 \times 6) - 10 = 170$
$(8 \times 1 \times 4 \times 9) - 10 = 278$, similarly
$(10 \times 6 \times 7 \times 2) - 10 = 830$.

22. *(d)* : The number inside the circle is the product of difference of two numbers above and difference of two numbers below, *i.e.*,
$(5 - 3)(12 - 9) = 6$
$(8 - 4)(2 - 1) = 4$, similarly
$(18 - 10)(17 - 14) = 24$.

23. *(a)* : Starting from number 1 anticlockwise the number in the diagonally opposite section is its multiplication by 4, *i.e.*,
$1 \times 4 = 4$, $7 \times 4 = 28$, $2 \times 4 = 8$, similarly
$6 \times 4 = 24$.

24. ***(a)*** **:** Square of the number on the left plus the number on the right is the number within brackets, *i.e.*,

$6^2+4=40$

$3^2+3=12$, similarly

$7^2+2=51$.

25. ***(b)*** **:** Letter H is 8th in order of alphabetical series. Taking the sum of numbers placed vertically outside the circle + 8; multiplying it by the number on the right; then subtracting from the product the number on the left, gives the number inside the circle, *i.e.*,

Step I $\rightarrow$ $4+8+4 = 16$

Step II $\rightarrow$ $16\times5 = 80$

Step III $\rightarrow$ $80-10 = 70$

Letter C is 3rd in order, so

Step I $\rightarrow$ $2+3+5 = 10$

Step II $\rightarrow$ $10\times3 = 30$

Step III $\rightarrow$ $30-4 = 26$

Similarly, J is 10th in order, so

Step I $\rightarrow$ $8+10+6 = 24$

Step II $\rightarrow$ $24\times ?$

Step III $\rightarrow$ $(24\times ?)-6=90$

Simplifying the above equation :

$24\times ? = 90+6$, *i.e.*, 96

$? = 96\div24=4$.

18. ALPHABET PROBLEMS

Alphabet problems are fun to attempt. They are based on alphabetical series in natural as well as reverse order.

Natural Order

A B C D E F G H I J K L M N O P Q R S T U V W X Y Z

Reverse Order

Z Y X W V U T S R Q P O N M L K J I H G F E D C B A

Note : The series starts from A on reaching Z and from Z on reaching A. Of these A E I O U are vowels and the rest are consonants.

EXERCISE

1. Which letter should be ninth letter to the left of ninth letter from the right if the first half of the alphabet is reversed?

(a) I *(b)* D
(c) F *(d)* E

2. Starting from the fifth letter from the left, if twelve letters are written in reverse order, then which letter will be the seventh to the left of the fourteenth letter from the right?

(a) N *(b)* H
(c) L *(d)* O

3. What letter will come in the centre of sixth letter from the right and thirteenth letter from the left?

(a) Q *(b)* R
(c) P *(d)* S

4. If in the word "DISTURBANCE", the first letter is interchanged with the last letter, the second letter is interchanged with the tenth letter and so on, which letter would come after the letter "T" in the newly formed word?

(a) I *(b)* U
(c) N *(d)* S

5. If it is possible to make a meaningful word with the third, the fifth, the seventh and the tenth letters of the word PROJECTION. If no such word can be made, give 'O' as the answer. If more than one such word can be made, give 'M' as the answer.

(a) T *(b)* N
(c) O *(d)* M

6. A meaningful word is made if we take the first, fourth, fifth, seventh, tenth, eleventh and the twelfth letters of the word "FELICITATIONS". Which of the following will be the fifth letter of that word from the right end of that word?

(a) T *(b)* C
(c) N *(d)* I

7. On rearranging the jumbled spelling of the word SKARTINS, a language is obtained. What is the fifth letter from the right of the rearranged word?

(a) N *(b)* K
(c) R *(d)* S

8. If the 1st, 3rd, 5th, 7th, 10th and 13th letters of the word "ENTERTAINMENT" are used to make a meaningful word, then what two letters will come in the centre?

(a) AM *(b)* TT
(c) RE *(d)* NA

9. On rearranging the jumbled spelling of the word GRUBY a sport is obtained. What is the letter in the centre?

(a) R *(b)* B
(c) G *(d)* U

10. If the letters 'ERVSECI' can be rearranged to form a meaningful word what will be the fifth letter from the right?

(a) R (b) V
(c) E (d) None of these

11. From the word HASTEN how many independent meaningful English words can be made without changing the order of the letters and using each letter only once?

(a) 1 (b) 2
(c) 3 (d) 4

EXPLANATORY ANSWERS

1. (d) : MLKJIGHFEDCBANOPQRSTUVWXYZ

9th 9th

2. (d) : ABCDPONMLKJIHGFEQRSTUVWXYZ

7th 14th

3. (a) : A M Q U Z

4th 4th

13th 6th

13th letter from left is 'M' and 6th letter from right is 'U'. The letter in the centre of 'M' and 'U' is 'Q'.

4. (d) : E C N A B R U T S I D

5. (d) : P R O J E C T I O N

The 3rd, 5th, 7th and 10th letters are OETN.

The words formed are TONE and NOTE.

6. (b) : F E L I C I T A T I O N S

The 1st, 4th, 5th, 7th, 10th, 11th and 12th lettes are FICTION.

The word is FICTION and 5th letter from right is 'C'.

7. (d) : The word is SANSKRIT and 5th letter from right is 'S'.

8. (b) : E N T E R T A I N M E N T

The 1st, 3rd, 5th 7th, 10th and 13th letters are ETRAMT.

The word formed is MATTER.

9. (c) : The sport is RUGBY. The letter in the centre is 'G'.

10. (a) : The word is SERVICE and fifth letter from right is 'R'.

11. (b) : The words formed are : HAS, TEN.

19. Logical Diagram

In these type of questions, a set of five different figures is given as options. Each figure represents a logical pattern of certain groups of related words wherein each word represents a class. One has to identify the most appropriate logical figure for the set of words given. Some of the relationships represented by these diagrams are given below. Understand the relationship patterns and then attempt the exercise following the explanation.

EXERCISE

Directions : *From the five logical Diagrams, select one which best illustrates the relationship among three given classes in the questions 1 to 10.*

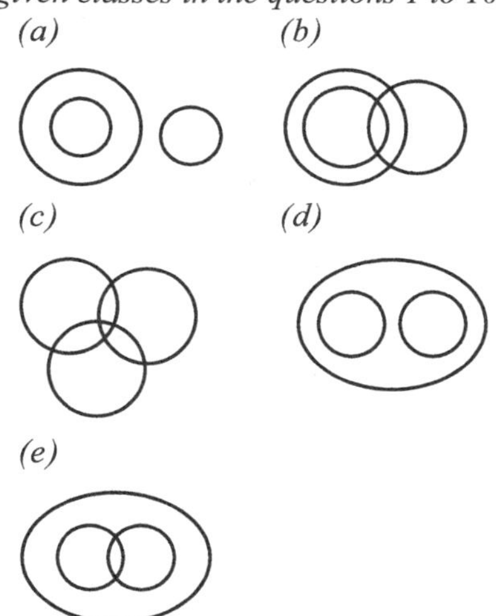

1. Birds, fruits, mangoes
2. Criminals, lawyers, bandits
3. Swimmers, bachelors, men
4. Smart, engineers, women
5. Vegetables, potatoes, brinjals
6. Grapes, sweet, fruit
7. Doctors, architects, humans
8. Scholars, people, Indians
9. Children, naughty, studious
10. Pens, pencils, stationery

Directions : *From the five logical diagrams select one which best illustrates the relationship among three given classes in questions 11 to 20.*

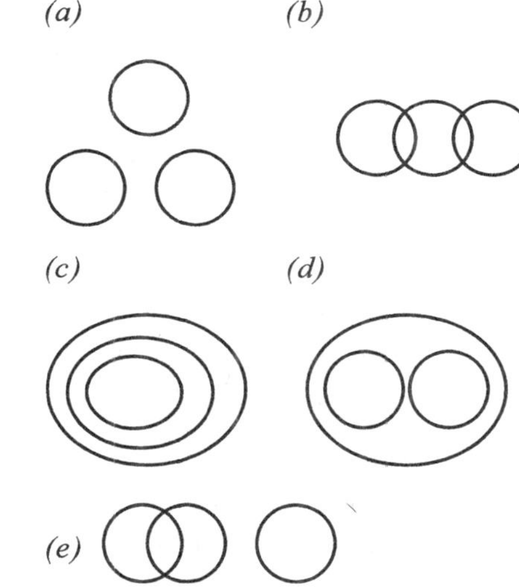

11. Ink, crayons, red
12. Canines, dogs, pups
13. Table, chair, stool
14. Ripe, mangoes, basket
15. Scholars, studious, illiterates
16. Cars, ships, means of conveyance
17. Age, number, thirteen
18. Country, state, continent
19. Father, parent, mother
20. Iron, metal, mercury

Directions : *From the five logical diagrams select one which best illustrates the relationship among three given classes in the questions 21 to 30.*

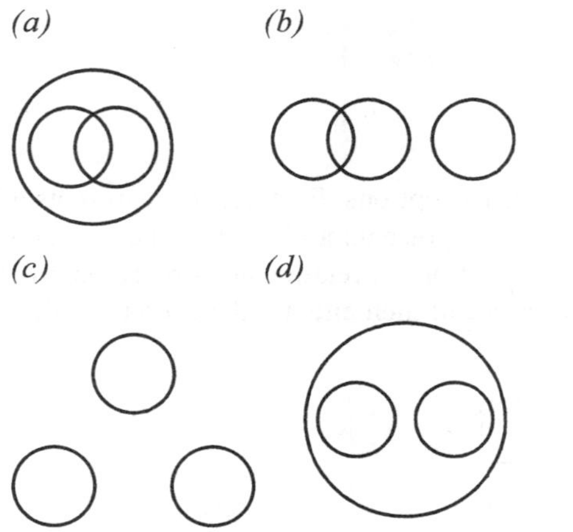

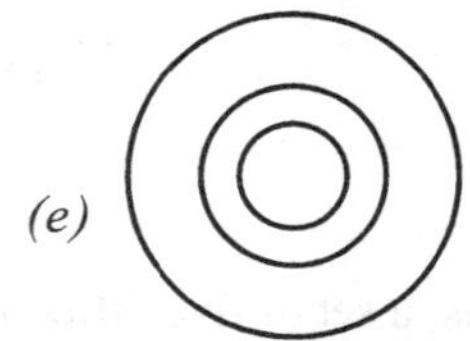

21. Lizards, Reptiles, Crocodiles
22. Whales, Tortoise, Fishes
23. Birds, Crows, Parrots
24. Sisters, Women, Mothers
25. Plants, Scientists, Men
26. Novels, Album, English
27. Sentences, Words, Paragraph
28. Beef, Mutton, Flesh
29. Principal, Student, Parent
30. Lily, Rose, Flower.

EXPLANATORY ANSWERS

1. *(a)* :

Fruits
Mangoes
Birds

All mangoes are fruits, but neither fruits, nor mangoes can be birds.

2. *(a)* :

Criminals
Bandits
Law-yers

All bandits are criminal, but neither criminals nor bandits can be lawyers.

3. *(b)* :

Men
Bache-lors
Swim-mers

All bachelors are men and some men and bachelors can be swimmers.

4. *(c)* :

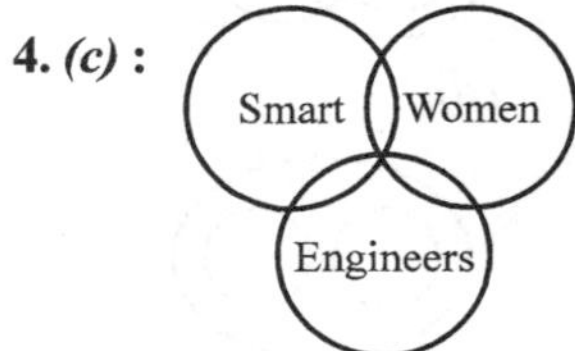

Some women can be smart and some women can be engineers and vice–versa. Some engineers can be women and some engineers can be smart and vice–versa.

5. *(d)* :

Vegetables
Potatoes
Brinjals

Potatoes and brinjals are vegetables but they have nothing in common. Some vegetables are potatoes and some are brinjals.

6. *(b)* :

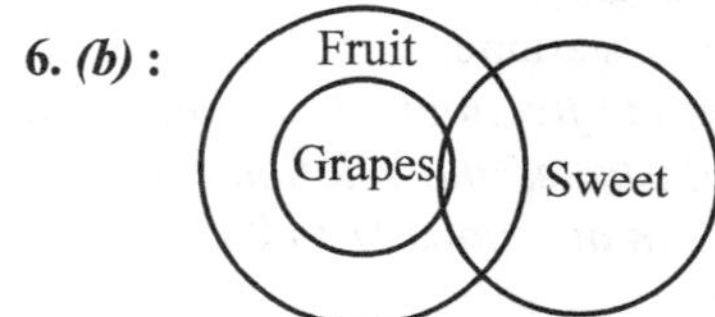

Some grapes are sweet and all grapes are fruit. But not all that is sweet is fruit.

7. *(d)* :

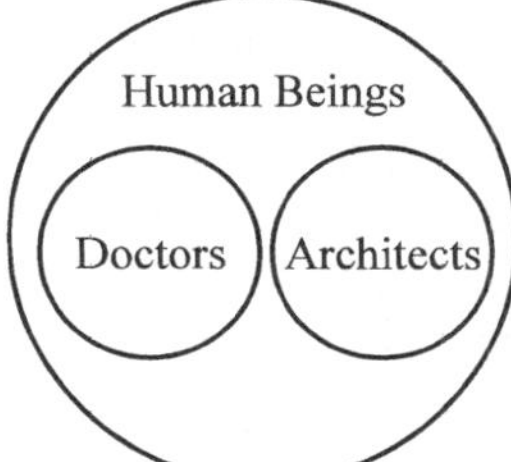

Doctors and architects are two separate classes, but all doctors and architects are humans and some humans are either doctors or architects.

8. *(e)* :

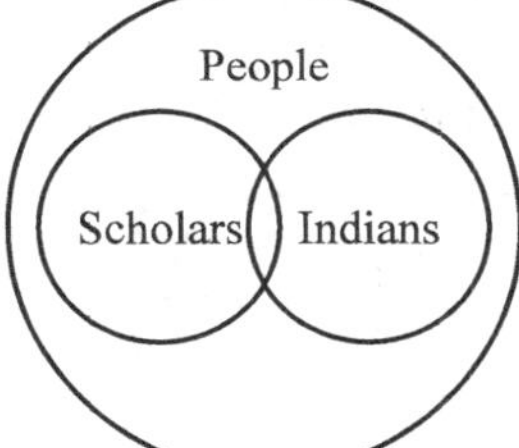

Some Indians can be scholars and some scholars can be Indians. All scholars and Indians are people.

9. *(c)* :

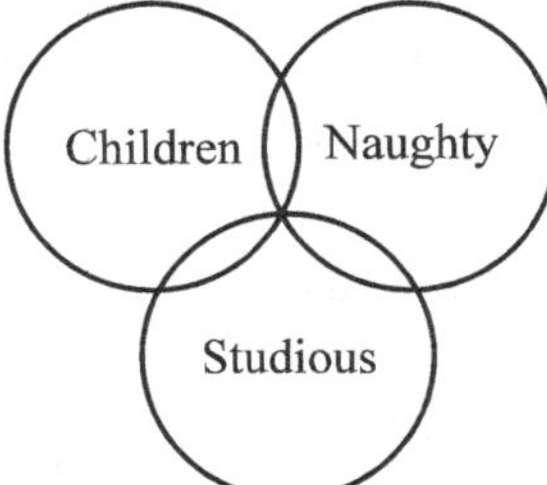

Some children can be naughty and some can be studious, some studious can be children and some naughty. Some naughty can be studious and some children.

10. *(d)* :

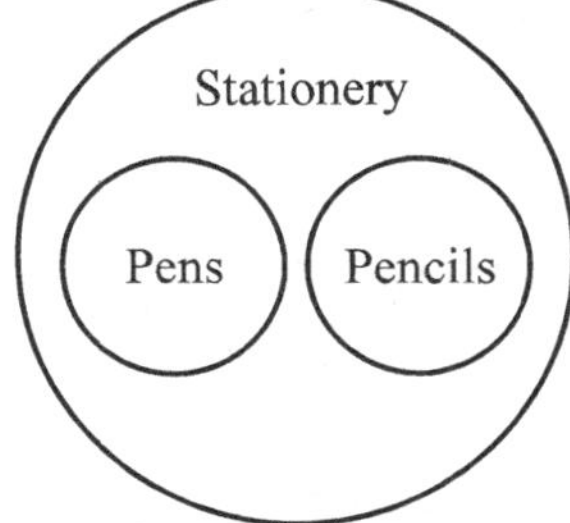

Pens and pencils both are items of stationery and some stationery is pens and pencils, but pens and pencils are two separate classes.

11. *(b)* :

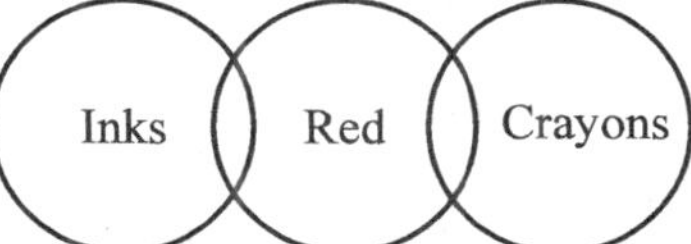

Some ink and some crayons can be red and some red units can be inks and crayons, but ink and crayon have nothing in common.

12. *(c)* :

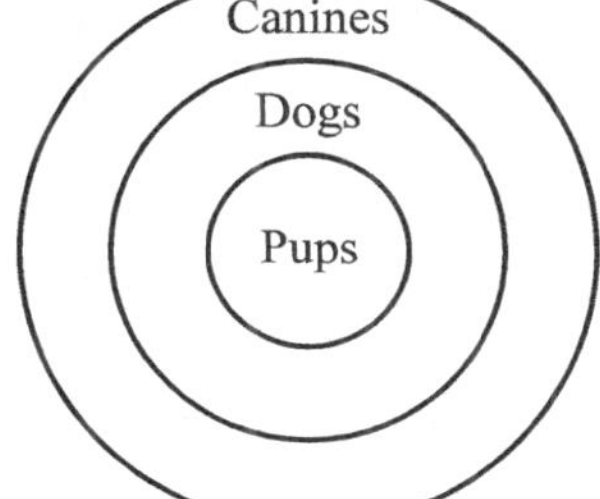

All pups are dogs and all dogs are canines. Some canines are dogs, of which some are pups.

13. *(a)* :

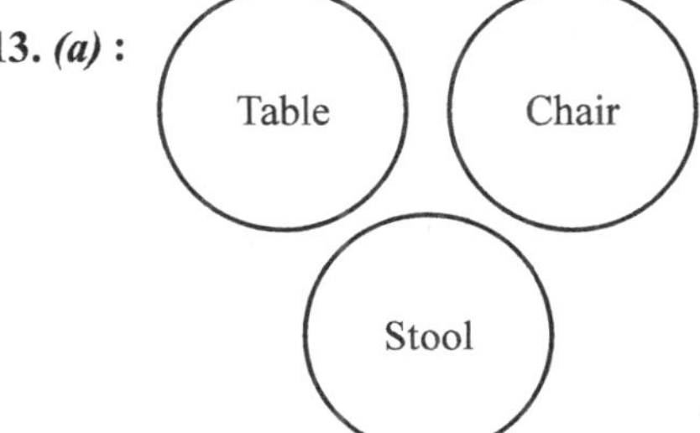

All three are different classes.

14. *(e)* :

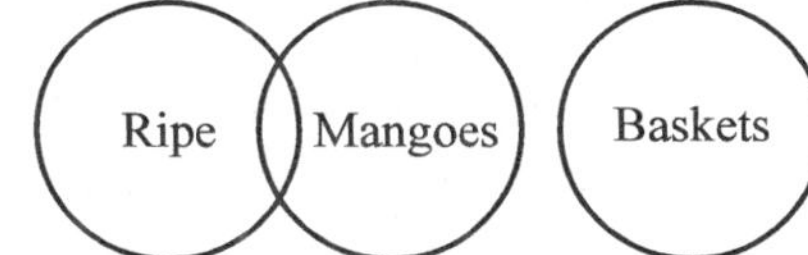

Some mangoes are ripe and some ripe units are mangoes, but neither ripe units nor mangoes can be baskets.

15. *(e)* :

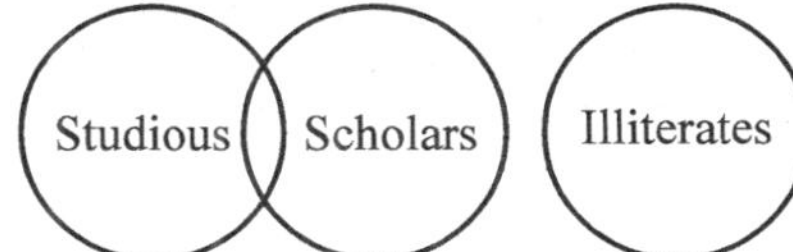

Some studious can be scholars and some scholars can be studious, but neither studious nor scholars can be illiterates.

16. ***(d)*** **:**

Means of Conveyance
Cars
Ships

All cars and all ships are means of conveyance, but neither is contained in the other. Some means of conveyance are cars and some ships.

17. ***(b)*** **:**

Age
Thirteen
Number

Some are aged thirteen and some numbers are thirteen. Some thirteen units are numbers and some ages. Age and number have nothing in common.

18. ***(c)*** **:**

Continents
Countries
States

All continents contain countries within it and each country contains states within it.

19. ***(d)*** **:**

Parents
Father
Mother

All fathers and mothers are parents, but they are two separate classes. Some of the parents are fathers and some are mothers.

20. ***(d)*** **:**

Metals
Iron
Mercury

Iron and mercury are metals, but they have nothing in common. Some metals are iron and some mercury.

21. ***(d)*** **:**

Reptiles
Lizards
Crocodiles

All lizards and crocodiles are reptiles, but neither is contained in the other. Some reptiles are lizards and some crocodiles.

22. ***(c)*** **:**

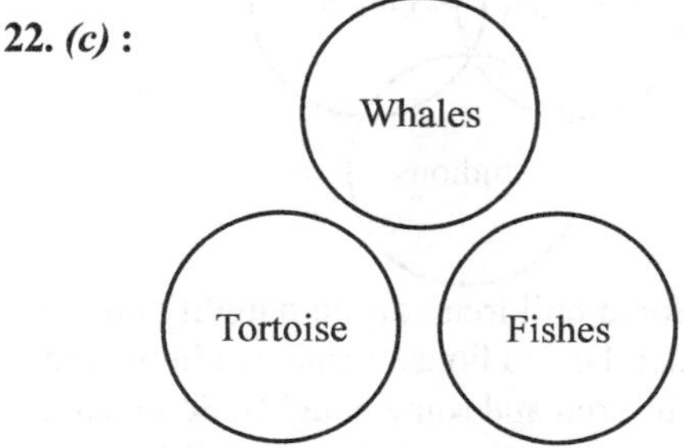

All three are different classes.

23. ***(d)*** **:**

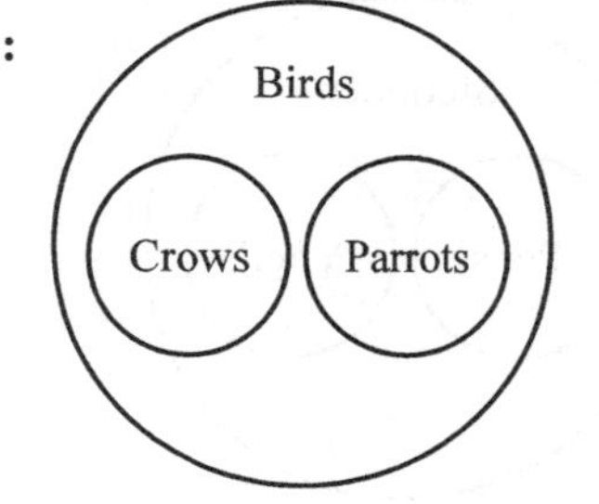

All crows and parrots are birds but neither is contained in the other. Some birds are crows and some parrots.

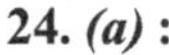

24. ***(a)*** **:**

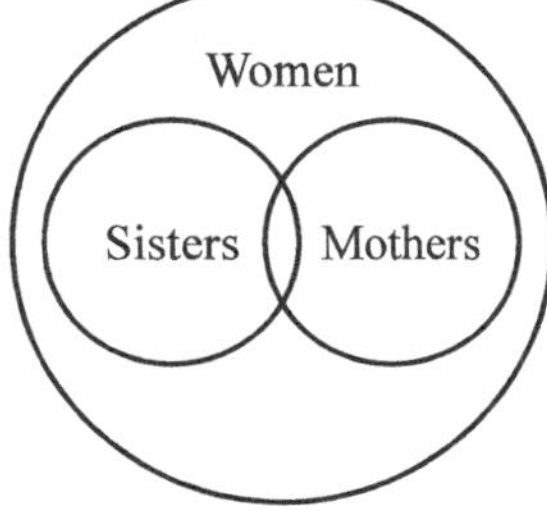

Some sisters can be mothers and some mothers can be sisters. All sisters and mothers are women.

25. ***(b)*** **:**

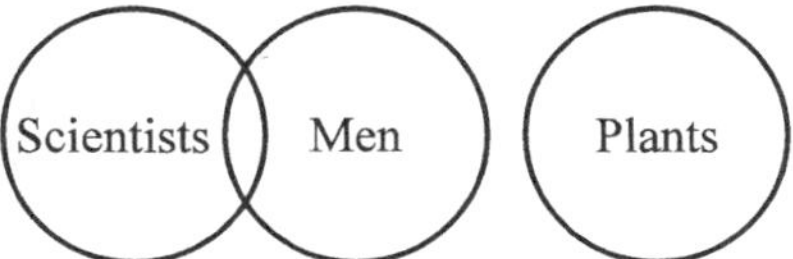

Some scientists can be men and some men can be scientists, but neither scientists nor men can be plants.

26. ***(b)*** **:**

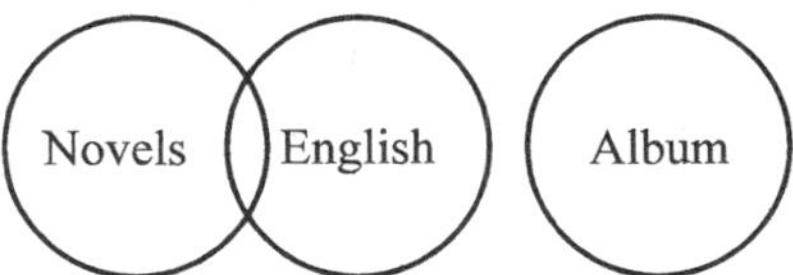

Some novels can be in English and some written material in English can be novels, but neither novels nor English can be album.

27. ***(e)*** **:**

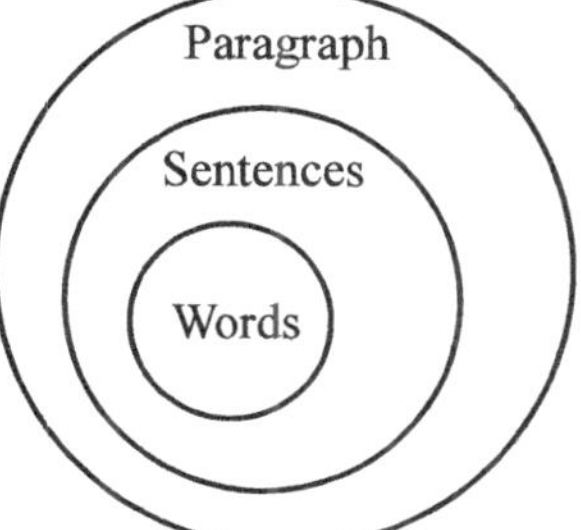

All paragraphs contain sentences within it and all sentences contain words within it.

28. ***(d)*** **:**

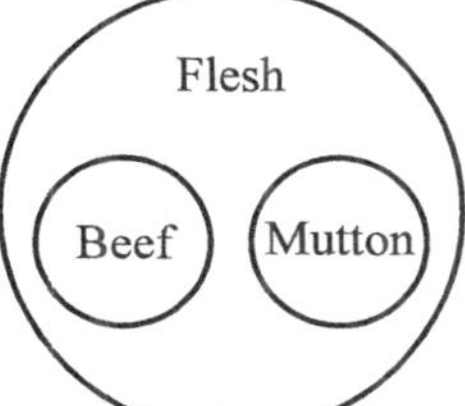

All beef and mutton is flesh of some animals. Some flesh is beef and some mutton.

29. ***(b)*** **:**

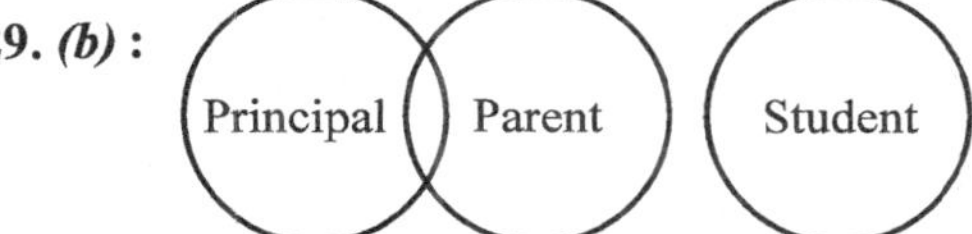

A Principal can be a parent and parent can be a principal. A student is a different class.

30. ***(d)*** **:**

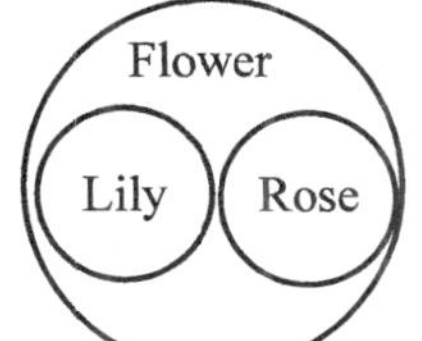

Both lily and rose are flowers. But neither is contained in the other.

20. SYLLOGISM

In this reasoning pattern, the two premises are followed by two conclusions drawn from them. Five options *(a)*, *(b)*, *(c)*, *(d)* and *(e)* are given as answers. Based on the two statements the candidate has to select the right option as answer.

EXERCISE

Directions (Qs. 1-10): *In each question below are given two statements followed by two conclusions numbered I and II. You have to take the two given statements to be true even if they seem to be at variance from commonly known facts and then decide which of the given conclusions logically follows from the two given statements, disregarding commonly known facts. Read both the statements and—*

Give answer (a) if only conclusion I follows; give answer (b) if only conclusion II follows; give answer (c) if either I or II follows; give answer (d) if neither I nor II follows and give answer (e) if both I and II follows.

1. *Statements* *I :* All tomatoes are red.
II : All grapes are tomatoes.
Conclusions *I :* All grapes are red.
II : Some tomatoes are grapes.

2. *Statements* *I :* All painters are smilling.
II : Some authors are painters.
Conclusions *I :* All smiling authors are painters.
II : Some authors are smiling.

3. *Statements* *I :* All peons in this office are efficient.
II : Ramu is not efficient.
Conclusions *I :* Ramu is not peon in this office.
II : Ramu should be more efficient.

4. *Statements* *I :* All weavers are hard working.
II : No hard working men are foolish.
Conclusions *I :* No weavers are foolish.
II : Some foolish are weavers.

5. *Statements* *I :* All fishes are cars.
II : All cars are vegetables.
Conclusions *I :* Some vegetables are cars.
II : Some vegetables are fishes.

6. *Statements* *I :* Some dogs are pups.
II : All horses are pups.
Conclusions *I :* Some dogs are horses.
II : Some horses are dogs.

7. *Statements* *I :* All beautiful women are mothers.
II : All mothers are understanding.
Conclusions *I :* All beautiful women are understanding.
II : All mothers are beautiful women.

8. *Statements* *I :* Some toys are tables.
II : No table is black.
Conclusions *I :* Some toys are black.
II : Some toys are not black.

9. *Statements* *I :* All rivers are mountains.
II : Some rivers are deserts.
Conclusions *I :* Some mountains are deserts.
II : Some deserts are not mountains.

10. *Statements* *I :* All men are horses.
II : All horses are elephants.
Conclusions *I :* All men are elephants.
II : All elephants are men.

Directions (Qs. 11-15): *In the following questions, select the set of conclusion which logically follows from the given statements.*

11. *Statements* *I*: All foxes are plates.
II: All plates are trees.
Conclusions *I*: All foxes are trees.
II: All trees are foxes.
III: Some trees are foxes.
IV: Some trees are plates.
(a) All conclusions are correct.
(b) Only conclusions I, III, and IV follow.
(c) Only conclusions II, III, and IV follow.
(d) Only conclusions I and IV follow.
(e) None of the above.

12. *Statements* *I*: Some cubes are squares.
II: All squares are circles.
Conclusions *I*: All cubes are circles.
II: Some circles are cubes.
III: Some circles are squares.
IV: All squares are cubes.
(a) Only conclusion I follows.
(b) Only conclusion I, II and III follow.
(c) All conclusions are correct.
(d) Only conclusions II and III follow.
(e) None of the above.

13. *Statements* *I*: All cups are goats.
II: All goats are tins.
Conclusions *I*: All goats are cups.
II: All tins are goats.
III: No cups are tins.
IV: No tins are cups.
(a) Only conclusions III and IV follow.
(b) Only conclusios I and II follow.
(c) Only conclusions I, II and III follow.
(d) All conclusions are correct.
(e) None of the above.

14. *Statements* *I*: All bombs are bags.
II: Some bags are jets.
Conclusions *I*: All bombs are jets.
II: All jets are bombs.
III: Some jets are bombs.
IV: Some bombs are jets.
(a) Only conclusion III follows.
(b) Only conclusions I and II follow.
(c) All conclusions are correct.
(d) Only conclusions III and IV follow.
(e) None of these.

15. *Statements* *I*: Some thorns are jackets.
II: Some jackets are boats.
Conclusions *I*: No thorns are boats.
II: All jackets are boats.
III: Some boats are thorns.
IV: No jackets are thorns.
(a) Either conclusion I or IV follows.
(b) Either conclusion I or II follows.
(c) Either conclusion I or III follows.
(d) No conclusion is correct.
(e) All conclusions are correct.

EXPLANATORY ANSWERS

1. *(e)*: When all tomatoes are red and all grapes are tomatoes, then all grapes are also red. When all grapes are tomatoes, then some tomatoes must be grapes. Therefore, both conclusions I and II are correct.

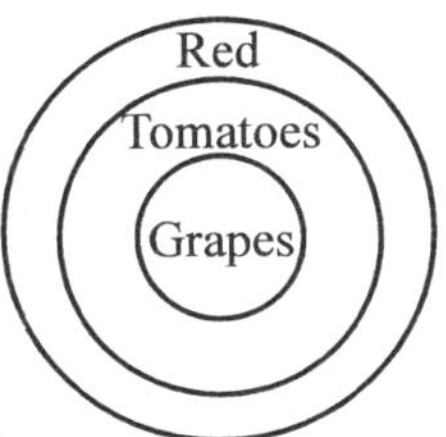

2. *(b)*: When all painters are smiling and some authors are painters, then some authors are smiling. Therefore, only conclusion II is correct.

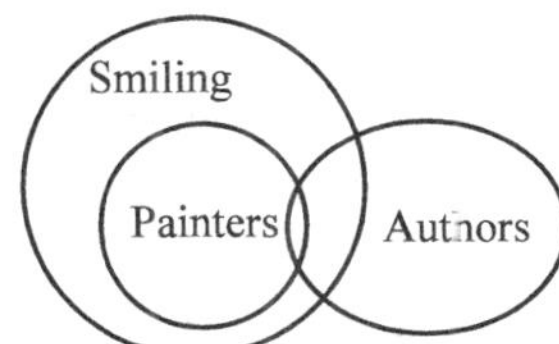

3. *(a)*: When all the peons of the office are efficient, then Ramu cannot be a peon in this office. Therefore, only conclusion I is correct.

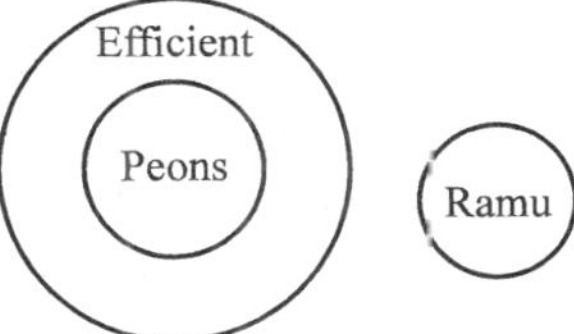

4. ***(a)* :** When all weavers are hardworking and no hardworking men are foolish, then no weavers are foolish. Therefore, only conclusion I is correct.

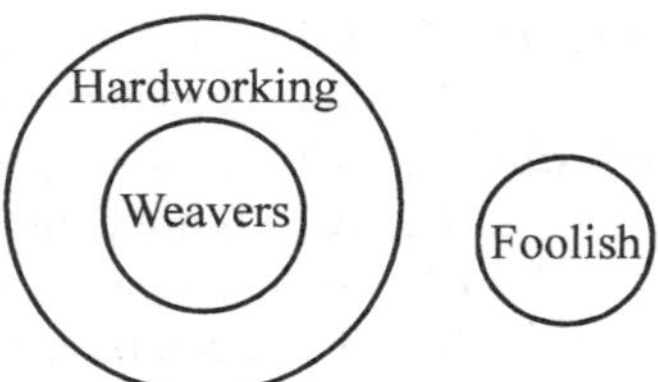

5. ***(e)* :** When all fishes are cars and all cars are vegetables, then all fishes will naturally be vegetables. This means that some vegetables are fishes. And when all cars are vegetables, then some vegetables will be cars naturally. Therefore, both the conclusions I and II are correct.

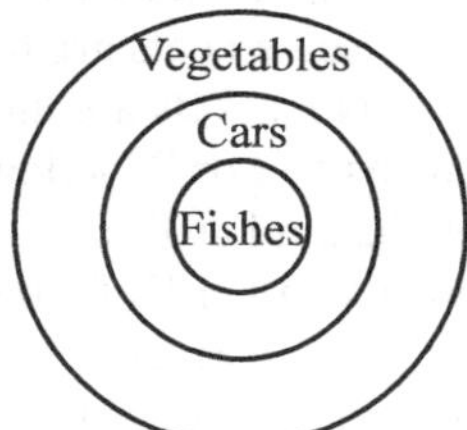

6. ***(d)* :** No relationship can be established between the two statements. Therefore, neither conclusion I nor conclusion II is correct.

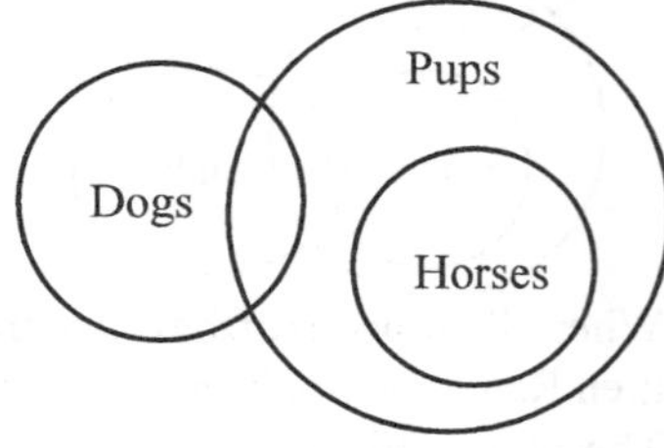

7. ***(a)* :** When all beautiful women are mothers and all mothers are understanding, then naturally all beautiful women are understanding. All mothers need not be beautiful women. Therefore, only conclusion I is correct.

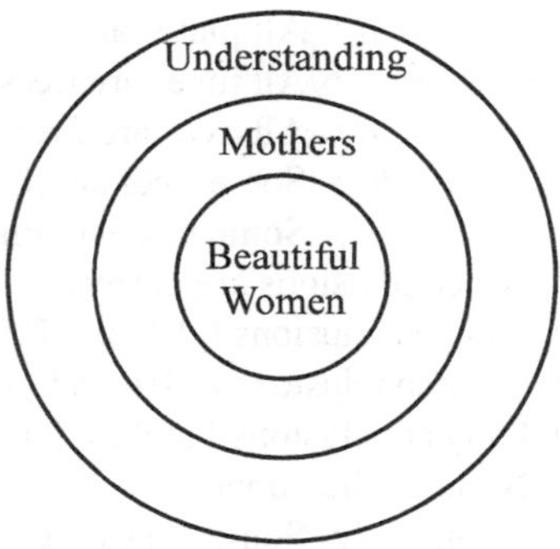

8. ***(c)* :** When some toys are tables and no table is black, then it is indicated that some toys can be black, as all toys are not tables. On the other hand, some toys may not be black. Therefore, there is a possibility that some toys may or may not be black. As such, either conclusion I or conclusion II can be correct.

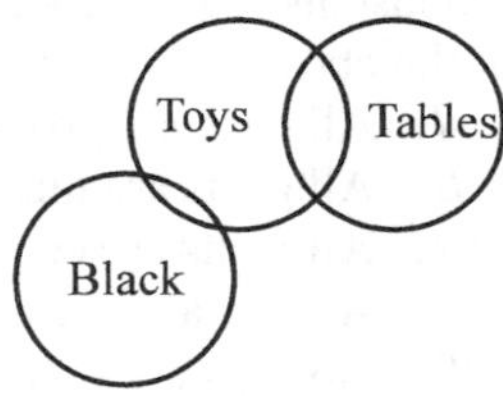

9. ***(e)* :** When all rivers are mountains and some rivers are deserts, then some deserts cannot be mountains and also, some mountains need not be deserts. Therefore, both conclusion I and conclusion II are correct.

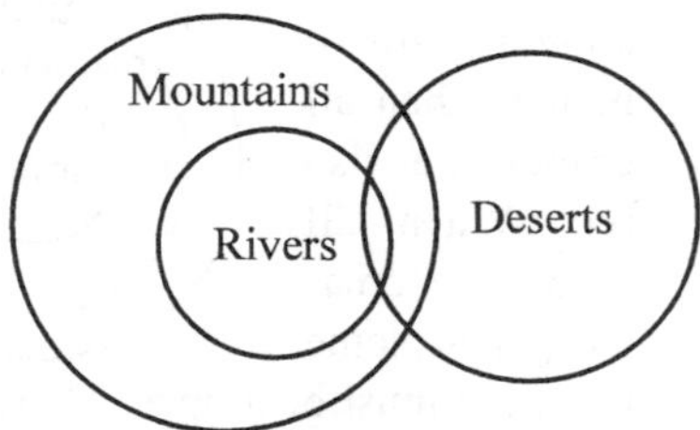

10. ***(a)* :** When all men are horses and all horses are elephants then, naturally all men are elephants, but all elephants need not be men. Therefore, only conclusion I is correct.

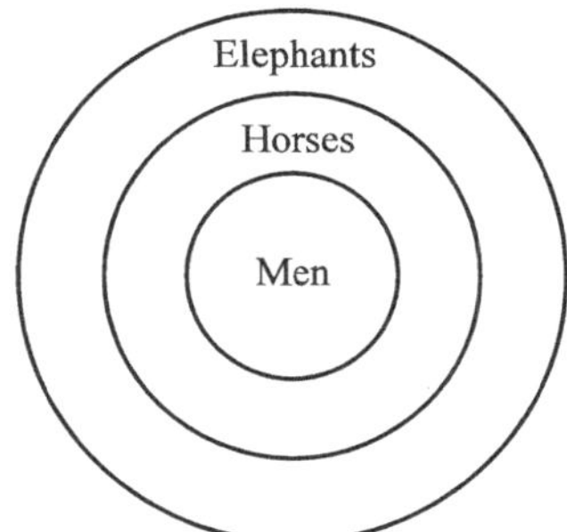

11. ***(b)*** **:**

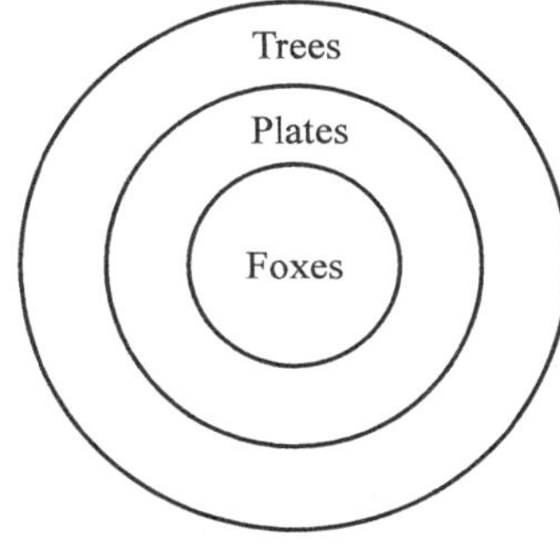

When all foxes are plates and all plates are trees, then naturally all foxes will be trees and some trees will then have to be foxes. And when all plates are trees then some trees will have to be plates. Therefore, only conclusions I, III and IV are correct.

12. ***(d)*** **:** When it is given that some cubes are squares and all squares are circles, then some cubes will naturally be circles, though all cubes cannot be circles. When some cubes are circles, then some circles will have to be cubes. And when all squares are circles, then some circles will have to be squares. As per given statement II, all squares are circles. Therefore all squares cannot be cubes. As such only conclusions II and III are correct.

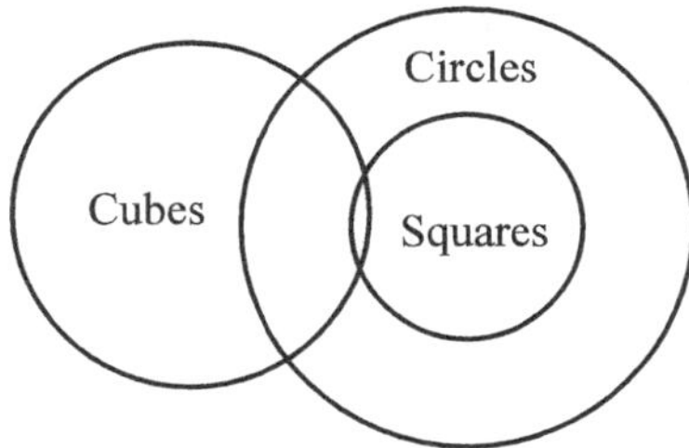

13. ***(e)*** **:** When all cups are goats, then only some goats can be cups. When all goats are tins, then only some tins can be goats. When all cups are goats and all goats are tins, then naturally all cups are tins and some tins must be cups. Therefore, all the conclusions are incorrect.

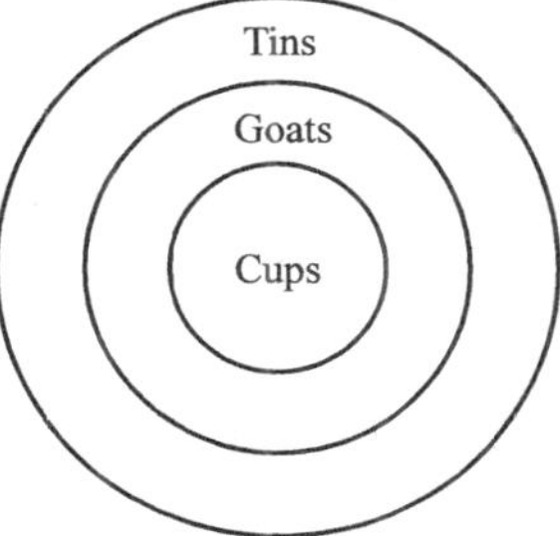

14. ***(e)*** **:** When all bombs are bags and some bags are jets then all bombs cannot be jets. 'Some bags' indicate that there is no chance of some bombs being jets, or some jets being bombs. Further all jets cannot be bombs. Therefore, all conclusions are incorrect.

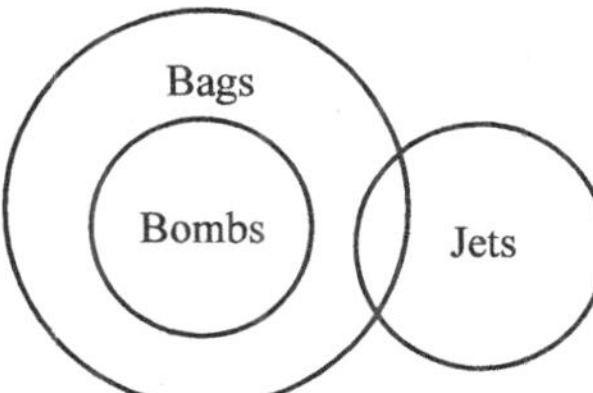

15. ***(d)*** **:** When some thorns are jackets and some jackets are boats, then some thorns may be boats but some boats cannot be thorns. As per Statement I, some thorns are jackets, some jackets need to be thorns. When Statement II conveys that some jackets are boats, then it is clear that all jackets cannot be boats. Therefore, no particular given conclusion can be drawn from the given statements.

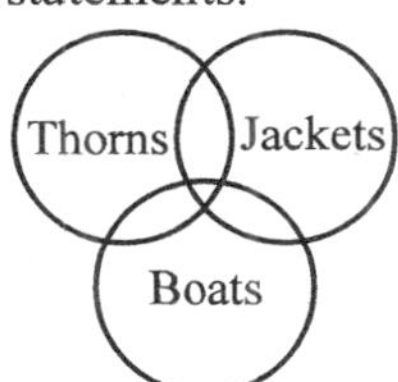

21. Venn Diagrams

In these type of questions, diagrammatic representation presents a logical illustration of particular class or statements based on which the questions are asked. A clear view of the diagram makes the concepts clear for attempting such questions.

EXERCISE

1. What is the number which is common to only two geometrical figures?

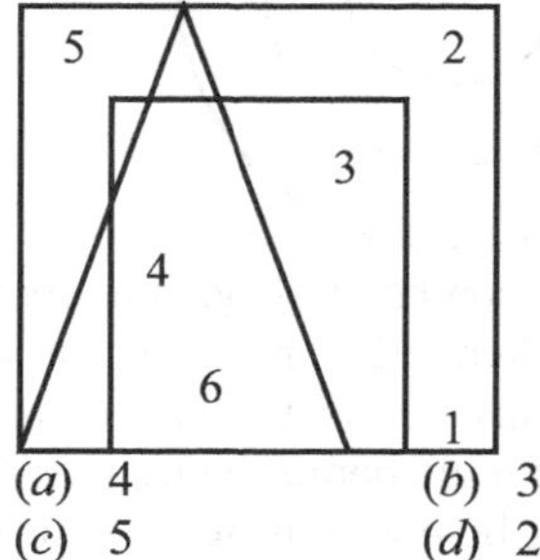

(*a*) 4 (*b*) 3
(*c*) 5 (*d*) 2

Directions (Qs. 2 and 3) : *In the following diagram, rectangle represents Hindi Announcers, circle represents English Announcers, square represents French Announcers, and triangle represents German Announcers.*

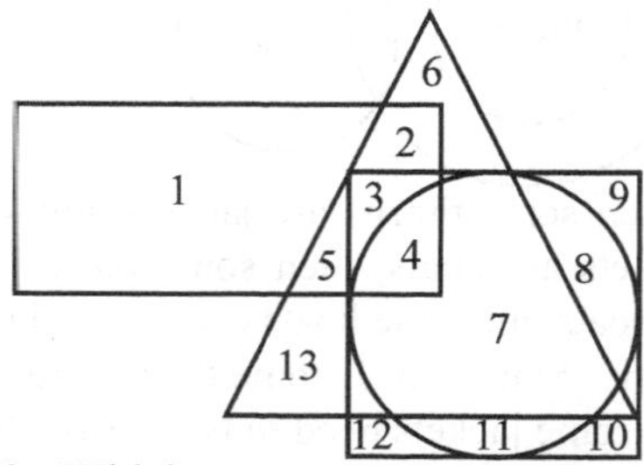

2. Which area represents those announcers who can present programmes in Hindi, French and German only?
(*a*) 1 (*b*) 2
(*c*) 3 (*d*) 4

3 Which area represents those announcers who can present programmes in French and English only?
(*a*) 7 (*b*) 9
(*c*) 11 (*d*) 13

Directions (Qs. 4 and 5) : *Study the diagram to answer these questions.*

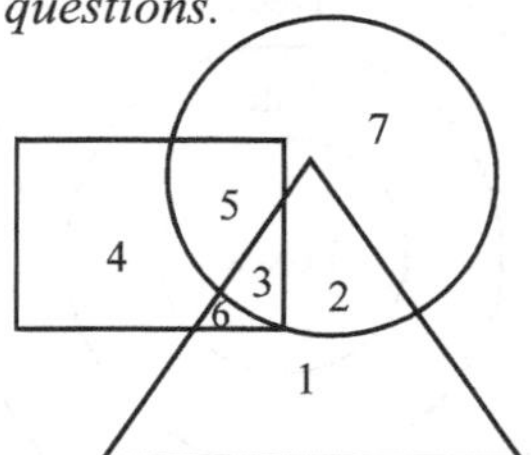

4. Which number is in all the geometrical figures?
(*a*) 5 (*b*) 6
(*c*) 2 (*d*) 3

5. Number 6 is in :
(*a*) Rectangle and triangle
(*b*) Circle and traingle
(*c*) Rectangle and circle
(*d*) Rectangle only

Directions (Qs. 6 to 9) : *In the following diagram*

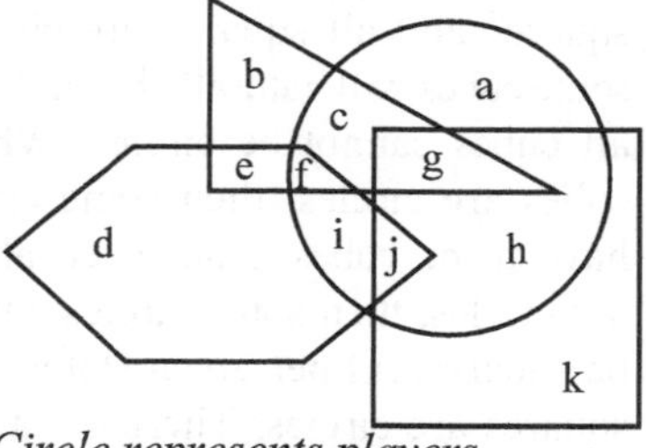

The Circle represents players
The Triangle represents outdoor games
The Hexagon represents indoor games and
The Square represents national level players
Study the diagram and answer the questions given below :

6. The letter in the section representing the players who play indoor games at national level is :
(*a*) f (*b*) i
(*c*) j (*d*) g

7. The letter representing the section of outdoor as well as indoor game players who do not play at the national level is :
   (*a*) c (*b*) f
   (*c*) e (*d*) i
8. The section representing national level players who do not play either outdoor or indoor games but still come under the category of players is :
   (*a*) k (*b*) g
   (*c*) c (*d*) h
9. Persons who play outdoor games but do not come under the category of players are represented in the section marked :
   (*a*) b (*b*) c
   (*c*) a (*d*) d

Directions (Qs. 10 to 13) : *Study the diagram given below.*

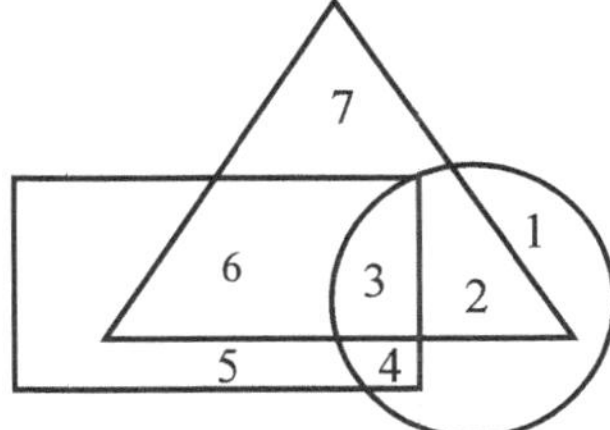

A college provides three different activities, students union represented by triangle, literary society represented by rectangle and social service league represented by circle.

10. Those who take part in both literary society and social service league but not in students union are represented by :
    (*a*) 3 & 4 (*b*) 5 & 6
    (*c*) 5 & 1 (*d*) 4
11. Those who take part in students union but not in social service league are represented by :
    (*a*) 2 & 7 (*b*) 6 & 7
    (*c*) 6 (*d*) 7
12. Those students who are members of literary society only and not of any other activity are represented by :
    (*a*) 2 (*b*) 5
    (*c*) 3 & 4 (*d*) 3
13. Those students who are members of all three groups are represented by :
    (*a*) 2 (*b*) 3
    (*c*) 4 (*d*) 6

EXPLANATORY ANSWERS

1. *(b)* :

Note : Numbers 4 and 6 are common to all three geometrical figures.

2. *(c)*, 3. *(c)* :

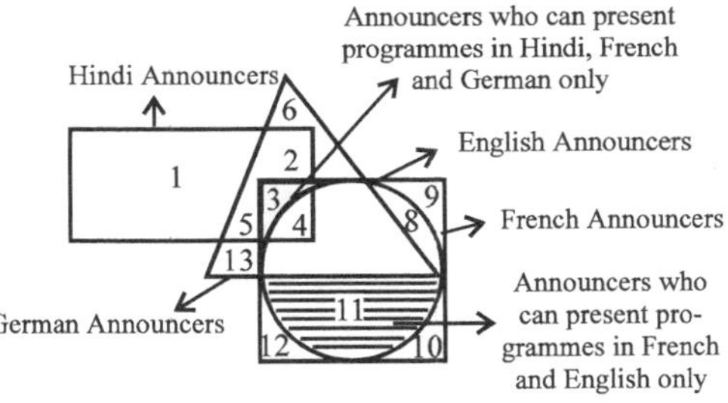

4. *(d)*, 5. *(a)* :

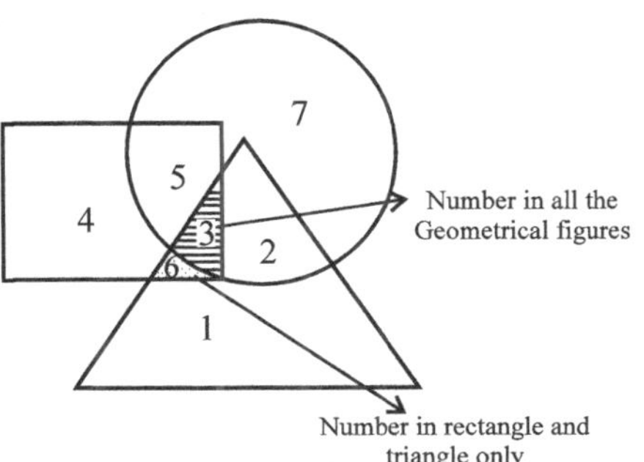

6. *(c)*,
7. *(b)*,
8. *(d)*,
9. *(a)* :

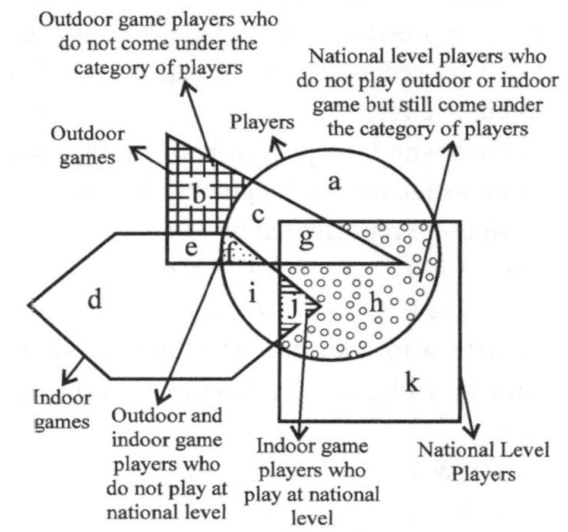

10. *(d)*, **11.** *(b)*, **12.** *(b)*, **13.** *(b)* :

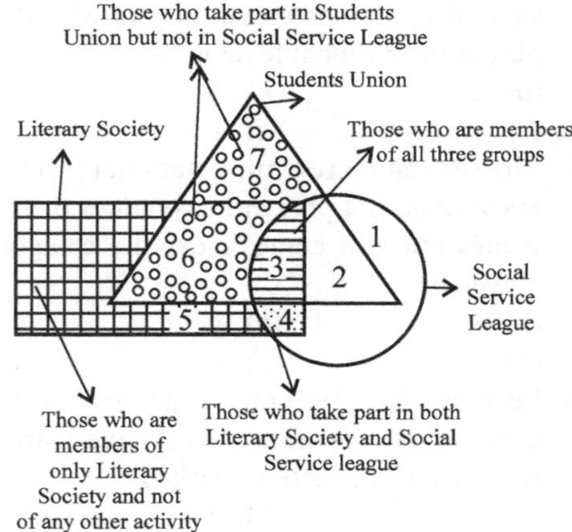

22. Non-Verbal Series

EXERCISE

Directions (Q. 1–10) : *In each of the following questions which one of the five answer figures given below should come after the problem figures if the sequence are continued?*

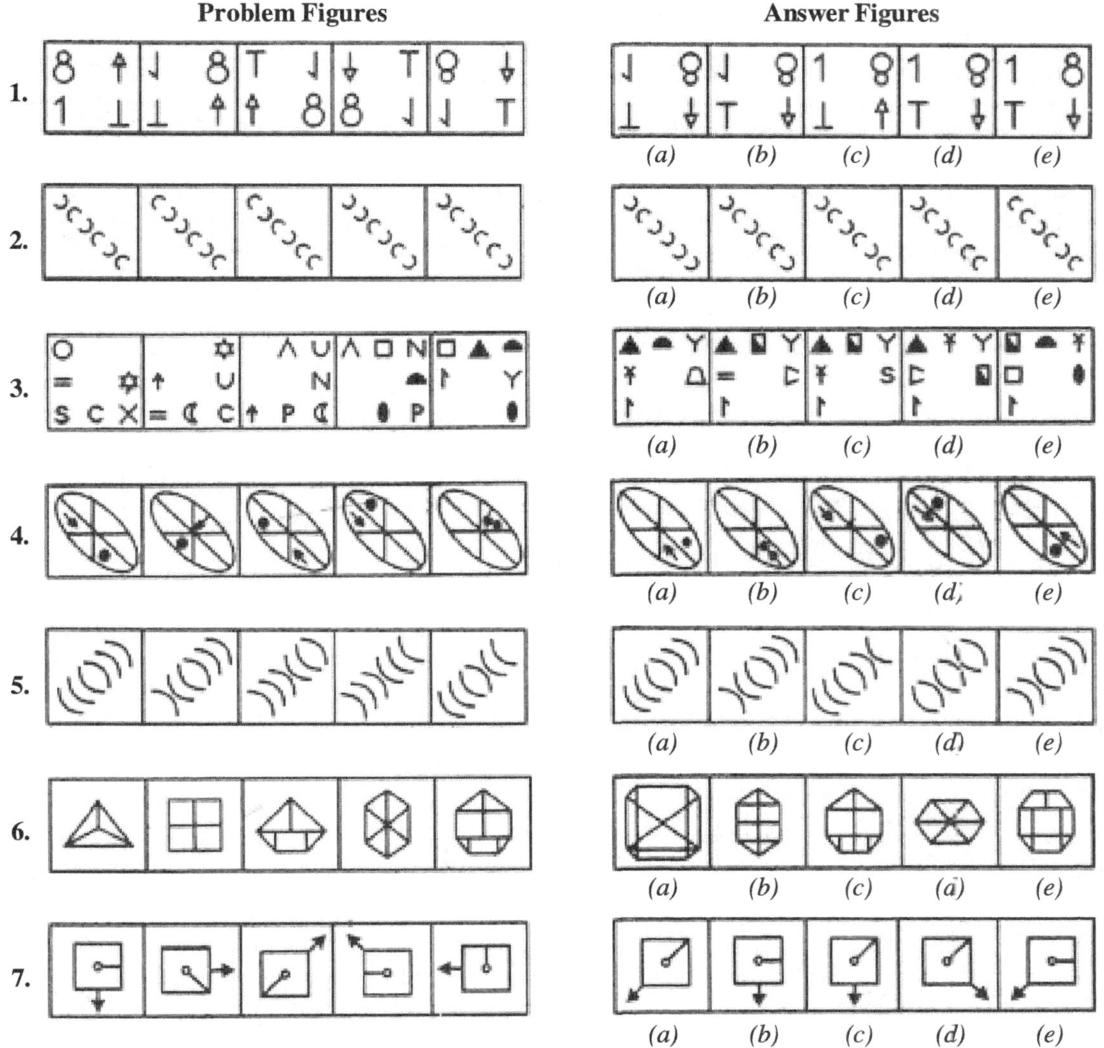

Problem Figures **Answer Figures**

8.

(a) (b) (c) (d) (e)

9.

(a) (b) (c) (d) (e)

10.

(a) (b) (c) (d) (e)

Directions (Q. 11-20) : *In each of these questions, a series begins with an unmarked figure on the extreme left in the row of figures. One and only one of the five lettered figures in the series does not fit into the series. The two unmarked figures, one on the extreme left and the other on the extreme right fit into the series. Take as many aspects into account as possible of the figures in the series and find out the one and only of the five marked figures which does not fit into the series. The letter of that figure is the answer.*

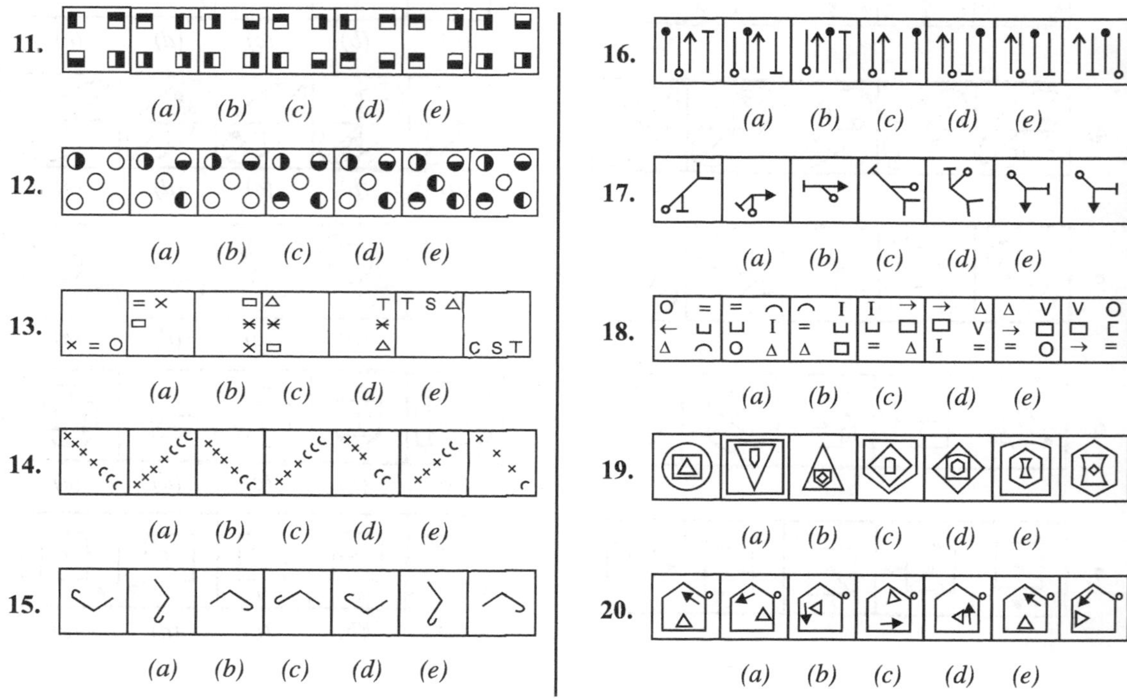

Directions (Q. 21–30) : *Each of the following questions consist of problem figures followed by answer figures. Select a figure from amongst the answer figures which will continue the same series or pattern as established by the problem figures.*

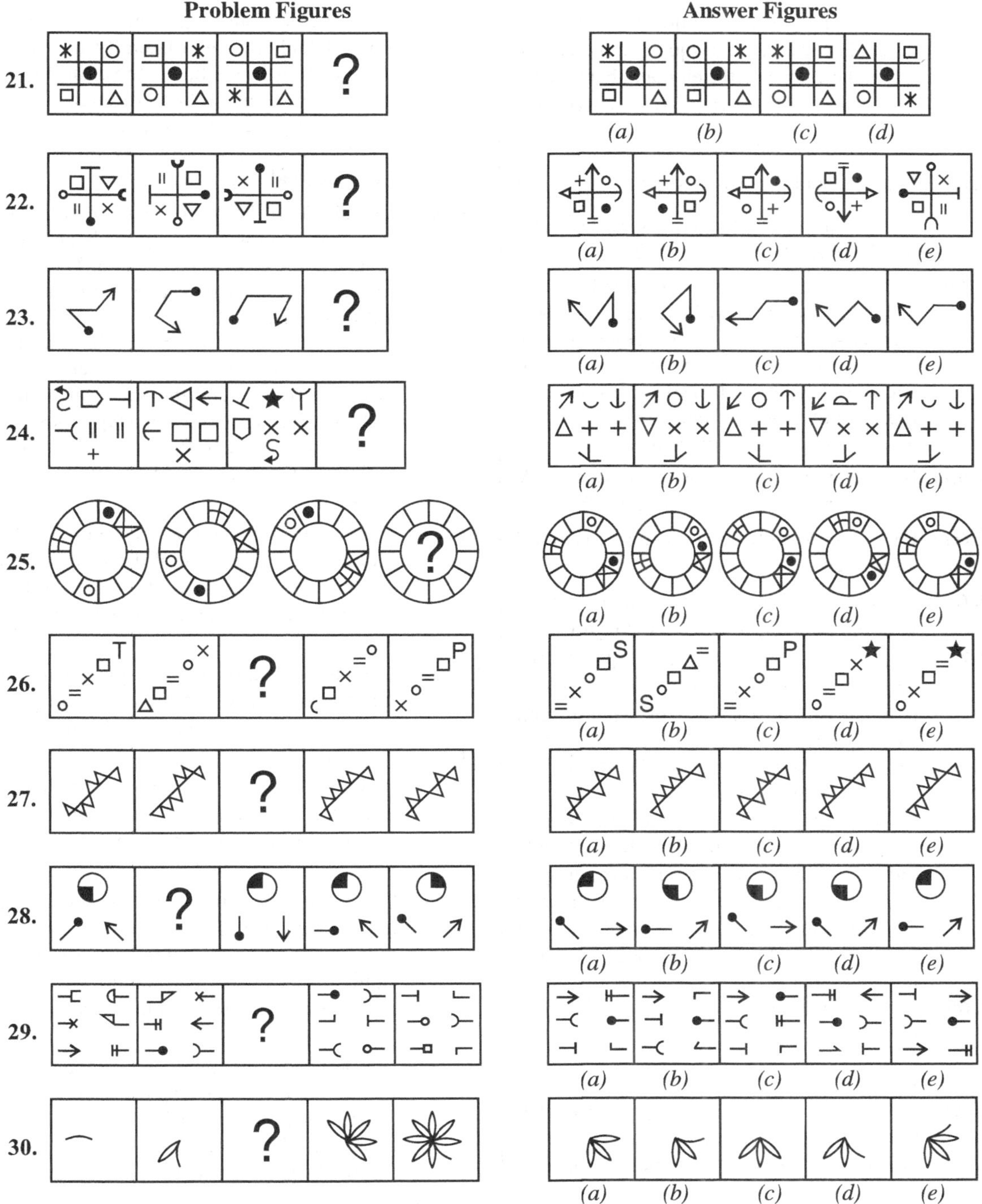

EXPLANATORY ANSWERS

1. *(d)* : In each step, all the elements move to the adjacent corner (of the square boundary) in a CW direction and the element that reaches the upper-left corner gets vertically inverted.

2. *(c)* : We can label the arcs as shown . The arcs get inverted in the sequence (1 & 2), (3, 4 & 5), (6 & 1), (2, 3 & 4), (5 & 6), ...

3. *(d)* : All the elements move half-a-side of the square boundary in ACW direction in each step. Also, first, third and fifth elements are replaced by new elements in one step and second, fourth and sixth elements are replaced by new elements in the next step. The two steps are repeated alternately.

4. *(a)* : In each step, the dot moves one space CW and the arrow moves two spaces CW.

5. *(c)* : One arc and four arcs get inverted alternately.

6. *(e)* : The number of parts increases by one along with the number of sides in the figure.

7. *(c)* : The pin rotates 45°CW and 90°CW alternately and moves one space (each space is equal to half-a-side of the square) and two spaces CW alternately. The arrow rotates 90°ACW and 45°ACW alternately and moves two spaces and one space.

8. *(e)* : In one step, the two elements interchange positions and the smaller element gets enlarged while the larger element gets reduced in size. In the next step, the smaller element is replaced by a new small element and the larger element is replaced by a new large element.

9. *(c)* : In each step, the elements move in the order

.

10. *(b)* : The upper-left element gets laterally inverted in first, third, fifth. .... steps; the upper-right element gets rotated through 180° is first, fourth, seventh,.... steps; the lower-left element gets laterally inverted in second, fourth, sixth, ... steps; the lower-right element gets rotated through 180° in third, sixth,... steps and the pin at the middle-right position gets laterally inverted in every second step.

11. *(a)* : The shade in the top left square is moved one step clockwise till figure B and then reversed, the process is repeated. The shade in the top right square is moved one step anticlockwise till figure D and then reversed. The shade in the bottom left square is moved one step clockwise in alternate figures and the shade in bottom right square is moved one step clockwise after two figures. In figure 'A' the rule is isolated by the shade in the bottom left square.

12. *(e)* : In alternate figures a new circle is shaded clockwise. The pattern of the shade is also moved clockwise. In figure 'E' right half of the circle in the centre should have been shaded.

13. *(a)* : The three elements are placed either horizontally or vertically. In option 'A' neither of the placements can be applied.

14. *(c)* : The placement of elements is same in alternate figures. The number and type of elements is same in two subsequent figures. In this manner, figure 'C' should have four crosses and two C shapes.

15. *(c)* : The element is moved one step anticlockwise and the arc at one end is turned outside and inside alternately. In figure 'C' the element should be on the right side with the arc turned outside on the top side.

16. *(e)* : The left most element, line segment with the dot is moved one step towards right till figure C where it reaches the extreme right position. This process is repeated from figure D where the element on the extreme left, line segment with a circle, is moved. In figure 'E' the placement of the elements does not follow the rule of the series.

17. *(e)* **:** The 'T' line is rotated 45° clockwise and the line with the circle 45° anticlockwise. The 'Y' shape and the arrow are repeated twice after two figures. In option E, the 'T' shape and the line with the circle are rotated by 90°.

18. *(e)* **:** First the elements in the four corners are moved one step anticlockwise, next the four elements from the top are moved one step anticlockwise and then the four elements from the bottom are moved one step anticlockwise. Of the remaining two elements, the one on the left is made new each time and then their places are interchanged. This process is repeated from figure D. In option 'E' open square should have been in place of circle to continue the series.

19. *(a)* **:** At each step the outermost figure is removed and a new figure is placed right in the centre of other two figures. In option 'A' the triangle is turned upside down, which violates the rule of the series.

20. *(a)* **:** The arrow is moved one step anticlockwise and the triangle one step clockwise. In figure 'A' the triangle should have been on the left side of the figure.

21. *(a)* **:** The places of star, circle and square are moved one step clockwise at each step.

22. *(e)* **:** The elements in the four quadrants are moved one step clockwise and the elements at the ends of the cross are moved one step anticlockwise in this series.

23. *(a)* **:** In alternate figures, the line with the dot is turned 90° clockwise and the arrow 180° clockwise.

24. *(e)* **:** In alternate figures, the element in the top left position is horizontally inverted and moved one and half steps anticlockwise, the top middle element is turned 90° clockwise and moved one step anticlockwise, the top right element is turned 135° clockwise and moved one step anticlockwise, the element at the bottom is replaced by a new element and moved to the top middle position, and the two identical elements are replaced by two new identical elements.

25. *(a)* **:** The cross and the circle move one and two steps clockwise respectively (at each step), the plus moves 3, 4 and 5 steps clockwise, and the dot 6, 5 and 4 steps clockwise.

26. *(a)* **:** At first step, the fifth or the bottom most element is moved to the second place from top, the second element moved to the fourth place, the fourth element is moved to the third place, the third element is moved to the first or the topmost place and the element on the top, which is made new, is moved to the last or the fifth place. At second step i.e., from second problem figure to third problem figure the above process is reversed. The bottom most element is the first and the top most element is the last or fifth. Hereafter, the process is repeated from the beginning. Option 'A' is the right answer.

27. *(c)* **:** Starting from the bottom, one triangle is moved to the opposite side at each step in upward order. Option 'C' fits into the question marked space.

28. *(c)* **:** The shade inside the circle is rotated clockwise in alternate figures; the line segment with a dot is rotated 135° clockwise in alternate figures and the arrow is rotated 135° anticlockwise in alternate figures. By this process answer figure 'C' completes the series.

29. *(a)* **:** At each step the elements are moved diagonally upward and then laterally inverted, and the top two elements are made new and placed at the bottom line. By this process, option figure 'A' completes the series.

30. *(a)* **:** The number of arcs making the petals of the flower are increased by one, one and half, two, two and half respectively at each step. Also, the flower is turned 45° anticlockwise. By this process, option 'A' is the right answer.

23. Non-Verbal Analogy

EXERCISE

TYPE-I

Directions (Q. 1-15): *The second figure in the first unit of the Problem Figures bears a certain relationship to the first figure. Similarly, one of the figures in the Answer Figures bears the same relationship to the first figures in the second unit of the Problem Figures. Locate the figure which would fit the questions marks.*

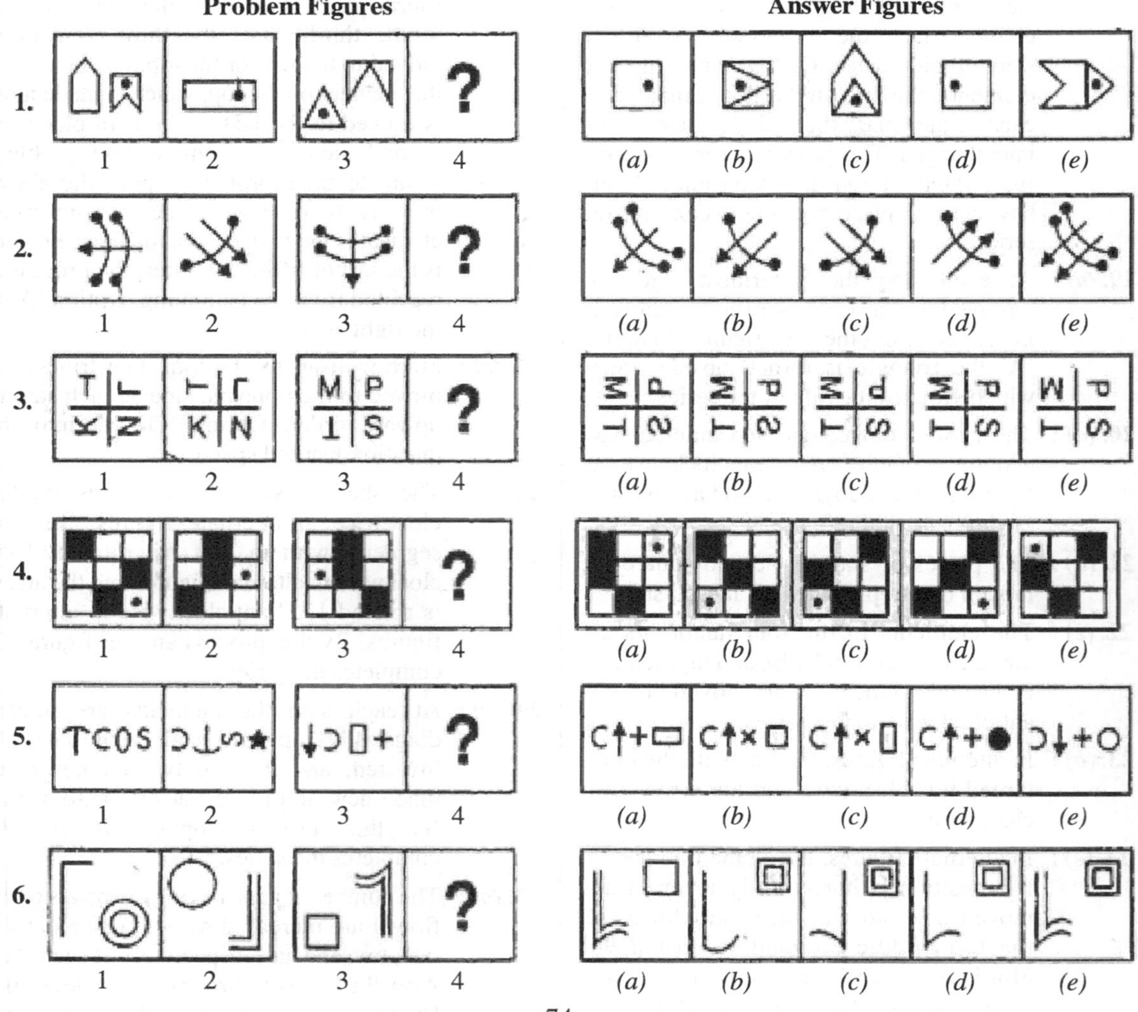

Problem Figures **Answer Figures**

7. 1 2 3 4  (a) (b) (c) (d) (e)

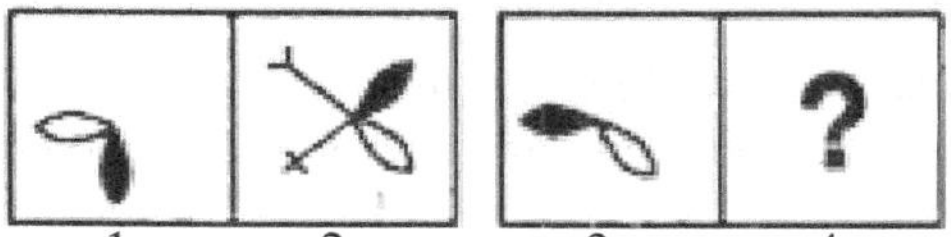

8. 1 2 3 4 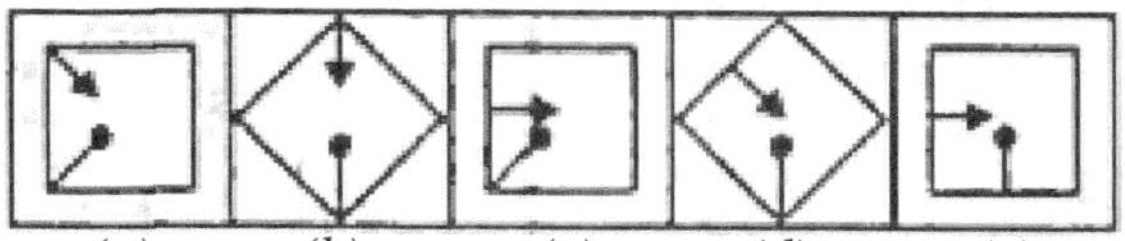 (a) (b) (c) (d) (e)

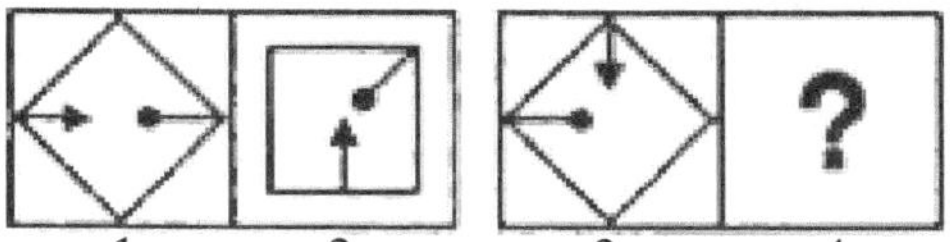

9. 1 2 3 4 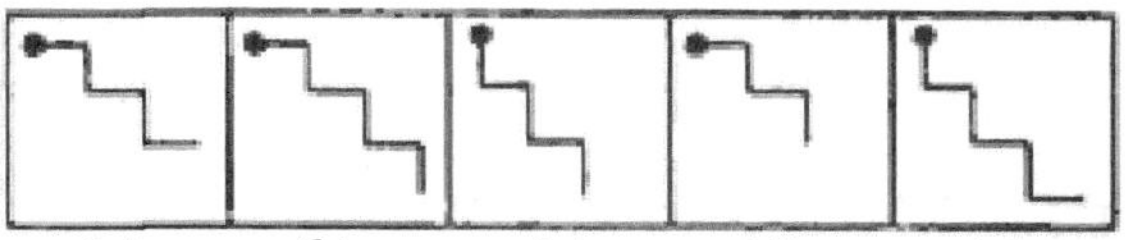 (a) (b) (c) (d) (e)

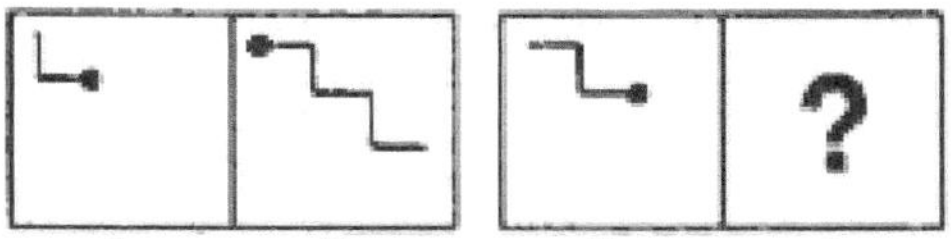

10. 1 2 3 4 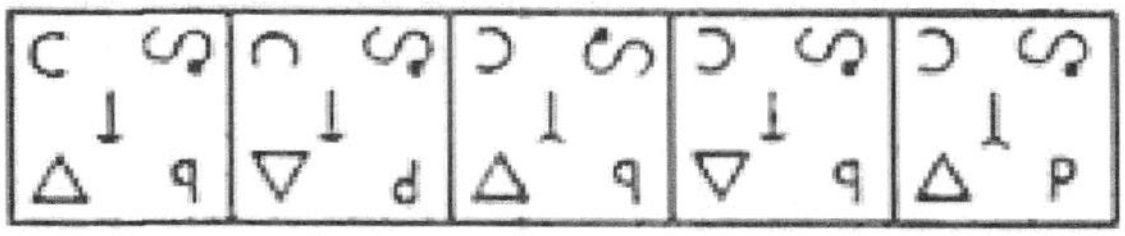 (a) (b) (c) (d) (e)

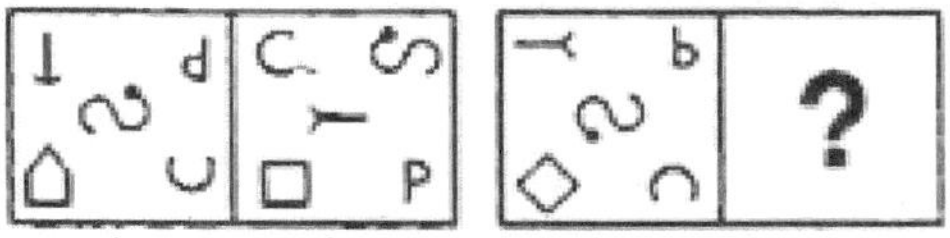

11. 1 2 3 4  (a) (b) (c) (d) (e)

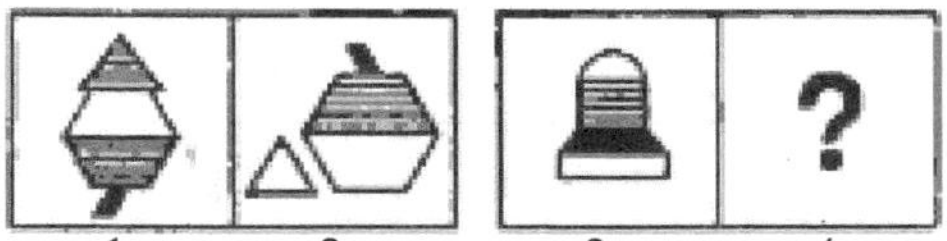

12. 1 2 3 4 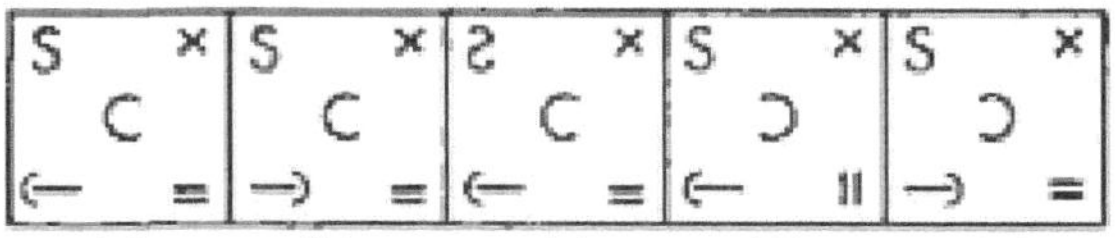 (a) (b) (c) (d) (e)

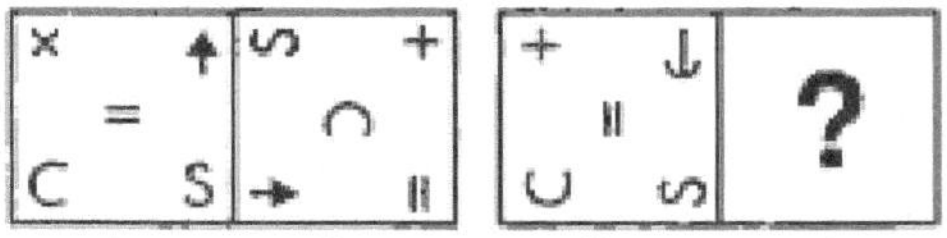

13. 1 2 3 4 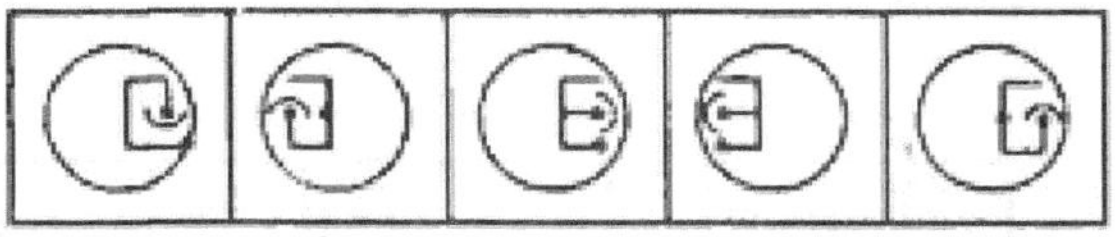 (a) (b) (c) (d) (e)

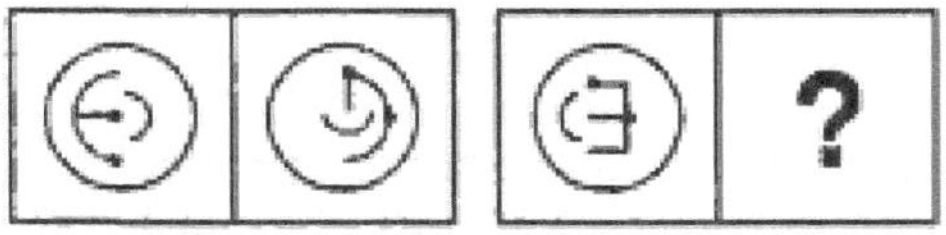

14. 1 2 3 4 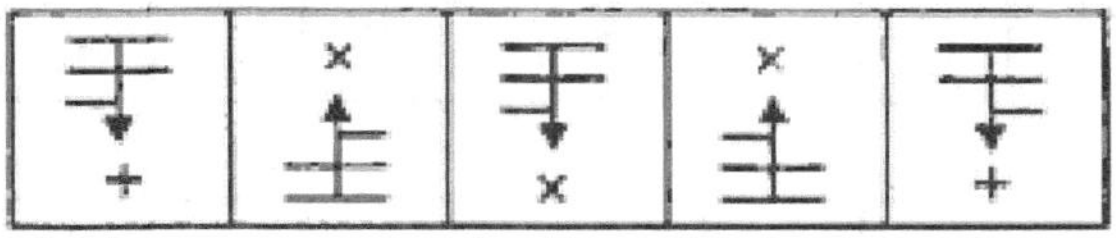 (a) (b) (c) (d) (e)

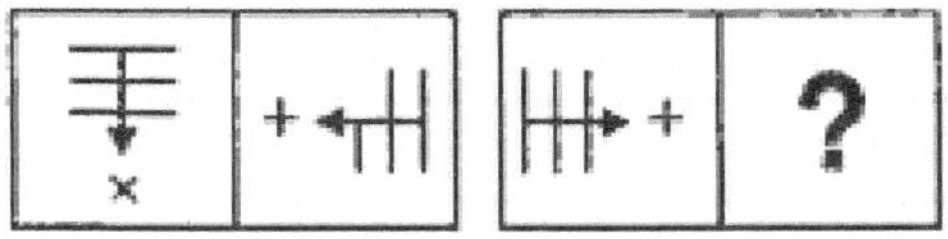

15. 1 2 3 4  (a) (b) (c) (d) (e)

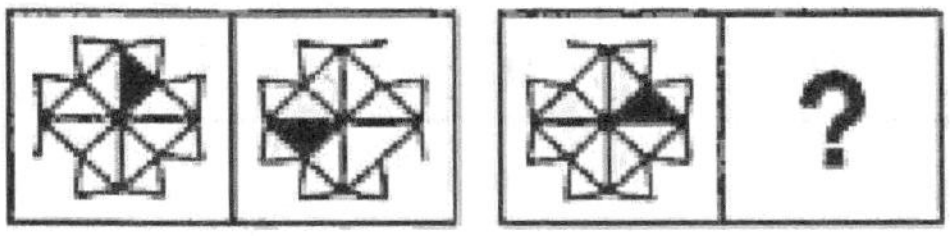

TYPE-II

Directions (Q. 16–30): *In each of the following questions, a related pair of figures is followed by five numbered pairs of figures. Select the pair that has a relationship* **similar** *to that in the unnumbered pair.*

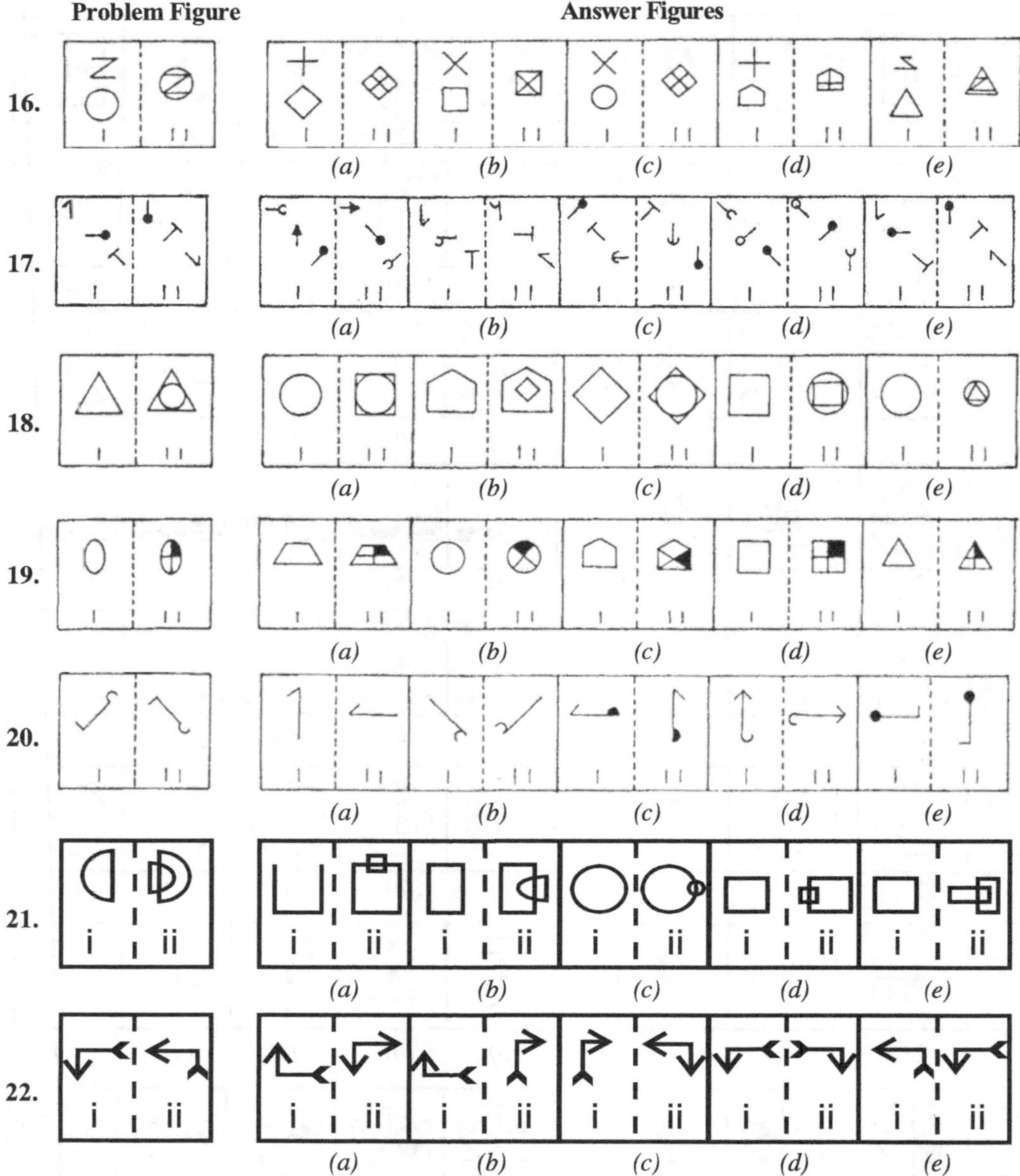

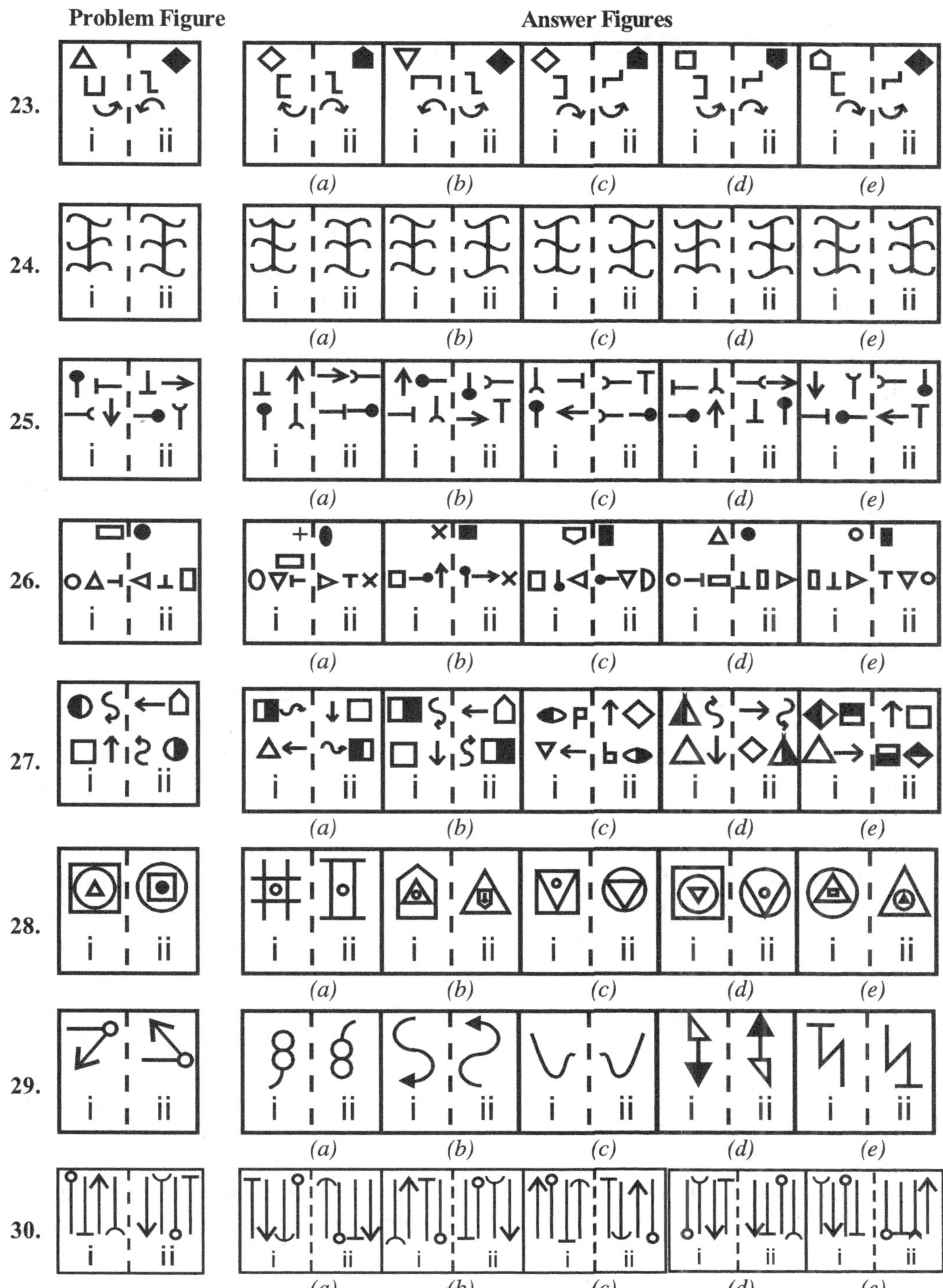
Problem Figure
Answer Figures
23.
24.
25.
26.
27.
28.
29.
30.
(a)
(b)
(c)
(d)
(e)

EXPLANATORY ANSWERS

1. *(b)* : The R.H.S. figure is fitted into the L.H.S. figure and the resulting figure is rotated 90° CW.

2. *(b)* : The figure rotates 45° ACW, the arrow changes to a curved line with dotted ends and the curved lines with dotted ends get converted to arrows.

3. *(d)* : The top left symbol rotates 90° ACW while all other symbols rotate 90° CW.

4. *(e)* : The black portion in top layer moves one step to the right; the black portions in the middle and the lower layers move one step to the left and the dot moves one step upwards.

5. *(d)* : The first and second symbols from the left interchange positions and the other two symbols also interchange positions. The symbol that reaches the first position from the left gets laterally inverted; the symbol that reaches the second position gets inverted, the third symbol rotates 90° CW and the fourth symbol gets replaced by a new one.

6. *(d)* : The single figure is replaced by a figure similar to the double figures and the double figures are replaced by figures similar to the single figure.

7. *(e)* : The figure rotates 135° ACW; a 'T' appears diagonally opposite to the black leaf and a 'Y' appears diagonally opposite to the white leaf.

8. *(c)* : The square rotates through 45°. The arrow moves 90° ACW and the pin moves 45° ACW.

9. *(b)* : The figure rotates through 180° and three lines forming a zig-zag, get attached to its lower end.

10. *(d)* : The symbols move in the order

The symbol that reaches the central position rotates 90° CW and its arc gets inverted; the 'P' shaped symbol rotates through 180°; the 'C' shaped symbol rotates 90° CW; the 'S' Shaped symbol gets laterally inverted and the fifth symbol gets replaced by a new one.

45°, the symbol that reaches the lower right corner rotates 90° ACW and a new symbol appears in middle-left position.

11. *(e)* : The upper and the lower parts of the figure get separated. Shading is removed from the upper part and the lower part is inverted. The two parts are then placed side by side.

12. *(a)* : The symbols move in the order

The symbol that reaches the top-left corner rotates 90° ACW; the symbol in the top-right corner rotates through 45°; the symbols in the lower-left corner and in the central positions rotates 90° CW and the symbol that reaches the lower-right corner rotates through 90°.

13. *(e)* : The figure gets laterally inverted. The dot on the larger arc, the pin and the small arc rotate 90° ACW. Also, the pin gets inverted.

14. *(c)* : The figure rotates 90° CW. One half of one of the lines on the arrow is lost. The figure in front of the arrowhead rotates through 45°.

15. *(d)* : The missing line segment in the first figure is replaced in second. Then moving ACW, the third line segment is removed along the two next consecutive sides of the square. Shaded portion in the first figure moves three steps ACW. Similarly, the third figure gives figure (D).

16. ***(b)*** **:** The uppermost design enters into innerside side of the lower design from Ist figure to the IInd figure.

17. ***(a)*** **:** In element I to II upper left design comes at lower right rotating 135° C.W. Middle design goes to upper left and rotates 90° CW. While lower right design goes to middle and it also rotates 90° C.W. The same changes occur in option A.

18. ***(e)*** **:** In element I to II and ellipse is put in the triangle. Similarly in option E a triangle is put in the ellipse.

19. ***(d)*** **:** From first figure to IInd figure, design is divided into four equal parts and right side of the upper portion becomes shaded.

20. ***(e)*** **:** From Ist figure to IInd figure, design is reversed after moving 90° anticlockwise direction.

21. ***(d)*** **:** The figure in the first part is laterally inverted and a similar but smaller design is placed on its left side in the second part.

22. ***(e)*** **:** The element in first part is moved by 90° and the places of short and long line segments are interchanged.

23. ***(c)*** **:** The number of sides making the top left figure is increased by one and a new figure is made, shaded and moved to the top right position. The element in the centre is turned 90° anticlockwise and the small line on the other side is turned by 180°. The element in the bottom right is turned upside down and moved to the bottom left position.

24. ***(a)*** **:** The direction of both arcs on the top, are on the middle right and arc on the bottom left in first part are turned to the other side in the second part.

25. ***(b)*** **:** From part one to part two, the element in the top left is turned 90° clockwise and the other three 90° anticlockwise, also the elements are moved one step anticlockwise.

26. ***(b)*** **:** From part one to part two, the top right element is turned by 90° and moved down, the lower right and middle elements are turned 90° clockwise and 90° anticlockwise respectively and moved to the left and the lower left element is shaded and moved up.

27. ***(a)*** **:** All the four elements exchange place diagonally and in doing so the top left element is laterally inverted, the top right element is horizontally inverted, the bottom right element is turned 90° anticlockwise and the number of lines making the element in bottom left is increased by one.

28. ***(e)*** **:** The innermost figure is removed and the new innermost figure also encloses the other two figures. The innermost and smallest figure is then shaded.

29. ***(b)*** **:** The design in the first part is horizontally inverted in the second.

30. ***(b)*** **:** All the elements in the first part are turned upside down and then 1st, 2nd, 3rd and 4th positioned elements become 3rd, 4th, 1st and 2nd elements in the second part.

---

24. Odd Man Out

In this type of reasoning a statement is followed by inferences drawn from it. From these inferences only one definitely follows which is the hidden proposition of the sentence and it is the right answer to the question.

EXERCISE

Directions (Q. 1–10) : *In each question below five figures are given. Four are similar in a certain way and so form a group. The question is— which one of the figures* **does not** *belong to that group?*

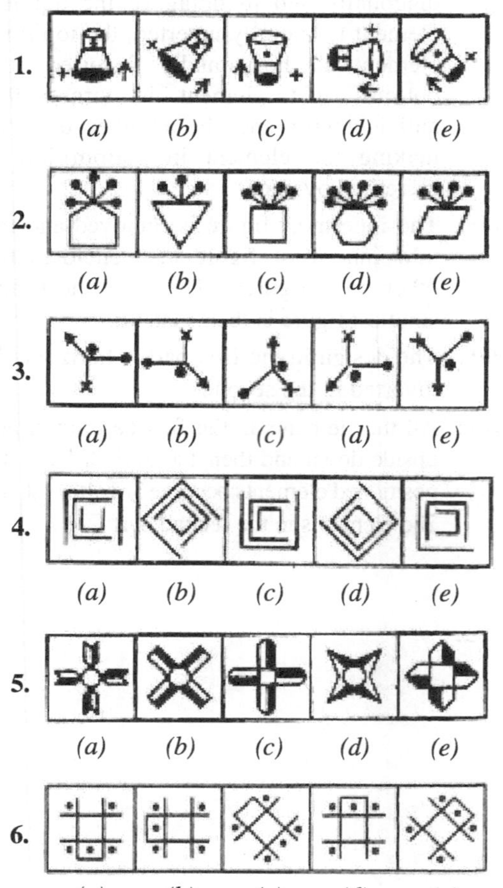

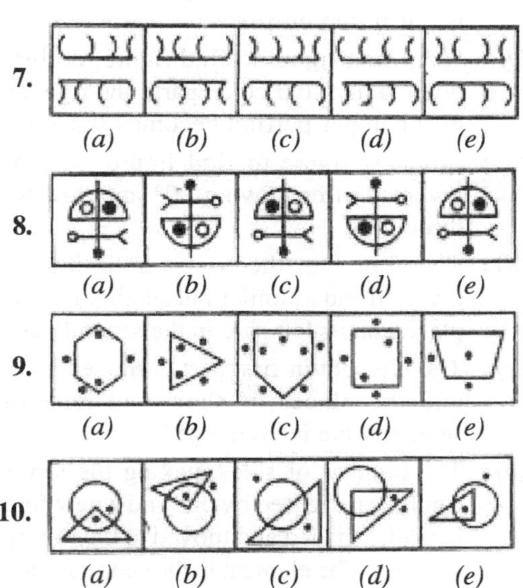

Directions (Q. 11–20) : *In each of the following questions, in four out of the five figures, element I is related to element II in the same particular way. Find out the figure in which the element I is* **not** *so related to element II.*

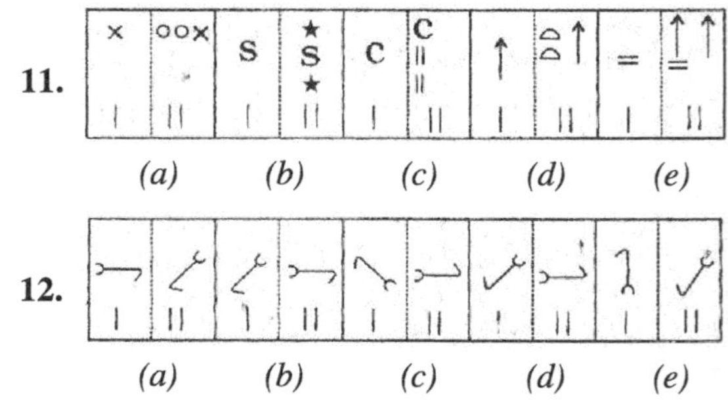

13.

(a) (b) (c) (d) (e)

14.

(a) (b) (c) (d) (e)

15.

(a) (b) (c) (d) (e)

16.

(a) (b) (c) (d) (e)

17.

(a) (b) (c) (d) (e)

18.

(a) (b) (c) (d) (e)

19.

(a) (b) (c) (d) (e)

20.

(a) (b) (c) (d) (e)

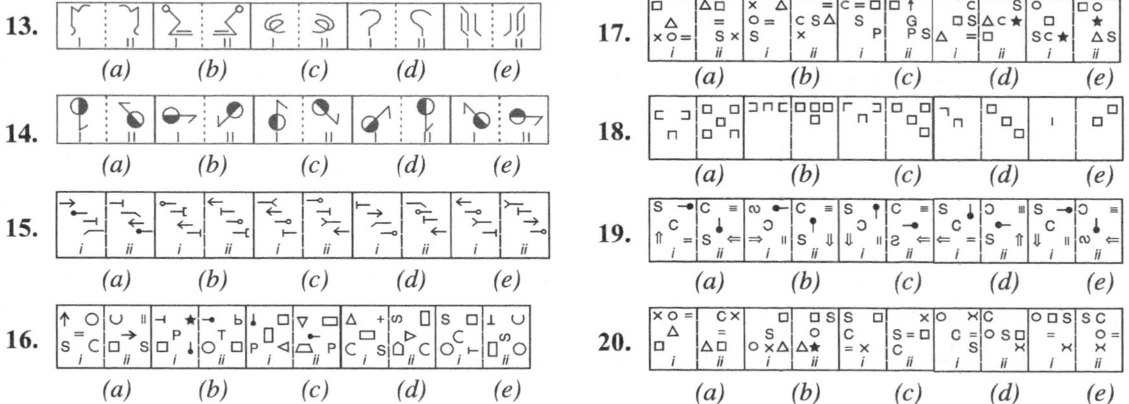

Directions (Q. 21–30) : *In each of the following questions, a related pair of figures (unnumbered) is followed by five numbered pairs of figures. Out of these five, four have relationship similar to that in the unnumbered pair. Only one pair of figures does not have similar relationship. Select that pair of figures which does not have a similar relationship to that in the unnumbered pair. Number of that pair is your answer.*

21.

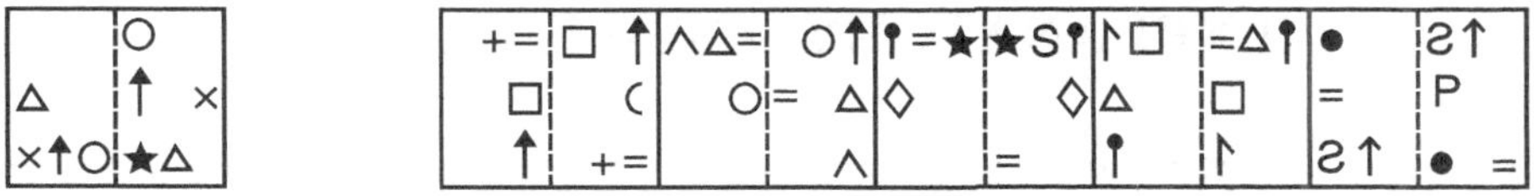

(a) (b) (c) (d) (e)

22.

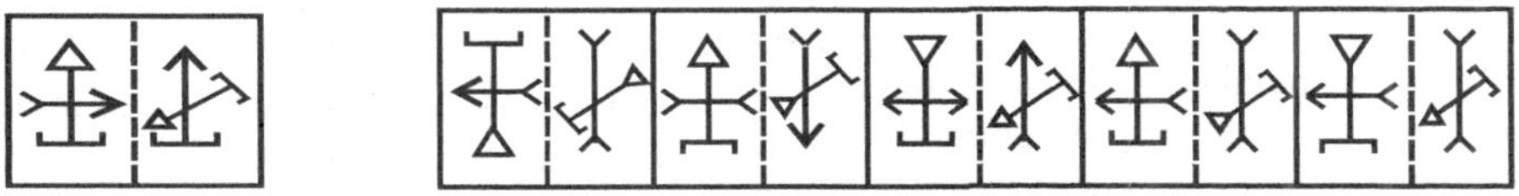

(a) (b) (c) (d) (e)

23.

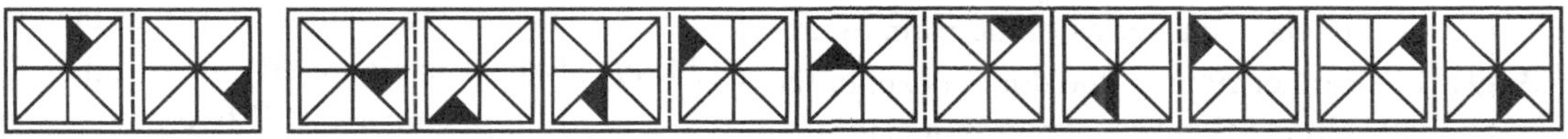

(a) (b) (c) (d) (e)

24.

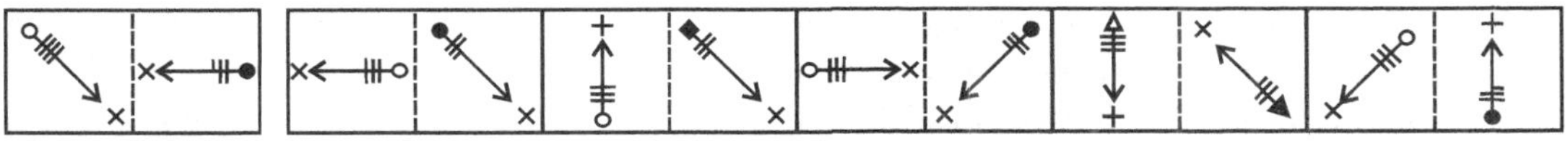

(a) (b) (c) (d) (e)

25.

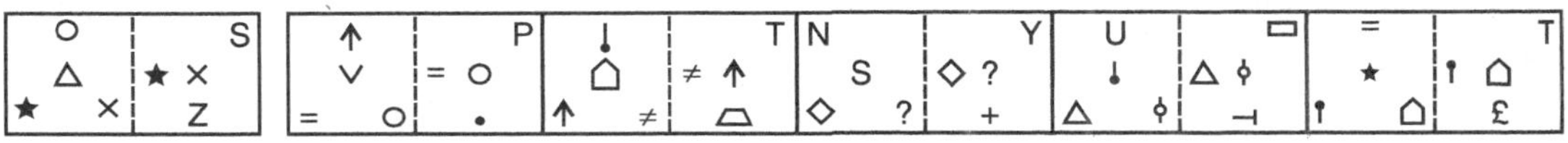

(a) (b) (c) (d) (e)

26.

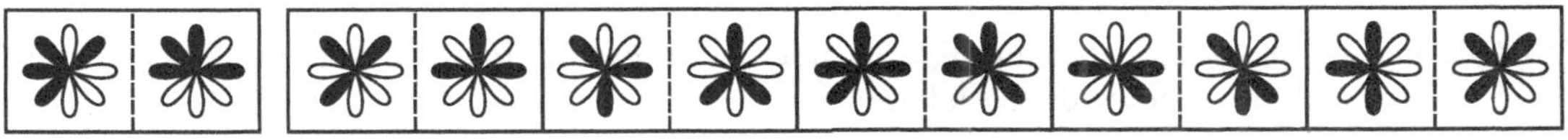

(a) (b) (c) (d) (e)

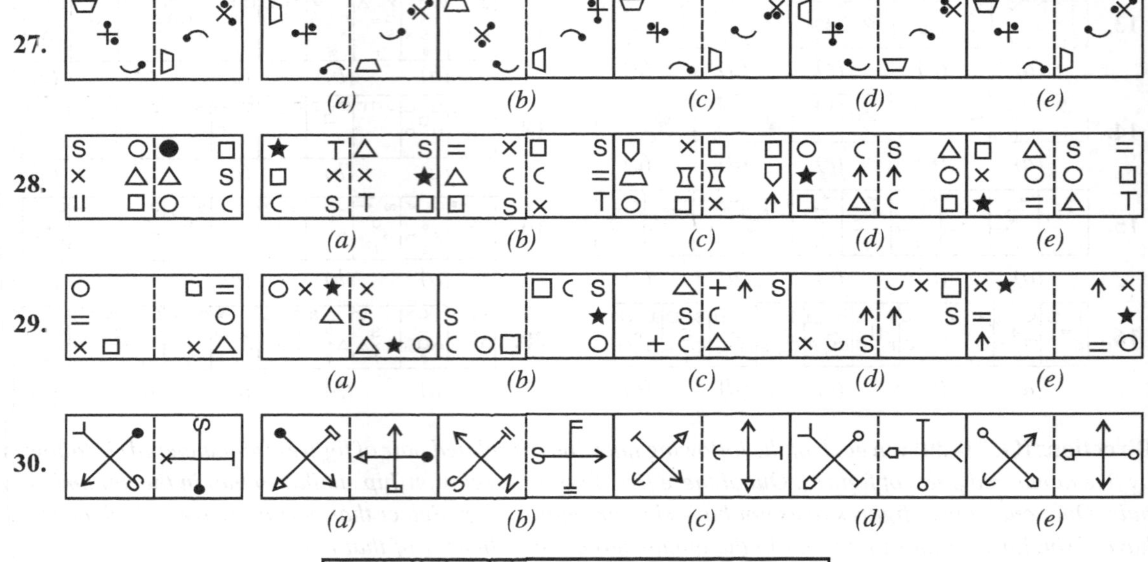

EXPLANATORY ANSWERS

1. *(d)* : In all other figures, the arrow and the + sign lie towards the black end of the main figure.

2.*(a)* : The pins, equal in number of sides in the main figure are attached to the midpoint of a side of the main figure in case of figures (B), (C), (D) and (E). In figure (A), these pins are attached to a vertex of the main figure.

3.*(c)* : In all other figures, the dot appears in the angle formed between the arrow and the pin.

4.*(a)* : All other figures can be rotated into each other. (In each figure except figure (A), the middle element is obtained by rotating the outer element through 90° CW and the inner element is obtained by rotating the middle element through 90° CW).

5.*(c)* : All other figures have at least one line of symmetry.

6.*(c)* : All other figures can be rotated into each other.

7.*(e)* : In each one of the other four figures, four arcs are curved towards the left and four other arcs are curved towards the right.

8.*(c)* : All other figures can be rotated into each other.

9.*(d)* : In all other figures, the number of dots outside the main figure is one more than the number of dots inside the main figure.

10.*(a)* : In all other figures, one of the dots lies outside the triangle as well as the circle.

11.*(e)* : Except in figure (B), in all other figures, from element I to II two new designs are added in one side of the main design.

12.*(c)* : In each figure from element I to II the main design rotates through 135° clockwise or anticlockwise. Except in figure (C), in all other figures, the smaller line segment moves to other side from element I to II.

13.*(a)* : In all other figures the element II can be obtained by the lateral inversion of the element I. In figure (A), the lower design has not been inverted.

14.*(b)* : In figure (B), the small segment is on the same side as that of the half shaded circle in both the elements.

15.*(d)* : The first design is inverted and moved to third place, the second design is moved to the fourth place, third design to the first place and fourth design is inverted and moved to the second place. Option (D) violates this.

16.*(b)* : In all other options the top-left element is moved to the centre with 90° clockwise rotation. Here, it is rotated anticlockwise.

17.*(d)* : All the designs are shifted in a set pattern one behind the other. The fourth design in all others is changed and placed in the last. Here, the fifth and last designs are changed.

18.*(a)* : In all other pair of figures, all incomplete squares in the first elements are completed and an extra square is added in the second element.

19.*(a)* : From element I to element II, the 'S' shape is turned 90° clockwise and moved down, the double arrow shape '⇒' is turned 90° clockwise and moved to the right, the two parallel lines one turned by 90°; one parallel line is added and all three lines are moved up, the line with a dot is turned 90° clockwise and moved to the centre and the 'C' shape in the centre is turned by 180° and moved to top left position. Here, the double arrow is turned anticlockwise.

20.*(c)* : Starting from one unit, all units are moved in a set pattern, the places of last two units moved are interchanged and the last unit is then made new. Here, no changes are made in the last two units.

21.*(d)* : From element I to element II clockwise the first unit is moved 2 steps forward, the second unit 1 step forward, the third unit 2½ steps forward and the fourth unit 3 steps forward. In option 'D' the third unit violates the rule.

22.*(e)* : From element I to element II, the horizontal bar is turned 135° anticlockwise and the unit at the lower end is turned by 180°. The vertical bar is turned 90° anticlockwise and the unit at the lower end is turned by 180°. In option 'E' one more unit at the top is turned by 180°.

23.*(e)* : In element II, the shade is moved two sections clockwise and shifted from the centre to the base. In option 'E' it is not so.

24.*(a)* : In element II, the arrow is turned 135° clockwise. In option 'A' it is turned anticlockwise.

25.*(b)* : From element I to element II, the bottom right unit and bottom left unit are moved to the centre and middle left position respectively. The other two units are removed and two new elements are placed in the top right and bottom centre position respectively. In option 'B' the placement of bottom right and left elements is not right.

26.*(c)* : In element II, the shades are shifted one petal clockwise. In option 'C' one of the shades is not moved.

27.*(b)* : From element I to element II, the unit on the top left is turned 90° anticlockwise and moved to the bottom right corner position, the unit in the centre is turned 135° anticlockwise and moved to the top right position, and the unit in the bottom right is turned by 180° and moved to the centre. In option 'B', the middle unit is turned 135° clockwise.

28.*(a)* : From element I to element II, a new unit is placed in the top left position, the top left unit is moved to the middle right position, the middle right unit is moved to the left position, the middle left unit is replaced by a new unit and placed in bottom right position, the bottom right unit is moved to the top right position, and the top right unit is moved diagonally to replace the bottom left unit. In option 'A', the middle left unit is not changed when moved to the bottom right position.

29.*(e)* : From element I to element II starting anticlockwise, the first and second units are moved 1½ steps clockwise respectively, the third unit ½ step anticlockwise, the fourth unit 2 steps clockwise, and a new unit is placed ahead of the first unit. Option 'E' violates the rules.

30.*(e)* : In element II, the cross is turned 135° clockwise and then the positions of left and top units on the cross are interchanged. In option 'E' it is not so.

YOUR SPACE

English Language & Comprehension

1

Comprehension Passages

Comprehension is a very important part of General English paper. The questions on comprehension lay particular stress on understanding a given passage. You are required to read a passage and answer a few questions based on it. Various comprehension questions are set solely with the objectives named below:

1. To test your ability to detect the central idea or the focal point in the given passage.
2. To test your ability to understand and interpret the given passage.
3. To judge your capability to pick out the various arguments put forward by the writer for or against something.
4. To test your accuracy and richness of vocabulary.
5. To test your academic ability to understand the implied and the clearly and fully expressed ideas of the writer of the passage.
6. To test, occasionally, your power of appreciating critically the views contained in the given passage.

While answering comprehension questions, you must comply with the following important points:

1. First, read the whole passage attentively, carefully and quickly.
2. Read it for the second time, slowly but steadily.
3. Work out the probable meaning of new words, from the context in which they have been used.
4. Underline and look for transitional words and phrases as an aid to comprehension.
5. The process of elimination should be used while selecting the correct answer.
6. Recheck your answers before marking in the answersheet.

Multiple Choice Questions

PASSAGE-1

Internet banking is the term used for new age banking system. Internet banking is also called as online banking and it is an outgrowth of PC banking. Internet banking uses the internet as the delivery channel by which to conduct banking activity, for example, transferring funds, paying bills, viewing checking and savings account balances, paying mortgages and purchasing financial instruments and certificates of deposits. Internet banking is a result of explored possibility to use internet application in one of the various domains of commerce. It is difficult to infer whether the internet tool has been applied for convenience of bankers or for the customers' convenience. But ultimately it contributes in increasing the efficiency of the banking operation as well providing more convenience to customers. Without even interacting with the bankers, customers *transact* from one corner of the country to another corner.

There are many advantages of online Banking. It is convenient, it isn't bound by operational timings, there are no geographical barriers and the services can be offered at a *minuscule* cost. Electronic banking has experienced explosive growth and has transformed traditional practices in banking.

Private Banks in India were the first to implement internet banking services in the banking industry. Private Banks, due to late entry into the industry, understood that the establishing network in remote corners of the country is a very difficult task. It was clear to them that the only way to stay connected to the customers at any place and at any time is through Internet applications. They took the Internet applications as a weapon of competitive advantage to corner the great *monoliths* like State Bank of India, Indian Bank etc. Private Banks are pioneer in India to explore the *versatility* of Internet applications in delivering services to customers.

Several studies have attempted to assess the relative importance of B2B and B2C business domains. There is wide difference in estimates of volume of business transacted over Internet and its components under B2C and B2B. However, most studies agree that volume of transactions in B2B domain far exceeds that in B2C. This is the expected result. There is also a growing opinion that the future of e-business lies in B2B domain, as compared to B2C. This has several reasons, like low penetration of PCs to households, low bandwidth availability etc., in a large part of the world. The success of B2C ventures depends to a large extent on the shopping habits of people in different parts of the world. A survey sponsored jointly by Confederation of Indian Industries and Infrastructure Leasing and Financial Services on e-commerce in India in 2010 the following observations. 62% of PC owners and 75% of PC non-owners but who have access to Internet would not buy through the net, as they were not sure of the product offered. The same study estimated the size of B2B business in India by the year 2011 to be varying between ₹ 1250 billion to ₹ 1500 billion. In a recent study done by Arthur Anderson, it has been estimated that 84% of total e-business revenue is generated from B2B segment and the growth prospects in this segment are substantial. It has estimated the revenues to be anywhere between US $ 8.1 trillion to over US $ 21 trillion within the next three years (2014).

1. Which bank(s) is/are pioneer in India to explore the versatility of Internet banking in serving customers?

A. State Bank of India
B. Indian Bank
C. Public Sector Banks
D. Private Banks
E. None of these

2. Which of the following is not an advantage of online banking?

A. It is convenient.
B. It is bound by operational timings.
C. The services can be offered at a minimum cost.
D. There is no geographical barrier.
E. None of these

3. What percentage of PC non-owners but who have access to Internet would not prefer to buy through the net, as they are not sure of the product offered?

A. 75% B. 62%
C. 84% D. 76%
E. None of these

4. Which type of activities are performed by Internet banking?

A. Paying bills
B. Transferring funds
C. Paying mortgages
D. Purchasing financial instruments and certificates of deposits
E. All of these

5. What estimate was made by Confederation of Indian Industries regarding the size of B2B business in India by the year 2011?

A. Between ₹ 250 billion to ₹ 500 billion
B. Between ₹ 1250 billion to ₹ 1500 billion
C. Between ₹ 850 billion to ₹ 1050 billion
D. Between $ 8.7 trillion to $ 21 trillion
E. None of these

Directions (Qs. 6 to 8) : *Choose the word which is MOST SIMILAR in meaning to the word printed in BOLD as used in the passage.*

6. VERSATILITY

A. multi-utility B. vesicle
C. dullness D. necessity
E. meanness

7. MONOLITHS
A. large blocks of stone
B. large organisations
C. monopoly
D. dwarfs
E. niche

8. TRANSACT
A. do business B. tranquillize
C. transcend D. exceed
E. transfer

Directions (Qs. 9 & 10) : *Choose the word which is MOST OPPOSITE in meaning to the word printed in BOLD as used in the passage.*

9. SUBSTANTIAL
A. meagre B. considerable
C. large D. submissive
E. sufficient

10. MINUSCULE
A. small B. minimum
C. minute D. large
E. maximum

PASSAGE-2

One could, in theory, conceive of a country "specialising" entirely in agriculture and obtaining all its industrial requirements from abroad. But it could never become a high income country simply because technologically developed agriculture could never absorb more than a fraction of the working population on the available land. Though in all underdeveloped countries the greater part of the working population is "occupied" in agriculture, most of this represents disguised unemployment; a rural community maintains all its members and expects everyone to share in the work. Much of the greater part of this labour could be withdrawn from agricultrue if alternative employment opportunities were available without any *adverse* effect, and probably with a beneficial effect, on total agricultural output. For the relief of the pressure of labour on the land is itself a most potent factor in *inducing* improvements in technology which raise yields per acre, as well as the yield per man. These improvements normally require an increase in the capital employed on the land; but the savings necessary for the increase in capital are themselves a by-product of reduced population pressure. The reduction in the agricultural population, and the increased use of capital in agriculture are thus different aspects of the same process. As there are fewer mouths to feed, the "agricultural surplus" rises (the excess of agricultural production over the self-consumption of the farming population). The rise in the "surplus" enables the farmers to plough back a higher proportion of their output—in the form of better tools, improved seeds, fertilisers, etc., and such improvements tend to both "labour saving" and "land saving"; they *diminish* the labour requirements at the same time as they increase the yield of the land.

1. According to the passage, it is theoretically possible to think of country
A. advanced both in agriculture and industry
B. specialised in industry but not in agriculture
C. backward both in agriculture and industry
D. specialised in agriculture but not in industry
E. borrowing all its requirements from abroad

2. What, according to the passage, will be the achievement of inducing improvement in technology?
A. Higher specialisation in agriculture
B. Better employment opportunities
C. Beneficial effects on quality of life of people
D. Relieving the pressure of employment in industry
E. None of these

3. What could be done, according to the passage, to induce improvement in agricultural technology?
A. Import of better agricultural technology
B. Providing better weather forecasts
C. To relieve pressure of labour on land
D. Providing irrigation facilities
E. None of these

4. According to the passage, in underdeveloped countries
A. agriculture is in a primitive stage
B. per acre yield is very high
C. land is available in plenty

D. alternative employment opportunities will have adverse effect on the lives of people
E. significant proportion of working population works in agriculture

5. Why, according to the passage, a country specialised in agriculture only cannot become a high income country?
A. It simply cannot borrow all its industrial requirements from abroad
B. It can absorb only a fraction of its working population
C. Agriculture needs huge investments and infrastructural facilities
D. Technological advancements in agriculture has limitations
E. None of these

6. Which of the following statements is TRUE in the context of the passage?
A. Underdeveloped countries are rapidly growing industrially
B. Technologically developed agriculture solves all the problems of unemployment
C. Relief of the pressure of labour on land raises yields per acre
D. Yield per acre and yield per man are unrelated
E. Surplus in agriculture is spent for domestic purposes

7. Which of the following statements is NOT TRUE in the context of the passage?
A. Theoretically there could be a country specialised entirely in agriculture
B. Capital is required to increase the per acre yield of the land
C. Agriculture surplus will rise if there are fewer mouths to feed
D. Technologically developed agriculture will absorb most of the working population on the available land
E. A rural community maintains all its members and expects everyone to share in the work

8. Which of the following is most OPPOSITE in meaning of the work ADVERSE as used in the passage?
A. Negative B. Facilitating
C. Supplementary D. Derogative
E. Decorative

9. Which of the following is most nearly the SAME in meaning as the word INDUCING as used in the passage?
A. Causing B. Augmenting
C. Reducing D. Developing
E. Increasing

10. Which of the following is most nearly the SAME in meaning as the word DIMINISH as used in the passage?
A. Reduce B, Shorten
C. Prohibit D. Increase
E. Worsen

PASSAGE-3

Morning and afternoon, all the young girls and maidens used to *gather* around the village well with their water pots. There they exchanged pleasantries, chatted and discussed. Lakshmi was the prettiest girl at the well. But, she was an orphan.

One day, a well-built man came to Lakshmi's house. He brought with him the richest clothes and jewels as presents for her, "I am your dead father's brother," he told the astonished girl. "You have not seen me before because I have been staying abroad. You must come and live with me now." Lakshmi believed his sweet words and in a short time, locked up her little house and set out with the man.

But a terrible surprise was in store for poor Lakshmi when she got to her new-found uncle's home. The man locked her in a room. "I am not your uncle, but a robber. And I am going to marry you," he told her. Lakshmi howled and wept when she heard this. Saying he would be back in a day or two after making arrangements for the wedding, the man went away. Lakshmi continued sobbing for a while and then stopped. "I must think of a plan to escape," she told herself. Lakshmi guessed that the robber would try to enter her room. So she kept near her bed a sharp knife which she could find in the room.

One night the robber did enter her room but Lakshmi did not make any sound. She just kept a tight hold of the knife and pretended to be sound asleep. When the robber was near her bed, she stood up suddenly, brandishing the knife. The robber was taken aback and with a loud cry, he ran out. Lakshmi *gave chase* and he climbed up the nearest tall tree. Lakshmi then gathered some dry figs and sticks around the foot of the tree and set them on fire. On seeing the rising flames, the robber gave a mighty yell and jumped down. But it was such a long way to the ground that he broke a couple of bones and was unable to move away from the place he fell.

In the mean time, the police was informed by someone about the robber. Very soon they reached the spot and arrested the robber. The people who had gathered at the spot were all praise for Lakshmi's courage and presence of mind,

1. The reason given by the man for his inability to meet Lakshmi was that
   A. he had not known earlier where she lived
   B. he was not friendly terms with her father
   C. he was living in a foreign country
   D. he was not sure whether she would recognise him
   E. he was staying in another village, far away from her place

2. Why did Lakshmi go with the man?
   A. She was convinced that the man was her uncle
   B. She wanted to accompany him and then get him arrested by the police
   C. She intended to teach him a good lesson
   D. She wanted the man to marry her
   E. She felt it necessary to verify his claim by accompanying him

3. Why did the robber run out of the room?
   A. He was stabbed by Lakshmi
   B. He got scared of the rising flames
   C. Lakshmi told him to go out as fast as possible
   D. He was afraid that Lakshmi would strike him with the knife
   E. He ran out to catch hold of Lakshmi and bring her back

4. How was the robber injured?
   A. Lakshmi stabbed him with the sharp knife
   B. He fell down accidently while climbing the tree
   C. He was beaten by Lakshmi and his bones were broken
   D. He jumped down from the tree to save his life
   E. He got burnt in the rising flames

5. "*But a terrible surprise was in store ..... uncle's home.*" What is the "terrible surprise" that is being referred to?
   A. The man told her that her father was dead
   B. The man refused to marry her
   C. The man took away her ornaments and locked her in a room
   D. The man told her that he was her real uncle
   E. The man turned out to be a robber interested in marrying her

6. Where did the robber apparently go after locking up Lakshmi?
   A. He went to her house to loot all the things
   B. He went out to bring a sharp knife
   C. He went away to bring clothes and jewels for her
   D. He went away to make preparations for his marriage
   E. He went out to bring the priest for performing the wedding ceremony

7. Which of the following is most nearly the SAME in meaning as the phrase, GAVE CHASE as used in the passage?
   A. escaped   B. continued
   C. followed   D. prevented
   E. raced

8. Which of the following is TRUE in the context of the passage?
   A. Lakshmi told the robber to climb up the tall tree
   B. At night, the robber entered Lakshmi's room with a knife
   C. Lakshmi had no near relatives and she stayed alone
   D. The robber started running after jumping from the tree
   E. The people who had gathered at the spot set fire to the tree

9. Which of the following is most OPPOSITE in meaning of the word GATHER as used in the passage?
A. Collect B. Reduce
C. Distribute D. Break
E. Disperse

10. Which of the following statements is NOT TRUE in the context of the passage?
A. The police was summoned by Lakshmi herself
B. The well-built man was not the real brother of Lakshmi's father
C. When the robber entered the room at night, Lakshmi was awake
D. Lakshmi used to go to the village well to collect water
E. Lakshmi's guess regarding the robber turned out to be correct

PASSAGE-4

Progress in life depends a good deal on crossing one threshold after another. Some time ago, a man watched his little nephew try to write his name. It was hardwork, very hardwork. The little boy had arrived at an effort threshold. Today he writes his name with comparative ease. No new threshold confronts him. This is the way with all of us. As soon as we cross one threshold, as soon as we conquer one difficulty, a new difficulty appears, or should appear. Some people make the mistake of steering clear of thresholds. Anything that requires genuine thinking and use of energy they avoid. They prefer to stay in a rut where thresholds are not met. Probably, they have been at their job a number of years. Things are easy for them. They make no effort to seek out new obstacles to overcome. Real progress stops under such circumstances.

Some middle-aged and elderly people greatly enrich their lives by continuing to cross thresholds. One man went into an entirely new business when he was past middle life and made success of it, De Morgan didn't start to write novels until he was past sixty. Psychologists have discovered that man can continue to learn throughout his life. And it is undoubtedly better to try and fail than not to try at all. There one can be placed in the category of the Swiss mountaineer of whom it was said, *"He died climbing"*. When a new difficulty arises to obstruct your path, do not complain. Accept the challenge. Determine to cross this threshold as you have crossed numerous other thresholds in your past. In the words of a poet, do not rest but strive *to pass from dream to grander dream.*

1. What obstructs real progress in life?
A. Remaining at one and the same post
B. Avoiding the thinking and energy
C. Shunning every work
D. Stopping education
E. Worrying about the future

2. What does progress in life depend upon?
A. Good habits
B. Hardwork
C. Overcoming one difficulty after another
D. Spirit of service and cooperation
E. None of these

3. What does '*He died climbing*' signify?
A. He died when he was climbing the hill
B. He died before getting at the top
C. He strove hard till the last moment of life
D. He climbed the hill and then died
E. He found it difficult to climb

4. What does '*to pass from dream to grander dream*' mean?
A. Always having greater and greater aspiration in life
B. Seeing one good dream and then greater aspiration in life
C. Making plan after plan
D. Seeing one dream after the other
E. None of these

5. What did the man entering a new business past middle life do of his business?
A. He miserably failed in it
B. He achieved partial success
C. He dropped the business after sometime
D. He achieved good success in it
E. He started writing novels

6. How can you accomplish the most difficult tasks?

A. By mobilizing all possible resources
B. By avoiding all obstacles
C. By sticking to hardwork
D. By getting other people to do your work for you
E. By doing it bit by bit and persisting in the effort

7. What does De Morgan's life teach?
A. That it is futile to learn many things
B. That one is never old in case he has vigour
C. That it is never too late to learn
D. That creative writing can be made even late in life
E. None of these

8. How do middle-aged and elderly people add brilliance to their lives?
A. By overcoming difficulty one after another
B. By getting sycophants to surround them
C. By making fine speeches
D. By acquiring resourcefulness
E. None of these

9. What should we do when a new difficulty obstructs our path?
A. Run away from it
B. Be bold and face it
C. Manoeuvre to get it removed
D. Enlist other people's help to get it over
E. None of these

10. When did De Morgan start to write novels?
A. When he was sixty years old
B. When he was below sixty
C. When he studied psychology
D. When he was a student
E. None of these

PASSAGE-5

In terms of the total energy consumed by different sectors, the largest consumer is understandably the industrial sector, which accounts for nearly half the total energy used in the country today. This is followed by the transport sector which consumes about 25%, the household sector (about 14%) and the agricultural sector (about 9%). This last sector has shown considerable increase in energy use over the last four decades. Among the primary fuels, the relative proportion of coal has dropped from nearly 80% to 40% and that of oil has gone up from 17% to 44% over the same period.

Total energy consumption in India today is equivalent to 291 million tons of oil of which 26% comes from wood. On a per capita basis it works out to about one litre of oil per day, which is extremely low by international standards. The future energy demand depends upon the level of development envisaged and also on the sections of people to be affected by it.

The energy disparity between the urban and the rural population is at present *as wide as* between nations on a *worldwide scale.* There is apparently a greater need to provide energy in the rural areas and to improve the efficiency of energy use than merely to increase the national figures for energy consumption limiting its use to those who are getting the bulk share already.

With the projected rate of population growth, improving upon the per capita energy consumption is a Herculean task as our coal reserves and the capacity to import oil cannot be increased beyond a point. *There is clearly no escape* from the utilisation of renewable energy sources in a big way if the gap between the desired levels of energy supply and available resources has to be kept at the minimum.

1. The author is laying greater emphasis on which of the following?
(*a*) Efficient use of energy
(*b*) Increasing national indices for energy consumption
(*c*) Controlling population growth
A. Only (*a*) B. Only (*b*)
C. Only (*c*) D. All the three
E. Both (*b*) and (*c*)

2. The author feels that increasing per capita use of energy is
A. rather difficult, but not impossible
B. not easy, but certainly achievable
C. not at all desirable
D. a matter of great difficulty
E. a routine matter

3. According to the passage, the energy requirement of the future will be decided on the basis of which of the following?

(*a*) Total energy already consumed by us in the past

(*b*) Level of development of oil industry

(*c*) Profile of the affected people

A. Only (*a*) B. Only (*b*)
C. Only (*c*) D. Both (*a*) and (*b*)
E. Both (*b*) and (*c*)

4. Which of the following shows correctly the different sectors consuming energy arranged in ascending order?

A. Agriculture, transport, household, industrial
B. Agriculture, household, transport, industrial
C. Industrial, transport, household, agriculture
D. Industrial, household, agriculture, transport
E. None of these

5. Which of the following has been suggested by the author as the best possible solution to overcome energy crisis?

A. Importing large quantities of coal
B. Exploration of oil reserves
C. Reducing share of bulk users
D. Maximisation of renewable sources
E. Reducing the energy disparity between urban and rural areas

6. Which of the following styles has been adopted by the author?

A. Unsubstantiated arguments and views
B. Data based, but coloured by socialism
C. Highly subjective with bias for rural people
D. Objective, descriptive, lacking clarity
E. Data based, objective, positive, solution oriented

7. Which of the following has been mentioned as a major hurdle in enhancing per capita consumption of energy in India?

A. Present level of development in India
B. Increased use of energy in agriculture sector
C. Disparity in use of energy in rural and urban areas
D. International norm of 1 litre of oil per day per person
E. None of these

8. Which of the following statements is TRUE in the context of the passage?

A. The household sector has shown considerable increase in energy use
B. Use of oil has increased from 40% to 80%
C. Industrial sector uses 50% of total energy used in India
D. Energy consumption in India is 26% of world consumption
E. Import of oil to the extent required is quite possible

9. *The energy disparity ..... as wide as ..... worldwide scale*, the first sentence of third paragraph means

A. disparity in urban and rural is observed in all nations
B. in no other nation such disparity is observed
C. developed countries consume more energy than developing countries
D. worldwide scale is different for rural and urban areas
E. None of these

10. *There is clearly no escape* ..... means.....

A. there is a way out, but it is ambiguous
B. there is a problem, but without solution
C. there is also no solution to this
D. there is hardly any alternative except
E. there is more than one way

PASSAGE-6

Peace and order are necessary, not just in our own country but also at the international level, if we are to secure national progress and development. The different countries in the world are coming closer today due to faster means of transport and communication. Economically, they are becoming increasingly interdependent. If peace is disturbed in one part of the world, it has adverse effects in other parts of the world as well. Nuclear weapons have already threatened the world with nuclear war. If the conflicts between different nations are not settled in time, they might *culminate* in a nuclear war destroying the whole world. It is therefore, in our own interest that the world is free of conflicts. If at all there are any, they must be settled promptly and peace should be restored. That is why we have declared the establishment of international peace and understanding as an objective of our foreign policy.

We need the help and cooperation of other countries for our scientific, industrial and economic development, especially in those fields where we have yet to achieve self-sufficiency. We obtain the latest machinery, technology and financial aid from the developed countries. On our part we too offer help to the under-developed countries. We are keen on maintaining friendly relations with other countries. Such friendly relations *foster* international understanding.

We have always exerted ourselves to see that the disputes arising between the different nations are settled through peaceful negotiations. We play an active role in the United Nations, the South Asian Association for Regional Cooperation, the Commonwealth of Nations and other such international organisations. We make it a point to participate in the international conferences on issues like energy crisis, environmental imbalance, nuclear arms race etc. We always offer a helping hand to other nations affected by natural calamities such as famines, earthquakes, floods and so on. We strive to maintain peaceful and friendly relations with our neighbouring countries. *Why do we do all this!* We sincerely believe that conflicts in today's world should be minimised, making way for better cooperation among the nations. If this is achieved, human resources will no longer be wasted in things like war or aggression. There will be no destruction of wealth. We believe that, in a peaceful world, there will be greater scope for the economic and cultural development of countries.

1. According to the passage, maintaining friendly relations with other countries facilitate
   A. developing international understanding
   B. exchange of scientists and technologists
   C. strategic planning in defence matters
   D. import and export of several vital commodities
   E. None of these

2. If conflicts between nations do not cease
   A. international bodies will have to take up these issues
   B. international understanding will not be fostered
   C. nuclear war will destroy the whole world
   D. the means of transport and communication will be disrupted

3. Which of the following is obtained by us from the developed countries, according to the passage?
   A. Fertilisers B. Foodgrains
   C. Leather Products D. Technology
   E. Crude Oil

4. Which of the following according to the passage, is facilitating the process of different countries coming together?
   A. Emerging world order
   B. Asian Association for Regional Cooperation
   C. Our participation in international conferences
   D. Need for self-sufficiency
   E. Faster means of transport and communication

5. Minimising the conflicts and making way for better cooperation among the nations will result in
   A. useful and purposive utilisation of human resources
   B. better utilisation of means of transport and communication
   C. culmination of nuclear war destroying the world
   D. keenness on maintaining friendly relations with other countries
   E. preservation of our national unity and integrity

6. Which of the following statements is NOT TRUE in the context of the passage?
   A. International conflicts must be settled promptly
   B. We try to maintain friendly relations with our neighbours
   C. We participate in many international conferences
   D. Friendly relations with other countries foster international understanding

E. Each country can be considered isolated and insulated from the effects of other countries

7. Which of the following words is largely SIMILAR in meaning of the word CULMINATE as used in the passage?

A. Reach the highest point
B. Stretch to the maximum
C. Absolute standards
D. Total destruction
E. Coming of age

8. Which of the following words is MOST OPPOSITE in meaning of the word FOSTER as used in the passage?

A. Advocate B. Hinder
C. Obviate D. Facilitate
E. Jettison

9. The question "Why do we do all this" is asked in the passage in which of the following contexts?

A We always offer a helping hand to other nations in improving their technology
B. We endeavour to maintain peaceful and friendly relations with our neighbours
C. We obtain the latest machinery, technology and financial aid from the developed countries
D. We have shaped our foreign policy in a balanced and purposeful manner
E. None of these

10. Does any of the following sentences contain any idea expressed in the passage?

A. We have to make conscious efforts to preserve our national unity
B. Our country is huge in size and population where many languages are spoken
C. We have adopted the objective of democracy in the interest of overall development of our country
D. Citizens must be well-informed about public issues in order to participate meaningfully in public
E. None of these statements contain any idea expressed in the passage

PASSAGE-7

There is a fairly universal sentiment that the use of nuclear weapon is clearly contrary to morality and that its production does not go far enough. These activities are not only opposed to morality but also to law and if the legal objection can be added to the moral, the argument against the use and the manufacture of these weapons will considerably be reinforced. Now the time is ripe to evaluate the responsibility of scientists who knowingly use their expertise for the construction of such weapons which has *deleterious* effect on mankind.

To this must be added the fact that more than 50 per cent of the skilled scientific manpower in the world is how engaged in the armaments industry. How appropriate it is that all this valuable skill should be *devoted* to the manufacture of weapons of death in a world of poverty is a question that must touch the scientific conscience.

A meeting of biologists on the Long-Term Worldwide Biological Consequences of Nuclear War added frightening dimensions to those forecasts. Its report suggested that the long biological effects resulting from climatic changes may at least be as serious as the immediate ones.

Subfreezing temperatures, low light levels and high dose of ionizing and ultraviolet radiation extending for many months, after a large-scale nuclear war, could destroy the biological support systems of civilization, at least in the Northern Hemisphere. Productivity in natural and agricultural ecosystems could be severely restricted for a year or more. Post-war survivors would face starvation as well as freezing conditions in the dark and be exposed to near-lethal dose of radiation. If, as now seems possible, the Southern Hemisphere were affected also, global disruption of the biosphere could ensue. In any event, there would be severe consequences, even in the areas not affected directly, because of the interdependence of the world economy. In either case the extinction of a large fraction of the earth's animals, plants, and microorganism seems possible. The population size of Homo Sapiens conceivably could be reduced to pre-historic levels or below and extinction of the human species itself cannot be excluded.

1. The author's most important objective of writing the above passage seems to
   A. highlight the use of nuclear weapons as an effective population control measure
   B. illustrate the devastating effects of use of nuclear weapons on mankind
   C. duly highlight the supremacy of the nations which possess nuclear weapons
   D. summarise the long biological effects of use of nuclear weapons
   E. explain scientifically the climatic changes resulting from use of nuclear weapons
2. The scientists possessing expertise in manufacturing destructive weapons are
   A. very few in number
   B. irresponsible and incompetent
   C. more than half of the total number
   D. engaged in the armaments industry against their desire
   E. not conscious of the repercussions of their actions
3. According to the passage, the argument against the use and manufacture of nuclear weapons
   A. does not stand the test of legality
   B. possess legal strength although it does not have moral standing
   C. is acceptable only on moral grounds
   D. becomes stronger if legal and moral considerations are combined
   E. None of these
4. Which of the following is one of the consequences of Nuclear War?
   A. Fertility of land will last only for a year or so
   B. Post-war survivors being very few will have abundant food
   C. Lights would be cooler and more comfortable
   D. Southern hemisphere would remain quite safe in the post-war period
   E. None of these
5. Choose the word which is MOST OPPOSITE in meaning of the word DELETERIOUS as used in the passage.
   A. Beneficial B. Harmful
   C. Irreparable D. Non-cognizable
   E. Revolutionary
6. The author of the passage seems to be of the view that
   A. utilization of scientific skills in manufacture of weapons is appropriate
   B. the evaluation of the scientists' expertise show their incompetence
   C. manufacture of weapons of death would help eradication of poverty
   D. spending money on manufacture of weapons may be justifiable subject to the availability of funds
   E. utilization of valuable knowledge for manufacture of lethal weapons is inhuman
7. Which of the following BEST EXPLAINS the word DEVOTED as used in the passage?
   A. dedicated for a good cause
   B. utilized for betterment
   C. abused for destruction
   D. underutilized
   E. overutilized
8. It appears from the passage that the use of nuclear weapons is considered against morality by
   A. only such of those nations who cannot afford to manufacture weapons
   B. almost all the nations of the world
   C. only the superpowers who can afford to manufacture and sell weapons
   D. a minority group of scientists who have the necessary skill and competence
   E. most of the scientists who devote their valuable skills to manufacture nuclear weapons
9. Which of the following statement(s) *(a)*, *(b)* and/ or *(c)* is/are definitely true in the context of the passage?
   (a) Living organisms in the areas which are not directly affected by the consequences of nuclear war would also suffer
   (b) There is a likelihood of extinction of the human species as a consequence of nuclear war

(c) The post-war survivors would be exposed to the risk of near-lethal radiation

A. Only *(a)* B. Only *(b)*
C. Only *(c)* D. Only *(a)* and *(b)*
E. All the three

10. The biological consequences of nuclear war as given in the passage include all the following except

A. fall in temperature below zero degree celsius
B. ultraviolet radiation
C. high dose of ionizing
D. low light levels
E. None of these

PASSAGE-8

Mahatma Gandhi has repeatedly called himself a truthseeker and has learned, in the course of his search, that truth is a condition of being, not a quality outside of oneself or a moral acquisition, that it is of the very essence of the divine in man. Though he saw deceit and falsehood all around him and knew that it was accepted as the standard of life by people occupying positions of authority and influence, he was never afterwards tempted to *yield to* it even when to have done so would have brought advantage and no condemnation.

For healing he always had a great love and some aptitude and when at the age of seventeen *his family in conclave* suggested his going to England to study law, he *begged* to be allowed to study medicine instead. This, however, was not permitted and law was chosen for him. But, the love of healing remained, and though he could not study in the *orthodox* schools of medicine, he *gratified* his desire by studying various forms of nature-cure treatment and by experimenting with these on his person and on his friends and relatives. Some of these experiments produced remarkable results possibly not only due to the treatment but also to his devoted and instinctive nursing.

1. On whom did Gandhiji practice nature-cure?

A. On sick patients in hospitals
B. On people occupying positions of authority and influence
C. Those who were in great need of the treatment
D. Those who were not cured by other medicines
E. None of these

2. Gandhiji studied law mainly because

A. he wanted to be an eminent lawyer
B. he wanted to go to England
C. his family thrust upon him the study of law
D. he knew he can make a good career in legal profession
E. he wanted to serve people by solving their legal problems

3. What was Gandhiji's idea of truth?

A. It should be assimilated as a personal quality
B. It should be observed with a healing touch
C. It should not be followed with an idea of sacrifice
D. It should be searched in the world around you
E. None of these

4. Mahatma Gandhi described himself as a man:

A. in search of divine qualities
B. who would like to serve people
C. who would like to set standard of life
D. who would not compromise on his principles
E. None of these

5. Choose the word that is MOST OPPOSITE in meaning of the word BEGGED as used in the passage.

A. Demanded B. Appealed
C. Suggested D. Requested
E. Protested

6. Choose the word which is MOST OPPOSITE in meaning of the word ORTHODOX as used in the passage.

A. Backward B. Non-conventional
C. Unpopular D. Modern
E. Customary

7. What temptation did Gandhiji always resist?

A. Getting attracted towards wordly comforts
B. Ignoring the dictates of elderly people
C. Healing the wound of other
D. Following deceit and falsehood
E. None of these

8. What was probably the real cause of Gandhiji's success in nature-cure?
A. His detailed study of various medicinal systems
B. His confidence and desire to help people
C. His skills and aptitude in nursing
D. His experiments in search of truth
E. None of these

9. What did Mahatma Gandhi learn in the course of his search?
A. Being truthful is a divine blessing
B. Truth is synonymous with one's existence
C. People are full of deceit and falsehood
D. Truth is a quality outside of oneself
E. None of these

10. What did Gandhiji see around him?
A. Sick and unhealthy people
B. People accepting proper standard of life
C. People suffering from poverty and disease
D. People not having love and aptitude for healing
E. Dishonesty and untruthfulness

11. Explain the meaning of expression '*his family in conclave*' as used in the passage.
A. Members of the family and relatives
B. Figurehead of the family
C. Private meeting of the family
D. Family meeting for celebrating Gandhiji's seventeenth birthday
E. None of these

12. Choose the word that is most nearly the SAME in meaning as the word GRATIFIED as used in the passage.
A. Purified B. Satisfied
C. Nurtured D. Glorified
E. Projected

13. Choose the word which is most nearly the SAME in meaning as the word YIELD as used in the passage.
A. Surrender B. Provoke
C. Confine D. Adapt
E. Adhere

14. Which of the following statements is NOT TRUE in the context of the passage?
A. Gandhiji did many experiments in the area of nature-cure
B. Gandhiji did not study medicine in the orthodox school
C. Studying law was Gandhiji's first love
D. Truthfulness is the condition of being
E. Gandhiji was always a truthseeker

15. Which of the following statement(s) is/are true in the context of the passage?
(a) Gandhiji had a love and aptitude for nursing
(b) Gandhiji experimented nature-cure on himself
(c) Gandhiji encouraged deceit and psychofancy
A. Only *(a)* B. *(a)* and *(c)*
C. Only *(c)* D. *(a)* and *(b)*
E. Only *(b)*

PASSAGE-9

Believe it or not, once a wonderful plate made of gold fell from heaven into the court of a temple at Banares. On the plate these words were inscribed: "A gift from Heaven to him who loves best." The priest at once made a proclamation that everyday, all those who would like to claim the plate should *assemble* at the temple to have their kind deeds *judged.*

Everyday for a whole year all kinds of holy men, hermits, scholars and nobles came and related to the priests their deeds of charity. The priests heard their claims. At last they decided that the one who seemed to be the greatest lover of mankind was a rich man who had every year given all his wealth to the-poor. So they gave him the plate of gold. But when he took it in his hand, it *turned* to worthless lead. When he dropped it in his amazement on to the floor, it became gold again.

For another year claimants came and the priests presented the heavenly gift three times. But the same thing happened, showing that Heaven did not consider these men *worthy* of the gift.

Meanwhile a large number of beggars came and lay about the temple gate, hoping that the claimants who came would give them alms to prove they were worthy of the golden plate. It was a good thing for the beggars because the pilgrims gave them money but showed no sympathy, nor even a look of pity.

At last a peasant who had heard nothing about the plate of gold came near the temple. He was so *touched* by the sight of the miserable beggars that he wept. When he saw a poor blind and maimed wretch at the temple gate, he knelt at his side and *comforted* him with kind words. When this peasant went inside the temple, he was shocked to find it full of men boasting of their kind deeds and quarrelling with the priests. The priest who held the golden plate in his hand saw the peasant standing there and beckoned to him to know what he wanted. The peasant went near the priest and knowing nothing about the plate, accidentally touched it. At once it shone out with three times its former splendour and the priest said: "Son, the gift is yours, for you are the one who loves best."

1. The gift from Heaven was meant for those who
   A. were scholars
   B. were highly religious and loved God best
   C. gave money to the poor
   D. loved others in the best way
   E. were poor peasants

2. What did the peasant see inside the temple?
   A. Miserable beggars and blind men
   B. Priests quarrelling among themselves
   C. People speaking high of their kind deeds and fighting with the priests
   D. The golden plate being converted to worthless lead
   E. None of these

3. For which of the following was the proclamation made by the priest?
   A. To find the richest person in the town
   B. To find the rightful owner of the plate
   C. To judge the worth of the golden plate
   D. To judge his own deeds with the help of the people

4. What happened to the plate when it was touched by the peasant?
   A. It started glowing with greater splendour
   B. It changed from gold to lead
   C. It became heavier and fell on the ground
   D. It turned into gold
   E. Not mentioned in the passage

5. The rich man dropped the golden plate to the floor as he was
   A. not intersted in possessing it
   B. afraid of holding it
   C. curious to know about its purity
   D. surprised to see it turning to lead
   E. the rightful owner of the plate

6. Why did the beggars stay near the temple gate? They
   A. wanted to prove their claim on the golden plate
   B. had come to pray in the temple
   C. knew that the visitors would give them alms
   D. wanted to seek the sympathy of the peasant
   E. wanted to have a glimpse of the golden plate

7. The priests could decide on the rightful owner of the plate when the peasant
   A. met with an accident
   B. entered the temple and stood there
   C. put forward his claim on the heavenly gift
   D. touched the plate unknowingly
   E. comforted the poor blind man with kind words

8. Which of the following statements is TRUE in the context of the passage?
   A. The rich man did not turn out to be the greatest lover of humanity
   B. The peasant touched the plate to know whether he was its rightful owner
   C. The priest told the peasant to narrate his kind deeds
   D. The plate shone out in splendour when the peasant dropped it on the floor
   E. The peasant went near the priest to ask for the golden plate

9. What made the peasant weep?
   A. The quarrel between the priests and some people

B. The greediness of the rich people
C. The boastful crowd inside the temple
D. The pitiable condition of the beggars
E. None of the above

Directions (Qs. 10 to 12): *Choose the word which is most nearly the SAME in meaning as the word given in BOLD as used in the passage.*

10. TURNED
A. bent B. moved
C. changed D. revolved
E. fell

11. WORTHY
A. useful B. promising
C. successful D. necessary
E. deserving

12. JUDGED
A. ordered B. justified
C. announced D. explainded
E. assessed

Directions (Qs. 13 to 15): *Choose the word which is most OPPOSITE in meaning of the word given in BOLD as used in the passage.*

13. COMFORTED
A. consoled B. ignored
C. advised D. scolded
E. controlled

14. ASSEMBLE
A. distribute B. gather
C. partition D. disperse
E. dismantle

15. TOUCHED
A. moved B. indifferent
C. disconnected D. excited
E. arrogant

PASSAGE-10

A struggle for power began with Bimbisara and Ajatshatru of the Kingdom of Magadha. In the 4th century BC, the Nandas came to power, with their capital at Pataliputra. The latter were replaced by the Mauryas at the close of the same century. This came about partly as a result of Alexander's invasion and the decline of Iranian strength in India. Chandragupta Maurya took advantage of the unsettled conditions and with the help of his adviser Kautilya, built the first great empire in India. Under him and his two great successors, Bindusara and Ashoka, almost the whole of India, with the exception of the farthest south, was unified into one empire.

Many important developments took place in the social, economic and cultural life of the Indian people in this period—322 to 184 BC. Particularly important was the spread of Buddhism, which had been introduced earlier.

The decline of the Mauryan Empire after the rule of Ashoka was followed by a long period of new invasions and the formation of small states. Of the foreign invasions, the first was that of the Greeks who were the rulers of Bactria. They conquered the Punjab and parts of Sind and their contact had a lasting influence on the culture of India. Gandhara style of art emerged and flourished. The greatest Greek ruler in India was Menander (Milinda) in the 2nd century BC, who became a Buddhist.

The Greek invasion was followed by that of the Sakas. The Sakas displaced the Greek in Bactria and spread their power in Western India. One of the Saka kings was Rudradaman who, as the name suggests, was a devotee of Siva. He was responsible for important irrigation works in Saurashtra. The Sakas, like other invaders, became a part of Indian life and played an important role in the development of Indian Culture. Another group of invaders from Central Asia was that of the Kushanas early in the first century AD. The greatest of the Kushana rulers was Kanishka who, according to some historians, started the Saka Era in AD 78. Kanishka ruled his vast empire in India and Central Asia from Purushapura (modern Peshwar) for 40 years. Kanishka's empire brought to India the cultural tradition of Iran, Greece and Rome. It also provided a stimulus to trade between India and other parts of the world Kanishka patronised the Mahayan form of Buddhism. It spread to Central Asia during this period and from there to China, Korea and Japan. The Kushana Empire declined in the third century AD.

1. A suitable title for the above passage is
A. Alexander's invasion of India
B. Kanishka, the great Kushana ruler
C. Development of India's Culture
D. India—the Period of Empires
E. None of these

2. The Kingdom of Magadha was ruled by the Nandas about
A. 2000 years ago
B. 2400 years ago
C. 2800 years ago
D. over 3000 years ago
E. None of these

3. The successors of the Nandas, whose capital was at Pataliputra, were the
A. Greeks B. Iranians
C. Mauryas D. Sakas
E. None of these

4. The cultural traditions of Iran, Greece and Rome came to India during the rule of
A. Ashoka B. Kanishka
C. Menander D. Rudradaman
E. None of these

5. Who, amongst the following, had their capital at Purushapura (modern Peshawar)?
A. The Mauryans B. The Nandas
C. The Kushanas D. The Sakas
E. None of these

6. The Saka Era is believed to have been established by
A. the Kushanas
B. Milinda, the Greek ruler
C. the Nandas
D. The Sakas
E. None of these

7. All of the following were foreign invaders of India, except
A. the Greeks B. the Kushanas
C. the Mauryas D. the Sakas
E. None of these

8. The greatest Greek ruler in India was
A. Ajatshatru B. Bimbisara
C. Bindusara D. Milinda
E. None of these

9. Who were the founders of the first great unified empire in India?
A. The Mauryans B. The Nandas
C. The Kushanas D. The Sakas
E. None of these

10. Which particularly important development took place in India between 322 to 184 BC?
A. The rulers of Bactria invaded India
B. Buddhism spread far and wide
C. The Sakas displaced the Greeks
D. Gandhara style of art attained its zenith
E. None of these

ANSWERS

PASSAGE-1

1	2	3	4	5	6	7	8	9	10
D	B	A	E	B	A	B	A	A	D

PASSAGE-2

1	2	3	4	5	6	7	8	9	10
D	E	C	E	B	C	D	B	B	A

PASSAGE-3

1	2	3	4	5	6	7	8	9	10
C	A	D	D	E	D	C	C	E	A

PASSAGE-4

1	2	3	4	5	6	7	8	9	10
A	C	C	A	D	E	B	A	B	E

PASSAGE-5

1	2	3	4	5	6	7	8	9	10
A	D	E	B	D	E	E	C	C	D

PASSAGE-6

1	2	3	4	5	6	7	8	9	10
A	C	D	E	A	E	A	B	B	E

PASSAGE-7

1	2	3	4	5	6	7	8	9	10
B	C	D	A	A	E	C	B	E	E

PASSAGE-8

1	2	3	4	5	6	7	8	9	10
E	C	A	A	E	B	D	C	B	E
11	**12**	**13**	**14**	**15**					
C	B	A	C	D					

PASSAGE-9

1	2	3	4	5	6	7	8	9	10
D	C	B	A	D	C	D	A	D	C
11	**12**	**13**	**14**	**15**					
E	E	D	D	B					

PASSAGE-10

1	2	3	4	5	6	7	8	9	10
C	D	C	B	C	A	C	D	A	B

2

Synonyms & Antonyms

There are thousands of words in English language. No one can remember their meanings easily but with regular practice one can memorise most of them. A number of words with their Synonyms and Antonyms are compiled here. Try to learn as many as you can and answer the questions thereafter.

Words	*Synonyms*	*Antonyms*
Abandon	Cease, Forsake	Continue
Abhor	Hate, Loathe, Detest	Like, Love
Abiding	Enduring, Durable	Fleeting
Able	Proficient, Competent	Incompetent, Unfit
Ability	Skill, Power	Disability, Inability
Abortive	Fruitless, Futile	Fruitful, Successful
Abolish	Destroy, Undo	Restore, Revive
Abridge	Shorten, Curtail	Lengthen, Expand
Absolve	Forgive, Pardon, Excuse	Condemn
Accelerate	Hasten	Retard
Accord	Agreement, Harmony	Discord, Disagreement
Accumulate	Collect, Store, Amass	Distribute, Scatter
Adamant	Hard, Inflexible	Flexible
Adversity	Misfortune, Distress	Prosperity
Adept	Expert, Skillful	Inexpert, Unskillful
Aggravate	Heighten, Intensify	Quell, Suppress
Agile	Nimble	Clumsy, Undeft
Alert	Vigilant	Heedless
Allay	Calm, Soothe, Assuage	Arouse
Ameliorate	Improve, Advance, Amend	Worsen, Deteriorate
Ambiguous	Vague, Unclear	Clear
Amiable	Lovable, Agreeable	Disagreeable
Annihilate	Destroy	Create
Arduous	Hard, Strenuous	Easy

Words	*Synonyms*	*Antonyms*
Attacks	Assault	Defend
Audacity	Boldness	Cowardice
Auspicious	Favourable, Propitious, Lucky	Ominous, Inauspicious, Unlucky
Austere	Harsh, Severe, Rigorous	Easy-going
Authentic	True, Genuine	Spurious, False
Avarice	Greed	Generosity
Averse	Unwilling, Loath, Disinclined	Willing, Inclined
Aversion	Hostility, Hatred	Affinity, Liking
Base	Low, Mean, Ignoble	Noble, Exalted
Boisterous	Noisy, Stormy	Calm, Quiet
Brave	Courageous, Daring, Bold, Plucky	Cowardly, Dastardly, Timid
Brief	Short, Concise, Laconic	Lengthy, Diffuse
Bright	Vivid, Radiant	Dull, Dark
Brutal	Savage, Cruel	Humane, Kindly
Callous	Hard, Cruel, Indifferent	Soft, Tender, Concerned
Cautious	Careful, Wary	Rash, Reckless, Foolhardy
Censure (*n*)	Blame, Condemnation	Praise
Censure (*vb*)	Blame, Condemn	Praise, Commend
Circumscribed	Restricted, Confined, Limited	Unconfined, Unrestricted
Civil	Polite, Courteous, Gracious, Urbane	Rude, Uncivil, Impolite, Ungracious
Coerce	Compel, Force	Volunteer
Compassionate	Pitiful, Sympathetic, Merciful	Unsympathetic, Merciless, Cruel
Compress	Condense, Abbreviate	Expand, Lengthen
Conspicuous	Noticeable, Manifest	Inconspicuous
Constant	Steady, Steadfast, Uniform	Inconstant, Variable
Cordial	Friendly, Warm, Hearty	Cold, Unfriendly
Covert	Hidden, Secret	Overt, Open
Cruel	Savage, Ruthless, Vicious	Kind, Gentle, Benevolent
Cursory	Rapid, Superficial	Thorough, Exhaustive, Intensive
Credible	Believable, Probable, Plausible	Incredible, Unbelievable, Fantastic
Crafty	Cunning, Sly	Artless, Simple, Ingenuous
Costly	Expensive, Dear	Cheap, Inexpensive
Confidence	Trust, Reliance	Distrust, Doubt
Death	Decease, Demise	Existence, Life
Dearth	Scarcity, Lack, Want, Paucity, Shortage	Plenty, Abundance
Decay	Dissolution, Decline, Decomposition, Disintegration	Regeneration

Words	*Synonyms*	*Antonyms*
Deference	Respect, Reverence	Disrespect, Irreverence
Deficient	Lacking, Inadequate	Complete, Sufficient
Desolate	Lonely, Deserted	Crowded, Occupied
Destitute	Wanting, Needy	Rich, Affluent
Diligence	Industry, Perseverance	Idleness
Disgrace	Dishonour, Discredit	Honour, Credit
Dwindle	Decrease, Shrink	Grow, Increase
Earthly	Terrestrial, Mundane	Celestial, Heavenly, Unearthly
Eligible	Qualified, Suitable	Ineligible, Unsuitable
Emancipate	Liberate, Free	Enslave
Excited	Impassioned, Stimulated	Composed, Cool, Impassive
Extraordinary	Uncommon, Remarkable, Marvellous	Commonplace, Ordinary
Extravagant	Lavish, Prodigal, Wastrel, Spendthrift	Thrifty, Economical, Frugal
Fabricate	Construct, Make	Destroy
Fabulous	Fictitious, Mythical	Actual, Real
False	Untrue, Mendacious	True, Genuine
Famous	Well-known, Renowned	Obscure, Unknown
Fantastic	Fanciful, Imaginative, Visionary	Practical, Down to earth
Fearful	Nervous, Anxious, Afraid, Scared	Fearless, Dauntless
Felicity	Happiness	Sorrow
Gaiety	Joyousness, Hilarity	Mourning, Dullness
Garrulous	Talkative, Loquacious	Taciturn, Silent, Reserved
Generous	Liberal, Magnanimous	Stingy, Miserly
Gigantic	Huge, Colossal	Minute, Small
Graphic	Vivid, Pictorial, Meaningful	Vague
Guest	Visitor	Host
Guile	Fraud, Trickery	Artlessness, Ingenuousness
Gratitude	Gratefulness	Ingratitude, Ungratefulness
Gratuitous	Voluntary, Spontaneous, Unwarranted	Involuntary, Forced
Hamper	Hinder, Obstruct	Facilitate, Ease
Haughty	Arrogant, Proud	Humble, Modest
Hazardous	Dangerous, Perilous	Safe, Secure Protected
Headstrong	Obstinate, Stubborn	Weak-willed, Flexible

Words	*Synonyms*	*Antonyms*
Hope	Belief, Conviction, Expectation	Despair, Hopelessness
Improvident	Prodigal, Carelessness	Provident, Economical
Incessant	Unceasing, Continuous	Discontinuous
Indolent	Slothful, Lethargic	Active, Energetic
Joy	Delight, Pleasure	Sadness, Gloom
Jolly	Jovial, Merry	Gloomy, Sad
Judicious	Discreet, Prudent	Indiscreet, Injudicious
Knowledge	Enlightenment, Learning	Ignorance, Stupidity
Laborious	Industrious, Assiduous	Slothful, Lazy
Laxity	Slackness, Looseness	Firmness
Lenient	Mild, Forbearing	Strict, Stern
Lethal	Deadly, Fatal, Mortal	Life-giving, Vital, Vivifying
Liberal	Generous, Tolerant	Intolerant, Illiberal
Liberty	Freedom, Independence	Slavery, Bondage
Lively	Animated, Active	Dull, Listless
Loyal	Faithful, Devoted	Treacherous, Disloyal, Unfaithful
Lucky	Fortunate	Unlucky, Unfortunate
Lucrative	Profitable	Unprofitable
Magnanimous	Generous, Largehearted	Ungenerous, Stingy
Malady	Illness, Ailment	Health
Manifest	Noticeable, Obvious	Obscure, Puzzling
Meagre	Small	Plentiful, Large
Mean	Low, Abject	Noble, Exalted
Mendacious	False, Untruthful	Truthful
Misery	Sorrow, Distress	Happiness, Joy
Morbid	Sick, Diseased	Healthy
Mournful	Sorrowful, Sad	Joyful, Happy
Negligent	Careless, Heedless	Careful
Notorious	Infamous, Disreputable	Reputable
Obedient	Submissive, Compliant, Docile	Disobedient, Recalcitrant, Wayward
Obsolete	Antiquated, Out-of-Date	Current, Modern
Opportune	Timely, Seasonable	Inopportune
Opulence	Wealth, Riches	Penury, Poverty
Onerous	Heavy, Burdensome	Light, Easy
Palatable	Tasty, Delicious	Unpalatable
Pathetic	Touching	Joyous, Cheery
Persuade	Urge, Induce	Dissuade
Praise (***vb***)	Applaud, Eulogise	Condemn

Words	*Synonyms*	*Antonyms*
Praise (*n*)	Applause, Eulogy	Condemnation
Precarious	Risky, Uncertain	Safe, Certain
Pretence	Pretext, Excuse	Candour, Frankness
Propagate	Breed, Circulate	Terminate, Restrict
Quaint	Odd, Singular	Usual, Ordinary
Quell	Suppress, Subdue	Agitate, Arouse
Rare	Uncommon, Scarce	Common, Ordinary
Refined	Polished, Elegant	Crude, Coarse
Remote	Distant	Near, Close
Renown	Fame, Reputation	Infamy, Notoriety
Rigid	Stiff, Unyielding	Flexible, Yielding
Remorseful	Regretful, Repentant	Unrepentant
Rebellion	Revolt, Mutiny, Insurgency	Loyalty
Scared	Holy, Consecrated	Profane, Unholy
Sane	Sensible, Sound	Insane
Scold	Chide, Rebuke	Praise
Serious	Grave, Earnest	Frivolous
Shy	Bashful	Bold, Impudent
Simple	Plain, Artless	Complex, Cunning, Shrewd
Solitary	Single, Lonely, Secluded	Numerous, Multitude
Shallow	Superficial	Deep
Solace	Comfort, Relief	Discomfort, Grief
Spurious	Sham, False	Genuine, Authentic
Stagnant	Still, Motionless	Moving
Surplus	Excess	Deficit, Shortage
Tame	Gentle, Mild, Domesticated	Savage, Wild
Teacher	Instructor, Educator	Student, Pupil
Tedious	Wearisome, Monotonous	Agreeable, Lively
Temporal	Worldly, Secular	Spiritual
Temperate	Moderate	Immoderate, Intemperate
Tortuous	Winding, Circuitous	Straight, Direct
Tough	Hard, Strong	Tender, Soft, Flexible
Transient	Temporary, Fleeting	Lasting, Durable, Permanent
Trusworthy	Reliable	Unreliable, Untrustworthy
Tranquil	Calm	Agitated
Ugly	Unsightly, Repulsive	Beautiful, Attractive
Useful	Advantageous, Serviceable	Useless
Vehemence	Passion, Force	Apathy, Indifference

Words	*Synonyms*	*Antonyms*
Vindictive	Revengeful	Forgiving
Wholesome	Healthy	Unwholesome, Morbid, Unhealthy, Diseased
Wicked	Evil, Impious	Pious, Good
Wise	Sagacious, Erudite	Foolish, Stupid
Wrath	Anger, Fury, Rage	Love, Peace, Calm
Wreck	Ruin, Destroy	Create, Construct
Yield	Surrender, Submit	Resist, Revolt
Yielding	Submissive, Supple	Inflexible, Intractable
Yoke	Oppression, Bondage	Freedom
Zeal	Passion, Fervour	Apathy, Indifference
Zest	Relish, Enthusiasm	Distaste, Disrelish

Multiple Choice Questions

Directions (Qs. 1 to 100): *In the following questions choose the words which best expresses the MEANING of the given words.*

1. INDICT
A. Condemn B. Reprimand
C. Accuse D. Allege
E. Trap

2. SCINTILLATING
A. Smouldering B. Glittering
C. Touching D. Warming
E. Glowing

3. REFECTORY
A. Restaurant B. Parlour
C. Living Room D. Dining Room
E. Factory

4. DISTINCTION
A. Diffusion B. Disagreement
C. Difference D. Degree
E. Honour

5. IMPROVEMENT
A. Advancement B. Betterment
C. Promotion D. Preference
E. Enhance

6. ADVERSITY
A. Failure B. Helplessness
C. Misfortune D. Crisis
E. Negativity

7. TURN UP
A. Land up B. Show up
C. Crop up D. Come up
E. Rotate

8. DEIFY
A. Flatter B. Challenge
C. Worship D. Face
E. Obstruct

9. ERROR
A. Misadventure B. Misgiving
C. Ambiguity D. Blunder
E. Flaw

10. SHALLOW
A. Artificial B. Superficial
C. Foolish D. Worthless
E. Deep

11. MASSACRE
A. Murder B. Stab
C. Assassinate D. Slaughter
E. Shoot

12. COMBAT
A. Conflict B. Quarrel
C. Feud D. Fight
E. Jostle

13. VORACIOUS
A. Wild B. Hungry
C. Angry D. Quick
E. Beautiful

14. IMPROMPTU
A. Offhand B. Unimportant
C. Unreal D. Effective
E. Punctual

15. RABBLE
A. Mob B. Noise
C. Roar D. Rubbish
E. Erase

16. TEPID
A. Hot B. Warm
C. Cold D. Boiling
E. Sticky

17. MAYHEM
A. Jubilation B. Havoc
C. Excitement D. Defeat
E. Movement

18. TIMID
A. Fast B. Slow
C. Medium D. Shy
E. Rapid

19. CANTANKEROUS
A. Quarrelsome B. Rash
C. Disrepectful D. Noisy
E. Obese

20. PRECARIOUS
A. Cautious B. Critical
C. Perilous D. Brittle
E. Sharp

21. TACITURNITY
A. Dumbness B. Changeableness
C. Hesitation D. Reserveness
E. Preserve

22. INEBRIATED
A. Dreamy B. Stupefied
C. Unsteady D. Drunken
E. Broken

23. HARBINGER
A. Massenger B. Steward
C. Forerunner D. Pilot
E. Performer

24. INTIMIDATE
A. To hint B. Frighten
C. Bluff D. Harass
E. Inform

25. IRONIC
A. Inflexible
B. Bitter
C. Good-natured
D. Disguisedly sarcastic
E. Hard

26. STRINGENT
A. Tense
B. Stringy
C. Strict
D. Causing to shrink
E. Liberal

27. ECSTATIC
A. Animated B. Bewildered
C. Enraptured D. Erratic
E. Gloomy

28. COMMENSURATE
A. Measurable B. Proportionate
C. Beginning D. Appropriate
E. Finish

29. DESTITUTION
A. Humility B. Moderation
C. Poverty D. Beggary
E. Orphanage

30. ASCEND
A. Leap B. Grow
C. Deviate D. Mount
E. Invite

31. UNCOUTH
A. Ungraceful B. Rough
C. Slovenly D. Dirty
E. Gracious

32. LYNCH
A. Hang B. Madden
C. Kill D. Shoot
E. Start

33. LAUD
A. Lord B. Eulogy
C. Praise D. Extort
E. Clap

34. CORRESPONDENCE
A. Agreements B. Contracts
C. Documents D. Letters
E. News

35. VENUE
A. Place B. Agenda
C. Time D. Duration
E. Ceremony

36. STERILE
A. Barren B. Arid
C. Childless D. Dry
E. Fertile

37. SYNOPSIS
A. Index B. Mixture
C. Summary D. Puzzle
E. End

38. GERMANE
A. Responsible B. Logical
C. Possible D. Relevant
E. Foreigner

39. PONDER
A. Think B. Evaluate
C. Anticipate D. Increase
E. Sprinkle

40. CANNY
A. Obstinate B. Handsome
C. Clever D. Stout
E. Container

41. ABUNDANT
A. Ripe B. Cheap
C. Plenty D. Absent
E. Closed

42. CONSEQUENCES
A. Results B. Conclusions
C. Difficulties D. Applications
E. Series

43. SHIVER
A. Shake B. Rock
C. Tremble D. Move
E. Cry

44. DILIGENT
A. Progressive B. Brilliant
C. Inventive D. Hard-working
E. Masculine

45. DISTANT
A. Far B. Removed
C. Reserved D. Separate
E. Unreachable

46. FORAY
A. Excursion B. Contest
C. Ranger D. Intuition
E. Light

47. FRUGALITY
A. Foolishness B. Extremity
C. Enthusiasm D. Economy
E. Weakness

48. GARNISH
A. Paint B. Garner
C. Adorn D. Abuse
E. Attract

49. VIGOUR
A. Strength B. Boldness
C. Warmth D. Enthusiasm
E. Vitality

50. CANDID
A. Apparent B. Explicit
C. Frank D. Bright
E. Sweet

51. BRIEF
A. Limited B. Small
C. Little D. Short
E. Compress

52. GARRULITY
A. Credulity B. Senility
C. Loquaciousness D. Speciousness
E. Misery

53. FURORE
A. Excitement B. Worry
C. Flux D. Anteroom
E. Noise

54. NEUTRAL
A. Unbiased B. Non-aligned
C. Undecided D. Indifferent
E. Unmoved

55. LAMENT
A. Regret B. Comment
C. Condone D. Console
E. Sadden

56. MASTERLY
A. Crafty B. Skillful
C. Meaningful D. Cruel
E. Rightfully

57. MOROSE
A. Annoyed B. Gloomy
C. Moody D. Displeased
E. Happy

58. BARE
A. Uncovered B. Tolerate
C. Clear D. Neat
E. Least

59. FEEBLE
A. Weak B. Vain
C. Arrogant D. Sick
E. Sleek

60. PRESTIGE
A. Influence B. Quality
C. Name D. Wealth
E. Strength

61. WARRIOR
A. Soldier B. Sailor
C. Pirate D. Spy
E. Juggler

62. ENTIRE
A. Part B. Quarter
C. Whole D. Half
E. Tiring

63. RESCUE
A. Command B. Help
C. Defence D. Safety
E. Problem

64. INFREQUENT
A. Never B. Usual
C. Rare D. Sometimes
E. Often

65. WRETCHED
A. Poor B. Foolish
C. Insane D. Strained
E. Broken

66. DIVERSION
A. Amusement B. Distortion
C. Deviation D. Bylane
E. Subway

67. AWAKENED
A. Enlightened B. Realised
C. Shook D. Waken
E. Walking

68. HESITATED
A. Stopped B. Paused
C. Slowed D. Postponed
E. Obstructed

69. PIOUS
A. Pure B. Pretentious
C. Clean D. Devout
E. Thirsty

70. TORTURE
A. Torment B. Chastisement
C. Harassment D. Terror
E. Beat

71. ATTEMPT
A. Serve B. Explore
C. Try D. Explain
E. Chance

72. RESTRAINT
A. Hindrance B. Repression
C. Obstacle D. Restriction
E. Tolerance

73. CHASTE
A. Honest B. Dignified
C. Virtuous D. Noble
E. Truthful

74. INSOMNIA
A. Lethargy B. Sleeplessness
C. Drunkenness D. Unconsciousness
E. Blindness

75. TRANSIENT
A. Transparent B. Fleeting
C. Feeble D. Fanciful
E. Flowing

76. MANDACIOUS
A. Full of confidence B. False
C. Encouraging D. Provocative
E. Thinkable

77. VORACIOUS
A. Truthful B. Gluttonous
C. Funny D. Venturous
E. Fearful

78. CONNOISSEUR
A. Ignorant B. Lover of art
C. Interpreter D. Delinquent
E. Officer

79. REPERCUSSION
A. Clever reply B. Recollection
C. Remuneration D. Reaction
E. Discussion

80. REPEAL
A. Sanction B. Perpetuate
C. Pass D. Cancel
E. Appeal

81. INFAMY
A. Dishonour B. Glory
C. Integrity D. Reputation
E. Beauty

82. FAKE
A. Original B. Imitation
C. Trustworthy D. Loyal
E. Lie

83. DEBACLE
A. Collapse B. Decline
C. Defeat D. Disgrace
E. Mistake

84. ADMONISH
A. Punish B. Curse
C. Dismiss D. Reprimand
E. Admit

85. EMBEZZLE
A. Misappropriate B. Balance
C. Remunerate D. Clear
E. Mix

86. CORPULENT
A. Lean B. Gaunt
C. Emaciated D. Obese
E. Corrupt

87. AUGUST
A. Common B. Ridiculous
C. Dignified D. Petty
E. Month

88. STRINGENT
A. Dry B. Strained
C. Rigorous D. Shrill
E. Thready

89. INSOLVENT
A. Poor B. Bankrupt
C. Penniless D. Broke
E. Unsoluble

90. EXTRICATE
A. Pull B. Free
C. Tie D. Complicate
E. Expel

91. INEXPLICABLE
A. Confusing
B. Unaccountable
C. Chaotic
D. Unconnected
E. Undesired

92. GRATIFY
A. Appreciate B. Frank
C. Indulge D. Pacify
E. Regard

93. ALERT
A. Energetic B. Observant
C. Intelligent D. Watchful
E. Smart

94. UNTIE
A. Unfold B. Unchain
C. Undo D. Unhinge
E. Free

95. OBJECT
A. Challenge B. Disapprove
C. Deny D. Disobey
E. Refuse

96. BROWSE
A. Heal B. Deceive
C. Examine D. Strike
E. Vision

97. SALACITY
A. Bliss B. Depression
C. Indecency D. Recession
E. Urban

98. ZANY
A. Clown B. Pet
C. Thief D. Magician
E. Virtuous

99. WARY
A. Sad
B. Vigilant
C. Distorted
D. Tired
E. Different

100. RECKLESS
A. Courageous
B. Rash
C. Bold
D. Daring
E. Disorganised

Directions (Qs. 101 to 200): *In the following questions choose the word which is the exact OPPOSITE of the given words.*

101. DEAR
A. Priceless
B. Free
C. Worthless
D. Cheap
E. Expensive

102. FLAGITIOUS
A. Innocent
B. Vapid
C. Ignorant
D. Frivolous
E. Stupid

103. LIABILITY
A. Property
B. Assets
C. Debt
D. Treasure
E. Responsibilty

104. VIRTUOUS
A. Wicked
B. Corrupt
C. Vicious
D. Scandalous
E. Dishonest

105. ENCOURAGE
A. Dampen
B. Disapprove
C. Discourage
D. Warn
E. Land

106. MORTAL
A. Divine
B. Immortal
C. Spiritual
D. Eternal
E. Strong

107. LEND
A. Borrow
B. Cheat
C. Pawn
D. Hire
E. Ask

108. COMIC
A. Emotional
B. Tragic
C. Fearful
D. Painful
E. Adult

109. ADDITION
A. Division
B. Enumeration
C. Subtraction
D. Multiplication
E. Minus

110. MINOR
A. Big
B. Major
C. Tall
D. Heavy
E. Adult

111. REPEL
A. Attend
B. Concentrate
C. Continue
D. Attract
E. Expel

112. ARTIFICIAL
A. Red
B. Natural
C. Truthful
D. Solid
E. Superficial

113. CAPACIOUS
A. Limited
B. Caring
C. Foolish
D. Changeable
E. Spacious

114. PROVOCATION
A. Vocation
B. Pacification
C. Peace
D. Destruction
E. Convocation

115. METICULOUS
A. Mutual
B. Shaggy
C. Meretricious
D. Slovenly
E. Ridiculous

116. ABLE
A. Disable
B. Inable
C. Unable
D. Misable
E. Probable

117. COMFORT
A. Uncomfort
B. Miscomfort
C. Discomfort
D. Uneasy
E. Luxury

118. GAIN
A. Loose
B. Fall
C. Lost
D. Lose
E. Again

119. SYNTHETIC
A. Affable
B. Natural
C. Plastic
D. Cosmetic
E. Pathetic

120. ACQUITTED
A. Freed B. Burdened
C. Convicted D. Entrusted
E. Predicted

121. STRINGENT
A. General B. Vehement
C. Lenient D. Magnanimous
E. Astringent

122. FLIMSY
A. Frail B. Filthy
C. Firm D. Flippant
E. Fat

123. BUSY
A. Occupied B. Engrossed
C. Relaxed D. Engaged
E. Free

124. ADAPTABLE
A. Adoptable B. Flexible
C. Yielding D. Rigid
E. Solid

125. LOVE
A. Villainy B. Hatred
C. Compulsion D. Force
E. Fight

126. BALANCE
A. Disbalance B. Misbalance
C. Debalance D. Imbalance
E. Unbalance

127. RELINQUISH
A. Abdicate B. Renounce
C. Possess D. Deny
E. Occupy

128. MOUNTAIN
A. Plain B. Plateau
C. Precipice D. Valley
E. Ocean

129. FICKLE
A. Courageous B. Sincere
C. Steadfast D. Humble
E. Strong

130. PERENNIAL
A. Frequent B. Regular
C. Lasting D. Rare
E. Often

131. RARELY
A. Hardly B. Definitely
C. Frequently D. Periodically
E. Barely

132. STARTLED
A. Amused B. Relaxed
C. Endless D. Astonished
E. Finished

133. ADHERENT
A. Detractor B. Enemy
C. Alien D. Rival
E. Follower

134. QUIESCENT
A. Indifferent B. Troublesome
C. Weak D. Unconcerned
E. Silent

135. CONDENSE
A. Expand B. Distribute
C. Interpret D. Lengthen
E. Lighten

136. BENIGN
A. Malevolent B. Soft
C. Friendly D. Unwise
E. Kind

137. OBSCURE
A. Implicit B. Obnoxious
C. Explicit D. Pedantic
E. Incurable

138. HYPOCRITICAL
A. Gentle B. Sincere
C. Amiable D. Dependable
E. Critical

139. EVASIVE
A. Free B. Honest
C. Liberal D. Frank
E. Invasive

140. INDUSTRIOUS
A. Indifferent B. Indolent
C. Casual D. Passive
E. Serving

141. EXTRICATE
A. Manifest B. Palpable
C. Release D. Entangle
E. Intricate

142. LUCID
A. Glory B. Noisy
C. Obscure D. Distinct
E. Clear

143. INSIPID
A. Tasty B. Stupid
C. Discreet D. Feast
E. Flavoured

144. OBEYING
A. Ordering B. Following
C. Refusing D. Contradicting
E. Insulting

145. VICTORIOUS
A. Defeated B. Annexed
C. Destroyed D. Vanquished
E. Triumphant

146. COMMISSIONED
A. Started B. Closed
C. Finished D. Terminated
E. Salaried

147. VANITY
A. Pride B. Humility
C. Conceit D. Ostentious
E. Grace

148. ZENITH
A. Acme B. Top
C. Nadir D. Pinnacle
E. Core

149. TANGIBLE
A. Ethereal B. Concrete
C. Actual D. Solid
E. Delicious

150. REPRESS
A. Inhibit B. Liberate
C. Curb D. Quell
E. Suppress

151. EPILOGUE
A. Dialogue B. Prelude
C. Post script D. Epigram
E. Monologue

152. FRAUDULENT
A. Candid B. Direct
C. Forthright D. Genuine
E. Real

153. LOQUACIOUS
A. Reticent B. Talkative
C. Garrulous D. Verbose
E. Verbatim

154. NIGGARDLY
A. Frugal B. Thrifty
C. Stingy D. Generous
E. Mean

155. PERTINENT
A. Irrational B. Irregular
C. Insistent D. Irrelevant
E. Inconsistent

156. FAINT-HEARTED
A. Warm-hearted B. Full-blooded
C. Hot-blooded D. Stout-hearted
E. Kind-hearted

157. VIOLENT
A. Humble B. Harmless
C. Gentle D. Tame
E. Pet

158. STATIONARY
A. Active B. Mobile
C. Rapid D. Busy
E. Unfixed

159. HONORARY
A. Dishonourable B. Reputed
C. Paid D. Official
E. Obligatory

160. COMMON
A. Rare B. Small
C. Petty D. Poor
E. General

161. FRUGAL
A. Copious B. Extravagant
C. Generous D. Ostentatious
E. Thrifty

162. MALICIOUS
A. Kind B. Boastful
C. Generous D. Indifferent
E. Harmful

163. FAMILIAR
A. Unpleasant B. Dangerous
C. Friendly D. Strange
E. Known

164. PRELIMINARY
A. Final B. First
C. Secondary D. Initial
E. Main

165. DOUBTFUL
A. Famous B. Certain
C. Fixed D. Important
E. Vague

166. REMISS
A. Forgetful B. Watchful
C. Dutiful D. Harmful
E. Break

167. INDISCREET
A. Reliable B. Honest
C. Prudent D. Stupid
E. Credible

168. FRESH
A. Faulty B. Sluggish
C. Disgraceful D. Stale
E. Old

169. ANNOY
A. Praise B. Rejoice
C. Please D. Reward
E. Happy

170. TRANSPARENT
A. Semi-transparent B. Muddy
C. Opaque D. Dark
E. Clear

171. REVEALED
A. Denied B. Concealed
C. Ignored D. Overlooked
E. Appealed

172. EXTRAVAGANCE
A. Luxury B. Poverty
C. Economy D. Cheapness
E. Vengeance

173. CROWDED
A. Busy B. Congested
C. Quiet D. Deserted
E. Empty

174. SHRINK
A. Contract B. Spoil
C. Expand D. Stretch
E. Droop

175. ENMITY
A. Important B. Unnecessary
C. Friendship D. Likeness
E. Infamy

176. EXODUS
A. Influx B. Home-coming
C. Return D. Restoration
E. Entry

177. CULPABLE
A. Defendable B. Blameless
C. Careless D. Irresponsible
E. Bailable

178. SUBSERVIENT
A. Aggressive B. Straightforward
C. Dignified D. Supercilious
E. Submissive

179. AWARE
A. Uncertain B. Ignorant
C. Sure D. Doubtful
E. Beware

180. GRACEFUL
A. Rough B. Expert
C. Miserable D. Awkward
E. Beautiful

181. AUTONOMY
A. Slavery B. Subordination
C. Dependence D. Submissiveness
E. Democracy

182. NADIR
A. Modernity B. Zenith
C. Liberty D. Progress
E. Horizon

183. CONCEDE
A. Object B. Refuse
C. Grant D. Accede
E. Exceed

184. SUPPRESS
A. Encourage B. Grow
C. Praise D. Permit
E. Swell

185. FAMOUS
A. Disgraced B. Notorious
C. Evil D. Popular
E. Ugly

186. EXPAND
A. Contract B. Condense
C. Congest D. Conclude
E. Compact

187. ARROGANT
A. Polite B. Cowardly
C. Meek D. Gentlemanly
E. Vibrant

188. ENORMOUS
A. Soft B. Average
C. Tiny D. Weak
E. Gigantic

189. URBANE
A. Illiterate B. Backward
C. Discourteous D. Orthodox
E. Villager

190. HOSTILITY
A. Courtesy B. Hospitality
C. Relationship D. Friendliness
E. Casualty

191. BELITTLE
A. Praise B. Flatter
C. Exaggerate D. Adore
E. Decry

192. HAPLESS
A. Cheerful B. Consistent
C. Fortunate D. Shapely
E. Hopeful

193. HAPHAZARD
A. Fortuitous B. Indifferent
C. Deliberate D. Accidental
E. Random

194. GREGARIOUS
A. Antisocial B. Glorious
C. Horrendous D. Similar
E. Affable

195. VALUABLE
A. Invaluable B. Worthless
C. Inferior D. Lowly
E. Worthy

196. ABSOLUTE
A. Deficient B. Faulty
C. Limited D. Scarce
E. Whole

197. CONFESS
A. Deny B. Refuse
C. Contest D. Contend
E. Profess

198. GULLIBLE
A. Incredulous B. Fickle
C. Easy D. Stylish
E. Credulous

199. HIRSUTE
A. Scaly B. Bald
C. Erudite D. Quiet
E. Hairy

200. HINDRANCE
A. Aid B. Persuasion
C. Cooperation D. Agreement
E. Encumbrance

ANSWERS

1	2	3	4	5	6	7	8	9	10
C	B	D	C	B	C	B	C	D	B
11	**12**	**13**	**14**	**15**	**16**	**17**	**18**	**19**	**20**
D	D	B	A	A	B	B	D	A	B
21	**22**	**23**	**24**	**25**	**26**	**27**	**28**	**29**	**30**
D	D	C	B	D	C	C	B	C	D
31	**32**	**33**	**34**	**35**	**36**	**37**	**38**	**39**	**40**
A	C	C	D	A	A	C	D	A	C
41	**42**	**43**	**44**	**45**	**46**	**47**	**48**	**49**	**50**
C	A	C	D	A	A	D	C	A	C
51	**52**	**53**	**54**	**55**	**56**	**57**	**58**	**59**	**60**
D	C	A	A	A	B	B	A	A	C

61	**62**	**63**	**64**	**65**	**66**	**67**	**68**	**69**	**70**
A	C	B	D	A	C	D	B	A	A
71	**72**	**73**	**74**	**75**	**76**	**77**	**78**	**79**	**80**
C	D	C	B	B	B	B	B	D	D
81	**82**	**83**	**84**	**85**	**86**	**87**	**88**	**89**	**90**
A	B	A	D	A	D	C	C	B	B
91	**92**	**93**	**94**	**95**	**96**	**97**	**98**	**99**	**100**
B	D	D	C	B	C	C	A	B	B
101	**102**	**103**	**104**	**105**	**106**	**107**	**108**	**109**	**110**
D	A	B	C	C	B	A	B	C	B
111	**112**	**113**	**114**	**115**	**116**	**17**	**18**	**19**	**20**
D	B	A	B	D	C	C	D	B	C
121	**122**	**123**	**124**	**125**	**126**	**127**	**128**	**129**	**130**
C	C	C	D	B	D	C	D	C	D
131	**132**	**133**	**134**	**135**	**136**	**137**	**138**	**139**	**140**
D	B	B	A	C	A	C	B	B	B
141	**142**	**143**	**144**	**145**	**146**	**147**	**148**	**149**	**150**
D	C	A	A	A	D	B	C	A	B
151	**152**	**153**	**154**	**155**	**156**	**157**	**158**	**159**	**160**
B	D	A	D	D	D	C	B	C	A
161	**162**	**163**	**164**	**165**	**166**	**167**	**168**	**169**	**170**
B	C	D	A	B	C	C	D	C	C
171	**172**	**173**	**174**	**175**	**176**	**177**	**178**	**179**	**180**
B	C	D	D	C	A	A	C	B	D
181	**182**	**183**	**184**	**185**	**186**	**187**	**188**	**189**	**190**
C	B	B	B	B	B	A	C	C	D
191	**192**	**193**	**194**	**195**	**196**	**197**	**198**	**199**	**200**
C	C	C	A	B	C	A	A	B	A

3

Fill in the Blanks

Fill in the blanks is such an exercise that starts with the primary education and continues at the highest level of examinations. One must practise it regularly to score well in competitive exams.

Multiple Choice Questions

Directions: *Pick out the most effective word(s) from the given words to fill in the blanks to make the sentence meaningfully complete.*

1. Leadership defines what the future should look like and ..... people with that vision.
A. aligns B. develops
C. trains D. encourages
E. transforms

2. We upset ourselves by responding in an ..... manner to someone else's actions.
A. unabashed B. irrational
C. arduous D. arguable
E. invalid

3. Nothing probably has more contributed to ..... the poverty and backwardness of India than the want of good roads.
A. alleviate B. circumvent
C. perpetuate D. accelerate
E. accentuate

4. The main objective of this dedicated institution is to ..... poverty.
A. enhance B. magnify
C. manifest D. entertain
E. alleviate

5. He feels that the ..... of his achievements goes to his father.
A. reward B. compensation
C. attribute D. credit
E. gist

6. Both the brothers are equally handsome but the elder ..... the two is more intelligent.
A. among B. than
C. of D. in
E. between

7. ..... being a handicapped person, he is very co-operative and self-reliant.
A. Because B. Although
C. Since D. Basically
E. Despite

8. The employees were unhappy because their salary was not increased .....
A. marginally B. abruptly
C. substantially D. superfluously
E. negligibly

9. No sooner did the bell ring, ... the actor started singing.
A. when B. than
C. after D. before
E. through

10. Unfavourable weather conditions can ..... illness.
A. cure B. detect
C. treat D. enhance
E. diagnose

11. They demanded a lot of things, but he cannot ..... to grant them for want of funds.

A. afford B. decide
C. permit D. buy
E. expect

12. The little child was so excited that he could not ..... the burning candle.

A. threw B. thrown
C. drift D. lights
E. throw

13. Though the brothers are twins, they look .....

A. alike B. handsome
C. indifferent D. identical
E. different

14. If I ..... realized it, I would not have acted on his advice.

A. was B. had
C. were D. have
E. being

15. Why don't you ..... your work in advance before commencing it.

A. start B. complete
C. finish D. plan
E. execute

16. The manager is to help his subordinates ..... their potential in their present as well as in their future assignment.

A. respect B. train
C. delegate D. judge
E. realise

17. All the employees in the company are entitled ..... reimbursement of medical expenses.

A. of B. for
C. on D. to
E. with

18. It is ..... in pursuit of these very objectives that our Government has made some basic changes in our economic policies.

A. greatly B. constantly
C. clearly D. largely
E. precisely

19. The Management of so many projects and of different nature ..... no common capacity and vigour.

A. demands B. require
C. permits D. urge
E. offers

20. He could ..... a lot of money in such a short time by using his intelligence and working hard.

A. spend B. spoil
C. exchange D. accumulate
E. pay

21. With his ..... income, he finds it difficult to live a comfortable life.

A. brief B. sufficient
C. meagre D. huge
E. adequate

22. The child broke ..... from his mother and ran towards the painting.

A. away B. after
C. down D. with
E. heavily

23. His interest in the study of human behaviour is indeed very .....

A. broad B. strong
C. vast D. large
E. deep

24. Finally, the thief ..... that he had stolen the ornaments.

A. argued B. decided
C. appealed D. admitted
E. obeyed

25. Since there was no evidence to prove him ..... he was acquitted.

A. innocent B. offence
C. guilty D. honest
E. accused

26. Marketing is one area in which our country has been particularly ..... and new strategies need to be evolved to strengthen it.

A. efficient B. deficient
C. strongest D. overemphasised
E. powerful

27. There is no doubt that one has to keep ..... with the changing times.

A. himself B. tuning
C. pace D. oneself
E. aside

28. The poor ones continue to ..... out a living inspite of economic liberalisation in that country.
A. eke B. go
C. manage D. bring
E. find

29. ..... eye witnesses, the news reporter gave a graphic description of how the fire broke.
A. Reporting B. Seeing
C. Examining D. Quoting
E. Observing

30. Before getting elected, he was ..... to the welfare of the people.
A. devoted B. attended
C. focussed D. neglected
E. concentrated

31. The union leader was very critical ..... the attitude of the management.
A. for B. at
C. on D. against
E. of

32. The passengers and crew members of the aeroplane had a ..... escape when it was taking off from the runway.
A. little B. narrow
C. brief D. large
E. better

33. Eight scientists have ..... the national awards for outstanding contribution and dedication to the profession.
A. picked B. conferred
C. bagged D. discovered
E. bestowed

34. There has been a ..... lack of efficiency in all the crucial areas of the working of Public Sector Undertakings.
A. conspicuous B. stimulative
C. insignificant D. surprising
E. positive

35. Rohan is too ..... as far as his food habits are concerned.
A. curious B. enjoyable
C. interesting D. involved
E. fastidious

36. Some people ..... themselves into believing that they are indispensable to the organisation they work for.
A. force B. delude
C. denigrate D. fool
E. keep

37. Arpan had to drop his plan of going to picnic as he had certain ..... to take of during that period.
A. transactions B. preparations
C. commitments D. urgencies
E. observations

38. No country can ..... to practise a constant, rigid foreign policy in view of the world power dynamics.
A. envisage B. anticipate
C. afford D. visualise
E. obliviate

39. After a recent mild paralytic attack his movements are ..... restricted; otherwise he is still very active.
A. not B. entirely
C. slightly D. nowhere
E. frequently

40. ..... he woke up, he saw that his bag was stolen.
A. If B. When
C. Where D. So
E. Neither

41. I am going to Bhopal today and plan to ..... by tomorrow evening.
A. returning B. returned
C. have returned D. be returning
E. return

42. Since the priest did not arrive in time, the ceremony was ..... late.
A. begins B. begun
C. began D. beginning
E. begin

43. He succeeded in getting possession ..... his land after a long court case.
A. to B. against
C. of D. with
E. for

44. The villagers have not ..... over the shock of losing everything in the earthquake.
A. got B. made
C. forgotten D. freed
E. felt

45. Ajay is the ..... head of the family and commands a lot of respect from the family members.
A. solely B. strongest
C. undisputed D. full
E. controversial

46. The blood donation camp was organised ..... the Naval Youth Club.
A. to B. by
C. from D. with
E. along

47. Last year the performance of this production unit was ..... .
A. tall B. staggered
C. fantastic D. below
E. upwards

48. We all must ..... that people are the most important assets of any organisation.
A. find B. look
C. realise D. involve
E. dispel

49. Since Vivek stays far away from our place, we do not meet each other ..... .
A. rarely B. shortly
C. timely D. frequently
E. momentarily

50. The lights ..... just as we sat down to watch the movie on television.
A. went off B. shut out
C. put out D. blew down
E. gave off

51. To ..... yourself from ..... wear warm clothes.
A. save, heat B. suffer, cold
C. prevent, ice D. protect, cold
E. prohibit, heat

52. He is ..... to ..... any kind of work with due sincerity.
A. determined, undertake
B. found, perform
C. eager, avoid
D. willing, ignore
E. reluctant, entrust

53. They wanted to ..... all these books, but they could not find ..... time to do so.
A. buy, some B. read, sufficient
C. dispose, some D. pursue, necessary
E. cover, almost

54. They started their ..... branch in this city today; their other ..... branches are in the next by-lane.
A. first, new B. first, old
C. second, old D. third, two
E. new, several

55. Due to ..... rainfall this year, there will be ..... cut in water supply.
A. meagre, least
B. abundant, considerable
C. enough, substantial
D. surplus, abundant
E. sufficient, no

56. The judge ..... him because he was found ..... on the basis of the evidence.
A. acquitted, criminal
B. punished, guilty
C. sentenced, innocent
D. suspended, involved
E. pardoned, innocent

57. The speaker's ..... over his subject was seen through his ..... discourse.
A. mastery, fluent
B. efficiency, thorough
C. lethargy, dull
D. grip, boring
E. skill, pleasant

58. Workers in earlier days were ..... because of which the industries ..... a lot.
A. honest, lost
B. rich, flourished
C. autocrats, developed
D. inefficient, suffered
E. idle, prospered

59. A close ..... of the bill shows that the provisions are ..... and there is a need to add certain crucial elements to them.

A. examination, sufficient
B. observation, helpful
C. scrutiny, inadequate
D. file, numerous
E. account, excellent

60. His ..... speech has seriously ..... the young minds.
A. audacious, delighted
B. maiden, flattered
C. humorous, damaged
D. irresponsible, misled
E. eccentric, questioned

61. On ..... of the enquiry, if it is found that the ..... are true, the enquiry officer will report the matter to the higher authority.
A. demand, findings
B. completion, allegations
C. instituting, charges
D. withdrawal, inferences
E. establishment, results

62. After the present tax holiday period ....., the power cost to users may become ..... .
A. starts, unreasonable
B. sets, perishable
C. ends, less
D. enhances, negligible
E. ends, intolerable

63. A good teacher-student relationship helps create a ..... and peaceful atmosphere where there is no room for any ..... of educational activity.
A. harmonious, interruption
B. congenial, development
C. quiet, confusion
D. cordial, education
E. delightful, exaggeration

64. No self-made person would ever like to ..... to any ..... .
A. take, task
B. yield, cause
C. submit, dimension
D. surrender, proposal
E. succumb, pressure

65. Though I had behaved with him very ....., he was ....., enough to forgive me.
A. nicely, unkind
B. rudely, indecent
C. nastily, reluctant
D. impolitely, kind
E. politely, generous

66. We cannot ..... up with your requirements for want of ..... facilities.
A. put, urgent
B. take, expert
C. cope, infrastructural
D. end, ancillary
E. give, deployable

67. He is too ..... to tolerate ..... .
A. humble, lethargy
B. impatient, delay
C. fast, speed
D. wicked, vices
E. lazy, sluggishness

68. The flood ..... in the State ..... to 261 with four more deaths reported today.
A. water, rose
B. level, aroused
C. toll, mounted
D. destruction, spread
E. catchment, increased

69. Right from the earliest ages, India's ..... developed a sense of unity and ..... among its people.
A. people, diversity
B. rulers, commitment
C. culture, commonness
D. population, diversification
E. heritage, disparity

70. ....., there is a widespread ..... among the educated youth which makes them increasingly alienated.
A. Luckily, dedication
B. Co-incidentally, feeling
C. Obviously, enthusiasm
D. Unfortunately, frustration
E. Nevertheless, optimism

71. The problem of ..... another war has assumed great urgency because of the ..... of nuclear weapons.
A. fighting, destruction
B. preventing, invention
C. precipitating, disarmament
D. stopping, need
E. winning, growth

72. In many countries, ... development arising out of fast technological ..... has led to some problems.
A. meagre, inventions
B. cultural, practices
C. agricultural, development
D. optimum, intervention
E. excessive, progress

73. Shyness is ..... through abnormal behaviour in various ..... .
A. manifested, ways
B. removed, people
C. shown, kinds
D. developed, things
E. enhanced, aspects

74. In that country, bureaucracy is ..... as a group of men and women that had arrogated to itself power ..... responsibility.
A. perceived, without
B. believed, within
C. held, into
D. known, unto
E. allowed, for

75. The employees of the factory owing ..... to the workers union have ..... of an agitation from next week in support of their demands.
A. allegiance, warned
B. respect, called
C. shelter, started
D. pressure, proposal
E. assurance, sought

76. Yesterday, around 400 huts were ..... in a major fire which ..... the slum area.
A. burn. hit
B. gutted, engulfed
C. fired, took
D. burning, blazed
E. demolished, entered

77. As a ..... of Chetan's rude behaviour he was ..... a memo by his boss.
A. sequel, issued
B. part, delivered
C. consequence, given
D. punishment, rewarded
E. reaction, presented

78. Deepak has ..... some unfinished work to ..... up before he can go home.
A. yet, get
B. since, come
C. still, clear
D. let, take
E. set, give

79. After careful ..... the thief ..... that he has committed the crime.
A. investigation, refused
B. questioning, divulged
C. consideration, felt
D. action, agreed
E. finding, insisted

80. The mining activity comes under the ..... of the forest conservation act and we must ..... that the law is followed strictly.
A. debate, see
B. course, observe
C. control, insist
D. purview, ensure
E. limits, stipulate

81. All the teachers ..... that Arpita would stand at the top in the examination, she ..... short of their expectation.
A. thought, fell
B. expected, ran
C. presumed, failed
D. dreamt, achieved
E. started, reached

82. In a ..... decision the government has announced that elementary education for children in the age group of six to fourteen would be ..... a fundamental right.
A. historical, obtained
B. landmark, deplore
C. clear, absolved
D. significant, made
E. rush, given

83. The researcher ..... information about the number of villages in each state which are ..... as problem villages to be covered by National Drinking Water Mission.
A. invested, found
B. got, designed
C. collected, identified
D. investigated, imagined
E. knows, gathered

84. The rules of the institute ..... that employees should not undertake any outside ..... work without seeking written permission of the institute.
A. conclude, devoted
B. strengthen, assignment
C. allow, important
D. stipulate, remunerative
E. direct, extra

85. The television boom might not ..... newspaper readership but magazines which are not leaders in their segment might ..... .
A. link, close
B. effect, prosper
C. reduce, encourage
D. attract, continue
E. affect, suffer

86. The other servants had to ..... since Appu alone ..... all the food.
A. leave, prepared B. eat, cooked
C. wait, spoiled D. cook, wasted
E. starve, consumed

87. If you do not ..... all your monthly expenses would ..... your income.
A. spend, gain B. save, outwit
C. economise, exceed D. think, swallow
E. realise, enhance

88. Ankur ..... me coming to his table, he smiled and ..... me a chair.
A. looked, gave B. welcomed, took
C. saw, offered D. found, signalled
E. met, sat

89. The counter clerk was very busy and ..... not pay any ..... to my request.
A. did, attention B. had, cash
C. could, respect D. can, help
E. certainly, acceptance

90. The speech ..... with subtle threats has resulted in ..... tension in the sensitive areas of the city.
A. full, escalating
B. started, reduced
C. followed, continuous
D. replete, increased
E. forced, dissolving

91. The State Government employees ..... threatened to launch an indefinite strike from next month to ..... their demands.
A. have, press B. did, get
C. were, meet D. nearly, fulfil
E. has, press

92. Virat ..... another feather ..... his cap by his wonderful preformance in the one day match.
A. created, by B. took, in
C. captured from D. kept, in
E. added, to

93. We are ..... to have him ..... here to make this function a great success.
A. happy, arrive B. wonderful, again
C. sure, come D. pleased, over
E. proud, leave

94. The charges made in the system were so ..... that they didn't require any ..... .
A. marginal, expenses
B. big, time
C. obvious, modifications
D. certain, expertise
E. genuine, intelligence

95. The police ..... any attempt of arson by ..... at the trouble spot quite in time.
A. predisposed, visiting
B. preempted, arriving
C. made, encircling
D. thwarted, presenting
E. squashed, surrounding

96. It is ..... for every tax-payer to ..... the tax returns to the Income Tax Department.
A. binding, pay B. possible, remit
C. worthwhile, evade D. obligatory, submit
E. necessary, lodge

97. ..... by long queues and bad weather the voters ..... their way to polling stations any way they could.
A. Undaunted, made
B. Worried, lost
C. Encouraged, prepared
D. Going, dropped
E. Satisfied, turned

98. The Chief Minister ..... the House that ..... action would be taken against all those found involved in corruption.
A. instructed, preventive
B. called, strict
C. assured, stringent
D. reiterated, strictly
E. informed, constructive

99. In his ..... he followed the ..... course.
A. ignorance, wrong
B. bewilderment, appropriate
C. hurry, diversified
D. agony, funny
E. predicament, proper

100. He is usually ..... but today he appears rather ..... .

A. tense, restless
B. quiet, calm
C. happy, humorous
D. strict, unwell
E. calm, distrubed

ANSWERS

1	2	3	4	5	6	7	8	9	10
D	B	D	E	D	C	E	C	B	D
11	**12**	**13**	**14**	**15**	**16**	**17**	**18**	**19**	**20**
A	E	E	B	D	E	D	E	A	D
21	**22**	**23**	**24**	**25**	**26**	**27**	**28**	**29**	**30**
C	A	E	D	C	B	C	A	D	A
31	**32**	**33**	**34**	**35**	**36**	**37**	**38**	**39**	**40**
E	B	C	A	E	B	C	C	C	B
41	**42**	**43**	**44**	**45**	**46**	**47**	**48**	**49**	**50**
E	B	C	A	C	B	C	C	D	A
51	**52**	**53**	**54**	**55**	**56**	**57**	**58**	**59**	**60**
D	A	B	D	E	B	A	D	C	D
61	**62**	**63**	**64**	**65**	**66**	**67**	**68**	**69**	**70**
B	E	A	E	D	C	B	C	C	D
71	**72**	**73**	**74**	**75**	**76**	**77**	**78**	**79**	**80**
B	E	B	A	A	B	A	C	B	D
81	**82**	**83**	**84**	**85**	**86**	**87**	**88**	**89**	**90**
A	D	C	D	E	E	C	C	A	D
91	**92**	**93**	**94**	**95**	**96**	**97**	**98**	**99**	**100**
A	E	D	C	B	D	A	C	A	E

4

Spotting Errors

The most common errors in English are of spellings, grammar and usage of words. By regular practice, the errors can be easily spotted and minimised. Read the following sentences and learn to spot the errors. Test your learning in the exercise that follows.

Common Errors with Nouns and Noun-Phrases

	Incorrect	*Correct*
1.	I have bought new *furnitures.*	I have bought new *furniture.*
2.	The wages of sin *are* death.	The wages of sin *is* death.
3.	She told these *news* to her mother.	She told her mother this *news.*
4.	He took *troubles* to do his work.	He took *trouble* (or pains) over his work.
5.	The *cattles* were grazing.	The *cattle* were grazing.
6.	He showered *many abuses* on me.	He showered *much abuse* on me.
7.	I spent the holidays with my *family members.*	I spent the holidays with my *family.*
8.	There is no *place* in this compartment.	There is no *room* in this compartment.
9.	Write this new *poetry* in your *copy.*	Write this new *poem* in your *note-book.*
10.	He took *insult* at this.	He took *offence* at this.
11.	Put your *sign* here.	Put your *signatures* here.
12.	She is my *cousin sister.*	She is my *cousin.*
13.	*Sunil's* my *neighbour's* house was burgled.	*Sunil* my *neighbour's* house was burgled.
14.	I lost a *ten-rupees* note.	I lost *a ten-rupee* note.
15.	Road closed for *repair.*	Road closed for *repairs.*
16.	His house is out of *repairs.*	His house is out of *repair.*
17.	What is the *reason* of an earthquake?	What is the *cause* of an earthquake?
18.	This building is made of *stones.*	This building is made of *stone.*
19.	I disapprove of *these kinds* of games.	I disapprove of *this kind* of games.
20.	Veena's and Sheela's father is ill.	Veena and Sheela's father is ill.
21.	His *son-in-laws* are doctors.	His *sons-in-law* are doctors.
22.	*Alms* is given to the *poor.*	*Alms* are given to the poor.
23.	He always keeps his words.	He always keeps his *word.*
24.	I carried the *luggages.*	I carried the *luggage.*
25.	*Two-third* of the work is left.	*Two-thirds* of the work is left.

Common Errors with Pronouns

	Incorrect	Correct
1.	Both did not go.	Neither went.
2.	We all did not go.	None of us went.
3.	Each of these boys play.	Each of these boys plays.
4.	Whoever does best he will get a prize.	Whoever does best will get a prize.
5.	One should not waste his time.	A man should not waste his time.
6.	I and she are sisters.	She and I are sisters.
7.	He is wiser than me.	He is wiser than I.
8.	Between you and I, Anil is not to be trusted.	Between you and me, Anil is not to be trusted.
9.	Nobody was there but I.	Nobody was there but me.
10.	Who is there ? It is me.	Who is there ? It is I.
11.	Only he and me can use this card.	Only he and I can use this card.
12.	Let you and I go now.	Let you and me go now.
13.	Everyone got one's pay.	Everyone got his pay.
14.	Everyone is frightened when they see a tiger.	Everyone is frightened when he sees a tiger.
15.	These two friends are fond of one another.	These two friends are fond of each other.
16.	I did not like him coming at that hour.	I did not like his coming at that hour.
17.	Who do you think I met?	Whom do you think I met?
18.	You should avail this opportunity.	You should avail yourself this opportunity.
19.	When you have read these books, please return the same to me.	When you have read the books, please return them to me.
20.	They that are humble need fear no fall.	Those that are humble need fear no fall.

Common Errors with Adjectives

	Incorrect	Correct
1.	These all oranges are good.	All these oranges are good.
2.	He held the book in the both hands.	He held the book in both hands.
3.	Both men have not come.	Neither man has come.
4.	That man should do some or other work.	That man should do some work or other.
5.	He is elder than I.	He is older than I.
6.	Shakespeare is greater than any other poets.	Shakespeare is greater than any other poet.
7.	He is a coward man.	He is a cowardly man.
8.	Many villagers cannot write his own name.	Many villagers cannot write their own name.
9.	Each of us loves our home.	Each of us loves his home.
10.	Much efforts bring their reward.	Much effort brings its reward.
11.	He found hundred rupees.	He found a hundred rupees.
12.	He had leave of four days.	He had four days leave.

Incorrect	Correct
13. This is a worth seeing sight.	This is a sight worth seeing.
14. He will spend his future life here.	He will spend the rest of his life here.
15. There is a best teacher in that class.	There is a very good teacher in that class.
16. Of the two plans this is the best.	Of the two plans this is the better.
17. He is becoming strong every day.	He is becoming stronger every day.
18. He is worst than I.	He is worse than I.
19. Jaipur is hot than Delhi.	Jaipur is hotter than Delhi.
20. In our library the number of books is less.	In our library the number of books is small.

Common Errors with Verbs

Incorrect	Correct
1. He asked had we taken our luggage.	He asked if we had taken our luggage.
2. She asked what are you doing.	She asked what we were doing.
3. Rama asked to Anil why he is angry.	Rama asked Anil why he was angry.
4. He does not care for his money.	He does not take care of his money.
5. He does not care for his work.	He takes no care over his work.
6. No one cared for him after his mother died.	No one took care of him after his mother died.
7. He got angry before I said a word.	He got angry before I had said a word.
8. I met a man who was my tutor 20 years ago.	I met a man who had been my tutor twenty years ago.
9. I had been for walking yesterday.	I went for a walk yesterday.
10. If I shall do this I shall be wrong.	If I do this I shall be wrong.
11. I have left trekking.	I have given up trekking.
12. I came to know as to how he did this.	I learnt how he did this.
13. I came to know why he was sad.	I found out why he was sad.
14. He knows to swim.	He knows how to swim.
15. The criminal's head was cut.	The criminal's head was cut off.
16. I said to him to go.	I told him to go.
17. I told the teacher to excuse me.	I asked the teacher to excuse me.
18. He is troubling me.	He is giving me trouble.
19. I have got a hurt on my leg.	I have hurt my leg.
20. She gave a speech.	She made a speech.

Common Errors in Subject-Verb Agreement

Incorrect	Correct
1. The owners of this factory *is* very rich.	The owners of this factory *are* very rich.
2. The pleasures of nature that one can experience at Shimla *is* beyond description.	The pleasures of nature that one can experience at Shimla *are* beyond description.

Incorrect	Correct
3. There *is* no street lights in our colony.	There *are* no street lights in our colony.
4. He and I *am* entrusted with the job.	He and I *are* entrusted with the job.
5. Rice and curry *are* his favourite dish.	Rice and curry *is* his favourite dish.
6. The honour and glory of our country *are* at stake.	The honour and glory of our country *is* at stake.
7. Time and tide *waits* for none.	Time and tide *wait* for none.
8. All the passengers with the driver *was* killed.	All the passengers, with the driver, *were* killed.
9. The teacher, with her students, *were* going out.	The teacher, with her students, *was* going out.
10. I as well as they *am* tired.	I as well as they *are* tired.
11. Not only the soldiers but their captain also *were* captured.	Not only the soldiers but their captain also *was* captured.
12. Neither you nor I *were* selected.	Neither you nor I *was* selected.
13. Either of these two applicants *are* fit for the job but neither want to accept it.	Either of these two applicants *is* fit for the job but neither wants to accept it.
14. One of these students are sure to stand first.	One of these students *is* sure to stand first.
15. Everyone of these workers want a raise.	Everyone of these workers wants a raise.
16. None of these letters has been answered so far.	None of these letters *have* been answered so far.
17. None of the girls were present at the party.	None of the girls *was* present at the party.
18. Many a battle were fought on Indian soil.	Many a battle *was* fought on Indian soil.
19. A lot of work remain to be done.	A lot of work *remains* to be done.
20. The majority of these girls likes music.	The majority of these girls *like* music.

Common Errors in the Use of Modals/Auxiliary Verbs

Incorrect	Correct
1. When I shall see him I shall tell him this.	When I *see* him, I shall tell him this.
2. If I should do wrong, he would punish me.	If I *did* wrong, he would punish me.
3. Until he will have confessed his fault, he will be kept in prison.	Until he *has* confessed his fault, he will be kept in prison.
4. She will obey me.	She *shall* obey me.
5. You would work hard.	You *should* work hard.
6. You shall find him in the garden.	You *will* find him in the garden.
7. He must have died of exposure, but we cannot be certain.	He *might* have died of exposure, but we cannot be certain.
8. You might not show disrespect to your elders.	You *must* not show disrespect to your elders.
9. You may take exercise in order to maintain good health.	You *must* take exercise in order to maintain good health.
10. He must be a crook for all we know.	He *may* be a crook for all we know.

Common Errors in the Use of Adverbs

	Incorrect	*Correct*
1.	He is very much angry.	He is *very* angry.
2.	She was very good enough to help me.	She was *good enough* to help me.
3.	She runs much fast.	She runs *very* fast.
4.	She runs very faster than Seema.	She runs *much* faster than Seema.
5.	It is bitter cold today.	It is *bitterly* cold today.
6.	He is a much learned man.	He is a very learned man.
7.	She is thinking very hardly.	She is thinking very hard.
8.	To tell in brief the film was boring.	*In short* the film was boring.
9.	He told the story in details.	He told the story *in detail.*
10.	I did it anyhow.	I *managed to do* it somehow.
11.	Aeroplanes reach Europe soon.	Aeroplanes reach Europe quickly.
12.	Before long there were dinosaurs on the earth.	*Long ago,* there were dinosaurs on the earth.
13.	This book is too interesting.	This book is *very* interesting.
14.	He lives miserly.	He lives in *a miserly* way.
15.	Just I had gone when she came.	I had just gone when she came.
16.	He sings good.	He sings *well.*
17.	He sings good than I.	He sings *better* than I.
18.	Really speaking it is cold.	*As a matter of fact* it is cold.
19.	He is enough tall to reach the ceiling.	He is *tall enough* to reach the ceiling.
20.	He went directly to his college.	He went *direct* to his college.

Common Errors in the Use of Conjunctions

	Incorrect	*Correct*
1.	As he is fat so he runs slowly.	As he is fat *he* runs slowly.
2.	If he is fat then he will run slowly.	If he is fat, he will run slowly.
3.	Though he is fat still he runs fast.	Though he is fat, *he runs* fast.
4.	*As* I pulled the trigger at the sametime he shook my arm.	As I pulled the trigger, he shook my arm.
5.	No sooner I had spoken than he left.	No sooner *had* I spoken than he left.
6.	Not only he will go, but also he will stay there.	Not only *will he* go, but he *will also* stay there.
7.	Neither he comes nor he writes.	Neither *does he* come nor *does he* write.
8.	Scarcely he entered the room than the telephone rang.	Scarcely *had* he entered the room *when the* telephone rang.
9.	Hardly she had left the house than it began to rain.	Hardly *had she* left the house *when* it began to rain.
10.	He is the fastest runner and he comes last.	He is the fastest runner *but* he comes last.
11.	She is as innocent as if she looks.	She is as innocent as she looks.
12.	Until he does not try he must be punished.	He must be punished unless he tries.
13.	I want to know as to why you are late.	I want to know why you are late.

Incorrect	Correct
14. I am fond of Chinese food as for example sweet and sour prawns.	I am fond of Chinese food, for example, sweet and sour prawns.
15. He was angry therefore I ran away.	He was angry so I ran away.
16. I was trying to work, at that time he was disturbing me.	While I was trying to work, he was disturbing me.
17. Supposing if he is late, what will happen?	Supposing he is late (or if he is late) what will happen?
18. He asked me that why I was late.	He asked me why I was late.
19. Let us catch a taxi lest we should not get late.	Let us catch a taxi lest we should get late.
20. She dresses herself like the teacher does.	She dresses herself as the teacher does.
21. Wait while I come.	Wait *until* (or *till)* I come.
22. Until, there is corruption in India, there can be little progress.	*As long* as there is corruption in India there can be little progress.
23. I have never told a lie nor cheated anybody.	I have never told a lie *nor have I* cheated anybody.
24. Both Mohan as well as Arun are responsible for this action.	Both Mohan *and* Arun are responsible for this action.
25. Hindus and Muslims both are to blame for the riots.	*Both Hindus* and Muslims are to blame for the riots.

Common Errors in the Use of Prepositions

Incorrect	Correct
1. I will not listen him.	I will not listen *to* him.
2. Copy this word by word.	Copy this word *for* word.
3. He enquired from her where she lived.	He enquired *of* her where she lived.
4. Sign here with ink.	Sign here *in* ink.
5. Has she come in train or by foot?	Has she come *by* train or *on* foot?
6. She said this at his face.	She said this *to* his face.
7. Open the book on page one.	Open the book *at* page one.
8. I was invited for lunch.	I was *invited to* lunch.
9. I am ill since three months.	I have been *ill for* three months.
10. This paper is inferior than that.	This paper is inferior *to* that.
11. This resembles to that.	This *resembles* that.
12. My brother is superior than you in strength.	My brother is superior *to* you in strength.
13. He wrote me.	He wrote *to* me.
14. I shall explain them this.	I shall explain this *to* them.
15. Send this letter on my address.	Send this letter *to* my address.
16. He suggested me this.	He suggested this *to* me.
17. He goes *on his* work.	He goes *to his* work.
18. He *reached to* Nagpur.	He *reached* Nagpur.
19. He told *to me* to go.	He told *me* to go.
20. The term begins *from* July 1st.	The term begins *on* July 1st.

Miscellaneous Errors

Incorrect	Correct
1. Many *homes* are lying vacant.	Many *houses* are lying vacant.
2. It is cool in the *shadow* of the tree.	It is cool in the *shade* of the tree.
3. She *keeps* good health.	She *enjoys* good health.
4. My leg is *paining.*	*I am feeling pain* in my leg.
5. *See* this word in the dictionary.	*Look up* this word in the dictionary.
6. The train will arrive *just now.*	The train will arrive *shortly.*
7. They are *pulling* on well.	They are *getting* on well.
8. The river has *over flown* its bank.	The river has *over flown* its banks.
9. He was appointed *on* the post.	He was appointed *to* the post.
10. Last but not *the least,* we have to discuss the problem of over population.	Last but not *least,* we have to discuss the problem of over population.
11. *Cities* after *cities* fell.	*City* after *city* fell.
12. What is the use Munir going there?	What is the use of Munir going there?
13. He *did many mischief.*	He *made much mischief.*
14. It is exact five *in* my watch.	It is exact five *by* my watch.
15. I will dine with them on *next Sunday.*	I will dine with them *Sunday next.*
16. Misfortunes when faced bravely and *manly* become less troublesome.	Misfortunes when faced bravely and *manfully* become less troublesome.
17. I am *laid down* with fever.	I am *laid up* with fever.
18. He is habituated to smoking.	He is *addicted* to smoking.
19. *According to my opinion* he is right.	*In my opinion* (or according *to me)* he is right.
20. Could you please *open* this knot?	Could you please *untie* this knot?

Multiple Choice Questions

Directions: *In each question below, a sentence is broken into four parts which are marked as (A), (B), (C) and (D). One of them may be grammatically or structurally wrong in the context of the sentence. The letter of that word is the answer. If there is no error, your answer will be (E), i.e., 'No error'. (Ignore the errors of punctuation, if any).*

1. (A) There is just not enough/(B) timing in my job to sit around/(C) talking about how we feel/(D) about each other./(E) No error.

2. (A) Reasonable ambition, if supported/(B) at persistent efforts,/(C) is likely to yield/(D) the desired results./(E) No error.

3. (A) Even after worked in the office/(B) for as many as fifteen years,/(C) he still does not understand/(D) the basic objectives of the work./(E) No error.

4. (A) Why some people don't get/(B) what they deserve/(C) and why others get what they don't deserve/(D) is a matter decided by luck./(E) No error.

5. (A) the five-member committee were/(B) of the view that the present service conditions/(C) of the employees of this company/(D) are quite good./(E) No error.

6. (A) If you would have/(B) gone to his house/(C) before 10 a.m., you would have/(D) got his autograph./(E) No error.

7. (A) His speech was/(B) judged by many/(C) as one of the most important speech/(D) given in the function./(E) No error.

8. (A) I am contacting you/(B) sometime in next week/(C) to explain to you/(D) my problem in detail./(E) No error.

9. (A) Whatever he was/(B) today is only because/ (C) of his mother who/(D) was a renowned scientist./(E) No error.

10. (A) The Head of the Department along with his colleagues/(B) are coming to attend/(C) the conference which is/(D) scheduled this afternoon./(E) No error.

11. (A) One of the most effective/(B) solutions is that/(C) she should work on Sunday/(D) and complete the assignment./(E) No error.

12. (A) He had to/(B) seek legal help in/(C) order for settling/(D) the dispute./(E) No error.

13. (A) Since I had been gone/(B) through the book/(C) long back, I could/(D) not remember the contents./(E) No error.

14. (A) We have to take/(B)him to the hospital yesterday/(C) because he was/(D) suffering from fever./(E) No error.

15. (A) The interviewer asked the actress/(B) how could she/(C) manage to attain fame/(D) in a short period./(E) No error.

16. (A) The Head of the Department/(B) advised all the staff/(C) to not to/(D) indulge in gossip./ (E) No error.

17. (A) I shall be able/(B) to complete the work in/ (C) stipulated time provide/(D) you do not disturb me./(E) No error.

18. (A) Having learn my lessons/(B) I was very careful/(C) in dealing with him/(D) in front of his room-mate./(E) No error.

19. (A) In spite of his/(B) being a Quiz Master/(C) show was/(D) a big flop./(E) No error.

20. (A) No sooner the/(B) clock strike six than/(C) all the employees/(D) rushed out of office./(E) No error.

21. (A) He could not/(B) decide as to which/(C) course he should do/(D) after obtaining his Degree./(E) No error.

22. (A) One of the objective/(B) of the meeting which/(C) was held today was to/(D) elect new office-bearers./(E) No error.

23. (A) She would have/(B) surely got the job/(C) if she would have/(D) attended the interview./ (E) No error.

24. (A) When the national/(B) anthem was being/ (C) sung, everyone were/(D) standing in silence./(E) No error.

25. (A) She herself wash/(B) all the clothes and/(C) never gives them/(D) to the laundry./(E) No error.

26. (A) But for your/(B) kind help this/(C) task could not/(D) have been completed./(E) No error.

27. (A) Since it was a memory test/(B) the students were instructed/(C) to learn the/(D) passage with heart./(E) No error.

28. (A) So longer as/(B) you are honest/(C) and forthright I will/(D) support you in this task./ (E) No error.

29. (A) The customer scarcely had/(B) enough money to pay/(C) to the cashier/(D) at the cash counter./(E) No error.

30. (A) Neither the earthquake/(B) nor the subsequent fire/(C) was able to dampen/(D) the spirit of the residents./(E) No error.

31. (A) Not one of the children/(B) has ever sang/ (C) on any occasion/(D) in public before./(E) No error.

32. (A) If the by-stander had not been/(B) familiar with first-aid techniques,/(C) the driver which had met/(D) with the accident would have died./(E) No error.

33. (A) Even after requesting/(B) him, he did not/ (C) tell us that how/(D) he solved the problem/ (E) No error.

34. (A) We never thought/(B) that he is/(C) oldest than the other/(D) players in the team./(E) No error.

35. (A) No sooner did he/(B) got up from bed/(C) than he was sent/(D) to the dairy./(E) No error.

36. (A) By arresting the local criminals/(B) and encouraging good people/(C) we can end/(D) hostilities of that area./(E) No error.

37. (A) The apparently obvious solutions/(B) to most of his problems/(C) were overlook by/(D) many of his friends./(E) No error.

38. (A) In spite of the difficulties/(B) on the way,/ (C) they enjoyed their/(D) trip to Gangotri./(E) No error.

39. (A) We decided not tell to/(B) the patient about/ (C) the disease he was/(D) suffering from./(E) No error.

40. (A) The principals of equal justice/(B) for all is one of/(C) the cornerstones of our/(D) democratic way of life./(E) No error.

41. (A) The Trust has succeeded/(B) admirably in raising/(C) money for/(D) its future programmes./(E) No error.

42. (A) Honesty, integrity and being intelligent/ (B) are the qualities which/(C) we look for when/(D) we interview applicants./(E) No error.

43. (A) In order to save petrol,/(B) motorists must have to/(C) be very cautious/(D) while driving along the highways./(E) No error.

44. (A) The committee is thankful to you/(B) for preparing not only the main report/(C) but also for preparing/(D) the agenda notes and minutes./(E) No error.

45. (A) All of you will agree with me/(B) that no problem faced by our society/(C) is as grave and intractable/(D) as this problem is/(E) No error.

46. (A) I would have lost/(B) my luggage and other belongings/(C) if I would have left the compartment/(D) and gone out to fetch drinking water./(E) No error.

47. (A) He did not like/(B) leaving his old parents alone in the house/(C) but he had no alternative/(D) as he has to go out to work./(E) No error.

48. (A) I was being astonished/(B) when I heard that/(C) he had left the country/(D) without informing anyone of us./(E) No error.

49. (A) According to one survey/(B) only those forests which were/(C) not under village management/(D) succumbed from fires recently./(E) No error.

50. (A) We can not handle/(B) this complicated case today/(C) unless full details are not given/ (D) to us by now./(E) No error.

51. (A) We will pack not only/(B) the material properly/(C) but will also deliver it/(D) to your valued customers./(E) No error.

52. (A) While he was away/(B) on a long official tour/(C) his office receive an important letter/ (D) which was marked 'Urgent'./(E) No error.

53. (A) We now look forward for/(B) some great achievements/(C) which to some extent/(D) can restore the country's prestige once again./(E) No error.

54. (A) Mahatma Gandhi did not solve/(B) all the problems of the future/(C) but he did solve/(D) problems of his own age./(E) No error.

55. (A) No country can long endure/(B) if its foundations/(C) were not laid deep/(D) in the material prosperity./(E) No error.

56. (A) Though he suffered of fever,/(B) he attended office/(C) and completed all the pending/(D) work by sitting late./(E) No error.

57. (A) As always have been said,/(B) parents should not/(C) impose their desires/(D) on their wards./(E) No error.

58. (A) Being a very fast worker,/(B) he is always liking/(C) by all his colleagues./(D) and superiors too./(E) No error.

59. (A) We fail to understand/(B) why do most educated people/(C) lose their temper even/(D) without any apparent reason./(E) No error.

60. (A) You may not always/(B) get whatever you deserve/(C) but that does not belittle/(D) the importance for your work./(E) No error.

61. (A) On resuming his duty,/(B) he asked his superiors/(C) that whether he would be/(D) permitted to leave early./(E) No error.

62. (A) We don't deny/(B) your right to know/(C) whatever happened while/(D) you were not in the office./(E) No error.

63. (A) He loved his mentor immensely/(B) and gave him fullest loyalty,/(C) yet he had his own/(D) independent way of thinking./(E) No error.

64. (A) We have done everything/(B) that could be done/(C) to avert the storm/(D) which is now coming on./(E) No error.

65. (A) Our school is making/(B) every possible effort/(C) to provide best facilities/(D) and personal attention for each child./(E) No error.

66. (A) They have been/(B) struggling with the management/(C) from the past five years/(D) but their demands are not considered./(E) No error.

67. (A) When I stood up spontaneously/(B) and questioned the speaker;/(C) someone commented that/(D) it was a boldly step./(E) No error.

68. (A) Their only demand/(B) for additional wages were/(C) considered sympathetically/(D) by the progressive management./(E) No error.

69. (A) He has been undergoing/(B) the special training course/(C) which each of the employees/(D) is required to./(E) No error.

70. (A) You must had/(B) a kind and gentle heart/(C) if you want/(D) to be a successful doctor./(E) No error.

71. (A) If you cannot/(B) sympathy with the poor,/(C) how will you be/(D) able to do social work?/(E) No error.

72. (A) He loosened his temper/(B) whenever he knows/(C) things do not take place/(D) as per his planning./(E) No error.

73. (A) They wanted money/(B) to purchase certain things/(C) for themselves and/(D) for donated to their colleagues./(E) No error.

74. (A) As the ticket was/(B) firm affixed/(C) on the envelope, he/(D) could not remove it./(E) No error.

75. (A) I asked him/(B) whom he thought/(C) would be able to/(D) get the first prize./(E) No error.

76. (A) He was too/(B) irritated to/(C) concentrate on his work/(D) for a long time./(E) No error.

77. (A) Both the brothers are/(B) so good-natured that/(C) they look at their/(D) old and aged parents very well./(E) No error.

78. (A) The observers felt that/(B) the stronger team had to face/(C) defeat because the players/(D) didn't play wholehearted./(E) No error.

79. (A) Every animal in the zoo/(B) is fed regularly/(C) and attended to/(D) very promptly./(E) No error.

80. (A) How you eat/(B) is as important/(C) as what/(D) you eat./(E) No error.

81. (A) All his relatives/(B) expect his daughter/(C) have gone on/(D) a month's vacation tour./(E) No error.

82. (A) All renew licences/(B) may be collected from/(C) the cashier's counter after/(D) paying the fees./(E) No error.

83. (A) We are happy/(B) to know that/(C) the project completed/(D) strictly as per the schedule./(E) No error.

84. (A) They would not/(B) have able to plan/(C) the details of the job,/(D) if you had no cooperated./(E) No error.

85. (A) Very few employees./(B) in our company are/(C) so dedicated as/(D) he will./(E) No error.

86. (A) He won the case as/(B) he argued very forcefully and/(C) in such the intelligent way/(D) that the judge changed his opinion./(E) No error.

87. (A) The basket of apples/(B) sent by the gardener/(C) contained a number of/(D) green mangoes also./(E) No error.

88. (A) In the absence of/(B) clear instructions/(C) one cannot be expected/(D) to be functioned effectively./(E) No error.

89. (A) They could have/(B) helped him/(C) had they approached by him./(D) for help well in advance./(E) No error.

90. (A) He has in/(B) his possession a/(C) price collection of very old coins,/(D) and some ancient paintings./(E) No error.

91. (A) Everyone is/(B) impress by/(C) his zeal/(D) and enthusiasm./(E) No error.

92. (A) The patient recover/(B) so fast that/(C) the expert doctors/(D) also were surprised/(E) No error.

93. (A) His father told me/(B) that though his son had/(C) worked very hard,/(D) but he had failed to make any mark in the examination./(E) No error.

94. (A) We must go/(B) and congratulate him for/(C) his brilliant/(D) performance./(E) No error.

95. (A) He deserted the path of honour/(B) in order to/(C) satisfy his ambition/(D) and then went down his doom very quickly./(E) No error.

96. (A) At last the rain ceased/(B) and the sky was/(C) cleared by clouds/(D) and lightening./(E) No error.

97. (A) He said that/(B) he had a difference/(C) with/(D) the chairman at his statement./(E) No error.

98. (A) The future is/(B) yet to come/(C) but you have a/(D) right to shape it./(E) No error.

99. (A) We have keep/(B) our promise and/(C) you can expect/(D) a lot from us in future./(E) No error.

100. (A) He has collected/(B) all the necessary documents/(C) and have written a good paper/(D) for this conference./(E) No error.

ANSWERS

1	2	3	4	5	6	7	8	9	10
B	B	A	A	A	A	C	B	A	B
11	**12**	**13**	**14**	**15**	**16**	**17**	**18**	**19**	**20**
E	C	A	A	B	C	C	A	C	A
21	**22**	**23**	**24**	**25**	**26**	**27**	**28**	**29**	**30**
E	A	C	C	A	E	D	A	A	C
31	**32**	**33**	**34**	**35**	**36**	**37**	**38**	**39**	**40**
B	C	C	C	B	C	C	E	A	A
41	**42**	**43**	**44**	**45**	**46**	**47**	**48**	**49**	**50**
E	A	B	C	B	C	D	A	D	C
51	**52**	**53**	**54**	**55**	**56**	**57**	**58**	**59**	**60**
A	C	A	B	C	A	A	B	B	D
61	**62**	**63**	**64**	**65**	**66**	**67**	**68**	**69**	**70**
C	E	D	A	D	C	D	B	D	A
71	**72**	**73**	**74**	**75**	**76**	**77**	**78**	**79**	**80**
B	A	D	B	B	E	C	D	C	E
81	**82**	**83**	**84**	**85**	**86**	**87**	**88**	**89**	**90**
C	A	C	B	D	C	E	D	C	C
91	**92**	**93**	**94**	**95**	**96**	**97**	**98**	**99**	**100**
B	A	D	B	D	C	D	A	A	C

5

Sentence Correction

A sentence will convey its true meaning and make the right impact if it is written in a grammatically correct way. One must learn the general rules of grammar and practise well to improve one's English regularly. Try your skills in this exercise.

Multiple Choice Questions

Directions: *Which of the phrases given below each sentence should replace the phrase printed in* **bold** *type to make the sentence grammatically correct? If the sentence is correct as it is, mark 'E' as the answer.*

1. The research study is an eye-opener and **attempts to acquaint** us with the problems of the poor nations.
   A. attempted to acquaint
   B. attempts at acquainting
   C. attempt to acquaint
   D. attempting to acquaint
   E. No correction required
2. The man who has committed such a serious crime must **get the mostly severe** punishment.
   A. be getting the mostly severely
   B. get the most severe
   C. have got the most severely
   D. have been getting the severemost
   E. No correction required
3. Acquisition of certain specific skills **can be facilitated from** general awareness, education and exposure to novel situations.
   A. can be facilitated by
   B. may facilitate through
   C. can be felicitated with
   D. may be felicitated with
   E. No correction required
4. He confidently asked the crowd if they thought he was right and the crowd shouted **that they did.**
   A. that he did
   B. that they had
   C. that he is
   D. that he didn't
   E. No correction required
5. If he has to spend five hours in the queue, it **was really a wastage.**
   A. is a really wastage
   B. is real a wastage
   C. has really a wastage
   D. is really a wastage
   E. No correction required
6. Why **did you not threw** the bag away?
   A. did you not throw
   B. had you not threw
   C. did you not thrown
   D. you did not thrown
   E. No correction required
7. They **are not beware of** all the facts
   A. are not aware for
   B. are not aware of
   C. are not to be aware
   D. must not to be aware for
   E. No correction required

8. **If I would have** realised the nature of the job earlier, I would not have accepted it.
A. If I have had
B. In case I would have
C. Had I been
D. Had I
E. No correction required

9. The moment they saw me, they **were delight**
A. had delighted
B. were delighted
C. are delighted
D. have been delighted
E. No correction required

10. The small child does whatever his father **was done.**
A. has done B. did
C. does D. had done
E. No correction required

11. It was unanimously resolved that the parties **should unitedly undertook** launching of popular programmes.
A. should be united undertook
B. should be unitedly undertaken
C. should be unitedly undertake
D. should unitedly undertake
E. No correction required

12. One of my drawbacks is that **I do not have to** tolerance of ambiguity.
A. do not have B. cannot have to
C. am not D. did not have to
E. No correction required

13. They **should have calmly thought of** the advantages that would accrue to them.
A. should have been calm in thinking about
B. should be calmly thought of
C. shall have to calmly thought of
D. should have calmly think of
E. No correction required

14. Their earnings are such that they find it difficult **to make both ends to meet**.
A. to making both ends meet
B. to make both ends for meeting
C. to make both ends meet
D. for making both ends to meet
E. No correction required

15. They **were all shocked at** his failure in the competition.
A. were shocked at all
B. had all shocked at
C. had all shocked by
D. had been all shocked on
E. No correction required

16. He is too impatient **for tolerating** any delay.
A. to tolerate B. to tolerating
C. at tolerating D. with tolerating
E. No correction required

17. Why **should the candidates be** afraid of English Language is not clear.
A. the candidates should be
B. do the candidates be
C. should be the candidates
D. are the candidates
E. No correction required

18. Rohan is **as tall if not,** taller than Arpan.
A. not as tall but B. not so tall but as
C. as tall as, if not D. as if not
E. No correction required

19. The easiest **of the thing to do** is to ask the address to the shopkeeper.
A. of the things to do
B. among the things did
C. of the thing to be done
D. of all the things done
E. No correction required

20. The player was asked **that why he had not** attended the prayer.
A. why had he not
B. that why had he not
C. why he was not
D. is hesitated to listen to
E. No correction required

21. He **hesitated to listen to** what his brother was saying.
A. listened to hesitate
B. hesitated listen to
C. hesitates to listening
D. is hesitated to listen to
E. No correction required

22. Hardly **does the sun rise** when the stars disappeared.
A. have the sun rose B. had the sun risen
C. did the sun rose D. the sun rose
E. No correction required

23. The police has **so far succeeded in recovering** only a part of the stolen property.
A. thus far succeeded for recovery
B. so far succeed in the recovery of
C. as far as succeeded in recovery of
D. so far succeed to recover
E. No correction required

24. **What happens to** all those travellers on the ship was not known?
A. What happened of
B. That is what happens to
C. What is that happens to
D. What happened to
E. No correction required

25. Because of his ill health, the doctor has advised him **not to refrain** from smoking.
A. to not refrain from
B. to resort to
C. to refrain from
D. to be refrained from
E. No correction required

26. The courts **are actively to safeguard** the interests and the rights of the poor.
A. are actively to safeguarding
B. have been actively safeguarding
C. have to active in safeguarding
D. are actively in safeguarding
E. No correction required

27. He is a singer of repute, but his **yesterday's performance was** quite disappointing.
A. performances for yesterday were
B. yesterday performance was
C. yesterday performances were
D. performances about yesterday were
E. No correction required

28. **Despite of their** differences on matters of principles, they all agree on the demand of hike in salary.
A. Despite their B. Despite of the
C. Despite for their D. Despite off their
E. No correction required

29. The orator **had been left** the auditorium before the audience stood up.
A. had been leaving B. was left
C. left D. would leave
E. No correction required

30. This is one of the most important **inventions of this century**.
A. invention of this century
B. invention of these centuries
C. inventions of centuries
D. inventions of the centuries
E. No correction required

31. Can you tell me **why did you not speak** the truth?
A. why did not you speak
B. that why did you not speak
C. why you did not speak
D. why did you not spoke
E. No correction required

32. The chemist **hadn't hardly any of those kind** of medicines.
A. had hardly any of those kinds
B. had hardly not any of those kind
C. had scarcely any of those kind
D. had hardly any of those kind
E. No correction required

33. She cooks, washes dishes, does her homework and **then relaxing.**
A. relaxing then B. then is relaxing
C. relaxing is then D. then relaxes
E. No correction required

34. Anyone interested in the use of computers can learn much if **you have access** to a personal computer.
A. they have access
B. access can be available
C. he or she has access
D. one of them have access
E. No correction required

35. **By such time** you finish that chapter, I will write a letter.
A. The time when B. By the time
C. By that time D. The time
E. No correction required

36. **Had I realised** how close I was to the edge of the valley, I would not have carried the bags there.
A. Had I been realised
B. If I would have realised
C. When I realised
D. Had I had realised
E. No correction required

37. Later he became unpopular because he tried **to lord it on** his followers.
A. to lord it for B. to lord over
C. to lord it over D. to lord it over on
E. No correction required

38. **The long or short of it** is that I do not want to deal with that new firm.
A. The long and short of it
B. The long and short for it
C. The long or short for it
D. The short and long of it
E. No correction required

39. The people generally try to **curry favour** with the corrupt but influential person.
A. cook favour B. seek favour
C. extract favour D. display favour
E. No correction required

40. My hair **stood off ends** when I saw the horrible sight.
A. stood at ends B. stood on ends
C. stood to ends D. stands on ends
E. No correction required

41. "Friends and comrades, the light has gone **away from** our lives and there is darkness everywhere."
A. off B. out of
C. out from D. out off
E. No correction required

42. We **can not always convey** ourselves in simple sentences.
A. cannot always convey
B. can not always express
C. cannot always express
D. can not always communicate
E. No correction required

43. **Shapes** of gods and goddesses are worshipped by people.
A. Images B. Reflections
C. Clay shapes D. Clay toys
E. No correction required

44. The crops are dying; **it must not had** rained.
A. must had not
B. must not be
C. must not have
D. must not have been
E. No correction required

45. It is always better to make people realise the importance of discipline than to **impose them on it.**
A. impose it with them
B. impose them with it
C. imposing them on it
D. impose it on them
E. No correction required

46. The performance of our players was rather **worst than I had expected.**
A. bad as I had expected
B. worse than I had expected
C. worse than expectation
D. worst than was expected
E. No correction required

47. For some days the new professor lectured **above the heads of** his pupils.
A. over the head of
B. over the heads of
C. on the heads of
D. through the heads of
E. No correction required

48. For many centuries in Indian history there was no city so famous **like** the city of Ujjain.
A. as B. such as
C. likewise D. so like
E. No correction required

49. Making friends is more rewarding than **to make enemies**.
A. to be unsociable B. to be sociable
C. being unsociable D. making enemies
E. No correction required

50. You need not come unless you want to.
A. You don't need to come unless you want to
B. You come only when you want to
C. You come unless you don't want to
D. You needn't come until you don't want to
E. No correction required

51. The drama had many scenes which were so humorous that it was **hardly possible to keep** a straight face.
A. hardly possible for keeping
B. hardly impossible keeping
C. hardly impossible to keep
D. hardly possible keeping
E. No correction required

52. The moment the manager came to know of the fradulent action of his assistant, he **order immediately dismissed him**.
A. immediately ordered his dismissed
B. ordered his immediate dismissal
C. immediately order dismissal of his
D. ordered for immediately dismissal him
E. No correction required

53. We met him immediately after the session in which he **had been given** a nice speech.
A. would be giving
B. has been given
C. will have given
D. had given
E. No correction required

54. The world has seen **small** real attempt at population and resource planning.
A. few
B. little
C. less
D. a few
E. No correction required

55. One of the most significant **phenomenons** of our time has been the development of the cinema.
A. phenomenon
B. phenomena
C. character
D. symptom
E. No correction required

56. It was until many years later that Gandhi became a rebel against authority.
A. It was not until many years
B. It was till many years
C. It was not many years
D. Until it was many years
E. No correction required

57. There are not many men who are so famous that they are frequently referred to by their **short names** only.
A. initials
B. signatures
C. pictures
D. middle names
E. No correction required

58. Though we **have kept in mind to try and maintain** most facilities, we would like to request you to kindly bear with us any inconvenience that may be caused.
A. must keep in mind to try and maintain
B. have kept in mind trying and maintain
C. would keep in mind to try and maintain
D. should have kept in mind to try and to maintain
E. No correction required

59. The tea-estate administration is **in such mess there** is no leader to set the things right.
A. in such a mess here
B. in a such mess that here
C. in such a mess that there
D. with such a mess that there
E. No correction required

60. My doctor knew that I would eventually recover and do the kind of work **I would be doing** before.
A. would have been doing
B. would have done
C. had been done
D. had been doing
E. No correction required

61. If you are thinking about investigation overseas, **isn't it makes** sense to find an experience guide?
A. it is not making
B. doesn't it make
C. does it make
D. is it making
E. No correction required

62. The **crime has growth rapidly** in Russia since the disintegration of the communist system.
A. rapid crime has grown
B. crime has grown rapid
C. crimes grow rapidly
D. crimes have been rapidly grown
E. No correction required

63. Technology **must use to feed** the forces of change.
A. must be used to feed
B. must have been using to feed
C. must use having fed
D. must be using to feed
E. No correction required

64. In addition **to enhanced their reputations** through strategic use of philanthropy, companies are sponsoring social initiatives to open new markets.
A. of enhancing their reputations
B. to having enhance their reputation
C. to enhancing their reputation
D. to have their reputation enhancing
E. No correction required

65. They failed **in their attempt to repair** the demolished portion of the building.
A. for their attempt to repair
B. in their attempting to repair
C. with their attempt to repair
D. in their attempt for repairs
E. No correction required

66. We don't know **how did the thief made** an escape.
A. how the thief did make
B. how the thief does make
C. how the thief made
D. how was the thief made
E. No correction required

67. They have a scheme of rewarding **the best of the performers** every year.
A. a best performer
B. the best among the performer
C. a best among performers
D. the best of the performer
E. No correction required

68. No sooner **do the bells ring** than the curtain rose.
A. did the bell ring
B. did the bells ring
C. had the bell rang
D. had the bell rung
E. No correction required

69. Most of the Indian workers are **as healthy as, if not healthier** than, the British workers.
A. as if healthy as and not healthier
B. healthier but not as healthy
C. as healthy, if not healthier
D. so healthy, if not healthier
E. No correction required

70. He admired the speed with which he completed the work and **appreciating the method adopted** by him.
A. appreciate the method being adopted
B. appreciated the method adopted
C. appreciate the method of adoption
D. appreciated the adopting method
E. No correction required

71. The population of Tokyo is **greater than that of any other** town in the world.
A. greatest among any other
B. greater than all other
C. greater than those of any other
D. greater than any other
E. No correction required

72. They examined both the samples very carefully but failed to detect **any difference** in them.
A. some difference in
B. some difference between
C. any difference between
D. any difference among
E. No correction required

73. Tax evaders **should heavily fined** as they do it intentionally.
A. should be heavy fined
B. should have heavily fined
C. shall have heavy fine
D. should be heavily fined
E. No correction required

74. He never **has and ever will take** such strong measures.
A. had taken nor will ever take
B. had taken and will ever take
C. has and never will take
D. had and ever will take
E. No correction required

75. The intruder stood quietly **for few moments**.
A. for few time
B. for the few moments
C. for moments
D. for a few moments
E. No correction required

76. He **should not had** done it.
A. had not
B. should had not
C. should not have
D. should have
E. No correction required

77. The meeting was **attended to by all** the invitees.
A. all attended to by
B. attended by all
C. fully attended to by
D. like attending to all
E. No correction required

78. I have got some tea, but I do not have **a** sugar.
A. some
B. got
C. more
D. any
E. No correction required

79. I need not offer any explanation regarding this incident—my behaviour **is speaking itself**.
A. will speak to itself
B. speaks for itself
C. has been speaking
D. speaks about itself
E. No correction required

80. Ankur has the guts **to rise from** the occasion and come out successfully.
A. in rising from
B. to raise with
C. to rise against
D. to rise to
E. No correction required

81. Mary unnecessarily **picked up** a quarrel with Rosy and left the party hurriedly.
A. has picked up
B. picked on
C. picked
D. picking up
E. No correction required

82. The train will leave at 8.30 p.m., we **have been** ready by 7.30 p.m. so that we can reach the station in time.
A. were
B. must be
C. are
D. should have
E. No correction required

83. He dislikes the word dislike, **isn't he**?
A. didn't he
B. doesn't he
C. hasn't he
D. does he
E. No correction required

84. The prosecution failed **in** establish in every case today.
A. to
B. on
C. as
D. upon
E. No correction required

85. We were still standing in the queue when the **film was beginning**.
A. film began
B. film had begun
C. beginning of the film was over
D. film begins
E. No correction required

86. I **earnestly believe that** you will visit our relatives during your forthcoming trip to Mumbai.
A. had hardly believe that
B. sincerely would believe
C. certainly believing that
D. could not believe
E. No correction required

87. We must **take it granted** that she will not come for today's function.
A. take it for granted
B. taking it granted
C. took it as granted
D. have it granted
E. No correction required

88. He has received no other message than an urgent telegram **asking him to rush his village** immediately.
A. asked him to rush his village
B. asking him to have rush his village
C. asking him to rush to his village
D. asking him rushing at his village
E. No correction required

89. They continued to work in the field **despite of the heavy rains**.
A. even though there is heavy rain
B. although heavily rains
C. in spite the heavy rains
D. even though it rained heavily
E. No correction required

90. **Had you been told** me about your problem, I would have helped you.
A. If you would have told
B. Had you have told
C. had you told
D. If you have told
E. No correction required

91. They felt humiliated because they realised that they **had cheated**.
A. have been cheated
B. had been cheated
C. had been cheating
D. were to be cheated
E. No correction required

92. He found the gold coin **as he cleans** the floor.
A. as he had cleaned
B. while he cleans
C. which he is cleaning
D. while cleaning
E. No correction required

93. Because of his mastery in this field, his suggestions **are wide accepted**.
A. are widely accepted
B. are wide acceptance
C. have widely accepted
D. have been wide accepted
E. No correction required

94. The man to **who I sold** my house was a cheat.
A. to whom I sell
B. to who I sell
C. who was sold to
D. to whom I sold
E. No correction required

95. **If I was you,** I would not have joined the party.
A. If I am you
B. If I be you
C. As you
D. Were I you
E. No correction required

96. You will be late if you **do not leave** now.
A. did not leave
B. left
C. will not leave
D. do not happen to leave
E. No correction required

97. All the allegations **levelled against** him were found to be baseless.
A. level against
B. level with
C. levelling with
D. levelled for
E. No correction required

98. What **does agonise me most** is not this criticism, but the trivial reason behind it.
A. most agonising me
B. agonises me most
C. agonising me most
D. I most agonised
E. No correction required

99. The accused now flatly denies **have admitted** his guilt in his first statement.
A. having admitted
B. had admitted
C. have been admitting
D. has admitting
E. No correction required

100. We demonstrated to them how we **were prepared** the artistic patterns.
A. are prepared
B. have prepared
C. are preparing
D. had prepared
E. No correction required

ANSWERS

1	2	3	4	5	6	7	8	9	10
B	B	A	E	D	A	B	D	B	C
11	**12**	**13**	**14**	**15**	**16**	**17**	**18**	**19**	**20**
D	A	E	C	E	A	A	C	A	D
21	**22**	**23**	**24**	**25**	**26**	**27**	**28**	**29**	**30**
E	B	E	D	C	B	E	A	C	E
31	**32**	**33**	**34**	**35**	**36**	**37**	**38**	**39**	**40**
C	A	D	C	B	E	C	A	E	B
41	**42**	**43**	**44**	**45**	**46**	**47**	**48**	**49**	**50**
B	C	A	C	D	B	B	A	D	A
51	**52**	**53**	**54**	**55**	**56**	**57**	**58**	**59**	**60**
E	B	D	B	B	A	A	E	C	D
61	**62**	**63**	**64**	**65**	**66**	**67**	**68**	**69**	**70**
B	B	A	C	E	C	E	B	E	B
71	**72**	**73**	**74**	**75**	**76**	**77**	**78**	**79**	**80**
E	C	D	A	D	C	B	D	B	D
81	**82**	**83**	**84**	**85**	**86**	**87**	**88**	**89**	**90**
C	B	B	A	B	E	A	C	D	C
91	**92**	**93**	**94**	**95**	**96**	**97**	**98**	**99**	**100**
B	D	A	D	D	E	E	B	A	D

6

Cloze Test

A cloze test is a procedure in which you are asked to supply words which have been removed from a passage. It is meant to test your ability to comprehend text. Try and practise it to master it in this exercise.

Multiple Choice Questions

Directions: *In the following passages there are some blanks, each of which has been numbered. These numbers are also printed below the passages and against each five words are suggested, one of which fits the blank appropriately. Find out the appropriate word in each case.*

PASSAGE-1

Mobile banking (M banking) involves the use of a mobile phone or any other mobile device to **...(1)...** financial transactions linked to a client's account. M banking is new in most countries and most mobile payment models even in developed countries, to date operate on a **...(2)...** scale. A mobile network offers a **...(3)...** available technology platform onto which other services can be provided at low cost with effective results. For example, M banking services which use **...(4)...** such as SMS can be carried at a cost of less than one US cent per message. The low cost of using existing infrastructure makes such services more **...(5)...** to use by customers with lower purchasing power and opens up access to services which did not reach them earlier due to **...(6)...** cost of service delivery. Although M banking is one aspect in the wider **...(7)...** of e-banking there are reasons to single it out for focus-especially because there are a lot more people with mobile phones than bank accounts in India.

M banking could provide a **...(8)...** solution to bring more "unbanked" people to the financial mainstream. Without traditional credit, individuals are **...(9)...** to exploitation by abusive lenders offering very high interest rates on short term loans. Also of considerable importance are public safety implications for the unbanked—they are often victims of crime because many operate on a cash only basis and end up carrying significant amounts of cash on their **...(10)...** or store cash in their homes.

1. A. Disburse B. Undertake C. Subscribe D. Lure E. Amass

2. A. Full B. Voluminous C. Substantial D. Limited E. Rapid

3. A. Readily B. Tangible C. Routinely D. Securely E. Unique

4. A. Process B. Waves C. Deliveries D. Connection E. Channels

5. A. Valuable B. Answerable C. Amenable D. Exposed E. Responsible

6. A. Waning B. Stable
C. Proportionate D. Marginal
E. High

7. A. Archive B. Domain
C. Purpose D. Component
E. Aspect

8. A. Law abiding B. Tried
C. Reassuring D. Cost effective
E. Stopgap

9. A. Inclined B. Immune
C. Vulnerable D. Surrendered
E. Pressured

10. A. Person B. Own
C. Relatives D. Purses
E. Self

PASSAGE-2

The world economy is in recession—the deepest and the most widespread ...**(1)**... the 1930s. There are ...**(2)**... of ...**(3)**... in the industrial countries, but most serious economic ...**(4)**... anticipate that rates of growth and levels of economic activity will remain low.

In all that has been written about world ...**(5)**..., the ...**(6)**... have been overwhelmingly and narrowly economic. Few have ...**(7)**... the human consequences in more than a superficial manner. Not a single international study has ...**(8)**... the recession's ...**(9)**... on the most vulnerable half of the world's population—the children.

The need for ...**(10)**... clearly the ...**(11)**... between world economic conditions and child welfare has thus become even more urgent in the last few years. The worldscale of current child distress also makes it artificial to restrict the analysis of causes to the ...**(12)**... level.

1. A. in B. for
C. by D. before
E. since

2. A. risks B. glimmers
C. studies D. tips
E. histories

3. A. development B. downfall
C. recovery D. slackness
E. impact

4. A. analysts B. journalists
C. surveys D. findings
E. students

5. A. development B. economy
C. wars D. recession
E. conflicts

6. A. emphasis B. aims
C. glimpses D. suppositions
E. preoccupations

7. A. delved B. taught
C. propagated D. investigated
E. manifested

8. A. understood B. analysed
C. highlighted D. prepared
E. planned

9. A. analysis B. undercurrents
C. impact D. overtures
E. study

10. A. chalking out B. curbing
C. bringing out D. implementing
E. propagating

11. A. linkages B. fallouts
C. dependence D. contrasts
E. similarities

12. A. international B. political
C. low D. national
E. highest

PASSAGE-3

Nowadays, under the ...**(1)**... system of education, however good it may be, when a young man comes out of the University, there seems to be this ...**(2)**... in him that the higher the standard of living rises, the less should a man work. Thus, mathematically higher the standard of living, according to this misconceived notion, the less the ...**(3)**.... Ultimately, what should be the highest standard of living then? ...**(4)**... work! This leads to an unhealthy ...**(5)**... among the workers. A typist who types over twenty letters a day asks his ...**(6)**... how many letters he had typed that day. The latter ...**(7)**... "fifteen". The former thinks, "Tomorrow I should type only fifteen or even ...**(8)**.... This tendency is quite ...**(9)**..., and may ultimately lead to ...**(10)**... . Even one's family life may be affected adversely due to such tendency.

1. A. developed B. extinct
C. outdated D. proposed
E. modern

2. A. anxiety B. misconception
C. realisation D. worry
E. apprehension

3. A. salary B. comfort
C. work D. energy
E. time

4. A. Minimum B. Maximum
C. Less D. No
E. Ample

5. A. competition B. dispute
C. delay D. jealousy
E. ambition

6. A. employee B. subordinate
C. boss D. client
E. colleague

7. A. suggests B. remembers
C. replies D. types
E. all

8. A. less B. all
C. more D. few
E. some

9. A. discouraging B. heartening
C. healthy D. unfortunate
E. unnatural

10. A. evil B. retardation
C. progress D. denial
E. complexity

PASSAGE-4

Four cases of burglary have been ...**(1)**... with the arrest of one ...**(2)**... criminal. The police have ...**(3)**... gold and silver jewellery from him. The police increased their public contacts with the residents of the area after following a spate of burglaries. They held corner meetings to ...**(4)**... the residents on steps to ...**(5)**... prevention. They were ...**(6)**... to inform their neighbours if they had to ...**(7)**... their houses unattended. Consequently, some ...**(8)**... of the locality observed one ...**(9)**... leaving an empty house. He was ...**(10)**... and a case was registered.

1. A. connected B. adjusted
C. solved D. deferred
E. dealt

2. A. notorious B. more
C. thief D. imprisoned
E. extremely

3. A. withdrawn B. amassed
C. sold D. recovered
E. stolen

4. A. harass B. arrest
C. probe D. threaten
E. educate

5. A. loss B. crime
C. its D. burglar
E. their

6. A. required B. forbidden
C. instructed D. entrusted
E. forced

7. A. paint B. sell
C. protect D. leave
E. build

8. A. criminals B. neighbours
C. burglars D. pedestrians
E. residents

9. A. stranger B. resident
C. neighbour D. entrant
E. alien

10. A. misled B. apprehended
C. neglected D. boycotted
E. informed

PASSAGE-5

...**(1)**... change is the ...**(2)**... of the day, a proper orientation to ...**(3)**... with the change becomes a natural necessity ...**(4)**... assured organisational stability. In this ...**(5)**... of organisational change and survival, the author brings in the concept of 'praxis', ...**(6)**... it as the dynamo of change and uses it for ...**(7)**... a conceptual and methodological ...**(8)**... for the identification of training needs. Training, ...**(9)**... perceived as only one of the many elements in the organisational reflection process, is believed to stand ...**(10)**... as the means for relevant learning.

1. A. Few B. Many
C. No D. If
E. Why

2. A. order B. scope
C. large D. direction
E. result

3. A. assist B. renew
C. become D. try
E. cope

4. A. in B. for
C. from D. which
E. but

5. A. end B. decision
C. context D. scope
E. focus

6. A. describes B. throws
C. rejects D. leaves
E. derives

7. A. neglecting B. developing
C. calculating D. experiencing
E. diluting

8. A. routine B. idea
C. book D. follow up
E. framework

9. A. be B. may
C. though D. gets
E. as

10. A. in B. against
C. through D. out
E. with

PASSAGE-6

Each year, middle class Indian children ...**(1)**... hundreds of crores of rupees in pocket money and ...**(2)**... a heavy burden on parental ...**(3)**... . Like adults, these kids have ...**(4)**... connected with budgeting and saving money. Unfortunately, basic money ...**(5)**... is ...**(6)**... taught in schools. At home, very few parents ...**(7)**... money matters with their children. Kids who ...**(8)**... about money ...**(9)**... have been found to be way ahead of their peers. Indeed, learning to ...**(10)**... with money properly fosters discipline, good work habits and self-respect.

1. A. spend B. steal
C. save D. give
E. invest

2. A. move B. take
C. risk D. put
E. lift

3. A. promises B. payments
C. demands D. attitudes
E. incomes

4. A. expenses B. experience
C. problems D. guidance
E. necessities

5. A. availability B. inflation
C. economics D. problem
E. management

6. A. carefully B. rarely
C. generally D. always
E. thoroughly

7. A. discuss B. understand
C. teach D. reveal
E. advise

8. A. quarrel B. ask
C. learn D. waste
E. spend

9. A. slowly B. early
C. timely D. lately
E. regularly

10. A. decide B. earn
C. control D. deal
E. pay

PASSAGE-7

Architecture is a unique ...**(1)**... of art and science that has ...**(2)**... out of man's primary need for shelter. It is concerned with the design and ...**(3)**... of buildings in their sociological, technological and environmental context. This field is not only ...**(4)**...but also provide the ...**(5)**... of designing and building pleasing and ...**(6)**... refined structures to serve various needs. ...**(7)**... the fairly large number of practising architects, the countrywide ...**(8)**... in building activity offers scope for more. And though the initial earnings in the field are relatively ...**(9)**... what you make thereafter will depend entirely on your ...**(10)**... .

1. A. procedure B. process
C. portion D. blend
E. subject

2. A. drifted B. fizzled
C. contrived D. earned
E. arisen

3. A. painting B. construction
C. decoration D. repairing
E. appearance

4. A. fatiguing B. strenuous
C. encouraging D. vast
E. rewarding

5. A. satisfaction B. facility
C. infrastructure D. amenities
E. decorum

6. A. practically B. ideologically
C. aesthetically D. principally
E. readily

7. A. Considering B. Having
C. Assuming D. Regarding
E. Despite

8. A. variation B. slack
C. lethargy D. spurt
E. deterioration

9. A. escalating B. modest
C. unpredictable D. negligible
E. exorbitant

10. A. ambition B. appearance
C. expectation D. experience
E. need

PASSAGE-8

Without science there is no future for any society. Even with science, ...(**1**)... it is controlled by some spiritual impulses, there is also no future. One great thing about science is that it does not accept anything on mere ...(**2**)... . Everything has to be ...(**3**)... beyond any doubt. All acceptance comes after experiement which has no room for any ...(**4**)... . This is the reason ...(**5**)... development of science and technology has revolutionised human life all over the world. There are very few spheres of human activity which have not experienced the ...(**6**)... of such development. However, despite its manifold ...(**7**)... science has not been ...(**8**)... to solve any of man's moral or spiritual problems. Society is still ...(**9**)... in the dark to find out what its future will be. The need, therefore, is to make science ...(**10**)... for the ultimate truth.

1. A. unless B. without
C. if D. before
E. because

2. A. principles B. conjecture
C. experiment D. research
E. experience

3. A. accepted B. demonstrated
C. proved D. performed
E. understood

4. A. precision B. exactness
C. confirmation D. speculation
E. apprehension

5. A. for B. how
C. that D. about
E. why

6. A. impact B. futility
C. causes D. problems
E. nature

7. A. limitations B. benefits
C. shortcomings D. researches
E. inventions

8. A. employed B. developed
C. able D. entrusted
E. taught

9. A. engulfed B. lost
C. enlightening D. investigating
E. groping

10. A. useful B. worthy
C. ready D. search
E. fit

PASSAGE-9

Faced with an ...(**1**)... number and variety of products on the market, managers are finding it more difficult to ...(**2**)... demand and plan production and order ...(**3**)... . As a result ...(**4**)... forecasts are increasing and, along with them, the costs of those errors. Many managers today, ...(**5**)... speed is the ...(**6**)..., have turned to one or another popular production scheduling system. But these tools tackle only part of the problem. ...(**7**)... really needed is a way to ...(**8**)... forecasts and simultaneously redesign planning processes to ...(**9**)... the impact of ...(**10**)... forecasts.

1. A. exact B. equal
C. optimum D. eccentric
E. unprecedented

2. A. meet B. predict
C. ignore D. accept
E. register

3. A. immediately B. quickly
C. accordingly D. positively
E. spontaneously

4. A. inaccurate B. buoyant
C. frequent D. inadequate
E. exorbitant

5. A. consider B. neglecting
C. visualising D. believing
E. notwithstanding

6. A. problem B. answer
C. source D. outcome
E. lacuna

7. A. What's B. That's
C. One D. Managers
E. Companies

8. A. ignore B. obtain
C. vitiate D. negate
E. improve

9. A. rationalise B. substantiate
C. minimise D. counter
E. tolerate

10. A. dangerous B. absolute
C. unpredicted D. erroneous
E. popular

PASSAGE-10

In view of the ...(1)... demand for personnel with commerce background, in the post-liberalisation period, courses in commerce have ...(2)... the attention of students and parents. There is growing ...(3)... for these courses not only in schools but also in colleges. But the ...(4)... of commerce education in schools leaves ...(5)... to be desired. Its popularity, importance and quality, to a large extent, depends much on the teaching methodology being ...(6)... in schools. Of course, the ...(7)... review and ...(8)... of syllabic also ...(9).... But this aspect is ...(10)... taken care of suitably, by the concerned organisations.

1. A. exaggerated B. unreasonable
C. tremendous D. increasing
E. diminishing

2. A. distorted B. ameliorated
C. attracted D. weighed
E. encouraged

3. A. demand B. contempt
C. dissatisfaction D. commotion
E. urgency

4. A. awareness B. intricacy
C. status D. necessity
E. quality

5. A. scope B. much
C. short D. everything
E. nothing

6. A. abandoned B. practised
C. contemplated D. assimilated
E. taught

7. A. unscrupulous B. partial
C. expert D. general
E. periodical

8. A. discussions B. perusal
C. reduction D. updating
E. formulation

9. A. matters B. flourishes
C. desires D. encompasses
E. needs

10. A. duly B. seldom
C. being D. often
E. never

ANSWERS

PASSAGE-1

1	2	3	4	5	6	7	8	9	10
B	D	D	A	D	E	B	D	C	A

PASSAGE-2

1	2	3	4	5	6	7	8	9	10
E	A	D	A	B	B	A	B	C	C
11	**12**								
D	D								

PASSAGE-3

1	2	3	4	5	6	7	8	9	10
E	B	C	D	E	C	C	A	A	B

PASSAGE-4

1	2	3	4	5	6	7	8	9	10
C	A	D	E	B	A	D	E	A	B

PASSAGE-5

1	2	3	4	5	6	7	8	9	10
D	A	E	B	C	A	B	E	C	D

PASSAGE-6

1	2	3	4	5	6	7	8	9	10
A	D	E	C	E	B	A	C	C	D

PASSAGE-7

1	2	3	4	5	6	7	8	9	10
D	E	B	D	C	C	E	D	B	D

PASSAGE-8

1	2	3	4	5	6	7	8	9	10
A	B	C	D	E	A	B	C	E	E

PASSAGE-9

1	2	3	4	5	6	7	8	9	10
E	B	C	A	D	B	A	E	C	E

PASSAGE-10

1	2	3	4	5	6	7	8	9	10
D	C	A	E	B	B	E	D	A	A

7

Idioms & Phrases

An idiom is a group of words established by usage having a meaning different from individual words.
A phrase is a small group of words standing together as an idiomatic expression.
Learn and practise as may as you can and test your knowledge in the exercise that follows.

Idioms and Idiomatic Phrases

- **ABC** (basic principles)
  I do not know the ABC of photography.
- **At one's beck and call** (ready to obey)
  He had a dozen men at his beck and call.
- **At sixes and sevens** (in disorder)
  The drawing room articles were lying at sixes and sevens on the floor.
- **A wet blanket** (a discouraging person)
  Don't allow him to accompany you to the hunting trip, he is a wet blanket.
- **A big gun** (an important person)
  Mr Tata is a big gun in our city.
- **At a stone's throw** (at a short distance from)
  My school is at a stone's throw from my house.
- **A man of word** (a person who keeps his promise)
  Mr Modi is a man of word.
- **A man of a few words** (a remarkable person)
  Gandhiji was a man of a few words.
- **At arm's length** (to keep away)
  We should always keep bad boys at arm's length
- **A bolt from the blue** (a sudden and unexpected event)
  The news of my friend's death came to me like a bolt from the blue.
- **A man of letters** (a scholar)
  Radha Krishnan was a man of letters.
- **A hard nut to crack.** (a puzzling problem)
  To get a win over American basket ball team is a hard nut to crack for India.
- **A yeoman's service** (service which is beneficial to the human beings)
  He did yeoman's service through his life.
- **A snake in the grass** (a hidden foe)
  Beware of him because he seems to be a snake in the grass.
- **Acid test** (hard test)
  The election will be an acid test for the ruling party.
- **A wolf in sheep's clothing** (a hypocrite)
  You should not keep company with him because he is a wolf in sheep's clothing.
- **At the eleventh hour** (at the last moment)
  The war was about to start but fortunately at the eleventh hour a messenger came to the PM with a message of peace.
- **A great card** (an important person)
  Mr Rajan is a great card in the ministry of finance.
- **A fool of the first water** (one completely foolish)
  Being a fool of the first water he could not solve even the simplest sum.
- **A bone of contention** (to be the cause of quarrel)
  Kashmir is the bone of contention between India and Pakistan.
- **A green hand** (not very much experienced)
  We shall pay a little to a green hand.
- **All in all** (completely)
  Rajesh is all in all in this office.

- **A bed of roses** (a comfort)
  Life is not a bed of roses.
- **An apple of discord** (to be the cause of)
  Kashmir is an apple of discord between India and Pakistan.
- **A white elephant** (of no use)
  This sort of glib talker always proves a white elephant in the end.
- **A red letter day** (an important day)
  15th August is a red letter day for the Indians.
- **By hook or by crook** (by any means fair or foul)
  You must complete this job by hook or by crook.
- **Black sheep** (a traitor)
  Later on the person proved a black sheep.
- **By dint of** (by means of)
  By dint of hard work, she earned a lot of money.
- **Break ones back** (to work hard to get something)
  He broke his back to earn his livelihood.
- **Break the back of** (accomplish the hardest part of a certain job)
  There is nothing to be worried about as we've already broken the back of the problem.
- **Beat about the bush** (to go on talking on some worthless topic)
  Stop this beating about the bush, come to the main task.
- **Beyond one's means** (beyond one's budget)
  He is living beyond his means, therefore, he is sure to get ruined.
- **Cut loose** (keep away)
  India should cut loose from bad politics.
- **Chips of the same block** (having the same taste)
  They are the chips of the same block.
- **Cut-throat competition** (a stiff competition)
  There is a cut-throat competition among the publishers in the market.
- **Come what may** (no matter what happens)
  I'll do it, come what may.
- **Drop someone a line** (send a letter, etc.)
  Please drop me a line of your well-being.
- **Dull the edge of** (reduce the intensity of)
  Take this pill and it will dull the edge of pain.
- **From hand to mouth** (without any saving)
  The poor factory worker is living from hand to mouth.
- **Fair and square** (clean)
  One must be fair and square in one's dealing.
- **Hard of hearing** (somewhat deaf)
  She is a bit hard of hearing.
- **In the good books of** (be good in one's mind)
  Jack is in the good books of his teachers.
- **In black and white** (in written)
  Don't give him anything in black and white.
- **In cold blood** (mercilessly)
  The old woman was murdered in cold blood.
- **In a crack** (all of a sudden or rapidly)
  The thief left the place in a crack.
- **In full swing** (in full force)
  The studies of the students are going on in full swing.
- **In the twinkling of an eye** (quickly)
  The monkey ate up grams in the twinkling of an eye.
- **Keep the ball rolling** (to maintain the progress of some activity)
  After the death of his father he had to take the charge of his office to keep the ball rolling.
- **Neck and neck** (even)
  There is a neck and neck fight between the two boxers.
- **Once in a blue moon** (seldom)
  She visits her brother once in a blue moon.
- **Slow and steady** (slowly but continually)
  Slow and steady wins the race.
- **To cut a sorry figure** (present oneself in a bad way)
  She cut a sorry figure on the stage.
- **To give a red carpet reception** (to give a warm welcome)
  The PM was given a red carpet reception in America.
- **To dance one's tune** (to follow someone submissively)
  He always dances to his brother's tune.
- **To turn a deaf ear to** (to disregard)
  She turned a deaf ear to her parents' advice.

- **To call a spade a spade** (to speak the truth) Gandhiji always called a spade a spade.
- **To bring to book** (to scold) The naughty boy was brought to book by the teacher.
- **To cut short** (to reduce) Smoking will cut short your life.
- **To grease the palm of** (to bribe) Rohit greased the palm of the clerk and got the file moved.
- **Through thick and thin.** (under all circumstances) We'll stand by you through thick and thin.
- **To die by inches** (to die a painful death) The old man died by inches.
- **To eat one's words** (to retract one's statement) You'll have to eat your words because you have spoken without thinking.
- **To burn the midnight oil** (to work hard) You'll have to burn the midnight oil if you want to get good marks.
- **To poke one's nose into** (to meddle with) It is bad to poke your nose into others' affair.
- **To fall flat** (to have no effect) His father's advice fell flat on him.
- **To make a clean breast of** (to confess) He made a clean breast of his involvement in the bomb blast.
- **To get the better of** (overcome) Anger got the better of him.
- **To break somebody's back** (to give too much work to him to do) She broke his back by giving him so much hard work to do.
- **Throw cold water on** (to discourage) She tried to throw cold water on his plan but he was well-determined.
- **The long and short of** (in brief) The long and short of his lecture is that we should live like brothers.
- **To burn one's fingers** (to get oneself in trouble) You have burnt your fingers by speaking against him.
- **To turn over a new leaf** (to change the course of life) He has turned over a new leaf in his life.
- **To have one's own axe to grind** (to have vested interest) He has his own axe to grind in this matter.
- **To take to one's heels** (to run away) The thief took to his heels as soon as he saw the policeman.
- **To move heaven and earth** (to make too much effort) The young man moved heaven and earth to find a job.
- **To be caught red handed** (to be caught at the time of committing a crime) The clerk was caught red handed when he was accepting bribe from Mr ABC.
- **To receive with open arms** (to give a warm welcome) The new president of the club was received with open arms by the members.
- **To be born with a silver spoon in one's mouth** (to be born in a rich family) Mr. J. L. Nehru was born with a silver spoon in his mouth.
- **To come to light** (to be known) A new disease has recently come to light.
- **To be the apple of one's eye** (be very dear) He is the apple of his parent's eye.
- **To make fun of** (laugh at) The children made fun of the waiter in the hotel.
- **To let the cat out of the bag** (to divulge secret) It was I who let the cat out of the bag by telling the real matter.
- **To open a new chapter** (to start some habit, etc.) By quitting drinking, you've opened a new chapter in your life.
- **To make the flesh creep** (to terrify) The story made my flesh creep.
- **To lose ground** (to retreat) After fighting for some time the Pakistani army began to lose ground.

- **To bring to book** (to punish)
The student was brought to book by the teacher.
- **To show a clean pair of heels** (to run away)
The thief showed a clean pair of heels as soon as he saw the policeman approaching.
- **To gain ground** (to be established)
He gained ground in India in a few years.
- **To get wind of** (to get information)
I got wind of his secret plans.
- **Under a cloud** (be in trouble or in a state of disgrace or suspicion)
His company seemed to be under a cloud as it had no funds to pay the wages to the workers.

Verbal Phrases

- **Act upon** (to follow)
I acted upon my father's advice.
- **Act upto** (to perform within limits)
He acted upto his conscience.
- **Act beyond** (to perform crossing limits)
We should not act beyond our capacity.
- **Act for** (to perform in place of someone else)
The vice principal acted for the principal.
- **Back up** (to make a queue)
The vehicles began to back up.
- **Back down** (withdraw claim in the presence of opposition)
The leader backed down from his previous statement.
- **Back off** (draw back some plan or action)
They backed off from building a flyover.
- **Back out** (withdraw from a promise, etc.)
The government backed out of its promise.
- **Break down** (stop working) My car broke down on the highway.
- **Break into** (enter in certain premises by breaking the door, etc.)
Last night a thief broke into my neighbour's.
- **Break off** (to detach by breaking)
The branch broke off from the tree.
- **Break out** (spread)
Cholera has broken out in the town.
- **Break out of** (escape from)
A prisoner broke out of the prison last night.
- **Break up** (disperse)
The cloud of fog began to break up as the sun rose.
- **Break something up** (cause something to break into small pieces)
She broke up the chocolate to distribute it among the children.
- **Break with** (cut off connection after quarrelling with someone)
He has broken with his brother.
- **Call on** (pay a visit to somebody)
I'll call on Mohan's today.
- **Call out** (to start)
The workers have called out a strike.
- **Call off** (to stop the strike etc.)
The workers have called off the strike.
- **Call at** (to visit someone's house)
I called at his house yesterday.
- **Call in** (send for)
Please call in the doctor.
- **Carry on** (continue)
Please carry on your work.
- **Carry something out** (perform a task)
Our company is carrying out a big deal with a foreign company.
- **Carry something over** (postpone)
The fancy dress competition had to be carried over till Monday)
- **Carry someone off** (kill somebody)
Cancer carried her off on the day of her 20th birthday.
- **Come of age** (get established)
As our company has come of age, so, there is no problem in selling our goods.
- **Come of** (belong to)
She comes of a royal family.
- **Come over** (surmount)
We at last came over all our problems.
- **Come off** (to take place)
The marriage of my brother comes off in the next month.

- **Come round** (agree)
At last he came round to my views.
- **Come under** (fall in the category of)
All these animals come under the same species.
- **Come down with** (suffer from)
She came down with whopping cough.
- **Come from** (be the native of)
She came from London.
- **Come about** (happen)
The explosion came about when the worker struck the match to light a cigarette.
- **Cut off** (die)
The cricketer is cut off in the prime of his life.
- **Cut down** (reduce)
The prices of consumer goods should be cut down.
- **Cut someone out** (exclude someone)
His father cut him out of his will.
- **Fall in**
She fell in love with the prince.
- **Fall down** (fail)
The deal fell down for lack of transparency.
- **Fall out** (quarrel)
She fell out with his elder brother.
- **Fall through** (fail)
The project fell through for lack of funds.
- **Get away** (escape)
She got away with her life.
- **Get by** (to accomplish something with great difficulty)
She is not rich. She has just enough to get by.
- **Get on** (perform)
How are you getting on with your studies?
- **Get out** (become known)
The news got out that the PM was paying a visit to Russia.
- **Get over** (overcome)
At last I got over all obstacles.
- **Get up** (rise)
When do you get up in the morning?
- **Give up** (stop)
He gave up smoking.
- **Give out** (emit)
Garlic gives out a pungent smell.
- **Give in** (collapse)
The bridge gave in under the heavy load.
- **Give away** (distribute)
The Principal gave away the prizes.
- **Give out** (announce)
It was given out that the President of India would visit the place soon.
- **Go off** (explode)
The gun went off suddenly.
- **Go on** (continue)
She went on about how she flew the aeroplane.
- **Go through** (examine)
I'll go through this book later on.
- **Go up** (be built)
The construction of the house is going up.
- **Grind on** (continue for a long time in a tedious way)
The discussion over political issues ground on.
- **Grind something out** (produce something a tedious way)
She will grind some more short stories.
- **Look out** (be careful)
Look out! there is a snake.
- **Look down upon** (hate)
We should not look down upon the poor.
- **Look at** (watch)
Look at the blackboard.
- **Look after** (take care of)
We ought to look after our old parents.
- **Look into** (investigate)
The new police inspector will look into the matter.
- **Look up** (rise)
The prices of consumer goods are looking up.
- **Look back** (think of the past)
It made her feel disolate when she looked back on things of the past.
- **Make up** (to fulfil)
I'll make up my deficiency in Mathematics.

✦ **Make out** (understand)
I could not make out what she said.

✦ **Make up one' mind** (to resolve)
I have made up my mind to settle in the USA.

✦ **Make off** (leave hurriedly)
She made off without informing anybody.

✦ **Make something over** (transfer)
She should make her property over to her sons.

✦ **Make over** (hand over)
He made over the charge of the file to Mr Robert.

✦ **Pull back** (retreat)
The government has pulled back from its previous policy.

✦ **Pull something down** (demolish)
The authorities concerned pulled down a few building which were illegally built on government land.

✦ **Pull out** (pluck)
The child pulled out a few petals of the flower.

✦ **Pull through** (recover)
The patient will pull through.

✦ **Push on** (continue a journey)
It was getting darker but we pushed on.

✦ **Push at** (exert force)
He pushed at the bell, but it did not ring.

✦ **Push for** (demand persistently)
The workers have been pushing for the installation of new machines for five years.

✦ **Put out** (extinguish)
She put out the light.

✦ **Put on** (wear)
He put on an overcoat.

✦ **Put off** (postpone)
The plan had to be put off.

✦ **Put by** (spare something for future)
We must put by some money for future.

✦ **Put up with** (stay)
Your aunt is out of town for a couple of days, you may put up with us till she comes.

✦ **Put something down** (record something)
She put a new idea down on the paper.

✦ **Take after** (resemble)
He takes after his father.

✦ **Take off** (remove)
He took off his shoes.

✦ **Take something out** (obtain)
You may take out some money from Rohit if you want to purchase this car.

✦ **Take to** (fall into the habit of)
He took to gambling.

✦ **Turn something down** (reject something)
The judge turned down his appeal.

✦ **Turn on** (attack)
The thief turned on him with a knife.

Multiple Choice Questions

Directions: *Some idioms/phrases are given below with their probable meanings. Select the options with their correct meanings.*

1. **Carry out**
   A. To take from one place to another
   B. To continue
   C. To obey
   D. To make efforts
   E. None of these

2. **In the same boat**
   A. A worn out choice
   B. Indifferent
   C. In identical circumstances
   D. Carry off
   E. None of these

3. **In one's good book**
   A. A costly book
   B. A priceless treasure
   C. In one's favour
   D. An enchanting beauty
   E. None of these

4. **Keep a straight face**
   A. To do make up
   B. To change clothes
   C. Assume responsibility
   D. To remain serious
   E. None of these

5. To be above board
A. To have a good height
B. To be honest in any business deal
C. To have no debts
D. To try to be beautiful
E. None of these

6. On the face of it
A. To agree B. From an action
C. More than enough D. Apparently
E. None of these

7. Let the bygones be bygones
A. In one's favour B. To pretend
C. To forget the past D. Other choice
E. None of these

8. To split hairs
A. Major distinctions
B. Hair with two ends
C. To make minute distinction
D. Without distinction
E. None of these

9. Bread and butter
A. Both bread and butter
B. Something essential
C. Livelihood
D. Relevant things
E. None of these

10. To bell the cat
A. To catch a cat and tie a bell round its neck
B. To make an effort
C. To be quick
D. To face a risk
E. None of these

11. Hard and fast
A. Strict B. Solid
C. Fast moving D. Some hard surface
E. None of these

12. Part and parcel
A. The part of a parcel
B. An essential part
C. A missing parcel
D. Some part of a machine sent by parcel
E. None of these

13. Null and void
A. Something invalid
B. Something that can be avoided
C. Something that can be nullified
D. Something evil
E. None of these

14. To make clean breast of
A. To gain prominence
B. To praise oneself
C. To confess without reserve
D. To destroy before it blooms
E. None of these

15. Trump card
A. A powerful means of achieving an object
B. Resourcefulness
C. The best gamble to attain success
D. A travel card
E. None of these

16. Tall talk
A. A discussion continued for a long time
B. A high sounding talk
C. A meaningful talk
D. A useless talk
E. None of these

17. Small talk
A. Gossip
B. A discussion carried on for a long time
C. A brief discussion
D. A talk of small children
E. None of these

18. Throw out of gear
A. To replace B. Hinder, disturb
C. To decide D. Take up tune
E. None of these

19. To and fro
A. Back and forth B. Puzzled
C. Amazed D. Reprove
E. None of these

20. To bell the cat
A. To do an easy job
B. To be indifferent to
C. To undertake a difficult job
D. To clarify
E. None of these

21. To be under cloud
A. Puzzle
B. Enjoy the favour
C. Talk thoughtlessly
D. To be under suspicion
E. None of these

22. A labour of love
A. A tragic end
B. A funny thing
C. Not fruitful
D. Work done without payment
E. None of these

23. Follow suit
A. Follow an example B. Wear a new dress
C. Irrelevant D. A gay person
E. None of these

24. Foul play
A. Bad intentions
B. A play not well acted
C. A play not liked by the audience
D. A foul scored at play
E. None of these

25. To pick holes
A. To find some reason to quarrel
B. To destroy something
C. To criticise someone
D. To cut some part of an item
E. None of these

26. To smell a rat
A. To see signs of plague epidemic
B. To get bad smell of a dead rat
C. To suspect foul dealings
D. To be in a bad mood
E. None of these

27. To put a spoke in one's wheel
A. To encourage
B. Act without restraint
C. Risk something
D. To obstruct one's progress
E. None of these

28. To pull one's leg
A. To give up B. Take care of
C. To befool D. To know
E. None of these

29. To play with fire
A. Grasp the truth
B. To handle something dangerous
C. To ridicule
D. To flee away
E. None of these

30. To reckon with
A. Take up time
B. Make an inventory
C. To deal with
D. Submit to punishment
E. None of these

31. To run short
A. Talk until one is tired at
B. Apply to oneself
C. To get rid of
D. To have or be too little
E. None of these

32. A man of letters
A. A postman B. A learned man
C. A hypocrite D. An ignorant man
E. None of these

33. A maiden speech
A. A speech made in the parliament
B. A speech made before unmarried girls
C. A speech made by a political leader
D. A speech made for the first time
E. None of these

34. Order of the day
A. An order passed on a particular day
B. A current law
C. Something common or general
D. A major order of court
E. None of these

35. To end in smoke
A. To make completely understand
B. To ruin oneself
C. To excite great applause
D. To die smoking
E. None of these

36. To give vent to
A. To allow to flow forth
B. To prove a failure
C. To amass wealth
D. To evade
E. None of these

37. To eat humble pie
A. To apologise or confess
B. To order
C. To flatter
D. To get a small share
E. None of these

38. A black sheep
A. An unlucky person
B. A negro
C. An ugly person

D. A man in animal skin
E. None of these

39. To catch a tartar
A. To trap wanted criminal with great difficulty
B. To catch a dangerous person
C. To meet with disaster
D. To deal with a person who is more than one's watch
E. None of these

40. Sit on fence
A. To remain neutral
B. To show contempt
C. To enjoy the surroundings
D. To become fond of
E. None of these

41. Pay off old scores
A. To repay the debt B. To have revenge
C. To invite D. Secretly
E. None of these

42. Turn turtle
A. To cheat
B. To be lopsided
C. To frustrate
D. To dance to the tune
E. None of these

43. Wash one's hands of
A. To refuse B. To assist
C. To abuse D. To refuse to be
E. None of these

44. Under duress
A. Under compulsion
B. Willing
C. To elicit information
D. To demand
E. None of these

45. To turn the tables
A. To ruin someone
B. To turn the situation to one's own side
C. To reverse the situation
D. To move from one point to another
E. None of these

46. On the cards
A. Possibly B. Probably
C. Openly D. Likely

47. To leave someone in the lurch
A. To come to compromise with someone
B. Constant source of annoyance to someone
C. To put someone at ease
D. To desert someone in his difficulties
E. None of these

48. To play second fiddle
A. To be happy, cheerful and healthy
B. To reduce importance of one's senior
C. To support the role and view of another person
D. To do backseat driving
E. None of these

49. To yearn for
A. To weep for B. To remember
C. To admire D. To long for intensely
E. None of these

50. Call off
A. To finish B. To withdraw
C. To postpone D. To cry
E. None of these

ANSWERS

1	2	3	4	5	6	7	8	9	10
C	C	C	D	B	D	C	C	C	D
11	**12**	**13**	**14**	**15**	**16**	**17**	**18**	**19**	**20**
A	B	A	C	C	B	A	B	A	C
21	**22**	**23**	**24**	**25**	**26**	**27**	**28**	**29**	**30**
D	D	A	A	C	C	D	C	B	C
31	**32**	**33**	**34**	**35**	**36**	**37**	**38**	**39**	**40**
D	B	D	C	D	A	A	D	B	A
41	**42**	**43**	**44**	**45**	**46**	**47**	**48**	**49**	**50**
B	B	D	A	C	D	D	C	D	B

8

Reordering Sentences

A paragraph is formed from sentences, it will convey its true meaning and purpose only when the sentences are arranged in a proper manner. One must try and practise it regularly to score well. Test your skills in this exercise.

Multiple Choice Questions

Directions (Qs. 1 to 60): *Each of these questions sets has a group of sentences marked with numbers. Rearrange them in proper sequence to form a meaningful paragraph and answer the questions given below each set.*

SET-1

1. After examining him, the doctor smiled at him mischievously and took out a syringe.
2. Thinking that he was really sick, his father summoned the family doctor.
3. That day, Banku wanted to take a day off from school.
4. Immediately, Banku jumped up from his bed and swore that he was fine.
5. Therefore; he pretended to be sick and remained in bed.

1. Which sentence should come **fourth** in the pargaraph?
A. 1 B. 2
C. 3 D. 4
E. 5

2. Which sentence should come **last** in the paragraph?
A. 1 B. 2
C. 3 D. 4
E. 5

3. Which sentence should come **first** in the paragraph?
A. 1 B. 2
C. 3 D. 4
E. 5

4. Which sentence should come **third** in the paragraph?
A. 1 B. 2
C. 3 D. 4
E. 5

5. Which sentence should come **second** in the paragraph?
A. 1 B. 2
C. 3 D. 4
E. 5

SET-2

1. In his literary work he spoke of that province of human life which mere intellect does not speak.
2. He has also given innocent joy to many children by his stories like 'Kabuliwalah'.
3. Thsese songs are sung not only in Bengal but all over the country.
4. Rabindranath's great works sprang from intensity of vision and feelings.
5. He sang of beauty and heroism, nobility and charm.

6. Which sentence should come **third** in the sequence?
A. 1 B. 2
C. 3 D. 4
E. 5

7. Which sentence should come **fourth** in the sequence?
A. 1 B. 2
C. 3 D. 4
E. 5

8. Which sentence should come **second** in the sequence?
A. 1 B. 2
C. 3 D. 4
E. 5

9. Which sentence should come **first** in the sequence?
A. 1 B. 2
C. 3 D. 4
E. 5

10. Which sentence should come **fifth** in the sequence?
A. 1 B. 2
C. 3 D. 4
E. 5

SET-3

1. I reached office at 11 o'clock after sending the money.
2. Some money had to be sent to my parents.
3. After that, I spent almost an hour at the post office.
4. Therefore, I went to the bank to withdraw some money.
5. However, I had no money with me.

11. Which statement should come **first** in the paragraph?
A. 1 B. 2
C. 3 D. 4
E. 5

12. Which statement should come **second** in the paragraph?
A. 1 B. 2
C. 3 D. 4
E. 5

13. Which statement should come **third** in the paragraph?
A. 1 B. 2
C. 3 D. 4
E. 5

14. Which statement should come **fourth** in the paragraph?
A. 1 B. 2
C. 3 D. 4
E. 5

15. Which statement should come **fifth** in the paragraph?
A. 1 B. 2
C. 3 D. 4
E. 5

SET-4

1. In fact, it prevents us from helping children to analyse conflict, to learn to cope with it and counter it.
2. Children have always known that there is conflict in the adult world.
3. However, the make-believe world that nineteenth century rationally imposed on childhood in Europe and which we impose in an institutionalised manner through our modern education system can hardly be described as related in this regard.
4. We may therefore conclude that conflict in an institutionalised manner is not a matter of faith in children's capacities, rather, it is a lack of faith in ourselves as adults.
5. Further, psychologists tell us and story tellers have always known that the child's desire to search for order and coherence gathers strength from the knowledge of conflict.

16. Which of the following should be the **last** sentence in the paragraph?
A. 1 B. 2
C. 3 D. 4
E. 5

17. Which of the following should be the **first** sentence in the paragraph?
A. 1 B. 2
C. 3 D. 4
E. 5

18. Which of the following should be the **fourth** sentence in the paragraph?
A. 1 B. 2
C. 3 D. 4
E. 5

19. Which of the following should be the **third** sentence in the paragraph?
A. 1 B. 2
C. 3 D. 4
E. 5

20. Which of the following should be the **second** sentence in the paragraph?
A. 1 B. 2
C. 3 D. 4
E. 5

SET-5

1. A case in point is the programme involving the Sardar Sarovar Dam which would displace about 2,00,000 people.
2. Critics decry the fact that a major development institution appears to absorb more capital than it distributes to borrowers.
3. For all its faults critics however, concede that the bank remains a relatively efficient instrument for distribution of development-aid money.
4. One of the key complaints focuses on this non-profit bank's recent "profitability".
5. Although the lives of millions of people around the globe have been improved by the bank's activities, it is now under fire.
6. The bank is also being blamed for large-scale involuntary resettlement to make way for dams and other construction projects.

21. Which sentence should come **third** in the paragraph?
A. 2 B. 5
C. 1 D. 4
E. 6

22. Which sentence should come **fourth** in the paragraph?
A. 6 B. 3
C. 5 D. 2
E. 1

23. Which sentence should come **first** in the paragraph?
A. 4 B. 6
C. 3 D. 2
E. 5

24. Which sentence should come **second** in the paragraph?
A. 3 B. 1
C. 4 D. 6
E. 5

25. Which sentence should come **last** (*i.e.* **sixth**) in the paragraph?
A. 5 B. 4
C. 2 D. 1
E. 3

SET-6

1. Akash was shocked when he realised that the leg had lost sensation.
2. When he tried to get up, he felt his left leg was very heavy.
3. He had to lie down hopelessly, till he saw a flashlight.
4. It was an odd night time and hence nobody heard his voice.
5. Due to sudden sprain Akash fell down.
6. Nervous with this realisation, he called out for help.

26. Which of the following should be the **third** sentence?
A. 1 B. 2
C. 3 D. 4
E. 5

27. Which of the following should be the **sixth (last)** sentence?
A. 6 B. 5
C. 4 D. 3
E. 2

28. Which of the following should be the **first** sentence?
A. 1 B. 2
C. 3 D. 4
E. 5

29. Which of the following should be the **second** sentence?

A. 1
B. 2
C. 3
D. 4
E. 5

30. Which of the following should be the **fourth** sentence?
A. 1
B. 2
C. 6
D. 4
E. 5

SET-7

1. The history of mankind is full of such fightings between communities, nation and people.
2. From the primitive weapons of warfare, man has advanced to the modern nuclear weapons.
3. Ever since the dawn of civilisation man has been fighting with man.
4. A modern war is scientific in character, but the effect is the same wiping human existence out of this earth.
5. The only difference now seems to be in the efficiency of the instruments used for killing each other.

31. Which of the following should be the **fifth (last)** sentence?
A. 1
B. 2
C. 3
D. 4
E. 5

32. Which of the following should be the **fourth** sentence?
A. 1
B. 2
C. 3
D. 4
E. 5

33. Which of the following should be the **first** sentence?
A. 1
B. 2
C. 3
D. 4
E. 5

34. Which of the following should be the **second** sentence?
A. 1
B. 2
C. 3
D. 4
E. 5

35. Which of the following should be the **third** sentence?
A. 1
B. 2
C. 3
D. 4
E. 5

SET-8

1. Its current was very powerful and could take away big tree trunks.
2. There were some children, playing on the bank of the waterway.
3. In the forest of Bharatpur, there is a big lake.
4. The excess water started flowing forcefully through the waterway.
5. Once there was a very heavy rain because of which the lake started overflowing.
6. A poor man noticed it and rushed to save them.

36. Which of the following should be the **first** sentence?
A. 6
B. 5
C. 4
D. 3
E. 2

37. Which of the following should be the **third** sentence?
A. 6
B. 5
C. 4
D. 3
E. 2

38. Which of the following should be the **sixth (last)** sentence?
A. 6
B. 5
C. 4
D. 3
E. 2

39. Which of the following should be the **fourth** sentence?
A. 5
B. 4
C. 3
D. 2
E. 1

40. Which of the following should be the **second** sentence?
A. 6
B. 5
C. 4
D. 3
E. 2

SET-9

1. The means and methods they employ to deal with public pressures are also different.
2. They will make no move unless the gallery is packed.
3. The poorest are over-hesitant, evasive and preoccupied with their relationships with others.

4. Enormous difference is generally observed in the ways in which various public officials respond to public pressures.
5. The best possess understanding of the forces that must be taken into account, determination not to be swerved from the path of public interest.
6. They confront all embarrasments with a stale general formula.

41. Which of the following should be the **third** sentence?
A. 1 B. 2
C. 3 D. 4
E. 5

42. Which of the following should be the **sixth (last)** sentence?
A. 2 B. 3
C. 4 D. 5
E. 6

43. Which of the following should be the **first** sentence?
A. 6 B. 5
C. 4 D. 3
E. 2

44. Which of the following should be the **second** sentence?
A. 1 B. 2
C. 3 D. 4
E. 5

45. Which of the following should be the **fourth** sentence?
A. 2 B. 3
C. 4 D. 5
E. 6

SET-10

1. A taxi was summoned and Raju was taken to Lifeline Hospital.
2. While hurrying home from school.
3. Since they did not succeed, they decided to take him to a hospital.
4. When Raju opened his eyes, he found himself surrounded by doctors and nurses.
5. Some people rushed towards him and tried to bring him to his senses.
6. He was thrown a couple of feet away and lost consciousness.

46. Which sentence should come **third** in the paragraph?
A. 6 B. 2
C. 5 D. 1
E. 4

47. Which sentence should come **fourth** in the paragraph?
A. 3 B. 5
C. 6 D. 2
E. 1

48. Which sentence should come **first** in the paragraph?
A. 4 B. 6
C. 2 D. 5
E. 3

49. Which sentence should come **last** (*i.e.*, **sixth**) in the paragraph?
A. 2 B. 3
C. 1 D. 4
E. 5

50. Which sentence should come **second** in the paragraph?
A. 5 B. 1
C. 4 D. 3
E. 6

SET-11

1. But by then it was too late to correct things.
2. It is impossible to steer such a large project to success without planning.
3. He had to stand by and watch helplessly.
4. The whole scheme was destined, to fail from the beginning.
5. Bhaskar started realising this only towards the end.

51. Which sentence should come **first** in the paragraph
A. 1 B. 2
C. 3 D. 4
E. 5

52. Which sentence should come **third** in the paragraph?
A. 1 B. 2
C. 3 D. 4
E. 5

53. Which sentence should come **last** in the paragraph?

A. 1 B. 2
C. 3 D. 4
E. 5

54. Which sentence should come **second** in the paragraph?

A. 1 B. 2
C. 3 D. 4
E. 5

55. Which sentence should come **fourth** in the paragraph?

A. 1 B. 2
C. 3 D. 4
E. 5

SET-12

1. John did not have the money to buy the beautiful clip.
2. After a while, Jane explained to John that she had sold her hair to buy a gold chain for his watch.
3. As it was Christmas, John wanted to give Jane a surprise present.
4. When Jane saw it, she felt like crying.
5. He decided to present her a clip made of ivory for her long flowing hair.
6. He, therefore, sold off his watch and brought home the present.

56. Which of the sentences should come **last** in the paragraph?

A. 5 B. 4
C. 1 D. 3
E. 2

57. Which of the sentences should come **first** in the paragraph?

A. 3 B. 6
C. 2 D. 5
E. 4

58. Which of the sentences should come **second** in the paragraph?

A. 6 B. 1
C. 5 D. 4
E. 3

59. Which of the sentences should come **third** in the paragraph?

A. 4 B. 5
C. 6 D. 2
E. 1

60. Which of the sentences should come **fourth** in the paragraph?

A. 1 B. 2
C. 3 D. 6
E. 5

ANSWERS

1	**2**	**3**	**4**	**5**	**6**	**7**	**8**	**9**	**10**
A	D	C	B	E	B	E	A	D	C
11	**12**	**13**	**14**	**15**	**16**	**17**	**18**	**19**	**20**
B	E	D	C	A	D	B	C	A	E
21	**22**	**23**	**24**	**25**	**26**	**27**	**28**	**29**	**30**
B	A	D	C	E	A	D	E	B	C
31	**32**	**33**	**34**	**35**	**36**	**37**	**38**	**39**	**40**
E	D	C	A	B	D	C	A	D	B
41	**42**	**43**	**44**	**45**	**46**	**47**	**48**	**49**	**50**
C	E	C	A	D	C	A	C	D	E
51	**52**	**53**	**54**	**55**	**56**	**57**	**58**	**59**	**60**
D	E	C	B	A	E	A	C	E	D

9

Spelling Errors

The most common errors in English are of spellings of words. Even the most learned men are sometimes confused about the correct spellings of some words. One must keep and use a dictionary religiously. Never ignore and let pass a new word casually.

A number of question to test your knowledge of spellings are compiled here. Try to solve as many as you can.

Multiple Choice Questions

Directions: *Find the correctly spelt word out of the four options in each question. If none of the words is correctly spelt, mark 'E' as your answer.*

1. A. Accompalish B. Ackmplesh C. Acomplush D. Accomplish E. None of these

2. A. Acommodation B. Acomodation C. Accomodation D. Accommodation E. None of these

3. A. Astonished B. Astronished C. Astoneshed D. Asstonished E. None of these

4. A. Benefeted B. Benefitted C. Benifited D. Benefited E. None of these

5. A. Belligerent B. Beligirent C. Belligarant D. Belligerrent E. None of these

6. A. Chancelery B. Chancellery C. Chancellary D. Chancelary E. None of these

7. A. Discriminate B. Discremineta C. Discrimenate D. Discriminat E. None of these

8. A. Damage B. Dammage C. Damaige D. Dammege E. None of these

9. A. Efficiant B. Effecient C. Efficient D. Eficient E. None of these

10. A. Extravagant B. Extreragent C. Extreregant D. Extravegent E. None of these

11. A. Efflorascence B. Eflorescene C. Effllorescence D. Efflorescence E. None of these

12. A. Equinimity B. Equanimmity C. Equannimity D. Equanimity E. None of these

13. A. Farmament B. Farmement C. Fermament D. Fremament E. None of these

14. A. Grieff B. Grief C. Grieef D. Grrief E. None of these

15. A. Guarantee B. Garuntee
C. Guaruntee D. Gaurantee
E. None of these

16. A. Hypocritical B. Hypocretical
C. Hypocriticel D. Hypocirticel
E. None of these

17. A. Humurous B. Humorous
C. Humoreus D. Humorrous
E. None of these

18. A. Itenerary B. Itinarery
C. Itinarary D. Itinerary
E. None of these

19. A. Indipenseble B. Indispansible
C. Indispensable D. Indipensable
E. None of these

20. A. Imprecticability B. Impracticebility
C. Impracticibility D. Impracticability
E. None of these

21. A. Incradulous B. Incredulous
C. Incridulous D. Incredalous
E. None of these

22. A. Juddicious B. Judiceous
C. Judicious D. Judiceus
E. None of these

23. A. Kleptomonia B. Kleptemonia
C. Kleptomania D. Klaptomania
E. None of these

24. A. Lackdaisical B. Lackadaisical
C. Lckadaisicle D. Lackadisical
E. None of these

25. A. Licentious B. Licontious
C. Licenttious D. Licientious
E. None of these

26. A. Meddicine B. Medicine
C. Medicene D. Medicinne
E. None of these

27. A. Meritricious B. Merefrecious
C. Meretricious D. Merritricious
E. None of these

28. A. Missunderstood B. Miesunderstood
C. Misunderstood D. Misunderstod
E. None of these

29. A. Occurad B. Occurred
C. Ocurred D. Occured
E. None of these

30. A. Osttentatious B. Ostentetious
C. Ostentatious D. Ostenttatious
E. None of these

31. A. Obnosious B. Obnoxeous
C. Obnoxious D. Obnoseous
E. None of these

32. A. Omenous B. Ominous
C. Ommineous D. Omineous
E. None of these

33. A. Pecification B. Pacification
C. Pecifacation D. Pecefication
E. None of these

34. A. Prograssive B. Progressive
C. Progresive D. Prograsive
E. None of these

35. A. Pasiveness B. Passiveness
C. Passeveniss D. Passivines
E. None of these

36. A. Polyendry B. Poliendry
C. Pollyendry D. Polyandry
E. None of these

37. A. Puerille B. Puerrile
C. Puerile D. Purrile
E. None of these

38. A. Pesanger B. Passenger
C. Pessenger D. Pasanger
E. None of these

39. A. Querrelsome B. Quarrelsame
C. Quarrelsome D. Querralsome
E. None of these

40. A. Rigourous B. Rigerous
C. Rigorous D. Regerous
E. None of these

41. A. Survellance B. Surveilance
C. Surveillance D. Survaillance
E. None of these

42. A. Schedule B. Schdule
C. Schedale D. Schedeule
E. None of these

43. A. Sepalchrle B. Sepalchral
C. Sepulchrle D. Sepulchral
E. None of these

44. A. Sympathetic B. Smypathetic
C. Sympothetic D. Sympethetic
E. None of these

45. A. Sincerely B. Sencerely
C. Sincerelly D. Sincerrely
E. None of these

46. A. Satellite B. Sattellite
C. Satelite D. Sattelite
E. None of these

47. A. Teracherous B. Treacherous
C. Treacheraus D. Treachereans
E. None of these

48. A. Uncivilized B. Uncevilized
C. Uncivillized D. Uncevelized
E. None of these

49. A. Vainglorious B. Vaniglorious
C. Vaniglerious D. Vaingloreus
E. None of these

50. A. Vulnarable B. Valnerable
C. Velnerable D. Vulnerable
E. None of these

51. A. Valuptuous B. Volluptous
C. Voluptuous D. Volupttuous
E. None of these

52. A. Veneration B. Venration
C. Venneration D. Venerration
E. None of these

53. A. Tacciturnity B. Taciturnity
C. Taciturrnity D. Tacitturnity
E. None of these

54. A. Tranquilitty B. Tranquility
C. Trenquility D. Tranquillity
E. None of these

55. A. Tranquil B. Trenquil
C. Tranquel D. Trinquil
E. None of these

56. A. Neggardly B. Nigardly
C. Niggerdly D. Niggardly
E. None of these

57. A. Quadruplets B. Quedruplets
C. Quadroplets D. Quadruplats
E. None of these

58. A. Schezophrenia B. Schizaphrenia
C. Schizophrenia D. Schizophrania
E. None of these

59. A. Transperency B. Transparency
C. Transpirency D. Tranporency
E. None of these

60. A. Superanuation B. Superennuation
C. Superannuation D. Superannuetion
E. None of these

ANSWERS

1	2	3	4	5	6	7	8	9	10
D	D	A	B	A	C	A	A	C	A
11	**12**	**13**	**14**	**15**	**16**	**17**	**18**	**19**	**20**
D	D	C	B	A	A	B	D	C	D
21	**22**	**23**	**24**	**25**	**26**	**27**	**28**	**29**	**30**
B	C	C	B	A	B	C	C	B	C
31	**32**	**33**	**34**	**35**	**36**	**37**	**38**	**39**	**40**
C	B	B	B	B	D	C	B	C	C
41	**42**	**43**	**44**	**45**	**46**	**47**	**48**	**49**	**50**
C	A	D	A	A	A	B	A	A	D
51	**52**	**53**	**54**	**55**	**56**	**57**	**58**	**59**	**60**
C	A	B	B	A	D	A	C	B	C

Computer Knowledge

Introduction

The term computer is derived from the Latin word compute, which means to calculate. A computer is an electronic machine, devised for performing calculations and controlling operations that can be expressed either in logical or numerical terms. In simple terms, a computer is an electronic device that performs diverse operations with the help of instructions to process the information in order to achieve the desired results. A Computer application extends to cover huge area including education, industries, government, medicine, scientific research etc.

A computer is one of the most influential forces available in modern times. Due to its memory, high speed and perfection, its application can be extended to almost infinite levels. Millions of complex calculations can be done in mere fraction of time. Difficult decisions can be made with accuracy for comparatively little cost. Computers are widely seen as instruments for future progress and as tools to achieve substantiality by way of improved access to information by means of video conferencing and e-mail. Indeed computers have left such on impression on modern civilization that we call this era as the information age.

CHARACTERISTICS OF COMPUTERS

The main characteristics of computers are:

(a) Speed *(b)* Storage

(c) Accuracy *(d)* Versatility

(e) Automation *(f)* Reliability

(a) **Speed :** Today's computers, according to their class, can perform from 4 MIPS (Millions of instructions per second) to 100 MIPS. What may take days for manual calculations may take only a few hours for computers to perform. Inside the computer the information signal travels at incredible electronic speed.

(b) **Storage:** This is expressed in terms of Kilobytes (or) Mega Bytes (MB) or Gega Bytes (GB) or Tera Bytes (TB). It is expressed as 'Main memory' or 'Primary storage' and through 'Auxiliary storage' or 'Secondary storage'. The Hard disks, Floppy disk, Compact Disc (CD) and Magnetic Tape storage are examples of secondary storages.

(c) **Accuracy:** The accuracy of a Computer is consistently high. In fact, this quality of the computers make them indispensable in various fields such as Scientific Research, Space Research, Weather Predictions and many other areas where precision of a high order is required.

(d) **Versatility:** Computers are versatile in that they can perform almost any task, provided they are given the appropriate logical steps. For example, they are capable of performing wide ranging tasks such as construction of a payroll, inventory management in a factory, hotel billing, hospital management, banking applications and any imaginable task in every walk of life.

(e) **Automation:** The biggest advantage of computers is that it is automatic in its operation. Once a programming logic is initiated the computer performs repeated operations without human interventions until program completion.

(f) **Reliability:** The computers give very accurate results with predetermined values. They correct and modify the parameters automatically, giving suitable signals. They give formatted results with high degree of precisions.

HISTORY OF COMPUTERS

Abacus

Abacus was probably the earliest of counting devices. It consists of rectangular wooden frame with two compartments and beads sliding along the steel wires for counting. Multiplication and divisions are done using repeated additions and subtractions. Even today in which cross strings are fixed. Beads are inserted on to the strings. There are a number of rows of beads.

Pascal's calculator

A French mathematician, Blaise Pascal invented a machine based on gear wheels. He was the son of tax collector who had to do lot of calculations as part of his job. Blaise Pascal wanted to make his job easier by inventing a calculator. You might be familiar with gear wheels in use in your bicycle which meshes with a driving chain. He used similar gear wheels with ten teeth for each digit position. He fixed them together so that one wheel drives the other. When the wheel corresponding to units position rotated by ten teeth, it drove the wheel corresponding to the next higher position by one tooth. Thus one could make calculations. Pascal provided dials, which indicated numbers stored on each wheel. He also used suitable "dialing system" to operate the gear wheels. Other people also made a number of such calculators.

Babbage difference and Analytical Engines

Babbage, a British National and the son of a wealthy banker wanted to correct the errors in the logarithm tables being used during his time. In 1822, he made a machine which calculated the successive difference of expressions ($x^2 + ax + b$ is an example of an expression) and prepared table which helped him in his calculations. He wanted to make an accurate calculating machine called "Babbage's Analytical Engine". He conceived that his machine would use input devices, would have a processing part called "mill" where you can perform calculations, would also incorporate. Because of his contributions Charles Babbage is known as the 'Father of Computing'.

Herman Hollerith's Machine

Dr. Herman Hollerith produced cards out of special paper pulp, designed punching machines to punch holes in the card to count census figures and invented sorting machines to read such punched card and collect data. He could complete the job within three years, achieving a speedup of about three times.

ABC Computer

In 1937, Dr. John Atanstoff with the help of his assistant Berry designed the Atanstoff Berry Computer (ABC). The machine laid the foundation for the development of electronic digital computer.

ENIAC- Electronic Numerical Integrator and Calculator

In 1947 John Mauchly and Eckart completed the first large scale Electronic Digital Computer, ENIAC. In this computer, each time a program was changed, the wiring had to be completely rearranged. It weighed 30 tons, contained 18,000 vacuum tubes and occupied a space of 30 by 50 feet.

UNIVAC-I – Universal Automatic Computers

In 1947, after ENIAC became operational Mauchly and Eckart formed their own Company—"The Eckart Mauchly Computer Corporation". Immediately after this they started the design of UNIVAC-I. This was purchased by US bureau of Census. UNIVAC was the first computer dedicated to business applications.

COMPUTER SYSTEM

A computer system is a combination of various components. It performs the system functions such as input, processing, output, storage and control. A computer system consists of the following components:

1. Hardware **2.** Software

Hardware

The physical components of the computer, such as electrical, electronics and mechanical unit are known as the hardware of the computer. That is, the input units, output units and CPU are called hardware. Thus hardware is the equipment involved in the function of a computer. It consists of the components that can be physically handled.

Software

The computer performs operations like addition, subtraction, multiplication and division only when the user instructs it to do so. The user issues instructions and the CPU acts in accordance with the instructions. The sets of instructions, which control the sequence of operations, are known as programs, and collectively programs are called software. The software can be broadly classified into two types. They are: (a) System Software (b) Application Software.

Few terms related to software are :

Firmware

The computer programs permanently stored in ROM or PROM are called firmware. These programs are provided by hardware manufacturer along with the computers. Generally these are booting programs which help in the starting of a computer. Such programs cannot be erased or overwritten.

Bridgeware

The computer components and programs used to translate instructions and information written for one type of computer into a format that another type of computer can understand is called bridge ware. This is necessary because different computers are made by different manufacturers.

Freeware

This is freely available in market. Anybody can use this without any license.

GENERATIONS OF COMPUTERS

First Generation (1940-1956) :

Vacuum Tubes

These computers used vacuum tubes for circuitry and magnetic drums for memory. A magnetic drum is a metal cylinder coated with magnetic iron-oxide material on which data and programs can be stored. Input was based on punched cards and paper tape, and output was displayed on printouts.

First generation computers relied on binary-coded language (language of 0s and 1s) to perform operations and were able to solve only one problem at a time. Each machine was fed with different binary codes and hence were difficult to program. This resulted in lack of versatility and speed. In addition, to run on different types of computers, instructions must be rewritten or recompiled.

Examples: ENIAC, EDVAC, and UNIVAC.

Characteristics of first generation computers:

- These computers were based on vacuum tube technology.
- These computers were very large, and required a lot of space for installation.
- Since thousands of vacuum tubes were used, they generated a large amount of heat. Therefore, air conditioning was essential.
- They were very expensive to operate and used a large amount of electricity.
- Since machine language was used, these computers were difficult to program and use.
- Each individual component had to be assembled manually. Hence, commercial appeal of these computers was poor.

Second Generation Computers (1956 - 1963) : Transistors

In the sixties, there was lot of development in semiconductor field—a field of materials. In 1946,Willam Shockley and a few of his colleagues invented transistors, which do not need any heating to liberate electrons in addition to being smaller in size, they saved power due to the absence of heating and hence the cooling needed. The smaller size resulted in smaller distances that the electrons have to travel to transmit information from one part of the computer to another. Hence calculations became faster. The reliability also increased.

Characteristics of second generation computers:

- These machines were based on transistor technology.

- Assemble language was used to program computers. Hence, programming became more time efficient and less cumbersome.
- Second generation computers still required air conditioning.

Third Generation Computers (1964-early 1970s): Integrated circuits

In second generation computers, one could recognize the circuit components such as transistors, resistors and capacitors distinctly. There were physically separate or 'discreet'. Slowly scientists started integrating these components together so that they are not separate. They were fused into the circuits. People called it large scale integrated circuits (LSI). Computers using such components were called third generation computers. Since components were packed together more densely, the size of computers became smaller. Programmers also developed more sophisticated software. By 1970, engineers developed a device called microprocessor. Lot of circuits was packed into it. Intel 4004 was one such chip.

Characteristics of third generation computers:

- These computers were based on integrated circuit (IC) technology.
- Extensive use of high-level languages became possible.
- Commercial production became easier and cheaper.

Fourth Generation Computers (Early 1970s – till date) : Microprocessors

More and more circuits were packed in a microprocessor. The components were integrated further and very large scale integration (VLSI) technology revolutionized computer field further. Intel Corporation made chips such as 8080 and 8086 to be followed by 80286, 80386, 80486 and now the Pentium processor. These chips perform calculations faster. They are not only used in computers, but also in measuring devices and even in house hold devices such as washing machines.

In course of time, the cost of these computers have come down so much that even individuals bought them so they came to be known as personal computers.

Characteristics of Fourth generation computers:

- Fourth generation computers are micro-processor-based systems.
- These computers are very small.
- These machines generate negligible amount of heat, hence they do not require air conditioning.
- GUI and pointing devices enable users to learn to use the computer quickly.
- Interconnection of computers leads to better communication and resource sharing.

Fifth Generation Computers (Present and beyond) : Artificial Intelligence

Up to fourth generation, the classification was based purely on hardware. Fifth generation computers are classified based on software also. VLSI technology is used in fifth generation computers. They have large main memories. The speed is also high. In addition to all this, Fifth generation computers run software called 'expert systems'.

VARIOUS TYPES OF COMPUTER SYSTEMS

Analog Computers

The analog computers operate by measuring instead of counting. The analog computer works on the supply of continuous electrical signals. The display is also continuous. Its output is in the form of graphs.

Analog Signal: An analog signal is a continuous variable electromagnetic wave. It can consume an infinite number of voltage or current values.

Characteristics of analog computer

The analog computer has the following important characteristics:

(a) It operates by measuring.

(b) It requires physical analog.
(c) It functions on continuously varying quantities.
(d) The output is usually represented in the form of graph.
(e) In analog, the calculations are first converted in equation and later converted into electrical signals.
(f) The accuracy of the output is poor.
(g) It has limited memory space.
(h) It is not versatile. *i.e.*, it has limited application.
(i) The speed of analog computer is low.

Digital Computers

These computers work with quantities represented as digits. They operate on discrete quantities. In digital computer, both numeric and non-numeric information are represented as strings of digits. These computers use binary codes, 0's and 1's, to represent the information. The information is given to the computer in the form of discrete electrical signals.

Characteristics of Digital Computer

The digital computer has the following characteristics:

(a) The calculations are converted into binary numbers *i.e.*, 1's and 0's.
(b) The output is represented in the form of discrete values.
(c) It is versatile in nature and is suitable for a number of applications
(d) In digital computers, the numbers, words and symbols can be used.
(e) Its processing speed is high.
(f) It is highly suitable for business application.

Hybrid Computers

The computer which possess the features of both analog and digital computers are called hybrid computers. That is, the hybrid computers have the good qualities of both analog and digital computer.

Micro Computers

Because of its small size and the use of microprocessor, this computer is called micro computer. All the computers have three units namely input, output and central processing unit, (CPU). The entire CPU is contained in a single or a few microchips. When equipped with memory and input/output control circuitry, it is called micro computer. Its storage capacity is low when compared to mini and main frame computers. It is able to accept most of the high level languages. Large numbers of these can be packed tightly on to a single tiny piece of silicon. Silicon is a material found in sand. The microchip is made by building up a series of very thin layers of silicon and of the tiny components which are held in it.

Workstation

Workstation is a type of computer used for engineering applications (CAD/ CAM), desk top publishing, software development, and other types of applications that required a moderate amount of computing power and relatively high quality graphics capabilities. Workstations generally come with a large, high-resolution graphics screen, at least 64MB (Mega bytes) of RAM, built - in network support, and a graphical user interface. Most workstations also have a mass storage device such as a disk drive, but a special type of workstation, called a diskless workstation, comes without a disk drive. The most common operating systems for workstations are UNIX and Windows NT.

Mini Computers

The size of the mini computer is in between the size of micro and main frame computers. It is more powerful than a micro computer. Mini computers are usually designed to serve multiple users.

Characteristics

1. It is a general purpose machine with a smaller CPU than a main frame
2. Its rate of acceptance and transfer of data is a maximum of 4 million bytes/seconds
3. It can support all high level languages
4. It can support many terminals i.e., more than 20 terminals

Super Computers

The super computers are very costly. Hence it is rarely used. Its capacity is abnormally high, it cannot be compared with any other computers in capacity, function, speed, accuracy, language etc., they have operations done in parallel, rather than sequential. They are employed for specialized applications that require immense amounts of mathematical calculations. The chief difference between a super computer and a main frame computer is that a super computer channels all its power into executing a few programs as fast as possible. But main frame uses its power to execute many programs concurrently. CRAY - 3, Cyber 205, and PARAM are some well known super computers.

Characteristics

(a) They use several processors working simultaneously.
(b) They process at a rapid speed.
(c) They have operations done in parallel, rather than sequentially. They are used in weather forecasting, supersonic aircrafts design and other works that require billions of calculations per second.
(d) They can be used for animated graphics-fluid dynamic calculations etc.

Laptop

This is a small mobile computer, which usually weighs 2-18 pounds (1-6 kilograms), depending on size, materials, and other factors.

As personal computers, laptops are capable of the same tasks as a desktop computer. They contain components that are similar to their desktop counterparts and perform the same functions, but are miniaturized and optimized for mobile use and efficient power consumption.

Basic Principles of Operation of Digital Computer

A computer is basically a device used for processing of data, it performs the following three operations in sequence:
(a) Receives the data and instruction.
(b) Processes the data as per the instructions.
(c) Output the result *i.e.*, information.

This cycle of operation of a computer is known as the input process—Output cycle.

The data are provided to the computer through the input devices. They are encoding such a way, which the computer can understand. The computer then processes the data with the help of instructions provided to it, then it produces a meaningful and desired output known as information.

The above functions are collectively known as the basic principles of operation of a digital computer. These can be expanded as follows:
(a) Accepting inputs
(b) Memory manipulation
(c) Arithmetic operations
(d) Decision making and
(e) Giving output

INPUT/OUTPUT DEVICES

Input Devices

An input device is any machine that feeds data into a computer. For example, a keyboard is an input device. Input devices other than the keyboard are sometimes called alternate devices. Trackballs and light pens are all alternate input devices.

Keyboard

Computer keyboards are similar to electric-typewriter keyboards but contain additional keys. The keys on computer keyboards are often classified as follows:

- **Alphanumeric Keys:** letters and numbers.
- **Punctuation Keys:** comma, period, semicolon, and so on.
- **Special Keys:** function keys, control keys, arrow keys, Caps Lock key, and so on.

The standard layout of letters, numbers, and punctuation is known as a QWERTY keyboard because the first five keys on the top row of letters spell QWERTY. Another keyboard design, which has letters positioned for speed typing, is the Dvorak keyboard.

There is no standard computer keyboard, although many manufacturers imitate the standards of PCs. There are actually three different PC standards: the original PC keyboard, with 84 keys; the AT keyboard, also with 84 keys; and the enhanced keyboard, with 101 keys. The three differ somewhat in placement of Function keys, the Control key, the Return key, and the Shift keys.

Mouse

Mouse is a device that controls the movement of the cursor or pointer on a display screen. Its name is derived from its shape, which looks a bit like a mouse, its connecting wire that one can imagine to be the mouse's tail, and the fact that one must make it scurry along a surface. As we move the mouse, the pointer on the display screen moves in the same direction. Mouse contains at least one button and sometimes as many as three, which have different functions depending on what program is running. Now-a-days, mouse is connected with computer through USB port.

Invented by Douglas Engelbart of Stanford Research Center in 1963.

Types of Mouse: There are three basic types of Mouse.

- **Mechanical:** It has a rubber or metal ball on its underside that can roll in all directions. Mechanical sensors within the mouse detect the direction the ball is rolling and move the Screen pointer accordingly.
- **Optomechanical:** It is same as a mechanical mouse, but uses optical sensors to detect motion of the ball.
- **Optical:** It does a laser to detect the mouse's movement. One must move the mouse along a special mat with a grid so that the optical mechanism has a frame of reference. Optical mice have no mechanical moving parts. They respond more quickly and precisely than mechanical and optomechanical mice, but they are also more expensive.

Trackball

This is another pointing device. Essentially, a trackball is a mouse lying on its back. To move the pointer, we rotate the ball with our thumb, our fingers, or the palm of our hand. There are usually one to three buttons next to the ball, which we use just like mouse buttons.

Joystick

With a joystick, the pointer continues moving in the direction the joystick is pointing. Most joysticks include two buttons called triggers. It has a lever that moves in all directions and controls the movement of a pointer or some other display symbols. A joystick is similar to a mouse, except that with a mouse the cursor stops moving as soon as we stop moving the mouse. Joysticks are used mostly for computer games, but they are also used occasionally for CAD/CAM systems and other applications.

Scanners

Scanner is an input device that can read text or illustrations printed on paper and translate the information into a form that the computer can use. A scanner works by digitizing an image-dividing it into a grid of boxes and representing each box with either a zero or a one, depending on whether the box is filled in. The resulting matrix of bits, called a bit map, can then be stored in a file, displayed on a screen, and manipulated by programs.

Optical scanners do not distinguish text from illustrations; they represent all images as bit maps. Therefore, we cannot directly edit text that has been scanned. To edit text read by an optical scanner, we need an Optical Character Recognition (OCR) system to translate the image into ASCII characters.

Magnetic Ink Character Recognition [MICR]

This allows the computer to recognize characters printed using magnetic ink. MICR is a direct-entry method used in banks. This technology is used to automatically read those frustrating-looking numbers on the bottom of the cheque. A special-purpose machine known as a reader/sorter reads characters made of ink containing magnetized particles. A related technology is the magnetic strip, used on the back of credit cards and bank debit cards, that allows readers such as Automated Teller Machines (ATMs) to read account information and facilitate monetary transactions. Another example of magnetic strip technology is in ID cards, which can be used for a variety of functions from attendance monitoring to restricting access to specific locations.

Optical Character Recognition [OCR]

It refers to the branch of computer science that involves reading text from paper and translating the images into a form that the computer can manipulate. An OCR system enables to take a book or a magazine article and feed it directly into an electronic computer file.

All OCR systems include an optical scanner for reading text, and a sophisticated software for analyzing images. Most OCR systems use a combination of hardware (specialized circuit boards) and software to recognize characters, although some inexpensive systems do it entirely through software. Advanced OCR systems can read text in a large variety of fonts, but they still have difficulty with handwritten text.

The potential of OCR systems is enormous because they enable users to harness the power of computers to access printed documents. OCR is already being used widely in the legal profession, where searches that once required hours or days can now be accomplished in a few seconds.

Optical Mark Recognition [OMR]

OMR also called mark sensing, is a technology where an OMR device senses the presence or absence of a mark, such as a pencil mark. OMR is used in tests such as aptitude tests for different competition/ entrance examinations.

Bar Code Reader

Most of the persons are probably familiar with the bar code readers in supermarkets, bookshops, etc. Bar code readers are photoelectric scanners that read the bar codes, or vertical zebra striped marks, printed on product containers. Supermarkets use a bar code system called the Universal Product Code (UPC).

The bar code identifies the product to the supermarket's computer, which has a description and the latest price of the product. The computer automatically tells the Point of Sales (POS) terminal what the price is.

Touch Screen

Touch screen is a type of display screen that has a touch sensitive transparent panel covering the screen. Instead of using a pointing device such as a mouse or light pen, we can use our finger to point directly to objects on the screen.

Light Pen

Light Pen is an input device that utilizes a light-sensitive detector to select objects on a display screen. A Light Pen is similar to a mouse, except that with a light pen we can move the pointer and select objects on a display screen by directly pointing to the objects by light pen.

Output Devices

Output is anything that comes out of a computer. Output can be meaningful information or gibberish, and it can appear in a variety of forms - as binary numbers, as characters, as pictures, and as printed pages. Output devices include display screens, loudspeakers, printers, plotters, etc.

Monitor

Monitor is another term for the display screen. The term monitor, however, usually refers to the entire box, whereas display screen can mean just the screen. In addition, the term monitor often implies graphics capabilities.

Classification of Monitors: There are many ways to classify monitors.

(i) **Based on Colour:** The most basic in terms of colour capabilities.

(ii) **Based on Signals:** Another common way of classifying monitors is in terms of the type of signal they accept: analog or digital.

- **Digital Monitor:** A digital monitor accepts digital signals rather than analog signals. A digital monitor then translates the digital signals into analog signals that control the actual display.

  Although digital monitors are fast and produce clear images, they cannot display variable colours continuously.

- **Analog Monitor:** This is the traditional type of colour display screen that has been used for years in televisions. In reality, all monitors based on CRT technology (that is, all monitors except flat-panel displays) are analog. Some monitors, however, are called digital monitors because they accept digital signals from the video adapter. EGA monitors, for example, must be digital because the EGA standard specifies digital signals. Digital monitors must nevertheless translate the signals into an analog form before displaying images.

Printer

Printer is a device that prints text or illustrations on paper and in many cases on transparencies and other media. There are many different types of printers. In terms of the technology utilized, printers fall into the following categories:

(i) **Daisy-wheel Printer:** Daisy-wheel printers are a type of printer that produces letter-quality type. A daisy-wheel printer works on the same principle as a ball-head typewriter. The daisy-wheel is a disk made of plastic or metal on which characters stand out in relief along the outer edge. To print a character, the printer rotates the disk until the desired letter is facing the paper.

(ii) **Dot-matrix Printer:** Dot-matrix printers create characters by striking pins against an ink ribbon. Each pin makes a dot, and combinations of dots form characters and illustrations.

These printers are inexpensive and relatively fast, but they do not produce high-quality output. Dot-matrix printers vary in two important characteristics:

- **Speed :** Measured in characters per second (cps), the speed can vary from about 50 to over 500 cps. Most dot-matrix printers offer different speeds depending on the quality of print desired.
- **Print quality :** Determined by the number of pins (the mechanisms that print the dots), it can vary from 9 to 24. The best dot-matrix printers (24 pins) can produce near letter-quality type, although we can still see a difference if we look closely.

(iii) **Ink-jet Printer:** Ink-iet printers work by spraying ionized ink at a sheet of paper. Magnetized plates in the ink's path direct the ink onto the paper in the desired shapes. Ink-jet printers are capable of producing high quality print approaching to that produced by laser printers. A typical ink-jet printer provides a resolution of 300 dots per inch, although some newer models offer higher resolutions.

(iv) **Laser Printer:** Laser printer utilizes a laser beam to produce an image on a drum. The light of the laser alters the electrical charge on the drum wherever it hits. The drum is then rolled through a reservoir of toner, which is picked up by the charged portions of the drum. Finally, the toner is transferred to the paper through a combination of heat and pressure. This is also the way copy machines work.

(v) **WD & LED Printers:** These are similar to a laser printer but uses liquid crystals or light-emitting diodes rather than a laser to produce an image on the drum.

(vi) **Line Printer:** Line printers are high-speed printers capable of printing an entire line at one time. A fast line printer can print as many as 3,000 lines per minute. The disadvantages of line printers are that they can print only one font, they cannot print graphics, the print quality is low, and they are very noisy.

Plotter

Plotter is a device that draws pictures on paper based on commands from a computer. Plotters differ from printers as they draw lines using a pen. As a result, they can produce continuous lines/ whereas printers can only simulate lines by printing a closely spaced series of dots. Multicolour plotters use different-coloured pens to draw different colors. In general, plotters are considerably more expensive than printers. They are used in engineering applications where precision is mandatory.

Sound Cards & Speakers

Sound card is an expansion board that enables a computer to manipulate and output sounds. Sound cards enable the computer to output sound through speakers connected to the board, to record sound input from a microphone connected to the computer, and manipulate sound stored on a disk. Nearly all sound cards support MIDI, a standard for representing music electronically.

HARDWARE & SOFTWARE

A computer system consists of hardware, the physical unit (parts) of the computer that are capable of computing and manipulating information and software (set of instructions or programs) that carries out predefined tasks to complete a given job. The computer performs operations like addition, subtraction, multiplication and division only when the user instructs it to do so. The user issues instructions and the CPU acts in accordance with the instructions. The sets of instructions, which control the sequence of operations, are known as programs, and collectively programs are called software.

Components of Hardware

I. **Input unit:** This unit accepts instructions and data.

II. **Output unit:** This unit communicates the results to the user.

III. **Storage unit:** This unit stores temporary and final results.

IV. **Central Processing Unit (CPU):** This unit performs processing of instructions and data inside the computer.

The CPU has three components:

(a) The Control Unit
(b) The Arithmetic Logic Unit (ALU) and
(c) The Memory Unit.

(a) Control Unit: It controls the overall operation of the computer system. It is considered as the heart of the computer system. It controls all the other units, directs them to operate in a proper way and co-ordinates various operations performed.

It instructs the input device to transfer the data and instructions to the main memory and then to the arithmetic and logic unit (ALU). Then, it sends the processed result from ALU to the memory unit for storage and transfers it to the visual display unit or to the printer.

The control unit coordinates the various parts of the computer system—the arithmetic logic unit, the memory unit and the peripheral units. Besides, it controls the flow of data into, from and within the main storage as per the program instructions.

To perform its control operations effectively and quickly, the control unit has four basic components. They are

(i) Instruction Register
(ii) Decoder
(iii) Address Register and
(iv) Instruction Counter

The instruction register receives one by one the instructions to be executed in the required sequence. Then, the operation code of the instructions is transferred to decoder, which decodes the operation code. And it activates the appropriate circuits of the arithmetic and logic unit to perform the operation. The address register enables the data in the location specified in the instruction to be transferred to a specified accumulator for the arithmetic and logic unit.

(b) Arithmetic Logic Unit (ALU): This unit performs two kinds of operations, the arithmetic processing and logical processing. In arithmetic processing, it performs all mathematical operations such as addition, subtraction, multiplication and division. In logical processing, it performs the relational and logical operations such as comparing larger or smaller values, true or false statements, etc.

(c) Memory Unit: This unit holds the intermediate results during the course of calculations and provides the data as and when required. This internal storage is also called primary memory or main memory. This memory takes the data from an input device and stores it until the computer is ready to process it. It also stores processed data and intermediate results. When the processing is finished, it transfers the results to an output device.

Software

Software is a generic term for organized collection of computer data and instructions. It is responsible for controlling, integrating, and managing the hardware components of a computer and to accomplish specific tasks. In other words, software tells the computer what to do and how to do it. For example, software instructs the hardware what to display on the user's screen, what kinds of input to take from the user, and what kinds of output to generate. Thus, software communicates with the hardware by organizing the control sequences, and the hardware carries out the instructions defined by the software.

A computer needs to be instructed to perform any task. These instructions are given in the form of computer programs, which are written in computer programming languages. A program controls the activity of the processor. The moment the hardware (processor, memory, etc.) acts as per the instructions of a program, the program is said to be in running or executing state.

A set of programs, which are specifically written to provide the user a precise functionality like solving a specific problem is termed as a software package. For example, word processing software package provides functionality to the computer so that it can be used to create text documents like letters and mailing lists. Similarly, an image processing software package assists a user in drawing and manipulating graphics.

Difference between Hardware & Software

Hardware

1. It is the physical unit of the computer
2. Hardware understands only machine language, lower level language or binary
3. It works with binary code, the presence or absence of Pulses as 1's or 0's.

Software

1. It is a collection of programs to bring the hardware system into operation
2. It is written by a well versed programmer and generally in higher level language which is readable by human being.
3. It is represented by the Higher Level Languages such as BASIC, COBOL, etc.,

COMPUTER MEMORY

There are two kinds of computer memory: primary and secondary. Primary memory is accessible directly by the processing unit. RAM is an example of primary memory. As soon as the computer is switched off the contents of the primary memory is lost. You can store and retrieve data much faster with primary memory compared to secondary memory. Secondary memory such as floppy disks, magnetic disk, etc., is located outside the computer. Primary memory is more expensive than secondary memory. Because of this the size of primary memory is less than that of secondary memory.

Computer memory is used to store two things: (i) instructions to execute a program and (ii) data. When the computer is doing any job, the data that have to be processed are stored in the primary memory. This data may come from an input device like keyboard or from a secondary storage device like a floppy disk. In computer's memory both programs and data are stored in the binary form.

Primary Memory

The primary memory as you know in the computer is in the form of IC's (Integrated Circuits). These circuits are called Random Access Memory (RAM). A bit is an acronym for binary digit, which stands for one binary piece of information. This can be either 0 or 1. The Primary or internal storage section is made up of several small storage locations (ICs) called cells. Each of these cells can store a fixed number of bits called word length. Each cell has a unique number assigned to it called the address of the cell and it is used to identify the cells.

Capacity of Primary Memory

Each cell of memory contains one character or 1 byte of data. So the capacity is defined in terms of byte or words. Thus 64 kilobyte (KB) memory is capable of storing 64 × 1024 = 65,536 bytes. (1 kilobyte is 1024 bytes). A memory size ranges from few kilobytes in small systems to several thousand kilobytes in large mainframe and super computer.

Types of Primary Memory

Random Access Memory (RAM): The primary storage is referred to as random access memory (RAM) because it is possible to randomly select and use any location of the memory directly store and retrieve data. It takes same time to any address of the memory as the first address. It is also called read/write memory. The storage of data and instructions inside the primary storage is temporary. It disappears from RAM as soon as the power to the computer is switched off. The memories, which loose their content on failure of power supply, are known as volatile memories. So, now we can say that RAM is volatile memory.

Read Only Memory (ROM): There is another memory in computer, which is called Read Only Memory (ROM). Again it is the ICs inside the PC that form the ROM. The storage of program and data in the ROM is permanent. The ROM stores some standard processing programs supplied by the manufacturers to operate the personal computer. The ROM can only be read by the CPU but it cannot be changed. The basic input/output program is stored in the ROM that examines and initializes various equipment attached to the PC when the switch is made ON. The memories, which do not loose their content on failure of power supply, are known as non-volatile memories. ROM is non-volatile memory.

Programmable Read Only Memory (PROM): There is another type of primary memory in computer, which is called Programmable Read Only Memory (PROM). You know that it is not possible to modify or erase programs stored in ROM, but it is possible for you to store your program in PROM chip. Once the programmes are written it cannot be changed and remain intact even if power is switched off. Therefore programs or instructions written in PROM or ROM cannot be erased or changed.

Erasable Programmable Read Only Memory (EPROM): This stands for Erasable Programmable Read Only Memory, which over come the problem of PROM & ROM. EPROM chip can be programmed time and again by erasing the information stored earlier in it. Information stored in EPROM exposing the chip for some time ultraviolet light and it erases chip is reprogrammed using a special programming facility. When the EPROM is in use information can only be read.

Cache Memory

The speed of CPU is extremely high compared to the access time of main memory. Therefore the performance of CPU decreases due to the slow speed of main memory. To decrease the mismatch in operating speed, a small memory chip is attached between CPU and Main memory whose access time is very close to the processing speed of CPU. It is called CACHE memory. CACHE memories are accessed much faster than conventional RAM. It is used to store programs or data currently being executed or temporary data frequently used by the CPU.

Registers

The CPU processes data and instructions with high speed, there is also movement of data between various units of computer. It is necessary to transfer the processed data with high speed. So the computer uses a number of special memory units called registers. They are not part of the main memory but they store data or information temporarily and pass it on as directed by the control unit.

Secondary Memory

Therefore additional memory is required in all the computer systems. This memory is called auxiliary memory or secondary storage.

In this type of memory the cost per bit of storage is low. However, the operating speed is slower than that of the primary storage. Huge volume of data are stored here on permanent basis and transferred to the primary storage as and when required. Most widely used secondary storage devices are magnetic tapes and magnetic disk.

Magnetic Tape

Magnetic tapes are used for large computers like mainframe computers where large volume of data is stored for a longer time. In PC also you can use tapes in the form of cassettes. It can be 12.5 mm to 25 mm wide plastic film-type and 500 meter to 1200 meter long which is coated with magnetic material. It is similar to cassette tape recorder.

Magnetic Disk

Magnetic disks used in computer are made on the same principle. It rotates with very high speed inside the computer drive. Data is stored on both the surface of the disk. Magnetic disks are most popular for direct access storage device. Each disk consists of a number of invisible concentric circles called tracks. Information is recorded on tracks of a disk surface in the form of tiny magnetic spots.

Floppy Disk

It is similar to magnetic disk discussed. They are 5.25 inch or 3.5 inch in diameter. They come in single or double density and recorded on one or both surface of the diskette. The capacity of a 5.25 inch floppy is 1.2 mega bytes whereas for 3.5 inch floppy is 1.44 mega bytes. It is cheaper than any other storage devices and is portable. The floppy is a low cost device particularly suitable for personal computer system.

Optical Disk

With every new application and software there is greater demand for memory capacity. It is the necessity to store large volume of data that has led to the development of optical disk storage medium. Optical disks can be divided into the following categories:

1. **Compact Disk/ Read Only Memory (CD-ROM):** CD-ROM disks are made of reflective metals. CD-ROM is written during the process of manufacturing by high power laser beam. Here the storage density is very high, storage cost is very low and access time is relatively fast. Each disk is approximately 4 1/2 inches in diameter and can hold over 600 MB of data. As the CD-ROM can be read only we cannot write or make changes into the data contained in it.
2. **Erasable Optical Disk:** These are optical disks where data can be written, erased and re-written. This also applies a laser beam to write and re-write the data. These disks may be used as alternatives to traditional disks. Erasable optical disks are based on a technology known as magnetic optical (MO). To write a data bit on to the erasable optical disk the MO drive's laser beam heats a tiny, precisely defined point on the disk's surface and magnetises it.

Central Processing Unit [CPU]

The Central Processing Unit [CPU] is the brain of any computer system. In a computer system all major calculations and comparisons are made inside the CPU. The CPU is also responsible for activating and controlling the operations of other units of a computer system.

The control unit primary memory and the arithmetic logic unit of a computer system are jointly known as the Central Processing Unit. While the control unit takes care of the flow of data from input unit to storage unit and the flow of final results to the output unit, the arithmetic logic unit is the place where the actual execution of instructions taking place during the processing operation.

SOFTWARE

The computer being a machine cannot perform on its own. It needs to be instructed to perform even a simple task like adding two numbers. Computers work on a set of instructions called computer software (programs), which clearly specify the ways to carry out a task. Software can be categorized as system software and application software. System software is a generic term for referring to any computer program whose purpose is to help the user to run the computer system, whereas application software employes the capabilities of a computer directly to a task that the user wishes to perform.

Categories of Software

System Software

System software consists of several programs, which are directly responsible for controlling, integrating, and managing the individual hardware components of a computer system.

In simple terms, system software makes the computer functional. They provide basic functionality like file management, visual display, and keyboard input which are used by application software to accomplish these functions. Some examples of system software are:

- OPERATING SYSTEM
- DEVICE DRIVERS
- LANGUAGE TRANSLATORS
- SYSTEM UTILITIES

Operating System

It is the first layer of software loaded into computer memory when it starts up. As the first software layer, all other software that gets loaded after it depends on it for various common core services. These common core services include disk access, memory management, takes scheduling, and user interfacing. In addition, the operating system ensures that different programs executing at the same time do not interfere with each other. It provides a software platform on top of which other programs can run. In simple words, the operating system organizes and controls the hardware. Examples of operating systems are Windows XP, UNIX, and LINUX.

Device Drivers

Device drivers are system programs, which are responsible for proper functioning of devices. Every device, whether it is a printer, monitor, mouse or keyboard, has a driver program associated with it for its proper functioning.

System Utility

System utility programs perform day-to-day tasks related to the maintenance of the computer system. They are used to support, enhance, and secure existing programs and data in the computer system. They are generally small programs, having specific tasks to perform:

(a) ***File Management:*** These utilities make it easier to manage data files. Many programs are written to help users to find the files, create and organize directions, copy, move, and remove files.

(b) ***Backup:*** It may happen that sometime data files are corrupted, or accidentally deleted. In such a case, data backups become very useful. A backup system utility is essential for those organizations, which want to keep their data intact.

(c) ***Data Recovery:*** It is the process of retrieving deleted or inaccessible data from failed electronic storage media such as computer hard disk drives, removable media, optical devices, and tape cartridges.

(d) ***Virus Protection:*** Anti-virus programs are essential system utilities for a computer system functioning in a network. They provide the security to the system from viruses that can damage the computer system.

(e) ***Disk Management:*** Disk management program includes various system softwares like disk defragmenter, data compressor and disk formatting tools. De-fragmentation implies putting fragments of files in a sequential order onto the disk which reduces the time to access the file.

(f) ***Firewall:*** It is commonly used to protect information such as e-mail and data files within a physical building or organization. Essentially, a firewall is designed to protect a computer from unauthorized access, especially via network.

(g) ***Disk Cleanup:*** To keep a computer running smoothly, regular maintenance is vital. Therefore, one should use the disk cleanup utility, which easily determines which files on hard drive are no longer needed, then delete those files.

WORD KEYBOARD SHORTCUTS

Action	Key Stroke
Open a file	Ctrl + O
New file	Ctrl + N
Close a file	Ctrl + W
Save As	F12
Save	Ctrl + S or Shift + F12
Print Preview	Ctrl + F2
Print	Ctrl + P
Show/Hide paragraph symbols	Ctrl + *
Spelling and grammar	F7
Help	F1
Find	Ctrl + F
Replace	Ctrl + H
Go To	Ctrl + G
Select all - entire document	Ctrl + A
Select from cursor to beginning of line	Shift + Home
Select from cursor to end of line	Shift + End
Go to beginning of line	Home
Go to end of line	End
Go to beginning of document	Ctrl + Home
Go to end of document	Ctrl + End
Cut	Ctrl + X
Copy	Ctrl + C
Paste	Ctrl + V
Undo	Ctrl + Z
Redo	Ctrl + Y
Format painter	Ctrl + Shift + C
Left alignment	Ctrl + L
Center alignment	Ctrl + E
Right alignment	Ctrl + R
Justified	Ctrl + J

Action	Key Stroke
Delete previous word	Ctrl + Backspace
Apply bulleted list	Ctrl + Shift + L
Indent	Ctrl + M
Page break	Ctrl + Enter
Font face	Ctrl + Shift + F
Font size	Ctrl + Shift + P
Bold	Ctrl + B
Italics	Ctrl + I
Underline	Ctrl + U
Double underline	Ctrl + Shift + D
Word underline	Ctrl + Shift + A
Change case	Shift + F3
Subscript	Ctrl + =
Superscript	Ctrl + Shift + =
Make web hyperlink	Ctrl + K
Go to next cell	Tab
Go to previous cell	Shift + Tab
Go to beginning of column	Alt + PageUp
Highlight to beginning of column	Alt + Shift + PageUp
Go to end of column	Alt + PageDown
Highlight to end of column	Alt + Shift + PageDown
Go to beginning of row	Alt + Home
Highlight to beginning of row	Alt + Shift + Home
Go to end of row	Alt + End
Highlight to end of row	Alt + Shift + End
Column break	Ctrl + Shift + Enter
Copyright ©	Alt + Ctrl + C
Date field	Alt + Shift + D
Go to footnotes	Alt + Ctrl + F
Show/Hide ¶	Ctrl + Shift + 8
Theasaurus	Shift + F7

Note: *A plus sign indicates that the keys need to be pressed at the same time.*

Application Software

The most often seen software by a user is the application software. It is used to accomplish specific tasks rather than just managing a computer system. For a user, the computer system has no specific use without application software. Application software may consist of a single program, such as Microsoft's Note pad (for writing and editing simple text). It may also consist of a collection of programs, often called a software package, which work together to accomplish a task, such as database management software. Application software may also include a larger collection of related but independent programs and packages (a software suite), which have a common user interface or shared data format, such as Microsoft Office suite.

Applications softwares are dependent on system softwares. A system software (like operating system) acts as an interface between the user and the computer hardware, while application software performs specific tasks. Applications are pieces of software that perform tasks for the user besides helping the computer operate, which is the tasks of system software. Applications softwares are controlled by system software, which manages hardware devices and performs background tasks for them. The distinction between the two is important. Without system software, the computer will not run, and without application software, the computer, no matter how powerful, will not be helpful in meeting user requirements. Think of it this way applications apply the computer's thinking power to business tasks such as tracking the general ledger or billing your customers.

Application software ranges from games, calculators, and word processors (document creating programs), to programs that "paint" images on screen (image editors). Applications represent real world tasks. They can be easily divided by looking at exactly what function they serve. Some of the most commonly used application software is discussed below:

1. Word processor

A word processor is software used to compose, format, edit, and print electronic documents. Word processing is one of the earliest applications for office productivity and the personal computer. It involves not only typing, but also checking the spelling and grammar of the text and arranging it correctly on the page.

2. Spreadsheets

One of the first commercial uses of computers was in processing payroll and other financial records, so the programs were designed to generate reports in the standard "spreadsheet" format book keepers and accountants used. A spreadsheet application is a rectangular grid, which allows text, numbers, and complex functions to be entered into a matrix of thousands of individual cells. The spreadsheet provides sheets containing cells each of which may contain text and / or numbers. Microsoft Excel and Lotus 1-2-3 are examples of spreadsheet applications.

3. Database management systems

Database management software is a collection of computer programs that allow storage, modification, and extraction of information from a database in an efficient manner. It supports the structuring of the database in a standard format and provides tools for data input, verification, storage, retrieval, query, and manipulation. FoxPro and Oracle are database management systems.

OPERATING SYSTEM

It is the first layer of software loaded into computer memory when it starts up. As the first software layer, all other software that gets loaded after it depends on it for various common core services. In simple words, the operating system organizes and controls the hardware. Examples of operating systems are Windows XP, UNIX, and Linux.

The operating system is a software program that acts as an interface between the user and the computer. It is used to control and manage the hardware components such as keyboard, monitor, printer, scanner etc.

Functions of an Operating System

(a) **Process Management:** It handles the creation,

deletion, suspension, resumption, and synchronization of process.

(b) **Memory Management:** It handles allocation and de-allocation of memory space as required by various programs.

(c) **File Management:** It is responsible for creation and deletion of files and directories. It also organizes, stores, retrieves, names, and protects all the files.

(d) **Device Management:** It manages all the devices of the computer system such as printers and modems. If any device fails, it detects the device failure and notifies the same to the user.

(e) **Security Management:** Protects system resources and information against destruction and unauthorized use.

(f) **User interface:** Provides the interface between the user and the hardware.

Types of Operating System

These are the different types of operating system :

DOS (Disk Operating System)

MS-DOS was the widely used operating system before the introduction of the Windows operating system. The DOS is a set of computer programs. The main functions of DOS are to manage files, allocate system resources according to the requirement.

DOS Commands

We can type all DOS commands in either upper or lower case letters. There are two basic types of DOS commands:

- **Internal commands**
  These commands, like COPY, DEL, and TYPE, are stored in computers memory. Many DOS commands fall into this category.
- **External commands**
  This group of commands is stored on the disk. To use them, either insert the DOS floppy disk, or change to the directory on hard disk which contains DOS external commands. Examples of external commands include FORMAT, DISKCOPY, and CHKDSK.
  Some commands can take several forms. These separate forms are used by including various parameters with the command. Parameters, which will be discussed with each command, are indicated by a / mark. Here is an example of command with an attached parameter:
  C:\>DIR/W
  [DOS command DIR is attached with parameter W]
  All DOS commands must be activated by pressing the <Enter> key after typing the command.

Windows Operating System

Microsoft Windows is the most popular operating system around the world. Even those who are new to computers can use it with a little practice. With the help of Windows, we can operate the computer just by clicking the mouse buttons, Windows95, Windows98, Windows2000 and Windows7 are the various versions of Windows.

Windows is an operating system. It is the extension of the disk operating system.

The Unix Operating System

Like DOS and windows, there's another operating system called UNIX.

PROGRAMMING LANGUAGES

Computers are machines. Unfortunately they cannot understand natural languages, such as Hindi, English, Tamil, etc. that human beings speak and understand. Therefore, to give instructions to computers, different languages have been developed. These languages are called computer languages. To get a particular work done by computers, programmers write instructions using these computer languages. Each computer language has its own vocabulary of a natural language that we speak. Each natural language has its rules and grammar. Similarly, each computer language too has its set of rules that are called as syntax. As computers are not intelligent, we have to use the exact syntax rules of the computer language whenever we write any computer program. Otherwise, the computer will not be able to understand our instructions.

Over the last few decades, several computer languages have developed. Different computer languages are suitable for different applications. For example, COBOL (Common business oriented Language) may be more suitable for business applications, whereas FORTRAN may be more suitable for scientific or engineering applications. We can classify all computer languages into three categories.

Programming Languages

Computer languages are classified into three categories:

1. Low Level Language / Machine Language
2. High level Languages:

Low Level Language / Machine language

The form in which information is denoted or represented by a combination of "1" and "0"s is called machine language. Programs and data are ultimately represented in machine language in memory and other hardware of the computer.

To start with computer programmers used machine language for programming. It was tedious since each operation that the computer has to perform is denoted by a particular combination of "1"s and "0"s. Also each computer had its own machine language code. One has to remember all these codes to write a program.

High Level Languages

During 1960s computers started to gain popularity and it became necessary to develop languages that were more like natural languages such as English so that a common user could use the computer efficiently. Since assembly language required deep knowledge of computer architecture, it demanded programming as well as hardware skills to use computers. Due to computer's widespread usage, early 1960s saw the emergence of the third generations programming languages (3GL). Languages such as COBOL, FORTRAN, BASIC, and C are examples of 3GLs and are considered high-level languages.

High level languages are similar to English language. Programs written using these languages can be machine independent. A single high-level statement can substitute several instructions in machine or assembly language. Unlike assembly and machine programs, highlevel programs may be used with different types of computers with little or no modification, thus reducing the re-programming time.

Translating High Level Language to Machine Language

Since computers understand only machine language, it is necessary to convert the highlevel language programs into machine language codes. This is achieved by using language translators or language processors, generally known as compilers, interpreters or other routines that accepts statements in one language and produces equivalent statements in another language.

Compiler

A compiler is a kind of translator that translates a program into another program, known as target language. Usually, the term compiler is used for language translator of high-level language into machine language. The compiler replaces single high-level statement with a series of machine language instruction.

Once the program has been compiled, the resulting machine code is saved in an executable file, which can be run on its own at any time. To be precise, once the executable is generated, there is no need for the actual source code file. Anyway, it is worthwhile to keep the source file(s) because if the source code is modified, it is necessary to recompile the program again to regenerate the executable file containing amendments.

Interpreter

Unlike compilers, an interpreter translates a statement in a program and executes the statement immediately, before translating the next source language statement. Similar to compilers, every interpreted language such as BASIC and LISP has its own interpreters.

Disadvantages of High Level Languages

The main disadvantages of this language are:

1. Poor Control on Hardware: High-level

languages are developed to ease the pressure on programmers so that they do not have to know the intricacies of hardware. As a result, sometimes the applications written in high-level languages cannot completely harness the total power available at hardware level.

2. **Less Efficient:** The HLL applications are less efficient as far as computation time is concerned. This is because, unlike low-level languages, high-level languages must be created and sent through another processing program known as a compiler. This process of translation increases the execution time of an application. Programs written in high-level languages take more time to execute, and require more memory space. Hence, critical applications are generally written in low-level languages.

Type of High-Level Languages

Languages are often referred to as generations, the idea being that machine languages were the first generation and assembly languages were the second generation. High-level languages are sometimes used to refer all languages above the assembly level. Here we will subdivide high-level languages into three generation.

1. Procedural-oriented or third generation
2. Problem-oriented or fourth generation
3. Natural or fifth generation

Procedural-oriented Languages

High-level languages are often classified according to whether they solve general problems or specific problems. General-purpose programming languages are called procedural languages or third generation languages. They are languages such as Pascal, BASIC, COBOL, and FORTRAN, which are designed to express the logic, the procedure, of a problem. Because of their flexibility, procedural languages are able to solve a variety of problems. Procedural languages have many advantages over machine and assembly languages:

1. The program statements resemble English and hence are easier to work with.
2. Because of their English-like nature, less time is required to develop a program for a given problem.
3. Once coded, programs are easier to understand and modify.
4. The procedural languages are machine-independent.

However, procedure-oriented languages still have some disadvantages compared to machine and assembly languages:

1. Programs are executed more slowly.
2. The languages use computer resources less efficiently.

Problem-oriented Languages and Application Generators

Third-generation languages, such as BASIC or Pascal, require you to instruct the computer in step-by-step fashion. Fourth-generation languages, also known as problem-oriented languages, are high-level languages designed to solve specific problems or develop specific applications by enabling you to describe what you want rather than step-by-step procedures for getting there. Fourth-generation languages may be categorized into several kinds of application development tools:

1. Personal computer applications software
2. Query languages and report generators
3. Decision support systems and financial planning languages
4. Application generators

Natural Languages

Two popular natural languages are LISP and PROLOG. Natural languages have two characteristics:

1. They are designed to make the connections that humans have with computers more natural - more humanlike.
2. They are designed to allow the computer to become "smarter"—to actually simulate the learning process by remembering and improving upon earlier information.

Structured Query Language (SQL) and other Query Languages

A query language is a set of commands to create, update and access data from a database allowing

The memory is measured by the following units

(*a*) **BIT (Binary digit):** It is the smallest possible unit of information. It can be either 0 or 1.

(*b*) **NIBBLE:** Four bits form one nibble.

(*c*) **BYTE:** It is a unit of information consisting of fixed number of bits. It is a combination of 8 bits.

(*d*) **CHARACTER:** It is represented by one byte. It can be a letter, digit, punctuation mark or special characters.

(*e*) **WORD:** The combination of 2 bytes or 4 bytes or 8 bytes is a word.

The data measurement is as follows:

8 bits	-	1 byte
1024 bytes	-	1 Kilo Byte (KB)
1024 KB	-	1 Mega Byte (MB)
1024 MB	-	1 Giga Byte (GB)
1024 GB	-	1 Tera Byte (TB)

(*f*) **SECONDARY STORAGE (Backing/Auxiliary Storage):**

(*a*) Magnetic disk – it includes the following:
Hard disk – Rigid, Floppy disk – Flexible

(*b*) Magnetic tape

(*c*) Magnetic drum

(*d*) Mass storage Device – cartridge

(*e*) Optical Disks – CD ROM (Compact Disk – ROM)

users to raise adhoc queries / questions interactively without the help of programmers. A structured query language (SQL) is a set of thirty (30) English like commands which has since become an adoptable standard. The structured query language syntax use some set of commands regardless of the database management system software like 'Select', 'From', 'Where'.

Some query languages have been designed in such a way that the command used is as close to Standard English text as possible. Query languages in a user-friendly way allow users to retrieve data from database without exposure to—

(i) file/record structure

(ii) processes that the system performs

(iii) Languages like Common Business Oriented Language (COBOL), Beginner's All-purpose Symbolic Instruction Code (BASIC) or such other standard programming languages. Data retrieving efficiency may be improved by gaining knowledge about query shortcuts, query strategies and the types of data used in the database. A training and development program for this purpose may prove useful for the end users.

Language Translator

A language translator is a system software which translates a computer program written by a user into a machine understandable form. The most elemental form of programming uses only the binary digits 0 and 1, which is directly understood by the electronic circuits. A program that have only binary digits is called a machine language program. It is difficult to write or understand machine language programs, as these consist of 0s and 1s.

Assemblers

Assemblers are used exclusively with assembly languages. They work similarly to compilers, translating an assembly language program into object code. Because assembly language programs are usually more machine efficient than those written in high-level languages, a two-step translation process may take place. First, the high-level language is translated to assembly language; then, using an assembler, it is converted to machine language.

CATEGORIES OF NETWORK

Network categories can be divided on the basis of its size, ownership, distance it covers and its physical architecture:

(i) LAN: LAN stands for Local Area Network. These networks evolved around the PC revolution. LANs enabled multiple users in a relatively small geographical area to exchange files and messages, as well as access shared resources such as file servers.

A local area network (LAN) is a network that connects computers and devices in a limited geographical area such as home, school, computer laboratory, office building, or closely positioned group of buildings. Each computer or device on the network is a node.

(ii) WAN: WAN stands for Wide Area Network. The interconnection of various LAN's through telephone network, which unites geographically distributed users, is achieved through WAN. In short when we log on to the internet, we become a part of a WAN.

Computers connected to a WAN are often connected through public networks, such as the telephone system (through a network service provider). Computers can also be connected through leased lines or satellites, also from a network service provider. The largest WAN in existence is the Internet.

(iii) MAN: MAN stands for Metropolitan Area Network. It is usually the interconnection between various LAN's in a particular geographical area like a metropolitan city like Bombay.

Internetworking evolved as a solution to three key problems: isolated LANs, duplication of resources, and a lack of network management. Isolated LANS made electronic communication between different offices or departments impossible. Duplication of resources meant that the same hardware and software had to be supplied to each office or department, as did a separate support staff. This lack of network management meant that no centralized method of managing and troubleshooting networks existed. A metropolitan-area network (MAN) is a data network designed for a town or city. A MAN can either be built as service provider or leased among multiple customers or a company can build its own private MAN. In terms of geographic breadth, MANs are larger than LANs, but smaller than WANs. MANs are usually characterized by high-speed connections using fiber-optic cable or other digital media and are often used by companies with several offices located within the same city. A corporation can extend the LAN services in each building across a metropolitan region by deploying a MAN to interconnect each corporate office.

(iv) Virtual private network: A virtual private network (VPN) is a computer network in which some of the links between nodes are carried by open connections or virtual circuits in some larger network (*e.g.*, the Internet) instead of by physical wires. The data link layer protocols of the virtual network are said to be tunneled through the larger network when this is the case. One common application is secure communications through the public Internet, but a VPN need not have explicit security features, such as authentication or content encryption. VPNs, for example, can be used to separate the traffic of different user communities over an underlying network with strong security features.

A VPN may have best-effort performance, or may have a defined service level agreement (SLA) between the VPN customer and the VPN service provider. Generally, a VPN has a topology more complex than point-to-point.

Communication Interface Devices

Network Interface Cards

Every computer in a network has a special card called a network interface card (NIC). An NIC first of all, provides the connector to attach the network cable to a server or a workstation. The on-board circuitry then provides the protocols and commands required to support this type of network card. An NIC has additional memory for buffering incoming and outgoing data packets, thus improving the network throughput. A slot may also be available for remote boot PROM, permitting the board to be mounted in a diskless workstation. Network interface cards are available in 8-bit bus or in faster 16-bit bus standards. Characteristics of NICs include following:

- NIC construct, transmits, receives, and processes data to and from a host to network.
- Each NIC has a manufacturer provided 8 bytes permanent and unique MAC(media access control) address. This address is also known as physical address.
- The NIC requires drivers to operate.

Switches and Routers

Switches and Routers are hardware devices used to direct messages across a network. Switches create temporary point to point links between two nodes on a network and send all data along that link. Router computers are similar to bridges but have the added advantage of supplying the user with network management utilities. A switch is a kind of multi port connecting device which makes intelligent routing decisions on the basis of hardware (physical) addresses. It regenerates incoming signals and forwards it.

Router is a kind of connecting device which makes forwarding decisions of data packet on the basis of network addresses. Routers are the backbone of the Internet, as they can be used to interconnect different types of networks. Routers help administer the data flow by such means as redirecting data traffic to various peripheral devices or other computers. In an Internet work communication, routers not only pass on the data as necessary but also select appropriate routes in the event of possible network malfunctions or excessive use.

The primary purpose of a router is to examine the source and destination IP addresses of data packets it receives and to direct those packets out the appropriate port and over the best path available at the time. Routers accomplish this by using routing protocols and routing algorithms.

Hubs

A hub is a multi port connecting device that is used to interconnect LAN devices. Each node is connected to the hub by means of simple twisted pair wires. The hub then provides a connection over a higher speed link to other LANs, the company's WAN, or the Internet. A hub can be used to extend the physical length of a network. Hubs can be active and passive. In case of passive hub incoming signal is sent as it as output. Active hub can regenerate incoming signal. It supports homogeneous network only.

Bridges, Repeaters and Gateways

Bridges: The main task of a bridge computer is to receive and pass data from one LAN to another. In order to transmit this data successfully, the bridge magnifies the data transmission signal. This means that the bridge can act as a repeater as well as a link.

Repeaters: Repeaters are devices that solve the snag of signal degradation which results as data is transmitted along the various cables. What happens is that the repeater boosts or amplifies the signal before passing it through to the next section of cable.

Gateways: Gateways are also similar to bridges in that they relay data from network to network. They do not, as a rule, possess the management facilities of routers but like routers they can translate data from one protocol to another. Gateways are usually used to link LANs of different topologies, *e.g.*, Ethernet and Token Ring, so enabling the exchange of data. The major point of distinction between gateways, bridge, and a router is that a gateway is a collection of hardware and software facilities that enables devices on one network to communicate with devices on another, dissimilar network. Bridges have the same general characteristics as gateways, but they connect networks that employ similar protocols and topologies. Routers are similar to bridges in that they connect two similar networks.

Modem

The coding/encoding device is called a modem. MODEM stands for Modulator/Demodulator. In the simplest form, it is an encoding as well as decoding device used in data transmission. It is a device that converts a digital computer signal into an analog telephone signal (*i.e.* it modulates the signal) and converts an analog telephone signal into a digital computer signal (*i.e.* it demodulates the signal) in a data communication system. Modems are used for handling data streams from a peripheral device to the CPU and vice versa through the common carrier network. Modems are required to telecommunicate computer data with ordinary telephone lines because computer data is in digital form but telephone lines are analogue. Modems are built with different ranges of transmission speeds.

Multiplexer

This device enables several devices to share one communication line. The multiplexer scans each device to collect and transmit data on a single line to the CPU. It also communicates transmission from the CPU to the appropriate terminal linked to the Multiplexer. The devices are polled and periodically asked whether there is any data to transmit. This function may be very complex and on some systems, there is a separate computer processor devoted to this activity and this is called a 'front-end-processor'.

Front-end Communication Processors

These are programmable devices which control the functions of communication system. They support the operations of a mainframe computer by performing functions, which it would otherwise be required to perform itself. These functions include code conversions, editing and verification of data, terminal recognition and control of transmission lines. The mainframe computer is then able to devote its time to data processing rather than data transmission.

Communication Channel (Medium)

Communication media comprises different types of cables and wireless techniques that are used to connect network devices in a Local Area Network (LAN), Wireless Local Area Network (WLAN) or Wide Area Network (WAN). Choice of correct type of media is very important for the implementation of any network. Communication media is divided into two groups:

(i) **Guided Media :** Twisted Pair, Coaxial cable and Optical fiber.

(ii) **Unguided Media** : Wireless.

Transmission Control Protocol/Internet Protocol

The protocols used on the Internet is called TCP/IP (Transmission Control Protocol/Internet Protocol). A TCP/IP protocol which has two parts.

(i) TCP deals with exchange of sequential data

(ii) IP handles packet forwarding and is used on the Internet.

Broad Band Networks (ISDN)

Integrated Services Digital Network (ISDN) is a system of digital phone connections to allow simultaneous voice and data transmission across the world. Such voice and data are carried by bearer channels (B channels) having a bandwidth of 64 kilobits per second. A data channel can carry signals at 16 kbps or 64 kbps, depending on the nature of service provided.

There are two types of ISDN service. Basic Rate Interface (BRI) and Primary Rate Interface (PRI). BRI consists of two 64 kbps B channels and one 16 kbps D channel for a total of 144 kbps and is suitable for individual users. PRI consists of twenty three B channels and one 64 kbps D channel for a total of 1536 kbps and is suitable for users with higher capacity requirements. It is possible to support multiple primary PRI lines with one 64 kbps D channel using Non Facility Associated Signaling (NFAS).

Intrusion Detection System (IDS)

ID stands for Intrusion Detection, which is the art of detecting inappropriate, incorrect, or anomalous activity. ID systems that operate on a host to detect malicious activity on that host are called host-based ID systems, and ID systems that operate on network data flows are called network-based ID systems. Sometimes, a distinction is made between misuse and intrusion detection. The term intrusion is used to describe attacks from the outside; whereas, misuse is used to describe an attack that originates from the internal network.

- The IDS is scalable so that the system grows with the organization, from smaller networks to enterprise installation.
- It provides automated network-based security assessment and policy compliance evaluation.

Techniques of Network Security

Firewall is a device that forms a barrier between a secure and an open environment when the latter environment is usually considered hostile, for example the Internet. It acts as a system or combination of systems that enforces a boundary between more that one networks. Firewalls protect network from an un-trusted one. In that effect it has a routing ability.

INTERNET

Internet is a communication network which bridges all the small computer networks worldwide as a whole. Internet is based upon Internet technology, in particular World Wide Web (WWW), to build Information System within organization or enterprise to accomplish standardization and automation. Fundamentally, it means network computing environments which let the users share the information through the Internet and Web browsers. Ultimately, it allows a certain organization to build a Groupware within Web environment at low cost on top of existing network infrastructure. By doing this, closed organization network would be interconnected with existing worldwide Internet, which results in diverse information that strengthens competitive advantages of the organization. Basically, it runs on top TCP/IP and HTTP and filters out any illegal access through firewall.

If a corporate web connects two or more trading partners, it is often referred to as a business-to-business web, or an Intranet.

Note that internal webs–also known as intranets –are only logically "internal" to an organization. Physically they can span the globe, as long as access is limited to a defined community of interest.

Internet Applications

The Internet has grown from a small project to today's biggest network of computers. Due to this colossal growth, the Internet has become the biggest domain of information. Now-a-days, an Internet user has access to a wide variety of services such as electronic mail, file transfer, vast information resources, interest group membership, interactive collaboration, multimedia displays, real-time broadcasting, shopping opportunities, and much more. Some of the important services provided by the Internet are briefed in the following few sections.

1. **World Wide Web: (WWW):** The World Wide Web (abbreviated as the web or WWW) is one of the most popular services available on Internet. Tim Berners Lee invented the World Wide Web (WWW) in 1989. It is a subset of the Internet and it presents text, images, animation, video, sound and other multimedia in a single interface. This greatly enhances the experience of the Internet surfer. Although the World Wide Web is often referred to as the Internet, they are actually two different concepts. The Internet is the decentralized global network of computers that transfer information and the bring that makes all this possible whereas the web is a collection of documents or websites, that users can access using the Internet and a web browser. The web is a part of the Internet and it refers to a system of Internet servers that supports hypertext using a specific Internet protocol called HTTP on a single interface (web browsers). In addition, almost every protocol type available on the Internet is accessible on the web. This includes e-mail, FTP, Telnet, and Usenet News. Since the WWW is a subset of the Internet, it stands to reason that the web could not exist without the Internet. However, the Internet would still be the Internet without the web.

The operation of the web relies primarily on hypertext, as it is a means of information retrieval. Hypertext is a document containing words that connect to other documents. These words are called links, which the user can select. A single hypertext document can contain links to documents and resources throughout the Internet. With the ability of the web to work with multimedia and advanced programming languages, the World Wide Web is the fastest growing and the most interesting part of the Internet. With video conferencing and wireless applications, the Internet is ready to take us to the new realm of communication and information exchange.

2. **Electronic Mail (e-mail):** Electronic mail, or e-mail, is a fast, easy, and inexpensive way to communicate with other Internet users around the world. It is one of the basic and earliest services of the Internet and the most used application on the Internet too. E-mail overcomes most of the problems and delays of getting a physical document from one person to another. Rather, it has the dual advantage of not only being faster but cheaper to sue as well.
3. **File Transfer Protocol (FTP):** FTP or File transfer Protocol is a system of rules and a software program that enables a user to log on to another computer and transfer information between it and his/ her computer. It was the first service developed for the Internet so that government and educational institutions could easily exchange files. FTP allows the user to get access to the files stored in the directory of a remote computer that is connected to the Internet. Using FTP, one can upload and download files from the remote computer (known as FTP servers), if he/she has access permission on the remote machine.
4. **Telnet:** The word 'telnet' is derived from telecommunications and network and is a protocol that allows a user to log on to a remote computer. Telnet is also known as remote login, which means connecting one machine to another in such a way that a person may interact with another machine as if it is being used locally.
5. **Internet Relay Chat (IRC):** IRC or Internet Relay Chat is a service on the Internet that allows people to communicate in real time and carry on conversations via the computer with one or more people. It provides the user with the facility to engage in simultaneous (synchronous) online "conversation" with other user from anywhere in the world.
6. **Chatting and Instant Messaging:** Chat programs allow users on the Internet to communicate with each other by typing in real time. They are sometimes included as a feature of a website, where users can log into chat rooms to exchange comments and information about the topics addressed on the site.
7. **Internet Telephony:** Internet telephone is the use of the Internet rather than the traditional telephone company infrastructure, to exchange spoken or other telephonic information. It consists of hardware and software that enable people to use the Internet as a transmission medium for telephone calls. There are many Internet telephony applications available. Some, such as Cool Talk and NetMeeting, come bundled with popular web browsers.
8. **Video Conferencing:** Video conferencing uses the same technology as IRC, but also provides sound and video pictures. It enables direct face-to-face communication across networks. A video conferencing system has to or more parties in different locations, which have the ability to communicate using a combination of video, audio, and data. A video conference can be person to person (referred to as "point-to-point") or can involve more than two people (referred to as "multipoint") and the video conferencing terminals are often referred to as "endpoints".
9. **Newsgroups (Usenet):** Newsgroups are international discussion groups that focus on a particular topic and helps in gathering information about that topic. The topics discussed here cover all the fields such as

politics, computers, technology, and many more. The information or articles that make up the "news" are written by people interested in a specific topic. These articles are posted to the newsgroup so that others can read, reply, and comment on them.

10. **Mailing Lists (List server):** The Internet is home to a large community of individuals who carry out active discussions, organized around topic-oriented forums that are distributed via e-mail. This method of Internet communications is known as mailing list and it enables people with similar interests from all over the world to communicate and share information with each other.

INTRANET AND E-MAIL

An Intranet is a private network that uses the internet protocol and the public telecommunication system to securely share part of business information or operations with-suppliers, vendors, partners, customers, or other businesses.

Through e-mail, documents are prepared and sent electronically. The recipients need not be present at the other end to send the message. The message gets stored in the electronic mailbox of the addressee. The recipient can open the mailbox whenever he is free and can read or print the message.

Intranet

An Intranet can be viewed a-part of a company's internal that is extended to users outside the company. It has also been described as a "state of mind" in which the internet is perceived as a way to do business with other companies as well as to sell products to customers. Intranet extends from one location to another across the internet by securing data flow, to another intranet to a business partner. In these way intranets of business partners, suppliers, creditors, distributors, customers, and the like are connected to Intranets by agreements.

An Intranet requires security and privacy. These require firewall server management, issuance and use of digital certificate or similar means of user authentication, encryption of messages, and the use of virtual private networks that tunnel through the public network.

Characteristics of Intranet

The following are the important characteristics of the Intranet.

(*a*) It is an extended internet-private business networks located outside of the corporate firewall.

(*b*) It can be referred to an intranet that is partially accessible to authorized outsiders.

(*c*) It is a network that uses the internet to link businesses with others that share the common goals.

Uses of Intranet

Companies can use an Intranet to:

(*a*) Exchange large volumes of data using Electronic Data Interchange.

(*b*) Share product catalogues exclusively with wholesalers or those in the Trade.

(*c*) Collaborate with other companies on joint development efforts.

(*d*) Jointly develop and use training programs with other companies.

(*e*) Provide or access services provided by one company to a group of other companies, such as an online banking application managed by one company on behalf of affiliated banks.

(*f*) Share news of common interest exclusively with partner companies.

(*g*) The manufacturing companies can coordinate the design manufacturing, scheduling and delivery across supply chain.

(*h*) With Intranet the technology firms can support for their customers and partners and makes it possible for remote access for employees.

(*i*) The financial services firms by using Intranet can reduce costs of proprietary networks.

(*j*) With Intranet the publishing companies can increase the speed of design and production cycles.

(*k*) Other benefits:

- Quicker turnaround time

- Improved communication
- Decreased paper flow
- Traceable correspondence
- Better service
- Lower overhead and expenses
- Improved employee morale
- Increased Margins
- Flexibility and scalability
- Reduced transitional barriers
- Versatility.

A brief list of examples of Intranet could include:

- Allowing suppliers access to relevant inventory levels
- Allowing clients to review their account records
- Allowing students to update address information in real time.

As with intranet, access is granted only where you establish that it is required. User access is controlled by the latest in security technologies, protecting sensitive material from intrusion.

What is the Relationship between Intranet and E-commerce?

The answer has three parts. First, Intranet, Intranet and e-commerce have in common the use of Internet (predominantly web) protocols to connect business users. Second, intranets are more localized and can therefore move data faster than more distributed Intranets. (Bandwidth limitations also apply to e-commerce.) Third, the amount of control that network managers can exert over users is different for the three technologies.

On an Internet, administrators can narrowly prescribe access and policy for a fixed group of users. For example, a company could specify Red Hat Linux as its standard desktop operating system, and Netscape Communicator 5 as its standard browser and mail client. The company could then write intranet workflow applications that leverage the uniform computing environment, over which it exercises strong control.

On a business-to-business Intranet, system architects at each of the participating companies must collaborate to ensure a common interface and consistent semantics (data meanings). Since one company cannot reasonably enforce standards on its trading partners, Intranet application developers must taken into account a wider range of technologies than is the case for intranets. For example, one company participating in an Intranet might be using Microsoft Internet Explorer, another Netscape Navigator 4.5 and another Navigator Gold 3.x. In order to collaborate via Intranet, the applications have to perform adequately on all represented platforms.

The same is true, even more, for e-commerce, in which the trading partners may be completely unknown to one another. This is the case when you walk into a supermarket: the common interest in communication is based on the need to transact business, and not necessarily on a long-term trust relationship. Thus, e-commerce applications often support a level of security and transactional integrity (for instance, non-repudiation of orders) not present in intranet or Intranet applications.

E-Mail

E-mail is an electronic message sent from one computer to another. We can send or receive personal and business-related messages with attachments, such as pictures or formatted documents. We can even send songs and computer programs.

The e-mail communication is incredibly simple. A person with a PC and a modem to connect to the network can communicate with the other(s) so connected to the network. The message can be prepared and sent instantly. The other person finds the e-mail when he checks his mailbox and may reply to the message in the same way. The message sent is private and no other person can read it.

Each user of e-mail service has a user ID or password serving as e-mail address. First thing to do is to get online using modem and communication software. The system requires userid and password. Now the user can prepare his message in the form of a document using a word processor. The e-mail address of the recipient has to be typed in before the message is sent.

With e-mail each person connected to the system is allotted a mailbox and the software required for sending and receiving e-mail. The mailbox is simply a file into which the e-mail system stores electronic documents. The user can check his mailbox for messages over the network. The sender specifies his identify and that of the recipient. The sender then prepares the document or retrieves the stored document and sends it.

E-mail is a document communication facility. To ensure that the recipient also understands the emotions as well, a set of special symbols is used to convey some non-verbal signals. A few of such symbols are given below.

E-mail is the transmission of information electronically from terminal to terminal. The document is prepared in a word processor and is mailed electronically. The basic facilities in e-mail include message creation, message transfer and post delivery service. The e-mail service may be traditional mainframe based or minicomputer based or LAN based system with PCS to access from.

How E-Mail Works?

The first thing to be done is to type the message and the e-mail address of the recipient. Once the 'send' button is clicked, this e-mail is sent through the telephone line after its conversion into analog signal by the modem. The e-mail message arrives at our service provider's server. If the server recognizes the e-mail address as valid, the mail will be sent either through the network of the service provider or through internet gateway to the service provider of the recipient.

To send e-mail, we need a connection to the internet and access to a mail server that forwards the mail. The standard protocol used for sending internet e-mail is called SMTP, short for Simple Mail Transfer Protocol. It works in conjunction with POP servers. POP stands for Post Office Protocol.

When we send an e-mail message, our computer routes it to an SMTP server. The server looks at the e-mail address (similar to the address on an envelope), then forwards it to the recipient's mail server. Once the message arrives at the destination mail server, It's stored until the addressee retrieves it. We can send e-mail anywhere in the world to anyone who has an e-mail address.

With the advent of MIME, which stands for Multipurpose Internet Mail Extension, and other types of encoding schemes, we can not only send messages electronically, but we can also send formatted documents, photos, sound files, and video files.

Infrastructure Requirement for E-Mail

- Personal Computer
- Telephone Connection
- Modem
- Mailing software viz., Outlook Express or Netscape communicator or Internet Explorer etc.

Advantages of E-mail

- Messages can be prepared and sent any time convenient for the sender.
- Message can be received at the convenience of the recipient.
- The transmission takes place instantly and the message gets stored in the mailbox of the recipient.
- The system can confirm delivery of message.
- Copies of message can be sent to multiple recipients.
- It reduces paper work.

Disadvantages

- Recipients must be having e-mail connectivity. They must have computer terminals, modem and telephone.
- They must be subscribing to the same e-mail service provider.
- Poor telecommunication affects the quality of message transmitted.
- Despite all the disadvantages e -mail is a cheap form of information transmission.

INDONET, NICNET, DARTMAIL and ICNET provide this service in India. A user can be a subscriber to such e-mail service providing agencies and use their facility.

GLOSSARY

Accumulator: A Storage area in memory used to develop totals of units or of aiounts being computed.

ActiveX: A Microsoft programming architecture that allows programs to interact with other programs over a network, such as the Internet. The controls created with ActiveX enable developers to add extra capabilities to Web sites, such as animation.

Address: A name, numeral, or other reference that designates a particular location in storage or some other data source or designation.

Note: Numerous types of addresses are employed in computer programming; for example; direct address, symbolic address.

ADSL: Asymmetric Digital Subscriber Line, a modem arrangement, connected to ends of a telephone line, that allows for high-speed transmissions of data — useful for interactive video and data communications. See also DSL, xDSL.

ALGOL (Algorithmic Language): A standard procedure oriented language for expressing computational algorithms developed as a result of international cooperation. ALGOL is designed to serve as a means for communicating computational procedures among humans, as well as to facilitate the preparation of such procedures for execution on any computer for which a suitable ALGOL compiler exists.

Note: The basic elements of ALGOL are arithmetic expressions containing numbers, variables and functions. These are combined to form self-containing units called assignment statements. Declarations are non-computational instructions which inform the compiler of characteristics such as the dimensions of an array or the class of a variable. A sequence of declarations followed by a sequence of statements, all enclosed within "begin" and "end" instruction, constitutes an ALGOL program block. ALGOL is very popular in Europe.

Alignment: Process of organising and fixing the position and order of words and lines in a document.

Analog Transmission: There are two ways that 'Information' can travel along a telecommunications network: either as an analog or a digital signal. Analog signals are like the spoken word - the signal is continuous and carried by a changing wavelength (pitch) and amplitude (loudness). A digital signal, on the other hand, is like the binary information which is stored in a computer. The signal consists of discrete on-off (1 and 0) bits. Although analog and digital information cannot be changed in form, the electronic signal the network uses to transmit it can. Analog information can be transmitted directly or encoded into digital bits; digital information can be transmitted directly or modulated into analog form. The choice between transmission systems depends upon the relative volumes of analog and digital information, the relative costs of codes (analog to digital coders-decoders) and modems (digital to analog modulators-demodulators) and the relative efficiencies of digital and analog transmission.

Applet: A small application program, made with the object-oriented programming language Java, which can be sent along the Web to a user. Applets can perform animations, calculations and other tasks without sending the user back to a server.

Application Program: A computer program used to perform a specific task, such as word processing, spreadsheet creation, or database management.

ASCII: Acronym for American Standard Code for Information Interchange. A standard set of characters used to enable compatibility between different computer devices.

Assemble: To prepare a machine language from a program written in symbolic coding by substituting absolute operation codes for symbolic operation codes and absolute or re-locatable addresses for symbolic addresses. For example, the symbolic instruction ADD TAX might be assembled into the machine instruction

24 1365, where 24 is the operation code of addition and 1365 is the address of the storage location labelled TAX. Contrast with compile.

Assembler: A computer program that assembles programs written in symbolic coding to produce machine language programs.

Note: Assemblers are an important part of the basic software for most computers and can greatly reduce the human effort required to prepare programs.

Asynchronous Communication: Transmission system in which the speed of operation is not related to any frequency in the system to which it is connected. In the transmission system each character is preceded by a start signal and succeeded by a stop signal. This means that 'asynch', as it is usually referred to, is rather slow.

Attachment: Content included in an e-mail, either as extra text or as a file.

Auxiliary Storage: Storage that supplements a computer's primary internal storage.

Note: In general, that auxiliary storage has a much larger capacity but a longer access time than the primary storage. Synonymous with mass storage. Same as secondary storage.

Backbone: The main pathway of a high-speed network.

Backup: Pertaining to equipment or procedures that are available for use in the event of failure or overloading of the normally used equipment or procedures.

Note: The provision of adequate backup facilities is an important factor in the design of all data processing systems and is especially vital in the design of real-time systems, where a system failure may bring the entire operation of a business to virtual standstill.

Bandwidth: How much data one can send through a connection. Usually measured in bits-per-second. A full page of English text is about 16,000 bits. A fast modem can move about 15,000 bits in one second. Full-motion, full-screen video would require roughly 10,000,000 bits per second, depending on compression.

BASIC (Beginner's All-purpose Symbolic Instruction Code): A programming language developed in the mid-1960's as an easy-to learn, easy-to-use language to teach students how to program. The language contains a limited set of powerful commands designed especially for use in a time sharing environment.

Batch file: It is like a mini program, a series of commands that are given to the personal computer to execute in sequence.

Batch processing: A technique in which items to be processed are collected into groups (batched) to permit convenient and efficient processing. **Note:** Most business applications are of the batch processing type; the records of all transactions affecting a particular master file are accumulated covering a period of time, (e.g., one day); then they are arranged in sequence and processed against the master file.

Baud: In common usage, the baud rate of a modem is how many bits it can send or receive per second. Technically, baud is the number of times per second that the carrier signal shifts value. For example, a 1200 bit-per-second modem actually runs at 300 baud, but it moves 4 bits per baud (4 × 300 = 1200 bits per second).

BBS: Bulletin Board System, a computer that creates a forum for sharing and exchanging messages and/or files. Most BBS's operate independent of the Internet, and must be reached with a modem or Telnet. But many BBS's have Web sites, as do service providers.

BCD (Binary Coded Decimal) : Pertaining to a method of representing each of the decimal digits zero through 9 by a distinct group of binary digits. For example, in the "8-4-2-1" BCD notation, which is used in numerous digital computers, the decimal number39 is represented as 0011 1001 (whereas in pure binary notation it would be represented as 100111).

Binary: Pertaining to the number system with a radix of 2, or to a characteristic or property involving choice or condition in which there are two possibilities. For example, the binary numeral 1101 means: $(1 \times 2^3) + (1 \times 2^2) + (0 \times 2^1) + (1 \times 2^0)$ which is equivalent to decimal 13.

Note: The binary number system is widely used in digital computers because most computer components, e.g., vacuum tubes, transistors, and integrated chips) are essentially binary in that they have two stable states.

BIOS (Basic Input Output System): Commands of function when a computer is switched on.

Bit: A binary digit; a digit (0 or 1) in the representation of a number in binary notation.

Booster Keys: Keys that do not perform actions by themselves but can be used with other keys to issue commands. The booster keys are Ctrl, Alt, and Shift.

Boot: To start a computer and load the operating system into RAM.

Bps–(Bits-per-Second): A measurement of how data is moved from one place to another. A 28.8 modem can move 28,800 bits per second.

Browser: A Client program (software) that is used to look at various kinds of Internet resources. Mosaic, Netscape Navigator and Internet Explorer are some of the commonly used browsers.

Buffer Memory: This is the internal memory of a microcomputer or word processor. Data is stored in this memory until transferred to its permanent store on a disk system. Buffer memories also hold the software used by the system.

Buffer: A storage device used to compensate for differences in the rates of flow of data or in the times of occurrence of events when transmitting data from one device to another. For example, a buffer holding the characters to print one line is associated with most line printers to compensate for the difference between the high speed at which the computer transmits data to the printer and the relatively low speed of the printing operation itself.

Bug: A mistake in the design of a program or a computer system, or an equipment fault.

BUS: Internal communication path in a computer.

Byte: A byte is eight bits.

Cell: The smallest unit of a spreadsheet filled with information.

Central Processor: The unit of a computer system that includes the circuits which controls the interpretation and execution of instructions. Synonymous with CPU (Central Processing Units) and main frame.

Chat: A chat, in general means talking to other people, by typing, who are using the Internet the same time as you. Most of this communication is done at a specific site. Chats can be ongoing or scheduled, group or one-to-one. Chats may also use sound and video where applicable.

Chip: An integrated electronic circuit consisting of miniature transistors and other circuit elements contained on a silicon wafer.

CIS development: The section of computer installation responsible for the analysis, design, and development of new systems and programs.

Client: A software program that is used to contact and obtain data from a Server software program on another computer, often across a great distance. Each Client program is designed to work with one or more specific kinds of Server programs and each Server requires a specific kind of Client. A Wed Browser is a specific kind of Client.

Clipart: These are pre-prepared graphic images that one can incorporate into a document with a word processor or a desktop publishing program.

COBOL (Common Business Oriented Language): A procedure-oriented language developed to facilitate the preparation and inter-change of programs which form business data processing functions.

Note: Designed in 1959 by a committee representing the U.S. Government and several computer manufacturers, COBOL has evolved through several versions (*e.g.*, COBOL-60, COBOL-61, COBOL 61-Extended, COBOL-65). Every COBOL source program has four divisions, whose names and functions are as follows: (1) Identification Division, which identifies the source program and the output of a compilation, (2) Environment Division, which specifies those aspects of a data processing problem that are dependent upon the physical characteristics of a particular computer, (3) Data Division, which describes the data that the object program is to accept as input, manipulate, create, or produce as output, and (4) Procedure Division, which specifies the procedures to be performed by the object program, by means of English-like statements such as: "Subtract tax from gross pay giving net pay".

Cold Boot: To start a computer and load the operating system into RAM.

Collage: A single picture formed by pasting parts of different pictures or objects.

Command Name: The component of a command that specifies what action DOS is to perform.

Command: An instruction for DOS to perform a specific action.

Compile: To prepare a machine language program (or a program expressed in symbolic coding) from a program written in another programming language (usually a procedure oriented language such as BASIC, COBOL or FORTRAN). The compilation process usually involves examining and making use of the overall structure of the program and/or generating more than one object program instruction for each source program statement. Contrast with assemble.

Compiler: A computer program that compiles. Compilers are an important part of the basic software for most computers permitting the use of procedure-oriented languages which can greatly reduce the human effort required to prepare computer programs.

Computer information system (CIS): A coordinated collection of hardware, software, people, data, and support resources to perform an integrated series of functions that can include input, processing, output, and storage.

Computer-aided instruction (CAI): Interactive use of a computer to deliver educational contents to individuals and to adjust presentations according to learner responses.

Console: A portion of a computer that is used for communication between operators or maintenance engineers and the computer, usually by means of displays and manual control.

Cookie: A type of text file given to a browser by a server, used to record specific information about a user's preferences.

Corel DRAW: An application software for vector drawing.

CR – Carnage Return: This is the most important key on a computer or word processor keyboard. It is used to activate most of the functions on the system. It is usually identified by a reverse L-symbol with an arrow on the end of the horizontal bar.

Current Directory: The directory that DOS is currently using.

Current Drive: The disk drive that DOS is currently using.

Cursor: A symbol on the screen that marks the location where characters will appear as they are typed from the keyboard. The cursor usually displays as a blinking vertical line in a word processor or as a blinking underscore.

Data Base Administrator (DBA): The person in charge of defining and managing the content of a data base.

Data Base Management System (DBMS) : Software to manage and control data resources.

Data Bus: The internal pathway in a computer on which data moves.

Data dictionary: A document listing and defining all items or processes represented in data flow diagrams or used within a system.

DDR (Double Data Rate): A mechanism used to produce computer memory.

Debug: To trace and eliminate mistakes in a program or faults in equipment. The process is often assisted by a diagnostic routine.

Decompression: Process of enlarging a compressed file in a computer to its original size. (Also called unzipping.)

Default: An assumed value or option the computer uses when none is specified. Synonymous with regular, normal, or primary (as in a printer). Or as in normal or standard settings in an application or software program. Default in computers has NOTHING to do with finances.

Density: The data storage capacity of a disk.

Desk checking: A manual checking process in which representative data items, used for detecting errors in program logic, are traced through the program before the latter is checked on the computer.

Dialog Box: A small window that opens up on the computer screen to the user request or put in information relating to a task (such as printing) or give the information to the user, such as when there is an error.

Digitize: The process of converting lines, drawings and pictures to digital form by scanning the drawings and pictures with a device that converts sensed highlights into numbers or horizontal and vertical coordinates.

Direct access device: A hardware unit that can read and write records from or to a file without processing all preceding records.

Direct data entry: Entry of data directly into the computer through machine-readable source documents or through use of on-line terminals. Direct entry is a by-product of source business transactions, without requiring manual transcription from original paper documents.

Directory: An area on a disk where you store a group of related files under an identifying name. Also a list of files contained on a disk.

Disk Drive: A mechanism that reads and writes data on a disk.

Disk Operating System (DOS): The name used for various operating systems. The primary function of a disk operating system is to control the flow of data to and from the CPU and peripherals.

Disk: A circular platter with a magnetic coating on both sides. The most common medium for storing computer data.

Diskette: A removable computer storage medium made of plastic and covered with a magnetic coating. Usually 3_" in size (5_" floppy diskettes are obsolete). See also *Disk* and *Hard Disk.*

Domain Name: The location or address of an entity on the Internet. They must contain a top level domain name (such as .com, .org or .net) and a second-level domain name, such as DigitalMadurai. Second level domain names for the root (top level) .edu, .com, .org, .gov and .net domains in North America must be registered with Internic.

Domain Name: The unique name that identifies an Internet site. Domain Names always have 2 or more parts, separated by dots. The part on the left is the most specific, and the part on the right is the most general. A given machine may have more than one Domain Name but a given Domain Name points to only one machine. For example, the domain names : matisse.net, mail.matisse.net, workshop.matisse.net, can all refer to the same machine, but each domain name can refer to no more than one machine.

Double-Density: The diskette type that holds 720 Kb of data in 3_" diskettes (360 Kb of data in obsolete 5_" diskettes).

Down time: Time at which the computer is not available for processing.

dpi – Dots Per Inch: The unit of resolution indicating the number of dots printed per inch of a raster picture.

Drag: To move something around the computer with the help of the mouse. This involves holding down one of the mouse buttons while user moves it.

DTP (Desk Top Publishing) : The process of making publication and taking printouts using specially designed computer software's.

Dump: (1) To copy the contents of a set of storage locations, usually from an internal storage device (such as disk storage) to an external storage medium (such as magnetic tape or floppy disk), and usually for diagnostic or rerun purposes.

(2) The data that results from the process defined in (1).

EBCDIC (Extended Binary Coded Decimal Interchange Code): An 8-bit code that represents an extension of a 6-bit "BCD" code that was widely used in computers of the first and second generations. EBCDIC can represent upto 256 distinct characters and is the principal code used in many of the current computers.

E-mail – (Electronic Mail): Messages, usually text, sent from one person to another via computer. E-mail can also be sent automatically to a large number of addresses (Mailing List).

Ethernet: A very common method of networking computers in a LAN. Ethernet will handle about 10,000,000 bits-per-second and can be used with almost any kind of computer.

External Commands: Commands stored in program files on a disk, which can only be executed when the program file is present in the current directory or in a directory, specified in a path statement.

Eye of Gnome: The GNU/Linux software to view pictures.

Facsimile Transmission System: Often abbreviated to 'Fax', this system is employed to relay alphanumeric and graphic data to other Fax machines at distant sites along a telephone or other telecommunications link. A fax device produces a facsimile copy of the original in the same manner as an office copier, except that the original is received electronically.

FAQ: Frequently Asked Question, a common format Web site authors use to answer questions.

File maintenance: The updating of a file to reflect the effects of period changes by adding, altering data; *e.g.*, the addition of new programs to program library on magnetic disk.

File processing: The periodic updating of master files to reflect the effect of current data, often transaction data contained in detail files; *e.g.*, a weekly payroll run updating the payroll master file.

File: A collection of related records, usually (but not necessarily) arranged in sequence according to key contained on each record.

Note: A record, in turn, is a collection of related items; an item is an arbitrary quantity of data that is treated as a unit. In payroll processing, an employee's pay rate forms an item; a group of items relating to one employee form a record, and the complete set of employee records forms a file.

Filter: Either a program that sorts data or a pattern that is used to determine which type of data is accepted. Often used with e-mail to separate messages.

Firewall: A system that protects a private network and its resources from unauthorized access.

Fixed length record: A record that always contains the same number of characters. The restriction to a fixed length may be deliberate, in order to simplify and speed processing or it may be dictated by the characteristics of the equipment used. Contrast with variable-length record.

Fixed word length: Pertaining to a machine word or operand that always has the same number of bits or characters. Contrast with variable word length. Most scientific computers are of the fixed word length type for maximum computational speeds, while many business oriented computers have variable word length to permit efficient handling of items and records of varying sizes. Some computers types have both fixed and variable words.

Floppy Disk: A removable computer storage medium made of plastic and covered with a magnetic coating. Usually 3_" in size (5_" floppy diskettes are obsolete).

Font: A character set in a particular style and size of type, including all alphanumeric characters, punctuation marks and special symbols.

Format: (Dual meaning) (a) To prepare a disk (or Drive) for data storage by creating sectors and cleaning (erasing) any and all files. (b) The layout or appearance of a document in terms of fonts, margins, etc. A special formula will have a certain format (sometimes also referred to as syntax), or appearance.

FORTRAN (Formula Translation): A procedure oriented language designed to facilitate the preparation of computer programs that performs mathematical computations. It was designed by IBM in the 1950's to use symbols and expression similar to those of algebra, FORTRAN was not originally intended to be a common language. However, it has evolved through several basic versions (*e.g.* FORTRAN II, FORTRAN IV) plus numerous dialects, has become largely machine-independent and has been approved as a USA standard programming language in two versions (FORTRAN and basic FORTRAN). FORTRAN is widely used procedure-oriented language in the United States and is being effectively employed in certain business as well as scientific applications. The essential elements of the FORTRAN is the assignment statement; *e.g.* Z = X + Y causes the current value of the variables X and Y to be added together and their sum to replace the previous value of the variable Z.

Fourth Generation Languages: These are infact sophisticated software packages that permit users to query data bases and extract the information needed to solve problems and prepare reports. With these languages, very complex operations are accomplished by just pressing a few keystrokes. Some examples of fourth generation languages are dBASE, FRED and PC/FOCUS.

FTP – (File Transfer Protocol): A very common method of moving files between two Internet sites. FTP is a special way to login to another Internet site for the purposes of retrieving and/or sending files. There are many Internet sites that have established publicly accessible repositories of material that can be obtained using FTP.

Function Keys : Keys from F1 to F12 of a keyboard, which has specific function in application programms (Eg. For Help press F1)

GUI (Graphical User Interface): A computer mode of interaction using graphics.

Hard Disk: A large built-in storage capacity medium for computer data.

Hardware: Any of the mechanical or electrical components of a computer such as the CPU, memory chips, disk drives, keyboard, and monitor.

Header label: A machine-readable record at the beginning of the file containing data identifying the file and data used in control.

Hollerith code: A widely used code for representing alphanumeric data on punched cards, named after Herman Hollerith, the originator of punched card tabulating. Each card column holds one character, and each decimal digit, letter, and special character is represented by one, two or three holes punched into designated row positions of the column.

Host: Any computer on a network that is a repository for services available to other computers on the network. It is quite common to have one host machine providing several services, such as WWW and USENET.

HTML – (Hyper Text Markup Language): The coding language used to create Hypertext documents for use on the World Wide Web. HTML looks a lot like old fashioned typesetting code, where you surround a block of text with codes that indicate how it should appear. Additionally, in HTML one can specify that a block of text, or a word, is linked to another file on the Internet. HTML files are meant to be viewed using a World Wide Web client Program, such as Netscape Navigator, Internet Explorer or Mosaic.

HTML Editors: Software for easy HTML page creation.

HTTP: Hypertext Transfer Protocol, the definitive manner in which messages are formatted, transmitted and received on the World Wide Web.

Hyper text: A text format with facilities like Link, Bold, Italics etc. like an HTML life.

Hyperlink: A pointer or reference to another document. Usually underlined text or a picture, it accesses another document when clicked on.

Hyperlink: A technique to open another page from a web page.

IDE Port: Port on motherboard to which Hard Disk, CD Drive, Floppy Drive etc. are connected.

IDP (Integrated Data Processing): Data processing by a system that coordinates a number of previously unconnected processes in order to improve overall efficiency by reducing or eliminating redundant data entry or processing operations. An example of IDP is a system in which data describing orders, production, and purchases is entered into a single processing scheme that combines the functions of scheduling, invoicing, inventory control, etc.

Input Device: A mechanism, such as a keyboard or a mouse, used to give instructions to a computer for processing.

Input: Any data entered into a computer for processing.

Integrated Circuit (IC): A device incorporating circuitry and semiconductor components within a single unit, usually a miniature chip. Circuit elements and components are created as part of the same manufacturing procedures.

Interface Card: Special utility cards like Sound card, Network card etc. connected to the mother board.

Interface Slot: Slot in mother board to connect interface cards.

Interlocked Gap: The distance on a magnetic tape between the end of one block and the beginning of the next. Within this distance, the tape can be stopped and brought up to the normal speed again. Since the tape speed is not constant when stopping, no reading or writing is permitted in the gap. Synonymous with inter-record gap and record gap, though the use of these two terms is not recommended because of the important distinction between blocks and records.

Internal Commands: Commands that are loaded into RAM with DOS when a computer is booted and which can be executed whenever the system prompt is displayed.

Internet – (Upper case I): The vast collection of inter-connected networks that all use the TCP/IP protocols and that evolved from the ARPANET of the late 60's and early 70's. The Internet now connects more than 70,000 independent networks into a vast global internet.

Interpreter: Language translator that converts source code to machine code and executes it immediately, statement by statement.

Intranet: A private network inside a company or organization that uses the same kind of software that one would find on the public Internet, but that is only for internal use. As the Internet has become more popular, many of the tools used on the Internet are being used in private networks. For example, many companies have web servers that are available only to employees. Note that an Intranet may not actually be an internet — it may simply be a network.

IP: Internet Protocol, specifies and addresses the packets that the messages transmitted on the Internet are composed of. It usually works with another protocol called TCP, or Transfer Control Protocol, which establishes a connection between a destination and a source.

IRC: Internet Relay Chat, a client/server-software chat system that allows people anywhere on the Internet to join in live discussions.

ISP – (Internet Service Provider): An institution that provides access to the Internet in some form, usually for money. For example, in India, VSNL (Videsh Sanchar Nigam Limited) is the Internet Service Provider.

ISP: Internet Service Provider, an outfit or company which offers access to the Internet, usually for a fee.

Java: Java is a network-oriented programming language invented by Sun Microsystems that is specifically designed for writing programs that can be safely downloaded to one's computer through the Internet and immediately run without fear of viruses or other harm to one's computer or files. Using small Java programs (called "Applets"), Web pages can include functions such as animations, calculations, and other fancy tricks. One can expect to see a huge variety of features added to the Web using Java, since a Java program can be written to do almost anything a regular computer program can do, and then include that Java program in a Web page.

Joystick: A vertical lever, usually in a ball socket, which can be tilted in any direction and is used to move a cursor around the screen or display unit of a computer.

JPEG: A format to save and keep picture files.

Kb or K or Kilobyte: 1,024 bytes or characters.

Label: A name attached to or written alongside the entity it identifies *e.g.,* a key that is attached to the item or record it identifies, or a name written alongside a statement on a coding sheet.

LAN: Local Area Network, a computer network for a relatively small geographic area. Each workstation or personal computer within the LAN has access to the devices shared by the LAN server or processor.

Layer Box: Dialogue box showing details of layers in a picture file.

Layer: A technique applied to prepare picture files.

Layout: Total design and positions of letters and graphics in a page.

Link: A pointer or reference to another document. Usually underlined text or a picture, it accesses another document when clicked on. (See also Hyperlink.)

Live Cam: A video camera attached to a computer. Its latest image is downloadable off the World Wide Web. Also called a Netcam.

Lock Up: When a computer does not accept input from the keyboard or any other input device, and the cursor does not move. A computer that locks up may have to be restarted again.

Login: Noun or a verb. ***Noun :*** The account name used to gain access to a computer system. Not a secret (contrast with Password). ***Verb:*** The act of entering into a computer system.

LOL: Laugh Out Loud, an e-mail or chat abbreviation.

Machine language: A language that is used directly by a computer. Thus, a "Machine language program" is a set of instructions which a computer can directly recognize and execute and which will cause it to perform a particular process. In Machine-oriented language there is a general (though not necessarily strict) one-to one correspondence between the statements of source program and the instructions of the object program (which will normally be a machine language program ready for executing on a particular computer). The input to an assembler is usually expressed in a machine-oriented language. Contrast with procedure-oriented language.

Maintenance (file): Process of changing a master file through the addition of new records, the deletion of old records and changing the contents of existing records.

Mark sensing: A technique for detecting pencil marks entered by hand in prescribed places on some preprinted documents. The marked data may be converted into light patterns and transmitted directly to a computer.

Master file: A file containing relatively permanent information which is used as source of reference and is generally updated periodically. Contrast with detail file.

Maximise Button: A button by which a software/ window under use can be maximised.

Media player: A software in Windows to watch movies.

Memory Slot: Part of a motherboard to connect memory cards.

Menu: Table that shows the available directions of a software.

Merge: To form a single sequenced file by combining two or more similarly sequenced files. Merging may be performed manually, by a collator, or by a computer system for which a "merge routine" is available. Repeated merging, splitting and remerging of strings of records can be used to arrange the records in sequence; this process, called a "merging sort," is frequently used as the basis for sorting operations on computer systems.

Message Switching System: A facility which uses computer techniques to transmit and receive, and store and retrieve textual information. It is a means of communicating in a fast, cost-effective and reliable way, using modern technology. These systems allow immediate access to any person or office using the facilities and all massages are transmitted and received instantly whether addressee is in the next office or the other side of the world.

MICR (Magnetic Ink Character Recognition): The automatic reading by machine of graphic characters printed with magnetic ink.

Module: In programming, a solution document representing a processing function that will be carried out by a computer.

Monitor: The visual display unit of a computer system.

Motherboard: The main circuit board of a microcomputer.

Mouse: A small, hand-held mechanism that controls the movement of the cursor or a pointer on a computer screen.

Move Tool: Tool to change the position of a picture.

MP3: MPEG-1 Audio Layer-3, a technology that compresses sound files from much larger files into very small files roughly one-twelfth of the size, while retaining sound quality. Usually download-and-play files rather than streaming audio, MP3 players are available for download at several MP3 sites.

MPEG: The Moving Pictures Experts Group, a consortium which develops standards for digital audio and video compression. To play an MPEG file a computer must have certain amounts of speed, hard disk space and memory, as well as an MPEG viewer or other software.

MS Backup: A utility program used to back up a large number of files.

MS-DOS Operating System or Microsoft Disk Operating System: The operating system used by most of the major personal computer systems, especially the IBM Personal Computer 'look-likes'. IBM personal computers used a variation known as PC-DOS.

Multiprocessing: The simultaneous execution of two or more sequences of instructions in a single computer system. Frequently refers to simultaneous execution accomplished by the use of a system with more than one central processor.

Multi-programming: A technique for handling two or more independent programs simultaneously by overlapping or interleaving their execution. The overlapping or interleaving of the execution of the various programs is usually controlled by an operating system which attempts to optimize the performance of the computer system in accordance with the priority requirements of the various jobs.

Nautilus: File manager in Linux.

Netscape: A WWW Browser and the name of a company. The Netscape browser was originally based on the Mosaic program developed at the National Center for Supercomputing Applications (NCSA). Netscape has grown in features rapidly and is widely recognized as the best and most popular web browser. Netscape Corporation also produces web server software. Netscape provided major improvements in speed and interface over other browsers.

Node: Any single computer connected to a network.

OCR (Optical Character Recognition): The automatic reading by machine of graphic characters through the use of light-sensitive devices.

Operating System: An organized collection of routines and procedures for operating a computer. These routines and procedures will normally perform some or all of the following functions —(1) Scheduling, loading, initiating and supervising the execution of programs; (2) allocating storage, input/output units and other facilities of the computer system; (3) initiating and controlling input/output operations; (4) handling errors and restarts; (5) coordinating communication between the human operator and the computer system; (6) maintaining a log of system operations, and (7) controlling operation in a multi-programming, multi-processing or time-sharing mode. Among the facilities frequently included within an operating system are an executive routine, a scheduler, an IOCS, utility routines, and monitor routines.

Output Device: A mechanism, such as a printer or a monitor, used to retrieve and view data after it has been processed by a computer.

Output: Data that is generated from a computer after processing.

Overflow: In an arithmetic operation, the generation of a quantity beyond the capacity of the register or storage location which is to receive the result.

Overlay: To transfer segment of program from auxiliary storage into internal storage for execution, so that two or more segments occupy the same storage locations at different times. This technique makes it possible to execute programs which are too large to fit into the computer internal storage at one time, it is also important in multi-programming and time-sharing operations.

Parallel Interface: Generally used to link a printer into a computer or word processor. This interface allows the printer to accept transmission of data which is sent in parallel bit sequences. (See also Serial Interface.)

Parallel Port: The port used to connect associated devices like a printer to a computer, which help speedy transfer of data.

Parity Bit: A bit (binary digit) appended to an array of bits to make the sum of all the 1-bits in the array either always even ("even parity") or always odd ("odd parity").

Parity Checks: A check that tests whether the number of 1-bits in an array is either even ("even parity check") or odd ("odd parity check").

Peripheral equipment: The input/output units and secondary storage units of a computer system. **Note:** The central processor and its associated storage and control units are the only units of a computer system which are not considered peripheral equipment.

Peripherals: Additional components which enhance computer performance.

Port: A device by which different component in and out of a system unit can be connected.

PPP – (Point to Point Protocol): Most well known as a protocol that allows a computer to use a regular telephone line and a modem to make TCP/IP connections and thus be really and truly on the Internet.

Printer: A device for generating computer output on paper.

Problem-oriented language: A language whose design is oriented toward the specification of a particular class of problems, such as numerical control of machine tools. Sometimes used as a general term to describe both procedure and problem-oriented languages.

Procedure-oriented language: A language designed to permit convenient specification, in terms of procedural or algorithmic steps, of data processing or computational processes. Examples include ALGOL, COBOL and FORTRAN. Contrast with problem-oriented language and machine-oriented language.

Program: A set of instructions that a computer follows to perform a task.

Programmable read-only memory (PROM): Computer memory chips that can be programmed permanently, by burning the circuits in patterns, to carry out predefined process.

Programming language/1: (PL/1) A general-purpose, high level language that is designed to combine business and scientific processing features and that can be easily learned by novice programmers, yet contains advanced features for experienced programmers.

Protocol Translator: A peripheral device which converts the communications protocol of one system into the protocols of another system so that the two systems are compatible enabling data to be transferred between them.

PSET: Command in BASIC to show a point on the screen.

QuickTime: A multimedia plug-in program from Apple. It can play sound, animation, text and video in a single file.

RAM: Randon Access Memory, the part of the computer which keeps operating system and applications' data. RAM is very fast to access, but it only stays as long as the computer is running.

Random Access Memory (RAM): Temporary memory that holds application programs and data which you create and manipulate.

Random access: Pertaining to a storage device whose access time is not significantly affected by the location of the data to be accessed, thus, any item of data which is stored online can be accessed within a relatively short time (usually in part of a second). Same as direct access. Contrast with serial access.

Read-Only Memory (ROM): Permanent memory that hold the programs which are responsible for the initial phases of starting a computer.

Reboot: To restart a computer by turning it off and then on again by pressing Ctrl, Alt, Del, or by pressing a reset button.

Redundancy check: A check based on the transfer of more bits or characters than the minimum number required to express the massage itself, the added bits or characters having been inserted systematically for checking purposes. The most common type of redundancy check is parity check.

Residue check: A check of numeric data or arithmetic operation in which each number A, is divided by the modulo, N, and the remainder, B, accompanies A as a check digits. For example, in modulo 4 checks, B will be either 0, 1, 2 or 3; if the remainder formed when A is divided by 4 does not equal B, an error is indicated. Synonymous with modulo N check.

Resolution: It indicates the degree of details—that can be perceived. The higher the resolution, the finer the detail.

Router: A special purpose computer (or software package) that handles the connection between 2 or more networks. Routers spend all their time looking at the destination addresses of the packets passing through them and deciding which route to send them on.

Run manual: A manual documenting the processing system, program logic, controls, program changes, and operating instructions associated with a computer run.

Run: A performance of a specific process by a computer on a given set of data *i.e.*, the execution of one routine or of several routines which are linked to form one operating unit, during which little or no human intervention is required.

Scanner: A device used to copy pictures from papers or photographs to computer.

Scroll: To move a graphics image or the text on the monitor up, down, right, or left, in a smooth, usually continuous and reversible action.

Search Engine: A program, or a system of programs, which uses keywords to find Web pages containing matching words, returning the results to the user.

Secondary storage: Storage that supplements a computer's primary internal storage. Synonymous with auxiliary storage.

Security program: Systems program that controls access to data in files and permits only authorized use of terminals and other equipments. Control is usually through various levels of pass words assigned on the basis of need to know.

Server: A computer, or a software package, that provides a specific kind of service to client software running on other computers. The term can refer to a particular piece of software, such as a WWW server, or to the machine on which the software is running *e.g.*, Our mail server is down today, that's why e-mail isn't getting out. A single server machine could have several different server software packages running on it, thus providing many different servers to clients on the network.

Shareware: Shareware is software that is initially free to download, with the agreement that the user may have to pay for it later.

SMPS (Switched Mode Power Supply) : The part of a system unit which distributes power supply to all segments of a computer.

Software: 1. A collection of programs and routines associated with a computer (including assemblers, compilers, utility routines, and operating systems) which facilitates the programming and operation of the computer. Contrast with hardware.

2. Any set of instructions or data a computer may use. The programs that tell a computer what to do and how to do it.

Sound Card: An electronic circuit card which can convert the data from computer on sound waves to pan it to speakers.

Source Program: A program written in a source language (*e.g.*, written in COBOL, C, FORTRAN, or symbolic coding for input to a compiler or assembler).

Spam: Internet slang for unsolicited, and often commercial, e-mail or newsgroup postings.

Spider: A program that automatically culls Web pages. Spiders are often used in search engines.

Spooling: Computer processing technique under which input and output files originating on and destined for slow-speed devices are written to high-speed storage devices prior to and following processing. Thus, processing can take place at high speeds while input and output can be handled separately at relatively slow speeds.

Spreadsheet An electronic grid of rows and columns used to enter, organize and analyze a collection of numbers or data.

SQL – (Structured Query Language): A specialized programming language for sending queries to databases.

Status line: An area–a strip–at the bottom of the screen that tells the user about the operations of a program he/she is working in. For instance, a status line could tell that the file is now being saved, or that it is being printed.

Storage allocation: The assignment of specific programs, program segments, and or block of data to specific portions of a computer's storage.

Streaming: Continuously playing audio (streaming audio) or video (streaming video). Users don't need to wait for large files to download before listening or viewing. Instead, the media plays as it arrives.

Subdirectory or Subfolder: A directory that is contained within or is subordinate to another directory.

Surf: Internet term for exploring the Internet without a pre-set agenda. See also Browse.

System development life cycle (SDLC): Activities required to develop, implement and install a new or revised system. Standard activity phases include investigation, analysis and general design, detailed design and implementation, installation, and review.

T-1, T-3: Bell introduced the T-carrier system, the first successful system to support digital transmission, in the 1960s. The original rate, T-1 (1.544 Mbps) is a higher-speed line commonly used by ISPs (Internet Service Providers). T-3 (44.736 Mbps) is an even higher speed line.

Tab: (1) Facility to move the curser at prefixed small distance between words, to prepare small tables. (2) The space given between two words using the tab key. (3) Mechanism in dialogue boxes like paragraph in word processors to organize more than one information in the same box.

Task Bar: The bottom portion of a window where the start button, time button etc. are usually placed.

TCP/IP – (Transmission Control Protocol/Internet Protocol): This is the suite of protocols that defines the Internet. Originally designed for the UNIX operating system, TCP/IP software is now available for every major kind of computer operating system. To be truly on the Internet, your computer must have TCP/IP software.

Template: A previously made model slide.

Toggle: A switch or control code that turns an event on or off by repeated action or use; to turn something on or off by repeating the same action.

Track: That part of a data storage medium that is influenced by (or influences) one head; *e.g.*, the ring-shaped portion of the surface of a disk, or one of several divisions (most commonly seven or nine) running parallel to the edges of a magnetic tape.

Translator: A device or computer program that performs translation from one language or code to another – *e.g.*, an assembler or compiler.

UNIX Operating System: Computer operating system developed by the Bell Telephone Laboratories in the USA. Currently considered to be the system of the future with many manufacturers adopting UNIX for their new ranges of equipments. Office automation software is, on the whole, not very well represented in the UNIX area. There are some world processing packages, such as Q-One from Quadratronic, an offering from Interplex within an integrated package, Crystalwriter from Syntactics and UNIX-option Multimate which will be available shortly.

UNIX: An operating system developed in the early '70s. It was the first operating system written with the C language, and was the first open or standard operating system. UNIX is popular with workstations, but not personal computers.

Unpack: To separate short units of data that have previously been packed *i.e.*, to reverse a packing operation.

Update: To incorporate into a master file the changes required to reflect recent transactions or other events.

URL – (Uniform Resource Locator): The standard way to give the address of any resource on the Internet that is part of the World Wide Web (WWW). A URL looks like this : http://www.icai.org/seminars.htnnl or telnet://well.sf.ca.in or newsmew.newusers.questions etc. The most common way to use a URL is to enter into a WWW browser program, such as Netscape, or Lynx.

USB Port (Universal Serial Bus Port): A way by which external equipments can be attached to a computer.

Utility routine: A standard routine used to assist in the operation of a computer by performing some frequently required processes such as sorting, merging, report program generation, data transcription, file maintenance, etc. Utility routines are important components of the software supplied by the manufacturers of most computers.

Vector File: A file stored with vector graphics or pictures.

Vector Image: Picture file madeup of geometric shapes like circuts, rectangles, ovals etc.

Very large scale integration (VLSI): Design and production techniques to place thousands of electronic components within small integrated circuit chips to reduce their sizes and costs.

Webmaster: Individual who creates and or manages a Web site. May also be the individual who manages the technical aspects of a Web site.

Wildcard Characters: Special characters that can be used in most DOS commands as substitutes for other characters. The asterisk (*) and the question mark (?) symbols are wildcard characters.

Word Length: The number of bits or characters in a word.

WWW: World Wide Web, all the resources on the Internet that use HTTP, or hypertext transfer protocol, *e.g.* Web pages.

Zip Drive: Durable disk drive that uses 100 MB disks. Popular for backing up hard drives, or transporting large files.

Zip File: File made up of several other files compressed into one.

Zoom: The command to see a thing on the screen as enlarged or as reduced.

ABBREVIATIONS

ACC	Accumulator
ACK	Acknowledge character
A/D	Analog to Digital
ADCCP	Advanced Data Communication Control Procedure
ADP	Automatic Data Processing
ALGOL	ALGOrithmic Language
ALU	Arithmetic Logic Unit
AM	Amplitude Modulation or Accounting Machine or Access Mechanism
ANSI	American National Standards Institute
APDOS	Apple DOS Operating System
AP	Attached Processor
APL	A Programming Language
ASCII	American Standard Code for Information Interchange
ASR	Automatic Send and Receive
ATM	Automatic Teller Machine
AU	Arithmetic Unit
BASIC	Beginner's All-purpose Symbolic Instruction Code
BCD	Binary Coded Decimal
BCS	British Computer Society
BDOS	Basic Disk Operating System
BIT	Binary digit
BIOS	Basic Input/Output System
BMC	Bubble Memory Control
Bps	Bits per second
BPI	Bytes per Inch
BROM	Bipolar Read Only Memory
BSAM	Basic Sequential Access Method
BSC	Binary Synchronous Communications
CAD	Computer Aided (Assisted) Design
CAD/CAM	Computer-Aided Design/Computer-Aided Manufacturing
CAFS	Contents Addressable File Store
CAI	Computer Aided (Assisted) Instruction
CAL	Computer Aided (Assisted) Learning
CAM	Computer Aided (Assisted) Manufacturing or Content Addressed Memory
CASE	Computer Aided Software Engineering
CAT	1. Computer Aided (Assisted) Training
	2. Computer Aided (Axial) Topography
CCD	Charge Coupled Device
CGA	Colour Graphics Adapter
CDAC	Centre for Development of Advanced Computing
CDROM	Computer Disk Read Only Memory
CICS	Computer Information Control System
CIM	Computer Input Microfilm
CLIP	Computer Language Information Processing
CMI	Computer Managed Instruction
CMOS	Complementary Metal Oxide Semiconductor
CML	Computer Managed Learning
CNC	Computer Numerical Control
COBOL	Common Business Oriented Language
CODASYL	Conference on Data System Languages
COM	Computer Output (Originated) Microfilm
COMAL	Common Algorithmic language
CORAL	Class Oriented Ring Associated Language
Cps	Characters per second
CPM	Control Program for Microprocessor

CPU	Central Processing Unit
CROM	Control Read Only Memory
CRT	Cathode Ray Tube
CSI	Computer Society of India
DS/HD	Double Sided, high density
DS/DD	Double Sided, double density
DAD	Direct Access Devices
DASD	Direct Access Storage Device
DBMS	Data Base Management System
DBTG	Data Base Task Group (of CODASYL)
DCE	Data Communications Equipment
DDL	Data Description (or Definition) Language
DDP	Distributed Data Processing
DOS	Disk (based) Operating System
DP	Data Processing
DPI	Dots per inch
DTP	Desktop Publishing
DPM	Data Processing Manager
DPS	Data Processing System
DRO	Destructive Read Out
DSS	Decision Support System
EBCDIC	Extended Binary Coded Decimal Interchange Code
ECMA	European Computer Manufacturers Association
ECOM	Electronic computer oriented mail
EDI	Electronic Data Interchange
EDS	Exchangeable Disk Store
EEPROM	Electrically Erasable Programmed Read Only Memory
EDP	Electronic Data Processing (equivalent to DP)
EFTS	Electronic Funds Transfer System
ENIAC	Electronic Numerical Integrator and Calculator
EPROM	Erasable Programmable Read Only Memory
FGCS	Fifth Generation Computer System
FEP	Front-End Processor
FORTRAN	Formula Translation
GB	Giga Bytes
GIGO	Garbage In/Garbage Out
GUI	Graphical User Interface
HIPO	Hierarchical Input/Process/Output
HLL	High Level Language
Hz	Hertz
IBG	Inter Block Gap
IC	Integrated Circuit
IDP	Integrated Data Processing
IFIP	International Federation for Information Processing
IMPLE	Initial Micro Program Load
I/O	Input/Output
IOCS	Input/Output Control System
IPS	Instructions per second
ISAM	Index(ed) Sequential Access method
ISDN	Integrated Services Digital Network
ISO	International Standards Organisation
ISR	Information Storage Retrieval
JCL	Job Control Language
K	Kilo-1000 in decimal; 1024 (210) in binary system
KBS	Kilo-Bytes per second
LAN	Local Area Network
LAP	Link Access Protocol
LCD	Liquid Crystal Display

LED	Light Emitting Diode
LISP	LIST Processing
LSI	Large Scale Integration
MB	Mega bytes.1 million in decimal; 1,048, 576 (220) in binary system
MAR	Memory Address Register
MCI	Magnetic Character Inscriber
MDR	Memory Data Register
MICR	Magnetic Ink Character Recognition
MIPS	Millions of instructions per second
MIS	Management Information System (or Services)
MPU	Micro-Processor Unit
MSI	Medium Scale Integration
MVS	Multiple Virtual Storage
NCC	National Computing Centre
NS	Nano Second
OCR	Optical Character Recognition (Reading)
OMR	Optical Mark Recognition (Reading)
OOF	Office of the Future
OOP	Object Oriented Programming
OS	Operating Systems
OPS	Operating per second
OSI	Open systems Interconnection
PBX	Private Branch Exchange
PCB	Printed Circuit Board
PC	Personal Computer
POS	Point-of Sale
PIN	Personal Identification Number
PL/1	Programming Language/1
PMOS	P-Channel Metal Oxide Semiconductor
PROLOG	Programming in Logic
PROM	Programmable Read Only Memory
PSE	Packet Switched System
PSTN	Public Switched Telephone network
QBE	Query By Example
RAM	Random Access Memory
RCS	Realtime Communication System
RJE	Remote Job Entry
ROM	Read Only Memory
RPG	Report Program Generator
RTL	Real Time language
RDBMS	Relational Data Base Management Systems
SOP	Standard Operating Procedure
SNOBL	String Oriented Symbolic Languages
SNA	Systems Network Architecture
SQL	Structured Query Language
SSI	Small Scale Integration
TDM	Time Division Multiplexing
TPI	Tracks Per inch
TRS	Tandy Radio Shack
T/S	Time Sharing
TSS	Time Sharing System
TTY	Tele Typewriter
UG	User Group
UNIVAC	Universal automatic computer
VDU	Visual Display Unit
VAN	Value Added Network
VLDB	Very Large Data Base
VGA	Video Graphics Adapter
VLSI	Very Large Scale Integration
WAN	Wide Area Network
WORM	Write Once, Read Memory
WP	Word Processing

❑ ❑ ❑

MULTIPLE CHOICE QUESTIONS

1. Machine language is different
   A. for some computer
   B. for each kind of computer c.p.u.
   C. Both A or B
   D. None of the above

2. A programmer if write instructions in machine language can specify an....... bit with the numerical 1.
   A. on B. off
   C. into D. None of these

3. Every operation that the computer is capable of performing is indicated by a specific
   A. code B. language
   C. binary code D. None of these

4. The assembly programmer must use the proper code for
   A. each operation
   B. each high level language
   C. all arithmetic operations
   D. all languages

5. Machine language is also called
   A. language
   B. machine
   C. binary representation
   D. None of the above

6. An 'on' bit indicates the presence of an
   A. electric current B. off
   C. address D. None of these

7. Programming language can be divided into.....categories.
   A. four broad B. three
   C. five D. six

8. The operating system contains
   A. same programs repetitively
   B. several types of programs
   C. a few programs
   D. None of the above

9. Utility programs performs
   A. specialized and useful functions
   B. all functions
   C. a few functions
   D. None of the above

10. The supervisor program is the major component of the
    A. system B. operating system
    C. all system D. language

11. When the computer is first turn on, the supervisor program is the..........to be used.
    A. last program B. first program
    C. middle program D. None of the above

12. A job is a unit of work to be processed by the
    A. CPU B. ALU
    C. TD D. memory

13. A computer can only execute instructions that are in
    A. secondary memory
    B. machine language
    C. pascal
    D. None of the above

14. English-like programs such as those written in Pascal must use for their execution, a
    A. language program
    B. language translation program
    C. Both A and B
    D. None of the above

15. Language translation program translates the English-like program into
    A. other language B. other program
    C. machine language D. None of the above

16. There are..........types of language translation programs.
    A. four B. two
    C. three D. five

17. A utility program can translate data from a format to
    A. another format
    B. any machine language
    C. Both A and B
    D. None of the above

18. The supervisor schedules the order of input and
A. other operations
B. a few operations
C. output operations
D. None of the above

19. When the computers were first developed, machine language was the only way they could be
A. used
B. programmed
C. Both A and B
D. None of these

20. Assembly language is also referred as
A. low-level language
B. high-level language
C. Both A and B
D. None of the above

21. Assembly language is easier for people to understand than
A. other languages
B. machine language
C. a few languages
D. None of the above

22. Assembly language instructions will execute faster than those written in
A. different language
B. a few languages
C. high level languages
D. None of the above

23. High level language is simpler to write a program than in
A. other languages
B. machine language
C. a few languages
D. None of the above

24. High-level-languages are strongly oriented towards the programmer rather than towards the
A. computer
B. other languages
C. Both A and B
D. None of these

25. A person who does not know a particular high level language can never determine the general purpose of the
A. computer
B. program statements
C. Both A and B
D. None of the above

26. COBOL is a
A. language program
B. machine program
C. high-level program
D. None of the above

27. Pascal is a fairly new
A. natural language
B. programming language
C. Both A and B
D. None of the above

28. Pascal was designed by
A. Niklaus Wirth
B. Blaise Pascal
C. Corrado Bohm
D. Guiseppe Jacopini

29. The Pascal languages was named after
A. Corrado Bohm
B. Blaise Pascal
C. Guiseppe Jacopini
D. Niklaus Wirth

30. The Pascal language was specifically developed to teach good
A. language
B. programming
C. structural programming
D. None of the above

31. An important feature of Pascal is that it is a general-purpose
A. language
B. programming learning language
C. Both A and B
D. None of the above

32. In Pascal, identifiers are used to name the parts of a
A. program
B. language
C. Both A and B
D. None of these

33. A valid Pascal identifier is any string of characters that begins with a letter (*a–z*) and contains letters (*a–z*) or digits
A. (0–10)
B. (0–9)
C. (0–11)
D. (0–12)

34. The primary storage unit also referred to as
A. internal storage
B. main memory, primary memory
C. Both A and B
D. None of the above

35. A given computer system can have
A. many different input devices
B. only one input device
C. two input devices
D. None of the above

36. Hardware consists of the actual
A. main memory B. control unit
C. Both A and B D. None of these

37. Programs and data that are entered into a computer to be processed are called
A. output B. input
C. Both A and B D. None of these

38. The communication between the CPU and external modules takes place via the
A. data B. address only
C. Both A and B D. None of these

39. Disk and tape drives are commonly used
A. hard copy
B. soft copy
C. secondary storage devices
D. None of the above

40. Mini Computers manufactured today are more powerful than
A. main frames B. super computers
C. micro computers D. none of these

41. Some programs direct the computer in its own internal operations. These are called
A. system programs
B. software
C. Both A and B
D. application programs

42. Which of the following computer is currently the smallest and least costly computer?
A. Super computer
B. Micro computer
C. Both A and B
D. None of the above

43. A computer is a device for automatically carrying out a/an
A. program of instructions
B. information
C. instructions
D. None of the above

44. One of the more modern programming language is called
A. higher language
B. assembly language
C. Pascal
D. None of the above

45. The arithmetic unit (ALU) performs
A. primary memory
B. mathematics computations
C. central processing unit
D. None of the above

46. Arithmetic and logic operations are the only types of instructions that the
A. ALU is able to execute
B. CPU is able to execute
C. hardware is able to execute
D. None of the above

47. Part of a record used to identify the record is called
A. language B. address
C. key D. None of these

48. The complete range of programs available for a computer is called
A. hardware B. software
C. Both A and B D. None of these

49. Set of instructions to the computer is called
A. language B. program
C. Both A and B D. None of these

50. Peripheral unit capable of writing or displaying output is called
A. output device B. input device
C. Both A and B D. None of these

51. A device with slowest switching speed is
A. LCD B. Nixie tubes
C. Octal code D. Both B and C

52. Which circuit is used for a clock generator?
A. JK flip flop
B. A free running MV
C. Both A and B
D. None of the above

53. A toggle operation is used
A. with a flip flop

B. with a gare circuit
C. Both A and B
D. None of the above

54. A memory used for storing variable quantities is
A. Erasable Programmable Read Only Memory (EPROM)
B. Programmable Read Only Memory (PROM)
C. Random Access Memory (RAM)
D. None of these

55. Which of the following is a temporary memory?
A. ROM B. RAM
C. Both A and B D. None of these

56. Which of the following is an electrostatic device?
A. PNP transistor B. MOSFET
C. both A and B D. None of these

57. In SQL the statement Expand Table can be used at any time
A. given relation B. combination
C. old relation D. None of these

58. A relation is in Third Normal Form (TNF) if and only if its non-key domains (if any) are mutually independent and fully independent on its.
A. key B. primary key
C. Both A and B D. None of these

59. A unit of data whose description appears with its occurrence. This is called
A. Defining data
B. Data
C. self defining data
D. None of the above

60. The process of reversing recent activities of the system to store some of or all of the database to its state at a previous point in time. This is known as
A. Roll B. address
C. Roll Back D. Both A and B

61. The operation of producing a subset of one relation which contains all tuples that are in common with a second relation. This is known as
A. Restriction B. Restructure
C. Both A and B D. None of these

62. Any large software project may be divided into
A. sub project B. project phases
C. hardware D. None of these

63. Program correctness has been a strong motivation for much of the work in software engineering and
A. programming language design
B. Pascal
C. high-level language programming
D. None of the above

64. The term "software engineering" implies the application of scientific knowledge and discipline to the construction of
A. computer hardware system
B. computer software system
C. database record
D. None of the above

65. Database software may be divided into
A. two distinct categories
B. four distinct categories
C. three distinct categories
D. None of the above

66. In hierarchical data model, the data base is represented by
A. tree structures B. relation
C. a directed graph D. None of these

67. An entity defines a block structure similar to
A. scheme
B. hierarchical structure
C. Pascal's record constructor
D. None of the above

68. The data model proposed by E.F. Codd in 1970 is called the
A. *n*-ary relational data model
B. network model
C. Codd model
D. None of the above

69. SQL is a relational language which has also been implemented in several
A. Advanced Peer-Peer Networking (APPN)
B. Database Management Systems (DBMS)
C. Both A and B
D. None of these

70. Relational algebra can be used to express
A. queries B. updates
C. Both A and B D. None of these

71. A transaction file is the unit of concurrence and
A. recovery control B. software system
C. system D. None of these

72. A great advantage of Modula-2 over Ada is that it is a
A. Pascal language B. greater language
C. small language D. Both A and B

73. The logical database design is a
A. two-stage process B. four-stage process
C. three-stage process D. None of the above

74. Program correctness has been a strong motivation for much of the work in software engineering and
A. assembly language B. hardware system
C. Both A and B D. None of the above

75. In software system, the data must be shared among
A. many different users
B. a very few users
C. Both A and B
D. None of the above

76. Concurrency control in database management systems, includes
A. transaction
B. alternatives to locking
C. database procedure
D. None of the above

77. An actual op-amp may have gain of about
A. 10^3 to 10^4 B. 10^4 to 10^6
C. 10^4 to 10^8 D. 10^4 to 10^7

78. Which of the following amplifier compensates for drift?
A. Differential amplifier
B. DC amplifier
C. Low gain amplifier
D. None of the above

79. Noise in op-amp may be due to
A. internal generation
B. pick up from main supply
C. Both A and B
D. None of the above

80. An ideal op-amp should have
A. high gain at all frequencies
B. low gain at low frequencies
C. Both A and B
D. None of the above

81. An ideal op-amp should have
A. infinite input
B. infinite input impedance
C. zero output impedance
D. Both B and C

82. The product AB for amplifier is known as
A. loop gain B. feedback factor
C. Both A and B D. None of these

83. An op-amp can be used for implementing which of the following mathematical operations?
A. Sign reversal B. Integration
C. Both A and B D. None of these

84. Which of the following systems is linear?
A. Voltage to current converter
B. Logarithmic amplifiers
C. Both A and B
D. None of the above

85. Which of the following systems is non-linear?
A. Sample and hold current
B. Logarithmic amplifier
C. Both A and B
D. None of the above

86. A linear system can be described by
A. dynamic equation
B. state transition equation
C. Both A and B
D. None of the above

87. The phenomenon of backlash is associated with
A. gear trains
B. servo motor
C. oscillators
D. None of these

88. For a differential amplifier, the common mode rejection ratio (CMRR) should be
A. as small as possible
B. as large as possible
C. zero
D. None of the above

89. A logarithmic amplifier can be used as
A. multiplier B. divider
C. Both A and B D. None of these

90. An operating system that allows the user to correct input data has
A. text editing
B. language processing
C. file storage
D. None of the above

91. Which of the following sorting algorithms has average-case and worst-case running time of 0 (*n* log *n*)?
A. Merge sort B. Quick sort
C. Bubble sort D. None of these

92. ALGOL is oriented to the solution of scientific language. ALGOL introduced the idea of
A. structural programming
B. nested procedures
C. Both A and B
D. None of the above

93. 13 bits are used for addressing the memory. The last storage address will be
A. 8133 B. 8188
C. 8191 D. 9225

94. Programming in a language that actually controls the path of signals or data within the computer is called:
A. instruction set
B. micro programming
C. machine language programming
D. None of the above

95. FORTRAN is a
A. Content-sensitive language
B. Regular language
C. Both A and B
D. None of the above

96. Which basic components comprise a machine instruction?
A. Operation part B. Address part
C. Both A and B D. None of these

97. A language in which a statement in a loop that runs 100 times and is decoded 100 times, is
A. FORTRAN B. COBOL
C. PASCAL D. BASIC

98. If no gaps or special formatting is assumed, then the nominal storage capacity, in bytes, of one such disk is
A. 218,750 B. 315,840
C. 450,35 D. 115,333

99. A general term denoting by collection of data, be it a data item, data aggregate, record, set or file. This is known as
A. Data structure B. Data privacy
C. Data unit D. Dead lock

100. The network model has been established by
A. IBM
B. ECA
C. CODASYL committee
D. None of the above

101. The word size of a microprocessor refers to—
A. The amount of information that can be stored in a byte
B. The amount of information that can be stored in a cycle
C. The number of machine operations performed in a second
D. The maximum length of an English word that can be input to a computer

102. Bar codes store information using—
A. Punch holes
B. Thick and thin lines
C. Magnetized spots
D. Bits

103. Below are examples of real security and privacy risks EXCEPT—
A. hackers B. identity theft
C. spam D. viruses

104. Which is an electronic device that can store temporarily a single bit of data.
A. Accumulator B. Buffer
C. Memory D. Latch

105. The first generation computers were characterised by—
A. Micro processor chips
B. Thermionic valves
C. Transistors
D. Integrated circuits

106. The ability to recover and read deleted or damaged files from a criminal computer is an example of a law enforcement specialty known as—
A. robotics
B. computer forensics
C. simulation
D. animation

107. A modern digital computer has—
A. Extremely high speed
B. Large memory
C. Almost unlimited army
D. All of these

108. What is the full form of COBOL?
A. Common Business Objective Language
B. Command Byte Oriented Language
C. Common Business Oriented Language
D. Character Business Oriented Language

109. Find the invalid combination.
A. Dot Matrix Printer - Impact Printer
B. Laser Printer - Non Impact Printer
C. Daisy Wheel Printer - Non Impact Printer
D. Inkjet Printer - Non Impact Printer

110. In which generation of computers transistors were used?
A. First generation computers
B. Second generation computers
C. Third generation computers
D. Fourth generation computers

111. Which computer system is mainly used in Weather forecasting and Disaster control?
A. Super computer
B. Mainframe computer
C. Micro computer
D. Personal computer

112. A factor which would strongly influence a business person to adopt a computer is its—
A. Accuracy B. Reliability
C. Speed D. All of these

113. The output quality of a printer is determined by—
A. Dot per sq. inch
B. Dot per inch
C. Dots printed per unit time
D. All of above

114. The first microprocessor built by the Intel Corporation was called—
A. 8008 B. 8080
C. 4004 D. 8800

115. When was the first minicomputer built?
A. 1965 B. 1962
C. 1971 D. 1966

116. The first digital computer built with IC chips was known as—
A. IBM 7090 B. Apple-1
C. IBM System/360 D. VAX-780

117. What is the name of the British gentleman who was the first to put forward in 1952 the idea for the integrated circuit?
A. Jack S. Kilby B. G.W. Dummer
C. William Shockley D. John Bardeen

118. The magnetic tape consists of a plastic type with a surface coating of magnetic material. When was it invented?
A. 1968 B. 1964
C. 1956 D. 1946

119. In the third generation of computers—
A. Distributed data processing first became popular
B. An operating system was first developed

C. High-level procedural languages were first used
D. On-line, realtime systems first became popular

120. In analog computer—
A. Input is first converted to digital form
B. Output is displayed in digital form
C. Input is never converted to digital form
D. All of above

121. Which of the following devices can be used to directly input 'Text books'?
A. OCR B. OMR
C. MICR D. None of these

122. Ascending order of a data hierarchy is—
A. Bit-byte-record field-file-database
B. Bit-byte-field-record-file-database
C. Byte-bit record file-database
D. None of the above

123. Personal computers are also called—
A. Desktop computers
B. Portable computers
C. Advanced computers
D. Palmtop computers

124. ENIAC stands for—
A. Electronic Number Instruction and Code
B. Electronic Numerical Integrator and Computer
C. Electronic Number Instruction Access Calculator
D. None of these

125. An IP address contains four sets of numbers ranging from—
A. 1 to 100 B. 1 to 1000
C. 0 to 255 D. 1 to 500

126. In 3rd generation computers, the instructions are executed—
A. Both sequentially and parallel
B. Parallel only
C. Sequentially only
D. All of above

127. EPROM consists of—
A. bipolar transistors B. easily erasable
C. MOSFETs D. Diodes

128. Which of the following is used only for data entry and storage, and never for processing?
A. Mouse B. Dumb terminal
C. Microcomputer D. None of these

129. Different components on the motherboard of a PC processor unit are linked together by sets of parallel electrical conducting lines. What are these lines called?
A. Conductors B. Buses
C. Connectors D. None of these

130. Where have the program and data to be located before the ALU and control unit of a computer can operate on it?
A. Internal memory
B. Secondary memory
C. Microprocessor
D. Magnetic types

131. Which chips are erasable by ultra-violet rays after removing them from the main circuit?
A. EPROM chips B. EEPROM chips
C. PROM chips D. All of these

132. A memory bus is mainly used for communication between—
A. processor and memory
B. processor and I/O devices
C. I/O devices and memory
D. input device and output device

133. A name or number used to identify a storage location is called—
A. A byte B. A record
C. An address D. All of these

134. Which of the following is not a primary storage devcie?
A. Magnetic tape B. Magnetic disk
C. Optical disk D. None of these

135. Which of the following is the user programmed semiconductor memory?
A. SRAM B. DRAM
C. EPROM D. All of the above

136. CD-ROM is a—
A. Semiconductor memory
B. Memory register

C. Magnetic memory
D. None of these

137. A characteristic of the ASCII code is—
A. its use of the zone code 1010, 1011 and 1100
B. its limitation to a maximum of 96 character configurations
C. its independence from the Hollerith code
D. All the above

138. A temporary storage area, attached to the CPU, for I/O operations is a—
A. Chip B. Buffer
C. Register D. Core

139. In magnetic disks, data is organized on the platter in a concentric sets of rings called—
A. Sector B. Track
C. Head D. Block

140. Who designed the first electronics computer - ENIAC?
A. Van-Neumann
B. Joseph M. Jacquard
C. J. Presper Eckert and John W Mauchly
D. Richard Davis

141. A code used for standardizing the storage and transfer of information amongst various computing devices is called—
A. CRT B. CPU
C. ASCII D. Dvorak

142. What is the name of the logic circuit which can add two binary digits?
A. Full adder B. Half adder
C. Buffer D. Register

143. Who invented the high level language C?
A. Dennis M. Ritchie B. Donald Kunth
C. Niklaus Writh D. Seymour Papert

144. Two new types of semiconductor memories are—
A. Magnetic disks
B. Charge-coupled devices
C. Magnetic bubble memory
D. Both B and C

145. Magnetic tape is used for—
A. Historical storage B. Computer input
C. Both A and B D. Neither A nor B

146. A byte is comprised of—
A. one bit B. four bits
C. eight bits D. sixteen bits

147. The CPU chip used in a computer is partially made up of—
A. copper B. iron
C. gold and silver D. silica

148. The silicon chips used for data processing are called—
A. RAM chips B. ROM chips
C. micro processor D. PROM chips

149. The hardware in which data may be stored for a computer system is called—
A. Registers B. Bus
C. Control unit D. Memory

150. A half byte is known is—
A. Data B. Bit
C. Half byte D. Nibble

151. The most common binary code in use today is the 8 bit ASCII code. What do the letters ASCII stand for?
A. American Standard Code for International Interchange
B. American Standard Code for Information Interchange
C. American Standard Code for Intelligence Interchange
D. American Scientific Code for Information Interchange

152. Personnel who design, program, operate and maintain computer equipment known as—
A. Console-operator B. Programmer
C. System Analyst D. Peopleware

153. Which of the following is an example of nonvolatile memory?
A. ROM B. VLSI
C. LSI D. RAM

154. Which is used for manufacturing chips?
A. Bus

B. Control unit
C. Semiconductors
D. A and B only

155. The computer code for the interchange of information between terminals is—
A. ASCII B. BCD
C. EBCDIC D. All of these

156. What is the name of the storage device which is used to compensate for the difference in rates of flow of data from once device to another?
A. Cache B. Concentrator
C. Buffer D. I/O device

157. Which is the most popular medium for direct-access secondary storage of a computer?
A. Magnetic tape B. Magnetic disk
C. RAM D. ROM

158. When did arch rivals IBM and Apple Computers Inc. join hands?
A. 1978 B. 1991
C. 1984 D. 1990

159. An error in software or hardware is known as bug. What is the alternative computer jargon for it?
A. Leech B. Squid
C. Glitch D. Slug

160. A type of semiconductor memory that usually has small capacity but very fast access is—
A. PROM B. RAM
C. scratchpad D. ROM

161. A single primary storage location in the processor unit—
A. can hold several different data items at the same time
B. can hold data items but not program instructions
C. is identified by a built-in and unique number called an address
D. is identified by a number that varies with the contents in the location

162. A storage device where the access time is dependent upon the location of the data is—
A. Random access
B. Serial access
C. Sequential access
D. Transaction access

163. Memory that holds microprograms is—
A. core memory B. ROM
C. RAM D. control memory

164. Octal numbers are used—
A. In computer hardware
B. When binary numbers are too long
C. Internal to the computer
D. In preference to 'hex' number

165. Binary numbers need more places for counting because—
A. They are always big numbers
B. Any no. of 0's can be added in front of them
C. Binary base is small
D. 0's and 1's have to be properly spaced apart

166. Any tape of storage that is used for holding information between steps in its processing is—
A. CPU
B. Primary storage
C. Intermediate storage
D. Internal storage

167. PROM is a type of computer memory. What does PROM stands for?
A. Powered Read Only Memory
B. Programmable Read Only Memory
C. Permanent Read Only Memory
D. Powered Read & Write Only Memory

168. Which one of the following is not a correct definition?
A. SRAM → Static Random Access Memory
B. PROM → Programmable Read Only Memory
C. DRAM → Dynamic Random Access Memory
D. SAM → Static Access Memory

169. Which of the following are the type of the secondary storage?

A. Floppy Disk & Hard Disk
B. Floppy Disk & ROM
C. Hard Disk & RAM
D. None of the above

170. Who defined the binary number system?
A. Pascal B. A.D. Leibniz
C. Newton D. Aristotle

171. Find the valid statements—
A. A floppy has more capacity than a hard disk
B. Hard disk is a primary memory device
C. RAM stands for Read Access Memory
D. ROM is a permanent memory

172. A set of programs that handle firm's data base responsibilities is called a—
A. Data Base Management System (DBMS)
B. Data Base Processing System (DBPS)
C. Data Management System (DMS)
D. All of the above

173. A computer will function only if it:
A. Has a control unit
B. Is given input data
C. Has a program in its memory
D. Has software package

174. The comparison of data inside the arithmetic logic unit is referred to as a—
A. Instruction
B. Data operation
C. Conditional question
D. Logical operation

175. Which of the following statement is false?
A. Generally, computers don't make mistake
B. Computers eliminate jobs
C. Computers can think
D. Maths is necessary to understand computers

176. Surgeons can perform delicate operations by manipulating devices through computers instead of manually. This technology is known as—
A. Computer forensics B. Simulation
C. Forecasting D. Robotics

177. A programme written in machine language is called—
A. Assembler B. Object
C. Computer D. Machine

178. Data transfer using telephone system is—
A. Time division multiplexing
B. Space division multiplexing
C. Frequency division multiplexing
D. All of the above

179. Software instructions intended to satisfy a user's specific processing needs are called_________.
A. Systems software
B. A microcomputer
C. Documentation
D. Application software

180. Which of the following is responsible for coordinating various operations using timing signals?
A. Arithmetic-logic unit B. Control unit
C. Memory unit D. Input/Output unit

181. A single but structure is primarily found in—
A. Main frames
B. Super computers
C. High performance machines
D. Mini and micro-computers

182. The study of molecules and structures whose size ranges from 1 to 100 nanometers.
A. Nanoscience
B. Artificial intelligence
C. Microelectrodes
D. Computer forensics

183. What is the term which represents the used of links between information of all softs whether text, graphics, video or audio-based?
A. Hypertext B. Hypermedia
C. HyperCard D. Wild Card

184. The two basic types of record-access methods are—
A. Sequential and random
B. Sequential and indexed
C. Direct and immediate
D. On-line and realtime

185. Modern Computer are very reliable but they are not

A. Fast B. Powerful
C. Infallible D. Economical

186. The language that the computer can understand and execute is called—
A. machine language
B. application software
C. system program
D. all of the above

187. Where was the India's first computer installed and when?
A. Institute of Social Science, Agra, 1955
B. Indian Institute of Statistics, Delhi, 1957
C. Indian Statistical Institute, Calcutta, 1955
D. Indian Institute of Science, Bangalore, 1971

188. The first electronic digital computer contained?
A. Electronic valves
B. Vacuum tubes
C. Transistors
D. Semiconductor memory

189. The first computer made available for commercial use was—
A. Mark-I B. ENIAC
C. EDSAC D. UNIVAC

190. The third generation of computer covers the period—
A. 1971-1982 B. 1982-1984
C. 1959-1964 D. 1964-1977

191. What was the computer conceived by Babbage?
A. Analytical Engine
B. Arithmetic Machine
C. Donald Knuth
D. All of the above

192. The process of starting or restarting a computer system by loading instruction from a secondary storage device into the computer memory is called—
A. Duping B. Booting
C. Padding D. All of the above

193. Who invented the microprocessor?
A. Marcian E. Huff
B. Herman H. Goldstein
C. Joseph Jacquard
D. All of the above

194. In which year were chips used inside the computer for the first time?
A. 1964 B. 1975
C. 1977 D. 1981

195. Computers on an internet are identified by—
A. E-mail address B. Street address
C. IP address D. All the these

196. Which one of the following is different from other members?
A. Google B. Windows
C. Linux D. Mac

197. The proper definition of a modern digital computer is—
A. an electronic automated machine that can solve problems involving words and numbers
B. a more sophisticated and modified electronic pocket calculator
C. any machine that can perform mathematical operations
D. a machine that words on binary code

198. Personal computers have number of chips mounted on a main circuit board. What is the common name for such boards?
A. Motherboard B. Fatherboard
C. Breadboard D. Daughterboard

199. In analog computer:
A. input is first converted to digital form
B. input is never converted to digital form
C. output is displayed in digital form
D. all of the above

200. Data processing computer built to conventional architecture is known as—
A. Super computer
B. Mainframe
C. Micro computer
D. Mini computer

201. Operatinng System concept started in _______
A. First generation computer

B. Second generation computer
C. Third generation computer
D. Fourth generation computer

202. A German mathematician who invented a calculator, for addition, subtraction, multiplication and division, His name was—
A. Napier B. Pascal
C. Leibniz D. Hollerith

203. Who invented analytical machine?
A. Charles Babbage B. Hollerith
C. Pascal D. Napier

204. Modern computers are very reliable but they are not—
A. Fast B. Powerful
C. Infallible D. Cheap

205. A complete microcomputer system consists of—
A. Microprocessor B. Memory
C. Peripheral equipment D. All of the above

206. Modem is a/an—
A. input device B. output device
C. both A and B D. storage device

207. Computer peripherals do not include—
A. UPS B. Speaker
C. Microphone D. Microwave

208. This device helps us to change our voice into electronic signals, is called—
A. Speakers B. Mouse
C. Microphone D. Motherboard

209. Which one of the following is Essential Peripheral?
A. Monitor B. Keyboard
C. Mouse D. All of the above

210. Which is not a 'Computer Peripherals—
A. Scanner B. Speaker
C. CPU D. Printer

211. ________ is an input device used for computer.
A. Scanner B. Joystick
C. Light pen D. All of these

212. In most IBM PCs, the CPU, the device drives, memory expansion slots and active components are mounted on a single board. What is the name of this board?
A. Breadboard B. Daughter board
C. Grandmother board D. Motherboard

213. The output that is printed on paper is called—
A. Hard copy B. Soft copy
C. Both A and B D. All of the above

214. In which kind of printers, a light beam is used to print?
A. Dot-matrix printers B. Line printers
C. Inkjet printers D. Laser printers

215. _______ printers are used for very good quality printout.
A. Dot-matrix B. Line
C. Inkjet D. Laser

216. Mouse, Keyboard, Monitor and Printer etc are examples of—
A. Software B. Memory
C. Peripherals D. CPU

217. A computer program that translates program instructions into machine language is called a/an
A. Interpreter B. Loader
C. Compiler D. Simulator

218. Which is not an input device?
A. CRT (Cathode Ray Tube)
B. Optical scanners
C. Voice recognition devices
D. COM (Computer Micro film)

219. Which is considered a direct entry input device?
A. Optical scanner B. Mouse
C. Light pen D. All of above

220. What of the following terms is related to a monitor?
A. Screen
B. Monochrome monitor
C. RGB monitor
D. Video display

221. The computer device primarily used to provide hardcopy is the—
A. CRT B. line printer
C. computer console D. card reader

222. Which of the following is a non-impact printer?
A. Daisy wheel printer B. Drum printer
C. Laser printer D. All of the above

223. The input unit of a computer _________
A. feeds data to the CPU or Memory
B. retrieves data from CPU
C. directs all other units
D. All of the above

224. Direct entry data devices include—
A. telephone, communications and bar codes
B. keyboards, cartridges and bar code reader
C. machine communication, key boards and data collection devices
D. analog computers, digital computers and time clocks

225. A disadvantage of the laser printer is—
A. It is quieter than an impact printer
B. It is very slow
C. The output is of a lower quality
D. None of these

226. Which of the following is used only for data entry and storage, and never for processing?
A. Mouse
B. Dumb terminal
C. Microcomputer
D. Dedicated data entry system

227. A small or intelligent device is so called because it contains within it a
A. Program B. Sensor
C. Computer D. Microcomputer

228. Compact discs, hold how many minutes of data?
A. 56 mins B. 60 mins
C. 60 mins D. 74 mins

229. Which of the following is a device that changes data from coded form to clear form—
A. Keyboard B. Decoder
C. Mnemonics D. Bar code

230. An input device that reads printed text employing optical character pattern matching is known as—
A. Scanner B. Magnetic disk
C. Mouse D. Magnetic tape

ANSWERS

1	2	3	4	5	6	7	8	9	10
B	A	C	A	C	A	A	B	A	B
11	**12**	**13**	**14**	**15**	**16**	**17**	**18**	**19**	**20**
B	A	B	B	C	C	A	C	B	A
21	**22**	**23**	**24**	**25**	**26**	**27**	**28**	**29**	**30**
B	C	B	A	B	C	B	A	B	C
31	**32**	**33**	**34**	**35**	**36**	**37**	**38**	**39**	**40**
B	A	B	C	A	C	B	C	C	A
41	**42**	**43**	**44**	**45**	**46**	**47**	**48**	**49**	**50**
A	B	A	C	B	A	C	B	B	A
51	**52**	**53**	**54**	**55**	**56**	**57**	**58**	**59**	**60**
A	B	A	C	B	B	A	B	C	C
61	**62**	**63**	**64**	**65**	**66**	**67**	**68**	**69**	**70**
A	B	A	B	C	A	C	A	B	C

71	**72**	**73**	**74**	**75**	**76**	**77**	**78**	**79**	**80**
A	C	A	D	A	B	C	A	C	A
81	**82**	**83**	**84**	**85**	**86**	**87**	**88**	**89**	**90**
D	A	C	A	C	C	A	B	C	A
91	**92**	**93**	**94**	**95**	**96**	**97**	**98**	**99**	**100**
A	B	C	B	D	C	D	A	C	C
101	**102**	**103**	**104**	**105**	**106**	**107**	**108**	**109**	**110**
B	B	C	D	B	D	D	C	C	B
111	**112**	**113**	**114**	**115**	**116**	**117**	**118**	**119**	**120**
A	D	B	C	A	C	B	C	D	C
121	**122**	**123**	**124**	**125**	**126**	**127**	**128**	**129**	**130**
A	B	A	B	C	D	C	A	B	A
131	**132**	**133**	**134**	**135**	**136**	**137**	**138**	**139**	**140**
A	A	C	D	C	D	C	B	B	C
141	**142**	**143**	**144**	**145**	**146**	**147**	**148**	**149**	**150**
C	B	A	D	C	C	D	C	D	D
151	**152**	**153**	**154**	**155**	**156**	**157**	**158**	**159**	**160**
B	D	A	C	A	C	B	B	C	C
161	**162**	**163**	**164**	**165**	**166**	**167**	**168**	**169**	**170**
C	B	C	C	C	C	B	D	A	B
171	**172**	**173**	**174**	**175**	**176**	**177**	**178**	**179**	**180**
D	D	C	D	C	D	B	B	D	B
181	**182**	**183**	**184**	**185**	**186**	**187**	**188**	**189**	**190**
D	A	B	A	C	A	C	A	D	D
191	**192**	**193**	**194**	**195**	**196**	**197**	**198**	**199**	**200**
A	B	A	B	C	A	A	A	B	B
201	**202**	**203**	**204**	**205**	**206**	**207**	**208**	**209**	**210**
B	C	A	C	D	C	D	C	D	D
211	**212**	**213**	**214**	**215**	**216**	**217**	**218**	**219**	**220**
D	D	A	D	D	C	A	D	D	D
221	**222**	**223**	**224**	**225**	**226**	**227**	**228**	**229**	**230**
B	C	A	B	D	A	D	A	B	A

Business & Management Aptitude

Business Organisation

Business

Business may be defined as an activity involving regular production or purchase of goods and services for sale, transfer and exchange with an object of earning profit.

Classification of Business Activities

We can classify business as Industry and Commerce.

Industry

Industry primarily refers to all such business activities concerned with production/raising or processing of goods and services. It processes raw materials or semi-finished goods into finished goods. Extracting raw materials from earth's surface, manufacturing goods and commodities, producing crops, fish, flowers, etc., constructing buildings, dams, roads etc. are all examples of industry.

Commerce

All goods and services produced are to be made available by those who need them. This involves a number of additional activities. For example when somebody produces bread, he has to make it available at convenient locations at right time. This involves activities like making people aware about the product, storing the product at right places, arranging retail outlets, packaging the product, transportation of the product, selling the product and so on. All these activities taken together are known as Commerce. It provides the necessary link between producers and consumers of goods and services and facilitates the purchase and sale of goods and services. In fact, it performs all functions, that are essential for maintaining a smooth and uninterrupted flow of goods and services to the customers. Thus, commerce involves:

(a) Buying and selling of goods and services; and

(b) Activities essential for the smooth and uninterrupted flow of goods and services from the point of production to the point of consumption.

The first activity, that is, purchase and sale of goods and services is termed as Trade, and the second activity i.e., the activities that ensure smooth flow of goods to customers are known as 'Auxiliaries to trade' or 'Aids to trade'. Thus, commerce is classified as:

(1) Trade; and

(2) Auxiliaries to trade.

Electronic Commerce

Commerce involves buying and selling and support services like transport, insurance, banking, communication etc. When all these activities are undertaken using information and communication technologies, it is termed as Electronic Commerce or e-Commerce. In other words, e-Commerce refers to the process of conducting business with the help of electronic devices using the computer and interconnected telecommunication network. Here, offer for sale and its acceptance are made electronically through Internet.

It does not require physical interaction between the parties concerned. It is also known as 'on-line trading', 'on-line shopping' and 'e-shopping'.

e-Commerce takes place between companies i.e., business to business (B2B), between companies and their customers (B2C), and customer to customer (C2C).

B2B, refers to interactions between a manufacturer and a supplier of materials and services, or between a manufacturer and a wholesaler, or between a wholesaler and a retailer. A network of computers is used for making enquiries seeking or placing orders, communicating supply of goods, making payments, and so on.

B2C, as the name implies, have business firms (manufacturer or retailers) at one end and its consumers on the other. It enables a business firm to be in touch with its customers on round the clock basis. It involves a wide range of marketing activities including promotion, seeking orders, intimating supply and so on.

C2C, usually involves consumers at both ends dealing in goods for which there is no established market mechanism as is the case with used books and household equipments.

Outsourcing of Services

Outsourcing is a management strategy by which an organisation contracts out its major non-core functions to specialised service providers with a view to benefit from their expertise, efficiency and cost effectiveness, and allow managers to concentrate on their core activities. The Information Technology (IT) is one area in which this approach is growing fast, and in recent years, outsourcing the operation of IT systems has been supplemented by a move to outsourcing the whole business processes such as payroll processing, cheque processing, etc. This is known as BPO (Business Process Outsourcing).

Entrepreneurship

Entrepreneur is a person who tries to do something new, visualises a business opportunity, organises the necessary resources for setting up the business and bears the risk involved. Thus, an entrepreneur may be termed as an innovator, an organiser and a risk bearer.

The term 'entrepreneurship' refers to the functions performed by an entrepreneur. It is the process involving various actions to be undertaken by the entrepreneur in establishing a new enterprise. In fact, what an entrepreneur does is regarded as entrepreneurship.

Qualities of Successful Entrepreneur

(a) Initiative
(b) Wide Knowledge
(c) Willingness to assume risk
(d) Open mind and optimistic outlook
(e) Adaptability
(f) Self-confidence
(g) Leadership Qualities
(h) Orientation towards hard work

Functions of an Entrepreneur

The functions of an entrepreneur can be summarised as follows:

(a) Conception of an idea
(b) Promotion
(c) Innovation
(d) Bearer of risks and uncertainty
(e) Arranging necessary capital
(f) Staffing

Business Organisation

To carry out any business and achieve its objective of earning profit it is required to bring together all the resources and put them into action in a systematic way, and coordinate and control these activities properly. This arrangement is known as business organisation.

Forms of Business Organisation

A business organisation usually takes the following forms in India:

(1) Sole proprietorship
(2) Partnership
(3) Joint Hindu Family
(4) Cooperative Society
(5) Joint Stock Company

Sole Proprietorship

The term 'sole' means single and 'proprietorship' means 'ownership'. So, only one person is the owner of the business organisation. This means, that a form of business organisation in which a single individual owns and manages the business, takes the profits and bears the losses, is known as sole proprietorship form of business organisation.

Characteristics of Sole Proprietorship form of Business Organisation

(a) Single Ownership
(b) No Separation of Ownership and Management
(c) Less Legal Formalities
(d) No Separate Entity
(e) No Sharing of Profit and Loss
(f) Unlimited Liability
(g) One-man Control

Partnership

'Partnership' is an association of two or more persons who pool their financial and managerial resources and agree to carry on a business, and share its profit. The persons who form a partnership are individually known as partners and collectively a firm or partnership firm.

Partnership form of business organisation in India is governed by the Indian Partnership Act, 1932 which defines partnership as "the relation between persons who have agreed to share the profits of the business carried on by all or any of them acting for all".

Characteristics of Partnership form of Business Organisation

(a) Two or More Persons
(b) Contractual Relationship
(c) Sharing Profits and Business
(d) Existence of Lawful Business
(e) Principal Agent Relationship
(f) Principal Agent Relationship
(g) Voluntary Registration

Types of Partners

(A) **Based on the extent of participation** in the day-to-day management of the firm partners can be classified as 'Active Partners' and 'Sleeping Partners'.

(B) **Based on sharing of profits,** the partners may be classified as 'Nominal Partners' and 'Partners in Profits'.

(C) **Based on Liability,** the partners can be classified as 'Limited Partners' and 'General Partners'. The liability of limited partners is limited to the extent of their capital contribution. The partners having unlimited liability are called as general partners or partners with unlimited liability.

(D) **Based on the behaviour and conduct exhibited,** there are two more types of partners besides the ones discussed above. These are (a) Partner by Estoppel; and (b) Partner by Holding out. A person who behaves in the public in such a way as to give an impression that he/she is a partner of the firm, is called 'partner by estoppel'. Such partners are not entitled to share the profits of the firm, but are fully liable if some body suffers because of his/her false representation. Similarly, if a partner or partnership firm declares that a particular person is a partner of their firm, and such a person does not disclaim it, then he/she is known as 'partner by Holding out'.

Formation of Partnership form of Business Organisation

The following steps are to be taken in order to form a partnership firm:

(a) Minimum two members are required to form a partnership. The maximum limit is ten in banking and 20 in other businesses.
(b) Select the like-minded persons keeping in view the nature and objectives of the business.
(c) There must be an agreement among the partners to carry on the business and share the profits and losses. This agreement must preferably be in writing and duly signed by all the partners. The agreement, i.e., the partnership deed must contain the following:
  (i) Name of the firm
  (ii) Nature of the business
  (iii) Names and addresses of partners
  (iv) Location of business
  (v) Duration of partnership, if decided
  (vi) Amount of capital to be contributed by each partner
  (vii) Profit and loss sharing ratio
  (viii) Duties, powers and obligations of partners
  (ix) Salaries and withdrawals of the partners
  (x) Preparation of accounts and their auditing
  (xi) Procedure for dissolution of the firm etc.
  (xii) Procedure for settlement of disputes

(d) The partners should get their firm registered with the Registrar of Firms of the concerned state. Although registration is not compulsory, but to avoid the consequences of non-registration, it is advisable to get it registered when it is setup or at any time during its existence.

Dissolution of Partnership Firm

Dissolution of partnership firm means putting an end to the relationship among the partners. This may be of two types: they are

(a) Dissolution of firm

(b) Dissolution of partnership

(a) Dissolution of firm

Dissolution of firm means dissolution of partnership. On dissolution of firm, partnership business comes to an end. Its assets are realised and the creditors are paid off. The business cannot be continued after dissolution of partnership firm.

(b) Dissolution of partnership

Dissolution of partnership means the termination of the original partnership agreement. A partnership is dissolved by insolvency, retirement, expiry or completion of the term of partnership. The business will continue after dissolution of partnership.

The various circumstances leading to dissolution of partnership firm can be summarised by taking the first letters used in the term "Dissolution".

D – Death of partner

I – Incapacity of a partner

S – Stipulated period of partnership completed in the case of particular partnership

S – Serious misconduct of a partner

O – Object is completed (Particular partnership)

L – Lunacy of a partner

U – Unavoidable continuous loss

T – Transfer of interest of the firm

I – Insolvency of a partner

O – Objectionable unlawful objectives

N – Notice of dissolution by a partner.

Modes of dissolution of Partnership

1. Dissolution by Agreement

2. Compulsory Dissolution

3. Dissolution on the happening of certain contingencies: A partnership may be dissolved on the happening of the following contingencies:

(a) Death of a partner.

(b) Expiry of the time, if partnership is for a fixed period.

(c) Completion of the venture for which the firm was formed.

(d) Adjudication of a partner as an insolvent.

4. Dissolution by notice of partnership-at-will

5. Dissolution through Court

Joint Hindu Family form of Business Organisation

The Joint Hindu Family (JHF) business is a form of business organisation run by Hindu Undivided Family (HUF), where the family members of three successive generations own the business jointly. The head of the family known as Karta manages the business. The other members are called co-parceners and all of them have equal ownership right over the properties of the business.

The membership of the JHF is acquired by virtue of birth in the same family. There is no restriction for minors to become the members of the business. As per Dayabhaga system of Hindu Law, both male and female members are the joint owners. But Mitakashara system of Hindu Law says only male members of the family can become the coparceners. While the Dayabhaga system is applicable to the state of West Bengal, Mitakshara system of Hindu Law is applicable to the rest of the country.

Formation of JHF form of Business Organisation

A Joint Hindu Family business is formed as per the provision of Hindu law. It comes into existence on the death of the person who established the business. His successor automatically become the coparceners if they decide to continue it as a joint family business. The children become its members by birth. The senior most member of the family will become the Karta of the business. No legal formalities are required for its establishment. But it has to be registered with the Income tax department to avail the tax concessions involved.

Cooperative Society

The term cooperation is derived from the Latin word 'co-operari', where the word 'co' means 'with' and 'operari' mean 'to work'. Thus, the term cooperation means working together. So those who want to work together with some common economic objectives can form a society, which is termed as cooperative society.

The Section 4 of the Indian Cooperative Societies Act 1912 defines Cooperative Society as "a society, which has its objectives for the promotion of economic interests of its members in accordance with cooperative principles."

Characteristics of Cooperative Society

(*a*) Voluntary Association

(*b*) Open Membership

(*c*) Number of Members: A minimum of 10 members are required to form a cooperative society. In case of multi-state cooperative societies the minimum number of members should be 50 from each state in case the members are individuals. The Cooperative Society Act does not specify the maximum number of members for any cooperative society.

(*d*) Registration of the Society: In India, cooperative societies are registered under the Cooperative Societies Act 1912 or under the State Cooperative Societies Act. The Multi-state Cooperative Societies are registered under the Multi-state Cooperative Societies Act 2002. Once registered, the society becomes a separate legal entity and attain certain characteristics.

(*e*) State Control: Since registration of cooperative societies is compulsory, every cooperative society comes under the control and supervision of the government.

(*f*) Return on Capital Investment: The members get return on their capital investment in the form of dividend.

(*g*) Distribution of Surplus: After giving a limited dividend to the members of the society, the surplus profit is distributed in the form of bonus, keeping aside a certain percentage as reserve and for general welfare of the society.

Types of Cooperative Societies

(a) Consumers' Cooperative Societies
(b) Producers' Cooperative Societies
(c) Marketing Cooperative Societies
(d) Housing Cooperative Societies
(e) Farming Cooperative Societies
(f) Credit Cooperative Societies

Joint Stock Company

A Joint Stock Company or simply a company is a voluntary association of persons generally formed for undertaking some big business activity. It is established by law and can be dissolved by law. The company has a separate legal existence so that even if its members die, the company remains in existence. Its members contribute money for some **common purpose.** The money so contributed constitutes the **capital** of the company. The capital of the company is divided into small units called **shares**. Since members invest their money by purchasing the shares of the company, they are known as **shareholders** and the capital of the company is known as **share capital**.

In India, the joint stock companies are governed by the Companies Act, 1956. According to the Act, a company means 'a company formed and registered under this Act or an existing company'. An existing company means a company formed and registered under any of the previous Companies Acts. This definition is not exhaustive enough to reveal the basic features of the company. However, based on the definition given in the previous Companies Act and various judicial decisions, it can be defined as 'an artificial person created by law, having a separate legal entity, with a perpetual succession'.

Characteristics of Joint Stock Company

(a) Artificial Person: A joint stock company is an artificial person in the sense that it is created by law and does not possess physical attributes of a natural person. It cannot eat or walk, smile or marry, read or write. However, it has a legal status like a natural person.

(b) Formation: The formation of a joint stock company is time consuming and it involves preparation of several documents and compliance of several legal requirements before it starts its operation. A company comes into existence only when it is registered under the Indian Companies Act.

(c) Separate Legal Entity: Being an artificial person, a company exists independent of its members. It can make contracts, purchase and sell things, employ people and conduct any lawful business in its own name. It can sue and can be sued in the court of law. A shareholder cannot be held responsible for the acts of the company.

(d) Common Seal: Since a company has no physical existence, it must act through its Board of Directors. But all contracts entered by them shall have to be under the common seal of the company. This common seal is the official signature of the company. Any document with the common seal and duly signed by an officer of the company is binding on the company.

(e) Perpetual Existence: The company enjoys continuous existence. Death, lunacy, insolvency or retirement of the members does not affect the life of the company. It goes on forever. Since it is created by law, it can only be dissolved by law.

(f) Limited Liability of Members: The company form of business is able to attract large number of people to invest their money in shares because it offers them the facility of limited risk and liability. The liability of a member is limited to the extent of the amount of shares he holds.

(g) Transferability of Shares: The members of the company (Public company) are free to transfer the shares held by them to others as and when they like. They do not need the consent of other shareholders to transfer their shares.

(h) Membership: To form a joint stock company, a minimum of two members are required in case it is private limited company and seven members in case of public limited company. The maximum limit is fifty incase of private limited company. There is no maximum limit of membership for a public limited company.

(i) Democratic Management: You know that people of different categories and areas contribute towards the capital of a company. So, it is not possible for them to look after the day-to-day management of the company. They may take part in deciding the general policies of the company but the day-to-day affairs of the company are managed by their elected representatives, called Directors.

KINDS OF COMPANIES

Statutory Companies

Companies established by Special Acts of Parliament or State Legislatures are called statutory companies.

Registered Companies

Companies which are registered under The Companies Act, 1956 are called registered companies.

Holding and Subsidiary Companies

A company becomes a holding company of another

(i) if it can appoint or remove all or majority of the directors of the latter company or

(ii) if it holds more than 50% of the equity share capital of the latter or

(iii) if it can exercise more than 50% of the total voting power of the latter.

The other company which is so controlled is called subsidiary company.

Government Companies

A Government company is one in which not less than 51% of the paid up capital is held by the Central Government or by any one or more State Governments or partly by the Central Governments and partly by one or more State Governments.

Public Limited Companies

The public is invited to subscribe to the shares of the company usually by issuing a prospectus. Shares are easily transferable. Minimum number of persons is seven and there is no limit to the maximum number of shareholders. The company's name must end with the word 'Limited'.

Private Limited Companies

A private limited company is a company which has a minimum paid up capital of rupees one lakh or such higher paid up capital, as may be prescribed.

The Articles of Association may prescribe the following:

(i) Restricts the right to transfer the shares, if any.
(ii) limits the number of its members to 50 not including its present or past employee-members
(iii) prohibits any invitation to the public to subscribe to any shares in or debentures of the company.

The name of the company must end with the words "Private Limited".

Stages in the Formation of a Joint Stock Company

It is very easy to establish a sole proprietorship business or a partnership firm as there are a few regulations to meet. But for the establishment of a company, a lot of formalities are to be complied with. The registration of the company is mandatory before starting its operation. The formation of a company, right from the origin of idea to establish a company goes through four different stages, like:

Stage –I Promotion
Stage- II Incorporation
Stage- III Raising of Capital
Stage- IV Commencement of Business

Important Documents Prepared While Forming a Company

There are three basic documents which are prepared and filed with the Registrar during the formation of a company. These are:

(1) Memorandum of Association (MOA)
(2) Articles of Association (AOA)
(3) Prospectus

Out of these three documents, MOA and AOA are filed with the Registrar of Companies before the registration along with other supporting documents while asking for certificate of incorporation. The prospectus is issued to the public at the time of subscription to capital.

Public Enterprises

The business units owned, managed and controlled by the central, state or local government are termed as public sector enterprises or public enterprises. These are also known as public sector undertakings. A pubic sector enterprise may be defined as any commercial or industrial undertaking owned and managed by the government with a view to maximise social welfare and uphold the public interest.

Public enterprises consist of nationalised private sector enterprises, such as, banks, Life Insurance Corporation of India and the new enterprises set up by the government such as Hindustan Machine Tools (HMT), Gas Authority of India (GAIL), State Trading Corporation (STC) etc.

Characteristics of Public Enterprises

(a) Government Ownership and Management
(b) Financed from Government Funds
(c) Public Welfare
(d) Public Utility Services
(e) Public Accountability
(f) Excessive Formalities

Forms of Organisation of Public Enterprises

There are three different forms of organisation used for the public sector enterprises in India. These are (1) Departmental Undertaking; (2) Statutory (or Public) Corporation and (3) Government Company.

Departmental Undertaking form of organisation is primarily used for provision of essential services such as railways, postal services, broadcasting etc. Such organisations function under the overall control of a ministry of the Government and are financed and controlled in the same way as any other government department.

Statutory Corporation (or public corporation) refers to a corporate body created by the Parliament or State Legislature by a special Act which defines its powers, functions and pattern of management. Statutory corporation is also known as public corporation. Its capital is wholly provided by the government. Examples of such organisations are Life Insurance Corporation of India, State Trading Corporation etc.

Government Company refers to the company in which 51 per cent or more of the paid up capital is held by the government. It is registered under the Companies Act and is fully governed by the provisions of the Act. Most business units owned and managed by government fall in this category.

Multiple Choice Questions

1. According to the Principle of Subrogation
(*a*) The insured must take all necessary steps to minimise the loss.
(*b*) The actual amount of loss, not exceeding the amount of the policy, shall be paid.
(*c*) The actual amount of loss should be distributed among the different insurers of the same risk.
(*d*) On making good the loss, the insurer is entitled to succeed to all the rights of the insured regarding the subject matter of insurance.

2. The persons who agree to insure cargo, hull or freight are called
(*a*) undertakers (*b*) caretakers
(*c*) underwriters (*d*) bookkeepers

3. Partnership is a form of business organisation in which business debts can be recovered
(*a*) the managing partners
(*b*) all the managers and partners
(*c*) the firm and the managers
(*d*) the firm and all the partners

4. Of the following organisations the easiest to wind up is the
(*a*) Public Limited Company
(*b*) Multinational Corporation
(*c*) Private Limited Company
(*d*) Partnership Firm

5. Match List-I with List-II and select the correct answer using the codes given below the lists:

List-I	List-II
I. Partners and Firms	A. agent and principle relationship
II. Sole Proprietorship	B. prospectus
III. Public Limited Company	C. personal supervision
IV. Nominal Partnership	D. firm image

Codes:
(*a*) I-A, II-B, III-C, IV-D
(*b*) II-B, II-C, III-A, IV-D
(*c*) I-A, II-C, III-B, IV-D
(*d*) I-D, II-B, III-A, IV-C

6. The main object of stock exchange is to
(*a*) Provided facilities for speculation
(*b*) Safeguard the interest of investors
(*c*) Help in the capital formation of the country
(*d*) Provide a ready market for securities

7. What is network form of organization called in Japan
(*a*) Keiretsu (*b*) Ransum
(*c*) Deptku (*d*) Seduku

8. 'Fishing Culture' is classified in
(*a*) Extractive Industry
(*b*) Genetic Industry
(*c*) Construction Industry
(*d*) None of these

9. If a partnership firm is not registered with the Registrar of firms,
(*a*) it has to pay penalty for non-registration
(*b*) the members can file suits against the third party
(*c*) the members can enforce their rights among themselves
(*d*) none of these

10. Which of the following is not an economic activity?
(*a*) A doctor practising
(*b*) A lawyer practising law
(*c*) A professional cricketer playing cricket
(*d*) A student playing cricket

11. In order an activity may be called business which of the following condition need not be satisfied?
(*a*) There should be exchange or transfer of goods or services

(*b*) There should be continuity of dealings
(*c*) Dealings may be either in goods or services
(*d*) There should be certainty of profit

12. Which among the following is a central problem of an economy
(*a*) What to produce
(*b*) How to produce
(*c*) Both (*a*) and (*b*)
(*d*) None of these

13. In a private business enterprise profit should be regarded as
(*a*) the legitimate reward for honest end labour
(*b*) the supreme objective of business
(*c*) the sole objective of business
(*d*) subsidiary to service motive

14. Which of the following should be regarded as the most important factor for deciding the form of business organisation?
(*a*) Types of business, trading manufacturing, etc
(*b*) Expected volume of business
(*c*) Financial requirements
(*d*) Area of operations

15. The liability of a sole proprietor is
(*a*) limited to the extent of his capital invested in the business
(*b*) limited to the extent of the value of business assets
(*c*) limited to the extent of the value of business assets and his all private assets
(*d*) none of these

16. The agreement of partnership
(*a*) must be in oral
(*b*) must be in writing
(*c*) can be either oral or in writing
(*d*) must be in writing on a stamp paper

17. Liability of partners in respect of the firm's debts is
(*a*) limited up to the amount of his capital in the business
(*b*) unlimited
(*c*) limited up to the amount of gurantee given by the partner
(*d*) limited up to the amount of his capital and loan to the firm if any

18. Partnership may come into existence
(*a*) by the operation of law
(*b*) by an express agreement only
(*c*) by an express or implied agreement only
(*d*) by inheritance of property

19. A partner has an implied authority to
(*a*) acquire immovable property on behalf of the firm
(*b*) enter into a partnership on behalf of the firm
(*c*) to borrow money on behalf of the firm
(*d*) to compromise or relinquish any claim or portion of a claim by the firm.

20. If a firm is not registered with the registrar of firms
(*a*) it has to pay penalty for non-registration
(*b*) it introduces certain disabilities which make registration necessary at one time or the other
(*c*) the members of the unregistered firm can enforce their rights between themselves
(*d*) the members of the unregistered firm can file suit against third parties.

21. Dissolution of firm takes place
(*a*) by the death or insolvency of anyone partner
(*b*) the retirement of any one partner
(*c*) by the expiry of the term
(*d*) by the insolvency of all but one partner

22. Registration of joint stock company is
(*a*) compulsory
(*b*) optional
(*c*) compulsory for public companies and optional for private company
(*d*) compulsory for companies with liabilities limited by shares and optional for companies with liabilities limited by guarantee

23. The minimum number of member require for registration of a co-operative society is
(*a*) two (*b*) seven
(*c*) ten (*d*) twenty

24. Co-operative and public companies are similar in respect of
(*a*) the liability of members
(*b*) the minimum number of members required for registration
(*c*) the maximum number of members
(*d*) none of these

25. Profits earned by a co-operative society are distributed.
(*a*) to members in the ratio of capital held by them
(*b*) to member in the ratio of purchases made by them
(*c*) by providing a nominal rate of interest on capital contribution by members and remaining in the ratio of purchases made by members
(*d*) by declaring dividend at a specific rate and remaining transfering to general reserves.

26. Management of a co-operative organisation is in the hands of
(*a*) persons nominated by the Registrar of co-operative societies
(*b*) an elected body by the members
(*c*) some persons nominated by Registrar of co-operative societies and other selected by the member
(*d*) the promoters of the co-operative organisation

27. Which of the following is an example of a company incorporated by a special act of parliament?
(*a*) Delhi Cloth Mills Ltd.
(*b*) Tata Iron and Steel Co. Ltd.
(*c*) Industrial Finance Corporation.
(*d*) Swadeshi Cotton Mills Ltd.

28. Which of the following documents need not be prepared and Registered with the Registrar of companies in public limited companies.
(*a*) Memorandum of Association
(*b*) Articles of Association
(*c*) Statutory Declaration
(*d*) Directors of undertaking to take up and pay for qualification shares.

29. The term, 'capitalisation' is used in relation to
(*a*) sole-proprietorship
(*b*) partnership
(*c*) joint stock companies
(*d*) co-operative societies

30. Which of the following methods provide a better basis of capitalisation for an establised concern?
(*a*) Add up the cost of fixed assets and working capital required
(*b*) Add up the cost of fixed assets, working capital and cost of promotion etc.
(*c*) Capitalise the profits to be earned.
(*d*) Estimate on the basis of financial position of other similar companies.

31. Watered capital means
(*a*) over capitalistation
(*b*) under capitalistation
(*c*) excessive capital
(*d*) part of the capital not reprensented by assets

32. Over capitalisation may be remedied by
(*a*) increasing the number of equity shares
(*b*) increasing the per value of shares
(*c*) issuing additional preference shares
(*d*) redemption of debentures

33. Under Capitalisation can be remedied by
(*a*) isssue of bonus shares
(*b*) redemption of preference shares
(*c*) redemption of debentures
(*d*) reduction of interest of debentures

34. Capital gearing means
(*a*) proper capitalisation
(*b*) watered capital
(*c*) fixation of a proper ratio between two or more types of securities
(*d*) trading on equity

35. A company is said to be low geared when the proportion of

(*a*) equity capital to the total capital is small
(*b*) preference capital to the total capital is small
(*c*) debentures capital to the total capital is small
(*d*) both preference and debentures capital to the total is small

36. Working capital can be used for the purchase of
(*a*) machinery (*b*) goodwill
(*c*) land and building (*d*) raw material

37. Which of the following sources is not used for medium term financing?
(*a*) Issue of equity shares
(*b*) Issue of preference shares
(*c*) Issue of debentures
(*d*) Terms loan from banks

38. Working capital is represented by
(*a*) current liabilities
(*b*) current assets minus current liabilities
(*c*) total assets minus current liabilities
(*d*) cash-in-hand plus stock-in-trade.

39. Participating preference shares are those which participate
(*a*) in the voting
(*b*) in the general meeting of the company.
(*c*) in the management of the company.
(*d*) in the profits over and above their fixed dividend.

40. In which of the following, rate of interest/ dividends is not fixed?
(*a*) equity capital (*b*) debentures
(*c*) preference capital (*d*) public deposits

41. To which of the following types of companies, debentures suit as a source of finance?
(*a*) companies with fluctuating earnings
(*b*) companies with stable earnings
(*c*) companies which cannot earn a rate of profit higher than the rate of interest, payable on debentures
(*d*) all of these

42. First debentures are those
(*a*) which are issued before share capital
(*b*) which are repayable before other debentures
(*c*) which are secured by a floating charges
(*d*) which are secured by a fixed charges

43. Underwriters are persons who
(*a*) purchase the shares and debentures of a company
(*b*) work as agents of the company for the sale of shares and debentures
(*c*) manage the issue of shares and debentures
(*d*) undertake to buy those shares and debentures not subscribed for by the public

44. Which of the following institutions under take underwriting of shares and debentures of companies?
(*a*) Unit Trust of India
(*b*) Industrial Development Bank of India
(*c*) State Finance Corporations
(*d*) All of these

45. Which of the following sources of finance do not pose a burden on the company?
(*a*) Public deposits
(*b*) Debentures
(*c*) Loans from financial institutions
(*d*) Retained earnings

46. Which of the following is not a component of the new issue market?
(*a*) Stock exchanges
(*b*) Unit Trust of India
(*c*) Financial Institution of India like IFC, IDBI
(*d*) LIC

47. When an existing company offers its shares for sale to the existing shareholders, it is known as
(*a*) private placing (*b*) bonus issue
(*c*) rights issue (*d*) offer for sale

48. The first stock exchange was set up in India in
(*a*) Kolkata (*b*) Mumbai
(*c*) Delhi (*d*) Chennai

49. The first stock exchange was set up in India in
(*a*) 1887 (*b*) 1905
(*c*) 1908 (*d*) 1923

50. Which of the speculators expects the price of securities to rise in the near future?
(*a*) bull (*b*) bear
(*c*) stag (*d*) lame duck

51. Which of the following speculative activities is based on disparity in quote prices in different markets?
(*a*) Option dealings (*b*) Arbitrage
(*c*) Margin trading (*d*) Blank transfers

52. Cantango charge is paid by a
(*a*) bull speculator to bear speculator
(*b*) bear speculator to bull speculator
(*c*) lame duck to bull speculator
(*d*) bull to lame duck speculator

53. Listing of securities in a stock exchange for the purpose of trading indicates that
(*a*) at the time of listing, the company is financially sound
(*b*) at the time of listing, the company is legally organised
(*c*) the stock exchange guarantees about the financial soundness of the company
(*d*) all of these

54. An existing company raising additional capital
(*a*) must offer the new shares to the existing shareholders
(*b*) need not offer the new shares to the existing shareholders
(*c*) issues share to debenture holders
(*d*) issue shares to preference share holders

55. Stock exchange deals with the
(*a*) second hand securities
(*b*) issues of equity shares
(*c*) issue of preference shares
(*d*) issue of debentures

56. One of the impelling causes of business combination is
(*a*) desire for bigness
(*b*) wasteful competition
(*c*) influence of tariffs
(*d*) rationalisation

57. When a cement mill, a steel mill and a chemical company combine, it is a case of
(*a*) horizontal combination
(*b*) vertical combination
(*c*) diagonal combination
(*d*) circular combination

58. Which of the following is an example of vertical integration?
(*a*) One small steel mill combines with a big steel mill
(*b*) Two steel mills of the same combine
(*c*) Iron ore firm combines with iron melting firm
(*d*) Paper mill combines with a publishing company

59. Combination of plants at the same stage of production or in the same trade or commerce is called a
(*a*) horizontal combination
(*b*) vertical combination
(*c*) diagonal combination
(*d*) allied combination

60. One of the main advantages of vertical combination is that
(*a*) it helps in avoiding competition
(*b*) it helps in controlling the market
(*c*) it helps in controlling the quality of raw material and finished output
(*d*) it brings about coordination between activities of combining units

61. Pools are a type of
(*a*) horizontal combinations
(*b*) vertical combinations
(*c*) allied combinations
(*d*) none of these

62. Cartel is a type of
(*a*) horizontal combination
(*b*) vertical combination
(*c*) allied combination
(*d*) mixed combination

63. FICCI was formed in the year
(*a*) 1920 (*b*) 1925
(*c*) 1927 (*d*) 1951

64. Business combinations are formed to derive the advantages of
(*a*) enabling the units to join hands and establish a monopoly
(*b*) avoiding wasteful competition
(*c*) enabling business units to withstand the rigours of a depression
(*d*) all of these

65. Match the following.

List-I	List-II
I. Trust	A. Company A holds more than 51% share capital of the company B
II. Merger	B. Existing companies A and B are merged into company C
III. Holding Company	C. Business of number of firms is entrusted to the care of Board of Trustees
IV. Amalgamation	D. Company A takes over Company B

Select the correct answer from the code given below :
Codes:
(*a*) I-B, II-C, III-A, IV-D
(*b*) I-A, II-B, III-C, IV-D
(*c*) I-C, II-D, III-A, IV-II
(*d*) I-B, II-A, III-D, IV-C

66. MRTP Act came into force in
(*a*) 1969 (*b*) 1970
(*c*) 1971 (*d*) 1980

67. Resale price maintenance is a
(*a*) restrictive trade practice
(*b*) monopolistic trade practice
(*c*) both of these
(*d*) none of these

68. When custom duty is levied according to the value of the goods, it is known as
(*a*) revenue duty (*b*) excise duty
(*c*) specific duty (*d*) ad-valorem duty

69. When custom duty is levied according to the weight of good, it is known as
(*a*) revenue duty (*b*) excise duty
(*c*) specific duty (*d*) ad-valorem duty

70. Import procedure begins with
(*a*) mate's reciept (*b*) marine insurance
(*c*) indent (*d*) shipping bill

71. Shipping order is issued by the owner of the ship when
(*a*) whole of the ship is hired
(*b*) major part of the ship is hired
(*c*) freight is reserved for the exporter
(*d*) ship starts its journey

72. A shipping bill is prepared when
(*a*) goods are damaged in the ship
(*b*) goods reach their destination in satisfactory condition
(*c*) goods are not cleared by the custom authorities
(*d*) none of these

73. Entrepot trade means
(*a*) import trade
(*b*) export trade
(*c*) foreign trade
(*d*) goods imported for re-export

74. A letter of credit means
(*a*) a letter sent by importer to exporter sanctioning credit deal
(*b*) a letter sent by exporter to importer sanctioning credit deal
(*c*) a letter containing conditions of credit purchase or sale
(*d*) a bank agreeing to accept and pay on due date

75. A bill of loading transferable to another person by
(*a*) mere delivery
(*b*) endorsement and delivery
(*c*) any of the above
(*d*) this one is not transferable

76. Charter party means
(*a*) an agreement by which the ship owner agrees to place the entire or part of the ship at the disposal of the merchant.

(*b*) the party who works as a middleman between shipper and shipping company.
(*c*) the party who performs loading or unloading operations on the ship.
(*d*) the party working as a middleman between importer and exporter.

77. State Trading Corporation of India was established
(*a*) by a special Act of Parliament
(*b*) under the companies Act, 1956 as a private limited company
(*c*) under the companies Act, 1956 as a public limited company
(*d*) as departmental undertaking

78. Which of the following is not a subsidiary of the State Trading Corporation of India?
(*a*) Indian Motion Picture Export Corporation of India
(*b*) Handicraft and a Handlooms Export Corporation of India Ltd.
(*c*) Project and Equipment Corporation of India Ltd.
(*d*) All of these

79. Mate's receipt is issued by
(*a*) the exporter
(*b*) the importer
(*c*) the captain of the ship or his assistant
(*d*) the bank

80. Under which of the following principles of insurance, parties to the contract must disclose the material facts known to them?
(*a*) Indemnity
(*b*) Utmost good faith
(*c*) Subrogation
(*d*) Insurable interest

81. A person can insure
(*a*) any body's property
(*b*) only his own property
(*c*) only that property in which he is interested
(*d*) only that property in which he has financial interest

82. In the case of fire insurance, the insured must have insurable interest in the thing insured at the time
(*a*) when policy is taken
(*b*) when loss is incurred
(*c*) through out the period of contract of insurance
(*d*) both when policy is taken and when loss is incurred

83. In marine insurance, the insured must have insurable interest at the time
(*a*) when policy is taken
(*b*) when the event happens
(*c*) when policy is taken as well as event happens
(*d*) when throughout the period of contract of insurance

84. According to the principle of cause proxima the assured can recover the loss from the insurer
(*a*) if it is proximatry caused by any of the perils insured against
(*b*) if it is caused by any of the remote cause
(*c*) if it is caused by any reason, whatsoever
(*d*) all of these

85. The principle of subrogation applies to
(*a*) all types of insurance
(*b*) fire insurance only
(*c*) marine insurance only
(*d*) fire and marine insurance

86. The principle of contribution applies when
(*a*) there are two or more insurance on one risk
(*b*) the insured does not take necessary steps to mitigate the loss
(*c*) the insured insures the same risk partly with other insurers
(*d*) the premium is not paid by the insured

87. Surrender value of a life policy is the amount payable by Life Insurance Corporation when
(*a*) the life policy matures by death
(*b*) the life policy matures after the expiry of the policy period
(*c*) the life policy is withdrawn before its maturity
(*d*) the payment of premiums is discontinued and the amount is payable at the maturity of the policy

88. Principle of subrogation states that
(*a*) the actual amount of loss should be distributed among the differented insurers of the same risk
(*b*) on making good the loss, the insurers is entitled to succeed to all the rights of the insured regarding the subject matter of insurance
(*c*) the insured must take all necessary steps to minimise the loss
(*d*) the actual amount of loss, exceeding the amount of the policy, shall be paid

89. Average clause in a fire policy is inserted in order to check mainly
(*a*) under-insurance
(*b*) over-insurance
(*c*) both other-insurance and under-insurance
(*d*) all of these

90. X mortgages certain property with Y who has insurable interest in property
(*a*) only X (*b*) only Y
(*c*) both X and Y (*d*) none of these

91. Principle of insurable interest applies to
(*a*) life insurance only
(*b*) fire insurance only
(*c*) fire and marine insurance only
(*d*) all types of insurance

92. In which of the following kinds of insurance, insurable interest should be present only at the time of loss subject-matter
(*a*) life insurance (*b*) fire insurance
(*c*) marine insurance (*d*) all of these

93. Unless the marine policy otherwise provides, insurer is liable
(*a*) if the loss is caused by ordinary wear and tear
(*b*) if the loss is caused by peril insured against.
(*c*) if the loss is caused by ordinary leakage and breakage
(*d*) if the loss is caused by inherent nature of the subject-matter

94. The life of a co-operative society is
(*a*) affected by the death of a member
(*b*) affected by the insolvency of a member
(*c*) affected by the withdrawal by a member from membership
(*d*) not affected by death, insolvency etc. of members

95. Non-registration of a partnership does not affect
(*a*) the right of a partner to sue the firm
(*b*) the right of the firm to sue third parties
(*c*) the right of the third party to proceed against the firm or its partners
(*d*) any of these

96. If a minor choose to continue as a partner on attaining the age of majority, he will be liable to the debts of the firm from the date of this
(*a*) attaining majority
(*b*) admission to profits of the firm
(*c*) choosing to become a partner at subsequent date
(*d*) guardian giving the option

97. The liability of the Karta in a joint Hindu family is
(*a*) limited to his interest in the joint family
(*b*) unlimited
(*c*) limited to the entire property of the family
(*d*) limited to the private properties of all the member

98. Match List-I with List-II and select the correct answer using the codes given below the lists:

List-I *(Organisation)*	**List-II** *(Associated with)*
I. Joint stock company	A. Memorandum of Association (M/A)
II. Co-operative society	B. Special Act
III. Statutory corporation	C. Mutual contract
IV. Partnership	D. Bye-laws

Codes:
(*a*) I-A, II-B, III-C, IV-D
(*b*) I-A, II-C, III-D, IV-B
(*c*) I-B, II-C, III-A, IV-D
(*d*) I-A, II-D, III-B, IV-C

99. Which one of the following is not the distinctive feature of the co-operative form of the business organisation?
(*a*) Service before self
(*b*) Democratic management
(*c*) Corporate status
(*d*) One-share one-vote system

100. Which one of the following does not constitute the purpose of setting up SEBI
(*a*) To protect the interest of the investors in securities
(*b*) To promote the development of the securities markets
(*c*) To regulate the global securities markets
(*d*) To deal with matters connected with fraudulent and unfair trade practices relating to securities market

101. Which one of the following best supports the theory that the stock exchange is a secondary market?
In a stock exchange
(*a*) Securities are bought and sold by way of transfer
(*b*) An existing holder of securities can dispose of the holding to another invest or who intends to buy them
(*c*) No new investment is created
(*d*) Securities are dealt in for dual purposes investment and speculation

102. Combination of printing and dyeing companies is a type of
(*a*) vertical combination
(*b*) horizontal combination
(*c*) circular combination
(*d*) allied combination.

103. In addition to consumer forums which one of the following looks after the interest of consumers?
(*a*) High Court
(*b*) Company Law Board
(*c*) M.R.T.P.
(*d*) Bureau of Industrial Costs and Prices

104. Which one of the following is not a commercial risk
(*a*) Insolvency of the buyer
(*b*) New restrictions placed on import export trade
(*c*) Damage to goods in transit
(*d*) Change in the exchange rate

105. The average clause in a fire policy states that the insured can get back.
(*a*) only that portion of the actual loss suffered as the sum insured bears to total value
(*b*) the entire amount of the total loss suffered
(*c*) the entire amount of partial loss suffered
(*d*) a fixed percentage of loss suffered

106. Consider the following statements :
The social responsibility of business is to:
I. Do a business as per the public policy.
II. Obey all the rules and regulations of the Government.
III. Make payment of the taxes imposed by the Government.
IV. Provide not necessarily adequate but good quality of goods.
of these statements:
(*a*) II and III are correct
(*b*) I and IV are correct
(*c*) I, II and III are correct.
(*d*) I, II, III and IV are correct.

107. One of the consequences of non-registration of a partnership firm is that
(*a*) a partner cannot sue the other partner to enforce a right arising from a contract
(*b*) the partner of such a firm cannot sue third parties
(*c*) third parties cannot sue the firm for claims exceeding ₹ 100
(*d*) the official Assignee or Receiver will have no power on the property of the dissolved firm

108. Consider the following rights:
I. Right to take part in the business.
II. Right to share profits.
III. Right to interest on advances in excess of capital
IV. Right to expel a non-cooperative partner

Codes:

(*a*) I and II (*b*) II and IV
(*c*) I, II and III (*d*) I, III and IV

109. Steps to be taken in a selling system include:

I. Receipt of order
II. Processing order
III. Shipment of merchandise
IV. Accounting for sale

The correct chronological sequence of these steps is

(*a*) I, IV, III, II (*b*) I, IV, II, III
(*c*) I, II, IV, III (*d*) I, II, III, IV

110. Match List-I with List-II and select the correct answer using the codes given below the lists:

List-I *(Type of combinations)*	List-II *(Illustrations)*
I. Association	A. Cartel
II. Federation	B. Chamber of commerce and industry
III. Partial	C. Holding Company
IV. Complete consolidation	D. Amalgamation

Codes:

(*a*) I-B, II-A, III-C, IV-D
(*b*) I-A, II-B, III-C, IV-D
(*c*) I-B, II-A, III-D, IV-C
(*d*) I-A, II-B, III-D, IV-C

111. Which one of the following is an example of a company incorporated by a special Act of Parliament?

(*a*) Life Insurance Corporation of India.
(*b*) Indian Oil Corporation.
(*c*) State Trading Corporation of India.
(*d*) Bharat Heavy Electricals Limited.

112. Match List-I with List-II and select the correct answer using the codes given below the lists:

List-I	List-II
I. Contract of uberrimal fidei	A. Public utility concern
II. Right of eminent domain	B. Co-operative society
III. Statement in lieu of prospectus	C. Partnership
IV. System of one man one vote	D. Sole trading concern
	E. Public limited company

Codes:

(*a*) I-A, II-C, III-E, IV-D
(*b*) I-C, II-A, III-E, IV-B
(*c*) I-C, II-B, III-A, IV-D
(*d*) I-A, II-B, III-E, IV-C

113. Match List-I (activity) with List-II (associated organisation) and select the correct answer by using the codes given below the lists:

List-I	List-II
I. Mutual fund	A. Stock exchange
II. Public issue of capital	B. Assets management company
III. Forward trading	C. Merchant banking
IV. Option pricing	D. Foreign market

Codes:

(*a*) I-C, II-B, III-D, IV-A
(*b*) I-C, II-B, III-A, IV-D
(*c*) I-B, II-C, III-A, IV-D
(*d*) I-B, II-C, III-D, IV-A

114. Integration of various limits of similar character producing similar products or engaged in the same sphere of business activity under a single form of management and control is called

(*a*) vertical combination
(*b*) horizontal combination
(*c*) circular or mixed combination
(*d*) lateral or allied combination

115. The scope of MRTP Act, since 1992, has been confined only to the regulation

(*a*) consumer monopolies
(*b*) monopolistic trade practices
(*c*) restrictive and unfair trade practices
(*d*) restrictive trade practices

116. EXIM bank can be described as a

(*a*) non-banking financial company
(*b*) commercial bank
(*c*) non-banking non-financial company
(*d*) schedule bank

117. Match List-I (document) with List-II (where used) and select the correct answer by using the codes given below the lists:

List-I	List-II
I. Shipping bill	A. to certify the origin of good's country
II. Bill of loading	B. for having loaded the cargo in the ship
III. Consular invoice	C. to transport cargo by ship
IV. Packing slip	D. to identify the cargo in transit

Codes:

(*a*) I-B, II-C, III-D, IV-A
(*b*) I-B, II-C, III-A, IV-D
(*c*) I-C, II-B, III-A, IV-D
(*d*) I-C, II-B, III-D, IV-A

118. In the context of foreign trade, the CIF cost may be obtained by

(*a*) adding freight and marine insurance premium to the FOB price
(*b*) deducting freight and marine insurance premium for the FOB price
(*c*) adding customs duties, freight and marine insurance premium to the cost
(*d*) deducting customs duties, freight and marine insurance premium from the price

119. Paid-up value is payable on a life insurance policy

(*a*) on the maturity of the policy
(*b*) when the policy lapses
(*c*) when the policy is surrendered
(*d*) on maturity or death which ever is earlier

120. A Co-partner partner is one who is

(*a*) an active member of a partnership
(*b*) a member of a joint Hindu family firm
(*c*) a member of a joint stock company
(*d*) a member of co-operative society

121. Every partner must account to the firm for any benefit derived by him without the consent of the other partners and thus make no secret profits. This is based on

(*a*) the general law of contract
(*b*) the general law of agency
(*c*) the law of sale of goods
(*d*) business ethics

122. In a broader sense, the activities of a co-operatives organisation are expected to ensure primarily.

(*a*) profitability to the members
(*b*) socialism in the economy
(*c*) equity to the members
(*d*) productivity to the society

123. Which of the following statements are correct?

I. A trust form of organisation cannot do business.
II. A society registered under the societies Registration Act can be formed only for non-profit purpose.
III. A partnership does not require registration.
IV. A company limited by guarantee is almost always registered for non-profit activities.

Codes:

(*a*) II, III and IV (*b*) I and IV
(*c*) II and III (*d*) I, II, III and IV

124. The basic characteristics of a partnership firm include.

(*a*) existence of relationship, plurality of persons, contract and profit maximisation.
(*b*) unlimited liability, contractual binding principal agent relationship and profit motive.
(*c*) existence of business, contractual relationship group of persons, task orientation and employment conditions.
(*d*) existence of business, plurality of persons contractual at relationship, profit motive and principle-agent relationship.

125. It is compulsory for a share broker to registered with the

(*a*) concerned stock exchange
(*b*) securities and exchange board of India
(*c*) department of company affairs
(*d*) concerned stock exchange in concurrence with the securities and exchange board of India

126. Who among the following is not a speculator in stock exchange?
(*a*) Broker (*b*) Bull
(*c*) Bear (*d*) Stag

127. The gilt edged market refers to the market for
(*a*) industrial securities
(*b*) Govt. and semi-govt securities
(*c*) shares and debentures
(*d*) public limited company securities

128. The combination of firms in successive stages of the same industry may be referred to as
(*a*) horizontal integration
(*b*) vertical integration
(*c*) forward integration
(*d*) backward integration

129. Which one of the following statements is true?
(*a*) Suppliers credit and buyers credit are one and the same thing.
(*b*) EXIM bank generally deals with export transaction above ₹ 5 crore.
(*c*) The main focus of EXIM bank is on export and import credit for short-term.
(*d*) ECGC provides no protection against hazards of nature.

130. Which one of the following statements are corrects?
I. Bill of loading is a document of title
II. Green shipping bill is used for export of goods entitled to duty draw back
III. An airway bill is not a document of title
IV. A consumer invoice and a proforma invoice are one and the same

Codes:
(*a*) II and IV (*b*) I, II and IV
(*c*) I, II and IV (*d*) I, II and III

131. Life insurance is a contract on the life of a man in which the insurer promises to pay a sum of money. For the consideration of a definite premium, to the insured person on his death or an attaining a particular age. Which one of the following assumptions is implicit in the above definition?
(*a*) It is a contract of indemnity
(*b*) It is a contract of guarantee
(*c*) It is a contract of compensation
(*d*) It is a contract of return on investment

132. "Causa promia" implies that the loss must arise from
(*a*) the nearest place
(*b*) an assertainable place source
(*c*) the cause insured against
(*d*) unforeseen source

133. Which one of the following risk are not covered by a marine insurance policy
I. Damage caused by delay in ships transit
II. Damage caued by unsuitable package
III. Loss due to sinking of the vessel
IV. Loss due to jettison

Select the correct answer using the codes given below:

Codes:
(*a*) I, III and IV
(*b*) I and II
(*c*) II and IV
(*d*) I, II, III and IV

134. Trading on equity takes place
(*a*) when capital other than that of equity share holders is also employed
(*b*) only when equity capital is employed
(*c*) only when debentures funds are employed
(*d*) when profits are ploughed back

135. Which one of the following statements is correct?
(*a*) Co-operative organisation are based on the principle of "one vote" one share
(*b*) A public limited company does not invite capital from the public
(*c*) Most of the public enterprises in India are organised on the pattern of private limited companies
(*d*) Registration of partnership is compulsory

136. Which of the following are the methods of marketing new issues of securities
I. Listing of securities
II. Jobbers and brokers
III. Private placement of securities
IV. Privileged subscriptions

Select the correct answer using the codes given below:

Codes:

(*a*) I and II (*b*) II and III
(*c*) III and IV (*d*) I, II, III and IV

137. Vertical combination helps to
(*a*) achieve economy by combination allied activities
(*b*) survive during the times of depression
(*c*) fight a common enemy
(*d*) add new product lines

138. Letter of credit is now becoming an increasingly popular method of financing
(*a*) fixed capital needs
(*b*) working capital needs
(*c*) redemption of debentures
(*d*) distribution of dividend

139. Import procedure begins with
(*a*) indent
(*b*) marine insurance
(*c*) mate's certificate
(*d*) shipping order

140. Which one of the following statements is correct?
(*a*) EXIM bank promotes Indian exports through a wide variety and range of lending programmes
(*b*) EXIM bank does not extent non-funded facility to Indian exports
(*c*) Overseas investment finance facility is not a part of the function of EXIM bank
(*d*) EXIM bank was established to provide assistance in raising capital in international markets

141. In which of the following types of insurance should insurable interest be present only at the time when policy is taken?
(*a*) Fire insurance
(*b*) Life insurance
(*c*) Marine insurance
(*d*) Life and Marine Insurance

142. Match list-I with list-II and select the correct answer using the codes given below the lists:

List-I	List-II
I. Causa proxima	A. Financial stake
II. Reinsurance	B. Main reason behind the event
III. Indemnity	C. Compensation for the loss
	D. Risking with other insurer

Codes:

(*a*) I-B, II-D, III-C (*b*) I-A, II-B, III-C
(*c*) I-B, II-C, III-A (*d*) I-B, II-D, III-A

143. Insurer is a person who has
(*a*) insured his life or goods
(*b*) helped a person to get an insurance policy
(*c*) undertaken to make good the loss of the subject matter of insurance
(*d*) filed a suit in a court of law to recover an insurance claim

144. In insurance contract uberimae fidie aspect is used as synonym of
(*a*) insurable interest
(*b*) free consent of parties
(*c*) utmost goods faith
(*d*) legality of consideration

145. Capital gearing ratio denotes the relationship between
(*a*) assets and capital
(*b*) loans and capital
(*c*) equity share holders, funds and long term borrowed funds
(*d*) debentures and share capital

146. Which one of the following is not applicable to a co-operative form of business organisation
(*a*) Membership is open to all having a common interest
(*b*) Transferability of shares is permitted among general public
(*c*) Policy decisions are taken by the members in a general meeting
(*d*) Major portion of profit is distributed to members by way of dividend

147. An enterprise incorporated by a special act of parliament or the state legislature intending to carry on some business of national importance is called

(*a*) Public company
(*b*) Statutory corporation
(*c*) Registered company
(*d*) Registered statutory company

148. Consider the following functions of a stock exchange

I. providing a ready market for securities.
II. helping capital formation.
III. regulating the capital structure of a company.
IV. regulating the public deposits with companies.

Of these statements

(*a*) I, II, III and IV are correct
(*b*) I, II, and III are correct
(*c*) I and II are correct
(*d*) none of these

149. Both 'securities' and 'investment' elements are available

(*a*) only in life insurance
(*b*) in both life and fire insurance
(*c*) in both marine and fire insurance
(*d*) in life, marine and fire insurance

150. Match List-I with List-II and select the correct answer using the codes given below the lists:

List-I	List-II
I. Bull	A. Buys the shares for sale but finds it difficult to meet his commitment
II. Bear	B. Buys the shares to sell them in future expecting a price rise
III. Lame duck	C. Neither buys nor sells but more applies for shares to sell at a premium
IV. Stag	D. Agree to sell on a fixed date expecting a fall in the price
	E. Buys and sells shares on the same date
	F. Agree to sell on a fixed date but finds it difficult to meet his commitment
	G. A genuine investor

Codes:

(*a*) I-D, II-B, III-A, IV-G
(*b*) I-D, II-B, III-C, IV-E
(*c*) I-B, II-D, III-E, IV-A
(*d*) I-B, II-D, III-F, IV-C

151. Which one of the following pair is not correctly matched?

List-I	List-II
I. Value of any security	A. The real value of any security is determined by the prior rights to the return of income.
II. Debentures	B. It possesses maximum safety and fixed income.
III. Prefernce share	C. It offers reasonable safety as well as regular and fixed income by way of dividend.
IV. Equity shares	D. It invites speculative tendency and the investors there is a risk of loss in such a share.

Select the correct answers using the codes given below:

Codes:

(*a*) I-A, II-B, III-C, IV-D
(*b*) I-B, II-A, III-C, IV-D
(*c*) I-A, II-B, III-D, IV-C
(*d*) I-B, II-A, III-D, IV-C

152. In stock exchange operations when the speculator buys the right to sell a certain number of shares on an agreed date at a specified time it is known as

(*a*) no option (*b*) put option
(*c*) call option (*d*) double option

153. The jurisdiction of the MRTP commission with respect to monopolistic trade practices is not exercisable upon / under

(*a*) a reference made to it by the central government
(*b*) an application made to it by the Director General

(*c*) its own knowledge or information
(*d*) any of the above mentioned circumstances

154. Complete consolidation as a class of business combination may include
(*a*) mergers and amalgamations
(*b*) pools and cartels
(*c*) trusts and holding companies
(*d*) trade association and chambers of commerce

155. Consider the following statements
The EXIM bank plays an active role in boosting exports by
I. civil constructions contract abroad
II. providing long term finance for export of capital goods
III. providing short term finance for import of capital goods
IV. providing short term finance for export of quality goods.
Of these statements :
(*a*) I and II are correct
(*b*) I and IV are correct
(*c*) II and III are correct
(*d*) III and IV are correct

156. Which one of the following is not in vogue now?
(*a*) REP licences
(*b*) Advance licences
(*c*) Special import licences
(*d*) Customs permit

157. Which one of the following items are not considered to be export promotion measures?
I. Quota certificate
II. Cash compensatory assistance
III. System of exchange control
IV. Marketing development funds

Select the correct answer from the codes given below
Codes:
(*a*) I and III (*b*) III and IV
(*c*) I and IV (*d*) II and IV

158. "Bill of loading" is issued by
(*a*) Indian commercial bank
(*b*) Foreign bank
(*c*) Shipping company
(*d*) Exporters

159. Which of the following conditions must be satisfied in a claim for loss by fire?
I. There must be actual fire
II. Fire must be a accidental
III. Cause of fire must be ascertainable
IV. The goods must have been destroyed, not damage by fire

Select the answer using the codes given below
Codes:
(*a*) I and II (*b*) I and III
(*c*) II and III (*d*) III and IV

160. A mixed marine policy means
(*a*) combination of fire and marine losses coverage
(*b*) combination of voyage and time policies
(*c*) combination of all types of risk on the sea
(*d*) combination of export credit insurance and marine insurance

161. A building worth rupees of five lakh is insured for one lakh of rupees. There is an average clause in the policy. A portion of the building valued one lakh of rupees is destroyed by fire. The owner can claim and recover.
(*a*) one lakh rupees
(*b*) twenty thousand rupees minus the sale of proceeds of the debris
(*c*) five lakh rupees
(*d*) one lakh rupees minus the sale of proceeds of the debris

162. In option dealings, speculation means
(*a*) buying in one market at cheaper price and selling the same in another at a higher price
(*b*) agreeing to illegitimate trading in securities outside the reorganised stock exchange
(*c*) acquiring right to buy or sell a certain quantity of securities at a stated price within a prescribed time
(*d*) postponing the payment to and delivery of securities if market conditions turn adverse

163. If the Broke Bond Company merges with the Lipton Company it would be an example of
(*a*) diagonal integration
(*b*) horizontal combination
(*c*) lateral integration
(*d*) vertical combination

164. Every person has insurable interest in his own life up to
(*a*) a maximum of ₹ 5,00,000
(*b*) twenty times his net salary drawn
(*c*) an unlimited extent provided the premium payable does not exceed 20% of his salary
(*d*) an unlimited extent

165. Plate-glass is typical type of accident insurance and it is mainly applicable to
(*a*) personal accident (*b*) motor cars
(*c*) retail trade (*d*) house burglary

166. Doctrine of subrogation, is used in
(*a*) life insurance
(*b*) fire insurance
(*c*) marine insurance
(*d*) joint life insurance

167. Match List-I with List-II select the correct answer using the codes given below the lists:

List-I	**List-II**
I. company X buys up company Y and shareholders of Y get share in X	A. amalgamation
II. company X and company Y join to form company Z	B. absorption
III. company X buys 51% of shares in company Y	C. cartel
IV. company X and company Y have the same directors	D. holding company
	E. community in India

Codes :
(*a*) I-A, II-B, III-E, IV-D
(*b*) I-B, II-A, III-D, IV-E
(*c*) I-B, II-A, III-D, IV-C
(*d*) I-A, II-B, III-D, IV-E

168. Which one of the following is the subsidiary of the state trading corporation of India meant for increasing exports?
(*a*) Minerals and Metals Trading Corporation of India
(*b*) Manufacturers Export Agents and Export Commission House
(*c*) Project and Equipment Corporation of India
(*d*) Mica Trading Corporation

169. The term duty draw-back means
(*a*) higher rate of import duty
(*b*) refund of import duty for the exporters
(*c*) handicap in the matter of export
(*d*) refund of export duty for exporters

170. A letter of credit is a
(*a*) letter of importer's bank agreeing to accept and pay on due date the exporter's bill
(*b*) letter containing conditions of a credit purchase or sale
(*c*) letter from an exporter to import sanctioning credit deal
(*d*) letter sent by importer to exporter sanctioning credit deal

171. The importer cannot take delivery of goods unless produces the
(*a*) bill of sight
(*b*) bill of loading
(*c*) shipping bill
(*d*) certificate of origin

172. Consider
I. export duty
II. export subsidy
III. liberal import entitlement
IV. revaluation of currency

Which of the above policy measures would lead to an expansion of exporters?
(*a*) I, II and IV (*b*) I and III
(*c*) III and IV (*d*) II and III

173. When an insurance company (other than Life Insurance Corporation) pays for the total loss to the insured, it has a right to take over all right and remedies, the insured may have

against the third parties. This right of an insurance company is based on
(*a*) causa proxima
(*b*) contract of indemnity
(*c*) scientific and actual calculation
(*d*) subrogation

174. Which one of the following is the true principle of insurance?
(*a*) All insurance contracts are contracts of indemnity
(*b*) Only marine and life insurance contracts are contracts of indemnity
(*c*) Only fire and life insurance contracts are contracts of indemnity
(*d*) Only fire and marine insurance contracts are contracts of indemnity.

175. The insurer will pay proportionately and the insured will be his own insurer for the balance if the value of the subject matter is greater than the insured amount in
(*a*) valued policy
(*b*) declaration policy
(*c*) average policy
(*d*) consequential loss policy

176. Average clause in a fire policy
(*a*) averages the claim on the different policies taken by the insured
(*b*) insures the property at average premium paid for the last three years
(*c*) insures the property at the average rate of premium received during the last year only
(*d*) penalises under-insurance

177. For the purposes of fire insurance, loss by fire means loss due to
I. ignition
II. accidental fire
III. causes arising from fire
IV. damage caused during extinguishment of fire

Of these statements:
(*a*) All are correct
(*b*) I and II are correct
(*c*) I, II and III are correct
(*d*) III and IV are correct

178. Economic oligarchy, fraudulent practices, bureaucratic management and difficulty in formation are the limitations of a
(*a*) Sale property concern
(*b*) Partnership firm
(*c*) Joint stock company
(*d*) Co-operative society

179. Consider the following statements:
I. Although purchasing department in a departmental store is a key department, only the sales department and not the purchasing department can be considered as line activities.
II. Line managers offer staff managers advice through research and analysis.
III. Functional authority is the authority of members of staff department to control the activities of other departments.

Which of the statements given above is/are correct?
(*a*) I and II (*b*) II only
(*c*) III only (*d*) I and III

180. Which of the following is/are the reason (s) for centralisation of authority in an organisation?
I. Specialised skills, talent and technology are neither affordable nor practical in multiple locations.
II. Decentralisation usually results in an increase in overhead and staff.
III. Recent improvments in communication technology facilitate the movement of money, credit information and data processing from a single centre of authority.

Select the correct answer using the codes given below.
(*a*) III only (*b*) I and II
(*c*) I and III (*d*) I, II and III

181. Consider the following statements about management of change
I. Job enlargement and job enrichment are examples of techno-structural approaches to change.
II. Organisational development is short range effort supported by top management to increase an organisation's problem solving and renewal processes.

Which of the statements given above is/are correct?

(*a*) I only (*b*) II only
(*c*) Both I and II (*d*) Neither I nor II

182. Consider the following statements about organisational structure:

I. Functional organisation is used by large, multi-product companies.
II. Product or market organisation is used by smaller firms that offer a limited line of products.
III. Matrix organisational structure is a hybrid.

Which of the statements given abvoe is/are correct?

(*a*) I and II (*b*) III only
(*c*) II and III (*d*) I, II and III

183. Export promotion is indispensable for overcoming disequilibrium in

(*a*) balance of payments
(*b*) balance of trade
(*c*) terms of trade
(*d*) all of these

184. Match List-I with List-II and select the correct answer using the codes given below the lists:

List-I	List-II
I. Horizontal combination	A. mixed combination
II. Vertical combination	B. service combination
III. Diagonal combination	C. industry combination
IV. Circular combination	D. trade combination

Codes:

(*a*) I-D, II-C, III-B, IV-A
(*b*) I-B, II-A, III-D, IV-C
(*c*) I-D, II-A, III-B, IV-C
(*d*) I-B, II-C, III-D, IV-A

185. Indentify the correct sequence of the following steps with regard to delegation of authority

I. creation of obligation
II. authorisation for actions
III. determination of the expected results
IV. assignment of duties

Select the correct answer using the codes given below

(*a*) III, II, IV, I (*b*) I, II, IV, III
(*c*) I, IV, II, III (*d*) III, IV, II, I

186. Burns and stalker model for categorising organisations by structural design uses the terms

(*a*) functional and geographic
(*b*) functional and organic
(*c*) geographic and mechanistic
(*d*) mechanistic and organic

187. One of the important weaknesses of the decentralised structure is

(*a*) unsuitability in a fast - changing environment
(*b*) difficulty in pinpointing responsibilities
(*c*) difficulty in coordinating common functions
(*d*) difficulty in promoting innovations

188. An organisational manual is designed to promote

(*a*) better clientele for a company
(*b*) better relationship betweeen the unit in an industry
(*c*) better understanding of basic organisational structures
(*d*) better information about business of the company

189. A planned sequence of operations for handling recurring business transactions uniformly and consistently is known as

(*a*) system (*b*) procedure
(*c*) routine (*d*) control

190. Which one of the following statements explains the concept of unity of command?

(*a*) all the workers focus on a common goal
(*b*) all the workers receive instructions from one authority
(*c*) all the workers are accountable to one authority
(*d*) all the workers aim at one objective at a time

191. The type of control that provides a means for taking corrective action even after viability of the programme is known as
(*a*) pre-action control
(*b*) post-action control
(*c*) screening control
(*d*) steering control

192. The mechanistic model of organisational design achieves high levels of production and efficiency because
(*a*) of its de-emphasis specialisation and its emphasis on increasing job range
(*b*) it is highly decentralised and informal
(*c*) both (*a*) and (*b*)
(*d*) it is highly complex, centralised and formalised

193. When there are large number of smaller projects and the activities of these project are to be accomplished by setting up some temporary department, the appropriate organisational structure should be
(*a*) project organisation
(*b*) functional organisation
(*c*) matrix organisation
(*d*) divisional organisation

194. Which one of the following is the major consideration for decentralisation?
(*a*) Organization's environment
(*b*) Nature of management function
(*c*) Size of organisation
(*d*) Ability of higher level managers

195. Which one of the following traits describes properly organic or behavioural structure of an organisation?
(*a*) Wider spans of control
(*b*) More centralisation
(*c*) Higher degree of specialisation
(*d*) Taller hierarchy

196. Centralising the office work is desirable mostly because it
(*a*) fixed responsibility
(*b*) avoids duplication
(*c*) permits better supervision
(*d*) permits better delegation

197. Social responsibility of business assumes considerable importance towards
(*a*) owner and workers
(*b*) consumer and community
(*c*) government and nation
(*d*) all the above

198. The most suitable form of business organisation for the people of weaker section is
(*a*) partnership firm
(*b*) cooperative society
(*c*) sole trading business
(*d*) joint stock company

199. A partner under his 'Implied Authority' can
(*a*) enter into partnership with others on behalf of the firm
(*b*) submit dispute relating to the business of the firm for arbitration
(*c*) defend any suit filed against the firm
(*d*) withdraw any suit or proceedings filed on behalf of the firm

200. E Commerce can be of following types
(*a*) B 2 B (*b*) B 2 C
(*c*) B 2 A (*d*) All of these

201. Mechanistic structures are designed to
(*a*) promote flexibility and quick responses to fast changing situations
(*b*) induce people to behave in predictable and accountable manner
(*c*) make people happy by assigning specific tasks to them
(*d*) perform assigned tasks within the scheduled time

202. The degree of decentralisation in an organisation depends most on
(*a*) technology
(*b*) size of work force
(*c*) volume of transactions
(*d*) competence of subordinates

203. Scalar principle refers to the
(*a*) responsibility of a subordinate to a superior
(*b*) conflict of instructions from two or more superior

(*c*) existence of a clear line of authority in all parts of the organisation
(*d*) delegation of authority at all levels of an organisation

204. 'Matrix organisation' refers to a form of
(*a*) organisation where authority and responsibility coexist
(*b*) organisation in which two or more basic types of departmentation are combined
(*c*) mathematical arrangement of events in columns and rows
(*d*) organisation where mathemetical simulation issued

205. Consider the following principles
I. harmony of objectives
II. unity of command
III. division of work
IV. responsibility

Which of these principles are not parts of 'Direction'?
(*a*) I and II (*b*) II and III
(*c*) III and IV (*d*) I and IV

206. Under which one of the following types of organisational structure does a person become accountable to two or more bosses at the same time?
(*a*) matrix structure
(*b*) centralised structure
(*c*) decentralised structure
(*d*) vertical structure

207. Consider the following stages in delegation of authority
I. creation of obligation
II. determination of results expected
III. assignment of duties
IV. authorisation for actions

The correct sequence of these stages is:
(*a*) I, II, III, IV
(*b*) II, I, IV, II
(*c*) II, III, IV, I
(*d*) I, III, IV, II

208. The delegation of authority from higher to lower levels of an organisation is called
(*a*) diminution of authority
(*b*) division of labour
(*c*) departmentalisation
(*d*) decentralisation

209. Which one of the following sets is correct with regard to liberalisation in financial sector?
(*a*) Globalisation, devaluation and privatisation
(*b*) Deregulation, moral suasion and branch expansion
(*c*) Privatisation, computerisation and standardisation
(*d*) Globalisation, deregulation and privatisation

210. Which one of the following is not the primary cause of India's chronic balance of payments problem?
(*a*) Value of imports not matched by value of exports.
(*b*) Deficits in merchandise trade
(*c*) Membership of WTO
(*d*) Pol imports

211. Globalisation of financial services is being promoted by
(*a*) World Trade Organisation
(*b*) International Finance Corporation
(*c*) International Bank for Reconstruction and Development
(*d*) International Monetary fund

212. According to Graicunas theory, total number of relations among superiors and subordinates can be found by the formula
(*a*) $n\left(2^{n}/_{2} + n + 1\right)$
(*b*) $n\left(2^{n-1}/_{2} + n - 1\right)$
(*c*) $n\left(2^{n-1}/_{2} + n + 2\right)$
(*d*) $n\left(2^{n}/_{2} + n - 1\right)$

213. Match List-I with List-II and select the correct answer using the codes given below the lists:

List-I	List-II
I. Line authority	A. Some people in an organisation are vested with primary source of authority.

II. Staff authority	B. Some people in an organisation have legitimate right to expert influence on others.
III. Functional authority	C. Some people in an organisation lack independent, formal authority.
IV. Formal authority	D. Some people have right to control activities of other departments as they relate to specific staff.

Codes:

(*a*) I-A, II-B, III-C, IV-D

(*b*) I-B, II-D, III-C, IV-A

(*c*) I-A, II-C, III-D, IV-B

(*d*) I-B, II-C, III-D, IV-A

214. Consider the given structure of an organisation. Which one of the following is represented by the same

(*a*) Durker's effective structure

(*b*) Span of effective control

(*c*) Functional form of organisation

(*d*) General Manager's view of the organisation

215. LIBOR refers to

(*a*) liberalised system of foreign exchange transfer between Banks

(*b*) inter-bank lending rate for Eurodollars at London

(*c*) lowest rate of interest at which banks in London lend pound sterling

(*d*) lowest rate of interest prescribed by the Reserve Bank of India

ANSWERS

1	2	3	4	5	6	7	8	9	10
(*d*)	(*a*)	(*d*)	(*d*)	(*c*)	(*b*)	(*a*)	(*b*)	(*d*)	(*d*)
11	**12**	**13**	**14**	**15**	**16**	**17**	**18**	**19**	**20**
(*d*)	(*c*)	(*d*)	(*d*)	(*c*)	(*c*)	(*b*)	(*c*)	(*c*)	(*b*)
21	**22**	**23**	**24**	**25**	**26**	**27**	**28**	**29**	**30**
(*d*)	(*a*)	(*c*)	(*a*)	(*d*)	(*b*)	(*c*)	(*b*)	(*c*)	(*c*)
31	**32**	**33**	**34**	**35**	**36**	**37**	**38**	**39**	**40**
(*d*)	(*d*)	(*a*)	(*d*)	(*d*)	(*d*)	(*a*)	(*b*)	(*d*)	(*a*)
41	**42**	**43**	**44**	**45**	**46**	**47**	**48**	**49**	**50**
(*b*)	(*b*)	(*d*)	(*d*)	(*d*)	(*a*)	(*c*)	(*b*)	(*a*)	(*a*)
51	**52**	**53**	**54**	**55**	**56**	**57**	**58**	**59**	**60**
(*b*)	(*a*)	(*b*)	(*a*)	(*a*)	(*b*)	(*d*)	(*c*)	(*a*)	(*c*)
61	**62**	**63**	**64**	**65**	**66**	**67**	**68**	**69**	**70**
(*a*)	(*a*)	(*c*)	(*d*)	(*c*)	(*a*)	(*a*)	(*d*)	(*c*)	(*c*)
71	**72**	**73**	**74**	**75**	**76**	**77**	**78**	**79**	**80**
(*c*)	(*d*)	(*d*)	(*a*)	(*c*)	(*a*)	(*b*)	(*d*)	(*c*)	(*b*)
81	**82**	**83**	**84**	**85**	**86**	**87**	**88**	**89**	**90**
(*d*)	(*d*)	(*b*)	(*a*)	(*d*)	(*a*)	(*c*)	(*b*)	(*a*)	(*b*)

91	92	93	94	95	96	97	98	99	100
(*d*)	(*c*)	(*b*)	(*d*)	(*c*)	(*b*)	(*b*)	(*d*)	(*d*)	(*c*)
101	**102**	**103**	**104**	**105**	**106**	**107**	**108**	**109**	**110**
(*b*)	(*c*)	(*c*)	(*b*)	(*a*)	(*d*)	(*b*)	(*d*)	(*d*)	(*b*)
111	**112**	**113**	**114**	**115**	**116**	**117**	**118**	**119**	**120**
(*a*)	(*b*)	(*d*)	(*b*)	(*c*)	(*a*)	(*b*)	(*c*)	(*d*)	(*b*)
121	**122**	**123**	**124**	**125**	**126**	**127**	**128**	**129**	**130**
(*b*)	(*c*)	(*d*)	(*b*)	(*d*)	(*a*)	(*b*)	(*b*)	(*c*)	(*b*)
131	**132**	**133**	**134**	**135**	**136**	**137**	**138**	**139**	**140**
(*b*)	(*c*)	(*b*)	(*b*)	(*a*)	(*c*)	(*a*)	(*b*)	(*a*)	(*a*)
141	**142**	**143**	**144**	**145**	**146**	**147**	**148**	**149**	**150**
(*b*)	(*a*)	(*c*)	(*c*)	(*c*)	(*b*)	(*b*)	(*c*)	(*a*)	(*d*)
151	**152**	**153**	**154**	**155**	**156**	**157**	**158**	**159**	**160**
(*a*)	(*c*)	(*d*)	(*a*)	(*c*)	(*b*)	(*a*)	(*c*)	(*a*)	(*b*)
161	**162**	**163**	**164**	**165**	**166**	**167**	**168**	**169**	**170**
(*b*)	(*c*)	(*b*)	(*d*)	(*b*)	(*b*)	(*b*)	(*d*)	(*b*)	(*a*)
171	**172**	**173**	**174**	**175**	**176**	**177**	**178**	**179**	**180**
(*b*)	(*d*)	(*d*)	(*d*)	(*c*)	(*d*)	(*a*)	(*c*)	(*c*)	(*a*)
181	**182**	**183**	**184**	**185**	**186**	**187**	**188**	**189**	**190**
(*d*)	(*d*)	(*d*)	(*d*)	(*d*)	(*b*)	(*c*)	(*d*)	(*a*)	(*b*)
191	**192**	**193**	**194**	**195**	**196**	**197**	**198**	**199**	**200**
(*d*)	(*d*)	(*b*)	(*c*)	(*c*)	(*b*)	(*d*)	(*b*)	(*c*)	(*d*)
201	**202**	**203**	**204**	**205**	**206**	**207**	**208**	**209**	**210**
(*d*)	(*d*)	(*c*)	(*b*)	(*d*)	(*a*)	(*b*)	(*d*)	(*d*)	(*a*)
211	**212**	**213**	**214**	**215**					
(*d*)	(*d*)	(*c*)	(*c*)	(*c*)					

Management

Management refers to the process of using men, money, machines, material and processes through proper direction, coordination and integration of several activities so as to produce desired results and attain predetermined goals. In other words, management consists of a series of activities classified into various functions like planning, organising, staffing, directing and controlling.

Characteristics of Management

The various characteristics of management are:

(a) Management is universal
(b) Management is goal directed
(c) Management is a continuous process
(d) Management is intangible
(e) Management is multi-disciplinary
(f) Management is a social process
(g) Management is situational

Nature of Management

The nature of management can be better appreciated by looking at it

1. as a process
2. as a discipline
3. as a group of individuals
4. as a profession, and
5. as a science as well as an art.

FUNCTIONS OF MANAGEMENT

(a) Planning

Planning is deciding in advance what is to be done, when it is to be done, how it is to be done. It is basically concerned with the selection of goals to be achieved and determining the effective course of action from among the various alternatives. This involves forecasting, establishing targets, developing the policies and programming and scheduling the action, procedure, etc. Thus, planning requires decisions to be made on what should be done, how it should be done, who will do it, where it will be done, and why it is to be done. The essential part of planning consists of setting goals and programmes of activities.

(b) Organising

After the plans have been drawn, management has to organise the activities, and physical resources of the firm to carry out the selected programmes successfully. It also involves determining the authority and responsibility relationships among functions, departments and personnel at various levels to ensure smooth and effective function together in accomplishing the objective. Thus, the organising function of management is primarily concerned with identifying the tasks involved and grouping them into units and departments, and defining the duties and responsibilities of people in different positions within each department for well coordinated and cooperative effort in the organisation.

(c) Staffing

Staffing is concerned with employing people for the various activities to be performed. The objective of staffing is to ensure that suitable people have been appointed for different positions. It includes the functions of recruitment, training and development, placement and remuneration, and performance appraisal of the employees.

(d) Directing

The directing function of management includes guiding the subordinates, supervising their performance, communicating effectively and motivating them. A manager should be a good leader. He should be able to command and issue instruction without arousing any resentment among the subordinates. He should keep a watch on the performance of his subordinates and help them out whenever they come across any difficulty. The communication system, i.e., exchange of information should take place regularly for building common understanding and clarity. The managers should also understand the needs of subordinates and inspire them to do their best and encourage initiative and creativity.

(e) Controlling

This function of management consists of the steps taken to ensure that the performance of work is in accordance with the plans. It involves establishing performance standards and measuring the actual performance with the standards set. If differences are noticed, corrective steps are taken which may include revision of standards, regulate operations, remove deficiencies and improve performance.

(f) Co-ordinating

Management has to ensure that all the activities contribute to the achievement of the objectives of the business as a whole. This requires integration of activities and synchronisation of efforts. The heads of different departments should not treat each other as competitors but should work as organs of one body. As the proper functioning of every organ of a human body is important for a healthy body, the work of every department is important for the organisation as a whole. Managers should, therefore, see that everybody in the organisation understands its objectives and works in co-operation with others to achieve these objectives. This function of management is called co-ordination. It consists of harmonising group effort so as to achieve common objectives.

VARIOUS APPROACHES TO MANAGEMENT PHILOSOPHY

Scientific Management

Frederick Winslow Taylor (1856-1915) is the father of scientific management. He exerted great influence on the development of management thought through his experiments and writings. During a career spanning 26 years, he arranged a series of experiments in three companies: Midvale Steel, Simonds Rolling Machine and Bethlehem Steel.

1. Time and motion study: Since Taylor had been an operator himself; he knew how piecework workers used to hold back production to one-third its level. The workers feared that their employers would cut their piece rate as soon as there was a rise in production. The real trouble, Taylor thought, was that no one knew how much work was reasonable for a man to do. Therefore, he established the time and motion study.

2. Differential payment: Taylor had founded the differential piecework system and the related incentives with production. Under this plan, a worker received a low piece rate if he produced the standard number of pieces and a high rate if he surpassed the standard. Taylor also comprehended that the attraction of a new high piece rate would encourage the workers to increase production.

3. Drastic reorganisation of supervision: Taylor developed two new concepts: (i) Division of planning and doing and (ii) Functional foremanship. In those days, it was customary for each worker to plan his own work. The worker himself used to select his tools and decide the sequence of performance of operations. The foreman essentially told the worker what jobs were to be performed, not how they were to be performed. Taylor suggested that the work should be designed by a foreman and not by the worker. He stated that there were distinctive functions involved in doing any kind of job and that each of the foremen should give orders to the worker in his specialised field.

4. Scientific recruitment and training: Taylor also gave importance to the scientific selection and development of the worker. He said that the management should develop and train every worker in order to bring out his best output and to enable him to perform a superior, more interesting and profitable class of work than he has done in the past.

5. Intimate and friendly cooperation between the management and workers: Taylor said that, "a complete mental revolution" on the part of management and labour was necessary to make the organisation successful. Rather than argue over profits, they should both try to increase production. Consequently, profits will also increase manifold, which will leave no room for further disagreements. Taylor realised that both, the management and labour, had a common interest in maximising production.

Contributions of Scientific Management

Firstly, through the time and motion studies we understand that the tools and physical activity concerned in a job can be made better balanced and organised. Secondly, scientific management discovered how important scientific selection of workers was and comprehended that without capability and training, a person cannot be expected to do his job properly. Finally, the significance that scientific management gave to work design encouraged managers to seek the 'one best way' of doing a job. Thus, scientific management has developed a rational approach to solve the organisation's problems and contributed a great deal to the professionalism of management.

Administrative Management

While Taylor is considered the father of scientific management, Henri Fayol (1841-1925) is considered as the father of the administrative management theory, with a focus on the development of broad administrative principles applicable to general and higher managerial levels.

Fayol opined that all actions of business enterprises could be divided into six groups: technical, commercial, financial, accounting, security and administrative or managerial. Fayol's primary focus was on this last managerial activity because he felt that managerial skills had been the most neglected aspect of business operations. He explained management in terms of five functions: planning, organising, commanding, coordinating and controlling.

Fayol's 14 principles of management are as under:

- Division of work
- Authority and responsibility
- Discipline
- Unity of command
- Unity of direction
- Subordination of individual interest to general interest
- Remuneration
- Centralisation
- Scalar chain
- Order
- Equity
- Stability of tenure of personnel
- Initiative
- Esprit de Corps

MATHEMATICAL AND BEHAVIOURAL SERIAL SCHOOLS OF MANAGEMENT

Behavioural Approach

This approach is an enhanced and more developed version of the human relations approach to management. Douglas McGregor, Abraham Maslow, Kurt Lewin, Chester Barnard, Mary Parker Follett, George Romans, Rensis Likert, Chris Argyris and Warren Bennis are some of the foremost behavioural scientists who made significant contributions to the development of the behavioural approach to management. These scientists were more rigorously trained in various social sciences (such as psychology, sociology and anthropology). They use more sophisticated research methods.

Behavioural scientists consider organisations as groups of individuals with objectives. They have, conducted extensive studies of human groups—large and small. They have studied the problems relating to groups, process, and group cohesiveness and so on. Behavioural scientists have completed vast studies on leadership. To behavioural scientists, the realistic model of human motivation is complex. This model suggests that different people react differently to the same situation or react the same way to different situations. The manager should alter and customise his approach to control people according to their individual needs.

The behavioural approach to organisational differences and change is quite practical. It recognises that (a) conflict is inevitable and sometimes is even desirable and should be faced with understanding and determination, (b) every organisational change involves technological and social aspects, also it is generally the social aspect of a change that people resist.

Management School of Thought

A new school of thought known as the management process school came into existence, which drew motivation from Fayol. According to Harold Koontz and Cyril O'Donnell, "Management is a dynamic process of performing the functions of planning, organising, staffing, directing and controlling". They also believe that these functions and the principles on which they are based have general or universal applicability. Managers, whether they are managing directors or supervisors, perform the same functions of planning and control, although the degree of complexity may differ. Similarly, management functions are not confined to business enterprises alone but are applicable to all organisations wherever group accomplishment and enterprise is involved. Management theory is not culture-bound but is adaptable and flexible from one environment to another.

The Human Relations Movement

Managers face many problems because employees do not follow predetermined and balanced patterns of behaviour. Thus, there is an increase in interest to help managers deal more effectively with the 'people side' of their organisations. The original inspiration for the movement, however, came from the Hawthorne experiments, which were done by Prof. Elton Mayo and his colleagues at the Western Electric Company's plant in Cicero, Illinois from 1927 to 1932.

Mathematical/Quantitative Approach

1. Management science and MIS: Management science (also called operations research) uses mathematical and statistical approaches to solve management problems. It originated during World War II, as strategists tried to apply scientific knowledge and methods to the complex problems of war. Industry began to apply management science after the war. George Dantzig developed linear programming, an algebraic method to determine the optimal allocation of scarce resources. Other tools used in industry include inventory control theory, goal programming, queuing models and simulation. The advent of the computer made many management science tools and concepts more practical and applicable for the industry. Increasingly, management science and management information systems (MIS) are interconnected. MIS focuses on providing needed information to managers in a useful format and at the proper time. Decision support systems (DSS) attempts to integrate decision models, data and the decision maker into a system that supports better management decisions.

2. Production and operations management: This school focuses on the operation and control of the production process that transforms resources into finished goods and services. It has its roots in scientific management but it developed into an identifiable area of management study after World War II. It uses many tools of management science.

Operations management emphasises the productivity and quality of both manufacturing and service organisations. W. Edwards Deming exerted tremendous influence in shaping modern ideas about improving productivity and quality. Foremost areas of study within operations management include capacity-planning, facilities location, facilities layout, materials requirement planning, scheduling, purchasing and inventory control, quality control, computer integrated manufacturing, just-in-time inventory systems and flexible manufacturing systems.

Systems Approach

A recurrent drawback of the classical, behavioural and quantitative schools is that they lay more emphasis on one aspect of the organisation at the expense of another.

However, it is difficult to know which aspect is most functional, constructive and appropriate in a given situation. What is needed is a singular expansive, detailed, conceptual framework that can help a manager diagnose a problem and decide which tool or combination of tools will accomplish the task best. The systems approach helps in obtaining an integrated approach to management problems. Some important contributors of the systems approach are Chester Barnard, George Homans, Philip Selznick and Herbert Simon. The following are the key concepts of this approach:

A system is a set of interdependent parts, which together form a unitary whole that performs some function. An organisation is also a system composed of four interdependent parts, namely, task, structure, people and technology.

Features of Systems Approach

1. An organisation comprises of many sub-systems.
2. All the sub-systems are inter-related.
3. The sub-parts should be studied in their inter-relationships rather than in isolation.
4. The organisation provides a demarcating line that separates it from other systems. It determines the internal and external parts.
5. The organisation is responsive to environmental effect. It is vulnerable to the changes in environment.
6. An organsiation is a system consisting of many interrelated and interdependent parts or sub-systems. These elements are then arranged in an orderly fashion.
7. As a system, an organisation draws inputs (energy, information, materials, etc) from its environment. It transforms these inputs and returns the output into the environment in the form of goods and services.
8. Every system is a part of a super system.
9. Organisation is an open system and it interacts with its environment. It is also a dynamic system as the equilibrium in it is always changing.
10. Management is expected to regulate and adjust the system to secure better performance.
11. Management is multidisciplinary as it draws and integrates knowledge from various disciplines.

Contingency Approach

According to this approach, management values and concepts of various schools have no universal applications. In other words, there is no optimal or single best way of doing things under all conditions. Methods and techniques, which are highly effective in one situation, may not work in other situations. Results differ because situations differ.

Accordingly, the contingency approach suggests that the task of managers is to try to identify which technique will best contribute to the attainment of management goals in a particular situation. Thus, managers have to employ a sort of situational sensitivity and practical selectivity.

Features of Contingency Approach

1. Management is externally situational: the conditions of the situation will determine which techniques and control system should be designed to fit the particular situation.
2. Management is entirely situational.
3. There is no best way of doing anything.
4. One needs to adapt himself to the circumstances.
5. It is a kind of "if" "then" approach.
6. It is practically suited.
7. Management policies and procedures should respond to environment.
8. Managers should understand that there is no best way of managing. It dispels the universal validity of principles.

PLANNING

Planning is a systematic way of deciding about and doing things in a purposeful manner. In the context of business organisations and their management it may be defined as the process of setting future objectives and deciding on the ways and means of achieving them. In the words of M.E. Hurley "planning is deciding in advance what is to be done in future. It involves the selection of objectives, policies, procedures and programmes from among the alternatives".

Importance of Planning

Planning is the most important of all the management functions. Some of the features of planning are as follows:

(a) Planning reduces uncertainty, risk and confusion in operation.
(b) Planning guides the decision making by the managers.
(c) Planning helps in achieving coordination and facilitates control.
(d) Planning with an element of flexibility makes the organisation adaptable.
(e) Planning leads to economy and efficiency in operations.
(f) Planning begins with the determination of objectives and directed towards their achievement.

The Planning Process/Steps in Planning

Planning in organisation follows a step-by-step process without which it may be difficult to build up proper plans and ensure their implementation. Such steps are as follows:

1. Establishment of Objectives
2. Making Assumptions (establishing premises) about the External and Internal Conditions
3. Development of Alternative Courses of Action
4. Evaluation of Alternatives
5. Selecting the Appropriate Course of Action
6. Arranging for implementation

ORGANISING

Organising is the next important function of management after the planning. Organising refers to the process of :

- Identifying and grouping the work to be performed.
- Defining and determining responsibility and authority for each job position.
- Establishing relationship among various job positions.
- Determining detailed rules and regulations of working for individuals and groups in organisation.

Process of Organising

The process of organising consists of the following steps:

1. Identification of activities
2. Grouping of activities
3. Assignment of Responsibilities
4. Granting authority
5. Establishing relationship

Formal and Informal Organisation

Formal organisation refers to the officially established pattern of relationship among departments, divisions and individuals to achieve well-defined goals and is a consciously designed structure of roles. In other words, formal organisation clearly spells what a person has to do, from whom he has to take orders and what rules, policies and work procedures are to be followed. Thus, it is a system of well-defined jobs, each bearing a definitive measure of authority, responsibility and accountability. This promotes order and facilitates planning and controlling functions.

Informal organisations on the other hand, refers to relationship between individuals in the organisation based on personal attitudes, likes and dislikes and originates to meet their social and emotional needs and develops spontaneously. It represents natural grouping of people in work situation and is supplementary to formal organisation as it serves the needs not satisfied by formal organisation. The formal organisation does not provide opportunity to members to exchange personal views and experiences and so they interact informally to fulfill such interest and needs. In fact, informal organisation comes into being because of the limitations of the formal structure and both are interlinked. However, they differ in respect of their origin, purpose, structure, authority, channels of communication and behaviour of members.

Delegation

In organisations, it is difficult on the part of a manager to complete all the jobs assigned to him. He thus, can take help from others by asking them to do some of the work in a formal way. It means, he can assign some of the work to his subordinates and give them authority to carry on the work and at the same time make them accountable. For example, a production manager may have the target to produce 1000 units in a weeks time. He can distribute his work to three of his subordinates to produce 250 units each and keep 250 units for self to produce. And then he must also give them enough authority to use organisational resources to produce. By doing so he also makes his subordinates answerable to him for non-performance.

This active process of entrustment of a part of work or responsibility and authority to another and the creation of accountability for performance is known as delegation. Thus, there are three elements of delegation as follows:

1. Assignment of Responsibility
2. Granting Authority
3. Creating Accountability

Decentralisation

Decentralisation refers to a systematic effort to delegate authority at all levels of management and in all departments. This shifts the power of decision making to lower level under a well considered plan. Decentralisation has number of benefits. Firstly, it reduces the workload of the top level management. Secondly, it motivates the employees and gives them more autonomy. It promotes initiative and creativity. It also helps employees to take quick and appropriate decisions. In the process the top management is freed from the routine jobs and it enables them to concentrate on crucial areas and plan for growth.

Distinction Between Delegations and Decentralisation

Decentralisation is not same as delegation. The points of differences are:

- While delegation is the process of assigning responsibility and authority and thereby creating accountability; decentralisation is the ultimate outcome of planned delegation.
- Delegation of authority takes place between the manager and his subordinates while decentralisation involves the entire organisation, and is between top management and divisions/departments.
- Delegation is done to speed up the work and is essential in trace; while decentralisation is optional and is usually done in large scale organisations.
- In case of delegation the responsibility and authority delegated may be withdrawn by the delegator; which is not so easy in case of decentralisation.

Authority Relationship

When a person is given certain duties to perform, he must be given necessary authority to carry on the activity successfully. Otherwise, he will not able to do the work. Similarly, in an organisation every member must have some sort of authority while performing individual job. In other words, there must be an authority relationship among the staff members. Thus, on the basis of nature, authority may be of three types:

(a) Line authority
(b) Staff authority and
(c) Functional authority

Line Authority

Line authority is the authority of a manager over his immediate subordinates. For example, the chief manager has line authority over production manager and the production manager has line authority over managers of workshops. Line authority is the right of a manager to issue order and to see that these orders are carried out.

Staff Authority

When the work of line managers increases, staff officers are appointed to help them. The job of staff officers is to give advice, information, suggestion and guidance. Staff officers can only advice. Their advice can be accepted or rejected by line managers. So staff authority refers to the responsibility and authority of providing advice and services to the line managers.

Functional Authority

Functional authority is similar to line authority, but it is exercised over a person who is not the immediate subordinate of a manager.

STAFFING

Staffing refers to the managerial function of employing and developing human resources for carrying out the various managerial and non-managerial activities in an organisation. This involves determining the manpower requirement, and the methods of recruiting, selecting, training and developing the people for various positions created in the organisation. This, in fact happens to be a continuous process because the organisation's need to retain and update its personnel is a never ending exercise.

It may be noted that staffing function is an integral part of human resource management and, in its wider sense, also includes the activities of determining the remuneration of workers, appraising their performance, and deciding on their promotion, transfers, etc.

Process of Staffing

The process of staffing starts with ascertaining the required number of various categories of employees for the organisation. This is known as manpower planning. It decides the kinds of staff and the number of staff required for the organisation. This is done through several methods like job analysis, workload analysis, etc. The next thing to be done in the staffing process is the recruitment exercise, i.e., finding out the available manpower from internal and external sources. The next step is to select the right person from the available manpower through tests and interviews and make appointments. This is followed by their placement on the jobs and necessary introduction of the work environment and the rules of compensation, promotion, transfer etc. Thus, the various steps involved in the process of staffing are as follows:

(a) Manpower Planning
(b) Job Analysis
(c) Recruitment
(d) Selection
(e) Placement
(f) Induction
(g) Training and Development
(h) Performance Appraisal
(i) Compensation
(j) Promotion and Transfer

DIRECTING

Directing is concerned with instructing, guiding, supervising and inspiring people in the organisation to achieve its objectives. It is the process of telling people what to do and seeing that they do it in the best possible manner. The directing function thus, involves:

- telling people what is to be done and explaining to them how to do it;
- issuing instructions and orders to subordinates to carryout their assignments as scheduled;
- supervising their activities;
- inspiring them to meet the manager's expectation and contribute towards the achievement of organisational objectives; and
- providing leadership.

Elements in Directing

Communication, Supervision, Motivation and Leadership are the four essential elements of directing. In the subsequent sections we shall discuss about the nature and significance of each of these components.

COMMUNICATION

Communication is a basic organisational function, which refers to the process by which a person (known as sender) transmits information or messages to another person (known as receiver). The purpose of communication in organisations is to convey orders, instructions, or information so as to bring desired changes in the performance and or the attitude of employees. In an organisation, supervisors transmit information to subordinates. Proper communication results in clarity and securing the cooperation of subordinates. Faulty communication may create problems due to misunderstanding between the superior and subordinates. The subordinates must correctly understand the message conveyed to them. Thus, in communication:

- there are two parties, one is known as the sender and the other is known as receiver;
- there is a message sent by the sender to the receiver; and
- the receiver receives the message and understands it.

Communication does not always flow from supervisor to subordinate. It can also be from a subordinate to a supervisor. For example, subordinates can pass information to the supervisor about the faults/problems at the assembly line. Thus, it is a two way process.

Elements of Communication Process: Communication, being a process must have some elements to complete the process. The elements of communication are given below:

1. Sender
2. Message
3. Encoding
4. Channel
5. Receiver
6. Decoding
7. Feedback

Types of Communication

Formal and Informal Communication

The path through which information flows is called channel of communication. The paths of communication which are based on relationship establish formally by management are the formal channels. For example, the General Manager communicates a decision to the production manager who may then issue orders or instructions to the foremen.

Communication, which takes place on the basis of informal or social relations among staff, is called informal communication. For example, any sharing of information between a production supervisor and an accountant, as they happen to be friends or so. Mostly informal channels are used due to friendly interaction of members of an organisation. In fact, it may be purely personal or related to organisational matters. The informal path of communication is also known as **Grapevine**.

Table : Differences Between Formal Communication and Informal Communication

Formal Communication	Informal Communication
1. It is based on formal organisational relationships.	It emerges out of social interactions among the people.
2. The channels of communication are prescribed.	Channels of communication depend on individuals' relationships.
3. It is rigid as deviations are not allowed.	It is quite flexible because nothing is prescribed.
4. The speed of message travel is slow because of formalisation.	Message travels faster.
5. Chances of message distortion are low.	Message are often distorted.
6. It is treated as authentic.	It is not authentic even if the message is correct.

Upward, Downward, Horizontal and Diagonal Communication

On the basis of the flow or direction of communication in organisations, it can be classified as upward, downward, horizontal or diagonal. When employees make any request, appeal, report, suggest or communicate ideas to the superior, the flow of communication is **upward** i.e., from bottom to top. For instance, when a typist drops a suggestion in the suggestion box, or a foreman reports breakdown of machinery to the factory manager, the flow of communication is upward. Upward communication encourages employees to participate actively in the operations of their department.

When communication is made from superiors down the hierarchy it is called a downward communication. For instance, when superiors issue orders and instructions to subordinates, it is known as downward communication. When the General Manager orders supervisors to work overtime, the flow of communication is downward i.e., from top to bottom. Similarly, communication of work assignments, notices, requests for performance, etc. through bulletin boards, memos, reports, speeches, meetings, etc, are all forms of downward communication.

Communication can also be amongst members at the same level in the organisation. For instance, production manager may communicate the production plan to the sales manager.

This is known as **horizontal flow of communication**. Here, the communication is among people of the same rank and status.

When communication is made between people who are neither in the same department nor at the same level of organisational hierarchy, it is called **diagonal communication**.

Barriers in Communication

The problem of communication arises because there are various obstacles which may entirely prevent a communication, filter part of it out, or give it incorrect meaning. These obstacles are known as communication barriers.

Semantic Barriers: Semantics is the science of meaning, as contrasted with phonetics, the science of sounds. All communications are symbolic, that is, these use symbols (words, pictures, action, etc.) that suggest certain meanings. Semantic barriers arise from limitations in the symbols with which we communicate. Following types of semantic barriers are more prominent:

1. Symbols with Different Meanings
2. Badly Expressed Message
3. Faulty Translations
4. Unclarified Assumptions
5. Specialist's Language

Emotional or Psychological Barriers

Emotional or psychological factors are the prime barriers in interpersonal communication. Some emotional barriers are as follows:

1. Premature Evaluation
2. Inattention
3. Loss by Transmission and Poor Retention
4. Undue Reliance on the Written Word
5. Distrust of communicator
6. Failure to communicate

Organisational Barriers

An organisation being a deliberate creation for the attainment of certain specified objectives; day-to-day happenings within it require being regulated in such a manner that they contribute to attain these objectives in the most efficient manner. Major organisational barriers may be as follows:

1. Organisational Policy
2. Organisational Rules and Regulations
3. Status Relationships
4. Complexity in Organisational Structure
5. Organisational Facilities

Personal Barriers

1. Attitudes of Superiors
2. Fear of Challenges to Authority
3. Insistence on Proper Channel
4. Lack of Confidence in Subordinates
5. Ignoring Communication
6. Lack of Time
7. Lack of Awareness

SUPERVISION

After the employees have been instructed regarding what they have to do and how to do, it is the duty of the manager to see that they perform the work as per instructions. This is known as **supervision**. Managers play the role of supervisors and ensure that the work is done as per the instructions and the plans. Supervisors clarify all instructions and guide employees to work as a team in co-operation with others.

MOTIVATION

Motivation is one of the important elements of directing. Issuance of proper instructions or orders does not necessarily ensure that they will be properly carried out. It requires manager to inspire or induce the employees to act and get the expected result. This is called motivation. It is a force that inspires a person at work to intensify his willingness to use the best of his capability for achievement of specific objectives. It may be in the form of incentives like financial (such as bonus, commission etc.) or, non-financial (such as appreciation, growth etc.), or it could be positive or negative. Basically, motivation is directed towards goals and prompt people to act.

The following are the features of motivation:

- Motivation is an act of managers
- Motivation is a continuous process
- Motivation can be positive or negative
- Motivation is goal oriented
- Motivation is complex in nature
- Motivation is an art
- Motivation is system-oriented
- Motivation is different from job satisfaction

Motivational Factors

There are several factors that motivate a person to work. The motivational factors can be broadly divided into two groups:

I. Monetary Factors:

- Salaries or wages
- Bonus
- Incentives

II. Non-Monetary Factors:

- Status or job title
- Appreciation and recognition
- Delegation of authority
- Working conditions
- Job security
- Job enrichment
- Workers participation

Need and Importance of Motivation

Motivation offers several importance to the organization and to the employees:

- Higher efficiency
- Reduce absenteeism
- Reduces employee turn over
- Improves a corporate image
- Good relations
- Improved morale
- Reduced wastages and breakages
- Reduced accidents
- Facilitates initiative and innovation

Motivational Theories

Maslow's-Hierarchy of Needs Theory:

This theory was proposed by Abraham Maslow and is based on the assumption that people are motivated by a series of five universal needs. These needs are ranked, according to the order in which they influence human behaviour, in hierarchical fashion.

- **Physiological needs** are deemed to be the lowest-level needs. These needs include the needs such as food and water.
- **Safety needs** — the needs for shelter and security — become the motivators of human behavior.
- **Social needs** include the need for belongingness and love.
- After social needs have been satisfied, **ego and esteem needs** become the motivating needs.
- The highest need in Maslow's hierarchy is that of **self-actualization**; the need for self-realization, continuous self-development, and the process of becoming all that a person is capable of becoming.

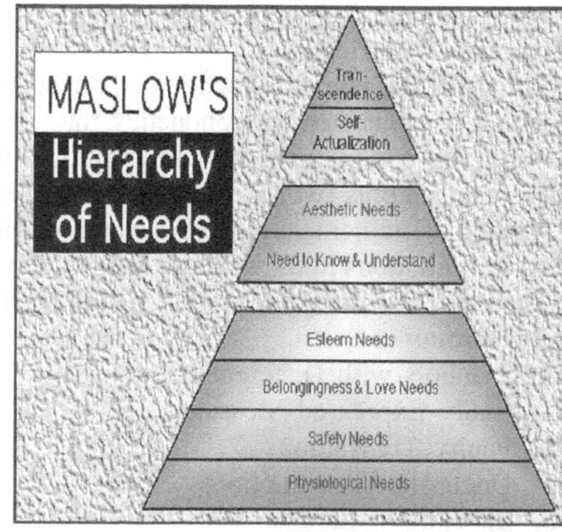

Alderfer's Hierarchy of Motivational Needs

Clayton Alderfer reworked Maslow's Need Hierarchy to align it more closely with empirical research. Alderfer's theory is called the **ERG theory** — **E**xistence, **R**elatedness, and **G**rowth.

1. Existence refers to our concern with basic material existence requirements; what Maslow called physiological and safety needs.
2. Relatedness refers to the desire we have for maintaining interpersonal relationships; similar to Maslow's social/love need, and the external component of his esteem need.
3. Growth refers to an intrinsic desire for personal development; the intrinsic component of Maslow's esteem need, and self-actualization

Alderfer's ERG theory differs from Maslow's Need Hierarchy insofar as ERG theory demonstrates that more than one need may be operative at the same time. ERG theory does not assume a rigid hierarchy where a lower need must be substantially satisfied before one can move on.

Alderfer also deals with frustration-regression. That is, if a higher-order need is frustrated, an individual then seeks to increase the satisfaction of a lower-order need.

In summary, ERG theory argues, like Maslow, that satisfied lower-order needs lead to the desire to satisfy higher-order needs; but multiple needs can be operating as motivators at the same time, and frustration in attempting to satisfy a higher-level need can result in regression to a lower-level need.

Two-factor Theory

Herzberg's Two Factor Theory, also known as the **Motivation-Hygiene Theory**, was derived from a study designed to test the concept that people have two sets of needs:

1. their needs as animals to avoid pain
2. their needs as humans to grow psychologically

Herzberg's study consisted of a series of interviews that sought to elicit responses to the questions:

(1) Recall a time when you felt exceptionally good about your job. Why did you feel that way about the job? Did this feeling affect your job performance in any way? Did this feeling have an impact on your personal relationships or your well-being?

(2) Recall a time on the job that resulted in negative feelings? Describe the sequence of events that resulted in these negative feelings.

Research Results: it appeared from the research, that the things making people happy on the job and those making them unhappy had two separate themes.

1. Satisfaction (Motivation): Five factors stood out as strong determiners of job satisfaction:

- achievement
- recognition
- work itself
- responsibility
- advancement

2. Dissatisfaction (Hygiene): The determinants of job dissatisfaction were found to be:

- company policy
- administrative policies
- supervision
- salary
- interpersonal relations
- working conditions

According to Herzberg, the factors leading to job satisfaction are separate and distinct form those that lead to job dissatisfaction. Therefore, managers who seek to eliminate factors that can create job dissatisfaction may bring about peace but not necessarily motivation. They will be placating their workforce rather than motivating them. As a result, conditions surrounding the job such as quality of supervision, pay, company policies, physical working conditions relations with others and job security were characterized by Herzberg as hygiene factors, when they're adequate, people will not be dissatisfied; neither will they be satisfied. If we want to motivate people on their jobs, Herzberg suggested emphasizing factors associated with the work itself or to outcomes directly derived form it, such as promotional opportunities, opportunities for personal growth, recognition, responsibility and achievement. These are the characteristics that people find intrinsically rewarding.

Expectancy Theory

In recent years, probably the most popular motivational theory has been the Expectancy Theory (also known as the Valence-Instrumentality-Expectancy Theory). Although there are a number of theories found with this general title, they all have their roots in Victor Vroom's 1964 work on motivation. The key elements to this theory are referred to as Expectancy (E), Instrumentality (I), and Valence (V).

Vroom suggests that an employee's beliefs about Expectancy, Instrumentality, and Valence interact psychologically to create a motivational force such that the employee acts in ways that bring pleasure and avoid pain.

McClelland's Theory of Needs

According to David McClelland, regardless of culture or gender, people are driven by three motives:

- achievement,
- affiliation and
- influence.

Since McClelland's first experiments, over 1,000 studies relevant to achievement motivation have been conducted. These studies strongly support the theory.

Achievement: The need for achievement is characterized by the wish to take responsibility for finding solutions to problems, master complex tasks, set goals, get feedback on level of success.

Affiliation: The need for affiliation is characterized by a desire to belong, an enjoyment of teamwork, a concern about interpersonal relationships, and a need to reduce uncertainty.

Power: The need for power is characterized by a drive to control and influence others, a need to win arguments, a need to persuade and prevail According to McClelland, the presence of these motives or drives in an individual indicates a predisposition to behave in certain ways. Therefore, from a manager's perspective, recognizing which need is dominant in any particular individual affects the way in which that person can be motivated.

Theory of "X" and Theory of "Y"

Douglas McGregor observed two diametrically opposing view points of managers about their employees, one is negative called "Theory of X" and one is positive called "Theory of Y"

(a) Theory of X: Following are the assumptions of managers who believe in the "Theory of X" in regard to their employees:

- Employees dislike work; if possible avoid the same
- Employees must be coerced, controlled or threatened to do the work
- Employees avoid responsibilities and seek formal direction
- Most employees consider security of job, most important of all other factors in the job and have very little ambition

(b) Theory of Y: Following are the assumptions of managers who believe in the "Theory of Y" in regard to their employees.

- Employees love work as play or rest
- Employees are self-directed and self-controlled and committed to the organizational objectives
- Employees accept and seek responsibilities
- Innovative spirit is not confined to managers alone, some employees also possess it.

LEADERSHIP

Leadership is the process, which influences the people and inspires them to willingly accomplish the organisational objectives. The main purpose of managerial leadership is to get willing cooperation of the workgroup in pursuit of the goals.

Importance of Leadership

The objectives of any organisation can only be fulfilled if its employees are working towards accomplishment of such objectives. To make people work in the desired manner, proper instructions and guidance are necessary. And this direction process becomes effective when the persons who give such direction have leadership qualities. Leadership is essential in functioning of any organisation and its importance and benefits are varied. Some of these importances are:

- leadership improves the performance of the employees. Leaders can motivate the followers to work and thereby increase their performance level.
- with continuous support and guidance, leaders are able to build confidence among the followers, thereby increasing speed and accuracy and decreasing wastage.
- with friendly and cooperative efforts the leader is able to build employees' morale which in turn contribute to higher productivity.

Leadership Qualities

In order to be successful, a leader must possess certain qualities. A good leader should be professionally competent, intelligent, analytical and he/she should have a sense of fair play, including honesty, sincerity, integrity, and sense of responsibility. He must possess initiative, perseverance, be diligent and realistic in his outlook. He must also be able to communicate his subordinates effectively. Human relation skills are a must for any leader.

Earlier, it was believed that the success or effectiveness of a leader depends upon his personal traits or characteristics, like physical appearance, intelligence, self-confidence, alertness, and initiative. This is no longer regarded as a correct approach. It has been established on the basis of experiments that the success or effectiveness of a person as a leader depends upon his behaviour pattern or leadership style in relation to the followers.

George R. Terry (Principles of Management) gives the following characteristics to a good leader:

- Energy
- Emotional stability
- Knowledge of human relations
- Empathy
- Objectivity
- Personal motivation
- Communication skill
- Teaching ability
- Social skill
- Technical competence

Viscount Slim gives the following six characteristics of leadership, which he considers common in a civil or military environment:

- Courage
- Will power
- Judgment
- Flexibility
- Knowledge
- Integrity

According to **Chester Barnard**, the qualities of a good leader are:

- Vitality and endurance
- Decisiveness
- Persuasiveness
- Stability in behaviour
- Intellectual ability
- Knowledge

Historical Evolution of Leadership

1776 - Adam Smith - A Wealth of Nations

- exchange will not occur voluntarily unless both people benefit.
- "I will follow you as long as I get some benefit in return."

1807 - Hegel - first book on leadership

- focused primarily on leadership as it related to the political process.

1847 - Thomas Carlyle - "Great Man Theory"

- the capacity for leadership is inherent – that great leaders are born, not made.
- only those men who are blessed with heroic qualities could ever emerge as leaders.
- portrays great leaders as heroic, mythic, and destined to rise to leadership when needed.

1910-1920 - first research on leadership conducted

- gave rise to **trait theories** - natural born leaders possess certain physical traits and personality characteristics which differentiate them from non-leaders.
- Similar in some ways to "Great Man" theory.
- People inherit certain qualities and traits that make them better suited to leadership.
- Trait theories often identify particular personality or behavioral characteristics shared by leaders.

1947-Jenkins - review of traits of military leaders

- concluded that traits were important but that the situation determined which traits were important and that expertise in the business at hand separated leaders from followers.

1948-Stogdil - review of traits of non-military leaders

- found that most important trait to possess was the trait most closely related to the task at hand.
- Max Weber - **charismatic leadership**
- descendant of thought from Hegel
- leaders emerge in a time of crisis due to their inherent charisma.

Situational Theory

Stogdil - proposed that leadership is a matter of situational demands emergence of a leader is a result of time, place, and circumstance

Behavioural Theories

The behavioural theorists identified determinants of leadership so that people could be trained to be leaders. They developed training programs to change managers' leadership behaviours and assumed that the best styles of leadership could be learned.

Path-Goal Theory – Robert House

- the successful leader shows followers the rewards available by meeting a goal and illustrates the path (behaviours) by which rewards may be obtained.

Contingency Theory – Fiedler

- dominated much of research in 1970's.
- suggested that there are two types of leaders-those who focus on tasks and those who focus on relationships.
- situation will determine which type of leader will be most effective.

Behavioural Theories

The behavioural theorists identified determinants of leadership so that people could be trained to be leaders. They developed training programs to change managers' leadership behaviours and assumed that the best styles of leadership could be learned.

Path-Goal Theory – Robert House

- the successful leader shows followers the rewards available by meeting a goal and illustrates the path (behaviors) by which rewards may be obtained.

Contingency Theory – Fiedler

- dominated much of research in 1970's.
- suggested that there are two types of leaders-those who focus on tasks and those who focus on relationships.
- situation will determine which type of leader will be most effective.

Leader-Participation Model - Vroom, Yetton & Jago

- provides a set of sequential rules to determine the extent to which followers participate in the decision making process in different situations.

Process Theories

(a) Transformational Leadership—James MacGregor Burns

- leader asks followers to put aside personal interests for the good of the group
- leaders focuses on followers' needs and input in order to transform everyone into a leader by empowering and motivating them.

(b) Relational Model of Leadership—Komives, Lucas & McMahon

- leadership is a relational process designed to accomplish a common goal to benefit all.
- leader must be inclusive, empowering, purposeful, ethical, and process-oriented to bind group together and achieve goal.

(c) Servant Leadership Theory—Robert Greenleaf

- successful leaders influence others as a result of dedicating their lives to serving others-individuals, groups, and organizations.

(d) Social Change Model of Leadership

- leadership is a process by which individuals and groups work toward the common goal of improving the quality of life for all by developing and promoting seven basic values.

Transactional Leadership

The transactional leader works through creating clear structures whereby it is clear what is required of their subordinates, and the rewards that they get for following orders. Punishments are not always mentioned, but they are also well-understood and formal systems of discipline are usually in place.

The early stage of Transactional Leadership is in negotiating the contract whereby the subordinate is given a salary and other benefits, and the company (and by implication the subordinate's manager) gets authority over the subordinate.

When the Transactional Leader allocates work to a subordinate, they are considered to be fully responsible for it, whether or not they have the resources or capability to carry it out. When things go wrong, then the subordinate is considered to be personally at fault, and is punished for their failure (just as they are rewarded for succeeding).

The transactional leader often uses management by exception, working on the principle that if something is operating to defined (and hence expected) performance then it does not need attention. Exceptions to expectation require praise and reward for exceeding expectation, whilst some kind of corrective action is applied for performance below expectation.

Whereas Transformational Leadership has more of a 'selling' style, Transactional Leadership, once the contract is in place, takes a 'telling' style.

The Managerial Grid

The dimensions identified at the University of Michigan provided the basis for the development of the managerial grid model developed by Robert Blake and Jane Mouton.

It identifies five various leadership styles that represent different combinations of concern for people and concern for production. Managers who scored high on both these dimensions simultaneously (labeled team management) performed the best. The five leadership styles of the managerial grid include impoverished, country club, produce or perish, middle-of-the road, and team.

CO-ORDINATION AND CONTROLLING

Co-ordination

In every organisation, different types of work are performed by various groups and no single group can be expected to achieve the goals of the organisation as a whole. Hence, it becomes essential that the activities of different work groups and departments should be harmonised. This function of management is known as 'co-ordination'. It ensures unity of action among individuals, work groups and departments, and brings harmony in carrying out the different activities and functions so as to achieve the organisational goals efficiently. Coordination is the orderly arrangement of individual and group efforts to provide unity of action in the pursuit of a common goal. In other words, coordination involves synchronisation of different activities and efforts of the various units of an organisation so that the planned objectives may be achieved with minimum conflict.

Controlling

Managerial planning results in the framing of objectives and laying down of targets. To achieve the objectives, a proper organisational structure is designed; people are assigned the various tasks; and are directed to perform their respective jobs. The actual performance is then assessed from time to time to ensure that what is achieved is in conformity with the plans and targets. This exactly is the controlling function. Thus, controlling as a function of management refers to the evaluation of actual performance of work against planned or standard performance and taking the corrective action, if necessary.

According to Henri Fayol, "Control consists in verifying whether everything occurs in conformity with the plan adopted, the instructions issued and principles established."

Planning and controlling are closely related and depend upon each other. Controlling depends upon planning because planning provides the targets or standards against which actual performance can be compared. Controlling, on the other hand, appraises planning.

It brings out the shortcomings of planning and helps to improve upon the plans.

Thus, controlling involves

(i) knowing the nature, quantum and time frame of the work;
(ii) comparing the performance with the plan;
(iii) analysing deviation, if any;
(iv) taking corrective steps; and
(v) suggesting revision of plans, if necessary.

Characteristics of Control

The following are the basic characteristics of control:

1. Planning is the basis of control
2. Control is a continuous process
3. Control is all pervasive
4. Action is the essence of control
5. Control is forward looking

Multiple Choice Questions

1. Which one of the following defines co-ordination?

(*a*) Actuating force which inspires a person to put his best for the fulfilment of a task
(*b*) Orderly arranged of group effort to provide unity of action in the pursuit of a common purpose.
(*c*) Process of transmitting information from one person to another or from one unit to another.
(*d*) Process of determining what is to be accomplished and what has been accomplished and if necessary applying corrective measures.

2. Consider the following basic steps involved in the process of control:

I. Identifying the strategic control points
II. Establish the standards
III. Measuring performance against standards.
IV. Correcting deviations from the standards.

The correct sequence of the above steps in the process of control is

(*a*) I, IV, III, II
(*b*) IV, III, II, I
(*c*) II, I, IV, III
(*d*) II, III, I, IV

3. Match List-I with List-II and select the correct answer using the codes given below the lists:

List-I *(Management thinkers)*	**List-II** *(Contribution/work)*
I. Elton Mayo	A. Importance of integrating the company's and employee's goal
II. Frederic W. Taylor	B. Social problems of Industrial Civilisation
III. Henri Fayol	C. General and Industrial management.
IV. Many Parker Follet	D. Principles of Scientific Management

Codes:

(*a*) I-A, II-D, III-C, IV-B
(*b*) I-D, II-C, III-B, IV-A
(*c*) I-B, II-D, III-C, IV-A
(*d*) I-C, II-D, III-A, IV-B

4. An organisation structure is effective if it enables individuals to contribute to the objectives of the enterprise. This is known as

(*a*) Scalar Principle
(*b*) Principle of functional definition
(*c*) Principle of unity of objectives
(*d*) None of these

5. Which one of the following orders indicates the correct logical order of managerial functions?
(*a*) Organising, planning, directing, staffing, coordination and control
(*b*) Planning, organising, staffing, directing, coordination and control
(*c*) Planning, directing, organising, staffing, control and coordination
(*d*) Organising, planning, staffing, directing, control and coordination

6. Effective direction does NOT depend on the
(*a*) Communication process
(*b*) Forces at the subordinate level
(*c*) Ability of the manager
(*d*) Deployment of human resources

7. Planning refers to
(*a*) Looking backward
(*b*) Looking forward
(*c*) Looking forward and backward
(*d*) Looking and actual performance to decide action to be taken

8. Leadership is a function of all the following factors except
(*a*) Workgroup (*b*) Product or service
(*c*) Leader (*d*) Situation

9. The main difference between delegation and decentralisation is that
(*a*) delegation refers primarily to transfer of authority from one individual to another while decentralisation refers to systematic delegation of authority to all units in an organisation.
(*b*) delegation of authority can take place without decentralisation where as there cannot be decentralisation without delegation of authority.
(*c*) delegation represents sharing of excessive burden of key managerial personnel while decentralisation refers to division of top managerial operations.
(*d*) delegation may take place due to administrative, technical and routine reasons while decentralisation involves deliberate action for the smooth functioning of the organisation.

10. Management by exception introduces
(*a*) selective, responsibility oriented reporting
(*b*) reporting of significant variances
(*c*) requirement of full reports on performance
(*d*) computation of actuals in different spheres of performance

11. Consider the following office equipments used in various offices:
I. Fax II. Typewriter
III. Dictaphone IV. Letter opener
The correct order in which they are used is
(*a*) I, II, III, IV (*b*) IV, III, II, I
(*c*) II, IV, III, I (*d*) III, II, IV, I

12. Control refers to
I. Establishment of standards
II. Measurement of actual performance against the set standards
III. Correction for deviation from standards
Of these statements:
(*a*) I alone is correct
(*b*) III alone is correct
(*c*) I and II are correct
(*b*) I, II, and III are correct

13. Which one of the following is not related to the trait theory of leadership?
(*a*) Physical factors such as height
(*b*) Intelligence and extroversion
(*c*) Self confidence and ambition
(*d*) Training and experience of employees

14. Match List-I with List-II and select the correct answer from the codes given below the lists:

List-I	**List-II**
I. Planning	A. Training
II. Staffing	B. Forecasting
III. Directing	C. Evaluating
IV. Controlling	D. Motivating
	E. Grouping

Codes :
(*a*) I-C, II-A, III-D, IV-E
(*b*) I-C, II-E, III-A, IV-B
(*c*) I-B, II-A, III-D, IV-C
(*d*) I-B, II-E, III-A, IV-C

15. Decentralisation of an organisation is commended on account of which of the following advantages?

I. Reduced burden on top executives
II. Executive development
III. Improvement of morale
IV. Solves problems of coordination

Select the correct answer from the codes given below and mark your answer sheet accordingly

Codes:

(*a*) II and III (*b*) I, II and IV
(*c*) I, II and III (*d*) III and IV

16. In a functional organisation
(*a*) There are no advisors, the executives alone having the authority and competence
(*b*) There are specialist advisors having no authority
(*c*) The entire organisation is divided into functions with specific role for specialists
(*d*) the organisation is divided into functions with specialists having authority

17. The process of grouping activities into units for the purpose of administration may be referred to as
(*a*) Departmentalisation
(*b*) Decentralisation
(*c*) Co-ordination
(*d*) Specialisation

18. Span of control means that
(*a*) an organisation consists of various departments
(*b*) each person's authority is clearly defined
(*c*) every subordinate has one superior
(*d*) a manager can supervise only a limited number of subordinates

19. If a general manager asks the sales manager to recruit some sales men on his behalf, it is an instance of
(*a*) division of authority
(*b*) decentralisation of authority.
(*c*) delegation of authority
(*d*) delegation of responsibility

20. Which one of the following principles states that recurring decisions should be handled in a routine manner by lower level managers whereas problems involving unusal matters only should be referred to higher levels?
(*a*) Principle of unity of command
(*b*) Scalar principle
(*c*) Principle of exception
(*d*) Principle of commitment

21. MBO is a technique which requires that the objectives of the enterprise
(*a*) be written and defined in board terms
(*b*) lay down the time period for achieving the results
(*c*) include a plan of action for achieving the desired results
(*d*) be defined in terms of measurable results

22. In the field of management some of the important techniques, relate to budgeting, cost accounting, planning and control are through
(*a*) Operational research
(*b*) PERT & CPM
(*c*) Budgetary control
(*d*) Financial Administration

23. Which of the following management functions are closely related?
(*a*) Planning and organising
(*b*) Staffing and control
(*c*) Planning and control
(*d*) Planning and staffing

24. "Human Relating Approach" to management was origined by
(*a*) Henery Fayol (*b*) Winslow Taylor
(*c*) Elton Mayo (*d*) Peter F. Drucker

25. The famous book "The Philosophy of Management" was written by
(*a*) Henery Fayol (*b*) Oliver Sheldon
(*c*) F. W. Taylor (*d*) Urwick

26. Policy making is an important part of the process of
(*a*) Planning (*b*) Co-ordinating
(*c*) Organising (*d*) Motivating

27. A firm has these characteristics : It is involved in the manufacture of custom built machinery, its products have shorter life span, the products are processed through different specialists and the products have a rigid time schedule to be met. In such a circumstance, which one of the following would be the form of organisation best suited to achieve the objectives?
(*a*) Functional organisation

(*b*) Line and staff organisation
(*c*) Project (Matrix) organisation
(*d*) Line organisation.

28. The managerial function of organising is
(*a*) To review and adjust plan in the light of changing conditions
(*b*) To establish a programme for the accomplishment of objections
(*c*) To create a structure of functions and duties to be performed by a group of people
(*d*) to get things done through and with the help of people

29. Span of management means
(*a*) A good organisation should consist of departments
(*b*) Authority of each person must be clearly defined
(*c*) Each subordinate should have one superior
(*d*) A manager can supervise a limited number of executives

30. Which of the following is the oldest type of organisation?
(*a*) Functional organisation
(*b*) Line organisation
(*c*) Line and staff organisation
(*d*) Committee organisation

31. 'Unity of command' principle of effective direction means
(*a*) Subordinates should be responsible to one superior
(*b*) Boosting the morale of the subordinates
(*c*) decreasing the productivity of subordinates
(*d*) All of these

32. In line organisation
(*a*) the organisation is divided according to the skill required to perform a work
(*b*) the organisation is divided according to the type of work involve
(*c*) the authority flows from the man at the top to the lowest man vertically
(*d*) each worker serves a number of supervisors

33. The function of 'staff' in 'line and staff' organisation is to
(*a*) take advice from the line
(*b*) advice the line
(*c*) hold authority and responsibility
(*d*) fix responsibility for performance of tasks in a definite manner upon certain individuals

34. Control function of management implies
(*a*) to bring harmony in various activities
(*b*) to keep the work force content
(*c*) taking corrective course of action
(*d*) to provide sufficient finance

35. The main advantage of line and staff organisation is
(*a*) Simplicity
(*b*) Specialisation
(*c*) Availability of expert advice
(*d*) Speedy decision making

36. The terms speed boss, route clerk etc. are used in relation to
(*a*) Line organisation
(*b*) Line and staff organisation
(*c*) Functional organisation
(*d*) None of these

37. General manager has delegated authority to production manager for achieving budgeted production. Who is responsible for low production to Board of Directors?
(*a*) Production Supervisors
(*b*) Production Manager
(*c*) General Manager
(*d*) None of these

38. Delegation can be
(*a*) upward (*b*) downward
(*c*) side ward (*d*) all of these

39. Unity of command is violated under
(*a*) Line organisation
(*b*) Line and staff organisation
(*c*) Functional organisation
(*d*) None of these

40. 'Theory Y' states that
(*a*) Workers prefer to be directed
(*b*) Workers exercise self-direction and self control
(*c*) Workers have inherent disliking for work and will avoid it if they can
(*d*) None of these

41. 'Theory X' and 'Theory Y' is given by
(*a*) Maslow (*b*) Herzberg
(*c*) Mc Gregor (*d*) Norman

42. The Need – Hierarchy Theory of Motivation is given by
(*a*) Maslow (*b*) Herzberg
(*c*) Vroom (*d*) Mc Gregor

43. Under the Need – Hierarchy Theory, When UDC designation is changed into 'Assistant', it is an example of
(*a*) Social needs
(*b*) Esteem needs
(*c*) Self – actualisation needs
(*d*) All of these

44. Maslow's Need – Hierarchy Theory of Motivation has classified the human needs into five categories as follows :
I. Safety needs
II. Esteem needs
III. Social needs
IV. Physiological needs
V. Self – actualisation needs

What is the sequence of domination of these needs?
(*a*) I, IV, III, II, V (*b*) IV, I, III, II, V
(*c*) V, III, II, IV, I (*d*) IV, I, III, II, V

45. Under Expectancy Theory of Motivation, increase in motivation results when
(*a*) Valence increases
(*b*) Valence decreases
(*c*) No effect on valence
(*d*) None of these

46. Which one of the following is a motivating factor as per Herzberg's Theory?
(*a*) Salary and allowances
(*b*) Job design
(*c*) Working conditions
(*d*) None of these

47. Which of the following functions of management are more closely related?
I. Planning
II. Co-ordination
III. Motivation
IV. Control
(*a*) I and II (*b*) II and III
(*c*) II, III, and IV (*d*) I, II, and IV

48. Staffing includes
I. Training
II. Appraisal
III. Placement
IV. Directing
(*a*) I and III (*b*) I, II and III
(*c*) II and III (*d*) I, II, III and IV

49. Match the following:

List-I	List-II
I. Need-Hierarchy Theory of Motivation	A. Taylor
II. M.B.O.	B. Maslow
III. Scientific Management	C. Herzberg
IV. Hygience Theory	D. Peter F. Drucker

Codes:
(*a*) I-B, II-A, III-D, IV-C
(*b*) I-C, II-B, III-D, IV-A
(*c*) I-A, II-B, III-C, IV-D
(*d*) I-B, II-D, III-A, IV-C

50. Decentralisation
(*a*) increases the importance of superiors
(*b*) decreases the importance of superiors
(*c*) increases the importance of subordinates
(*d*) decreases the importance of subordinates

51. When management pays attention to more important areas and when day today routine problems are looked after by lower level of management, this is known as:
(*a*) MBO
(*b*) Management by exception
(*c*) Unity of command
(*d*) Critical path method

52. A leader uses the following methods.
I. Uses criticism
II. Encourages growth
III. Sets objectives
IV. Gives orders and directions

Which of these methods are used by a democratic leader
(*a*) I and II (*b*) III and IV
(*c*) II and III (*d*) I, II and IV

53. Span of control is narrow when the
(*a*) posts in the top management increases
(*b*) posts in the middle management increases
(*c*) posts in lower management increases
(*d*) all of these

54. The delegation of authority results in
I. Decentralisation of branches at places.
II. Avoiding responsibility by top management.
III. Delegation of authority by top management without avoiding responsibility

Codes:
(*a*) I and III (*b*) I, II and III
(*c*) III only (*d*) I and II

55. In Taylor's functional organisation there are eight foremen
I. Time and cost clerk
II. Route clerk
III. Speed boss
IV. Gang boss
V. Shop disciplinarian
VI. Instruction card clerk
VII. Repair boss
VIII. Inspector

Which of these foremen operate at the shop level?
(*a*) I, II, III and IV
(*b*) V, VI, VII, and VIII
(*c*) III, IV, VII and VIII
(*d*) IV, V, VI and VII

56. Match the following

List-I	**List-II**
I. Staff executives	A. Advisory function
II. Directing	B. Manpower development
III. Line executives	C. Guiding function
IV. Staffing	D. Management authority

Codes:
(*a*) I-A, II-D, III-C, IV-B
(*b*) I-A, II-C, III-C, IV-B
(*c*) I-B, II-C, III-D, IV-A
(*d*) I-B, II-A, III-C, IV-D

57. "Grapevine" is a term used in relation to
(*a*) formal communication
(*b*) informal communication
(*c*) both formal and informal communications
(*d*) this term is not used in relation to communication

58. Which of the following pairs are correctly matched?

List-I	**List-II**
I. Henri Fayol	Administration Industrial Generate
II. F.W. Taylor	The functions of the Executive
III. Douglas Mc Gregor	The Human side of Enterprise
IV. Peter Drucker	Management: Tasks, Responsibilities and Practices

Select the correct answer using the codes given below:
Codes:
(*a*) I, II, III and IV (*b*) III and IV
(*c*) II and IV (*d*) I and III

59. According to the Peter Principle, managers tend to
(*a*) Work late as they go higher up the hierarchy
(*b*) Work even beyond their retirement age
(*c*) Get promoted to the level of their incompetence
(*d*) Lose their competence with successive promotions

60. Which of the following constitute manpower planning?
I. Determining human resource requirements both quantitatively and qualitatively.
II. Finding the sources of talented individuals.
III. Planning for the human resource needs of an organisation.
IV. Reaching out to the right source for procuring the right people.

Select the correct answer using the codes given below:
Codes:
(*a*) I, II and IV (*b*) II and III
(*c*) I and III (*d*) I, II, III and IV

61. Which one of the following may not necessarily be an advantage of co-ordination?
(*a*) Effective supervision
(*b*) Unity of direction
(*c*) Creative force
(*d*) Summarisation of all management functions

62. Understanding control does not signify under standing
(*a*) How one controls
(*b*) What is meant by control
(*c*) Who controls
(*d*) What is controlled

63. Consider the following statements :
Strategic management process comprises
I. Goal setting, strategy formulation, administration and strategic control.
II. Setting courses of action attaining objective, process of seeking key areas and strategy formulation.
III. Integrating the organisation with culture.
IV. Strategic planning and acting on these plans.
Of these statements :
(*a*) I, II and III are correct
(*b*) II, III and IV are correct
(*c*) I, II and IV are correct
(*d*) I, III and IV are correct

64. Match List-I with List-II and select the correct answer using the codes given below the Lists:

List-I	List-II
I. Line authority	A. Some People in an organisation are vested with primary sources of authority
II. Staff authority	B. Some people in an organisation have legitimate right to expert influence on others.
III. Functional authority	C. Some people in an organisation lack independent.
IV. Formal authority	D. Some people have right to control activities of other departments as they relate to specific staff.

Codes :
(*a*) I-A, II-B, III-C, IV-D
(*b*) I-B, II-D, III-C, IV-A
(*c*) I-A, II-C, III-D, IV-B
(*d*) I-B, II-C, III-D, IV-A

65. Which is the most fundamental function of Management
(*a*) Planning (*b*) Organising
(*c*) Staffing (*d*) Controlling

66. Match List-I with List-II and select the correct answer using the codes given below the lists:

List-I	List-II
I. Span of control	A. The superior helps, through continuous guidance, the subordinate to reach his goals.
II. M.B.O.	B. Numerical limit of subordinates to be supervised by an executive
III. M.B.E.	C. Subordinate remains accountable to his superior and the superior has the authority to demand accountability from his subordinate
IV. Delegation of authority	D. The management will concern itself and confine its activities to those areas and operations where the actual performance is short of the target

Codes:
(*a*) I-A, II-B, III-C, IV-D
(*b*) I-A, II-B, III-D, IV-C
(*c*) I-B, II-A, III-C, IV-D
(*d*) I-B, II-A, III-D, IV-C

67. Consider the following statements:
I. MBO is a control technique in which managers devote time only on the areas of deviation.
II. MBO integrates the individual with the organisation and the organisation with the environment.
III. In MBO the control over people is Shifted to control over operations
IV. The MBO Principle must be accompanied in practice by the principle of critical – point control
Of these statements:
(*a*) I and II are correct
(*b*) II and III are correct
(*c*) III and IV are correct
(*d*) I and IV are correct

68. Which one of the following statements is correct?
(*a*) Planning and controlling are essentially one and the same.
(*b*) Controlling is a part of the planning process.
(*c*) Controlling is a substitute for planning.
(*d*) A control process is meaningless without pre-set goals.

69. When jobs are broadened in scope and complexity so that the person's over all area of job responsibility increases, it is a case of
(*a*) Job rotation (*b*) Job enrichment
(*c*) Job specification (*d*) Job enlargement

70. Consider the following statements :
Planning involves
I. forecasting
II. choice among alternative courses of action
III. wishful thinking
IV. decision only by production manager
Of these statements
(*a*) I, II, III and IV are correct
(*b*) I, III and IV are correct
(*c*) I and II are correct
(*d*) II and III are correct

71. Techniques of managerial control are useful in
(*a*) Selection of plant location
(*b*) Identifying appropriate technology.
(*c*) Profit planning
(*d*) Conducting share holder's meetings.

72. Motivational process and not the motivators as such is associated with the
(*a*) Need hierarchy theory
(*b*) Two – factor theory
(*c*) ERG theory
(*d*) Expectancy theory

73. "Perceived equity in reward results in satisfaction". Which one of the following motivation theories take this into account?
(*a*) Porter and Lowler model
(*b*) Victor Vroom's Expectancy model.
(*c*) F.W. Taylor's incentive scheme
(*d*) Herzberg's Two-factor theory.

74. One of the steps that may be required for achieving effective coordination is
(*a*) reporting on performance and taking remedial measures
(*b*) training in leadership and supervisory abilities of controllers of activity.
(*c*) transmission of messages in a full line communication channel.
(*d*) making an honest appraisal and initiating rewards/ punishments.

75. An important aspect of control is that the
(*a*) manager motivates his subordinates to give better performance
(*b*) manager sets as effective management in formation system
(*c*) plans are checked before implementation against predetermined measures of performance
(*d*) performance is checked against predetermined standards

76. Delegation of authority takes place when a manager thinks that
(*a*) the job is too difficult and hazardous
(*b*) the job requires the high skill that he does not possess

(*c*) he cannot look after all the demanding tasks by him self
(*d*) He needs to punish his subordinate

77. According to the principle of "Span of control", there is
(*a*) A tendency to overload supervisors with too much of work
(*b*) A limit to the number of subordinates a supervisor can effectively supervise
(*c*) No limit to the number of subordinates a supervisor can supervise
(*d*) A limit to delegation of authority to the subordinate

78. Establishment of management by objectives pre-supposes
(*a*) That limits of authority are not defined
(*b*) That the employees are provided with result expected
(*c*) Unlimited freedom to operate in the assigned task
(*d*) Unlimited freedom to set goals

79. Each subordinate should have only one superior whose command he has to obey. This is known as
(*a*) Scalar principle
(*b*) Exception principle
(*c*) Unity of command principle
(*d*) Authority responsibility principle

80. Which one of the following is the oldest form of organisation?
(*a*) Functional organisation
(*b*) Line organisation
(*c*) Line and staff organisation
(*d*) Departmentation

81. Which of the following pairs are correctly matched?

List-I	**List-II**
I. Planning	Sets out the objectives and complete set of policies
II. Organisation	Enables the owner or top executive of a business to arrange, money, materials and methods.
III. Co–ordination	Orderly arrangement of group effort to provide unity of action.
IV. Control	Verifying whether everything occurs in conformity with the plan adopted, the instructions issued and principles established.

Select the correct answer using the codes given below:
Codes:
(*a*) II, III and IV (*b*) II and IV
(*c*) I, III and IV (*d*) I, II and III

82. A written statement of the main duties and responsibilities which a particular job entails is called?
(*a*) Job analysis (*b*) Job specification
(*c*) Job description (*d*) Job evaluation

83. Selection process in any organisation is usually proceeded by the preparation of
(*a*) human resources audit
(*b*) operations audit
(*c*) human resources inventory
(*d*) human resources accounting

84. Which one of the following monitors critical inputs and suggests preventive measures in the form of corrective action to correct inputs and processes?
(*a*) Feed back control
(*b*) Feed forward control
(*c*) Budgetory control
(*d*) Operational control

85. If the span of control is narrow, a number of managers would be required in each unit of the organisation and there would be many managerial levels or layers. Such an organisational structure is referred to as
(*a*) Flat structure (*b*) Tall structure
(*c*) Matrix structure (*d*) Project structure

86. The following steps are involved in the process of organising:
I. Forming supportive objectives
II. Delegating to the head of each group the authority necessary to perform the activities

III. Establishing enterprise objectives
IV. Identifying and classifying activities

The correct sequence of these steps is

(*a*) III, I, II, IV (*b*) III, I, IV, II
(*c*) I, III, IV, II (*d*) I, III, II, IV

87. When management pays attention to more important areas and when the day-to-day routine problems are looked after by lower level management, it is known as
(*a*) Management by Objectives
(*b*) Management by Exception
(*c*) Participative Management
(*d*) Critical Path Method

88. The following steps are involved in managing by objectives:
I. Preliminary setting of objectives at the top
II. Setting subordinates objectives
III. Tying resources with the goals
IV. Clarifying the organisational steps is
(*a*) I, II, III, IV (*b*) I, II, IV, III
(*c*) I, III, II, IV (*d*) I, IV, II, III

89. Match List-I (types of securities) with List-II (Special features) and select the correct answer using the codes given below the lists:

List-I	List-II
I. Blue Chip	A. Issued by a private limited company
II. Deep Discount Bonds	B. Highly Profitable investments in a stock exchange
III. Commercial paper	C. Issued by finally sound companies
IV. Debentures	D. Small investments and big yielding.
	E. Issued by companies having large reserves
	F. Issued in lieu of loans

Codes:
(*a*) I-B, II-A, III-C, IV- F
(*b*) I-A, II-D, III-F, IV- E
(*c*) I-B, II-C, III-A, IV-E
(*d*) I-B, II-D, III-C, IV-F

90. Match List-I (Management experts) with List-II (sequence of functions advocated by them) and select the correct answer using the codes given below the lists:

List-I	List-II
I. Newman and Summer	A. Organising, planning, leading and controlling
II. Henry Fayol	B. Planning, organising, commanding, coordinating and controlling
III. Luther Gulick	C. Planning, organizing, staffing, directing and controlling
IV. Koontz and O' Donnel	D. POSDCORB

Codes:
(*a*) I-A, II-B, III-D, IV-C
(*b*) I-B, II-A, III-C, IV-D
(*c*) I-A, II-B, III-C, IV-D
(*d*) I-B, II-A, III-D, IV-C

91. Which among the following are sub-systems of business firms
(*a*) Production system
(*b*) Finance system
(*c*) Research a development system
(*d*) All of the above

92. An economy which comprises the combination of capitalism and communism with a state ownership and control of business along with private enterprises is called
(*a*) Mixed Economy
(*b*) Financial Economy
(*c*) Dual Economy
(*d*) Organized Economy

93. Match List-I (Motivation theory) with List-II (Management Expert) and select the correct answer using the codes given below the lists:

List-I ***(Motivation Theory)***	List-II ***(Management Expert)***
I. Hygiene Theory	A. Abraham H. Maslow
II. Theory 'X' and theory 'Y'	B. Victor Vroom
III. Expectancy theory	C. Fredrick Herzberg
	D. Douglas Mc Gregor

Codes:
(*a*) I-C, II-D, III-B
(*b*) I-A, II-D, III-B
(*c*) I-C, II-B, III-D
(*d*) I-A, II-B, III-D

94. In management principles, grid refers to
(*a*) Diverse managerial styles
(*b*) Coordination
(*c*) Communication
(*d*) Motivation

95. The process of determining how to pursue long term goals with the expected resources available to the organisation is called
(*a*) Operational planning
(*b*) Strategic planning
(*c*) Intermediate planning
(*d*) Tactical planning

96. Which one of the following is the most appropriate management control technique for timely completion of a project?
(*a*) Organisation chart
(*b*) Management by objectives
(*c*) PERT
(*d*) Span of control

97. Which of the following pairs are correctly matched?

I. Frederick Herzberg	Scientific management
II. Henry Fayol	Modern management
III. Max Weber	Bureaucracy
IV. Philip Kotler	Marketing

Select the correct answer using the codes given below:
(*a*) I and II (*b*) II and III
(*c*) I and III (*d*) II, III and IV

98. Hawthorne studies have underlined the significance of which of the following?
(*a*) System approach to management
(*b*) Contingency approach to management
(*c*) Modern approach to management
(*d*) Human relations approach to management

99. Is management by exception, one of the important principles of control?
(*a*) Yes; because only the unusual deviations from standards should be brought to the notice of the management
(*b*) No; because less significant deviations and the actual performance according to the standards are not brought to the notice of the management
(*c*) Yes; because exception principle saves time of the subordinates staff
(*d*) No; because the manager can attend too operative decisions, and the strategic problems can be left to the technocrats

100. Job evaluation is used for
(*a*) study of progress of production
(*b*) study of job composition
(*c*) determining wage-rate differentials
(*d*) rating the merit of an employee

101. The first step of the control process actually gets initiated in the managerial function of
(*a*) Staffing (*b*) Planning
(*c*) Communication (*d*) Coordination

102. Which one of the following statements is correct?
(*a*) Business policy is another name for long range planning
(*b*) Strategic planning is the function of middle management
(*c*) Operational planning is the function of top management
(*d*) Strategic planning is largely influenced by external environment

103. The concept 'Management by Exception' implies
(*a*) exceptional contributions by the top management
(*b*) achievement of objectives by participation of all concerned
(*c*) that the immediate superior has to deal with deviations only and not with details of the work assigned to the subordinate
(*d*) that the highest officer need not worry about the results if he/she has delegated his/her authority

104. The most complex and widely used method of job evaluation is
(*a*) the job ranking method
(*b*) the job classification method
(*c*) the market pricing method
(*d*) the points method

105. Consider the following
I. Measurement
II. Projection
III. Selection
IV. Observation
V. Comparison
VI. Decision making

The correct sequence of the above ingredients of management by exceptions is
(*a*) I, II, III, IV, V, VI
(*b*) I, II, III, V, IV, VI
(*c*) I, II, III, VI, IV, V
(*d*) I, II, III, IV, VI, V

106. The Psychologist A.H. Maslow has developed a widely acclaimed conceptual frame work for understanding human motivation. Human needs, according to Maslow, tend to follow the classification of five categories of needs given as under:
I. Egoistic needs
II. Safety needs
III. Social needs
IV. Physiological needs
V. Self-fulfillment needs

These needs, according to Maslow, follow a basic hierarchical pattern from the most basic to the highest level needs as follows:
(*a*) I, II, III, IV, V (*b*) IV, II, III, I, V
(*c*) V, IV, III, II, I (*d*) I, III, II, IV, V

107. Douglas Mc Gregor made five basic assumptions about people in his theory Y. First four assumptions are:
I. People are ambitious.
II. They seek responsibility
III. They are dynamic
IV. They recognize and accept organisational goals

The fifth assumption is
(*a*) People are always cooperative and cheerful at their work
(*b*) People are not self-centred
(*c*) People are by nature resistant to change
(*d*) People are intelligent and possess creative potential

108. Kurt Lewins' three phases of organizational change consist of
(*a*) Unfreezing, changing, feedback
(*b*) Changing, refreezing, feedback
(*c*) Unfreezing, evaluation, refreezing
(*d*) Unfreezing, changing, refreezing

109. Which one of the following statements is not correct?
(*a*) Management by objectives is a philosophy of management
(*b*) Management by objectives is an approach of management
(*c*) Management by objectives is a process of participative management
(*d*) Management by objectives is a control technique

110. Consider the following two statements and select the correct answer using the codes given below:
I. The office supervisor is concerned with the overall managerial functions of the office activities.
II. The office manager is concerned with guiding and directing the routine work assigned to his subordinates.

Codes:
(*a*) Only I is correct
(*b*) Only II is correct
(*c*) Both I and II are correct
(*d*) Neither I nor II is correct

111. Which one of the following functions does not relate to O & M Division?
(*a*) To enlarge the organisation
(*b*) To improve organisation
(*c*) To simplify methods
(*d*) To create and maintain an efficient administrative machinery

112. The traditional concept is that authority flows from top to bottom. But a new concept of authority has been developed. This is known as acceptance theory. Who is the exponent of this view?
(*a*) Herbert A. Simon
(*b*) Douglas Mc Gregor
(*c*) Chester Barnard
(*d*) Keith Davis

113. Contingency school of management says that management is
(*a*) Practice – oriented
(*b*) Principle – oriented
(*c*) Result – oriented
(*d*) Profit and loss – oriented

114. Which among the following is the oldest and simplest device for achieving coordination?
(*a*) Hierarchy (*b*) Planning
(*c*) Incentives (*d*) Rules

115. Which one among the following is an instance of participative management?
(*a*) Board of Directors
(*b*) Trade Unions
(*c*) Work committees
(*d*) Task force

116. Which one of the following is the correct sequence in terms of the four management functions, first identified by Henry Fayol?
(*a*) Planning, organising, staffing and coordinating
(*b*) Planning, organising, leading and controlling
(*c*) Planning, motivating, directing and reporting
(*d*) Planning, staffing, communicating and leading

117. According to behavioural scientists, organisation means the structure of
(*a*) Physical facilities
(*b*) Tasks and relationships
(*c*) Behaviour of the management with the working force
(*d*) Attitude of workers with the management

118. Which one of the following styles of leadership is the most effective for a job order firm?
(*a*) Participative leadership
(*b*) Authoritarian leadership
(*c*) Transformational leadership
(*d*) Free-rein leadership

119. Match List-I with List-II and select the correct answer using the codes given below the lists:

List-I	**List-II**
I. F.W. Taylor	A. Principles of Management
II. Maslow	B. Team work
III. Esprit decorps	C. Scientific Management
IV. Henry Fayol	D. Theory of Human Motivation

Codes :
(*a*) I-A, II-D, III-B, IV-C
(*b*) I-C, II-B, III-D, IV-A
(*c*) I-A, II-B, III-D, IV-C
(*d*) I-C, II-D, III-B, IV-A

120. The managerial function of organising involves
(*a*) Reviewing and adjusting plan in the list of changing conditions
(*b*) Establishing programme for the accomplishment of objectives
(*c*) Creating a structure of functions and duties to be performed by a group
(*d*) Getting things done through others

121. Which one of the following is the most important function of a manager?
(*a*) Communication
(*b*) Directing
(*c*) Supervising
(*d*) Decision making

122. Organisations require narrow span of control if there are
(*a*) mature subordinates within
(*b*) competent and trained managers
(*c*) unclear plans for non-repetitive operations
(*d*) well-defined plans for repetitive operations

123. Which among the following is the most popular approach for accomplishing the results?

(*a*) Management by exception
(*b*) Reward system
(*c*) Management by objectives
(*d*) Mentor system

124. A systematic and orderly process of determining the worth of a job in relation to other jobs is known as
(*a*) Job analysis
(*b*) Job evaluation
(*c*) Job specification
(*d*) Job description

125. Which among the following is a direct advantage of incentive compensation?
(*a*) Mutual cooperation among the workers
(*b*) Decrease in absenteeism
(*c*) Increase in productivity
(*d*) Better industrial relations

126. Among the following 'change management' methods, which one is the most appropriate when the employees are unwilling to accept change?
(*a*) Participative method
(*b*) Directive method
(*c*) Leading by example
(*d*) Negative reinforcement

127. People resist change in organisation because of
(*a*) fear of unemployment
(*b*) increase in responsibility
(*c*) need for new social adjustments
(*d*) all the above

128. The term "organisational climate" best represents
(*a*) human environment prevailing in an organisation
(*b*) union - management relations with an organization
(*c*) problems introduced by faulty organisational structure
(*d*) Socio - cultural environment in an organization

129. Which one of the following is NOT a useful tool in decision making?
(*a*) Annual return
(*b*) Linear programming
(*c*) Sales forecasts
(*d*) Operation research

130. Which one of the following indicates the correct chronological order of management approaches in the History of management thoughts?
(*a*) Classical, Human Relations, Behavioural, Systems, Contingency
(*b*) Contingency, Systems, Behavioural, Human Relations, Classical
(*c*) Classical, Behavioural, Human Relations, Systems, Contingency
(*d*) Classical, Human Relations, Behavioural, Contingency, Systems

131. David C. Mc Clelland's motivating needs are
(*a*) Needs for power, affiliation and growth
(*b*) Needs for affiliation, achievement and security
(*c*) Needs for power, achievement and relatedness
(*d*) Needs for power, affiliation and achievement

132. Which one of the following gives the correct sequence with respect to communication process?
(*a*) Sender, Message, Encoding, Receiver, Channel, Decoding and Feedback
(*b*) Message, Sender, Encoding, Receiver, Channel, Decoding and Feedback
(*c*) Encoding, Message, Sender, Decoding, Feedback, Receiver and Channel
(*d*) Sender, Message, Encoding, Channel, Receiver, Decoding and Feedback

133. Wider span of control is effective in organisations where
(*a*) authority delegation is inadequate
(*b*) tasks are complex
(*c*) through subordinate training scheme exists
(*d*) the leadership style is authoritarian

134. Management by Exception is to improve
(*a*) Control over personnel
(*b*) Strategic management

(*c*) Steady flow of information
(*d*) High morale

135. Job evaluation is carried on mainly for
(*a*) identifying geographical locational factors of business enterprise
(*b*) promoting job satisfaction
(*c*) simplifying wage administration
(*d*) meeting competition effectively

136. Consider the following stages of planned change:
I. Moving
II. Refreezing
III. Unfreezing

According to Kurt Lewin, the correct sequence of these is
(*a*) I, II, III (*b*) II, III, I
(*c*) III, I, II (*d*) I, III, II

137. In which one of the following, crisis management is reflected?
(*a*) Future expansion plans of business
(*b*) Organisation Development programme
(*c*) Short-term manpower planning
(*d*) Prudent managerial leadership.

138. The most important advantage of centralisation of office services is
(*a*) specialisation
(*b*) higher departmental loyalty
(*c*) no delay in providing services
(*d*) less burden of work

139. Consider the following elements:
I. Policies
II. Objectives
III. Programmes
IV. Procedures

The correct sequence of these elements in the planning process is
(*a*) I, II, III, IV (*b*) I, II, IV, III
(*c*) II, I, IV, III (*d*) II, I, III, IV

140. TQM's major emphasis is on
(*a*) product quality
(*b*) company profitability
(*c*) customer delight
(*d*) employee training

141. The approach that considers an organisation to be in a dynamic relationship with its environment, is called
(*a*) Contingency approach
(*b*) Scientific approach
(*c*) Societal approach
(*d*) Systems approach

142. Consider the following stages in Management by Exception:
I. Setting criteria that the management will use to follow progress towards organistional objectives.
II. Measurement of current performance in the organisation.
III. Making comparison of actual and planned performance and identifying the exceptions.
IV. Decision making prescribing the action to be taken

The correct sequence of these stages is
(*a*) II, III, IV, I (*b*) II, I, III, IV
(*c*) I, III, II, IV (*d*) I, II, III, IV

143. In an organisation, performance appraisal is not expected to
(*a*) integrate and coordinate the endeavour of individuals.
(*b*) monitor the effects of individuals
(*c*) provide a means of correcting or commending the efforts of individuals
(*d*) calculate the living wage of the worker

144. A collection of duties, tasks and responsibilities assigned to a single individual is
(*a*) Occupation (*b*) Position
(*c*) Job (*d*) Grade

145. Computerised communication system existing within an organisation is called
(*a*) Internet
(*b*) Extranet
(*c*) Local Area Network
(*d*) Intranet

146. Scalar principle of organisation implies that
(*a*) all subordinates have only one supervisor.
(*b*) line of authority is defined clearly.

(*c*) manager can directly supervise only a limited number of persons.
(*d*) the subordinates need not necessarily have a supervisor.

147. To indicate the functions of management, the catch word POSDCORB was coined by
(*a*) Luther Gulik
(*b*) Henry Fayol
(*c*) Ernest Dale
(*d*) None of the above

148. Consider the following statements.
The social responsibility of business is to:
I. do a business as per the public policy
II. obey all the rules and regulations of the Governement
III. make payment of the taxes imposed by the Governement
IV. provide not necessarily adequate but good quality of goods
Of these statements
A. II and III are correct
B. I and IV are correct
C. I, II and III are correct
D. I, II, III and IV are correct

149. The integration of different economies of the world leading to emergence of global economy is called
(*a*) Globalization (*b*) Privatisation
(*c*) Liberalisation (*d*) None of these

150. The process of carrying out business transaction through internet for buying and selling of products through electronic means is known as
(*a*) Service (*b*) E-commerce
(*c*) Trade (*d*) Core Banking

151. Which among the following is not a limitation of e-commerce
(*a*) System and Data Integrity
(*b*) Vulnerability to Competition
(*c*) Shortage of Talent
(*d*) Less speed

152. The resources of e-commerce that can be required are
(*a*) Technically Qualified and Responsive Workforce
(*b*) Reliable Payable System
(*c*) Effective Telecommunication System
(*d*) All of the above

153. Strategic Planning refuse to
(*a*) Comprehensive and integrate Planning
(*b*) Formulate derivative Plans
(*c*) Develop planning premises
(*d*) Evaluating alternative courses

154. The network of horizontal and recital relationships among the members of a group designed to accomplish some common objective is called
(*a*) Organization structure
(*b*) Networking
(*c*) Organization process
(*d*) Path formation

155. Which among the following is/are type of departmentation
(*a*) Departmentation by function
(*b*) Combined departmentation
(*c*) Departmentation by process or equipment
(*d*) All of the above

156. Which among the following is an advantage of customer departmentation
(*a*) Special attention can be given to the particular tastes and preference of each class of customers
(*b*) It may lead to duplication of activities
(*c*) There may be under utilisation of facilities and manpower
(*d*) Managers of customer departments may put pressure for special facilities and benefits

157. Which among these are steps of Delegation
(*a*) Authority
(*b*) Responsibility
(*c*) Accountability
(*d*) All of the above

158. Brain storming is used by the management for
(*a*) work allocation on the shop floor
(*b*) generating alternative for problem solving
(*c*) the promotion of research and development
(*d*) training employees

ANSWERS

1	2	3	4	5	6	7	8	9	10
(*b*)	(*b*)	(*d*)	(*c*)	(*b*)	(*c*)	(*d*)	(*b*)	(*a*)	(*b*)
11	**12**	**13**	**14**	**15**	**16**	**17**	**18**	**19**	**20**
(*b*)	(*d*)	(*d*)	(*c*)	(*c*)	(*d*)	(*a*)	(*d*)	(*c*)	(*c*)
21	**22**	**23**	**24**	**25**	**26**	**27**	**28**	**29**	**30**
(*d*)	(*b*)	(*c*)	(*c*)	(*b*)	(*a*)	(*c*)	(*c*)	(*d*)	(*b*)
31	**32**	**33**	**34**	**35**	**36**	**37**	**38**	**39**	**40**
(*a*)	(*c*)	(*b*)	(*a*)	(*c*)	(*d*)	(*c*)	(*b*)	(*c*)	(*a*)
41	**42**	**43**	**44**	**45**	**46**	**47**	**48**	**49**	**50**
(*b*)	(*a*)	(*b*)	(*d*)	(*a*)	(*c*)	(*d*)	(*b*)	(*d*)	(*c*)
51	**52**	**53**	**54**	**55**	**56**	**57**	**58**	**59**	**60**
(*b*)	(*c*)	(*b*)	(*c*)	(*c*)	(*b*)	(*b*)	(*d*)	(*a*)	(*c*)
61	**62**	**63**	**64**	**65**	**66**	**67**	**68**	**69**	**70**
(*a*)	(*a*)	(*c*)	(*c*)	(*a*)	(*c*)	(*b*)	(*d*)	(*d*)	(*c*)
71	**72**	**73**	**74**	**75**	**76**	**77**	**78**	**79**	**80**
(*c*)	(*d*)	(*a*)	(*c*)	(*d*)	(*c*)	(*b*)	(*b*)	(*c*)	(*b*)
81	**82**	**83**	**84**	**85**	**86**	**87**	**88**	**89**	**90**
(*c*)	(*c*)	(*c*)	(*b*)	(*b*)	(*b*)	(*b*)	(*a*)	(*d*)	(*a*)
91	**92**	**93**	**94**	**95**	**96**	**97**	**98**	**99**	**100**
(*d*)	(*a*)	(*b*)	(*c*)	(*a*)	(*c*)	(*d*)	(*d*)	(*a*)	(*c*)
101	**102**	**103**	**104**	**105**	**106**	**107**	**108**	**109**	**110**
(*b*)	(*d*)	(*a*)	(*c*)	(*a*)	(*c*)	(*d*)	(*d*)	(*c*)	(*d*)
111	**112**	**113**	**114**	**115**	**116**	**117**	**118**	**119**	**120**
(*a*)	(*d*)	(*c*)	(*b*)	(*c*)	(*a*)	(*b*)	(*a*)	(*d*)	(*c*)
121	**122**	**123**	**124**	**125**	**126**	**127**	**128**	**129**	**130**
(*b*)	(*c*)	(*c*)	(*b*)	(*c*)	(*a*)	(*d*)	(*a*)	(*a*)	(*d*)
131	**132**	**133**	**134**	**135**	**136**	**137**	**138**	**139**	**140**
(*a*)	(*d*)	(*c*)	(*b*)	(*c*)	(*c*)	(*d*)	(*a*)	(*c*)	(*a*)
141	**142**	**143**	**144**	**145**	**146**	**147**	**148**	**149**	**150**
(*d*)	(*d*)	(*a*)	(*b*)	(*d*)	(*b*)	(*a*)	(*d*)	(*a*)	(*b*)
151	**152**	**153**	**154**	**155**	**156**	**157**	**158**		
(*d*)	(*d*)	(*a*)	(*a*)	(*d*)	(*a*)	(*d*)	(*b*)		

General Awareness

NATIONAL SYMBOLS

STATE EMBLEM

State Emblem of India is an adaptation from the Sarnath Lion Capital of Ashoka. It was adopted by the Government of India on January 26, 1950. In the adapted form, only three lions are visible, the fourth being hidden from the view. The wheel (Dharma Chakra) appears in relief in the centre of the abacus with a bull on the right and a horse on the left.

The bell-shaped lotus has been omitted. The words ''Satyameva Jayate'' meaning ''Truth alone triumphs'' are inscribed below the Emblem in Devanagari script.

NATIONAL FLAG

The National Flag of India is a horizontal tricolour of deep saffron (Kesari), white and dark green in equal proportion. In the centre of the white band there is a wheel in navy blue colour. It has 24 spokes. The ratio of the length and the breadth of the flag is 3 : 2. Its design was adopted by the Constituent Assembly of India on July 22, 1947.

NATIONAL ANTHEM

Rabindranath Tagore's song 'Jana-gana-mana' was adopted by the Constituent Assembly as the National Anthem of India on January 24, 1950.

Jana-gan-mana-adhinayaka jaya he, Bharata-bhagya-vidhata
Punjab-Sindh-Gujarat-Maratha-Dravida-Utkala-Banga
Vindhya-Himachala-Yamuna-Ganga Uchhala-jaladhi-taranga.
Tava subha name jage, Tava subha asisa mange, Gahe tava jaya gatha,
Jana-gana-mangala-dayak, jaya he Bharata bhagya vidhata,
Jaya he, jaya he, jaya he, Jaya jaya jaya, jaya he.

NATIONAL SONG

Bankim Chandra Chatterji's 'Vande Mataram' which was a source of inspiration to the people in their struggle for freedom, has been adopted as National Song. It has an equal status with the National Anthem.

Vande Mataram
Sujalam, suphalam, malayaja-shitalam,
Shasya shyamalam, Mataram
Shubhrajyotsna,pulkita yaminim,
Phulla kusumita drumadalashobhinim,
Subhasinim sumadhura—bhashinim,
Sukhadam, Varadam, Mataram.

NATIONAL CALENDAR

It is based on the Saka era with Chaitra as its first month and a normal year of 365 days. It was adopted from March 22, 1957. Dates of the national calendar have a permanent correspondence with dates of Gregorian calendar as Chaitra I falls on March 22 in a normal year and March 21 in a leap year. In official communications, both Saka and Gregorian calendar dates are written. Months of the national calendar are Chaitra, Vaishakha, Jaishtha, Ashada, Shravan, Bhadra, Ashvina, Kartika, Margashirsha, Pausha, Magha and Phalguna.

NATIONAL ANIMAL

The magnificent tiger — Panthera tigris (Linnaeus) is the national animal of India. Tiger is found in several parts of the country and is known for its grace, strength, agility and enormous power. 'Project Tiger' was launched in 1973 to check their dwindling population in India.

NATIONAL BIRD

The Indian Peacock — Pavo Christatus (Linnaeus) is the national bird of India. It is a colourful, swan-sized bird with a fan-shaped crest of feathers on its head and a long-slander neck. The male species is more colourful with blue breast and a spectacular bronze-green train of around 200 elongated feathers.

National Flower—Lotus

National Tree—Banyan

National Fruit—Mango

National Currency—Rupee '₹'

(One Rupee = 100 Paise)

National Aquatic Animal—Dolphin

BOOKS AND AUTHORS

Name of Book	Author
Ain-e-Akbari	Abul Fazal
Anand Math	Bankim Chandra Chatterjee
An Unknown Indian	Nirad C. Chaudhuri
Arthshastra	Kautilya
Coolie	Mulk Raj Anand
Das Kapital	Karl Marx
Discovery of India	Jawaharlal Nehru
Eternal India	Mrs. Indira Gandhi
Godan	Prem Chand
Gitanjali	Rabindranath Tagore
Gora	Rabindranath Tagore
Geet Govinda	Jayadeva
Harsha Charit	Bana Bhatta
Hindu View of Life	Dr. S. Radhakrishnan
India Wins Freedom	Maulana Abul Kalam Azad
Jobs of Millions	V.V. Giri
Jungle Book	Rudyard Kipling
Kamayani	Jai Shankar Prasad
Kadambari	Bana Bhatta
Life Divine	Sri Aurobindo
Last days of Netaji	G.D. Khosla
Les Miserables	Victor Hugo
Mahabharat	Veda Vyas
Macbeth	William Shakespeare
Mein Kempf	Hitler
Meghduta	Kalidas

Name of Book	Author
Mother (Maa)	Maxim Gorky
Mother India	Katherine Mayo
My Experiments with Truth	Mahatma Gandhi
My Presidential Years	R. Venkataraman
Neeti Shatak	Bhartrihari
Nehru and His Vision	Dr. K.R. Narayanan
Old Man and the Sea	Ernest Hemingway
One World	Wendell Wilkie
Panchtantra	Vishnu Sharma
Paradise Lost	John Milton
Ramayana	Valmiki (in Sanskrit)
Raghuvansham	Kalidas
Rajtarangini	Kalhan
Ram Charit Manas	Tulsi Das
Abhijnan Shakuntalam	Kalidas
Satanic Verses	Salman Rushdie
Saket	Maithili Sharan Gupta
Speed Post	Shobha De
The God of Small Things	Arundhati Roy
Treasure Island	R.L. Stevenson
Twelfth Night	William Shakespeare
Train to Pakistan	Khuswant Singh
Uttara Ram Charitra	Bhava Bhuti
Vanity Fair	W.M. Thackeray
War and Peace	Leo Tolstoy
Wealth of Nations	Adam Smith
Wake up India	Annie Besant

INVENTIONS AND DISCOVERIES

Geographical Discoveries

Discovery	Discoverer
America	Columbus
Brazil	Cabral
North Pole	Robert Peary
Everest (Conquered)	Tabie Junko
Planetary Motion	Kepler
Hawaiian Islands	Captain Cook
South Pole	Amundsen
Solar System	Copernicus

Chemistry and Physics

Discovery	Discoverer
Atom Bomb	Otto Hahn
Atomic Theory	Dalton
Atomic Numbers	Moseley
Cosmic Rays	R.S. Millikan
Dynamite	Alfred Nobel
Electrons Theory	Bohr
Electricity (current)	Volta
Electric Telegraphy (Code)	S. Morse

Discovery	Discoverer
Gravitation	Newton
Gas Light	Murdock
Oxygen	J. Priestly
Photography	L. Daguerre
Printing for the blind	Louis Braille
Radium	Madame Curie
Telegraph	Samuel Morse
Television	J.L. Baird
Telephone	Graham Bell
Wireless	G. Marconi
X-rays	W.K. Roentgen
Mechanical	
Aeroplane	Wright Brothers
Bicycle	Macmillan
Computer	Charles Babbage
Dynamo	Michal Faraday
Diesel Engine	Rudolf Diesel
Engine (Railway)	Stephenson
Fountain Pen	Waterman
Gramophone	Edison
Locomotive Power of Steam	James Watt
Helicopter	Brequet
Life Boat	Henry Greathead

Discovery	Discoverer
Microscope	Z. Jansen
Printing Press	Gutenberg
Revolver	Colt
Sewing Machine	Elias Howe
Thermometer	Fahrenheit
Transistor	W. Shockley
Typewriter	Sholes
Telescope	Hans Lippershey
Tank (Military)	Swinton
Medical	
Antiseptic Surgery	Lord Joseph Lister
Bacteria	Leeuwenhock
Circulation of Blood	William Harvey
Homoeopathy (Discovered)	Hahnemann
Insulin	F. Banting
Penicillin	Alexander Flemming
Malaria Parasite	Dr. Ronald Ross
Stethoscope	Laennec
Vitamins	Funk
Anti-Rabies Treatment	Pasteur
General	
Nylon	Carouthers
Science of Geometry	Euclids

WORLD'S GEOGRAPHICAL SURNAMES

• City of Sky-scrapers—New York • City of Seven Hills—Rome • City of Dreaming Spires—Oxford • City of Golden Gate—San Francisco • City of Magnificent Buildings—Washington D.C. • City of Eternal Springs—Quito (S. America) • China's Sorrow—Hwang Ho • Cockpit of Europe—Belgium • Dark Continent—Africa • Emerald Isle—Ireland • Eternal City—Rome • Empire City—New York • Forbidden City—Lhasa (Tibet) • Garden City—Chicago • Gate of Tears—Strait of Bab-el-Mandeb • Gift of the Nile—Egypt • Granite City—Aberdeen (Scotland) • Hermit Kingdom—Korea • Herring Pond—Atlantic Ocean • Holy Land—Jerusalem • Island Continent—Australia • Islands of Cloves—Zanzibar • Isle of Pearls—Bahrein (Persian Gulf) • Key to the Mediterranean—Gibralter • Land of Cakes—Scotland • Land of Golden Fleece—Australia • Land of Maple Leaf—Canada • Land of Morning Calm—Korea • Land of Midnight Sun—Norway • Land of the Thousand Lakes—Finland • Land of the Thunderbolt—Bhutan • Land of White Elephant—Thailand • Land of Thousand Elephants—Laos • Land of Rising Sun—Japan • Loneliest Island—Tristan De Gunha (Mid-Atlantic) • Manchester of Japan—Osaka • Pillars of Hercules—Strait of Gibraltar • Pearl of the Antilles—Cuba • Playground of Europe—Switzerland • Quaker City—Philadelphia • Queen of the Adriatic—Venice • Roof of the World—The Pamirs, Central Asia • Sugar bowl of the world—Cuba • Venice of the North—Stockholm • Windy City—Chicago • Whiteman's grave—Guinea Coast of Africa • Yellow River—Huang Ho (China) • Sickman of Europe—Turkiye

CAPITALS AND CURRENCIES OF COUNTRIES

Country	Capital	Currency
Afghanistan	Kabul	Afghani
Algeria	Algiers	Dinar
Angola	Luanda	New Kwanza
Argentina	Buenos Aires	Peso
Armenia	Yeravan	Dram
Australia	Canberra	Dollar
Austria	Vienna	Euro
Azerbaijan	Baku	Manat
Bahrain	Manama	Dinar
Bangladesh	Dhaka	Taka
Barbados	Bridgetown	Dollar
Belgium	Brussels	Euro
Bhutan	Thimphu	Ngultrum
Bolivia	La paz	Boliviano
Brazil	Brasilia	Cruzeiro
Bulgaria	Sofia	Euro
Belarus	Minsk	Ruble
Cambodia	Phnom-Penh	Riel
Canada	Ottawa	Dollar
Chile	Santiago	Peso
China	Beijing	Yuan
Colombia	Bogota	Peso
Congo (Republic)	Brazzaville	Franc (CFA)
Croatia	Zagreb	Euro
Cuba	Havana	Peso
Cyprus	Nicosia	Euro
Czech Republic	Prague	Koruna
Denmark	Copenhagen	Krone
Egypt	Cairo	Pound
Estonia	Tallinn	Euro
Ethiopia	Addis Ababa	Birr
Fiji	Suva	Dollar
Finland	Helsinki	Euro
France	Paris	Euro
Georgia	Tbilisi	Lari
Germany	Berlin	Euro
Ghana	Accra	Cedi
Greece	Athens	Euro
Guatemala	Guatemala City	Quetzal
Hong Kong	Victoria	Dollar
Hungary	Budapest	Forints
Iceland	Reykjavik	Krona
India	New Delhi	Rupee

Country	Capital	Currency
Indonesia	Jakarta	Rupiah
Iran	Teheran	Rial
Iraq	Baghdad	Dinar
Ireland	Dublin	Euro
Israel	Jerusalem	Shekel
Italy	Rome	Euro
Jamaica	Kingston	Dollar
Japan	Tokyo	Yen
Jordan	Amman	Dinar
Kazakhstan	Astana	Tenge
Kenya	Nairobi	Shilling
Korea (S)	Seoul	Won
Korea (N)	Pyongyang	Won
Kyrgyzstan	Bishkek	Som
Kuwait	Kuwait City	Dinar
Laos	Vientiane	Kip
Latvia	Riga	Euro
Lebanon	Beirut	Pound
Libya	Tripoli	Dinar
Lithuania	Vilnius	Euro
Malaysia	Kuala Lumpur	Ringgit
Maldives	Male	Rufiyya
Mauritius	Port Louis	Rupee
Moldavia	Chisinau	Leu
Mexico	Mexico City	Peso
Morocco	Rabat	Dirham
Mozambique	Maputo	Metical
Myanmar	Nay Pyi Taw	Kyat
Nepal	Kathmandu	Rupee
Netherlands	Amsterdam	Euro
New Zealand	Wellington	Dollar
Nigeria	Abuja	Naira
Norway	Oslo	Krone
Oman	Muscat	Rial
Pakistan	Islamabad	Rupee
Philippines	Manila	Peso
Poland	Warsaw	Zloty
Portugal	Lisbon	Euro
Qatar	Doha	Riyal
Romania	Bucharest	Leu
Russia	Moscow	Ruble
Saudi Arabia	Riyadh	Rial

Country	Capital	Currency
Slovakia	Bratislava	Euro
Spain	Madrid	Euro
Sri Lanka	Colombo	Rupee
Sudan	Khartoum	Dinar
Sweden	Stockholm	Krona
Switzerland	Berne	Swiss Francs
Syria	Damascus	Pound
South Africa	Capetown (Legislative) Pretoria (Administrative)	Rand
Tajikistan	Dushanbe	Somoni
Taiwan	Taipei	Dollar
Tanzania	Dodoma	Shilling
Thailand	Bangkok	Baht
Turkiye	Ankara	Turkish Lira
Turkmenistan	Ashgabat	Manat
Uganda	Kampala	Shilling
Ukraine	Kiev	Hryvna
United Arab Emirates	Abu Dhabi	Dirham
U.K.	London	Pound Sterling
U.S.A.	Washington	Dollar
Uzbekistan	Tashkent	Som
Vietnam	Hanoi	Dong
Yemen	Sana'a	Rial/Dinar
Zimbabwe	Harare	Dollar
Congo (Democratic Republic)	Kinshasa	Franc (CDF)
Zambia	Lusaka	Kwacha

INDIAN CITIES AND THEIR RIVERS

City	State	River
Agra	U.P.	Yamuna
Ahmedabad	Gujarat	Sabarmati
Alwaye	Keralam	Periyar
Kolkata	West Bengal	Hooghly
Cuttack	Odisha	Mahanadi
Delhi	Delhi	Yamuna
Haridwar	Uttarakhand	Ganga
Kanpur	Uttar Pradesh	Ganga
Ludhiana	Punjab	Sutlej
Lucknow	Uttar Pradesh	Gomati
Nasik	Maharashtra	Godavari
Patna	Bihar	Ganga
Prayagraj	U.P.	Confluence of the Ganga, Yamuna, and invisible Saraswati
Srinagar	J & K	Jhelum
Surat	Gujarat	Tapti
Tiruchirapally	Tamil Nadu	Kaveri
Ujjain	Madhya Pradesh	Shipra
Vijayawada	Andhra Pradesh	Krishna
Varanasi	Uttar Pradesh	Ganga

WONDERS OF THE WORLD

Seven Wonders of the Ancient World: (1) the Pyramids of Egypt, built in approximately 2700 BC; (2) the Hanging Gardens at Babylon; (3) the temple of Artemis at Emphesus; (4) the statue of Zeus at Olympia; (5) the tomb of Mausolus at Halicarnassus, built in nearly 350 BC; (6) the Colossus of Rhodes, built in nearly 280 BC; (7) the Pharos Lighthouse at Alexandria.

Seven Wonders of the Medieval World: (1) the Colosseum of Rome; (2) the Great Wall of China; (3) the Porcelain Tower of Nanking; (4) the Mosque at St. Sophia (Constantinople); (5) Stonehenge; (6) the Catacombs of Rome; (7) the Leaning Tower of Pisa.

Seven New Wonders of the World: (1) Taj Mahal of Agra (India); (2) Pyramid at Chichen Itza (Mexico); (3) Machu Picchu (Peru); (4) Statue of Christ The Redeemer (Brazil); (5) Great Wall of China; (6) Roman Colosseum, Italy; (7) Ruins of Petra, Jordan.

STATES & UNION TERRITORIES OF INDIA (CAPITALS, PRINCIPAL LANGUAGES)

States & Union Territories	Capitals	Principal Languages
Andhra Pradesh	Amravati	*Telgu and Urdu*
Arunachal Pradesh	Itanagar	*Monpa, Adi, Nissi etc.*
Assam	Dispur	*Assamese and Bengali*
Bihar	Patna	*Hindi and Maithili*
Chhattishgarh	Raipur	*Hindi*
Goa	Panaji	*Konkani*
Gujarat	Gandhinagar	*Gujarati*
Haryana	Chandigarh	*Hindi*
Himachal Pradesh	Shimla	*Hindi and Pahari*
Jharkhand	Ranchi	*Hindi*
Keralam	Thiruvananthpuram	*Malyalam*
Karnataka	Bengaluru	*Kannada*
Madhya Pradesh	Bhopal	*Hindi*
Maharashtra	Mumbai	*Marathi*
Meghalaya	Shillong	*Khashi, Jayantia and Garo*
Manipur	Imphal	*Manipuri*
Mizoram	Aizawl	*Mizo and English*
Nagaland	Kohima	*Naga, Assamese and English*
Odisha	Bhubaneshwar	*Odia*
Punjab	Chandigarh	*Punjabi*
Rajasthan	Jaipur	*Hindi, Rajasthani*
Sikkim	Gangtok	*Sikkimese and Gorkhali*
Tamil Nadu	Chennai	*Tamil*
Tripura	Agartala	*Bengali, Tripuri*
Uttar Pradesh	Lucknow	*Hindi*
Uttarakhand	Dehradun	*Hindi*
West Bengal	Kolkata	*Bengali*
Telangana	Hyderabad	*Telgu and Urdu*
Jammu & Kashmir	Srinagar/Jammu	*Kashmiri, Dongri, Urdu, Dardi and Pahari*
Andaman and Nicobar Islands	Shri Vijaya Puram	*Hindi, Nicobarese, Bengali, Malayalam, Tamil, Telugu*
Chandigarh	Chandigarh	*Hindi, Punjabi, English*
Dadar and Nagar Haveli and Daman and Diu	Daman	*Gujarati, Hindi*
Delhi	Delhi	*Hindi, Punjabi*
Lakshadweep	Kavaratti	*Malayalam*
Puducherry	Puducherry	*Tamil, Telugu, Malayalam, English and French*
Ladakh	Leh	*Ladakhi*

HIGH COURTS IN INDIA

Name	*Territorial Jurisdiction*	*Seat*
Allahabad	Uttar Pradesh	Prayagraj (Bench at Lucknow)
Andhra Pradesh	Andhra Pradesh	Amaravati
Bombay	Maharashtra, Goa, Dadar and Nagar Haveli and Daman and Diu	Mumbai (Benches at Nagpur, Panaji, and Aurangabad)
Calcutta	West Bengal and Andaman & Nicobar Islands	Kolkata (Circuit Benches at Port Blair and Jalpaiguri)
Chhattisgarh	Chhattisgarh	Bilaspur
Delhi	New Delhi	NCT of Delhi
Gauhati	Assam, Nagaland, Mizoram and Arunachal Pradesh	Guwahati (Benches at Kohima, Aizawl and Itanagar)
Gujarat	Gujarat	Sola (Ahmedabad)
Himachal Pradesh	Himachal Pradesh	Shimla
Jammu & Kashmir and Ladakh	Jammu & Kashmir/Ladakh	Srinagar and Jammu
Jharkhand	Jharkhand	Ranchi
Karnataka	Karnataka	Bengaluru (Circuit Benches at Dharwar and Gulbarga)
Kerala	Keralam & Lakshadweep	Kochi
Madhya Pradesh	Madhya Pradesh	Jabalpur (Benches at Gwalior and Indore)
Madras	Tamil Nadu & Puducherry	Chennai (Bench at Madurai)
Orissa	Odisha	Cuttack
Patna	Bihar	Patna
Punjab and Haryana	Punjab, Haryana and Chandigarh	Chandigarh
Rajasthan	Rajasthan	Jodhpur (Bench at Jaipur)
Sikkim	Sikkim	Gangtok
Uttarakhand	Uttarakhand	Nainital
Tripura	Tripura	Agartala
Meghalaya	Meghalaya	Shillong
Manipur	Manipur	Imphal
Telangana	Telangana	Hyderabad

FAMOUS HILL STATIONS

Hill Station	State/UT
1. Almora, Mussoorie, Nainital	: Uttarakhand
2. Cherrapunji (Shillong), Khasi Hills (Shillong)	: Meghalaya
3. Ooty, Kodaikanal, Yercaud	: Tamil Nadu
4. Dalhousie, Kassauli	: Himachal Pradesh
5. Darjeeling	: West Bengal
6. Gulmarg, Srinagar	: Jammu and Kashmir
7. Mahabaleshwar	: Maharashtra
8. Mt. Abu	: Rajasthan
9. Pachmarhi	: Madhya Pradesh

FAMOUS NATIONAL PARKS

1. Corbett National Park : Nainital, Uttarakhand
2. Dudhwa National Park : Lakhimpur Kheri, Uttar Pradesh
3. Kaziranga National Park : Jorhat, Assam
4. Kanha National Park : Jabalpur, Bhedaghat
5. Gir National Park : Rajkot, Junagarh, Gujarat
6. Guindy National Park : Guindy, Chennai, Tamil Nadu
7. Nagairhole National Park : Coorg, Karnataka
8. Bandipur National Park : Mysore, Karnataka

FAMOUS NATIONAL WILDLIFE SANCTUARIES

1. Dachigam Wildlife Sanctuary : Srinagar, Jammu and Kashmir
2. Sariska : Alwar, Rajasthan
3. Hazaribagh Wildlife Sanctuary : Hazaribagh, Jharkhand
4. Tiger Project : Sawai Madhopur, Rajasthan
5. Mudhumali Wildlife Sanctuary : Mudhumalia, Nilgiri, Tamil Nadu
6. Periyar Wildlife Sanctuary : Idukki, Kottayam, Keralam

HOLY PLACES IN INDIA

1.	Amarnath	Jammu and Kashmir
2.	Ayodhya	Uttar Pradesh
3.	Badrinath	Uttarakhand
4.	Dwarka	Gujarat
5.	Haridwar	Uttarakhand
6.	Kancheepuram	Tamil Nadu
7.	Kedarnath	Uttarakhand
8.	Mathura	Uttar Pradesh
9.	Puri	Odisha
10.	Rameswaram	Tamil Nadu
11.	Tirupati	Andhra Pradesh
12.	Ujjain	Madhya Pradesh
13.	Varanasi	Uttar Pradesh
14.	Bodh Gaya	Bihar

SPORTS

Terms Associated With Sports :

Cricket : Ashes, Bye, Bodyline, Bowling, Break, Cover-point, Creases, Chinaman, Chucker, Drive, Duck, Follow on, Googly, Hit-Wicket, Hat-trick, Leg-before-wicket, Leg break, Leg-bye, Maiden over, No ball, Night-watchman, Runner, Run-out, Stumped, Silly-point, Slip.

Football : Handball, Corner kick, Dribble, Free Kick, Hat-trick, Off-side, Penalty Kick, Try, Throw in, Wembley.

Hockey : Bully, Carry, Corner kick, Corner, Penalty stroke, Off-side, Penalty, Roll in scoop, Sticks, Sudden death, Striking circle, Short Corner, Scoop, Tie-breaker, Under-cutting, Hat-trick.

Tennis : Backhand drive, Deuce, Fault, Half-volley, Net, Let, Volley, Smash, Service.

Billiards : Break, Cannons, Cue, Pot, Jigger, Scratch, In Bauk, In, Off.

Bridge : Dummy, Finesse, Grand-slam, Little Slam, Revoke, Ruff slam, Trump, Tricks, Vulnerable.

Volley Ball : Booster, Love, Service, Volley, Smasher.

Badminton : Smash, Drop, Let.

Chess : Check, Checkmate, Gambit, State-mate.

Golf : Bogy, Caddie, Hole, Links, Stymie, Tee, Put.

Polo : Chukker, Mallet, Bunder.

Baseball : Bunting, Diamond, Pitcher, Put-out, Strike, Home.

Boxing : Knockout, Punch, Upper-cut, Jab, Hook.

FAMOUS TROPHIES

Agha Khan Cup	Hockey
Beighton Cup	Hockey
Corbillion Cup	World Table Tennis (Women)
Davis Cup	Lawn Tennis
Duleep Trophy	Cricket
Durand Cup	Football
Ezra Cup	Polo
I.F.A. Shield	Football
Irani Cup	Cricket (India)
Jayalaxmi Cup	Table Tennis (Women)
Lady Rattan Tata Trophy	Hockey (Women)
Nehru Cup	Hockey (India)
Obaidullah Cup	Hockey
Ranji Trophy	Cricket (India)
Rangaswamy Cup	Hockey (India)
Rovers Cup	Football (India)
Santosh Trophy	Football (India)
Subroto Cup	Football
Thomas Cup	Badminton
Uber Cup	Badminton (Women)
Wellington Trophy	Rowing (India)

BIGGEST, LARGEST, TALLEST OF THE WORLD

Airport, *Largest*—King Fahd International Airport, Dammon (Saudi Arabia)

Animal, *Tallest*—Giraffe (Average height 6.09 m); *Largest and Heaviest*—Blue Whale (190 tonnes)

Longest recorded Animal—Boot lace Worm (55 m); *Fastest*—Cheetah (Approximately 100 km/hr)

Bay, *Largest*—Bay of Bengal

Continent, *biggest*—Asia (31,845,872 km^2); *Smallest*—Australia Mainland (Area 76,17,930 km^2)

Desert, *Largest*—Sahara (N. Africa; maximum length 5,150 km EW; maximum width 3,200 km NS)

Dome, *Largest*—Singapore National Stadium (310 m)

Fish, *Largest fresh water*—Plabeuk (China, Laos and Thailand); *Most abundant*—Bristle mouth; *Most venomous*—Stone Fish (Indo-Pacific Waters)

Fountain, *Tallest*—King Fahd's Fountain (Jeddah, Saudi Arabia)

Gulf, *Largest*—Gulf of Mexico (1,544,000 sq. km)

Island, *Biggest*—Greenland (Kalaatdlit Nunaat- 2,175,000 sq km)

Lake, *Largest*—Caspian Sea (Azerbaijan, Russia, Iran border: 37.18 lakh km^2); *Deepest*—Baikal (Siberia); *Largest (fresh water)*—Superior Lake (USA---Canada border: 82,350 km^2)

Mountain, *Highest peak*—Mt. Everest (8848 m; Nepal); *Highest range*—Himalayas, Asia (upto 4200 m); *Greatest mountain range*—Himalaya-Karakoram (96 out of 109 peaks over 7315 m are here)

Museum, *Largest*—American Museum of Natural History, New York

Ocean, *Largest and Deepest*—The Pacific (Area: 166,240,000 km^2; Depth: 10,924 m)

Platform, *Longest (rail)*—Shri Siddharoodha Swamiji Railway Station, Hubballi (Karnataka; India, 1507 m. long)

Railway Station, *Largest*—Grand Central Terminal (New York City; 19 hc)

Rivers, *Longest*—(i) Nile (6650 km) (ii) Amazon (6437 km)

Sea, *Largest*—Philippine Sea (5,695,000 sq. km)

Star, *Brightest*—Sirius A (also called Dog Star)

Temple, *Largest*—Angkor Vat (Cambodia: 402 acres)

Tunnel, *Longest (railway)*—Gotthard Base Rail Tunnel (Switzerland; 57.1 km); *Largest (road)*—Laerdal, Norway (24.51 km)

FIRST IN INDIA

Governor General of Independent India — Lord Mountbatten

Cosmonaut — Sq. Ldr. Rakesh Sharma

Field Marshal — S.H.F.J. Manekshaw

Indian Governor General of Indian Union — C. Rajagopalachari

Indian I.C.S. Officer — Satyendra Nath Tagore

Indian to swim across English Channel — Mihir Sen

Indian Women to swim across English Channel — Miss Arti Saha

Man to climb Mount Everest — Tenzing Norgay

Man to climb Mount Everest without Oxygen — Phu Dorjee

Man to climb Mount Everest twice — Nwang Gombu

Nobel Prize Winner — Rabindra Nath Tagore

President of Indian National Congress — W.C. Banerjee

President of Indian Republic — Dr. Rajendra Prasad

Talkie Film — Alam Ara (1931)

Test Tube Baby (Documented) — Indira

Viceroy of India — Lord Canning

Woman Minister of Indian Union — Rajkumari Amrit Kaur

Woman Governor — Mrs. Sarojini Naidu

Woman President of Indian National Congress — Dr. Annie Besant

Woman Prime Minister — Mrs. Indira Gandhi

Woman Speaker of a State Assembly — Mrs. Shanno Devi

Prime Minister of India — Pt. Jawaharlal Nehru

Muslim President of Indian Union — Dr. Zakir Hussain

Speaker of Lok Sabha — G.V. Mavlankar

Women to Climb Mount Everest — Bachhendri Pal

Woman Judge in Supreme Court — Mrs. Meera Sahib Fatima Biwi

Women Chief Justice of a High Court — Smt. Leela Seth

The First Indian Weightlifter to Win bronze medal in Olympics — Karnam Malleshwari (Sydney, in 2000)

Chief of Defence Staff (CDS) —General Bipin Rawat

World Chess Champion — Vishwanathan Anand

India's First Woman Merchant Navy Officer — Sonali Banerjee

The First Woman Air Vice-Marshal — P. Bandopadhyaya

The First Indian to be appointed as United Nations Civilian Police Advisor — Ms. Kiran Bedi

The First Women to be appointed Deputy Governor of Reserve Bank of India — K.J. Udeshi

The First Indian Lady to win a medal in World Athletic Championship — Anju Bobby George

The First Sikh Prime Minister of India — Dr. Manmohan Singh

IMPORTANT DAYS

15th January	—	Army Day
26th January	—	Republic Day
30th January	—	Leprosy Eradication Day/ Martyr's Day
28th February	—	National Science Day
8th march	—	International Women's Day
15th March	—	World Consumer's Day
21st March	—	World Disabled Day
5th April	—	National Marine Day
7th April	—	World Health Day
18th April	—	World Heritage Day
22nd April	—	International Earth Day
Ist May	—	Worker's Day
3rd May	—	International Sun Day
21st May	—	Anti-Terrorism Day
24th May	—	Commonwealth Day
31st May	—	World No Tobacco Day
5th June	—	World Environment Day
21st June	—	World Yoga Day
26th June	—	International Day against Drug Abuse
11th July	—	World Population Day
15th August	—	Independence Day
24th August	—	Sanskrit Day
5th September	—	Teacher's Day
8th September	—	World Literacy Day
27th September	—	World Tourism Day
1st October	—	World Elder's Day
4th October	—	World Animal Day
8th October	—	Air Force Day
10th October	—	National Solidarity Day
16th October	—	World Food Day
24th October	—	U.N. Day
14th November	—	World Diabetes Day
14th November	—	Children's Day
19th November	—	National Integration Day
26th November	—	Law Day
1st December	—	World AIDS Day
4th December	—	Navy Day
7th December	—	Flag Day
10th December	—	Human Rights Day

PARLIAMENTS OF IMPORTANT COUNTRIES

Afghanistan	—	Shora
Britain	—	Parliament House of Commons, House of Lords
Denmark	—	Folketing
The Netherlands	—	States General
India	—	Sansad
Israel	—	Knesset
Iran	—	Majlis
Ireland	—	Airetann
Iceland	—	Althing
Japan	—	Diet
Norway	—	Storting
Russia	—	Supreme Soviet
Spain	—	Cortes
Sweden	—	Riksdag
U.S.A.	—	Congress Senate
Germany	—	Bundestag

MINERAL RESOURCES OF THE WORLD

Mineral	Largest Producers
Iron Ore	China, Japan, Russia
Tin	China, Indonesia, Peru
Lead	China, Australia, U.S.A.
Zinc	China, Australia, Peru
Manganese	South Africa, Brazil, Australia
Aluminium	China, Russia, Canada
Petroleum	Saudi Arabia, Russia, USA
Silver	Peru, Mexico, China
Coal	China, USA, India

WORLD'S LARGEST PRODUCERS

Articles	Producers	Articles	Producers
Carpets	Iran	Cheese	USA
Cocoa	Cote d'Ivoire	Coffee	Brazil
Copper	Chile	Cotton	China
Diamonds	Russia	Jute	India
Rice	China	Rubber	Thailand
Silk	China	Steel	China
Sugar	Brazil	Tea	China
Tin	China	Wheat	China
Wool	Australia		

TEN LARGEST COUNTRIES BY AREAS

Rank by Area	Country	Area (sq. km.)
1.	Russia	17,075,400
2.	Canada	9,976,139
3.	China	9,561,000
4.	U.S.A.	9,363,123
5.	Brazil	8,511,965
6.	Australia	7,686,848
7.	India	3,287,263
8.	Argentina	2,776,889
9.	Kazakhstan	2,724,900
10.	Algeria	2,381,741

PRESIDENT OF INDIA

He is the constitutional head of the Republic but not the real executive.

Qualifications: (1) Indian citizen; (2) age not less than 35 years; (3) should have qualifications for election to Lok Sabha; (4) should not hold any office of profit; (5) should not be a Member of Parliament or State Legislature.

Election: He is elected by the elected Members of Parliament and State Legislative Assemblies in accordance with the system of proportional representation by means of single transferable vote.

Powers: He makes appointment to all the Constitutional posts. He can address either House of Parliament and send message to them. He can summon and prorogue either House of Parliament and dissolve Lok Sabha. All Bills passed by Parliament must receive his assent to become an Act. He issues Ordinance when Parliament is not in session. No money Bill can be introduced in Lok Sabha without his recommendation. He can grant pardon, reprieve or remit punishment and he can commute death sentences. He can declare national emergency, state emergency and financial emergency.

VICE-PRESIDENT OF INDIA

The Vice-President acts as the ex-officio Chairman of Rajya Sabha and acts as the President when the latter is unable to discharge his functions due to illness, absence or any other reason, or till the election of a new President when a vacancy is caused by the death, resignation or removal of the President.

The Vice-President is elected by an electoral college consisting of the members of both Houses of Parliament in accordance with the system of proportional representation by means of the single transferable vote. He must be a citizen of India, not less than 35 years of age, and should be eligible for election as a member of the Council of States.

PRIME MINISTER OF INDIA

The Prime Minister is the leader of the majority party in the Parliament and the President cannot exercise his discretion in the appointment of the Prime Minister. He stays in office till the majority of the members of Lok Sabha has confidence in him. He occupies an important posi-tion in relation to the council of Ministers. He recommends the names of the persons to be included in the Council of Ministers. He allocates portfolios among them and can ask any minister to tender resignation. He can drop a minister while reshuffling the ministry. He coordinates the administration of various departments. He is the chief link between the President and the Council. He is the leader of the majority party and so, he has a great influence on the Parliament and the party. The Prime Minister enjoys such extensive powers as have been described as the virtual ruler of the country.

THE SOLAR SYSTEM: SOME FACTS

Number of Planets: 8—Mercury, Venus, Earth, Mars, Jupiter, Saturn, Uranus and Neptune.

Largest most

Massive planet .... Jupiter
Brightest planet .... Venus
Brightest star .... Sirius
Fastest orbiting planet .... Mercury
Longest (Synodic) day .... Mercury
Planet with largest moon .... Jupiter
Greatest average density .... Jupiter
Tallest mountain .... Earth
Strongest magnetic fields .... Jupiter
Most circular orbit .... Venus
Shortest (synodic) day .... Jupiter
Hottest planet .... Venus
No moons .... Mercury, Venus
Planet with moon with most eccentric orbit .... Neptune
Lowest average density .... Saturn
Deepest Oceans .... Jupiter
Greatest amount of liquid on the surface .... Earth

THE EARTH: FACTS AND DATA

Composition of the Earth: Aluminium (0.4%), Sulphur (2.7%), Silicon (13%), Oxygen (28%), Calcium (1.2%), Nickel (2.7%), Magnesium (17%), Iron (35%)

Surface area	: 510100500 sq km
Land Surface (29.1%)	: 148950800 sq km
Ocean Surface (70.9%)	: 361149700 sq km
Type of water	: 97% salt, 3% fresh
Total area of water	: 382672000 sq km
Equatorial diameter	: 12753 km
Equatorial Circumference	: 40066 km
Polar Circumference	: 39992 km
Polar diameter	: 12710 km
Equatorial radius	: 6376 km
Polar radius	: 6335 km
Mass (estimated weight)	: 594×10^{19} metric tons
Mean distance from the Sun	: 149407000 km

Earth's orbit speed (around sun)	: 107320 kmph	Time of Rotation (on its axis)	: 23 hrs 56 min 4.09 seconds
Period of Revolution (round the sun)	: 365 days 5 hrs 48 min. 45.51 seconds	Inclination of the axis (to the plane of the ecliptic)	: 23°27'

PRINCIPAL MOUNTAIN PEAKS OF THE WORLD

Mountains	Height in Metres	Range	Date of First Ascent
1. Mount Everest	8,848	Himalayas	May 29, 1953
2. K-2 (Godwin Austen)	8,611	Karakoram	July 31, 1954
3. Kanchenjunga	8,597	Himalayas	May 25, 1955
4. Lhotse	8,511	Himalayas	May 18, 1956
5. Makalu I	8,481	Himalayas	May 15, 1955
6. Dhaulagiri I	8,167	Himalayas	May 13, 1960
7. Mansalu I	8,156	Himalayas	May 9, 1956
8. Chollyo	8,153	Himalayas	Oct. 19, 1954
9. Nanga Parbat	8,124	Himalayas	July 3, 1953
10. Annapurna I	8,091	Himalayas	June 3, 1950
11. Gasherbrum I	8,068	Karakoram	July 5, 1958
12. Broad Peak I	8,047	Karakoram	June 9, 1957
13. Gasherbrum II	8,034	Karakoram	July 7, 1956
14. Shisha Pangma (Gosainthan)	8,014	Himalayas	May 2, 1964
15. Gasherbrum III	7,952	Karakoram	Aug. 11, 1975

POPULAR NICK NAMES OF SOME FAMOUS PERSONALITIES

Andhra Kesari	T. Prakasam
Anna	C.N. Anna Durai
Bang Bandhu	Sheikh Mujibur Rehman
Bapu	Mahatma Gandhi
Bard of Avon	William Shakespeare
Chachaji	Jawaharlal Nehru
Desh Bandhu	C.R. Das
Frontier Gandhi	Khan Abdul Gaffar Khan
Fuhrer	Adolf Hitler
G.B.S.	George Bernard Shaw
Grand Old Man of India	Dadabhai Naoroji
Grand Old Man of Britain	Gladstone
Guru Dev	Rabindra Nath Tagore
Guruji	M.S. Golwalkar
Iron Man of India	Sardar Patel
Lok Nayak	Jayaprakash Narayan
Lady with the Lamp	Florence Nightingale
Lal, Bal, Pal	Lala Lajpat Rai, Bal Gangadhar Tilak, Bipin Chandra Pal
Little Corporal	Napoleon Bonaparte
Lokmanya	Bal Gangadhar Tilak
Mahamana	Pt. Madan Mohan Malaviya
Maid of Orleans	Joan of Arc
Maiden Queen	Queen Elizabeth I
Missile Man	A.P.J. Abdul Kalam
Man of Destiny	Napoleon Bonaparte
Netaji	Subhash Chandra Bose
Nightingale of India	Sarojini Naidu
Panditji	Jawaharlal Nehru
Punjab Kesari	Lala Lajpat Rai
Shastriji	Lal Bahadur Shastri
Uncle Ho	Ho Chi Minh
Wizard of the North	Walter Scott

FAMOUS INTERNATIONAL ORGANISATIONS, HEADQUARTERS	
International Organisations	***Headquarters***
United Nations Organisations (U.N.O.)	New York
International Monetary Fund (I.M.F.)	Washington D.C.
World Health Organisation (W.H.O.)	Geneva
Food & Agricultural Organisation (FAO)	Rome
International Labour Organisation (ILO)	Geneva
UNESCO	Paris
International Court of Justice	The Hague
Universal Postal Union (UPU)	Berne
International Civil Aviation Organisation (ICAO)	Montreal
UNIDO	Vienna
International Atomic Energy Agency (IAEA)	Vienna
International Finance Corporation (IFC)	Washington
United Nations Development Programme (UNDP)	New York
UNICEF	New York
International Maritime Organisation (IMO)	London
World Meteorological Organisation (WMO)	Geneva
International Telecommunication Union (ITU)	Geneva
Arab League	Cairo
Commonwealth of Nations	London
World Trade Organisation (WTO)	Geneva
International Development Association (IDA)	Washington D.C.
International Bank for Reconstruction and Development (IBRD)	Washington D.C.
World Intellectual Property Organisation (WIPO)	Geneva
Organisation of Islamic Conference (OIC)	Jeddah (Saudi Arabia)
European Union	Brussels
Red Cross	Geneva
Interpol	Lyons (France)
Asian Development Bank (ADB)	Manila
North Atlantic Treaty Organisation (NATO)	Brussels
Association of South East Asian Nations (ASEAN)	Jakarta

AWARDS

NOBEL PRIZES

- These Prizes were instituted in 1901 by a Swedish scientist, Dr. Alfred Nobel; the discoverer of Dynamite.
- Six prizes are awarded annually for (*i*) Chemistry, (*ii*) Physics, (*iii*) Medicine, (*iv*) Literature, (*v*) Peace and (*vi*) Economics —started since 1969.
- The following Indians so far have been awarded these prizes: (*i*) Dr. Rabindra Nath Tagore (1913) for his "Geetanjali". (*ii*) Dr. C.V. Raman for Physics in 1930, (*iii*) Mother Teresa for Peace in 1979, (*iv*) Prof. Amartya Sen in 1998 for Economics and (*v*) Kailash Satyarthi in 2014 for Peace.
- In addition, four non-resident Indians have also been awarded the Nobel Prize. They are: (*i*) Hargobind Khurana for Medicine in 1968, (*ii*) Subramanian Chandrasekhar for Physics in 1983, (*iii*) Venkatraman Ramkrishnan for Chemistry in 2009, (*iv*) Abhijit Vinayak Banerjee for Economics in 2019.

BHARAT RATNA

- Bharat Ratna is India's highest Civilian Award. It was first awarded in 1954.
- The actual award is designed in the shape of a *peepal* leaf with Bharat Ratna inscribed in Devanagri script in the Sun Figure.
- This is India's highest civilian award. It is given for exceptional work on art, literature, science and recognition of public service of the highest order.
- The emblem, the Sun and the rim are of platinum. The inscriptions are in burnished bronze.
- Government servants are not eligible for it.

ART AND CULTURE

☞ Classical Dances

Dance	State	Famous Artists
Bharat Natyam	Tamil Nadu	Yamini Krishnamurthy, Rukmini Devi Arundale, Swapna Sundari, Sonal Mansingh, Vaijanti Mala, Mrinalini Sarabhai, Chandralekha, Indrani, Ram Gopal, Bal Saraswati
Kathakali	Keralam	Gopinath, K.K. Nayar, Kunju-Kurup, T.K. Chandu
Kuchipudi	Andhra Pradesh/ Telangana	Sapna Sundari, Raja Reddy, Shobha Nayar, Radha Reddy, Vedantam Satyanarayan, Vimpanti Chinna Satyam.
Kathak	North India	Birju Maharaj, Gopi Krishna, Shambhu Maharaj, Sitara Devi, Vishnu Sharma, Durga Lal, Shobhana Narayan
Odissi	Odisha	Kelucharan Mahapatra, Indrani Rehman, Madhavi Mudgal, Pratima Bedi, Samyukta Panigrahi, Sonal Mansingh, Debudas
Manipuri	Manipur	Uday Shankar, Bipin Singh, Suryamukhi, Darohra Jhaveri

☞ Famous Folk Dances

State/UT	Folk Dance	State/UT	Folk Dance
Andhra Pradesh/ Telangana	Dandari, Banjara	Keralam	Mohini Attam, Padayuni
Assam	Bihu, Keli Gopal, Sataria	Madhya Pradesh	Lota Nritya, Jawara
Bihar	Chhau, Magahi, Durga dance	Maharashtra	Tamasha, Dahi Handi, Gof, Deepak Dindi
W. Bengal	Kirtan, Kalatri, Asweabadh, Brita, Kalidance	Manipur	Dhol Cholam
Chhattisgarh	Saila, Karama, Bhagoria	Meghalaya	Nongakarem
Gujarat	Garba, Rasalila, Tippani, Dandia,	Nagaland	Bamboo dance
Haryana	Damyal, Lahoor	Odisha	Chhau, Maya Shabari, Dalachai
Himachal Pradesh	Dussehra dance, Hikat, Notio	Punjab	Gidda, Bhangra, Panihari
Jammu & Kashmir	Dumhal	Rajasthan	Thumar, Kathaputali, Tera Tali
Jharkhand	Jhau, Ghumakudia, Jadur, Sarhul, Soharai, Karama, Vaima, Loojhari, Jat-Jatin, Vidayat	Tamil Nadu	Terukalathu, Kabalatam, Kargam, Pulivesham
Karnataka	Yakshagan, Dolu Kunitha	Tripura	Hazagiri
		Uttar Pradesh	Rasalila, Nautanki, Thali, Dhurang, Jhumela, Huraka, Bol.
		Uttarakhand	Kajari, Karan
		Goa	Dhode Modini

MUSIC

Main Schools of Classical Music

- There are two main schools of classical music, namely, the Hindustani and the Carnatic. The Hindustani school of classical music is in vogue in north-western India, eastern India and northern parts of the South India.

Musical Instruments

- ***They are:*** Tabla, Mridangam, Pakhawaj, Chandai, Dholak, Veena, Sitar, Sarod, Gootuvachyam, Sarangi, Flute, Nadaswaram, Shehnai, Shringi and Turahi.

FAMOUS INTERNATIONAL AIR SERVICES

Air Service	*Name of Country*	*Air Service*	*Name of Country*
Air India	India	Lufthansa Airlines	Germany
British Overseas Airways Corporation	Britain	Iraqi Airways	Iraq
Trans World Airlines	America	National Airlines	Iran
Russian Airlines	Russia	Quantas Airlines	Australia
Japan Airlines	Japan	Hong-Kong Airlines	Hong-Kong
Pakistan International Airlines	Pakistan	Egypt Airlines	Egypt
Malaysia Airlines	Malaysia	Slovak Airlines	Slovakia
Royal Nepal Airlines	Nepal	S.I.A.	Singapore
Swiss Airways	Switzerland	Garuda Airways	Indonesia
Air France	France	Bangladesh Viman Sewa	Bangladesh
Kuwait Airways	Kuwait	Air Lanka	Sri Lanka
Pan American World Airways	America	Elitalia Airlines	Italy
K.L.M. Royal Airlines	The Netherlands (Holland)	Air Canada	Canada

FAMOUS RELIGIONS, FOUNDERS, HOLY BOOKS & PLACES OF WORSHIP

Religion	*Founder*	*Holy Books*	*Place of Worship*
Hinduism	Hinduism has no one Founder. (This religion is based upon the religion of original Aryan Settlers)	Ramayan, Vedas, Puranas and Geeta	Temple
Sikh	Guru Nanak Dev	Guru Grantha Sahib	Gurdwara
Christianity	Jesus Christ	Bible	Church
Islam	Prophet Mohammed	Koran (Quran)	Mosque
Parsi	Zoroaster	Zend Avesta	Fire Temple
Jainism	Adinath Rishavdev	Jain Granth	Jain Temple
Buddhism	Gautam Buddha	Tripitaka	Buddha Temple
Jew	Moosa	Torah	Synagogue

INTELLIGENCE AGENCIES OF SOME PROMINENT COUNTRIES

Country	*Intelligence Agency*	*Country*	*Intelligence Agency*
India	Research & Analysis Wing (RAW), Intelligence Bureau (I.B.), Central Bureau of Investigation (C.B.I.)	Russia	K.G.B. (Komitel Gosudarstvennoy Bezopasnosty) (Committee for State Security)
Pakistan	Inter Service Intelligence (I.S.I.)	Canada	Security Intelligence Service
U.S.A.	Central Intelligence Agency, Federal Bureau of Investigation	S. Africa	Bureau of State Security
		Iran	Sabak
Britain	Military Intelligence (M.I.)-5 and 6, Special Branch, Ultra, Joint Intelligence Organisation	Iraq	Al-Mukhabarat
		Australia	Australian Security and Intelligence Organisation
Israel	Mosad	France	S.D.E.C.E.
Egypt	Mukhabarat	Spain	C.E.S.I.D.
Japan	Nicho	Cuba	D.G.I.

SOME PROMINENT RACES OF THE WORLD

Races	Country/Area	Races	Country/Area	Races	Country/Area	Races	Country/Area
Veddas	Sri Lanka	Pygmy	Congo Basin	Eskimo	Canada, Tundra Region	Bushman	Kalahari Desert
Somaid	West Siberia	Bantu	Central and South Africa	Lapps	European Tundra	Red Indian	North America
Masai	East Africa	Tartars	Siberia	Hausa	Nigeria		
Muree	New Zealand	Baddu	Arab's Desert	Kirghiz	Steppes (Russia)		
Yakoot	Russian Tundra	Semang	Malaysia				
Papuans	New Guyana						

FAMOUS STRAITS OF THE WORLD

Strait	Between	Country
Malacca Strait	Andaman Sea and South China Sea	Indonesia
Palk Strait	Mannar and Bay of Bengal	India-Sri Lanka
Magellan Strait	Pacific and South Atlantic Ocean	Chile
Dover Strait	English Channel and North Sea	England-France
Berring Strait	Berring Sea and Chukasi Sea	Alaska-Russia
Sugaroo Strait	Japan Sea and Pacific Ocean	Japan
Sunda Strait	Java and Indian Ocean	Indonesia
Gibralter Strait	Mediterranean Sea and Atlantic Ocean	Spain
Harmuj Strait	Persia and Bay of Oman	Oman-Iran
Hudson Strait	Bay of Hudson and Atlantic Ocean	Canada

FAMOUS NEWSPAPERS OF THE WORLD

Newspaper	Place of Publishing	Language
Daily News	New York (America)	English
Guardian	London (Britain)	English
Pravada	Moscow (Russia)	Russian
Al-Ahram	Cairo (Egypt)	Arabic
Merdeca	Jakarta (Indonesia)	Indonesian
Times	London (Britain)	English
People's Daily	Beijing (China)	Chinese
New Statesman	Britain	English
Daily Mirror	Britain	English
Hindu, Hindustan, Times of India, Tribune, Statesman, Indian Express, Economic Times	India	English
Hindustan, Nav Bharat Times, Dainik Bhaskar, Dainik Jagaran, Punjab Kesari	India	Hindi

IMPORTANT BOUNDARY LINES

Boundary Line	Countries
Durand Line	Pakistan and Afghanistan
Hindenberg Line	Germany-Poland
Maginot Line	France and Germany
Mannerhein Line	Russia-Finland
Mc Mahon Line	India-China
Order Niesse Line	Germany-Poland
Radcliff Line	India-Pakistan
Seigfrid Line	Germany-France
24th Parallel	India-Pakistan
17th Parallel	The line which defined the boundary between North Vietnam and South Vietnam before the two were united.
38th Parallel	North Korea and South Korea
49th Parallel	U.S.A. and Canada

SIGNALS/SIGNS AND MEANING

Signal/Sign	*Meaning*	*Signal/Sign*	*Meaning*
Red Triangle	Family Planning	White Flag	Treaty or Surrender
Red Cross	Medical Help	Yellow Flag	Vehicles with patients of contagious diseases
Red Light	Danger, 'Stop' for the movement of vehicles	Two Bones across with a Skull	Danger of electricity
Green Light	Go		
Olive Branch	Peace	Half mast flown Flag	National mourning
White Pigeon or Dove	Peace	Lotus and culture	Sign of civilization
Black Strip on Arm	(i) Opposition (ii) Sorrow	Wheel (Chakra)	Sign of Progress
Black Flag	Opposition	A blind folded woman with scale in hand	Sign of Justice
Red Flag	(i) Danger (ii) Revolution	Reversed flown	National calamity flag

NATIONAL EMBLEMS OF IMPORTANT COUNTRIES

Country	*National Emblem*	*Country*	*National Emblem*
America	Golden Rod	New Zealand	Kiwi, Fern Southern Cross
Australia	Kangaroo	Norway	Lion
Ireland	Shamrock	Nepal	Kukri
Italy	White Lily	Pakistan	Crescent
Israel	Candelabrum	Poland	Eagle
Iran	Rose	France	Lily
Canada	White Lily	Belgium	Lion
Great Britain	Rose	Bangladesh	Water Lily
Chile	Candor and Huemul	Mongolia	The Soyombo
Germany	Corn Flower	Russia	Double headed eagle
Japan	Chrysanthemum	Lebanon	Cedar Tree
Zimbabwe	Zimbabwe Bird	Sudan	Secretary Bird
Denmark	Beach	Syria	Eagle
Turkiye	Crescent and Star	India	Lioned Capital
The Netherlands	Lion		

THE CONTINENTS OF THE WORLD

Name	*Population (2021) (In million)*	*Per cent of the world's population*
Asia	4,584	59.1
Africa	1,375	17.4
Europe	747	9.8
North America	373	4.8
South America	651	8.4
Australia	41.66	0.5
Antarctica	NA	NA

COMPUTER

The computer is the system of that electronic device through which various informations are processed on the basis of a definite set of instructions called program and mathematical (numerical) and non-mathematical both types of informations are processed.

The first mechanical computer was composed or fabricated by Blaise Pascal in 1642 and it is called Pascalene. But in 1833, Charles Babbage first time conceived an automatic calculator or computer. Charles Babbage is called the father of modern computer. Herman made an electronic tabulating machine based on punch cards which operates automatically.

In 1937, first mechanical computer mark-I was fabricated by Howard Akeen. The most outstanding contribution in the development of modern computer goes to John Wan Newmaan who brought the 2nd revolution in the area of computer in 1951. He discovered EDVAC (Electronic Discrete Variable Automatic Computer) and utilised the stored program and the binary number system in the computer.

FUNCTIONS OF COMPUTER

1. Collection and composition (input) of datas;
2. Storage of datas.
3. Processing of datas.
4. Retrieval or output of the proccessed informations and datas.

UNITS OF COMPUTER

1. Input unit.
2. Central processing unit–CPU.
3. External Memory unit.
4. Output unit.

The CPU of the computer is called brain of the computer and sometimes CPU is also called Micro Processor of the computer. The data is entered through the input unit in the computer and through the central processing unit with the help of External Memory Unit datas are arranged and processed. Ultimately by the output unit these datas or informations are issued or released.

PARTS OF COMPUTER

- **Monitor :** The monitor of the computer is like a television in which the picture appears in the form of doted points on the screen and these are called pixcels.
- **Hard Disc and Floppy Disc :** The Hard Disc is the permanent disc in the computers while the Floppy Disc is the disc utilised when datas or informations are to be transferred from one computer to another.
- **Mouse :** The mouse of the computer is like the remote control of TV through which computer is directly regulated or controlled without utilising the key-board.
- **Printer :** The printer is a device which prints any documents or processed informations of the computer.

SOME HIGH LEVEL LANGUAGES

1. **FORTRAN :** This language was developed for solving the mathematical formulae very quickly and conveniently.
2. **COBOL :** This language was developed for the commerical purposes. For the processing of this language a group of sentences is selected called paragraph and all paragraphs composed are called a section, while all sections composed are called a division.
3. **BASIC :** In basic a definite part of the prescribed instruction is only inserted in the computer.
4. **ALGOL :** This was basically fabricated and designed for the complex algebraic calculations.
5. **PASCAL :** It is an amplified and modified form of ALGOL.
6. **COMAL :** This computer language is used for the students of secondary level.
7. **LOGO :** This language is used for children and kids for drawing Graphic line diagrams.
8. **PROLOG :** This language is developed in 1973 in France and this language is used for Artificial Intelligence which is capable and equivalent to the logical program.

9. **FORTH :** This language was invented by Charles Mure which is frequently used in all types of the works in the computer.

COMPUTER VIRUS

The computer virus is an electronic code which is used to abolish or erradicate the inclusive informations or programs of the computer. Some important computer viruses are Micheleanjalo, Dork Avangor, kilo, filip, Macmug, Scores, Casecade, Jeruslem, Date crime, Coloumbs crime, Internet virus, Pachcom, Pach EXE, COM-EXE, Marizuana, C-brain, bloody, Chenge Mungu and Desi etc.

COMPUTER NETWORKING

There are two types of networkings which are usually occur—Local Area Networking (LAN) and Wide Area Networking (WAN). By LAN all the computers of the same buildings are connected like the computers of university premises, computers of offices etc.

By WAN all the comptuers of a large area are connected like the computers of all the offices of a city or town etc. In India a very large computer network namely INDONET has been installing through which all the main towns and cities has to be interlinked.

COMPUTER TERMINOLOGY

- **Bit :** The bit is a unit of measurement of the electronic data. One bit is either 0 or 1 but not both. On composing 8 bits, 1 byte is formed.
- **Bug :** The Bug is the error in the computer program or system and its eradication is called Debug.
- **Byte :** Total eight bits compose a byte. Thus 8 bits = 1 byte.
- **CD-ROM :** A CD like of music CD in which data can be stored substantially called CD-ROM. In a CD with comparison to floppy extremely more datas can be stored but one problem in it is that one time recorded data can not be deleted or modified.
- **Chip :** It is a thin slice on which by a special mechanism a circuit is designed which is normally made from Silicon.
- **Memory System :** The place where computer data and program are temporarily kept is called Memory system. Usually memory is implied from RAM.
- **Modem :** The device which converts digital signals into analogue signals and vice-versa is called Modem.
- **RAM :** It is Random Access Memory (a place) where datas to be processed are kept temporarily and it is unstable memory.
- **ROM :** It is Read Only Memory and it is stable or Non-valatile memory which doesn't ended after power off.
- **Scanner :** It is a device through which graphic image is transformed to digital image and the scanners are of usually two types one desktop and another hand operating.

PROGRAMING

Computers perform phenomenal feats of calculation, but they do not do so in a complicated way. They actually carry out very simple operations, such as addition and subtraction. They achieve their fantastic computing power by carrying out these operations at incredible speed.

The programme, or set of instructions for operating the computer, is therefore written as a sequence of very simple steps. (See box below) Several computer languages have been developed for different applications, including BASIC, COBOL, FORTRAN and PASCAL. Writing programmes is very skilled and time-consuming work. But for most typical computer applications ready-written programmes are available, called "packages".

☞ How A Programme Works

Without a programme to tell it what to do and how to do it, a computer is unable to function. If, for example, you wanted to know how many times the word 'the' appears in this paragraph, or in the whole book, it would not be enough merely to put the text into a computer and then ask it how many times the word appears. For the computer to accomplish the calculations it has to be told what to do in simple steps. The instructions might be:

1. Scan the text until a space followed by 'T' or 't' is found.
2. If the next letter is not 'h', go back to step 1.
3. If the letter is 'h', is the next letter 'e'?
4. If not, go back to step 1. If it is, go to step 5.
5. If 'e' is followed by a space, add 1 to the total.
6. Go back to step 1.

A full computer programme for this operation would need to be broken down into even more simple steps, but a series of such programmes could enable a computer to analyse any amount of text in great detail.

DEFENCE

The Supreme Command of the Armed Forces is vested in the hands of the President of the Country. The responsibility for national defence, however, rests with the Cabinet. All important questions having a bearing on defence are decided by the Cabinet Committee on Political Affairs, which is presided over by the Prime Minister. The Defence Minister is responsible to Parliament for all matters concerning the Defence Services. All the administrative and operational control of Armed Forces are exercised by the Ministry of Defence. The three services – Army, Navy and Air Force function through their respective service headquarters headed by the chief of Staff.

COMMISSIONED RANKS IN DEFENCE SERVICES

Army	*Navy*	*Air Force*
General	Admiral	Air Chief Marshal
Lieutenant-General	Vice-Admiral	Air Marshal
Major-General	Rear-Admiral	Air Vice-Marshal
Brigadier	Commodor	Air Commodor
Colonel	Captain	Group Captain
Lieutenant-Colonel	Commander	Wing Commander
Major	Lt.Commander	Squadron Leader
Captain	Lieutenant	Flight Lieutenant
Lieutenant	Sub-Lieutenant	Flying Officer

INTERNAL SECURITY ORGANISATIONS OF INDIA

S. No	*Name of Organisation*	*Year of Creation*	*Headquarters*
1.	Assam Rifles (A.R.)	1835	Shillong
2.	Central Reserve Police Force (C.R.P.F.)	1939	New Delhi
3.	National Cadet Corps (N.C.C.)	1948	New Delhi
4.	Territorial Army	1948	In different States
5.	Indo-Tibetan Border Police	1962	New Delhi
6.	Home Guard	1962	In different States
7.	Coast Guard	1978	New Delhi
8.	Border Security Force (B.S.F.)	1965	New Delhi
9.	Central Industrial Security Force (C.I.S.F.)	1969	New Delhi
10.	National Security Guard	1984	New Delhi
11.	Police	—	In different States

COMMANDER-IN-CHIEFS OF INDIA

1. General Sir Rob Lockhart	Aug. 15, 1947 — Dec. 31, 1947
2. General Sir Roy Bucher	Jan. 1, 1948 — Jan. 14, 1949
3. General K. M. Kariappa	Jan. 15, 1949 — Jan. 14, 1953
4. General Maharaj Rajendra Sinhji	Jan. 15, 1953 — March 31, 1955

FIRST INDIAN CHIEFS OF STAFF OF INDIAN FORCES

1. General Maharaj Rajendra Sinhji (Army Staff)	April 1, 1955 — May 14, 1955
2. Vice Admiral R.D. Katari (Naval Staff)	April 22, 1958 — June 4, 1962
3. Air Marshal S. Mukherjee (Air Staff)	April 1, 1954 — Nov. 8, 1960

ARMY INSTITUTES

1. Sainik Schools upto +2 Level	33 places in India
2. Rashtriya Indian Military College (prepare for entrance to N.D.A)	Dehradun
3. National Defence Academy (three services)	Khadakwasla, Pune
4. Indian Military Academy (Army)	Dehradun
5. Officers Training Academy (3 services) Short Courses	Chennai
6. National Defence College	New Delhi
7. The College of Combat	Mhow
8. The College of Military Engineering	Kirkee
9. Military College of Telecommunication Engineering	Mhow
10. The armoured Corps Centre and School	Ahmed Nagar
11. The School Artillery	Deolali
12. The Infantry School	Mhow and Belgaum
13. College of Material Management	Jabalpur

AIR FORCE INSTITUTIONS

Air Force Academy	Hyderabad
Helicopter Training School	Hakimpet
Flying Instructors School	Tambaram, Chennai
The College of Air Warfare	Secunderabad
Air Force Administrative College	Coimbatore
Air Force Technical College	Jalahalli

DEFENCE PRODUCTION UNITS

1. Bharat Dynamites Ltd.	Hyderabad
2. Praga Tools	Hyderabad
3. Mishra Dattu Nigam	Hyderabad
4. Bharat Electronics Ltd.	Bangalore
5. Bharath Earthmovers Ltd.	Bangalore
6. Heavy Vehicles Ltd.	Avadi, Chennai
7. Garden Reach Ship Builders and Engineers Ltd.	Kolkata
8. Mazagaon Dock	Mumbai
9. Goa Shipyard	Marmugao
10. Hindustan Shipyard Ltd.	Vishakhapatnam
11. Hindustan Aeronautics Ltd.	Bangalore, Hyderabad, Nasik, Koraput, Kanpur, Lucknow

☞ Indian Army Commands

Command	HQ Location	Command	HQ Location
Eastern Command	Kolkata	Western Command	Chandigarh
Northern Command	Udhampur	Southern Command	Pune
Central Command	Lucknow	Training Command	Shimla
South-Western Command	Jaipur		

☞ Indian Air Force Commands

Command	HQ Location	Command	HQ Location
Western Air Command	New Delhi	South-Western Air Command	Gandhinagar
Central Air Command	Prayagraj	Eastern Air Command	Shillong
Southern Air Command	Thiruvananthapuram	Training Command	Bengaluru

☞ Indian Navy Commands

Command	HQ Location	Command	HQ Location
Eastern Naval Command	Vishakhapatnam	Western Naval Command	Mumbai
Southern Naval Command	Kochi		

☞ Missile and Other Weapons

Name	Class	Range
✶ Agni I	SRBM	850 km
✶ Agni II	MRBM	2500 km
✶ Agni III	IRBM	3500 km-5500 km
✶ Agni IV *or* Agni II Prime	IRBM	4000 km
✶ Agni V	ICBM	5000 km-6000 km
✶ Agni VI	ICBM	8000 km-10000 km
✶ Agni 3SL	ICBM	5200 km-11600 km
✶ Dhanush	SRBM	350 km
✶ Nirbhay	Subsonic Cruise Missile	1000 km

Name	Class	Range
✶ Brahmos	Supersonic Cruise Missile	290 km
✶ Brahmos 2	Hypersonic Cruise Missile	290 km
✶ Prithvi I	SRBM	150 km
✶ Prithvi III	SRBM	350 km
✶ Sagarika	SLBM	700 km-2200 km
✶ Shaurya	TBM	700 km-2200 km
✶ Astra	Air to Air Missile	80 km-100 km
✶ Barak-I	SRSAM	12 km
✶ Barak-8	SRSAM	90 km

☞ Chief of Defence Staff (CDS)

To bring in reform in higher defence management in the country, the post of Chief of Defence Staff (CDS) was created in the rank of a four-star General with salary and prerequisites equivalent to a Service Chief. The Chief of Defence Staff will also head the Department of Military Affairs (DMA), to be created within the Ministry of Defence and functions as its Secretary. Gen. Bipin Rawat was the first CDS of the country from January 1, 2020 to December 08, 2021.

MULTIPLE CHOICE QUESTIONS

1. Match List-I with List-II and select the correct answer from the codes given below the lists:

List-I

(*a*) Napoleon Bonaparte
(*b*) Jean Jacques Rousseau
(*c*) Croce
(*d*) Madame Roland

List-II

1. 'A history is contemporary history'
2. 'Liberty what crimes are committed in thy name'
3. 'Man is born free but everywhere he is in chains.'
4. 'I am the Child of Revolution'

Codes :

	(*a*)	(*b*)	(*c*)	(*d*)
A.	1	2	3	4
B.	4	3	1	2
C.	3	4	2	1
D.	3	4	1	2

2. Abraham Lincon was elected the President of United States in:
A. 1862 B. 1860
C. 1875 D. 1855

3. Who was known as the 'Prince of Humanists'?
A. Francisco Petrarch B. Dante
C. Boccacio D. Erasmus

4. D-Day is the day when:
A. Germany declared war on Britain
B. US dropped the atom bomb on Hiroshima.
C. Allied Troops landed in Normandy
D. Germany surrendered to the allies

5. Whose teachings inspired the French Revolution?
A. Locke
B. Rousseau
C. Hegel
D. Plato

6. At a time when empires in Europe were crumbling before the might of Napoleon which one of the following Governor-Generals kept the British flag flying high in India?
A. Warren Hastings B. Lord Cornwallis
C. Lord Wellesley D. Lord Hastings

7. Which one of the following statements regarding Fascism in Italy is *not* true?
A. The Fascists came to power as a result of popular uprising
B. In 1926, all political parties except Mussolini's party were banned
C. The Fascists suppressed the Socialist movement
D. The Fascists were hostile to the Communists

8. The fall of Czar Nicholas-II is known as:
A. Bloody Sunday
B. Bolshevik Revolution
C. February Revolution
D. October Revolution

9. Industrial Revolution took place first in:
A. France B. Germany
C. United Kingdom D. Japan

10. The British Prime Minister at the outbreak of World War II was :
A. Churchill B. Baldwin
C. Attlee D. Chemberlain

11. The 'Great Depression' (1929) economic crisis was met by adopting the policy of
A. Stimulus B. Marshall Plan
C. New Deal D. Open Door

12. The slogan "No taxation without representation" was raised during the:
A. American War of Independence
B. Russian Revolution
C. French Revolution
D. Indian Freedom struggle

1741 (GA)–4

13. In the nineteenth century the people of Europe started moving from the villages to the cities due to the impact of :
A. Epidemics
B. War
C. Industrialisation
D. Population explosion in villages

14. The important cause of the Civil War in America was:
A. Abolition of slavery
B. Quest for freedom
C. Industrialisation
D. Rebellion by the native Americans

15. Industrial Revolution could not have come about without:
A. Merchant capitalism
B. The Enclosure Movement
C. The services of the proletariat class
D. An agricultural revolution

16. Consider the following statements :
The French Revolution came about mainly due to the :
1. Extreme poverty of the people
2. Impact of the works of great writers
3. Cruelty of the rulers
4. Impact of impulsive reaction
Which of the above statements are correct?
A. 1, 2 and 4 B. 2 and 3
C. 1, 3 and 4 D. 1, 2, 3 and 4

17. Asia's oldest and largest Buddhist monastery is situated in :
A. Tawang (Arunachal Pardesh)
B. Lhasa (Tibet)
C. Trincomallee (Sri Lanka)
D. Ulan Bator (Mongolia)

18. Who was the main architect of the Russian Revolution?
A. Karl Marx B. Lenin
C. Stalin D. Tolstoy

19. V.I. Lenin is associated with :
A. Russian Revolution of 1917
B. Chinese Revolution of 1949
C. German Revolution
D. French Revolution of 1789

20. Which one of the following statements is *not* correct?
A. Voltaire believed in Natural Religion
B. Rousseau wrote *Social Contract*
C. Montesquieu authored *The Spirit of Laws*
D. Necker believed in 'General Will'

21. 6th April, 1930 is well known in the history of India because this date is associated with...........
A. Dandi March by Mahatma Gandhi
B. Quit India Movement
C. Partition of Bengal
D. Partition of India

22. Which ruler enforced the system of 'Price Control' in India?
A. Mohammad Tughlak
B. Razia Begum
C. Alauddin Khilji
D. Sher Shah Suri

23. The concept of 'Din-e-Elahi' was founded by which king?
A. Dara Shikoh B. Akbar
C. Sher Shah Suri D. Shahjahan

24. Who are supposed to be the earliest inhabitants of India? Where did they come from?
A. Aryans from Central Asia
B. Dravidians from Mediterranean
C. Negroids from Africa
D. Bhils and the Santhals from West Asia

25. The one chief characteristic of temple architecture of the Gupta Age was :
A. Absence of dome
B. Huge size
C. Beautiful carvings
D. absence of a covered courtyard for the gathering of worshippers

26. The Rigveda consists of :
A. 1000 hymns B. 2028 hymns
C. 1028 hymns D. 1038 hymns

27. The central point in Ashoka's dharma was :
A. royalty to kings
B. peace and non-violence
C. respect to elders
D. religious tolerance

28. The social evil which was conspicuously absent during ancient India was :

A. *Sati*-System B. *Devadasi*-System
C. Polygamy D. *Purdah*-System

29. Which, among the following, can be accepted as a novelty introduced by Mughal emperors to their buildings?

A. Domes B. Minarets
C. Arches D. Attached gardens

30. The first ruler of India who defeated Muhammud of Ghur was :

A. Mularaja II of Gujarat
B. Prithviraja Chauhan of Delhi
C. Jayachand of Kannauj
D. Parmaldeva of Bundelkhand

31. What important event happened in India in 1911?

A. Bengal was partitioned
B. Non-Cooperation movement was launched
C. India's capital was shifted from Calcutta to Delhi
D. Mahatma Gandhi presided over the Congress session

32. The first phase of the Congress Party (1885-1905) was characterized by its efforts to secure:

A. limited independence
B. complete freedom
C. Indianization of services
D. constitutional reforms

33. The Muslim League demanded a separate homeland for the Indian Muslims openly for the first time at its annual session held in Lahore in the year :

A. 1931 A.D. B. 1936 A.D.
C. 1940 A.D. D. 1941 A.D.

34. Under whose governorship did the East India Company secure the Diwani Rights in Bengal, Bihar and Odisha from Emperor Shah Alam?

A. Lord Cornwallis
B. Lord William Bentinck
C. Lord Clive
D. Lord Wellesley

35. The Simon Commission was generally boycotted by the Indian political parties. What was the reason for this general non-cooperation?

A. the Commission aimed at dividing the people
B. it was an 'all white' Commission
C. it came after the Jallianwala Bagh carnage
D. it was an eye wash

36. Aligarh Muslim University was founded by :

A. Dr. Saifuddin Kitchlu
B. Mohammad Ali Jinnah
C. Sir Syed Ahmed Khan
D. Maulana Mohammad Ali

37. Ibn Batutah was an African traveller visiting India during the time of :

A. Alivardi Khan
B. Ala-ud-din Khalji
C. Iltutmish
D. Mohammad-bin-Tughlaq

38. The battle of Wandiawash was fought in :

A. 1726 B. 1760
C. 1818 D. 1857

39. The abolition of *Sati* by government regulation was at the time of :

A. Warren Hastings B. Lord Wellesley
C. Lord Bentinck D. Lord Ahmerst

40. Pick out the wrong combination :

A. Dilwara Temple : Mt. Abu
B. Pashupati Temple : Kathmandu
C. Padmanabh Temple : Bangalore
D. Minakshi Temple : Madurai

41. Match the following:

(*a*) Chanhudaro (*b*) Kalibangan
(*c*) Lothal (*d*) Surkotada

1. Alleged discovery of the skeleton of horse.
2. Bead making.
3. Traces of a dock and ship on seal.
4. Evidence of ploughing the fields.

The Correct code is :

	(*a*)	(*b*)	(*c*)	(*d*)
A.	2	4	3	1
B.	2	1	3	4
C.	1	2	3	4
D.	2	1	4	3

42. Match the Harappan settlements with the banks of rivers on which they were located :

(*a*) Harappa	1. Ravi
(*b*) Mohenjodaro	2. Indus
(*c*) Ropar	3. Sutlej
(*d*) Kalibangan	4. Ghaggar
(*e*) Lothal	5. Bhogava

Codes :

	(*a*)	(*b*)	(*c*)	(*d*)	(*e*)
A.	1	2	3	4	5
B.	1	2	3	5	4
C.	2	1	3	5	4
D.	2	1	4	3	5

43. The Goddess 'Kannagi' whose many temples were erected during the 'Sangam Age' was the goddess of :

A. Chastity B. Love
C. Prowess D. Wisdom

44. The Jain goal of life is to attain deliverance from the fetters of mudane existence, the way to which lies through three jewels. Which one of the following was not included among the 'three jewels' of Jainism?

A. Right faith B. Right action
C. Right knowledge D. Right conduct

45. The most striking feature of the Ashokan pillar is polish. Name the Ashokan pillar which is considered to be the most graceful of all Ashokan pillars.

A. Sarnath
B. Rampurva
C. Laurya-Nandangarh
D. Rummindei

46. Which are the correct statements?

1. The land grants, started in Satavahana period, paved the way for feudal developments in India.
2. Silk and spices were the Chief Indian export articles of Indo-Roman trade.
3. The Guptas issued the largest number of gold coins in ancient India.
4. The first memorial of a 'SATI' dated 510 A.D. is found at Eran in Madhya Pradesh.

A. 1 and 2 B. 1, 3, and 4
C. 1 and 4 D. 1, 2, 3 and 4

47. Who among the following patronised the 'Gandhara' (Indo-Greek style) School of Art?

A. Ashoka, the Great
B. Harsha Vardhana
C. Kanishka
D. Chandragupta Vikramaditya

48. The Sultanate of Delhi had five ruling dynasties. The dynasty having longest and shortest period were :

A. Ilbari and Khalji
B. Tughlaq and Khalji
C. Tughlaq and Sayyid
D. Ilbari and Lodis

49. Which one of the following events took place at the last during reign of Muhammad-bin-Tughlaq?

A. Introduction of token currency
B. Increase of land-revenue in Doab
C. Transfer of Capital from Delhi to Devagiri.
D. Conquest of Khurasan and Iraq

50. The most learned medieval Muslim ruler who was well versed in various branches of learning including astronomy, mathematics and medicine was :

A. Jalaluddin Khilji
B. Sikander Lodi
C. Ghiyasuddin Tughlaq
D. Muhammad-bin-Tughlaq

51. The 'Sufis' had 12 silsilas. They propounded the idea of Union with God through:

A. Love B. Rituals
C. Fasts D. Prayers

52. Match the following:

(*a*) Peshwa	1. Foreign affairs
(*b*) Panditrao	2. Audit and accounts
(*c*) Amatya	3. Providing grants to scholars
(*d*) Sumant	4. General supervision
	5. Military affairs

Select the correct code :

	(*a*)	(*b*)	(*c*)	(*d*)
A.	2	3	4	5
B.	4	1	2	3
C.	4	3	2	1
D.	3	1	4	2

53. The Regulating Act of 1773 can be regarded as the first measure to :
A. assert the right of British Parliament to legislate for India
B. separate the legislature from the executive
C. separate the judiciary from the executive
D. centralise law-making

54. What was the exact constitutional status of the Indian Republic on 26th January, 1950?
A. A Democratic Republic
B. A Sovereign, Democratic Republic
C. A Sovereign, Secular, Democratic Republic
D. A Sovereign, Socialist, Secular, Democratic Republic

55. When the British obtained the grant of Diwani of Bengal, Bihar and Odisha they acquired the right to :
A. maintain law and order in these territories
B. administer civil justice and collect revenue in these territories
C. collect revenue and establish revenue administration in these territories
D. militarily defend these territories

56. Which of the following were responsible for the growth of nationalism in India during the British rule?
1. Economic exploitation of India.
2. Impact of western education.
3. Role of the Press.
Select the correct answer using the codes given below :
Codes:
A. 1, 2 and 3 B. 1 and 2
C. 2 and 3 D. 1 and 3

57. Which one of the following nationalist leaders has been described as being radical in politics but conservative on social issues?
A. G.K. Gokhale
B. B.G. Tilak
C. Lala Lajpat Rai
D. Madan Mohan Malviya

58. Provincial Autonomy in British India was envisaged by the :
A. Act of 1909 B. Act of 1919
C. Act of 1935 D. Act of 1947

59. Dyarchy means :
A. double government
B. a government in which the centre is very powerful
C. a government based on division of power between centre and provinces
D. None of the above

60. The Indian National Congress observed 'Independence Day' for the first time on 26th January in :
A. 1920 B. 1925
C. 1930 D. 1947

61. ....is situated near the banks of Sabarmati River
A. Bhavnagar B. Aurangabad
C. Ahmedabad D. Rajkot

62. Sericulture is:
A. science of the various kinds of serum
B. artificial rearing of fish
C. art of silkworm breeding
D. study of various cultures of a community

63. The most abundant constituents of earth's crust are:
A. Igneous rocks
B. Sedimentary rocks
C. Metamorphic rocks
D. Granite

64. Indian Standard Time is based on:
A. 80°E longitude B. 82½°E longitude
C. 110°E longitude D. 25°E longitude

65. Tides in the oceans are caused by :
A. Gravitational pull of the moon on the earth's surface including sea water
B. Gravitational pull of the sun on the earth's surface only and not on the sea water
C. Gravitational pull of the moon and the sun on the earth's surface including the sea water
D. None of these

66. Nagarjunasagar Project is situated on the river:
A. Tungabhadra
B. Cauvery
C. Krishna
D. Godavari

67. The difference between the Indian Standard Time and the Greenwich Mean Time is:
A. – 3½ hours B. + 3½ hours
C. – 5½ hours D. + 5½ hours

68. Which of the following dams is not on Narmada river?
A. Indira-Sagar Project
B. Maheshwar Hydel Power Project
C. Jobat Project
D. Koyna Power Project

69. Which of the following statements is **not true** about the availability of water on the earth, the crisis for which is going to increase in the years to come?
A. About 97.5 per cent of the total volume of water available on the earth is salty
B. 80 per cent of the water available to us for use comes in bursts as monsoons
C. About 2.5 per cent of the total water available on the earth is polluted water and cannot be used for human activities
D. Possibility is that some big glaciers will melt in the coming ten-fifteen years and sea level will rise by 3-4 metres all over the earth

70. Which of the following is **not** a cash crop?
A. Jute B. Paddy
C. Cashewnut D. Sugarcane

71. Through which States does Cauvery River flow?
A. Gujarat, M.P., Tamil Nadu
B. Karnataka, Keralam, Tamil Nadu
C. Karnataka, Keralam, Andhra Pradesh
D. M.P., Maharashtra, Tamil Nadu

72. Indian Standard Time is the local time of 82½ºE which passes through :
A. Guntur B. Delhi
C. Prayagraj D. Kolkata

73. The 17th parallel defines the boundary between:
A. North and South Korea
B. USA and Canada
C. North and South Vietnam
D. China and Russia

74. During the period of south-west monsoon, Tamil Nadu remains dry because:
A. the winds do not reach this area
B. there are no mountains in this area
C. it lies in the rain shadow area
D. the temperature is too high to let the winds cool down

75. Which country does top in producing cocoa?
A. Cote d'Ivoire B. Brazil
C. Croatia D. Nigeria

76. The biggest reserves of thorium are in :
A. India B. China
C. The Soviet Union D. U.S.A.

77. The Girnar Hills are situated in which of the following states?
A. Gujarat B. Karnataka
C. Madhya Pradesh D. Maharashtra

78. During December 22nd the sun is vertically over:
A. Tropic of Cancer
B. Tropic of Capricorn
C. The Equator
D. None of the above

79. Photosphere is described as the :
A. Lower layer of atmosphere
B. Visible surface of the sun from which radiation emanates
C. Wavelength of solar spectrum
D. None of the above

80. Broadly, there are three layers of the earth of the crust, the mantle and the core. The crust forms what percentage of the volume of the earth?
A. 0.5% B. 2.5%
C. 7.5% D. 12.5%

81. The grassland of Argentina is known as :
A. Pampas B. Campos
C. Savanna D. None of the above

82. Different seasons are formed because :
A. Sun is moving around the earth
B. of revolution of the earth around the Sun on its orbit
C. of rotation of the earth around its axis
D. All of the above

83. Eskers and Drumlins are features formed by:
A. underground water
B. running water
C. the action of wind
D. glacial action

84. Match List-I and List-II and select the correct answer using the codes given below the Lists :

List-I *(Rivers)*	**List-II** *(Towns)*
(*a*) Ghaghara	1. Lucknow
(*b*) Brahmaputra	2. Hoshangabad
(*c*) Narmada	3. Ahmedabad
(*d*) Sabarmati	4. Guwahati
	5. Ayodhya

	(*a*)	(*b*)	(*c*)	(*d*)
A.	4	5	1	2
B.	5	4	2	3
C.	5	4	3	1
D.	3	5	2	1

85. Which of the statements as regards the consequences of the movement of the earth is not correct?
A. Revolution of the earth is the cause of the change of seasons.
B. Rotation of the earth is the cause of days and nights.
C. Rotation of the earth causes variation in the duration of days and nights.
D. Rotation of the earth effects the movement of winds and ocean currents.

86. The world is divided into :
A. 12 time zones
B. 20 time zones
C. 24 time zones
D. 36 time zones

87. The 'Kiel' canal links the :
A. Pacific and Atlantic Oceans
B. Mediterranean Sea and Red Sea
C. Mediterranean Sea and Black Sea
D. North Sea and Baltic Sea

88. Match the following :

List-I	**List-II**
(*a*) Himadri	1. Outer Himalayas
(*b*) Shivalik	2. Inner Himalayas
(*c*) Himanchal	3. Middle Himalayas
(*d*) Sahyadri	4. Western Ghats

Codes:

	(*a*)	(*b*)	(*c*)	(*d*)
A.	1	2	3	4
B.	4	2	3	1
C.	2	1	3	4
D.	1	2	3	4

89. The term 'Regur' refers to:
A. Laterite soils
B. Black Cotton soils
C. Red Soils
D. Deltaic Alluvial Soils

90. Location of sugar industry in India is shifting from north to south because of:
A. cheap labour
B. expanding regional market
C. cheap and abundant supply of power
D. high yield and high sugar content in sugarcane

91. Consider the following statements :
1. Ozone is found mostly in the Stratosphere.
2. Ozone layer lies 55-75 km above the surface of the earth.
3. Ozone absorbs ultraviolet radiation from the Sun.
4. Ozone layer has no significance for life on the earth.

Which of the above statements are correct?
A. 1 and 3 B. 2 and 4
C. 2 and 3 D. 1 and 4

92. Match List-I with List-II and select the correct answer using the codes given below the Lists :

List-I *(Crops)*	**List-II** *(Producer)*
(*a*) Banana	1. Brazil
(*b*) Cocoa	2. Cote d'Ivoire
(*c*) Coffee	3. India
(*d*) Tea	4. China

Codes :

	(*a*)	(*b*)	(*c*)	(*d*)
A.	2	3	1	4
B.	3	2	1	4
C.	3	2	4	1
D.	2	3	4	1

93. Darjeeling and Dharamsala would be the right places to visit if one wanted to get a clear view respectively of :
A. Kanchanjunga and Dhauladhar ranges
B. Nandadevi and Dhauladhar ranges
C. Kanchanjunga and Nandadevi ranges
D. Nandadevi and Nanga Parvat

94. Atmosphere exists because:
A. The Gravitational force of the Earth
B. Revolution of the Earth
C. Rotation of the Earth
D. Weight of the gases of atmosphere

95. Victoria lake is located in the continent:
A. Africa
B. Asia
C. North America
D. South America

96. The famous Lagoon Lake of India is :
A. Dal Lake B. Chilka Lake
C. Pulicat Lake D. Mansarover

97. Where are most of the earth's active volcanoes concentrated?
A. Indian Ocean B. Pacific Ocean
C. Aral Sea D. Atlantic Ocean

98. Through which of the following states does the river Chambal flow?
A. U.P., M.P., Rajasthan
B. M.P., Gujarat, U.P.
C. Rajasthan, M.P., Bihar
D. Gujarat, M.P., U.P.

99. Which country is called the sugar bowl of the world?
A. Cuba B. India
C. Argentina D. USA

100. The area covered by forest in India is about:
A. 46% B. 33%
C. 23% D. 21.76%

101. A closed economy is the one which :
A. does not permit emigration or immigration
B. permits emigration but no immigration
C. engages in no foreign trade
D. engages in no foreign and domestic trade or transit

102. In a developed economy the major share of employment originates in the :
A. primary sector B. tertiary sector
C. secondary sector D. any of the above

103. The Economic and Social Commission for Asia and Pacific (ESCAP) is located at :
A. Bangkok B. Kuala Lumpur
C. Manila D. Singapore

104. Commercial vehicles are not produced by which of the following companies in India?
A. TELCO B. Ashok Leyland
C. DCM Daewoo D. Birla Yamaha

105. In India, the Public Sector is most dominant in:
A. transport
B. steel production
C. commercial banking
D. organised term-lending financial institutions

106. The main argument advanced in favour of small scale and cottage industries in India is that:
A. cost of production is low
B. they require small capital investment
C. they advance the goal of equitable distribution of wealth
D. they generate a large volume of employment

107. The most serious economic problems of India are:
A. Poverty and unemployment
B. Stagnation, not poverty
C. Unemployment, not poverty
D. Underdevelopment, not poverty

108. Which of the following is not one of the three central problems of an economy?
A. What to produce
B. How to produce
C. When to produce
D. For whom to produce

109. If saving exceeds investment, the national income will:
A. fall B. rise
C. fluctuate D. remain constant

110. In which of the following industries in India are the maximum number of workers employed?

A. Sugar B. Jute
C. Textiles D. Iron and Steel

111. Terrace Cultivation is practiced mostly:

A. in urban areas
B. on slopes of mountains
C. on tops of hills
D. in undulating tracts

112. Which of the following is a Selective Credit Control method?

A. Bank Rate
B. RBI directives
C. Cash Reserve Ratio
D. Open market operations

113. Which of the following taxes is not shared by the Central Government with the States?

A. Union excise duties
B. Customs duty
C. Income tax
D. Estate duty

114. ICICI is the name of a:

A. Financial Institution
B. Chemical Industry
C. Cotton Industry
D. Chamber of Commerce and Industry

115. Structural Unemployment arises due to

A. Deflationary conditions
B. Heavy industry bias
C. Shortage of raw material
D. Inadequate productive capacity

116. Which Commission replaced the Planning Commission in 2015?

A. NIYAM Aayog
B. NAGRIK Aayog
C. NITI Aayog
D. Jan Aayog

117. The largest public sector bank in India is:

A. Central Bank of India
B. Punjab National Bank
C. State Bank of India
D. Indian Overseas Bank

118. Which of the following statements best explains the term contraband goods?

A. Goods produced only for exports
B. Goods produced in joint sector only
C. Goods for the trading of which licence is not required
D. Goods that are forbidden, from export, import or even possession, by law

119. Price in the market is fixed by:

A. Stock exchange rates
B. The demand and supply ruling in the market at a particular time
C. The Finance Minister
D. None of the above

120. Devaluation of currency helps to promote:

A. National Income
B. Savings
C. Imports at lower cost
D. Exports

121. Balanced economic growth can be achieved only if:

A. All the sectors of economy grow at the same rate
B. Population growth is arrested
C. All the inter dependent sectors grow in harmony
D. Basic and heavy industries are assigned highest priority

122. P.V. Sindhu is associated with which of the following sports?

A. Badminton
B. Weightlifting
C. Swimming
D. Tennis

123. 'MODVAT' stands for:

A. Modified Value Added Tax
B. Deduction of cost of inputs from the value of output
C. Reduction in import duties
D. Imposition of tax on professions

124. Who among the following is the first to receive 'Dada Saheb Phalke' award?

A. Shivaji Ganeson B. Devika Rani
C. Dr. Raj Kumar D. None of the above

125. The term 'devaluation' means:
A. Reducing the value of a currency in terms of another currency
B. Increasing the value of a currency
C. Revising the value of a currency
D. None of the above

126. Per capita net availability of pulses has shown a tendency of:
A. Increase over time
B. Decrease over time
C. Constant over time
D. First increase then decrease

127. National Income is the same as:
A. Net national product at market price
B. Net domestic product at market price
C. Net national product at factor cost
D. Net domestic product at factor cost

128. Which one of the following is not an example of indirect tax?
A. Sales tax B. Excise duty
C. Customs duty D. Expenditure tax

129. The major aim of devaluation is to:
A. encourage imports
B. encourage exports
C. encourage both exports and imports
D. discourage both exports and imports

130. Structural unemployment arises due to:
A. deflationary conditions
B. heavy industry bias
C. shortage of raw materials
D. inadequate productive capacity

131. When was the Family Planning Programme officially started in India?
A. 1950 B. 1952
C. 1956 D. 1962

132. When was the Reserve Bank of India nationalised?
A. 1947 B. 1949
C. 1950 D. 1951

133. Which of the following is *not* a feature of the Indian economy?
A. High rate of population growth
B. Disguised unemployment
C. Lowest rate of adult literacy
D. High rate of exports

134. The 'Relative Deprivation' approach for measuring poverty has been adopted by:
A. developing countries
B. developed countries
C. under-developed countries
D. None of the above

135. One of the main factors that led to rapid expansion of Indian exports is:
A. Imposition of import duties
B. Liberalisation of the economy
C. Recession in other countries
D. Diversification of exports

136. Sustainable economic development means an increase in the rate of growth of real:
A. total and per capita product
B. total and per capita product and level of literacy rate
C. total and per capita product and life expectancy at birth
D. total and per capita product, taking into account the cost of degradation of the quality of environment in this process

137. Functional unemployment occurs when:
A. unemployed have no qualification for job
B. people frequently change their job
C. people were thrown out from job due to recession
D. None of these

138. Which among the following does **not** have a 'free trade zone'?
A. Kandla B. Mumbai
C. Visakhapatnam D. Thiruvanantpuram

139. Sun Belt of USA is important for which one of the following industries?
A. Cotton textile
B. Petrochemicals
C. Hi-tech electronics
D. Food Processing

140. Commercial banking system in India is
A. unit banking B. branch banking
C. mixed banking D. None of the above

141. Who gives recognition to political parties in India?
A. Parliament

B. President
C. Supreme Court
D. Election Commission

142. The Quorum of the Legislative Council is :
A. one-fourth of its total membership
B. one-third of its membership
C. one-tenth of its membership
D. 25

143. The Indian Constitution is:
A. federal
B. unitary
C. a happy mixture of the federal and unitary
D. federal in normal times and unitary in times of emergency

144. Universal adult franchise implies a right to vote to all:
A. adult residents of the State
B. adult male citizens of the State
C. residents of the State
D. adult citizens of the State

145. When a resolution prefering a charge against the President has been passed by a specified majority in the House, it is sent to the other House for investigation. If, as a result of such an investigation, a resolution is passed through a specified majority by the other House, declaring that the charge has been sustained, the President shall leave his office. The specified special majority must not be less than :
A. two-third of the members present and voting
B. one-third of the members present and voting
C. three-fourth of the members present and voting and two-third of the total membership
D. two-third of the total membership

146. Which one of the following judicial powers of the President of India has been *wrongly* listed?
A. he appoints the Chief Justice and other judges of the Supreme Court
B. he can remove the judges of the Supreme Court on grounds of misconduct
C. he can consult the Supreme Court on any question of law or fact which is of public importance
D. he can grant pardon, reprieves and respites to persons punished under Union Law

147. The Vice-president of India can be removed from his office before the expiry of his term if :
A. the Rajya Sabha passes a resolution by a majority of its members and the Lok Sabha agrees with the resolution
B. if the Supreme Court of India recommends his removal
C. the President so desires
D. None of the above

148. The Chief Justice of a High Court in India is appointed by the :
A. Governor of the State
B. Prime Minister of India
C. Chief Justice of the Supreme Court
D. President of India

149. Which of the following statements is constitutionally not true about the passing of the Union Budgets, Railway Budgets and Finance Bill in India?
1. Under the law, Finance Bill should be adopted by both the Houses of the Parliament within 45 days of its introduction.
2. If the Finance Bill is not adopted within specified period, the government loses its authority to levy the taxes proposed in the budgets.
3. In the absence of full budget, a vote-on-account gives the power to the government to spend.
4. Government cannot raise revenues without a proper approval of the Finance Bill

A. Only 2 B. Only 3
C. Only 4 D. Only 1, 2 and 3

150. Normally, on whose advice the President's Rule is imposed in a State?
A. Chief Minister
B. Legislative Assembly
C. Governor
D. Chief Justice of High Court

151. Which Article of the Indian Constitution deals with Amendment procedure?
A. Article 368 B. Article 358
C. Article 367 D. All of these

152. Government is the agency through which the will of :
A. the state is expressed
B. the people is expressed
C. the head of the state is expressed
D. the majority is expressed

153. In a unitary system of government :
A. The centre is all powerful
B. The centre is weaker than the states
C. The centre and states stand at par
D. The states and centre are supreme in their respective spheres

154. In Cabinet System of Government the real executive authority rests with :
A. The Council of Ministers
B. The Prime Minister
C. The Constitution
D. The Parliament

155. The Head of the State under a parliamentary government:
A. is an elected representative
B. is a hereditary person
C. is a nominated person
D. may be any one of the above

156. In the event of a ministerial proposal being defeated on the floor of the legislature, under the parliamentary system :
A. the government waits for a general no-confidence motion
B. the minister concerned is taken to task by the Prime Minister
C. the minister is forced to resign
D. the whole Council of Ministers resign

157. The "due process of law" is an essential characteristic of the judicial system of:
A. UK B. France
C. USA D. India

158. Under the Constitution it is :
A. obligatory for the President to accept the advice of the Council of Ministers but is not obliged to follow it
B. obligatory for the President to accept the advice of the Council of Ministers
C. not obligatory for the President to seek or accept the advice of the Council of Ministers
D. obligatory for the President to seek the advice of the Council of Ministers if his own party is in power

159. Which one of the following statements is correct?
A. the Presiding Officer of Rajya Sabha is elected every year
B. the Presiding Officer of Rajya Sabha is elected for a term of two years at a time
C. the Presiding Officer of Rajya Sabha is elected for a term of six years
D. the Vice-President of India is the ex-officio Presiding Officer of Rajya Sabha

160. The introduction of "no confidence" motion in the Lok Sabha requires the support of at least:
A. 50 members B. 70 members
C. 60 members D. 80 members

161. The High Court comes under :
A. State List B. Union List
C. Concurrent List D. None of the above

162. Which one of the following has been wrongly listed as a Fundamental Duty of the Indian citizens?
A. to develop scientific temper, humanism and spirit of inquiry and reform
B. to work for raising the prestige of the country in the international sphere
C. to protect and improve the natural environment
D. to strive towards excellence in all spheres of individual and collective activity

163. Which one of the following is not a Fundamental Duty as outlined in Article 51A of the Constitution?
A. to abide by the Constitution and respect its ideals
B. to defend the country and render national service when called upon to do so

C. to work for the moral upliftment of the weaker sections of society
D. to preserve the rich heritage

164. The main characteristics of the Directive Principles of State Policy given in the Indian Constitution are :
A. not enforceable by any court
B. fundamental in the governance of the country
C. 'Like instruments, instructions, political manifesto and a code of moral precepts which have to guide governors of the country'
D. no law can be passed, which is opposed to these principles

165. Of the following which are true?
A. In a State, the Legislative Council is dominant with regard to non-financial bills and the Legislative Assembly with regard to financial (money) bills
B. Vidhan Parishad can virtually block legisla-tion even if the same is passed by the Vidhan Sabha
C. In case of a tie between the two Houses, the Governor is duty-bound to call a joint session of the two Houses to have the issue settled on a majority verdict
D. If a Bill is twice approved by the Vidhan Sabha, it becomes law even if rejected by the Vidhan Parishad

166. Which one of the following types of emergency can be declared by the President?
A. Emergency due to threat of war and external aggresion
B. Emergency due to break-down of constitu-tional machinery in a State
C. Financial emergency on account of threat to the financial credit of India
D. all the three emergencies

167. The chairman of which of the following parliamentary committees is invariably from the members of ruling party?
A. Committee on public undertakings
B. Public accounts committee
C. Estimates committee
D. Committee on delegated legislation

168. Which of the following is not a formally prescribed device available to the members of parliament?
A. Question hour
B. Zero hour
C. Half-an-hour discussion
D. Short duration discussion

169. Which of the following is not a tool of executive control over public administration?
A. Power of appointment and removal
B. Line agencies
C. Appeal to public opinion
D. Civil services code

170. If the Speaker of the State Legislative Assembly decides to resign, he should submit his resignation to the:
A. Judges of the High Court
B. Deputy Speaker
C. Chief Minister
D. Finance Minister

171. Who was the first Home Minister of Independent India?
A. Rajendra Prasad
B. Jawahar Lal Nehru
C. B.R. Ambedkar
D. Sardar Vallabh Bhai Patel

172. India is a Federal State because of:
A. dual judiciary
B. dual citizenship prevalent here
C. share of power between the Centre and the States
D. rigid Constitution

173. Residuary Subjects are those subjects which are:
A. contained in the State list
B. contained in the Union list
C. contained in the Concurrent list
D. not covered by any of the three lists

174. Which of the following writs can be issued, by the Supreme Court, to enforce Fundamental Rights?
A. Writ of Habeas Corpus
B. Writ of Mandamus
C. Writ of Quo Warranto
D. All of these

175. When the offices of both the President and the Vice-President of India are vacant, who will discharge their functions?
A. Prime Minister
B. Home Minister
C. Chief Justice of India
D. The Speaker

176. The Supreme Court tenders advice to the President of India on a matter of law or fact:
A. on its own
B. only when such advice is sought
C. only if the matter relates to some basic issue
D. only if the issue poses a threat to the unity and integrity of the country

177. Six months shall **not** intervene between two sessions of the Indian Parliament because :
A. it is the customary practice
B. it is the British convention followed in India
C. it is an obligation under the Constitution of India
D. None of the above

178. The States of the Indian Union can be recognised or their boundaries altered by:
A. the Union Parliament by a simple majority in the ordinary process of legislation
B. two-thirds majority of both the Houses of Parliament
C. two-thirds majority of both the Houses of Parliament and the consent of the legislatures of concerned States
D. an executive order of the Union government with the consent of the concerned State governments

179. The Basic Feature theory of the Constitution of India was propounded by the Supreme Court in the case of :
A. Minerva Mills Vs. Union of India
B. Golaknath Vs. State of Punjab
C. Maneka Gandhi Vs. Union of India
D. Keshavananda Vs. State of Kerala

180. Which one of the following writs is issued by a court in case of illegal detention of a person?
A. Habeas corpus B. Mandamus
C. Certiorari D. Quo-warranto

181. Name the instrument with the help of which a sailor in a submarine can see the objects on the surface of the sea.
A. Telescope B. Periscope
C. Gycroscope D. Stereoscope

182. 'HEMOPHILLIA' is the disease of ....
A. liver B. blood
C. brain D. bones

183. Vitamin A is abundantly found in ....
A. Brinjal B. Tomato
C. Carrot D. Cabbage

184. .... is not soluble in water.
A. Vitamin A B. Vitamin B
C. Vitamin C D. None of these

185. The blood vessels with the smallest diameter are called ....
A. capillaries B. arterioles
C. venules D. lymphatics

186. Out of the following .... has the greatest elasticity.
A. steel B. rubber
C. aluminium D. annealed copper

187. Cooking gas is a mixture of which of the following two gases?
A. Carbon Dioxide and Oxygen
B. Butane and Propane
C. Carbon Monoxide and Carbon Dioxide
D. Methane and Ethylene

188. The substance most commonly used as a food preservative is:
A. sodium carbonate B. tartaric acid
C. acetic acid D. benzoic acid

189. Normally, the substances that fight against diseases in human systems are known as:
A. dioxyribonucleic acids
B. carbohydrates
C. enzymes
D. antibodies

190. The SI unit of temperature is ....
A. Kelvin B. Celsius
C. Fahrenheit D. None of the above

191. One of the common fungal diseases of man is :
A. plague B. ringworm
C. cholera D. typhoid

192. A clear sky is blue because:
A. red light is scattered more than blue
B. ultraviolet light has been absorbed
C. blue light is scattered more than red
D. blue light has been absorbed

193. Jenner introduced the method of making people immune to :
A. small pox B. rabies
C. cholera D. polio

194. The largest cell in the human body is :
A. Nerve cell B. Live cell
C. Muscle cell D. Kidney cell

195. What is the device that steps up or steps down the voltage?
A. Dynamo B. Conductor
C. Inductor D. Transformer

196. The protein deficiency disease is known as :
A. Kwashiorker B. Cirrhosis
C. Eczema D. Clycoses

197. Iron deficiency causes :
A. rickets B. anaemia
C. cirrhosis D. goitre

198. Blood group of an individual is controlled by :
A. Haemoglobin B. Shape of RBC
C. Shape of WBC D. Genes

199. In a normal man the amount of blood pumped out by the heart per minute is about :
A. 1 litre B. 3 litres
C. 4 litres D. 5 litres

200. Red/green colour blindness in man is known as :
A. Protanopia
B. Deutetanopia
C. Both A and B above
D. Marfan's syndrome

201. The blue colour of the water in the sea is due to :
A. Reflection of the blue light by the impurities in sea water
B. Reflection of the blue sky by sea water and scattering of blue light by water molecules
C. Absorption of other colours by water molecules
D. None of the above

202. The image formed on the retina of the eye is:
A. upright and real
B. larger than the object
C. small and inverted
D. enlarged and real

203. Unit of loudness of sound is:
A. bel B. decibel
C. phon D. none of these

204. Oil rises up the wick in a lamp :
A. because oil is volatile
B. due to the capillary action phenomenon
C. due to the surface tension phenomenon
D. because oil is very light

205. The 'stones' formed in human kidney consist mostly of :
A. calcium oxalate
B. sodium acetate
C. magnesium sulphate
D. calcium

206. We hear the sound later, while the light is seen earlier:
A. because light's speed is more than that of sound
B. because lights travel in a straight direction while sound in a zigzag direction
C. because sound's frequency is lower than light
D. All of the above

207. Which part of an eye is transplanted?
A. Cornea B. Retina
C. Iris D. Sciera

208. The Universal donor group of blood is:
A. O B. A
C. B D. AB

209. The green colour of the leaf is due to :
A. Presence of Chloroplast
B. Presence of Chromium
C. Presence of Nicoplast
D. Presence of excess of oxygen

210. Voice of a child is more shrill than that of an elderly person because:
A. the pitch of the child's voice is higher than that of the person
B. the pitch is lower
C. the child is more energetic
D. None of the above

ANSWERS

1	2	3	4	5	6	7	8	9	10
B	C	D	C	B	C	A	C	C	D
11	**12**	**13**	**14**	**15**	**16**	**17**	**18**	**19**	**20**
C	A	C	A	A	D	A	B	A	D
21	**22**	**23**	**24**	**25**	**26**	**27**	**28**	**29**	**30**
A	C	B	C	D	C	B	D	D	B
31	**32**	**33**	**34**	**35**	**36**	**37**	**38**	**39**	**40**
C	D	C	C	B	C	D	B	C	C
41	**42**	**43**	**44**	**45**	**46**	**47**	**48**	**49**	**50**
A	A	A	B	C	D	C	B	B	D
51	**52**	**53**	**54**	**55**	**56**	**57**	**58**	**59**	**60**
A	C	A	B	B	A	B	C	A	C
61	**62**	**63**	**64**	**65**	**66**	**67**	**68**	**69**	**70**
C	C	B	B	C	C	D	D	D	B
71	**72**	**73**	**74**	**75**	**76**	**77**	**78**	**79**	**80**
B	C	C	C	A	A	A	B	B	A
81	**82**	**83**	**84**	**85**	**86**	**87**	**88**	**89**	**90**
A	B	D	B	C	C	D	C	B	D
91	**92**	**93**	**94**	**95**	**96**	**97**	**98**	**99**	**100**
A	B	A	A	A	B	B	A	A	D
101	**102**	**103**	**104**	**105**	**106**	**107**	**108**	**109**	**110**
C	B	A	D	D	D	A	C	D	C
111	**112**	**113**	**114**	**115**	**116**	**117**	**118**	**119**	**120**
B	B	B	A	D	C	C	D	B	D
121	**122**	**123**	**124**	**125**	**126**	**127**	**128**	**129**	**130**
C	A	A	B	A	D	C	D	B	D
131	**132**	**133**	**134**	**135**	**136**	**137**	**138**	**139**	**140**
B	B	D	A	B	D	B	D	D	C
141	**142**	**143**	**144**	**145**	**146**	**147**	**148**	**149**	**150**
D	C	D	D	D	B	A	D	C	C
151	**152**	**153**	**154**	**155**	**156**	**157**	**158**	**159**	**160**
A	B	A	A	A	D	C	B	D	A
161	**162**	**163**	**164**	**165**	**166**	**167**	**168**	**169**	**170**
B	B	C	B	D	D	C	B	B	B
171	**172**	**173**	**174**	**175**	**176**	**177**	**178**	**179**	**180**
D	C	D	D	C	B	C	A	D	A
181	**182**	**183**	**184**	**185**	**186**	**187**	**188**	**189**	**190**
B	B	C	A	A	A	B	D	D	A
191	**192**	**193**	**194**	**195**	**196**	**197**	**198**	**199**	**200**
B	C	A	A	D	A	B	D	D	A
201	**202**	**203**	**204**	**205**	**206**	**207**	**208**	**209**	**210**
B	B	B	B	A	A	A	A	A	A